Why Do You Need This New Edition?

If you're wondering why you should buy this new edition of *The Adolescent,* here are 10 good reasons!

1 The thirteenth edition has been shortened from 18 to 15 chapters, and the content has been restructured and reorganized so that related topics flow more naturally from one to the next.

2 All data and terminology have been updated to be as current as possible.

3 The Cross-Cultural Concerns boxes have been updated to reflect recent research into the cultural issues and cultural conflicts that adolescents deal with—for example, there is a new box entitled *An Example of Cross-Cultural Conflict: Chinese American Adolescent Dating.*

4 This edition contains approximately 500 new reference citations, taken from the most up-to-the-minute research on adolescents' growth, development, and behavior.

5 Newly-updated content is included in many of the Research Highlight boxes. In addition, two Research Highlight box topics are new in this edition: *The Effects of Maternal Ethnic Socialization on Sons and Daughters* and *Does This Generation Have Higher Self-Esteem?*

6 This edition provides an expanded research methods section, including updated content discussing cross-sectional vs. longitudinal vs. cross-sequential designs. In addition, there is more coverage of the limitations of quasi-experimental research.

7 Much new research on adolescent thinking and reasoning has been added.

8 Discussions on adolescents' interactions within the family unit have been expanded. Topics include: father-only families; successful stepfamilies; importance of family closeness and warmth; and sources of parental knowledge about their teens.

9 This edition expands upon the twelfth edition's discussions of adolescents' cell phone and Internet use.

10 The revised Epilogue discusses recently conceptualized positive youth development programs, which guide adolescents to avoid delinquency and become well-functioning adults.

PEARSON

THIRTEENTH EDITION

The Adolescent

Development, Relationships, and Culture

KIM GALE DOLGIN

Ohio Wesleyan University

Allyn & Bacon

Boston ■ Columbus ■ Indianapolis ■ New York ■ San Francisco ■ Upper Saddle River
Amsterdam ■ Cape Town ■ Dubai ■ London ■ Madrid ■ Milan ■ Munich ■ Paris ■ Montreal ■ Toronto
Delhi ■ Mexico City ■ Sao Paulo ■ Sydney ■ Hong Kong ■ Seoul ■ Singapore ■ Taipei ■ Tokyo

Executive Editor: *Jeff Marshall*
Editorial Assistant: *Courtney Elezovic*
Marketing Manager: *Nicole Kunzmann*
Marketing Assistant: *Amanda Olweck*
Senior Production Project Manager: *Liz Napolitano*
Manufacturing Buyer: *Debbie Rossi*
Cover Designer: *Kristina Mose-Libon*
Editorial Production and Composition Service: *Laserwords Maine*
Interior Design: *Laserwords Maine*
Photo Researcher: *Debbie Needleman*

Photo credits appear on page 489, which constitutes an extension of the copyright page.

Library of Congress Cataloging-in-Publication Data

Dolgin, Kim Gale.
  The adolescent : development, relationships, and culture / Kim Gale Dolgin, F. Philip Rice. — Thirteenth ed.
      p. cm.
  Prev. ed. published under author: F. Philip Rice.
  ISBN-13: 978-0-205-73136-7
  ISBN-10: 0-205-73136-8
  1. Teenagers—United States—Social conditions. 2. Adolescent psychology—United States. 3. Adolescence. I. Rice, F. Philip. II. Rice, F. Philip. Adolescent.
III. Title.
  HQ796.R543 2011
  305.2350973—dc22

                                                                                    2010012903

10 9 8 7 6 5 4 3 2 CIN 14 13 12 11

**Allyn & Bacon
is an imprint of**

www.pearsonhighered.com

ISBN 13: 978-0-205-73136-7
ISBN 10:   0-205-73136-8

For my mother, Florence

Contents

PART THREE THE SELF

Chapter 6 Self-Concept, Identity, Ethnicity, and Gender 149

Chapter 7 The Development of Moral Values 175

PART FOUR SOCIAL RELATIONSHIPS

Chapter 8 Relationships with Family Members 199

Features

IN THEIR OWN WORDS

Preface

It is almost impossible for me to believe that I have now had the privilege to complete my fourth edition of *The Adolescent: Development, Relationships, and Culture*. (My fourth go-around, the text's thirteenth.) Even in the near-decade since I have been associated with Philip Rice's masterpiece, the field of adolescent psychology has undergone enormous changes—it is almost incomprehensible how much more we know now, and how different our perspective on adolescents is, than when Philip completed his first edition of the text in 1975. In the 1970s, the notion that gender might play a significant role in development was a new, emergent idea; any conception of the importance of ethnic or cross-cultural influences was lacking. The field of neuroscience had barely been invented, and we had no idea of the biological underpinnings of adolescent behavior. The past thirty-five years have seen a flurry of research activity into the lives, desires, needs, strengths, and stresses faced by adolescents.

Plan for the Thirteenth Edition

In part because of the accumulation of these advances, the thirteenth edition has undergone a major restructuring: the number of chapters has been reduced from 18 to 15, so that certain topics could be reorganized to flow more naturally from one to the other. In addition, this change has the benefit of making the book fit more neatly into a standard college semester.

The Adolescent begins, as before, with three introductory chapters that make up the first Part. Chapter 1 places adolescent development, relationships, and culture in a social context, and discusses the significant ways in which our society has evolved and how these changes affect the lives of adolescents. Seven changes are discussed: the prolongation of adolescence, the introduction of new information technologies, changes in the world of work and consumerism, the ever-increasing need for prolonged education, the changing nature of the family, evolving sexual standards, and the increased presence of violence in adolescents' lives. An overview of the research designs commonly used to study adolescent development is also introduced.

Chapter 2 places adolescence in a theoretical context and introduces multidisciplinary views of adolescence. Chapter 3 examines adolescence from both an ethnic and a socioeconomic context. It considers adolescents of low socioeconomic status along with adolescents who belong to these ethnic/racial groups: African Americans, Hispanic Americans, Native Americans, and Asian Americans. There is also a section on immigrants and refugees.

Part Two deals with *growth*. Chapter 4 addresses physical change, such as the anatomical and biochemical aspects of puberty, and also topics such as physical attractiveness, weight, nutrition, and exercise. Chapter 5 details the cognitive development that occurs during the adolescent years. The foundational contributions of Piaget are introduced, and the more current information-processing perspective is examined. The newest information about the physical bases for cognitive development is also presented.

The third Part describes changes to a person's sense of self. Personal and ethnic identities, as well as gender roles, are discussed in Chapter 6. The development of a moral ethic, so necessary to a mature self-concept, is discussed in Chapter 7.

Next, Part Four turns to examining adolescent social relationships, and looks at the kinds of interactions that teenagers have with others whose opinions and behaviors are meaningful to them. The first two chapters in this section (Chapters 8 and 9) detail the relationships that adolescents have with members of their families. Topics such as parenting style, family conflict, sibling interactions, divorce, and remarriage are reviewed. Since the other significant relationships adolescents have largely involve peers, the text continues by describing adolescent–adolescent interactions. The first of the two chapters that do this (Chapter 10) describes adolescent friendships and the unique aspects of the adolescent subculture. The following chapter (Chapter 11) is concerned with adolescent sexual activity.

The text's fifth Part is concerned with adolescents' preparations for their futures as adults. Chapter 12 covers the adolescent secondary school experience, whereas Chapter 13 discusses the many issues involved in career choice. The book's last major division, consisting of Chapters 14 and 15, examines the psychosocial problems that beset many youth: depression, eating disorders, substance abuse, and delinquency.

Finally, the text concludes with a brief Epilogue that discusses positive youth development, the newly described stage of life termed "emerging adulthood," and the major life tasks of young adulthood.

New Content for This Edition

I hope that you will find this new, amalgamated thirteenth edition of *The Adolescent* even better than previous editions. I have added approximately 500 new references in this edition (a follow-up to the approximately 700 new references I added to the twelfth edition) and have, of course, updated all data and terminology to be as current as possible. In addition, the following new topics have been included or expanded upon in the thirteenth edition:

- Greatly expanded methods section (including information on cross-sectional vs. longitudinal vs. cross-sequential designs) and more on the limitations of quasi-experimental research
- Biological mechanisms by which the chronic stress of poverty negatively impacts teens
- Asian American adolescent dating patterns
- Risky decision making
- Adolescent egocentrism
- Much new research on adolescent thinking and reasoning
- Self-esteem levels in the current adolescent cohort
- Cross-cultural moral development
- Adolescents' views of political and human rights
- Importance of family closeness and warmth
- Sources of parental knowledge about their teens
- Developmental change in adolescent sibling relationships
- Sibling relations post-divorce
- Father-only families
- Successful stepfamilies
- Global teen culture
- Academic success and popularity
- Early mixed-group dating
- Age changes in dating habits
- Effects of cohabitation on later marriage
- Adolescents as consumers
- Cell phone use by teens
- Adolescent Internet use
- Current downward trends in adolescent sexual activity
- Father absence and sexual activity
- The current sexual "double standard"
- Gardasil
- Current adolescent abortion laws by state
- Abstinence-only sex education
- High schools with very poor graduation rates
- High school dropouts
- Changing issues of school safety
- Social cognitive career theory
- International perspectives on youth employment
- Role of self-efficacy in career determination
- Depression
- Juvenile delinquency
- Adolescent children of alcoholic parents
- Prescription drug abuse
- Genetics of susceptibility to addiction
- Effective smoking prevention programs
- Drinks of choice for teens
- Positive youth development

Features

Many important features, highly praised by adopters of the book, have been retained from previous editions, including five different types of boxes that present many new topics and examples.

Personal Issues features discuss topics of individual interest to students.

PERSONAL ISSUES   WHEN DO ADOLESCENTS BECOME ADULTS?

Adulthood is the stage of life recognized by cultures all over the world. In many nontechnological societies, the major criterion for attaining adulthood is that one has married (Schlegel & Barry, 1991). In addition, in Western societies, significant life changes, such as completing one's education, becoming a full-time worker, and establishing one's own home, have been assumed to be markers of social maturity (Goldscheider & Goldscheider, 1999). Are these the criteria used by adolescents and young adults?

The answer appears to be, largely, "no." A number of studies have shown that adolescents are more likely to believe that psychological, cognitive traits are more important than these social role markers. For example, Arnett (2001) found that almost 90 percent of the adolescents in his study believed that "accepting responsibility for one's actions" was necessary for adulthood, whereas fewer than 15 percent believed that "marriage" was needed. Similarly, the single most commonly cited marker for adulthood given by adolescents in Barker and Galambos's (2005) study was "the ability to act responsibly"; this beat out living independently, being financially independent, or being out of school.

When do adolescents think that they will begin to accept responsibility and hence become adults? That depends upon their age. Generally, the older the teen, the older the person believes that adulthood will strike (Galambos & Vitunski, 2000). Most adolescents think that adulthood will descend upon them at an earlier age—perhaps 20 or 21—than they later would. Arnett (2001), however, discovered that somewhat fewer than half of the individuals in their twenties that he sampled believed they were "adults."

The findings of these studies are consistent with research suggesting that adulthood is an emerging process. This is a period of time (often in mid-adolescence) when youths begin to consider themselves adults—cognitively, emotionally, and behaviorally.

Cross-Cultural Concerns boxes show comparisons between different racial and ethnic groups on a wide variety of subjects.

CROSS-CULTURAL CONCERNS AN EXAMPLE OF CROSS-CULTURAL CONFLICT: CHINESE AMERICAN ADOLESCENT DATING

Traditional Chinese values concerning adolescent dating are in conflict with those of present-day America. Parents raised in the Chinese culture generally believe that it is inappropriate for teenagers to date or to be interested in the opposite sex (Tang & Zuo, 2000). Dating is viewed as a distraction from the important job of doing well in school and getting good grades (Kim & Ward, 2007). In keeping with their parents, in the main Chinese American adolescents have more conservative sexual attitudes than their peers and begin sexual explorations at a later age (Feldman, Turner, & Araujo, 1999), although this is less true the more they are Westernized (Yu, 2007). Still, first- and second-generation Chinese American youths who have been raised in the United States and who have non-Asian peers with more liberal views toward adolescent sexuality are caught between two cultures.

How, then, do they navigate this culture clash? A recent study found that 70 percent of Chinese American youth dated without their parents' knowledge (Lau, Markham, Lin, et al., 2009). The teenagers expressed concern that their parents would disapprove if they found out, mostly citing fears that their academic achievement would suffer. Many parents, for their part, seemed to turn a blind eye to their children's dating as long as they continued to get high grades; they instituted a "no ask, no tell" policy. The Chinese American adolescents in the study also differed from Caucasian peers in being more likely to move quickly into an exclusive, steady dating relationship.

Research Highlight boxes continue the discussion of current research issues of special interest.

RESEARCH HIGHLIGHT DOES THIS GENERATION HAVE HIGHER SELF-ESTEEM?

The present generation of youth is often portrayed as content and self-satisfied. A recent study suggests that this is an accurate depiction. Twenge and Campbell (2008) analyzed data from the 2006 Monitoring the Future survey, a questionnaire given to about 15,000 high school students from across the United States each year. They pulled out a subset of items that related to self-esteem and confirmed that current U.S. high schoolers feel better about themselves and their futures than did high schoolers in 1975. In particular, today's students like themselves more and are considerably more likely to believe that they will make good spouses, parents, and employees than did those in 1975. They do not, however, believe that they are generally more competent, although they do believe they are a little more intelligent.

Why all this optimism? Perhaps, the authors suggest, it is because they are getting better grades than students in the past. Twice as many students who were in high school in 2006 reported having an A average than those in 1975, and nearly twice as many reported having an A- average. As Baumeister, Campbell, Kreuger, et al. (2003) noted, a combination of grade inflation and an increasing emphasis upon enhancing self-esteem by schools could act together to produce individuals who would like themselves. Given that individuals with high self-esteem tend to be optimistic, this could explain this cohort's rosy predictions about their future personal successes.

In Their Own Words boxes—first-person narratives written by adolescents about their experiences that exemplify and personalize the information—illustrate concepts in the text.

> **IN THEIR OWN WORDS**
>
> *"As far as I can remember, my body weight has been tightly connected to my self-esteem. This started while I was in high school. Dieting was something every girl practiced at some time or another. Not eating was something to be proud of! I must say that I was a normal weight, and this was true for all the other girls in my class, but we all thought we were extremely fat. Going to the gym after classes was a must, even though we all hated it.*
>
> *"There was this notion that as long as you are skinny, you are beautiful. Plus, the boys were constantly making jokes about the overweight girls in school. Well, I do not think that what the boys thought of us was what motivated us the most. What motivated us was the thought that being skinny means being beautiful and sexy. When I was not eating, I was feeling good about myself, and when I ate, I was miserable. There were days when I could not think of anything else but food. If I ate a sandwich, I used to feel guilty and be mad at myself. I had these nightmares about becoming fat and everyone laughing at me.*
>
> *"I used to buy these magazines with skinny girls in them, and every time I looked at them, even though I was hungry, my appetite disappeared. I wanted to look like them so much! I cannot believe I was so stupid—thinking that being thin would solve all my problems and make me happy.*
>
> *"Even nowadays, I still watch my weight very closely. I don't think I suffer from an eating disorder, but this feeling of guilt when I eat a piece of pizza is still there. But I've learned to live with it."*

Wouldn't You Like to Know . . . boxes ask and answer questions intended to stimulate students' interest in the course material. Together, these boxed features add variety and interest to the text.

WOULDN'T YOU LIKE TO KNOW . . .

- Why is a good self-concept important?
- Do adolescents become delinquent because they have low self-esteem?
- What kinds of parents raise children with high levels of self-esteem?
- Do adolescent girls and boys have different levels of self-esteem?
- What identity status is most common among college students?
- How does the development of an ethnic identity affect self-esteem?
- What is the difference between *sex* and *gender*?
- Why is it good to have a blend of masculine and feminine traits?

> **ANSWERS WOULDN'T YOU LIKE TO KNOW . . .**
> **Why is a good self-concept important?**
>
> A positive self-concept not only makes it easier for a person to be friendly and outgoing, but it also gives him or her the confidence to try new activities and take on challenges. Having a positive self-concept leads to having high self-esteem, as well.

Other valuable features include the following:

Broad Research Base

The discussions are substantiated with over 3,000 citations, most of which are original research studies; however, the emphasis in the text is on discussing the subjects, not summarizing one research study after another.

Attention-Grabbing Chapter Introductions

Each chapter begins with a series of interesting "Wouldn't You Like to Know . . ." questions that highlight some of the most intriguing information in the chapter. As mentioned above, answers to these questions are provided in boxes at relevant points throughout the chapter.

Pedagogical Aids

This book has been written with the teaching-learning process in mind. Each chapter begins with a detailed outline as well as the interest-inducing **"Wouldn't You Like to Know . . ."** questions). **Key terms** appear in the text in bold type and are defined in the margin on or near the same page where first mentioned; they appear again in the **Glossary** at the end of the book and at the end of each chapter that first introduces them. Each chapter discussion is followed by a detailed, numbered **Summary. Thought Questions** at the end of each chapter may be used in class discussions, in essay assignments, or to foster debate. The **Suggested Reading** list that concludes each chapter enables students and instructors to do extra reading on topics, as desired. Similarly, the addition of **Useful Web Sites** to many chapters provides readers with more source materials.

Eclectic Orientation

This text presents not one theory of adolescence but many, discussing the contributions, strengths, and weaknesses of each. Information is presented not only from the field of psychology, but sociology, education, economics, communications, public health, anthropology, and medicine.

Comprehensive Coverage

The book is as comprehensive as possible within the confines of one text. The adolescent is discussed within the context of contemporary society. Material includes both theory and life experiences of adolescents and discusses physical, intellectual, emotional, psychosexual, social, familial, educational, and vocational aspects of adolescent development and behavior. It also reviews psychosocial problems of adolescents.

Adolescents in Contemporary Society

How modern society and social forces shape the lives of adolescents today is an important topic. Adolescents are discussed in social, theoretical, and ethnic contexts, not as though they were isolated from the social forces around them.

Cultural Diversity

Adolescents are not all alike, any more so than are adults. A wide variety of ethnic, racial, and cultural groups are discussed, both from within the United States and from around the world.

Adolescent Society and Culture

This book includes not only adolescent development and relationships but also group life and culture. Subjects include cultural versus subcultural societies, dress, social activities, and group life in and out of school. The importance of the automobile, cell phones, and music in adolescents' lives is also emphasized.

Gender Issues and Concerns

Gender issues are raised in relation to a wide range of topics: physical attributes and body image, cognitive abilities and intelligence, eating disorders, social development and dating, sexual values and behavior, education, work and vocation, and others.

Personal Applications

The **Thought Questions** at the end of each chapter are designed to bring out students' attitudes, feelings, and responses to the subjects discussed. The questions have been subdivided into three sections. The first contains **Personal Reflection** questions, in which students are encouraged to reflect on their own adolescent years, to think about adolescents they know (either their own friends or their children), and to react in a critical way to the issues discussed. The next section is composed of **Group Discussion** questions, which can be used to facilitate small-group interaction in or out of class. The questions could also be posted in a chat room or electronic bulletin board. The final section contains **Debate Questions;** these are controversial statements that are intended to be springboards for discussion and dispute.

The **"In Their Own Words"** boxes also bring a personal focus to the topics discussed.

Supplements

MyDevelopmentLab

MyDevelopmentLab is a learning and assessment tool that enables instructors to assess student performance and adapt course content—without investing additional time or resources. Students benefit from this easy-to-use site where they can test themselves on key content, track their own progress, and utilize individually tailored study plans.

For more information on MyDevelopmentLab and MyVirtualTeen, go to www.mydevelopmentlab.com.

MyVirtualTeen, available in MyDevelopmentLab, is an interactive simulation that allows students to raise a child from birth to age 18, with a specific focus on the teenage years, and monitor the effects of their parenting decisions over time. This engaging Web site helps students to apply the key concepts that they are learning in the adolescent development class.

Instructor's Manual/Test Bank

This Instructor's Manual/Test Bank includes a wealth of resources. The Instructor's Manual contains detailed outlines, objectives, discussion questions, and media resources for each chapter of the text. The Test Bank contains over 50 test items per chapter in multiple-choice and essay formats. A page reference to the text discussion, a skill level, and a difficulty rating scale are included for each item. This supplement is available for download from the Instructor's Resource Center. Contact your Pearson Arts & Sciences representative for more details.

Pearson MyTest Computerized Test Bank (www.pearsonmytest.com)

The Test Bank The test item file comes with the NEW Pearson MyTest, a powerful assessment generation program that helps instructors easily create and print quizzes and exams. Questions and tests can be authored online, allowing instructors ultimate flexibility and the ability to efficiently manage assessments anytime, anywhere.

PowerPoint Presentation Package

This PowerPoint package is an excellent tool for enhancing lectures. This supplement is available for download from the Instructor's Resource Center. Contact your Pearson Arts & Sciences representative for more details.

Acknowledgments

I gratefully acknowledge the special help of Jeff Marshall and Amy Trudell at Pearson Education, who provided valuable guidance in writing and producing this edition.

I would also like to thank the following individuals, who reviewed this edition's text or Instructor's Manual/Test Bank and offered useful suggestions: David Bell, St. Xavier University; Kim Brown, California State University, Bakersfield; Carmen Davis, California State University, Hayward; Patricia Janca, University of Houston, Victoria; Hsin-Hui Lin, University of Houston, Victoria; Laura Pannell, Itawamba Community College, Tupelo; Ian Payton, Bethune Cookman University; Gareth Phillips, University of Technology, Jamaica; Trudean Scott, Kent State University, Tuscarawas Campus; Michael Shields, Texas Tech University; Pat Somers, College of DuPage; Theresa Stahler, Kutztown University of Pennsylvania; Gisele Tchamba, University of the Southern Caribbean; Steve Trotter, East Tennessee State University; Fabian Vega, Baltimore City Community College, Liberty Campus; Cathy Wong, California State University, Stanislaus.

Finally, I would like to thank my family for putting up with a wife and mom who always goes a little nuts when revising this text. Thanks for all your understanding and for not complaining when we had catch-as-catch-can dinners. I'd also like to especially thank my mom who sees me less than she'd like to during the summers that I work on the book. I love you all.

Kim Gale Dolgin

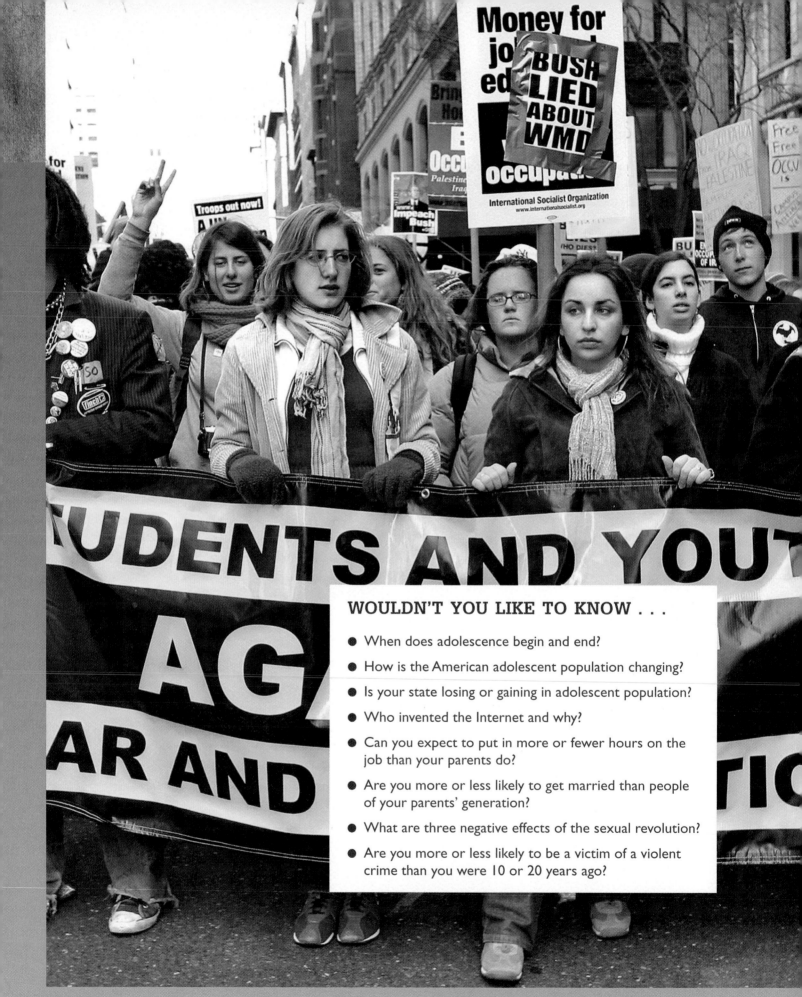

WOULDN'T YOU LIKE TO KNOW . . .

- When does adolescence begin and end?

- How is the American adolescent population changing?

- Is your state losing or gaining in adolescent population?

- Who invented the Internet and why?

- Can you expect to put in more or fewer hours on the job than your parents do?

- Are you more or less likely to get married than people of your parents' generation?

- What are three negative effects of the sexual revolution?

- Are you more or less likely to be a victim of a violent crime than you were 10 or 20 years ago?

The Social Context of Adolescence

The word *adolescence* comes from the Latin verb *adolescere,* which means "to grow" or "to grow to maturity." **Adolescence** is the period of growth between childhood and adulthood. The transition from one stage to the other is gradual and uncertain, and although the time span is not the same for every person, most adolescents eventually become mature adults. In this sense, adolescence is likened to a bridge between childhood and adulthood over which individuals must pass before they take their places as full-grown, responsible adults.

Most people place the beginning of adolescence at the time at which children *begin* to physically mature into individuals capable of reproduction—that is, when they begin to sexually mature. People call this "hitting puberty." Actually, this is a misnomer, since **puberty** actually means to be physically capable of procreating, and the physical changes that are associated with "hitting puberty" begin quite a few years before children become fertile. In any case, most children reach puberty when they are between ages 11 and 13, and this is considered the lower boundary of adolescence. (By the way, in Latin, the word *puberty* means "to grow hair," which is a great descriptor of this maturation process!)

The upper boundary of adolescence is less clear. Different criteria can be used, and none are universally agreed upon. Some people believe that adolescence ends once physical maturity is reached. Others believe that it ends once an individual attains full legal status and can thereby vote, drink alcohol if desired, be drafted, get married, and so on. (A problem with this designation is that these legal markers do not occur at the same age: in most states, you can freely marry at 18 but are prohibited from freely drinking alcohol until 21.) Another, more vague criterion puts the end of adolescence at the age when most others treat the individual as an adult, according him or her respect and independence in decision making.

Adolescents themselves tend to focus on achieving emotional independence from their parents and taking responsibility for their own actions (Arnett, 1997). Most adults tend to think of adolescence as ending with a combination of attaining financial independence, emotional independence, and a change in focus onto issues that are less related to adolescence and more related to adulthood. Therefore, in this text, we consider full-time college students as adolescents and discuss them periodically.

Adolescence, then, is not monolithic and uniform. There is a tremendous difference between an insecure, gangly, 12-year-old middle school student and a fully grown, confident, 20-year-old college sophomore. Because of this, we distinguish early adolescence from middle adolescence and late adolescence. *Early adolescence* refers to individuals who are about ages 11

● **ANSWERS WOULDN'T YOU LIKE TO KNOW …**

When does adolescence begin and end?

Adolescence begins at about age 12, when the body starts maturing toward puberty. The end of adolescence is much less clearly delineated: Some individuals leave home at 17 and support themselves (adults?), whereas others live at home and are supported by their parents well into their twenties (adolescents?).

---

to 14, and *middle adolescence* refers to those who are ages 15 to 17. We use the term *late adolescence* to mean those adolescents who are 18 or older, with full recognition that some 18-, 19-, and 20-year-olds are truly adults. Adults are (theoretically) mature in all ways—physically, emotionally, socially, intellectually, and spiritually—whereas adolescents still have significant growth to achieve in some areas.

When do adolescents believe they fully become adults? Some think they have to wait too many years to "get into the club." Whereas many middle-aged and elderly adults say they feel younger than they really are and young adults typically "feel their age," adolescents most commonly feel older and more mature than their chronological age (Galambose, Kolaric, Sears, et al., 1999). Since their parents and teachers usually do not share this assessment, however, many adolescents chafe under what they perceive to be excessive control by the adults around them.

Two other words that we use frequently in this text are *teenager* and its shortened form, *teen.* Both of these terms, strictly speaking, mean someone in the teen years: ages 13 to 19. The word **teenager** is of fairly recent origin. It first appeared in the *Readers' Guide to Periodical Literature* in the 1943–1945 issue. However, because children (especially girls) sometimes mature physically before age 13, there are some discrepancies. An 11-year-old girl may look and act like a teenager, but a 15-year-old boy, if not yet sexually mature, may still act and look like a child. In this text, the words *teenager, teen,* and *adolescent* are used interchangeably.

The word **juvenile** is generally used in a legal sense to signify one who is not yet considered an adult in the eyes of the law—in most states, anyone up to age 18. The legal rights of 18-year-olds are confusing, however, for they vary from state to state. The Twenty-sixth Amendment gave 18-year-olds the right to vote, and in some areas, they are called for jury duty. They may obtain credit in their own names at some stores and banks; at others, they have to obtain cosigners. Many landlords still require the parents of 18-year-olds to cosign leases.

Finally, for variety's sake, we also frequently use the words **youth** or **youths.** These two terms are used synonymously with *adolescent(s).*

Approaches to Studying Adolescents

There are numerous approaches to the study of adolescents. In Chapter 2, we review the work of many of the most influential thinkers who studied and wrote about this age group. In some cases these perspectives are complementary, in that they fundamentally agree with one another or address different, non-overlapping issues. In other instances, the researchers' ideas are in stark conflict with each other. These disagreements stem from the fact that these researchers were writing at different points in time and, hence, had different knowledge sets from which to work. They also had different backgrounds and theoretical orientations.

The approach taken in this book is an *eclectic approach* to the study of adolescents. That is, the approach is interdisciplinary, emphasizing not one aspect of adolescent development but all of them, recognizing that no single discipline has a monopoly on the truth. As such, the contributions of biologists, psychologists, educators, sociologists, economists, anthropologists, and medical personnel are all important. If we are to get a complete view of adolescence, we must stand in different places and look at adolescents from different perspectives.

The first standpoint presented is a sociological, cultural one. Much of this chapter discusses some of the current cultural conditions that are affecting today's youths. Since American adolescents are a diverse group, Chapter 3 examines some of the most important contributors to this diversity: socioeconomic status and ethnicity. It also discusses the unique experiences of immigrant adolescents.

Next is the *biological* approach, which focuses on the process of sexual maturation and physical growth that takes place during puberty. It involves the maturation and functions of the male and female organs; the development of secondary sexual characteristics; neurological development; and the growth trends in height, weight, and body composition that take place during adolescence. As their bodies change, adolescents develop new concerns about their nutrition, size, and physical attractiveness. In short, they are not always pleased with what is happening to their bodies. We focus on the biological approach in Chapter 4.

This is followed by a chapter devoted to the *cognitive* approach to the study of adolescence. It deals with both the *qualitative* changes that take place in the way adolescents think and reason and the *quantitative* changes that take place in attention, memory, and intelligence. Of concern also is the effect that these cognitive changes have on the adolescent's personality and behavior. Researchers interested in cognition study topics such as learning, problem solving, decision making, and IQ. We take up the cognitive approach in Chapter 5.

The fourth perspective in the study of adolescence is the *psychosexual* approach, which deals with the development of emotions and of the self, including the development of self-concept, gender role, and identity. It is concerned also with mental health and the effects of stress on the adolescent. During adolescence, individuals must integrate newfound sexual feelings into their self-concept and learn to manage their sexuality. Many begin thinking about their ethnic heritage in new and more meaningful ways and begin to develop a mature ethical code. We examine the psychosexual approach in Chapters 6 and 7.

The fifth way to view adolescents is to examine them in the context of their *social relationships*. We do this in Chapters 8 through 11. Chapters 8 and 9 are concerned with the ways that teenagers interact with members of their families. We look at parent-adolescent communication and conflicts, sibling relationships, and parenting styles. The effects of different family constellations—single-parent families, blended families, and adoptive families—are also considered. Chapter 10 deals with peer, friendship, and romantic relationships and the peer subculture as a whole. Topics such as conformity, fads, and cliques are discussed. Finally, sexual behavior is discussed in Chapter 11.

Some of the most important connections that adolescents have with the broader social world are introduced in Chapters 12 and 13. Adolescents spend many of their waking hours in school, interacting with teachers and administrators as well as peers. The school is the institution that provides adolescents with many of the skills they need to function as independent adults, including social and job-related skills. The special needs of school dropouts are also considered here. Often while in school, and certainly after they graduate, most adolescents are employed. Pathways to career decisions, career education, the costs and benefits of youth employment, and youth unemployment are discussed in Chapter 13.

The text's penultimate section deals with many of the serious problems faced by today's adolescents: suicide, delinquency, eating disorders, running away from home, and substance abuse. (Another serious concern, teenage pregnancy, is discussed with sexuality in

adolescence   the period of growth from childhood to maturity.

puberty   the developmental stage at which one becomes capable of reproduction.

teenager   in a strict sense, includes only the teen years: ages 13 to 19.

juvenile   one who is not yet considered an adult in the eyes of the law.

youth(s)   a term that will be used synonymously with "adolescent(s)."

Chapter 11.) Although certainly not all adolescents encounter these problems, surprisingly high percentages do. And even if they do not experience these problems themselves, they almost certainly know someone who does. Thus, a text on adolescent psychology would not be complete without an examination of the causes, symptoms, and treatments of these problems.

Finally, in order to provide a sense of closure, the text ends with an epilogue. In that chapter, the discussion begins with what we have learned about helping adolescents successfully negotiate this stage of life. The epilogue also contains a description of "what comes next." *Emerging adulthood,* the stage that describes individuals who are in some ways between adolescence and adulthood, is presented. Emerging adulthood has become an increasingly more common bridge stage between adolescence and young adulthood in modern times and is now normative enough that it deserves discussion since it, not young adulthood proper, will be the next phase of life for many adolescents. We then conclude by talking about the differences between adolescence, emerging adulthood, and young adulthood.

The Changing Face of American Adolescence

Because of fluctuations in immigration rates and birthrates, the absolute size of the juvenile population in the United States is continuously changing. Between the late 1960s and the mid-1980s, the number of Americans ages 14 to 24 steadily declined. Since that time, it has been slowly but steadily increasing. In 1990, there were 40 million Americans in this age range. If the forecasts are accurate, this slow but steady increase will continue at least through 2050, such that there will be about 58 million American 14- to 24-year-olds at that time (U.S. Bureau of the Census, 2008a). This represents a 25 percent increase in the juvenile population between 2000 and 2050 (see Figure 1.1).

Although this change seems large, it is actually small in comparison to the increases in some other age groups. The change in the number of elderly individuals—those over the age of 65—in particular, has been and will be greater. Therefore, over the next 30 or 40 years, adolescents will make up a slightly smaller fraction of the U.S. population, despite their increase in absolute numbers. In 2010, those aged 14 to 24 accounted for 15.8 percent of the American population; in 2050, it is estimated that they will comprise 14.6 percent of the population.

Again, as a result of different immigration rates and birthrates, the racial and ethnic makeup of American adolescents is also changing. During the next 25 years, the relative increases in the numbers of Asian American, African American, Hispanic American, and Native American juveniles will greatly outstrip the number of non-Hispanic Caucasian juveniles. The American adolescent population is becoming increasingly multiracial and multiethnic. (Adolescent diversity is discussed in Chapter 3.)

Juveniles and their families are also on the move. Whereas many states have experienced significant increases in their juvenile populations, numerous others have shown declines (see Figure 1.2). These changes reflect the overall movement of the U.S. population away from the north-central and northeastern states to the western and southern states.

> **ANSWERS WOULDN'T YOU LIKE TO KNOW …**
>
> **How is the American adolescent population changing?**
>
> Although there are increasingly more adolescents in the United States, they now make up a smaller proportion of the total population because people are living longer and the birthrate is dropping. The racial/ethnic makeup of American adolescents is also changing. More and more are of African, Hispanic, or Asian descent.

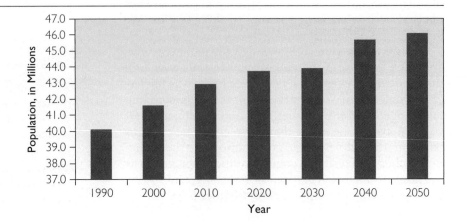

FIGURE 1.1   U.S. JUVENILE POPULATION PROJECTION

Source: Data from U.S. Bureau of the Census (2008a).

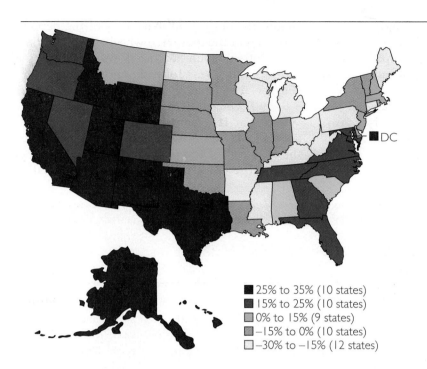

FIGURE 1.2 PROJECTED CHANGE IN U.S. JUVENILE POPULATION: 1995 TO 2015 (IN PERCENTAGES)

Source: Snyder and Sickmund (2006).

- ■ 25% to 35% (10 states)
- ■ 15% to 25% (10 states)
- □ 0% to 15% (9 states)
- ▨ −15% to 0% (10 states)
- □ −30% to −15% (12 states)

Our Evolving Society

The society in which adolescents grow up has an important influence on their development, relationships, adjustments, and problems. The expectations of society mold their personalities, influence their roles, and guide their futures. The structure of the society either helps them fulfill their needs or creates problems for them by stimulating tension and frustration. Because adolescents are social beings who are part of a larger culture, we need to understand this social order and some of the ways it influences them.

Certainly, much of the adolescent experience is reasonably constant. After all, for eons individuals have had to cope with reaching puberty and all that goes with it. But not everything about being an adolescent is so predictable. The world is constantly changing—sometimes quite rapidly and sometimes more gradually. Today's adolescents are facing a number of new conditions that are different from those faced by past generations. Some of these conditions are the result of gradual evolution and thus outgrowths of what has come before; others would have been unanticipated even 50 years ago. These societal changes are interrelated, each change playing off of and influencing the others.

Because of these sometimes rapid changes and singular events, different historical groups, or **cohorts,** of adolescents have had different characteristics. It is easier to speak definitively about those cohorts from the past than about more current ones, as there is not yet enough historical distance to know absolutely what events and issues will have been most important in shaping present-day and near-present-day adolescents. The following are the descriptors most frequently given to the major adolescent cohorts since the early 1900s.

The Lost Generation: These individuals were adolescents or young adults during or just after World War I and hence were born between the mid-1880s and 1900. They were traumatized by the large number of casualties caused by the war and disdainful of their parents' Victorian ideas about morality and propriety.

The G.I. Generation: This is the generation of Americans who were children during the Great Depression and adolescents or young adults during World War II. An enormous percentage of young men either enlisted or were drafted into the armed services, and many young women enlisted as well. The women who remained in the United States took on many formerly male occupations. (A popular song of the day was "Rosie the Riveter."

ANSWERS WOULDN'T YOU LIKE TO KNOW . . .

Is your state losing or gaining in adolescent population?

Check Figure 1.2 to see if your home state is gaining or losing in adolescent population. If you live in the West, it is likely gaining; if you live in the Midwest or the Northeast, it is likely losing.

cohort   a group of individuals who are born at approximately the same time and who share traits because they experienced the same historical events.

"Rosie" was even immortalized in a trendy poster of the day showing a muscular woman with her hair in a bandana flexing her bicep.) Our country had been attacked, and patriotism ruled the day.

The Silent Generation: Born between 1925 and 1940—too late to serve in World War II and too early to be unconventional and antiauthoritarian—this group is characterized as conservative and traditionalist. However, it

should be recognized that many of the heroes and icons of the more free-wheeling groups that came after—such as the Reverend Martin Luther King Jr., John Lennon, and Jerry Garcia—were actually members of this cohort.

The Baby Boomers: This group was born after World War II, when the soldiers came home and began their adult civilian lives. They are the children of the G.I. generation. Boomers are a large cohort because of the unusually

CROSS-CULTURAL CONCERNS   THE MAJOR CRISES FACING THE WORLD'S ADOLESCENTS

According to the United Nations Population Fund, the largest adolescent generation in all of history—1.5 billion individuals—is coming of age. The most pressing global needs of this group include the promotion of gender equality and universal access to education, health services, and reproductive and sexual health information. Meeting these goals will not only improve the lives of the youth themselves but will also help stem the AIDS pandemic and reduce worldwide poverty. (More than half of the world's youth live on less than $2/day.) Even though some of the issues faced by adolescents in other nations are different from those faced by American youth, some are eerily similar. For example, it is a global, not an American, concern that adolescents are leaning too much upon peers and the media for advice on how to survive in the "new" world they are facing rather than relying upon tradition.

Gender inequality is one pervasive theme; female adolescents face discrimination in much of the world. In many societies, families do not invest as much in their daughters' health or education as they do in their sons'. In many geographic areas, females are not allowed to own property. Because of poverty and a lack of employment opportunities, girls and women are vulnerable to sexually exploitive practices such as child marriage, sexual coercion, and sexual trafficking. Child brides almost never continue their education and, because of the large age difference between themselves and their husbands, have subordinate positions in the household and are usually not allowed to socialize outside the family. They have little opportunity to leave abusive husbands. In societies in which women have few rights and little social standing, sexual coercion is commonplace and females are held responsible for its occurrence. Annually, between 700,000 and 4,000,000 adolescent girls are forced into the sex trade and have bleak existences filled with degradation and illness.

Because premarital sexual activity has become more commonplace around the globe, HIV/AIDS and other

sexually transmitted diseases (STDs) have become diseases of the young. Half of all new cases of AIDS occur among people between the ages of 15 and 24; this translates to 6,000 young people each day becoming infected, most of them female. The highest rates are in sub-Saharan Africa. Another way that the AIDS epidemic has affected adolescents is that many have lost family members to the virus. If a family member is ill, it is likely that a child (usually a daughter) will have to drop out of school to care for the family member. If a child or adolescent is left an orphan, he or she often must turn to theft or prostitution to survive.

It is important to provide reproductive health information to adolescents to help prevent the spread of STDs. Schools cannot be relied on to provide this information since many youth in developing nations do not attend classes. Different countries have tried different approaches, often using the mass media to get the message out. The most common themes involve abstinence, faithfulness to a single partner, and condom use.

These practices would also, of course, help reduce the number of adolescent pregnancies. Early pregnancy is a serious health risk for young adolescent girls. It is the leading cause of death for young women ages 15 to 19 worldwide. Most of these deaths are due to complications from labor and delivery, but a significant minority are due to botched abortions. Some young adolescents who survive childbirth are permanently disabled from the experience.

The good news is that issues of adolescent well-being are being taken seriously. The biggest problems have been identified, steps are being taken, and globally progress is being made to improve adolescent outcomes. Real strides have been made in the past decade.

Source: Data from the United Nations Population Fund, 2003 and 2007.

high birthrate after the returning WWII soldiers started families. Boomers, born from the mid-1940s until the early- to mid-1960s, were fortunate to grow up in a largely prosperous economic time. They comprised the first rock-and-roll generation in the 1950s and the hippie nation in the late 1960s.

Generation X: The name reflects this generation's feelings of cynicism and alienation. It is a small cohort that was born from the mid-1960s until about 1980. Members of Generation X were therefore adolescents in the 1980s and 1990s. They are generally the children of baby boomers; as a group, they were not enamored of the world their parents left to them. They often felt neglected by their parents, who were searching for personal self-fulfillment, and pessimistic about their own economic opportunities and abilities to make positive changes in the world.

Generation Y: Also known as the Millennial Generation, these are individuals born from about 1980 until 2000. They (most of you) are too young to personally remember the Cold War and young enough that computers, the Internet, and cell phones are integral parts of your lives. Many members of generation Y were raised by attentive "helicopter parents," who were very child centered.

Generation ?: Members of the most recent living generation, consisting of those born after 2000 are, of course, not adolescents yet. They will be the first generation raised solely in the post–9/11 era, a time that feels quite different from the more optimistic era that came just before it. They will take it for granted that America can have an African American president. Only time will tell what impact that event and others will have on this generation.

Let's briefly consider seven societal changes that are affecting or will affect the contemporary adolescent experience: the prolongation of adolescence, the presence of the Internet and other new communication tools, the changing economy, the ever-increasing need for a prolonged education, alterations in the makeup of the family, shifting sexual values and practices, and new concerns for health and safety. Each of these issues is considered in more depth later in the textbook. The purpose of presenting them here, right up front, is to get you thinking about the social forces that are working to shape the current (and did work to shape recent) cohorts of adolescents. The world of today's adolescents is considerably different from that of their grandparents or great-grandparents.

The Evolving Prolongation of Adolescence

Since the 1970s, individuals' full entrance into adulthood has been more and more delayed, as youth have taken longer to complete their education, settle on a career, move out of their parents' home, marry, and have children (Arnett, 2000). In other words, adolescence has expanded and become increasingly prolonged. It is not unusual to be at least partly financially dependent upon one's parents well into one's twenties or to marry when close to 30. With this delay has also come not only a pushing back of significant life events but also a disruption of the lockstep sequence in which these events have traditionally occurred (Fussell, 2002). For example, it is less likely that a female will have a child prior to marriage if she marries at 19 instead of at 27. Also, someone who completes his or her education at age 20 is less likely to work at a full-time job before leaving school than someone who keeps working toward a degree until he or she is 28.

Many reasons can explain this prolongation: more skills are needed to get a good job; there is increased societal permissiveness toward premarital sexual activity; inexpensive, effective birth control is available; parents are more willing to continue to support their children for longer; and so on. Some youths' maturity and lifestyle really does remain largely "adolescent" for quite some time; others move into a "betwixt and between" state termed **emerging adulthood,** in which they lead a life midway between that of adolescents and young adults. Emerging adulthood is discussed in the epilogue of this text.

Evolving Communication and Information Technologies

Adolescents today live in a society undergoing rapid technological changes. Probably no other society has so revered technological innovation while placing so little restraint on it than that of the United States. During the past 100 or so years, Americans have witnessed unprecedented advances: the introduction of radio, television, automobiles, airplanes, nuclear energy, robots, and satellite communication.

Of all these changes, perhaps none has had as profound an effect as the introduction of the computer. The first computers were less powerful than today's personal

emerging adulthood   the stage of life between adolescence and young adulthood.

computers, yet they occupied whole rooms and cost millions of dollars. It's easy to forget that the first personal computer was introduced in 1980. Since that time, their use has skyrocketed. More than half of all U.S. workers today use computers on the job (Bureau of Labor Statistics, 2005). More than 90 percent of American adolescents have access to and use computers both at home (Nielson Company, 2009) and at school (U.S. Bureau of the Census, 2003). Even more than half of prekindergarten and kindergarten students are using computers at school.

The Internet

One of the most important reasons for using the computer is the Internet. The military researchers who created the Internet needed a safe way to store and communicate sensitive government information in the event of a nuclear war. The solution was a network that lacked a central computer to store its billions of bytes of information or to direct the actions of remote computers. Each computer site on the network stands alone but is also interconnected to the others. Thus, the destruction of one site (in the event of war) would not prevent the free interchange of information or destroy the data stored at other sites. Today, the result is a decentralized network of data stored on thousands of computers that make up the network and speak a common language. If a particular computer breaks, the rest of the computers connected to the network can use any number of other connections to maintain their links.

Estimates put more than 1.5 billion users on the Internet worldwide (Internet World Stats, 2009). The Internet is open 24 hours a day, 365 days a year. It's a way to meet people; find adventure; share ideas and experiences; look for a job, a date, or a mate; ask questions; or give advice. The information resources of thousands of universities, government agencies, and researchers are at your fingertips. It's like a shopping mall that never closes where you can shop for everything from automobiles to food. It's cyberspace: the final frontier. Cyberspace has no borders or defined boundaries; it is a system to which you can go to meet people, communicate, learn, explore, and get information. Cyberspace is the place for those who connect to one another electronically to share their thoughts and feelings. Once online, you can have private and group conversations, join in lively discussions with nationally known experts, play online games, browse through the articles of hundreds of periodicals and online magazines, read movie reviews, make flight or hotel reservations, or track investments with the latest stock market quotes and investment advice.

About 60 percent of American teens say that they connect to the Internet at least once per day; about one-third say they get on several times per day (Lenhart, Madden, MacGill, et al., 2007). Almost all use the Web at

ANSWERS WOULDN'T YOU LIKE TO KNOW . . .

Who invented the Internet and why?

The Internet was invented by the U.S. military as a way of protecting its computer network from sabotage. Since the Web is diffuse and decentralized, it is hard to destroy.

least occasionally. The most common reasons adolescents get on the Web is to find information, communicate with others (via social-networking sites, instant messaging, or e-mails), visit entertainment sites, and play games.

Since only 16 percent of the world's Internet users live in North America (Internet World Stats, 2009), and youth are generally technologically savvy, it is apparent that the Internet provides adolescents from around the world the opportunity to interact with one another directly or indirectly. They can visit the same Web sites, download the same music and films, compete at online gaming sites, watch each other on YouTube, and so on. Because of these interactions, some researchers believe that the Web is contributing to a global youth culture, with universal tastes and values (e.g., United Nations, 2005).

As is obvious from the Internet's explosive growth, there is much good to be gained from spending time online. The sheer quantity of available information is staggering: you can learn about almost anything. It is like having a fantastic library at your fingertips, one in which you can check out any books, pictures, or sound clips you'd like. You can take virtual tours of the world's great museums and watch and listen to video clips of policy makers announcing important decisions. (Of course, the information on the Web is of uneven quality, and users must learn how to judge the accuracy of sites and weigh the value of the information they find.) This informational benefit is especially important to more isolated individuals who otherwise might not have access to educational materials. The Internet also lets you inexpensively keep in touch with others, even those far away. For example, posting pictures to your Web page is a way to let your friends see what you did on your vacation or what your new girlfriend or boyfriend looks like. The Web allows you to purchase esoteric items that might not be available in your community, or listen to a livestream radio program from a city on another continent.

There are, however, a number of potential downsides to Internet use.

Potential Hazards of Internet Use

One unfortunate downside to the Internet is that it makes a wide variety of inappropriate materials readily available to children and adolescents. For instance, one can find sexually explicit materials such as photographs and videos of singles, couples, and groups

One drawback of Internet use is the opportunity for adolescents to view pornography and other objectionable material.

involved in various sex acts. Some photographic and artistic materials contain examples of bestiality and pedophilia. Fictional and nonfictional accounts of sexual encounters may include incest or sadism. Users can find personal ads of individuals seeking partners for one-night stands. Catalogs for sexual devices and clothing as well as advertisements for pay-for-service organizations ranging from phone sex to escort services are also offered.

There's nothing on the Internet that isn't available in other places, but the Internet is not as controllable and thus online materials are more accessible to adolescents and children than from most other sources. Furthermore, sometimes even searches intended to visit only innocuous sites result in matches that contain graphic and explicit materials. Mitchell, Wolak, and Finkelhor (2007) found that one-third of the adolescents they sampled had been exposed to Web-based pornography, *even when they were not looking to do so,* an increase from only a few years before, and 20 percent had received a sexual solicitation online (Finkelhor, Mitchell, & Wolak, 2005).

Violent and destructive materials are also found on the Internet, including recipes for bombs and other destructive devices. The Internet may also contain posts encouraging drug use, self-mutilation, or eating-disordered behavior. Radical activist groups provide materials on the Internet. Such materials may come from neo-Nazi groups or state militia organizations or include information on gang-related activity.

Parents and lawmakers have sought to pass legislation that will help protect children from these kinds of materials. The Communications Decency Act was passed into law in February 1996. Within days, several civil rights organizations challenged the law on the grounds that it violated the First Amendment. A U.S. federal court in New York overturned the law, and on June 26, 1997, the U.S. Supreme Court, in a 7–2 decision, concurred that it violated the right of free speech and upheld the lower court's finding. A second version of the law, the Child Online Protection Act, was passed in 1998 but was also struck down by the Supreme Court in 2004. A much narrower statute, the Children's Internet Protection Act (CIPA), was passed by Congress in 2000. It was directed not at Internet site producers, but at libraries and public schools. It directed these institutions to ensure that children would not be exposed to "harmful" material if the institutions wished to continue receiving federal funds; what is "harmful" would be determined by local community standards. The act was jointly challenged by the American Civil Liberties Union (ACLU) and the American Library Association, although in 2003, the U.S. Supreme Court upheld the law. Libraries and schools have complied with the law by installing blocking software, which they are permitted to remove for adult users who request that they do so (American Library Association, 2006).

Another potential risk of Internet use stems from the fact that communication can be anonymous. People can invent screen names for themselves that give little clue to their true identities. You can present yourself any way you wish on the Web: you can develop multiple screen personalities with different races and genders and describe your appearance in an untruthful fashion. You can be rude or hostile with little real consequence. Many Internet users develop multiple "virtual selves" (Anderson, 2002), and the impact of doing so on the development of a teen's true identity is unclear at this time.

A final issue is that differential access to the Internet will increase the divide between rich and poor (U.S. Department of Commerce, 1999). Lack of familiarity with computers, networking, and information accessing will put lower-income adolescents further behind their middle-class peers and could make it even more difficult for them to get high-paying jobs.

Cell Phones

More than three-quarters of American teenagers own their own cell phone (Nielson, 2009), and the percentage has been growing each year. Adolescents use these phones to call and send text messages to their friends, staying in near constant contact in a way never before possible. It has changed the nature of social relationships in several ways. For example, cell phones (with friends' circles and unlimited texting plans) allow friends to communicate readily even when they are physically separated, even by a substantial distance. This might, for instance, make it more likely that a college student keeps in close touch with friends from high school. In addition, get-togethers can be more spontaneous and fluid if you can check on a friend's availability at the last minute or cancel because you are running late. There is less need to plan ahead than there was in the past.

Cell phones have also influenced family relations. Just as adolescents can keep in closer touch with their friends, they can also keep in closer contact with their parents and siblings. And, their parents can more closely monitor them. As a result of the security that comes (on both sides) from a teen's having a means of calling for help if it is needed, many parents say they are granting their adolescent child more freedom than they would if he or she did not possess a cell (Ribak, 2009).

Evolving World of Work and Consumption

The United States is a rather materialistic society. Most individuals believe that it is important to own a nice home and to have many possessions in order to lead a good life. Materialism often increases when children become adolescents and then declines as they move through adolescence (Chaplin & John, 2007). Many adolescents, especially early and middle adolescents, are very concerned about wearing the right clothes or having the right possessions so that they fit in. Given this acquisitive ethic and the corresponding drive to accommodate ever-increasing consumer needs, the employment situation in this country continues to evolve in ways that will affect today's youth.

Longer Workdays

Americans keep putting in more and more hours at work; nevertheless, some of them are in hard financial straits. Others are forced to work overtime by their employers. Yet others desire a higher standard of living than they can afford working one 40-hour-a-week job. The recent past has seen increases in the number of workers who hold two jobs—usually one full-time job and a secondary part-time job—as well as increases in the amount of overtime put in by workers with single jobs. Americans spend more time working than most of their European counterparts; in fact, most Europeans spend less time working now than they did in 1970, whereas Americans spend about 20 percent more time working (Office of Economic Cooperation and Development, 2004). We work longer hours each week than most Europeans and we take less vacation time.

The Internet has further lengthened the average American's workday. Twenty-one percent of American workers now say that they "take their jobs home" and participate in business activities while at home (U.S. Bureau of Labor Statistics, 2009). A significant part of this is due to the fact that people with a PC, laptop, or BlackBerry can check their e-mails while at home (or in a restaurant, or standing in line . . .) and then reply. There is thus less distinction between work and leisure time than ever before.

Obviously, working these long hours cuts down on the amount of time workers can spend with their families and children. In addition, the frequent interruption of taking phone calls and checking e-mails, even when at dinner or on family outings, often decreases the quality of that time as well.

Working Women

Another indicator of Americans' attempting to keep up with the high cost of living is the increase in the number of women, even women with young children, who are working outside the home. In 2007, 59 percent of women worked outside the home. Some 71 percent of women with children ages 6 to 17 were employed, as were 63 percent of all women with children younger than age 6. Single mothers were even more likely to be employed than married mothers: 76 percent vs. 69 percent (U.S. Bureau of the Census, 2009b). If you look

---

ANSWERS WOULDN'T YOU LIKE TO KNOW . . .

Can you expect to put in more or fewer hours on the job than your parents do?

If current trends continue, you will likely spend more hours on the job than your parents do or your grandparents did. (So much for technology ensuring increased leisure!)

closely at the numbers, you will see that mothers are actually more likely to work than women who are not mothers. (This is in part due to the high costs associated with raising children.)

Increasing employment among mothers has intensified the demand for child care. In some cases, the adolescents or older children in the family are expected to take over child-rearing duties while their parents are at work. It also means that women are less likely to be home to supervise and monitor their adolescent children in the late afternoons and early evenings. Finally, these women are providing role models for their daughters, who will most likely go on to work outside the home when they become adults as well.

Adolescent Employment

One reason that Americans work longer hours than Europeans is that vastly more American adolescents are employed than European adolescents. The proportion of high school students who work has been rising rapidly and steadily. Generally speaking, working students have had the support of parents, teachers, and social scientists. The conventional wisdom argues that employment is good for students. With the blessing of society, then, American youths have gone to work. Nearly 3 million 15- to 17-year-olds are employed during the school year, and 4 million are employed during the summer months. These adolescents work an average of 17 hours per week while school is in session and 29 hours per week during the summer (Herman, 2000; Stringer, 2003).

Many experts, however, are beginning to believe that many adolescents are devoting too much time to their jobs and not enough to school (e.g., Marsh & Kleitman, 2005). Furthermore, most "waste" the money they earn on unimportant items such as concert tickets, fast food, and DVDs. These spending patterns feed materialism and do not help prepare adolescents for adult self-sufficiency.

The effects of adolescent employment are fully reviewed in Chapter 13, but for now, suffice it to say that credible data suggest that working after school is associated with lowered school achievement and with increased delinquency and substance abuse rates (e.g., Lee & Staff, 2007). Employed teenagers are also less likely than their nonworking peers to get adequate sleep and sufficient exercise. Most adolescents who work may be somewhat at risk for negative outcomes, but this is particularly true of those adolescents who work long hours.

Adolescent Consumption

Teens work in such large numbers because they feel the need to earn money. The mass media are partly responsible for creating a generation of consuming adolescents. Today's children have been surrounded, as no other generation before, by messages in magazines, on the radio, and on television (not to mention pop-ups on their computers) urging the purchase of the newest antiperspirant, breakfast food, or shampoo. More than 99 percent of U.S. households own televisions, and more than two-thirds of adolescents have television sets in their bedrooms (Rideout, Roberts, & Foehr, 2005).

The number of adolescents who hold part-time jobs has been rising steadily. An after-school job often conflicts with schoolwork and responsibilities at home, especially if the job takes more than 20 hours per week.

Today's youths constitute a huge consumers' market. The increasing wealth of this age group has caused more and more businesses to cater directly to youths. Clothes, cosmetics, DVDs, sunglasses, grooming aids, sports equipment, electronic goods, and thousands of other items are given the hard sell to attract the dollars of adolescents.

Adolescent buying power has been growing at an enormous rate. Adolescents are not only earning more money themselves because they are working more, but parents are increasingly giving them cash. Most of their money (about one-third) goes for clothing, accessories, and food (Coinstar, 2003). Adolescent girls spend more time shopping than either adult women or men: the average teenage girl goes to a mall 54 times a year and spends 90 minutes per visit, 40 percent more time than other shoppers (Voight, 1999). Furthermore, adolescents are exercising more and more influence in regard to family purchases. American teens directed the spending of $190 billion in 2006, a 25 percent increase since 2001 (MarketResearch.com, 2006).

Families that have not been able to keep up with the struggle for money, status, and prestige seem poorer than ever. As a result, adolescents in those families often feel rejected. Youths who come from extremely poor families are more likely to be nonjoiners in school activities, are seldom elected to positions of prestige, and often seek status through antisocial behavior (U.S. Bureau of the Census, 2005). These youths struggle for identity and sometimes become problems because they find an identity that middle-class society rejects.

Evolving Educational Imperatives

Expanding technology and social complexity have increased the need for higher education and thus lengthened the period of adolescent dependency. It is vital that adolescents graduate from high school and even college if they are to get well-paying jobs. If American adolescents wish to be economically competitive with their peers in other nations, they must spend more days and years in school, put in more hours doing homework, and tackle more complex information. It is essential that they devote more time to learning new technological skills.

This increased need for education has contributed to the lengthened period of dependency on parents. In 2008, more than two-thirds (69 percent) of unmarried men between ages 18 and 24 lived at home with one or both parents; more than 63 percent of unmarried 18- to 24-year-old women did as

well (U.S. Bureau of the Census, 2009b). The result has been the delay of full independence for these young people.

Educational Attainment

Considerable progress has been made in educating U.S. students through high school age. In 2007, 85 percent of the population age 25 and older had completed at least four years of high school. This figure represents 89 percent of non-Hispanic Whites, 80 percent of African Americans, and 60 percent of Latinos (Crissey, 2009). The percentage of students who complete high school has doubled in the past 40 years. The number of students earning college degrees has not kept pace, however. In 2007, 28 percent of people age 25 and older had completed four or more years of college. This number represents 30 percent of non-Hispanic Whites but only 17 percent of African Americans and about 13 percent of Latinos. (A full 50 percent of Asian Americans have earned at least a bachelor's degree.) Still, the percentage of students of all races who have completed four years or more of college has tripled since 1960. (See Figure 1.3). There is still a long way to go, however.

Part of the problem of raising higher educational levels is the rapid increase in costs. Although the amount of financial aid available in the forms of grants and loans has also increased, it has not kept pace with tuition. The cost of a college education is rising faster than the standard of living. Many students are burdened with repaying huge loans years after they graduate from college.

Embracing the New Technology

One of the most exciting changes in education is happening as teachers become more experienced with computers and the Internet and introduce new uses for them. Educators across the nation continue to embrace the new electronic technologies. Many are developing dynamic lesson plans that include significant uses of online resources. In addition to using computers for research, many teachers employ computers in science classrooms as test equipment, in foreign-language labs for interactive work with students in other countries, in virtual field trips to the countries students are studying, in art classes to create 3-D images and videos, and in math labs to model complex mathematical equations. Students can send e-mail messages worldwide in minutes to correspond with those in other lands. In Internet chat rooms, individuals can participate in live, interactive discussions via the keyboard; video conferencing over the Web lets people speak face-to-face even when separated by a continent. The changes that

I FIGURE 1.3 EDUCATIONAL ATTAINMENT BY AGE 25: 1960–2008

Source: Data from U.S. Bureau of the Census, Current Population Survey Historical Tables.

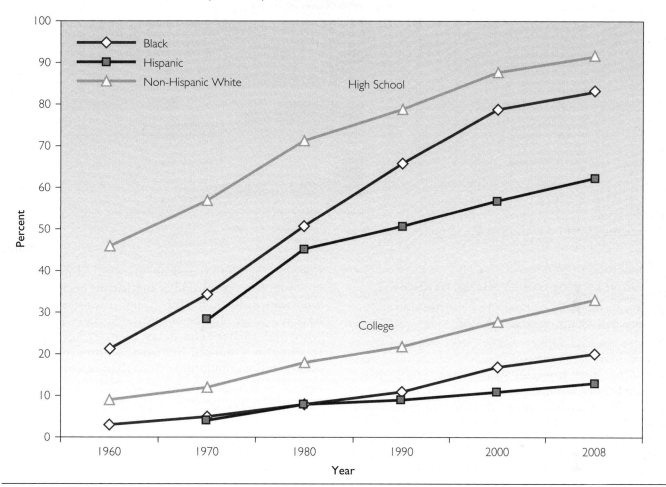

have been made in education over the past 30 years have been significant and inspiring, but none will likely have more effect on educational processes than classroom computers.

Innovations in Career Education

Another educational trend that will affect adolescents is an increasing awareness of the need for career preparation while in high school. Not all students graduate from high school, and of those who do, many do not go on to college. As good-paying jobs require ever more specialized skills, schools are positioning themselves to provide those skills to students.

At the present time, American schools still do far less to facilitate graduates' entrance into the working world than do the schools in many European nations (Kerckhoff, 2002). However, increased opportunities for apprenticeships, as well as other innovations, may someday close that gap. (These new approaches are discussed more fully in Chapter 13.)

The Evolving Family

Changes in the Likelihood of Marriage and Parenthood

The likelihood of getting married and/or becoming a parent has changed over the past few decades. The marriage rate has declined, the age at which people marry has gone up, and the number of children per family has decreased. As shown in Figure 1.4, more and more adults are electing to remain single than was true in the past. Today's adolescents are more likely to remain single for quite a few more years than either their parents or their grandparents, if they marry at all.

Age at Marriage

Even when individuals choose to marry, they are waiting longer before doing so. The median age of marriage for men in 1970 was 23.2; in 2008, it was 27.4. The median age of marriage for women in 1970 was 20.8; in 2008, it was 27.6 (U.S. Bureau of the Census, 2009).

FIGURE 1.4 PERSONS NEVER MARRIED BY AGE AND SEX: 1970 AND 2008

Source: Data from U. S. Bureau of the Census.

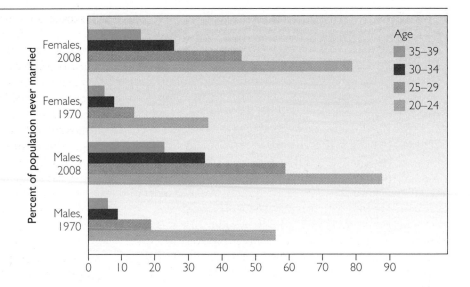

ANSWERS **WOULDN'T YOU LIKE TO KNOW . . .**

Are you more or less likely to get married than people of your parents' generation?

Fewer individuals are marrying than in the past, and they are waiting longer before they do so.

Furthermore, the gap in median age of marriage for men and women has narrowed substantially.

The reasons for the trend to delay marriage include an increase in permissiveness toward premarital sex, more need and opportunities for higher education, decreased negative attitudes toward singlehood, and an increase in nonmarital cohabitation. This trend is significant because those who wait until their mid- to late-twenties to marry have a greater chance of marital success than those who wed earlier. The delay of marriage has also resulted in a marked increase in unmarried young adults in the population. More than one-third of the men and one-fourth of the women in the United States have not married by age 30.

In any case, even those adolescents who do eventually marry (which are the majority of them) will spend more years as single adults than those in previous generations. They will spend more years living alone, with their parents, with nonmarital partners, or with platonic roommates than those in earlier cohorts.

The characters in HBO's popular TV series *Entourage* illustrate the trend to delay marriage. More than one-third of American men and one-fourth of American women have not married by age 30.

Family Size

Declining birthrates since 1965 have resulted in smaller families. The average number of people per household was 3.67 in 1960, 3.19 in 1985, and 2.56 in 2008. More than half of families in 2008 had no children of their own younger than age 18 at home. An additional 20 percent of families had only one child of their own at home who was younger than age 18. These figures seem almost incredible: more than 70 percent of U.S. families had one or no children younger than age 18 living at home. The fact is that women in the United States are having fewer children. At the beginning of the twentieth century, the average married woman had five children. Today, the average number of total births to an ever-married woman between ages 15 and 55 has declined to 1.8 (Dye, 2005). Marital delay and smaller family size go hand in hand since couples tend to have fewer children if they wait until they are older to wed.

Adolescents who come from smaller families enjoy several advantages. Their parents are more likely to give ample attention and care to each child. Adolescents who come from small families also have a greater opportunity to continue higher education, since parents' resources are not as stretched as they would be with additional children. On the other hand, they have fewer siblings with whom to interact.

Changes in Family Dynamics

Not only has the likelihood of marriage changed, but also the expectations that individuals bring to marriage. For example, adolescents today have grown up in a time when the fulfillment of romantic love and companionship—not economic necessity—are considered to be the primary reasons to get married. In some ways, this emphasis on personal relationships has placed more of a burden on the family unit. When people establish a family for love, companionship, and emotional security but do not find this fulfillment, they become disappointed and experience feelings of failure and frustration. This is one reason for the high rate of divorce in the United States. Rather than stay together for the sake of the family, couples often separate if their personal needs and expectations are not met.

The family has also gradually become more democratic. Throughout most of our nation's history, the American family was patriarchal, with the father considered the head of the household, having authority over and responsibility for other members of the family. Since he was head of the household and owner of the property, his wife and children were expected to reside with him or near his family, according to his choice. One characteristic of the traditional patriarchal family was a clear-cut distinction between the husband's and the wife's roles in the family. The husband was the breadwinner and was usually responsible for clearly defined chores that were considered "man's work." The wife was responsible for "woman's work," such as housecleaning, cooking, sewing, child-rearing, and other responsibilities. Children were expected to be submissive and obedient to their parents and to follow their directions, including assuming a considerable responsibility in the performance of family chores.

Gradually, a more democratic form of the family gradually evolved. This change came about for several reasons. First, the rise of the feminist movement brought greater economic power and freedom to women. In the 1870s, women gained the power to own property and to borrow money. Second, increasing educational opportunities for women and the gradual increase in the percentage of married women working outside the home encouraged the adoption of more egalitarian gender roles in the family. As more wives earned incomes, more husbands were asked to take on greater responsibilities for homemaking and child care. The general trend was toward a more equal voice in decision making and a more equitable distribution of family responsibility. Third, the recognition of the sexual capabilities of women in the 1960s and 1970s increased the demand for equality of sexual expression and fulfillment. With such recognition, marriages could be based on the mutual exchange of love and affection. The development of efficient contraceptives also freed women from unwanted pregnancies and enabled them to have personal lives as well as social lives with their husbands.

The child-study movement after World War II catalyzed the development of the child-centered family. No longer was the focus on what a child could do to serve his or her family but rather what the family could do to contribute to the total development of the child. The rights and needs of children as important members of the family were emphasized. As children matured, they demanded a greater voice in family decision making, which sometimes led to rebelliousness against their parents. Today's adolescents expect to have freedoms and degrees of influence that would have astounded their grandparents.

Nonmarital Cohabitation

Another significant change in marriage trends in the United States is the increase in the number of couples who cohabit before marriage. According to the government, there were 5.1 million unmarried cohabiting couples in the United States in 2004, which represents a 170 percent increase since 1980 (Fields, 2004). In excess of half of today's young adults will live with someone prior to marriage (Stanley, Whitton, & Markman, 2004). About 40 percent of these cohabiting couples have children (Fields, 2004). (A complete discussion of nonmarital cohabitation is found in Chapter 10.)

Adolescents will be affected by this rise in cohabitation for two main reasons: (1) they will be more likely to be raised by nonmarried, cohabiting couples than in the past, and (2) they will be more likely to cohabit someday themselves.

Out-of-Wedlock Births

Another, related, trend worth noting is the dramatic rise in the number of births to unwed and never-wed mothers. This means that teens are more likely to become parents themselves prior to marriage and that they are also more likely to have been raised by single, never-wed mothers. (These issues are discussed more fully in Chapters 9 and 11.) Suffice it for now to say that unwed mothers are more likely to experience significant stress and to have a low standard of living than wed mothers. Moreover, their children are less likely to receive adequate prenatal care and to attend high-quality schools, and they are more likely to develop a variety of problems than children raised by married mothers.

Divorce

The divorce rate in the United States has been declining slightly since 1980 (U.S. Bureau of the Census, 2004; see Figure 1.5). In spite of this downward trend, the United States has one of the highest divorce rates in the world. Almost one-third of American adults have been divorced at least once (Krieder & Fields, 2002), and more than two-thirds of American children have experienced their parents' divorce (Fields, 2003).

The high divorce and separation rates, plus a rise in out-of-wedlock births, means that more than one-half of all children who were born in the 1980s and 1990s will spend a considerable amount of time living with only one parent. Today's adolescents will most likely have less contact with their fathers than those in previous cohorts. Since most divorced adults remarry, these teenagers are more likely than those from previous generations to live in a blended, stepfamily situation.

The Evolving Sexual Landscape

The "sexual revolution" began in earnest in the 1970s with the development of the birth control pill and the rise of the feminist movement. This revolution has had both positive and negative effects upon adolescents.

Positive Effects of the Sexual Revolution

Acceptance of Sexual Desire

One benefit of the sexual revolution was a more open acknowledgment that humans are sexual beings. Individuals became more open, and presumably felt less guilty, about having sexual thoughts and feelings. Sex was something that could be discussed (although most parents still had trouble talking about it with their adolescent children). More comprehensive sex education courses began to be taught in schools. Now that sexuality was more widely accepted, teens could take some comfort in knowing that they weren't abnormal in their longings or behaviors.

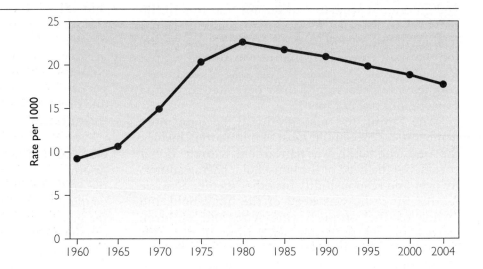

FIGURE 1.5   DIVORCE RATES: 1960–2004

Source: Data from U.S. Bureau of the Census (2006).

Development of Scientific Knowledge About Sexual Functioning

Although biologists and physicians had studied the human body for centuries, little was known about the human sexual response prior to the 1960s. The mechanics of reproduction were rather well understood, as were malformations and diseases of the reproductive organs. Virtually no attention, however, had been paid to learning about sexual arousal, response, and expression. This all changed when the husband-and-wife research team of William Masters and Virginia Johnson began to conduct their well-known laboratory studies of the physical details of human sexual arousal. For the first time, the physiological changes in human sexual responses that occur under sexual stimulation were described. Since the pioneering work of Masters and Johnson (1966), other clinicians have made significant contributions to the field.

This knowledge of the sexual response system enables individuals to understand human sexual functioning better. In turn, this increased understanding can be used to enhance the pleasure of sexual relationships and to help solve many sexual problems. Knowing exactly what is to take place, medical personnel are now better able to assist individuals in dealing with sexual dysfunction. The study of the human sexual response system also exploded some sexual myths, one of which was that human females are not really sexual beings and are not able to respond sexually to the extent that males are. This fact tended to free females from the harmful philosophy that sex is a woman's duty and a man's pleasure.

Development of Contraceptives

The acceptability of sex for pleasure's sake (as opposed to for procreation) spurred the development and availability of new forms of birth control. These include pills, implants, spermicides, condoms, diaphragms, patches, and less invasive sterilization techniques. The development of contraceptives freed women from the necessity of bearing one child after the other and enabled couples to plan their families rather than having them by chance. It also contributed to many individuals becoming more willing to be sexually active outside of marriage.

Willingness to Deal with Unwanted Sexual Behavior

Since the sexual revolution, people have become more willing to openly discuss sexual harassment and rape. Individuals who used to suffer the pain and humiliation of rape in silence can now come forth to confront their aggressors. The sexual abuse of children is also being faced and dealt with in a more helpful and healthful manner. Although American society still has a long way to go in reducing the incidence of sexual abuse of women and children, much progress has been made.

Flexibility of Gender Roles

Due in part to the sexual revolution, gender roles have undergone some drastic changes. Traditionally, society strictly defined what was meant by *femininity* and *masculinity*. People were stereotyped and pressured to live up to certain roles according to their genders. These gender-role stereotypes placed limitations on the relationships that people were capable of forming and on career and personal achievements. Today, gender roles have become more flexible and men and women are interchanging roles. Similarly, housekeeping and child care roles have expanded to include both sexes. Gender roles regarding choice of vocation have also changed, so that many women now occupy positions of leadership that were formerly reserved for men.

Negative Effects of the Sexual Revolution

Unfortunately, the more open sexual topics have become, the more opportunity there has been for this freedom to be abused. The media expose children to sexual images and violent materials before they learn to ride tricycles. Children have scant protection from sexual messages that 20 years ago would have been taboo for grown-ups. Adolescents are certainly affected by watching sexually explicit images on television and in the movies, and, as noted before, the Internet has made these images even more available. It is hardly uncommon to hear of parents' reports of their 13-year-old children attending parties where they experiment sexually as part of the party games. A girl from Kansas said, "In fifth grade, my friends and I decided we would have sex with boys. Now we can't get our reputations back. Now we're the sluts of the school." Another girl remarked, "It's confusing, you're pressured to have sex but when you do, you're a whore" (Pipher, 1996).

An Earlier Beginning to Premarital Sexual Behavior

Researchers have noticed significant changes in premarital sexual attitudes and behavior over the past 540 years. Not only are youths more likely to have premarital intercourse, but also the age of their initial intercourse is younger than in the past. Research indicates that more than half of American teens have lost their virginity by their senior year in high school (Centers for Disease Control and Prevention [CDC], 2006c). In addition, oral sex has become a common activity among even younger adolescents (Remez, 2000).

Unfortunately, many early and middle adolescents are not emotionally prepared to deal with intercourse. They are emotionally devastated when a relationship sours, they are not knowledgeable about birth control, they are not sufficiently concerned about sexually transmitted diseases, and they are uncertain as to how to set limits. Much early sexual behavior is therefore either unwanted or unsatisfactory.

Nonmarital Pregnancy

About 750,000 adolescent pregnancies, most of them unplanned, occur each year in the United States (Guttmacher Institute, 2006). Although this number is substantially lower from peak rates in the early 1990s, the American adolescent pregnancy rate is still far higher than that found in most of the rest of the industrialized world (Singh & Darrock, 2000). Almost half a million babies are born to adolescent girls annually, most of them to unwed, single mothers. More than 95 percent of these mothers keep their children and raise them themselves rather than giving them up for adoption (Henshaw, 2003).

Almost no one considers this an ideal situation. Adolescent mothers are more likely households than other adolescent females to face continuing economic hardship, to fail to continue their education, and to fail to establish their own independent households. In addition, their children are similarly likely to be impoverished, to be deprived of prenatal care, and to have poor developmental outcomes. We must continue working to find ways to further reduce adolescent pregnancy rates.

Sexually Transmitted Diseases and AIDS

Since the sexual revolution, the average person has more sexual partners in his or her lifetime than did those before it occurred. One of the most important consequences of the sexual revolution has been the rapid spread of STDs. In today's world, gonorrhea is more common than chicken pox, measles, mumps, whooping cough, tetanus, rubella, tuberculosis, and trichinosis combined. The Centers for Disease Control and Prevention (CDC) estimates that 19 million

new sexually transmitted infections develop each year in the United States, half of them to persons younger than age 25 (Centers for Disease Control and Prevention [CDC], 2004b). Adolescents are at high risk for STDs because they have multiple sex partners, do not consistently use safer sexual practices, and are frequently ignorant of STDs' symptoms. Many are unaware that several of the disorders are often asymptomatic (meaning that you might have an STD even though you exhibit no symptoms) and so unknowingly pass them on to their partners.

Unfortunately, although many STDs are merely unpleasant and uncomfortable, some can have serious consequences—ranging from serious illness through infertility to death. A number of them are becoming harder to treat since the organisms that cause them are becoming resistant to the available treatments. As with adolescent pregnancy, the adolescent STD situation is a national crisis that cannot be trivialized or ignored.

Confusion About Sex

Adolescents are more and more confused about their sexuality. They are encouraged to learn about and discuss it, and some are stimulated to sexual arousal, but they are not quite certain how and if they should express their sexuality when they are confronted with the dangers of losing their reputations, having their hearts broken, or contracting a dangerous STD.

Sex has been demystified, which may be a good thing, but it is also being marketed, which is not. Adolescents have moved from viewing sex as forbidden and terrifying to seeing it as accessible and interesting but still terrifying. Sex education and counseling are needed more than ever.

Evolving Safety Concerns

Another social change taking place in the United States is the increased fear of violence experienced by many individuals—adolescents as well as children and adults. Even before the tragedy of 9/11, there was a growing perception among many Americans that their neighborhoods and schools were not as safe as they would like. New fears of terrorism and global unrest have only augmented this anxiety.

Violent Crime

The violent crime rate in the United States fell precipitously during the mid- to late-1990s and, in fact, is now lower than at any time in the past 30 years (Snyder & Sickmund, 2006). Even so, there is an overall perception that the United States is becoming an ever

---

ANSWERS WOULDN'T YOU LIKE TO KNOW . . .

What are three negative effects of the sexual revolution?

Unfortunately, the sexual revolution has brought with it a number of negative effects: high rates of STDs and adolescent pregnancies, a too-early onset of sexual activity (for which most teens are unprepared), and a proliferation of sexual messages on television and in movies. As a result, adolescents are confused about sexuality.

more dangerous place to live. Well-publicized shootings in a number of high schools have made many adolescents fearful for their own safety; there is a sense that violence can erupt anytime, anywhere and that there is nowhere to hide from it. In fact, adolescents have some reason to be afraid: even though crime rates have decreased, teenagers are more likely to be assaulted, raped, and robbed than persons in all other age groups (Snyder & Sickmund, 2006).

Violence in Society

Not only are significant percentages of adolescents involved in violent crime, but all of them have been exposed year after year to physical violence and disturbances in the world: the murders or attempted assassinations of national leaders, the bombings of embassies, terrorism at home and on a global scale, and war in more than a dozen countries. Television and the press have provided constant exposure to violence. The mass media have created an age of instant news: television viewers share in the experiences of starving Africans, bombings, tsunamis, wars, and massive earthquakes. Today's youths have not just heard about killings, they have also seen them on the nightly news. They have been bombarded with sensory information that affects emotions and feelings as well as cognitive perceptions. As a result of this constant exposure to violence, many adolescents become insensitive to the

RESEARCH HIGHLIGHT COMPUTER GAMES

Computer games first appeared in the 1970s. Since then, their use has skyrocketed as they incorporated more complex themes and better graphics. Given the perception that many of these games have also become increasingly violent—for instance, requiring players to use weapons to kill large numbers of sometimes innocent opponents—many parents and educators are concerned about their effects on adolescents. Concern is ubiquitous enough that in 2000 the U.S. Senate held hearings on the topic, and a number of prominent researchers testified about the harm that violent games could cause (e.g., Funk, 2000).

No doubt, many of the most popular video and computer games are violent. A study conducted in 2001 found that 89% of the video games sold contained significant violence, including more than 3/4s of the games labeled "E" for "Everyone" (Children Now, 2001). Killing is almost always seen as justified in the games and players are almost always rewarded for their acts of violence. Furthermore, the negative consequences of violence are rarely depicted, and most victims appear unaffected by the aggressive acts committed against them.

There is much less research about the harmful effects of violent video and computer games than there is about the effects of violent television. However, since the data clearly indicate that watching violent television promotes aggression in children and adolescents, there is legitimate cause for concern about the effects of violent computer games. Anderson and Dill (2000) suggest three reasons that playing violent games might be even worse than watching violent TV:

1. When playing a violent computer game, the player takes on the role of the hero, who succeeds by killing "the bad guys." Because the player and the hero are one and the player sees the world through the hero's eyes, he or she identifies with the hero. Much previous research has shown that the more a television viewer identifies with an aggressive hero, the more deleterious the effects of televised violence.

2. Computer and video games require active participation, which is not part of regular television viewing. This increased participation promotes the development of aggressive scripts and develops the habit of selecting violent responses.

3. Computer and video games actively reward a player's aggressive actions. By killing, the player earns points and moves closer to succeeding at his or her goal.

Still, as Kirsh (2006) points out, the data are so scanty as to make any definitive claims impossible at this time. Unfortunately, much of the little research that does exist was collected using old gaming systems whose graphics were much less realistic than today's and whose levels of violence were considerably lower. Also, as of yet, no one has systematically examined the effects of the different types of violent games on youth. For example, games with a first-person perspective may be more or less harmful than those with a third-person perspective, and games in which the objective is to avoid being violent might have different effects than those in which the entire point is to kill as many creatures as possible. We simply do not know yet. However, most psychologists who work with adolescents believe that further research will provide conclusive and overwhelming evidence that playing violent computer and video games is harmful to teenagers.

violence that goes on around them, and they begin to believe that violence is a necessary and accepted part of their lives.

Violence in the Home

Part of the violence that adolescents are exposed to may be traced back to violence in the home. Adolescents who are brought up in violent families in which spousal abuse and child abuse are common tend to become abusive mates and parents themselves. Youths generally model the marital aggression that they witness in their homes. Children who observe their fathers hitting their mothers are more likely to be perpetrators as well as victims of severe marital aggression. The greater the frequency of violence, the greater the chance that the young victims will grow up to be violent parents or partners. Moreover, teenagers who are exposed to violence are more likely to use violence against their parents (Holden, Geffner, & Jouriles, 1998).

Violence in Schools

There has recently been an increased awareness of the degree to which students are subjected to bullying at school. Although bullying generally does not entail much serious physical harm, it can be psychologically traumatizing. Many adolescents report that they are afraid to go to school for fear of being taunted and harassed by fellow students. The resulting stress can result in poor grades, depression, or psychosomatic symptoms or in the victims' lashing

ANSWERS WOULDN'T YOU LIKE TO KNOW ...

Are you more or less likely to be a victim of violent crime than you were 10 or 20 years ago?

The violent crime rate has dropped significantly, such that you are now less likely to be assaulted or murdered than you were in the 1980s and early 1990s. Even so, the publicity given to school and gang shootings, as well as terrorist incidents, has increased adolescents' level of fear.

out in turn. Larger numbers of students than previously thought are involved in bullying, either as victims, active perpetrators, or bystanders, and this seems to be across a broad range of countries (e.g., Due, Merlo, Harel-Fisch, Damsgaard, Holstein, et al., 2009).

Violent Deaths

The most disturbing development in recent years relates to adolescent mortality. Among adolescents ages 15 to 24 who die, more than three-fourths die violently. Death from accidents, suicides, and homicides has exceeded disease as the leading cause of death for youths (Centers for Disease Control and Prevention [CDC], 2009). Young people are the only age group in the United States that has not enjoyed improved mortality over the past 30 plus years; the reason is the increase in violent deaths.

A greater percentage of adolescents have become involved in violent crime in recent years. This 15-year-old is accused of opening fire inside a California school, killing two classmates and wounding thirteen others.

Understanding Adolescence: Research Methods

Correlations

Throughout this text and already in this chapter, we have made statements such as "Adolescents who work long hours do less well in school than those who do not" and "Adolescents who watch a lot of violent television are more aggressive than those who do not." Statements such as these describe **correlations,** or relationships between factors or situations. A correlation can be **positive,** meaning that as one factor increases, so does the other. For example, the sentence "Income level and years of schooling are positively correlated" means that the higher someone's income, the more years he or she probably attended school. A correlation can also be **negative,** meaning that as one factor increases, the other decreases. For example, the statement "Weight and popularity are negatively correlated in Caucasian adolescent girls" means that the heavier a girl is, the less likely she is to be popular. Negative correlations are just as meaningful, and can be just as strong, as positive correlations: the difference between them lies in the direction of the relationship, not in its magnitude or certainty.

The most important thing to understand about correlations is that they do not imply *causation*. Many individuals will read a statement such as "Adolescents with high IQ scores do well in school" to mean that having a high IQ score *causes* someone to get good grades. This is a common mistake in interpretation.

Whenever a correlation exists, there are four possible explanations for its occurrence. One is that A might cause B. Having a high IQ score might indeed help you get good grades. Equally possible, however, is that B might cause A. That is, getting good grades and learning a lot in school might help you do well on an IQ test. There is a third possibility as well: that A and B mutually reinforce each other, that A causes B *and* B causes A. Having a high IQ score helps you do well in school, and because you do well in school you enjoy it and work hard at your studies, further increasing your IQ score. The fourth possibility, and the one that must always be kept in mind, is that A and B are not directly related to each other. Instead, some other factor, C, might cause both A and B. For example, an adolescent whose parents spend a good deal of time talking with him or her about how to solve problems might do well in school and have a high IQ. Having these discussions might independently promote getting good grades and might also help a teen do well on an IQ test. It is only coincidental that A and B occur together.

FIGURE 1.6   FOUR POSSIBLE CAUSAL PATHWAYS RESPONSIBLE FOR A CORRELATION

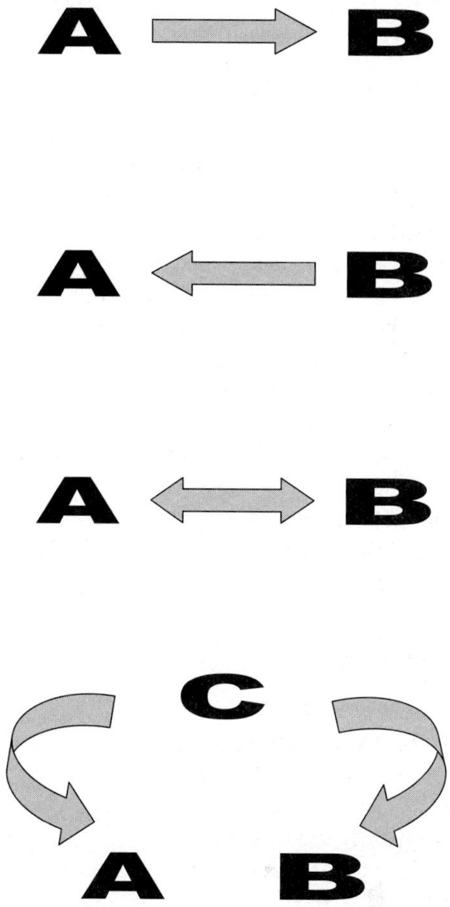

An example I often use in my intro psych class is this: there is a strong positive correlation between the number of ice cream cones purchased on a given day and the number of persons rushed to the hospital for heat stroke. Do you seriously believe the waffle cone I buy causes your uncle Fred to develop heat stroke? Of course not. The reason for the correlation is that there is a third, up-until-now unidentified factor—the temperature—that is independently causing both my desire for ice cream and your uncle Fred's heat stroke. The lesson is this: when you read this text (or another text or a newspaper or magazine article), do not make the mistake of assuming that the factor described in the first half of a correlation caused the second factor. (See Figure 1.6.)

correlation   a description of a relationship between two factors that does not imply a causal relationship between them.

positive correlation   a description of a relationship in which when one factor increases, so does the other.

negative correlation   a description of a relationship in which when one factor increases, the other decreases.

True vs. Quasi-Experiments

Why do we describe so many correlations if we cannot draw causal conclusions from them? The answer is twofold. First, correlations do provide valuable information. In particular, they let us make predictions about which adolescents are or are not likely to have a particular experience. For example, because I know that there is a negative correlation between academic success and dropping out, I will concentrate my dropout prevention dollars on students who are doing poorly in school, not those with B+ averages.

Second, many of the issues we are most interested in—gender differences, age differences, ethnic differences, and socioeconomic differences—cannot be studied in such a way as to make reaching a causal conclusion possible. In order to be able to validly draw a causal conclusion, the researcher must have conducted a **true experiment.** In a true experiment, the researcher has control over the situation and its participants. He or she can ensure that the groups of participants are identical in all relevant ways before the study begins and that they have the same experiences while the study is ongoing (with the exception of the one issue being examined).

For example, if an educational psychologist wanted to determine whether viewing a particular "Don't drink and drive" film would decrease adolescents' inebriated driving behavior, she could set up an experiment. She could go to a high school and randomly divide all the students into two groups. (This is how researchers usually ensure that the participant groups are comparable before the intervention is performed.) She could then show one group of students the drunk-driving film and the other group a film about car maintenance. After waiting a period of time, perhaps two months, the researcher could survey all of the students, asking how often within the past month they had driven while intoxicated. If the students who watched the alcohol-related film were less likely to have driven while inebriated than the students who saw the neutral film, she could then validly conclude that watching the film *caused* a decrease in driving while drinking.

Much of the time, however, researchers do not have this degree of control. In particular, they cannot be sure that the participant groups they have identified (rich versus poor, males versus females) are the same in all ways except for the issue being examined. Why? In a true experiment, the participants are randomly assigned to conditions, but in a

RESEARCH HIGHLIGHT   TEENS WHO KILL FAMILY MEMBERS

Another kind of family violence is perpetrated by the adolescent himself or herself. It includes *parricide*, the killing of a parent (which includes both *patricide*, the murder of a father, and *matricide*, the killing of a mother) and *siblicide*, the murder of a sibling. Although literary examples abound of such behavior—for example, Oedipus Rex, Cain and Abel—in fact, such behavior is sensational but uncommon. About 300 to 400 deaths per year are due to parricide (Sacks, 1994); roughly equal numbers of siblicides occur (Underwood & Patch, 1999).

Most parricides—90 percent—are committed by White males ages 14 to 17 (Shon & Targonski, 2003). Matricides are less common than patricides and matricides by females are especially rare. The most common profile of a perpetrator is a 17- or 18-year-old male from a middle- or upper-middle-class family who has no history of violent behavior. He usually acts alone and not in immediate self-defense, although most typically he has been repeatedly abused by his parent(s) (Hart & Helms, 2003). Research is contradictory as to whether these perpetrators are likely to have a psychological disorder, as some studies find that they do (e.g., Bourget, Gagne, & Labelle, 2007), while others find they do not (e.g., Hart & Helms, 2003).

Adolescents use different weapons when attacking their mothers or fathers, most likely because their fathers are usually bigger and stronger than themselves whereas their mothers are not. Guns are used more consistently in father homicides: they are more quickly lethal and can accomplish their task from a distance. Mothers are attacked with a broader range of weapons (Heide & Petee, 2007).

Siblicides are similar to and different from parricides. Perpetrators and victims tend to be older, so that adolescents are not the individuals most commonly involved. Whatever the age, brothers are more likely to be involved as both the victim and the murderer; when sisters are involved, they are more likely to be victims than perpetrators. As with parricide, guns are the weapon of choice. Usually the murder closely follows an argument; alcohol or other drugs are unlikely to be in use (Underwood & Patch, 1999).

quasi-experiment, preexisting groups of individuals are studied. The researcher cannot say to a 14-year-old girl, "OK, for the purposes of my experiment, today you are a 14-year-old boy. Get in that group over there." If 14-year-old girls end up scoring differently than 14-year-old boys because experimental control was not maintained, the researcher will not be able to infer that this difference is caused by gender. For example, if we give 14-year-old girls and boys a math test, we might find that the boys do better than the girls. Does this have anything to do with gender directly? Maybe yes, maybe no. It might be that the boys, as a group, have taken more math classes, been more encouraged by their teachers, or not been teased by their peers for doing well in math. Without maintaining control, we cannot determine that gender per se caused the observed difference between the groups; other unspecified circumstances might have been more responsible. Again, it's essential not to jump to causal conclusions when you read quasi-experimental or correlational data.

Research Designs That Measure Developmental Change

Although there are an unlimited number of questions we might wish to ask about adolescents, in some ways the most fundamental one involves age change. We want to know whether adolescents differ from children, whether early adolescents differ from late adolescents, and whether late adolescents differ from young adults. We are interested in whether there is stability across the lifespan, both within individual persons (will Stan be the same at 16 as he is at 11?) and between groups of individuals (as a group, are 16-year-olds different from 11-year-olds?). There are a number of research techniques that are specifically designed to answer one or both of these questions, all of them *quasi-experimental.* Again, you cannot randomly assign individuals to age groups and so do not have experimental control.

Cross-Sectional Research

The simplest of these designs is the **cross-sectional study,** which compares a group of persons who are one age with a group of persons who are another age. For example, imagine that I was interested in the issue of whether teens become less anxious as they move through adolescence. One way I could study this is to go out and find 100 thirteen-year-olds, 100 sixteen-year-olds, and 100 nineteen-year-olds. I would have 300 participants in my research, 100 in each of three age groups. I could then measure their

anxiety levels in some way, giving the same test to all of my subjects.

Being a professional researcher, I would surely employ all sorts of fancy statistical analyses, but in essence what I would do next is compare the average scores of each group of subjects to one another. I would begin by calculating the mean scores for each group; imagine I found that the 13-year-olds averaged 70 on my test, whereas the 16-year-olds averaged a 55, and the 19-year-olds averaged a 32. Looking at the data, and assuming that a higher score indicates elevated anxiety levels, it seems that anxiety decreases from age 13 to age 19.

Not so fast, however. What if I looked more closely at the individual scores and realized that the 13-year-olds' scores ranged from 10–180, the 16-year–olds' scores ranged from 5–180, and the 19-year-olds' scores ranged from 0–140. Would I be as confident now in my conclusions? Would I be as confident had the scores ranged from 70–72, 50–60, and 27–32, respectively? I hope not! Determining that the groups' scores are different actually depends both upon the magnitude of the differences of their averages *and* the degree to which the scores in each group are similar to one another. (If you've taken statistics, you know this and understand that I am talking about examining means and standard deviations or variance.)

There is an obvious benefit to conducting cross-sectional research: you can get your results quickly. If my test is brief, I might be able to test all 300 of my subjects in a matter of a few weeks. However, there are limitations to this kind of research as well. One major drawback is that this design can never tell you whether traits are stable within individuals. Even if it were true that 20 percent of the subjects in each of my three age groups were highly anxious, I would have no way of knowing if the fretful 13-year-olds were the ones who were fretful at 16 or 19. Maybe, instead, many adolescents have short bouts of anxiety.

---

true experiment   a study in which the researcher maintains control to ensure there are no significant differences among his or her groups of participants before the study begins and that the different groups of participants have identical experiences (except for the one issue of interest).

quasi-experiment   a study in which the researcher compares preexisting groups.

cross-sectional study   a quasi-experimental study in which a group of persons who are one age is compared with a group of persons who are another age.

In addition, it is difficult to separate out true developmental differences from **cohort effects** in cross-sectional research. In the data set presented earlier, the 13-year-olds have the highest anxiety scores. Assuming that my measurement of anxiety was a good one, did I get this finding because younger adolescents truly are more anxious than older ones? Perhaps, instead, the 13-year-olds, who all attend middle school rather than high school, as do my other subjects, had an experience that my older subjects did not. Maybe there was a bomb scare or a school shooting in a middle school in a neighboring community that was highly publicized several weeks before I made my assessment. It would be possible that the middle schoolers were more affected by this incident than high schoolers. Cohort effects tend to increase between group differences and may make it seem that a true developmental difference exists when it does not.

Longitudinal Research

A very different approach to studying development is to conduct a **longitudinal study.** Longitudinal research begins with a single group of subjects and follows them as they age and mature. If, for instance, we were interested in determining whether individuals become more stubborn and dogmatic as they move through adolescence, we might find a group of 150 sixth-graders and give them a test to see how rigidly they cling to their ideas in the face of conflicting information. We could then wait several years and retest them, and then even call them back for a third testing when they were seniors in high school. (See Chapter 5 to see what our data might look like.)

There are two enormous benefits of conducting longitudinal research. First, because we are tracking the same individuals across time, we can get an idea of the temporal sequence by which events occur. These studies can help answer "chicken or egg" questions, such as whether teens are bullied because they are socially awkward or if they become socially awkward because they have been bullied. Although, as stated before, one must always be cautious about drawing firm causal conclusions from quasi-experimental data, one factor can cause another only if it precedes it in time. Therefore, if it turns out that teens are socially awkward before they are bullied, then we can logically conclude that the bullying did not cause their awkwardness. (We are on shakier ground if we try to conclude that their awkwardness caused them to be bullied.)

The second benefit of longitudinal research is that you can track trait stability within an individual. Using this technique, we can ascertain, as we could not with a cross-sectional study, if the anxious 13-year-old becomes the anxious 16-year-old who becomes the anxious 19-year-old. This is enormously important to know, as it has tremendous implications for the timing of and need for intervention.

There are downsides to longitudinal research as well. The first is that longitudinal research is, as its name implies, *long*. If a researcher is going to follow individuals from the time they are 12 to the time they are 20, she must wait eight years to collect her data. Another is that it is difficult to keep track of subjects over many years, and so fewer subjects are tested at the end than at the beginning of the study. This is not a large problem if the subjects withdraw randomly, but often this is not the case. Adolescents from lower-income families, for example, move more frequently than middle-class adolescents; this is also true of teens whose parents have divorced. The result is that the pool of subjects tested at the end of the study might be different in some significant ways than it was in the beginning, and this can result in misleading data. In addition, depending upon the nature of the study, sometimes there is a question of whether repeated participation in the study itself (**testing effects**) is coloring the results obtained in later years. Finally, cohort effects can also occur: it is possible to see the same surge in anxiety described earlier in a longitudinal study as well as in a cross-sectional one, and the question remains whether the occurrence is a true age effect or a result of a specific environmental condition that occurred at that precise time.

Cross-Sequential Research

Beginning in the 1990s, a new research design began to be used that was a hybrid of cross-sectional and longitudinal approaches. It was termed **cross-sequential design** or time-sequential research (Schaie, 1996). Although it takes longer to complete than cross-sectional studies, it is more efficient than longitudinal research and eliminates most of the problems associated with both of those two designs. Cross-sequential research begins by recruiting and testing subjects who are different ages—for example, 11, 14, and 17. These subjects are then retested at a later time or perhaps several different times, ideally until the age groups overlap: in this example, until the 11-year-olds are at least 14 and the 14-year-olds are at least 17. This does take three years, but at the end of that period, the researcher has collected data from subjects ranging in age from 11 to 20. Furthermore, the researcher can track individual differences and trait stability (something he couldn't have done with cross-sectional research) and there is less of a problem with subject dropout and testing effects (as there would be with longitudinal research). Also, examination of the data allows one to determine

Design	2011 Who is tested	2015 Who is tested
Cross-sectional	Group 1 (12 years old) Group 2 (14 years old) Group 3 (16 years old)	No testing done
Longitudinal	Group 1 (12 years old)	Group 1 (16 years old)
Cross-sequential	Group 1 (12 years old) Group 2 (14 years old) Group 3 (16 years old)	Group 1 (16 years old) Group 2 (18 years old) Group 3 (20 years old)

FIGURE 1.7 A COMPARISON OF CROSS-SECTIONAL, LONGITUDINAL, AND CROSS-SEQUENTIAL RESEARCH DESIGNS

whether group differences are truly due to maturation or are cohort effects (a potential confound in both of the other designs). Cross-sequential designs truly are the best of both worlds!

As you read descriptions of various studies throughout the text, keep in mind the benefits and limitations of the research design used. (See Figure 1.7 for an illustration of the differences of these three designs.)

cohort effects differences amongst individuals that are caused by historical events rather than by maturation or development.

longitudinal study a quasi-experimental study in which a group of people are tracked over time as they age.

testing effects a change in subject performance due not to age or maturation, but to repeated exposure to test materials.

cross-sequential design a research method in which subjects at several different ages are tracked over time.

SUMMARY

1. *Adolescence* is the period of growth between childhood and adulthood. It is usually considered to begin with puberty, but its ending is less clearly defined. It is often divided into early adolescence (ages 11 to 14), middle adolescence (15 to 17), and late adolescence (18 and older).

2. The various approaches to the study of adolescence include the biological, the cognitive, the psychosexual, and the social approaches.

3. The number of juveniles in the United States has been slowly but steadily increasing and will continue to do so. For a number of years, the increase had been less rapid, however, than that for other age groups, which means adolescents have been making up an ever smaller segment of the population. The relative size of the adolescent population has now stabilized. The American adolescent population is becoming increasingly diverse.

4. Because individuals born at about the same time experience the same historic events, different generations sometimes take on a predominant characteristic. There have been a number of identifiable cohorts since the beginning of the twentieth century, including the Lost Generation, the G.I. Generation, the Quiet Generation, the Baby Boomers, the members of Generation X, and the Millennial Generation.

5. Seven current societal changes are affecting the adolescent experience: the prolongation of adolescence, the presence of the Internet and other communication technologies, the changing job market, the need for a prolonged education, the changing family constellation, the sexual revolution, and the increased amount of exposure to violence.

6. In recent decades, adolescence has become greatly prolonged. Individuals in their twenties are less likely to be financially independent, to live in their own homes, to be married, or to have children than were adolescents in the past.

7. The Internet has had a profound effect on U.S. society. Cyberspace has opened up the world to adolescents in a way that would have been unimagined in the past. Almost any fact can be found, and people around the globe can be contacted.

8. Unfortunately, many materials that are inappropriate for children and adolescents have also become available on the Internet. Unintended exposure to pornography can be unsettling.

9. The world of work continues to evolve. The average employed full-time worker puts in more hours now than at any other time in the past 50 years. An increasingly greater number of women, even mothers, are employed outside the home. Adolescents are ever more likely to hold down jobs after school. These

changes all have the potential of decreasing contact among family members.

10. Adolescents today have more money of their own to spend, and the consumer industry has responded by directing marketing and products their way.

11. Because high-paying jobs demand increasingly sophisticated skills, education is becoming more prolonged. More and more adolescents are graduating from high school, and to a lesser degree, more are graduating from college. Career-focused education is becoming more common.

12. Fewer individuals are marrying, and more are remaining single longer before they marry. Those who do marry are having fewer children. Most families have become more democratic and child centered.

13. More adolescents are being raised for at least part of their lives in a single-parent home. This is due to increases in both the nonmarital birthrate and the divorce rate.

14. Members of U.S. society are more open today about sexuality than they were in the past. This has had some positive effects—for example, the increased availability of information and contraception—but it has had some negative consequences, as well—such as increases in the prevalence of adolescent pregnancy and sexually transmitted diseases.

15. In part due to terrorism and school shootings, Americans have an increased awareness of the violence around them. Even though the crime rate is not climbing, individuals are more fearful of their personal safety than in the past.

16. It is important to understand that a *correlation* between two factors does not imply that they are causally related. Much of the research about adolescence is quasi-experimental, not true experimental research.

17. Three main research methods are used to measure developmental change: cross-sectional studies, longitudinal studies, and cross-sequential studies. Of the three, cross-sequential studies provide the most benefits and have the fewest shortfalls.

KEY TERMS

adolescence 4	longitudinal study 26
cohort effects 26	negative correlation 23
cohorts 7	positive correlation 23
correlation 23	puberty 4
cross-sectional study 25	quasi-experiment 25
cross-sequential design 26	teenager 4
	testing effects 26
emerging adulthood 9	true experiment 24
juvenile 4	youth(s) 4

THOUGHT QUESTIONS

Personal Reflection

1. Are you an adolescent? If not, when did your adolescence end and why? If you are an adolescent, when do you anticipate adolescence ending? Why then?
2. How has the Internet affected your life? How much time do you spend online and what activities do you do? Do you always accurately portray yourself or do you perform identity experiments?
3. Did you ever consider *not* going to college? Why did you choose to continue your education?
4. Ideally, how many hours per week would you like to work? Would you be willing to work 45 hours per week on a regular basis if your job was otherwise good? 50 hours per week?
5. Have you ever cohabitated? Would you? Why or why not?

Group Discussion

6. What criteria should be used to determine when adolescence ends? Why are these criteria important? Is there an upper age limit to adolescence?
7. How greatly will the so-called "graying of America" affect the adolescent experience?
8. Who is affected by adolescence becoming more prolonged? Who benefits? Who is harmed?
9. What can society do to encourage more students to go on to college?
10. The nuclear family was the standard in U.S. society for a long time. Why have so many alternative family structures become common in recent decades?
11. What have been the most important social changes during the years you've been growing up? How have these changes affected your life?

Debate Questions

12. Today's adolescents have too much independent spending money.
13. The sexual revolution has been more positive than negative.
14. Many young people are taking too long to become true adults.
15. Society is not any more violent than in the past.
16. The adolescent experience of the present generation is quite unique.

SUGGESTED READING

Arnett, J. J. (2004). *Emerging Adulthood: The Winding Road from the Late Teens through the Twenties.* New York: Oxford University Press.

Buckingham, D., and Willett, R. (Eds.). (2006). *Digital Generations: Children, Young People, and the New Media.* Mahwah, NJ: Erlbaum.

Chilman, C. S. (2001). *Adolescent Sexuality in a Changing American Society: Social and Psychological Perspectives.* Westport, CT: Greenwood Press.

Cornbleth, C. (2003). *Hearing America's Youth: Social Identities in Uncertain Times.* New York: Peter Lang.

Hoffman, A. M., and Summers, R. W. (2000). *Teen Violence: A Global Perspective.* Westport, CT: Greenwood Press.

Mortimer, J. T., and Larson, R. W. (2002). *The Changing Adolescent Experience: Societal Trends and the Transition to Adulthood.* Cambridge, England: Cambridge University Press.

WOULDN'T YOU LIKE TO KNOW...

- How did the first psychologist who studied adolescents characterize them?

- What did Sigmund Freud think about adolescents?

- What do most psychologists believe is *the* most important task of adolescence?

- In what ways are adolescents more intelligent than children?

- To what extent does merely observing others' behavior influence adolescents?

- How does modern American society marginalize adolescents?

- How does modern American culture make the adolescent transition to adulthood more difficult than it otherwise might be?

- Is adolescence inevitably a difficult time of life?

chapter 2

Adolescents in Theoretical Context

Biological Views of Adolescence
G. Stanley Hall: *Sturm und Drang* ▪ Arnold Gesell: Spiral Growth Patterns

Psychoanalytical and Psychosocial Views of Adolescence
Sigmund Freud: Individuation ▪ Anna Freud: Defense Mechanisms ▪ Erik Erikson: Ego Identity

Cognitive Views of Adolescence
Jean Piaget: Adaptation and Equilibrium ▪ Lev Vygotsky: Social Influences on Cognition

Social Learning View of Adolescence
Albert Bandura: Social Learning Theory
Social-Cognitive Theory
RESEARCH HIGHLIGHT *Scaffolding in Course-Related Bulletin Boards*

The Impact of Culture on Adolescents
Robert Havighurst: Developmental Tasks ▪ Kurt Lewin: Field Theory ▪ Urie Bronfenbrenner: Ecological Systems Theory
▪ Margaret Mead and Ruth Benedict: Anthropological Views
PERSONAL ISSUES *When Do Adolescents Become Adults?*
RESEARCH HIGHLIGHT *How Troubled Are Adolescents?*

Another way to answer the question from Chapter 1 *What is adolescence?* is to look at it from different points of view. In this book, we draw on the studies of biologists, psychiatrists, psychologists, economists, sociologists, social psychologists, and anthropologists. This chapter begins by surveying the views of a few representative and influential scholars from these disciplines. Later on, we revisit some of these views as we take a closer look at various aspects of adolescence. By understanding different viewpoints, we gain a truer, more complete picture of adolescence.

The theories presented in this chapter are arranged in order from most to least biologically based. Biological theorists—primarily biologists and psychologists—believe that adolescents are the way they are because of their genes, hormones, or evolutionary history. These theorists downplay environmental influences and tend to believe that the adolescent experience is similar regardless of where someone is raised. The less biologically based theorists—behaviorally oriented psychologists, anthropologists, and sociologists—believe that both immediate personal experience and culture shape adolescence. It follows that they believe that adolescents may be different from one another, depending on the specific events that have occurred during their lives.

Biological Views of Adolescence

A strictly *biological view* of adolescence defines this period as one of physical and sexual maturation, during which important growth changes take place in the child's body. In this section, we outline these physical, sexual, and physiological changes; their reasons (when known); and their consequences.

The biological view emphasizes biogenetic factors as the primary cause of any behavioral and psychological changes in the adolescent. Growth and behavior are under the control of internal maturational forces, leaving little room for environmental influences. Development occurs in an almost inevitable, universal pattern, regardless of the sociocultural environment. According to some theoreticians, these patterns were formed as a result of evolutionary pressures and natural selection.

G. Stanley Hall: *Sturm und Drang*

If there is a "father of adolescent psychology," it is G. Stanley Hall (1844–1924), as he was the first person to take a scientific approach to the study of adolescence. His two-volume book—*Adolescence: Its Psychology and Its Relation to Physiology, Anthropology, Sociology, Sex, Crime, Religion, and Education*,

published in 1904—is considered by many to be the first serious work in the field.

Hall was captivated by Charles Darwin's theory of evolution: namely, that humans evolved from more primitive life-forms through a process of *natural selection* ("the survival of the fittest"). Like Darwin, Hall believed that "ontogeny recapitulates phylogeny," which means that an individual's growth and development (ontogeny) mirrors or parallels (recapitulates) the evolutionary history (phylogeny) of its species. Hall applied this idea to the study of human, particularly adolescent, behavior.

According to Hall, after moving through the animal, hunter, and savagery stages—infancy, childhood, and preadolescence, respectively—adolescents found themselves in a period of **sturm und drang.** This German phrase means "storm and stress," and it reflects Hall's view of the turbulent nature of adolescence. He believed that adolescents are on an emotional seesaw: giddy one moment and depressed the next, apathetic today and impassioned tomorrow. These vacillations between emotional extremes, Hall thought, lasted until a person was in his or her early twenties. Furthermore, little could be done to prevent them since they were genetically based.

Although psychologists no longer subscribe to Hall's views that adolescence is inevitably difficult, he was instrumental in inspiring others to study adolescence. Moreover, his negative views of the adolescent experience were picked up by others, such as Sigmund Freud (see pp. 34–35).

Arnold Gesell: Spiral Growth Patterns

Arnold Gesell (1880–1961) is known for observations of human development from birth to adolescence that he and his staff made at the Yale Clinic of Child Development and later at the Gesell Institute of Child Development. His best-known book on adolescence is *Youth: The Years from Ten to Sixteen* (Gesell & Ames, 1956). Gesell was a student of G. Stanley Hall's and learned much from him.

Gesell was interested in the behavioral manifestations of development. He observed the actions and behavior of children and youths at different ages and constructed descriptive summaries of the stages of

ANSWERS WOULDN'T YOU LIKE TO KNOW . . .

How did the first psychologist who studied adolescents characterize them?

G. Stanley Hall, the "father of adolescent psychology," thought that adolescents were by nature emotionally volatile and unstable.

Hall theorized that adolescence is a turbulent time of life—one characterized by vacillations between emotional extremes.

development. In his summaries, he described what he believed were the norms of behavior in their chronological sequences.

Gesell believed that genes determine the order of appearance of behavioral traits and developmental trends. Thus, abilities and skills appear without the influence of special training or practice. This concept implies a sort of biological determinism that prevents teachers and parents from doing anything to influence human development. Because maturation is regarded as a natural ripening process, it is assumed that time alone will solve most of the minor problems that arise in raising children. Difficulties and deviations will be outgrown, claimed Gesell, so parents were advised against overreacting to misbehavior.

Gesell did try to allow for individual differences, accepting that each child is unique, born with his or her own "genetic factors or individual constitution and innate maturation sequences" (Gesell & Ames, 1956, p. 22). But he emphasized that "acculturation can never transcend maturation" because maturation is of primary importance. In spite of accepting individual differences and some influence of environment on individual development, Gesell nevertheless considered many trends and sequences to be universal among humans.

Although Gesell tried to emphasize that changes are gradual and overlap, his descriptions often indicate profound and sudden changes from one age to the next. He emphasized also that development is not only upward but also spiral, characterized by both upward and downward changes that cause some repetition at different ages. For example, he believed that both 11- and 15-year-olds are generally rebellious and quarrelsome, whereas 12- and 16-year-olds are fairly stable.

One of the chief criticisms of Gesell's work concerns his sample. He drew his conclusions from boys and girls of high socioeconomic status in New Haven, Connecticut. He contended that such a homogeneous sample would not lead to false generalizations. (This is in keeping with his belief that environmental influences are unimportant.) However, even when only physical factors are considered, children differ so greatly in the level and timing of their growth that it is difficult to establish precise norms for any age. Nevertheless, Gesell's books were used by thousands of parents and exerted tremendous influence on child-rearing practices during the 1940s and 1950s. The books were considered the "child-development bibles" for many students and teachers during those years.

Psychoanalytical and Psychosocial Views of Adolescence

Sigmund Freud was a Viennese physician who became interested in neurology, the study of the brain and nervous disorders. He was the originator of psychoanalytical theory. His daughter, Anna Freud, applied his theory to adolescents. Freud's perspective, although intrinsically psychological in nature, has a strong biological flavor because he believed that

sturm und drang   "storm and stress"; used to describe the volatile adolescent temperament.

"biology is destiny." That is, he believed that males and females, because of differences in the anatomy of their genitals, would necessarily have dissimilar experiences and hence turn out different from each other.

Sigmund Freud: Individuation

Sigmund Freud (1856–1939) was not greatly involved with theories on adolescence, for he considered the early years of a child's life to be the formative ones. He did, however, deal briefly with adolescence in his *Three Essays on the Theory of Sexuality* (Freud, 1953b). He described adolescence as a period of sexual excitement, anxiety, and sometimes personality disturbance. According to Freud, puberty is the culmination of a series of changes destined to give infantile sexual life its final, adult form. During the period of infancy, when pleasure is linked with oral activities (the **oral stage**), children derive pleasure from objects outside their own bodies: their mother's breasts. From these objects, they derive physical satisfaction, warmth, and security. While the mother feeds her infants, she also cuddles, caresses, kisses, and rocks them (Freud, 1953b).

Gradually, children's pleasures become autoerotic; that is, children begin to derive pleasure and satisfaction from activities that they can carry on by themselves. As they give up sucking at their mother's breasts, they find they can still derive pleasure from other oral activities. They learn to feed themselves, for example. At around age 2 or 3, much concern and pleasure centers on anal activities and elimination (the **anal stage**). This period is followed by a developing interest in their own bodies and in the examination of their sex organs during the **phallic stage** (ages 4 and 5) of development.

During the next period, which Freud termed the **latency stage** (roughly from age 6 to puberty), children's sexual interests do not appear to be as intense. Although Freud believed that children's sexual urges had temporarily dried up, more recent research suggests that they merely go underground (e.g., Thanasiu, 2004). Children's source of pleasure gradually shifts from self to other people. They become more interested in cultivating the friendship of others, especially those of the same sex.

At puberty (the **genital stage**), this process is brought to completion. Along with maturation of the external and internal sexual organs comes a strong desire to resolve the sexual tension that follows. This resolution demands a love object; therefore, Freud theorized, adolescents are drawn to other people—usually members of the opposite sex—who can resolve their tensions.

Freud believed that beginning with the phallic stage (ages 4 to 6), males and females have different personalities and engage in different behaviors because of differences in their anatomy. Their progression through

the phallic stage is necessarily dissimilar. Boys undergo what Freud termed the *Oedipal complex*. (The name comes from the protagonist in the Greek tragedy *Oedipus Rex*. In that play, Oedipus is a king who kills his father and marries his mother.) Essentially, boys become jealous of their mothers' attention toward their fathers and believe, unconsciously, that their fathers must be equally jealous of their mothers' attention toward them. Boys fear that their fathers will try to hurt them and remove them as sexual rivals (which is called *castration anxiety*). In order to reduce this anxiety, they *identify* with their fathers. **Identification** involves absorbing their fathers' beliefs, behaviors, and values and serves two functions: (1) It reduces castration anxiety, since such imitation is flattering to the fathers and reduces conflict between father and son and (2) it teaches the boy how to behave like a man, enabling him to find a wife of his own when he matures. Because castration anxiety is so stressful, boys work very hard at identification and develop well-rounded personalities.

Girls do not become jealous of their fathers, nor do they experience the Oedipal complex; instead, they must work their way through the *Electra complex*. (Electra was also a character in a Greek tragedy. She incited her brother to kill her mother to avenge her father's murder.) According to Freud, girls at this age are attracted to their fathers because they are seen as strong and powerful and because they are male. Once girls come to recognize the differences between male and female genitals, they become envious of boys because of their perception that penises are better than vulvas (which is called *penis envy*). Girls become hostile toward their mothers, whom they blame for their inferior genitals and because they resent the attention that their fathers give to their mothers. Girls only reluctantly identify with their mothers: they have attracted husbands, which is good, but they are only females, which is bad. Freud blamed the Electra complex and its resulting weak identification for the many negative personality traits—such as a low level of morality, excessive modesty, and lack of sex drive—that he thought were intrinsic to women.

Freud believed that by the end of childhood, children have identified with their same-sex parents and are emotionally dependent on them. A central task of adolescence, then, is to break these close emotional ties so that adolescents can become independent adults. This process, termed **individuation,** involves a differentiation of an individual's behavior, feelings, judgments, and thoughts from those of his or her parents. At the same time, the parent-child relationship moves toward growing cooperation, equality, and mutuality as the child becomes an autonomous person within the family context (Mazor & Enright, 1988).

Few psychologists endorse Freud's views today. He was a product of Victorian times, in which it was presupposed that women were weak, inferior beings. His theory, although groundbreaking in its willingness to acknowledge the importance of human sexuality, swung too far in the other direction and overemphasized the role of sexual urges in controlling behavior. In addition, **psychoanalytic theory** has a negative bias, claiming that people are ruled by selfish, hostile, demanding urges. This negativism most likely arose because Freud developed his theory by working with hospitalized mental patients, rather than more typical individuals. Also, most psychologists would say that Freud exaggerated the importance of early experiences and saw personality as more fixed than it really is.

Still, it is important to recognize Freud's enormous contribution to our understanding of behavior. If he had done nothing except invent the concept of the unconscious, he would be remembered for centuries.

Anna Freud: Defense Mechanisms

Anna Freud (1895–1982), daughter of Sigmund Freud, was more concerned with the period of adolescence than her father was. She elaborated more on the process of adolescent development and the changes in the psychic structure of the child at puberty (Freud, 1946, 1958).

Anna Freud characterized adolescence as a period of internal conflict, psychic disequilibrium, and erratic behavior. Adolescents are, on the one hand, egoistic, regarding themselves as the sole object of interest and the center of the universe but, on the other hand, also capable of self-sacrifice and devotion. They form passionate love relations, only to break them off suddenly. They sometimes desire complete social involvement and group participation and at other times solitude. They oscillate between blind submission to and rebellion against authority. They are selfish and materialistic but also full of lofty idealism. They are ascetic yet indulgent, inconsiderate of others yet touchy themselves. They swing between optimism and pessimism, between indefatigable enthusiasm and sluggishness and apathy (Freud, 1946).

According to Anna Freud, the reasons for this conflicting behavior are the psychic disequilibrium and internal conflict that accompanies sexual maturation at puberty, with its most obvious change being an increase in the instinctual drives. This is due partly to sexual maturation, with its accompanying interest in genitalia

vidual. The ego is the evaluative, reasoning p
the individual. By **superego,** Anna Freud meant the conscience that results from identification with the

oral stage   the first psychosexual stage in Sigmund Freud's theory of development: from birth to one year, during which the child's chief source of pleasure and satisfaction comes from oral activity.

anal stage   the second psychosexual stage in Sigmund Freud's theory of development: the second year of life, during which the child seeks pleasure and satisfaction through anal activity and the elimination of waste.

phallic stage   the third psychosexual stage in Sigmund Freud's theory of development: from about the fourth to the sixth year, during which the genital area is the chief source of pleasure and satisfaction.

latency stage   the fourth psychosexual stage in Sigmund Freud's theory of development: from about ages 6 to 12, during which sexual interests remain hidden while the child concentrates on school and other activities.

genital stage   the last psychosexual stage in Sigmund Freud's theory of development, during which sexual urges result in seeking other persons as sexual objects to relieve sexual tension.

identification   the taking on of parental values, beliefs, and behaviors.

individuation   the formation of personal identity by the development of the self as a unique person separate from parents and others.

psychoanalytic theory   Freud's theory that the structure of personality is composed of the id, ego, and superego and that mental health depends on keeping the balance among them.

id   according to Sigmund Freud, those instinctual urges that a person seeks to satisfy according to the pleasure principle.

ego   according to Sigmund Freud, the rational mind that seeks to satisfy the id in keeping with reality.

superego   according to Sigmund Freud, that part of the mind that opposes the desires of the id by enforcing moral restrictions that have been learned to try to attain a goal of perfection.

ANSWERS WOULDN'T YOU LIKE TO KNOW …

What did Sigmund Freud think about adolescents?

Sigmund Freud believed that adolescents are anxious and moody because they are plagued by newly awakened sexual urges.

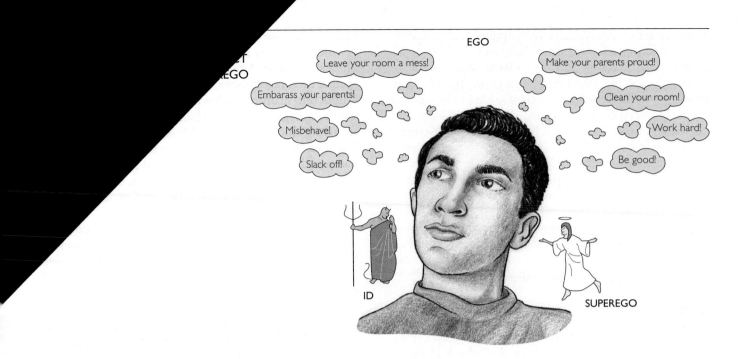

same-sex parent (see Figure 2.1). Therefore, the renewed vigor of the instincts at adolescence directly challenges the reasoning abilities and the conscience of the individual. The careful balance achieved between these psychic powers during latency is overthrown as open warfare breaks out between the id and superego. The ego, which previously had been able to enforce a truce, has as much trouble keeping the peace now as does a weak-willed parent when confronted by two strong-willed children who are quarreling. If the ego allies itself completely with the id, "no trace will be left of the previous character of the individual and the entrance into adult life will be marked by a riot of uninhibited gratification of instinct" (Freud, 1946, p. 163). Conversely, if the ego sides completely with the superego, the id's impulses will be confined within the narrow limits prescribed for the child, but a constant expenditure of psychic energy will be needed to hold these impulses in check.

If this id-ego-superego conflict is not resolved at adolescence, the consequences can be emotionally devastating to the individual. Anna Freud discussed how the ego uses **defense mechanisms** to win the battle. The ego represses, displaces, denies, and reverses the instincts and turns them against the self. According to Anna Freud, the rise of asceticism and intellectualism at adolescence is a symptom of mistrust of all instinctual wishes. She did believe, however, that harmony among the id, ego, and superego is possible and does occur finally in most normal adolescents. This balance is achieved if the superego is sufficiently developed during the latent period—but does not inhibit the instincts too much, which would cause extreme guilt and anxiety—and if the ego is sufficiently strong and wise to mediate the conflict (Freud, 1946).

Erik Erikson: Ego Identity

Erik Erikson (1902–1994) became interested in psychoanalysis after meeting Anna Freud. He trained at Freud's Vienna Psychoanalytic Institute but later modified Freud's theories. Although Erikson retained many of Freud's concepts, including the id-ego-superego triangle of personality components, he placed considerably less emphasis on the id's basic biological urges than did Freud. Instead, Erikson believed that the ego was the driving force behind much of behavior.

Erikson described eight stages of human development (Erikson, 1950, 1968, 1982). In each stage, the individual has a psychosocial task to master. Confronting each task produces conflict, with two possible outcomes. If the conflict is resolved successfully, a positive quality is built into the personality and further development takes place. If the conflict persists or is resolved unsatisfactorily, the self is damaged because a negative quality is incorporated into it. According to Erikson, the overall task of the individual is to acquire a *positive ego identity* as he or she moves from one stage to the next (Erikson, 1959). Table 2.1 lists Erikson's eight stages, along with the age at which each stage occurs and a description of its possible positive and negative outcomes.

Although we are most concerned with *identity formation*—the event associated with stage 5, adolescence—it is useful to understand the four stages that come before it. Each stage builds on the previous ones, and the positive resolution of a stage is more ensured if the previous stages have been successfully negotiated. Adolescents who feel optimistic and secure, who are independent and curious, and who feel pride in their accomplishments—all qualities learned earlier in life in

TABLE 2.1   ERIKSON'S STAGES OF PERSONALITY

AGE GROUP	STAGE	OUTCOMES
1. **Infants** (birth–2 years)	Basic trust vs. mistrust	Optimism and serenity vs. pessimism and anxiety
2. **Toddlers** (2–4 years)	Autonomy vs. shame and doubt	Self-trust and independence vs. dependency and fear
3. **Preschoolers** (4–6 years)	Initiative vs. guilt	Curiosity and energy vs. boredom and apathy
4. **Grade-schoolers** (6–11 years)	Industry vs. inferiority	Ability to feel pride in accomplishment and to work hard vs. shame at lack of accomplishment
5. **Adolescents** (11–early 20s)	Identity vs. diffusion	A sense of one's current and future self vs. lack of commitment and instability
6. **Young adults** (early 20s–40)	Intimacy vs. isolation	Close, meaningful relationships vs. loneliness
7. **Middle-aged adults** (40–65 years)	Generativity vs. stagnation	Growth and giving to others vs. stasis and meaninglessness
8. **Elderly adults** (65+ years)	Ego integrity vs. despair	Acceptance of mortality vs. fear of death

previous stages—are more likely to be able to form an identity effectively.

Identity formation neither begins nor ends with adolescence but is a lifelong process. Its roots go back in childhood to the experiences a child has with his or her parents. Children begin to form self-concepts through these interactions: if their parents love them and treat them as worthy, they feel worthy; if their parents neglect or reject them, they are likely to believe themselves flawed. As children mature, interactions

defense mechanisms   according to Anna Freud, unrealistic strategies used by the ego to protect itself and to discharge tension.

The areas of interest shown in this girl's bedroom demonstrate that she has established a sense of personal identity, as defined by Erikson.

with peers and other meaningful adults continue to shape their sense of who they are. The community both molds and gives recognition to newly emerging individuals.

Erikson emphasized that the identity search is a normative crisis, a normal phase of increased conflict. During this time, the individual must establish a sense of *personal identity* and avoid the dangers of **identity diffusion,** or lack of personal identity. To establish identity requires individual effort in evaluating personal assets and liabilities and using these to achieve a clearer concept of who one is and what one wants to become. Adolescents who are actively engaged in identity exploration are more likely to evidence a personality pattern characterized by self-doubt, confusion, impulsivity, and conflict with parents and other authority figures (Kidwell, Dunham, Bacho, et al., 1995).

One intriguing aspect of Erikson's theory is his concept of adolescence as a **psychosocial moratorium,** a societally sanctioned intermediary period between childhood and adulthood, during which through free role experimentation the individual may find a niche in society (Erikson, 1959). Adolescence becomes a period of analyzing and trying various roles without the responsibility for assuming any one of them. Erikson acknowledged that the duration and intensity of adolescence vary in different societies, but that eventually a failure to establish identity results in deep suffering. It is interesting that, at present, the length of time it takes many individuals to create an identity has been increasing until well into their late twenties, so that a new stage of life—**emerging adulthood**—is being established. This newly recognized stage of life is discussed in the epilogue.

The adolescent who fails in the search for an identity will experience self-doubt and role confusion; such an individual may indulge in a self-destructive, one-sided preoccupation or activity. He or she will likely be preoccupied with the opinions of others or may turn to the other extreme of no longer caring what others think. He or she may withdraw or turn to drugs or alcohol in order to relieve the anxiety that identity diffusion creates.

Erikson emphasized that although the identity crisis is most pronounced at adolescence, a redefinition of one's ego identity may also take place at other periods of life—when individuals leave home, marry, become parents, get divorced, or change occupations, for example. The extent to which people are able to cope with these changes in identity is determined partly by the success with which they have first mastered the adolescent identity crises (Erikson, 1959).

Erikson's work on identity is extensively discussed in Chapter 6.

ANSWERS WOULDN'T YOU LIKE TO KNOW …

What do most psychologists believe is *the* most important task of adolescence?

Most psychologists believe that forming a personal identity is the single most important task of adolescent development.

Cognitive Views of Adolescence

Cognition is the act or process of knowing. It is the mental activity or thinking involved in understanding. The cognitive theorists are discussed here (after the more biologically based theorists) because enhanced thinking skill depends in part on physical brain development. (No one believes that a 6-month-old could be taught to play chess.)

Jean Piaget, who began his career as a field biologist, retained a biological flavor in his views. He is often described as an **organismic psychologist;** that is, he believed that both brain maturation and personal experience drive cognitive development. Lev Vygotsky, the second cognitive theorist discussed, is known for his emphasis on the environmental determinants of cognitive growth.

Jean Piaget: Adaptation and Equilibrium

Jean Paul Piaget (1896–1980) was a Swiss psychologist who became interested in human cognitive development. More than anyone before him, Piaget changed people's conceptions and understandings of the cognitive resources of children. Piaget showed that from birth onward, children actively interact with their surroundings to make sense of their world.

Piaget began his work in Alfred Binet's Paris laboratory, where modern intelligence tests originated. He disagreed with Binet's insistence that intelligence is fixed and innate and began to explore higher-level thought processes (Piaget & Inhelder, 1969). Piaget became more interested in how children reached conclusions than in whether their answers were correct. Instead of asking questions and scoring them right or wrong, Piaget questioned children to find the logic behind their answers. Through painstaking observation of his own, as well as other, children, he began to construct his theory of cognitive development (Piaget, 1951, 1967, 1972).

Piaget taught that cognitive development is the combined result of environmental influences and the maturation of the brain and nervous system. He used five terms to describe the dynamics of development. A **schema** represents an original pattern of thinking, or a mental structure that a person uses when interacting with the environment. For example, when children see something they want, they learn to reach out to grasp it. They form a schema that is called for by the situation. By forming new schema and linking them together, children learn to adapt to their environment.

Adaptation means including and adjusting to new information that increases a person's understanding of the world around him or her. Adaptation takes place through two means: assimilation and accommodation. **Assimilation** means acquiring new information by integrating it into already existing structures in response to new environmental stimuli. **Accommodation** involves adjusting to new information by creating new schema to replace the old. For example, a child's pet golden cocker spaniel might give birth to a litter of black puppies. The child will thereby learn that cocker spaniels can be black as well as golden (assimilation). And if the child tries to pet a new puppy and it nips at him or her (something the mother dog would never do), he or she will learn that some dogs bite and some do not (accommodation).

Equilibrium involves achieving a balance between assimilation and accommodation. It means feeling comfortable because the reality that a person experiences is compatible with what he or she has been taught to believe. *Disequilibrium* arises when there is dissonance between reality and a person's comprehension of it; when disequilibrium occurs, further accommodation is necessary. Children resolve the conflict by acquiring new ways of thinking so that what they understand agrees with what they observe. The desire for equilibrium becomes the motivation that pushes children through the stages of cognitive development.

Piaget outlined four stages of cognitive development, which are discussed next.

Sensorimotor Stage (Birth to 2 Years)
During the sensorimotor stage, children learn to coordinate their physical actions and sensory experiences. Infants' senses of touch, hearing, vision, taste, and smell bring them into contact with various objects. As a result, they learn to reach for their bottles, move their arms and hands to pick up an object, and move their head and eyes to follow a moving object.

Preoperational Stage (2 to 7 Years)
During the preoperational stage, children acquire language and learn to use symbols, such as maps, to represent the environment. Preoperational children can deal with the world symbolically but still cannot think logically. The stage is termed *preoperational* because young children have not yet developed the mental operations needed for logical thought.

Concrete Operational Stage (7 to 11 Years)
During the concrete operational stage, children show some capacity for logical reasoning, although it relates only to things actually experienced. They intuitively understand a number of **mental operations,** overarching logical principles. For example, they understand that two glasses might contain the same amount of water even if they are different shapes because the fact that one is taller than the other *compensates* for the fact that it is thinner than the other. They also have learned that objects can belong to more than one category—a woman can be both a mom and a teacher—and that some categories are nested inside one another. Children are not as easily fooled by appearances as they previously were.

Formal Operational Stage (11 Years and Older)
During the formal operational stage, adolescents move beyond concrete, actual experiences and begin to think in more logical, abstract terms. They are able to engage in introspection, thinking about their thoughts. They are able to use systematic, propositional logic in solving problems and drawing conclusions. They are also able to use inductive reasoning, bringing a number of facts together and constructing theories on the basis of these facts. Adolescents can also use deductive reasoning in scientifically testing and proving theories and can use algebraic symbols and metaphorical speech as symbols. Additionally, they can think beyond what is to what might be, projecting themselves into the future and planning for it.

We discuss Piaget's stages of cognitive development in detail in Chapter 5.

identity diffusion   the failure to establish a personal identity.

psychosocial moratorium   a socially sanctioned period between childhood and adulthood during which an individual is free to experiment to find a socially acceptable identity and role.

emerging adulthood   the stage of life, generally extending through one's twenties, in which one is between adolescence and full adulthood.

cognition   the act or process of knowing.

organismic psychologist   someone like Piaget, who believes that both brain maturation and environmental experience are needed for cognitive development.

schema   the original patterns of thinking; the mental structures that people use for dealing with what happens in the environment.

adaptation   including and adjusting to new information that increases understanding.

assimilation   incorporating a feature of the environment into an existing mode or structure of thought.

accommodation   adjusting to new information by creating new structures to replace old ones.

equilibrium   according to Piaget, achieving a balance between schemas and accommodation.

mental operations   abstract reasoning principles that allow children to think logically.

FIGURE 2.2   COMPARISON OF PIAGET'S, FREUD'S, AND ERIKSON'S STAGES

The life cycle	Piaget's cognitive stages	Freud's psychosexual stages	Erikson's psychosocial stages
Late adulthood	↑	↑	Ego integrity vs. despair
Middle adulthood			Generativity vs. stagnation
Early adulthood			Intimacy vs. isolation
Adolescence	Formal operational	Genital	Identity vs. identity confusion
↑	↑	↑	↑
Middle and late childhood	Concrete operational	Latency	Industry vs. inferiority
↑	↑	↑	↑
Early childhood	Preoperational	Phallic	Initiative vs. guilt
Infancy	Sensorimotor	Anal Oral	Autonomy vs. shame, doubt / Trust vs. mistrust

ANSWERS WOULDN'T YOU LIKE TO KNOW ...

In what ways are adolescents more intelligent than children?

Adolescents are more intelligent than children because they can think abstractly and hypothetically. They are also more logical and can imagine things and events they have not actually experienced.

Lev Vygotsky: Social Influences on Cognition

Lev Vygotsky (1896–1934), a Russian psychologist who was originally trained as a teacher, had a view of cognitive development very different from that of Piaget. Whereas Piaget thought that cognitive development is an individual achievement brought about by the child's private explorations of his or her environment, Vygotsky (1978) believed that cognitive skill is developed through social interaction. According to Vygotsky, children learn best when they are paired with a more skilled partner with whom they work collaboratively to solve some problem. Learning is most rapid when the task is beyond the child's grasp but not so hard as to be overwhelming. This level of learning is called the **zone of proximal development.** Learning is also enhanced if the more expert helper provides **scaffolding** for the child—that is, if he or she provides assistance and then gradually withdraws that help as the child becomes able to complete the task alone. Vygotsky's theory has clear implications for teaching in that it strongly suggests that cooperative, group learning is a useful adjunct to or should even replace solitary, individual endeavors.

Social Learning View of Adolescence

Social learning theory is concerned with how the individuals around us shape our tendency to perform or not perform various behaviors.

Albert Bandura: Social Learning Theory

Albert Bandura (1925–) first developed social learning theory and has also been concerned with its application to adolescents. His view emphasizes that children learn through observing the behavior of others and by imitating this pattern—a process referred to as **modeling.** As children grow, they imitate different models from their social environment. In many studies, parents are identified as the most significant adults in the lives of adolescents and hence the persons most likely to be modeled. Siblings are also mentioned as significant others, as are friends and peers.

Many aspects of behavior may be modeled from parents. Some of these are good, constructive behaviors; for example, adolescents are more likely to participate in community service activities if their parents do so (Perry, Coursey, Brudney, et al., 2008). In other instances, however, adolescents copy the destructive behaviors that they observe their parents do. For example, adolescents whose fathers gamble heavily are more likely to gamble heavily themselves (Vachon, Vitaro, Wanner, et al., 2004), and it is well known that parents who physically discipline their offspring are likely to raise children who hit others when they are angry (e.g., Barry, 2007).

The Role of Reinforcement

The most well-known learning theory, Skinner's (1938) *operant conditioning theory,* emphasizes the dual roles of **reinforcement** (reward) and punishment on influencing the behaviors we perform. It is common sense that if a teenager is praised by his or her friends for skipping class, he or she will be more likely to skip class in the future. On the other hand, if the teen is caught and gets two weeks' worth of detention, that punishment might be sufficient to prevent him or her from skipping class again.

Bandura expanded on this idea, speaking of **vicarious reinforcement** and **self-reinforcement.** Vicarious reinforcement consists of the positive or negative consequences that one observes *others* experiencing. Observing that others are rewarded for aggressive behavior increases the possibility that the observer will also show aggression. Bandura (1973) observed that self-reinforcement was as effective as external reinforcement in influencing behavior. Once the performance of a desired response pattern, such as shooting and making baskets with a basketball, acquired a positive value, adolescents could administer their own reinforcement by producing the baskets and then feeling good afterward. Adolescents who set reasonable goal levels of performance and reach that level feel proud and satisfied internally and become less dependent on parents, teachers, and bosses to give them rewards.

The work of social learning theorists is of great importance in explaining human behavior. It is especially important in emphasizing that *what adults do and the role models they provide are far more important in influencing adolescent behavior than what they say.* Teachers and parents can best encourage human decency, altruism, moral values, and a social conscience by exhibiting these virtues themselves.

Social-Cognitive Theory

In the 1980s, Bandura expanded his social learning theory to include the role of cognition (Bandura, 1986, 1989). Rather than describing individuals as determined strictly by environmental influences, Bandura emphasized that they, in large measure, *determine their own destinies* by choosing their future environments as well as the goals they wish to pursue. People reflect on and regulate their own thoughts, feelings, and actions to achieve their goals. In short, the way they interpret environmental influences determines how they act. For example, consider again the behavior of aggressive boys. Research has shown that aggressive boys are biased in favor of attributing hostile intent to others in various situations (Crick & Dodge, 1996). Aggressive boys are not careful in processing information that would help them to determine whether the

zone of proximal development   the level of learning at which a task that is too difficult for a child to complete by himself or herself is manageable with help.

scaffolding   the assistance provided to help a child master a task; it is gradually withdrawn as the child gains competence.

modeling   learning by observing and imitating the behavior of another.

reinforcement   positive reinforcements are influences that increase the probability that the preceding response will occur again; negative reinforcements are influences that increase the probability that the preceding response will stop.

vicarious reinforcement   learning from observing the positive or negative consequences of another person's behavior.

self-reinforcement   the act of learners rewarding themselves for activities or responses that they consider of good quality.

intent of the action against them was hostile or benign. They pay less attention to information that would help them reach a more accurate inference about someone else's motives. Therefore, they are more likely to infer hostile intent when they come to conclusions quickly. In other words, it is not just what happens to these boys that determines the level of their aggression; it is also the way they interpret others' intentions.

Social-cognitive theory emphasizes that individuals can actively control the events that affect their lives, rather than having to passively accept whatever the environment provides; they partially control the environment by the way they react to it. A placid, pleasant, easy-to-care-for adolescent may have a positive influence on parents, encouraging them to act in a friendly, warm, and loving manner. However, an overactive, temperamental, hard-to-care-for adolescent who is easily upset may stimulate parents to be hostile, short-tempered, and rejecting. From this point of view, children—however involuntarily—are partly responsible for creating their own environments. Because of individual differences, different people, at different developmental stages, interpret and act on their environments in differing ways that create different experiences for each person (Bandura, 1986).

The Impact of Culture on Adolescents

We now consider a set of theorists who hold the perspective that adolescents' development is strongly influenced by the culture and society in which they are raised. (Vygotsky could easily have been placed in this section, and Erikson, too, wrote of the importance of culture on development.) If you recall, Hall and Gesell underscored the importance of biology in influencing development, Freud and Piaget wrote of the interplay between biology and experience, and Bandura was concerned with the effects of those individuals who directly interact with the adolescent. This next set of researchers stresses the importance of cultural norms, traditions, and values in influencing behavior.

Robert Havighurst: Developmental Tasks

In *Developmental Tasks and Education* (1972), Robert Havighurst (1900–1991) outlined what he believed were the major developmental tasks of adolescence. His developmental task theory is an eclectic one, combining previously developed concepts.

RESEARCH HIGHLIGHT   SCAFFOLDING IN COURSE-RELATED BULLETIN BOARDS

More and more college professors are using chat rooms and bulletin boards to facilitate discussions among the students in their classes (Berge, 2000). This is usually done in the hope that the students will learn from one another, and that the questions they pose will trigger a greater understanding of the course material. However, Vygotsky (1978) was quite clear in stating that individuals learn best from *experts* who *scaffold* their attempts at problem solving, not from other novices. Do online peer discussions foster learning? Can they?

The answers seem to be "Not always" and "Yes, they probably can, but only if the professor sets up the situation correctly." Students do not always know how to ask the kinds of questions that promote learning (van der Meij, 1998), and they may not have enough knowledge to be helpful (Land, 2000; van der Meij, 1990). Still, a number of studies have shown that it is possible for a teacher to provide external scaffolds that help students ask one another useful questions in a face-to-face classroom environment (e.g., King, Staffieri, & Adelgais, 1998), and so it seemed possible that online interactions could be similarly facilitated.

Choi, Land, and Turgeon (2005) attempted to do so for an online college course that contained several mandatory online discussion sessions. They developed scaffolds in the form of prompts to help students ask three different types of questions of one another during these sessions (clarification/elaboration questions; counterarguments/disagreements; and probing, hypothetical questions); the intent was to prompt the students to ask the sorts of questions that would help their peers gain a deeper understanding of the course material. Although the prompts succeeded in getting the students to ask *more* questions, the questions were not of higher quality. The authors explained the lack of positive effects by the limited knowledge that the students had of the subject material (they were novices, not experts) and the fact that the initial answers that the students were responding to were already of high quality, with few obvious flaws. Perhaps most important, many of the students failed to utilize the prompts; previous research has shown that this is a common problem (e.g., Greene & Land, 2000). Azevedo and his colleagues (e.g., Azevedo, Cromley, Winters, et al., 2005) have shown that dynamic, rather than static, prompts can significantly aid self-directed computer-assisted learning, and so interactive, individualized prompts might be the key to improving the quality of student-student chat room or bulletin board interactions. In any case, as Vygotsky believed, without intervention and guidance, novices are not as helpful to one another as are trained experts.

Havighurst sought to develop a psychosocial theory of adolescence by combining a consideration of individuals' needs with societal demands. What individuals need and society demands constitute the **developmental tasks.** They are the skills, knowledge, functions, and attitudes that individuals must acquire at certain points in their lives as a result of physical maturation, social expectations, and personal effort. Mastery of the tasks at each stage of development results in adjustment and preparation for the upcoming stage's tasks. Mastery of adolescent tasks results in maturity. Failure to master the adolescent tasks results in social disapproval and the inability to function as a mature person.

According to Havighurst, there exists a teachable moment—a correct time for teaching any task. Some of the tasks arise out of biological changes, others from societal expectations at a given age or the individual's motivation at certain times to do particular things. There are significant differences in developmental tasks in the upper, middle, and lower socioeconomic classes of the United States. Also, the demands and opportunities differ in various cultures, so that success is culturally defined, and the competencies required may differ (Brown, Larson, & Saraswathi, 2002).

Havighurst (1972) outlined eight major tasks that American youths face during the adolescent period:

1. *Accepting one's physique and using the body effectively:* One characteristic of adolescents is their emerging, often extreme, self-consciousness about their physical selves as they reach sexual maturity. Adolescents need to accept their physiques and the pattern of growth of their own bodies, to learn to care for their bodies, and to use their bodies effectively in sports, recreation, work, and everyday tasks.

2. *Achieving new and more mature relations with age-mates of both sexes:* Adolescents must move from the same-sex interests and playmates of middle childhood to establish cross-sex friendships. Becoming an adult also means learning the social skills and behaviors required in group life.

3. *Achieving a masculine or feminine social sex role:* What is a man? What is a woman? How should they behave? What are they supposed to be? Psychosexual social roles are established by each culture, but because masculine-feminine roles in Western culture have undergone rapid changes, part of the adolescent maturational process is to reexamine the changing sex roles of our society and decide which aspects of masculinity-femininity they wish to adopt.

4. *Achieving emotional independence from parents and other adults:* Adolescents must develop understanding, affection, and respect without emotional dependence. Typically, the frequency and duration of contacts between parents and adolescents decrease (Mooney, Laursen & Adams, 2006), and closeness with parents declines (McGue, Elkins, Walden, et al., 2005).

developmental tasks   the skills, knowledge, functions, and attitudes that individuals have to acquire at certain points in their lives in order to function effectively as mature persons.

One of the major developmental tasks during the adolescent period, as defined by Havighurst, is accepting one's physique and using it effectively.

5. *Preparing for an economic career:* One of the primary goals of adolescents is to decide on a career, prepare for that career, and then become independent by earning their own living. Part of the task is to discover what they want out of life.

6. *Preparing for marriage and family life:* Patterns of marriage and family living are being readjusted because of the changing economic, social, and religious characteristics of our society. The majority of youths desire a happy marriage and parenthood as one important goal in life and so they need to develop the positive attitudes, social skills, and emotional maturity to make marriage work.

7. *Desiring and achieving socially responsible behavior:* This goal includes the development of behavior that takes into account societal values. The goal also includes participation in the adult life of the community and nation. Adolescents must find their place in society in a way that gives meaning to their lives.

8. *Acquiring a set of values and an ethical system as a guide to behavior—developing an ideology:* This goal includes the development of a principled ideology and the adoption and application of meaningful values, morals, and ideals in one's personal life. Havighurst believed that many modern youth have not been able to achieve identity and therefore suffer from aimlessness and uncertainty.

Kurt Lewin: Field Theory

Kurt Lewin's (1890–1947) theory of adolescent development is outlined in his article "Field Theory and Experiment in Social Psychology: Concepts and Methods" (1939). This field theory attempts to explain why adolescents vacillate between mature and childish behavior and why they are so often unhappy.

Lewin's core concept is "that behavior (B) is a function (f) of the person (P) and of his environment (E)" (p. 34). To understand an adolescent's behavior, you must consider the individual's personality and the environment as interdependent factors. The sum total of all possible behaviors is called the life space (LSp). Unfortunately, not all areas of the life space are available to individuals.

Lewin compared the life space of a child with that of an adult. The child's life space is structured by what is forbidden and what is beyond his or her ability. As the child matures and becomes more capable, fewer restrictions are placed on his or her freedom, so the life space expands into new regions and experiences. By the time the child reaches adolescence, more regions have become accessible, but it is unclear which ones the adolescent is supposed to enter. Thus, the life space remains undefined and uncertain. The adult's space is

considerably wider, but it is still bounded by activities beyond ability or forbidden by society.

According to Lewin, adolescence is a period of transition during which group membership changes from childhood to adulthood. The adolescent belongs partly to the child group and partly to the adult group. Not only the adolescent, but the adults around him or her are unclear as to the adolescent's status. The result is that sometimes the teen is treated like an adult and given respect and responsibility, whereas at other times he or she is treated like a child and expected to obey without questioning and to be silent. The result is confusion and apparent willful misbehavior.

This bewilderment helps explain uncertainty in adolescent behavior. Lewin referred to the adolescent as the "marginal man," represented in Figure 2.3 by the overlapping area (Ad) of the child region (C) and the adult region (A). Being a marginal man implies that the adolescent may at times act more like a child, often when he or she

FIGURE 2.3　THE ADOLESCENT AS A MARGINAL MAN

(a) During childhood and adulthood, the "adults" (A) and "children" (C) are viewed as relatively separated groups. The individual child (c^1, c^2) and the individual adult (a^1, a^2) are sure of their belonging to their respective groups. *(b)* In adolescence, the adolescent is seen as belonging to a group (Ad) that can be viewed as an overlapping region of the children's (C) and the adults' (A) groups, belonging to both of them, or the adolescent is seen as standing between them, not belonging to either one.

Source: K. Lewin, "Field Theory and Experiment in Social Psychology: Concepts and Methods," *American Journal of Sociology, 44* (1939): 868–897. Copyright © the University of Chicago Press. Used by permission of the University of Chicago Press.

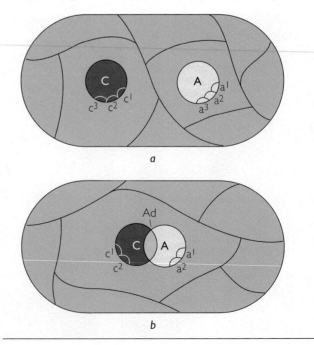

wants to avoid adult responsibilities; at other times, he or she acts more like an adult and requests adult privileges.

One of the strengths of Lewin's field theory is that it assumes both personality and cultural differences, so it allows for wide individual variations in behavior. It also allows for varying lengths of the adolescent period from culture to culture and from social class to social class within a culture.

Urie Bronfenbrenner: Ecological Systems Theory

Adolescents develop within the multiple contexts of their families, communities, and countries. They are influenced by peers, relatives, and other adults with whom they come in contact, and by the religious organizations, schools, and groups to which they belong. They are also influenced by the media, the cultures in which they are growing up, national and community leaders, and world events. They are partly a product of environmental and social influences.

Urie Bronfenbrenner (1917–2005) developed an ecological model for understanding social influences (1979, 1987). His perspective has firmly taken root over the past 30 years, and at present, it is one of the most widely accepted and influential approaches. As you can see in Figure 2.4, social influences may be grouped into a series of nested systems extending beyond the adolescent. The adolescent is at the center of the arrangement.

The Microsystem

The most immediate influences on the adolescent are within the **microsystem,** which include those with whom he or she has immediate contact. For most adolescents, the immediate family is the primary microsystem, followed by friends and school. Other components of the microsystem are health services, religious groups, neighborhood play areas, and various social groups to which the adolescent belongs.

microsystem   includes those persons with whom the adolescent has immediate contact and who influence him or her.

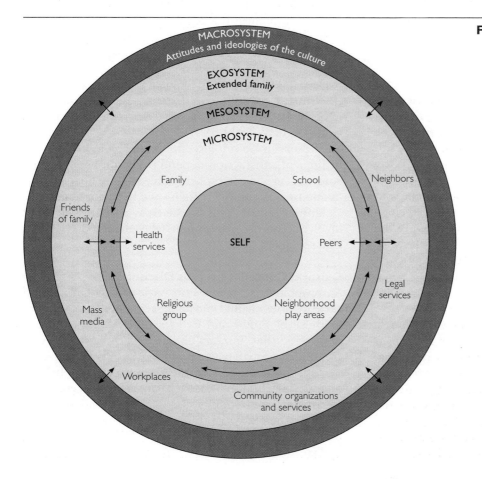

FIGURE 2.4 BRONFENBRENNER'S ECOLOGICAL SYSTEMS MODEL FOR UNDERSTANDING SOCIAL INFLUENCES

Microsystems change as the adolescent moves in and out of different social settings. For example, the adolescent may change schools, stop going to a particular church, mosque, or synagogue, drop out of some activities, and join others. In general, the peer microsystem increases in influence during adolescence, providing powerful social rewards in terms of acceptance, popularity, friendship, and status. The peer group may also exert negative influences, encouraging irresponsible sex, drug use, theft, or cheating. A healthy microsystem offers positive learning and development that prepares the adolescent for success in adult life.

The Mesosystem

The **mesosystem** involves reciprocal relationships among microsystem settings. For example, what happens at school influences what happens at home and vice versa. An adolescent's social development is understood best when the influences from many sources are considered in relation to one another. A mesosystem analysis would look at the frequency, quality, and influence of interactions, such as how family experiences are related to school adjustments, how family characteristics are related to peer pressures, or how religiosity is related to intimacy with the opposite sex.

The Exosystem

The **exosystem** is composed of those settings in which the adolescent does not play an active role but that nevertheless influence him or her. For example, what happens to the parents at work influences the parents, and they, in turn, influence the adolescent's development. The parents' bosses determine the rate of pay, work and vacation schedules, and the community in which the work will take place. If the company decides to move an employee, it affects the whole family. All of these factors influence the parents' relationships with their adolescent.

Similarly, community organizations affect the adolescent in many ways. For instance, the school board establishes the curriculum and the school calendar and hires the teachers. The town government may open or close a youth center or a swimming pool. Those in the exosystem make decisions that affect the adolescent, whose parents are concerned that their adolescent's best interests are kept in mind.

The Macrosystem

The **macrosystem** includes the ideologies, attitudes, mores, customs, and laws of a particular culture. It includes a core of educational, economic, religious, political, and social values. The macrosystem determines who is an adult and who is an adolescent. It sets standards of physical attractiveness and gender-role behavior and influences health practices such as smoking. It also influences educational standards and relationships between races and ethnic groups.

Macrosystems differ in various countries and in racial, ethnic, or socioeconomic groups. There are also differences within each group. In Sweden, for example, it is against the law for parents to hit children, yet the practice is condoned by some groups in the United States. Middle-class parents in the United States often have different goals and philosophies of child-rearing than do those in low-socioeconomic-status groups; rural families may have different parenting values than urban families. These values and customs have differential effects on adolescents. In talking about social development, then, we have to discuss issues and concerns in the contexts in which adolescents are growing up.

Margaret Mead and Ruth Benedict: Anthropological Views

The theories of Margaret Mead (1901–1978), Ruth Benedict (1887–1948), and other cultural anthropologists have been called **cultural determinism** and **cultural relativism** because, like Bronfenbrenner, anthropologists emphasize the importance of the broader *social environment* in determining the personality development of the child. Since social institutions, economic patterns, habits, rituals, and religious beliefs vary from society to society, culture is relative.

Anthropologists emphasize that the sociocultural milieu determines the course of adolescence and strongly influences the degree to which adolescents feel welcomed by the adult community. In modern society, adolescence has become a prolonged stage of development; its completion is imprecise and its privileges and responsibilities are often illogical and confused. This is in contrast to nontechnological societies, in which puberty rites mark a definite and early introduction into adulthood (Weisfeld, 1997).

Research on adolescents has revealed that their feelings of satisfaction depend partly on having some control over their lives, being able to have choices, and taking responsibility for their own behavior (Barker & Galambos, 2005). This is exactly what being an adult involves. This process is often delayed in modern industrial societies.

Cultural Continuity versus Discontinuity

Anthropologists challenge the basic truths of all age and stage theories of child and adolescent development (such as those of Freud and Erikson). Mead, for example, discovered that Samoan children followed a relatively continuous growth pattern, with no abrupt changes from one age to the other. They were not expected to behave one way as children, another way as adolescents, and yet another way as adults. Samoans never had to change abruptly their ways of thinking or acting, they did not have to unlearn as adults what they learned as children, and so adolescence did not represent an abrupt change

PERSONAL ISSUES   WHEN DO ADOLESCENTS BECOME ADULTS?

Adulthood is the stage of life recognized by cultures all over the world. In many nontechnological societies, the major criterion for attaining adulthood is that one has married (Schlegel & Barry, 1991). In addition, in Western societies, significant life changes, such as completing one's education, becoming a full-time worker, and establishing one's own home, have been assumed to be markers of social maturity (Goldscheider & Goldscheider, 1999). Are these the criteria used by adolescents and young adults?

The answer appears to be, largely, "no." A number of studies have shown that adolescents are more likely to believe that psychological, cognitive traits are more important than these social role markers. For example, Arnett (2001) found that almost 90 percent of the adolescents in his study believed that "accepting responsibility for one's actions" was necessary for adulthood, whereas fewer than 15 percent believed that "marriage" was needed. Similarly, the single most commonly cited

marker for adulthood given by adolescents in Barker and Galambos's (2005) study was "the ability to act responsibly"; this beat out living independently, being financially independent, or being out of school.

When do adolescents think that they will begin to accept responsibility and hence become adults? That depends upon their age. Generally, the older the teen, the older the person believes that adulthood will strike (Galambos & Vitunski, 2000). Most adolescents think that adulthood will descend upon them at an earlier age—perhaps 20 or 21—than they later would. Arnett (2001), however, discovered that somewhat fewer than half of the individuals in their twenties that he sampled believed they were "adults."

The findings of these studies are consistent with research suggesting that adulthood is an emerging process. This is a period of time (often in mid-adolescence) when youths begin to consider themselves adults—cognitively, emotionally, and behaviorally.

or transition from one pattern of behavior to another. This principle of *continuity of cultural conditioning* is illustrated with three examples from Benedict (1938) and Mead (1950):

1. *Responsible versus nonresponsible roles:* The responsible roles of children in nontechnological societies can be contrasted with the nonresponsible roles of children in Western culture. Children in nontechnological societies learn responsibility quite early. Play and work often involve the same activity; for example, by "playing" with a bow and arrow, a boy learns to hunt. His adult hunting "work" is a continuation of his youthful hunting "play." In contrast, children in Western culture must assume drastically different roles as they grow up. They shift from nonresponsible play to responsible work and must do it rather suddenly.

2. *Submissive versus dominant roles:* The submissive role of children in Western culture is contrasted with a more dominant role of children in many nontechnological societies. Children in Western culture must replace their childhood submission and adopt its opposite—dominance—as they become adults. Mead (1950) showed that Samoan children were not taught submission as children and then suddenly expected to become dominant when reaching adulthood. On the contrary, a 6- or 7-year-old Samoan girl dominated her younger siblings and in turn was dominated by the older ones. The older she got, the more she dominated and disciplined others and the fewer there were to dominate her. When she

became an adult, she did not experience the dominance-submission conflict that the adolescent in Western society generally does.

3. *Similar versus dissimilar sex roles:* The similarity of sex roles of children and adults in many nontechnological cultures is contrasted with the dissimilar sex roles of children and adults in Western culture. Mead indicated that the Samoan girl experienced no real discontinuity of sex roles as she passed from childhood to adulthood. She had the opportunity to experiment and become familiar with sex with almost no taboos (except against incest). Therefore, by the time she reached adulthood, the Samoan female was able to assume a sexual role in marriage very easily. By contrast, in Western culture, infant sexuality is denied and adolescent sexuality is

mesosystem   the reciprocal relationships among microsystem settings.

exosystem   that part of an ecological system that includes settings in which the adolescent does not have an active role as a participant but that influence him or her nevertheless.

macrosystem   the ideologies, attitudes, mores, customs, and laws of a particular culture that influence the individual.

cultural determinism   the influence of a particular culture in determining the personality and behavior of a developing individual.

cultural relativism   variations in social institutions, economic patterns, habits, mores, rituals, religious beliefs, and ways of life from one culture to another.

Adolescents in many non-Western societies are given important responsibilities. This Cambodian girl is harvesting rice to help feed her family.

ANSWERS WOULDN'T YOU LIKE TO KNOW . . .

How does modern American culture make the adolescent transition to adulthood more difficult than it otherwise might be?

Modern American culture is discontinuous, which means that adolescents must change their behaviors as they mature. Change is more difficult to cope with than continuity.

repressed; sex is considered sinful and dangerous. When adolescents mature sexually, they must unlearn those earlier attitudes and taboos to become sexually responsive adults.

Storm and Stress Revisited

Although the research on which Mead based her conclusions has been criticized by some (e.g., Freeman, 1983), her 1950 book, *Coming of Age in Samoa,* rocked the academic world. Since Hall's time, it had been taken for granted that adolescence was inevitably troublesome. Evidence of the existence of even one society in which adolescence was tranquil severely undermined

any and all biologically based interpretations of adolescent behavior.

In showing the continuity of development of children in some cultures, in contrast to the discontinuity of development of children in Western culture, anthropologists and some psychologists cast doubt on the universality of ages and stages of growth of children in all cultures.

Anthropologists challenge the inevitability of the storm and stress of adolescence by minimizing the impact of physical changes and by focusing on the interpretation of those changes. Menstruation is a case in point. One tribe may teach that the menstruating girl is a danger to the tribe (she may scare the game or dry up the well); another tribe may consider her condition a blessing (she could increase the food supply or the priest could obtain a blessing by touching her). A girl taught that menstruation is a blessing will react and act differently from a girl who is taught that it is a curse. Therefore, the stress and strains of pubescent physical changes may be the result of certain cultural interpretations of those changes and not to any inherent biological tendencies.

RESEARCH HIGHLIGHT   HOW TROUBLED ARE ADOLESCENTS?

Early theoreticians, philosophers, and writers almost unanimously declared that adolescents were disrespectful, angry, immoderate, and disruptive. Even today, many American adults certainly believe that adolescents are more problematic than younger children (Buchanan, Eccles, Flanagan, et al., 1990), and they believe teens to be lazy, rude, and selfish (Public Agenda, 1999). How accurate are these views?

After reviewing the available literature, Arnett (1999) concluded that those who believe in adolescent storm and stress are usually referring to one or more of three different types of behavior: (1) conflicts with others, especially parents and other authority figures; (2) mood swings; and (3) participation in risky behaviors. In each case, it appears that these problems are *more common* among adolescents than among persons of other ages. Certainly, this doesn't mean such behaviors are universal. Not all adolescents are

depressed, but a disproportionate number are. Not all adolescents engage in unsafe sexual practices or drive without seatbelts, but too many do. Nonetheless, this finding does, in part, substantiate the notion of *sturm und drang*.

Perhaps the more correct conclusion is that adolescents are *more likely* to experience significant difficulties than either children or adults. The opposite is also likely true: if a person was moody or behaved recklessly during some part of his or her life, it was most likely during adolescence. Yet there is little reason to fear, as some adolescents do, that life will be one long downhill slide after reaching adulthood. At the same time, though, it is important to keep in mind that the majority of adolescents do not get into serious trouble and that even when problems occur, they are often sporadic or transitory (Offer & Schonert-Reichl, 1992).

As another example, anthropologists believe that specific conditions within Western society, not biology, prompt parent-adolescent tension (Mead, 1974). In particular, the furious pace of social change, the diversity of available opinions, and the rapidity of technological development all converge, Mead and others would argue, to devalue parental views. Furthermore, early physiological puberty and the need for prolonged education allow many years for the development and assimilation of a peer-group culture in which adolescent values, customs, and mores may be in conflict with those in the adult world (Finkelstein & Gaier, 1983).

It might interest you to know that Mead believed adolescents should be given more freedom to make their own choices and live their own lives. By requiring less conformity and less dependency and by tolerating individual differences within the family, adolescent-parent conflict and tension could be minimized (Mead, 1950). Also, Mead wrote that youths can be accepted into adult society at younger ages. Gainful employment, even part time, would promote greater financial independence. Parenthood should be postponed, advocated Mead, but not necessarily sex or marriage. Adolescents should be given a greater voice in the social and

political life of the commu
would eliminate some of the c
cultural conditioning of children g
Western society and would allow for a s.
easier transition to adulthood.

The later writings of Mead (1970, 1974) and others were modified to show an appreciation of universal aspects of development and more acknowledgment of the biological role in human development. Today, extreme positions are generally disregarded by both geneticists and anthropologists. They basically agree that a composite view that acknowledges both biogenetic factors and environmental forces comes closest to the truth.

SUMMARY

1. G. Stanley Hall was the "father of adolescent psychology." He believed that adolescent behavior was shaped by evolutionary forces and that adolescents were destined to be disrespectful and temperamental. He said that adolescence was a time of *sturm und drang,* or "storm and stress."

2. Arnold Gesell emphasized the importance of genetics and maturation in development.

3. Sigmund Freud made a significant contribution in his emphasis on early childhood experiences and unconscious motivations in influencing behavior. The desire to satisfy sexual instincts and psychic needs for affection is a strong motivating factor in influencing adolescent behavior. Similarly, Freud's explanations of the need to separate emotionally from parents, to establish heterosexual friendships with peers, and to find a love object for emotional fulfillment are helpful.

4. Anna Freud proposed that adolescents enter into a period of psychic disequilibrium when they enter puberty because the id becomes stronger and dominates behavior. Because of this unbalance, adolescents are forced to employ psychological defense mechanisms to reduce tension.

5. Erik Erikson outlined an eight-stage sequence of personality development over the lifespan. He coined the term *identity* to describe the adolescent's search for

goals, self-understanding, and sense of unity. The identity search is now considered one of the major tasks that adolescents face.

6. Jean Piaget believed that individuals learn by developing new cognitive structures that help them adapt to their environment. He outlined four stages of cognitive development. Preadolescents are in the *concrete operational stage*; they can think logically about things they have actually experienced. Adolescents are in the *formal operational stage* and can think abstractly.

7. Lev Vygotsky believed that learning is a social, rather than an individual, process. He suggested that cognitive development proceeds most quickly if novices are teamed with experts to solve problems together.

8. Albert Bandura's social learning theory emphasized the importance of modeling and vicarious reinforcement in the learning process. His later emphasis on cognitive factors in shaping the environment was an important contribution.

9. Robert Havighurst outlined the major developmental tasks of adolescence. They include accepting one's changing body, developing more meaningful relationships with others, achieving emotional independence from parents, and exhibiting socially responsible behavior.

10. Kurt Lewin believed that adolescents are unhappy and confused because they are unclear as to what they are

...ust give up many of the pleasures ...ut yet gaining the benefits that come

...nner described the adolescent's world as ...ted environments. He urged researchers ...nd the adolescent's immediate contacts ...ctions and examine the effects of more dis-...cts of the environment. He believed that over-...tural values greatly influence adolescent ...opment.

...garet Mead and Ruth Benedict and other anthro-...logists provide evidence that there are few univer-...al patterns of development and that adolescent ...turmoil is not universal. Cultural comparisons emphasize the positive and negative elements in each culture that aid or prevent the adolescent from becoming an adult.

KEY TERMS

accommodation 39	macrosystem 46
adaptation 39	mental operations 39
anal stage 34	mesosystem 46
assimilation 39	microsystem 45
cognition 38	modeling 41
cultural determinism 46	oral stage 34
cultural relativism 46	organismic psychologist 38
defense mechanisms 36	phallic stage 34
developmental tasks 43	psychoanalytic theory 35
ego 35	psychosocial moratorium 38
emerging adulthood 38	reinforcement 41
equilibrium 39	scaffolding 40
exosystem 46	schema 38
genital stage 34	self-reinforcement 41
id 35	*sturm und drang* 32
identification 34	superego 35
identity diffusion 38	vicarious reinforcement 41
individuation 34	zone of proximal development 40
latency stage 34	

THOUGHT QUESTIONS

Personal Reflection

1. Would you describe your own adolescence as a period of storm and stress? Why or why not?
2. Think of the Eriksonian stages that you have already passed through in your lifespan. Did you have a favorable or an unfavorable outcome at each stage? What experiences seemed to contribute to these outcomes?
3. What aspects of your identity have you formed? Which are you still working on? Which have you put off for the time being?
4. Give specific examples of how you adapted cognitively through assimilation and accommodation.
5. Give several examples of the ways in which you have modeled yourself after your parents. Did you consciously try to do this or did it just happen?

Group Discussion

6. To what extent do basic biological urges, such as sexual desire and aggression, underlie behavior? Support your idea with examples.
7. Why is adolescence the time when most individuals begin to feel the need to break away from their parents? Why not earlier or later?
8. How might increased skill at perspective taking influence interpersonal relationships? Do you see any downside to having this skill? Explain.
9. Do you figure out problems best when working alone or when working with others? Do the characteristics of the people you are working with matter? Support your answers with examples.
10. Which of Havighurst's developmental tasks should be accomplished during early adolescence? Which should take longer? Why?
11. Drawing from as many theories as possible, explain why some adolescents act aggressively.
12. What cultural values do you believe can ease the transition from childhood to adolescence and from adolescence to adulthood?

Debate Questions

13. Adolescent development is more a matter of physical maturation than environmental experience.
14. Adolescence is a more difficult period of life than other developmental stages.
15. Only ill comes from generating developmental norms as Gesell did.
16. Emerging sexuality underlies most adolescent stress.
17. Adolescents really are "marginalized," as Lewin suggested.
18. The micro- and mesoenvironments have a greater effect on adolescents' school achievement than the macro- and exoenvironments.

SUGGESTED READING

Bronfenbrenner, U. (2006). *Ecology of Human Development: Experiments by Nature and Design.* Cambridge, MA: Harvard University Press.

Coté, J. E. (1994). *Adolescent Storm and Stress: An Evaluation of the Mead-Freeman Controversy.* Hillsdale, NJ: Erlbaum.

Erikson, E. H. (1994). *Identity and the Life Cycle.* New York: W. W. Norton.

Muuss, R. E. H., and Porton, H. (1998). *Adolescent Behavior and Society: A Book of Readings.* New York: McGraw-Hill.

Rieber, R. W., and Robinson, D. K. (Eds.). (2004). *The Essential Vygotsky.* New York: Kluwer Academic Press.

Serulniko, A. (2000). *Piaget for Beginners.* London, England: Writers and Readers.

WOULDN'T YOU LIKE TO KNOW . . .

- How is the racial/ethnic composition of the United States changing?

- What is the *cycle of poverty*?

- How do the lives of low-socioeconomic-status (SES) adolescents differ from the lives of middle-class adolescents?

- In what ways have the lives of African Americans improved over the past 20 years?

- How do African American families differ from White families?

- What is arguably the greatest problem facing American Latinos?

- Are most Mexican Americans farmers or migrant workers?

- What values and beliefs distinguish Native American culture?

- How did U.S. immigration law disrupt the family lives of Chinese immigrants?

- From which area of the world have the most recent immigrants to the United States come? From which area have the most recent refugees to this country come?

Adolescent Diversity: Socioeconomic Status and Ethnicity

One of the most common myths about adolescents is that they are all alike. Adolescents cannot be discussed as one homogeneous group any more than any other group of people. Not only do youth come from a wide variety of ethnic and cultural backgrounds, but also the environments in which they are raised are different and the circumstances of their lives are quite varied.

Many sections of this book refer to cultural differences among adolescents. Differences between low-socioeconomic-status and middle-class adolescents are highlighted, as are some differences between non-White and White adolescents. Unfortunately, a disproportionate amount of the research with adolescents has been conducted with White, middle-class youths. Although these are the majority in the United States, they are not representative of all. So before we get into a more detailed discussion of adolescence, let's look at the wide cultural diversity that exists among our adolescent population.

We begin with low-socioeconomic-status adolescents of whatever race or national origin. The low-socioeconomic-status category cuts across racial and ethnic boundaries, affecting 13 percent of the population (Bishaw & Semega, 2008). In terms of sheer number, because there are more Caucasian Americans than any other group, there are more poor White adolescents than either Asian American, African American, Hispanic American, and Native American adolescents. A greater *proportion* of non-White adolescents are poor, however. For example, while about 9% of Caucasian American adolescents lives below the poverty line, 30% of African American and 15% of Asian American adolescents do (Wright & Chau, 2009).

The discussion continues with a consideration of the adolescents in four racial/ethnic groups: African Americans, Hispanic Americans/Latinos, Asian Americans, and Native Americans. Figure 3.1

ANSWERS WOULDN'T YOU LIKE TO KNOW …

How is the racial/ethnic composition of the United States changing?

The United States is becoming more Asian and more Latino. Whereas the percentages of Americans in these groups are increasing, the Black and Native American populations are expected to remain stable and the relative size of the Caucasian population is expected to decrease.

shows the sizes of these groups. There are almost equal numbers of Latinos and Black Americans, at approximately 14 percent and 13 percent respectively. (Note that the term *Latino* does not denote people of a given skin color but those with a Spanish-speaking heritage; Latinos can be Black or White, and about 0.5 percent of Americans are both Black and Latino.) There are many fewer Asian Americans (4.5 percent) and a very small proportion of Native Americans (about 1 percent). The remaining 66 percent of the U.S. population consists of White non-Latinos. Figure 3.1 also shows that as a result of differences in both immigration and birthrates among the groups, the percentage of non-Latino White Americans is expected to decrease. By the year 2050, Whites are expected to make up just over half of the U.S. population.

A word of caution is in order as we begin. Even though we will be making general statements about various minority groups, all individuals within a minority group are not alike. Tremendous diversity exists within minority groups, just as it exists within the White middle-class majority. In describing minority groups, the intent is to provide the background for better understanding, *not* to create or reinforce stereotypes.

FIGURE 3.1 RACIAL/ETHNIC MAKEUP OF THE UNITED STATES: 2008 AND 2050

Source: Data from U.S. Bureau of the Census (2009).

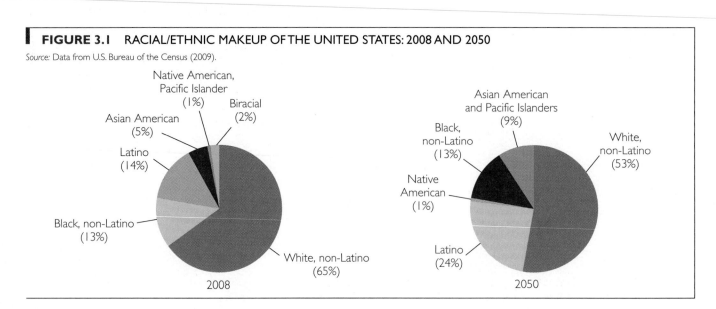

You likely know individuals from these minority groups to whom these descriptions apply only partially or perhaps not at all.

Adolescents of Low Socioeconomic Status

Various terms have been applied to youths who are members of lower social classes and poor, among them *disadvantaged, poverty class,* and *low socioeconomic status.* In this book, the term **low socioeconomic status (low SES)** is used because it refers to two important aspects of the living condition: low social standing and low income.

These two factors do not always go together. Someone with a relatively low income may have a fairly high social standing (an artist or a poet, for example), and conversely, someone with a high income might be disfavored socially (a drug dealer, for instance). Generally, though, individuals who have very little money are marginalized by society in terms of status. Thus, they have only limited access to leisure facilities, educational advantages, work opportunities, health and medical care, and desirable living conditions.

Compared with the general U.S. population, low-SES adolescents are disproportionally from non-White families (see Figure 3.2). In addition, these families are typically larger than average, have fewer wage earners, and have more female heads of household. They reside more often in the South, and in rural areas or in inner cities rather than in the suburbs (DeNavas-Walt, Proctor, & Smith, 2007).

Socioeconomic status plays an important role in the lives of adolescents. Awareness of different levels of SES influences adolescents' self-perceptions as well as their perceptions of the external world. Children, adolescents, and adults learn their worth, in part, by comparing themselves with others. Also, their self-attitudes are influenced greatly by the attitudes held by others toward them (Pearlman, 1995).

Limitations of Low Socioeconomic Status

Four important limitations are imposed on the lives of adolescents who have low socioeconomic status.

Limited Alternatives

Youths with low-SES are not exposed to a variety of social and cultural settings. Poverty limits their educational and career attainments. They and their families have few choices about where to live or which schools to attend. Vocationally, they have fewer opportunities. They lack the funds to take advantage of enriching experiences, and they usually lack transportation away from their immediate neighborhoods. They are "stuck," physically and metaphorically. Limited experience restricts the possibilities and opportunities in their lives (McLoyd, 1998).

Helplessness, Powerlessness

Individuals with low-SES backgrounds are usually unskilled workers. As such, they can exercise little autonomy or influence in improving their conditions, and they have little opportunity or knowledge to receive additional training. They are the most easily replaced personnel and often dare not complain if they are being treated unfairly. These individuals have little political or social influence and, sometimes, inadequate legal protection of their rights as citizens.

low socioeconomic status (low SES)   those persons who are of low social class and status and experience cultural deprivation and low incomes.

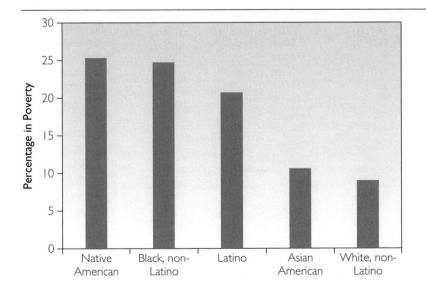

FIGURE 3.2   POVERTY RATES BY RACE AND ETHNICITY: 2008

Source: Data from Bishaw & Semega, 2008.

Deprivation and Hardship

Economically disadvantage adolescents are quite aware of the affluence around them and the benefits received by others. The media make them constantly aware of their own abject status and "failure," often resulting in bitterness, embarrassed withdrawal and isolation, and social deviation and rebellion (Wadsworth & Compas, 2002). In addition, they are far more likely to be immersed in unhealthy, objectionable environments: they may be near fetid city dumps, drink polluted water, or be surrounded by deserted buildings and graffiti. Similarly, they may be surrounded by less tangible aspects of what James Garbarino (2008) calls *social toxicity*, which includes exposure to violence and lack of adult supervision.

Insecurity

Low-SES individuals are at the mercy of life's unpredictable events: sickness, loss of work, injury, family difficulties, evictions, and so on. The lower their socioeconomic status, the more vulnerable they are to the stresses of life. And, in addition, one crisis—such as an unexpected major car repair bill—is more likely to provoke another—loss of heat because of failure to pay an electric bill. Poor persons have no cushion, no rainy day funds to fall back upon. They strive just to provide themselves with the daily basic necessities of life and they can never feel secure.

Cycle of Poverty and Deprivation

The net effect of the limitations imposed on the lives of low-socioeconomic-status youths is to perpetuate poverty (e.g., Abelev, 2009). Figure 3.3 illustrates this cycle of poverty. The cycle begins at the top, with a low level of education. Moving clockwise, having little education results in earning a low income, which results in having a low standard of living, which results in having a limited ability to manage or control the external environment. Therefore, adolescents are socialized to expect low education, a low level of living, and powerlessness. Their worldview perpetuates the lifestyle to which they have become accustomed.

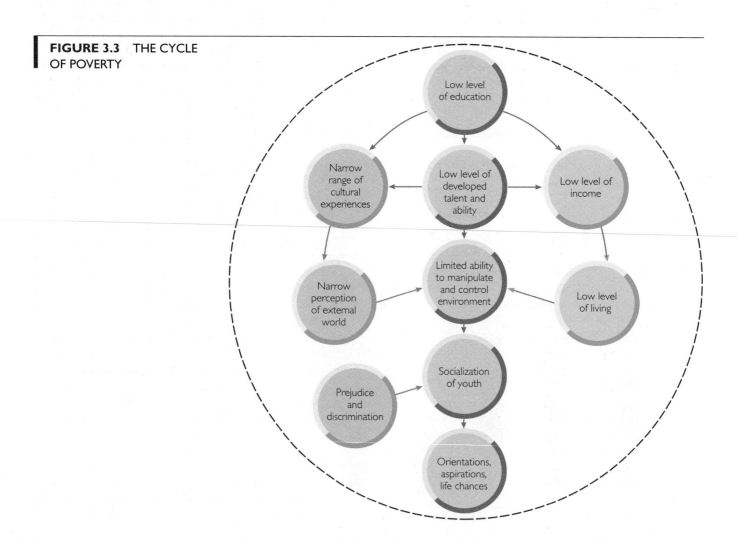

FIGURE 3.3 THE CYCLE OF POVERTY

Starting at the top of Figure 3.3 again and moving counterclockwise, having a low level of education results in a low level of developed talent and ability and a narrow range of cultural experiences. This, in turn, results in a narrow perception of the external world, which, along with the low level of living, contributes to limited ability to manage and control the environment. Because of discrimination and limitations imposed on them, parents, in one way or another, teach their children not to expect a high income or level of living or much education. Low-SES adolescents tend to be caught in a self-perpetuating cycle of poverty. This is especially true if adolescents' parents have themselves been poor for their entire lives. Individuals who start off being economically advantaged and then fall into poverty tend to be more optimistic about their children's future. Given that, they are more likely to socialize their children in ways that will help them succeed scholastically and economically.

Low Level of Education

The abilities to read and understand, to analyze situations and think critically about them, and to perform numerical calculations are important both to the individual and to society. Individuals with sound basic skills are more likely to attend and complete high school, perhaps go on to college, secure employment, earn higher wages, and live generally productive lives. Individuals who are frustrated by deficiencies in their abilities to read and write are less likely to complete school, less likely to succeed in the labor market, and more likely to engage in behaviors with negative social consequences, such as depending on public assistance or committing crime.

A meta-analysis that examined the findings from 74 studies looking at the relationship between educational achievement and poverty found a moderate influence of socioeconomic status and student achievement at the student level and a very large influence at the school level (Sirin, 2005). This confirms that families who live in areas of concentrated poverty are likely to have children who do not do well in school. Although the effect at the individual student level was smaller, it was still one of the best overall predictors of academic achievement. These SES effects were even stronger for Caucasian than for non-Caucasian students. Schools in higher-SES neighborhoods provide better materials and more experienced teachers and have less teacher turnover and lower teacher-student ratios than those in lower-SES neighborhoods (McLoyd, Kaplan, Purtell, et al., 2009): all of these help students learn more effectively. Coupled with the facts that lower-income parents often have lower expectations for their children and fewer personal resources to help them academically

---

ANSWERS WOULDN'T YOU LIKE TO KNOW ...

What is the *cycle of poverty?*

The term *cycle of poverty* refers to the vicious circle that characterizes the experiences of impoverished people, who find it difficult to move into the middle class. For example, if you are poor, you will likely go to an inadequately funded high school. Even if you work hard, you will likely learn less than your middle-class peers. Because of this, you will be less likely to go to college or get a good job. And if you can't get a good job, you will have no legitimate way to earn enough money to raise your standard of living.

(Wood, Kaplan, & McLoyd, 2007), at present this relationship is almost inevitable.

Family Instability

Largely as a result of early marriages and economic struggles, low-SES families are much less stable than families of higher SES. The rates of divorce and separation increase as one goes down the socioeconomic scale (Bramlett & Mosher, 2002). Pregnancy rates, especially unintended pregnancy rates, also are higher among those of lower socioeconomic status. Poor pregnant teenagers are less likely to obtain abortions than middle-class teens. These two factors mean that more economically disadvantaged teenage girls than middle-class teenage girls become mothers. Entering into single parenthood at an early age greatly increases the risk that the person will remain impoverished (U.S. Bureau of the Census, 2007a).

High divorce and out-of-wedlock pregnancy rates result in the prevalence and persistence of female-headed households among the poor. Much research indicates that although a single-parent family is not necessarily disadvantaged relative to a two-parent family (a father may be a financial burden or a source of friction), the overall effects of the absence or only occasional presence of a father are usually detrimental to the emotional and social development of adolescents. The fact that being raised in a one-parent family is a risk factor for a variety of problems (e.g., Jablonska & Lindberg, 2007) is discussed quite fully in Chapter 8. For now, suffice it to say that being poor increases the chances of being raised in a one-parent home, and that being raised in a one-parent home increases the chances of ending up economically disadvantaged both as a child and as an adult.

Homelessness

A large number of people who are poor are also homeless. Homelessness has increased in recent years for several reasons. First, there has been a decrease in the

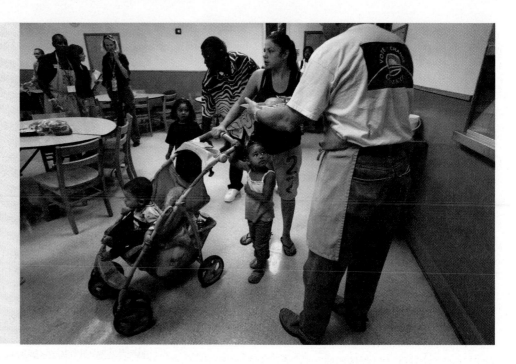

Given the shortage of low-cost housing in some cities, many poor families must turn to homeless shelters to house and feed their children.

availability of low-cost housing; older, less expensive units have been torn down and replaced with far more expensive ones. Second, there has been a decline in the amount of government aid directed at housing assistance. Third, escalating health care costs have pushed many families over the edge so that they can no longer afford the housing they have (National Coalition for the Homeless, 2006).

Homelessness affects adolescents in many ways. Homeless adolescents are subject to both physical and emotional stress. Many turn to panhandling, drug dealing, or stealing in order to survive. A number are in need of psychiatric treatment. School performance is low because of irregular attendance (Kennedy, 2007). Many homeless youths have multiple problems and they face a bleak future without some direct intervention.

Child-Rearing Goals and Philosophies
Low-SES families tend to be hierarchical, with strained parent-adolescent relationships. Most parents become more rigid and punitive when placed under stress (Abell, Clawson, Washington, et al., 1996), and economic deprivation is a chronic stressor. Parents react to this strain by becoming less warm and nurturant (Grant, Compas, Stuhlmacher, et al., 2003) and less involved in their children's lives (Gutman & Eccles, 1999). Adolescents see their parents as closed and inaccessible, and the home atmosphere is one of imperatives and absolutes, physical discipline, and psychological distancing by

the adults. Parent-child interaction patterns are oriented toward maintaining order, obedience, and discipline. The discipline—which is generally harsh and inconsistent—emphasizes physical punishment (even of adolescents) rather than verbal explanations and requests (Berger, 2007). As a group, adolescents from low-SES families report more problems with parents than do those from more privileged families.

Peer Orientation
Because adolescents from low-SES families tend to maintain weaker ties with parents than do youths from middle-class families, they form stronger, more influential peer relationships. Those who report a low evaluation of parents and low self-esteem tend to be more peer oriented than those who have a high evaluation of parents (Vitaro, Brendgen, & Tremblay, 2000). This may be so for at least three reasons.

First, adolescents do not gain status through their familial identifications. The parents of these youths are not doctors, professors, or business executives. The adolescents, then, do not acquire status from the identity of their parents. In fact, they are keenly aware of their parents' lack of status in the community and, therefore, their own lack of status. When a group in an achievement-oriented society cannot gain status in socially acceptable ways, then theft, narcotics, assault, vandalism, and other antisocial expressions may become the means of gaining status and recognition. The peer group replaces the family as the adolescent's primary reference group.

Second, everyone needs emotional support. If a teenager's parents appear cold and rejecting, then they are not being emotionally supportive or meeting their child's belongingness needs (Maslow, 1943). Third, low-SES adolescents may become more peer oriented than parent oriented because of their need for security. In the roughest neighborhoods, teens need their gangs for self-protection.

Social Outcasts

Many low-SES adolescents are socialized differently from middle-class youths. They have their own manner of dress, speech, and behavior. Those who seem loud, ill mannered, or aggressive are scorned by middle-class society. On the other hand, those who withdraw, have low self-esteem, and are shy do not participate in many social functions and groups and are often ignored. In addition, inappropriate or hand-me-down clothing invites criticism from middle-class peers.

Ordinarily, school is an important part of the social world of adolescents, but prejudicial treatment by middle-class adults and students can make low-SES adolescents social outcasts (Wadsworth & Compas, 2002). They are likely to find themselves more and more socially isolated as they proceed through the grades and, as a result, tend to seek friendships with out-of-school youths. Sometimes the association with these youths influences adolescents to drop out of school.

Mental Health

The stresses, social stigma, lack of emotional security, and lack of stability in low-SES homes all contribute to a high rate of psychological problems and mental illness among low-income adolescents (Najman, Aird, Bor, et al., 2004). This is especially true for adolescents exposed to longer durations of poverty (Goosby, 2007).

Recent research has begun to explore the underlying mechanisms by which these factors and poor mental health are linked. For example, as discussed in Chapter 5, we now know that the prefrontal cortex—the area of the brain responsible for problem solving, judgments, and complex decision making—develops greatly during the adolescent years (Arnsten & Shansky, 2004). We also now know that its development is impaired under conditions of chronic stress (Bar-On, Tranel, Denburg, et al., 2003), and that this can lead to problems such as substance abuse (Fishbein, Herman-Stahl, & Eldreth, 2006).

> **ANSWERS WOULDN'T YOU LIKE TO KNOW …**
>
> How do the lives of low-socioeconomic-status (SES) adolescents differ from the lives of middle-class adolescents?
>
> Low-SES adolescents are less likely than middle-class youths to be raised by both their biological parents. In addition, their parents are less likely to be home after school and more likely to be strict when they are home. Low-SES adolescents are more likely than middle-class teens to experience both physical and psychological illnesses, and they are also less likely to finish high school.

Furthermore, if low-SES adolescents are hospitalized due to a psychological condition, they are less likely to receive adequate treatment, are assigned less-skilled staff members, and are treated for shorter periods with less intensive techniques. It is not surprising, then, that their psychiatric symptoms are less likely to improve than those of middle-class patients (Tarnowski, Brown, & Simonian, 1999).

Physical Health

Poverty also leads to physical health problems. Poor health care, substandard nutrition, and exposure to environmental toxins are all more common when income is inadequate. These problems can lead to increased school absenteeism, as well as fatigue, which creates an inability to pay attention even when in attendance. Among students with these problems, academic performance is likely to suffer, and students who do poorly in school frequently rebel, drop out, begin using drugs, or father or bear a child. The stresses can cause poor adolescents to have chronically increased blood pressure (Evans, Kim, Ting, et al., 2007), a condition that can have negative health consequences later in life.

What should you take from the prior discussion? You should come away with an understanding that being raised in a family with meager economic resources is stressful and that impoverished adolescents are more likely than middle-class youths to have grappled with a variety of problems while growing up. Later chapters will detail the basic fact that poor adolescents are substantially more likely to exhibit problem behavior than middle-class adolescents. Understand that this is not due to bad genes or poor moral values but rather to the strain of living in a family that can barely make ends meet. Also remember, however, that many poor adolescents beat the odds. They avoid problem behaviors, maintain high levels of physical and psychological well-being, graduate from high school, and move successfully into adult roles (Werner & Smith, 2001).

Minority Adolescents

The backgrounds of adolescents from minority groups are quite varied: some are first-generation Americans who do not speak English in their homes; others have relatives who fled war or persecution in their homelands several generations ago; others have ancestors who were brought to the United States as slaves; and still others have parents who arrived here as wealthy, well-educated professionals. They may be rich or poor or middle class, and they may live on a farm or in a suburb or in the inner city.

Despite these differences, minority adolescents share one important quality: they are readily identifiable because they look different from Caucasian Americans and may be targeted for prejudice and hostility. Even when they are not, minority youths are often acutely aware of the potential for prejudice to rear its ugly head at any moment. They feel different and sometimes marginalized—and this feeling of difference often affects them more than the specifics of their cultural backgrounds.

Much research suggests that it is the experience of being in the minority, rather than cultural differences per se, that most strongly influences African, Asian, Latino, and Native American youths in the United States. If a White American adolescent were to move, say, to Japan or Nigeria, he or she would experience many of the same strains that an adolescent from a minority group does in the United States. It is difficult to have others view you as different from them—especially when their behavior suggests that *different* means "not quite as good as us." It is also difficult when others are oblivious to cultural differences and expect you to behave in ways that are foreign to what you have been taught at home.

RESEARCH HIGHLIGHT   THOSE WHO MAKE IT

A tremendous amount of research has focused on the factors that contribute to **resiliency,** the ability of a person to bounce back despite much hardship (e.g., Sandler, 2001). The traits and protective factors that have been identified as promoting resiliency cut across ethnic and socioeconomic groups. Some of the ones most commonly identified include the following:

Individual Characteristics

1. Resilient personalities: Resilient adolescents are often found to be assertive, verbally expressive, energetic, creative, and self-confident (Hart, Atkins, & Fegley, 2003). They are warm and outgoing, responsible, and reflective rather than impulsive and believe that they are masters of their own fates (Werner, 1998).
2. Genetic endowment: Research has shown a substantial genetic component to resiliency, often at or above the 50 percent mark (e.g., Kim-Cohen, Moffett, Caspi, et al., 2004). Presumably, some people's nervous systems are designed to withstand stress more effectively than others.
3. High goal setters: Resilient youth are achievement oriented, do well in school, and have set high career goals for themselves (Lewis, 2004).
4. Intelligent: Resilient youth tend to be bright (Asendorph & van Aken, 1999). Their intelligence allows them to think of solutions to the obstacles before them and to be flexible.

5. Possess sustained, intense interests: These interests give them joy and feelings of accomplishment and may provide them access to a mentor (Dolgin, 2006).
6. Use appropriate coping strategies (Compas, Connor-Smith, Saltzman, et al., 2001).
7. Are spiritual or are involved in a religious organization: Religious institutions provide mentorship, moral guidance, and support to vulnerable teens (Crawford, Wright, & Masten, 2004).

Family Characteristics

1. Parents provide emotional support: Resiliency is fostered when children know that their parents are there for them and express approval of them.
2. Parents foster self-sufficiency and independence.
3. Children are expected to assume responsibility (Werner, 1998).
4. Good role models are present: Parents behave in ways that encourage success.

Community Resources

1. Involved, caring teachers
2. Stable friendships
3. Presence of mentors
4. Presence of safe havens

It is important to keep in mind that there are many adolescents who are raised under difficult conditions who overcome their own backgrounds and who break out of the cycle of poverty.

Because minority youths are more likely than White youths to be poor, they are more likely to experience the stressors described earlier in this chapter. Furthermore, they are more likely to experience *persistent* poverty than their White counterparts, even their poor White counterparts, and they are more likely to *live in areas of concentrated poverty*. In addition to substandard living conditions, minority youths often face neighborhood and school violence, drug and alcohol abuse, academic underachievement, delinquency, and adolescent pregnancy (Leventhal, Dupéré, & Brooks-Gunn, 2009).

The following sections describe some of the issues of particular relevance to individuals in specific minority groups. Keep in mind that diversity is just as great within ethnic groups as between them and that poverty and discrimination are more responsible for ethnic-group differences than are differences in values and culturally prescribed behaviors.

African American Adolescents

Most Blacks have been in the United States for generations, having descended from enslaved Africans. More recently, Black immigrants have arrived from Latin America and the Caribbean. Each of these groups has its own culture. Here we concentrate on African Americans.

Legacy of Discrimination

For generations, African American families, especially those of lower SES, were forced to assume an inferior role in order to get along in White society. In the not-so-distant past, getting along meant sitting in the back of the bus and avoiding all "Whites-only" restaurants, restrooms, recreational facilities, theaters, and playgrounds. African American parents had to teach their children the so-called "Black role." African American children left their homes for school at their own peril if they had not learned where they could sit and what they could or could not do. At 5 years old, just as surely as at 15 or 25 years old, they had to know their place. One of the important lessons to learn was that no matter how unjustly they were treated, they had to control anger and conceal hostility. They had to be subservient and polite in the face of provocation and walk with their eyes straight ahead, unmoved by taunts and jeers. Above all, they had to ignore insults and never argue or get in a fight with a White person. Black parents believed that they had to use severe measures to instill fear in their children as their best protection, or White society would punish them more severely.

Richard Wright (1937) wrote of his "first lesson in how to live as a Negro." Describing how he was badly cut as a result of a fight with White boys who threw bottles at him and his friends, he wrote:

> I sat brooding on my front steps, nursing my wound and waiting for my mother to come home from work. . . . I could just feel in my bones that she would understand. . . . I grabbed her hand and babbled out the whole story. She examined my wound, then slapped me.
> "How come yuh didn't hide?" she asked me. "How come yuh always fightin'?"
> I was outraged and bawled. Between sobs I told her that I didn't have any trees or hedges to hide behind. . . .
> She grabbed a barrel stave, dragged me home, stripped me naked, and beat me till I had a fever of one hundred and two. She would smack my rump with the stave, and, while the skin was still smarting, impart to me gems of Jim Crow wisdom. I was never to throw cinders any more. . . . I was never, never under any conditions to fight white folks again. And they were absolutely right in clouting me with the broken milk bottle.

New Realities

In November 2008, Americans elected Barack Obama to be the first Black president of the United States. African Americans have served as secretaries of state and U.S. Supreme Court justices. They have managed the largest, most prestigious companies in America and created some of our finest works of art and music. Clearly, the reality of the Black experience has changed greatly and continues to evolve. In the second half of the twentieth century, a series of sweeping judicial decisions that began to desegregate the United States and grant African Americans their due rights encouraged the emergence of a significant Black middle class, allowed for the rise of political leadership among Blacks, promoted a sense of enfranchisement, and opened the doors of opportunity for more Black citizens.

Today, 85 percent of Black adults have graduated from high school, and about 15 percent have gone on to earn college degrees (U.S. Bureau of the Census, 2009). (This is slightly higher than the national average for high school graduation, but significantly lower for higher degrees.) The upward trend toward higher education is continuing, as more and more African Americans are entering and graduating from college. Poverty rates among Blacks are down compared to historic highs, but they are still about twice as high as for Whites. Still, 40 percent of African American families have annual incomes in excess of $55,000 (U.S. Bureau of the Census, 2009b).

resiliency an individual's ability to succeed in spite of adversity and hardship.

Many factors determine the level of self-esteem and self-image of African American adolescents, including graduating from high school, having positive relationships with their families, and enjoying family approval.

Contemporary Segregation

On May 17, 1954, in the landmark *Brown vs. the Board of Education* decision, the U.S. Supreme Court overruled the principle of "separate but equal" opportunity in education. In 1955, Dr. Martin Luther King Jr., launched his passive resistance movement against the segregated bus system of Montgomery, Alabama. Although the court battles have been fought and won, there is still considerable disparity today between White and Black income, education, and other standards of living. Segregation continues, unfortunately, to be a fact of life.

More African Americans live in the South than in the Northeast, Midwest, or West. This is part of the legacy of slavery. In many cases, families have lived in particular areas for generations. In terms of absolute numbers, more African Americans live in New York, California, Texas, Florida, and Georgia than in other states. However, as a percentage of the total population, Blacks are most heavily represented in Mississippi, Louisiana, South Carolina, Georgia, and Maryland. In addition, African Americans are more likely to live in metropolitan areas, especially in central cities, than are non-Hispanic Caucasians (55 percent versus 22 percent) (McKinnon & Bennett, 2005). In many communities, neighborhoods are still segregated.

Unequal Education

In spite of the legal efforts to ensure equal education for all citizens, African American adolescents still do not enjoy that privilege. In terms of the total number of years of schooling, young African Americans have been catching up with Whites, especially in terms of high school graduation rates. (See Figure 3.4.) If quality of education is considered, however, African Americans still lag far behind Whites.

This difference is largely due to the socioeconomic differences between Blacks and Whites. If income levels are equated, there is much less racial difference in educational attainment. African American parents who are financially better off, close to their children, and involved in their schooling are much more likely to have adolescents who remain in school and do well (Brody, Stoneman, & Flor, 1995).

Occupational Aspirations

Although an increasing number of African Americans have reached higher socioeconomic levels in recent decades, several authors have pointed out that the actual *percentage* of Blacks who have moved into the

FIGURE 3.4 EDUCATIONAL ATTAINMENT AMONG AFRICAN AMERICANS AND WHITES, AGES 25 AND OLDER: 1960 TO 2004

Source: Data from U.S. Bureau of the Census (2005b).

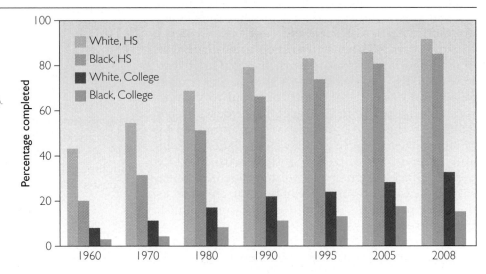

middle class has declined and that, given the nation's current poor economy, there is a substantial risk that their children will fall back into a lower socioeconomic class (e.g., Isaacs, 2007).

African American college students appear aware of the fragility of their socioeconomic stability. Much research has confirmed that, as a group, they are more prone to consider future earning potential when selecting a career than their White counterparts; they are also more likely to select careers that will enhance their social prestige, such as law or medicine (e.g., Daire, LaMothe, & Fuller, 2007; Hwang, Echols, & Vrongistinos, 2002). (Conversely, African American students are not more likely than Caucasian students to consider the degree to which they will help others or benefit society when making a career selection.) Although they feel capable of surmounting the barriers they will face, Black college students believe that they will be presented with fewer career opportunities and face more hurdles than do White students (Fouad & Byars-Winston, 2005).

Desegregation Efforts

Traditionally, most African Americans lived in segregated neighborhoods and had little opportunity for interracial contact. But changes in public attitudes and legislation paved the way for decreased segregation. Since 1980, the segregation of African Americans declined by all five of the measures used by the U.S. Census Bureau to assess segregation (Iceland, Weinberg, & Steinmetz, 2002). Despite this decline, however, residential segregation is still higher for African Americans than for the other groups across all measures. Segregation remains strongest in large urban areas in the Midwest and Northeast.

Unemployment Rates

Unemployment rates are considerably higher for Black men and for Black teenagers than they are for the population at large. (Black women are actually

ANSWERS WOULDN'T YOU LIKE TO KNOW ...

In what ways have the lives of African Americans improved over the past 20 years?

African Americans are less likely to live in segregated housing, less likely to be poor, and more likely to attend college than they were 20 years ago. On the other hand, the wage gap between Blacks and Whites has widened, and it is often the case that the public schools Blacks attend are less well funded than those attended primarily by Whites.

slightly more likely to be employed than women at large; McKinnon & Bennett, 2005.) In fact, in the summer of 2006, whereas the overall teenage unemployment rate was at 15 percent, almost 28 percent of African American teens who were seeking jobs could not find them (Employment Policies Institute, 2006). These higher rates are due to a complicated interaction of lower education, physical distance to available jobs, lack of transportation, discrimination, and lack of skills.

Income

In spite of the fact that the incomes of both Whites and African Americans have been increasing, the income gap between Whites and non-Whites has *widened*, not closed, especially for those with college degrees (see Figure 3.5). In every occupational category, African Americans are paid less than Whites for the same work. Blacks who had a four-year bachelor's degree earned $46,502, or about 78 percent of the salary for comparably educated Whites (U.S. Bureau of the Census, 2009a). Unequal income is the result of unequal education, segregation, disproportionate layoffs because of lack of seniority, and discrimination, and it is still a reality.

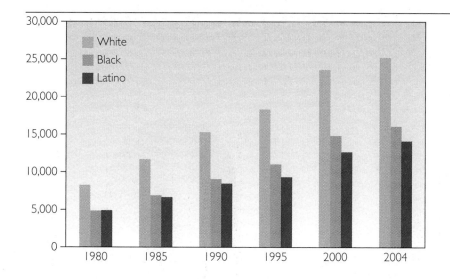

FIGURE 3.5 AVERAGE FULL-TIME WAGES BY RACE AND HISPANIC ORIGIN: 1980–2004

Source: Data from U.S. Bureau of the Census (2000b).

Adolescent Pregnancy

Teenage pregnancy and motherhood (issues that will be discussed at length later in this text) are generally harmful to the adolescents involved. Adolescent mothers are less likely to graduate from high school and more likely to become or remain impoverished than other adolescent girls (Hofferth, Reid, & Mott, 2001). Since African American adolescent girls are about two and a half times as likely to get pregnant as Caucasian girls—51 percent conceive at least once prior to their 20th birthday (The National Campaign to Prevent Teenage Pregnancy, 2008)—adolescent pregnancy is a particularly crucial issue for the Black community. Approximately two-thirds of all births to Black women are to unwed mothers (National Center for Health Statistics, 2002).

Family Strengths

African American families are beset by many problems resulting from racial discrimination and the economic conditions under which many live. These families struggle to survive against the backdrop of high unemployment, high rates of poverty, and the retrenchment of social programs important to them. However, African American families also show a number of positive characteristics that have enabled them to function and survive in a hostile social environment.

Strong Kinship Bonds   Extended families are common in many minority populations. African Americans, in general, are exposed to more stress than Whites, but family members rely on one another for care, strength, and mutual support (Taylor, 2000). Extended family members tend to live near one another, and they share a strong sense of family obligation. There is a fluidity of household boundaries such that households absorb relatives and friends in need. There is much interaction, and a good deal of direct help and aid is given.

Favorable Attitude Toward the Elderly   At all socioeconomic levels, African Americans have a more favorable attitude toward the elderly than do Whites (Slaughter-Defoe, Kuehne, & Straker, 1992). One reason for this is the strong kinship bond just discussed.

ANSWERS WOULDN'T YOU LIKE TO KNOW . . .

How do African American families differ from White families?

When most African Americans think of the family in which they were raised, that group likely includes their aunts, uncles, cousins, grandparents, and even their parents' close friends. Their family likely had flexible gender roles, and it was more likely that they regularly attended church than their White peers.

Adaptable Roles   Husband-wife relationships in African American families are more egalitarian than in other races, with African American husbands sharing significantly in the performance of household tasks (Landry, 2000). Roles of all family members are flexible. For instance, an uncle or grandfather can assume the vacated position of a father or mother.

Strong Religious Orientation   Religion has been a source of solace for downtrodden people, as well as a vehicle for rebellion and social advancement. The African American church—through preaching and teaching, symbols, belief systems, and rituals—remains the glue that binds families and communities together. Young people who attend church have a relatively high level of faith and support that helps them deal with the stresses in their lives (King, 2008).

Latino Adolescents

Hispanic Americans, or Latinos, are those whose families came from geographic areas in which Spanish is spoken; they can be of any race. About 14 percent of Americans are Latino (U.S. Bureau of the Census, 2008a); considerably more than half are citizens (Pérez, 2004). Figure 3.6 shows a breakdown of the world areas from which Hispanic Americans' families originally emigrated. As you can see, about 60 percent of Latino families came from Mexico and about 10 percent came from Puerto Rico. Given this, these two ethnic groups are discussed in the following sections.

First, however, it's essential to discuss an over-arching problem in the Latino community: inequities in educational attainment.

Educational Concerns

Hispanic Americans are less likely to graduate from high school than other American citizens (Fuligini & Hardway, 2004). Since educational attainment is essential to

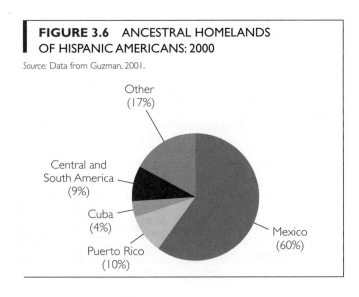

FIGURE 3.6   ANCESTRAL HOMELANDS OF HISPANIC AMERICANS: 2000

Source: Data from Guzman, 2001.

Other (17%)

Central and South America (9%)

Cuba (4%)

Puerto Rico (10%)

Mexico (60%)

getting a good job, it is not surprising that the poverty rate is high among Latinos. The main reason that Latinos as a group struggle in school is because English is not the primary language spoken in most Hispanic students' homes. More than three-fourths of Hispanic families speak Spanish at home (Ramirez, 2004). Spanish-speaking children and adolescents must fight to understand teachers and textbooks not written in their native tongue; they must also try to put their thoughts on paper in a language with which they may not be comfortable.

Because of this difficulty, Latino students are more likely than others to be held back in elementary school. And by middle school, Latino students are likely to be several years behind in reading and math. Therefore, they are more likely to be tracked into general high school curricula, which do not prepare them for college. It is hardly surprising, then, that the dropout rate for Latino students in high school is double the rate for Blacks and four times that for non-Hispanic Whites (U.S. Bureau of the Census, 2009a), and they are more likely to drop out of school at an earlier age than youths from other ethnic groups. As a consequence, Latino youths are less likely to go to college and graduate school than other adolescents (see Table 3.1). They receive only about 6 percent of the nation's B.A. degrees and 3 percent of its Ph.D.s (U.S. Bureau of the Census, 2009a).

In addition to the obvious language barrier, other issues that contribute to Latinos' lower level of academic achievement include inequities in school funding, school segregation, low numbers of Hispanic school personnel, lack of multicultural training for teachers, misplacement of students in special education classes, lack of availability of postsecondary financial assistance, and lack of school safety (President's Advisory Commission on Educational Excellence for Hispanic Americans, 1996).

Health

An additional serious issue that confronts many Latino families is that Latino children and adolescents are disproportionately likely to suffer from ill health. For example, they have high rates of asthma (National Center for Health Statistics, 2004), diabetes (American

ANSWERS WOULDN'T YOU LIKE TO KNOW ...

What is arguably the greatest problem facing American Latinos?

The most pressing problem for the Latino community is the mismatch between Latino children and the schools they attend. As a result of language difficulties, inadequate funding, and cultural misunderstanding, needed skills are not being learned and diplomas are not being earned. This situation only perpetuates the levels of social isolation and high unemployment.

Diabetes Association, 2009), and HIV (Hall, Song, Rhodes, et al., 2008). These health concerns are made worse by the fact that Latinos are much less likely to be insured than other American children (DeNavas-Walt, Proctor, & Smith, 2007). This lack of medical coverage is due to a combination of poverty, immigrant status, fear of using government services, lack of Spanish-speaking health care providers, and employment in occupations that fail to provide health care benefits.

Mexican American Adolescents
Mexican Americans are the second-largest minority group in the United States. They are also a young group: 35 percent of the Mexican American population is younger than 18 years old (Guzmán, 2001). Mexican Americans are concentrated in the Southwest in the states of California, Texas, New Mexico, and Arizona, but they are also moving in large numbers to cities in the Northeast and Midwest.

Segregation and Housing   Mexican American youths are primarily urbanized: about 80 percent live in urban areas, but a significant number are migrant workers on farms. The majority of Mexican Americans are segregated in residential ghettos called **colonias** or **barrios** (neighborhoods) (Hobbs & Stoops, 2002).

colonias or barrios   colonies or districts of Spanish-speaking people.

TABLE 3.1   ACADEMIC ACHIEVEMENT BY RACE AND ETHNICITY: 2008

	WITHOUT HIGH SCHOOL DIPLOMA	HIGH SCHOOL GRADUATE	AT LEAST SOME COLLEGE	BACHELOR'S DEGREE	PH.D. OR PROFESSIONAL DEGREE
Latinos	37.7%	62.3%	32.8%	13.3%	1.0%
Blacks	15.0%	85.0%	43.9%	15.3%	1.3%
Asians	10.8%	89.2%	69.1%	52.6%	6.4%
Non-Hispanic Whites	8.5%	91.5%	59.8%	32.6%	3.1%

Source: Data from U.S. Bureau of the Census (2009a).

ANSWERS WOULDN'T YOU LIKE TO KNOW ...
Are most Mexican Americans farmers or migrant workers?

Neither. Most Mexican Americans live in urban areas. Only a minority are migrant workers. And not all migrant workers are Mexican American or even Latino; there are a significant number of Black migrant workers.

Families Mexican American marriages are more stable than those of either Whites or African Americans (U.S. Bureau of the Census, 2002). The greater stability holds true even when statistical allowances are made for differences in age, age at first marriage, education, and place of residence. Apparently, the traditional Mexican American family is highly cohesive. The mother is especially warm to her children, close to them, and plays an important role in their care (Crickettt, Brown, Russell, & Shen, 2007). Extended families are common. There is some evidence, however, that the traditional emphasis on the family is beginning to decline. Mexican American women, especially those who are more acculturated and who do better in school, are showing increasing interest in having time-consuming, well-paying careers (Reyes, Kobus, & Gillock, 1999).

Culture The traditional Mexican culture, and hence the Mexican American culture, is different from that of the American mainstream in several ways:

1. Families are more patriarchal and traditional sex roles are emphasized (Raffaelli & Ontai, 2004).

2. There is a greater emphasis on **familialism:** devotion to one's family and respect for one's parents and grandparents (Niemann, Romero, Arredondo, et al., 1999).

3. There is a strong commitment to Catholicism (Valentine & Mosley, 1999).

Familialism is expressed by keeping children emotionally and physically close. Children in Mexican American families are given less freedom than those in non-Hispanic families, and Mexican American parents have the right to discipline their children as they see fit. Even as adults, children ask their parents for advice and listen respectfully to them. There are many positive aspects to familialism, but one downside is a lack of trust in people outside one's extended family. Maintaining this attitude can make it more difficult for Mexican Americans to succeed in the broader American society (Chandler, Tsai, & Wharton, 1999). Fortunately, this distrust of outsiders seems to be diminishing.

Niemann and colleagues (1999) asked Mexican Americans to compare their culture with that of their non-Hispanic neighbors. In addition to the differences

Mexican American culture places a strong emphasis on familialism, or devotion to one's family. The traditional Mexican American family is highly cohesive, and extended families are common.

already noted, they mentioned a love of celebration, a strong work ethic, and pride in their bilingualism. Unfortunately, the majority also mentioned being treated with discrimination and hostility by individuals such as store clerks and police.

Socialization of Adolescents Traditional Mexican American parents may emphasize values that hinder the advancement of adolescents in the individualistic, highly competitive, materialistic U.S. society. An emphasis on family ties and dependency, submission to authority, living in the present, and politeness are not conducive to independence, achievement, deferred gratification, and success. For example, the older son's role in the Mexican American family is often an extension of that of the father: protector, supervisor, and guardian of the younger children. Family dependency is antithetical to initiative and autonomy. Mexican

American daughters are closely monitored and taught to take their place in the home (Villarruel, 1998). The emphasis on honor and respectful conduct leads to extraordinary courtesy and politeness. Young people are taught to show respect, obedience, and humility (Delgado-Gaitan, 1994). (In traditional homes, the answer to the parent's call is *"Mande usted"*—"At your command.")

In school or work, Mexican American adolescents are not prodded to take risks but to be careful not to bring shame on themselves or their families. This is one reason comparisons between Mexican American and White American adolescents show that the latter are much more competitive (Lucas & Stone, 1994). Mexican Americans are concerned with personal gain but more often avoid overtly competitive behavior. Furthermore, reflecting a broader Latino value, Mexican American children are not expected to defer gratification but to live in the present (Altarriba & Bauer, 1998). Such an orientation is not conducive to upward mobility.

Heterosexual Relationships When Mexican American males reach adolescence, they are expected to take an active interest in females and to talk and act in ways that demonstrate their virility. There are those girls whom the males may exploit for sexual purposes to prove their ***machismo*** (manhood) and those whom they might someday think to marry. Whereas boys are given a degree of sexual freedom (Huerta-Frano, de Leon, & Malacara, 1996), dating is frowned on for Chicanas, and parents typically lecture their daughters about what they can and cannot do with boys.

The importance of modesty is highly emphasized for girls, who are not supposed to learn about sexual relations from either conversation or experience. The result is a low level of knowledge about human sexuality. Mothers do not discuss sex with their daughters, and many do not even discuss menstruation (Meneses, Orrell-Valante, Grendelman, et al., 2006). Mexican American females are encouraged to preserve their virginity until marriage. This socialization partially explains the later age of first premarital sex of Mexican American adolescent women relative to their non-Hispanic White counterparts (Browning, Leventhal, & Brooks-Gunn, 2004). However, because of a lack of information about birth control, religious prohibitions against many forms of birth control, and fear of parental disapproval for sexual activity, adolescent pregnancy and birthrates are high (Ventura, Abma, Mosher, et al., 2008).

Puerto Rican Adolescents

About 4 million Puerto Ricans live in the United States. About 70 percent live in the Northeast, with New York City having the largest population. One-fifth of the Puerto Ricans living in the United States are adolescents. Although Puerto Rican Americans are more likely than Mexican Americans to have graduated from both high school and college, they are more likely to live in poverty. Puerto Rican Americans also have the highest rates of both divorce and births to adolescents of any ethnic or racial group (Pew Hispanic Center, 2009).

As United States citizens, Puerto Ricans may enter the country and travel freely within it. This fact, combined with overpopulation and much poverty on their island, contributed to a rapid immigration of Puerto Ricans to the mainland in the decades following World War II. In recent years, immigration has declined, however.

The island of Puerto Rico lies near Cuba. It was a Spanish colony from the 1500s until 1898, when it was ceded to the United States at the end of the Spanish-American War. Puerto Rico is a commonwealth; so even though its residents enjoy many of the privileges of American citizenship, they are not allowed to vote in presidential elections or to elect senators or congresspersons.

The Puerto Rican culture is derived from the cultures of several historic populations: the native Taíno Indians, the African slaves who began settling there in the 1500s, and the Spanish explorers. The most important cultural values include **fatalism** (the belief that one cannot change one's destiny or fate), acceptance of hierarchies, masculine superiority, and a need for personal respect and dignity (Gibbons, Brusi-Figueroa, & Fisher, 1997).

Family Life Puerto Ricans have a profound sense of family. Most traditional women view motherhood as their central role. Their concept of motherhood is based on the female capacity to bear children and on the notion of ***marianismo,*** which presents the Virgin Mary as a role model. *Marianismo* implies that a woman finds her identity and derives her life's greatest satisfaction through motherhood.

Ideal family relations are described by two interrelating themes—family interdependence and family unity. Family interdependence fits within the Puerto Rican orientation to life, which stresses that the individual cannot do everything and still do it well. Older Puerto Rican women especially adhere strongly to the value of family interdependence. It influences patterns of mutual

familialism devotion to one's family and respect for one's parents and grandparents.

machismo Spanish term for maleness or manhood.

fatalism the belief that one cannot change one's destiny or fate.

marianismo in Puerto Rican society, the implication that a woman finds her greatest satisfaction through motherhood.

assistance with their children as well as expectations of support. The older women expect their adult children to take care of them during old age.

Family unity emphasizes the desirability of close and intimate kin ties—members get along well and keep in frequent contact during separations. Puerto Ricans believe that the greater the degree of unity in the family, the greater emphasis family members will place on interdependence and familial obligation.

Still, Puerto Rican Americans are less likely to be married than other Latinos, both because they are less likely to marry at all and because their marriages are more likely to end in divorce. Often when individuals are under stress, their idealized situation and the one they find themselves in are not the same.

Education, Employment, and Income The problems confronting Puerto Rican families are partly a result of the adverse economic and social conditions under which they live. In 2000, 25 percent of adult Puerto Ricans had less than 12 years of schooling. Only 13 percent had 4 years of college or more. Puerto Ricans had the highest rate of unemployment of all Hispanics (Ramirez, 2004). As a consequence, income was low.

Implications for Adolescents Considering the prevalence of single-parent households, Puerto Rican adolescents often lack parental role models with whom they can identify. Identity formation among minority adolescents includes discovering, on a personal basis, what it means to be a member of a specific group. But characteristics of the group are changing or often confusing (McLoyd, 1990). Puerto Rican adolescents experience an identity crisis compounded by strong intercultural and intergenerational conflicts. They experience conflict between the cultural values represented by their parents and the cultural values they experience on the city streets. They also face language and socioeconomic barriers to acculturation.

Many Puerto Rican youths are compelled to live in abject poverty, in the poorest slum areas of the city, where crime rates are high, drug use is rampant, and good schools and quality education are scarce. These realities are often the reason why many disillusioned families return to Puerto Rico. The problems these youths face have been linked to their higher prevalence of mental disorders, anxiety and depression, drug and alcohol abuse, delinquency, and lower self-esteem, compared with populations of African Americans and Whites (Hajat, Lucas, & Kington, 2000).

Native American Adolescents

In 2000, about 2.4 million Native Americans lived in the United States; they represent more than 500 diverse tribes. Although their number is growing faster than the U.S. population as a whole, Native Americans still constitute just over 1 percent of the population. About half of all Native Americans live in rural areas, including their own reservations, with the remaining half split between urban and suburban areas. Most Native Americans live in the western half of the United States. California, Oklahoma, Arizona, New Mexico, Washington, and Alaska are home to more Native Americans than any other states (Hobbs & Stoops, 2002; Ogunwole, 2006).

Arizona and Oklahoma represent two extremes in tribal representation. Arizona has the second largest number of Native Americans, as well as the largest single tribe—the Navaho, who live on the largest reservation in the United States. Oklahoma, in contrast, has the largest number of tribes—about 60. This land was once Indian Territory, to which Native Americans from all over the country were moved when their tribal lands were confiscated by Whites. Because these displaced Native Americans were newcomers living on land next to their White neighbors (who had also recently immigrated), most Oklahoma Native Americans lived among the general population, although there are some remote reservations in the state. In states such as New Mexico and the Dakotas, the majority of Native Americans are still living on their original reservations. In other states—such as North Carolina, California, and New York—the majority either resisted movement to reservations or now lives on land for which government control has terminated.

Since the beginning of World War II, there has been a rapid migration of Native Americans to urban areas. In 1940, only 7.2 percent of the total Native American population lived in cities; in 1999, the figure was 50 percent. This rapid migration was the result of youths leaving reservations during World War II to join the armed services and adults going to work in wartime factories. The government encouraged migration and offered assistance through a relocation program that sought to promote rapid integration into White American life (Fixico, 2000). This relocation created many problems. Even though urbanization increased Native Americans' level of employment, quality of housing, and perceived quality of life, it has not been a panacea for poverty, discrimination, and alienation. One of the major problems of contemporary Native American youths is their inability to reconcile the cultural conflict between the way of life on the reservation and the way of life in urban America.

Health and Standard of Living
Native Americans have the lowest standard of living of any minority group in the United States, with unemployment high and income low. Approximately one-quarter live below the poverty level (U.S. Bureau of the Census, 2007c). Unemployment on some reservations runs as high as 80 to 90 percent. In most Native American

communities, the pattern is one of bare subsistence, with the result that some of the worst slums in the United States are on reservations.

Although treaty agreements entitle federally recognized tribes to health services from the national government, many Native Americans cannot or do not take advantage of these services. First, the Indian Health Service operates out of tribal lands and reservations, and many Native Americans do not live in these areas. In addition, factors such as poverty, inadequate sewage disposal, suspicion toward authorities, and cultural barriers increase the probability of illness and decrease the chances of adequate treatment (Office of Minority Health, 2006).

Native American individuals are more likely than others to die from a variety of causes, including all types of accidents, liver disease, diabetes, pneumonia and influenza, suicide, homicide, and tuberculosis (National Center for Health Statistics, 2001). Suicide is a leading cause of death among Native American youths ages 15 to 19, with a rate two to three times the national average (CDC, 2003). The rate varies tremendously from tribe to tribe, however. Eating disorders, particularly bulimia, are common among Native American girls (Lynch, Heil, Wagner, et al., 2007). Substance abuse, particularly alcoholism, is rampant among Native Americans, resulting in a high rate of *fetal alcohol syndrome* (*FAS*) in babies of both adult and adolescent mothers (Kaskutas, 2000). FAS is the leading cause of preventable mental retardation in the United States. Even though the alcoholism rate among the Native American population as a whole is comparatively high, the fact remains that only a relatively small minority of Native Americans are alcoholics.

Despite these negative conditions, there is much room for optimism that economic strides can be made. Native American lands include many beautiful areas as well as valuable ones. They contain, for example, much needed timber and uranium. In addition, in excess of 40% of the nation's Indian tribes operate casinos and bingo halls, scattered across 28 states. In 2008, these gaming ventures took in revenues of more than $26 billion (National Indian Gaming Commission, 2009). Barriers to economic growth include a lack of financial capital to invest in new initiatives, a lack of skilled workers on the reservation, a lack of experience with entrepreneurial enterprises, a large distance from markets and the high cost of transportation to them, and a recent Supreme Court decision that (if not reversed by Congress) will limit Native Americans' abilities to build new casinos (Cornell & Kalt, 2004; The Oyez Project, 2009).

Education

The record of Native American education is one of broken promises; inadequate resources; poor teachers; and, worst of all, the use of education as a tool to destroy a culture and a way of life. By the beginning of the twentieth century, the Bureau of Indian Affairs (BIA) was operating reservation day schools, reservation boarding schools, and off-reservation boarding schools for Native Americans in various parts of the country as part of the government's legal trust responsibility. However, the goal was complete assimilation. "Kill the Indian and Save the Man" was the motto. Regimentation, reading, writing, arithmetic, the manual trades, and home economics were drilled into the students.

Life at boarding schools was regimented, as well. Estranged from family, under the rule of an alien culture, and unable to talk to teachers (who did not know their dialects), Native American students' academic performance was poor. As many as 75 percent of the children in boarding schools were far from home and had school-related social or emotional problems. About one-third of the children in these schools were physically disabled (McShane, 1988).

In addition, the BIA operated a number of day schools located on or near the reservations. These schools also presented problems. Physical facilities were notoriously inadequate, texts and supplies were scarce and outdated, and little money was available to hire competent staff. The schools conducted all classes in English, yet some of the children spoke little or no English. The dropout rate was very high.

At the secondary level, the school curriculum did not acknowledge ethnic diversity. A report on education in Native American schools in Alaska stated that "education which gives the Indian, Eskimo, and Aleut knowledge of—and therefore pride in—their historic and cultural heritage is non-existent" (Henninger & Esposito, 1971). The Indian Education Act of 1972 (known as Title IV) resulted in some improvements. This legislation established funding for special bilingual and bicultural programs, culturally relevant teaching materials, proper training and hiring of counselors, and establishment of an Office of Indian Education in the U.S. Department of Education. Most important, the act required participation of Native Americans in the planning of all relevant educational projects (O'Brien, 1989).

Native American education has improved remarkably in the past 40 years or so. During the 2007–2008 school year, the Office of Indian Education Programs directly served more than 48,000 students in 184 schools scattered over 23 states and more than 60 reservations. At present, more than 125 of these schools are controlled and operated by the tribes, not the federal government. More than 400,000 additional students were served indirectly, in good part through the provision of financial aid and scholarships. Twenty-six tribal colleges and universities were also funded. Navajo Community College, on the Navajo Reservation in Arizona, and Sinte Gleska (Spotted Tail) University, on the Rosebud

Reservation in South Dakota, are two of the better-known of these institutions (Bureau of Indian Education, 2009). Native American enrollment at the nation's colleges and universities in aggregate—native-run and non-native combined—more than doubled in the past quarter century. By 2002, almost 166,000 Native American students were enrolled in higher education, and more than half of these students were enrolled at 4-year, degree-granting institutions. Much of this increase has been because of a rise in young *female* Native American enrollment: there are currently approximately 40,000 more female Native American college students than male Native American college students (National Center for Education Statistics, 2005a).

Family Life

Since there are more than 550 federally recognized Native American tribes, there is no such institution as a typical Native American family. Despite the attempt to impose Western family models on them, various family forms still exist among the different tribal groups. Some families are **matrilineal** (with descent through the mother's line) (Keshna, 1980). For many Native Americans, the extended family is the basic unit for carrying out family functions (LaFromboise & Dixon, 2003). This is often true despite the absence of extended kin in the same household. Children may be raised by relatives residing in different, noncontiguous households. The existence of multiple households sharing family functions is quite common.

Children

Most Native Americans view children as assets to the family. Children are taught that family and tribe are of the utmost importance. Grandmothers are especially important; in fact, people who are aged, in general, are looked up to for wisdom and counsel. The aged occupy the important position of relating traditions, beliefs, and customs through their role as storyteller. Children are taught that listening, rather than speaking, is a sign of respect and the best way to learn. They are also taught to be independent (there are no rigid schedules for eating and sleeping), to be patient and unassuming, and to maintain a rather severe reserve rather than to show emotions. The ability to endure pain, hardship, hunger, and frustration is emphasized, as are bravery and courage (Gilliland, 1995).

Cultural Conflict

For years, official U.S. government policy was assimilation—that is, the ultimate goal of full absorption of Native Americans in the U.S. society by the dominant group. However, acceptance was to come about as members of the minority group became more like members of the majority. Native Americans were considered heathens and savages, and so White Americans sought to civilize them so that they could find acceptance in the dominant society (Williams, Himmel, Sjoberg, et al., 1995). Today, however, Native Americans are making a determined effort to retain and to teach their cultural values to their young people. Religion has

For many Native American tribes, the extended family is the basic family structure. Elderly family members, especially grandmothers, are often teachers of traditions and customs.

ANSWERS WOULDN'T YOU LIKE TO KNOW ...

What values and beliefs distinguish Native
American culture?

Native Americans value cooperation and modesty more
than individual achievement and bravado. They also show
great respect for the elderly. Native Americans are not
materialistic. They believe in focusing on the here and now,
rather than worrying about the future.

always been important, but many practices were
banned when the federal government conducted its
60-year (1870–1930) program of enforced encultur-
ation ("The Denial of Indian Civil and Religious
Rights," 1975).

Puberty rites or equivalent rites of passage are still
practiced by some tribes and form part of religious
rituals today. When the federal government banned all
Native American assemblies from 1870 to 1930, except
between July 1 and July 4, the Apache changed the
individual rite that marked a girl's first menstruation to
a group rite in which all girls who had come of age
during the year participated. The mandatory rite marks
a transition in status from childhood to adulthood and
makes the young woman eligible for marriage. Navaho
boys and girls go through a religious ceremony at about
the time of the appearance of secondary sex characteristics. Through this ceremony, they are introduced to full
participation in ceremonial life.

Native American values are often at variance
with White American culture. The Native American is
present oriented, not concerned about the future or with
time; Whites are future oriented, concerned about time
and planning ahead. Native Americans see human life
as being in harmony with nature; Whites tend to seek
conquest over nature. Native American life is group
oriented, emphasizing cooperation, whereas Whites
emphasize individualism and competition. Native
Americans value the wisdom that comes with experience and old age, whereas Whites idealize youth (Joe &
Malach, 1992). The qualities of friendliness, humor, and
dependability are especially esteemed (Stiffman, Brown,
Freedenthal, et al., 2007).

As a result of conflicting cultures, Native American
youths today are faced with an identity crisis: whether to
accommodate to the White world and learn to compete
in it or to retain traditional customs and values and live
apart from the White world (Markstrom-Adams, 1990).
More than 150 years of determined government effort
have not succeeded in destroying Native American
culture and society. Yet the longer Native American
youths are isolated, the greater their chances are
of remaining the most deprived minority in the
United States. Certainly, one answer is to help all people

appreciate and understand the values of Native
American culture and the importance of preserving a
rich heritage. The adolescent who is proud of being
a Native American, as many are, and who is respected by
White society, can contribute richly to a Western culture
that prides itself on being culturally diverse.

Asian American Adolescents

Asian Americans, in general, differ from Hispanic
Americans and African Americans in that they have
been more successful at achieving the American
Dream; in fact, as a group they have done so well that
they have been termed the "model minority" (Yang,
2004). Asian Americans have a higher average family
income than all other groups, including non-Hispanic
Whites (Reeves & Bennett, 2004). Asian and Pacific
Americans are also more likely to have earned college
degrees. Even though they comprise only about 4 percent of the U.S. population, they earn 10 percent of
the nation's doctorate degrees and more than 20 percent of the doctorates in engineering and computer
science. This is not to suggest that Asian Americans
have not faced discrimination—they have and still do
(e.g., Sue, Bucceri, Lin, et al., 2009). Nonetheless, they
have managed to find their way into mainstream society in spite of hardships. Some of this success may be
due to the fact that many of their own cultural values
are sufficiently compatible with those of mainstream
American society to allow upward mobility.

Another explanation may be that marriages among
Asian Americans tend to be stable. More than 80 percent
of Asian American children live with both of their biological parents. More than half of all Asian Americans
are foreign born; it is therefore not surprising that most
live in the Western states near where they entered
the United States. Many Asian American immigrants
came from educated, middle-class backgrounds; many
others, however, were peasants looking for a better way
of life or fleeing political oppression.

The families of Asian Americans originally immi-
grated from all over the Asian continent. As shown in
Figure 3.7, the largest numbers trace their ancestries to
China, the Philippines, or India. About two-thirds of
Asian Americans are foreign born; about half of those
are naturalized citizens (Reeves & Bennett, 2004).

Chinese American Adolescents

There are about 2 million Chinese Americans in the
United States. A minority of modern Chinese Americans
are descendants of those who immigrated to the United
States during the period of open immigration from
1820 to 1882; many more are new or second-generation

---

matrilineal   descent through the mother's line.

FIGURE 3.7 COUNTRIES OF ANCESTRAL ORIGIN OF CURRENT ASIAN AMERICANS

Source: Reeves and Bennett, 2004.

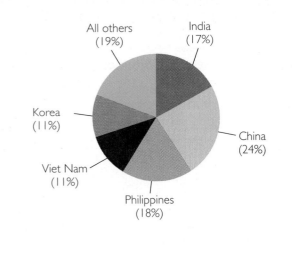

All others (19%)
India (17%)
Korea (11%)
China (24%)
Viet Nam (11%)
Philippines (18%)

ANSWERS WOULDN'T YOU LIKE TO KNOW ...

How did U.S. immigration law disrupt the family lives of Chinese immigrants?

For 50 years, U.S. immigration law forbade Chinese women to immigrate to the United States, with few exceptions. Therefore, Chinese men would come to this country to work, leaving their wives, children, and parents at home.

immigrants. After 1882, a series of exclusion acts restricted Asian immigration. It was not until 1965 that the national origin quota system that discriminated against Asians was abolished. Since that time, Chinese have immigrated in large numbers.

Until then, Chinese men entered the United States without their wives and children. Custom required that a man marry before he left China and that his wife remain in the house of her husband's parents. The man's duty was to send money to his waiting family and to return home eventually. Frequently, years passed before

he returned. Many hoped to earn enough to bring their families to the United States, but under the Immigration Act of 1882, no Chinese women, except a minority of exempt classes and wives of U.S. citizens, were permitted to enter. This restriction continued until 1943. As a result, Chinese men who remained in the United States were condemned to a life without intimate family relations (Chan, 1991).

Family and Children   Well-educated Chinese Americans have lower rates of divorce, mental illness, and public assistance—and higher family incomes—than the general U.S. population. In comparison to other minorities, Chinese Americans have more conservative sexual values (see Cross-Cultural Concerns box), a lower fertility rate, fewer out-of-wedlock births, and more conservative attitudes toward the role of women.

Most Chinese Americans today have a strong sense of family ties. They feel a high sense of duty to family, responsibility for relatives, and self-blame when a young person fails to live up to expectations. A child who misbehaves brings shame to the family name. They value **collectivism** (the belief that

Many Chinese American families emphasize the importance of intergenerational family ties. Even adolescent children place a great deal of value on the family unit.

an individual is less important than the family as a whole), conformity, emotional self-control, academic achievement, filial piety, and modesty (Kim, Yang, Atkinson, et al., 2001). Chinese American parents tend to be more controlling than Caucasian parents. However, because of their cultural heritage, their adolescent children are generally more accepting of this intrusion than Caucasian adolescents would be (Lam, 2003). Harmony and absence of conflict within the home are highly valued, more so than openness and communication (Shek, 2001).

Chinese children are taught that everyone has to work for the welfare of the family. They are given a great deal of responsibility and are assigned specific chores. Adolescents are responsible for supervising young children and for working around the house or in the family business. In spite of the effects of acculturation, even second-generation Chinese youths still place a great deal of emphasis on the family as the most important unit (Feldman, Mont-Reynaud, & Rosenthal, 1992).

Youths   Traditionally, rebellion among Chinese youths was almost unknown. Respect for elders was so deeply ingrained that youths never questioned their parents' authority or broke rules to bring dishonor on their families. If parents forbade something, it was wrong.

Contemporary Chinese American youths are more vocal than previous generations, more inclined to speak out and to rebel against authority than in the past. As this happens, the risk of antisocial behavior increases (Chiu, Feldman, & Rosenthal, 1992). Young and newly arrived immigrants from Hong Kong and Taiwan and American-born Chinese high school dropouts can become estranged from both the Chinese American community and White America and become involved in delinquent activity or join gangs (Tsunokai, 2005).

Education   Chinese Americans have always stressed the importance of education and hard work as the means of getting ahead. A study was conducted of the school performance of first- and second-generation Chinese American students and their Westernized peers in Australia and the United States. Results indicated that Chinese American high schoolers of both generations reported that they put more effort into school and reported higher grades than did their White American and Australian peers. Family factors were associated with both high achievement and greater effort (Rosenthal & Feldman, 1991). The emphasis is on becoming able to earn a good deal of money and to gain prestige from entering technical professions such as engineering, pharmacy, and dentistry (Leong, 1991).

About two-thirds of today's Asian Americans who are age 25 or older have a bachelor's degree or higher—almost twice the rate among all Americans (U.S. Bureau of the Census, 2009a). So great is the drive for educational accomplishment that Asian Americans outscore all other groups on standardized math exams and are well represented at the nation's top universities (National Center for Education Statistics, 2001).

---

collectivism   an emphasis on the family rather than on the individual.

CROSS-CULTURAL CONCERNS   AN EXAMPLE OF CROSS-CULTURAL CONFLICT: CHINESE AMERICAN ADOLESCENT DATING

Traditional Chinese values concerning adolescent dating are in conflict with those of present-day America. Parents raised in the Chinese culture generally believe that it is inappropriate for teenagers to date or to be interested in the opposite sex (Tang & Zuo, 2000). Dating is viewed as a distraction from the important job of doing well in school and getting good grades (Kim & Ward, 2007). In keeping with their parents, in the main Chinese American adolescents have more conservative sexual attitudes than their peers and begin sexual explorations at a later age (Feldman, Turner, & Araujo, 1999), although this is less true the more they are Westernized (Yu, 2007). Still, first- and second-generation Chinese American youths who have been raised in the United States and who have non-Asian peers with more liberal views toward adolescent sexuality are caught between two cultures.

How, then, do they navigate this culture clash? A recent study found that 70 percent of Chinese American youth dated without their parents' knowledge (Lau, Markham, Lin, et al., 2009). The teenagers expressed concern that their parents would disapprove if they found out, mostly citing fears that their academic achievement would suffer. Many parents, for their part, seemed to turn a blind eye to their children's dating as long as they continued to get high grades; they instituted a "no ask, no tell" policy. The Chinese American adolescents in the study also differed from Caucasian peers in being more likely to move quickly into an exclusive, steady dating relationship.

Filipino American Adolescents

The Philippine Islands were under U.S. rule for 44 years and gained independence in 1946. There has therefore been a substantial American presence in the Philippines for more than 100 years, and there has been much interaction between the two peoples. However, the inequality of the relationship, the fact that the United States ruled the Philippines, led many Filipinos to feel shamed and to have less ethnic pride than is found among persons from other ethnic groups (Rotheram-Borus, Lightfoot, Moraes, et al., 1998). Nonetheless, it is relatively common for Filipino American children to spend time living with relatives in the Philippines to experience that part of their heritage (Agbayani-Siewart, 2002). Unlike the majority of other Asians, most Filipinos are Catholic, a result of Spanish influence dating from the 1500s. Not surprisingly, Filipino Americans less strongly adhere to traditional Asian values than do other Asian Americans, as their culture is a blend of Spanish, native, and Asian traditions (Kim, Yang, Atkinson, et al., 2001).

Immigrants and Refugees

The United States is a country of **immigrants** and **refugees.** Ninety-nine percent of Americans can trace their ancestry to a foreign land. In 2005, more than 35 million foreign-born individuals resided in the United States, representing about 12.5 percent of the total U.S. population (Batalova & Terrazas, 2007). Approximately one out of every five American children is from an immigrant family (Hernandez, 2004). Historically, most immigrants to the United States came from Europe, but today Mexico, by itself, accounts for 39 percent of immigrants to the United States. (No other country contributes more than 4 percent of the total.) In addition, more than half of immigrants to this country were born in Latin America; the next largest group comes from Asia. Immigrants are a diverse group of individuals, not only in their place of birth and ethnic background but in socioeconomic levels as well. Many, for example, are well educated: in 2007, 27 percent of foreign-born adults in the United States had at least a bachelor's degree (Batalova & Fix, 2008).

Almost all immigrants come to the United States because they believe they can find better lives here. A subset, refugees, are fleeing political persecution or dire poverty. Since 1975, the United States has admitted, if not always welcomed, more than 2 million refugees—more than all the other countries in the world combined (United Nations High Commissioner for Refugees, 2005). Figure 3.8 illustrates the areas from which the most recent refugees have arrived. As you can see, more than 40 percent were from Africa. This is a change from the trend seen for most of the past 40 years, during which the majority of refugees came from Southeast Asia.

Regardless of country of origin, immigrants and refugees—along with their adolescent children—face many difficulties. They have come to a country where most people speak a different language, behave in different ways, practice different traditions, and hold somewhat different values. Even individuals who were educated in their homelands may face difficulty, as their degrees might not be considered equivalent to those earned in the United States. Refugees face the added stress of the trauma they endured before arriving in the United

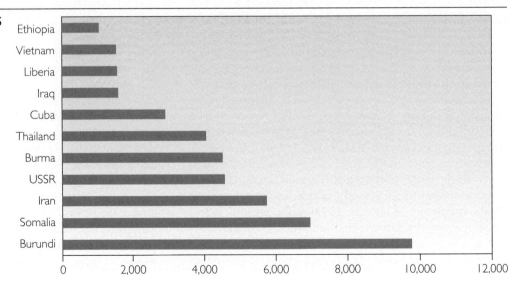

FIGURE 3.8 COUNTRIES OF ORIGIN OF REFUGEES RESETTLED IN THE UNITED STATES: 2007

Source: Data from U.S. Department of Heath and Human Services (2009).

States—perhaps seeing their home destroyed or living through starvation or war. They may even feel guilty because they survived to make their journey whereas many of their friends and family members did not. Immigrants may desperately miss those family members they lost or left behind.

One problem at least initially faced by many immigrants is poverty. Poverty rates for children in immigrant families are 50 percent higher than for children in native-born families (21 percent vs. 14 percent; Hernandez, 2004). They are often forced to live in areas of concentrated poverty with schools that lack the resources to help them make the transition to their new lives (Suárez-Orozco & Suárez-Orozco, 2001). Although immigrant fathers are almost as likely to be employed as native-born fathers, they work fewer total hours and earn less income. Immigrant mothers, conversely, are quite a bit less likely to work than native-born women (Hernandez, 2004): although this provides the positive benefit of increased parental presence and availability, it decreases family earnings.

Although immigrants and refugees come from all over the world, in the next section, we focus on the experiences of those from Southeast Asia. More research has been conducted on the experiences of Southeast Asian immigrants than on other immigrant groups because, as noted, a large percentage of refugees to the United States during the past 40 years have been from that region. Many of the issues they have faced are typical of the issues faced by all refugees, regardless of country of origin.

Southeast Asian Refugee Experience

The Southeast Asian refugee exodus from the countries of Vietnam, Thailand, Cambodia (now Kampuchea), and Laos is one of the largest such movements in modern history. Today, more than 1.8 million former Southeast Asian refugees live in the United States; they have almost 700,000 children (Yang, 2004).

There were two different waves of Southeast Asian immigration to the United States. The first was prompted by the fall of the South Vietnamese city of Saigon in 1975. Refugees from Saigon were almost entirely Vietnamese. They were generally well educated, young, urban dwellers, in good health, and in the company of family. The second wave of refugees included a much greater proportion of Hmong, Khmer, Lao, and Chinese Vietnamese ethnic groups. They were generally less well educated, less literate, and of rural origin. Escape attempts from the countries of origin were typically long and traumatic (Kinze, Frederickson, Ben, et al., 1984).

immigrants   people who leave their native land to come to live in the United States for any reason.

refugees   people who leave their native land to come to live in the United States because they are fleeing political oppression or death.

Immigrants and refugees face many difficulties, including learning a new language, behaving in different ways, practicing new traditions, and even holding different values.

Acculturation Stress of Adolescents

Major research findings indicate that most newly arrived refugees experience acculturative stress, primarily in the areas of speaking English, employment, and limited formal education (e.g., Nwadiora & McAdoo, 1996). Acculturation is a multifaceted phenomenon. The degree of acculturation of each adolescent depends on the following variables: (1) number of years in the United States, (2) cultural compatibility of the country of origin and the new culture, (3) age at time of immigration, (4) language use at home, (5) school environment, and (6) acculturation rate of parents and family members. The acculturation rate of refugee adolescents is influenced by the interplay of the culture of the country of origin, the U.S. culture, the refugee culture, the U.S. adolescent culture, and the refugee adolescent culture. Refugee adolescents, and the children of refugees, are confronted with traditional values from the old country, contemporary values from the new country, and transitional values that represent a mixture of some traditional and contemporary traits. A Vietnamese American adolescent girl born in the United States to refugee parents may be perceived as "too Vietnamese" by her American friends, "too old-fashioned" by her Vietnamese peers, and "too American" by her parents. Her American friends may expect her to go out after school, to date American boys, to drive a car, and to be more independent. Her parents may expect her to speak only Vietnamese at home, to take care of her grandparents and younger siblings after school, to clean the house, and to marry someone chosen by the family. Many such adolescents deal with the conflict by rejecting both the new and the old cultures and establishing a "third culture" with a combination of the two and their refugee experiences.

Southeast Asian youth often disagree with their parents about whom they should date and marry: parents are more likely than teenagers or young adults to believe that a person should marry within one's own ethnic group. They are also likely to believe that marriage should be delayed. Many of these parents, who have journeyed far to give their children better opportunities in life, are heavily invested in their children entering prestigious, high-paying careers; this may or may not be in keeping with the child's own desires. In addition, there can be stress at the role reversal that may occur because the children in the family speak better English and are more familiar with American cultural practices than are their parents. Adolescents may become the "cultural brokers" who deal with the outside world. Such dependence can evoke anger and resentment on both parts and may lead to family stress.

CROSS-CULTURAL CONCERNS AND URBAN INDUSTRIAL VALUES
COMPARISON OF TRADITIONAL ASIAN VALUES

Traditional Asian Values	Urban Industrial Values
Group/community emphasis	Individual emphasis
Extended family	Nuclear family/blended family
Interdependence	Independence
Person-to-person orientation	Person-to-object orientation
Past → present → future	Future → present → past
Age	Youth
Conformity/cooperation	Competition
Harmony with nature	Conquest over nature
Fatalism	Master of one's own fate
Logic of the heart	Logic of the mind
Balance	Change
Patience/modesty	Aggression/assertion
Pragmatic outlook	Theoretical outlook
Suppression of emotion	Expression of emotion
Rigidity of role and status	Flexibility of role and state

Source: E. Lee, "Cultural Factors in Working with Southeast Asian Refugee Adolescents," *Journal of Adolescence, 11* (June 1988): 167–179. Reprinted by permission.

Educational Struggles

Southeast Asian American youth overall have not had the stellar success in the classroom that has been characteristic of adolescents whose parents have emigrated from other parts of Asia (Yang, 2004). One reason is that many, even those born in this country, do not speak English well. In addition, their parents' limited English abilities, cultural norms, and lack of information prevent them from being closely engaged in their children's education. A significant number of Southeast Asian teens believe that their teachers discriminate against them, and this contributes to a sense of alienation from school that undermines achievement.

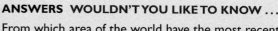

ANSWERS WOULDN'T YOU LIKE TO KNOW ...

From which area of the world have the most recent immigrants to the United States come? From which area have the most recent refugees to this country come?

Within the past decade, most immigrants to the United States have come from Latin America whereas most refugees have come from Africa. Both of these trends will likely change as the political and social situations in other nations fluctuate.

SUMMARY

1. American adolescents are a diverse group. Experiential and subcultural differences can be identified between high-socioeconomic-status and low-socioeconomic-status groups. People of different ethnicities also have different histories and somewhat different values.

2. Low socioeconomic status cuts across ethnic boundaries, affecting more than 10 percent of U.S. families. Low-SES youths are both culturally disadvantaged and have low incomes. There are at least four limitations on their lives: limited experience and opportunities; little autonomy or influence, which results in a sense of helplessness and powerlessness; hardship caused by lack of resources; and feelings of insecurity and being at the mercy of life's unpredictable events. The net effect of these limitations is to perpetuate a cycle of poverty.

3. Adolescents from low-SES families often achieve only a low level of education; they therefore do not possess the basic skills to acquire high-paying jobs.

4. Low-SES families are more unstable, resulting in large numbers of female-headed households. Parents tend to be harsh disciplinarians and more concerned with keeping children out of trouble than with personal growth.

5. Impoverished adolescents are more likely than their middle-class peers to suffer from both physical and mental health problems.

6. Lower-SES youth who are fortunate to have protective factors that buffer them from their harsh experiences may be resilient and overcome their adverse backgrounds.

7. Adolescents from minority groups have a wide variety of lifestyles and backgrounds. However, they share a legacy of prejudice and discrimination and are more likely to live in areas of concentrated poverty and to be chronically poorer than non-Hispanic White adolescents.

8. African American adolescents are gradually overcoming the legacy of prejudices and discrimination against them. Nevertheless, many African Americans still live in segregated neighborhoods and have not achieved equality of education, rates of employment, and income, although some achieve a high level of success in spite of the handicaps they face. Unwed adolescent pregnancy among African Americans continues at high rates.

9. African American family strengths include strong kinship bonds, respect for the elderly, adaptable roles, and a strong religious orientation.

10. Mexico is the ancestral home of most of American Latinos. The most outstanding issue facing Latino children and youths is the educational difficulty they face if they are not proficient in English.

11. Mexican American families are very stable. Familialism, or devotion to one's family, is a strong cultural ethic. Traditionally, the culture favors strong, well-defined gender roles. "Good" girls are expected to be modest and to remain sexually inexperienced until marriage.

12. The second-largest group of Latinos came to the United States mainland from Puerto Rico. Cultural values include fatalism, the need to maintain dignity, and a belief in strongly delineated gender roles. Puerto Rican Americans have a high poverty rate.

13. Native Americans comprise the smallest minority group in the United States, making up about 1 percent of the country's population. As a group, they are the least well-off Americans. They have the highest poverty rate of any culture group.

14. There are many Native American tribes, each with a unique culture. Common values, however, include matrilinealism, a strong sense of responsibility to one's extended family, respect for the elderly and for nature, and greater concern for the present than the future.

15. The ancestors of Asian Americans immigrated to the United States from countries as disparate as India, China, Korea, and Vietnam. Although they have

experienced discrimination, as a group, many Asian Americans are highly educated and financially well off.

16. Chinese American families are extremely cohesive; individuals are expected to act in a manner consistent with their family's best interest.

17. More than 35 million foreign-born individuals currently reside in the United States. Approximately 2 million of them are refugees who have been admitted during the past 35 years. New immigrants must cope with language barriers, cultural differences, and often economic hardship. Refugees face the additional difficulty of having experienced trauma and loss.

18. Many Southeast Asian immigrants were refugees. The stresses that they face include the difficulties of acculturation because of the major differences between traditional Asian values and contemporary urban industrial values. Conflicts arise over dating and marriage, career choices, and role reversal.

KEY TERMS

collectivism 72	*machismo* 67
colonias or barrios 65	*marianismo* 67
familialism 66	matrilineal 70
fatalism 67	refugees 74
immigrants 74	resiliency 60
low socioeconomic status (low SES) 55	

THOUGHT QUESTIONS

Personal Reflection

1. Were you ever financially poorly off as a child or adolescent? If so, do you remember how that made you feel? If not, did you notice that other children were not as well off financially? How did you feel about their situation?

2. Did you ever experience discrimination for any reason at any point in your life? Why? How did it make you feel? Could you successfully resolve the situation?

3. To what extent do you think that poverty is due to individuals' personal lack of ability or responsibility as opposed to lack of opportunity?

4. Think about having been raised in a home with uncaring, dysfunctional parents who didn't monitor your behavior or care about your education. Imagine that you lived in a neighborhood where many of the families were much the same. Do you think you would be as successful as you are today?

5. How important is your ethnicity to you? How different were your family's values from the cultural mainstream? Did you ever feel tugged in two directions?

6. How long ago did your family immigrate to the United States? Under what circumstances did they come? Do the stories your family tells emphasize the opportunities or the challenges they faced when they arrived in America?

Group Discussion

7. How is it possible for adolescents from poor families to break the cycle of poverty and deprivation?

8. Why are low-SES parents more likely than middle-class parents to harshly discipline their children?

9. Describe the discrimination faced by ethnic minorities in the community in which you were raised. Use examples to support your answer.

10. Do you believe that reparations are due to African Americans because of past slavery and discrimination? How about to Native Americans, for broken treaties and confiscated lands?

11. What should the government do, if anything, to ease immigrants' transition to life in the United States?

Debate Questions

12. All immigrants should be required to take classes in English.

13. There is adequate opportunity so that no one has to remain impoverished.

14. Discrimination is not a major problem anymore.

15. Poor parenting and dysfunctional family life are the primary causes of adolescent maladjustment.

16. It is the government's responsibility to help raise people out of poverty.

SUGGESTED READING

Benokraitis, N. V. (Ed.). (2001). *Contemporary Ethnic Families in the United States: Characteristics, Variations, and Dynamics*. Englewood Cliffs, NJ: Prentice Hall.

Coleman, J., and Hagell, A. (2008). *Adolescence, Risk and Resilience: Against the Odds*. New York: John Wiley & Sons.

Garbarino, J. (2008). *Children and the Dark Side of Human Experience: Confronting Global Realities and Rethinking Child Development*. New York: Springer.

Garrod, A., and Kilkenny, R. (Eds.). (2007). *Balancing Two Worlds: Asain American College Students Tell Their Life Stories*. Ithaca, NY: Cornell University Press.

Hefner, K., and Longhine, L. (Eds.). (2009). *Growing Up Latino: Teens Write About Hispanic-American Identity*. New York: Youth Communication Center.

Iceland, J. (2003). *Poverty in America: A Handbook*. Berkeley: University of California Press.

Kelen, J. A., and Kelen, L. G. (2002). *Faces and Voices of Refugee Adolescents.* Logan: Utah State University Press.

Piper, M. (2003). *The Middle of Everywhere: Helping Refugees Enter the American Community.* New York: Harcourt Brace Jovanovich.

Rumbaut, R. G., and Portes, A. (Eds.). (2001). *Ethnicity: Children of Immigrants in America.* Berkeley: University of California Press.

Suárez-Orozco, C., and Suárez-Orozco, M. M. (2001). *Children of Immigration.* Cambridge, MA: Harvard University Press.

WOULDN'T YOU LIKE TO KNOW . . .

- Why does puberty start?

- Which hormones are adults referring to when they describe adolescence as a time of "raging hormones"?

- What is the major difference between males' and females' sex hormones?

- What is usually the first sign of puberty?

- Why are girls often taller than boys during early adolescence?

- Besides the obvious, what are the differences between males' and females' bodies?

- Are most adolescents happy with their bodies?

- Do most teens think they are fat?

- Is it hard to reach puberty earlier or later than everyone else?

- How healthy are adolescents?

- Why don't adolescents take better care of themselves?

- What kinds of foods should adolescents eat?

- Why are more and more teens obese?

- Why can't you and your friends stay awake during 8 A.M. classes?

chapter

4

Body Issues: Physical Growth and Health-Related Behaviors

Imagine that you are taking a walk in your local park and are observing people running, walking, biking, and skateboarding by you. Being a people watcher by nature, you check each one out as he or she passes by. It takes you no time at all to figure out each person's general age: that one's a kid, that one's old, that one's a teen, that one's grown up but young. How do you do it so quickly?

Certainly, there are contextual clues, such as behavior and clothing style, but mostly you can tell by looking at people's bodies. Children just don't look like adolescents, and until late adolescence, adolescents don't look like adults. Why not? What kinds of changes happen to the body so that its shape and size change so much? Look again, and you'll notice that except for clothing and hair style, male and female children don't look very different from each other. That's certainly not true of adolescent boys and girls and adult men and women!

In this chapter, we examine how and why female and male bodies grow, change, and become so different from each other. We also talk about less obvious, internal changes that occur during puberty and set the stage for understanding the changes in behavior that occur during adolescence. We discuss the attitudes that adolescents typically have about their bodies, and how they are influenced by their shape and by the age at which they physically mature. Finally, we examine several issues that relate to adolescent health: these issues are important not only because they influence adolescents' current well-being, but also because many of the habits that we establish during adolescence linger into adulthood and help determine our health for the rest of our lives.

Biochemical Basis of Puberty

Ultimately, the physical changes associated with adolescence occur because the brain starts directing various **endocrine glands** to increase their production of **hormones**—chemical messengers that flow through the bloodstream and affect what other cells do (see Figure 4.1). We still do not know exactly what triggers the brain to do this, but it is surely a complex interplay between heredity and environmental factors such as food availability and stress (Sisk & Foster, 2004). For whatever reason, the **hypothalamus**—a part of the brain intimately connected with puberty and sexuality—becomes more active and begins to direct the body to produce more sex hormones.

The Hypothalamus

The hypothalamus is a small area of the forebrain about the size of a marble. It is the motivational and emotional control center of the brain, regulating functions such as hunger, hormonal production, menstrual cycles, and sexual behavior. We are most concerned here with the role of the hypothalamus in hormonal production and regulation. It produces a chemical called **gonadotropin-releasing hormone (GnRH),** which controls the secretion of the hormones LH and FSH by the pituitary.

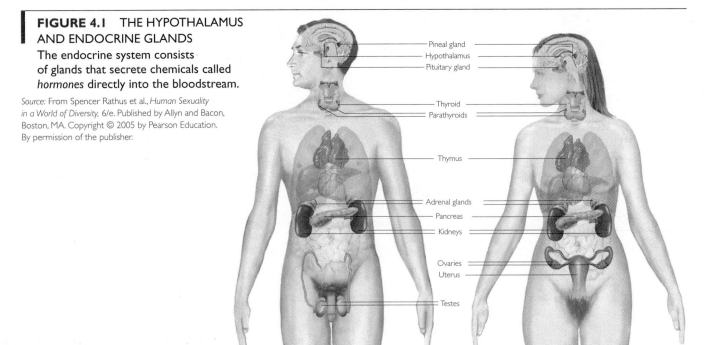

FIGURE 4.1 THE HYPOTHALAMUS AND ENDOCRINE GLANDS

The endocrine system consists of glands that secrete chemicals called *hormones* directly into the bloodstream.

Source: From Spencer Rathus et al., *Human Sexuality in a World of Diversity,* 6/e. Published by Allyn and Bacon, Boston, MA. Copyright © 2005 by Pearson Education. By permission of the publisher.

Male

Female

The Pituitary Gland

The **pituitary gland** is a small gland about the size of a pea that is located in the brain just beneath the hypothalamus. It consists of three lobes: anterior, intermediary, and posterior. The anterior pituitary lobe is known as "the master gland of the body," for it produces several hormones that control the action of the other glands.

Gonadotropic hormones secreted by the anterior pituitary are so named because they influence the gonads, or sex glands. The two gonadotropic hormones are **follicle-stimulating hormone (FSH)** and **luteinizing hormone (LH).** FSH stimulates the growth of egg cells in the ovaries and sperm in the testes. FSH and LH in the female control the production and release of female sex hormones by the ovary. LH in the male controls the production and release of male sex hormones by the testes (Susman & Dorn, 2009).

An additional important pubertal pituitary hormone is the **human growth hormone (HGH),** also called the *somatotropic hormone (SH).* It affects the growth and shaping of the skeleton. An excess causes giantism; a deficiency causes dwarfism.

The Gonads

The **gonads,** or sex glands, secrete a number of sex hormones. The **ovaries** in the female secrete a whole group collectively known as **estrogens** (from the Greek, meaning "producing mad desire") that stimulate the development of female secondary sex characteristics such as breasts and the distribution of fat on the hips and thighs. These hormones also maintain the normal size and function of the uterus and the vagina. By interacting with the pituitary, they control the production of various pituitary hormones. Studies have shown that estrogens also influence olfactory sensitivity, which is greatest midway between menstrual periods when estrogen levels are the highest (e.g., Doty, 2001).

A second female hormone, **progesterone,** is produced in the ovaries by a cell mass called the **corpus luteum** (meaning "yellow body"). The corpus luteum forms when LH from the pituitary interacts with ovarian cells following ovulation, and so levels are higher during the second half of a woman's menstrual cycle. Progesterone is an extremely important hormone. It controls the length of the menstrual cycle from ovulation until the next menstruation. It is of primary importance in preparing the uterus for pregnancy and for maintaining a pregnancy. A proper amount of progesterone is necessary to inhibit premature uterine contractions; it is often prescribed when there is a danger of spontaneous abortion.

The **testes** in the male, under the stimulation of LH from the pituitary, trigger the production of the male sex hormones, or **androgens** (meaning "to make male"). One male hormone, **testosterone,** is

---

endocrine glands   structures in the body that produce hormones.

hormones   biochemical substances secreted into the bloodstream by the endocrine glands that act as an internal communication system that tells different cells what to do.

hypothalamus   a small area of the brain that controls motivation, emotion, pleasure, and pain in the body; that is, it controls eating, drinking, hormonal production, menstruation, pregnancy, lactation, and sexual response and behavior.

gonadotropin-releasing hormone (GnRH)   a hormone secreted by the hypothalamus that controls the production and release of FSH and LH from the pituitary.

pituitary gland   master gland of the body located at the base of the brain.

gonadotropic hormones   hormones that are secreted by the pituitary and that influence the gonads, or sex glands.

follicle-stimulating hormone (FSH)   a pituitary hormone that stimulates the maturation of the follicles and ova in the ovaries and of sperm in the testes.

luteinizing hormone (LH)   a pituitary hormone that stimulates the development of the ovum and estrogen and progesterone in females and of sperm and testosterone in males.

human growth hormone (HGH)   a pituitary hormone that regulates body growth.

gonads   the sex glands: testes and ovaries.

ovaries   female gonads, or sex glands, that secrete estrogen and progesterone and produce mature egg cells.

estrogens   feminizing hormones produced by the ovaries and, to some extent, by the adrenal glands.

progesterone   a female sex hormone produced by the corpus luteum of the ovary.

corpus luteum   a yellow body that grows from the ruptured follicle of the ovary and becomes an endocrine gland that secretes progesterone.

testes   the male gonads that produce sperm and male sex hormones.

androgens   a class of masculinizing sex hormones produced by the testes and, to a lesser extent, by the adrenals.

testosterone   a masculinizing sex hormone produced by the testes and, to a lesser extent, by the adrenals.

ANSWERS WOULDN'T YOU LIKE TO KNOW . . .

Why does puberty start?

No one knows why puberty begins precisely when it does, but it has to do with changes in the region of the brain called the *hypothalamus.*

responsible for the development and preservation of masculine secondary sexual characteristics—including facial and body hair, voice change, and muscular and skeletal development—and for the development of the male sex organs—the seminal vesicles, prostate gland, epididymis, penis, and scrotum.

Estrogens and androgens are found in both boys and girls but in negligible amounts prior to puberty. They are produced by the adrenals and the gonads in modestly increasing amounts during childhood. As the ovaries mature, the production of ovarian estrogens increases dramatically and begins to show the cyclic variation in level during various stages of the menstrual cycle. The level of androgens in the female's bloodstream also increases but not as much. As the testes mature in the male, the production of testosterone increases dramatically, whereas the level of the estrogens in the male's bloodstream increases only slightly. Figure 4.2 shows the increases in hormones at puberty.

It is the ratio of the levels of the male to female hormones that is largely responsible for developing and maintaining male or female characteristics. An imbalance in the natural hormonal state in a growing child can produce deviations in primary and secondary sexual characteristics and affect the development of expected masculine or feminine physical traits. For example, a female with an excess of androgens may grow a mustache and body hair, develop masculine musculature and strength, and go bald (Redmond, 1998). A male with an excess of estrogens or with an androgen deficiency may show decreased potency and sex drive and an enlargement of the breasts (Vincenzo, Bruno, Matteo, et al., 2005).

The Adrenal Glands

If the testes produce the male hormones, androgens, and the ovaries produce the female hormones, estrogen and progesterone, how is it that adolescents of both genders have both androgens and estrogens in their bodies? Males get their estrogens primarily from converting some testosterone into estrogen. Females get most of their androgens from their adrenal glands. The **adrenal glands,** located just above the kidneys (the term *adrenal* means "on the kidneys"), are capable of producing small amounts of relatively weak male sex hormones. The ovaries also produce small amounts of androgens (Nussey & Whitehead, 2001).

Sex Hormone Regulation in Males

The hypothalamus, pituitary gland, and testes function in the male to control hormone production. Under the influence of GnRH from the hypothalamus, the pituitary secretes FSH and LH. The follicle-stimulating hormone stimulates sperm growth in the testes (**spermatogenesis**), as does LH. Without the luteinizing hormone, sperm production begins but the cells fail to fully mature. However, the chief function of LH is to stimulate the testes to produce testosterone.

The level of testosterone is kept fairly constant by a phenomenon known as a *negative feedback loop* (see Figure 4.3). The GnRH stimulates the production of LH, which, in turn, stimulates secretion of testosterone. As the level of testosterone builds, the hypothalamus, sensitive to the amount of testosterone present, reduces the production of GnRH, which, in turn, reduces the production of LH and testosterone. When the level of testosterone declines, the hypothalamus picks up this signal to increase secretion of GnRH, which stimulates greater production of LH and testosterone. The system acts much like a furnace with a thermostat to control the temperature of a room: an increase in temperature shuts the furnace down; a decrease turns it on.

An additional substance, **inhibin,** regulates FSH levels in another negative feedback loop (vanZonneveld, Broekmans, Blankenstein, et al., 2003). Inhibin is produced in the testes by cells called **Sertoli cells.** As the level of inhibin builds, FSH production is suppressed, which results in a decline of sperm production. Researchers have shown considerable interest in the possibility of using inhibin as a male contraceptive because of this effect. Whether the idea is practical remains to be seen.

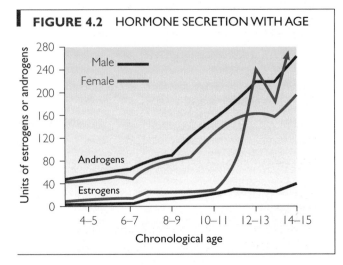

FIGURE 4.2 HORMONE SECRETION WITH AGE

FIGURE 4.3   NEGATIVE FEEDBACK LOOPS

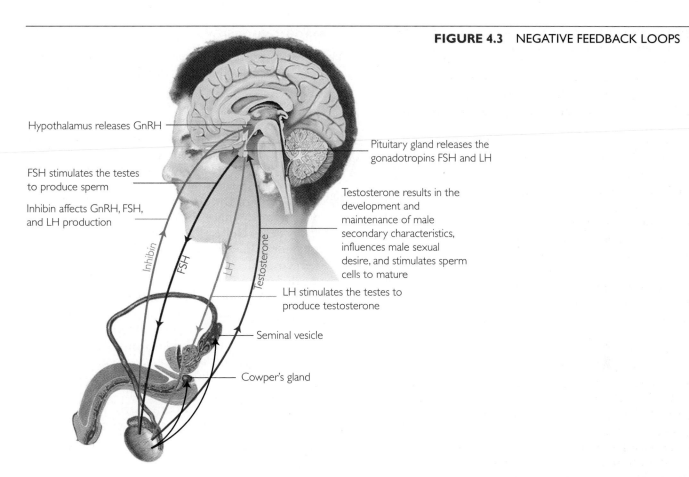

Hypothalamus releases GnRH

Pituitary gland releases the gonadotropins FSH and LH

FSH stimulates the testes to produce sperm

Inhibin affects GnRH, FSH, and LH production

Testosterone results in the development and maintenance of male secondary characteristics, influences male sexual desire, and stimulates sperm cells to mature

Inhibin

FSH

LH

Testosterone

LH stimulates the testes to produce testosterone

Seminal vesicle

Cowper's gland

Sex Hormone Regulation in Females

The hypothalamus, pituitary gland, and ovaries also work together in a negative feedback loop to control hormonal production in females. The gonadotropin-releasing hormone from the hypothalamus stimulates the pituitary to produce FSH and LH. These hormones act on the ovaries to stimulate the growth of follicles and egg cells and the secretion of ovarian estrogen and progesterone. As the level of estrogen builds, it inhibits the production of GnRH, which, in turn, reduces the production of FSH. Estrogen and progesterone levels of females vary with different stages of the menstrual cycle, as we discuss later in this chapter.

The increased presence of human growth hormone, the gonadotropic hormones, and the sex hormones in the bloodstream has a profound effect on the size and shape of the body. Since the purpose of puberty is, after all, to physically mature the body so that it will be capable of reproduction, it makes sense to begin with the changes that occur in the sex organs.

ANSWERS WOULDN'T YOU LIKE TO KNOW ...

Which hormones are adults referring to when they describe adolescence as a time of "raging hormones"?

When frustrated adults say that adolescence is a time of "raging hormones," they are probably thinking of androgens, the male sex hormones, and estrogens and progesterone, the female sex hormones. The other hormones involved include gonadotropin-releasing hormone, luteinizing hormone, and follicle-stimulating hormone.

adrenal glands   ductless glands, located just above the kidneys, that secrete androgens and estrogens in both men and women, in addition to the glands' secretion of adrenaline.

spermatogenesis   the process by which sperm are developed.

inhibin   a hormone produced in the testes to regulate FSH secretion and sperm production.

Sertoli cells   cells in the testes that produce the hormone inhibin.

Maturation and Functions of Male Sex Organs

Figure 4.4 depicts the primary male sex organs: the testes, scrotum, epididymis, seminal vesicles, prostate gland, Cowper's glands, penis, vas deferens, and urethra. A number of important changes occur in these organs during adolescence (Styne, 2002). The growth of the testes and **scrotum** (the pouch of skin containing the testes) accelerates when a boy is age 11 or 12, becomes fairly rapid by age 13 or 14, and slows thereafter. These ages are averages. Rapid growth may start between 9½ and 13½ years, ending between ages 13 and 17. During this time, the testes increase 2½ times in length and about 8½ times in weight. The **epididymis** is a system of ducts, running from the testes to the vas deferens, in which sperm mature and are stored. Before puberty, the epididymis is relatively large in comparison with the testes; after maturity, the epididymis is only about one-ninth the size of the testes.

> ### ANSWERS WOULDN'T YOU LIKE TO KNOW . . .
> **What is the major difference between males' and females' sex hormones?**
>
> The major difference between the hormonal systems of males and females is that the level of testosterone in males stays fairly constant, whereas the secretion of estrogen and progesterone in females is cyclic.

Spermatogenesis

The most important change within the testes themselves is the development of mature sperm cells. Again, this begins when FSH and LH from the pituitary stimulate their production and growth. The total process of spermatogenesis, from the time the primitive, undeveloped sperm ares formed until they are ready to leave the seminipherous tubules where they rest inside the testes, is about 10 days.

Following spermatogenesis, the sperm migrate by contraction of the seminiferous tubules to reach the epididymis, where they may remain for as long as eight weeks (Heller & Clermont, 1963). During ejaculation, muscle contractions and cilliary action conduct the sperm from the scrotum into the male's trunk through the **vas deferens.** They eventually reach the **seminal vesicles** and **prostate gland.** It is here that they are made more mobile by the addition of the *seminal fluid,* passing with through the **urethra** and out of the penis. The seminal fluid—a nutrient-rich alkaline fluid with a milky appearance—keeps the sperm alive, healthy, and mobile and serves as a vehicle for carrying the sperm out of the penis. About 70 percent of the seminal fluid comes from the seminal vesicles; the remaining 30 percent comes from the prostate gland.

The Developing Penis

The **penis** doubles in length and girth during adolescence, with the most rapid growth taking place between ages 14 and 16. Genital growth usually takes

FIGURE 4.4 THE MALE REPRODUCTIVE SYSTEM
The external male sex organs include the penis and the scrotum.

Source: From Spencer Rathus et al., *Human Sexuality in a World of Diversity,* 6/e. Published by Allyn and Bacon, Boston, MA. Copyright © 2005 by Pearson Education. By permission of the publisher.

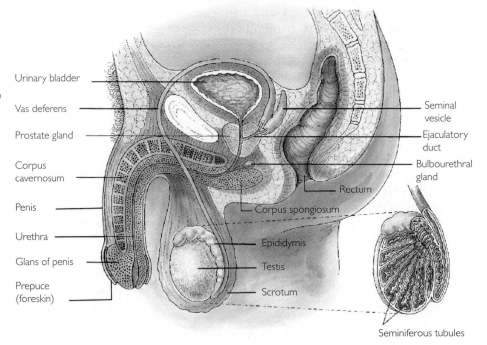

PERSONAL ISSUES   USE OF STEROIDS BY ATHLETES

Athletes sometimes take synthetic male hormones called **anabolic steroids** to increase their strength and endurance. Ever since several competitors were disqualified from the 1988 Olympics because of the illegal use of anabolic steroids, attention has focused on the use of these drugs by athletes of all ages. It is feared that the use of androstenedione—a nonprescription, over-the-counter food supplement thought to help build muscle mass—by baseball greats Mark McGwire, Barry Bonds, and Alex Rodriguez will further increase adolescent interest in these drugs. Steroids can be taken in pill form, rubbed on in cream form, or injected through a syringe.

There is no question that steroids increase muscle mass and reduce body fat. Unfortunately, they produce many serious physical side effects, as well. All abusers risk the development of liver tumors, jaundice, high blood pressure, weakening of tendons (resulting in tears and ruptures), heart attacks, strokes and blood clots, headaches, muscle cramps, severe acne, and baldness. And athletes who share needles are at increased risk for contracting hepatitis and HIV (human immunodeficiency virus), which causes AIDS (acquired immune deficiency syndrome). Males who abuse steroids are also likely to experience reduced sperm count, impotence, enlargement of the prostate gland, and increased breast size. Females who take steroids often find that their breasts shrink, their clitorises enlarge, they develop menstrual irregularities, their voices deepen, and their body and facial hair becomes more profuse. Adolescents who use steroids are at great risk for permanently shortened stature, since the presence of so much excess male hormone shuts down the production of human growth hormone (National Institute on Drug Abuse, 2006).

Steroids also have emotional side effects. Abusers are subject to severe mood swings, paranoia, depression, and anxiety. They often exhibit hostile, irritable moods and are prone to fits of rage. Sometimes, these feelings result in fighting and other types of destructive behavior, such as property destruction (Daly, Su, Schmidt, et al., 2003).

The number of adolescents who use steroids is, fortunately, low. Although the number of twelfth-graders who used steroids had been steadily rising from 1.1 percent in 1991 to 2.5 percent in 2000, the most recent figures (2008) indicate a decline back to 1.5 percent. Most teenagers who use steroids are male. High school students perceive these drugs as risky (about 60 percent), and most (about 90 percent) disapprove of their use. Teenagers believe that steroids are easy to obtain, although perhaps not quite as easy as they were a few years ago (Johnson, O'Malley, Bachman, et al., 2009).

---

3 years to reach the adult stage, but some males complete this development in about 2 years and others take more than 4½ years. In the adult male, the flaccid (limp) penis averages from 3 to 4 inches in length and slightly more than 1 inch in diameter. The tumescent (erect) penis, on the average, is 5½ to 6½ inches in length and 1½ inches in diameter; sizes vary somewhat from male to male. The head of the penis (*glans*) is covered by a loose fold of skin, the *prepuce* or *foreskin,* often removed surgically through *circumcision* for hygienic or religious reasons.

Adolescent boys are often concerned with the dimensions of their penis, for they incorrectly associate masculinity and sexual capability with penis size. These insecurities are often heightened because the scrotum starts to develop before the penis does. Mistakenly believing that their testes and penis should grow in sync, many young male teens fear that their penis will remain small forever.

Erection of the penis occurs beginning in infancy; it may be caused by tight clothing, local irritation, the need to urinate, or manual stimulation. Sexual thoughts and masturbation are added to this list during puberty. Furthermore, erections become much more obvious and potentially embarrassing once the penis begins to grow. It is common for adolescent males to experience undesired, uncontrollable erections, which they hope nobody else notices.

scrotum   the pouch of skin containing the testes.

epididymis   a system of ducts, running from the testes to the vas deferens, in which sperm mature and are stored.

vas deferens   the tubes running from the epididymis to the urethra that carry semen and sperm to the ejaculatory duct.

seminal vesicles   twin glands that secrete fluid into the vas deferens to enhance sperm viability.

prostate gland   gland that secretes a portion of the seminal fluid.

urethra   the tube carrying the urine from the bladder to the outside; in males, it also carries the semen to the outside.

penis   the male organ for coitus and urination.

anabolic steroids   the masculinizing hormone testosterone taken by athletes to build muscle mass.

The Cowper's Glands

The **Cowper's glands,** which also mature during adolescence, secrete an alkaline fluid that lubricates and neutralizes the acidity of the urethra for easy and safe passage of the semen. A drop or two of this fluid may be observed at the opening of the glans during sexual excitement and before ejaculation. Because the fluid often contains sperm, conception is possible whenever intercourse occurs, even if the male withdraws prior to ejaculation.

Nocturnal Emissions

Although male infants and children get erections, ejaculation isn't possible until puberty. Most adolescent boys experience **nocturnal emissions,** or "wet dreams," as do most adult men. In fact, even way back in 1948, Kinsey and colleagues reported that almost 100 percent of men have erotic dreams, and about 83 percent of them have dreams that culminate in orgasm. These dreams occur most frequently among males in their teens and twenties, but about half of all married men continue to have them.

Research has revealed that a boy's first ejaculation—termed **semenarche** or *spermarche*—is a memorable event (Janssen, 2007). Many boys are surprised at the occurrence because it often happens earlier than they imagine it will—most boys begin to ejaculate sometime before their thirteenth birthday—and because it is not often discussed. In addition to confusion, boys report feelings of pleasure and maturity. Still, most boys do not tell anyone that they have begun ejaculating. Those boys who are most informed about pubertal changes express the most positive feelings about semenarche.

Maturation and Functions of Female Sex Organs

The primary internal female sex organs are the ovaries, fallopian tubes, uterus, and vagina. The external female sex organs are known collectively as the **vulva.** They include the mons veneris (a fatty pad covering the pubic bone), the labia majora (major or large outer lips), the labia minora (small inner lips), the clitoris, and the **vestibule** (the cleft region enclosed by the labia minora). The **hymen** is a fold of connective tissue that partly closes the vagina in the virginal female. The **Bartholin's glands,** situated on either side of the vaginal orifice, secrete a small amount of fluid during sexual excitement. Figure 4.5 depicts the female sexual organs.

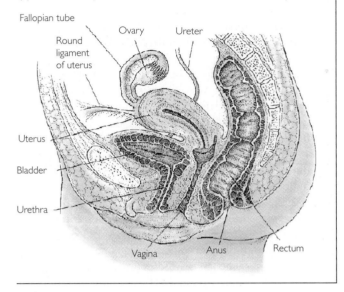

FIGURE 4.5   THE FEMALE REPRODUCTIVE SYSTEM
This cross-section locates many of the internal sexual organs that comprise the female reproductive system. Note that the uterus is normally tipped forward.

Source: From Spencer Rathus et al., *Human Sexuality in a World of Diversity,* 6/e. Published by Allyn and Bacon, Boston, MA. Copyright © 2005 by Pearson Education. By permission of the publisher.

The Developing Vagina

The **vagina** matures at puberty in a number of ways. It increases in length and its mucous lining becomes thicker and more elastic and turns a deeper color. The Bartholin's glands begin to secrete their fluids, and the secretions from the inner walls of the vagina change from basic to acidic.

Changes in the Vulva and Uterus

The **labia majora,** practically nonexistent in childhood, enlarge greatly, as do the **labia minora** and the **clitoris.** The **mons veneris** becomes more prominent through the development of a fatty pad.

A dramatic change also takes place in the **uterus,** which doubles in length, showing a straight-line increase in size from ages 10 to 18. The uterus of the mature nonpregnant female is a hollow, thick-walled, muscular organ shaped like a pear, about 3 inches long, 2½ inches at the top and narrowing to a diameter of 1 inch at the cervix. Note from Figure 4.5 that the uterus sits at a right angle, tilted forward, to the vagina, not straight up and down.

Ovarian Changes

The ovaries increase greatly in size and weight. Every infant girl is born with about 400,000 follicles in each ovary. By puberty, this number has declined to about

80,000 in each ovary. Ordinarily, one follicle ripens into an ovum (egg) every 28 days for about 40 years, which means that only about 500 ova ripen during the woman's reproductive years (Crooks & Baur, 2007). The **fallopian tubes**—each only a little larger than a human hair in diameter—transport the ova from the ovaries to the uterus.

Menarche and the Menstrual Cycle

On average, the adolescent girl begins her menstrual cycle at about age 12, although she may mature considerably earlier or later (9 to 15 years is the extreme range). **Menarche** (the onset of menstruation) usually does not signal the beginning of puberty in girls; it is in the middle of the process and does not occur until after maximum growth rates in height and weight have been achieved. The timing of menarche is partly due to genetic makeup (Demerath, Towne, Chumlea, et al., 2004) and partly to environmental factors. Because of enhanced nutrition and health care, girls start menstruating earlier today than in former generations (Gluckman & Hanson, 2006). An increase in body fat may stimulate menarche; vigorous exercise tends to delay it (Ellis, 2004). There are racial and ethnic differences in the timing of menarche. Parent and her colleagues (2003), for example, found that girls with Northern European ancestry hit puberty several months earlier than girls with Southern European ancestry.

The menstrual cycle may vary in length from 20 to 45 days, averaging about 28 days (Hilliard, 2008). There is considerable difference in the length of the cycle when women are compared, and any one woman may show widespread variations. A truly regular cycle is quite rare.

The menstrual cycle has four phases: the menstrual phase, the follicular phase, the ovulatory phase, and the luteal phase. As Figure 4.6 shows, hormones control the cycle. During the *menstrual phase*—which begins with the first day of menstrual bleeding—estrogen, progesterone, FSH, and LH levels are all at their minimums. This signals the hypothalamus to resume production of GnRH. GnRH, in turn, stimulates the pituitary gland to begin production of FSH. The *follicular phase* extends from just after menstruation until a follicle ripens and an egg matures. During this phase, the pituitary continues to secrete FSH. The follicle-stimulating hormone stimulates development of the follicles and one or more ova and induces the secretion of increasing levels of estrogen. When estrogen levels are at a peak, the hypothalamus acts on the pituitary to reduce the level of FSH and to secrete a surge of LH. The high estrogen level results in a thickening of the inner lining of the uterus (the endometrium) to receive a possible fertilized egg.

Approximately 14 days before the onset of the next menstrual period, the spurt in LH production results in *ovulation*, during which a mature ovum erupts from its follicle and passes into the fallopian tube. The *ovulatory phase* is the shortest of the cycle.

The *luteal phase* follows ovulation and continues to the beginning of the next menstrual period. During the luteal phase, LH secretion from the pituitary stimulates growth of the follicle from which the ovum has erupted. This follicle develops into the *corpus luteum,* which secretes progesterone during the remainder of this phase (see Figure 4.7).

A high progesterone level causes the pituitary to cease its production of LH, and the LH level drops. But without LH, the corpus luteum degenerates and dies. Without a corpus luteum to produce progesterone, the level of this hormone drops as well. At the conclusion of the luteal phase, a woman's body contains relatively little FSH, LH, estrogen, or progesterone. This triggers menstruation, and the cycle begins anew.

Whereas many, but by no means all, adolescents know that ovulation occurs on about day 14 of a 28-day menstrual cycle, they have no idea when it occurs during a cycle that is longer or shorter. Many believe that ovulation always occurs in the middle of a girl's cycle—that is, on day 17 of a 34-day cycle or on day 12 of a 24-day cycle. This is a serious

Cowper's glands   small twin glands that secrete a fluid to neutralize the acid environment of the urethra.

nocturnal emissions   male ejaculation during sleep.

semenarche   a recently coined term for a boy's first ejaculation; derived from the term *menarche*.

vulva   collective term referring to the external genitalia of the female.

vestibule   the opening cleft region enclosed by the labia minora.

hymen   the tissue partly covering the vaginal opening.

Bartholin's glands   glands on either side of the vaginal opening that secrete fluid during sexual arousal.

vagina   the canal from the cervix to the vulva that receives the penis during intercourse and acts as the birth canal through which the baby passes to the outside.

labia majora   major or large lips of tissue on either side of the vaginal opening.

labia minora   smaller lips or tissue on either side of the vagina.

clitoris   a small shaft containing erectile tissue, located above the vaginal and urethral openings, that is highly responsive to sexual stimulation.

mons veneris   mound of flesh (literally "mound of Venus") in the female located above the vagina, over which pubic hair grows.

uterus   the womb in which the baby grows and develops.

fallopian tubes   tubes that transport the ova from the ovaries to the uterus.

menarche   first menstruation.

FIGURE 4.6 HORMONAL CHANGES
DURING THE MENSTRUAL CYCLE

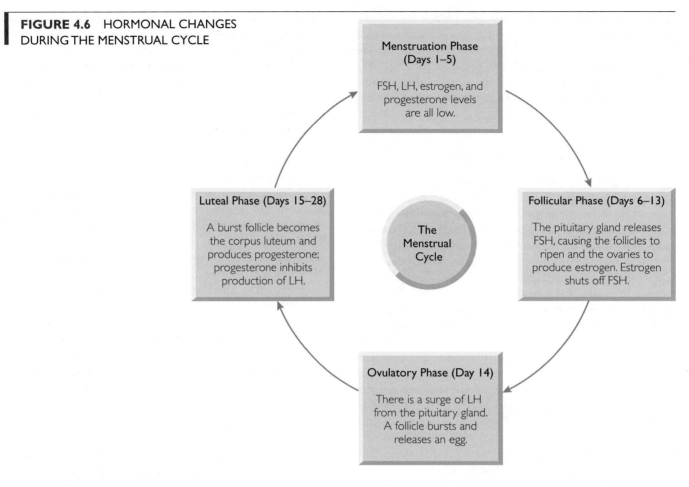

Menstruation Phase (Days 1–5)

FSH, LH, estrogen, and progesterone levels are all low.

Luteal Phase (Days 15–28)

A burst follicle becomes the corpus luteum and produces progesterone; progesterone inhibits production of LH.

The Menstrual Cycle

Follicular Phase (Days 6–13)

The pituitary gland releases FSH, causing the follicles to ripen and the ovaries to produce estrogen. Estrogen shuts off FSH.

Ovulatory Phase (Day 14)

There is a surge of LH from the pituitary gland. A follicle bursts and releases an egg.

misconception! Ovulation almost always occurs 14 days before the beginning of the *next* menstrual period; that would be day 20 of a 34-day cycle or day 10 of a 24-day cycle. Ovulation is *not* closely tied to the beginning of the current menstrual cycle. This is

an important piece of information because although pregnancy can occur at any point in the cycle, it is most likely to occur on the day of ovulation or one day later. If a girl's periods are at all irregular (which is true for most adolescent girls), then she cannot

FIGURE 4.7 FORMATION
OF THE CORPUS LUTEUM

Source: J. W. Hole, *Anatomy and Physiology,* 6th ed. (New York: McGraw-Hill, 1992). Copyright © 1992 McGraw-Hill Publishing Company. Adapted by permission of The McGraw-Hill Companies.

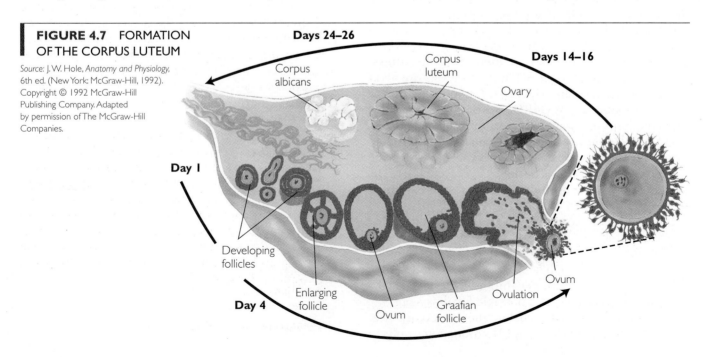

Days 24–26

Corpus albicans

Corpus luteum

Days 14–16

Ovary

Day 1

Developing follicles

Enlarging follicle

Ovum

Graafian follicle

Ovulation

Ovum

Day 4

PERSONAL ISSUES   STRESS, FAMILY DISCORD, AND PUBERTAL TIMING

For almost twenty years, research has consistently uncovered links between the age at which girls first get their periods and characteristics of their home environment. For example, we know that

1. Girls whose parents are warm and supportive undergo puberty at later ages than do girls whose parents are cold and rejecting (e.g., Romans, Martin, Gendall, et al., 2003).

2. Compared with girls from intact families, those from divorced families have an earlier onset of menarche (e.g., Bogart, 2008).

3. Girls raised in families with stepfathers undergo puberty at earlier ages than girls who are raised by their biological fathers (Mendle, Turkheimer, & Emery, 2007)

4. Higher maternal reports of interparental conflict are significantly related to earlier menarche (e.g., Jorm, Christensen, Rogers, et al., 2004).

5. As indicated above, several lines of research suggest that the absence of a girl's father hastens the onset of menarche. To confirm that the absence of a highly involved father promotes early puberty in girls, Kanazawa (2001) found that girls in polygynous cultures—cultures in which men are typically less involved with their children—reach menarche earlier than girls in more monogamous societies.

6. Depressive mood and poor family relations decrease the age of menarche. This has been found in American samples (e.g., Ellis & Garber, 2000) and replicated elsewhere. For example, Hulanicka (1999) described the same pattern occurring among girls in Poland.

How do family stress and family conflict lead to early menarche? Researchers propose that family conflict predisposes girls to lower metabolism and hence hasten weight gain, triggering the early onset of menarche (Ellis & Essex, 2007). In addition, stress during childhood has been shown to provoke changes in the hypothalamus, the part of the brain that triggers puberty (Dobson, Ghuman, Prabhakar, et al., 2003).

---

predict when she will ovulate. To do so, she would have to be able to count backward from a date that she does not yet know.

A girl's cycles are usually **anovulatory** (without ovulation) when her menstrual cycle begins. The first periods may be scanty and irregular, spaced at varying intervals until a rhythm is established. It is not uncommon for the flow to last only a day or so for the first few periods. Later, it may last from two to seven days, with the mean usually about five days. The total amount of blood lost averages 1.5 ounces (3 tablespoons). A normal range is from 1 to 5 ounces. Only part of the menstrual fluid is blood. The total discharge amounts to approximately 1 cup (6 to 8 ounces) and is composed partly of mucus and broken-down cell tissue (Warner, Critchley, Lumsden, et al., 2004).

Menstrual Concerns

Menarche is a big event in a girl's life. It signals as nothing else can that she is growing up. Some girls—especially those who feel they have been waiting a long time for menstruation to start—view the event in a highly positive light. As one student explained:

> When it happened, I thought FINALLY! It seemed like all of my friends had had their periods for years. I felt very left out when they'd sit around and talk

about it (even though they didn't make it sound very pleasant). I even practiced wearing pads so I'd be ready. When I woke up on a Saturday morning with a tell-tale stain, I called my three best friends right then and there—at 7:30 in the morning. I was so happy! I giggled on and off all day, because I felt I wasn't a kid anymore.

Contrary to this report, many girls have a negative view of menstruation. This is more common among early maturers, who are generally less informed about what to expect and how to manage than their peers who mature later (Chrisler & Zittel, 1998). Negative views typically stem from three sources: off-putting messages received from others, fear of embarrassment, and anticipated discomfort (Stubbs, 2008).

Unfortunately, many girls are pessimistically conditioned even before menses begins (Teitelman, 2004). Studies of advertisements of menstrual products showed that the ads depicted menstruation as a "hygienic crisis" that is managed by an "effective security system" that affords protection and "peace of mind." Failure to provide adequate protection places the woman at risk for soiling, staining, embarrassment, and odor. Such ads encourage guilt, insecurity, and diminished self-esteem (e.g., Simes & Berg, 2001).

anovulatory without ovulation.

Regardless of whether they are privately pleased that they are physically maturing, many girls do not want to share this information with the world at large. This taboo is especially strong in regard to males, even fathers (Kalman, 2003). Many college-age women can laughingly recall how they timed bathroom trips so that no one would suspect they had their period or how they would buy pads or tampons only from a female cashier, even if they had to wait in a much longer line. Fortunately, this desperation to hide one's periods seems to wane by late adolescence.

Some adolescent girls do experience physical difficulties with their menstrual periods (McEvoy, Chang, & Coupey, 2004). These physical problems usually fall into one of four categories. *Dysmenorrhea* is painful or difficult menstruation: menstrual cramps or abdominal pain, with or without other symptoms such as backache, headache, vomiting, fatigue, irritability, sensitivity of the genitals or breasts, pain in the legs, swelling of the ankles, or skin irritations such as pimples. *Menhorrhagia* is excessive bleeding. Both of these conditions are believed to be caused by an excess of **prostaglandins:** hormones that cause smooth muscle contractions. Therefore, almost all girls who experience these conditions can be helped by taking **antiprostaglandins,** which are drugs that destroy or inhibit these hormones. Ibuprofen is an antiprostaglandin that is available without prescription; aspirin, too, is a mild prostaglandin inhibitor (Mehlisch, Ardia, & Pallotta, 2003). *Amenorrhea* is absence of flow. This may be due to a physical cause, such as vigorous exercise that changes the percentage of body fat and alters hormonal secretion. It may also be caused by an endocrine disorder or a change of climate, overwork, emotional excitement, and other factors. *Metrorrhagia*—bleeding from the uterus at times other than during a menstrual period—is not common. It demands a medical checkup to determine its cause.

Generally, girls who have been menstruating for some time have more positive attitudes about menstruation than do premenstrual young women (McGrory, 1990). This suggests that the reality of managing one's period is not as bad as it is reputed to be. Still, some adolescent girls experience new mood swings with the onset of their menstrual period. Although not nearly as ubiquitous as most people imagine (most women experience only mild symptoms), many adolescent girls will find themselves more irritable or depressed in the few days before they get their period. Some may also find that they retain fluid, gain weight, have an increased appetite, or feel their breasts swell and ache (Claman, Miller, Cromwell, et al., 2006). There is a tendency, however, to mistakenly attribute a premenstrual sour mood with hormonal fluctuations. It is important to remember that all people, male and female, have emotional ups and downs. A girl who feels low the day before she gets her period might be experiencing the effects of low hormone levels or she might be reacting to breaking up with her boyfriend, just as she would mid-cycle. Many people attribute *all* bad moods during the premenstrual period to biology, when that is certainly not always the case (Baines & Slade, 1988).

Development of Secondary Sexual Characteristics

We began this chapter by observing that it is easy to tell the differences between male and female bodies, even when they are clothed. The physical differences in the

RESEARCH HIGHLIGHT   MENSTRUAL IRREGULARITY IN ATHLETES

Extensive research has established that *amenorrhea*, or cessation of menstruation, is common in female athletes: in fact, as many as 25 percent may have this condition (e.g., Misar, 2008). It is generally believed that a lack of body fat causes amenorrhea, since menstruation will begin only when a girl has attained 17 percent body fat (Warren & Perlroth, 2001). It has also been suggested that the amenorrhea is caused by the elevated cortisol levels that can result from prolonged physical stress (Reid, 2008). The current evidence suggests that exercise-induced amenorrhea rapidly reverses once training is discontinued. When physical training is reduced or stopped, either as a result of a vacation or an injury, amenorrheic athletes report a resumption of normal menstrual cycles.

However, in recent years there has been a growing concern over what has been termed the "female athlete triad": a combination of disordered eating behavior, amenorrhea, and **osteoporosis** (Reinking & Alexander, 2005). The bone mineral loss in athletes who have sustained amenorrhea can be quite dramatic and resemble that of postmenopausal women (Tietz, Hu, & Arendt, 1997). The bone loss can lead to increased bone fragility and risk of fracture, and the lost bone mass may be irreplaceable and irreversible.

It should be noted that *moderate* exercise has been found to reduce menstrual problems such as cramps and discomfort (Golub, 1992).

reproductive organs, however, are largely invisible in clothed individuals. The same sex hormones that cause changes in the reproductive structures during puberty also cause the **secondary sexual characteristics** to develop. These are the features that, although not absolutely necessary for reproduction, differentiate male and female bodies. They include the presence or absence of body hair, an enlarged or smaller larynx (voice box), and increased muscle mass or body fat.

Table 4.1 gives the sequence of development for boys and girls. The development of some of the primary sexual characteristics is also included to give a picture of the total sequence of development (primary characteristics are marked with an asterisk). The ages provided in the table are averages; actual ages may extend several years before and after. Although the average girl matures about two years before the average boy, the rate of development is not always consistent.

Generally speaking, the average age of sexual maturity has been decreasing over the years (Gluckmn & Hanson, 2006), primarily because of both the better health care of today's generation of youth and the fact that today's youths are heavier. Although many studies have found an overall link between increased body mass and early puberty (e.g., Anderson, Dallal, & Must, 2003), that link appears stronger for girls than for boys (Biro, Khoury, & Morrison, 2006). In addition, African American girls hit puberty earlier on average than Caucasian girls, possibly because of the combination African American girls' greater likelihood of having higher levels of body fat (Kaplowitz, Slora, Wasserman, et al., 2001) and their bodies' production of more **leptin,** a hormone associated with the onset on puberty (Susman & Dorn, 2009).

Males

The development of secondary sexual characteristics in boys is a gradual process. The appearance of pubic hair starts with sparse, straight hair at the base of the penis, and then the hair gradually becomes more profuse and curled, forming an inverse triangle and spreading up to the umbilicus (belly button). Figure 4.8 shows the developmental process. Axillary (underarm) hair usually first appears about two years after the appearance of pubic hair, with the growth of the beard coming near the end of the total sequence, and the indentation of the hairline (this does not occur

prostaglandins   hormones that cause smooth muscle contractions and contribute to dysmenorrhea and menhorrhagia.

antiprostaglandins   drugs that destroy prostaglandins and can reduce menstrual distress.

osteoporosis   a condition in which the bones become brittle due to calcium loss.

secondary sexual characteristics   features not directly related to reproduction that distinguish male from female bodies.

leptin   a hormone that helps trigger puberty.

TABLE 4.1   SEQUENCE OF DEVELOPMENT OF PRIMARY AND SECONDARY SEXUAL CHARACTERISTICS

BOYS	AGE SPAN		GIRLS
Beginning growth of testes, scrotum, pubic hair Some pigmentation, nodulation of breasts (later disappears) Height spurt begins Beginning growth of penis*	11.5–13	10–11	Height spurt begins Slight growth of pubic hair Breasts, nipples, elevated to form "bud" stage

Development of straight, pigmented pubic hair
Early voice changes
Rapid growth of penis, testes, scrotum, prostate,
    seminal vesicles*
First ejaculation of semen*
Kinky pubic hair
Age of maximum growth
Beginning growth of axillary hair
	13–16	11–14	Straight, pigmented pubic hair
			Some deepening of voice
			Rapid growth of vagina, ovaries, labia, uterus*
			Kinky pubic hair
			Age of maximum growth
			Further enlargement, pigmentation, elevation
			    of nipple, areola to form "primary breast"
			Menarche*

Rapid growth of axillary hair Marked voice change Growth of beard Indentation of frontal hairline	16–18	14–16	Growth of axillary hair Filling out of breasts to form adult conformation, secondary breast stage

*Primary sexual characteristics are marked with asterisks.

FIGURE 4.8 STAGES OF PUBIC HAIR DEVELOPMENT IN ADOLESCENT BOYS

Stages are (1) prepubertal (not shown), in which there is no true pubic hair; (2) sparse growth of downy hair mainly at base of penis; (3) pigmentation, coarsening, and curling with an increase in amount of hair; (4) adult hair, but limited in area; (5) adult hair with horizontal upper border and spread to thighs.

Source: Adapted from J. M. Tanner, *Growth at Adolescence,* 2nd ed. (Oxford: Blackwell Scientific Publications, 1962), as reprinted in H. Katchadourian, *The Biology of Adolescence* (San Francisco: W. H. Freeman, 1977), p. 67.

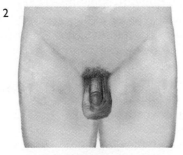
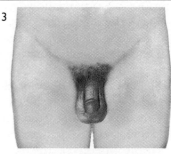
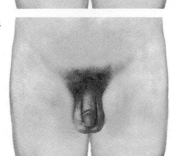
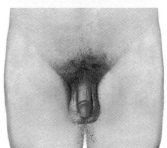

in girls) arriving as the final development. Muscular development, widening of the shoulders and chest, and other changes in body contours continue. Usually, a boy has reached 98 percent of his adult height during his seventeenth year.

Changes in the boy's voice are due to the rapid growth of the larynx (the Adam's apple) and the lengthening of the vocal cords across it. The vocal cords nearly double in length, lowering the voice's pitch one octave. Volume also increases, and the tonal quality is more pleasant. Roughness of tone and unexpected pitch changes may last until ages16 to 18.

Before and during the period when sexual maturation takes place, some boys (and girls!) suffer what has been referred to as the *locker-room syndrome.* After physical education class, middle schoolers are herded into the showers, where they have to undress and bathe in front of others. The range in normal developmental rates is great enough so that some boys are completely underdeveloped while others are substantially ahead of their classmates. The adolescent boy with little pubic or axillary hair, a small penis, or undeveloped muscles feels uncomfortable around his more fully developed friends. Those who have started to develop may feel self-conscious at their new more sexual physique. Involuntary erections in front of others are especially embarrassing, as is noticeable body odor. Furthermore, as many as 70 percent of boys experience **gynecomastia:** a temporary enlargement of their breasts resulting from an excessive amount of estrogen in their systems (Lee & Houk, 2008). In fact, almost everything having to do with body development can become a source of embarrassment.

Females

Girls also grow more body hair during adolescence. Development of pubic hair in girls is similar to the process that occurs with boys. On average, girls are about age 12 when straight, pigmented pubic hair begins to grow, first along the labia, then becoming more abundant and kinky, spreading over the mons in an inverted triangular pattern. By late adolescence, pubic hair spreads to the medial surface of the thighs. Figure 4.9 shows the developmental sequence (Katchadourian, 1977). Axillary hair grows about two years after pubic hair and is generally coarser and darker in brunettes than in blonds. Body hair, especially on the arms and legs, is the last to develop.

One of the most noticeable changes in girls is the development of the breasts. It takes place in five stages (Tanner, 1990):

1. *Prepubertal stage:* There is a flat appearance to the breasts.

2. *Bud stage:* Elevation, enlargement, and pigmentation of the nipple and surrounding areola begin, usually starting about 2½ years before menarche.

3. *Primary stage:* An increase in the underlying fat surrounding the nipple and areola causes the areola to project in a mound above the level of the chest wall.

4. *Secondary or mature stage:* The mammary gland tissue develops, producing larger, rounder breasts. The areola recedes and is incorporated

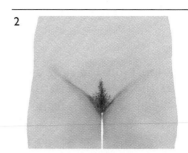

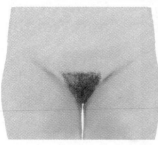

FIGURE 4.9 STAGES OF PUBIC HAIR DEVELOPMENT IN ADOLESCENT GIRLS

(1) Prepubertal (not shown), in which there is no true pubic hair; (2) sparse growth of downy hair mainly at sides of labia; (3) pigmentation, coarsening, and curling with an increase in the amount of hair; (4) adult hair, but limited in area; (5) adult hair with horizontal upper border.

Source: Adapted from J. M. Tanner, *Growth at Adolescence,* 2nd ed. (Oxford: Blackwell Scientific Publishers, 1962), as reprinted in H. Katchadourian, *The Biology of Adolescence* (San Francisco: W. H. Freeman, 1977), p. 57.

IN THEIR OWN WORDS

"I think that most of my friends were envious of my chest, but they didn't have a clue. I hated the stares—I still do. I can't walk down the street in the summer without some jerk making a comment. It was worse when I was in middle school. I grew really big by seventh grade, and I was the only one in my class who was so developed. I especially hated when we had to do laps in gym because I bounced so much. It was pretty uncomfortable, and the guys would watch me and crack jokes. I even quit soccer because I didn't like to run with anyone watching me. I wore tight sports bras all the time, trying to make myself look smaller. I couldn't wear tube tops or spaghetti straps like the other girls, and I always resented that because they are so cute!"

"I was really scrawny and small back in middle and high school—definitely a late bloomer. I'd played lots of baseball as a kid but couldn't make the team even in seventh grade because I was just too small. There was this group of guys who rode the same bus I did, and they gave me a hard time. There were three of them, and they were all bigger than me. They were on me all the time for being a sexless wimp (and worse). One day, their horsing around got worse. As we started fighting, one grabbed my shirt and it tore and half fell off. One of the guys laughed and said, 'He's all right! Look at all that pit hair!' After that, they started called me 'Pit,' but they stopped hassling me. I guess you could say my armpit hair proved I was a real man."

in the breast itself so that only the papilla (nipple) protrudes. This mature stage usually comes after menarche. Regardless of when development starts, it usually takes three years before the papilla projects out from the surrounding breast.

5. *Adult stage:* Development is complete.

Many adolescent girls are concerned about the size and shape of their breasts. Some girls who are flat chested feel self-conscious because they are influenced by society's emphasis on full breasts as a mark of beauty and sexuality. Girls who have unusually large breasts are also self-conscious when they suffer unkind remarks and stares.

Results of Sexual Maturation

One of the most immediate results of sexual maturation is a developing preoccupation with sex. Attention becomes focused on new sexual sensations, and on others found enticing and attractive. Adolescent boys and girls spend a lot of time thinking about sex, looking at pictures of sexy individuals, and talking about the opposite sex.

These awakening sexual interests motivate adolescent boys to devote much time and attention to grooming and clothes, to body building and care, or to various attempts to attract the attention of girls.

gynecomastia   a phenomenon experienced by some young male adolescents in which their breasts temporarily swell as they enter puberty.

Many adolescent girls are concerned about the size and shape of their breasts, due in large part to society's scrutiny of women's physiques.

Growth in Height and Weight

One of the earliest and most obvious physical changes of adolescence is the growth spurt that begins in early adolescence. This growth in height is accompanied by an increase in weight and changes in body proportion.

Growth Trends

As you can see in Figure 4.10, girls grow most in height and weight at approximately age 12; boys grow most in height and weight at approximately age 14 (Abassi, 1998). Girls are usually a little shorter and lighter than boys during childhood; however, because they start to mature earlier, they are, on average, taller than boys between ages 12 and 14 and heavier than boys between ages 10 and 14. Girls reach 98 percent of their adult height by the time they are almost 17, but boys do not until they are close to 18.

Determinants of Height

What determines the mature height of an individual? A number of factors are believed to be important (Rowe, 2002), but one of the most important is heredity. Tall parents tend to have tall children; short parents tend to have short children. The most

They may read pornography or go on the Web to find sexually explicit sites. Girls worry about their hair, experiment with makeup, flirt, and sigh over romantic movies or "chick flicks." They also spend endless hours discussing the hottest boys in class with their best friends.

Needless to say, it doesn't end there—with thoughts and fantasies. Most adolescents engage in some form of sexual behavior, including kissing, petting, masturbation, and intercourse. (These topics are fully discussed later in the text.)

ANSWERS WOULDN'T YOU LIKE TO KNOW ...

What is usually the first sign of puberty?

In most boys, the first sign that puberty is beginning is that their testes and scrotum begin to grow. The first obvious sign in girls is that they start sprouting and growing taller, but in fact the first indication is the appearance of breast buds.

FIGURE 4.10   INCREASE IN HEIGHT

Source: Adapted from J. M. Tanner, *Growth at Adolescence,* 2nd ed. (Oxford: Blackwell Scientific Publishers, 1962), as reprinted in H. Katchadourian, *The Biology of Adolescence* (San Francisco: W. H. Freeman, 1977), p. 55.

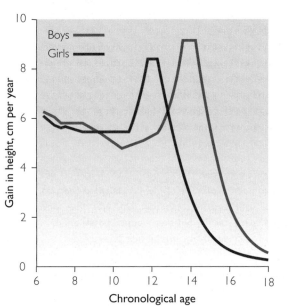

important environmental factor is nutrition. Children who are better nourished during the growth years become taller adults than those who are not nourished as well. Studies have shown that children from higher socioeconomic groups grow taller than those from poorer families (e.g., Mascie-Tayor & Lasker, 2005). The primary reason is better nutrition—although better health may also play a role.

The age when sexual maturation begins also affects the total height finally achieved. Boys and girls who are early maturers tend to be a little shorter as adults than those who are later maturers. Sexual maturation results in the secretion of sex hormones from the gonads; those hormones inhibit the pituitary from producing human growth hormone. A later maturer has a longer time to grow before the sex hormones stop the pituitary from stimulating further growth. In addition, because limb bones tend to grow longer faster than they grow wider, late maturers are usually relatively narrower and less stocky than those who stop growing sooner.

Evidence indicates that the process of physical growth has sped up. Children and adolescents in industrialized nations today experience the growth spurt earlier, grow faster, attain a greater total adult height, and attain this height earlier than did children and adolescents 100 or even 30 or 40 years ago. For example, a recent study found that Belgian adolescents are significantly taller in 2005 than they were in 1979 (Matton, Duvigneaud, Wijndaele, et al., 2007). In 1880, males did not reach their final height until ages 23 to 25; today, their adult height is reached at age 18 (Tanner, 1968). The average height of U.S. sailors in the war of 1812 is estimated at 5 feet, 2 inches, which explains why the decks of the U.S.S. *Constitution* did not need to be more than 5 feet, 6 inches high.

This accelerated growth pattern, referred to as the **secular trend,** has recently tapered off, at least in the United States (Sun, Schubert, Liang, et al., 2005) and other developed countries (e.g., Simsek, Ulukol, & Gulnar, 2005). Apparently, there is a limit to the ultimate size of human beings.

Other Physical Changes

There are yet other ways in which mature male and female bodies are different. The high level of testosterone in males prompts their bodies to develop differently from those of females, who have a lower level of testosterone (Wells, 2007). Testosterone causes bones to grow thicker and to become more prominent. Men, therefore, have a relatively larger chin and more pronounced eyebrow ridges than women. Men's voices are deeper because their larynx enlarges more. Testosterone also encourages muscle growth, and so men generally have larger muscles than women.

Finally, testosterone fosters the growth of hair over a wide range of the body: men typically have hairier arms, legs, chests, and backs than women. Paradoxically, testosterone causes the hairline on the forehead to recede, leaving men with a more exposed forehead than women. Since adolescent females do have testosterone in their systems, they experience increased bone and muscle growth and become hairier but to a lesser degree than adolescent males.

Conversely, a high estrogen level causes girls' bodies to become more feminine. Most obviously, estrogen encourages breast development and prompts the body to lay down a layer of *subcutaneous* ("under the skin") fat that men lack (Gloria-Bottini, Cervelli, Giarrizzo, et al., 2007). In addition, girls' hips widen to facilitate childbirth.

Internally and thus invisibly, there are other changes, too. Men's heart and lungs are relatively larger for their body size than are women's. Thus, men tend to have higher blood pressure. Their blood contains more oxygen-carrying hemoglobin. Men have relatively more "fast-twitch" muscle fibers than women—muscle cells that are strong but do not sustain their contraction as long. Women have relatively more "slow-twitch" fibers—muscle cells that contract with less initial force but can sustain their pull (Mannion & Dolan, 1994).

ANSWERS WOULDN'T YOU LIKE TO KNOW ...
Why are girls often taller than boys during early adolescence?
Your sixth-grade class photo didn't lie: girls are typically taller than boys throughout much of middle school because they hit their adolescent growth spurt about two years earlier.

ANSWERS WOULDN'T YOU LIKE TO KNOW ...
Besides the obvious, what are the differences between males' and females' bodies?
By the end of middle adolescence, it's not just the genitals that are different anymore. Girls' bodies are smaller, less boney, less muscular, and less hair covered than male bodies. Girls also have developed breasts and wide hips, whereas boys have developed broad shoulders.

secular trend   the trend to mature sexually at earlier ages.

Together, t
adolescent boy
women. (Of c
and factors su
than some me
quick bursts c
and carry mo
fuel their larg
bodies are bui
ogy lessens th
and stroke.

Body Ima

The health-r
are linked to
Those who f
to avoid han
do not, may i
a large part o
physically at
nate, the sta
are often uni
sion focuses
attractivene
own bodies.

Physical A

Physical att
important re
self-evaluati

Adolescents
and sizes. Th
is a muscula
whereas the
is endomor
to him is a
ectomorphi

ANSWERS WOULDN'T YOU LIKE TO KNOW …

Are most adolescents happy with their bodies?

Most adolescents are not that happy with their bodies, especially late-adolescent Caucasian and Asian girls.

and ethnicities to judge themselves as being overweight (White, Kohlmaier, Varnado-Sullivan, et al., 2003). Latinas, too, are relatively comfortable with "curves" (Rubin, Fitts, & Becker, 2003). Caucasian girls are often quite dissatisfied with their body shapes, as are Asian American girls (Mintz & Kashueck, 1999).

In contrast, boys are most likely to prefer having a mesomorphic body type (Ricciardelli & McCabe, 2004). In contrast to girls, generally only quite heavy adolescent boys believe that they are overweight (Jones & Crawford, 2005). Body dissatisfaction in more slender boys results from a lack of sufficient muscularity (Carlson Jones & Crawford, 2005). Tall men with good builds are considered more attractive than short men, and boys who are short or heavy are subjected to stigmatization and other psychosocial stressors (Barker & Galambos, 2003). Boys' preoccupation with muscularity appears in part media driven, since exposure to models in men's magazines (Baird & Grieve, 2006) increases body dissatisfaction in adolescent boys.

Adolescent males tend to feel better and better about their bodies as they move through adolescence, whereas adolescent females do not (Bearman, Martinez, & Stice, 2006). Therefore, not only are boys more satisfied with their bodies than girls during early adolescence (Rosenblum & Lewis, 1999), but these differences are even greater during late adolescence (Yuan, 2007).

Early and Late Maturation

As noted previously, there is a great deal of variation in the age at which adolescents undergo puberty. Figure 4.11 further illustrates this point. The timing

ANSWERS WOULDN'T YOU LIKE TO KNOW …

Do most teens think they are fat?

Adolescent girls tend to think that they are fat because their ideal is to be extremely slender. Adolescent boys are more divided about feeling too fat or too thin; their preference is to be lean but athletic.

In an attempt to be slim and attractive, many adolescent girls constantly diet. Unfortunately, carrot sticks and diet soda do not provide adequate nutrition.

with which an adolescent experiences the physical changes of puberty can have a profound effect on how he or she feels about his or her body and self. For good or ill, it can also affect how others treat him or her and the expectations that they have of him or her. This is especially true for someone who matures either earlier or later than average. Much research has been devoted to understanding the effects of the timing of puberty on adolescents' self-esteem and behavior, including upon health-related behavior.

Early-Maturing Boys

There has been a long-standing belief, based on older data, that early maturation is a positive experience for boys (Ge, Conger, & Elder, 2001). It seems logical that this would be the case. After all, early-maturing boys are large for their age, stronger, more

FIGURE 4.11   VARIATIONS IN PUBESCENT DEVELOPMENT
All three girls are 12³/₂ years and all three boys are 14³/₄ years of age but in different stages of puberty.

Source: Adapted from J. M. Tanner, *Scientific American* (Sept. 1973): 38.

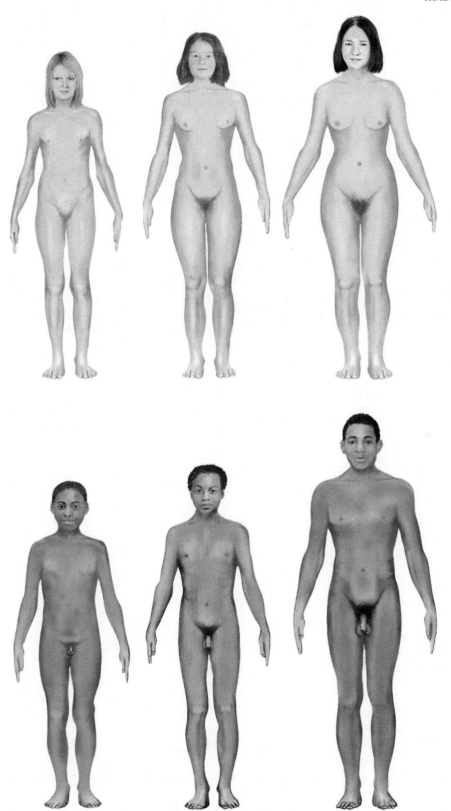

muscular, and better coordinated than later-maturing boys, so they enjoy a considerable athletic advantage. Early-maturing boys are better able to excel in competitive sports, and their athletic skills enhance their social prestige and position. They enjoy considerable social advantages in relation to their peers, participate more frequently in extracurricular activities in high school, and are often chosen for leadership roles. Early-maturing boys also tend to show more interest in girls and to be popular with them because of their mature appearance. Early sexual maturation thrusts them into heterosexual relationships at an early age.

More recent data highlight the fact that some early-maturing boys cannot handle the freedom they are granted, nor perhaps, the pressure they feel to conform to older peers. The strongest linkages are with smoking (van Jaarsveld, Fidler, Simon, et al., 2007) and alcohol use (Wichstrøm, 2001). These problems seem most likely to appear when the boys are experiencing detectable stressors in their lives. These problems by no means affect all early maturers, but they are common enough to raise the group average above that of later-developing males.

Late-Maturing Boys

Although this phenomenon has been much less studied, it is logical to assume that late-maturing boys experience socially induced inferiority. A boy who has not reached puberty at age 15 may be 8 inches shorter and 30 pounds lighter than his early-maturing male friends. Accompanying this size difference are marked differences in body build, strength, and coordination. Because physical size and motor coordination play such an important role in social acceptance, late maturers develop body dissatisfaction and negative self-concepts (Alsaker, 1992; Richards & Larson, 1993). They are characterized as less attractive and are less popular. They may become self-conscious and withdraw because of their social rejection. Some studies have found that late-maturing boys drink (Andersson & Magnusson, 1990) and engage in antisocial behavior, perhaps in an attempt to appear older and more mature.

The undesirable behaviors that result from off-time maturation may be superficially similar, but the same activity may be differently motivated for late and early maturers. Williams and Dunlop (1999), who found high delinquency rates in both early- and late-maturing boys, suggest that early maturers are motivated to misbehave when egged on by older peers, whereas late maturers misbehave in order to raise their self-esteem and gain social status. *All* adolescents want to be liked and admired by their peers, and they will engage in compensatory behaviors to ensure their acceptance.

In fact, it might be the presence or lack of acceptance that determines whether off-time maturers will have problems. In a more recent study, Nadeem and Graham (2005) found that it was the early-maturing boys who were perceived as misfits or victims by peers. Apparently, the combination of being physically developed while at the same time not behaving in a sufficiently "masculine" fashion encouraged peer bullying, and the stress of this bullying provoked problematic behavior. Similarly, the small size of late-maturing boys can make them easy targets for bullies (Olweus, 1991). Off-time maturation may therefore interact with peer acceptance to affect adjustment.

Early-Maturing Girls

Early maturation is not a positive experience for female adolescents (Susman & Dorn, 2009). Since girls usually reach puberty about two years before boys, the earliest-maturing girls are considerably out of step with the rest of their peers. Because they are taller and more developed sexually, they tend to feel awkward and self-conscious. Early maturers are also *heavier* than their friends, which, as discussed earlier, is perceived negatively by most female adolescents. Being so different from their peers adversely affects these girls' self-esteem and distances them from their peers (Ge, Conger, & Elder, 2001).

Given these stresses and the fact that early-maturing girls are more likely to hang around with older boys, they are at increased risk for a variety of problems. Early-maturing females are more likely to experience internalizing disorders, such as anxiety and depression (Ge, Conger, & Elder, 2001; Graber, Seeley, Brooks-Gunn, et al., 2004), and they are more likely to develop eating disorders (McCabe & Ricciardelli, 2004). They are more likely to perform delinquent acts, including violent ones (Haynie, 2003). They are more likely to engage in early sexual behavior (Ellis, 2004), and they are more likely to drink (Lanza & Collins, 2002). As with early-maturing boys, early maturation makes girls susceptible to other stressors in their lives (Ge, Conger, and Elder, 1996).

These effects are not limited to girls in the United States but have been replicated in Europe and in Asia. For example, in a Slovakian study, Prokopcakova (1998) found that early-maturing girls were more likely to drink alcohol, smoke cigarettes, smoke marijuana, and spend more time with boys than their on-time or late-maturing peers.

Late-Maturing Girls

Late-maturing girls are at a social disadvantage in middle school and high school. They look like little girls and resent being treated as such. They are largely bypassed and overlooked in invitations to boy-girl parties and social events. Girls who experience menarche at ages 14 to 18 are especially late daters. As a consequence, late-maturing girls may be envious of their friends who are better developed. They are generally on the same level with normal-maturing boys and so have much in common with them as friends. However, their activities reflect the interests of those of the younger age groups with whom they spend their time.

One advantage is that late-maturing girls do not experience the sharp criticism of parents and other adults as do girls who develop early. The chief disadvantage seems to be the temporary loss of social status because of their relative physical immaturity.

ANSWERS WOULDN'T YOU LIKE TO KNOW …

Is it hard to reach puberty earlier or later than everyone else?

It's easiest to deal with puberty if you are in the middle of the pack. Early maturers may get teased and find themselves in trouble because they often hang out with misbehaving older peers. Late maturers may also get teased and may be excluded by peers because they appear immature and childlike.

Health Status

Mortality

One of the most common ways to understand health concerns is to examine **mortality** or death rates. The *number* of deaths tells us how relatively healthy a certain group is, and the *causes* of death tell us where the most significant problems lie. Figure 4.12 shows the death rates of American children, adolescents, and adults. As you can see, the rate for younger adolescents (ages 10 to 14) is low, but the rate for older adolescents (ages 15 to 19), although still less than that of adults, is quite a bit higher (Centers for Disease Control and Prevention [CDC], 2009).

The reason for this rise can be inferred from Figure 4.13, which depicts the leading causes of death of American adolescents. The single most common reason that adolescents die is car accidents. (Note, however, that adolescents who wear seatbelts and drive only when sober are much less likely to die or be seriously injured in motor vehicle accidents.) About three-fourths of adolescent deaths are due to nonmedical reasons: accidents, taken together, account for just about half of the deaths, and violence (homicide and suicide) accounts for about one-fourth (Centers for Disease Control, 2005). This pattern is a change from the past, when most adolescent deaths were due to natural causes (Ozer, Park, Paul, et al., 2003). Older adolescents are more likely to die from both accidents and violence

mortality   the probability of dying.

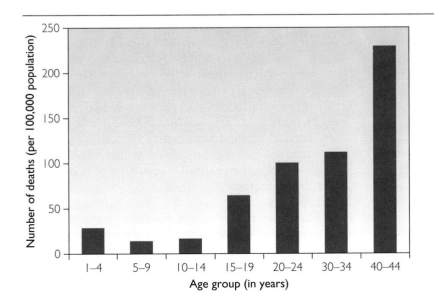

FIGURE 4.12   DEATH RATES OVER THE LIFESPAN: 2006

Source: Data from Centers for Disease Control (2009).

PERSONAL ISSUES   AUTOMOBILE CASUALTIES

Adolescents are not very safe drivers. In fact, they are more likely to be in accidents than drivers of any other age, including the elderly. Youths are especially accident prone in these situations: right after they get their license, at night, after they have been drinking, and when they are horsing around with their passengers (McCartt, Shabanova, & Leaf, 2003).

Accident fatality rates for teens followed several clear trends in the 1990s. The good news was that the overall fatality rate fell during this period. The bad news was that the fatality rates for African American teens, Asian American teens, and Hispanic American girls rose slightly during the same period (Ozer, Park, Paul, Brindis, et al., 2003).

Adolescents can take several steps to reduce their risk of becoming a motor vehicle fatality. First, they should wear a seat belt, whether driving or riding. The death rate is about twice as high for those who don't wear a seat belt compared to those who do. Most teens (about 85 percent) now report that they "usually" or "always" wear a seat belt, especially females (NHTSA, 2001), so "buckling up" should carry no sense of social stigma.

Second, teens should avoid driving after drinking alcohol. Males are more likely than females to perform this risky behavior. Similarly, teens should avoid being a passenger in a car being driven by someone who has been drinking. Males and females report this behav-

ior with equal frequency. Studies have shown that it is even more risky to ride with someone who is drunk than to drive while drunk yourself; the passenger seat is a more dangerous place to sit than the driver's seat, in part because cars are less likely to have passenger-side airbags. Almost 30 percent of adolescent traffic fatalities involve a collision resulting from drunk driving (NHTSA, 2001).

Although it has become commonplace, drivers should avoid both talking on a cell phone or, even worse, text messaging while driving. Researchers at the University of Utah (Strayer, Drews, & Crouch, 2006) found that college students who spoke on cell phones, even if they used hands-free devices—drove as badly as those who had been given alcohol to drink before being placed in the driving simulator; in fact, they were in more accidents. Similarly, researchers at the Virginia Tech Transportation Institute found that while texting, drivers were 23 times as likely to be involved in an accident as when they were focused on the road (Richtel, 2009).

Finally, the 25 percent of adolescents who sometimes ride on motorcycles should wear a helmet, as doing so greatly increases the likelihood of surviving a motorcycle crash. Only about two-thirds of adolescents who ride on motorcycles do wear a helmet (Ozer, Park, Paul, et al., 2003).

---

than younger adolescents, hence, their increased mortality rate. Males, who are more likely to be violent and to take risks, are more likely to die than females. Remember, too, that accidents and violence can result in injury and disability as well as death and so greatly contribute to the health concerns of living adolescents.

Health Decisions

Every day, each of us makes decisions that affect our well-being. We can make good decisions, such as following a healthy diet, exercising regularly, keeping medical appointments, and getting adequate sleep, or we can make bad decisions and engage in risky behaviors, such as using drugs, practicing unsafe sex, and performing thrilling but risky stunts. The health decisions adolescents make result from a complex interplay of factors:

1. *Their knowledge of the health consequences of particular behaviors.* This knowledge is, of course, based on what parents, peers, doctors, and teachers have taught teens, as well as the messages they have received from the media and society at large.

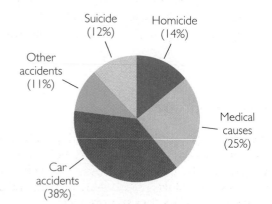

FIGURE 4.13   LEADING CAUSES OF DEATH OF AMERICAN ADOLESCENTS

Source: Data from Centers for Disease Control (2005).

Suicide (12%)
Homicide (14%)
Other accidents (11%)
Medical causes (25%)
Car accidents (38%)

2. *Their ability to judge risks and make rational decisions.* Cognitive development is taken up in a later chapter of this book, but it is important to state here that adolescents' ability to think abstractly, to appreciate the long-term consequences of actions, to evaluate information, and to weigh personal risk is not fully developed.

3. *Their parents' behaviors.* Adolescents mimic their mothers' and fathers' actions and values. So if parents are unconcerned about their own health, then their adolescents are likely to be lackadaisical, as well. Another factor is that parents who closely monitor and supervise their children do not give them as much opportunity to engage in dangerous behaviors.

4. *The resources available to teens and their families.* Some families may have the desire to lead a healthy lifestyle but not the means. For instance, some families have no choice but to live in a dangerous, polluted, or violent neighborhood. Likewise, some cannot afford to get regular medical and dental checkups.

5. *Peer pressure.* Peers can convince one another to be sexually active, to drink alcohol or use drugs, or to do something dangerous, such as swim where there is a strong current. Conversely, peers can encourage one another to use condoms, to avoid drugs, and to participate in sports or exercise.

6. *Societal values.* Adolescents receive messages that it's important, for instance, to be slender and that it's cool to smoke and drink. The images they see on television and in movies and the advertisements directed at them in magazines and other media often encourage less-than-ideal health behaviors.

Adolescent Health in the Third World

The health issues facing adolescents living in the less developed parts of the world are quite different from those confronting American teenagers (Call, Aylin, Hein, et al., 2002). Some of the problems of Third World teens stem directly from poverty and political instability. For example, adolescents in much of Asia, Africa, and Latin America are more likely than American youths to be malnourished and to contract illnesses. In many parts of the world, where political instability is the reality, war and terrorism take their toll on lives and health and disrupt the government's ability to provide needed health services. In addition, numerous children and adolescents in sub–Saharan Africa are infected with the human immunodeficiency virus (HIV) that leads to AIDS (acquired immune deficiency syndrome). Countless more have been left orphans because their parents have succumbed to this disease.

Other negative health consequences can be attributed to Westernization and rapid cultural change. For example, Third World youths today are smoking in greater and greater numbers. This is due, in good part, to the fact that American tobacco companies, which are facing ever greater restrictions in the United States, are increasingly turning their marketing efforts overseas (Verma & Saraswathi, 2002). And as sexual values change, adolescents from Southeast Asia, China, the Indian subcontinent, Latin America, and Africa (not to mention North America and Europe) are engaging in more nonmarital sex and beginning at earlier ages (Brown, Larson, & Saraswathi, 2002). This has greatly increased the likelihood that these teens will develop sexually transmitted infections.

Health Concerns

Being healthy requires not only avoiding unhealthy behaviors but also practicing healthy behaviors. In order to stay healthy, adolescents must eat well, exercise sufficiently, maintain a reasonable weight, and get enough sleep. But what does that mean?

Nutrition

Adults sometimes think that adolescents are constantly eating. The fact is that during the period of rapid growth, adolescents *need* greater quantities of food, as well as certain nutrients, to take care of bodily requirements.

The stomach increases in size and capacity in order to be able to digest the increased amount of food needed by adolescents. Research shows that the caloric requirement for girls may increase, on average, by 25 percent from ages 10 to 15 and then decrease slightly and level off. The caloric requirement for boys may increase, on average, by 90 percent from ages 10 to 19. Active adolescent boys need between 2,500 and 3,000 calories a day; girls, with their smaller stature and lower basal metabolic rate, need about 2,200 (DiMeglio, 2000).

Adolescents also need the right nutrients. Most studies of nutrition during adolescence show that many adolescents have inadequate diets (Venkdeswaran, 2000). The deficiencies may be summarized as follows:

1. Insufficient calcium, due primarily to the inadequate intake of milk and dairy products—adolescents need 1,200 to 1,500 milligrams of calcium daily, which is equivalent to about three servings of dairy products.

2. Insufficient iron, especially in girls—girls need more iron than males (15 milligrams versus 12 milligrams) because of the blood loss that occurs with menstruation. Iron can be found in red meat, eggs, beans, and dark green vegetables such as spinach.

3. Inadequate protein, primarily in girls who are dieting.

4. Too little vitamin A, which can be found in yellow and green fruits and vegetables.

5. Insufficient vitamin B6, which can be found in seeds, whole grains, and legumes.

Adolescent girls have nutritional deficiencies more often than boys. One reason is that girls eat less and so are less likely to get the necessary

Media images of excessively slender women encourage adolescent girls to be overly critical of and dissatisfied with their own weight.

nutrients; another reason is that they are so frequently on diets (Adams, Sargent, Thompson, et al. 2000). The additional need for some nutrients because of menstruation or pregnancy may cause special problems. In any case, about 20 percent of boys but only 7 percent of girls get all the nutrients they need (DiMeglio, 2000).

Why do so many adolescents, both boys and girls, have inadequate diets? Here are some of the reasons:

1. They *skip breakfast* because of lack of time in the morning, because they would rather sleep late, or to save calories.

2. They rely on *snacks,* which make up about one-fourth of their daily intake of food. Snacks do not compensate for missed meals because they are composed primarily of fats, carbohydrates, and sugars.

3. They eat only *small quantities of nutritious foods,* especially fruits, vegetables, milk, cheese, and meat. Girls usually need more eggs and whole-grain cereal than they eat. One-quarter of

---

● **ANSWERS WOULDN'T YOU LIKE TO KNOW . . .**

What kinds of foods should adolescents eat?

The healthiest diet for adolescents includes a lot of fruits and vegetables (the green, red, and yellow kinds), whole grains (brown rice, not white bread), lean meats and fish, and lowfat dairy products. It includes little processed sugar, saturated fats (butter and ice cream), and starches (potatoes).

all vegetables eaten by teens are french fries (Washington State Department of Health, 2000)—hardly the most nourishing choice. Very few adolescents (20 percent) eat enough fruits and vegetables (Grunbaum, Kann, Kirchen, et al., 2002). Since a diet low in fruits and veggies poses significant long-term health risk (Frazao, 1999), adolescents should be encouraged to eat more of these foods.

4. *Inadequate knowledge of nutrition* influences the development of poor nutrition practices. Many times, high school boys and girls know so little about nutrition that they cannot select a well-balanced meal in a cafeteria.

5. *Social pressures* may cause poor eating habits. Girls, in particular, may encourage one another to follow extreme, controversial diets in order to lose weight (Page & Suwanteerangkul, 2007). Friends may also pressure one another to follow strict vegan and macrobiotic diets. Although it is certainly possible to eat healthy under these regimens, adolescents need to consciously work to ensure an adequate protein intake.

6. *Troubled family relationships and personal adjustments* seem to accompany poor eating habits. Adolescents from broken or troubled homes may not have parents at home to cook for them or to see that they get an adequate diet. Those with emotional problems may have nervous stomachs, ulcers, or eating disorders and hence not eat properly.

7. The *family is poor* and cannot afford to buy proper food.

How can teens be encouraged to eat better? Parents and other adults can model good eating habits and prepare nourishing meals. Since most teens cannot be bothered to count milligrams of calcium and other nutrients, they need to be taught guidelines that will help them take in the good (vitamins, minerals, protein) and leave out the bad (saturated fats, sugars). One widely used model is the U.S. Department of Agriculture's My Pyramid (see Figure 4.14). Adolescents who follow this model will take in all the nutrition they need. Also, making sensible selections within each food group will provide the proper nutrients without excess calories.

Exercise

American adolescents as well as adults are in the midst of a nationwide fitness craze—or at least, we say we are. Working out and staying in shape have become immensely popular—to talk about. The trendiest clothes include active wear and expensive athletic shoes. Every sizable community has fitness centers, gyms, pools, tennis courts, and bike trails.

Unfortunately, all the talk and attention has not translated into increased activity. Only about one-half

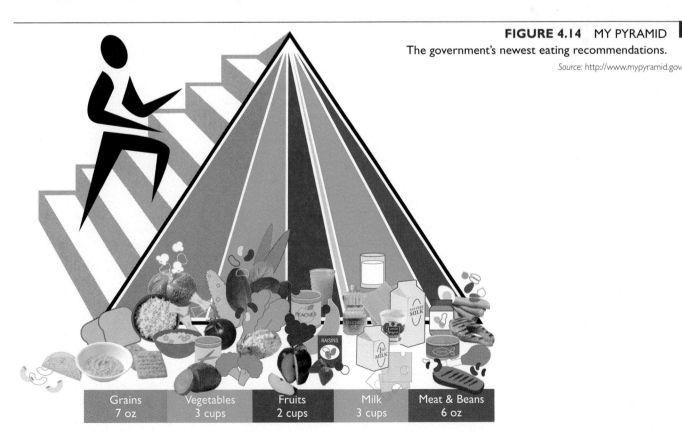

FIGURE 4.14 MY PYRAMID
The government's newest eating recommendations.

Source: http://www.mypyramid.gov.

Grains	Vegetables	Fruits	Milk	Meat & Beans
7 oz	3 cups	2 cups	3 cups	6 oz

of American adolescents regularly participate in vigorous physical activity. About 25 percent report no vigorous activity, and about 14 percent get no exercise at all. Adolescent girls are less likely to be physically active than adolescent boys, and Black females are even less likely to exercise than White females. The overall amount of physical activity declines during the course of adolescence, which means older teens get even less exercise than younger ones (Aaron, Stortin, Robertson, et al., 2002; U.S. Department of Health and Human Services, 2008).

Benefits of Exercise

People are finding that exercising is fun and beneficial in a variety of ways. One most obvious benefit is to *build physical fitness.* Exercise tones up the body system, builds muscles, strengthens the heart and lungs, and improves circulation. It also relieves nervous tension, depression, and anxiety. Similarly, a desire to *lose weight* motivates many adolescents to exercise. Nearly everyone knows that exercising consumes calories and that exercise can also depress the appetite (Vartanian & Herman, 2006).

In addition, exercise *promotes psychological and mental health* (Birkeland, Torsheim, & Wold, 2009). Possessing a physically fit body that meets the cultural ideals of thinness and beauty can enhance body image and self-esteem and help promote feelings of competence and mastery (Grieve, Jackson, Reece, et al., 2008). Also, physically active adolescents are less likely than less-active youth to feel depressed or anxious (Kirkcaldy, Shephard, & Siefen, 2002). Boys and girls seem to benefit equally in this way from participation in sports and exercise (Gore, Farrell, & Gordon, 2001).

There is evidence that physical activity patterns developed in adolescence may continue into adulthood.

A comparison of the physical activity levels of 453 young adult men, ages 23 to 25, with their childhood fitness scores revealed that those who were physically active as adults had better childhood physical fitness test scores than those who were not physically active (Friedman, Martin, Tucker, et al., 2008).

How much exercise do adolescents need? According to the U.S. Surgeon General, they should average at least 30 minutes of moderately intense physical activity on all or most days of the week (U.S. Department of Health and Human Services, 2001). How can they best be encouraged to do this? The best way appears to be to enroll them in organized, after-school physical activities (Sallis, Prochaska, Taylor, et al., 1999). This suggests that schools should place an emphasis on intramural as well as varsity sports. In addition, girls' participation could be increased by providing them environments in which they can be both awkward and sweaty without fear of embarrassment, since embarrassment is a barrier to athletic participation (Grieser, Vu, Bedimo-Rung, et al., 2006).

Obesity

Few adolescents want to be obese, and even many children are concerned about their weight. For example, Ricciardelli, McCabe, Holt, et al. (2003) asked 500 Australian 8- to 11-year-olds whether they worried about their weight and whether they had ever dieted to lose weight. The boys' and girls' answers were almost identical: about 45 percent sometimes, often, or always thought about their weight, and virtually the same number had attempted to lose weight by dieting. Almost as many young children report exercising to lose weight (Ricciardelli & McCabe, 2001).

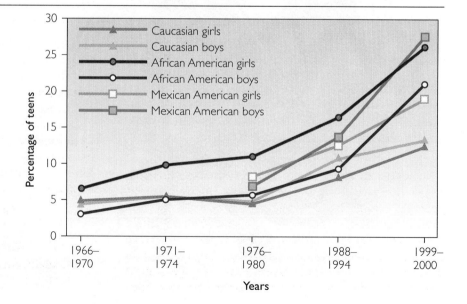

FIGURE 4.15 TEENAGE OBESITY RATES: 1966 TO 2000

Source: Data from Centers for Disease Control (2006).

Even so, adolescent **obesity** is on the rise in the United States: the obesity rate rose significantly between the years of 1999 and 2004 (Ogden, Carroll, Curtin, et al., 2006). Furthermore, the amount by which adolescents are overweight continues to rise; that is, overweight adolescents weigh more than they used to (Jolliffe, 2004).

Teenage obesity rates began climbing rapidly in the mid-1970s. African American girls and Mexican American boys have the highest rates (18 and 20 percent, respectively), and Caucasian girls have the lowest rates (about 7 percent) (Centers for Disease Control and Prevention [CDC], 2008). Even these rates are too high, however, as they represent a tripling of obesity among teens since the mid-1960s (Ozer, Park, Paul, et al., 2003). (See Figure 4.15.)

As most people know, obesity carries numerous serious health risks, even for children and adolescents. In particular, adolescent obesity is associated with a significantly increased risk for Type 2 diabetes, a disease previously almost unknown in children. Also, overweight adolescents are more likely than their slender peers to develop high blood pressure and a high cholesterol level, both of which are precursors to heart disease (Katzmarzyk, Tremblay, Pérusse, et al., 2003). In addition, of course, overweight adolescents face social rejection and have lowered self-esteem.

The causes of obesity and the reasons it is becoming more common are complex. In order to understand this health crisis, we need to look (1) within individual adolescents, (2) at their interactions with others, (3) at the environments in which they spend their time, and (4) at broader societal influences.

Personal Contributors to Being Overweight

A number of personal characteristics make individuals more likely to become overweight. These characteristics include genetic makeup, motivation to eat excessively, eating patterns preference for high-calorie foods, and their lack of physical activity.

Genetic Contributors to Obesity   Several studies have provided clear evidence for a genetic link to body weight. For example, we know that biological siblings raised in different households are nearly as similar to each other in weight as pairs raised together and that adopted children are more similar in weight to their biological parents than to their adoptive parents (Hebebrand & Hinney, 2009).

Motivation to Eat   Obese individuals often eat for different reasons than their more normal-weight peers. Braet and her colleagues, for example, recently found that obese adolescent girls were more likely than average-weight girls to eat when they were unhappy. In contrast, obese adolescent boys did not do this, but they were more likely than average-weight boys to eat when they were not hungry because they

were influenced by the sight or smell or tempting food (Braet, Claus, Goossens, et al., 2008).

Eating Patterns   Since most heavy teens are unhappy with their weight, they frequently try to control their eating. For instance, they may not allow themselves to eat breakfast and have only a small lunch (Keski-Rahkonen, Viken, Kapiro, et al., 2004), but then they get so hungry later in the day that they binge and eat late at night. Others frequently snack, even when they are not especially hungry. Some eat rapidly and so consume more food than normal in a set period of time (Marcus & Kalarchian, 2003).

Food Preferences   Most of us have a variety of foods to select from when we are hungry. Those of us who reach for ice cream and potato chips are more likely to gain weight than those who enjoy fruits and other less calorie-laden alternatives. Some of the increase in average adolescent weight can be attributed to increased consumption of fast food. American adolescents now eat in fast-food restaurants almost one day out of every three (Bowman, Gortmaker, Ebbeling, et al., 2004). Research has shown that overweight teens eat more in fast-food restaurants than their more slender counterparts, and that their total calorie intake is greater on days in which they eat at fast-food establishments than on days they do not (Ebbeling, Sinclair, Pereira, et al., 2004).

Lack of Exercise   Adolescents' low levels of physical activity have already been discussed. Suffice it here to say that exercising both burns calories while you are doing it and increases the body's **metabolic rate** (the rate at which it burns calories) for a period of time even after you have finished, and so contributes to maintaining a healthy weight.

Interpersonal Interactions and Being Overweight

Parents and peers can influence adolescents' tendency to gain weight.

Family Contributors   Parents greatly influence what foods their children eat and how much they participate in physical activity (Faith, Scanlon, Birch, et al., 2004). For example, parents can insist that the entire family eat dinner together and prepare healthy meals; alternatively, parents can leave their adolescents to fend for themselves, with the result that they live on peanut butter sandwiches, hot dogs, and fast food. Some parents use high-caloric foods as rewards and inadvertently train their children to expect cookies and

---

obesity   overweight; excessively fat.

metabolic rate   the rate at which the body utilizes food and oxygen.

IN THEIR OWN WORDS

"As far as I can remember, my body weight has been tightly connected to my self-esteem. This started while I was in high school. Dieting was something every girl practiced at some time or another. Not eating was something to be proud of! I must say that I was a normal weight, and this was true for all the other girls in my class, but we all thought we were extremely fat. Going to the gym after classes was a must, even though we all hated it.

"There was this notion that as long as you are skinny, you are beautiful. Plus, the boys were constantly making jokes about the overweight girls in school. Well, I do not think that what the boys thought of us was what motivated us the most. What motivated us was the thought that being skinny means being beautiful and sexy. When I was not eating, I was feeling good about myself, and when I ate, I was miserable. There were days when I could not think of anything else but food. If I ate a sandwich, I used to feel guilty and be mad at myself. I had these nightmares about becoming fat and everyone laughing at me.

"I used to buy these magazines with skinny girls in them, and every time I looked at them, even though I was hungry, my appetite disappeared. I wanted to look like them so much! I cannot believe I was so stupid—thinking that being thin would solve all my problems and make me happy.

"Even nowadays, I still watch my weight very closely. I don't think I suffer from an eating disorder, but this feeling of guilt when I eat a piece of pizza is still there. But I've learned to live with it."

candy when they have had success. Similarly, parents can model athletic participation by taking walks or playing sports with their children, or they can spend their time watching television with them.

Peer Contributors   Peers influence one another's weight, as well (Field & Kitkos, 2009). For example, they help set behavioral norms, such that teenagers whose friends participate in sports are more likely to do so, as well. Conversely, teens whose friends hang out at fast-food restaurants or who make snacking a large part of the social scene will be discouraged from maintaining a normal weight.

Environmental Influences

The places in which adolescents find themselves may or may not be conducive to weight gain.

Schools   Adolescents spend much of their lives in school. School policies can therefore determine what they eat during those hours. What foods are served at lunch? Are vending machines available? If so, what

foods do they contain? Are students allowed to leave the building to eat lunch elsewhere? (If they are, they are likely headed to a fast-food restaurant.) In 2006, America's largest beverage distributors agreed to halt sales of sodas to elementary and middle schools, and they agreed to sell only diet sodas in high schools. These steps help ensure that younger adolescents drink more water, juice, and low-fat milk and will likely reduce high schoolers' sugar consumption.

School policies can also promote students' physical activity levels. For example, they encourage students who live within a close radius to the school to walk by discontinuing bus service. Alternatively, they can ensure that students regularly enroll in physical education classes that make them sweat.

Community   Communities can also encourage or discourage obesity. Do they provide parks and rec centers? Do they offer public basketball courts? Are these facilities open for extensive hours? Are there sidewalks, which encourage walking, and bike paths, which encourage riding?

Broader Social Influences

Obesity has increased, in part, because food (and especially calorie-dense food) is far more available than in the past. In addition, we can now buy foods that are already or almost entirely prepared and ready for consumption, and this convenience encourages impulsive eating. What's more, the portion sizes served in restaurants have increased enormously (Nielsen & Popkin, 2003).

Lack of activity is also an issue. Adolescents today spend more time in front of the TV and computer monitor than they did in the past, burning relatively fewer calories as they do. We have also become more and more dependent on automobiles to take us where we wish to go and as a result spend less time walking.

Sleep

Not only do adolescents need exercise to remain healthy, but they need adequate sleep, as well. In fact, however, many teenagers do not get as much sleep as they should.

ANSWERS WOULDN'T YOU LIKE TO KNOW . . .

Why are more and more teens obese?

Ever greater numbers of teens are obese, in part, because not only is junk food more available (even in school and at home), but it also comes packaged in larger portions. In addition, adolescents get less exercise than they did in the past because they spend more time sitting in front of the television, playing video games, and visiting chat rooms.

Mary Carskadon and her colleagues have intensely studied adolescent sleep patterns and their consequences. In one study, they compared the sleep habits of students doing poorly in school (earning mostly Cs or lower) with those of students doing well. They found that compared to the A and B students, the C and D students got about 40 minutes less sleep per night and stayed up later on weekends (Wolfson & Carskadon, 1998). And no wonder: the participants who reported getting less sleep were both more tired and depressed during the day than those who reported getting more sleep. Students who lack sleep are also more inattentive (Fallone, Acebo, Arendt, et al., 2001), which surely cannot help school performance. The seriousness of adolescent sleep deprivation was underscored even more strongly in one of Carskadon's later studies. About two-thirds of the adolescents she sampled reported driving badly due to tiredness, and 20 percent claimed that they had actually fallen asleep while behind the wheel! Males were more likely than females to drive while excessively tired (Carskadon, 2002b).

Although most adolescents believe that they should stay up later than they did when they were children, teenagers actually need *more* sleep than preteens (9 hours), not less (Carskadon, Harvey, & Duke, 1980). Yet adolescents stay up later than children—and older adolescents stay up later than younger adolescents—because they are under increasing pressure to juggle the responsibilities of homework, sports, and jobs (Carskadon, 2002a). They are also more likely to socialize during late hours and to stay up late to play video games or watch TV (Owens, Stohl, Patton, et al., 2006). Another issue is that parents become less likely to enforce early bedtimes as their children age (Mercer, Merritt, & Cowell, 1998).

Why do so many adolescents, even those who are not especially busy, stay up late? Carskadon's research indicates that there is a real biological underpinning to this behavior. She found that an adolescent's peak secretion of **melatonin**—the hormone that your brain produces to make you sleepy—occurs two hours later than that of a child or an adult (Carskadon, Wolfson, Acebo, et al., 1998). This delay has been tied directly to pubertal status. When girls of the same age who had and had not entered puberty were compared, only the ones who had begun to develop had later melatonin surges (Carskadon, Vieira, & Acebo, 1993).

Ironically, as bedtimes get later, waking times get earlier. Middle schools generally start earlier in the morning than elementary schools, and high schools begin earlier yet, often before 8:00 A.M. (Most school districts have staggered starting times so that they can use the same school buses for students at all three levels.) Since adolescents' biological clocks are

set so as to encourage them to sleep late, it is not surprising that middle school and high school students are not often alert during their first few class periods. These adolescent sleep experts, therefore, advocate starting adolescents' school days later and enforcing an earlier "lights out" (Carskadon, Wolfson, Acebo, et al., 1998).

Acne

Although **acne** is not a serious medical concern, it is often an upsetting aspect of adolescent development. Many teens spend countless dollars purchasing and then endless hours applying creams, astringents, and special soaps to try to control their acne. In addition, having acne can lead to self-consciousness and social withdrawal, particularly when youths are teased or otherwise embarrassed by the condition of their skin (Goodman, 2006). As such, having acne is an important adolescent phenomenon.

Skin Gland Development
Three kinds of skin glands can cause problems for the adolescent:

1. **Merocrine** sweat glands, distributed over most of the skin surfaces of the body

2. **Apocrine** sweat glands, located in the armpit, mammary, genital, and anal regions

3. **Sebaceous** glands, which are the oil-producing glands of the skin

melatonin   the hormone that the brain produces to induce sleep.

acne   pimples on the skin caused by overactive sebaceous glands.

merocrine glands   sweat glands distributed over the entire body.

apocrine glands   sweat glands located primarily in the armpits and groin whose secretions cause body odor.

sebaceous glands   oil-producing skin glands whose secretions can cause acne if the glands' pores become blocked.

During the adolescent years, the merocrine and apocrine sweat glands secrete a fatty substance with a pronounced odor that becomes more noticeable. The result is body odor. The sebaceous glands develop at a greater speed than the skin ducts through which they discharge their skin oils. As a result, the ducts may become plugged and acne can develop. Almost 85 percent of adolescents develop acne at some point (UCLA Medical Center, 2000).

Acne can take a variety of forms, depending on its severity. Whiteheads and blackheads result when oil glands become blocked. In the case of blackheads, the plugs oxidize and turn dark. (Blackheads are not dark because they contain embedded dirt.) If the plug becomes infected, then a **papule**—a tender, inflamed, pink bump—or a **pustule**—a pus-filled pimple—will form. Large pustules, called **cysts,** can leave permanent scars. Acne is most common on the face, upper back, and chest.

Causes

Acne is triggered by the increased amount of testosterone present during adolescence. Boys tend to develop acne more than girls because they have more testosterone in their systems. Acne has little to do with personal hygiene, since most people wash their faces once or twice per day. Masturbation does not cause acne, either. And contrary to popular belief, most people can eat chocolate without exacerbating their acne. On the other hand, oily cosmetics, the friction caused by rubbing the skin, and stress can make acne worse.

Treatment

Mild cases of acne often respond to over-the-counter medications. Creams containing benzoyl peroxide kill the bacteria that cause pustules and can reduce oil production. Salicylic acid helps keep pores from becoming clogged. More severe cases of acne require prescription medication. Topical vitamin A solutions (Retin-A) are one option; oral antibiotics, such as tetracycline and erythromycin, are another. Estrogen-containing birth control pills are usually effective, as well, because estrogen counters the effects of testosterone.

Individuals with acne tend to want to scrub with harsh, abrasive soaps and douse their faces with harsh astringents in an attempt to wash away blackheads and dry out the skin. Neither remedy is desirable, however, since both will irritate the skin and often make acne worse. Instead, individuals with acne should treat their skin gently by using mild soap and avoiding scouring (National Institute of Arthritis and Musculoskeletal and Skin Diseases, 2006).

---

papules   tender, raised red bumps that are precursors to pimples.

pustules   the medical term for *pimples.*

cysts   large, deep pimples that can cause scarring.

SUMMARY

1. Adolescence is a period of sexual maturation and physical growth. The changes that occur prepare the body for reproduction and cause female and male children's bodies (which are quite similar except for the reproductive organs) to become distinctly different.

2. Puberty is triggered by changes in the hypothalamus that cause it to release GnRH and signal particular endocrine glands to secrete hormones that stimulate and regulate the growth process.

3. The pituitary gland secretes HGH, the gonadotropic hormones FSH and LH, and LTH. FSH and LH stimulate the growth of egg cells in the ovaries, sperm in the testes, and the sex hormones. HGH affects the growth and shaping of the skeleton.

4. The ovaries secrete the hormones estrogen and progesterone. Estrogen stimulates the development of female sex characteristics and progesterone regulates the menstrual cycle and acts on the breasts.

5. The testes secrete the male hormone testosterone, which stimulates the development of male characteristics.

6. The adrenal glands also secrete androgens.

7. The level of testosterone and estrogen is regulated by negative feedback of these hormones, which tells the hypothalamus and gonads when enough of the hormones has been secreted.

8. Numerous changes occur in the male sex organs at puberty. The testes, scrotum, penis, prostate gland, and Cowper's glands enlarge. The testes increase the production of testosterone and begin the production of mature sperm.

9. Once boys become teenagers, it is quite normal for them to have nocturnal emissions, or spontaneous ejaculations, while they sleep at night.

10. Numerous changes occur in the female sex organs. The vagina, labia, clitoris, uterus, and Bartholin's glands enlarge and mature. The ovaries increase the secretion of estrogen and progesterone and begin the production of mature ova.

11. Most girls begin to menstruate early in adolescence. The menstrual cycle is controlled by rising and ebbing hormonal levels. FSH and estrogen levels are higher in the first half of the monthly cycle; later, a surge of LH causes the progesterone level to rise as the FSH and estrogen levels drop off.

12. It is important for parents to provide good information about menstruation to their daughters before they get their period. Doing so will alleviate anxiety and help girls develop a good attitude about their maturing bodies.

13. Sexual maturation at puberty also includes the development of secondary sexual characteristics. In males this includes the appearance of pubic hair, voice changes, muscular development, and the growth of axillary and facial hair. In women, this includes the appearance of pubic hair, developed breasts, and a more rounded female figure. Boys and girls can become self-conscious about their development, especially if they do not believe their growth is normal.

14. One of the most obvious physical changes of adolescence is the growth spurt that begins in early adolescence. The growth in height is accompanied by changes in body proportion. Both heredity and environmental factors determine the total mature height achieved. Girls usually begin their growth spurt about two years earlier than boys.

15. Both boys and girls today are maturing at younger ages than did those of previous generations. This secular trend is due primarily to better nutrition and health care.

16. The three body types are ectomorph, mesomorph, and endomorph. Boys prefer to be mesomorphic: solid and muscular. Girls hope to be ectomorphic: tall and slender. A soft, round, endomorphic build is least preferred by both genders.

17. Most adolescents are not happy with their bodies. This is truer of girls than boys, and their discontentment increases over the course of adolescence. Unfortunately, not liking one's body can have a negative effect on one's overall level of self-esteem.

18. The timing of physical maturation is important. Some adolescents mature earlier or later than average, with a differential effect. Current research suggests that off-time maturation—whether relatively early or relatively late—puts adolescents at risk for poor psychological and behavioral adjustment.

19. Adolescence is intrinsically a healthy time of life. Most of the health concerns that teens face are due to their own behaviors and are thus preventable. The three leading causes of death for American adolescents are car accidents, homicide, and suicide.

20. Adolescents often make poor health-related decisions because they lack knowledge and fail to perceive the hazards that risky behaviors entail. They may also bow to peer pressure and societal messages that glorify unhealthy and even dangerous activities.

21. Adolescents in developing countries face different health risks than American adolescents. Malnutrition, lack of medicine and health services, and war-related violence are of more concern in the Third World than in the United States.

22. Nutrition is extremely important to individual health. Adolescents may suffer a variety of deficiencies: calcium; iron; protein; and vitamins A, C, and

B6. There are a number of reasons for deficiencies: adolescents skip breakfast, snack excessively, and eat only small quantities of nutritious foods; social pressures and chaotic family lives result in poor eating habits; and many families cannot afford to buy good food.

23. Exercise is not only fun but physically and psychologically beneficial. Too many American youths do not get sufficient exercise.

24. An ever-increasing number of American adolescents are obese, which poses health risks and increases their likelihood of social rejection. Obesity is on the rise because adolescents are eating more and exercising less than they did in the past.

25. Most adolescents do not get enough sleep because they stay up late and get up early. This sleep deprivation has both psychological and academic ramifications.

26. Adolescents worry about body odor and acne caused by the increased secretion by skin glands during puberty. Prompt attention and treatment of acne may prevent its becoming severe.

KEY TERMS

THOUGHT QUESTIONS

Personal Reflection

1. To men: When you had your first nocturnal emission, did you understand what was happening? Were you prepared for it? How did you feel? With whom did you discuss it?
2. To women: When you first started to menstruate, did you understand what was happening? Were you prepared for it? How did you feel? With whom did you discuss it?
3. When did you first become self-conscious about your body? Was it timed with the onset of puberty?
4. When you were an adolescent, were you shorter or taller than your classmates? How did you feel? Explain.
5. Do you ever think about your own health? What steps do you take to ensure that you stay healthy? What changes could you make to stay healthy or become healthier?
6. Did you mature earlier or later than your classmates? How did you feel? How did it affect you?
7. Have you ever been overweight? What helped you deal with this condition?
8. What changes should you make in your diet and why? What are you eating too much or too little of?
9. Do you eat breakfast? Lunch? Why or why not?
10. Do you follow a regular exercise routine? Why or why not?
11. Do you usually get enough sleep? If not, why not? What effects have you noticed when you fail to get enough sleep?

Group Discussion

12. Explain why there is no completely safe period of the month when a woman cannot get pregnant.
13. Comment on the attitudes in U.S. society toward female breasts. What effect do these attitudes have on adolescent girls? Boys?
14. Have you known anyone who died during adolescence? If so, what was the cause? Was it either accidental or violence related?
15. What are the similarities and differences between the health issues faced by American adolescents and those in the developing world?
16. Why is adolescents' self-esteem so tied to their feelings about their appearance? Why does that change as youths move into adulthood?
17. How can we get adolescents to eat a more balanced diet?

Debate Questions

18. Both female and male athletes should be allowed to take testosterone to improve their abilities if they wish.
19. American families should formally celebrate an adolescent's menarche or first ejaculation.
20. Schools should be required to educate students about the physical changes that will accompany puberty before these changes happen.
21. In order to improve adolescent health, schools should require that all students participate in more extensive physical education activities.
22. Adolescents who desire it should be permitted to have plastic surgery procedures.
23. In order to decrease adolescent obesity, school cafeterias should serve only healthy, nutritious foods.
24. The media can be held responsible for the widespread body dissatisfaction and high prevalence of eating disorders found in today's adolescents.
25. Cigarette companies are not allowed to advertise on television. Fast-food commercials should also be banned.

SUGGESTED READING

Carskadon, M. A. (Ed.). (2002). *Adolescent Sleep Patterns: Biological, Social, and Psychological Influences.* New York: Cambridge University Press.

Hayward, C., Hurrelmann, K., Curie, C., and Rasmussen, V. (2003). *Gender Differences at Puberty.* New York: Cambridge University Press.

Heffner, L. J., and Schust, D. J. (2006). *The Reproductive System at a Glance.* Oxford, UK: Blackwell.

Hefner, K., and Longhine, L. (Eds.). (2009). *Through Thick and Thin: Teens Write About Obesity, Eating Disorders, and Self Image.* New York: Youth Communication.

Jelalian, E., and Steele, R. G. (Eds.). (2008). *Handbook of Childhood and Adolescent Obesity.* New York: Springer.

Kaplowitz, P. B. (2004). *Early Puberty in Girls.* New York: Random House.

Rew, L. (2004). *Adolescent Health: A Multidisciplinary Approach.* Thousand Oaks, CA: Sage.

Romer, D. (Ed.). (2003). *Reducing Adolescent Risk: Toward an Integrated Approach.* Thousand Oaks, CA: Sage.

Thompson, J. K., and Smolak, L. (Eds.). (2001). *Body Image, Eating Disorders, and Obesity in Youth: Assessment, Prevention, and Treatment.* Washington, DC: American Psychological Association.

USEFUL WEB SITES

ACNE.org
www.acne.org

> *This site contains "Answers to Frequently Asked Questions" about acne, a list of common myths about acne, and many links to other related sites.*

Kansas State University Nutrition Links
www.oznet.k-state.edu/humannutrition/nutlink/n2.htm

> *This site provides numerous links to other sites concerned with all aspects of nutrition.*

National Institute of Arthritis and Musculoskeletal and Skin Diseases (NIAMS)
www.niams.nih.gov/hi/topics/acne/acne.htm

> *This site is an up-to-date, comprehensive information source about acne.*

WOULDN'T YOU LIKE TO KNOW . . .

- Why do preschoolers sometimes seem so selfish?
- Why are children in grade school smarter than those in preschool?
- Why are adolescents sometimes described as "junior scientists"?
- Why do adolescents often have extreme political views?
- Why do adolescents often say one thing and then do another?
- Why are adolescents so self-conscious?
- Are adults actually smarter than adolescents, or do they just know more?
- What can be done to promote high levels of reasoning in adolescents?
- How are adolescents' memory skills better than children's?
- Why can adolescents think more quickly than children?
- How does reasoning improve during adolescence?
- Why do adolescents take greater risks than adults do?
- Why do adolescents sometimes become skeptical of authority?
- Why are adolescents sometimes more emotional than adults?
- How well do IQ tests measure intelligence?

chapter 5

Cognitive Development: Improvements in Thinking, Reasoning, and Decision Making

The word *cognition* literally means "the act of knowing or perceiving." So, in discussing the cognitive development of adolescents, we seek to discuss the process by which they grow in knowledge. More specifically, we look at their ability to understand, think, and analyze and to utilize these abilities in solving the practical problems of everyday living.

There are basically three approaches to this study of cognition. The first is the *Piagetian approach,* which emphasizes the broad patterns and qualitative changes in the way adolescents think. The second is the *information-processing approach,* which examines the progressive steps, actions, and operations that take place when the adolescent receives, perceives, remembers, thinks about, and uses information. The third approach is the *psychometric approach,* which measures quantitative changes in adolescent intelligence. We will examine each in turn.

Piaget's Stages of Cognitive Development

As introduced in Chapter 2, Jean Piaget was the most important early researcher of cognitive development. He divided cognitive development into four major stages (Piaget, 1963):

- The *sensorimotor stage* lasts from birth to about age 2.
- The *preoperational stage* lasts from about ages 2 to 7.
- The *concrete operational stage* lasts from about ages 7 to about 11 or 12.
- The *formal operational stage* lasts from age 11 or 12 on.

The differences among the four stages have to do primarily with (1) what one can think about, (2) how flexible one's thinking is, and (3) how correctly one can use logic. In the sensorimotor stage, the individual cannot think without performing movement: to think *is* to move. Thought, therefore, is quite inflexible and so the infant does not engage in logic. In the preoperational stage, the young child can think entirely in his or her mind; he or she doesn't have to take physical action in order to imagine or consider. Thinking is *pre*operational, however, as the child at this age lacks the **mental operations** needed for flexible thinking. His or her logic is inadequate, frequently leading to erroneous conclusions. Once the child enters the concrete operational stage, those mental operations are in place. As the name of the stage indicates, however, the individual can use these mental operations only when thinking about real, concrete objects or actual behavior. Such thought is flexible and logical. Finally, with the onset of the formal operational stage, adolescents can think abstractly and hypothetically. They can reason and draw logical

conclusions even when thinking about things that they have not actually experienced.

Let's look at each stage in more depth.

Sensorimotor Stage

During the **sensorimotor stage,** learning is related to the mastery of sensory-motor sequences. The infant moves from a self-centered, body-centered world to an object-centered world as the senses of vision, touch, taste, hearing, and smell bring him or her into contact with objects having various properties and relationships to other objects. The child becomes intrigued with simple motor activities such as picking up objects, falling backward on a pillow, and blowing air out of his mouth. Thinking, if there is any, occurs as a stimulus-response connection with the physical world, although the latter part of this period marks a transition to symbolic play, imitation, and the mental representation of objects.

During Piaget's sensorimotor stage, children under age 2 begin to move from a body-centered world to an object-centered world, where simple motor activities, such as picking up objects, become intriguing.

Preoperational Stage

The **preoperational stage** is the period when language is acquired. Children begin dealing with their world by learning and manipulating symbols, as well as through motor activity and direct interactions with the environment. Symbolic play, or *internalized imitation,* emerges.

During this period, there is evidence of transductive reasoning rather than more mature inductive or deductive reasoning. **Transductive reasoning** occurs when the child proceeds from particular to particular, without generalization, rather than from the particular to the general **(inductive reasoning)** or from the general to the particular **(deductive reasoning).** Transductive reasoners tend to infer cause and effect when none exists. If, for example, a 4-year-old girl meets a mean man who has a beard, she may assume that all men with beards are mean because beards make people mean. She would then worry if her father said he was planning on growing a beard because doing so would make him mean. Similarly, a young boy who once noticed he had a sore throat as he was combing his hair might thereafter believe that brushing his hair would make him sick. These examples also illustrate the concept of **syncretism,** or trying to link ideas that are not always related. For example, Mommy had a baby the last time she went to the hospital, so the next time she goes to the hospital, the child mistakenly expects Mommy to bring home another baby.

Preoperational thinking is also *egocentric;* that is, children have difficulty understanding why someone else cannot see something in the same way they do. For example, suppose you have already had three cookies and your sister has had only one. There is one more cookie on the plate. If you are in the preoperational stage, who do you believe should eat the last cookie? You, of course, because you are still hungry. At this stage, you cannot put yourself in your sister's place and imagine how she feels. Syncretism coupled with egocentrism leads to a related phenomenon called **animism.** Young children assume that inanimate objects—especially those that share features such as eyes and faces with animals—have feelings and are, in essence, alive. Since children get lonely when they are left alone, they assume that their dolls and teddy bears get lonely, too.

Related to all the preceding characteristics is **centering,** which refers to children's tendencies to focus

attention on one detail and their inability to shift attention to other aspects of a situation. For example, a preoperational child may conclude there is more water in a shallow dish than in a glass because the dish is wider, even though you have already seen all the water poured from the glass into the dish (see Figure 5.1). She ignores the greater height of the glass and the demonstration of pouring. As a result of their inability to maintain more than one relationship in their thinking at a time, children frequently make errors of judgment. There is evidence of thinking but still an absence of operational thinking.

Concrete Operational Stage

Piaget described pre- and early adolescents as being in the **concrete operational stage** of cognitive development. And as we will see, even older adolescents and adults sometimes think in ways characteristic of concrete, rather than formal, operations. It is therefore important to understand what individuals in this stage can and cannot do.

During the concrete operational stage, children show a greater capacity for logical reasoning, although at a concrete, rather than abstract, level. One of the reasons they can think more logically is that they are able to arrange objects into **hierarchical classifications** and comprehend **class inclusion relationships** (the mental manipulation of objects in different levels of a hierarchy at the same time). This gives children the

mental operations   logical processes that allow for flexible thought.

sensorimotor stage   the first stage of cognitive development, according to Piaget, lasting from birth to about age 2.

preoperational stage   the second stage of cognitive development, according to Piaget, lasting from ages 2 to 7.

transductive reasoning   proceeding from particular to particular in thought, without making generalizations.

inductive reasoning   gathering individual items of information and putting them together to form hypotheses or conclusions.

deductive reasoning   beginning with a hypothesis or premise and breaking it down to see if it is true.

syncretism   the act of trying to link ideas.

animism   the preoperational belief that inanimate objects have humanlike properties and emotions.

centering   the tendency of children to focus attention on one detail and their inability to shift attention to other aspects of the situation.

concrete operational stage   the third stage of cognitive development, according to Piaget, lasting from ages 7 to 11 or 12.

hierarchical classification   the ability to divide objects into nested series of categories.

class inclusion relationships   understanding that objects can be fit into different levels of hierarchies.

ANSWERS WOULDN'T YOU LIKE TO KNOW ...

Why do preschoolers sometimes seem so selfish?

Preschoolers can seem selfish because they are egocentric. They simply cannot imagine what is going through another person's mind. Rather, they assume that what they want is what you want and that what they like is what you like. They are not deliberately ignoring others' feelings, however.

FIGURE 5.1 UNDERSTANDING THE PRINCIPLE OF CONSERVATION OF VOLUME

(a) The child agrees that glasses A and B have the same amount of water. *(b)* The water from B is poured into the dish. The child is unable to understand that glass A and the dish still have the same amount of water, because the dish appears broader even though it is shallower. The child is unable to retain one aspect (the amount) when another aspect changes (the height of the water column and the width of the column).

a   *b*

ability to understand the relations of the parts to the whole, the whole to the parts, and the parts to the parts.

For example, suppose you are given a randomly organized array of blue and red squares and black and white circles. If you understand inclusion relationships, you discover there are two major collections (squares and circles) and two subtypes of each (blue versus red squares and black versus white circles). The higher level of the hierarchy is defined by shape and the lower level by color. This enables you to say that all squares are either blue or red; that there are more squares than blue squares; that there are more squares than red squares; that if the red squares are taken away, the blue ones are left; and so on.

Children at this stage learn that different objects may be grouped by size, by alphabetical order, by age, and so on, or that an object may simultaneously belong to more than one class. A child may be a girl, a fourth-grader, an athlete, and a redhead, all at the same time. Children learn that some relationships are *symmetrical*, or *reciprocal*—such as two brothers are brothers to each other—while some others are not—for example, I am Florence's daughter but she is my mother. In dealing with numbers, children learn that different combinations of numbers make the same total and that *substitutions* may be made with the same result. In dealing with liquids and solids, they learn that a change in shape does not necessarily change volume or mass.

For the first time, children can make **transitive inferences.** Transitive inference problems can be easy or difficult, but they all have a similar form. A typical transitive inference problem is "Oranges cost more than

grapefruit, and grapefruit cost more than apples. Do apples cost more than oranges?" In order to solve such a problem, you must be able to **seriate,** or mentally arrange items in order from large to small or small to large. Preoperational children can seriate (although it is often difficult for them), but they cannot perform the mental manipulations necessary for transitive inferences.

Piaget calls this stage the *concrete operational stage* of cognitive development because it involves concrete elements (objects, relations, or dimensions) and mental operations (such as addition or subtraction) that describe the way the operations may be performed. Four mental operations are especially important:

1. *Reversibility:* All actions, even mental actions, have an opposite. For example, "canaries" and "turtles" can be lumped together into the category of "pets," and "pets" can be divided into the subcategories of "canaries" and "turtles." Understanding reversibility, in effect, lets you think backward, imagining an item's state before some action was performed on it. For example, when we see a wet washcloth, we know that it must have been dunked in water, since removing the water would make it dry again.

2. *Identity or nullifiability:* This operation involves understanding that if we do something to an object and then do its opposite, the net effect is that the object is unchanged. For example, imagine that you have six pennies. If your brother gives you two more but then your sister takes two of them away, you will be back to having six pennies. Another

way of thinking about identity is that anything plus zero stays the same. So, if you take a glass of water and pour it into a differently shaped container, you will still have the same amount you started with (assuming you didn't add or spill any water).

3. *Associativity:* This operation involves understanding that the same outcome can result from different combinations or clusterings or actions. For instance, if we want to make fruit salad, we can mix blueberries and strawberries and then add some pineapple. If we instead mix the strawberries and pineapple and only later add the blueberries, the results will be identical.

4. *Combinativity:* Classes can always be combined to form larger, broader categories. For example, "boxes" and "jars" can be conceptually combined to form the category "containers."

Piaget used **conservation problems** to determine whether children had entered the concrete operational stage of cognitive development. *Conservation* refers to the recognition that properties of things such as weight and volume are not altered by changing their shape or the container they are in. Conservation tasks involve some manipulation of the shape of matter that does not alter the mass or volume of the matter (Piaget & Inhelder, 1969). Look again at Figure 5.1. Whereas a preoperational child would tell you that there is more water in the glass than in the petrie dish ("It's taller!"), a child in concrete operations would recognize that both containers have the same amount of liquid regardless of their appearance.

It is important to remember that the child's thinking is still linked to empirical reality (Piaget, 1967). Children have made some progress toward extending their thoughts from the actual toward the potential, but the starting point must still be real because concrete operational children can logically reason only about those things with which they have had direct, personal experience. When children have to start with any hypothetical or contrary-to-fact proposition, they have difficulty.

Formal Operational Stage

The last stage of cognitive development, the **formal operational stage,** begins during early adolescence. Piaget subdivided this stage further into substages III-A, almost full formal function (ages 11 or 12 to 14 or 15), and III-B, full formal function (ages 14 or 15 and up). Substage III-A is a preparatory stage in which adolescents may make correct discoveries and handle certain formal operations, but their approach is crude and they are not yet able to provide systematic and rigorous proof of their assertions; these early adolescents are able to exhibit formal operations in some situations but not in others. Many adolescents and adults never truly reach the second substage. They seem to remain fixated in substage III-A, often thinking formally only in situations with which they are familiar (Flavell, Miller, & Miller, 1993).

Formal operational thinking differs radically from that of concrete operations. Although the concrete operational child can perform mental operations and has some understanding of classes and relations, his or her ability to use induction and deduction is significantly limited. A child at this stage will get lost when asked to juggle multiple dimensions of a problem at the same time or to ignore his or her own past experiences in problem solving. Conversely, adolescents are able, through inductive reasoning, to systematize their ideas and deal critically with their own thinking and so are able to construct theories about it. Furthermore, they can test these theories logically and scientifically, considering several variables, and are able to discover truth through deductive reasoning (Inhelder & Piaget, 1958). In this sense, adolescents are able to assume the role of scientists because they have the capacity to construct and test theories.

This is illustrated by one of the experiments Piaget conducted that led him to discover the strategies adolescents use in solving problems. Adolescent participants were shown a pendulum suspended by a string (see Figure 5.2). The problem was to discover which factors would affect the speed by which the pendulum

transitive inferences the ability to solve problems such as "Tom is taller than Fred, and Fred is taller than Marty. Is Tom taller than Marty?"

seriate the act of lining things up in order from large to small or small to large.

conservation problems tests used by Piaget to determine whether children had mastered concrete operations, such as understanding that changing an object's appearance does not alter its fundamental properties.

formal operational stage the fourth stage of cognitive development, according to Piaget, during which people develop abstract thought independent of concrete objects.

FIGURE 5.2   THE PENDULUM PROBLEM

This simple pendulum consists of a string, which can be shortened or lengthened, and a set of varying weights. The other variables that at first might be considered relevant are the height of the release point and the force of the push given by the subject.

Source: "The Pendulum Problem" from *The Growth of Logical Thinking: From Childhood to Adolescence* by Jean Piaget. Copyright © 1958 by Basic Books, Inc. Reprinted by permission of Basic Books, a member of Perseus Books, L.L.C.

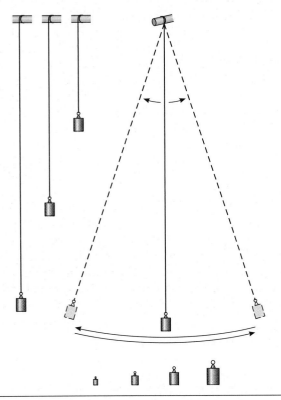

would swing. The participants were asked to investigate four possible effects: changing the length of the pendulum, changing its weight, releasing the pendulum from various heights, and starting the pendulum with various degrees of force. The adolescents were allowed to solve the problem in any way they chose.

The adolescents showed three basic characteristics in their problem-solving behavior. First, they planned their investigations systematically. They began to test all possible causes for variation in the pendulum swings: long or short string, light or heavy weight, high or low heights, and various degrees of force of push. Their search was *exhaustive*. Second, they recorded the outcomes accurately and with little bias under the different experimental conditions. Third, they were able to draw logical conclusions based upon their observations. The adolescents intuitively knew to vary only one feature of the pendulum at a time—for instance, the length of the string, the force with which they pushed the pendulum, or the weight. They realized that if they changed more than one feature at a time, then they would be unable to ascertain which feature caused any observed change in speed. Psychologists call this approach **hypothetico-deductive reasoning,** but it is more often referred to as *the scientific method.*

Younger subjects given the same problem may come up with the right answer by trial and error, but they will not use systematic and scientific procedures or be able to give a logical explanation of the solution. Children tend to form conclusions that seem warranted by the facts, but often these conclusions are premature and false because the children have not considered all of the important facts and are not able

During Piaget's formal operational stage, which begins in early adolescence, the teen's thinking begins to differ radically from that of a child. He or she becomes able to construct theories and can test these theories using scientific methods.

to reason logically about them. Even when presented with contrary evidence, younger children tend to hold tenaciously to the initial hypothesis and try to make the circumstances fit these preconceived notions.

One striking characteristic of adolescents' thinking is the ability to be flexible. They can be quite versatile in their thoughts and in dealing with problems. They can also devise many interpretations of an observed outcome. Because they can anticipate many possibilities prior to an actual event, they are not surprised by unusual outcomes. They are not stuck with their preconceptions. In contrast, younger children are confused by atypical results inconsistent with their perceptions of events.

It has already been stated that the preoperational child begins to utilize symbols. The formal operational adolescent, however, now begins to utilize a second symbol system: *a set of symbols for symbols*. For example, metaphorical speech or algebraic symbols are symbols for other words or numbers. The capacity to symbolize symbols makes the adolescent's thought much more flexible than the child's. Words can now carry double or triple meanings. Cartoons can

represent a complete story that would otherwise have to be explained in words.

Another important difference between concrete operational children and formal operational adolescents is that the latter are able to orient themselves toward what is abstract and not immediately present. They are able to escape the concrete present and think about the hypothetical and the possible. This facility enables adolescents to project themselves into the future, to distinguish present reality from possibility, and to think about what might be. Not only do adolescents have the capacity to accept and understand what is given, but they also have the ability to conceive of what might be possible and reflect on the blatantly impossible. Because they can construct ideas, they have the ability to elaborate on what they have been taught, generating new or different ideas and thoughts. They become inventive, imaginative, and original in their thinking. Possibility dominates reality.

In summary, formal thinking, according to Piaget, involves five major aspects: (1) introspection (thinking about thought), (2) abstract thinking (going beyond the real to the possible), (3) combinatorial thinking (being able to consider all important facts and ideas), (4) logical reasoning (the ability to form correct conclusions using induction and deduction), and (5) hypothetical reasoning (formulating hypotheses and examining the evidence for them, considering numerous variables). See Figure 5.3 for an overview of the abilities that distinguish the concrete operational and formal operational stages.

hypothetico-deductive reasoning a way to solve problems using the scientific method; only one factor at a time is varied while all else is held constant.

FIGURE 5.3   CHARACTERISTICS OF CONCRETE OPERATIONAL AND FORMAL OPERATIONAL THOUGHT

Effects of Adolescent Thought on Personality and Behavior

Parents and siblings alike often bemoan the fact that their sweet, polite son/daughter/brother/sister turned into a brat once he or she became a teenager. This stereotype is the stuff of sitcoms and comic strips. But how accurate is this perception? Does the adolescent personality take a turn for the worse? In Chapter 2, we noted that teenagers are often moodier and even more depressed than children and adults. In this chapter, we describe common changes in adolescent personality and behavior that have commonly been tied to cognitive development. David Elkind (1967, 1975) developed most of these concepts.

Idealism

As they become more cognitively mature, adolescents' powers of reflective thinking enable them to better evaluate what they learn. They become more capable of moral reasoning (see Chapter 7). Furthermore, their ability to differentiate the possible from the real enables them to distinguish not only what the adult world is but also what it *might* be like. This ability of adolescents to grasp what is and what might be makes them **idealistic.** They compare the possible with the actual and discover that the actual is less than ideal; as a result, many become critical observers of things as they are and ultracritical of adults. Often this displeasure is limited to verbal complaints and snide remarks; sometimes it motivates teens to participate in service activities that benefit others.

Hypocrisy

The behavior of these adolescents was hypocritical in that it revealed a discrepancy between idealism and behavior. This occurs because young adolescents are unable to relate general theory to specific practice. Early adolescents have the capacity to formulate general principles, such as "Thou shalt not pollute," but lack the experience to see the application of these general rules to specific practice. Youths tend to believe that if they can conceive and express high moral principles, then they have attained them, and nothing concrete need be done. This attitude confuses and upsets adults, who insist that ideals must be actualized. This attitude is, in turn, considered cynical and hypocritical by youths (Elkind, 1978).

The ability of adolescents to think about themselves, their own thoughts, and society also leads to another manifestation of **hypocrisy:** pretending to be what they are not. Teenagers are expected to like school yet they rarely do. They are expected to conform to parental beliefs even when they do not agree with them. They are

Idealism in adolescents results from their newfound ability to distinguish between what is and what might be. They become champions of the underdog and often become involved in helping people with problems.

ANSWERS WOULDN'T YOU LIKE TO KNOW ...

Why do adolescents often say one thing and then do another?

While adolescents' minds are focusing on lofty ideals, their bodies are performing mundane, everyday behaviors, and they don't always see the connection between the two. Adults unknowingly encourage hypocrisy by asking adolescents to pretend to have feelings that they do not have.

ANSWERS WOULDN'T YOU LIKE TO KNOW ...

Why are adolescents so self-conscious?

Adolescents are self-conscious because they believe that everyone else is looking at them all the time. And not only do they believe that others are paying attention to them, but they believe that they are playing to a tough, critical audience. Being subject to such scrutiny is enough to make almost anyone feel insecure.

expected not to express hurt or anger when they really are upset. They are expected not to engage in behavior that will hurt or disappoint parents, so they do not dare talk to them. They are pressured to deny themselves and so they behave hypocritically. Their newly achieved capacity to envision what *should be* enables them to go beyond their real selves and to pretend to be what others expect them to be.

Pseudostupidity

Elkind (1978) pointed out that young adolescents often demonstrate what he has called **pseudostupidity:** the tendency to approach problems at much too complex a level and fail, not because the tasks are difficult but because they are too simple. It's as if they approach most problems as if they are trick multiple-choice test questions. They overanalyze the situation, searching for nuances that are probably not to be found, and they can become paralyzed because tasks seem so difficult. For instance, a young adolescent might spend 20 minutes staring at a restaurant's menu, unable to decide what to have. Likewise, a high-schooler might find choosing which classes to take or what clothes to wear overwhelming.

In other words, the ability to perform formal operations gives young adolescents the capacity to consider alternatives, but this newfound capacity is not completely under control. Thus, adolescents appear stupid because they are, in fact, bright but not yet experienced.

Egocentrism

The most well studied of Elkind's constructs is **egocentrism,** which is manifested in two ways: through the development of what have been termed the *imaginary audience* and the *personal fable* (Alberts, Elkind, & Ginsberg, 2007).

As adolescents develop the capacity to think about their own thoughts, they become egocentric, self-conscious, and introspective. They turn their thoughts toward themselves rather than toward others and become so concerned about themselves that they may conclude that others are equally obsessed with their appearance

and behavior. As a result, adolescents feel they are "on stage" much of the time. Thus, a great deal of their energy is spent reacting to this **imaginary audience.**

The need to react to an imaginary audience helps account for the extreme self-consciousness exhibited by many, even most, adolescents (Peterson & Roscoe, 1991). Whether in the lunchroom or on the bus going home, most youths believe that they are the center of attention. Sometimes, groups of adolescents react to this audience by loud and provocative behavior because they believe everyone is watching them and they want to look cool. Reacting to an imaginary audience also contributes to conformity. For example, peers can't laugh at your shoes if they are wearing the same shoes that you are. Finally, the concept of the imaginary audience drives many adolescents to exhibit an increased need for privacy; the only time they can relax and feel at ease is when they are literally unobservable and by themselves.

Elkind (1967) also described what he termed the **personal fable:** adolescents' beliefs in the uniqueness of their own experiences. Because of their imaginary audiences and their beliefs that they are important to so many people, adolescents come to regard themselves as special and unique. They believe that their emotions are stronger and more intense than those of other people, and that they have more profound insights. In addition, they have a unique sense of their own immortality and invulnerability (Alberts, Elkind, & Ginsberg, 2007). This, these researchers believe, is why so many

idealistic   insisting upon high standards of behavior.

hypocrisy   discrepancy between what people say and do.

pseudostupidity   the tendency to approach problems at much too complex a level and to fail, not because the tasks are difficult, but because they're too simple. Adolescents appear stupid when they are, in fact, bright but not yet experienced.

egocentricism   the inability to take the perspective of another or to imagine the other person's point of view.

imaginary audience   adolescents' belief that others are constantly paying attention to them.

personal fable   adolescents' belief that they are invulnerable and that their feelings are special and unique.

IN THEIR OWN WORDS

"The concept of the imaginary audience was certainly something I experienced as an adolescent. I think that this was in part due to the fact that I was a very late-maturing boy and thus pretty self-conscious about my looks. Excessive grooming was often a part of my routine. I can remember that before dances, I would spend so much time messing with my hair that my arms would actually begin to hurt!"

"I was never much of a diary or bad-poetry girl, but I was a big fan of writing horrible, horrible letters to celebrities and sometimes even sending them. I remember writing to some of the Friends cast members about how much I could relate to the show and how I totally understood the characters and thought I could be much better friends with them than I could with my classmates. I was thirteen!"

"At my house, I had a basketball hoop on my garage. When I would go out to play alone, I would imagine how all of my classmates showed up and watched as I played against someone famous like Michael Jordan. Every time that I made a shot, I would act like the crowd was going wild. When I began to grow tired, I would do a countdown, as if the clock was running out and I was trailing by 2 points with 5 seconds left. Then I would try to make the shot that would either win the game for me or send me 'to the showers' in defeat. It was obvious that I had a serious case of an imaginary audience!"

adolescents suppose that unwanted pregnancies happen only to others, never to them, or that they won't be in a car accident, even if they drive very aggressively.

Because of its potential link to risky behavior, adolescent egocentrism has received much interest and has been examined by myriad researchers. A critique of the concept is offered later in this chapter, when risky decision making is considered.

Introspection

As adolescents gain the ability to think abstractly and hypothetically, as they become more interested in society's ills, as they come to believe that everyone is staring at them, and as they develop a personal fable that says they are deeper and more sensitive than the people around them, they begin to spend more time in **introspection.** When we add up all of these other cognitive changes, it makes sense that adolescents become fascinated with their own thoughts and feelings. They *are* smarter than they used to be, and they *can* now think about complex issues that were formerly beyond them. Moreover, their thoughts are worth examining in detail because they are undoubtedly better than other people's thoughts. In their minds, adolescents replay interactions they have had with friends and non-friends: Was there some subtle meaning to the way Carrie said hi this morning? Would it have been better if I had passed a note to Tony in geometry instead of asking Marcy to speak to him for me? The adolescent world is full of intricate problems that careful thought can help solve.

RESEARCH HIGHLIGHT   IS A PERSONAL FABLE ENTIRELY A BAD THING?

When Elkind (1967) first described the personal fable, he emphasized its negative qualities. If you believe you are *unique*, you may feel lonely and misunderstood. If you suppose yourself *invulnerable*, then you don't think that bad things can happen to you and you engage in risky behaviors. If you think you are *omnipotent*, then of course you are right and others are wrong. But is the personal fable entirely a bad thing? Recent research suggests that it is not, or at least that not all of it is.

Aalsma, Lapsley, and Flannery (2006) examined the correlations among the strengths of the different aspects of the personal fable and various aspects of mental health in sixth- through twelfth-graders. On one hand, their findings indicate that feelings of *uniqueness* are negatively associated with mental health; in particular, those

adolescents who felt most unique were most likely to be depressed and to have suicidal thoughts. On the other hand, adolescents who felt omnipotent had positive mental profiles: they viewed themselves worthy, strong, and able to cope and were well adjusted. The relationship of invulnerability to mental health was more complex. Teenagers who believed they were invulnerable were more prone to engage in dangerous, risky behavior and to use drugs. However, they also tended to feel good about themselves.

The researchers were careful to note that these relationships may well hold true for adults as well as adolescents. Their study was not designed to compare adolescent and adult egocentrism. Future research will be needed to see if these patterns are exclusive to teenagers.

Critique of Piaget's Theory

Piaget did his research in the early part of the twentieth century, so it is not surprising that at the beginning of the twenty-first century, criticisms of his work have evolved and the field of cognitive development has moved on to new theories. Although no one doubts Piaget's assertion that adolescent thinking greatly surpasses that of younger children, and that they are better at solving the kinds of tasks that Piaget used to assess formal operations better than those younger than themselves (Keating, 2004), the specifics of his claims about formal operational thought have been questioned on several fronts (Kuhn, 2009).

Age and Universality

Investigators have questioned the age at which formal operational thought replaces the concrete operational stage and whether it inevitably does so. Piaget (1972) himself advanced the possibility that in some circumstances, the appearance of formal operations may be delayed to ages 15 to 20 and "that perhaps in extremely disadvantageous conditions, such a type of thought will never really take shape" (p. 7). He acknowledged that social environment can accelerate or delay the onset of formal operations (Piaget, 1971). In fact, fewer economically deprived adolescents achieve formal thought than do their more privileged counterparts, and there is a complete absence of formal operations among the mentally challenged. The percentage of adolescents demonstrating formal operational thinking has often been found to be below 50 percent (Lapsley, 1990).

Cross-cultural studies have shown that formal thought is more dependent on social experience than is sensorimotor or concrete operational thought. The attainment of the first three Piagetian stages appears to be more or less universal, but full attainment of formal thinking, even in college students and adults, is far from guaranteed (Cole, 1990). Some cultures offer more opportunities than others to adolescents to develop abstract thinking, by providing a rich verbal environment and experiences that facilitate growth by exposure to problem-solving situations. Similarly, more immediate environments such as the family or school can accelerate or retard the development of formal operations (Ardila, Rosselli, Matute, et al., 2005). Parents who encourage exchanges of thoughts, ideational explorations, academic excellence, and the attainment of ambitious educational and occupational goals promote high-level reasoning abilities in their children; schools that encourage students to acquire abstract reasoning and develop problem-solving skills enhance cognitive development.

In sum, it appears that formal operational abilities do not emerge at a set time, nor is their emergence guaranteed.

Consistency

Even those individuals who can use formal operations don't consistently do so. In particular, people regress when they are angry, upset, or rushed (Neimark, 1975). Someone who looks under his or her bed 15 times for a lost set of keys is hardly gathering data and using it in a logical, systematic way. Likewise, the person who repeatedly pushes the button on a vending machine that has eaten his or her dollar bill has not accepted that this particular strategy is not working and is thus failing to operate at the formal operational level.

The lack of consistency by which individuals who are capable of using formal operations in fact use them is particularly problematic because it undermines Piaget's assumption that formal operational thinking rests on an understanding of formal propositional logic. Piaget believed that early in adolescence, individuals grasp the rules by which logical propositions can be manipulated and that this is the primary reason that their thinking becomes more sophisticated. We now know, however, that even young children can handle questions involving easy propositional logic and that even most adults have trouble with more difficult applications of those rules; furthermore, there is little improvement in this ability during adolescence itself (Klaczynski, Shuneman, & Daniel, 2004).

Beyond Formal Operations

Piaget believed that the formal operational stage was the fourth and final level of cognitive development. Although people would continue to learn more and to make better decisions as they matured—presumably because they had collected more experiences and had more data to draw on—all the "hardware" they would ever have would be in place by mid-adolescence. Many, if not most, researchers now disagree with this contention (e.g., Commons, Richards, & Kuhn, 1982).

There is currently no one, consistent, uniform conception of post-formal cognitive development. Indeed, stage theories of development have fallen out of favor. I am, however, fond of a description of advanced reasoning called **dialectics,** which was proposed by Riegel (1973) and Basseches (1980). Although couched in different terms, it meshes well with current research on epistemological development (discussed later in this chapter). A dialectical thinker is one who can integrate two or more conflicting pieces of data; a formal thinker, in contrast, tends to assume that one argument is right and the other is wrong. A dialectical thinker also understands that

introspection   thinking about one's thoughts and feelings.

dialectics   an advanced form of reasoning that allows one to create new and better insights by integrating conflicting data.

many aspects of the world are interconnected—that if you make a change in one place, it might have ramifications elsewhere. A formal thinker tends to wear mental "blinders" and hone in on the specific problem with which he or she is concerned, ignoring the ripple effects of solutions. This approach often leads to the extreme stances associated with idealism.

For example, imagine that both a formal reasoner and a dialectical reasoner are asked their opinions about a new law allowing unrestricted logging on state-owned land. The formal reasoner might say, "It's a terrible law; think of the wildlife that will be killed!" or he or she might say, "Great! We need that lumber for houses. It will help the economy." The dialectical thinker will more likely say, "Well, it's good in that it will help decrease unemployment among loggers, but on the other hand, that habitat is irreplaceable and beautiful. Maybe we can work something out that will allow more logging but still protect the forest." The world appears more simple and straightforward to formal operations thinkers than it does to dialectical thinkers. The positive side of this formal operations simplicity is that it allows individuals to make decisions and take action, rather than be paralyzed by complexities. The negative aspect of this simpler approach is that people risk being wrong and shortsighted in the solutions they enact. (This last point provides another example of dialectical reasoning about an issue.)

Parents can create a stimulating and supportive home environment that facilitates their child's cognitive development.

ANSWERS WOULDN'T YOU LIKE TO KNOW ...

Are adults actually smarter than adolescents, or do they just know more?

Although it's true that adults have had more time than teens to learn facts and gain experiences, they also seem to think in better ways. They better appreciate the complexity and murkiness of many issues, and they can better deal with conflicting information. Also, many adults (but certainly not all) tackle problems before they become crises. Thus, most experts agree that adults *are* smarter than adolescents.

ANSWERS WOULDN'T YOU LIKE TO KNOW ...

What can be done to promote high levels of reasoning in adolescents?

The highest levels of reasoning are attained when individuals are given the chance to discuss, argue, and debate with people whose views are different from their own. Giving adolescents the opportunity to formulate their own ideas and opinions and then gently challenging them is one way to promote such reasoning. (Socrates taught this way thousands of years ago.) Giving teens the opportunity to actively learn by doing, experimenting, and questioning is extremely helpful, as well.

What Can We Retain from Formal Operations?

The substantive list of criticisms presented here may seem to suggest that Piaget was just plain wrong about cognitive development and that his work is now irrelevant. Although movement into the formal operational stage as originally conceived by Piaget cannot account for all of the changes that occur in adolescent reasoning (Moshman, 1997), his work cannot be completely discounted. Piaget was correct about these crucial aspects of adolescent cognition:

● Children become significantly and qualitatively more intelligent beginning at about age 11. (These changes are discussed more fully later in the chapter.) This change takes time and develops throughout much of adolescence.

- Deductive reasoning greatly improves during adolescence and leads to finding better answers in shorter periods of time (Foltz, Overton, & Ricco, 1995).
- Being able to think about hypothetical or even blatantly untrue situations improves substantially during adolescence (Morris & Sloutsky, 2002).
- Use of prepositional logic increases, albeit modestly, during adolescence (Ward & Overton, 1990).
- Exhaustive combinatorial reasoning improves during adolescence, as documented by evidence from studies of probabilistic reasoning (Dixon & Moore, 1996).
- Metacognition—the ability to think about one's own thoughts—improves during adolescence (Moshman, 1994).

And even though the field of cognitive development has moved on, much of the research currently being conducted about adolescent cognition was inspired by issues and questions first raised by Piaget. Even though many of his specific findings have been called into question, his work is the bedrock upon which more modern research rests.

Information Processing

In the first part of this chapter, we discussed Piaget's views of cognitive development. Now we will build on that discussion and consider more contemporary perspectives. Much of the current research concerning cognitive development is based on the **information-processing approach,** in which scientists study how individuals perceive, attend to, retrieve, and manipulate information (hence the name). Other researchers are trying to discover how adolescents reason and make difficult decisions. In addition, there has recently been a surge of interest in the effects of brain development on adolescent cognitive ability.

Overall, the current research differs from that done by Piaget in a number of consistent ways. First, whereas Piaget was most interested in developing an overview of cognitive development—a broad description of the intellectual gains that we make as we mature—researchers today are more focused on a micro-level analysis of the processes underlying those grand changes. They have taken this route because the mechanisms proposed by Piaget do not (to most psychologists' satisfaction) adequately account for the great intellectual differences observed between individuals at different stages in Piaget's scheme.

A second point about which current researchers disagree with Piaget is the stage concept itself. Piaget strongly believed in a stage approach to cognitive development, proposing that individuals grow in a steplike fashion. According to the stage theory, individuals

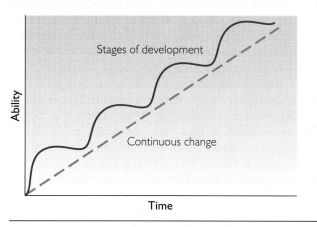

FIGURE 5.4 DISCONTINUOUS VERSUS CONTINUOUS GROWTH: STAGES OF DEVELOPMENT VERSUS GRADUAL CHANGE

mature rapidly for a period of time, and then their growth greatly slows and their achievement levels off. Most of today's researchers believe that change is more gradual and continuous. Also, what appear to be major strides are actually the gradual accumulation of smaller accomplishments (see Figure 5.4).

A third point of departure between most of current researchers and Piaget is a belief that knowledge and skills are *domain specific*. Piaget believed that once a person had acquired a cognitive skill, he or she could apply it broadly in a wide range of circumstances. The current thought, however, is that many skills can be used only in contexts similar to the ones in which they were acquired (e.g., Wellman & Gellman, 1998). Researchers today believe that cognitive structures are specialized, rather than general.

Finally, whereas Piaget believed that the central feature of adolescent cognitive development was the ability to think abstractly, the most current conceptualizations emphasize increased executive control (Kuhn, 2006). In other words, older adolescents are better able to monitor and control their own learning and thinking behaviors than are children and younger adolescents. Because of this, they are more efficient and more likely to succeed at cognitive tasks.

The information-processing approach emphasizes the progressive steps, actions, and operations that take place when the adolescent receives, perceives, remembers, thinks about, and utilizes information. One way we can understand information processing in humans is to compare the workings of the human mind with the actions of a computer. Information is

information-processing approach an approach to studying cognition that focuses on the perception, attention, retrieval, and manipulation of information.

coded and fed, in an organized way, into a computer, where it is stored in memory. When any of that information is required, the computer is asked to produce it. The machine searches for the relevant information and displays or outputs the items requested. It can then operate on that information, ranking, weighing, or combining the data in some fashion. Information processing by adolescents is similar in fashion but far more sophisticated. The adolescent receives information, organizes it, stores it, retrieves it, thinks about it, and combines it in such a way as to answer questions, solve problems, and make decisions. The most elaborate computer used in creating *artificial intelligence* cannot match the capacity of the human mind and nervous system in the input and output of information.

Steps in Information Processing

Figure 5.5 illustrates how information processing can be divided into a series of logical steps. The diagram shows information flowing in one direction only, from the time a stimulus is received until an action is begun. The general flow is in one direction, but there may be some movement backward as well as forward. For example, an adolescent may receive and select some information and take it in and out of memory to think about it over a long period of time before making a decision and initiating action. Nevertheless, the flow-chart helps us understand the total process. Next we'll look at the steps in more detail.

Stimuli

Every person is constantly bombarded with audible, visual, and tactile stimuli. As you walk down the street, for instance, you are exposed to sounds, sights, and even physical contact when someone bumps into you or touches you. Your senses are your *receptors,* your contacts with the world outside yourself. Through them, you receive all information. The sensory organs mature early in life and develop little during adolescence in terms of their raw abilities to take in information.

Selection

People do not really hear, see, or feel all of the stimuli they are exposed to, primarily because they cannot focus attention on everything at once, and they may not be interested in much of what is happening. For example,

you may dimly hear a horn honking, but you may not notice the color and make of the car from which the sound is emitted or care about who is doing the honking. However, if you hear someone call your name, your attention is directed immediately to the source, and you see that the person calling your name is your good friend, driving her familiar blue car. Your friend pulls over, you walk over to talk, and your attention is directed to the conversation rather than to the hundreds of other sights and sounds around you. Thus, people are interested in some happenings but not others, so they are motivated to direct their attention to that which they select.

Although a person's automatic attention to unexpected, demanding signals (e.g., a loud noise) does not change from childhood into adolescence (Rueda, Fan, McCandliss, et al., 2004), the ability to direct one's attention does (Vakil, Blachstein, Sheinman, et al., 2009). Eighteen-year-olds are better than younger children at sustaining attention and ignoring distraction (Wetzel & Schroger, 2007). They are also better at ignoring irrelevant information and focusing on the important aspects of what they are attending to (Lehman, Morath, Franklin, et al., 1998).

Interpretation

People make judgments about everything they are exposed to, partly according to their past experiences. For instance, an adolescent girl brought up by an alcoholic father may perceive her boyfriend as drunk when he has one beer. Another girl may not consider him inebriated at all. These two girls will interpret information differently according to their perceptions of it. Adolescents, as well as adults, may sometimes make faulty judgments because of inaccurate perceptions or insufficient information. Therefore, there is often the need to make additional inquiry, to gain further information, or to check perception against fact to make sure the perception is accurate.

The interpretational biases of adolescents are one of the factors that have been implicated in their well-established tendency to engage in risky behavior (Halpern-Felsher, 2009). Because the potentially life-altering consequences that can result from making poor decisions in regard to sexual behavior, drug use, reckless driving and the like, risky decision making is discussed in its own section later in this chapter. Interpretational biases will be revisited then.

FIGURE 5.5 STEPS IN INFORMATION PROCESSING

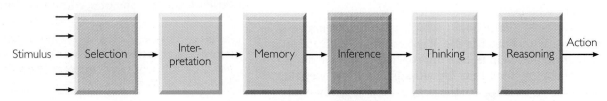

Memory

Information that is useful must be retained so that it can be used in the future or undergo additional processing. The process of remembering involves a series of steps. The most widely accepted model is a three-stage one (Gray, 2007): sensory storage, short-term storage, and long-term storage. Information is seen as passing from one compartment to another, with decreasing amounts passed on at any one time to the next stage. Figure 5.6 illustrates the three-stage model of memory.

Information is held only briefly (as little as a fraction of a second) in the mind before the image begins to decay and/or is blocked out by other incoming sensory information. Information that has not already faded from the **sensory storage** is read out to **short-term storage.** Because of the limited capacity of the short-term store, information to be held longer must be transferred to the relatively permanent **long-term storage.** For all practical purposes, long-term storage capacity is infinite. In the process of retrieval, stored information is obtained by searching, finding, and remembering, either through recall or recognition. *Recall* refers to memory retrieval in the absence of cues or hints—such as occurs when answering an essay question—whereas *recognition* refers to memory retrieval when cues are present, as would be the case when answering a multiple-choice question. Memory efficiency depends on all three of these processes and is usually at a maximum during adolescence and young adulthood (Li, Naveh-Benjamin, & Lindenberer, 2005).

Information received by the senses is held briefly in one of several specific types of sensory storage. Auditory information is held in an auditory sensory store, referred to as *echoic memory.* Visual information is held in a visual sensory store, called *iconic memory.* Other sensory stores include those for tactile information and for smells. Research evidence indicates that *the ability to retrieve information from the sensory store does not change much* as children and adolescents mature (e.g., Wickens, 1974).

There is often some confusion about the difference between short-term and long-term memory. Short-term memory involves information still being rehearsed and

focused on in the conscious mind. Long-term memory is characterized by how deeply the information has been processed, not by how long the information has been held. Deep processing, in which perceived information has been passed into layers of memory below the conscious level, constitutes long-term memory. For example, when you memorize a word list, the words under immediate consideration are in short-term memory. Words already looked at, memorized, and tucked away are in long-term memory, even though they were learned only a short time before. Specific words recalled several days or months later are recalled from long-term memory; information in long term memory can remain there for 30 seconds or for years. Once you are actively thinking about the words, they are again in short-term memory.

When measuring short-term memory, subjects are presented with short strings of digits, letters, or words and then tested for the total that can be recalled immediately. Research indicates that short-term memory continues to improve during adolescence and into early adulthood (e.g., Fry & Hale, 1996). For example, Kail (2000) found that one's short-term memory span increases throughout adolescence. This seems to be true of both verbal and visuospatial memories (Swanson, 1999; Zald and Iacono, 1998).

The most significant changes in memory storage occur in long-term ability or in the capacity to shift information from short- to long-term storage. Long-term memory improves not only from childhood into adolescence, but also throughout adolescence into young adulthood. Adolescents, for example, take longer to retrieve information from memory than young adults do (Kail, 1991). They are also less likely than young adults to use effective memory strategies; in particular, teenagers don't use retrieval cues as efficiently as adults do (Lehman, Morath, Franklin, et al., 1998). Some of the changes that occur in memory during adolescence can be attributed to the fact that compared to children, older adolescents are less likely to clutter up their memories with irrelevant information. For example, Bjorklund and Harnishfeger (1990) presented children and adolescents with sentences whose last words were missing; each sentence was constructed in such a way

---

| **FIGURE 5.6**   THREE-STAGE MODEL OF MEMORY

sensory storage (sensory memory)   the process by which information is received and transduced by the senses, usually in a fraction of a second.

short-term storage (short-term memory)   the process by which information is still in the conscious mind, being rehearsed and focused on (also called *primary memory*).

long-term storage (long-term memory)   the process by which information is perceived and processed deeply so it passes into the layers of memory below the conscious level (also called *secondary memory*).

that there was only one sensible, obvious choice for the last word (e.g., *Bananas are the color* . . .). Each subject was asked to supply the missing last word. Sometimes, the correct answer was the obvious choice, but other times, the subject was told that his or her answer was wrong and that another, unexpected word was correct. Each subject was told to remember the correct last word for each sentence. At the end of the procedure, each subject was asked to list the correct ending words and also the words that he or she had guessed, even if they were incorrect. The older subjects generally remembered only the correct words, as they had been instructed; the younger subjects remembered both the correct words and their incorrect guesses. Because the older subjects had concentrated on remembering the correct words only, they recalled more of the correct ending words than did the children.

Processing Speed

Age changes in both attention span and memory are likely accounted for by the same mechanism: mental processing speed. **Processing speed** refers to how fast the brain perceives and utilizes information. It influences how fast you notice the details of a stimulus and how fast you think. Kail (1991) found that 12- and 13-year-old adolescents were substantially slower—a full standard deviation slower—than adults on a wide variety of processing speed tasks, including mental addition, mental rotation, memory search, and the performance of simple motor skills. By mid-adolescence, teens process information about as fast as young adults (Hale, 1990). This simple change in processing speed, which is probably linked to neural development and myelinization (Kail, 2000), causes improvements in short-term memory (Kail, 1997). (*Myelin* is a fatty covering that helps nerve impulses travel more quickly.) Enhanced short-term memory, in turn, leads to increases in intelligence, reasoning, and problem-solving abilities (Demetriou, Christou, Spanoudis, et al., 2002). Fry and Hale (1996) labeled this series of enhancements a "developmental cascade."

ANSWERS WOULDN'T YOU LIKE TO KNOW . . .

How are adolescents' memory skills better than children's?

Adolescents can store more bits of information in their working memory than children. Also, adolescents are better at laying down new memories than children, in part because they can better focus their attention on the information that they want to remember.

ANSWERS WOULDN'T YOU LIKE TO KNOW . . .

Why can adolescents think more quickly than children?

Adolescents can think more quickly than children because more of their neurons are *myelinated*, or covered with an insulating fatty material. This coating speeds up neural transmission and results in quicker thinking.

Higher-Order Thought Processes

After information has been retrieved from memory, it must be manipulated in some way. In a lengthy review of the literature, Moshman (1997) differentiates among three higher-order thought processes: inference, thinking, and reasoning. Each improves during adolescence.

Inference—the most basic of the thought processes—is the ability to generate new thoughts from old information. Even very young children make unconscious inferences, but the ability to draw on what one already knows to infer new facts continues to improve with age. For example, Barnes, Dennis, and Haefele-Kalvaitis (1996) asked 147 six- to fifteen-year-olds to make inferences after having been read a story. The adolescents were better able to infer information not explicitly stated than the younger children were.

Thinking is more advanced in that it is the conscious, deliberate coordination of information. You are thinking when you struggle with a problem, try to decide between two options, or plan the itinerary of your vacation. Adolescents think more clearly than children; for example, they are more planful (Lachman & Burack, 1993). Several studies have demonstrated that older adolescents are more deliberative and systematic than younger adolescents when using information (e.g., Nakajima & Hotta, 1989), and that—as Piaget claimed—they are more likely to manipulate one variable at a time when solving problems (Kuhn & Dean, 2005).

One way that adolescents' thinking improves is that they are better able than younger children to use *negative information*—that is, information that refutes their hypotheses. During early and middle childhood, children search for and base their decisions on the confirming evidence that they find; during adolescence, teens search for and rely more on disconfirming evidence. For example, imagine that you have been asked to decide whether all pears are green. To help you, you have been given a large stack of pictures of pear trees. If you were 8 or 9 years old, you would point to a lot of pictures of green pears and gleefully say that they are *all* green. If you were 15, you would either indicate those same pictures and say, "They seem to be but I'm not certain," or you would find the one picture at the bottom of the stack that showed a red pear. You would then conclude that not all pears are green because you would understand that one counterexample is enough to disprove a premise, even if there are hundreds of confirming pieces of evidence. Adolescents rely on **negation** rather than **affirmation** (Mueller, Sokol, & Overton, 1999), and they use an **elimination strategy** rather than the younger child's **confirmation strategy** (Foltz, Overton, & Ricco, 1995).

Adolescents may be more able than children to incorporate negative information into their judgments, but like adults, adolescents are not very good at doing this when they are personally or emotionally involved in the situation (Kuhn, 1989). Klaczynski and Gordon (1996), for example, found that adolescents were better able to find logical flaws in arguments that were inconsistent with their religious beliefs than those that were in accord with them. This **self-serving bias** probably serves the same function in adolescence that it does in adulthood: seeing the data as more consistent with your opinion than it really is enhances self-esteem, allows one to feel self-righteous, and promotes optimism (Schaller, 1992).

The most sophisticated cognitions involve the third type of thought process: **reasoning.** Reasoning occurs when you constrain and limit your thinking along lines that you believe are rational and useful. You do this based on prior experiences with both successful and unsuccessful thinking strategies.

Finding parallels between similar problems is one form of reasoning known as reasoning by *analogy: Grass is to green as sky is to* . . . . As with many cognitive skills, young children have some ability to form analogies, but this skill improves during adolescence (Nippold, 1994).

A second form of reasoning involves deliberately following the rules of logic, or making *deductions.* This is the type of reasoning that Piaget (1963) focused on in his discussions of formal operations. The fact that formal operational thinking begins in adolescence indicates a growth in logical, deductive reasoning ability. This increased use of deduction has been confirmed by other researchers, such as Moshman and Franks (1986), who demonstrated that older adolescents can better follow a logical argument than younger adolescents, and Byrnes

and Overton (1988), who showed that older adolescents better comprehend *if/then* statements than younger ones.

Although adolescents use deduction best when solving problems in which the content is familiar (Klaczynski & Narasimhan, 1998), they can create and test hypotheses when the content is unfamiliar or counterfactual (Ward & Overton, 1990). In fact, Moshman (1999) concluded that most of the deductive improvement that occurs during adolescence comes from an increasing ability to suspend one's own beliefs. A third form of reasoning, *induction* (the ability to drawing general conclusions from a series of examples), also appears to improve during adolescence (e.g., Galotti, Komatsu, & Voelz, 1997).

Although reasoning improves during adolescence, it remains far from perfect. Adolescents do not use data as effectively as young adults (Kuhn & Pease, 2006), and they will more often twist and distort information to fit their preconceptions (Klahr, 2000). For example, teens in one study were willing to attribute improvement in student performance to a single cause—smaller classes, teaching assistants, or a change in curriculum—even though several changes were instituted at once and causality could not be disentangled and conclusions should not be made based upon a single data point (Kuhn, Katz, & Dean, 2004). To be fair, even adults are not very good at coordinating and juggling multiple potential causes for an outcome, although they are better than adolescents (Kuhn & Dean, 2004).

One of the practical results of thinking and reasoning is *problem solving.* Some of the differences between adolescents and children in problem-solving ability can be attributed to the nature of adolescents' information processing. As has been mentioned, adolescents are better able than children to remember more information, consider all possible relationships, think about them logically, and generate and evaluate different variables and solutions ahead of time before deciding on a solution and course of action. Children usually do

---

● **ANSWERS WOULDN'T YOU LIKE TO KNOW . . .**

How does reasoning improve during adolescence?

Adolescents are better than children at seeing similarities between problems; this lets them use their past experiences to solve current dilemmas more effectively. Adolescents are also better than children at *deducing* answers, or beginning with general truths and logically deriving specific answers to problems. Adolescents are better able to do the opposite, too: drawing general conclusions from specific examples.

---

processing speed   the pace at which the brain perceives and manipulates information.

inference   to develop new thoughts from old information.

thinking   the conscious, deliberate manipulation of information.

negation   a strategy used to disprove.

affirmation   a strategy used to confirm.

elimination strategy   looking for evidence that disproves a hypothesis.

confirmation strategy   looking for examples that match a hypothesis.

self-serving bias   looking at the world in a way that favors one's own opinion.

reasoning   logical, constrained, useful thinking.

not get sufficient information, remember enough of it, think about it logically enough, or consider all possible relations before arriving at solutions. Their information-processing ability is limited in relation to that of adolescents and they are not as good at solving problems (Kuhn, 2006).

Finally, an advanced type of reasoning occurs when one uses **principles** to solve problems. Principles differ from rules in that rules are more precise. For example, the statement *"Any number times 0 equals 0"* is a rule because it is always true. If you apply the rule, you will always get the same, correct answer. Principles are more abstract; thus, two individuals using the same principle might propose different solutions to a dilemma. Two people who believe in the principle "One should be kind to others" might easily treat their neighbors differently. Whereas one might conclude that kindness involves doing extensive favors, the second might believe that exchanging pleasantries is sufficient. Adolescents are much more likely than children to engage in principle-based reasoning (Moshman, 1993). The development of principled moral reasoning has been extensively studied and is discussed further in Chapter 7.

The Role of Knowledge

"Garbage in, garbage out" is an apt saying when it comes to problem solving. In order to accurately manipulate facts in your mind, you must *know* those facts. Part of the reason that adolescents are smarter than children is simply that they know more and have had more experiences (Byrnes, 2003). They can thus draw on that information and those experiences to find analogies to new problems they are facing. For example, suppose you get a new pie recipe from a friend but forget to ask how long it needs to be baked. If you have made a lot of pies in your lifetime, you can guess that the baking time is about an hour. But if you have never baked one before, you will be clueless.

As noted earlier, adolescents do better at solving problems when the content is familiar. Obviously, as we get older, more and more content is familiar to us and so our problem-solving ability is enhanced.

Decision Making

One of the characteristics of an intelligent, mature person is the ability to make good decisions. Some decisions made during adolescence may have lifelong consequences. Important decisions may pertain to education, career, choice of partner, and health habits. Adolescence is a period of challenge and change—a time when both deliberate and unintentional decisions are made that affect the course of the adolescents' lives. The consequences of these decisions depend in good part on the degree to which good judgment is exercised.

The Process

Decision making is a complicated process involving information search and processing to understand available options (Moore, Jensen, & Hauck, 1990). It involves problem solving to find novel or creative solutions. Ross (1981) proposed that decision makers must master five skills: (1) identifying alternate courses of action, (2) identifying appropriate criteria for considering alternatives, (3) assessing alternatives by criteria, (4) summarizing information about alternatives, and (5) evaluating the outcome of the decision-making process. One often must make decisions when there are no easy answers, when one is faced with conflicting information, and when all choices involve a mixture of positive and negative attributes. Making good decisions, then, involves all of the skills previously discussed and others as well.

Older adolescents are more aware of the process than are younger adolescents. One study revealed that whereas mid-adolescents understand very well what is involved in the activity of decision making, early adolescents have little recognition that decision-making activity involves clearly specifying goals, considering options, and checking before taking action to implement a decision. They are less likely than older adolescents to generate options, to anticipate the consequences of decisions, and to evaluate the credibility of sources (Ormond, Luszez, Mann, et al., 1991).

This awareness of and ability to think about one's own thinking has often been refered to as **metacognition.** If you know that you study better with soft music than with loud music or that it will take you longer to get through a chapter in your physics text than it will to read a chapter in a best-selling novel, you have some metacognitive skills. Metacognition is now also referred to as **executive control.** As mentioned earlier, many researchers believe that advances in executive control are largely responsible for the cognitive advances seen during adolescence (e.g., Keating, 2004). For example, monitoring how well one is succeeding at a task and changing strategies accordingly increases from childhood across adolescence (Crone, Somsen, Zanolie, et al., 2006). As people mature, they become more and more able to inhibit maladaptive strategies and limit themselves to those that work (Kuhn, 2009).

Another reason for improvement is that, in general, older adolescents have had more experience in making decisions than younger adolescents, and breadth of experience plays an important role in the quality of decisions that one makes. There is an old saying that "Experience is the world's best teacher." Adolescents who have had many opportunities to make decisions for themselves are better at doing so than adolescents who have not (Quadrel, Fischoff, & Davis, 1993). Parents who involve their adolescents in family decision making are helping to prepare them for mature adult life. So important is this opportunity for practice that many schools have developed programs to help teach adolescents critical-thinking skills.

Barriers to Good Decision Making

Unfortunately, neither adolescents nor even adults always make good decisions. Sometimes this occurs from lack of information or from inexperience. Sometimes it is because we rely too much on **heuristics,** or rules of thumb, when making decisions.

A good example involves the "sunk-cost fallacy," a situation that arises when people do more of a disliked activity if they paid for it than if it were free. In one study, 63 percent of adults watched a boring movie longer if they paid for it than if it were shown gratis; 73 percent of 16-year-olds and a whopping 84 percent of 12-year-olds did the same (Klaczynski & Cottrell, 2004). Clearly, then, the tendency to avoid this mistake increases as we get older, but most individuals, even adults, still make a poor choice.

Similarly, adolescents (just like adults) are mistakenly likely to conclude that a pretty, cheerful girl is more likely to be a cheerleader than to be in the band even though there are far more female band members than cheerleaders (Jacobs & Potenza, 1991) because they judge according to stereotypes. They also rely too much upon anecdotal evidence and too little upon more rigorous evidence (Klaczynski, 2001), even by the end of adolescence. Ignoring base-rate data, or usual frequency, is a common logical fallacy (Kahneman & Tversky, 1973).

Risky Decision Making

It is widely recognized that adolescents are more likely than adults to take risks (Steinberg, 2007). For many years, this was attributed to Elkind's *personal fable,* introduced earlier in this chapter. The explanation was that adolescents engaged in potentially harmful activities because they felt invulnerable and because they believed that the odds of anything bad happening to them were small to vanishingly rare. Although many decades of research have found correlations between that egocentrism and risky behavior (e.g., Schwartz,

Maynard, & Uzelac, 2008), current research indicates that the underlying explanation for the linkage is incorrect. In truth, new data show that adolescents often *overestimate* the rate of negative consequences from risky actions (Reyna & Farley, 2006). Why, then, are they willing to take risks?

Strangely, risk taking is not strongly correlated with risk perception. Whereas some studies find that teens who judge risks to be high avoid engaging in dangerous behaviors, others find the opposite: that some teens, at least, are *more* likely to perform a behavior if they believe it to be risky (Mills, Reyna, & Estrada, 2008). A number of authors (e.g., Holland & Klaczynski, 2009) have suggested that rather than concentrating on the risks, adolescents appear to be focusing on the *benefits* they will get from actions. They rely upon *intuitive* rather than analytic reasoning. These researchers advocate a **dual process theory** of decision making (Reyna & Rivers, 2008) in which intuitions and use of heuristics often trump logic and deliberation. Intuitive decision making, and its resulting poorer outcomes, is apt to kick in when teens are emotionally involved rather than dispassionate (Sequin, Aresenault, & Tremblay, 2007).

Similarly, teens are also influenced by how they conceptualize risks. If they view a behavior as so dangerous as to be avoided under any circumstances, in the absolute terms of "it's bad," they will likely avoid it. Conversely, if they view behaviors in a more complex fashion ("It has these costs, but it has these benefits"), they will more likely choose to do it (Mills, Reyna, & Estrada, 2008).

Other factors that contribute to making the decision to engage in risky behaviors include that the harm that can result from risks is not always viewed as being as significant by adolescents as it is by adults and so is seen as having less consequence (Millstein & Halpern-Felsher, 2002b). In addition, some adolescents may engage in risky behaviors because they are pessimistic about their chance of leading a long, healthy, happy life (Chapin, 2001). Apparently, these adolescents' interpretation of the importance of the consequences, not a sense of low risk itself, is what allows them to smoke, drink excessively, and drive without wearing a seat belt.

---

principles   abstract, theoretical guidelines.

metacognition   the ability to think about one's own thought processes.

executive control   the ability to monitor and direct one's thought processes.

heuristics   rules of thumb, general strategies or principles.

dual process theory   a theory of decision making that says that adolescents can logically and analytically make choices, but that they often rely upon intuition and short-term benefits instead.

ANSWERS WOULDN'T YOU LIKE TO KNOW ...

Why do adolescents take greater risks than adults do?

Some adolescents take risks because they feel invulnerable and charmed (the personal fable). Others are willing to take greater risks than adults because they are less upset at the thought of negative consequences. These adolescents are fatalistic and assume that bad things are likely to occur regardless of what they do. Why, then, bother to be careful?

Epistemological Understanding

A major change in reasoning that occurs during adolescence involves how teenagers think about *facts* and *truth.* As adolescence progresses, individuals become much more sophisticated in how they perceive and reason about information and knowledge. They come to understand that truth is not objective but subjective. More specifically, they discover that one *constructs* his or her understanding of the truth rather than *uncovers* it. The great strides in thinking about knowledge—**epistemology**—that occur during adolescence rely on the abstract reasoning capacity and the metacognitive abilities that emerge during the formal operations stage.

Boyes and Chandler (1992) have devised a four-level scheme of epistemic development that is appealing because it speaks to a diverse set of changes that occur during childhood and adolescence.

Level 1

In early childhood—through the age of 6 or 7—children are **naive realists.** They believe that there are absolute, universal truths in the world, and they have difficulty distinguishing fact from opinion. Naive realists believe that when people have diverging opinions, it is because they are working with different pieces of information. The 4-year-old who says "Just try my vanilla ice cream; you'll think it's better than chocolate" after you announce that chocolate is your favorite flavor is demonstrating naive realism.

ANSWERS WOULDN'T YOU LIKE TO KNOW ...

Why do adolescents sometimes become skeptical of authority?

Some adolescents lose respect for authority because they realize that what comprises truth sometimes changes and that experts can be wrong. In a sense, they view all opinions as equally valid because they understand that our knowledge of truth is imperfect.

Level 2

During middle childhood, when children are in elementary school, they become **defensive realists.** They are still realists because they continue to cling to the belief that there are absolute, universal truths, but they now recognize that people can hold different opinions and draw different conclusions even when they are working with the same information. They defend their belief in realism by arguing that people are biased (and hence misrepresent and distort the truth) and by differentiating between fact and opinion. Defensive realists see facts as unambiguously, universally true and opinions as variable. Some individuals never progress beyond this epistemic stage.

Level 3

Once adolescents can think abstractly and hypothetically, they become either **dogmatists** or **skeptics,** at least in the short run. Boyes and Chandler see these opposite types as being rooted in the same awareness: that truth is always constructed and that facts are open to multiple valid interpretations. This is an unsettling revelation at best, and adolescents feel beset by uncertainty. They wonder: "If you can't tell the true from the false, if you cannot be certain who is right and who is wrong, how can you make good choices?"

Skeptical adolescents react to this uncertainty by rejecting rationality. They take the attitude that if they cannot be certain about what to do or whom to believe, then all opinions and positions are equally valid and they don't have to listen to anyone (or to anyone in particular). They lose respect for authority and have little patience for those who parade around as experts. Because they have lost faith in logic, these adolescents behave *impulsively* (without reasoning through situations), *intuitively* (doing what their emotions, rather than their logic, tells them to do), and *indifferently* (without attempting to choose a good course of action, "going with the flow"). They are apt to *conform* to others, letting the majority make their decisions for them, and they become rebellious or disengaged.

In contrast to the skeptics, *dogmatists* flee from their uncertainty, rigidly clinging to one set of beliefs. They are intolerant of other views because they find them threatening, and they do not want to question their own beliefs. They conform to the views of those they have chosen as allies. They insist that their way of thinking is right and that any who disagree with them are wrong.

Whereas skeptics believe that anyone who believes too deeply in anything is foolish, dogmatists believe that anyone who espouses something different from them is misguided. Clearly, neither of these positions is desirable. Boyes and Chandler view skepticism and dogmatism as short-term costs associated with entry into formal operations. However, many people never outgrow this stage of reasoning.

Level 4

Finally, some individuals progress to the stage of **post-skeptical rationalism.** Post-skeptical rationalists understand that absolute certainty of the truth is not needed for rational behavior. Although one cannot be completely certain what is right, it is clear that some possibilities are more likely right than others. Post-skeptical rationalists believe that you do the best you can with the information available. You recognize, however, that others may draw different conclusions from that data or reject as false some of the data that you use.

Other researchers have developed schemes very similar to Boyes and Chandlers'. For example, Kuhn (2009) describes children as *absolutists* who believe that knowledge is a reflection of absolute reality, and adolescents as most frequently *relativists* who believe that all knowledge is essentially opinion. Only some individuals become *evaluativists* who understand that some opinions are more valid than others because they are more in keeping with the available data. There is some disagreement, though, as to how quickly individuals can move through the levels of epistemic development. For example, Boyes and Chandler (1992) found evidence of rationalism in some of the high school juniors they studied, but King, Kitchener, Davidson, et al. (1983) found that it took several years of college experience before rationalism emerged.

Brain Development During Adolescence

Why do adolescents make these cognitive gains? It might be, in part, because they have had time to acquire a substantial amount of knowledge. It might be, in part, that they have had time to practice their cognitive skills or that they have learned which cognitive strategies are most successful. Or it might be, in part, due to physical maturation of the brain (Byrnes, 2003).

For many years, scientists believed that brain development was largely completed during early childhood (Straugh, 2003). They now know that this is not the case and that a number of key brain structures do not mature until the individual is in his or her twenties (Casey, Giedd, & Thomas, 2000). Most of the identified changes occur in the **cerebrum.** As the largest structure in the human brain, the cerebrum is mostly what you see when you look at an intact brain. The cerebrum is divided into two hemispheres (or halves) that are connected by the

IN THEIR OWN WORDS

"I definitely saw the world in dichotomies. I thought that the world had a few truths, such as Good/Evil and Just/Unjust. At the time, it was surprising to me that adults did not view things the same way. To me, it was obvious that problems existed in the world and that solutions were easy. Becoming dogmatic in my religion and my beliefs, I held firm to the fact that I was right and those who disagreed with me were wrong. I was very argumentative with my mom, family, and friends. I was not afraid to be controversial if it meant that I held onto my beliefs. I felt that my faith and my thoughts were truth in the world."

"Boy, was I a skeptic! In some ways, I still am. I used to argue with my dad and my teachers and say stuff like 'You don't really know that; you just think that.' I thought that my opinion was just as good as anyone else's. I got into a huge fight with my English teacher. She loved Shakespeare, and I thought his plays sucked. She told me that most scholars agreed that he was one of the greatest writers of all time. I told her that I thought his plays were stupid and boring and that I didn't care what anyone else thought. I didn't think that anyone had anything worthwhile to tell me. I needed to figure it all out for myself. I still think that a lot of so-called experts are just full of bullshit. I like to think things out for myself."

corpus callosum, a band of nerve fibers that transmits information back and forth. Each hemisphere is divided into four lobes (or sections; see Figure 5.7).

Each type of lobe contributes to thinking in a different way, and three of the lobes—the **parietal lobe,**

epistemology   one's beliefs about knowledge.

naive realists   believing that there are absolute, universal truths; creates difficulty in distinguishing fact from opinion.

defensive realists   believing that there are absolute truths but people are biased; differentiates between opinion and fact.

dogmatists those who   cling rigidly to one belief.

skeptics those who reject   rationality.

post-skeptical rationalism   the belief that truth is constructed but that some beliefs are more valid than others.

cerebrum   the largest part of the human brain.

corpus callosum   a fibrous band of tissue that connects the two cerebral hemispheres of the brain.

parietal lobe   the cerebral lobe that is the center for solving problems involving spatial relationships.

FIGURE 5.7   THE CEREBRAL LOBES

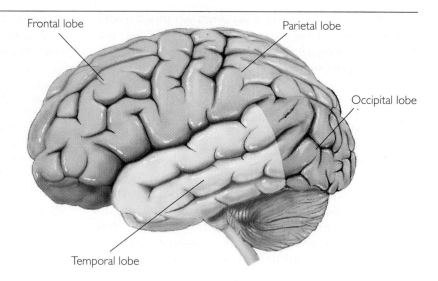

the **frontal lobe,** and the **temporal lobe**—continue to develop into adolescence. The cells in the parietal lobe become active when a person is working on problems involving *spatial reasoning*, such as figuring out whether a car will fit into that small parking space or which way to turn in order to get to a friend's house. The frontal lobe is involved in higher-order thought processes, such as planning and impulse control. People whose frontal lobe has been damaged act before they think and are unconcerned with long-term consequences. In contrast, if you bite your tongue instead of telling off your boss when he or she is being unreasonable or if you begin studying for finals more than a week before they occur, you have a well-functioning frontal lobe. Its maturation allows for the increased executive control discussed previously. The most well-known function of the temporal lobe (or in most people, the left temporal lobe) is language. (The right hemisphere of the temporal lobe is more concerned with interpreting nonverbal communication.)

Not only do these lobes continue to mature throughout adolescence, but the connections among them continue to develop, as well; for example, the nerve fibers running between the frontal and temporal lobes become thicker and more myelinated (Paus, Zijdenbos, Worsley, et al., 1999). The corpus callosum also thickens (Giedd, Blumenthal, Jeffries, et al., 1999). This enables different areas of the brain to share information more efficiently.

Deep inside the temporal lobe are two other structures that are now known to mature during adolescence: the hippocampus and the amygdala. The **hippocampus** is involved with learning, memory, and motivation. The **amygdala** interprets incoming sensory information and causes us to respond in primal, emotional ways to that information. It is also concerned with memory, especially emotional

memory. An individual who has a strong amygdala and a weak frontal lobe may, for example, anger easily and lash out at others or perhaps cry at a small setback. It is interesting that the hippocampus matures more quickly in girls and the amygdala matures more quickly in boys (Giedd, Castellanos, Rajapakse, et al., 1997).

Maturation of these brain structures is a two-step process. First, the cells rapidly grow and proliferate. This growth is so rapid that the resulting interconnections are termed *exuberant synapses*. Growth continues until the adolescent is about 16. At that point, the number of cells and interconnections are cut back. Some cells grow larger and stronger, and the surrounding, less-used cells die off. (Imagine a fast-growing oak sapling creating so much shade that its slower-growing siblings die off; it now has more room to expand and get even larger.) The cell loss that occurs can be quite dramatic. The brain actually loses 7 to 10 percent of its cells, and in some specific areas, half of all cells disappear (Durston, Hulshoff, Hilleke, et al., 2001). To repeat the theme that inhibition is associated with maturity, the number of excitatory synapses that are eliminated is much greater than the number of inhibitory synapses. In fact, the ratio of excitatory to inhibitory synapses drops from 7:1 to 4:1 during adolescence. This, in turn, highlights the importance of the environment in adolescent brain development, since which interconnections are strengthened and which are lost is a function of the experiences that the adolescent is having.

A number of researchers have hypothesized that the kinds of brain changes just described could account for much of the cognitive advancement seen during adolescence (e.g., Kail, 2000). Increased processing speed, increased processing capacity, memory improvements, more sophisticated use of language, enhanced self-awareness, and increased executive control are the sorts of cognitive effects to be expected from these types of brain changes. At the same time, some of the less positive aspects of adolescent behavior—such as increased risk taking, moodiness, and impulsiveness—also correlate with the uneven growth of the brain (e.g., Galvan, Hare, Parra, et al., 2006).

Assessing Cognition

In addition to the Piagetian and information-processing approaches already described, there is a third perspective from which we can study cognitive development: the **psychometric approach.** Psychometricians are interested in the measurement of knowledge and thinking ability. To this end, they have devised many tests, some of which are given to enormous numbers of children and adolescents. Tests that are designed to measure intelligence, which are usually termed *IQ tests* (for **intelligence quotient**), are widely used by schools to determine students' eligibility for special academic programs. The other main type of test, **achievement tests,** is intended to measure mastery of particular subject matter, such as reading comprehension or geometry.

Questions about these types of tests and the utility of testing in general have become the subject of public debate, in large part because the Bush administration made the frequent, mandatory achievement testing of all American schoolchildren part of its "No Child Left Behind" educational agenda. Although tests are usually labeled as being either *intelligence* or *achievement* tests, many are, in fact, blends of the two. In order to do well on such a test, you must be bright and capable of quick thought *and* you must possess relevant knowledge.

Theories of Intelligence

Intelligence has almost as many definitions as experts who try to measure it. It has been described as an innate capacity to learn, think, reason, understand, and solve problems. At the present time, two very different theories of intelligence are generally accepted. Let's describe each in turn.

Triarchic Theory of Intelligence

Sternberg (1997) and his colleagues at Yale University arranged abilities into the following three major groupings in his triarchic theory of intelligence:

1. *Analytic intelligence:* Analytic intelligence includes general learning and comprehension abilities, such as good vocabulary; high reading comprehension; the ability to do test items such as analogies, syllogisms, and series; and the ability to think critically. This is the traditional concept of intelligence as measured on tests.

2. *Creative intelligence:* Experiential intelligence includes the ability to select, encode, compare, and combine information in meaningful ways to produce new insights, theories, and ideas.

3. *Practical intelligence:* Contextual intelligence includes adaptive behavior in the real world, such as the ability to size up situations, achieve goals, and solve practical problems (Sternberg & Wagner, 1986).

Research has demonstrated that adolescents who are taught in a manner that taps into each of these three types of intelligence learn more than those who are taught in a more traditional, memory-based fashion (Sternberg, Torff, & Grigorenko, 1998).

Eight (or Ten?) Frames of Mind

Harvard professor Howard Gardner objects to narrow views of intelligence. In his classic book *Frames of Mind* (1993), he outlined seven types of reasoning ability:

1. *Linguistic intelligence*

2. *Logical-mathematical intelligence*

3. *Spatial intelligence:* Spatial intelligence is the ability to form spatial images and to find one's way around

---

> **ANSWERS WOULDN'T YOU LIKE TO KNOW …**
>
> Why are adolescents sometimes more emotional than adults?
>
> Adolescents may be more emotional than adults because the amygdala (the emotional center) develops faster than the frontal lobes (the center of planning and impulse control). This is even more true of boys than girls.

---

frontal lobe   the cerebral lobe that is the center for higher-order thought processes, such as planning and impulse control.

temporal lobe   the cerebral lobe that is the center for producing and understanding language.

hippocampus   the part of the brain involved with learning, memory, and motivation.

amygdala   the part of the brain that creates primitive emotional responses to the environment.

psychometric approach   an approach to cognitive development that focuses on the measurement of knowledge and thinking ability.

intelligence quotient (IQ)   calculated by dividing the mental age (MA) by the chronological age (CA) and multiplying by 100.

achievement tests   tests designed to assess mastery of specific subject matter or skills.

in an environment. The sailors in the Caroline Islands of Micronesia navigate among hundreds of islands using only the stars and their bodily feelings. Intelligence testers in Micronesia would have to come up with an entirely different list of intelligences and testing methods.

4. *Musical intelligence:* Musical intelligence is the ability to perceive and create pitch and rhythmic patterns. There are individuals who are otherwise classified as mentally challenged who can play a song on a piano after hearing it once, or who have an extraordinary talent as a trombonist yet are not able to read a newspaper.

5. *Body-kinesthetic intelligence:* Body-kinesthetic intelligence is the gift of fine motor movement, as seen in a surgeon or dancer.

6. *Interpersonal intelligence:* Interpersonal intelligence is the ability to understand others: how they feel, what motivates them, how they interact. Certain people interact well with others because of their empathetic understanding; others, such as politicians, are highly skilled at understanding others and manipulating them.

7. *Intrapersonal intelligence:* Intrapersonal intelligence centers on the individual's ability to know himself or herself and to develop a sense of identity.

In his more recent works, Gardner (1999, 2006) considers the possibility of three additional types of intelligence: existential, spiritual, and naturalistic. He most clearly endorses **naturalistic intelligence,** which is the ability to identify plants and animals.

Gardner insists that psychologists have to develop a completely different concept of who is bright and how to measure brightness. His concept is unique because he claims independent existence for different intelligences in the human neural system. He would like to stop measuring people according to some unitary dimension called "intelligence." Instead, he would like to think in terms of different intellectual strengths.

Do these various types of intelligence improve between childhood and adulthood? Verbal, spatial, and mathematical abilities surely do. Interpersonal intelligence improves, too; the effects this change has on friendship and other relationships are discussed in Chapter 10. Dramatic changes also occur in self-awareness, which are discussed in Chapter 6. Musical intelligence appears to increase sharply during adolescence (Hassler, 1992), and kinesthetic ability also increases until early adulthood (Visser & Geuze, 2000).

According to Gardner, one of the dimensions for assessing intelligence involves music and the ability to perceive and create pitch and rhythmic patterns.

Intelligence Testing

The most well-known intelligence tests are the Stanford-Binet and the Wechsler Scales. Neither is based on Sternberg's or Gardner's theory of intelligence, as both tests predate these theories. Although aspects of each theory are captured by the questions on the tests, the tests measure a much narrower swath of abilities than either theory proposes. (See Table 5.1 for subtests in the Wechsler Scale.) In Sternberg's terms, the tests measure largely *analytic intelligence;* in Gardner's terms, they measure *linguistic intelligence* and *logical-mathematical intelligence.* They both provide IQ scores whose average value is 100.

Although IQ can change greatly from earlier in childhood into adolescence (Schneider, Perner, Bullock, et al., 1999), by the time individuals reach the teenage years their IQ scores have usually stabilized (Kaufman & Lichtenbeger, 2002). The differences in

TABLE 5.1 SUBTESTS OF THE WECHSLER ADULT INTELLIGENCE SCALE (WAIS-III)

VERBAL SUBTESTS	PERFORMANCE SUBTESTS
Arithmetic—Perform mathematical calculations	Block Design—Arrange colored blocks to mimic specific patterns
Comprehension—Give solutions to social and practical problems	Digit Symbol—Use a key to translate symbols into numbers
Digit Span—Repeat a set of digits either forward or backward	Object Assembly—Assemble a puzzle
Information—Answer questions about general information and common knowledge	Picture Arrangement—Arrange a set of pictures into a coherent story
Similarities—Use inductive reasoning skills (How is A similar to B?)	Picture Completion—Find the missing part in a picture (e.g., a dog without a tail)
Vocabulary—Define words	
Letter-Number Sequencing—Remember the order of presented numbers and letters	Matrix Reasoning—Fill in a missing element in a symbolic sequence

Source: Adapted from L. R. Aiken, *Psychological Testing and Assessment* (7th ed., pp. 163–164). Copyright © 1991 Pearson Education. Used with permission.

childhood IQ and adolescent IQ can be explained by the experiences that the individual has had. For example, if he or she has experienced significant stress (such living in poverty, experiencing a parent's protracted illness or death, or having parents who are chronically fighting), his or her IQ is likely to decrease over time (e.g., Gutman, Sameroff, & Cole, 2003). This underscores that IQ score is a product not only of biology, but also of the environment. Both past experiences and immediate circumstances can affect how well one does on an IQ test.

Factors Influencing Test Results

One reason for variations in IQ and other measures of intelligence is that it is sometimes difficult to get valid test results. Scores differ not only because intelligence may vary but also because of immediate factors influencing test scores (Richardson, 2002). One of the most important influences is the presence of *anxiety* in the subjects tested. Anxious youths do not do as well on tests as those with greater emotional security (Zeidner, 1995). Motivation also has a marked influence on test results. An otherwise bright student who is poorly motivated to do well on a test will not measure up to his or her capacity and will do much worse than he or she is capable of (Goff & Ackerman, 1997). Alternatively, a student might not be feeling well on testing day or might be distracted by construction noises outside.

Furthermore, the tests are not free of cultural bias. Tests to measure IQ were originally designed to measure innate general intelligence apart from environmental influences. But research over a long

period has shown that sociocultural factors play a significant role in the outcome of the tests (Richardson, 2002). The tests' language, illustrations, examples, and abstractions are designed to measure intelligence according to middle-class standards (Martinez, 2000). Thus, some adolescents do poorly not because they are less intelligent but because they do not comprehend language or concepts foreign to their backgrounds and experiences.

Efforts to develop culturally unbiased tests have been frustrating. The general approach has been to use language familiar to the particular minorities for which the test is designed or to make the test completely nonverbal. The most well-known example of such a test is the Raven Progressive Matrix Test, or the RPM. Items in this test are composed of several rows of symbols; the rightmost symbol of the bottom row is missing, and the test taker's job is to select which symbol would complete that row so that its pattern matches that of the rows above. Although its nonverbal nature was thought to ensure that it was culturally fair, many researchers now disagree with that assertion (e.g., Carpenter, Just, & Shell, 1990).

A relatively new approach that is being endorsed by some is termed *dynamic testing* (Lidz, 2001). It is based on Vygotsky's approach to intelligence in that it taps ability to improve performance based on social interaction. Children are first tested on their ability to perform some task; they are then coached in as helpful a manner as possible and, finally, asked to try

naturalistic intelligence   the ability to identify plants and animals.

The amount of anxiety and motivation are factors that influence test results. There is also the effect of cultural bias, in which cultural standards and language favor the students from middle-class, nonminority backgrounds.

the task again on their own. Dynamic testing differs from traditional intelligence testing in that each child is treated as an individual rather than in a fixed, consistent manner and in that the children are given feedback as to how they initially did. Researchers who have used dynamic testing assessments have found that the results are good predictors as to how well children can learn in school (Sternberg & Grigorenko, 2002).

Uses and Misuses of IQ Tests

Great caution must be used when interpreting intelligence test scores. First, as stated earlier, a test score reflects, at best, a snapshot of a person's ability at a particular point in time. If you have ever had to take an exam when you were tired or grumpy or didn't feel well, then you know that people do not always perform their best when test taking. Second, even if a person's score is an accurate reflection of how well he or she can perform on a particular test, it may not reflect his or her intelligence per se but instead his or her attitude or background. How do you think your score would change if you were given an IQ test in a language in which you were not completely fluent or that contained questions about a culture with which you were not familiar? Clearly, you would do worse on such a test than on one more reflective of your own background.

At the same time, IQ tests can be put to good use. In fact, an adolescent who does poorly on an IQ test probably has *some* issue that is keeping him or her from doing well. Whatever that issue is—be it worry over personal problems, lack of motivation,

a background that has failed to provide expected learning opportunities, or low intelligence—it is important to identify it so that appropriate services can be provided to the student. Thus, IQ tests can serve as screening devices and call attention to adolescents in need.

In addition, IQ tests do predict—even if the means are indirect and not causally related to intelligence—various important aspects of a person's situation. For instance, IQ scores do, to a certain degree, predict an adolescent's popularity with peers (Scarr, 1997). And, as one might expect, IQ does predict school achievement (e.g., Chamorro-Premuzic, & Furnham, 2006). In good part because of this, IQ also predicts occupational status (Nyborg & Jensen, 2001).

Achievement Tests

An achievement test is designed to measure the mastery of a set of facts or skills. Most of the tests that you took in elementary, middle, and high school were achievement tests, as will be most of the tests that you will take in college. For instance, midterms and final exams are usually designed to assess whether you have learned the course material (although if they require you to draw inferences beyond what was actually taught, they may be tapping into intelligence, as well). The mandatory competency tests that are now given to American schoolchildren as a result of federal education legislation are also examples of achievement tests; so are the SAT area tests in biology, literature, and the like.

The Scholastic Reasoning Test (SAT)

One of the most widely used tests in the United States is the *SAT*. (It used to be called the *Scholastic Assessment Test* and, prior to that, the *Scholastic Aptitude Test*. It is now named the *Scholastic Reasoning Test*, and the abbreviation *SAT* is still used even though it no longer fits.) The SAT is used by a majority of colleges as one basis for admission. More than 1.5 million high school seniors took the test in 2007–2008 (College Board, 2008).

The combined verbal and math scores often determine eligibility not only for college admission but also for scholarships and financial aid. The Educational Testing Service (ETS), which produces the SAT, claims that in combination with high school records, the SATs have proved to be better predictors of students' first-year performances in college than any other measurement. Nevertheless, the protests against the use or misuse of this test are significant (e.g., Zwick & Green, 2007).

There are two primary objections to the SAT. First, the test is not neutral in terms of race/ethnicity, socioeconomic status, and gender (e.g., Freedle, 2003). Asian Americans consistently outscore Caucasians, and both of these groups outscore African Americans and Hispanic Americans. In addition, males outscore females on both the verbal and quantitative sections of the test (Jackson & Rushton, 2006). SAT test scores are higher for individuals who come from higher-level socioeconomic backgrounds (College Board, 2008).

The second primary objection has to do with the claim that the test measures basic abilities acquired over a student's lifetime and is thus immune to last-minute cramming and is "coach proof." Several studies (e.g., Kaplan, 2005) have shown that special coaching can significantly improve SAT scores. In contrast, a study sponsored by the College Board, the parent organization of the SAT, found that students who were coached were only slightly more likely to show large score gains

RESEARCH HIGHLIGHT   INTELLECTUALLY DIFFERENT ADOLESCENTS

The IQ scores of about 95 percent of the population fall between 70 and 130. The remaining 5 percent are evenly divided between top and bottom, such that 2.5 percent have IQs above 130 and 2.5 percent have IQs below 70. Those with IQs above 130 are referred to as *gifted*, whereas those with the lowest scores are *mentally challenged*. Adolescence can be an especially challenging time for an individual in either group.

Individuals with cognitive limitations are subjected to increased pressures during adolescence. They find school more challenging than ever, since they have fallen even further behind their peers. These students will remain locked into preoperations or concrete operations while their classmates move into formal operations. Students with cognitive disabilities also have low self-esteem and feel less in control of their own lives than intellectually normal adolescents (Wehmeyer & Palmer, 1997). Adolescents who are mentally challenged and have been integrated into schools with typical adolescents (i.e., *mainstreamed*) are more content with their social lives than mentally challenged adolescents in segregated schools (Heiman, 2000), but they are still less socially accepted than the average teenager (Freeman & Alkin, 2000). Individuals who are mentally challenged are sometimes shunned by former friends who, because of the insecurities of adolescence, have become concerned about how being friends with a mentally challenged individual would affect their own social standing.

Sexuality is another issue that confronts adolescents with cognitive disabilities to an even greater degree than average adolescents. Many adults view mentally challenged individuals as perpetually childlike and asexual. Because of this erroneous assumption, parents and teachers are unlikely to discuss puberty and sexuality with these adolescents. Unschooled as to the appropriate channels for their sexual feelings and having been taught to do what others tell them to do, mentally challenged adolescents are particularly vulnerable to sexual exploitation.

Although the issues confronting gifted teenagers are less severe than the issues confronting those with mental challenges, they stem from the same roots: stereotyping by others and the desire to conform and fit in. There is the widespread presumption that gifted adolescents are perfectionistic, nerdy, or teachers' pets. In fact, gifted adolescents are as well or better adjusted on the whole than intellectually average teens (Garland & Zigler, 1999; Nail & Evans, 1997) and no more perfectionistic (LoCicero & Ashby, 2000). Students who are gifted also find that other students try to take advantage of them by wanting to copy their schoolwork and that teachers ignore them in class (Moulton, Moulton, Housewright, et al., 1998). The desire to fit in makes some gifted teens— especially females—try to hide their talents and to drop out of activities in which they excel (Patrick, Ryan, Alfeld-Liro, et al., 1999).

All adolescents have a tremendous need to be liked and understood by their peers and the adults who are important to them. Being intellectually different can make this more difficult to accomplish. When conformity is king, being different in *any* way can be problematic.

than uncoached students (Powers & Rock, 1999). The SAT measures both aptitude and achievement. The fact is, any timed test measures mental quickness (aptitude), and a student must have learned specific mathematical principles in order to do well on the quantitative section and specific vocabulary words to do well on the verbal section (achievement). It seems obvious that reviewing mathematical formulas that one has forgotten or becoming familiar with the instructions on a timed test—whether one is formally coached or spends time on one's own—should be able to influence one's score. In addition, although aptitude itself may not be coachable, learning certain test-taking skills may help one do better on aptitude tests.

If coaching can raise a student's score, should the SAT be relied on as a basic measure of scholastic aptitude? Should admission to college depend partly on a skill gained by those who can afford a coaching course? In all fairness, the College Entrance Examination Board has long issued warnings against making admissions decisions on the basis of the SAT score alone. ETS itself has stated that an individual's score can vary plus or minus 30 to 35 points, a spread of 60 to 70 points. For these reasons, most schools rely equally or more on student essays, interviews, and other admission procedures (Laird, 2005). In addition, more and more colleges and universities are making the SAT optional rather than required; at this writing, more than 800 have made them optional (Fairtest.org, 2009).

SUMMARY

1. Piaget divided cognitive development into four major periods: the sensorimotor stage, the preoperational stage, the concrete operational stage, and the formal operational stage.

2. During the sensorimotor period, children learn about the effects that their actions have on their senses and perceptions; during the preoperational stage, language is acquired and children begin to use symbolic representation.

3. During the concrete operational stage, children show a greater capacity for logical reasoning but only when they are thinking about reality and experiences they have actually had. They come to understand hierarchical relationships, to be able to make transitive inferences, and to understand mental operations such as reversibility and identity.

4. Piaget attributed adolescent cognitive gains to their entrance into formal operations. He believed that teenagers, but not children, are able to use logic correctly and apply it to abstract concepts. They become capable of introspection (thinking about thought), abstract thinking (going beyond the real to what is possible), logical thinking (being able to consider all important facts and ideas and to form correct conclusions), and hypothetical reasoning (formulating hypotheses and examining the evidence for them).

5. At the same time that adolescents develop formal operational thought, their behavior often changes; for example, they often become idealistic, rebellious, and hypocritical. David Elkind and others linked cognitive maturation and personality change causally together, believing that the one induced the second.

6. Sometimes adolescents demonstrate pseudostupidity—the tendency to approach problems at too complex a level.

7. Elkind proposed that adolescents become egocentric and so develop an imaginary audience and a personal fable. This means that teens are very self-conscious and feel as if they are on stage much of the time, and they believe that they are unique and invulnerable.

8. Adolescents spend a lot of time in introspection, thinking about their own thoughts and feelings.

9. Not all adolescents attain formal operations, and the age at which they do varies. One's cultural, educational, and family backgrounds all contribute to whether one develops this mode of thinking.

10. Even those individuals who can sometimes solve formal operational problems do not do so consistently.

11. Many researchers believe that formal operations do not represent the most sophisticated form of thought. One conceptualization of more advanced thinking is called dialectics. Dialectical thinkers can handle conflicting information, lack of clarity, and complexity.

12. Although adolescent cognitive development is not precisely as Piaget described it, his basic findings are fundamentally correct—namely, that adolescents show qualitative cognitive change, that they think more abstractly than younger children, that they reason in a more deductive fashion, that they more exhaustively generate solutions to problems and more logically evaluate those solutions, and that they are more aware of their own thought processes.

13. Current views on adolescents' cognitive development differ from Piaget's views in four main ways: (a) they are more process oriented, (b) they see cognitive development as more continuous, (c) they see abilities as domain specific, and (d) they believe that increased executive control is largely responsible for the cognitive advances of adolescence.

14. Information processing is concerned with attending to and interpreting stimuli; memory; and the ability to make inferences, think, reason, and solve problems.
15. Both the ability to sustain attention and the ability to ignore distractions improve during adolescence.
16. Sensory storage improves only slightly during adolescence. Short-term memory does improve. The long-term memory of adolescents is better than that of children, in part because adolescents have learned to ignore irrelevant information. Young adults' memory, however, is better than that of adolescents.
17. Improvements in mental-processing speed likely account for adolescents' improved attention span and memory ability.
18. After information has been retrieved from memory, it is used to make inferences, to think, and to reason. Each of these thought processes improves during adolescence.
19. Decision makers must master five skills: identify alternate courses of action, identify appropriate criteria for considering alternatives, assess alternatives, summarize information about the alternatives, and self-evaluate the outcome of the decision-making process.
20. Adolescents perceive risk differently than adults. Although (contrary to Elkind) they do not view themselves as being at less risk than adults do, they are more likely than adults to engage in risky behavior.
21. Adolescents become increasingly able to reason about the nature of truth and knowledge. They pass through four levels of development—naive realism, defensive realism, dogmatism or skepticism, and post-skeptical rationalism—as they come to better understand the constructed nature of knowledge.
22. Three of the four cerebral lobes mature during adolescence: the parietal, the temporal, and the frontal lobes. The corpus callosum, which connects the cerebrum's two hemispheres, also grows at this stage. These changes in the brain may account for the development of spatial reasoning, language abilities, and impulse control in adolescence and adulthood.
23. During adolescence, more neurons in the brain become myelinated. This results in faster and more selective neural transmission.
24. The hippocampus—the part of the brain involved in setting down new memories—continues to develop throughout adolescence. The amygdala—a part of the brain that reacts emotionally to stimuli—matures earlier in adolescence than the frontal lobe, which moderates emotional response.
25. There is no single agreed upon definition of *intelligence*.
26. Sternberg groups intelligence into three categories: analytic intelligence, creative intelligence, and practical intelligence.
27. Gardner identifies eight types of intelligence: linguistic, logical-mathematical, spatial, musical, body-kinesthetic, interpersonal, intrapersonal, and naturalistic.
28. IQ tests measure subsets of the intellectual abilities that comprise intelligence. The two most commonly used individual IQ tests are the Stanford-Binet and the Wechsler Scales.
29. Although often stabilized by adolescence, IQ scores should be considered only as a result on a test taken at a particular time.
30. Anxiety, the degree of motivation, and sociocultural factors, among others, may influence test results.
31. Achievement tests differ from aptitude tests in that they measure actual mastery of specific skills and knowledge rather than learning potential.
32. The SAT is the most widely used college admission test; it provides a common yardstick for evaluating students from across the United States. However, questions about fairness and the fact that students' scores can be improved by taking test preparation courses have led to criticism as to the SAT's fairness.

KEY TERMS

achievement tests 139
affirmation 133
amygdala 138
animism 119
centering 119
cerebrum 137
class inclusion relationships 119
concrete operational stage 119
confirmation strategy 133
conservation problems 121
corpus callosum 137
deductive reasoning 119
defensive realists 136
dialectics 127
dogmatism 136
dual process theory 135
egocentrism 125
elimination strategy 133
epistemology 136
executive control 134
formal operational stage 121
frontal lobe 138
heuristics 135
hierarchical classification 119
hippocampus 138
hypocrisy 124
hypothetico-deductive reasoning 122
idealistic 124
imaginary audience 125
inductive reasoning 119
inference 132
information-processing approach 129
intelligence quotient (IQ) 139
introspection 126
long-term storage 131
mental operations 118
metacognition 134

THOUGHT QUESTIONS

Personal Reflection

1. Think of personal examples in which you, a sibling, or a friend demonstrated three or more of the following: the imaginary audience, the personal fable, adolescent hypocrisy, idealism, and pseudostupidity.

2. Do you believe that the imaginary audience inhibited your own personal creativity when you were younger? Does it still do so?

3. Are you satisfied with your level of cognitive sophistication? In what ways would you like to become smarter or wiser? Do these match the ways of thinking associated with dialectics?

4. Are you a risk taker? Why or why not?

5. Do you use the confirmation strategy or the elimination strategy when solving a problem? If you go back and forth, when do you use each?

6. When was the last time you can remember using deduction to solve a problem? Induction? Provide examples.

7. When you are faced with problems, which techniques do you find most helpful in making decisions or arriving at solutions?

8. Are you an epistemological realist or rationalist? Explain how so.

Group Discussion

9. Come up with several real-life, practical examples of how the cognitive limitations of the preoperational stage would affect a 5-year-old's behaviors and decisions.

10. Describe how a preschooler, a grade-schooler, and a middle schooler would each go about playing Twenty Questions. How would their choice of questions differ from one another?

11. Another test that Piaget used to assess whether adolescents were capable of formal operational thinking that is not described in the text is the *chemistry experiment*. It involves showing a child five test tubes, each filled with a colorless liquid. Behind a screen, the tester pours some of the tubes' contents together. She then holds up a beaker filled with a yellow liquid. The child is asked to make a yellow liquid himself or herself. What would be the differences between how a concrete operational child and a formal operational child would approach this task?

12. What if any are the drawbacks of being in the dialectical-reasoning stage?

13. How could middle and high schools apply Piaget's ideas in the classroom?

14. Were you and your friends more impulsive when you were younger? If so, why do you think your rash tendencies have diminished?

15. How would you describe an intelligent person? What factors distinguish a person who is intelligent from one who is not?

16. Imagine going through a school day as an adolescent who is cognitively impaired. How would other students treat you? How would teachers treat you? What would you find particularly difficult? Which part of your day would you enjoy most?

Debate Questions

17. Many adolescents are functioning at a cognitive level that renders them unable to practice most forms of birth control effectively.

18. Idealism is, in balance, more good than bad.

19. Componential intelligence is more important than experiential or contextual intelligence.

20. Some of Gardner's types of intelligence are more important than others.

21. All students should be given intelligence tests and then they and their parents should be told their test scores.

22. The SAT or ACT should be required for admission to all colleges.

SUGGESTED READING

Elkind, D. (1981). *Children and Adolescents: Interpretive Essays on Jean Piaget,* 3rd ed. New York: Oxford University Press.

Gardner, H. (2006). *Multiple Intelligences: New Horizons in Theory and Practice.* New York: Basic Books.

Jacobs, J. E., and Klaczynski, P. A. (Eds.). (2005). *The Development of Judgment and Decision Making in Children and Adolescents.* Mahwah, NJ: Erlbaum.

Pass, S. (2004). *Parallel Paths to Constructivism: Jean Piaget and Lev Vygotsky.* Greenwich, CT: Information Age Publishing.

Serulinkov, A. (2000). *Piaget for Beginners.* New York: Writers & Readers;

Sternberg, R. J. (2007). *Wisdom, Intelligence, and Creativity Synthesized.* Cambridge, England: Cambridge University Press.

USEFUL WEB SITES

Human Intelligence
http://www.indiana.edu/~intell/

This site is produced by Indiana University, and contains information on standardized testing, giftedness, significant researchers in the field, controversies, and a historical timeline.

Jean Piaget Society
www.piaget.org

The Jean Piaget Society is a scholarly organization devoted to furthering the work begun by Piaget. It contains a short *biography of Piaget, extensive reference lists for students and professionals, and links to many other valuable pages about cognitive development.*

Psi Café: Jean Piaget
www.psy.pdx.edu/PsiCafe/KeyTheorists/Piaget.htm

Includes links to biographies of Piaget, descriptions of his work, critiques of his theory, reprints of some of his most important works, and other Piaget cites.

WOULDN'T YOU LIKE TO KNOW . . .

- Why is a good self-concept important?
- Do adolescents become delinquent because they have low self-esteem?
- What kinds of parents raise children with high levels of self-esteem?
- Do adolescent girls and boys have different levels of self-esteem?
- What identity status is most common among college students?
- How does the development of an ethnic identity affect self-esteem?
- What is the difference between *sex* and *gender*?
- Why is it good to have a blend of masculine and feminine traits?

chapter **6**

Self-Concept, Identity, Ethnicity, and Gender

Since Erik Erikson first proposed that finding an identity was *the* major life task of adolescence, researchers have been examining the ways in which teenagers go about this process of self-discovery. Even before they have developed identities, however, adolescents bring from childhood certain views of themselves. How someone would describe himself or herself is a good indication of this self-view.

The **self** is that part of an individual's personality of which he or she is aware. **Self-concept** is a conscious, cognitive perception and assessment by an individual of himself or herself; it is one's thoughts and opinions about oneself. Self-concept is more limited in scope than *identity*, which is more complete, more coherent, and more forward projecting, as it includes long-term goals. Self-concept, and later identity, form the basis for **self-esteem**, a related term that refers to how one feels about oneself; it is more evaluative in nature. My self-concept informs me that I am reasonably athletic; my self-esteem rises as a result. People with high self-esteem like themselves; people with low self-esteem do not.

This chapter begins by reviewing the research on changes in self-concept and self-esteem that occur during adolescence. A detailed discussion of the identity search then follows. Since in modern American society ethnicity and gender play such a significant role in an individual's self-concept, this chapter concludes with sections examining ethnic and gender differences in self-perception and identity.

Self-Concept and Self-Esteem

The first step in the development of a self-concept occurs when a person recognizes that he or she is a distinct, separate individual. This awareness begins in early childhood. Self-concept also implies a developing awareness on a person's part of who and what he or she is. It describes what individuals see when they look at themselves, in terms of their self-perceived physical characteristics, personality skills, traits, roles, and social status. It might be described as the system of attitudes they have about themselves. It is the sum total of their self-definitions or self-images (Harter, 1990).

Self-concept is often described as a *global entity:* how someone feels about himself or herself in general (DuBois, Felner, Brand, et al., 1996). But it has also been described as being made up of *multiple self-conceptions*, with concepts developed in relation to different roles (Griffin, Chassin, & Young, 1981). Thus, a person may rate himself or herself as a son or daughter, student, artist, friend, and so forth. Self-concept is similarly composed of beliefs about different aspects of the self, such as social skills, intelligence, and morality. These conceptions of different aspects of the self

may differ, which helps explain how behavior varies in different circumstances.

Adolescents gather evidence that helps them evaluate themselves: Am I competent? Am I attractive to others? Am I a good person? From this evidence, they form hypotheses about themselves and check out their feelings and opinions through further experiences and relationships. They compare themselves with their own ideals and use the reactions of others as a mirror for self-reflection.

Whether individuals' self-concept is accurate is significant. As Figure 6.1 illustrates, all people have six different selves: the person they are, the person they think they are, the person others think they are, the person they think others think they are, the person they think they will become, and the person they think others want them to become. Self-concepts may or may not be close approximations of reality, and self-concepts are always in the process of change, particularly during childhood and adolescence. Allport (1950) emphasized that personality is less a finished product than a transitive process. It has some stable features, but at the same time, it undergoes change. Allport coined the word **proprium,** which he defined as "all aspects of personality that make for inward unity." This is the self that is at the core of personal identity.

In the late 1950s, Strang (1957) outlined four basic dimensions of the self that are still used today. First, there is the *overall, basic self-concept,* which is the adolescent's view of his or her personality and "perceptions of his abilities and his status and roles in the outer world" (p. 68).

Next are the individual's *transitory self-concepts.* These ideas of self are influenced by the mood of the moment or by a recent or continuing experience. A recent low grade on an examination may leave a person

FIGURE 6.1 SIX DIFFERENT SELVES

Who others think I am

Who I think others think I am

Who I think I am

Who I think I will become

Who I really am

Who I think others want me to become

with a temporary feeling of being stupid; a critical remark from parents may produce a temporary self-evaluation of laziness.

Third, there are the adolescent's *social selves*—the selves he or she thinks others see, which, in turn, influence how the individual sees himself or herself. If youths have the impression that others think they are boring or socially unacceptable, they tend to think of themselves in these negative ways. Their perceptions of others' feelings color their views of themselves (Harter, Stocker, & Robinson, 1996). Self-concept comes partly from an involvement of the self with others. It evolves through social interactions, encompassing both continuity of self and identification with something beyond the self.

Part of self-concept is one's sense of social status, the positions in which individuals place themselves in the social system in the present or the future. For example, adolescents from low-socioeconomic-status backgrounds who see themselves as not belonging there but as members of a higher socioeconomic class are molding new identities because of their higher aspirations.

The fourth dimension is the **ideal self,** which is the kind of person an adolescent would like to be. His or her aspirations may be realistic, too low, or too high. An ideal self that is too low impedes accomplishment; one that is too high may lead to frustration and self-depreciation. Having a realistic concept of one's ideal self leads to self-acceptance, mental health, and the attainment of realistic goals.

Importance of a Good Self-Concept

Why is having a good self-concept important? It motivates and directs one's behavior. If you believe that you are athletic and coordinated, you are more likely to try to learn to ski than if you view yourself as clumsy and graceless. Likewise, if you view yourself as intelligent and hard working, you are more likely to sign up for hard courses than if you think you are limited in these areas.

In their discussion of the link between motivation and self-concept, Oyserman and Markus (1990a, 1990b) focus on an adolescent's **possible selves.** These are the people he or she might be someday; they refer to the future, not to the present. Each of us has **hoped-for selves,** or the people we wish to become; **expected selves,** the people we think we will likely become; and **feared selves,** the people we dread becoming. For example, you may hope to become a world-famous violinist, expect to become a high school music teacher, and fear becoming an unemployed street musician.

self   a person's personality or nature of which that person is aware.

self-concept   a person's conscious, cognitive perception and evaluation of himself or herself; one's thoughts and opinions about oneself.

self-esteem   a person's impression or opinion of himself or herself.

proprium   the self-identity that is developing in time.

ideal self   the kind of person an individual would like to be.

possible selves   the different selves we envision ourselves becoming.

hoped-for selves   the people we hope to be in the future.

expected selves   the people we think we will likely be in the future.

feared selves   the people we are afraid of becoming in the future.

RESEARCH HIGHLIGHT   DOES THIS GENERATION HAVE HIGHER SELF-ESTEEM?

The present generation of youth is often portrayed as content and self-satisfied. A recent study suggests that this is an accurate depiction. Twenge and Campbell (2008) analyzed data from the 2006 Monitoring the Future survey, a questionnaire given to about 15,000 high school students from across the United States each year. They pulled out a subset of items that related to self-esteem and confirmed that current U.S. high schoolers feel better about themselves and their futures than did high schoolers in 1975. In particular, today's students like themselves more and are considerably more likely to believe that they will make good spouses, parents, and employees than did those in 1975. They do not, however, believe that they are generally more competent, although they do believe they are a little more intelligent.

Why all this optimism? Perhaps, the authors suggest, it is because they are getting better grades than students in the past. Twice as many students who were in high school in 2006 reported having an A average than those in 1975, and nearly twice as many reported having an A- average. As Baumeister, Campbell, Kreuger, et al. (2003) noted, a combination of grade inflation and an increasing emphasis upon enhancing self-esteem by schools could act together to produce individuals who would like themselves. Given that individuals with high self-esteem tend to be optimistic, this could explain this cohort's rosy predictions about their future personal successes.

PERSONAL ISSUES   PERFECTIONISM

Generally, the wish to excel is an admirable attribute. Well-adjusted perfectionists derive real pleasure from their accomplishments, but they feel free to be less precise if a situation permits. *Maladaptive perfectionists* pursue excellence to an unhealthy extreme. They hold the irrational belief that they must be perfect to be accepted. Their standards are beyond reason—they strain toward impossible goals that are never reached. Plagued by self-criticism, their self-worth is constantly lowered with every perceived failure. Because in their own eyes they never measure up, they become defensive and angry when faced with possible criticism, a behavior that frustrates and alienates others and causes the very disapproval that they fear. They are plagued by anxiety and emotional turmoil and experience more pain than rewards. Even academic success, which many attain, does nothing to promote self-confidence (Flett & Hewitt, 2002). Perfectionism is closely associated with the development of eating disorders (Pearson & Gleaves, 2006). Developing a healthy identity, then, involves wanting to be a good person while at the same time not demanding flawlessness from oneself.

ANSWERS WOULDN'T YOU LIKE TO KNOW …
Why is a good self-concept important?

A positive self-concept not only makes it easier for a person to be friendly and outgoing, but it also gives him or her the confidence to try new activities and take on challenges. Having a positive self-concept leads to having high self-esteem, as well.

Oyserman and Markus assert that adolescents who lack positive expected selves drift into unproductive, antisocial behavior. It seems that if one has no hope for happy outcomes, then one will engage in self-destructive activities. If the most optimistic future you envision for yourself is none too good, why bother trying? Conversely, if you believe that you can attain your dreams, then you will be willing to work hard at improving your chances. In addition, having a balancing set of feared selves can also prompt responsible behavior. Being aware that bad outcomes can occur is energizing, and acknowledging negative consequences can help one avoid antisocial actions. For instance, you may wish to get rich (a hoped-for self) but robbing a bank may land you in jail and make you a convict (feared self). Researchers have shown that an adolescent's possible selves influence his or her delinquency, tobacco use, and alcohol consumption (Aloise-Young, Hennigan, & Leong, 2001).

Self-Esteem

Having built concepts of themselves, adolescents then must deal with the esteem with which they view themselves. When they examine themselves, what value do they place on the selves they perceive? Does this appraisal lead to self-acceptance and approval, to a feeling of self-worth? If so, then they have enough self-esteem to accept and live with themselves. For people to have high self-esteem, there must be a correspondence between their self-concepts and their self-ideals.

With the onset of puberty, most young people begin to make a thorough assessment of themselves, comparing not only their body parts but also their motor skills, intellectual abilities, and social skills with those of their peers and their ideals or heroes. This critical self-appraisal is accompanied by self-conscious behavior that makes adolescents vulnerable to embarrassment. It can lead to having an imaginary audience. As a consequence, teenagers are preoccupied with attempting to reconcile their selves as they perceive them with their ideal selves. By late adolescence, most have managed to sort themselves out—to determine what they can most effectively be and to integrate their goals into their ideal selves.

Carl Rogers (1961) was one of the most important theorists in the development of a theoretical and practical structure of self-ideals. He pictured the end point of personality development as a basic congruence between objective reality and one's self-perception. This result allows freedom from internal conflict and anxiety; when individuals discover who they are and what they perceive themselves to be and want to begin to merge those two concepts, they are then able to accept themselves, without conflict. Their self-perceptions and relationships with others elicit self-acceptance and self-esteem. Psychological maladjustment occurs when there is a divergence between the selves they are being in relationship to others and the selves they perceive they are or want to be.

Self-esteem is so important that a number of life outcomes are correlated with it. Several of these are discussed next.

Mental Health

A positive self-perception, or high self-esteem, is a desired outcome of the human developmental process. It has been linked to long-term mental health and emotional well-being, and individuals whose self-esteem has never sufficiently developed manifest a number of symptoms of emotional ill health. There is a well-established link between low self-esteem and depression in adolescence (Martyn-Nemeth, Penckofer, Gulanick, et al., 2009) and a separate, equally strong link between low self-esteem and suicidal behavior (Chatard, Selimbegović, & Koman, 2009). Individuals with low self-esteem may evidence psychosomatic symptoms and anxiety (Byrne, 2000). It has also been found to be a factor in both drug abuse (Donnelly, Young, Pearson, et al., 2008) and in unwed pregnancy (Parker & Benson, 2005). In fact, unwed pregnancy is often an effort on the part of young women to enhance their self-esteem. Low self-esteem is also associated with the eating disorders anorexia nervosa and bulimia (Sassaroli & Ruggiero, 2005). These associations have been found in many nations, not just in the United States.

Sometimes, an adolescent with low self-esteem tries to develop a false front or facade with which to face the world. This is a compensating mechanism used to overcome feelings of worthlessness by convincing others that one is worthy. The teen tries to put on an act to impress people. Putting on an act, however, is a strain. To act confident, friendly, and cheerful when one feels the opposite is a constant struggle. The anxiety around making a false step and letting one's guard slip creates considerable tension.

Another reason for anxiety is that people with low self-esteem show a shifting and unstable identity. Adolescents with low self-esteem are self-conscious and overly vulnerable to criticism or rejection, which testifies to their sense of inadequacy (Rosenthal & Simeonsson, 1989). They may be deeply disturbed when laughed at, when blamed, or when others have a poor opinion of them. The more vulnerable they feel themselves to be, the higher are their anxiety levels. Such adolescents report, "Criticism hurts me terribly" or "I can't stand to have anyone laugh at me or blame me when something goes wrong." As a result, they feel awkward and uneasy in social situations and avoid embarrassment whenever they can.

Interpersonal Competence and Popularity

Those with poor self-concepts are often rejected by other people. Acceptance of self is positively and significantly correlated with acceptance by others (de Bruyn & van den Boom, 2005). Thus, there is a close relationship between self-acceptance and popularity.

Poor social adjustment, which is related to low self-concept and self-esteem, manifests itself in a number of ways. Adolescents with low self-esteem are often socially invisible. They are not noticed or selected as leaders, and they do not participate often in class, clubs, or social activities. They do not stand up for their own rights or express their opinions on matters that concern them. These adolescents more often develop feelings of isolation and loneliness. A vicious cycle can develop when these feelings reinforce negative self-concepts and low self-esteem.

The other problem faced by low-self-esteem adolescents is that they experience a good deal of **role strain** (Fenzel, 2000). Role strain is the stress experienced by people when they are tugged in different directions by competing demands. For example, role strain occurs when a teen gains status with his peers by excelling in sports, but his parents pressure him to devote himself solely to getting good grades. Most young adolescents experience stress when they make the transition to middle school, with its new expectations; enlarged peer group; and larger, more impersonal size. But whereas more popular teens can lean on friends for social support, less popular adolescents—those with low self-esteem—find themselves being picked on, teased, and bullied by their peers (Jankauskiene, Kardelis, Sukys, et al., 2008). Thus, teenagers with low self-esteem experience the double strain of transition stress and peer neglect or hostility.

Delinquency

For many years, psychologists and sociologists believed there was a close relationship between low self-esteem and delinquency. Namely, it was thought that being delinquent was an attempt to compensate for having negative feelings about oneself. This idea was first proposed by Kaplan (1980) as the **self-enhancement thesis.** He argued that individuals who were unsuccessful at following the so-called straight-and-narrow path would not receive positive reinforcement for their behavior and would therefore have lowered self-esteem. Thus, teens who got bad grades, didn't get along with better adjusted peers, and couldn't seem to do anything right would feel bad about themselves and suffer from low self-esteem. In order to feel better about themselves, they would associate with deviant teens who would reinforce and praise them for these same delinquent behaviors. Association with deviant peers would encourage their behavior to become even more deviant and, with further reinforcement, their self-esteem would rebound. In sum, Kaplan suggested that adolescents with low self-esteem would become delinquents and that after they had done so, their self-esteem would rise.

Research conducted in the 1990s, however, failed to find this link. In fact, findings varied dramatically. Delinquents' self-esteem was found to increase, decrease, and not change; it was found to be low and

---

self-enhancement thesis an explanation for delinquency based on the need for troubled youths to enhance their self-esteem.

role strain the stress individuals experience when they are faced with competing demands and expectations.

high and unremarkable. Most often, though, self-esteem was found to be weakly negatively correlated with delinquency (Baumeister, Campbell, Krueger, et al., 2003); that is, most studies found that delinquents' self-esteem was on the low side.

However, results from more recent studies may finally provide an explanation for the contradictory findings. Donnellan and his colleagues (2005) conducted research in which they separated out the effects of self-esteem and **narcissism** (a personality trait that denotes an overly vain and self-absorbed person). They found a strong relationship between *low* self-esteem and delinquent behavior and aggression. High self-esteem did not predict delinquency: narcissism did. Similar results were found by Barry and his colleagues (2007). Since previous research did not distinguish between normal, healthy high self-esteem and pathological narcissism, in a number of studies it appeared that high self-esteem was related to aggression when in fact it was not.

Development of a Positive Self-Concept

How can a positive self-concept be developed? Let's look at several factors that contribute to its achievement.

Significant Others

The idea that self-concept is determined in part by others' views of us, or the way we think others view us, is generally accepted. However, not all people exert an equally strong influence. *Significant others* are those individuals who occupy a high level of importance; they are influential and their opinions are meaningful. Their influence depends on their degree of involvement and intimacy and the social support they provide and the power and authority given to them by others.

Parents A variety of researchers have found that the quality of family relations during adolescence is associated with their levels of self-esteem, not only in the United States, but in many other nations as well (e.g., Farruggia, Chen, Greenberger, et al., 2004). Adolescents with higher self-esteem report greater intimacy with their mothers and fathers; in other words, they feel close to and get along with their parents (Field, Lang, Yando, et al., 1995). Adolescent self-esteem has

been associated with parental willingness to grant autonomy (Linver & Silverberg, 1995); acceptance and warmth (Dusek & McIntyre, 2003); authoritative parenting style (Dekovic & Meeus, 1997); communication (Caughlin & Malis, 2004); and parental support, participation, and control (Robinson, 1995).

The quality of *mother*-adolescent relationships is clearly an important factor in adolescent self-esteem (Turnage, 2004). For example, older adolescent girls who feel close to their mothers see themselves as confident, wise, reasonable, and self-controlled. Those who feel distant from their mothers perceive themselves in negative terms: rebellious, impulsive, touchy, and tactless. These findings indicate that the degree of maternal identification influences self-concept.

Fathers are important, too, in an adolescent's development. Although in the past it had been assumed that children's relationships with their mothers were more important to their psychological adjustment than their relationships with their fathers, more recent research finds that this is not the case (Rohner & Veneziano, 2001). Studies generally show that both relationships serve the same functions or that father-child relationships serve different but equally vital roles in adolescent development (e.g., Arbona & Power, 2003)

When children perceive conflict between parents or between themselves and their parents, lower self-esteem can be expected. Amato (1986) found lower self-esteem among adolescents from conflicted families and from those in which the parent-adolescent relationship was poor. One study found that adolescents who had experienced parental divorce were significantly more likely to have encountered lowered parental expectations, lessened parental trust, fewer family discussions, and greater financial hardship. In turn, lower self-concepts and/or level of social skills were found to be associated with these kinds of life experiences (Sun & Li, 2002). However, loss of self-esteem when parents divorce is usually temporary. Goodman and Pickens (2001), for example, found no significant association between an *adult's* self-esteem and having experienced parental divorce or death as a child.

Socioeconomic Status

Socioeconomic status has a small but significant effect on self-esteem (Twenge & Campbell, 2002). Generally, low-SES students have lower self-esteem than high-SES

A positive relationship with his father will help the adolescent boy develop high self-esteem and a stable self-image. This is also true of the adolescent girl's relationship with her father.

students, and the effects of SES appear to be stronger with increasing age.

The effects of socioeconomic status appear to be more indirect than direct (Dusek & McIntyre, 2003). It is not so much that teenagers view themselves harshly *because* they are poor but rather that they are doing poorly because of their economic situation. Also, economic hardship can reduce positive affective parental support and may thus convey a negative appraisal of the adolescent, thereby lowering his or her self-esteem (Ho, Lempers, & Clark-Lempers, 1995). In addition, teenagers from low-income families are unlikely to be able to afford the latest fashions, nor are they as able as more wealthy peers to join the kinds of clubs and organizations that can lead to increased popularity. They have a legitimate reason to worry about how they are being judged by their classmates, and this, of course, can decrease self-esteem.

Race/Ethnicity

In the 1950s, eminent psychologist Kenneth Clark (1953) reported the results of groundbreaking research that indicated that African American children had lower levels of self-esteem than Caucasian children. He presented young Black children with both Black and White dolls and asked them to indicate which of the dolls were nice, which were pretty, which they would like to play with, and so on. The Black children preferred the White dolls, indicating that they felt bad about themselves and about Black individuals in general. Clark's research was instrumental in convincing the members of the U.S. Supreme Court to declare segregation unconstitutional in their seminal 1954 decision *Brown v. Board of Education*.

Does race still factor into self-esteem today? Research findings suggest that with the increase of racial pride brought about by the civil rights movement, self-esteem among African Americans has risen. In fact, most research now shows that African American adolescents have higher self-esteem than adolescents from any other group, including Caucasians (Twenge & Crocker, 2002). (This is generally not found to be true for adolescents from other racial minorities.)

Overall, there is some evidence that African American youths have higher self-esteem primarily when they are not exposed to White prejudices. When surrounded chiefly by those with similar physical appearance, social-class standing, family background, and school performance, African Americans rate themselves much higher in self-esteem than when they are surrounded by Whites (Ward, 2000). African American students in schools with largely or entirely African student bodies have higher self-esteem than those in more integrated schools. The desegregated school has many advantages, but enhancing self-esteem is not one of them.

The self-esteem of African American adolescents is enhanced if they have a positive ethnic identity. (This is discussed more fully later in this chapter.) Adolescents who have a healthy dose of racial pride are apt to have higher self-esteem (Harris-Britt, Valrie, Kurtz-Costes, et al., 2007).

What about adolescents of other races/ethnicities? Asian American youth are often found to have the lowest self-esteem levels (Way & Chen, 2000). This may be due to the fact that they experience more verbal and

narcissism   the trait of being excessively vain and self-absorbed.

physical harassment from peers than other adolescents (Rosenbloom & Way, 2004). Latino adolescents' self-esteem is midway between these two groups (Greene & Way, 2005). It may also be true that adolescents from different ethnic backgrounds may base their overall self-esteem on different factors. One study (Erkut, Marx, Fields, et al., 1999) found that African American girls based their self-worth predominately on their scholastic abilities, that Chinese American girls based their self-worth primarily on their close friendships, and that Caucasian and Puerto Rican American girls derived their self-worth mainly from their appearance.

Gender

Most research on the effects of gender on self-esteem finds that in adolescence, girls' global self-esteem is somewhat lower than boys'. This was most recently confirmed in a meta-analysis of more than 100 studies on this topic conducted by Gentile and her colleagues (2009). Rather than look at overall self-esteem, they looked at domain specific aspects of self-esteem. They found that males had moderately higher levels of personal self-esteem and self-satisfaction than females—measurements similar to global self-esteem—and that males also felt better about their physical appearance and athletic abilities. Conversely, female adolescents had moderately higher behavioral conduct and moral-ethical self-esteem scores. There were no gender differences in academic, family, social acceptance, or emotional self-esteem ratings. This pattern of lower self-esteem in girls is not limited to the United States but has been replicated in other countries. For example, Bolognini, Plancherel, Bellschart, et al. (1996) found that Swiss adolescent girls had lower self-esteem than Swiss adolescent boys.

Girls' self-esteem, therefore, appears to be based on different attributes than boys'. Girls' self-esteem is tied much more strongly to their perceived physical attractiveness (Furnham, Badmin, & Sneade, 2002) and to their feelings of interconnectedness—their social networks (Thomas & Daubman, 2001). Boys' self-esteem is most strongly related to their feelings of achievement and their athletic abilities (Wigfield, Eccles, MacIver, et al., 1991).

ANSWERS WOULDN'T YOU LIKE TO KNOW …

Do adolescent girls and boys have different levels of self-esteem?

Although there are few gender differences in self-esteem during childhood, in adolescence, boys often have higher overall self-esteem than girls. This is probably because adolescent girls are more preoccupied and less satisfied with their appearance than boys are at this age.

Why do adolescent girls have lower self-esteem than adolescent boys? Some researchers point to the fact that traits viewed as masculine are seen by American society as more desirable than those seen as feminine (Markus & Kitayama, 1994). Other researchers point to the negative effects of the media on girls' body image (van den Berg, Paxton, Keery, et al., 2007), and still others suggest that it is harder to maintain high self-esteem when it is largely based on others' impressions of you (Gentile, Grade, Dolan-Pascoe, et al., 2009). In any case, these differences are important since self-esteem helps determine one's moods, goals, and life plans.

Disabilities

As might be expected, individuals with physical disabilities have negative body images and hence have more difficulty developing positive self-concepts and self-esteem than do those who are not disabled (Nosek, Hughes, Swedlund, et al., 2003). The same is true of adolescents with cognitive limitations such as learning disabilities (Conley, Ghavami, VonOlen, et al., 2007). It is difficult to feel good about yourself if you have a trait that not only makes you different from your peers, but also makes it more difficult to do all the things that they can do.

Stress

Stress and self-esteem are negatively correlated in teens: as stress goes up, self-esteem goes down (Gerber & Puhse, 2008). Stress can have many causes, such as the death of a loved one, failing an exam, changing schools or residence, illness, relationship problems, or family changes such as gaining a new family member or divorce. Adolescence is often a time of great stress, and so it is not surprising that many adolescents are plagued with low self-esteem. This low self-esteem may, in turn, contribute to adjustment problems (Tevendale, DuBois, Lopez, et al., 1997).

Changes in Self-Concept During Adolescence

To what extent does self-concept change during adolescence? Generally, the overall level of one's self-concept gradually stabilizes (Cole, Maxwell, Martin, et al., 2001) and at the same time it becomes more differentiated so that older adolescents tend to evaluate themselves "piece by piece" rather than globally (Shapka & Keating, 2005). As noted earlier, though, adolescents are extremely sensitive to important events and changes in their lives and so self-esteem is generally lower in early adolescence than in childhood; this appears to be true across lines of race/ethnicity, gender, and socioeconomic status. Numerous changes account for this drop. With cognitive development comes the ability to see oneself

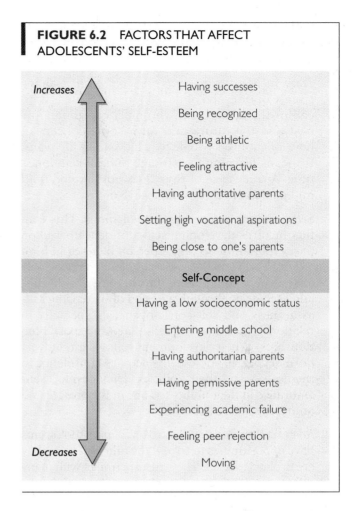

FIGURE 6.2   FACTORS THAT AFFECT ADOLESCENTS' SELF-ESTEEM

more realistically, rather than in the inflated way that is typical of younger children (e.g., Young & Mroczek, 2003); therefore, in adolescence, one may all of a sudden feel that one isn't as great as one had thought. In addition, once puberty has occurred, adolescents become very interested in finding girlfriends or boyfriends, and so they become concerned about and dissatisfied with their own appearance. This is more true of girls than of boys, contributing to the greater decline in girls' self-esteem at this time (Cole, Maxwell, Martin, et al., 2001).

Most important, perhaps, is the fact that students leave elementary school for middle school at this time. The move from a protected elementary school, where a child had few teachers and one set of classmates, to a much larger, more impersonal middle school, where teachers, classmates, and even classrooms are constantly shifting, can be disturbing to youths' self-image. Research has shown that school level is a more critical factor than age. In one study, sixth-graders in elementary schools felt better about themselves than sixth-graders who attended middle schools (Wigfield & Eccles, 1994). Many studies have reinforced the finding that the transition from elementary to middle school can be a stressful event in the lives of early adolescents (e.g., Fenzel, 2000).

In summary, the concept of the self is not completely solidified by adolescence, although recognizable trends and traits persist. With increasing age, these recognizable traits become more stable. However, self-concept is subject to change under the influence of powerful forces, both positive and negative (see Figure 6.2). Assisting the adolescent who has a negative identity to find a mature and positive image of self is a major undertaking, but it can be done. It is certain that the change is easier during adolescence than in adulthood.

Identity

No doubt, one of the most important tasks an adolescent faces is to form an identity. As you may recall from Chapter 2, the concept of identity was first proposed by Erik Erikson (see pp. 36–38). Identity is, in a sense, one's life story (McAdams, 2001). Society expects young people to decide on a college and/or a job, to become romantically involved, and to make choices regarding political philosophies and religious practices. Erikson described the task of identity formation as one of making choices by exploring alternatives and committing to roles (Adams, Gulotta, & Montemayor, 1992). Then, as one moves through adolescence, if these values, beliefs, goals, and practices are no longer appropriate, one can engage in a task of identity redefinition and refinement. Identity is clearly not stable but is instead an ongoing process of self-reflection and change as one moves through life.

Seven Conflicts

You must make scores of decisions before you develop a fully formed identity: Where should you live? Do you want to have children? How important is religion in your life? Even so, Erikson (1968) believed that seven issues were of primary importance, some of which may seem more obvious than others:

1. *Temporal perspective versus time confusion:* Gaining a sense of time and of the continuity of life is critical for the adolescent, who must coordinate the past and the future and form some concept of how long it takes people to achieve their life plans. It means learning to estimate and allocate one's time. A true sense of time does not develop until mid-adolescence—around age 15 or 16.

2. *Self-certainty versus self-consciousness:* This conflict involves developing self-confidence based on past experiences so that a person believes in himself or herself and believes that there is a reasonable chance of accomplishing future aims. To do this, adolescents go through a period of increasing self-awareness and self-consciousness, especially in relation to their physical self-image and social relationships. When development follows a relatively normal course, adolescents acquire confidence in themselves and their abilities. They develop self-assurance in their ability to cope in the present and anticipate future success.

3. *Role experimentation versus role fixation:* Adolescents have opportunities to try out the different roles they are to play in society. They can experiment with many different identities, personality characteristics, ways of talking and acting, ideas, goals, and types of relationships. Identity comes through opportunities for such experimentation. Those who have developed too much inner restraint and guilt, who have lost initiative, or who have prematurely experienced role fixation never really find out who they are.

4. *Apprenticeship versus work paralysis:* Similarly, teenagers have the opportunity to explore and try out different occupations before deciding on a vocation. The choice of career plays a large part in determining a person's identity. A negative self-image and its accompanying feelings of inferiority can prevent a person from mustering the necessary energy to succeed at school or on the job.

5. *Sexual polarization versus bisexual confusion:* Adolescents continue to attempt to define what it means to be male or female, a process begun in childhood. Erikson believed it is important that adolescents develop a clear identification with one sex or the other as a basis for future heterosexual intimacy and as a basis for a firm identity. Furthermore, he emphasized that for communities to function properly, men and women must be willing to assume their so-called proper roles; he viewed sexual polarization as necessary. Much

present-day analysis (and much criticism!) of Erikson relates to his emphasis on the need for sexual polarization.

6. *Leadership and followership versus authority confusion:* As adolescents expand their social horizons through school, social groups, and new friends, they begin to learn to take leadership responsibilities as well as how to follow others. At the same time, they discover there are competing claims on their allegiances. The state, employer, parents, and friends all make demands, with the result that adolescents experience confusion in relation to authority. To whom should they listen? Whom should they follow? To whom should they give their loyalty? Sorting out the answers requires an examination of personal values and priorities.

7. *Ideological commitment versus confusion of values:* One's ideology guides, or should guide, many aspects of one's behavior. Erikson referred to this struggle as the "search for fidelity." He emphasized that individuals need something to believe in or to follow.

Identity Status

When Erikson described the concept of identity, he furthered our understanding of adolescent development and inspired an incredible amount of research on the development of the sense of self that emerges during adolescence. Of all that research, the most influential was conducted by James Marcia (1966, 1976, 1991, 1994). According to Marcia, there are dual criteria that must be met before one can attain a mature identity: one must undergo *crises* and make *commitments*: "*Crisis* refers to the adolescent's period of engagement in choosing among meaningful alternatives, *commitment* refers to the degree of personal investment the individual exhibits" (Marcia, 1966, p. 551; emphasis added). A *mature identity* is achieved only after the individual has experienced a crisis and has become committed to an ideology.

Marcia (1966) identified four basic identity statuses: identity diffused, foreclosure, moratorium, and identity achieved. Table 6.1 shows the four identity statuses, which we examine in more detail in the following sections.

Identity Diffused

Subjects who are **identity diffused** have not experienced a crisis period, nor have they made any commitment to an occupation, a religion, a political philosophy, sex roles, or personal standards of behavior (Archer & Waterman, 1990). They have not experienced an identity crisis in relation to any of these issues, nor have they gone through the process of reevaluating, searching, and considering alternatives.

TABLE 6.1	THE FOUR IDENTITY STATUSES AS DERIVED FROM THE EGO IDENTITY DIMENSIONS	
	COMMITMENT DIMENSION	
EXPLORATION DIMENSION	**MADE FIRM COMMITMENTS**	**NOT MADE FIRM COMMITMENTS**
Have explored or are exploring alternatives	Identity achievement	Moratorium
Have not explored alternatives	Foreclosure	Identity diffusion

Diffusion is developmentally the most unsophisticated identity status and is usually a normal characteristic of early adolescents. ("Where do you want to live when you grow up?" "I don't know; I never thought about it.") Given time and increasing pressure from parents, peers, and schools, most young people eventually begin to grapple with these issues. Adolescents who continue to express no interest in commitment may be masking an underlying insecurity about identity issues (Berzonsky, Nurmi, Kinney, et al., 1999). Lacking self-confidence, they mask their feelings with expressions of apathy. Diffused individuals usually have low self-esteem, are unduly influenced by peer pressure, and lack meaningful friendships. They drift from interest to interest, relationship to relationship. They are selfish and hedonistic.

If an adolescent has tried to make identity commitments and has failed, the response may be anger directed against parents or religious or political leaders. Older adolescents who become social dropouts, who are rebelling against all established values, and who have adopted a nihilistic attitude often fall into this category. Some identity-diffused adolescents try to avoid anxiety, crisis, and commitment by using alcohol and drugs.

Foreclosure

Subjects in **foreclosure** have not experienced a crisis, but they have made commitments to occupations and ideologies that are not the result of their own searching but are ready-made and handed down to them, frequently by parents. It is a typical pattern found in children. Foreclosures often have identified closely with their same-sex parent (Cella, DeWolfe, & Fitzgibbon, 1987). They become what others want them to become, without really deciding for themselves. An example of someone with this type of identity status is the youth who wants to be a doctor because his or her parent is a doctor. Foreclosed adolescents are not able to distinguish between their own goals and the ones their parents plan for them. Foreclosed adolescents report a strong emotional bond within the family, but it is such a close relationship that it reflects enmeshment and lack of independence. Foreclosed adolescents exhibit significantly

lower levels of healthy separation than do others (Papini, Mucks, & Barnett, 1989).

Foreclosed individuals are often authoritarian and intolerant. They are conformists and conventional thinkers (Kroger, 2003). They seek security and support from significant others or familiar settings (Kroger, 1990) and they have high approval needs (Kroger, 1995). When put under stress, however, they perform poorly. Their security lies in avoiding change or challenge. As one researcher observed, the "total lack of conflict during adolescence is an ominous sign that the individual's psychological maturity may not be progressing" (Keniston, 1971, p. 364). Foreclosure may be a means of reducing anxiety. Persons who are too uncomfortable with uncertainty make choices without a lengthy process of consideration. They may marry while still in school, as well as make early decisions about vocations without lengthy consideration.

Other adolescents adopt a **negative identity** that is at odds with the cultural values of the community. In a sense, a negative identity is a variant of the foreclosure status. Whereas a foreclosure may be thought of as slavishly following authority figures' desires, someone with a negative identity will sit when told to stand. He or she derives satisfaction from rebelling against and defying more obedient, mainstream individuals. The individual with a negative identity can be viewed as a "reverse foreclosure" in that he or she bases his or her behavior on what parents, teachers, and members of society at large want—but does the opposite. Slackers, truants, juvenile delinquents, and those with oppositional defiant disorder are the types of individuals who might have a negative identity.

Do individuals in cultures that neither encourage nor support identity crises have identities?

identity diffused   according to Marcia, those adolescents who have not experienced a crisis and explored meaningful alternatives or made any commitments in finding an acceptable identity.

foreclosure   according to Marcia, establishing an identity without search or exploration, usually according to what has been handed down by parents.

negative identity   an identity based on rejecting parental and societal values.

IN THEIR OWN WORDS

"I am fully immersed in the moratorium stage—a not-altogether fun place to be! Coming into college, I remember people around me telling me how much time I had to figure out what I wanted to do in life. Well . . . time is rapidly running out and I still don't know what I want to do with myself. I was encouraged when I learned that nobody usually gets stuck in this stage, because right now, it feels like I may never know what to do with myself. I am consumed with thoughts of my future and where I will be in 10 years. So, basically to sum up the last 10 years, I have gone from worrying about looks and popularity to worrying about a job and money. The fact that there is no one clear answer to this is what makes it so hard, I think. I have a good amount of self-esteem."

Of course, but the identity is a foreclosed one. An identity does not have to be achieved in these cultures to be functional. Going through the decision-making process necessary to achieve an identity is unnecessary if one has no choices to make. If there is only one possible occupation (say, farmer), if everyone has the same beliefs, and if everyone marries, for instance, then there will be no real crises to face. It is certainly easier to remain foreclosed in a foreclosure society.

Moratorium

Moratorium means a period of delay granted to someone who is not yet ready to make a decision or assume an obligation. Adolescence is a period of exploration of alternatives before commitments are made. Some individuals with a moratorium identity status are involved in continual crises. As a consequence, they seem confused, unstable, and discontented (Schwartz, Zamboanga, Weisskirch, et al., 2009). They are often rebellious and uncooperative. Some moratorium-status individuals avoid dealing with problems, and they may have a tendency to procrastinate until situations dictate a course of action (Berzonsky, 1989). Because these individuals are experiencing crises, they tend to be anxious (Meeus, Iedema, Helsen, et al., 1999). One study even showed that death anxiety is higher in moratorium-status adolescents than in those in the other three statuses (Sterling & Van Horn, 1989). Adolescents in this status category are often uncertain they have selected the right major in college and may be unhappy with their college experience and education. Granted, it is not uncommon or even especially undesirable for adolescents to "try on" a variety of identities (even radically

different ones) before finding the one that best fits them. Thus, they may dabble in exotic religions, wear unusual and attention-getting clothing, and choose impractical careers. However, most individuals become reasonably conventional by the end of this identity search (Bosma & Kunnen, 2001).

Why do adolescents move from being foreclosed or diffused into a state of moratorium? Going to college encourages exploration. Students in college are actively and thoughtfully confronted with the crisis of making an occupational commitment and stimulated to rethink their ideologies. In addition, college is an environment in which individuals meet people who are different from themselves. Being confronted with persons who have dissimilar values and desires often triggers a rethinking of your own views and may make you less certain of your beliefs. Being met with conflicting opinions—especially those of people whom you respect—stimulates identity growth (Bosma & Kunnen, 2001).

Much less is known about the identity formation process of those late adolescents who move on directly to employment without attending college (Schwartz, 2005). One recent study, however, found that young workers in Belgium had made more identity commitments than Belgian college students (Luyckx, Schwartz, Goossens, et al., 2008). This suggests that they remain in a state of identity moratorium for a briefer period of time.

Identity Achieved

Subjects whose status is **identity achieved** have experienced a psychological moratorium, have resolved their identity crises by carefully evaluating various alternatives and choices, and have come to conclusions and decisions on their own. Once an identity has been achieved, there is self-acceptance; a stable self-definition; and a commitment to a vocation, religion, and political ideology. There is harmony within oneself and an acceptance of capacities, opportunities, and limitations. There is a more realistic concept of goals (Waterman, 1999).

Research with high school students indicates that few have achieved an identity by the time of graduation: in fact, most college seniors have not (van Hoof, 1999). Living at home or in a dorm and possessing limited life and work experiences are not conducive to identity achievement. Most but not all 18- to 21-year-olds know that they have yet to find an identity. As one student wrote in her journal:

When I was a senior in high school, I just knew that I was going to be a doctor. I had planned on a career in medicine as long as I could remember. I would have bet a million dollars that that's what I was going to do. What a joke! I hated all the science courses

According to Erikson, a coherent self-identity is formed as the adolescent chooses values, beliefs, and goals. These choices are made by exploring alternatives and committing to roles.

I had to take in college, and I struggled to even pass. Now that I'm a junior, I'm still not sure what I want to do with my life—but it's not to be a doctor! I want to do something where I work with people, but that's all I'm sure of.

Adolescents who have a foreclosure status are often certain of their career plans and believe that they have achieved their identities. If they move on to a moratorium status, however, they usually rethink and reject their initial plans. At the college level, 80 percent of students change their majors during their four years (Waterman, 1992). In general, however, the percentage of adolescents who are identity achievers increases with age (Waterman, 1999).

Critique

Since Marcia's four-status scheme was first developed in the 1960s, criticisms have been raised. Some have come from the fact that his four identity statuses do not capture the entirety of the identity concept as envisioned by Erikson. Namely, critics say that Marcia focuses too much on the crisis/commitment aspect of identity and too little on its other crucial components. For example, van Hoof (1999) states that Marcia's scheme is inadequate because it fails to address the sense of personal

continuity so central to Erikson's description of identity. Similarly, Glodis and Blasi (1993) believe that the four statuses do not adequately capture the integration of different parts of the self or the sense of unity that comes with having an identity.

In addition, it is now recognized that identity statuses do not always develop in an exact sequence. It was originally believed that a specific developmental progression would be the norm: most adolescents would enter the identity crisis from the foreclosure status, moving through a moratorium phase, out of which achievement status would be attained. The diffusion status during adolescence was seen as an aberration in this natural progression, hopefully a transient one.

Note that there are three important variations from this developmental sequence. First, a significant number of individuals enter adolescence in the diffusion status; some of them remain there. Second, some individuals never seem to make the transition to the moratorium and achievement statuses, remaining firmly entrenched within the foreclosure status. Third, certain individuals who attain an achievement status appear to regress to a lower status years later (Marcia, 1991). This suggests that individuals may

moratorium according to Marcia, a period of time in the life of adolescents who are involved in a continual crisis, who continue to search for an identity, and who have not made any commitments.

identity achieved according to Marcia, those adolescents who have undergone a crisis in their search for an identity and who have made a commitment.

go through the developmental sequence of identity more than once during a lifetime. A person may have found identity achievement at a certain period of life, then later in life go through another moratorium stage or stage of identity diffusion before identity achievement is accomplished (Stephen, Fraser, & Marcia, 1992). Finally, it is quite normative for an individual to remain in a state of moratorium for many years. This, in fact, is one of the hallmarks of the new stage of life termed "emerging adulthood" (see the epilogue).

Identity as a Process

Erikson's and Marcia's approaches to identity are status, or *outcome,* approaches. Their research did not concentrate on the *process* by which adolescents find their identities. Much of the later research about adolescent identity formation—and hence, much of the criticism of Erikson's and Marcia's work—focuses on this process.

Grotevant (1992) was one of the first researchers (and one of the most influential) to discuss identity from this process perspective. He emphasizes that exploration is the key to finding an identity; one needs to gather information about oneself and about the environment in order to make life choices. (This certainly does not contradict Erikson's view.)

Burke (1991) envisions an **identity control system** that consists of two interpersonal and three intrapersonal components. The interpersonal components include one's *social behavior* and the *interpersonal feedback* one gets from others. The intrapersonal factors are *self-concept,* one's **identity standards (or beliefs about how one *should* behave),** and a **comparator** that assesses the similarity between the two. As individuals behave and get feedback on their behavior, their self-concept is affected. The comparator matches one's self-perceptions against the standards one has about who one wants to be. If there is a discrepancy between the two, then one's behavior, standards, or self-concept must be modified to increase consistency.

Adolescents in the different identity states handle discrepancies in different ways. Diffused individuals have yet to develop identity standards and so do not experience discrepancies. Foreclosed youths overemphasize the feedback from their parents and significant others and form standards too early on; they discount discordant feedback if it does not match their already established identity standards. Moratoriums are actively seeking feedback and are willing to adjust their identity standards. Like those in foreclosure, individuals who are identity achieved have solidified their identity standards, but they developed these standards more slowly and based them more on broad-based feedback (Kerpelman, Pittman, & Lamke, 1997).

Berzonsky and Kuk (2000) identified three styles of identity searching. Youths with an *informational style* seek out diagnostic information and modify their plans and behaviors, if necessary, to match it. This style characterizes moratorium and identity-achieved individuals. Others have a *normative style;* they are resistant to change and block out discrepant information. This style is characteristic of foreclosured adolescents. Diffused individuals are most likely to exhibit an *avoidant style* of identity searching. They put off making decisions and evade feedback; when they do make changes, these changes are superficial and short-lived. These styles appear consistent across both genders and among youths in at least three different countries: the United States, Finland, and the Czech Republic (Berzonsky, Macek, & Nurmi, 2003).

Components of Identity

Identity has many components—*physical, sexual, social, vocational, moral, ideological,* and *psychological* characteristics—that make up the total self (Grotevant, 1987). Thus, individuals may identify themselves by their physical appearance, their gender, their social relationships and membership in groups, their vocations and work, and their religious and political affiliations and ideologies. It is personal because it is a sense of "I-ness," but it is also social, for it includes "we-ness," or one's collective identity. Identity is intrinsically both an individual and a social process (Adams & Marshall, 1996). Adolescents who have a positive identity have developed a sense of accepting themselves; furthermore, identity development is associated with the development of intimacy and an acceptance of others. Identity achievement also helps in developing committed relationships: intimacy alters identity—it helps people grow (Kacerguis & Adams, 1980).

Some aspects of identity are more easily formed than others. Physical and sexual identities seem to be established earliest. Young adolescents become concerned with their body image before they become interested in choosing a vocation or examining their moral values and ideologies. Similarly, they must deal with their own sexual identity both before and after puberty.

Vocational, ideological, and moral identities are established more slowly. These identities depend on adolescents reaching more advanced levels of cognitive growth and development that enable them to explore alternative ideas and courses of action. In addition, reformulation of these identities requires independence of thought. The exploration of occupational alternatives is the most immediate and concrete task as adolescents finish high school or enter college. Religious and political ideologies are usually examined during late adolescence, especially the college years, but identities in these areas may be in a state of flux for years (Coté & Levine, 1992).

Ethnic Identity

Ethnic identity is the sum total of group members' feelings about those symbols, values, and common histories that identify them as a distinct group. It is an individual's sense of self as a member of an ethnic group and the attitudes and behaviors associated with that sense (Helms, 1990). Ethnic development is the process of development from an unexamined ethnic identity through a period of exploration to arrive at an achieved ethnic identity (Yeh & Huang, 1996). The development of an ethnic identity is an essential human need. It provides a sense of historical continuity and a sense of belonging (Smith, 1991). It positively influences academic achievement (Arellano & Pedilla, 1996), helps individuals stand up to the strains of discrimination (Phinney & Chavira, 1995), and bolsters psychological well-being (Umaña-Taylor, Diversi, & Fine, 2002).

Acculturation Options

Acculturation is the adjustment of minority groups to the culture of the dominant group (Sodowsky, Lai, & Plake, 1991). A problem experienced by adolescents from ethnic-minority families and from immigrant families is that the culture into which they were born does not always match, and is not always valued or appreciated by, the culture in which they are raised. In the early stages of forging an identity, ethnic minorities and immigrants often find conflict between their ethnic cultures and the values of the larger society in which they live.

There are four possible ways in which ethnic group members can participate in a culturally diverse society. *Separation* involves exclusive focus on the cultural values and practices of the ethnic group and little or no interaction with the dominant society. *Assimilation* is the opposite; it occurs when an ethnic group member chooses to identify solely with the culture of the dominant society and to relinquish all ties to his or her ethnic heritage. *Integration* is characterized by strong identification and involvement with both the dominant society's culture and the traditional ethnic culture. *Marginality* is defined by the absence or loss of one's culture of origin and the lack of involvement with the dominant society.

Which type of participation contributes most to the positive development of identity and self-esteem in adolescents? One study of high school and college students from diverse inner-city schools sought an answer to this question. The students were from mixed backgrounds: Asians, African Americans, Hispanics, and Whites (Phinney, Chavira, & Williamson,

1992). Results indicated that among the four acculturation options, integration is the most adaptive, resulting in better psychological adjustment and higher self-esteem. A healthy relationship between endorsement of integration and self-esteem indicates that a more positive self-concept is associated with identification with a person's mainstream culture as well as his or her own culture. In contrast, endorsement of assimilation was found to be related to lower self-esteem among the Asian and foreign-born participants. Thus, giving up one's ethnic culture can have a negative impact on self-concept. The idea of separation (an ethnic group should keep to itself and not mix with mainstream society) was given little support by the students, with no difference among ethnic groups or by socioeconomic status. Of all four alternatives, marginality—in which a person identifies neither with his or her own ethnic group nor the dominant culture—is the least satisfactory alternative (Phinney, 1992).

Some years later, Phinney and Devich-Navarro (1997) revised the concept of integration by dividing it into two new types: **blended biculturalism** and **alternating biculturalism.** In addition, they posited a third new acculturation option, **fusion.** A blended bicultural person finds commonalities between his or her ethnic culture and the mainstream society; this individual usually acts in ways congruent with both cultures. An alternating bicultural is someone who moves back and forth between the two cultures, sometimes acting in the way the ethnic culture proscribes and sometimes in the way the mainstream culture proscribes. Fusion occurs when someone truly merges both cultures into a new, coherent whole. Figure 6.3 illustrates these different acculturation patterns.

A large majority of the African American and Mexican adolescents in Phinney and Devich-Navarro's study were bicultural. The blended bicultural teenagers felt both American and ethnic. They believed the United States to be a diverse country and felt generally

identity control system a construct that describes the process of developing an identity.

identity standards one's beliefs about how one should behave.

comparator the component of the identity control system that compares one's self-concept with one's identity standards.

blended biculturalism the state in which one finds the commonalities between one's ethnic and mainstream identities.

alternating biculturalism the state in which one vacillates between following one's ethnic beliefs and those of the societal mainstream.

fusion the state in which one has merged one's ethnic traditions and those of the cultural mainstream into a new whole.

FIGURE 6.3   ETHNIC ACCULTURATION PATTERNS

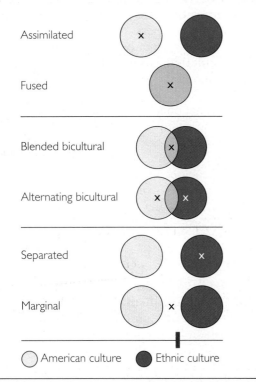

Assimilated

Fused

Blended bicultural

Alternating bicultural

Separated

Marginal

American culture   Ethnic culture

positive toward people in other ethnic groups. Ethnicity was not especially salient for them, and they did not perceive their biculturalism to be problematic. The teenagers who had chosen an alternating bicultural pattern felt more ethnic than American. They took

pleasure in their ethnicity but experienced more conflict in negotiating between their ethnic culture and mainstream American society. Separated adolescents felt distant from the mainstream culture, which they perceived as more exclusively White. They felt they were actively excluded from full membership in society at large and were negative about people from other ethnic groups. The authors found no assimilated, fused, or marginal individuals in their sample of 98 tenth- and eleventh-graders.

Developing an Ethnic Identity

Children are not born understanding the concept of ethnicity; it must be learned. Tse (1999) proposed a four-stage model of ethnic identity development. Very young children are *ethnically unaware.* They don't know that people have different ethnicities and assume everyone is just like them. This period is typically short and ends by the time a child enters school. Children in the second stage are *ethnically ambivalent.* They downplay the importance of their ethnic background and don't strongly identify with their ethnic group. During adolescence, *ethnic emergence* develops. In this stage, individuals realize that they can't fully join the mainstream. This can lead to feelings of anger and resentment and motivates many to immerse themselves in their ancestral culture. For instance, they may take courses or read books about their cultural history, spend most of their time socializing with others who share their ethnicity, and visit their ancestral homeland. Finally, when individuals realize that they are a product of two cultures—their ethnic culture and the mainstream American culture in which they were

Adolescents who are experiencing an ethnic identity search typically segregate themselves by ethnicity, at least temporarily.

raised—they *incorporate* their ethnic identities, feeling both American and ethnic.

Quintana, Casañeda-English, and Ybarra (1999) base their conception of developing ethnic awareness on Selman's (1977) model of social cognition. Initially, young children believe that race/ethnicity is based solely on physical characteristics, such as skin color and eye shape. When they enter school, children come to know that other traits—such as native language, preferred foods, and countries of origin—distinguish groups, as well. At some point during elementary school, children become sensitive to more subtle differences between groups. They note socioeconomic differences and become aware of discrimination.

During early adolescence, they learn the attitudes and perspectives of their particular groups; they see the world through these ethnic lenses. Eventually, many individuals develop a multicultural perspective and a bicultural identity. They come to understand the views of other groups.

Ethnic Identity and Multiracial Teens

Early theoretical research on multiracial adolescents painted a bleak picture of their situation: they were thought to be betwixt and between, marginalized by members of both of their parent ethnicities and as a result having low self-esteem and a poor sense of self (Bracey, Bámaca, & Umaña-Taylor, 2004). Other empirical research has provided a more mixed view: some studies have found that multiracial adolescents have high self-esteem (e.g., Brown, 2001), whereas others have found no consistent differences in the self-concepts of monoracial and multiracial youth (e.g., Phinney & Alipuria, 1996). Those multiracial adolescents who have a well-developed sense of ethnic identity are the ones most likely to have high self-esteem (Bracey, Bámaca, & Umaña-Taylor, 2004) and less likely to engage in problem behaviors (Choi, Harachi, Gillmore, et al., 2006).

ANSWERS WOULDN'T YOU LIKE TO KNOW …

How does the development of an ethnic identity affect self-esteem?

Adolescents who are integrated—either blended biculturals or fused biculturals—have higher self-esteem than adolescents who have assimilated.

RESEARCH HIGHLIGHT   THE EFFECTS OF MATERNAL ETHNIC SOCIALIZATION ON SONS AND DAUGHTERS

As the numbers of ethnic minority children continue to increase, the socialization of these children in adolescence has become a topic of growing interest. On the basis of research, it appears that minority parents face three distinct challenges. Their children need to be socialized both to their own culture and to the mainstream culture, and they need to understand prejudice and discrimination. The first challenge, the learning of one's own culture, would seem to be the least problematic, in that it is presumably learned naturally in the home. Yet we know from several studies of ethnic minority families that some explicit cultural teaching is needed. A second socialization theme involves teaching children to get along in the mainstream culture or helping them to succeed in society at large. Minority parents generally teach their children to be bicultural. Part of getting along in society involves developing the skills necessary to be successful; to accomplish this, children are encouraged to work hard and do well. The final theme common to the research on minority child socialization is explicit teaching to prepare children to be aware of prejudice and discrimination. Racial barriers and blocked opportunities need to be emphasized.

A recent study by Hughes and her colleagues (Hughes, Hagelskamp, Way, et al., 2009) examined the relationships between mothers' and early adolescents' self-reports of ethnic-racial socialization and ethnic identity in a sample of Black, Puerto Rican, Dominican, and Chinese Americans. Mothers and adolescents in each of the four groups reported more emphasis on positive cultural knowledge than on preparation for bias. Consistent with previous research, Black mothers spent relatively more time discussing discrimination with their children than did mothers from the other groups. The adolescents were for the most part proud of their ethnic heritages, although they had not yet fully explored their ethnicity. It is interesting that mothers' reports of ethnic socialization were more strongly related to their daughters' levels of ethnic identity but their sons' perceptions of bias. This suggests that teenage boys and girls may attend to parental information differently. Overall, there were few differences across the four minority groups, suggesting a similarity in ethnic socialization across cultural boundaries.

Ethnic Identity and Caucasian Adolescents

Do Caucasian students have an ethnic identity? Many, if not most, do not have a strong one (St. Louis & Liem, 2005) because their own ethnicity is often not salient or important to them. (Self-esteem is generally tied to White adolescents' ethnic identity only when they find themselves in the minority [Roberts, Phinney, Masse, et al., 1999]—a situation analogous to that of most minority adolescents, who find themselves surrounded by the majority culture.) Of course, some Caucasian adolescents do strongly identify themselves as being part of an ethnic or religious group (the author fondly remembers her years in Minnesota, where many individuals are fervently and proudly *Norwegian American*), and their ethnic identities can be important sources of pride.

In sum, the research on ethnic identity strongly demonstrates that having a positive ethnic identity is strongly related to healthy self-esteem in non–Caucasian American adolescents (Smith, Walker, Fields, et al., 1999). Integration—that is, feeling good about and comfortable with both the ethnic and mainstream aspects of one's heritage—is most closely associated with having a positive self-concept. Furthermore, feeling good about one's own ethnicity allows one to be positive about people whose ethnic backgrounds are different from one's own (Phinney, Jacoby, & Silva, 2007).

Sex and Gender

The word **sex,** when used by psychologists and sociologists, refers to a person's anatomical attributes. If you have a penis and a scrotum, you are male; if you have a vagina and labia, you are female. Sex is determined by chromosomes and prenatal hormones; it is a biological phenomenon. Thus, each person is born having a biological sex.

From his or her first day of life, each person is assigned a **gender.** Gender is a much more inclusive concept than sex. It entails all of the cultural associations and expectations that go along with one's biological sex. It is a psychological and social phenomenon. Some of these cultural expectations are directly based on biology: for instance, the fact that only women can get pregnant and give birth and the fact that male athletes are apt to have more muscle mass than female athletes are biological. Some cultural expectations are more indirectly tied to biology: for example, that women should be nurturing in order to care for children and that males should compete with one another to attract mates. Still other cultural expectations have little or nothing to do with biology or evolutionary history: that only women should enjoy wearing skirts (but not in

ANSWERS WOULDN'T YOU LIKE TO KNOW …

What is the difference between *sex* and *gender*?

Sex is a purely biological concept: male or female. *Gender* is a social construction that includes expectations about what males and females should be like.

Scotland) and that only men should participate in contact sports.

How one feels about his or her sex and gender is an important part of identity. Understanding society's characterization of your gender and developing your own personal code as to how someone of your gender should behave are therefore central components of the identity search.

Biological Sex

Biological sex is genetically and hormonally determined. The fetus becomes a male or female depending on whether it has one X and one Y chromosome (male) or two X chromosomes (female) and on the prenatal balance between the male and female hormones in the bloodstream. Hormones can have a definite influence on physical characteristics even after birth. Male hormones can be administered to a woman, encouraging the growth of a beard, body hair, and the clitoris and the development of masculine muscles, build, and strength. Similarly, female hormones can be administered to a man, encouraging breast development, increasing voice pitch, and leading to other feminine traits. Femaleness or maleness, then, is somewhat tenuous and may be partially altered.

Hormones alter physical characteristics, but do they influence sex-typed behavior? If human females are exposed to excessive androgenic (masculinizing sex hormones) influences prior to birth, they become more tomboyish, more physically vigorous, and more assertive than other females. They will prefer boys rather than girls as playmates and will choose strenuous activities over the relatively docile play of most prepubertal girls (Meyer-Bahlburg, Dolezal, Baker, et al., 2006). Similarly, adolescent boys born to mothers who receive estrogen and progesterone during pregnancy tend to exhibit less assertiveness and physical activity and may be rated lower on general masculine-type behavior (Rabin & Chrousos, 1991). This suggests that changes in prenatal hormonal levels in humans may have marked effects on gender-role behavior; after birth, however, hormonal changes have much less effect on masculine/feminine characteristics already evident.

Cognitive-Developmental Theories

Cognitive-developmental theories suggest that gender identification has its beginning in the gender that is assigned to the child at birth and subsequently accepted by him or her while growing up. At the time of birth, gender assignment is made largely on the basis of genital examination. From that point on, the child is considered a boy or a girl. If genital abnormalities are present, gender assignment may prove to be erroneous if it is not in agreement with the child's sex chromosomes and his or her gonads. However, even if erroneous, gender identification usually follows the sex assignment in which the child is reared.

The assignment of gender influences how the child feels about herself or himself and how others feel about the child. The cognitive theories, of course, focus on the child's self-perceptions. They hold that the child's self-categorization as a boy or girl is the basic organizer of the gender identification attitudes that are developed. For example, the child who recognizes that he is a male begins to act consistently with male gender expectations. He begins to structure his own experiences according to his accepted gender and to act out appropriate sex roles. Sex differentiation takes place gradually as children learn to be masculine or feminine according to culturally established gender identification expectations and their interpretations of them (Ruble, Martin, & Berenbaum, 2006).

The most widely accepted variant of the cognitive-developmental perspective on gender is called **gender schema theory.** It proposes a multistep developmental process. First, children learn that they are boys or girls (even if they are unclear as to exactly what those labels mean). Next, children recognize that not only people but things and behaviors are also labeled as "boy things" or "girl things." Children are naturally more curious about items and behaviors that match their labels than they are about items and behaviors that do not. They therefore pay more attention to and learn more about gender-appropriate objects and behaviors than gender-inappropriate ones. It is a well-established aspect of human nature that we come to like things that we are familiar with; they make us feel comfortable. It follows, then, that children will begin to prefer gender-appropriate actions and will perform them more frequently than gender-inappropriate ones (Martin, Ruble, & Szkrybalo, 2002).

Societal Influences

Children do not develop their attitudes about gender in a vacuum; they are surrounded by parents, teachers, other adults, friends, and less-than-friendly peers who make their views of appropriate masculine and feminine behaviors known. Even people whom children don't know and with whom they don't directly interact—such as the producers of TV shows and movies and musicians whose songs are heard on the radio and whose videos are seen on TV—bombard them with images of men and women. Through these observances and interactions, children learn the **gender roles** prescribed by their society: that is, the behaviors that men and women are expected to engage in with different frequencies. For example,

A child's sex-role identity begins with the cognitive assignment of gender made at birth. However, society also plays an important role, ascribing certain qualities of femininity or masculinity to the child.

sex   one's biological endowment as a male or a female.

gender   the psychological/sociological construct of what it means to be a man or a woman.

gender schema theory   a revised cognitive-developmental approach to gender that emphasizes the effects of labeling, attention, and interest in developing gender beliefs.

gender roles   the behaviors that are supposedly characteristic of men and women.

being aggressive is part of the American male gender role, whereas being emotional is part of women's. Eating is not part of anyone's gender role because males and females eat with more or less equal frequency. (Eating or avoiding eating certain foods, however, may be part of one's gender role. In some social circles, it is perceived as more masculine to eat bratwurst than to eat crustless cucumber sandwiches.) Individuals are described as **masculine** or **feminine** based on how consistently they fulfill gender-role expectations.

Masculinity

Traditionally, masculine men were supposed to be aggressive, strong, forceful, self-confident, virile, courageous, logical, and unemotional. Pleck (1976) captured the traditional American male gender role in four directives. A man is supposed to be "The Big Wheel"; that is, he must be successful and have a high status. He is also expected to be "The Sturdy Oak"; like Christian Bale and Arnold Schwartzenegger, he is required to constantly evidence toughness, self-confidence, and self-reliance. A man is allowed and expected to "Give 'Em Hell" as well—to be daring and ready to solve his problems with violence if needed. Finally, a man is told "No Sissy Stuff"; in other words, any interest or behavior that is in any way feminine should be shunned at all costs. It is especially important for a man to avoid any expression of caring or gentleness toward other men (Salt, 1991).

Although many members of American society have moved away from this rigid conceptualization of masculinity, some subgroups have not. For example,

male youths who join delinquent street gangs tend to be very concerned about appearing masculine. Many of the practices that form their initiation rites—such as having to fight and needing to demonstrate their courage by engaging in dangerous acts (such as running along subway tracks)—are reminiscent of old-fashioned masculine ideals (Hunt & Laidler, 2001).

Femininity

What are the traditional concepts of femininity as taught by middle and upper-middle classes of U.S. society? In the past, women were supposed to be submissive, sensitive, tender, affectionate, sentimental, dependent, and emotional. A feminine female was never aggressive, loud, or vulgar in speech or behavior. She was expected to be soft-hearted, to cry easily, and to like frivolous things. She was expected to be dependent and submissive and to be interested primarily in her home. Today, few social groups hold these stereotypes of femininity, indicating that significant changes have taken place in people's concepts.

Social Learning Theory

Social learning theory suggests that a child learns sex-typed behavior the same way he or she learns any other type of behavior: through a combination of reward, punishment, direct instruction, and modeling. From the beginning, boys and girls are socialized differently. Boys are expected to be more active, hostile, and aggressive. They are expected to fight when teased and to stand up to bullies. When they act according to expectations, they are praised; when they refuse to fight, they are criticized for being a "sissy."

Trying to be a macho man is sometimes harmful and has been associated with suicide, health and emotional problems, stress, and substance abuse. Do these adolescents fit the macho stereotype?

TABLE 6.2   HOW CHILDREN LEARN SEX-TYPED BEHAVIORS

MECHANISM	MALE EXAMPLE	FEMALE EXAMPLE
Reward	A boy is cheered by his team for making the winning tackle in a football game. The next day, he practices running fast so that he can make more tackles in the future.	A girl is praised by her teacher for working so quietly at her desk. The girl continues to work without getting up and speaking to others.
Punishment	A father ridicules his son for crying when his pet dies. The boy subsequently avoids crying in front of others.	Other girls refuse to play with a pre-schooler who plays too rough. The preschooler plays more gently the next day.
Instruction	A grandfather teaches his grandson how to fish. The boy spends his afternoons fishing in the stream behind his house.	A mother teaches her daughter how to knit. The girl makes a scarf for her aunt on her birthday.
Modeling	A boy watches an interview of a sports star who uses foul language. The boy begins cursing when speaking to his friends.	A girl overhears her older sister putting down some girls who dress unfashionably. She later criticizes unfashionable girls to her own friends.

Similarly, girls are condemned or punished for being too boisterous and aggressive and are rewarded when they are polite and submissive. As a consequence, boys and girls grow up manifesting different behaviors (see Table 6.2).

Traditional gender roles and concepts are taught in many ways as a child grows up. For instance, television plays a significant role in the socialization process (for both young and old). Television commercials and programming contain considerable gender bias and sexism (Signorielli, 2001). Another way of reinforcing gender roles is giving children gender-specific toys that may influence vocational choices. For example, boys might be persuaded to be scientists, astronauts, and football players, and girls might be inclined to be nurses, teachers, and flight attendants by the toys they are given (Blakemore & Centers, 2005).

Without realizing it, many teachers still develop traditional masculine/feminine stereotypical behavior in school. Studies of teachers' relationships with boys and girls reveal that teachers, in general, encourage boys to be more assertive in the classroom (e.g., Sadker & Sadker, 1995). When the teacher asks questions, the boys call out comments without raising their hands, literally grabbing the teacher's attention. Most girls sit patiently with their hands raised, but when a girl calls out, the teacher reprimands her: "In this class, we don't shout out answers; we raise our hands." The message is subtle but powerful: boys should be assertive academically; girls should be quiet.

Children also find appropriate gender roles through the processes of identification and modeling, especially with parents. Parental **identification** is the process by which a child adopts and internalizes parental values, attitudes, behavioral traits, and personality characteristics. Identification begins shortly after birth because of the child's early dependence on parents. This dependency, in turn, usually leads to close emotional attachment. Gender-role learning takes place almost unconsciously and indirectly in this close parent-child relationship. Children model their parents: they listen and observe how each parent behaves, speaks, dresses, and acts differently in relation to the other parent, to other children, or to people outside the family. Thus, children learn what a mother, a wife, a father, a husband, a woman, and a man *is* through example and through daily contacts and association.

Parents also influence their children's gender role by providing them with sex-typed opportunities and encouragement (Fredricks & Eccles, 2004); for example, they are more likely to sign their sons up for computer camp than they are their daughters. Parents with traditional values are more likely to assign household chores to their daughters than to their sons (McHale, Updegraff, Shanahan, et al., 2005). Intentionally or not, parents often steer their children in sex-typed directions.

Peers may play a particularly important role in the development of children's gender identities. Eleanor Maccoby (1990) observed that boys and girls behave

masculine having the personality and behavioral characteristics of a male according to culturally defined standards of maleness.

feminine having the personality and behavior characteristics of a female according to culturally defined standards of femaleness.

identification the process by which an individual ascribes to himself or herself the characteristics of another person.

quite similarly when viewed alone, but in same-sex play groups, they behave very differently. Same-sex play groups are formed because from a young age, when left to their own devices, most children prefer to play with others of the same sex. Girls gravitate toward other girls because boys play too roughly for them and don't listen to their suggestions; boys prefer to play with other boys because girls don't like to play fun games. These male and female same-sex groups develop distinct cultures. Boys play competitively and physically; they like to win and to show who is the best. Girls like to talk, take turns, and cooperate. The messages that boys and girls get from their peers are different, and Maccoby believes that many gender differences in behavior can be traced to these early social groupings.

Gender Stereotypes

Gender stereotypes are harmful to the people being stereotyped as well as the people doing the stereotyping. Individuals may feel pressured to live up to stereotypes that do not suit their personalities or abilities. Adolescents may feel this pressure especially intensely, since they value conformity and peer opinions more than children and adults do. Trying to be someone you are not is stressful and unsatisfying, and trying to do things that do not suit you usually leads to failure. Belief in rigid gender roles is also limiting in that it prevents one from exploring supposedly inappropriate behaviors that one might, in fact, enjoy.

Fortunately, during the past quarter century, gender stereotypes have broken down somewhat and individuals have gained more freedom to pursue their interests, regardless of whether those interests are typical of their gender. Because of peer pressure, however, this remains less true during early and mid-adolescence than at other points in the lifespan. Even so, teenagers grant each other somewhat more gender-role flexibility today than they did in the past.

Androgyny

A gradual mixing of male and female traits and roles seems to be emerging as the ideal, thereby producing **androgyny,** or male and female in one (Bem, 1974). Androgynous people are not sex-typed with respect to gender roles (although they are distinctly male or female in gender). They match their behavior to the situation rather than being limited by what is culturally defined as male or female. An androgynous male feels comfortable cuddling and caring for a young child; an androgynous female feels comfortable pumping gas and changing the oil in her car. Androgyny expands the

range of human behavior, allowing individuals to cope effectively in a variety of situations.

Being androgynous has more benefits for females than for males because many masculine traits are valued more highly than feminine traits. For instance, women who take on masculine characteristics such as assertiveness and independence are generally rewarded for these traits; however, men who are emotionally expressive or passive or who embrace nontraditional occupations are generally devalued. Men therefore have less reason to become androgynous than women (Skoe, 1995).

Although the concept of androgyny was an improvement over exclusive notions of femininity and masculinity, it has turned out to be less of a panacea than many of its early proponents envisioned (Doyle & Paludi, 1995). Some theorists believe androgyny should be replaced with *gender-role transcendence*— the belief that when an individual's competence is at issue, it should not be conceptualized on the basis of masculinity, femininity, or androgyny but rather on a personal basis. Thus, rather than merging gender roles or stereotyping people as masculine or feminine, we should begin to think about people as people.

Gender in Adolescence

What happens to an individual's sense of gender when he or she hits adolescence? Usually the teenager becomes *more* gendered; that is, he or she begins to act in a more gender-stereotypical way and to hold more stereotypical beliefs. This is termed the **gender intensification hypothesis** (Ruble, Martin, & Berenbaum, 2006). This effect is stronger in girls than in boys, probably because girls' sex-role behavior is less stereotypical in middle childhood than boys' and so they have more ground to make up (Huston & Alvarez, 1990). Also, once they hit puberty, girls tend to be concerned that boys will find them attractive, and "femininity" is seen as part of attractiveness.

How do these findings relate back to identity? If girls are shaped by biology, societal messages, and reinforcement to have stereotypically feminine traits—or to believe that they *should* have stereotypically feminine traits—then they will limit their identity choices to conform to those qualities. They will therefore shy away from choosing careers that require assertiveness and competition and believe that they must necessarily become wives and mothers. If boys believe they will be valued only if they are stereotypically masculine, they will throw themselves into their work and undervalue the relationships in their lives. Clearly, the choices we make are done so against a backdrop of gender.

ANSWERS WOULDN'T YOU LIKE TO KNOW ...

Why is it good to have a blend of masculine and feminine traits?

People who possess both traditionally masculine and traditionally feminine traits have the flexibility to act appropriately in more circumstances than those who do not. It is thus a good thing to be androgynous, especially if you are female.

confined to two issues: family-career priorities and sexual values (Kroger, 2003), perhaps because more and more individuals are androgynous or gender transcendent. Indeed, gender-role orientation may be more influential than gender per se in influencing identity formation.

There appear to be few gender differences in the *processes* individuals use to form an identity. In fact, a review of the literature concluded that gender differences in identity formation were small and mainly

androgyny   a blending of male and female characteristics and roles.

gender intensification hypothesis   the proposal that adolescents feel more pressure than children to behave in gender-stereotypical ways.

SUMMARY

1. Self-concept is one's perception of oneself; it is who a person thinks he or she is. Having a good self-concept allows you to like yourself, to feel comfortable around others, and to participate willingly in a variety of activities.

2. Self-esteem refers to how much you like yourself; it is based on your self-concept.

3. Self-esteem influences mental health, interpersonal competence, and social adjustment.

4. Warm, authoritative, involved parents raise children with the highest levels of self-esteem.

5. In general, adolescents from lower-SES families have somewhat lower self-esteem than do those from higher-SES families.

6. Adolescent girls' self-esteem is lower than that of boys. Girls' self-esteem relies more on their perceived physical attractiveness and social relationships than does boys'.

7. Self-esteem decreases in early adolescence and then later rises. This decrease is associated most strongly with the move to middle or junior high school.

8. The central developmental task of adolescence is the formation of a coherent identity.

9. Erikson outlined seven major conflicts that are central to the self-identity search.

10. Marcia described four basic identity statuses: identity diffused, foreclosed, moratorium, and identity achieved.

11. Adolescents who are identity diffused have not experienced a crisis, explored alternatives, or made a commitment in a given area.

12. Foreclosure status is typical of adolescents who have made a commitment without exploring alternatives. They are not able to distinguish between their own values and goals and those of their parents.

13. Adolescents in a moratorium status are exploring alternatives with the expectation of making a decision. Using adolescence as a period of moratorium can be a positive experience.

14. Adolescents who are identity achieved have experienced a crisis and moratorium, have evaluated various alternatives, and have come to conclusions and decisions on their own.

15. The newest research on identity focuses on the process of identity development. Burke has suggested that an individual compares his or her self-concept with his or her identity standards based on feedback from others. Berzonsky has compared individuals with informational, normative, and avoidant styles of information gathering.

16. Part of one's identity is one's ethnic identity. Acculturation options for ethnic minorities include separation, assimilation, integration, and marginality. Integration can take the form of blended biculturalism or alternating biculturalism. Integration is more related to higher self-esteem than are the other options.

17. Ethnic identity develops by progressing through several stages. Individuals begin by being ethnically unaware; next, they are ambivalent. Their ethnicity then emerges, and they finally incorporate their ethnicity into their self-concept. Changes in thinking about ethnicity may parallel changes in social cognition.

18. Sex is a biological endowment: anatomy determines whether one is male or female. Gender is the sum of biology and cultural beliefs; it is a way of categorizing people and is more psychological and behavioral in nature.

19. The biological basis of gender includes both heredity and hormonal influences. Both affect physical characteristics. Hormones can accentuate or minimize certain masculine/feminine traits already in evidence.

20. Gender schema theory emphasizes the role of self-labeling on the attention a child pays to objects and behaviors and his or her resulting interest in, and competence with, those objects and actions.

21. Cultural influences are a major determinant of gender identity and roles. Concepts of masculinity and

femininity vary from culture to culture and have undergone changes in the United States.

22. Social learning theory says that children learn sex-typed behavior through a combination of rewards, punishment, instruction, and modeling. Boys and girls learn sex-typed behavior as defined by their culture and as taught and exemplified by significant others.

23. Parental identification says that children learn appropriate gender roles by identifying with parents and internalizing parental values, attitudes, traits, and personality characteristics.

24. Traditional concepts of gender roles are changing. Men are becoming more expressive and women more independent and assertive. What is emerging is a gradual mixing of male and female traits and roles to produce androgyny, which has advantages for both sexes.

25. There are few differences in the process used by persons of each gender to form an identity, although women and men often come to different decisions regarding sexual values and the relative importance of family and career.

KEY TERMS

alternating biculturalism 163	identity achieved 160
androgyny 170	identity control system 162
blended biculturalism 163	identity diffused 158
comparator 162	identity standards 162
expected selves 151	masculine 168
feared selves 151	moratorium 160
feminine 168	narcissism 154
foreclosure 159	negative identity 159
fusion 163	possible selves 151
gender 166	proprium 150
gender intensification hypothesis 170	role strain 153
gender roles 167	self 150
gender schema theory 167	self-concept 150
hoped-for selves 151	self-enhancement thesis 153
ideal self 151	self-esteem 150
identification 169	sex 166

THOUGHT QUESTIONS

Personal Reflection

1. In what ways does your concept of yourself differ from what you want it to be?

2. Have your feelings about yourself changed much as you have become older? Why or why not?

3. How do your parents feel about you? How do their views affect your feelings about yourself?

4. What events in your life have most influenced how you feel about yourself?

5. Everyone has an ethnic heritage. Is yours important to your identity and self-concept? Why or why not?

Group Discussion

6. In which of Marcia's identity statuses are most of your friends? Can you come up with specific issues for which they are in each of the four identity statuses?

7. Of the four possible ways in which ethnic group members can participate in a culturally diverse society (separation, assimilation, integration, and marginality), which one appeals most to you? Why do you think that that is the best way of participating in a culturally diverse society?

8. How do people learn sex-typed behavior according to (a) cognitive-developmental theory, (b) social learning theory, and (c) parental identification theory?

9. What changes should be made in traditional sex roles?

10. Will equality result in people having identical personalities and gender roles? Explain.

11. Do you think it is harder for women to find identity achievement than it is for men? Why or why not?

Debate Questions

12. All children should be encouraged to be androgynous.

13. There is no such thing as too much self-esteem.

14. Being an identity foreclosure is better than being identity diffused.

15. Society would benefit if Caucasian adolescents were encouraged to develop ethnic identities.

SUGGESTED READING

Gauntlett, D. (2008). *Media, Gender, and Identity: An Introduction,* 2nd ed. New York: Routledge.

Harter, S. (1999). *The Construction of the Self: A Developmental Perspective.* New York: Guilford Press.

Kimmel, M. (2000). *The Gendered Society.* Oxford, England: Oxford University Press.

Kimmel, M., and Aronson, A. (2003). *Men and Masculinities: A Social, Cultural, and Historical Encyclopedia.* Santa Barbara, CA: ABC-CLIO.

Kroger, J. (2000). *Identity Development: Adolescence through Adulthood.* Newbury Park, CA: Sage.

Leary, M. R., and Tangney, J. P. (Eds.). (2005). *Handbook of Self and Identity.* New York: Guilford Press.

Simon, B. (2004). *Identity in Modern Society: A Social Psychological Perspective.* Oxford, England: Blackwell.

Winters, L. I., and De Bose, H. L. (2002). *New Faces in a Changing America: Multiracial Identity in the 21st Century.* Thousand Oaks, CA: Sage.

USEFUL WEB SITES

National Association for Self-Esteem
www.self-esteem-nase.org

This Web site provides research summaries, a booklist, an online newsletter, and a discussion forum. It also contains pages directed toward parents who wish to ensure their children develop high self-esteem.

The Psi Café: Erik Erikson Page
www.psy.pdx.edu/PsiCafe/KeyTheorists/Erikson.htm

This Web page provides a good deal of information on Erik Erikson and his theory of identity formation. It provides multiple links to other pages.

WOULDN'T YOU LIKE TO KNOW . . .

- How is a child's moral thinking different from that of an adult?

- What can be said about the moral development of someone who bases his or her behavior on what other people think?

- Are truly moral people ever willing to break the law?

- Do men and women think differently about moral issues?

- Do teens and their parents often disagree about basic moral issues?

- What should parents do to help their children grow into moral adults?

- How religious are most American teenagers?

- Does watching violence on television really affect people?

- How commonly do students cheat on exams and papers?

The Development of Moral Values

This chapter discusses the development of moral judgments, behaviors, and values. I've moved this topic here in this edition, after the chapter on identity, to reflect my belief that morality and values are (or should be!) at the center of a person's sense of self. Your values should ideally guide many of the important decisions you make. For example, your sense of the importance of helping others could help determine whether you choose a career in social work, nursing, or education. Your beliefs about a person's responsibilities toward future generations might determine how diligently you work to "go green" and conserve resources. Your views on the acceptability of aggression might determine whether you purchase tickets to watch a professional boxing match or what decision you would come to if you ever serve on a jury. Morality regulates the way in which we behave toward others and how we expect them to behave toward us. Our moral code delineates both our rights and our responsibilities toward those around us.

The process by which adolescents develop moral judgment is extremely interesting. Jean Piaget, Lawrence Kohlberg, and Carol Gilligan all produced theories that emphasize the development of moral judgment as a cognitive process stimulated by the increasingly complex, changing social relationships of children as they get older. These stage theories have been gradually supplanted by the social-cognitive domain model of moral behavior, which emphasizes the multiple influences that direct moral decision making. Yet other researchers have concentrated on an examination of various family correlates that influence moral development. In this chapter, we discuss parental warmth, parent-teen interaction patterns, discipline, parental role models, and independence opportunities outside the home in relation to their influence on moral learning. The transmission of religious beliefs and practices from parents to children is also an important consideration and rests upon a number of religious and family variables. Finally, we examine the effects of other social influences, such as peer groups, television, and schools, on moral development. The effects of all these factors on the development of values and behavior are important and complex.

Cognitive-Socialization Theories of Development

The most important early research on the development of moral judgment was that of Piaget (1948) and Piaget and Inhelder (1969). Although some details of Piaget's findings have not been substantiated by subsequent research, his ideas formed the theoretical basis for many important later studies. Piaget's work was with children, but the theoretical framework that outlines his stages of development may be applied to adolescents and adults as well. It is important, therefore, to understand his discoveries.

Piaget and Children's Moral Development

Piaget's (1948) research into morality involved two types of studies. In one, he observed and questioned children about the need for rules when playing games: Could these rules be changed? If so, under what circumstances? In the second type of research, Piaget told children stories and required them to make moral judgments about the characters in them; for example, is a child more naughty if he or she intentionally breaks one cup or accidentally breaks several? On the basis of this work, Piaget uncovered quite a number of issues for which there was developmental change.

In studying children's attitudes about the rules of the game of marbles, Piaget concluded that there is first a **morality of constraint** and second a **morality of cooperation.** In the early stages of moral development, children are constrained by the rules of the game. These rules are coercive because children regard them as inviolable and because the rules reflect parental authority. Rules constitute a given order of existence and, like parents, must be obeyed without question. Later, as a result of social interaction, children learn that rules are not absolute; instead, they can be altered by social consensus. Rules are no longer external laws to be considered sacred because they are laid down by adults but are social creations arrived at through a process of free decision and consent.

Piaget's story-based research gave him additional insights into the reasoning behind children's moral judgments. He said that there are first judgments based solely on the consequences of wrongdoing (**objective judgments**) and later judgments that take into account intention or motive (**subjective judgments**). Therefore, whereas his younger subjects thought that the child who had accidentally broken several cups was more deserving of punishment than the one who had intentionally broken one cup, the older subjects did not.

Piaget (1948) spoke of children moving from a stage of **moral realism** to one of **moral relativism.** Moral realism is *received* morality, in which you do what authority figures tell you to do. You do not question—just obey. You think that rules are absolute and unchallengeable, and because you believe in the omniscience of those who make rules (parents, God, teachers), you believe that you will inevitably be caught and punished if you transgress. Piaget termed this **immanent justice.** Moral relativism, conversely, is both *independent* and *cooperative.* It is independent in the sense that you believe that you own your own moral beliefs; they come from within you, rather than having been given to you by others. It is cooperative in that it is based on mutual decisions made with others.

ANSWERS WOULDN'T YOU LIKE TO KNOW ...

How is a child's moral thinking different from that of an adult?

There are two major differences between the moral thinking of children and adults. One is that children believe that rules are set and unchangeable, whereas adults see rules as open to discussion and change. Children also believe that behaviors should be judged by their consequences, whereas adults are more likely to consider the intentions behind behaviors.

For example, if we all agree that the person who rolls the lowest number, not the highest number, on the dice should go first before we start playing a board game, there is no reason that the rule cannot be changed.

As children move toward moral realism, their conception of fairness changes. They begin to develop a sense of *reciprocity*. Initially, they come to believe in cooperation but only because they understand that they will benefit if they behave cooperatively. Ultimately, they appreciate that they should treat others as they wish to be treated because that is what is moral and correct.

Piaget (1948) believed that morality progresses because children are developing on two fronts. On one front, they are becoming smarter and more cognitively sophisticated. This increased thinking ability lets them consider alternatives, recognize inconsistencies, and better understand others so that they can experience empathy. On the other front, they are immersed in an ever more complicated social world. Whereas very young children interact mostly with adults, older children interact with peers as well. These interactions with age-mates provide more opportunities for cooperation and negotiation. When alone, with no adults present, groups of children make their own rules and set their own standards. Piaget believed that these kinds of interactions were crucial to the development of autonomous morality.

Although Piaget's conclusions were deduced from research with children up to age 12, they are relevant to the moral life of adolescents. It has been noted that Piaget said that children move from a morality of constraint (or obedience) to a morality of cooperation (or reciprocity), and they move from objective to subjective responsibility. Piaget has said that the second stage of moral development gradually supersedes the first as children grow older, and that by early adolescence individuals should be firmly in the stage of moral relativism.

Of course, there are adolescents and even adults who obey certain laws and rules only because of the threat of external punishment. They are constrained by authority, not by an inner conscience. If they break the rules, their concern is not remorse at doing wrong but at having been caught. In other words, they never move from a morality of constraint to a morality of cooperation. They remain, like young children, at an immature

stage of moral development, for the rules have never been internalized, and they never desire to do the right thing from mutual respect and concern for the feelings and welfare of others.

It is unreasonable, then, always to attach fixed age categories to the stages of moral development. There are children, adolescents, and adults at early stages of moral growth. This is one reason that Piaget's findings may be applied to adolescents as well as children.

Kohlberg's Levels of Moral Development

One of the principal deficiencies of Piaget's work was his exclusive concern with children up to age 12. Kohlberg compensated for this deficiency by using adolescents in a series of studies (e.g., Kohlberg, 1963, 1970; Kohlberg and Gilligan, 1971; Kohlberg and Turiel, 1972). Kohlberg greatly extended Piaget's work and over time developed his own theory of moral development.

Kohlberg's (1963) initial study included 72 boys ages 10, 13, and 16. All groups were similar in IQ; half of each group came from the upper middle class. Data were collected through taped interviews in which 10 moral dilemmas were presented to each boy. In each dilemma, acts of disobedience to legal-social rules or the commands of authority figures conflicted with human needs or the welfare of others. The most famous of Kohlberg's stories involves a man named Heinz:

> In Europe, a woman was near death from a very bad disease, a special kind of cancer. There was one drug the doctors thought might save her. It was a form of radium that a druggist in the same town had recently discovered. The drug was expensive to make, but the druggist was charging ten times what the drug cost him to make. He paid $200 for the radium and

morality of constraint   conduct that is coerced by rules or authority.

morality of cooperation   conduct that is regulated by mutual respect and consent.

objective judgments   judgments based solely on the consequences of wrongdoing.

subjective judgments   judgments that take into account intentions or motives.

moral realism   the earlier of Piaget's two stages of moral development, in which individuals slavishly follow the rules they are given.

moral relativism   the latter of Piaget's two stages of moral development, in which individuals make their own moral judgments rather than blindly follow rules.

immanent justice   the child's belief that immoral behavior inevitably brings pain or punishment as a natural consequence of the transgression.

charged $2,000 for a small dose of the drug. The sick woman's husband, Heinz, went to everyone he knew to borrow the money, but he could get together only about $1,000, which was half of what the drug cost. He told the druggist that his wife was dying and asked him to sell it cheaper or let him pay later. But the druggist said, "No, I discovered the drug and I'm going to make money from it." Heinz got desperate and broke into the man's store to steal the drug for his wife.

Should the husband have stolen the drug? Was doing so right or wrong? (Kohlberg, 1963)

Each boy was asked to select one of two acts as the more morally correct solution and was then questioned about the reasons for his choice. In this study, Kohlberg was concerned not with moral behavior but with moral judgment and the process of thought by which the individual made his judgment. There were no right or wrong answers; the individual was scored according to mode of reasoning, regardless of his conclusion.

From an analysis of the interviews, Kohlberg (1970), and then Kohlberg and Gilligan (1971), identified three major levels of moral development, each level having two stages of moral orientation or judgment. The levels and stages are outlined in Figure 7.1. Kohlberg found that Level I *preconventional moral reasoning* declined sharply from the younger to the older age groups. Level II *conventional moral reasoning* increased until age 13 and then stabilized. Level III *postconventional moral reasoning* was essentially absent during the teenage years. Figure 7.2 shows the mean percentage of moral reasoning at each stage for males through age 36.

In outlining his stages, however, Kohlberg was careful not to equate each type with a particular age. Within any one age group, individuals are at different levels of development in their moral thinking: some are delayed and others are advanced. Furthermore, no person fits neatly into any one of the six types. Kohlberg and Gilligan (1971) indicated that the development of moral

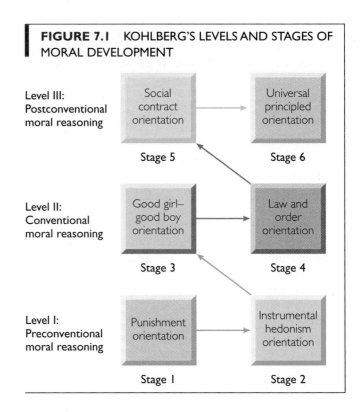

FIGURE 7.1   KOHLBERG'S LEVELS AND STAGES OF MORAL DEVELOPMENT

thought is a gradual and continuous process as the individual passes through a sequence of increasingly sophisticated moral stages.

The three major levels of morality are quite different from one another, whereas the two stages within each level are more similar. Let's consider each in turn.

Level I

Preconventional moral reasoning is characterized by selfishness—it is, in fact, premoral rather than moral. People acting at this level of moral reasoning are motivated by self-interest. They "look out for number one": what's good for them is good and to be embraced, and what's bad for them is bad and to be avoided. In Stage 1, the **punishment orientation,** people act so as to avoid negative consequences. They obey not

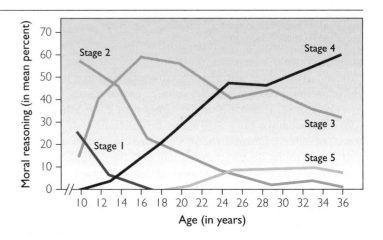

FIGURE 7.2   MORAL REASONING STAGE AND AGE LEVEL (FROM THE 20-YEAR LONGITUDINAL FOLLOW-UP OF KOHLBERG'S FIRST STUDY OF ADOLESCENT BOYS)

Source: From L. Kohlberg, *Moral Reasoning in Adolescence* (Boston: Allyn and Bacon, 1994), p. 200. Copyright © 1994 Pearson Education. Used with permission.

because of guilt or the desire to be nice but because they are afraid they will get into trouble if they don't. When presented with the Heinz dilemma, someone in Stage 1 might answer, "Heinz was foolish to steal the drug; if he had gotten caught, he would have surely gone to prison." He or she could also say, "Of course Heinz should have taken the drug. Think how miserable he would have been if his wife had died." These different responses illustrate that for most of the stages, it does not matter whether a person believes Heinz should or should not have taken the drug; rather, what matters is the explanation used to justify the decision.

When in the higher of the two preconventional stages—Stage 2, the **instrumental hedonism orientation**—people are motivated by the thought of payback and future gain. They do favors with the thought that favors will be returned. They obey because there is more gain than harm in doing so. An instrumental hedonist would think that Heinz should have taken the drug, reasoning that "If he saved his wife, think how grateful she would be. She'd treat him like a king forever." Almost all children are preconventional moral reasoners, as are many, if not most, young adolescents.

Level II

People at the **conventional moral reasoning** level of Kohlberg's sequence act so as to gain others' approval. They do what others think is right. In the lower of the two stages, Stage 3, or the **good girl–good boy orientation,** those others are family members, friends, teachers, coworkers, and other people important to the individual. Should Heinz have taken the drug? Of course not: "Think how embarrassed his family must have been when he got caught and his name was in the newspaper." On the other hand, maybe his action was justified: "His children must have been so proud that he was so brave and risked himself to save his wife."

Those in the **law and order orientation,** Stage 4, have a broader, more abstract conception of the term *others.* They are concerned with what members of society at large will say about their conduct, not just with how their circle of acquaintances will respond. They are motivated to follow rules and obey laws because that is

what *others* have said is correct and moral. It is hard to imagine an individual in Stage 4 saying that Heinz should have stolen the medicine. A far more typical response would be: "Of course he shouldn't have taken the drug! It's against the law to steal! If everyone broke the law anytime it was convenient for them to do so, we'd have chaos and anarchy! None of us would be safe!" Most adolescents—and in fact, most adults—are conventional moral reasoners.

Level III

The highest level of moral reasoning, **postconventional moral reasoning,** occurs when people don't necessarily do what is best for themselves or what others think they should do but instead do what they believe is right and just. This is also termed *principled moral reasoning.* During the first of the two principled stages—Stage 5, **social contract orientation**—individuals understand that the purpose of rules and laws is to serve the greater societal good. At this stage, individuals define morality in terms of general principles such as individual rights, human dignity, equality, and mutual obligation. They believe that if a law doesn't further these aims, it should be changed. Stage 5 moral reasoners believe in *extenuating circumstances:* factors that allow one to violate a rule for valid moral grounds. They believe in following the spirit of the law. (In contrast, Stage 4 moral reasoners believe in following the letter of the law.) A Stage 5 moral reasoner might respond to the Heinz scenario by saying: "Stealing is wrong, but

preconventional moral reasoning   according to Kohlberg, the first level of development of moral thought, based on reward and punishment.

punishment orientation   the more primitive level of preconventional moral reasoning, in which one acts so as to avoid negative consequences.

instrumental hedonism orientation   the more advanced of the two preconventional reasoning levels, in which one acts so as to gain a future reward.

conventional moral reasoning   according to Kohlberg, the second level of development of moral thought, based on the desire to conform to social convention.

good girl–good boy orientation   the first of the two levels of conventional moral reasoning, in which one acts so as to win others' approval.

law and order orientation   the more advanced type of conventional moral reasoning, in which one unquestioningly obeys society's rules and laws.

postconventional moral reasoning   according to Kohlberg, the third level of development of moral thought, based on adherence to universal principles.

social contract orientation   the type of postconventional moral reasoning in which one believes that individual actions should serve the greater good.

allowing someone to die is worse. The law shouldn't apply in this circumstance. Heinz did the right thing." The U.S. Declaration of Independence and Constitution both reflect a social contract morality.

Kohlberg originally included a sixth stage of moral reasoning in his scheme, that of **universal principled reasoning.** This type of reasoner behaves so as to avoid self-condemnation. The approach to moral issues is based not on selfish needs or conformity to the existing social order but on autonomous, universal principles of justice that are valid beyond existing laws, social conditions, and peers' valves. Thus, individuals governed by universal ethical principles may break unjust civil laws because they recognize a morality higher than existing law.

The Reverend Martin Luther King Jr. (1964) eloquently expressed Kohlberg's highest form of moral reasoning in his letter from a Birmingham jail:

> I do not advocate evading or defying the law. . . . That would lead to anarchy. One who breaks an unjust law must do so openly, lovingly, and with a willingness to accept the penalty. An individual who breaks the law that conscience tells him is unjust, and willingly accepts the penalty of imprisonment in order to arouse the conscience of the community over its injustice is, in reality, expressing the highest respect for the law. (p. 86)

Since very few persons employ Stage 6 moral reasoning, Kohlberg stopped discussing it in his later writings.

The Relation Between Kohlberg's Stages and Thinking Ability

Since Kohlberg's theory is concerned with moral reasoning, it follows that advances in overall reasoning ability should open the door to higher levels of moral thought. Thus, there should be a relationship between cognitive level and moral reasoning. Kohlberg (Kuhn, Langer, Kohlberg, et al., 1977) believed that a high level of cognitive development was necessary for a high level of moral reasoning. He thought that advanced reasoning skills were necessary *but not sufficient* to ensure sophisticated moral reasoning. In other words, you must be able to think in a mature way to be a postconventional moral reasoner, but having mature thought processes does not guarantee this outcome.

ANSWERS WOULDN'T YOU LIKE TO KNOW ...

Are truly moral people ever willing to break the law?

Yes. Truly moral people *are* willing to break the law if they believe the law is unjust and violates their moral principles. Whereas immoral people break the law for their own benefit, moral people break the law to benefit others.

Was Kohlberg correct in making this argument? It appears so. Cognitive level and moral reasoning level are certainly correlated (e.g., Walker & Henning, 1997). In addition, researchers who have attempted to train children to morally reason above their cognitive level have failed in their efforts (e.g., Walker & Richards, 1979). Still, some who study moral development believe that the influence between cognitive development and moral development is more bidirectional: that each influences the other. These researchers (e.g., Gibbs, 2003) believe that children and adolescents can develop new cognitive capabilities if they continually grapple with difficult moral dilemmas.

One construct that has received little attention in the moral development literature is **metacognition.** Metacognition, or knowing about knowing, refers to insights children have about their own cognitive processes. By analogy to the discussions of metacognition, *moral metacognition* would refer to the knowledge that children have about their own morality. One investigation described the relationship between metamoral knowledge, moral reasoning, and moral behavior in three age groups: adolescents in grades 7, 9, and 12 (Swanson & Hill, 1993). These researchers found that older children had more accurate understanding of moral judgmental processes than did younger children and that the higher levels of moral metacognition were closely tied to more advanced moral reasoning and behavior. In regard to moral judgment, the researchers assumed and found that children who were better able to think about their moral reasoning processes were more likely to be aware of inconsistencies in this reasoning and were also more likely to attempt to resolve these inconsistencies. Likewise, moral metacognition affected behavior in that children who were better able to reason about their actions were more likely to recognize moral aspects of their behavior and thus employ moral reasoning in formulating plans for that behavior. Finally, moral metacognition served as a correlate between moral action and moral reasoning and as a prerequisite to using moral judgment to direct one's actions.

A more recent research study has succeeded in linking moral reasoning with epistemological development. (If you don't recall what that is, refer back to Chapter 5.) Krettenauer (2004) questioned 200 German seventh-through thirteenth-graders about their beliefs as to the certainty of moral judgments, whether they perceived moral judgments as relative or absolute, the reasons they believed justified changes in moral beliefs, and the kinds of information that should be taken into account when making moral assessments. Most of the subjects were quite consistent in their responses, falling neatly into one of the established epistemological categories. Krettenauer's youngest subjects were primarily *intuitionists*, or "realists" as they were termed in Chapter 5. They believed that moral judgments were either right or wrong, that you "just know" whether something is moral or not, and that you should listen to experts. High schoolers were primarily *subjectivists*, or "skeptics." They believed that moral judgments were completely subjective and that no moral position was more valid than any other. *Transsubjectivism*, or "post-skeptical rationalism," emerged gradually after ninth grade. Transsubjectivists believed that moral judgments are more or less well founded, that all views are somewhat subjective, and that one should adjust one's views according to all of the available evidence.

Criticisms of Kohlberg's Theory

Criticisms of Kohlberg's theory raise three issues: (1) whether his stages are universal among humans or limited to people in Western cultures, (2) whether moral reasoning should be conceptualized as stagelike, and (3) whether his ideas are gender biased.

Are Kohlberg's Stages Universal?   Kohlberg emphasized that a stage concept implies universality of sequence under varying cultural conditions (Jensen, 1995). That is, the development of moral judgment is not merely a matter of learning the rules of a particular culture but instead reflects a universal process of development. In order to test this hypothesis, Kohlberg (1966) used his technique with boys 10, 13, and 16 years old in a Taiwanese city, in a Malaysian (Atayal) aboriginal tribal village, and in a Turkish village, as well as in Great Britain, Canada, and the United States. The results indicated similar age trends across nationalities.

More recent studies with children and adolescents have confirmed these findings. Gibbs, Basinger, Grime, et al. (2007) reviewed 75 moral development studies conducted in 23 diverse nations and concluded that Stages 1 through 4 appeared universally. Furthermore, they found that Stage 3 reasoning typically emerges during early adolescence and is the most common form of moral reasoning by late adolescence. However, although these earlier stages showed a similar sequence of development in all cultures, the last two stages of moral thought—which normally do not emerge until adulthood—do not develop clearly in preliterate village or tribal communities (Snarey, 1995). Principled moral reasoning develops only when individuals are exposed to differing, conflicting points of view. Therefore, cross-cultural studies indicate that only those societies that have been urbanized or that provide formal education are likely to have citizens who develop principled moral reasoning (De Mey, Baartman, & Schulze, 1999).

In addition, some cultures have values that put them into conflict with Kohlberg's hierarchy. Persons raised in collectivist societies—those that emphasize each individual's responsibilities to the others around him or her—tend to find structural, macro-explanations for Kohlberg's dilemmas and do not blame the specific characters in the scenarios (Miller, 1997). For example,

someone raised in such a culture might say that the problem lay not with Heinz but with the fact that he was placed in an awkward position because of such a limited supply of the drug.

Is Moral Development Stagelike?   In order to term any type of development *stagelike*, it must meet two criteria. First, the stages must be finite and consistent; for instance, someone must be either in Stage 1 or in Stage 2, not waffling back and forth between them. Second, the stages must emerge in an invariant, progressive sequence; Stage 1 must always come before Stage 2, Stage 2 must always come before Stage 3, and so on. Does moral reasoning meet these two criteria?

From early on, the data (even Kohlberg's own data) have indicated that people do *not* give consistent moral responses to Kohlberg's dilemmas (Boyes, Giordano, & Galperyn, 1993) nor do they always move upward through his sequence. Kohlberg and Kramer (1969), for example, found that many of their participants regressed from Stage 4 to Stage 2 over time. In fact, a number of studies have found that premoral reasoning reemerges in mid- and late-adolescence, especially in circumstances in which personal cost is high (e.g., Eisenberg, 1998). In addition, when newer, alternative methods are used to test moral thought, individuals' answers tend to be inconsistent and dependent on the context of the situation (Smetana & Turiel, 2003).

Critics have also argued that it is not correct or fair to say that the higher the stage, the greater the level of morality (e.g., Callahan & Callahan, 1981). Stage 6 reflects liberal and radical political reasoning. Does this mean that liberals are more advanced morally than conservatives? There is little basis in empirical fact to conclude that this is so.

The most pervasive and serious challenge to Kohlberg's theory, however, is that it is biased against females.

Gilligan and Gender Differences in Moral Reasoning

Carol Gilligan (1977), an associate of Kohlberg, pointed out that Kohlberg conducted his research about moral development on male subjects. The scoring method was developed from male responses, and some of the later research using this scoring system indicated that females used lower levels of moral reasoning than males. (They were more likely to

universal principled reasoning   the highest form of moral reasoning, in which one acts according to his or her abstract moral principles.

metacognition   the ability to think about one's own thought processes.

IN THEIR OWN WORDS

"I was really blown away when I read Carol Gilligan's work. In my house, my mother is a doormat: She cooks and cleans and fixes everyone else's problems. She puts up with my brother being rude to her. She always asks everyone else what they want; it's never about what she wants. My family all praise her all the time and say what a great mother she is, and so I grew up thinking that this is what you were supposed to do for your husband and kids. So ... this is how I used to act toward my boyfriends. We'd hang with their friends and do what they wanted to do. During the past few years, I've started to think that I never wanted to get married—I mean, why be someone else's slave? It was terrific to read that it's OK to put limits on what you give to other people."

remain in Stage 3 than to move on to Stage 4.) Gilligan did not believe that females' level of moral judgment is lower than that of males but instead that the test results reflected the fact that females approach moral issues from a different perspective than males. Men emphasize justice—preserving rights, rules, and principles. Women emphasize concern and care for others and sensitivity to their feelings and rights. Women emphasize responsibility to human beings rather than to abstract principles. Thus, in her words, men and

women speak with two different voices (Gilligan, 1982). In summarizing six studies, including four that were longitudinal, Gilligan (1984) concluded that men rely more heavily on a justice orientation, and women on a caring orientation.

As a result of the difference in the way men and women think, Gilligan proposed a female alternative to Kohlberg's stages of moral reasoning. Table 7.1 compares Kohlberg's and Gilligan's levels.

At Level I, women are preoccupied with self-interest and survival, which requires obeying restrictions placed on them. Gradually, they become aware of the differences between what they want (selfishness) and what they ought to do (responsibility). This leads to Level II, in which the need to please others takes precedence over self-interest. The woman becomes responsible for caring for others, even sacrificing her own preferences. Gradually, she begins to wonder whether she can fulfill the needs of others and still remain true to herself. Still, she does not give her own needs full equality with those of others. At Level III, which many never attain, the woman develops a universal perspective, in which she no longer sees herself as submissive and powerless but active in decision making. She becomes concerned about the consequences for all, herself included, in making decisions.

Gilligan's work is not without its own critics. Many researchers have concluded that Kohlberg's tests are not, in fact, biased against women (e.g., Greeno & Maccoby, 1986). And although numerous studies have verified the

TABLE 7.1   KOHLBERG'S VERSUS GILLIGAN'S UNDERSTANDING OF MORAL DEVELOPMENT

KOHLBERG'S LEVELS AND STAGES	KOHLBERG'S DEFINITIONS	GILLIGAN'S LEVELS
Level I: Preconventional morality		**Level I: Preconventional morality**
Stage 1: Punishment orientation	Obey rules to avoid punishment	Concern for the self and survival
Stage 2: Instrumental hedonism orientation	Obey rules to get rewards, share in order to get returns	
Level II: Conventional morality		**Level II: Conventional morality**
Stage 3: Good girl–good boy orientation	Conform to rules that are defined by others' approval/disapproval	Concern for being responsible, caring for others
Stage 4: Law and order orientation	Rigid conformity to society's rules, law-and-order mentality, avoid censure for rule-breaking	
Level III: Postconventional morality		**Level III: Postconventional morality**
Stage 5: Social contract orientation	More flexible understanding that we obey rules because they are necessary for social order, but the rules could be changed if there were better alternatives	Concern for self and others as interdependent
Stage 6: Universal principled orientation	Behavior conforms to internal principles (justice, equality) to avoid self-condemnation, and sometimes may violate society's rules	

Source: Adapted from J. S. Hyde, Half the Human Experience (Lexington, MA: D. C. Heath, 1985). Reprinted with permission from Cengage.

existence of a caring moral orientation, it appears that both males and females use legalistic as well as caring reasoning (Wark & Krebs, 1996), with women utilizing caring somewhat more than men (Jaffee & Hyde, 2000). Any gender differences that appear are often due to the content of the dilemma that is chosen for discussion, with females selecting scenarios that are more personal (Walker, 2006). Since both women and men exhibit more of a caring orientation when speaking of personal concerns and more of a legalistic orientation when speaking of impersonal issues, this could account for the gender differences found in some studies. Perhaps, too, Gilligan's open-ended interview technique—which required much interpretation on the part of the researcher—allowed her own biases to accentuate gender differences rather than gender similarities (Colby & Damon, 1983).

The Social-Cognitive Domain Approach to Moral Reasoning

As a result of the problems with the stage theories described in the previous sections (especially that individuals don't proceed through the stages in a consistent fashion), a new approach to moral thinking has emerged. This **social-cognitive domain model** goes beyond moral reasoning per se and analyzes social reasoning more broadly, but much of what its proponents discuss is relevant to moral development (Killen, Lee-Kim, McGlothlin, et al., 2002). Whereas Piaget believed that a rule was a rule was a rule and that all rules are moral in nature, we now know that not all rules are treated equivalently by children, adolescents, and adults.

The social-cognitive domain model holds that there are three types of rules, only one of which is similar to

those studied by Piaget and Kohlberg (Turiel, 1998). That type of rule is a **moral rule,** which has to do with how people should behave toward each other; it is not okay, for example, for people to hurt one another. The second type of rule is a **social convention.** Such a rule has been agreed on by everyone and helps ensure that society runs smoothly; it guarantees that people know what to expect from one another. Social conventions are less universal in nature than moral rules. For example, in some cultures, it is considered impolite to burp after eating; to do so signals disrespect for those around you. In other cultures, burping after a meal is seen as a sign that the food was ample and delicious; it indicates respect for the food that your host prepared. Both moral rules and social conventions serve to regulate social interactions, but they have different essences. It is worse to transgress against a moral rule than a social convention. Finally, the third type of rule is a **personal preference.** This type of rule governs behaviors that are in the private sphere. No one else has the right to tell you how to behave in the personal domain. The color of clothing you like to wear, your taste in music, and the length of your hair are all personal preferences. From an early age, children can distinguish among these three types of rules (Smetana & Turiel, 2003).

The social-cognitive domain approach emphasizes that social decisions are complex and that individuals must often juggle moral, social, and personal concerns when making decisions. The context in which a decision is made and the weight given to each factor is what determines moral judgment, not the identification of a stage of reasoning. If adolescents seem to regress in moral development, it is because they weigh these competing factors differently as they age (Killen, Lee-Kim, McGlothlin, et al., 2002).

Adolescents tend to believe that adults have the right to make rules about truly moral behavior and that those rules should be obeyed (Smetana, 1995; Smetana & Turiel, 2003). Adults are allowed, however, to make and enforce moral rules only in their own sphere of influence; teachers, for example, are not allowed to tell youths how to behave outside of school. Parents and adolescents rarely argue about topics they agree involve basic moral issues—such as whether it is alright to steal or

social-cognitive domain model an approach to moral development that stresses the contextual nature of moral decisions and distinguishes social conventions from moral rules.

moral rules social rules that are concerned with how people behave toward one another.

social conventions social rules that dictate what is appropriate and expected.

personal preferences aspects of behavior that involve independent choices with which others have no right to interfere.

cheat—but adolescents have much less respect than adults for social conventions. Early adolescents view social conventions as ways for authority figures to needlessly control adolescent behavior, and late adolescents see social conventions as superfluous, old-fashioned societal expectations (Smetana & Turiel, 2003). Parents and their adolescent children also frequently disagree as to whether an issue should be considered a personal choice or a social convention, and as an adolescent ages, he or she is more likely to believe that an issue falls into the realm of personal choice (Smetana, Crean, & Campione-Barr, 2005). A teenager, for example, may think that wearing revealing clothing is in the personal realm, whereas her parents may believe that doing so violates social norms. Adolescents universally agree—even those in traditional, non-Western cultures—that parents do not have the right to interfere in their personal choices (Smetana, 2002). Their parents, of course, often disagree with this premise.

Moral Reasoning and Prosocial Behavior

As the previous sections have indicated, most of the early research about morality focused on *moral reasoning*—the ability to make correct moral decisions. Although many studies are still being conducted about the development of moral-reasoning skills, the field has expanded to include the study of prosocial behavior. **Prosocial behavior** consists of actions that benefit, help, and bolster others; it is the opposite of antisocial behavior. Examples of prosocial behavior include complimenting a friend, doing a favor for a neighbor, helping a parent wash the dishes, and volunteering to clean up a local park.

There is a strong link between moral reasoning and prosocial behavior, but they don't always go together. On one hand, someone may make a good moral decision but then not carry through and act on it because of laziness, fear, or vested interest. Thus, good moral decision making is necessary but not sufficient to promote prosocial behavior. On the other hand, people can be selfishly motivated to act prosocially. For instance, an adolescent boy might help his dad fix the car only so that he can borrow it or help a friend with her math homework today so that she will help him with chemistry next week. Still, there is no doubt that people are more likely to behave in a prosocial manner if they are good moral reasoners (Eisenberg, Carlo, Murphy, et al., 1995).

Fabes and Carlo and their colleagues collected and summarized the major factors that influence adolescents' tendencies to perform prosocial and moral behaviors (Carlo, Fabes, Laible, et al., 1999; Fabes, Carlo, Kupanoff, et al., 1999):

1. *Pubertal status:* Postpubertal adolescents are larger and stronger, and so more actions are open to them. Also, with puberty come feelings of sexual

Adolescents who have attained higher levels of moral maturity are less selfish than their more immature peers. Moral maturity may be expressed in a desire to help others.

arousal and romantic love, both of which might prompt prosocial or antisocial actions.

2. *Perspective taking:* Cognitive maturation, combined with new kinds of experiences, allows adolescents to better understand others' points of view (Bosacki, 2003).

3. *Moral reasoning:* The more advanced an adolescent's moral-reasoning skills, the more likely he or she will make moral decisions.

4. *Empathy:* The more an adolescent can feel empathic toward others, the more likely he or she will engage in both moral and prosocial actions.

5. *Personality:* Anger-prone individuals are more likely to behave antisocially (Carlo, Roesch, & Melby, 1998).

6. *High self-esteem:* Adolescents who like themselves are more likely to behave prosocially than those who do not (Lerner, Lerner, Almerigi, et al., 2005).

7. *Family relationships:* Having a supportive family background promotes moral development.

8. *Peer relationships:* Peers can encourage either prosocial or antisocial actions.

9. *Schooling:* School size, class size, and school climate can influence prosocial tendencies. Schooling encourages the development of higher levels of moral reasoning.

10. *Culture and ethnicity:* Adolescents are influenced by the norms and values of their cultures. For example, in one study of British and Chinese adolescents, the Chinese teens were more likely to risk their lives to save someone else than were the British teens (Ma, 1989).

In addition, the neural systems that control how individuals respond to social stimuli (such as facial expressions) mature during adolescence, providing new abilities to make subtle discriminations as to others' feelings and needs (Nelson, Leibenluft, McClure, et al., 2005).

Several of these issues are discussed more in the following sections; others are discussed in later chapters.

How does prosocial functioning change from childhood into adolescence and then during adolescence itself? There are reasons to believe that it should increase (Eisenberg, Cumberland, Guthrie, et al., 2005). First, adolescents consider selfish behavior inappropriate and immature (Galambos, Barker, & Tilton-Weaver, 2003). Second, prosocial reasoning has long been linked with the ability to empathize and take another's point of view, and we know that perspective-taking abilities increase well into adolescence (Eisenberg, 1986). Third, cognitive development allows adolescents to increasingly empathize *abstractly* with those they do not know and those who are different from themselves, thus broadening their motivation to perform altruistic actions (Hoffman, 2000). For, as just discussed, moral reasoning itself improves as individuals mature, making it more likely that adolescents will make prosocial rather than selfish decisions.

Recent research has shown that some but not all aspects of prosocial functioning improve from childhood into adolescence (Eisenberg, Morris, McDaniel, et al., 2009). In particular, the willingness to share and display empathy toward others increases, but the tendencies to offer comfort or to actually help others do not. The evidence that prosocial behavior improves from childhood through mid-adolescence is not strong: it appears only in lab studies (not naturalistic observations) and only when the target of the concern is a child, not an adult. Similarly, as adolescents move from mid- to late adolescence, and from late adolescence into early adulthood, their prosocial tendencies improve in some ways but not in others. Although prosocial moral reasoning and perspective taking do show development, helping behavior itself actually declines in the early twenties. Sympathetic responses do not always lead to systematic changes. Still, individuals show reasonable rank order consistency over time (Eisenberg, Guthrie, Cumberland, et al., 2002); in other words, a person who is a highly prosocial child will be a high prosocial adolescent and adult, whereas a person who is selfish as a child will remain so.

Family Factors and Moral Learning

The Family's Role

Studies of family socialization have demonstrated repeatedly that parents have a tremendous impact on the development of their children. Parents play a fundamental role in the development of their children's basic social, religious, and political values and in encouraging them to adopt prosocial actions and empathetic responses to those in distress (e.g., Eisenberg & Murphy, 1995). Much of the important research about the moral development of children and adolescents emphasizes the importance of parents and the family in the total process. A number of family factors correlate significantly with moral learning:

- The degree of parental warmth, acceptance, mutual esteem, and trust shown the child
- The frequency and intensity of parent-teen interaction and communication
- The type and degree of discipline used
- The role model parents offer the child
- The independence opportunities the parents provide

Each of these factors deserves elaboration. (For additional information on parent-adolescent relationships, see Chapter 8.)

Parental Acceptance and Trust

One important aid to moral learning is a warm, accepting relationship of mutual trust and esteem between parent and child. Young children who are emotionally dependent on their parents and have a strong emotional attachment to them develop strong consciences, whereas nondependent children grow up more lacking in consciences (Eisenberg & McNally, 1993).

There are a number of explanations for the correlation between parental warmth and moral learning. In a warm, emotional context, respected parents are likely to be admired and imitated by youths, resulting in similar positive traits in the adolescents. Youths learn consideration for others by being cared for, loved, and trusted by their parents (Pratt, Hunsberger, Pancer, et al., 2003). In fact, supportive parenting not only encourages moral beliefs, it also is most likely to instill **moral courage,** the tendency to stand up for one's values in the face of opposition (Eisenberg, Morris, McDaniel, et al., 2009).

prosocial behavior actions that benefit, help, and bolster others.

moral courage the ability to stand up for one's values, especially those concerning fairness.

Frequency and Intensity of Parent-Teen Communication

Role-modeling theory maintains that the degree of identification of the child with the parent varies with the amount of interaction the child has with the parent. Frequent interaction offers opportunities for the communication of meaningful values and norms, especially if the exchange is democratic and mutual. A one-sided form of authoritarian interaction results in poor communication and less learning for the adolescent. It is important, therefore, for the channels of communication between parents and youths to be kept open. Certain types of communication appear to be especially good at fostering moral reasoning. Research has discovered, for example, that fathers who engage in Vygotskian/Socratic–style "transactive dialogues" with their adolescents—who push their thinking by challenging their reasoning—have adolescents who are more morally advanced than their peers (Pratt, Arnold, Pratt, et al., 1999).

Type of Discipline

Research on the influence of parental discipline on the moral learning of youths indicates that discipline has the most positive effect when it is (1) consistent rather than erratic; (2) accomplished primarily through clear, verbal explanations to develop internal controls rather than through external, physical means; (3) just and fair and avoids harsh, punitive measures; and (4) democratic rather than permissive or authoritarian (Zelkowitz, 1987).

One of the most important requirements is that discipline be consistent, both *intraparent* (within one parent) and *interparent* (between two parents). Erratic parental expectations lead to an ambiguous environment and thus to poor moral learning, anxiety, confusion, disobedience, and sometimes hostility and delinquency in the adolescent.

Parents who rely on clear, rational, verbal explanations to influence and control behavior—induction—have a more positive effect than those who use power assertion (Lopez, Bonenberger, & Schneider, 2001). This is primarily because cognitive methods result in the internalization of values and standards, especially if explanations are combined with affection so that the adolescent is inclined to listen and accept them. Reasoning or praise used to correct or reinforce behavior enhances learning, whereas physical means of discipline, negative verbal techniques such as belittling and nagging, or infrequent explanations are more often associated with antisocial behavior and delinquency.

Parents who rely on harsh, punitive methods are defeating the true purposes of discipline: to develop a sensitive conscience, to socialize, and to foster cooperation (Hoffman, 1994). Cruel punishment, especially when accompanied by parental rejection, develops an insensitive, uncaring, hostile, rebellious, unkind person. Instead of teaching children to care about others, it deadens their sensitivities, so that they learn to fear and hate others and no longer care about them or want to please them. They may obey, but when the threat of external punishment is removed, they are antisocial.

Parents who are overly permissive also retard the moral development of their children (Boyes & Allen, 1993), for they give the children no help in developing inner controls. Without external

Although no one involved enjoys it, parents must sometimes discipline their adolescent children. The best kind of discipline involves a clear explanation as to why a certain behavior is unacceptable. When handled correctly, these interactions can enhance youths' moral development.

Extrafamilial Influences on Morality

Peers

Sets of adolescent friends tend to behave in similar ways. This is true in regard to prosocial and antisocial behavior as well as to more morally neutral behaviors. Given this, there is great societal concern about the degree to which peers influence one another to engage in risky or deviant acts such as drug use and delinquency. In fact, many youth intervention programs incorporate *peer-resistance training* as part of their curricula. Although this similarity among peers is caused, in part, by the fact that adolescents choose friends akin to themselves, it can also be explained by how peers directly and indirectly influence one another's actions.

Brown and Theobald (1999) have identified four ways that peers can influence one another's behavior: (1) peer pressure, (2) normative expectations, (3) structuring opportunities, and (4) modeling. Sometimes, all four of these forces act at once. For example, consider the case of a teenage girl, Lori, who had recently moved to a new high school and made a new group of friends. When they went to the movies together on a Friday night, Lori was in for a shock. She discovered that her new friends never paid for the movies they watched. Instead, they would pool their money and buy one girl a ticket; she would legitimately enter the theater and then hold open an out-of-the-way door, through which the other girls would enter. Lori felt stuck, because although she disapproved of her friends' behavior, they clearly thought it was normal (normative expectations), they had worked out the means to avoid paying and did this weekly (opportunity), they all took turns entering illegally (modeling), and they gave her a hard time when she refused to join in (peer pressure).

Peers can encourage one another to engage in positive, prosocial actions as well. In fact, there is a reciprocal relationship between peers and prosocial activities: peers can encourage doing good deeds, and doing good deeds can make one more popular with peers (Wentzel & McNamara, 1999). Since, contrary to stereotype, peers more often encourage and facilitate prosocial rather than antisocial behavior, the more close friends an adolescent has, the higher his or her level moral reasoning is likely to be (Schonert-Reichl, 1999).

Religion

Religion certainly plays an important part in the lives of many Americans, including adolescents, and it is one avenue through which adolescents can learn a

---

authority, the child will remain amoral. Adolescents want and need some parental guidance. Without it, they may grow up to be spoiled brats, disliked by their peers because of their lack of consideration for others, and lacking self-discipline, persistence, and direction.

Parental Role Models

It is important for parents to be moral people themselves if they are to offer positive role models for their children to follow. Children—even adolescent children—have a natural tendency to copy their mothers' and fathers' behaviors. And so no matter what parents may say about honesty, if they are observed cheating on their taxes, stealing a tip that was left on a table for a waiter, or walking out of a store knowing that they were given too much change, they will be teaching their children to be dishonest. Adolescents are much more likely than children to recognize and be affected by adult hypocrisy, and so it is even more important for parents to model moral behavior as their children get older. Parents can also encourage positive, prosocial actions in their children by behaving in caring, generous ways. Talk is not enough.

Opportunities for Independence

The number and kinds of opportunities that parents give their children to make independent moral judgments also affect moral development. As we discussed in Chapter 5 (the cognitive development chapter), making good decisions of any sort is a learned skill, for which practice is required. Adolescents need to be given chances to make decisions that affect their moral behavior and then to observe the results of their actions.

Of course, parents who provide too much independence—that is, who fail to monitor their children and provide guidance—cause their children to look to outsiders for moral guidance. A charismatic peer, for example, might encourage antisocial behavior. External forces of all sorts have greater impact if a moral vacuum is created by parental neglect and indifference.

Some adolescents engage in decidedly antisocial actions, often because of the influence of peers. Youths may turn to peers as a reaction against parental neglect and rejection.

moral code. What determines how religious an adolescent is? Which religion is he or she likely to follow? How religious is the average adolescent? Does religion influence adolescents to behave more morally? We will try to answer these questions in the sections that follow.

What Determines How Religious an Adolescent Is?
The main determinant of an adolescent's religiosity is the strength and quality of the relationship with his or her family (Ream & Savin-Williams, 2003). Religious parents are the ones most likely to raise religious offspring (King, Elder, & Whitbeck, 1997). Religious parents tend to expose their children to religion (whether the children want this or not) by making them attend religious services and Sunday school (Ozarak, 1989). Doing so provides the children with a sense of familiarity and comfort that facilitates their continued religiosity

in later life. Children are most likely to become religious if their parents practice the same faith than if they are of different faiths (Myers, 1996). Harmonious homes, in which the parents are nurturing and there is little parent-child or spousal conflict, tend to produce the most religious children (King & Furrow, 2004). Mothers appear to influence their adolescents' religious beliefs more than fathers (Boyatzis, Dollahite, & Marks, 2006).

Gender, race/ethnicity, place of residence, and denomination also influence religiosity. Girls are more religious than boys over a wide range of measures (Smith & Denton, 2005). African American teens are more likely to be religious than teens of other races and ethnic groups. Adolescents from the southern states are, as a group, more religious than adolescents from other parts of the United States. Teens who belong to theologically conservative churches are more likely to claim that religion is important to them than are those who are either Catholic or belong to more liberal Protestant denominations (Smith, Faris, & Denton, 2003).

Which Religion Are Adolescents Likely to Follow?
Adolescents who have a close relationship with their parents usually remain in the faith in which they were raised, maintaining their parents' religion. Rejection

of parents' religious values is often symptomatic of a strained parent-adolescent relationship (Dudley, 1999). In fact, adolescents who convert to a different religion may do so because they crave forming a close attachment—something that seems to have been lacking in their lives (Streib, 1999). Additionally, adolescents may change faiths because they believe that their current faith is not adequately helping them cope with their problems (Ream & Savin-Williams, 2003).

How Religious Is the Average Adolescent?

According to a major study, American teenagers are fairly religious (Smith, Faris, & Denten, 2003). About 60 percent say that religion is either "very" or "pretty" important to them. Eighty percent pray at least some of the time; 40 percent report daily prayer. Very few appear to be disaffected from religion. Only about 10 percent say that churches are doing a poor job serving the nation, and only about 20 percent would like to see religion exert less influence on society. All of these figures have remained nearly constant over the past 25 years, and so there is little basis on which to claim that today's teens are any more or less religious than those of one or two generations ago.

Nonetheless, as people move into their late teens and early twenties and leave home, their religious participation tends to decline (Gallup & Lindsey, 1999) and doubts increase (Levenson, Aldwin, & D'Mello, 2005). For most individuals, this lapse is temporary. Once they marry, have children, and become a part of a permanent community, their religious affiliation will again increase (Stolzenberg, Blair-Loy, & Waite, 1995).

Does Religion Influence Adolescents' Moral Behavior?

The majority of research suggests that religion has a positive effect on adolescent behavior (Smith, 2003). For example, religious youths have been found to be less likely to drink or use drugs than their less-religious counterparts (Barkowski & Xu, 2007), and they also appear to engage less in other types of delinquent behavior, such as vandalism or fighting (Regnerus & Elder, 2003). Religious teens tend to be less sexually active and to have fewer sexual partners than nonreligious teens (Regnerus, Smith, & Fritsch, 2003). In addition to protecting against harmful behaviors, religiosity also promotes positive, prosocial

concerns (Furrow, King, & White, 2004). It is associated with good academic achievement (Regnerus, 2000), a healthful lifestyle (Wallace & Forman, 1998), and overall thriving (Dowling, Gestsdottir, Anderson, et al., 2004).

Why does being involved in religion provide such benefits? Many reasons have been proposed. First, being involved in an organized church provides a teenager with a good deal of **social capital,** or other persons willing to be there for him or her (King & Furrow, 2004). Second, it provides opportunities for helping others (Mattis, Jagers, Hatcher, et al., 2000), and third, it surrounds teenagers with individuals who will praise and reinforce them for their good works (Ellison, 1992). Fourth, religious involvement provides opportunities for skill and leadership development (Smith, 2003). Finally, many (although not necessarily all) religions promote positive, prosocial values such as kindness (Hardy & Carlo, 2005).

Television and Other Screen Time

The increasingly large impact of the mass media on adolescents is discussed elsewhere in this book. But since so much attention has been devoted to worrying about the potentially harmful effects of televised content on adolescents' characters, it is worth examining those effects here. Adolescents spend an enormous amount of time watching video: approximately 4.5 hours/day. About 3 hours are spent watching a television set (which actually represents a decline in recent years), about half an hour is spent watching clips or programs on-line, another half an hour is spent watching DVDs, and about 15 minutes/day is spent watching video on both MP3 players and cell phones (Rideout, Foehr, & Roberts, 2010). By the time the typical teen graduates from high school, he or she will have spent considerably more time in front of the tube than in a classroom (Comstock & Paik, 1999)—20,000 versus 14,000 hours—and that doesn't take into account all of the time that youths played video games or watched movies. Almost 70 percent of American 8- to 18-year-olds have a television in their own bedrooms (Roberts, Foehr, & Rideout, 2005).

Is it, then, any wonder that the public is worried about the effects of such a steady television diet on adolescent values? Their unease centers on three issues: (1) the effects of viewing televised violence, (2) the effects of being exposed to sexually provocative stimulation, and (3) the effects of advertising on adolescents' material desires.

● **ANSWERS WOULDN'T YOU LIKE TO KNOW ...**

How religious are most American teenagers?

Most are reasonably religious. They believe in God, pray on a regular basis, and believe that religion benefits society.

---

social capital   the resources available to an individual through his or her interpersonal connections.

Violence

Public concern over the content of television shows has focused on the effects on children and youths of watching so much violence. Back in 1992, Althea Huston and her colleagues estimated that the average American child would see an average of 200,000 violent acts on television—rapes, assaults, murders—by the time he or she was 18 years old. Given that it is well established that American television has grown increasingly violent (in part because of cable networks), the number surely far surpasses that now. American television is the most violent in the world (Strasburger, 1995).

Almost all researchers and child advocacy groups who have examined the issue conclude that exposure to television violence *does* contribute to increased aggressiveness (Anderson & Bushman, 2002). Most of the classic studies on the relationship between television violence and aggression in children and adolescents support this association. In fact, more than 1,000 separate studies have linked television viewing with adolescent antisocial activity (Strasburger, 1995).

Violent television promotes violence in several ways. It makes aggression seem less shocking and more acceptable—even typical and normal (Krcmar & Hight, 2007). In many cases, it presents likable, attractive role models who are acting aggressively (Wilson, Smith, Potter, et al., 2002), and often, these characters are rewarded and admired for their aggressive behavior. In addition, action-oriented programming excites and arouses viewers, which makes them more prone to react aggressively in the short run if provoked (Cantor, 2000). Repeated exposure to violent actions, on the other hand, desensitizes people such that their arousal in the face of violence begins to decrease rather than increase. This results in less distress at the thought of violence and less sympathy for the victims of violence (Molitor & Hirsch, 1994). Violence becomes more acceptable.

Another effect of watching violent television is that viewers come to believe that the world is a place in which others are out to harm them (Gerbner, 1994). Children and adolescents may become frightened because of what they see on television, with the result that some have nightmares and recurring thoughts that can last for years. Adolescents are especially troubled by scenes depicting supernatural forces and sexual assault (Harrison & Cantor, 1999). Many adults (including the author) can recall lingering fears after seeing such movies as *Psycho* and *Silence of the Lambs*. After even brief exposure to aggression, **cognitive priming**—the activation of neural pathways so that ambiguous or neutral stimuli are perceived as similar to what has been

RESEARCH HIGHLIGHT   ADOLESCENTS' VIEWS OF POLITICAL AND HUMAN RIGHTS

Early research on the early growth of one's understanding of government suggested a three-step model of change: children viewed the government as a punitive entity whose role was to make sure that people behaved; early adolescents' views were fragmented but more positive; by late adolescence, individuals understood that the government provides services to its citizens and keeps society running smoothly (Gallatin, 1980). More recent studies have examined the views held by adolescents from around the globe concerning several topics related to politics.

One issue is about the value of democracy. Not surprisingly, Canadian adolescents judged direct and representative democracy as superior to nondemocratic systems of government such as oligarchies or meritocracies on the basis of the fact that they give everyone a voice and let the majority rule. On a more interesting note, both urban and rural Chinese teenagers also felt this way (Helwig, Arnold, Tan, et al., 2007). This was true even for youth who had not been greatly exposed to Western culture or ideas.

Cross-culturally, adolescents are also strikingly similar in their endorsement of certain basic human rights. In particular, young persons across the globe believe that people, including children, are entitled to be guided and protected by society (**nurturance rights**) and to the right of **self-determination** (the right to make up their own minds about issues and express their opinions) (Cherney & Shing, 2008). As might be expected, Western youth from individualistic societies are somewhat more supportive of self-determination rights, which are associated with individual autonomy, than Eastern youth from more collectivist cultures.

Similarly, an adolescent's religious background influences his or her views of the relative importance of nurturance and self-determination. In one study, Jewish teenagers were more sympathetic to children's rights than were Muslim Palestinian teenagers (Ben-Arieh, Khoury-Kassabri, & Haj-Yahia, 2006). In another, Buddhist early adolescents were more supportive of self-determination rights than were Christian early adolescents (Cherney & Shing, 2008). These differences may be due to varying levels of paternalism in the different religions (Cherney, Greteman, & Travers, 2008).

Watching violent television promotes violence in several ways. For instance violence seems commonplace and acceptable and even admirable when likable, attractive characters are rewarded for their violent actions.

previously perceived—can occur (Strasburger, Wilson, & Jordan, 2009).

The sum of the data leaves little doubt that there is a *causal* link between watching violent television and behaving aggressively (Kirsch, 2006). Numerous laboratory and field experiments conclusively show, especially in aggregate, that television violence is a social pollutant that actively contributes to violent behavior. Many persons have trouble accepting this, because *they* watch violent TV but believe that *they* are not aggressive. However, remember that there are some people who smoke two packs of cigarettes each day and yet do not develop lung cancer. Does that mean that smoking does not increase your cancer risk? No. Similarly, although not everyone who watches violent television is affected (although you may have been affected more than you realize), on a population level the amount of aggression has increased because of its prevalence.

ANSWERS WOULDN'T YOU LIKE TO KNOW …

Does watching violence on television really affect people?

The data on the negative effects of watching violence on television are strong and compelling. Viewers who regularly see appealing characters save the day by using aggression eventually come to see aggression as commonplace and acceptable. Moreover, some become more likely to react aggressively themselves when provoked.

Sexual Content

Just as television inundates youths with violent images, it also presents an abundance of sexual ones. The average American adolescent is exposed to almost 15,000 sexual references or behaviors each year while watching TV (Strasburger & Donnerstein, 1999). Sexual content on television has increased significantly, even during prime family-viewing time (Kunkel, Keven, Finnety, et al., 2005). Nearly one-third of the shows that air during the so-called family hour (from 8 to 9 P.M. Eastern Standard Time) contain sexual content, averaging eight or more such references per hour. Even worse, sex is usually presented either as exploitive or as trivial, harmless fun; the potential emotional and health consequences are rarely mentioned. In fact, only about 1 percent of the sexual incidents portrayed on television deal with issues such as the risk of pregnancy or sexually transmitted diseases, birth control, and abstinence (Zillmann, 2000). The number of sex scenes shown on television has doubled since 1997–1998, and the shows that adolescents watch have even more sexual content than those that adults watch (Kunkel, Finnety, Biely, et al., 2005). The number of portrayals of sexual risk has not, however, increased in that time.

cognitive priming the activation of neural pathways so that ambiguous or neutral stimuli are perceived as similar to what has been previously perceived.

nurturance rights the right to be protected by adults and societal institutions.

self-determination the right to have one's own opinions and make one's own decisions.

This is troubling for the same reason that violence on television is troubling: adolescents *are* affected by television's sexual content. Even watching programs in which sex is merely discussed, not portrayed, has been shown to influence adolescents' beliefs as to what constitutes normative sexual behavior (Ward, 2002) and their attitudes about casual sex (Taylor, 2005). At least one well-designed, longitudinal study has demonstrated a link between heavy consumption of sexual television programming and early sexual activity, including intercourse (Collins, Elliot, Berry, et al., 2004).

Since studies parallel to those done on televised violence show that adolescents' concept of normal sexual activity can be skewed by what they view, the National Commission on Adolescent Sexual Health (SEICUS, 1996) recommends the following guidelines for the portrayal of sexuality in the media. The commission believes these changes will promote more beneficial adolescent sexual attitudes and behaviors. According to this group, society would benefit if the media would do the following:

1. Stop portraying only physically attractive people as desirable and capable of being involved in sexual relationships.

2. Depict sexually abstinent teens as well as sexually active ones.

3. Depict typical sexual relations as nonexploitive.

4. Represent the typical sexual encounter as planned, rather than impulsive.

5. Portray the use of contraceptives and display the negative consequences of failing to do so.

6. Depict scenes of parent-child communication about sexuality.

Materialism

American children and adolescents see about 40,000 commercials on television each year (Wilcox, Cantor, Dowrick, et al., 2004); in fact, teens usually see 10 to 14 minutes of ads for each hour of television that they watch (Gantz, Schwartz, Angelini, et al., 2007). Some children and adolescents even view commercials while at school, since it is now quite common for schools to present packaged "current event" video programs that contain commercials. The fact that companies are willing to spend millions of dollars to buy air time to advertise their products suggests that these ads must be effective in changing people's consumer behavior.

RESEARCH HIGHLIGHT   WHY DO WE LIKE SCARY MEDIA?

Television executives wouldn't put violent television shows on the air, and movie executives wouldn't spend tens of millions of dollars producing horror movies, if people didn't watch them. At some level, then, people must enjoy frightening programs and movies. (And there are some data suggesting that adolescents like scary shows more than children or older adults; e.g., Cantor, 1998.) Why do teens and the rest of us like to be scared?

Several theories have been proposed. Zillmann (1996) suggested that the physiological arousal produced by the empathic distress we feel at seeing another in danger heightens the positive emotional response we feel when it all ends positively; the distress up front is worth the relief at the end. (This theory has trouble accounting for the fact that sometimes people enjoy frightening films even when there is no happy ending.) Conversely, Tamborini (1996) proposed that only those low in empathy could enjoy horror films, since those high in empathy would be too distressed at the protagonists' plight. Slater (2003) believes that frightening films satisfy a need for sensation seeking, and Sparks (2001) views watching scary films as a means of escapism—a way to temporarily forget one's everyday problems. Cantor (1998) likens watching scary films to "forbidden fruit," stating that its appeal comes from the fact that it is not quite appropriate. Goldstein (1999) states that it is done for companionship, since the majority of the time these shows and movies are watched in groups. Many (e.g., Selah-Shayovtis, 2006) have suggested that watching death and mayhem is a means of vicarious aggression—which would explain why aggressive individuals tend to prefer violent media more than nonviolent individuals.

Hoffner and Levine (2005) conducted a meta-analysis of the research studies that have been conducted on this topic to date. They found that the bulk of the data suggests that males enjoy violent media more than females, and that adolescents enjoyed watching violence more than older adults did. (They did not include studies that examined children.) They also found that the more frightening a show was found to be, the more enjoyable it was rated, whether or not there was a positive resolution. Highly empathic individuals did enjoy these programs less than others, whereas aggressive individuals and sensation seekers enjoyed them more.

Unfortunately, much of the advertising directed at children and adolescents is for products that are not especially beneficial to them (e.g., sugary snack foods) or that are expensive (e.g., name-brand sports clothing). These ads help create a demand for these products and encourage teens to want to buy them.

Because they have been well studied, we know that advertisements for certain products (i.e., cigarettes, alcohol) do convince teenagers to go out and use these products. For example, one study found that for each ad for alcohol above the average number that an adolescent saw, he or she was 1 percent more likely to drink alcohol (Snyder, Milici, Slater, et al., 2006). Similarly, a study with early adolescents found that 12-year-olds who were more aware of televised beer advertisements had more favorable views of drinking and expressed more of an intention to drink as adults than did other young adolescents (Grube, 1995).

On a more general level, television commercials promote the concept that living "the good life" entails having many material possessions. The message is that there is a product out there that will solve any and all of your problems. Unpopular? Try this acne cream or mouthwash or buy this car. Dissatisfied with your appearance? Try this shampoo and that brand of clothing. The role of possessions in bringing happiness is overemphasized in the media. In one study, Sirgy, Lee, Kosenko, et al. (1998) found that the more television that American undergraduate students watched, the more materialistic they were and the more dissatisfied they were with their standard of living. It therefore appears that television advertising does have an effect upon viewers.

Other Concerns
Violence, promiscuity, and materialism are not the only complaints that have been raised about television. As discussed in Chapter 4 in the section on body image, media portrayals of excessively slender individuals contribute to body dissatisfaction, especially in girls. In addition, the several hours a day spent watching television could be spent doing something else, such as exercising, being with friends, talking with family members, working on a hobby, or reading. Even watching good television is problematic if done to excess, since it siphons hours away from more beneficial activities.

Moral Education

Because we all are affected by the moral behavior of others, American schools have historically been concerned with instilling morality in their students. A number of the nation's founders—for example, Thomas Jefferson and John Adams—advocated public education as a means of transmitting democratic values to young citizens (Wynne, 1989). In the 1800s, as waves of immigrants who had not grown up in the democratic tradition

came to the United States, the sense that the schools needed to teach democratic values increased (Titus, 1994). Over time, as societal concerns and values have evolved and changed, the approaches to moral education have changed, as well.

One of the earliest of approaches (which became fashionable again within the past decade) involves **inculcation,** or teaching specific values and norms to students so that they will come to identify with these values and follow them. In a pluralistic society, an obvious question arises: whose values will you teach? Proponents of inculcation insist that there are universally agreed-upon values that transcend culture, religion, and race/ethnicity. Numerous yet similar lists of universal values have been developed, including this one from the Josephson Institute of Ethics (2002), which proposes six pillars of morality:

1. *Trustworthiness,* which includes honesty, integrity, reliability, and loyalty
2. *Respect,* which includes treating others with dignity, civility, courtesy, and tolerance
3. *Responsibility,* which assumes that one is accountable for one's actions, perseveres, is diligent, and shows self-restraint
4. *Fairness,* which involves following due process, being impartial, and refusing to take unfair advantage of others
5. *Caring,* or the concern for others' welfare
6. *Citizenship,* or giving to the community and obeying its rules

The second approach to moral education, known as **moral development,** grew directly out of Kohlberg's theories and research and first became popular in the early 1970s. The approach is based on the belief that adolescents must be exposed to higher-level reasoning in order to develop it themselves (Harding & Snyder, 1991). In this type of approach, the primary method used is to present case studies, or moral dilemmas, for the students to solve (Mills, 1988). Here is the kind of dilemma used to promote thinking and discussion:

> Trisha is a 16-year-old girl whose best friend's name is Cassie. Yesterday, Cassie told Trisha that she was planning to run away from home. Cassie said that she had taken all of the money that she had in her bank

inculcation an approach to moral education that teaches students to accept specific moral values, such as honesty and trustworthiness.

moral development an approach to moral education that uses moral dilemmas and the like to give youths experience in higher-level reasoning.

PERSONAL ISSUES   ACADEMIC CHEATING IN COLLEGE

By all counts, cheating in college has reached epidemic proportions. Estimates range from a *low* of just more than 50 percent of students (Pino & Smith, 2003) to a high in excess of 80 percent of students (Cochran, Wood, Sellers, et al., 1998). In addition, plagiarism appears to occur at least as frequently as cheating on exams (Wilson, 2001). Equally bad, more than 70 percent of students report making fraudulent excuses so as to have extra time to prepare for exams or to complete papers (Roig & Caso, 2005).

Given how many students cheat, at least occasionally, it might be better to ask who *doesn't* cheat rather than to ask who does. Women claim that they cheat less often than men (e.g., Jensen, Arnett, Feldman, et al., 2002), but there are few gender differences when cheating is measured more objectively (McCabe, Trevino, & Butterfield, 2001). Independent students—those not affiliated with fraternities or sororities—are less likely to cheat than those involved in the Greek system (Storch & Storch, 2002), perhaps because they have less opportunity to do so. Furthermore, the more heavily involved a student is with a fraternity or sorority, the more likely he or she is to cheat. In general, the brightest, most able students are less likely to cheat than those who are academically weaker—and by quite a margin (Nathanson, Paulhus, & Williams, 2006). Perhaps because so many students cheat, only weak associations have been found between personality variables and cheating (Whitley & Keith-Spiegel, 2002). Szabo and Underwood (2004) conjecture, however, that students who have a sincere desire to learn will be less likely to cheat.

Cheating can also be encouraged or discouraged by situational factors. Faculty can discourage cheating by making it difficult for students to cheat, so that it is simply not worth the effort (Szabo & Underwood, 2004). Teachers can give specific rather than broad, general assignments (Davis, 1994). They can make the students believe that there is a real probability that they will be caught and that the penalties will be severe if that happens (Szabo & Underwood, 2004). They can make sure that students understand exactly what the rules governing cheating and plagiarism are (Roig, 1999) so that no one unintentionally misbehaves. They can be sure that students have adequate time to complete assignments (Szabo & Underwood, 2004), and they can make sure that they teach in such a way that their students believe that the course material is valuable to them and relevant to their lives (Kibler, 1993).

Fear of failure remains the most common reason for cheating. Math and science are the courses in which cheating most often occurs. The home is considered the best place and school the worst place to inculcate honesty. Over the past three decades, dishonesty has been viewed as increasingly necessary. More students now admit to cheating on tests and homework (Garavalia, Olson, Russell, et al., 2007). Research has underscored the fact that students usually blame others—parents, teachers, school, and even society—for their cheating (Anderman, Griesinger, & Westerfield, 1998; McCabe, 1999). In addition, students are unlikely to believe that they will get caught for cheating and do not think they will be punished severely even if they are caught (McCabe & Trevino, 1997). The problem of cheating will not likely disappear soon, especially since the wealth of resources available on the Internet has created new opportunities for plagiarism: in one study, 60% of British college students admitted to at least moderate levels of cyber cheating within the past month (Selwyn, 2008).

account and used some of it to buy a bus ticket to Los Angeles. Trisha asked Cassie if she knew anyone there, and Cassie said "no." Trisha also asked Cassie why she was running away from home, and Cassie said that her parents were too strict and never let her go anywhere or have any fun, and that she thought things would get worse after they saw her latest report card. Trisha is worried about Cassie, and tried unsuccessfully to talk her out of running away. After Cassie leaves, Tricia wonders about whether she should tell a teacher or Cassie's parents about Cassie's plans. What do you think she should do?

The students are then presented with several questions:

- Should Tricia tell Cassie's parents about Cassie's plans? Why or why not?

- Should Tricia do anything else or tell anyone else? What? Why or why not?
- Is it Tricia's responsibility to prevent Cassie from doing anything reckless?
- Should one always keep a friend's secrets?

ANSWERS WOULDN'T YOU LIKE TO KNOW ...
How commonly do students cheat on exams and papers?

All forms of student cheating are distressingly common. The most common reason given for cheating is the fear of failing or doing poorly.

The third approach to moral education is **values clarification.** It is not concerned with the *content* of values but with the *process* of valuing. It does not aim to instill any particular set of values; rather, the goal is to help students become aware of the beliefs and behaviors they prize and would be willing to stand up for, to learn to weigh the pros and cons and consequences of various alternatives, to choose freely after considerations of consequences, and to learn to match their actions with their beliefs in a consistent way. A significant part of values clarification education, which can be viewed as either a strength or a weakness, is that students are allowed to choose their own values. Those who favor this approach assert that in a free, democratic society, individuals should be allowed to hold whatever values they wish; the state should not tell people what to think. Critics of this method argue that some moral choices are superior to others and that it is irresponsible to teach adolescents that all moral choices are equally valid.

Teachers who employ values clarification use a variety of methods. Students may be asked to think about their values and discuss them with one another; they may also be given real and hypothetical ethical dilemmas to consider. Another method is to ask students to make forced moral choices—for example, to decide whether people should be allowed to make as much noise as they want (individual freedom) or have their right to be noisy curtailed if they disturb others. Similarly, students are often asked to rank-order their priorities (Rice, 1980).

The fourth approach, **analysis,** has never become as popular as the others. In it, students are taught to employ critical thinking and reasoning when making moral decisions. Generally, lessons concentrate more on broad social values than on personal dilemmas. As is often the case with critical-thinking instruction, students are given practice in clarifying the issue, assembling and evaluating the truth of the facts used to support different positions on the issue, appraising the relevance of the facts, drawing appropriate conclusions, and thinking through the implications of their decision (Huitt, 2003).

The final approach to moral education, **service learning,** is the newest but has become extremely widespread (Reinders & Youniss, 2006). It involves giving students the opportunity to participate in community service projects, thus bridging the gap between moral reasoning and moral action. The idea behind service learning is that adolescents will come to value moral, caring behavior and develop enhanced social consciousness if they observe social problems (e.g., poverty, pollution) firsthand and experience the self-satisfaction that comes from knowing that they have helped their community. More and more high schools are incorporating community service obligation into their set of graduation requirements. This issue is discussed more fully in Chapter 13.

values clarification   a method of teaching values that helps students become aware of their own beliefs and values.

analysis   an approach to moral education that emphasizes using logical reasoning to solve social dilemmas.

service learning   an approach to moral education that emphasizes community service.

SUMMARY

1. This chapter has discussed four major aspects of moral development: (a) theories of development of moral judgment, represented by Piaget, Kohlberg, Gilligan, and those who take a social-cognitive approach; (b) family correlates to moral development; (c) transmission of religious beliefs and practices; and (d) the social influences of peers, television, and education on moral values and behavior.

2. Piaget outlined two stages of moral development: a morality of constraint (or obedience) and a morality of cooperation (or reciprocity). In between is a transitional stage during which rules become internalized as the individual moves from realism to relativism.

3. Kohlberg outlined three major levels of moral development: (a) preconventional, (b) conventional, and (c) postconventional.

4. Like Piaget, Kohlberg emphasized that the level of morality at which individuals operate depends on their *motives* for doing right. Piaget said that as children become more moral, they depend less on outside authority to constrain them and more on an inner, subjective desire to cooperate and to consider the rights and feelings of others.

5. Essentially, Kohlberg said the same thing: children's motives change gradually from a desire to avoid punishment, gain the reward of others, and avoid disapproval or censure to a more positive motive of desire for individual and community respect and a desire to avoid self-condemnation.

6. Sufficient cognitive development is a prerequisite for advanced moral reasoning but does not guarantee it.

7. Kohlberg's later stages of moral development describe individuals from Western countries better than those raised in other cultures. Also, people are not as consistent in their development of moral reasoning as a stage theory would suggest.

8. Kohlberg based his theory on his research with male subjects. Later researchers raised the question of how applicable the theory was to females' moral development. One of Kohlberg's students, Carol Gilligan, made this issue the focus of her research.

9. Whereas Gilligan believes that women are more likely to resolve moral dilemmas using a caring perspective and men using a legalistic perspective, most researchers believe that the perspective both men and women take is a function of the particular dilemma being discussed and that both men and women use both caring and legalistic reasoning.

10. Moral progression is similar in all three theories: from amorality to outer control to inner control; from negative, selfish motivations to positive, altruistic motivations; from a desire to escape external punishment to a desire to escape self-condemnation.

11. The social-cognitive model identifies three types of rules: moral rules, social conventions, and personal preferences. Many of the disagreements between adolescents and adults stem from the fact that they view specific situations as fitting differently into these domains.

12. Moral reasoning is needed for moral behavior but does not guarantee it. Many factors—such as pubertal status, degree of empathy, cultural background, and personality—act together to determine whether a person will behave morally.

13. Some, but not all, aspects of prosocial functioning improve during adolescence.

14. Moral growth and development cannot be isolated from other aspects of the adolescent's life. They have many correlates in the parent-child relationship especially and, to a lesser extent, in adolescent peer relationships. What happens to children at home, with peers, and in the neighborhood will affect their moral development.

15. The majority of American teenagers believe in God and are fairly religious. Teens are most likely to be religious if their parents are religious and both follow the same faith. Although religiosity declines during late adolescence/young adulthood, it reemerges once a person marries and has children. Religious participation tends to positively influence adolescent behavior.

16. Teenagers spend more than 20 hours per week watching television. There is concern about this behavior, since many television shows promote violence, portray sex as impersonal and exploitive, and present commercials that encourage adolescents to spend their money unwisely.

17. An increasing number of people believe that schools should play a significant role in moral education. Some think that schools should teach selected moral values; others emphasize reasoning, values clarification, and learning through community service.

18. Cheating in school is widespread, and the practice seems to have gained more acceptance. Fear of failure is the most common reason given for cheating.

KEY TERMS

analysis   195

cognitive priming   190

conventional moral reasoning   179

good girl–good boy orientation   179

immanent justice   176

inculcation   193

instrumental hedonism orientation   179

law and order orientation   179

metacognition   180

moral courage   185

moral development   193

moral realism   176

moral relativism   176

moral rules   183

morality of constraint   176

morality of cooperation   176

nurturance rights   190

objective judgments   176

personal preferences   183

postconventional moral reasoning   179

preconventional moral reasoning   178

prosocial behavior   184

punishment orientation   178

self-determination rights   190

service learning   195

social capital   189

social-cognitive domain model   183

social contract orientation   179

social conventions   183

subjective judgments   176

universal principled reasoning   180

values clarification   195

THOUGHT QUESTIONS

Personal Reflection

1. Do you remember believing in immanent justice? Do you ever still feel that punishment is inevitable if you transgress?

2. Reflect on your own past and think of instances in which you and your parents disagreed as to whether a behavior was a personal preference or a social convention.

3. Think about an instance in which you behaved morally. Why did you behave that way? Think about an instance in which you behaved immorally. Why did you behave that way? Can you generalize about when and why you choose one path over the other?

4. Are you religious? By what criteria? Do your religious views influence the behavioral decisions that you make? If so, how?

5. Do you think that American teenagers watch too much television? Why or why not?

6. What are some of the specific concerns that psychologists have about the portrayal of sex on television? Do you agree with their characterizations?

Group Discussion

7. Compare and contrast the moral reasoning of a child who is a moral realist with one who is a moral relativist.

8. Do adults really make subjective moral judgments instead of objective moral judgments? If so, why does the crime of attempted murder carry a lighter sentence than that of a completed murder?

9. How would the thought processes of individuals at the preconventional, conventional, and postconventional moral levels differ if they were deciding whether to borrow their sibling's bicycle after having been told they could not?

10. Which criticisms of Kohlberg's theory do you agree with? Disagree with? Why?

11. How should one behave when one sees someone violate a moral rule? A social convention? Use examples to make your point.

12. Which family practices contribute positively to moral learning?

13. How does the type of discipline that parents use influence moral development?

14. What are the different ways in which peers can influence one another's moral behavior?

15. Identify some issues for which adolescents should be allowed to exercise self-determination rights. Identify some in which it is more important to protect them.

16. Imagine that your roommate mentions that he or she does not believe that televised violence really affects anyone. How would you respond?

17. What values are taught through television ads?

18. Which approach to moral education do you favor? Why?

19. What should schools do about academic cheating?

Debate Questions

20. Carol Gilligan was correct: A certain amount of self-protection is more moral than continual self-sacrifice.

21. A legalistic moral orientation is superior to a caring one.

22. Adolescents should be made to attend religious services whether or not they wish to go.

23. Television viewing should be strictly limited in terms of both time and content.

24. Schools should teach moral values as part of their curricula.

25. It is impossible for schools to be morally neutral.

SUGGESTED READING

Goodman, J. F., and Lesnick, H. (2000). *The Moral Stake in Education: Contested Premises and Practices.* Boston: Allyn & Bacon.

Hamilton, J. T. (2000). *Channeling Violence.* Princeton, NJ: Princeton University Press.

Kirsh, S. J. (2006). *Children, Adolescents, and Media Violence: A Critical Look at the Research.* Thousand Oaks, CA: Sage.

Lapsley, D. K., and Power, F. C. (2005). *Character Psychology and Character Education.* South Bend, IN: University of Notre Dame Press.

Nucci, L. P., and Narvaez, D. (2008). *Handbook of Moral and Character Education.* New York: Routledge.

Palmer, E. L., and Young, B. M. (Eds). (2003). *Faces of Televisual Media: Teaching, Violence, and Selling to Children.* Mahwah, NJ: Erlbaum.

Roehlkepartain, E. C., King, P. E., Wagener, L., and Benson, P. L. (Eds). (2006). *The Handbook of Spiritual Development in Childhood and Adolescence.* Thousand Oaks, CA: Sage.

Ryan, K., and Bohlin, K. E. (2003). *Building Character in Schools: Practical Ways to Bring Moral Instruction to Life.* San Francisco: Jossey-Bass.

USEFUL WEB SITES

Center for the Advancement of Ethics and Character
www.bu.edu/education/caec

The center is located in the College of Education at Boston University. Its Web site contains information about character education, a suggested reading list (including books appropriate for children as well as adults), and links to other sites.

Character Counts!
www.charactercounts.org

Character Counts! is an offshoot of the Josephson Institute of Ethics, a consortium of prestigious organizations (e.g., the Red Cross, Big Brothers/Big Sisters, the Police Athletic League) that are concerned with fostering moral development. It was developed in the early 1990s to promote moral education in schools. The group's Web site describes its beliefs and details the six moral virtues that it believes are most important; it also includes free educational materials and links to other sites.

Character Education Partnership
www.character.org

This nonpartisan organization hosts an e-mail newsletter about character education and publishes a quarterly print newsletter. The site has a useful Question & Answer section and contains many links to other moral education sites.

National Study of Youth and Religion
http://www.youthandreligion.org

The National Study of Youth and Religion is conducted by researchers out of the University of North Carolina at Chapel Hill. The Web site includes many reports of the researchers' data and includes links to other Web pages about this topic. It contains information about a wide variety of topics related to adolescents and religion, and the quality of the reported research is very high.

WOULDN'T YOU LIKE TO KNOW . . .

- Which traits characterize the best parents?
- Do most teens find it easier to talk with their mothers or their fathers?
- Do adolescents want their parents to be affectionate and demonstrative?
- How can teens get their parents to trust them?
- Is it possible to be *too close* to one's family?
- What is the best way to discipline adolescents?
- How much say should adolescents have in making family plans?
- Are adolescent–parent conflicts mostly due to adolescents' desire for greater freedom?
- What are most parent–adolescent arguments about?

chapter

Relationships with Family Members

Virtually all adolescents find themselves part of a family. The specific makeup of that family may be unique. For instance, a teen might be raised by both of his biological parents, by only his father or only his mother, or by a biological parent and a stepparent. He may or may not have interactions with siblings, aunts, uncles, grandparents, or cousins. Yet regardless of makeup, the function and importance of every family is the same. The family is probably the single most important influence in an adolescent's life.

Relationships with kin tend to be more long lasting and intense than those with nonkin. The older members of your family have most likely known you since your birth. When children are young, their parents or their parents' surrogates have almost complete control over their behavior; these elders set the rules and provided the opportunities. Because many family members typically share the same physical space, they come into frequent contact with one another (whether they want to or not). And since families share financial resources as well as space, the behavior of one family member often affects one or more of the others. If you share a bathroom with your sister, for instance, when she leaves it a mess, it will inconvenience you. And if your brother damages the family car, it will likely cause real hardship for your whole family. Therefore, interactions with family members are frequently impassioned.

This chapter begins by describing what adolescents need and expect from their parents. After that, the focus turns to parent-adolescent conflict. The next section focuses on adolescent-sibling relationships and the relationship of youths with their grandparents. Finally, discussion on the maltreatment of adolescents includes the topics of child abuse, sexual abuse, incest, and neglect.

Parenting Adolescents

Almost all research indicates that parents have an enormous influence on adolescents' behavior (Laursen & Collins, 2009). Parents vary in their behavior, however, and some patterns of behavior are more beneficial than others.

What Kind of Parents Do Adolescents Want?

What kind of parents do adolescents want and need? A sample of adolescents said the following:

"Be interested in us and what we do."
"Listen to us."
"Give us lots of love."
"Always be there for us."
"Accept us for who we are, not who they want us to be."
"Trust us."

"Don't treat us like little kids."
"Make time for us."

These comments map well onto the three key components of parenting identified by researchers. The first is **connection,** or the presence of a warm, stable, loving, and attentive bond between parents and child. Connection provides a sense of security that allows an adolescent to explore the world outside the family. The second component is **psychological autonomy,** the freedom to form one's own opinions, have privacy, and make decisions for oneself. If autonomy is lacking, adolescents are vulnerable to problem behavior and have trouble becoming independent adults. Finally, children (even adolescent children) must have **regulation.** Successful parents monitor and supervise their children's behavior and set rules that limit that behavior. Regulation teaches children self-control and helps them avoid antisocial behavior (Barber, 1997).

Let's examine these qualities in more detail.

Connection

Parental Interest and Help

Some of the ways adolescents know that their parents care about them include the interest their mothers and fathers show in them, the amount of quality time parents spend with them, and their parents' willingness to stand beside them and help them as needed (Meeus, Iedema, Maasen, et al., 2005). Positive parental support is associated with close relationships with both parents and siblings, high self-esteem, academic success, and advanced moral development (e.g., Barber, Maughan, Olsen, et al., 2002). Lack of parental support may have exactly the opposite effect: low self-esteem, poor schoolwork, impulsive behavior, poor social adjustment, and involvement in deviant and antisocial behavior or delinquency (Herman, Dornbusch, Herron, et al., 1997). For instance, consider this reaction expressed by a high school athlete:

I'm the star player on the school basketball team, but never once has either parent come to see me play. They're either too busy or too tired or can't get a baby sitter for my younger sister. The crowds cheer for me, the girls hang around my locker, some kids even ask me for my autograph. But it doesn't mean much if the two most important people in my life don't care. (Rice, counseling notes)

Adolescents want attention and companionship from their parents. However, some parents overdo the companionship. Adolescents want to spend time with their own friends and do not want their parents to be pals. They need adult interest and help, not adults trying to act like adolescents. Adolescents need time to be alone, and to be alone with their peers.

In general, parents spend less time with their adolescents as their teens get older (Mooney, Laursen, & Adams, 2006). Although they continue to provide emotional support and warmth, they are less involved in their children's activities. Adolescents and their parents are less likely to express warmth to each other than children and their parents, with the steepest declines being in early adolescence. The decline for daughters is greater than that for sons, mostly because daughters have higher baseline rates in childhood (McGue, Elkins, Walden, et al., 2005). Adolescents tend to remain closer to their mothers than to their fathers (Smetana, Metzger, Gettman, et al., 2006). How much familial closeness declines over the course of adolescence appears to be a function of its strength at the onset of adolescence: in close-knit families, the decline is small; in more distant families, the decline is much greater (Allen, McElhaney, Kupermine, et al., 2004).

The amount of attention adolescents get from their parents depends partially on the birth order and spacing of the children within the family. Eldest children have the closest, warmest relationships with their parents throughout adolescence (Shanahan, McHale, Crouter, et al., 2007). Middle-born adolescents sometimes feel cheated of parental attention and support and express a sense of being "pushed around" in terms of family rules and regulations. Middle-born adolescents are less likely than first- or last-borns to say that they would turn to their parents for help (they are more likely to nominate a sibling), and they are less likely than their older and younger siblings to identify themselves as being a member of their family when asked an open-ended question (Salmon & Daly, 1998).

In general, parents view their relationship with their adolescent children as closer than do those adolescent children (Silverberg & Steinberg, 2000). Parents, especially mothers, view their family as more harmonious (Laursen & Collins, 2004). Discrepancies between parents' and adolescent children's views of family support and cohesion decrease as the teens get older (Seiffge-Krenke, 1999).

Listening and Empathetic Understanding

Empathy refers to the ability to identify with the thoughts, attitudes, and feelings of another person. It is *emotional sensitivity* to others, the vicarious sharing of experiences had by another person and the emotions associated with them (Decety & Jackson, 2004).

Some parents are completely insensitive to their adolescents' feelings and moods. They are unaware of what their adolescents are thinking and feeling and so act without taking those thoughts and feelings into account. When their adolescents are upset, they have no idea why. One possible consequence of this insensitivity is that children grow up as insensitive as the parents. The children's own feelings have never been considered, so they don't learn to consider other people's feelings. Older adolescents perceive their parents as more empathic than younger adolescents, perhaps because the worst conflicts are behind them (Drevets, Benton, & Bradley, 1996).

Communication with parents deteriorates to some extent during adolescence. Teens disclose less information to their parents and communication with parents is often difficult (Beaumont, 1996). Perhaps one reason for this lack of communication is that many parents do not listen to their teens' ideas, accept their opinions as relevant, or try to understand their feelings and points of view. Adolescents want parents who will talk *with* them, not *at* them, in a sympathetic way:

"We want parents we can take our troubles to and be sure they'll understand. Some parents won't listen or let their children explain. They should try to see things a little more from our point of view."
"We wish our parents would lose an argument with us once in a while and listen to our side of problems." (Rice, counseling notes)

Basically, adolescents are saying that they want sympathetic understanding, an attentive ear, and parents who believe that their children have something worthwhile to say (Noble, Adams, & Openshaw, 1989). Research indicates that the respect parents show for adolescent opinions contributes greatly to the climate and happiness of the home (e.g., Jackson, Pratt, Hunsberger, et al., 2005).

A number of studies have found that adolescents spend more time talking with their mothers than with their fathers and that they are more likely to go to their mothers for advice on a wide variety of topics (e.g., Ackard, Neumark-Sztainer, Story, et al., 2006). This is especially true of daughters. Mothers are more likely than fathers to be available to talk and are perceived

connection the presence of a warm, stable, loving, attentive bond between parents and child.

psychological autonomy the freedom to form one's own opinions, have privacy, and make decisions for oneself.

regulation parental monitoring, supervision, and rule setting.

empathy the ability to identify with the thoughts, attitudes, and feelings of another person.

as listening with more sympathy and less judging. Open-minded communication is one key to harmonious parent-youth relationships (Masselam, Marcus, & Stunkard, 1990).

Some parents feel threatened when their adolescent disagrees, does not accept their ideas, or tries to argue. Parents who refuse to talk and close the argument by saying, "I don't want to discuss it; what I say goes," are closing the door to effective communication, just as are adolescents who get angry, stamp out of the house, or go into their rooms to pout. As discussed later, arguments can be constructive and beneficial if well handled.

Given the often limited communication between parents and adolescents—along with the fact that parents and adolescents frequently have different perceptions of the same event—even empathic, caring parents are often unaware of the stresses that their adolescent children are experiencing. Several studies (e.g., Hartos & Power, 2000) have shown that mothers consistently underestimate the magnitude of the stressors felt by their adolescent children. Since parents cannot help their children deal with problems that they don't know exist, it's not surprising that the greater the awareness gap, the more problems exhibited by the adolescent.

Love and Positive Affect

Affect, which refers to the emotions or feelings that exist among family members, may be positive or negative. **Positive affect** between family members refers to relationships characterized by emotional warmth, affection, love, and sensitivity. Family members show that they matter to one another and are responsive to one another's feelings and needs. **Negative affect** is characterized by emotional coldness, rejection, and hostility. Family members don't seem to love one another—or even like one another. In some families, hate or indifference is the norm. In these families, there is little affection, positive emotional support, empathy, or understanding.

Most adolescents need a great deal of love and demonstration of affection from parents. Sometimes, however, parents themselves were brought up in unexpressive families in which affection was seldom bestowed. As a consequence, the parents seldom hug their children, hold them, or kiss them. They don't express positive, warm feelings at all. As one girl

Most adolescents need a great deal of love and affection from their parents. Perceptions of parental support, both intrinsic and extrinsic, correlate positively with life satisfaction for adolescents.

expressed it: "I don't remember my parents ever telling me that they loved me. They just assumed I knew, but I wish they could have told me, and showed it once in a while."

Two possibilities may result: Either the adolescents are so starved for love and affection that their needs become very great when they become adults or they remain cold and aloof themselves, finding it difficult to express affection to their own spouses or children. Adolescents emphasize that they need both intrinsic support (encouragement, appreciation, shared pleasure, trust, and love) and extrinsic support (external expressions of support, such as hugging and kissing, taking the child to dinner or a movie, or buying the child something special). Adolescents' perceptions of parental support, particularly intrinsic support and closeness, are positively correlated with life satisfaction for the adolescents (Young, Miller, Norton, et al., 1995).

Adolescents use a variety of tactics to elicit demonstrations of the love they crave (Flint, 1992). They demonstrate mutual trust (by being honest, by discussing times they did the wrong things), they are polite (they listen and don't talk back), they show concern and caring (they compliment their parents and help them out), and they demonstrate affection. Older adolescents rely on mutual trust-enhancing behaviors more than younger adolescents, and they demonstrate more concern and caring. Adolescents are typically more polite to their fathers and more demonstrative to their mothers. Research consistently shows that parental demonstrations of warmth decrease from early to middle adolescence and then stabilize (e.g., Shanahan, McHale, Crouter, et al., 2007).

Acceptance and Approval

An important component of love is unconditional acceptance. One way to show love is to know and accept adolescents exactly as they are, faults and all. Adolescents need to know they are valued, accepted, and liked by their parents. They also want parents to have tolerance for individuality, intimacy, and interpersonal differences (Bomar & Sabatelli, 1996). There must be a determined effort by parents both to show approval and to achieve enough objectivity to see the child as a human being, entitled to flaws. Adolescents do not want to feel that their parents expect them to be perfect before they will love them, nor can they thrive in an atmosphere of criticism and displeasure.

Negative feelings between parents and adolescents may exist for a variety of reasons. Some children are resented, rejected, and unloved by parents from the time they are born because they were unplanned and unwanted in the first place. One girl explained:

> My mother always tells me how upset she was when she found out she was pregnant with me. She had to give up a successful career when I was born. Carrying me destroyed her figure. Giving birth was painful. I was a fussy baby who cried a lot and kept her awake nights. Growing up, I was a pain in the butt most of the time, according to her. She's resented me all these years and she lets me know it. (Rice, counseling notes)

Other parents may be upset at the way their children have turned out. One father complained:

> I hate to admit it but I'm very disappointed in my son. He's not at all like me. When I was in school, I played football and other sports. My son prefers music and books. He has long hair, an earring in his left ear, and looks like a sissy. I wish I could be proud of him but I'm not. He really embarrasses me. (Rice, counseling notes)

Trust

> "Why are our parents always so afraid we are going to do the wrong thing? Why can't they trust us more?" (Rice, counseling notes)

Some of the most annoying manifestations of distrust are parents' opening the children's e-mail, reading their diaries, and listening in on their phone conversations. One girl complained:

> My mother is forever going through my room under the pretense of "cleaning." I don't like to have my desk straightened up (it's where I keep my diary) or my bureau rummaged through. . . . Don't you think a 16-year-old girl needs privacy? (Rice, counseling notes)

Some parents seem to have more difficulty trusting their adolescents than others do. Such parents tend to project their own fears, anxiety, and guilt onto the adolescent. The most fearful parents are usually those who are the most insecure or who had difficulties themselves while growing up. Mothers who themselves have conceived or borne children out of wedlock are those most concerned about their own daughters' dating and sexual behavior. Most adolescents believe that parents should trust them completely unless they have given the adults reason for distrust.

Research suggests that parents' trust is based primarily on the amount and kind of knowledge they have about their adolescent. Knowledge of their child's daily activities accounts for more trust than knowledge of their child's past misbehaviors. Adolescents who spontaneously tell their parents about their daily lives elicit the most trust of all (Kerr, Stattin, & Trost, 1999).

affect   feelings that exist among family members.

positive affect   a relationship characterized by emotional warmth, affection, love, empathy, care, sensitivity, and emotional support.

negative affect   a relationship characterized by negative feelings of emotional coldness, rejection, hostility, anger, and insensitivity among family members.

Autonomy

One goal of every adolescent is to be accepted as an autonomous adult. This is accomplished through a process called **separation-individuation,** during which the parent-adolescent bond is transformed but maintained (Josselson, 1988). The adolescent establishes individuality yet maintains connectedness with parents at the same time (Grotevant & Cooper, 1985; Reis & Buhl, 2008). Thus, adolescents seek a differentiated relationship with parents, while communication, affection, and trust continue (Quintana & Lapsley, 1990). For example, they develop new interests, values, and goals and may develop points of view that are different from their parents' in order to experience distinctiveness. Nevertheless, the adolescents are still part of a family. Adolescents and their parents continue to expect emotional commitment from each other (Newman, 1989). Individuation is a fundamental organizing principle of human growth (Gavazzi & Sabatelli, 1990). It involves the ongoing efforts of an individual to build self-understanding and identity in relation to other people. In making the transition from childhood to adulthood, adolescents need to establish a degree of **autonomy** and identity in order to assume adult roles and responsibilities. Adolescents who remain too dependent on their parents are not as able to develop satisfactory relationships with peers (Schneider & Younger, 1996).

There are two aspects of autonomy. **Behavioral autonomy** involves becoming independent and free enough to act on your own without excessive dependence upon others for guidance. **Emotional autonomy** means becoming free of childish emotional dependence on parents. Research indicates that behavioral autonomy, the ability to make decisions for oneself, increases sharply during adolescence (e.g., Feldman & Wood, 1994). Adolescents desire behavioral autonomy in some areas, such as clothing selection or choice of friends, but they follow their parents' leads in other areas, such as formulating educational plans. Adolescents want and need parents who will grant them behavioral autonomy in slowly increasing amounts as they learn to use it, rather than all at once. Too much freedom granted too quickly may be interpreted as rejection. Youths want to be given the right to make choices, to exert their own independence, to argue with adults, and to assume responsibility, but they do not want complete freedom. Those who have it worry about it because they realize they do not know how to use it.

The shift to emotional autonomy during adolescence is not as dramatic as the shift to behavioral autonomy. Much depends on parental behavior. Some parents continue to encourage overdependency. Parents who encourage dependency needs that become demanding and excessive, even into adulthood, are interfering with their child's ability to function as an effective adult. Some adolescents who have been dominated by their parents begin to accept and to prefer being dependent. The result is prolonged adolescence. Some adolescents, for example, may prefer to live with their parents after marriage or may never achieve mature social relationships; establish a vocational identity of their own choosing; or develop a positive self-image as a separate, independent person. The opposite extreme from overdependence is detachment by parents, so that the adolescent cannot depend on them at all for guidance and advice. As in so many other areas of life, a middle ground should be established.

Connectedness and autonomy may at first seem to be mutually exclusive. How can one feel close to one's parents yet be independent from them? Most researchers, however, see the two traits as complementary (e.g., Montemayor & Flannery, 1991) and believe that the healthiest families balance independence and emotional support. Families whose members lean too heavily toward connectedness—they spend most of their time together, expect to know details about every aspect of one anothers' lives, and so on—are described as **enmeshed.** Conversely, families whose members are isolated from one another—no one knows what the others do during the day, who their friends are, what they think about important events—are termed **disengaged** (Olson, 1988).

Regarding adolescents and family **cohesion,** then, more is not necessarily better. Much depends on the adolescent's age and the stage of the family life cycle. Ordinarily, family cohesion is tightest in the early stages of marriage while the children are young. Children like to feel that they are part of a closely knit family unit. As the children become adolescents, most families become less cohesive (Ohannesian & Lerner, 1995).

The lower level of family cohesion in adolescence is due to the adolescent striving to become autonomous, to carve out a life for himself or herself in the process of separation-individuation. At the same time, parents are separating from the adolescent in their increasing need for privacy as they create a new life for themselves

(Demick, 2002). The result of these simultaneous separating processes is a lower level of cohesion at the adolescent stage of the family life cycle.

Furthermore, research indicates that the spatial distance in parental-adolescent dyads is greater for older adolescent families compared with younger adolescent families (e.g., Bulcroft, Carmody, & Bulcroft, 1996). This lends support to the idea that older adolescents strive for more autonomy and separateness, and for more personal space, compared with younger adolescents. Thus, there is a clear and important relationship between the developmental stage of the family and its spatial distance. This conclusion is even more evident in the research of Larson and Lowe (1990), who found that older adolescents and their parents maintained, on average, a 70 percent greater physical distance between themselves than did younger adolescents and their parents.

Regulation

Guidance and Control
More than 40 years ago, Diana Baumrind (1971) described four basic patterns by which parents exercise control over their children. These four patterns arise from two different, independent dimensions of parenting: control and warmth. The first dimension, **control,** has to do with the degree to which parents manage their children's behavior. At one extreme are parents who exercise a lot of control: they dictate many aspects of their children's behavior, and they expect their children to unquestioningly obey their commands. At the other end of the control continuum are parents who set few rules and impose few consequences if those rules are violated. The second dimension, **warmth,** reflects the degree to which parents are affectionate and supportive as opposed to rejecting and unresponsive.

When these two dimensions are combined in different ways, four separate parenting styles are determined (see Figure 8.1):

- **Authoritative parents** listen to their children and take their wants and desires into account when making rules and decisions. These parents are not really democratic, however; if consensus cannot be reached, the parents have the ultimate say. If you were raised in a family that had frequent family conferences, in which issues were hashed out and everyone's opinion was solicited, then you were most likely raised in an authoritative home.
- **Authoritarian parents** are strict disciplinarians. They make decisions based on what *they* want and what *they* believe is right; there is little discussion about rules and family practices. Children find themselves in big trouble if they do not live up to their parents' expectations. If your parents frequently said "You'll do it because I said so," without offering any other explanation for their demands, you were likely raised in an authoritarian home.
- **Permissive parents** are overindulgent. They believe that the best way to express their love is to give in to their children's wishes. They permit their children to decide almost everything for themselves and tend to avoid monitoring their children too closely. They don't like to say no or to disappoint their children. It follows that not much happens to the children if they do something that goes against their parents' preferences. If your parents let you stay up as late as you wanted (even when you were only 7 or 8) and didn't give you any chores to do (or did them for you), you were probably raised in a permissive home.

separation-individuation the process by which the adolescent becomes separated from parents and becomes a unique individual.

autonomy independence or freedom.

behavioral autonomy becoming independent and free enough to act on one's own without excessive dependence on others.

emotional autonomy becoming free of childish emotional dependence on parents.

enmeshed families those whose members are too heavily connected with one another.

disengaged families those whose members are isolated from one another.

cohesion the degree to which family members are connected to one another.

control the degree to which parents manage their child's behavior.

warmth the love, approval, and emotional support that parents give their children.

authoritative parents parents who respect their children's wishes but who maintain control in the home.

authoritarian parents parents who set many rules and harshly enforce them.

permissive parents parents who exercise little control over their children's behavior.

FIGURE 8.1 THE FOUR PRIMARY PARENTING STYLES

Source: Based on Baumrind (1971).

	Controlling	Undemanding
Warm	Authoritative parents	Permissive parents
Cold	Authoritarian parents	Uninvolved parents

- **Uninvolved parents** do not seem to care about their children, as they let their children do whatever they (the children) wish. However, these parents do so out of indifference rather than (misguided) love. They seem to want to be bothered as little as possible. Often, parents are uninvolved because they are overwhelmed by the stresses in their own lives or because their children were unwanted.

What effect does each style of control have on the adolescent? Which styles are best?

Few ideas are agreed upon more readily by developmental psychologists than the assertion that authoritative parenting is best (Steinberg, 2001). In fact, it is better to have one parent who is authoritative and one who is not (even though this means there will be parental disagreement) than it is to have two parents who use another parenting style (Fletcher, Steinberg, & Sellers, 1999). Authoritative parents exercise authority but express concern through guidance. **Induction** (Hoffman, 2000) is the discipline technique most frequently used by authoritative parents. Induction involves talking with the child, explaining why the action in question was inappropriate and how it affected others in a negative way. The purpose of the discussion is to induce feelings of guilt over the behavior so that it will not be repeated. Not only is induction the most effective disciplinary technique, but it is one that adolescents are most receptive to: they may not enjoy these discussions, but they believe them appropriate responses on their parents' part and the discussions do not make them angry (Padilla-Walker & Carlo, 2004).

Authoritative parents also encourage individual responsibility, decision making, and autonomy. Adolescents are involved in making their own decisions while listening to and discussing the reasoned explanations of their parents. Adolescents are also encouraged to detach themselves gradually from their families. As a result, the authoritative home atmosphere is likely to be one of respect, appreciation, warmth, acceptance, and consistent parenting (Necessary & Parish, 1995). This type of home is associated with conforming, trouble-free nondelinquent behavior in both boys and girls.

This finding about the effectiveness of authoritative parenting is so robust that it not only holds true for American adolescents, but also cross-culturally, as well

RESEARCH HIGHLIGHT   IS IT OKAY TO MISLEAD ONE'S PARENTS?

Adolescence is a time when individuals actively seek autonomy and independence, when they strive to grow up and experience new things. Parents frequently disagree with their teenage children as to the pace at which this maturation should take place and the specific activities appropriate for them. Given this, and the perceived need for conformity to peers and for being cool, it is almost inevitable that adolescents will find themselves in the situation of wanting to do something of which their parents may disapprove. One "solution" to this dilemma is to mislead one's parents, either by outright lying or by neglecting to tell them about the upcoming activity. Recently, as an outgrowth of interest in parental monitoring, there has been a burst of research activity concerning the issue of adolescent deception.

Perhaps the most basic question asks whether it is common for adolescents to lie to their parents. The answer appears to be "yes." Jensen and his colleagues (2004) asked high school and college students whether they had lied to their parents about six issues (e.g., parties, alcohol) during the previous year. Between one-third and two-thirds of the high school students and 28 to 50 percent of the college students reported lying about each issue; approximately 80 percent of the students had lied at least once during the previous year. Sons lied somewhat more than daughters.

Do adolescents think that it is morally acceptable to lie to their parents? Sometimes. It depends both on the issue and the motivation for lying. Adolescents feel most obligated to tell their parents about those issues that they believe to be legitimately their parents' concern and least obligated to tell them about issues that are purely personal, and hence not their parents' business (Smetana, Metzger, Gettman, et al., 2006). Of course, parents and adolescents do not always agree about into which realm issues fall, but these disagreements become smaller as adolescents age. Lying is more acceptable when the motives are altruistic or prosocial rather than spiteful (Jensen, Arnett, Feldman, et al., 2004).

Still, what may be acceptable and normative in small doses is not necessarily good in larger ones. Consistent with most previous research, Frijns, Frinkenauer, Vermilst, et al. (2005) found that adolescents who made a habit of keeping secrets from their parents were more likely to have low self-esteem, exhibit depressed moods, be stressed, be aggressive, and have low levels of self-control than their more honest peers. They suggested three possible reasons for these negative associations. First, keeping secrets is stressful, hard work. Second, parents can't help their adolescents as well as they should if they are uninformed about what is really going on in their lives. Third, keeping secrets undermines feelings of belongingness and cohesiveness with the family.

In any event, honesty is generally the best policy!

PERSONAL ISSUES   CORPORAL PUNISHMENT

Corporal punishment or *physical punishment* refers to the use of physical force with the intention of causing a child pain, but not injury, for purposes of correction or control of the child's behavior. Corporal punishment of children by parents is a normative form of discipline in U.S. society and in many places around the world. More than half of American parents employ physical punishment (Wissow, 2001), including 20 percent of those with teenage children. Its use has become more controversial, however, and a number of countries—including Sweden, Germany, and the United Kingdom—have either banned its practice or legally restricted its use (Ben-Arieh & Haj-Yahia, 2008). Widely accepted or not, it is important to note that a meta-analysis of 70 studies of the effects of corporal punishment (studies conducted between 1961 and 2000) indicated that physical discipline had both negative behavioral and negative emotional consequences (Paolucci & Violata, 2004). Other forms of discipline are more effective and do not yield these negative effects.

ANSWERS WOULDN'T YOU LIKE TO KNOW …

What is the best way to discipline adolescents?

The best way to discipline adolescents is to talk to them about the reasons that their actions are unacceptable. Making threats and handing out punishments tend to make children and adolescents aggressive, and withdrawing love and affection makes them insecure.

(Rohner & Britner, 2002). For example, in their comparative study of American, Swiss, Hungarian, and Dutch adolescents, Vazsonyi, Hibbert, and Snider (2003) found that parents who were relatively authoritative had adolescent children who were better adjusted than did those parents who were relatively authoritarian or permissive. This pattern also holds true for families from non-Western cultures (e.g., Feldman & Rosenthal, 1994), and for ethnic minorities within the United States as well (Steinberg, 2001).

The usual effect of *authoritarian parenting* is to produce a combination of rebellion and dependency. Adolescents are taught to follow their parents' demands and decisions without question and not to try to make decisions themselves. Adolescents in such environments usually are more hostile to their parents, often deeply resent their control and domination, and less often identify with them. The teens may become rebellious and are sometimes overtly aggressive and hostile—especially if the parents' discipline has been harsh, unfair, or administered without much love and affection. The effects on children growing up in authoritarian homes varies according to their dispositions: the meeker offspring are cowed and remain dependent; the stronger ones are rebellious. Both usually show some emotional disturbances and have both social and emotional problems.

Authoritarian parents are usually inflexible, believing that there is only one right way, and that is their way. Such parents are unyielding and refuse to change their ideas and behavioral responses. They won't discuss different points of view or allow disagreements, so they and their adolescents can never understand one another. They expect all of their children to fit narrow molds, to act, think, and be alike. They are intolerant of children who are different from themselves.

Inflexible parents are often perfectionists and thus are regularly critical and displeased with their adolescents' performance on most things. The results are the destruction of the adolescents' self-esteem and the creation of considerable tension and stress. Many such adolescents grow up with a great deal of anxiety and fear they will be doing something wrong or not be able to measure up.

Authoritarian parents rely heavily on punishment, and the effect of using punitive measures to exercise control is usually negative. Adolescents can get (metaphorically) beaten down by their parents' harshness, and adolescents with authoritarian parents are more likely to become clinically depressed than other adolescents (Aquilino & Supple, 2001). Furthermore, adolescents who grow up in homes in which parents use harsh and physical punishment will usually model their parents' aggressive behavior. Family violence seems to beget more violence in and outside the home (Walker-Barnes & Mason, 2004).

ANSWERS WOULDN'T YOU LIKE TO KNOW …

How much say should adolescents have in making family plans?

Parents should definitely allow adolescents to have a say in making family plans. Doing so demonstrates respect for their opinions and gives them practice in decision making. However, adolescents should not have as much as or more say in these decisions than their parents.

uninvolved parents   parents who seem disinterested in their children and thus do not supervise them or give them much affection.

induction   parental control through offering alternative choices.

There is also a relationship between harsh discipline in the home and adolescents' relationships with their peers. Adolescents who exercise little restraint in their social behavior, partly because they model the aggressive behavior of their parents, are not as well liked by peers as adolescents who have learned restraint from positive models at home (Kaufmann, Gesten, & Santa Lucia, 2000).

Although, as noted before, the evidence strongly suggests that authoritative parenting works best across a broad array of cultural and ethnic groups, it is also true that the negative effects of authoritarian parenting are not as consistent in some groups as in others (e.g., Asian Americans and African Americans). This may be in part because the broad term *authoritarian* does not capture the subtle differences in how parents in different ethnic groups exercise strict control. Brooks-Gunn and Markman (2005), for example, found evidence that older African American mothers sometimes use a strategy they termed "tough love," a variant of authoritarianism different from that used by younger African American mothers, that can be quite successful. It is also likely due to the fact that the different cultural backgrounds of individuals from these groups mean that these adolescents and parents have different expectations about normative behavior and hence attribute different meanings to the parents' disciplinary behaviors than Caucasian adolescents would; this could serve to mitigate the negative effects of authoritarianism (Mason, Walker-Barnes, Tu, et al., 2004). For example, Asian American adolescents with authoritarian parents tend to do well in school, although in one recent study they did not do as well as those who had more authoritative parents (Lee, Daniels, & Kissinger, 2006).

At the other extreme is the *permissive* home, in which adolescents receive little guidance and direction, are given few restrictions from parents, and are expected to make most decisions for themselves. There are actually three forms of overindulgence: (1) material overindulgence, in which children are given nearly every possession they desire, regardless of the cost or their need for it; (2) relational overindulgence, which occurs when parents excessively attend to their child's every whim so that the child never learns to do anything independently for himself or herself; and (3) structural overindulgence, which results when parents set no rules or limits on a child's behavior (Clarke, Dawson, & Bredehoft, 2004). Often these types of permissiveness occur together.

The specific effects of the different sorts of permissiveness vary, of course, but the overall outcome is the same: pampered adolescents will be ill prepared to accept frustrations or responsibility or show proper regard for others. They often become domineering, self-centered, and selfish and get into trouble with those who will not indulge them the way their parents have. Without limits on their behavior, they feel insecure, disoriented, and uncertain. If adolescents interpret the parents' lack of control as disinterest or rejection, they blame the parents for not wanting or guiding them. Lax discipline, rejection, and lack of parental affection have also been associated with delinquency. In fact, in one study, juvenile delinquents from permissive homes were less empathic, had lower grades, and were more likely to use drugs than were those from authoritarian homes (Steinberg, Blatt-Eisengart, & Cauffman, 2006). Adolescents raised by uninvolved parents are similar to those raised by permissive parents, but the effects are more extreme.

In addition to setting rules and meting out punishments, parents regulate their children's behavior by *monitoring* them. Successful parents know what their children do, where they go, and with whom they spend their time (Jacobson & Crockett, 2000). Moreover, adolescents are less likely to get into trouble if they believe that their parents will find out about it. Monitored adolescents are less likely to participate in delinquent behavior, engage in sexual behavior, and use drugs (Crouter & Head, 2002). Permissive parents, of course, expend less effort in monitoring their children than either authoritarian or authoritative parents.

Although agreeing that there is a strong correlation between parental knowledge of their adolescents' behavior and the quality of that behavior, some researchers have questioned the *source* of that knowledge. Does it come from monitoring per se, or does it come from voluntary self-disclosure on the part of the teen? There are, after all, different ways of knowing what another is doing. Stattin and Kerr (2000) examined three sources of knowledge: parental control (rules structuring the adolescent's behavior so that the parents knew their child's whereabouts and actions), parent solicitation of information (direct questioning), and child self-disclosure. In their study, it was self-disclosure that best predicted both parental knowledge and lack of antisocial behavior. Similarly, Waizenhofer, Buchanan, and Jackson-Newsom (2004) studied four sources of knowledge: asking others about the child, child self-disclosure, unsolicited information from the spouse, and extrapolation from usual routine ("if this is 6 P.M. Thursday at, then . . ."). They found that parents knew more about their daughters' activities than their sons' and that mothers knew more about adolescents' activities than did fathers. Mothers were also more likely than fathers to gain information by active supervision or voluntary disclosure from the adolescent, whereas fathers tended to receive information from their spouses.

Parent–Adolescent Tension

The amount of tension between parents and adolescents is greater than that between parents and younger children (Kim, Conger, & Lorenz, 2001). Even so, most parents who enjoy good relationships when their children are small will continue to do so when their children become teens (Noack & Buhl, 2004). Given that adolescents are striving to increase their autonomy, a certain amount of conflict is normal and inevitable. One might even argue that conflict contributes to healthy development. Working out disagreements forces adolescents to clarify their identities, to take others' perspectives, to grapple with moral issues, to learn how to compromise, and to handle frustration and anger (Walker & Taylor, 1991). In the following sections, we discuss some of the major causes of parent-adolescent tension.

Differences in Outlook

Parent-adolescent misunderstandings arise from the two types of outlooks that adults and youths typically have. Table 8.1 shows a comparison of these outlooks. Although not all adults or youths fit the types described, enough are similar to the two descriptions to make these differences a major source of conflict. The table reveals some significant differences between middle-aged parents and adolescent children. From a vantage point reached after many years of experience, parents believe that youths are irresponsible, reckless, and naive, too inexperienced even to recognize that they are foolish to take chances. Parents worry that their teenaged children will have accidents, get hurt, or get in trouble with the law. Youths believe their parents are overly cautious and worry too much.

Middle-aged parents tend to compare today's youths and lifestyles with those of their own past. Parents often suffer from a perennial *cultural lag*—a situation that renders them relatively poorly informed. Children and teenagers show a tendency to overgeneralize the ineffectiveness of parents as instructors of current cultural norms and thereby question their reliability as educators in general. In fact, adolescents sometimes think they have to socialize parents to bring them up to date on modern views.

Parents also become a little cynical about human character and somewhat disillusioned about trying to change the world and everybody in it; they realistically learn to accept some things as they are. Adolescents are still extremely idealistic and impatient with adults who are part of the establishment and accept and like things as they are. Adolescents want to reform the world overnight and become annoyed when their parents do not agree with them.

Recall from Chapter 5 (Cognitive Development) that adolescents are enthralled with their new cognitive abilities. They can now think abstractly, hypothetically, and counterfactually. They can imagine alternatives that do not, in fact, exist. Parental behaviors that were once taken for granted are now questioned. Adolescents often believe that they have intuited solutions to problems that are better than those proposed by their elders. Although sometimes they have, more often, their solutions are not realistic because they lack experience and do not yet comprehend the complexities of the world. Adolescents may feel misunderstood, however, when their suggestions are not embraced.

Adolescents also grow to be wary of adults, primarily because they believe that most adults are too critical and will not understand them. Youths think they have good ideas, too, and know more about some things than their parents do, and, because they feel grown up, they may scoff at parental suggestions or ideas. Adults—like adolescents—react to criticism and rejection with anger and hurt.

Finally, some aging adults become oversensitive about growing old or being considered aged. Because they hate to think of getting old, they focus more and more attention on staying young. If parents carry this insecurity to extremes in their dress and behaviors, they succeed mostly in attracting the embarrassed shame of their own teenagers and the amused ridicule of other youths.

TABLE 8.1   MIDDLE-AGED ADULT VERSUS ADOLESCENT OUTLOOKS

MIDDLE-AGED GENERATION	ADOLESCENT GENERATION
Tends to be restrictive on views as to what is age-appropriate behavior	
Is careful/experienced	Tends to be more accepting than adults of actions that violate behavioral and social expectations of age-appropriate behavior
	Is daring and adventurous; sometimes takes foolish chances
Holds to past; has tendency to compare present with yesterday	Considers past irrelevant; lives in present
Is realistic; sometimes skeptical about life and people	Is idealistic, optimistic
Is conservative in manners, morals, and mores	Is liberal; challenges traditional ideas; experiments with new customs
Is generally contented and satisfied; accepts status quo	Is critical with things as they are; desires to reform, change
Wants to stay youthful; fears age	Wants to be grown up, but dislikes idea of ever being old

ANSWERS WOULDN'T YOU LIKE TO KNOW ...

Are adolescent–parent conflicts mostly due to adolescents' desire for greater freedom?

Although adolescent-parent arguments are due, in part, to adolescents' wanting greater freedom, they are also due to the fact that middle-aged parents are fighting their own psychological battles and have different perspectives on life than their teenage children.

Focus of Conflict

In spite of personality differences, research indicates that parent-adolescent relationships are usually harmonious (Laursen & Collins, 2009). When conflict occurs, arguments usually involve one or more of five broad topics (Holmbeck, Paikoff, & Brooks-Gunn, 1995). In the main, arguments are about mundane, trivial issues.

Social Life and Customs

Adolescents' social lives and the social customs they observe probably create more conflict with parents than any other area (Smetana & Asquith, 1994). The most common sources of friction include choice of friends or dating partners, going out on school nights, where the teen is allowed to go and the type of activity in which he or she can participate, curfew, going steady, and choice of clothes and hairstyles. One of the most common complaints of parents is that adolescents are never home and do not spend any time with the family.

Responsibility

Parents become critical of adolescents who do not evidence enough responsibility. Parents and adolescents disagree as to the extent that the adolescent should perform family chores; earn and spend money; care for personal belongings, clothes, and room; use the family car; incur cell phone or texting charges; do work for others outside the home; and care for family property or belongings (furniture, tools, etc.).

School

Adolescents' school performance, behavior at school, and attitude toward school receive much attention from parents. Specifically, parents are concerned about grades, study habits and homework, regularity of attendance, general attitude toward school studies and teachers, and conduct in school.

Family Relationships

As parents and their adolescent children negotiate new standards of relationships during adolescence, some tension is likely. Conflict often arises over perceived immature behavior; general attitude toward and level of respect shown to parents; quarreling with siblings; relationships with other relatives, especially aged grandparents in the home; and degree of orientation toward family.

Social Conventions

Parents are often especially concerned with these behaviors: drinking, smoking, and drug use; vulgar language and speech; sexual behavior; rule violations; and church or Sunday school attendance.

As discussed in Chapter 7 (The Development of Moral Values), parents and their teenage children rarely disagree about basic moral values, such as whether it is wrong to cheat or hurt others (Reisch, Bush, Nelson, et al., 2000). Instead, they disagree about behaviors that are socially acceptable to one group (adolescents) but not to the other (adults). For example, adolescents usually find it more acceptable to curse and use coarse language than adults.

Adolescents and their parents can come into conflict over many different issues: choice of friends, curfews, chores, grades, and use of inappropriate language, among others.

Conflicts usually occur when people's expectations are violated. These violations are especially likely during adolescence because the adolescent is changing rapidly (hence, parental expectations may be out of date) and because the adolescent may have an inflated sense of his or her own maturity and abilities (Collins, Laursen, Mortensen, et al., 1997). Adolescents expect to be granted autonomy at an earlier age than their parents believe is appropriate (Feldman & Quatman, 1988); this is perhaps because they feel older than they really are (Montepare & Lachman, 1989).

Variables Affecting Conflict

The focus of conflict in any one family will depend on a number of factors. The three most obvious ones are the *adolescent's gender*, the *parent's gender*, and the *adolescent's age*.

The first of these, adolescent gender, does not by itself seem to contribute greatly to the overall amount of conflict in a family (Bosma, Jackson, Zijsling, et al., 1996), although it does interact with the other two factors to produce different patterns. For example, girls argue with their fathers most often in early adolescence, whereas sons argue most with their fathers in late adolescence (Comstock, 1994). Also, adolescent girls and boys may argue with their parents about somewhat different issues; one study found that sons argued more with their parents about behavioral problems than did daughters, who argued more (with fathers, at least) about peer and friend issues (Renk, Liljequist, Simpson, et al., 2005).

Adolescents have different types of conflicts with their mothers than with their fathers because they tend to have different kinds of relationships with them. Adolescents typically perceive their fathers to hold more authority than their mothers (Youniss & Smollar, 1985). This, coupled with the fact that they usually spend more time with their mothers, means that they tend to argue more with their mothers (Laursen & Collins, 1994a). But again, conflict does not necessarily imply dislike or lack of closeness. As mentioned before, most adolescents feel closer to and communicate more openly with their mothers than with their fathers (Ackard, Neumark-Sztainer, Story, et al., 2006), and mothers exert more influence over adolescents (Greene, 1990).

As adolescents age, they are apt to agree more and argue less with their parents. By the time a child is 18 or 19, his or her parents are usually willing to grant the

autonomy and freedom he or she desires. It is earlier, during middle and especially early adolescence, that conflict is more likely. At those ages, adolescents likely desire freedoms that their parents believe are inappropriate and want to shrug off responsibilities that their parents think they are ready to assume. A meta-analytic review of the literature confirmed this trend: the conflict rate does decrease over the course of adolescence. However, the conflicts become more intense and emotional as the adolescents mature (Laursen, Coy, & Collins, 1998).

The total *atmosphere within the home* influences conflict. Conflicts of all types are more frequent in authoritarian homes than in authoritative homes. In authoritarian homes, there is more conflict over spending money, social life, activities outside the home, and home chores. Conflict between parents also affects the home atmosphere and has a detrimental effect on adolescents. A family atmosphere of warmth and supportiveness promotes successful negotiation of disagreements between parents and adolescent children and thereby helps keep conflict at a low to moderate level. Under hostile, coercive conditions, however, parents and adolescents will be unlikely to resolve disagreements and conflict will escalate to dysfunctional levels (Rueter & Conger, 1995).

The *socioeconomic status* of the family is another variable affecting the amount and causes of conflict. Low-socioeconomic-status families are more often concerned about obedience, politeness, and respect, whereas middle-income families are more concerned with developing independence and initiative. Low-socioeconomic-status families may also worry more about keeping children out of trouble at school; middle-class parents are more concerned about grades and achievement (Hoff, Laursen, & Tardif, 2002). Poverty-class parents are more likely to be authoritarian and to use harsh and inconsistent discipline practices (Leyendecker, Harwood, Comparini, et al., 2005), leading to increased conflict levels.

As previously mentioned, *ethnicity* is also correlated with family interaction patterns. For example, since Asian American adolescents are likely to believe that their parents have more of a right to supervise their studying habits and academic progress than other teens, they are less likely to fight over these issues (Lee, Daniels, & Kissinger, 2006).

The *community environment* in which the child grows up will determine what parents worry about. An adolescent growing up in an area where there is high delinquency or considerable drug abuse will find their parents more concerned with these problems.

Another factor influencing conflict is *parental workload*. Adolescent conflict is highest when both parents are stressed. This is particularly true in dual-career families, in which both the mother and father may be stressed because of their jobs (Galambos, Sears, Almeida, et al., 1995). When both parents work outside the home to support the family, there is often a reduction of parental attention and monitoring provided to the adolescent. This lack of proper supervision is the major cause of difficulty in some families. Some parents do a good job in parenting their adolescents even though both work; other parents virtually neglect this responsibility almost entirely, and their adolescents are left on their own to fend for themselves.

The variables influencing parent-adolescent conflict are almost countless, but the ones mentioned here indicate how many factors may be involved.

Conflicts with Parents Versus Conflicts with Peers

Adolescents spend more time arguing and fighting with their parents than they do with their peers (Fuhrman & Buhrmester, 1992), and their arguments with their parents are more emotional and heated (Laursen, 1993). Arguments with parents tend to involve clear winners and losers, whereas with friends the resolution is more likely to include a compromise (Adams & Laursen, 2001). These differences likely stem from two sources. First, parents and adolescents have more things to argue about—more divergent expectations—than friends and adolescents. Second, friendships are voluntary alliances that can be terminated, whereas family ties are intrinsically more permanent (Collins, Laursen, Mortensen, et al., 1997). In short, you can yell at your mother without worrying that she will abandon you for some other child, but you can't yell at your friend because he or she may likely end the relationship.

Results of Conflict

Again, it is important to emphasize that constant, intense adolescent-parent conflict is abnormal (Laursen & Collins, 2009). Research with families of adolescents not under clinical treatment has consistently shown that despite arguments with parents, adolescents characterize their family relationships as close, positive, and flexible. Studies on the frequency and intensity of family conflict, however, including both marital conflict and parent-adolescent conflict, emphasize that high levels of conflict affect family cohesion and have an adverse effect on adolescent development. Adolescents in families with high levels of conflict are more likely to evidence antisocial behavior, immaturity, and low self-esteem than those in families with low levels of conflict (Barber & Delfabbro, 2000).

Parents actually seem to experience more stress from having arguments with their adolescents than the adolescents do. In one study, 40 percent of parents reported experiencing two or more negative effects—decreased self-esteem, increased anxiety, and so on—as a result of conflict with their teenage children (Steinberg & Steinberg, 1994; Steinberg, 2001). It is the parents, not the children, who cannot easily stop thinking about these disputes.

Relationships with Other Family Members

Parents, of course, are usually not an adolescent's only relatives. Most adolescents have siblings, grandparents, aunts, uncles, and cousins. They may also have stepparents and half- and stepsiblings. (These relationships are discussed in the next chapter.) The influence of siblings and grandparents, in particular, can be quite significant.

Adolescent-Sibling Relationships

Research efforts have concentrated on exploring parent-adolescent relationships in the family, and less information is available on adolescent-sibling relationships. Yet the relationships between brothers and sisters are vitally important because they may have a lasting influence on development and serve as a model for other, future close adult relationships (Conger, Cu, Bryan, et al., 2000). Let's examine the number of ways in which sibling relationships are important.

First, older siblings are likely to serve as role models for younger brothers and sisters. They have a strong influence on the development of younger brothers and sisters. This influence can be good or bad. For example, economically disadvantaged inner-city youths who had close relationships with supportive, well-adjusted, older siblings were less likely to be delinquent and did better in school than similar youths who did not have comparable older siblings (Widmer & Weiss, 2000), whereas having a delinquent sibling increases the risk that a youth will become delinquent (Williams, Conger, & Blozis, 2007) . Similarly, adolescent girls whose older sisters were teenage mothers were more likely to be sexually active themselves than girls whose older sisters were not mothers as teens (East, Reyes, & Horn, 2007), and teens whose older siblings use drugs are more likely to do so themselves (Rende, Slomkowski, Lloyd-Richardson, et al., 2005). Having deviant older siblings may be an even stronger influence on an adolescent's proclivity toward deviant behavior than having antisocial parents (Ardelt & Day, 2002).

Next, older siblings often serve as surrogate parents and caregivers (Dunn, Slomkowski, & Beardsall, 1994). If older children feel useful, accepted, and admired because of the care they give younger children, this added appreciation and sense of usefulness contributes positively to their own sense of self-worth. Older siblings nurture and give advice (Tucker, Barber, & Eccles, 1997), and they are also often expected to protect younger siblings from the aggression of older children (Tisak & Tisak, 1996). Many adolescents learn adult roles and responsibilities by having to care for younger brothers and sisters while growing up. Still, sibling relationships become more egalitarian during adolescence and lose much of their imbalance; during the teenage years, older and younger siblings give support to each other (Branje, van Lieshout, van Aken, et al., 2004).

Adolescents frequently serve as role models and teachers to their younger siblings.

Third, siblings often provide companionship and friendship and meet one another's needs for affection and meaningful relationships. For example, Sherman, Lansford, and Volling (2006) found that adolescents who were not popular with their peers developed especially close ties with their siblings. Furthermore, these close sibling relationships partially compensated for the lack of close peer ties, and the unpopular adolescents who had warm, affectionate relationships with siblings were less lonely than those who did not (Milevsky, 2004). In some studies, adolescents have been found to self-disclose more to their siblings than to their parents (e.g., Furman & Buhrmeister, 1992).

What is the most typical nature of adolescent siblings' relationships? Perhaps they can best be described as "love/hate"; although there are frequently elements of support and caring, there is also often a degree of rivalry and competition (East, 2009). Siblings spend less time together in adolescence than during childhood, and their interactions are usually less intense (Kim, McHale, Osgood, et al., 2006). Overt conflict decreases, but feelings of rivalry may actually increase because age differences become less important. (The difference in a

parent's expectations of a 4- and a 7-year old is much greater than the difference between his or her expectations for a 13- and a 16-year-old.). Sibling intimacy and closeness drop during early adolescence but climb again during mid-adolescence (Cole & Kerns, 2001). Girls tend to remain closer to their siblings than do boys (Moser, Paternite, & Dixon, 1996).

Relationships with Other Relatives

Relationships with grandparents can also have positive effects on adolescents. Three of the most important are these:

1. Grandparents may be significant agents in providing a sense of continuity in an adolescent's life, in linking the past to the present, and in transmitting knowledge of culture and family roots, and thus having a positive impact on the adolescent's search for identity (Kopera-Frye & Wiscott, 2000).

2. Grandparents may have a positive impact on parent-adolescent relations by conveying information about the parents to the adolescent. Adolescents also turn to grandparents as confidants and arbiters when they are in conflict with their parents (Lussier, Deater-Deckard, Dunn, et al., 2002).

3. Grandparents help adolescents understand aging and accept the aged. Adolescents who see their grandparents frequently and have a good relationship with them are more likely to have positive attitudes toward the elderly (Harwood, Hewstone, Paolini, et al., 2005).

Mueller, Wilhelm, and Elder (2002) have identified five different grandparenting styles. The closest grandparents they labeled *influential;* as the term implies, these grandparents are highly involved in their grandchildren's lives, the majority of them see their grandchildren almost daily. They serve as confidants, friends, and mentors, and they tend to provide financial resources to their grandchildren. The next-closest relationship is held by *supportive* grandparents. The largest difference between supportive grandparents and influential grandparents is that supportive grandparents do not play a role in disciplining their grandchildren and do not see themselves as authority figures to them. *Passive* grandparents see their grandchildren less frequently (generally at least once/month) and enjoy them, but they do not materially help them nor do they assume quasi-parental responsibilities for them. *Authority-oriented* grandparents are more distant fonts of family wisdom who have less direct involvement with their grandchildren. Last, *detached* grandparents do not know their grandchildren well, and although they may have fond feelings for them, they are largely uninvolved in their lives.

In addition, with increases in both the divorce rate and births to never-married women, it is becoming more common for grandparents to actively help parent or even

Grandparents often have positive effects in relationships with their adolescent grandchildren. A grandparent may help in the adolescent's search for identity by linking the past to the present and may serve as an arbiter in conflicts with the adolescent's parents.

solely raise their grandchildren. This phenomenon is discussed more fully in the next chapter.

What determines the nature of the grandparent-grandchild relationship? Physical proximity certainly makes it easier to maintain contact (Uhlenberg & Hammill, 1998). The relationship of parent and grandparent is also of key importance, as parents are generally the gatekeepers of grandchild-grandparent contact. Since daughters usually remain closer to their parents than sons, grandchildren often spend more time with their mothers' parents than with their fathers' (Chan & Elder, 2000). Also, relationships with grandparents tend to improve during the course of adolescence (Crosnoe & Elder, 2002), most likely as autonomy issues are resolved and family relations as a whole improve.

Maltreatment

Maltreatment of children may include either child abuse or child neglect. **Child abuse** means nonaccidental physical injury and assault, sexual abuse, and/or mental and emotional injury of the child. The child may be physically attacked, burned, hit, beaten, banged against a wall or the floor, or battered, leading to fractures, lacerations, or bruises. **Sexual abuse** includes suggestive language, use of pornography, fondling, petting, masturbation, exhibitionism, voyeurism, oral sex, or full vaginal or anal intercourse. **Emotional abuse** includes constant screaming at the child, calling him or her foul names, criticizing, ridiculing the child, unfavorably comparing the child with siblings, or ignoring the child. **Child neglect** means failure to provide even minimal care of the child, including adequate food, clothing, shelter, and medical care, as well as failure to

provide for a child's emotional, social, intellectual, and moral needs. Thus, maltreatment is a multidimensional concept that includes both attack and neglect.

Physical Abuse

Parents who physically attack and hurt their children have a devastating emotional and physical effect on them. Some children die of the abuse; others are permanently maimed. The children are hurt and terrified and are deeply scarred emotionally by the rage and hatred directed against them. Pathological fear; shyness; passive dispositions; deep-seated hostility; sullenness; and a cold, indifferent inability to love others are often the results. Adolescents who are physically abused are more likely to use violence themselves, even as adults. Fagan (2005) found that adolescents who had been physically abused while teenagers were 50 percent more likely than non-victims to engage in general crime and to use drugs. Even more startlingly, she found a doubling or tripling in the amount of violent crime that physically abused individuals committed against the general public or against intimate partners. Adolescent girls who have been physically abused often continue to find themselves on the receiving end of violence: they choose abusive dating partners and are traumatized in their romantic relationships (Sappinton, Pharr, Turnstall, et al., 1997). They also are more likely than other adolescent girls to engage in risky sexual behavior (Elliott, Avery, Fishman, et al., 2002). Finally, adolescents who have been physically abused are more likely to develop clinical depression and to have suicidal thoughts than adolescents without a history of abuse (Danielson, de Arellano, Kilpatrick, et al., 2005).

Children of all ages, including adolescents, are sometimes the victims of physical abuse, sexual abuse, emotional abuse, and neglect.

Sexual Abuse

The effects of sexual abuse on children and adolescents have been well documented. Researchers in the area of child sexual abuse have noted that the constellation of symptoms observed among abuse survivors matches the diagnostic criteria for post-traumatic stress disorder (PTSD) (Kingston & Raghaven, 2009).

Both clinical and community studies have found high levels of depression, anxiety, sexual problems, and suicidal threats and behavior in sexual abuse victims (Paolucci, Genius, & Violato, 2001). In addition, sexual abuse victims appear highly susceptible to substance abuse (Martin, Peters, Amos, et al., 2005), eating disorders (Johnson, Cohen, Kotler, et al., 2002), and self-injurious behavior (Cyr, McDuff, Wright, et al., 2005).

Sexual abuse also seems to be an important background factor in some patterns of adolescent antisocial behavior (Lowenstein, 2006). People who are sexually abused—primarily females—have been found to score higher than controls on measures of hostility and

aggression and are more likely to become delinquent. They have also been reported to manifest elevated levels of school problems, including truancy and dropping out before completing high school. In addition, they are more likely than controls to run away from home during adolescence. There is evidence that many prostitutes have been sexual abuse victims, particularly those abused at relatively young ages and with greater violence (Stoltz, Shannon, Kerr, et al., 2007). Females are more often sexually abused than males, but much sexual abuse of both males and females remains undetected and underreported. Because of this underreporting, estimates of the prevalence of child sexual abuse vary from 8 to 32 percent in women and 1 to 16 percent in men (Sikkema, Hansen, Meade, et al., 2009).

Incest

The long-term consequences of incest are similar to those of other forms of sexual abuse. However, because of the intense sense of betrayal that they experience, victims of incest are generally more strongly affected by the experience than are victims of non-incestuous sexual abuse (Rind & Tromovitch, 1997). Common reactions include an inability to trust others; low self-esteem; increased risks for developing depression, eating disorders, and substance abuse; and diffuse physical symptoms such as stomach pain (Holifield, Nelson, & Hart, 2002). It is not unusual for incest survivors to find it difficult to trust others, and so they often have trouble forming intimate relationships. It appears that men who were incest victims as boys are even more strongly affected than women who were incest victims as girls (Garnefski & Diekstra, 1997).

Neglect

Neglect is the most common form of maltreatment of children and adolescents. It may take many forms. *Physical neglect* may involve failure to provide enough food or a proper diet, adequate clothing, health care,

child abuse   may include not only physical assault of a child but also malnourishment, abandonment, neglect, emotional abuse, and sexual abuse.

sexual abuse   may include suggestive language, use of pornography, fondling, petting, masturbation, exhibitionism, voyeurism, oral sex, or full vaginal or anal intercourse.

emotional abuse   may include constant screaming at the child, calling him or her foul names, giving constant criticism and put-downs, making fun, constantly comparing the child with siblings, ignoring the child, and refusing to talk or listen to him or her.

child neglect   failure to provide even minimal care of a child, including adequate food, clothing, shelter, and medical care, as well as for the child's emotional, social, intellectual, and moral needs.

adequate shelter, or sanitary conditions in the home or to require personal hygiene. *Emotional neglect* may include showing inadequate attention, care, love, and affection or failing to provide for the child's need for approval, acceptance, and companionship. *Intellectual neglect* may include allowing the child to stay out of school frequently for no reason, failing to see that the child goes to school or does homework, or failing to provide intellectually stimulating experiences and materials. *Social neglect* may include inadequate supervision of social activities, lack of concern about the child's companions and playmates, unwillingness to get the child involved in social groups and activities, or failure to socialize the child to get along with others. *Moral neglect* may include the failure to provide a positive moral example for the child or any type of moral education and guidance.

The stories of parental neglect are legion. One couple went on vacation for several weeks at a time and left their 12-year-old daughter alone in the house unsupervised. Another mother spent days with her boyfriend, leaving her 15-year-old son to care for himself. One mother let her daughter's teeth decay until they fell out without making any attempt to get dental care (Rice, counseling notes).

Some cases of neglect are more subtle. The parents reject their children emotionally and fail to show that they love or care for them. Such situations can be just as devastating as physical abuse. For example, emotional abuse has been linked to substance abuse (Moran, Vuchinich, & Hall, 2004). Children who have been emotionally abused tend to have low self-esteem, to be depressed, to have difficulties in school, and to have poor peer relations (Sneddon, 2003).

SUMMARY

1. Good parents are emotionally connected to their children, give them opportunities for psychological autonomy, and monitor their behavior.
2. Parents express the love they have for their children by being interested in them, helping them, listening to them, being sensitive to their needs, trusting them, and accepting them for who they are.
3. Adolescents want parents who will accept them as autonomous adults and let them establish individuality and independence through the process of separation-individuation. Autonomy consists of two aspects: behavioral autonomy and emotional autonomy. The desire for behavioral autonomy arises during adolescence before the shift to emotional autonomy.
4. *Cohesion* refers to the degree to which family members are connected or separated. Families on the extremes—either completely disengaged or completely enmeshed—function less adequately than do families that are nearer the center of the scale. Family cohesion is greatest when children are young and declines as adolescents grow up and seek to become autonomous adults.
5. There are four basic patterns of family control: authoritative, authoritarian, permissive, and uninvolved.
6. The authoritative pattern of control has the most positive effect on adolescents.
7. Authoritarian control tends to produce a combination of rebellion and dependency. The effect of punitive measures is usually negative.
8. Adolescents raised by permissive parents are often selfish and irresponsible.
9. Uninvolved parents typically produce adolescent children who feel rejected and insecure.
10. The most functional families are those in which the parents are flexible, adaptable, and tolerant in their ideas and behavior.
11. Parents and adolescents often find themselves in conflict because they are in the midst of different stages of life.

They have different perspectives on the issues they are confronting, which makes misunderstandings inevitable.
12. Overall, parent-adolescent relationships are usually harmonious, but when conflict occurs, it may be in any one of the following five areas: social life and customs, responsibility, school, family relationships, and social conventions.
13. A number of variables affect conflict: age and sex of the adolescent, the atmosphere within the home, the socioeconomic status of the family, ethnicity, the community environment in which the child grows up, and parental workload.
14. Whereas moderate levels of conflict are normal, high levels are not. Still, conflicts with parents are often more intense than those with peers.
15. Older siblings affect the development of children: they serve as role models and surrogate parents, provide companionship, and meet one another's needs for affection and meaningful relationships.
16. Siblings also are sometimes jealous, compete for parental affection, and have conflicts with one another.
17. Relationships with grandparents can have a positive effect on adolescents. Grandparents can be influential, supportive, passive, authority oriented, or detached.
18. *Child abuse* includes non-accidental physical injury and assault, sexual abuse, and/or mental and emotional injury of the child. *Sexual abuse* may include suggestive language, pornography, fondling, petting, masturbation, exhibitionism, voyeurism, oral sex, or vaginal or anal intercourse. *Emotional abuse* may include screaming at the child, calling names, criticism and put-downs, making fun, unfavorable comparisons of the child, and refusal to talk or to listen. *Child neglect* means failure to provide even minimal care of the child; failure to provide adequate food, clothing, shelter, and medical care; and failure to provide for the child's emotional, social, intellectual, and moral needs.

19. Adolescents who have been abused are more likely to be depressed, anxious, and violent than other teenagers. They are more likely to use drugs and to develop eating disorders. Without treatment, many of these problems carry on into adulthood.

KEY TERMS

affect 202	empathy 201
authoritarian parents 205	enmeshed families 204
authoritative parents 205	induction 206
autonomy 204	negative affect 202
behavioral autonomy 204	permissive parents 205
child abuse 214	positive affect 202
child neglect 214	psychological autonomy 200
cohesion 204	regulation 200
connection 200	separation-individuation 204
control 205	sexual abuse 214
disengaged families 204	uninvolved parents 206
emotional abuse 214	warmth 205
emotional autonomy 204	

THOUGHT QUESTIONS

Personal Reflection

1. Were your parents authoritative, authoritarian, permissive, or uninvolved? Why do you characterize them that way? Provide examples to support your answer.
2. Do you want to be the same kind of parent that your mother was? That your father was? What do you think you will do differently than they did? Why?
3. How did your parents express their warmth and concern for you? Which means of expression meant the most to you? Why?
4. When you were an adolescent, what sort of discipline did your parents use on you? Was it effective? Why or why not?
5. Did you find it easier to talk to your mother or your father? Were there some topics you discussed more with one than with the other?

Group Discussion

6. What issues did you and your parents most frequently argue about? Did the same issues come up over and over again, or were they constantly changing?
7. What keeps parents from listening to adolescents and understanding them?
8. What sorts of home responsibilities or family chores should be expected of adolescents? Should they be paid for doing these chores? Why or why not?
9. If you have an adolescent brother or sister living at home, what are the major sources of conflict between him or her and your parents?

10. Do you know any adult who was abused as a child? What have been some of the effects?
11. What do you think is the ideal role for grandparents to play within the family?

Debate Questions

12. Parents should unquestioningly act as if they trust their adolescent children unless they have been given clear reason to do otherwise.
13. Teenagers should always obey their parents.
14. Parents should give their adolescent children advice, whether or not their children want to hear it.
15. Siblings should be required to "be friends" and spend a lot of time together.

SUGGESTED READING

Barber, B. K. (Ed.). (2002). *Intrusive Parenting: How Psychological Control Affects Children and Adolescents*. Washington, DC: American Psychological Association.

Crosson-Tower, C. (2001). *Understanding Child Abuse and Neglect* (5th ed.). Boston, MA: Allyn & Bacon.

Ferrara, F. F. (2001). *Childhood Sexual Abuse: Developmental Effects across the Lifespan*. Pacific Grove, CA: Brooks-Cole.

Glasser, W. (2003). *For Parents and Teenagers: Dissolving the Barrier between You and Your Teen*. Chatsworth, CA: Quill.

Lipinski, B. (2001). *Heed the Call: Psychological Perspectives on Child Abuse*. Seattle: Pacific Meridian.

USEFUL WEB SITES

Child Abuse Prevention Network
http://child-abuse.com/

This site is primarily designed to help professionals in the field of child abuse. However, it contains a listing of useful e-lists and support groups for laypersons with an interest in this topic.

Child Welfare Information Gateway
www.childwelfare.gov

This site, created and maintained by the U.S. Department of Health and Human Services, was designed to be useful to parents as well as educators and other professionals. It is full of current information about child abuse; namely, it provides information about individual state statutes, the steps to take if you suspect child abuse or neglect, information about how to seek help, national statistics of abuse, a database, and links to other sites. It also provides information about adoption.

Ohio State University Family and Consumer Sciences Extension Service
www.hec.ohio-state.edu/famlife/adolescence/parads.htm

The Department of Family and Consumer Sciences at Ohio State University provides this site, which contains a series of articles written to help parents learn to better interact with their teenage children. Topics include Communicating with Your Teen, Monitoring: Staying Involved in Your Teen's Life, and Understanding Teens.

WOULDN'T YOU LIKE TO KNOW . . .

- What are the short-term effects of divorce on adolescents, and how long do these effects last?

- How many adolescents have divorced parents?

- Are children from divorced families more likely to have long-term behavioral problems than children from intact families?

- Are children whose parents divorced more likely to get divorced themselves someday?

- In terms of the children's well-being, should unhappy parents stay together or get divorced?

- Which is better for adolescents: if their parents have joint custody or if one parent has sole custody?

- How well do children fare when they are raised by never-married mothers?

- Do adolescents benefit when their mothers get remarried?

- How well do adolescents in blended families get along with their stepsiblings?

Different Family Patterns

Fewer and fewer American adolescents have the experience of living in the same home as both of their biological parents for the duration of their childhood. In fact, while it is still the norm to be raised in a single house by both one's biological mother and biological father, it is *barely* so, and it is even less typical to be raised in what has historically been known as a "traditional" family, in which one's biological father goes off to work while one's biological mother stays home and minds the kids. Because so many adolescents have undergone their parents' divorce, are being raised by single parents, or are part of a blended, reconstituted family, it is worthwhile to consider the impact of these events on adolescent

development. In this chapter, we examine each of these family constellations.

With Whom Do American Adolescents Live?

As Figure 9.1 illustrates, almost all American adolescents (about 95 percent) younger than age 19 reside with at least one of their biological parents, and somewhat more than half (about 60 percent) live with both of their biological parents (Kreider, 2008). Almost 30 percent live with only their biological mothers, and

FIGURE 9.1 ADOLESCENT/BIOLOGICAL PARENT RESIDENTIAL PATTERNS BY RACE AND ETHNICITY

Source: Data from U.S. Bureau of the Census (2009).

Both biological parents · Biological mother only · Biological father only · Neither biological parent

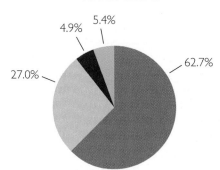

All Adolescents
5.4%
4.9%
62.7%
27.0%

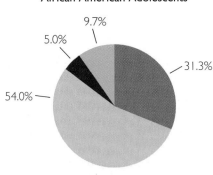

African American Adolescents
9.7%
5.0%
31.3%
54.0%

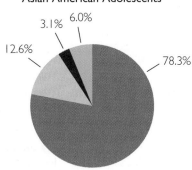

Asian American Adolescents
6.0%
3.1%
12.6%
78.3%

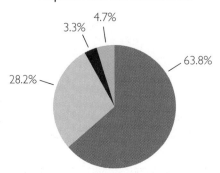

Hispanic American Adolescents
4.7%
3.3%
63.8%
28.2%

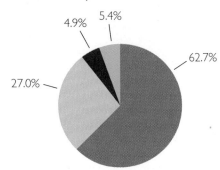

White, Non-Hispanic American Adolescents
5.4%
4.9%
62.7%
27.0%

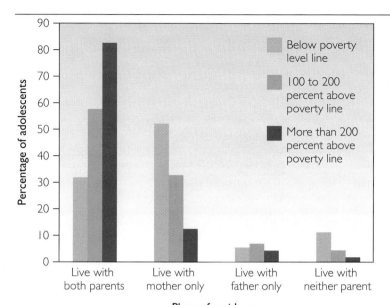

FIGURE 9.2 ADOLESCENT RESIDENCE AS A FUNCTION OF FAMILY INCOME LEVEL

Source: Data from U.S. Bureau of the Census (2002).

less than 5 percent live with only their biological fathers. Residential patterns vary considerably by race and ethnicity. Asian American teens, for example, are very likely to live with both biological parents, whereas nearly two-thirds of all African American adolescents live apart from their biological fathers.

These racial/ethnic differences are, in part, a result of the economic disparities among cultural subgroups. As shown in Figure 9.2, middle-class adolescents are far more likely to live with both biological parents than are those from lower socioeconomic levels. Conversely, lower-income youths are far more likely to live with only their mothers or with neither

parent than are middle-income youths (U.S. Bureau of the Census, 2002).

There are four possible reasons why an adolescent might live with only one of his or her biological parents. First, the parents might be married but living apart because of idiosyncratic circumstances, such as one parent working in another city or state. Second, a parent may have died. Third, the parents might be divorced or legally separated. Finally, the child might have been born to a single mother who has never been wed to the child's father. As Figure 9.3 depicts, the latter two reasons are by far more common than the first two (U.S. Bureau of the Census, 2009b). Again, there is significant

CROSS-CULTURAL CONCERNS   EXTENDED FAMILIES

When Americans of European descent hear the word *family*, they will most likely envision what anthropologists and sociologists call the *nuclear family*, a family composed of a married couple and any children they might have together. Of course, in modern American society—with its proliferation of out-of-wedlock births, divorces, and remarriages—many White Americans think of *single-parent families*, *split families*, and *blended families*, as well. Individuals with other ancestral backgrounds, however, may find that the *extended family* more quickly comes to mind.

The extended family structure is common throughout much of the world. Families in many parts of Asia, Africa, and Latin America follow an extended family model. Many

Native American people have also traditionally followed and continue to embrace this pattern. Some extended families are three generational: grandparents, parents, and children share the same household. Other extended families are composed of adult siblings and their spouses and children. In some parts of the world, extended families consist of a husband, his several wives, and their children.

The extended family has the advantage of involving more adults in the sharing of economic burdens, household labor, and child care. Because of this, extended families are more common among low-socioeconomic-status Americans than among middle-class Americans. This trend is most apparent among African Americans, who have enjoyed the benefits of the extended family for generations.

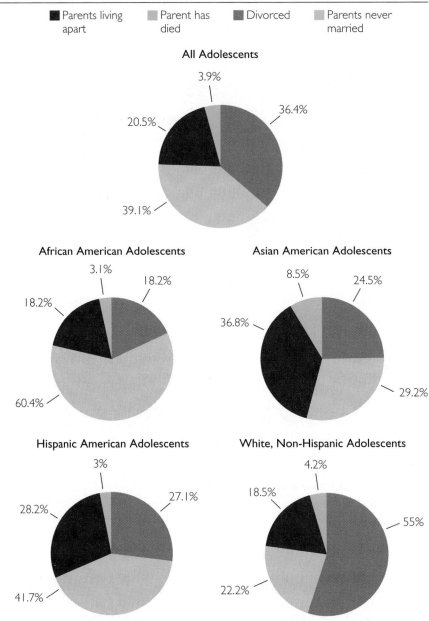

FIGURE 9.3 REASONS ADOLESCENTS LIVE WITH ONE BIOLOGICAL PARENT BY RACE AND ETHNICITY

Source: Data from U.S. Bureau of the Census (2009b).

racial/ethnic variation in the reasons for living with one parent. Divorce is the most common reason in non-Hispanic Caucasian homes, whereas out-of-wedlock birth is the most common reason in Hispanic and African American homes. And as noted earlier, family income level correlates with the reason for parental absence: the higher the income level, the more likely the parents were divorced as opposed to never wed (see Figure 9.4).

Divorce and Adolescents

Since divorce has become so common, the question arises as to how it affects adolescents. A range of factors are involved.

Attitudes Toward Divorce

Data indicate that nearly half of all American marriages end in divorce (National Marriage Project, 2005). The great majority of these marriages involve children, some of whom are already adolescents and some of whom have yet to grow into adolescents.

A large number of mental health practitioners view divorce as a major, negative event that stimulates insecurity, confusion, and painful emotions in the children involved. Although the majority of these practitioners believe that most children are not permanently harmed by divorce, others insist that the upset interferes with long-term emotional and social growth (e.g., Wallerstein & Lewis, 2004).

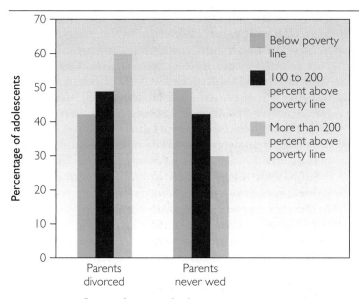

FIGURE 9.4   REASONS ADOLESCENTS LIVE WITH ONE BIOLOGICAL PARENT BY FAMILY INCOME LEVEL

Source: Data from U.S. Bureau of the Census (2002).

Short-Term Emotional Reactions

Immediate emotional reactions to parents' divorce have been well documented (Kelly, 2003). Sometimes they involve shock and disbelief if adolescents have not realized the extent of their parents' marital problems. Another reaction is a combination of fear, anxiety, and insecurity about the future: "Will my father move away? Will I get to see him?" "Will I have to go to another school?" "Who am I going to live with?" "How am I going to be able to go to college?"

Anger and hostility are also common emotional reactions among adolescents, especially toward the parent they blame for the divorce. One girl asked her mother, "Why did you make daddy leave?" Another, age 12, asked, "Why did you leave my father all alone?" A son told his father, "I hate you for leaving mom for that other woman" (Rice, counseling notes). Sometimes the anger is directed toward both parents: "You've ruined my whole life. I have to leave all my friends and my school." Some youths are so caught up in their own pain that they forget (at least temporarily) the distress that their parents are feeling.

Other typical feelings among adolescents are self-blame and guilt. If parental conflict has been about the children, they may feel partly responsible for their parents breaking up or that the parent is leaving because he or she wants to get away from them rather than the spouse. They may also feel self-conscious and bewildered that their parents are getting divorced, and they try to hide that fact from their friends.

After separation occurs, adolescents have to adjust to the absence of one parent, often one on whom they have depended deeply for affection and help. One adolescent girl remarked, "The hardest thing for me was to get used to being without my father. I never realized how

ANSWERS WOULDN'T YOU LIKE TO KNOW ...

What are the short-term effects of divorce on adolescents, and how long do these effects last?

Most adolescents whose parents divorce experience a range of emotions—among them fear, anger, depression, guilt, and resentment—and are, at times, entirely overwhelmed by the experience. (A minority of youths, however, feel relieved and happy.) It is not uncommon for youths to lose interest in school and other activities during this time of upheaval. It usually takes one to two years for adolescents to adjust to their parents' divorce.

much I needed him until he left" (Rice, counseling notes). Divorce is often followed by a period of mourning and grief, not unlike the feelings that arise when a parent dies. Feelings of sadness, dejection, and depression are common.

If parents begin to date again and get emotionally involved with another person, adolescents may become jealous and resentful because they have to share their parent with another adult. If parents remarry, as the majority of them do, the adolescents are confronted with a new adjustment to a stepparent.

Burns and Dunlop (1999) found that these negative emotions, which were almost universal near the time of divorce, do not last. Three years after their parents divorced, most of the adolescents studied reported that their sadness and shock had greatly diminished; these feelings were replaced with those of relief and gladness that the conflict was over. Ten years after the divorce, gladness and relief dominated the teens' emotions, although many still retained anger toward one of their parents (usually their father).

Long-Term Effects

Many people believe that children whose parents divorce can be scarred for life by the experience. This common conviction was reinforced by Judith Wallerstein's best-seller *Second Chances: Men, Women, and Children a Decade after Divorce* (Wallerstein & Blakeslee, 1989), based on a 15-year follow-up to a landmark clinical investigation. Wallerstein found that almost half of the subjects in her California study were, on reaching young adulthood, "worried, underachieving, self-deprecating, and sometimes angry young men and women. Many were involved in maladaptive pathways, including multiple relationships and impulsive marriages that ended in divorce" (Wallerstein, 1991, p. 354). Later follow-up indicated that the negative outcomes were visible even a quarter century after the divorce occurred (Wallerstein & Lewis, 2004). There were among these young adults some who had seemed calm and untroubled at earlier ages. This led Wallerstein to remark that the long-term effects of divorce on children cannot be predicted from how the children react earlier in life.

These rather pessimistic conclusions were challenged because other studies produced different results. Critics noted the limitations of the California study, such as its small size, the lack of a non-divorced control group, and the fact that the sample was not selected on a probability basis and was overrepresented by families that sought clinical help (Cherlin & Furstenberg, 1989). Others claimed that Wallerstein failed to take into account the harm caused by living in the conflict-ridden situation that preceded the divorce (Gordon, 2005).

Given the continued high rate of marital disruption and ongoing controversy over what impact it has on children, scholars called for better evidence to test

Wallerstein's and others' hypotheses about the long-term effects of parental divorce. In the intervening 15 to 20 years, much more research on this topic has been conducted—most of it confirming and extending Wallerstein and Blakeslee's findings: children and adolescents whose parents divorce are at heightened risk for a variety of problem behaviors, both when they are minors and when they are adults.

A meta-analysis of divorce-outcome studies published in the 1990s found that compared to children with continuously married parents, children with divorced parents scored significantly lower on measures of academic achievement, acceptable conduct, psychological adjustment, self-concept, and social relations, although the differences were not always large (Amato, 2001). These negative outcomes are likely regardless of the child's age at the time of the divorce (Wallerstein & Lewis, 1998). Many studies have concluded that boys' behavior is more affected than girls' (e.g., Trinder, 2008).

Furthermore, the influence of having experienced parental divorce extends into adulthood. Compared to adults raised in intact families, adults whose parents divorced when they were children are less likely to attend college and more likely to cohabitate without marriage, to have children at an early age, and to suffer from poor mental health. These differences are not all merely continuations of the problems that emerge during adolescence. In fact, the gap between individuals raised in intact families and those raised by divorced parents increases during adulthood (Cherlin, Chase-Lansdale, & McRae, 1998).

This pattern is not confined to the United States but has been validated cross-culturally. For example, in a large European study, Huurre, Junkkari, and Aro (2006) tracked nearly 1,500 individuals as they moved through adolescence into their early thirties. Adults whose parents had divorced were less likely to attend college and more likely to be unemployed than those whose parents had not divorced. They were also less likely to be married themselves and more likely to smoke and use alcohol excessively. In addition, women (but not men) whose parents had divorced were more likely to suffer from depression and psychosomatic symptoms than women from intact families. These effects held even when socioeconomic status and other factors were controlled.

One specific aspect of Wallerstein and Blakeslee's (1989, 2004) findings that has been confirmed by other researchers is the long-term effect of parental divorce on children's future marital relationships. In 2001, Amato and DeBoer reported the results of a large, longitudinal study of adults that found that those who were the children of divorced parents were at twice the risk of getting divorced themselves compared to those who were raised in intact families. The adults raised by parents who had low levels of marital satisfaction but did not divorce were not at such risk. More recently, Whitten and her colleagues (2008) studied women from intact and divorced families who were engaged to be married and found that women's parental divorce was associated with both lower commitment to their fiancé and lower confidence in their relationship with him. The men they studied did not show this lack of confidence.

Researchers have been trying to sort out causes for this phenomenon. One explanation is suggested by the previously mentioned study by Whitten et al.: when children of divorce marry, they are highly apprehensive about it and have a lower commitment to their marriages, and their marriages are more likely to fail than those of offspring from intact families. They tend to be hesitant and cautious about marriage. However, they are just as likely to marry as are other people. They are strongly impelled toward marriage but often hedge their bets against failure by withholding full commitment to it.

A second explanation is offered by social learning theory. Children tend to model their behavior after that of their parents. Thus, children may imitate parental behavior that is detrimental to successful marriage and be more prone to divorce. Finally, a third explanations is that children of divorced parents marry at an earlier age than children from intact families. This may be because of emotional need or the desire to escape an unpleasant home situation. Marriage at early ages has been found to be significantly related to marital failure (DiCario, 2005).

Relationships with siblings, too, seem to suffer in divorced families. Studies by Riggio (2001) and Milevsky (2004) found sibling relations to be less supportive after a parental divorce. Sheehan, Darlington, Noller, et al. (2004) found them to be more hostile and conflict laden.

It is important to underscore that most adolescents whose parents divorce have no long-term adjustment problems. Divorce is a risk factor; it increases the odds that problems will develop, but it by no means guarantees that they will (Amato, 2000). In general, children whose parents have divorced are two to three times as likely to develop problems as children from intact families (Kelly, 2003), so that whereas approximately 10 percent of children from never-divorced families have serious adjustment problems, approximately 20 to 25 percent of children whose parents have divorced do (Hetherington & Kelly, 2002).

Moreover, the alternative to divorce—that is, for the parents to remain in a conflict-ridden, unhappy marriage—is no better for children's development. Numerous studies (e.g., Morrison & Coiro, 1999) have indicated that children whose parents have divorced are better off than those raised in intact but discordant households. Furthermore, children brought up in intact homes fraught with conflict are no more likely to experience stable marriages themselves than those whose parents chose to divorce (Amato & Booth, 2001).

Factors Influencing the Effects of Divorce

Many factors contribute to the lower well-being of adolescents who have experienced parental divorce. First, there is the trauma and conflict leading up to the divorce. Since adults who are happily married and content with their lives do not divorce, children whose parents divorce have witnessed parental battles and experienced significant tension within the home. Next is the trauma of the divorce itself. Even in the most harmonious of circumstances, divorce brings pain and uncertainty. Children ask themselves questions such as: Where will we live? Will Dad still love me? Whom will I stay with? Finally, there are the long-term lifestyle changes that result from divorce. Children will likely spend far less time with one of their parents, or they will move back and forth between two households. Moreover, the family's financial situation usually deteriorates following divorce, and the family may move to a new home in a new neighborhood. The parents' behavior toward their children likely changes, as well. (Each of these issues will be discussed in more detail later in this section.)

Many but not all of these issues revolve around *conflict*. Multiple forms of family conflict—including frequent disagreements with parents, marital conflict, parental aggression, and conflict between nonresidential fathers and mothers—consistently and adversely affect adolescent outcomes. For many adolescents in divorced families and stepfamilies, conflict had been a routine part of their lives. Many adolescents suffer lingering effects from sustained pre-divorce marital discord

ANSWERS WOULDN'T YOU LIKE TO KNOW . . .

Are children whose parents get divorced more likely to get divorced themselves someday?

Again, yes: children whose parents get divorced are more likely to divorce themselves someday.

ANSWERS WOULDN'T YOU LIKE TO KNOW . . .

In terms of the children's well-being, should unhappy parents stay together or get divorced?

The most important factor in determining the children's well-being is the amount of discord that they experience at home. If parental divorce will diminish the conflict in the home, then that is preferable to subjecting the children to an ongoing hostile family situation. But if getting divorced does not relieve or increases the parents' acrimony, then it is not the better solution.

and accompanying changes in family process, including inconsistent parenting, interspousal aggression, parent-child aggression, and deteriorating parent-child relationships. These problems are compounded by persistent post-divorce tensions and hostilities between parents as adolescents are drawn into conflicts, feel caught between parents, and are either pressured to take sides or try to remain close to both parents and subsequently experience loyalty conflicts. In other words, the data corroborate mounting evidence that family conflicts—manifested in diverse ways, and persisting over stages of the life course—impair adolescent well-being (e.g., Bing, Nelson, & Wesolowski, 2009).

Heredity and Temperamental Differences

Individuals vary in their ability to adapt to change—namely, the quality of their coping skills, their level of self-esteem, and their willingness to go to others for help. These personality attributes may well affect how a given child will adjust to his or her parents' divorce (Hetherington & Stanley-Hagan, 1999). Some children are simply more resilient than others. There is substantial evidence that personality traits such as these are, in part, genetic and that they do contribute to psychological well-being and adjustment. Monroe and Reid (2008), for example, report that genetic differences influence one's tendency to respond to stress with depression. Even more directly, D'Onofrio and colleagues (2006) found that an inherited, genetic susceptibility was responsible for a number of the effects usually attributed causally to divorce, such as increased substance abuse and increased risk of cohabitation.

Pre-Divorce Economic Circumstances

As a whole, families that are headed for divorce are qualitatively different from families that are destined to remain intact. In particular, individuals who have a low level of education, earn less money, and marry at a young age (characteristics that frequently occur together) are more likely to divorce than are those who do not fit this profile (Pryor & Rogers, 2001). Furthermore, declining economic circumstances (or becoming less wealthy, regardless of one's starting point) also increase the probability of divorce (O'Connor, Pickering, Dunn, et al., 1999). This means that children whose parents have divorced are more likely than children whose families are stable to have experienced poverty or a decline in their standard of living. Moreover, the stressful economic circumstances that were experienced prior to the divorce will likely contribute to any negative outcomes seen after the divorce.

Pre-Divorce Parental Behavior

In addition to parental conflict, as mentioned earlier, additional aspects of parents' pre-divorce behavior are detrimental to the children living in the household.

For example, even prior to a divorce, mothers whose marriages will end behave more negatively toward their children than mothers whose marriages will succeed, and neither mothers nor fathers in marriages destined to dissolve exercise as much control over their children as those whose marriages will continue (Hetherington, 1999a). In addition, adults are generally physically and psychologically distressed for a period of time leading up to a divorce, and being under stress decreases the quality of parenting. Alcohol or substance abuse on the part of one spouse may also be involved, as it is frequently cited as a reason for divorce (Ostermann, Sloan, & Taylor, 2005). It follows that children whose parents have divorced are more likely to have been raised by a substance-abusing parent than children whose parents have remained married. Again, the fact that these stressors were present in a household prior to a divorce can help explain the origin of any problems displayed by a child after the fact.

Post-Divorce Economic Resources

In most cases, children's economic status worsens after their parents' divorce. Most children live full or part time with their mothers after their parents have separated, and women's standard of living declines by an average of 36 percent post-divorce (Bianchi, Subaiya, & Kahn, 1999). This drop in income frequently means that children lose not only the security of their family as they have known it, but also the lifestyle to which they have become accustomed. It is not unusual, for instance, for children to move to a smaller home after a divorce, often in a different neighborhood or school district. They may also have to give up music lessons or need to take a job to help with expenses.

Post-Divorce Parental Behavior

The effect of divorce on adolescents depends partly on how their parents are affected. The psychological adjustment of parents, especially of the custodial parents, greatly influences the adjustment of their adolescents (Hetherington, 1999a). The more upset the parents are, the more likely adolescents will be disturbed. Some parents are very relieved by the divorce and this has a positive effect on adolescents.

Divorce is a difficult experience for couples, even under the best circumstances. Under the worst circumstances, it results in emotional trauma and a high degree of shock and disorientation. The newly divorced face loneliness and social readjustment as they seek new friendships and companionship (Pinquart, 2003). The divorced woman with children is faced with role strain and an overload of work, now that she must perform all family functions herself. Contacts with an ex-spouse may continue to be troublesome. Positive support from one's own parents is helpful, and grandparents can have an important effect on the adolescent's adjustments, as well.

It is generally agreed that after a divorce, the quality of parenting goes down. For example, right after the divorce, parents may become less affectionate and more authoritarian with their children; they may be inconsistent in their demands and enforcement of rules (Hetherington, 1991). In the long run, divorced custodial mothers tend to engage in less monitoring of their children's behavior and use less effective discipline strategies (Simons, Lin, Gordon, et al., 1999).

Some parents feel guilty about the divorce and want to make it up to their children (Raphael, Cubis, Dunne, et al., 1990). If this desire leads to a parent's spoiling his or her child, the intent may be good but the outcome is not. Adolescents may enjoy being spoiled at the time, but being plied with expensive gifts, being allowed to stay out until 3:00 A.M., and being excused from chores do not help teenagers become mature, responsible adults. Often, it is the noncustodial parent who tries to make the most of the limited time he or she has with the child and, in effect, buy the child's affection.

Any understanding of the effects of divorce on adolescents must take into account the parents' changed position following a divorce. If a parent is quite upset, if her income is severely reduced, if she must often leave her adolescents alone while she goes to work outside the home, the children are going to be affected, not because of the divorce, as such, but because of the subsequent effect on that parent and her changed relationship with her children.

Amicability of the Divorce

As stated earlier, children benefit from their parents' divorce if it removes them from a conflict-ridden situation (Morrison & Coiro, 1999). Unfortunately, the conflict between parents does not always cease once their divorce has been finalized. The stress often continues and the children may feel caught in the middle. Adolescents are particularly upset over the fighting if their parents are trying to get them to take sides or to exploit them as spies, go-betweens, and informers to find out about the other parent. In most cases, adolescents love both of their parents and do not want to have to choose sides.

Relocation and Relationship Loss

Although custody arrangements are discussed in the next section, it is worth mentioning here that *post* divorce, most adolescents do not see one of their parents—usually their fathers—nearly as often as they formerly did. In addition, they are less likely to spend as much time with members of the noncustodial parent's extended family: if you see your father only six days a month, then you most likely see your paternal grandparents and your cousins from his side of the family less often as well. In

RESEARCH HIGHLIGHT ADOLESCENT CHILDREN RAISED BY GAY AND LESBIAN PARENTS

Many people assume that adolescent children raised by gay and lesbian parents will more likely have problems than children raised by heterosexuals, including (1) an abnormal sexual identity, (2) adjustment and personality problems, (3) impaired relationships, and (4) increased likelihood of being sexually abused. Are these concerns legitimate? Let's examine each in turn:

1. *Abnormal sexual identity: Sexual identity* is a broad term that encompasses gender identity (positive feelings about being male or female), sex-typed behavior (doing and enjoying so-called masculine activities if male and feminine activities if female), and sexual orientation (one's sexual preference in a partner). Contrary to popular belief, there is *no* evidence that children raised by homosexuals are more likely to develop an abnormal sexual identity than children raised by heterosexuals. Most children raised by gay parents are themselves heterosexual.

2. *Adjustment problems:* Researchers have compared the personalities, autonomy, behavioral problems, depression rates, moral development, and intelligence of children raised by gay versus straight parents. *No* meaningful differences have been found (Tasker, 2005).

3. *Social relationships:* Although many children of gay parents are undoubtedly teased and harassed about their parents' sexual orientation, overall, the peer relationships of these youths are fine (Wainright & Patterson, 2008). Just as having heterosexual parents doesn't shield children from teasing, having homosexual parents doesn't guarantee it either. Also, a bully who wishes to tease can always find something to belittle in another person.

4. *Sexual abuse:* There is no reason to believe that children of gay parents are more likely to be sexually abused than other children. The notion that gay men are more likely to be child molesters than straight men is an erroneous assumption and is simply untrue (Finkelhor, 2003).

In sum, children raised by gays and lesbians do not behave any differently from children raised by heterosexuals. Although there has been little long-term research in this area, it appears that these children remain as normal and well adjusted as other children into adulthood.

addition, many children and adolescents lose contact with their friends because their custodial parent physically relocates them (they move). In one study (Braver, Ellman, & Fabricius, 2003), approximately 30 percent of the respondents said they moved more than an hour's drive away from their former home with their custodial parent, and there were numerous negative outcomes associated with those moves. Also, Hetherington and Kelly (2002) reported that the custodial mothers in their study moved an average of four times in the six years following their divorce. Even if some of those moves are within the same relatively small geographic area, the likelihood of a child's having to change schools, thereby losing contact with friends and teachers, is great.

Custody and Living Arrangements

Some of the most difficult decisions made during a divorce are those concerning child custody. Custody is composed of two separate issues: **legal custody** refers to the right of a parent to make decisions affecting a child, and **residential custody** refers to where and with which parent the child will live. Emotional attachments, fairness, and economic consequences for children and parents are among the issues involved in arriving at a custody disposition.

Until the 1980s, in the majority of the cases, it was assumed that the mother would receive both legal and residential custody unless there were circumstances that would keep her from being a competent parent. Today, the odds of father custody are enhanced when children are older, especially when the oldest child is male, when the father is the plaintiff, and when a court investigation has occurred during divorce proceedings. Odds of the father getting custody are reduced by higher educational levels of mothers, higher earnings by the mother, and

support delinquency prior to final divorce judgments. It is not surprising that substantial policy debates concerning legal and residential custody arrangements at divorce are common (Fox & Kelly, 1995).

The greatest fear of adolescents who have good relationships with both parents is that divorce will result in their losing contact with a parent. This is not an unreasonable fear: between 18 and 25 percent of children lose all contact with their fathers within two to three years after a divorce occurs (Kelly, 2003). This is clearly not beneficial. The data are quite compelling that adolescents who remain in close contact with their noncustodial fathers, especially when those fathers are authoritative, involved in their schoolwork, and support them financially, do better scholastically and have fewer behavioral problems than adolescents whose fathers do not (King & Sobolewski, 2006). Research has shown that in cases of **joint custody**, fathers are more likely to be active in parenting than are noncustodial fathers and that children are often, as a result, better adjusted (e.g., Bauserman, 2002). Quantity of contact does not appear to be as important as quality of contact (Dunn, 2005). For this reason, parents need to make it clear that they are not divorcing their children and that they will continue to be active, concerned, and caring parents. Of course, if a parent is poorly adjusted, extremely immature, or abusive in any way, tight restrictions on child visitation may be necessary (Warshak, 1986). Under the best circumstances, disturbance is minimized if the adolescent can see a parent any time he or she needs or wants to.

Divorce often results in reduced attachment to the noncustodial parent. In general, adolescents from intact families view themselves as more positively emotionally attached to their fathers than do those from divorced

Until recently, the mother automatically was granted custody of the children, unless there were concerns about her competency. Today, the father's chances of custody are enhanced. Rallies such as the one shown have helped change this pattern.

and remarried families. This seems to be especially true for daughters, as sons spend more time with their fathers post-divorce and report feeling closer to them (King, Harris, & Heard, 2004). Thus, divorce may have an impact on the emotional bonds adolescents have with their fathers, and remarriage does not seem to mediate this impact (McCurdy & Scherman, 1996).

Joint custody arrangements require a high degree of maturity and flexibility on the part of the parents, or discussions will result in squabbles and a continuation of the marital stress, to the detriment of the children (McIntosh & Chisholm, 2008). If desired by both parents, and if they are able to get along together, there is general agreement that joint custody is a helpful solution to a difficult problem.

Which type of arrangement is best? There is no clear-cut answer to this question. For most of twentieth century, it was assumed that mothers made better parents than fathers, and so almost all custody decisions were made in the mother's favor. The research comparing adolescents in joint custody with those in single-parent custody have had mixed results: some have shown little overall difference in outcomes as a function of type of custody (Hines, 1997), whereas others have shown benefits (Bauserman, 2002). Breivik and Olweus (2006), for example, found that adolescents involved in joint custody arrangements fared better than those in single-custody situations; the authors note, however, the significant possibility of selection being at play here. In other words, parents choose joint custody only if they get along well, and it may well be the lack of conflict, rather than the custody arrangement per se, that causes the positive outcome. What matters more is the quality of the relationship of the child with each parent and the quality of the relationship of the parents with each other after the divorce. The benefits of joint custody are largely negated if the situation is strained and the parents argue and fight (Lee, 2002).

What appears to be most important is not the amount of time spent with both parents but the degree to which both parents remain actively engaged in the adolescent's life and continue to function *as parents* (Simons, Lin, Gordon, et al., 1999). Functioning as a parent involves more than having fun, going on outings, and providing economic support. It also means providing discipline, giving advice, and fostering maturity. Engaged parents share in the negative as well as the positive aspects of the parental role.

Single-Parent/Grandparent-Headed Families

As we have seen, divorce may have different effects on different adolescents, depending on a number of factors. What do we know about adolescents raised in other types of single-parent homes? Far less than we should, especially since almost 40 percent of the births in the United States in 2006 were to an unmarried woman (Martin, Hamilton, Sutton, et al., 2009). Given this fact, it is surprising that so little of the research literature has specifically examined the differences between adolescents raised by single mothers who were never wed and those raised by mothers who were married but later divorced (Amato, 2000).

Furthermore, the literature that does look at this issue is often confounded by parental age: much of the research concerning the children of unwed mothers focuses on the children of unwed *adolescents,* whereas the divorce research usually examines children of *older parents.* Since adolescent mothers are generally less successful than older mothers, whatever their marital status, it is hard to separate the effects of being raised by an unwed mother from those of being raised by a teenage mother.

Racial and economic factors are involved, as well. Most single Black mothers have never been married, whereas most single White mothers have been married and then divorced; never-wed mothers, as a whole, are worse off economically than divorced mothers (Amato, 2000). These two factors may be related.

In any event, in 2000, more than 4.5 million American children and adolescents lived in households headed not by parents, but by grandparents. About 5 percent of White, non-Hispanic children and adolescents, 9 percent of Hispanic children, and 15 percent of Black children had these living arrangements. Most of the time the mother is present as well as the grandparent(s), but 25 percent of the time she is not (U.S. Bureau of the Census, 2000c). Therefore, although it is common for women in all ethnic groups to turn to their own mothers for

legal custody the parent has the right to make important decisions about the child's life, such as which school he or she will attend.

residential custody where and with which parent the child will live.

joint custody when two parents share decision-making privileges (joint legal custody) and/or living with a child (joint residential custody).

"I came from a wonderful family—living proof that single parenthood does not automatically lead to endless despair and troubles. My mom is my role model. She provided a wonderful home for my brother and I to grow up. She sacrificed her own needs and wants for ours. We are indebted to her for life.

"After the divorce, my mother was committed to family each hour of the day. While we were sleeping, she was studying to pass her certification for public accounting. During the days, she was an at-home mom who was there when we got home from school and willing to drive us to a friend's house or sports game. She would help us with homework and talk to us in the evenings. My mom did such a great job that things were never out of step—I never actually realized how bad our family's situation was until just a few years ago.

"Yet extended family support was also key for our successful development. I knew from an early age that I belonged to my family. My maternal grandparents have always been there for us. My grandfather pulled his double-duty, while my grandmother was always willing to take some burden off of my mom. Aunts and uncles would take us on vacation. They gave us a childhood full of experiences that my mother could not provide alone."

support when they find themselves single mothers (Szinovacz, 1998), this phenomenon is most strongly practiced in African American families. African Americans are more likely than Caucasian Americans to emphasize extended family ties (Hill, 1998), as such ties are a part of their African cultural heritage (Hunter, 1997). In addition, first-time African American mothers are apt to be younger than first-time Caucasian mothers (Hamilton, Ventura, Martin, et al., 2005) and so have less experience with child-rearing and are less likely to have resources of their own.

Apfel and Seitz (1991) studied the helping arrangements of 120 inner-city Black adolescent mothers and their own mothers and found that they fell into one of four types. The most common arrangement was a *parental supplement* pattern; it occurred in about half of the families. In these homes, mothers and grandmothers essentially co-parented, although the grandmothers did not necessarily share a residence with their daughters and grandchildren. The grandchildren benefited from the situation in that they had the care of two parents, one of them quite experienced; the adolescent mothers benefited because they could continue their education and they had a helpmate to assume a good deal of the child care burdens. On the downside, Apfel and Seitz found that the coequal nature of the relationship could cause tension between mother and daughter

when there were disagreements and could lead to the child/grandchild's confusion about whom to obey.

Twenty percent of families followed a *supportive primary parenting model*. In this arrangement, the mothers were responsible for the full-time care of their children. Grandmothers helped with expenses, occasionally babysat, and sometimes lent a hand with the mothers' household responsibilities. Family members might all share a residence, or they might live near one another. Some of the families settled into this arrangement because it was the mother's wish to do so: some of the young mothers wanted to live with their boyfriends or assume an adult, independent lifestyle. In other cases, it was more the choice of the grandmothers, who were uninterested in assuming the task of full-time child-rearing or did not want to make things too easy for their daughters and hence encourage additional pregnancies. The benefits of this model are that the mother is provided some support, and the child is provided some additional care; the risk of this model is that the young mother will be overwhelmed when trying to manage so much on her own. The child may be poorly cared for or neglected, and the mother may find that she cannot finish her education or find time for job training.

The third arrangement was for the grandmother to be a *parental replacement* for her daughter; this occurred in about 10 percent of the families. As the name suggests, in these families the grandmothers assumed total parental responsibilities and the mother herself played a rather insignificant role. Sometimes this model was chosen by mutual agreement; for example, both mother and grandmother wanted the mother to go off to college. Sometimes the grandmother took over, gradually or abruptly, because her daughter was negligent. Some families drifted into this pattern, whereas others consciously chose to adopt it. Both mother and child may benefit from this model, the child by having a more competent, nurturing parent than he or she might otherwise have and the mother by being able to concentrate on her own development. However, families run the risk of conflict (if the grandmother does not wish to become the full-time parent or if the mother does not wish to relinquish her role completely), and the child may have to make a wrenching adjustment in the future if the mother returns to resume her parental role.

Apfel and Seitz termed the final pattern the *parental apprentice* model; it, too, occurred in about 10 percent of the families. In this situation, the grandmother acted as mentor to her daughter. These grandmothers believed that although their daughters had the potential to be good parents, they did not yet have the skills and knowledge needed to do a good job. The grandmothers acted as teachers and gradually turned responsibility over to the mothers. This model appeared to have numerous benefits: the adolescent mother was given the training she needed, the child became strongly attached to his or her mother, the mothers and grandmothers were not in conflict about who was the primary parent, and the child received high-quality care. Furthermore, grandmothers and mothers following the *apprentice* model tended to have warm, close relations. (Of course, they could have entered into this relationship *because* they had warm relations rather than developing these relations as a result of it.) The risk of this approach is that the emphasis in these homes was so strongly on parenting that the young mother's education and economic future may have been jeopardized. It is also possible for resentments to develop between grandmother and mother.

It is clear, then, that not all children raised by never-wed mothers are raised solely (or even primarily) by these mothers. The presence of grandparents in these children's lives—and, in fact, in any child's life—can make a profound difference in their development and well-being. For example, using a British sample, Attar-Schwartz and colleagues found that greater grandparent involvement was associated with fewer emotional problems and increased prosocial behavior on the part of adolescents, especially those from single-parent families (Attar-Schwartz, Tan, Flouri, et al., 2009).

Although there are definite benefits to the grandchild to having a highly involved grandparent, there are often costs to that grandparent. Many studies have shown that raising grandchildren often takes a strong toll on the grandmother's well-being (e.g., Ross & Aday, 2006). Custodial and near-custodial grandparents (corresponding to the *parental supplement* and *primary supportive parenting* models) exhibit higher rates of depression and worse physical health and report being under more stress than noncustodial grandparents (e.g., Minkler & Fuller-Thomson, 1999). This is especially true if their grandchild has emotional or behavioral difficulties, as is often the case if the child had been previously raised by an inattentive mother (Emick & Hayslip, 1999). Many experience unwanted feelings of responsibility, obligation, and call for sacrifice (Erbert & Aleman, 2008). Still, most custodial grandparents report immense satisfaction from their role, stating that their grandchildren give them a renewed reason for living and that they feel content knowing that their grandchild is being well cared for (Pruchno, 1999).

Single-Parent Families Resulting from Parental Death

Another type of family that has not been well studied is the single-parent family that results from parental death. More than 2 million American children and adolescents younger than age 18 have experienced a parent's death (Christ, Siegel, & Christ, 2002). Although experiencing a parent's death is in some ways similar to experiencing parental divorce—there are feelings of separation and loss, the child's life is disrupted, economic circumstances

likely change—with parental death, the loss is complete and permanent and there is no hope for continued contact (at least in this lifetime). On the other hand, unless the parent committed suicide, there is less of a sense of betrayal, as the separation was not voluntary. Children's attitudes about their fathers often go down after a divorce, whereas they rise after his death (Spruijt, Degoede, & Vandervalk, 2001). How similar, then, are the effects of divorce and parental death on children?

Surprisingly little is known about the effects of parental death on adolescent adjustment, and most of what is known relates to short-term changes rather than long-term outcomes. Adolescents are likely to experience sadness (*dysthymia*) for up to a year after the death of a parent, but only a minority will become clinically depressed (Dowdney, 2000). They often develop fears about the safety of their remaining parent, and many develop symptoms of post-traumatic stress syndrome, especially if the death was a violent, unexpected one (Cerel, Fristad, Weller, et al., 2000). Not surprisingly, interest in school work and other activities drops (Abdelnoor & Hollins, 2004). Adolescent boys are more likely than girls to react aggressively and to act out (Dowdney, Wilson, Maughan, et al., 1999). One of the most important determinants of the adolescents' reactions is the success

IN THEIR OWN WORDS

"My dad died when I was eleven. Things were worse than awful—Dad was gone and we moved out of state so that my mom could be close to her family. So much went wrong all at the same time! I lost all my friends, my school, my neighborhood, and my dad in one week. For months, I was obsessed with guilt for not being a better daughter while I had the chance; to this day I still kick myself for turning down his invitation to go see a ball game with him a few days before he died. I was miserable and lonely. I had had lots of friends in my old school but was a social loser in my new one because I was unfriendly and cried a lot.

"Over time, though, I began to realize that if I had to lose my dad, I'd rather lose him the way I did—because he died, not because of divorce. There's no anger or sense of betrayal when someone dies, or at least only irrational anger. We were sad and worried, but I didn't feel abandoned. My situation wasn't anyone's fault. I didn't have to watch my dad remarry and love other kids and be with them. I didn't have to watch him choose to move away from us for a better-paying job. I mean, it would have been better to have had my parents get a happy divorce—the kind where they live next door to each other and you see both of your folks all the time and they stay friends. But I don't know any people who ended up in that situation for more than a little bit of time."

that their surviving parent has with his or her own coping: having a strong, calm parent to rely on makes the grieving interval more bearable (Cerel, Fristad, Verducci, et al., 2006). Another important variable is the degree to which the child's life remains similar to the way it was prior to the parent's death (Hope & Hodge, 2006).

There has been much less research on the long-term effects of parental absence because of death versus other causes. Therefore, Hetherington's classic (1972) study, which found that daughters of widows have more positive views of men than daughters of divorcees, is still of interest. One study compared the long-term depression and alcohol abuse rates of children who had lost a parent through death or divorce and found no link between alcohol abuse and parental death (although there was a linkage with divorce) and found a shorter time course for elevated depression rates for the children whose parents had died; the authors speculatively attributed these differences to less family discord in the families that experienced parental death and to a lack of genetic contribution to psychological difficulties in these families (Kendler, Sheth, Gardner, et al., 2002).

Effects of Being Raised in a One-Parent Family

Being raised in a one-parent family, of any sort, is a risk factor for a variety of problems (McLanahan, 1999). Adolescents raised in single-parent families are more likely than those raised in two-parent homes to exhibit emotional and personality problems, to engage in delinquent acts, to be involved in early pregnancies, to use drugs, to do poorly in school, and to be aggressive. This research has been replicated outside of the United States, notably in Australia and Great Britain (Pryor & Rogers, 2001) and in several Scandinavian countries (e.g., Nævdal & Thuen, 2004).

Two issues, the development of masculinity/femininity and school achievement, have received the most attention.

Development of Masculinity/Femininity

The common assumption has been that boys who lack an effective father figure and who are raised by their mothers are more likely to score lower on measures of masculinity; to have less masculine self-concepts and sex-role orientations; and to be more dependent, less aggressive, and less competent in peer relationships than those whose fathers are present (Mandara, Murray, & Joyner, 2005). The younger a boy is when he is separated from his father and the longer the separation, the more the boy will be affected in his early years. As a boy gets older, however, the early effects of father absence decrease. By late childhood, father-absent boys may score as high as their father-present counterparts on measure of sex-role adoption and preference.

RESEARCH HIGHLIGHT   SINGLE FATHERS

About one in seven American children who live with only one parent live with their fathers (Krieder, 2008). Fathers are far less likely than mothers to be single parents because they nearly never raise children born out of wedlock and because 85 percent of sole-custody decisions grant custody to mothers. Usually, a father will retain custody because the mother has died, is deemed an unfit parent, or doesn't get along well with her children. Adolescents are more likely than younger children to live with their fathers, and sons are more likely than daughters to live with their fathers (Cancian & Meyer, 1998).

Single fathers have one clear advantage over single mothers: they are more likely to have an adequate income (Richards & Schmeige, 1993). They are therefore more likely to avoid the numerous stresses that come with poverty. Instead, single fathers' stress more often comes from learning to take on responsibilities that were formerly assumed by their wives (Maccoby & Mnookin, 1992).

Much early research suggested that children raised by their fathers turn out similarly to those raised by their mothers (Amato & Keith, 1991); for example, they do equally well in school (McLanahan & Sandefur, 1994) and exhibit comparable levels of internalizing problems (i.e., depression and anxiety) (Downey, Ainsworth-Darnell, & Dufur, 1998). However, a growing body of data suggests that they are more likely to exhibit externalizing problems and engage in substance abuse (e.g., Breivik, & Olweus, 2006). These behavioral problems might exist because there are differences in how single mothers and fathers rear their children. Mothers, for instance, more closely supervise and monitor their children than do fathers (Cookston, 1999), and we know that lack of parental monitoring is associated with antisocial behavior (Demuth & Brown, 2004). It is also possible that any additional behavioral problems exhibited by adolescents raised by custodial fathers are a result of selection factors: children are disproportionately likely to live with their fathers if their families were highly dysfunctional prior to a divorce.

In single-parent families, many children are faced with being on their own at home because their parents work. Although this is associated with many negative effects on the adolescent, the development of independence and autonomy may be one positive result.

The effect of father absence depends largely on whether boys have male surrogate role models (Ruble & Martin, 2000). Father-absent boys with a father substitute such as an older male sibling are less affected than those without a father substitute. Male peers, especially older ones, may become important substitute models for paternally deprived boys. Young father-absent male children seek the attention of older males and are strongly motivated to imitate and please potential father figures. Still, surrogates are not usually as close to them or as available as a father (Hofferth & Anderson, 2003).

The effects of father absence on daughters seem to be just the opposite. In one study (Mandara, Murray, & Joyner, 2005), African American girls raised by single mothers were *more* masculine than those raised in two-parent families. (Their brothers were less masculine.) In addition, a lack of meaningful male/female relationships in childhood can make it more difficult for adolescent girls to relate to the opposite sex later on. One of the most well-known studies in the field of adolescent psychology was conducted by Mavis Hetherington in 1972. She was the first researcher to explicitly compare the cross-sex relationships of adolescent girls raised by married women, divorced women, and widows. She found that daughters of divorcées were more flirtatious than girls raised by the other two types of women and that they were more likely to begin dating at an early age. These girls had likely interpreted their mothers' unhappiness at being divorced as the result of not having a romantic attachment. The daughters of widows, in contrast, were stiff and cautious in their dealings with males. They set high standards that had to be met before they were willing to get involved, perhaps because their mothers had glorified their dead husbands.

 ANSWERS WOULDN'T YOU LIKE TO KNOW . . .

How well do children fare when they are raised by never-married mothers?

Never-wed mothers are often young when they have children and thus face ongoing financial struggles. But when income levels are equated between never-married mothers and divorced mothers, few differences are observed in their children.

Influences on School Performance, Achievement, and Vocation

Adolescents raised by single parents are less likely to do well in school than adolescents raised in two-parent homes (e.g., Sun & Li, 2008). This is especially true for girls, and especially true for mathematics (Murray & Sandqvist, 1990). Partly because of this, and partly because of twin economic issues—single-mother households typically have lower incomes, and absent fathers are frequently unwilling or unable to contribute financially to their children's education (Popenoe, 1996)—adolescents from one-parent homes are less likely than other teenagers to attend college. This is even truer for adolescent girls than boys (Krohn & Bogan, 2001). Other factors, such as lowered self-esteem and decreased belief in one's ability to succeed academically, doubtless also contribute to this phenomenon.

Furthermore, since doing well in school is vital to obtaining interesting, well-paying jobs, it follows that children, especially girls, raised in one-parent families are less likely to obtain satisfactory employment after they have finished their education.

Blended Families

More than 50 percent of divorced women who have children remarry within 5 years of their divorce, and more than three-fourths do so within 10 years of the divorce (Bramlett & Mosher, 2002). The high rate of divorce and remarriage means that nearly half of marriages are now second marriages for one or both of the partners. Unfortunately, the divorce rate for second marriages is higher than that for first marriages. As a result, many children end up undergoing more than one parental divorce and remarriage. It is no longer unusual for children to have several sets of stepparents and perhaps multiple set of stepsiblings and half-siblings, as well. In 2004, 8 percent of American children lived with a stepparent, and 17 percent lived with a stepsibling (Kreider, 2008). The most recent estimate (although it is now somewhat dated) concluded that almost one-fourth of all American children younger than age 18 will spend some time living in a stepfamily; if unmarried, cohabiting families are counted, the estimate rises to almost one-third (Bumpass, Raley, & Sweet, 1995).

There are many different combinations of blended families. Family relationships in remarriage can become quite complicated. Children may have natural parents and siblings, stepparents and stepsiblings, grandparents and stepgrandparents, plus other relatives. Adult spouses relate to one another, to their own natural parents and grandparents, and to their new in-laws, and they may continue to relate to their former in-laws and other family members. It is understandable why family integration is difficult.

ANSWERS WOULDN'T YOU LIKE TO KNOW ...

Do adolescents benefit when their mothers get remarried?

Boys tend to benefit, as they once again have a male role model in the home. Girls do not adjust as well; they often feel that their stepfather intrudes on their relationship with their mother.

Children are usually not pleased when their biological parents remarry (Stoll, Arnaut, Fromme, et al., 2005), and so they do not gladly welcome their new stepparents. Their behavior often puts a strain on the newlyweds. In fact, the presence of children from prior marriages increases the possibility of divorce among remarried couples (Kreider & Fields, 2002). When remarried couples divorce, it is often because they want to leave the stepchildren, not the new spouse (Meer, 1986).

In a majority of cases, at least one spouse has children when the remarriage begins. The mother most often gets residential custody, so her children are living with her and her new husband, who becomes a stepfather (Bramlett & Mosher, 2002). The husband's children are usually living with his ex-wife, creating family ties with her household and the possibility of hostility and conflict. The wife's ex-spouse as noncustodial father usually comes to visit his children, so he has contact with his ex-wife and her new husband, which may also result in problems and tension. Being a stepparent is far more difficult than being a natural parent, because children have trouble accepting a substitute parent.

Stepmothers, more often than stepfathers, experience greater difficulties in rearing their stepchildren than in rearing their biological children. This is true regardless of whether their biological children are from a previous marriage or from the current marriage. Several reasons explain stepmothers' difficulties. First, biological fathers often expect stepmothers (i.e., their new wives) to do more of the child-rearing than vice versa; stepfathers are thus able to remain uninvolved when there is disciplining to be done. A second reason is that noncustodial biological mothers tend to stay more involved with their children than noncustodial biological fathers; this creates the potential for greater conflict between stepmothers and biological mothers than is typical between stepfathers and biological fathers (Hetherington, 1999a). Finally, fairytales and folklore have developed the stereotype of the cruel stepmother—a myth that may be hard to overcome (Claxton-Oldfield & Butler, 1998).

Despite these issues, stepmothers must try to develop friendly relationships with their stepchildren, often during infrequent visits—a difficult task at best. All of the adults are co-parenting, with three or four parental figures as opposed to two. The children are continually adjusting to those in two households—three or four authority figures and two or more models of relationship patterns. Both children and adults must contend with the attitudes and influences of other family members.

A great deal of research has confirmed that daughters tend to have a harder time than sons adjusting to their parents' remarriage. Girls tend to be more resistant to both stepmothers and stepfathers, and their adjustment difficulties are both more severe and more sustained (e.g., Hetherington & Jodl, 1994). Rather than acting out, they often withdraw and behave in a sullen, uncommunicative fashion (Hetherington, 1993). A preadolescent girl who is close to her mother is especially likely to resist the addition of a new stepfather.

Adolescent stepchildren have particular difficulty accepting their new stepfather or stepmother. They may be jealous of the attention their own parent gives his or her new mate (the stepparent). They may view the stepparent as an intruder or as just one more adult who will try to curtail their freedom (Hetherington, 1999a). They may also believe that their primary loyalty is toward their biological parent and that the stepparent is an interloper (Moore & Cartwright, 2005). This was dramatically illustrated in the case of a new wife who was greeting her husband's older daughter for the first time. The woman was anxious to make a good impression. "I'm your new mother," she cooed. "The hell you are," replied the daughter and stamped out of the room (Rice, counseling notes).

This case is not unusual. One of the typical reactions of a stepchild to a stepparent is rejection: "You're not my father" or "You're not my mother." This dismissal is hard for the stepparent to take and sometimes leads to a battle of wills. In many cases, the stepparent who initially tried to be kind and concerned will pull back in the face of continued hostility. He or she may display less warmth and support and give up trying to control or monitor the adolescent's behavior (Anderson, Greene, Hetherington, et al., 1999).

Another source of conflict is that parents and children may have different perceptions about how well the family is functioning as well as different expectations as to how it should function. For example, Koerner and her colleagues (2004) found that more than half of the mother-adolescent dyads they sampled had different views of the quality of the adolescent/stepfather relationship, the degree to which the remarriage had affected the adolescent's life, and the degree to which the adolescent thought that the remarriage had affected his or her relationship with his or her mother; the mothers cast their family situations in a more favorable light. Moore and Cartwright (2005) found that adolescents clearly expected that their biological mothers would maintain primary responsibility for their discipline; parents (biological and step) might believe that the duties should be shared between them.

Given these strains and the fact that the relationships between the children and both their biological parents and stepparents will cool down for some time after a remarriage (Hetherington, 1993), it is no wonder that stepchildren look much more like children raised in single-parent homes than like those raised in intact homes (Amato, 2001). Like the children whose parents divorced but did not remarry, stepchildren are more likely than children from intact families to do poorly in

Because of the high rate of divorce and remarriage, there are many second marriages. In most blended families, it takes time and effort to work out problems and build good stepparent/stepchildren relationships.

PERSONAL ISSUES STEPPARENTS VERSUS NATURAL PARENTS

Many stepparents are disappointed, surprised, and bewildered when they find few similarities between being stepparents and natural parents. Let's review important differences between the two:

- *Stepparents may have unrealistic expectations of themselves and of their stepchildren.* After all, they have been parents before, so they anticipate that they will fit into the stepparent role very easily. They are bewildered if their stepchildren don't accept them immediately and show them due respect. This creates anger, anxiety, guilt, and low self-esteem. They believe there is something wrong with the stepchildren or they blame themselves. They need to realize it may take several years before they and their stepchildren accept one another and develop satisfactory relationships.
- *Parents and stepparents may enter into their new families with a great deal of regret and guilt over their failed marriages.* They are sorry that they have put their children through the trauma of divorce. As a result, parents tend to be overindulgent and not as strict as they would be otherwise, so they have more trouble controlling and guiding the children's behavior (Amato, 1987). Often, they try to buy the children's cooperation and affection.
- *Stepparents are faced with the necessity of dealing with children who have been socialized by another set of parents.* They don't have a chance to bring them up from infancy as they see fit (unless a stepchild is quite young). The children resent the stepparent coming in and trying to change things.
- *Stepparent roles are not clearly defined.* Stepparents are neither parents nor friends. In the beginning,

efforts to take over the parental role may be rejected by older children. Stepparents can't be just friends, because they are confronted with parental responsibilities and hope to make a contribution to the lives of these children. They are required to assume many of the responsibilities of parents: support, physical care, recreational opportunities, and attendance at sports events and school functions. They may have the responsibilities of parents but few of the privileges and satisfactions.
- *Stepparents expect thanks and gratitude for all of the things they do but may get criticism and rejection instead.* They usually offer the same care as they give their own biological children, yet most biological children and stepchildren seem to take such help for granted. One stepfather complained, "I would like to have a little appreciation and thanks once in a while" (Rice, counseling notes).
- *Stepparents are faced with unresolved emotional issues from their prior marriages and divorces.* Stepparents are still influenced by what happened in their previous families. They may still have a lot of anger, resentment, and hurt, which can come out in destructive ways in their new families. They may need therapy to resolve some of the negative feelings that were created by the separation and divorce.
- *Family cohesion tends to be lower in stepfamilies than in intact families.* Life in reconstituted families tends to be stressful and chaotic during the years following remarriage. Fortunately, things usually settle down in time.

school, to be involved in a teenage pregnancy, to drop out of school, to use drugs, and to eventually divorce themselves (Hanson, McLanahan & Thomson, 1996). As before, *more likely* does not mean *usually:* even so, the rates at which children whose parents have divorced (and remarried or not) experience these problems are roughly double the rates for adolescents from intact families, or 20 to 25 percent (Amato, 2001).

Does a parent's remarriage change sibling relationships? How well do half-siblings and stepsiblings get along? Let's begin with the effects on the relationship between the siblings who lived together before the remarriage—the full biological siblings from the original marriage. A number of studies have shown than full biological siblings who are raised in stepfamilies tend to be less close than those raised in intact homes

(e.g., Hetherington & Clingempeel, 1992; Baham, Weimer, Braver, et al., 2008). Boys are especially likely to become more distanced from their siblings, male and female. This distance carries over into adulthood, such that full siblings raised in blended families are more estranged than full siblings raised in intact homes even after they move out of their childhood households (Hetherington, 1999a).

A majority of children whose parents remarry either immediately or eventually gain either a half-sibling or a stepsibling, which clearly has the potential to be unsettling. For example, the adolescent who is used to being the oldest child in the household may lose that status and the privileges that go with it. Still, most stepsiblings get along reasonably well (Beer, 1992). Their relationships tend to be more casual and less intense than those of full or half-siblings

(Hetherington, 1999b), however, and involve fewer positive and fewer extremely negative interactions. Half-siblings are most often treated the same as full siblings, and they have the same kinds of relationships (Anderson, 1999).

The most successful stepfamilies are those in which the parents proactively deal with the stresses that will almost certainly crop up (Michaels, 2006). These stresses include feelings of loss, change, and divided loyalties (Freisthler, Svare, & Harrison-Jay, 2003). This involves giving adolescents a reasonable amount of time to adjust to changes; the opportunity to be heard; building in time alone with the biological, custodial parent; working to maintain extended

> **ANSWERS WOULDN'T YOU LIKE TO KNOW …**
>
> How well do adolescents in blended families get along with their stepsiblings?
>
> The relationships between stepsiblings are usually cordial and friendly but rather superficial. Stepsiblings generally coexist without a lot of tension, but they do not become very close to one another.

family ties; providing verbal acknowledgments of the difficulties everyone is experiencing; and minimizing changes to routine as much as possible.

Adopted Adolescents

Another kind of family involves adopted adolescents and their parents. Approximately 1 million American children are adopted; this figure does not count children who have been adopted by stepparents (Kreider, 2008).

How well do these adolescents fare? It depends on to whom they are compared. Adopted adolescents, as a whole, have fewer problems and better educational attainment than adolescents raised in single-parent families (Fergusson, Lynskey, & Horwood, 1995). They tend to be better off economically and hence go to better schools and receive higher-quality health care than adolescents raised by single parents. Moreover, adopted families tend to be more stable than single-parent families, and interactions between adoptive parents and their children tend to be warm and nurturing. Adopted adolescents, as a group, are not as successful, however, as children raised by their biological parents in intact

RESEARCH HIGHLIGHT   OPEN AND CLOSED ADOPTIONS

From the 1930s until the 1980s, most adoptions were *closed* adoptions; that is, birth records were sealed, all parties were advised to minimize the fact of the adoption, and children were usually placed with parents who looked similar to themselves so as to maintain the illusion that the child was biologically related to the adoptive family (Bussiere, 1998). Although practices still vary by state to some degree, the trend has clearly been to move toward *open* adoption (which was the common practice prior to the 1930s). *Open adoption* has numerous meanings, ranging from providing the adoptive parents biographical and medical information about the biological mother through third-party letter exchange all the way to visitations between adoptive parents and biological mother or biological mother and child (McRoy, Groteant, Ayers-Lopez, et al., 2007). Openness has become more the norm as the number of infants available for adoption has decreased as a result of the availability of abortion and an increase in the number of women who are willing to raise a child as a single parent. Biological mothers now have a greater ability to negotiate prior to adoption the terms that they, rather than the adoptive parents, would like (Hartman & Laird, 1990). In many states, adopted children are legally permitted to view their adoption records when they reach the age of majority.

Are adopted adolescents interested in obtaining information about their birth parents? A study by Wrobel, Grotevant, and McRoy (2004) suggests that they are. Approximately two-thirds of the adopted adolescents Wrobel and colleagues studied indicated that they had at least some interest in searching for their birth parents. There was some indication that girls were more interested in searching than boys, and older adolescents were more likely than younger ones to have actively begun to take steps. There was no evidence that the adolescents who were interested in finding their birth parents were more poorly adjusted or less happy with their adopted families than those adopted adolescents who did not wish to search. The more information that the adolescents already had about their birth parents, the more eager they were to search; in other words, information piqued rather than slaked their curiosity. Most of the adoptive parents in this study were supportive of their children's desires to search. Wrobel, Grotevant, and McRoy concluded that a desire to search for one's birth parents is a normative state for adoptive teenagers and is not indicative of unhappiness or maladjustment. A later study by these and other researchers (Grotevant, Wrobel, Von Korff, et al., 2007) found that the adolescents were very satisfied with having made contact and found interaction with their birth mothers a positive experience.

families (Weinberg, Waldman, van Dulmen, et al., 2004). A subset of adopted youths do not do as well in school, are more prone to conduct disorders, and are not as popular with their peers (Kirschner, 1996; Bimmel, Juffer, van IJzendoorn, et al., 2003); however, most adoptees are well adjusted (Juffer & van IJzendoorn, 2005).

What explains any less successful adjustment? There may be both pre-adoption and post-adoption contributing factors. The birth mothers of many adopted adolescents likely received inadequate prenatal care, as there is an increased likelihood that these mothers were young, impoverished, or substance abusers. Adopted children may also have been neglected or abused after birth and prior to having been adopted (Haugaard & Hazan, 2003). Once they have been adopted, adolescents may face more complex attachment issues and experience more conflict over regulation issues than other teenagers, as indicated by statements such as "You can't tell me what to do—you're not really my mother!" Adopted individuals may also find it more difficult to cope with increasing autonomy if they feel they have been abandoned before. They may also face added social stigma because of their adopted status. Most important, having been adopted often makes the identity search more difficult. It is harder to form an identity—to figure out who you are—when pieces of information are missing (Grotevant,

1997). This is especially true of adolescents whose adoptions were closed and know little or nothing about their birth parents. Adolescents whose adoptions were open and have had contact with their birth parents will not have this problem but may instead experience conflicted loyalties to relatives with different values and lifestyles. Finally, adoptive parents may be quicker to acknowledge that their teenager in fact has a behavioral or emotional problem and may be more likely to make a mental health referral (Juffer & van IJzendoorn, 2005).

One group that might seem particularly at risk is transracially adopted adolescents. After all, their identity searches will be that much more disrupted than those of intra-racially adopted adolescents, and their adopted parents may be ill equipped to help them become comfortable with their ethnic identities. Contrary to this argument, transracial adoptees are just as successful as intra-racial adoptees. A recent meta-analysis by Juffer and van IJzendoorn (2007) found that transracially adopted youths feel just as good about themselves and have resolved their ethnic identifications as well as those adopted intra-racially. Furthermore, they fare significantly better than adolescents raised in institutions, which would be the alternative if there were no families available to adopt them.

SUMMARY

1. About one-third of American adolescents live with only one of their biological parents, more often their mother. About 35 percent of these teenagers have parents who are divorced, and about 40 percent have mothers who were never married to their biological fathers.
2. Most experts agree that divorce has both short-term and long-term effects on adolescent development.
3. Short-term emotional reactions include shock and disbelief, fear, anxiety, insecurity about the future, anger and hostility, self-blame and guilt, mourning and grief, and jealousy and resentfulness.
4. Although the large majority of children whose parents divorce grow up well adjusted, experiencing parental divorce often impairs family relationships and increases the probability of a wide variety of adjustment problems during adolescence and young adulthood.
5. A number of factors influence the effects of divorce: the individual adolescent's temperament, the behavior and economic circumstances of the family before the divorce, the quality of parenting after the divorce, the economic resources available to the child after the divorce, and the amicability of the parents after the divorce.
6. Joint custody is not uniformly better or worse than single-parent custody. Joint custody can work very well if the parents get along; it does not work well if the adolescent is caught between fighting parents.
7. There is little research directly comparing children raised by never-wed mothers and divorced mothers,

and the research that does exist often compares children from different socioeconomic statuses and races/ethnicities. Still, it appears that the effects of being raised by a single parent—whether as the result of a divorce or out-of-wedlock birth—are similar.
8. Single fathers are in most ways as successful as parents as single mothers. There is some data, however, suggesting that their children are more likely to drink or use drugs.
9. Many adolescents raised by single mothers, especially African American children, are cared for exclusively or in good part by their grandmothers.
10. Most divorced adults eventually remarry, which means large numbers of adolescents will grow up in blended families.
11. The biggest complication in remarriage is children. Being a stepparent is far more difficult than being a natural parent because children have trouble accepting a substitute parent.
12. Relations are typically more strained between stepmothers and stepchildren than between stepfathers and stepchildren, primarily because stepmothers are more involved in their stepchildren's lives.
13. While a son is more likely to have trouble adjusting to his parents' divorce, a daughter is more likely to have trouble adjusting to her parents' remarriage.
14. Adolescents raised in blended families are more similar to those raised by single parents than to adolescents raised in intact, two-parent homes.

15. Full-sibling relationships often become less supportive if siblings' parents remarry. Relations with step-siblings are usually cordial but not close.
16. Adopted adolescents fare better than adolescents raised in single-parent homes, but a significant minority have more adjustment problems than adolescents raised by both of their biological parents.

KEY TERMS

joint custody 228   residential custody 228
legal custody 228

THOUGHT QUESTIONS

Personal Reflection
Think about questions 1–5 if your parents are divorced; if they are not, ask these questions of a friend whose parents are. Think about questions 6–7 if your mother and father were never married; if your parents were married, ask these questions of a friend raised by an unwed mother.

1. How did your parents' divorce affect you as it was happening? What emotions did you experience? Give some examples to illustrate your explanation.
2. What upset you the most when your parents were first divorced? Compile a list of do's and don'ts for parents who are divorcing.
3. What custody arrangements did you have? Were they, in your opinion, ideal? Why or why not?
4. Looking back, did you benefit from your parents' divorce in any ways? Explain.
5. Are you a different person because of your parents' divorce? Why or why not?
6. Were you content with your family situation (i.e., having an unwed mother) as you were growing up? Did you feel different or ostracized in any way? Use examples to explain.
7. Did you have close relationships with any adult men as you were growing up (uncles, grandfathers, etc.)? Was the fact that these relationships were with men as opposed to women important to you? Why or why not?

Group Discussion
8. Did your peers have negative stereotypes about an adolescent raised in a one-parent home? Did you? If so, what were they?
9. What are the appropriate roles for residential stepmothers and stepfathers? Nonresidential stepmothers and stepfathers? What should characterize the relationship each has with his or her stepchildren?
10. Draw up a list of the advantages and disadvantages of having stepsiblings.
11. If you were adopted, when did you begin to have an interest in your birth family? How strongly interested were you? How did your adoptive parents react? Was any of the information you received helpful?
12. If you were not adopted, do you think you would want to develop a relationship with your birth parents? What would be the possible costs and benefits?

Debate Questions
13. Society should make it more difficult for married couples to divorce.
14. Parents who divorce should not be permitted to relocate far from their children's other biological parent.
15. The main reason for the decreased outcomes for adolescents raised in single-parent families is poverty and economic hardship.
16. Stepparents should leave disciplining to a child's biological parents.

SUGGESTED READING

Bernet, W., and Ash, D. R. (2007). *Children of Divorce: A Practical Guide for Parents, Therapists, Attorneys, and Judges*, 2nd ed. Malabar, FL: Krieger.

Ganong, L. H., and Coleman, M. (2003). *Stepfamily Relationships: Development, Dynamics, and Interventions*. New York: Springer.

Hetherington, E. M. (1999). *Coping with Divorce, Single-Parenting, and Remarriage: A Risk and Resiliency Perspective*. Mahwah, NJ: Lawrence Erlbaum.

Howard, J. A., and Smith, S. L. (2003). *After Adoption: The Needs of Adopted Youth*. Washington, DC: Child Welfare League of America.

Mason, M. A., Skolnick, A., and Sugarman, S. D. (2002). *All Our Family: New Policies for a New Century. A Report of the Berkeley Family Forum*, 2nd ed. Oxford, England: Oxford University Press.

Papernow, P. L. (2002). *Becoming a Stepfamily: Patterns of Development in Remarried Families*. Hillsdale, NJ: Analytic Press.

Steinberg, G., & Hall, B. (2000). *Inside Transracial Adoption*. Indianapolis, IN: Perspectives Press.

Tasker, F. L., and Golombok, S. (1998). *Growing Up in a Lesbian Family: Effects on Child Development*. New York: Guilford Press.

Teyber, E. (2001). *Helping Children Cope with Divorce*, 2nd ed. Lexington, MA: Lexington Books.

Volkman, T. A. (Ed.). (2005). *Cultures of Transnational Adoption*. Durham, NC: Duke University Press.

USEFUL WEB SITES

Family Pride Coalition
www.familypride.org

The Family Pride Coalition is a nonprofit organization whose purpose is to "advance the well-being of lesbian, gay, bisexual and transgender parents and family members." The site contains news articles, advocacy information, a newsletter, a bookstore, contact information for local parents' support groups, and links to other sites of interest to gay and bisexual parents.

Stepfamily Association of America
www.saafamilies.org

The Web site of this nonprofit organization is geared to both laypersons and professionals interested in stepfamilies. It contains a large list of recommended books and articles and is home to a number of forums in which individuals can share ideas about different aspects of stepparenting.

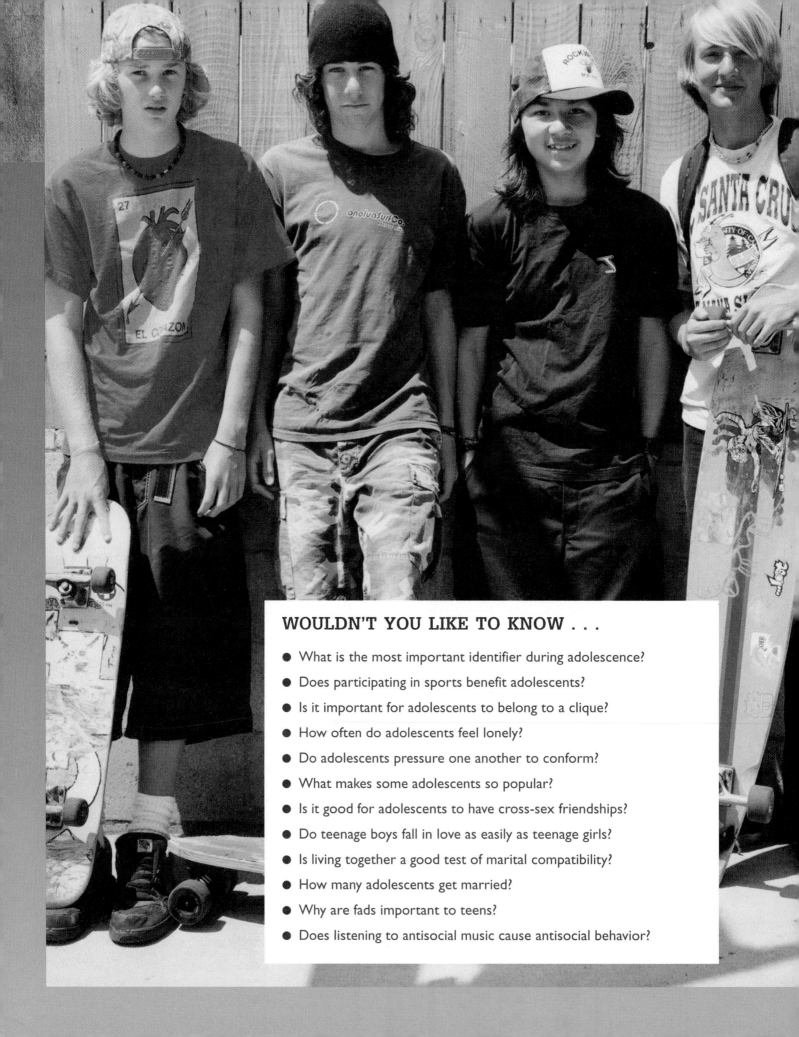

WOULDN'T YOU LIKE TO KNOW . . .

- What is the most important identifier during adolescence?
- Does participating in sports benefit adolescents?
- Is it important for adolescents to belong to a clique?
- How often do adolescents feel lonely?
- Do adolescents pressure one another to conform?
- What makes some adolescents so popular?
- Is it good for adolescents to have cross-sex friendships?
- Do teenage boys fall in love as easily as teenage girls?
- Is living together a good test of marital compatibility?
- How many adolescents get married?
- Why are fads important to teens?
- Does listening to antisocial music cause antisocial behavior?

chapter 10

Being a Member of the Adolescent Subculture: Activities and Interactions with Peers

Adolescence is a time of profound changes in relationships with peers. As teenagers break away from their families, they spend increasingly more time with their friends. And because their social cognitive skills are more sophisticated than when they were younger, they have a better understanding of others, and their peers have a better understanding of them. This opens the door to more intimate, meaningful interactions. What's more, when adolescents change schools—going from elementary school to middle school and then from middle school to high school—they are usually exposed to a new, larger, more diverse group of peers. With physical maturation and emerging sexual interests comes the desire for romantic as well as platonic attachments.

This chapter is concerned with the nature of peer interactions during adolescence. It begins at the macrolevel, by examining the organization and preoccupations of the peer cohort as a whole. We then discuss larger social networks and work our way down to friendship and then to romantic attachments. Because nonmarital cohabitation has become quite common during late adolescence, that phenomenon is also discussed, and since some adolescents marry, the experience of early marriage is considered, as well. We conclude by looking at some of the activities that preoccupy adolescents and fill their time.

Adolescent Culture and Society

Some researchers would assert that adolescents have both their own *society* and their own *culture*. **Adolescent society** refers to the organized network of relationships among adolescents. **Adolescent culture** is the sum of the ways that adolescents behave; it refers to the body of norms, values, attitudes, and practices shared by members of the adolescent society. Adolescent society consists of the interrelationships of adolescents within their social systems; their culture describes the way they think, act, and live.

Adolescent culture is not a single, monolithic structure that includes all young people. There is wide variation among age groups, socioeconomic levels, and ethnic or national backgrounds; there are different groups that have different values and styles. Some researchers, however, believe that a more uniform global teenage culture is forming as a result of the homogenizing influence of the Internet and satellite television (Wang, Holloway, Beatty, et al., 2007). In any event, adolescent society is only loosely structured. It exists without any formal, written codification and without long-standing traditions. Individuals move into and out of the adolescent cohort within a few short years, contributing to change and instability.

Before we can analyze adolescent society or culture, an important question should be addressed: Is adolescent culture unique and different from that of the adult world? According to one point of view, adolescents are a relatively uniform group whose ethics are contrary to adult ethics. To those who hold this view, youths form a distinct subculture. This happens because teenagers are set apart in schools, where they engage in peer-focused activities. Largely segregated from the adult world, they develop a subculture with its own language, fads, and, most important, value system that differ from those of adults. As a result, the adolescent lives in a segregated society and establishes behaviors that meet with peer, but not necessarily adult, approval.

An opposing stance is that the notion of an **adolescent subculture,** segregated and different from adult culture, is a myth. This view—that adolescents reflect adult principles, beliefs, and practices—is substantiated by many studies. For example, when they are deciding what to do with their lives, adolescents turn to their parents for advice more than they turn to their friends or to the media (Malmberg, 2001). When conflict *does* arise between the generations, it is usually centered on mundane, day-to-day issues such as noisiness, tidiness, punctuality, and social custom, rather than on fundamental values such as honesty, perseverance, and concern for others (Smetana, 2002).

There continues to be disagreement, then, as to whether adolescent culture is different enough from adult culture to be distinct from it. This may occur in part because some generations are more divergent from—and critical of—their parents' generation than are other generations.

The more studies that are conducted and the more closely these studies are analyzed, the more evident it becomes that adolescents choose to follow neither parents nor friends exclusively. One explanation is that, in many instances, parents and friends are quite alike, so the peer group serves to reinforce rather than violate parental values. Adolescents tend to choose friends whose values are like their own (Aloise-Young, Graham, & Hansen, 1994); thus, there may be considerable overlap between the values of parents and peers because of commonalities in their backgrounds—social, economic, religious, educational, and even geographic similarities.

And, as has been discussed previously, some teenagers are relatively more influenced by peers and others by parents—age, gender, socioeconomic status, and the quality of the relationship between parent and child all come into play—but most of the basic values that adolescents hold are similar to those of their parents. In particular, parents' values in the realms of finance, education, career plans, and prejudices are often followed (Ritchey & Fishbein, 2001). In contrast, activities that are intrinsic to peer life are heavily influenced by peer guidance. Such matters as style of dress, taste in music, language, preference of movie and recording stars, dating customs, and behavior at youth hangouts are particular to the adolescent subculture, and they may sometimes run counter to adult inclinations. In addition, adolescents tend to value popularity, nonconformity with tradition, and hedonism (Boehnke, 2001) more than their parents do. It is therefore possible to point to certain aspects of adolescent culture that are identifiable as separate, for they are developed and practiced predominantly by adolescents, sometimes in contradiction to adult norms.

Two especially notable areas of adolescent-adult disagreement involve drugs and sexual behavior. The primary reason adolescents and adults disagree in these matters is that cultural change has been so rapid and so great that youthful behavior *is* different from adult values. For example, several attitude surveys have revealed that in some ways the sexual attitudes of adolescents diverge from those of adults (e.g., Le Gall, Mullet, & Shafighi, 2002). For example, today's teens are less likely to view oral sex as "having sex" than are adults (Remez, 2000). These youthful attitudes, therefore, may be regarded as subcultural. Parents do, however, continue to exert some influence on their adolescent children's sexual behavior. For instance, adolescents whose mothers are fundamentalist Protestants and those whose parents attend church regularly are significantly less likely than others to approve of premarital sexual intercourse (Regnerus, 2005).

Thus, whether a youth subculture exists depends on what areas of concern are being examined. Overall, youth culture reflects adult culture. In specific areas, however, youth culture is a distinct subculture. Eventually, as adolescents age and become adults, many aspects of youth culture are absorbed into mainstream adult society. (Nowadays, most adults enjoy rock music and wear blue jeans.) What is novel and rebellious at first becomes staid and commonplace with the passage of time.

Adolescent Societies

Adolescent societies may be divided into two types of groups: formal and informal. Formal adolescent societies primarily include groups based at or located in school. Links to peers are determined by whether adolescents are enrolled in school, which school they attend, and which student organizations they join. Some teens, of course, participate in supervised, out-of-school religious or youth groups as well. Informal adolescent societies generally describe those loosely structured groups of youths who get together socially, without adult supervision. Most of these meetings take place outside of school grounds, on weekends or in the evenings.

Formal Systems

The Formal Academic Subsystem

Adolescents are involved in a formal academic **subsystem** shaped by the school administration, faculty, curriculum, grade level, and classrooms. As students, adolescents are concerned with intellectual pursuits, knowledge, achievement, and making the honor roll. In this system, seniors outrank first-year students, and the honor roll student outranks the D student. In general, there is a positive correlation between academic success and popularity, especially for younger children (O'Neil, Welsh, Parke, Wang, et al., 1997). However, the degree to which students subscribe to this academic ranking varies according to gender, neighborhood, and socioeconomic status.

Many but not all studies suggest that female adolescents value academic success more than male students (e.g., Steinmayr & Spinath, 2008) and rate peers more highly if they do well in school than if they do not. Socioeconomic status also plays a role: middle-class students are more likely than poverty-class students to value academics (Guay, Boivin, & Hodges, 1999). Still, academic success by itself is not a good predictor of popularity; instead it interacts with adolescents' other personal characteristics, especially their willingness to engage in norm-breaking and aggressive behaviors (Dijkstra, Lindenberg, Verhulst, et al., 2009). In other words, you can be both smart and popular if you don't always follow the rules and can defend yourself; on the other hand, if you always behave and are perceived as weak, you won't be considered popular.

The Activities Subsystem

Most teens are involved in a semiformal activities subsystem, which includes sponsored organizations and activities, such as athletics, drama, music, and departmental

adolescent society   the adolescent social system.

adolescent culture   sum of the ways that adolescents behave.

adolescent subculture   values and way of life that are contrary to those found in adult society.

subsystems   smaller segments of adolescent society within the larger social system.

clubs. There are dozens of independent formal school organizations, ranging from varsity basketball to the community services club. Each group has a prestige ranking in the eyes of the students, and membership conveys a certain status to its members. Each group has specific offices, and an individual's standing is determined partly by which of these offices he or she holds; for example, the captain of the football team is accorded higher status than a benchwarmer. The amount of prestige that any position bestows depends on its rank within each respective group and the prestige of the group in relation to other groups.

As many as 75 percent of middle-school students participate in structured extracurricular activities (Mahoney, Schweder, & Stattin, 2002). The most common activities for high school students involve athletics; this is followed by arts, which is in turn followed by journalism (yearbook, the school newspaper or television program), and then vocational clubs (National Center for Education Statistics, 2002). Girls are more likely to participate in athletic activities than boys, although boys are more likely to participate in organized team sports (Eccles & Barber, 1999).

Is it good for youths to be involved in these structured after-school activities? The answer is, in the main, yes (Feldman & Matjasko, 2005). Although there are some conflicting data, students who participate in structured extracurricular activities tend to do better in school than those who do not (Marsh & Kleitman, 2003), are less likely to drop out (Mahoney, 2000), and are more likely to go on to and graduate from college (Mahoney, Cairns, & Farmer, 2003). Participants are also less likely to use drugs (Gottfredson, Gerstenblith, Soulé, et al., 2004) or engage in sexual intercourse (Miller, Sabo, Farrell, et al., 1998). Participants tend to carry enhanced self-esteem with them into young adulthood (Barber, Eccles, & Stone, 2001).

Why should participation in structured extracurricular activities be so beneficial? One can imagine several contributors. First, the self-confidence that comes from success in an extracurricular activity could spill over into other areas of endeavor. Another possibility is that participants must develop time management skills that help them juggle all of their responsibilities. Participants also have greater access to supportive coaches, teachers, or other adults who mentor them (Grossman & Bulle,

2006). Most research (e.g., Eccles & Barber, 1999), however, has concentrated on the fact that involvement in extracurricular activities puts adolescents in the company of high-quality peers (i.e., those who are academically focused, avoid using drugs, don't break the law). Adolescents tend to spend a lot of time with the teens who are on their team or in their club, both during meetings and after hours; therefore, joining an extracurricular group helps ensure that peer influence will be positive rather than negative.

As mentioned before, more students participate in athletics than in any other activity. Given the obesity crisis facing our country, it is surely good for adolescents to have an outlet in which to be physically active. However, the positive benefits associated with athletic involvement are not quite as clear as the positive benefits of other types of extracurricular activities, as the data are more mixed. For example, some studies show that academic achievement *is not* increased by being on a sports team. Crosnoe (2001) found that there were two types of athletes, those whose friends were academically successful and those whose friends were more interested in partying. Not surprisingly, those who ran with an academically disinterested crowd did not do well in school

Involvement in extracurricular activities, such as athletics, can enhance the adolescent's development of sociability, popularity, competency, self-esteem, and commitment to goal achievement.

ANSWERS WOULDN'T YOU LIKE TO KNOW ...

Does participating in sports benefit adolescents?

For the most part, yes. Being on sports teams enhances adolescents' status and helps them feel good about themselves. Such participation instantly makes them part of a group. It is less clear, however, whether sports participation improves academic performance.

themselves. Other research has found that athletes are more likely, not less likely, to drink and use drugs (e.g., Crosnoe, 2002). In addition, some studies show that male athletes are more likely than nonathletes to engage in sexual activity and have more sexual partners (Miller, Sabo, Farrell, et al., 1999). In general, girls seem to benefit more clearly from sports participation than boys do.

Again, much of the research concludes that being on a sports team is highly beneficial for the students involved; it is probable that the outcomes depend upon which sport is being considered, the characteristics of the students who select each sport, and the status that each sport has in a given school. We know more about this at the college level than we do at the high school level. It is well established that college athletes as a whole drink considerably more frequently than nonathletes (Nelson & Wechsler, 2001). They also drink more heavily than nonathletes, are more likely to report doing something they regret while drunk, are more likely to drive after heavy drinking, and are more likely to get into trouble for drinking. College athletes at large universities also exhibit high rates of pathological gambling behavior (Kerber, 2005). Athletes at Division I schools have high status and may develop a sense of entitlement, which increases the chance that they engage in problematic behaviors. In addition, these athletes are under a good deal of stress and pressure to win.

The Informal System

Adolescent students are also involved in an informal network of friendship subsystems. Friendship choices are directed overwhelmingly to other students in the same school, and the majority of these choices are directed to members of the same grade and gender. Of the three subsystems, membership in the informal friendship system is most important in the eyes of other students. This is the only subsystem unencumbered by adult sponsorship. This is the adolescent's world, and the status an individual enjoys in this world is of major importance.

The friendship system has a structure: it is composed of cliques, crowds, and friends. **Cliques** are relatively small, tightly knit groups of three to ten friends who spend considerable and often exclusive time with one another. Virtually all observational studies of adolescents have shown that the clique is the most prevalent and important friendship structure for adolescents. Studies also have indicated that cliques are characterized by similarities among members in age, gender, race/ethnicity, social status, and enjoyment of the same kinds of activities (Ennett & Bauman, 1996). In particular, members tend to be equally disposed toward or against antisocial behavior (Cairns & Cairns, 1994).

Cliques, especially female cliques, have a definite status hierarchy (Adler & Adler, 1995). The high-status members ridicule outsiders and low-status members to keep them in line. The high-status members also determine who is permitted to join the clique. Membership changes are frequent. In one study, only about 10 percent of the cliques showed no change of membership over a one-year period (Engles, Knibble, Drop, et al., 1997).

Not everyone belongs to a clique; in fact, fewer than half of adolescents do. About 30 percent of students are **liaisons**—individuals who have friends from several different cliques but belong to none (Ennett & Bauman, 1996). These youths are generally well thought of, and many prefer their peripheral position. As one tenth-grader explained:

> If you're in a clique, you have to hang with everyone in the group. I always find that I like some of them but not others. Since I'm not in the clique, I can just be with the girls I like. It does make having parties difficult, because my friends don't like each other!

Liaisons serve as bridges between cliques. Liaisons become increasingly common as adolescents get older (Shrum & Cheek, 1987).

Schools also contain **crowds.** A crowd is larger than a clique, often having about 20 members. Crowds are loose associations of cliques; it is unusual to be in a crowd if you are not in a clique. Whereas cliques get together all the time, crowds usually get together on weekends. They may all attend the same party, for instance, or meet at a mall. During the week, the cliques process and discuss what transpired at the crowd event (Urberg, Degirmencioglu, Tolson, et al., 1995).

In large part because of the shootings at Columbine and other high schools, there has been a resurgence of interest in the clique and crowd structures of schools. Past and current data (and almost everyone's personal experiences) leave little doubt that cliques vary dramatically in status. Aronson (2000) compared the informal

ANSWERS WOULDN'T YOU LIKE TO KNOW ...

Is it important for adolescents to belong to a clique?

Belonging to a clique is very important to adolescents. In fact, the clique is the most prevalent and significant friendship structure for this age group. Even so, only about half of all adolescents belong to a clique. Some have friends from several different cliques but don't belong to any of them.

cliques relatively small, tightly knit groups of friends that spend a lot or even all of their time together.

liaisons individuals who have friends from several cliques but belong to none.

crowds loose associations of cliques that usually meet on weekends.

social structures at three high schools—one in Missouri, one in Arizona, and one in California—and found them to be nearly identical. In those schools, like most others, "jocks" and "preppies" (well-dressed, obedient students who are active in school government and other sanctioned activities) ruled the schools. Lower down in the pecking order were "techno nerds," and below them were the "Goths" (short for "gothics"), "skaters" (skateboarders), and the "dirts" (drug users). The lowest of the low were those students who were loners, belonging to no crowd.

The observation that there are status differences among middle and high school students is old news. The surprising findings from these new studies are (1) how great these differences are, (2) the magnitude of the unhappiness and anxiety experienced by subordinate students, and (3) the number of students who feel put down and hassled by popular crowds.

RESEARCH HIGHLIGHT   TWO NOTABLE YOUTH SUBCULTURES

Because adolescents need to distinguish themselves from their elders, youth subcultures come and go. There have been a number of interesting, distinctive youth subcultures in the past 100 years. Two of the more interesting ones from the 1900s are described here.

Flappers

> We are the Younger Generation. The war tore away our spiritual foundations and challenged our faith. We are struggling to regain our equilibrium. The times have made us older and more experienced than you were at our age. It must be so with each succeeding generation if it is to keep pace with the rapidly advancing and mighty tide of civilization.

Ellen Welles Page, *Outlook* magazine, December 6, 1922

This modern-sounding plaint was written by a young flapper who was trying to explain her generation to her parents. **Flapper** is a term used to describe a certain type of rebellious teenage girl in the late 1910s–1920s. The war Welles Page refers to is World War I, an event that truly shocked the world's citizens and caused a rise of cynicism and pessimism about the future. Flappers were scandalous, especially compared to their Gibson Girl mothers and Victorian grandmothers. (Those women wore tight corsets, were never seen without long sleeves, and wore floor-length dresses.) They went to jazz clubs (with men!) where they danced in highly inappropriate ways. They smoked cigarettes and wore makeup (something associated only with loose women). They cut their hair into short bobs and (gasp) dyed it. They wore skirts so short that their knees showed when they walked, they threw away their corsets, and they went sleeveless. They openly drank alcohol (even though it was against the law at the time). They threw "petting parties" where much societally frowned upon sexual activity took place.

Although the flapper era didn't last very long—the Great Depression put an end to it in the 1930s—it had a lasting impact. Women would never be viewed in quite the same way again, nor would they ever go back to their bustles.

Hippies

As almost everyone knows, the word **hippie** refers to a particular kind of 1960s teenager. Hippie values were distinct from those of mainstream America: hippies were against the war in Vietnam, were interested in Eastern religions more than Christianity, were antimaterialistic, and were suspicious of government and what was commonly referred to as the "military-industrial complex." Because of these values, hippies held sit-ins to protest the war and burned their draft cards. They became vegetarians, meditated, and burned incense. They preferred to earn money by making crafts or by panhandling rather than by getting traditional jobs.

Hippies also believed in sexual freedom, interracial dating, communal living, and recreational drug use. They freely and openly cohabited. It was common to allow strangers to "crash" at your place if they needed a place to stay. Marijuana and LSD use were extolled. Hippie values were summed up well by the title of Timothy Leary's book *Turn On, Tune In, Drop Out*. *Turn on* referred to using drugs, *tune in* referred to getting in touch with one's inner self, and *drop out* meant refusing to participate in the negative aspects of our culture.

Hippies had a distinct appearance. Both sexes tended to have long hair (often kept out of their faces with headbands), and men usually sported beards or mustaches. Women wore floor-length peasant skirts. Individuals of both sexes often wore flowers in their hair and bell-bottom or very wide blue jeans. Tie-dyed fabric was popular, as were other items that were handmade, such as beaded necklaces or crocheted vests. Clothing tended to look old and well worn rather than newly purchased.

San Francisco, especially the Haight-Ashbury district, was the spiritual home of the hippie movement. Tens of thousands of hippies gathered there during the summer of 1967 ("the summer of love"). The movement itself was really over by the early 1970s, but its legacy can be seen in the sexual revolution, health food stores, large outdoor rock concerts, and the punk movement that followed it.

The Darker Side of Peer Interactions: Bullying

Bullying is unprovoked aggressive behavior that is intended to hurt another. It is usually repeated over and over, and it can occur only when there is a perceived power difference between the bully and his or her victim (Rigby, 2002). It is distressingly common in schools: more than half of adolescents report having both bullied another student and having been a victim of bullying themselves (Bond, Carlin, Thomas, et al., 2001). Bullying can take many forms, including physical aggression, ridicule, or shunning (Tanaka, 2001). It can be done by a lone individual, but it is usually done in the presence of peers who either actively support it or passively condone it (Karatzias, Power, & Swanson, 2002).

Victims of bullies are insecure, quiet, and shy (Olweus, 1994). They have few friends and are physically weak (Card, 2003). They may be physically unattractive (Sweeting & West, 2001) or come from a different ethnic or racial group than those who bully them (Siann, Callaghan, Glissov, Lockhart, et al., 1999). They are often either very weak or very strong students (Horowitz, Vessey, Carlson, et al., 2004).

Bullying has a major effect on the victims. In the short run, they lose friends because others are afraid that they will become targets if they associate with those who are being victimized (Batsche & Knoff, 1994). They may begin to avoid school (Kochenderfer & Ladd, 1997) and attempt or complete suicide (Tanaka, 2001). Even long afterward, they are more likely to become depressed (Bond, Carlin, Thomas, et al., 2001).

Bullies, especially male bullies, frequently have cold, rejecting, authoritarian parents (Baldry & Farrington, 2000). Those who use physical aggression are likely to continue to do so as they get older (Olweus, 1993). A minority of bullies are also victims themselves. These adolescents look worse than either pure bullies or pure victims (Wolke, Woods, Bloomfield, et al., 2000); not only are they hostile to others, but they are also so disliked that they are picked on as well. A disproportionate number of these youth have attention deficit hyperactivity disorder (Griffin & Gross, 2004).

Fortunately, some effective school-based anti-bullying programs have been devised. When fully implemented, these programs have reduced the rates of bullying by 50 to 75 percent (Olweus, 1994). Greene (2006) recently summarized the characteristics of the most effective interventions:

1. *All students must be actively involved, not just the bullies and victims.* All students need to be familiar with anti-bullying rules, they need to know whom to go to if bullying does occur and to develop

---

flappers   teenage girls in the late 1910s–1920s who dated, wore short skirts, and drank alcohol.

hippies   youth in the late 1960s who held pro-drug, pacifistic, antimaterialistic values.

bullying   repetitive, unprovoked aggression against another.

RESEARCH HIGHLIGHT   CYBERBULLYING

Although computers and the Internet have the potential to enhance student learning and foster positive communication among people, they also bring the potential for a new form of harassment: cyberbullying (Beran & Li, 2005). According to Willard (2004), cyberbullying involves sending or posting harmful or cruel text or images using the Internet or other digital communication devices. Specific examples include (1) sending derogatory or threatening messages, (2) posting stories or pictures that ridicule named others, (3) sending embarrassing or pornographic material to the one you wish to harass, (4) spreading rumors on a Web page about another, and (5) copying personal information that has been sent to you via e-mail or instant messaging from the person you wish to harass to others.

Cyberbullying has not yet been well studied, but it appears to be prevalent. Beran and Li (2005) found that one-fourth of the Canadian adolescents they studied had been cyberbullied, and 50 percent claimed to know at least one teenager who had been harassed online. A study done in Great Britain had comparable findings (National Children's Home, 2002). There is a strong correlation between face-to-face bullying and cyberbullying: it is those adolescents who are bullied at school who are also victimized online (Katzer, Fetchenhauer, & Belschak, 2009).

Males are more likely to bully, in the conventional sense, than females. Is this true in cyberspace? It appears that it is. Li (2006) found that adolescent boys were about twice as likely as girls to admit to cyberbullying.

In addition, Li (2006) found that about one-third of the victims were repeatedly harassed online. Most victims did not tell an adult, even when the harassment occurred at school. It is likely that the students did not believe that the cyberbullying could be stopped. Unfortunately, they are likely correct: it is very difficult to stop online harassment because of laws protecting freedom of speech.

anti-bullying attitudes themselves. It helps if students can learn strategies that help diffuse potential bullying situations.

2. *Teachers must participate.* Not only must they control behavior within their classrooms, but they must teach social skills and monitor what is going on.

3. *Fair, schoolwide policies must be enforced.* Administrators must be sure that teachers are trained to take bullying seriously and not view it as inevitable, normative behavior. They must be sure that teachers receive adequate training to handle bullying incidents. There must be consistent, meaningful sanctions for those who bully.

4. *The best programs get parents and other members of the community involved.* Schools can directly address only what happens on their own turf; others must take over after hours.

5. *The specific motivations for bullying must be addressed in each individual school.* If the primary cause is racial, then that topic must be dealt with; if it is sexual harassment, then programs need to focus on that issue. Schools must also address the specific forms of bullying that occur (e.g., shunning).

6. *The efforts must be continued over time.* Short-term interventions rarely have lasting results.

Friendship

The smallest social unit is the friendship pair, and the need for close friends becomes crucial during adolescence. Until adolescence, children's dependence on friends is rather shallow. Children seek out playmates of their own ages with whom they share common interests or activities. They spend time together, but emotional involvement with them is not intense. Children do not depend primarily on one another for emotional satisfaction, instead looking to their parents for fulfillment of their emotional needs and seeking their praise, love, and tenderness. Only if they have been unloved, rejected, and excessively criticized by parents will they turn to friends or parent substitutes for emotional satisfaction. During adolescence, this picture changes: adolescents now turn to their peers to find much of the emotional support formerly provided by their families (Helsen, Vollebergh, & Meeus, 2000).

The potential benefits of peer relationships among adolescents are well documented. Involvement with peers has been found to be positively related to many indicators of psychological and social adjustment. For example, Erath, Flanagan, and Bierman (2008) found that students with close friends do better in school. Other research indicates that teens with close friends exhibit

fewer behavioral problems than those who do not (e.g., Laursen & Mooney, 2008). Many studies have found that having good friends enhances self-esteem (e.g., Keefe & Berndt, 1996); conversely, associating with abusive "friends" who bully or taunt you decreases self-esteem and adjustment (Guroglu, van Lieshout, Haselager, et al., 2007). Peer conformity increases during the early adolescent years to maximize acceptance.

Early adolescents form relationships with others based upon common interests (Hortacsu, 1989). As they grow older, they desire closer, caring relationships that involve sharing affection, problems, and their most personal thoughts (Berndt, 2004). Adolescents need close friends who stand *beside* them and *for* them in an understanding, caring way. As one boy said, "He is my best friend. We can tell each other things we can't tell anyone else; we understand each other's feelings. We can help each other when we are needed" (Rice, counseling notes).

One of the reasons friendships are crucial is that adolescents are insecure and anxious about themselves (Hartup & Stevens, 1999). They lack personality definition and secure identities. Consequently, they gather friends around them from whom they gain strength. From friends, they learn the necessary personal and social skills and societal definitions that help them become part of the larger adult world. They become emotionally bound to others and become comrades in a hostile world.

Research has indicated that young adolescents prefer to disclose their emotional feelings to parents. However, as they get older, adolescent self-disclosure to friends increases and becomes greatest among older adolescents. Females of all ages exhibit greater emotional disclosure to both parents and a broader range of peers than do males (Brendgen, Markiewicz, Doyle, et al., 2002). This finding is consistent with traditional masculine stereotypes that emphasize that males are not to express emotional concerns and feelings. Adolescents desire to disclose to their friends because they believe they are more likely to empathize with them and to be less critical than their parents would be.

Loneliness

One of the greatest detractors from happiness is loneliness (Chipuer, Bramston, & Pretty, 2003). Adolescents describe their loneliness in terms of emptiness, isolation, and boredom. They are more likely to describe themselves as lonely when feeling rejected, alienated, isolated, and not in control of a situation (Woodward & Kalyan-Masih, 1990). Adolescent boys seem to have a greater problem with loneliness than adolescent girls (Koenig & Abrams, 1999), probably because it is more difficult for boys to express their feelings.

PERSONAL ISSUES   BEING ALONE VERSUS BEING LONELY

There is a tremendous difference between *being alone* and *being lonely*, although sometimes people—especially adolescents—confuse the two. *Being alone* literally means to be physically apart from others. *Being lonely* reflects the subjective feeling that one is not receiving enough support or companionship; one can feel lonely when standing in a crowd.

Loneliness in adolescence is most strongly tied to feelings of distance from peers, rather than from parents. Both not having a best friend and feeling distant from the larger peer network can contribute to a youth's feelings of loneliness (Hoza, Bukowski, & Beery, 2000).

Adolescents generally do not prefer to be alone (Buchholz & Catton, 1999), and they are less happy when they are alone (Larson, Csikszentmihalyi, & Graef, 1982) than when they are with others. Still, numerous benefits can be gleaned from solitude. For example, one can use time alone for private reflection (crucial to the adolescent identity search), for concentrating on a difficult task, or for rest and renewal (Corsano, Majorano, & Champretavy, 2006).

Many teenagers seem to think that they should spend all of their free time socializing with friends and that there is something wrong with a teen who chooses to be alone. This idea should be more actively discouraged. It is not only possible but desirable for an individual to enjoy the company of others yet enjoy private time, as well.

Adolescents are lonely for a variety of reasons. Some have trouble knowing how to relate to others; they have high levels of social anxiety (Goossens & Marcoen, 1999). Some have a poor self-image and are especially vulnerable to criticism. They anticipate rejection and avoid actions that might cause them embarrassment (Cacciopo, Ernst, Burleson, et al., 2000). Given this, a vicious cycle can develop: an adolescent may become depressed because he or she is lonely, and the depression makes it even more difficult to establish new relationships, essentially ensuring further loneliness (Brage, Meredith, & Woodward, 1993). Some adolescents have had a history of victimization and so have been conditioned to mistrust peers and are therefore cynical about relating to them (Boivin, Hymel, & Bukowski, 1995). Still other adolescents have experienced a lack of support from parents (Mahon, Yarcheski, Yarcheski, et al., 2006), which makes it harder to make friends. Whenever adolescents perceive the social risks of forming friendships to be greater than the potential benefits, they have difficulty establishing meaningful relationships.

For the most part, youths are lonelier than either children or older people (Snell & Marsh, 2008). Part of loneliness is situational; it is socially conditioned because the youth culture emphasizes that if you are alone on a weekend, you will be miserable. Believing this to be true, adolescents end up feeling the pain (Meer, 1985). It becomes a self-fulfilling prophesy.

It is important to realize that *almost all* adolescents, including college students, feel lonely some of the time and that many feel lonely a good part of the time. Also, objectively, lonely adolescents are, as a whole, no less attractive or socially desirable than more socially embedded adolescents (Cacciopo, Ernst, Burleson, et al., 2000). They are as bright, as good looking, and as athletic. They are, however, more likely to be shy and to have low self-esteem (Mahon, Yarcheski, Yarcheski,

ANSWERS WOULDN'T YOU LIKE TO KNOW ...

How often do adolescents feel lonely?

Adolescents commonly experience feelings of loneliness. In fact, feeling lonely is more common in adolescence than in childhood or adulthood.

---

et al., 2006). Loneliness comes from inside, from a tendency to withdraw and disengage rather than reach out to others. It is therefore important for all adolescents to develop strategies to help deal with bouts of loneliness in positive, productive ways. Some good choices include keeping busy with enjoyable activities (for example, favorite hobbies or exercising), reaching out to friends and loved ones, and helping others who are in need.

Family and Peer Relationships

The ability to form close friendships is partly learned in the family. There are significant correlations between particular aspects of an adolescent's relationship with his or her parents and his or her success with peers (Markiewicz, Doyle, & Bregden, 2001). For example, many studies have tied the quality of parent-child attachments to the quality of peer relationships (e.g., Zimmerman, 2004). **Attachments** are the earliest form of love that children experience, usually between themselves and their parents. Adolescents who had healthy, secure attachments have intrinsic trust in others and so relate warmly to them (Waters &Cummings, 2000). On the other hand, adolescents

attachment   the early emotional bond formed between child and parent.

who never developed healthy attachments to their parents are often rigid and hostile in their dealings with peers (Zimmerman, 1999). The effect of parent-child closeness can also be explained by the fact that teens who are close to their parents tend to have high self-esteem (Sim, 2000). Having high self-esteem, in turn, allows one to be outgoing and to think of oneself as likeable, thus allowing one to approach and be open to peers.

A second example is that parents can influence friendship by actively encouraging or discouraging it. For example, Way and her colleagues (Way & Chen, 2000; Way & Greene, 2005) have found that Asian American parents are less likely to encourage their adolescent children to have close nonfamilial relationships than are Latino or African American parents. Hence, Asian American youth are less likely to spend as much time with friends or to be as close to them as are teens from these other groups.

Age Changes in Adolescent Friendships

The need for companionship causes young adolescents to choose a best friend or two, almost always of the same sex. The adolescent will spend long hours conversing with this friend on his or her cell phone; will attend school, club, and athletic events with him or her; and will strive to dress like, look like, and act like this person. Usually, this best friend is from a similar socioeconomic, racial, and home background; from the same neighborhood, school, and school grade; of the same age; and with numerous interests, values, and friends in common. Best friends usually get along well because they are similar and thus compatible.

Why are adolescent friends so similar? One reason is that adolescents consciously select friends who are like themselves (Urberg, Degirmencioglu, & Tolson, 1998). Those who are like us affirm who we are and what choices we make; they bolster our self-confidence. Next, once someone is our friend, he or she has multiple ways of influencing us (Brown & Larson, 2009). Friends can encourage or reinforce a behavior; they can provide opportunities for a behavior to occur; they can engage in a behavior themselves, modeling it for us to see. However, contrary to many adults' imaginings, friends rarely actively coerce each other into doing things (Bradford-Brown & Klute, 2003). Friendships usually end if one friend puts too much unwanted pressure on the other.

Early adolescent friendships are intense, emotional, and sometimes stormy. Adolescents expect that their close friends will be there for them, and they—especially girls—react with anger, jealousy, and frustration when their friends are not (Parker, Low, Walker, et al., 2005). Because early adolescents are often somewhat egocentric, they may have unrealistic expectations about the level of support their friends should give them. They may

fight with their friends or even break off friendships if they are unsatisfied with how well their friends came to their aid. (When I was in middle school, my best friend and I didn't speak for weeks because I had the audacity to eat lunch with another girl—once.) The friendships of young adolescents really can be tempestuous and unstable.

Although the rigid single-sexed structure of friendship gradually breaks down during adolescence (Connolly, Furman, & Konarski, 2000), adolescents continue to have predominantly same-sex friends (Hartup, 1983). Intimacy truly begins to distinguish friendships between males and females by middle adolescence (Radmacher & Azmitia, 2006). Adolescent girls report that their same-sex friendships are more intimate than boys' and that they disclose more than boys do (Dolgin & Kim, 1994). Boys believe that they will be teased if they disclose much to their friends (Berndt, 1990); so when boys do talk, it

Adolescents need close friends who will share secrets, plans, and feelings and who will help with personal problems. These best friends are usually quite similar, coming from the same type of socioeconomic and racial/ethnic background, living in the same neighborhood, going to the same school, and sharing interests and values.

"My best friend is a male [writes a female student]. We have been through so much together that I feel he has always been a part of my life. When we were not together, we spoke on the phone for hours. There was only one awkward moment in our relationship: when we thought we wanted something more than to just be friends. We had just broken up with our girlfriend/boyfriend, and I guess we both needed to be loved. So we decided to love each other. We kissed and I felt like I was kissing my brother and he told me he felt like he was kissing his sister. So, we ended the whole thing before it began and went back to normal.

"I lived with him through every love affair he ever had. He was seeking my advice and I was happy to give it to him. One girl left him once and he called me, crying. I tried to convince him that it wasn't his fault.

"He, on the other hand, was my conscience releaser. At home, I was a good girl, but outside, I was quite wild. He was always covering my back and supporting me in my initiatives. When I smoked my first cigarette, he was the first to know and he just accepted it as something I did."

"I was known as a dork ever since the time that I got glasses and braces in the same year. I hung out with the cool kids but was never really accepted into their group. Once, one guy I hung out with called me and asked for my X-box controller—but then didn't invite me over to play video games at his house. At the lunch table, I usually sat at the end closest to the garbage cans so that everyone could pass down their trash to me to throw it away for them. On the few occasions that I didn't sit by the garbage cans, trash was still passed to me and I had to get up and walk it to the trash cans. Now that I'm in college, I'm at least somewhat popular, and at least if I put anyone's trash in the garbage, it's because I want to be a nice guy."

largely takes the form of bragging about their achievements (Stapley & Haviland, 1989). Adolescent girls are more likely than boys to turn to friends for emotional support (Lederman, 1993). When males seek support, they expect concrete, material help from their friends; they also expect their friends to stand by them when they are in trouble with authority figures (Douvan & Adelson, 1966). During mid-adolescence, girls begin to experience increased stress in their friendships and are increasingly concerned about their friends' faithfulness (Schneider & Couts, 1985).

As already noted, friendships during early adolescence are volatile. However, they become calmer and more stable as teens move through adolescence. This increased stability is due to social-cognitive development, decreased egocentrism, and improved relationship management skills (Erwin, 1993). After age 18, friendships again typically fluctuate because students leave home for college, jobs, or the armed services. In addition, friendships become less intense as more time and emotional energy are expended upon romantic attachments.

Group Acceptance and Popularity

As their number of acquaintances broadens, adolescents become increasingly aware of their need to belong to a group. By mid-adolescence, it is important to most that they be befriended by members of a clique or crowd they admire. At this stage, they are sensitive to criticism or to others' negative reactions to them. They are especially concerned about what people think because their concepts of who they are and their degrees of self-worth are partly a reflection of the opinions of others.

What Does It Take to Be Popular?

When my daughter was just starting high school, she was often upset because she didn't perceive herself as being popular. This surprised me no end, since she had literally dozens of friends, more invitations to go places and do things than she could possibly take advantage of, and her cell phone never stopped buzzing. To me she appeared quite the social butterfly! When I tried to speak with her about the disconnect between her perceptions and mine, she would say, "But Mom, the *popular* kids don't like me; not that I really like them, either. So I'm not popular." Three years later, it was déjà vu all over again, as I listened to my equally well-liked son say the exact same things. My children were apparently not alone: many well-liked adolescents yearn to be popular, and middle and high school students spend a good deal of time talking about the popular kids (Eder, Evans, & Parker, 1995).

The discrepancy comes from the fact that adults (and, until recently, psychologists) did not mean the same thing as teenagers when they used the word *popular*. Popular people, to adults and (formerly) psychologists, are those whom everyone else likes. Popular kids are those who have a lot of friends. They are *nice*: friendly, sociable, helpful, cooperative, generous, and trustworthy (Rubin, Bukowski, & Parker, 1998). When adolescents refer to "the popular kids," they mean something else entirely: they mean the socially dominant leaders. These students may or may not be liked at all, but they are the social center of the school. They are the trendsetters, the ones with whom others wish to be seen (de Bruyn & van den Boom, 2005). Psychologists now refer to the "nice kids" as having **sociometric popularity,** and the high-status crowd as having **perceived popularity** (Cillessen & Rose, 2005).

So what are the perceived popular teens like? They are usually physically attractive (Lease, Musgrove, & Axelrod, 2002). Also, they spend a good deal of money on clothing and so are fashionable and look good (LaFontana & Cillessen, 2002). Everyone knows who they are, they mingle with the other popular teens, and they are considered hot by members of the opposite sex. They spend most of their time in groups and shun solitary activities (deBruyn & Cillessen, 2008). They have good leadership skills and can be quite manipulative (Farmer, Estell, Bishop, et al., 2003). They know how to turn on the charm, but they are not above using coercion to get what they want (Hawley, 2003). In other words, although they are always socially successful, they are not always nice. Many of their peers, while longing to be part of their crowd, at the same time consider them stuck up and mean.

Two tools that perceived popular adolescents often employ to hold onto their high status are *relational* and *reputational aggression* (Xie, Swift, Cairns, et al., 2002). **Relational aggression** involves using your friends to keep someone in line; for example, you may get your friends to promise that they will snub that other person until you tell them to stop. **Reputational aggression** involves spreading lies and rumors about another to damage her or his social standing; for example, you might say that you know that Sarah had sex with the entire basketball team after last weekend's big game. Reputational aggression appears to be used first; if it proves insufficient, then relational aggression is used to ensure that the other is firmly put in her or his place. Girls are somewhat more likely to use relational aggression than boys, who more often resort to more direct verbal insults and physical aggression (Crick, 1997). Also, adolescents are more likely to use relational and reputational aggression than younger children (Rose, Swenson, & Waller, 2004): The social scene really does get more vicious when you enter middle school.

Routes to Social Acceptance

Conformity
Adolescents choose their friends so as to maximize the similarity within the friendship pair (Urberg, Degirmencioglu, & Tolson, 1998). If there is a state of

imbalance such that the friend's attitude or behavior is incongruent, the adolescent will either break off the friendship and seek another friend or keep the friend and modify his or her own behavior. Cliques and crowds operate in the same way.

Achievement
One way of finding group acceptance and approval is through achievement—in sports, recreational activities, or academic subjects. The recognition and acceptance the individual achieves depend on the status accorded the activity by the peer group. Sports are given particularly high status; for example, a youth who wears team clothing is perceived favorably by peers (St-James, de Man, & Stout, 2006).

Data as to the relationship between academic achievement and popularity are mixed, probably in part because of a confounding in many studies between perceived and sociometric popularity (de Bruyn & Cillessen, 2006). Quatman, Sokolik, and Smith (2000), for example, found that academic achievement only weakly increased popularity and that its effect was less than all but one of the other traits they studied (music). Their work, like that of others, suggests that academic achievement enhances girls' popularity more than boys' (e.g., Van Houtte, 2004). One potential downside of academic success is that the hours spent studying take time away from peer interaction and decrease a teen's ability to be spontaneous, which is valued by youths (Landsheer, Maasen, Bisschop, et al.,1998).

Participation
Joining in-school clubs and participating in a variety of out-of-school social activities are other ways the adolescent has of finding social acceptance (Dubois & Hirsch, 1993), and the desire to belong was the most important motive for participating in out-of-school activities. The most popular students are often joiners, usually in multiple activities in schools, but also as members of out-of-school, community-sponsored youth groups and every conceivable type of social and recreational activity among friends.

The group life of adolescents has been characterized as *herd life.* The herd assembles at the local hangout for snacks and small talk. The herd goes joyriding in the car or to a movie, a dance, or a rock concert. The herd goes on a hayride, skiing, or to the beach. The herd hangs out at the local shopping mall. To be part of the social scene, one has to join and be with the herd.

Physical Attractiveness
Physical attractiveness also influences popularity. In one study, 270 ninth-graders were asked to rate the acceptability of hypothetical same-sex peers with whom they might be paired to complete a school assignment. Participants consistently ranked the physically attractive partners as more acceptable than the less attractive

---

ANSWERS WOULDN'T YOU LIKE TO KNOW ...

Do adolescents pressure one another to conform?

Yes, but not usually in overt or threatening ways. Instead, adolescents use nonverbal signals, approval, attention, and teasing to encourage one another to conform.

ones, regardless of whether the attractive partner was presented as having high or low grades. Boys and girls were equally likely to value having a good-looking partner (Boyatzis, Baloff, & Durieux, 1998).

Even teachers have been found to rate physically attractive students as more academically competent than less attractive students (Lerner, Delaney, Hess, et al., 1990). After getting to know less attractive students better, however, both adolescents and adults begin to place less emphasis on physical attractiveness and more emphasis on other qualities. The older they become, the more adolescents emphasize interpersonal factors and deemphasize achievement and physical characteristics in friendship bonds.

Deviance

Thus far, little has been said about achieving group acceptance through deviant behavior—that is, behavior different from that of the majority of youths but considered acceptable in a particular group that itself deviates from the norms. Whereas overtly aggressive, hostile behavior may be unacceptable in society as a whole, it may be required in a gang as a condition of membership. Likewise, what might be considered a bad reputation in the local high school (fighter, troublemaker, uncooperative) might be a good reputation among a group of delinquents.

Although it might seem that antisocial adolescents would be incapable of being good friends, this is not true. In fact, the friendships among deviant youths are frequently quite close (Hussong, 2000). Unfortunately, because of the mechanisms described earlier—modeling, opportunity, and normative expectations—adolescents who are involved in friendships with delinquents often end up behaving badly themselves.

Heterosociality

Psychosocial Development

One of the most important social goals of mid-adolescence is to achieve heterosociality (Miller, 1990). During the course of psychosocial development, children pass through three stages:

1. **Autosociality:** The first stage, autosociality, is the early preschool period of development in which the child's chief pleasure and satisfaction is himself or herself. This is most typical of the 2-year-old who wants to be in the company of others but who plays alongside them, not with them.

2. **Homosociality:** The second stage, homosociality, is the primary school period of development in which the child's chief pleasure is in being with others of the same sex, not for sexual purposes but for friendship and companionship. Every normal child passes through this important stage of forming same-sex friendships (Martin & Fabes, 2001). Establishing same-sex friendships in preadolescence is crucial to identity formation. During this stage, children actively avoid interacting with members of the opposite sex (Adler, Kleiss, & Adler, 1992), and sex segregation is pronounced, even when children are engaged in gender-neutral activities. When excursions into the "enemy camp" do occur in middle childhood, they often have romantic overtones. Thorne (1986) termed this "border work" and believes that it serves to further emphasize the boundaries between the sexes. This marked sex segregation is a near-universal phenomenon, occurring in cultures as disparate as those found in Sweden (Tietjen, 1982) and Botswana (Bock, 2005)

3. **Heterosociality:** The final stage, heterosociality, is the adolescent and adult stage of development in which the individual's pleasure and friendships are found with those of both sexes (Goff, 1990). Relationships may be platonic or romantic. Failure to achieve close relationships with a member of the opposite sex may result in anxiety, fears about one's sexuality, and lower self-esteem. Older adolescents are particularly sensitive and vulnerable to feelings of heterosocial inadequacy.

sociometric popularity a measure of how many friends you have, how many people like you.

perceived popularity a measure of your social dominance and status.

relational aggression using your friends to help hurt another socially.

reputational aggression spreading rumors or doing other actions to hurt another's reputation.

autosociality the period during which a child plays alongside other children, not with them.

homosociality the period during which children prefer the company of those of the same sex.

heterosociality the period during which adolescents and adults enjoy the company of both sexes.

ANSWERS WOULDN'T YOU LIKE TO KNOW ...

Is it good for adolescents to have cross-sex friendships?

Yes. Having cross-sex friendships is good for both adolescent girls and boys. Girls benefit by becoming comfortable around members of the opposite sex and by learning what boys think. Boys enjoy these benefits and also have the opportunity to disclose their feelings.

With sexual maturity comes a biological-emotional awareness of the opposite sex and a decline in hostile attitudes. The girl who was looked upon before as a giggly, pain-in-the-neck kid now takes on a new allure. On the one hand, the now-maturing male is fascinated and mystified by this young woman; on the other hand, he is awed, terrified, and bewildered. No wonder he ends up asking "How do you go about talking to a girl?" The boy's first effort is to tease by engaging in some sort of physical contact: swipe her books, pull her hair, hit her with a snowball. Her response is often a culturally conditioned, predictable one: scream, run (either away or after him), and pretend to be upset. The boy is not very good at talking to girls, but he knows how to roughhouse, so he uses this time-honored method of making his first emotionally charged heterosocial contacts.

Gradually, these initial contacts take on a more sophisticated form. Teasing is now kid stuff. To be "cool"—confident, poised, unemotional, a good conversationalist, and comfortable in social situations—is the order of the day. The group boy/girl relationships change into paired relationships and these deepen into affectionate friendships and romance as the two sexes discover each other. Table 10.1 lists the usual stages of psychosocial development.

Overall, the average age for choosing opposite-sex companionship has been declining, probably because of earlier sexual maturity and changing social customs. A boyfriend/girlfriend relationship at early stages may not be reciprocal, and the object of affection may not be aware of the love affair. (I knew a preadolescent boy who sold his girlfriend to another boy for 100 gaming cards, but the girl was never aware of the fact that she had been a girlfriend in the first place.) With advancing age, however, expected and actual reciprocity begin to converge.

Some gay and lesbian teens are aware of their sexual orientations from early adolescence. They, of course, may not feel the desire or need to develop romantic attachments to persons of the opposite sex. Still, all adolescents need to develop friendships and other comfortable relationships with persons of the other gender. They also must learn to pursue same-sex romantic relationships. As a result of prejudice and increased fear of rejection, gay and lesbian youths often find doing so even more difficult than do teens who are negotiating cross-sex romantic attachments.

Cross-Sex Friendships

Cross-sex friendships provide benefits above and beyond those found in same-sex friendships: opposite-sex companionship, insights into the other sex, and a boost to self-esteem because someone of the opposite sex finds you appealing (Monsour, 2002). They can also raise your social standing (Bleske & Buss, 2000). Still, teenagers spend more time with their same-sex friends and prefer their company, especially in early and mid-adolescence (Richards, Crow, Larson, et al., 1998). They are generally happier with their same-sex friends and find them more supportive and intimate (Furman & Buhrmester, 1992). This may because they usually have known their same-sex friends longer and are more committed to those relationships (Johnson & Durell, 2004). Cross-sex friendships may be more important to female adolescents than to male adolescents (Blyth, Hill, & Thiel, 1982).

Adolescent Love and Crushes

Love and romance are common interests for adolescents. In one study, more than half of American 12- to 18-year-olds reported having been in a romantic

TABLE 10.1 AGES AND STAGES IN PSYCHOSOCIAL DEVELOPMENT	
AGE	**STAGE**
Infancy	Autosocial: Boys and girls are interested only in themselves.
About ages 2–7	They seek companionship of other children regardless of sex.
About ages 8–12	Homosocial: Children prefer to play with others of the same sex; some antagonism exists between the sexes.
Ages 13–14	Heterosocial: Girls and boys become interested in one another.
Ages 15–16	Some boys and girls pair off.
Ages 17–18	The majority of adolescents "go with" someone.

relationship within the past 18 months (Furman & Shaffer, 2003). Most American teens fall in love for the first time in early adolescence (Montgomery & Sorrell, 1998), often with someone they barely know and to whom they have rarely spoken. Boys begin falling in love at a younger age than girls, are more likely to have been in love at some time than girls, and as adolescents are more likely to currently be in love than girls, perhaps because boys base their love for girls more on physical attractiveness than girls do (Feiring, 1996). Even when alone, high-schoolers report spending at least five hours per week thinking about a real or imagined romantic partner (Richards, Crowe, Larson, et al., 1998).

Falling in love serves as a positive need in the lives of most people. If the love is reciprocated, it is associated with fulfillment and ecstasy. College dating couples who report they are in love are also the ones who report the greatest happiness. In addition, romantic involvement can foster the identity search and help adolescents break away emotionally from their parents (Gray & Steinberg, 1999).

Intense love can be risky business. Success sparks delight but failure invites despair. Unrequited love is associated with emptiness and anxiety. The loss of love can be a devastating experience for the adolescent.

ANSWERS WOULDN'T YOU LIKE TO KNOW ...

Do teenage boys fall in love as easily as teenage girls?

Teenage boys fall in love more easily than teenage girls. They report falling in love more quickly and more often.

Loss of Love

The loss of a romantic relationship constitutes a major life change, and adolescents are thus often devastated when a boyfriend or girlfriend leaves them. Parents and other adults commonly underestimate the grief that an adolescent feels over a breakup. From the adults' point of view, the relationship was brief and unimportant. Adults may seek to make various types of comforting statements: "You're too young to understand what love is; this wasn't the real thing." "You'll feel better tomorrow." "You're young; you have plenty of time to find a relationship." "You'll look back and wonder what you ever saw in this person." But from the adolescent's perspective, this may have been the relationship of a lifetime. Adolescents are also especially vulnerable to loss because their egos are still evolving and their range of coping skills may not be fully developed. It is unsurprising, therefore, that experiencing a romantic breakup is among the most common causes of adolescent depression, suicide, and murder (Joyner & Udry, 2000).

Emotionally disengaging from a relationship takes considerable time and effort. Youths often experience grief, which may result in reduced academic performance and health problems, as well as carelessness about home duties, employment responsibilities, schoolwork, and attire. Adolescents may withdraw and spend more time alone, even taking meals to their rooms. They may be thinking and fantasizing about the former partner while listening to sentimental music. They may express hopelessness of ever loving anyone else. They may also attempt to self-medicate with drugs or alcohol. Of equal concern are adolescents who exhibit no typical reaction to the loss but

---

RESEARCH HIGHLIGHT   GAY AND LESBIAN ADOLESCENTS' ROMANTIC RELATIONSHIPS

Because gay and lesbian youths are in the minority and because of the prejudice they face, negotiating intimate relationships is even more difficult for them than for straight youths. Certainly, the majority of gay and lesbian adolescents would like to have same-sex romances (Savin-Williams, 1990), but it is difficult for them to do so. Fearing rejection, most are willing to approach only openly gay or lesbian peers, and there are not likely to be many in their school or even in their community. Even if they know two or three other same-sex homosexual teens, they face a range of issues: (1) they might not be attracted to those other teens, (2) the other teens might not be attracted to them, (3) they might not be interested in the same type of relationship (e.g., exclusive or open, intensive or casual), and (4) they may be afraid to risk losing the few friends to whom they can really relate (Diamond & Savin-Williams, 2003).

Given these difficulties, many homosexual adolescents date persons of the opposite sex, even though that is not their preference (Russell & Consolacion, 2003). In addition, adolescent lesbians may form extremely intense, passionate platonic friendships with other girls (Diamond, Savin-Williams, & Dubé, 1999). Gay adolescent boys may also form emotionally supportive platonic friendships with girls, who are generally less threatened by and more supportive of their sexual orientation than their straight male peers.

who start living at a hectic pace and initiate new, intense relationships too quickly.

The following techniques, summarized from Kaczmarek and Backlund (1991), are steps adults can take to help adolescents get past such a loss:

- Help them to view the intense feelings as normal, to be expected. Adolescents need to be given permission to feel and to grieve.
- Encourage them to express feelings and thoughts.
- Teach them about the process of grief.
- Encourage them to rely on a network of family and friends—those who will accept their pain and not offer comforting clichés. Friends who have also lost a love may prove empathetic and insightful.
- Give them permission to slow down and allow the healing process to begin.
- Encourage a balance between the need for connectedness and the need for withdrawal.
- Encourage them to take care of themselves physically through rest, diet, and exercise.
- Suggest that they put away mementos. Doing this indicates that they relinquish some of the fantasy of being reunited.
- Help them view themselves as survivors who understand that the hurt will become less intense with the passage of time.
- Help them to understand that there will be up-days and down-days and to anticipate sadness occasionally.
- Suggest that they postpone major decisions and avoid other significant changes in their lives, that the period of grief is not the time to make major changes.

- Encourage them to find new ways to enjoy the extra time and new freedom. Propose ways to do this, such as taking up a hobby, making new friends, or engaging in additional work or activities. These can help rebuild confidence and self-esteem.

Dating

Dating is not a universal phenomenon. Many societies actually prohibit dating or even close premarital contact with members of the opposite sex (Hatfield & Rapson, 1996). In fact, dating as American adolescents practice it—by freely and independently choosing romantic partners and having no sense that the experience will necessarily culminate in marriage—is a recent cultural custom. What purpose, then, does dating serve? Why do adolescents (and adults) date? A number of reasons can be cited:

1. *Recreation:* One major purpose of dating is to have fun. Dating provides amusement; it is a form of leisure and source of enjoyment. It can be an end in itself.

2. *Companionship:* Wanting the companionship of others is a strong motive for dating. Desiring the friendship, acceptance, affection, and love of others is a normal part of growing up.

3. *Status:* Higher-status youths date more frequently than lower-status youths, and some teens use dating partly to achieve, prove, or maintain status. Membership in certain cliques is associated with the status-seeking aspects of dating. Although

The purpose of dating among adolescents ranges from platonic recreation, to companionship, to mate selection, to intense sexual and/or romantic involvement.

there has been a significant decline in dating as a means of gaining or proving status, there are still significant prestige dimensions to cross-sex socializing, especially with the "right" person.

4. *Socialization:* Dating is a means of personal and social growth. It is a way of learning to know, understand, and get along with many different types of people. Through dating, youths learn cooperation, consideration, responsibility, numerous social skills and matters of etiquette, and techniques for interacting with other people. This may not often be a reason for dating, but it is certainly a benefit often gained from that activity.

5. *Sexual experimentation or satisfaction:* Dating has become more sex oriented as more adolescents have sexual intercourse. Whether dating is used to have sex or sex develops out of dating depends on the attitudes, feelings, motives, and values of the youths involved. Most research, however, indicates that males want sexual intimacy in a relationship sooner than do females, and this discrepancy is a potential source of conflict.

6. *Intimacy:* The development of intimacy is the primary psychosocial task of the young adult, but adolescents crave intimacy, as well. *Intimacy* is the development of openness, sharing, mutual trust, respect, affection, and loyalty with another. The capacity to develop intimacy varies from person to person. Research indicates that intimacy is valued more by females than by males, although gender differences decrease in later adolescence as males become closer to and more supportive of their partners (Eaton, Mitchell, & Jolley, 1991).

7. *Partner selection:* Whether or not this is a conscious motive, partner selection is eventually what happens, usually among older adolescents and young adults. The longer a couple dates, the less they tend to overidealize each other and the greater are their chances of knowing each other well. Dating provides an opportunity for two people to become a pair. If they are similar in role preferences, leisure interests, and personality characteristics, they are more likely to develop a compatible relationship than if they are dissimilar.

Dating affects and is affected by the others in youths' lives. One study found that daters had more autonomy from their parents and experienced more conflicts with them than did non-daters (Dowdy & Kliewer, 1998). A second study determined that adolescents who felt emotionally distant from their parents were less satisfied with their dating relationships than those who were close to their parents (Larson, Peterson, Health, et al., 2000). An additional study found that casual daters felt closer to their other friends than those who had a steady boyfriend or girlfriend (Davies & Windle, 2000).

The Development of Dating

By late adolescence, most American teenagers have had at least one romantic relationship. Furthermore, about 25 percent of early adolescents, 50 percent of mid-adolescents, and 70 percent of late adolescents reported having had a romantic relationship within the past 18 months (Carver, Joyner, & Udry, 2003). Within the United States, there are ethnic variations in the onset and prevalence of dating. Due to family influence, Asian Americans and Latinas, for example, are less likely to date than teens from other ethnic backgrounds (Connolly, Craig, Goldberg, et al., 2004; Raffaelli, 2005).

The dating process slowly begins with teens participating in mixed-sex group activities (Poulin & Pedersen, 2007). These groups go to movies, dances, basketball games, and parties where cross-sex interaction can occur. Next, some members—usually the most popular teens—of these mixed-sex groups begin to date and stick closely together in these mixed-sex groups (Carlson & Rose, 2007).

The benefits of this gradual immersion into the world of dating are obvious. First, because the teen is in a group, many of whom are the teen's friends, the teen is surrounded by supportive individuals whom he or she likes. There is little chance for rejection by the group. Second, the teen has the opportunity to observe others of the opposite sex, to "size them up" and see who is of interest. Third, the teen can gently test the waters and see if the person he or she is interested in seems at all interested in him or her as well; if not, the teen can casually move off. Fourth, the burden of carrying on a conversation and of being amusing is spread among many people; there are fewer awkward gaps to fill. Fifth, there is only limited opportunity for intimacy—physical or emotional—for which the younger teen is likely unready. With increasing comfort and maturity, these crutches are needed less, and adolescents gradually desire to spend more time alone with their romantic partner.

In middle adolescence, dating evolves in two separate ways (Connolly & McIsaac, 2009). First, some adolescents form brief, casual dating relationships, lasting between a few weeks and a few months (Seiffge-Krenke, 2003). Second, some teens engage in "group dating," in which several established couples go out together (Nieder & Seiffge-Krenke, 2001).

Dating in late adolescence is more typically characterized by exclusive, intense relationships (Seiffge-Krenke, 2003). These relationships are relatively long-lasting, often enduring for a year or longer. They are important and central to the adolescents' lives and take

Dating violence occurs more commonly than many adolescents realize. Girls, in particular, are at significant risk of being physically or sexually assaulted in the context of a dating relationship.

up so much of their time that involvement with platonic friends diminishes (Kuttler & LaGreca, 2004).

Although this depiction had originally been construed as a rigid, fixed sequence of events, most researchers now recognize that the events are more fluid; there is more back-and-forth movement in terms of a teen's behavior (Connolly, Craig, Goldberg, et al., 2004).

Violence

Upon conducting a literature search to find current articles about adolescent romantic experiences, I was appalled to find that 50 percent of the articles written since 2004 that were retrieved using the search term "adolescence + dating" were about dating violence. Therefore, even though rape is discussed in Chapter 11, it seems worthwhile to introduce the broader topic of dating violence in this chapter, as well.

Aggression—physical, emotional, and sexual—is all too common when adolescents date. Approximately one in six high-schoolers reports being a victim of physical dating violence (Marquart, Nannini, Edwards, et al., 2007); the incidence is similar for male and female teens (Howard, Wang, & Yan, 2008). Although the numbers among boys and girls may be similar, the nature of the violence they experience is not. Males are more likely to report being shoved, kicked, or pushed, whereas females are more likely to report being forced to engage in unwanted sexual activities (although not necessarily intercourse). Boys are more likely to initiate violence, usually because they are jealous or angry. Girls who engage in violence most often do so because they are angry or want to "get back" at a boy who has hurt them. Girls react to the violence they experience with fear or by having hurt feelings; boys' reactions are closely divided

between anger and thinking that the girls' attempts to hurt them were "funny" (O'Keefe & Treister, 1998).

Different behaviors predict dating violence victimization in girls and boys. Male victims are likely to have been in fights or to have carried a weapon in the past (suggesting a history of participation in violent behavior), whereas females are likely to have engaged in binge drinking or used drugs (Howard & Wang, 2003). After having experienced dating violence, girls exhibit elevated rates of depression (Ackard, Eisenberg, & Neumark-Sztainer, 2007).

Dating violence is not confined to teens in the United States. One study conducted in the United Kingdom found that almost half of the 13- to 19-year-olds sampled had experienced some form of aggression while on a date (Hird, 2000). Similarly, a study of New Zealand teens found that almost 80 percent of the girls and 67 percent of the boys had engaged in unwanted sexual activity and that most had been subjected to emotional violence at least once. As in the American study, boys were less likely than girls to be troubled by these incidents (Jackson, Cram, & Seymour, 2000).

Nonmarital Cohabitation

To many older adolescents and young adults, nonmarital cohabitation is just an extension of steady dating.

Incidence

The rise in nonmarital sex has been accompanied by an increase in cohabitation. In 2004, there were 5.1 million unmarried cohabiting couples in the United States. About 20 percent of these couples included individuals

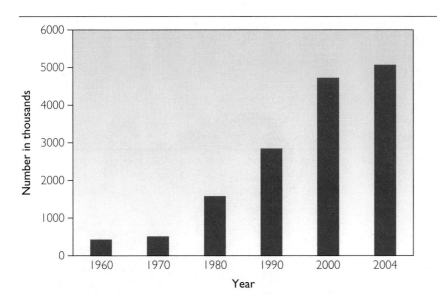

FIGURE 10.1   NUMBER OF COHABITATING U.S. COUPLES

Source: Data from Popenoe and Whitehead (2005).

who were younger than 25 (Fields, 2004). A large number of adolescents anticipate that they will cohabit prior to getting married (Manning, Longmore, & Giordano, 2007).

In fact, more than half of young adults will live with someone prior to marriage (Stanley, Whitton, & Markman, 2004). Living together is more common among African Americans, among people who are poor, and among people who are not religious. Cohabiting is also more prevalent among young adults whose parents were divorced or who are from single-parent homes. As Figure 10.1 illustrates, the number of cohabiting couples has increased astronomically during the past 40 years. Although many people view cohabiting couples as never-married, childless young adults, this image is not entirely accurate. Almost half of all cohabiting couples have one or more children (Fields, 2004), and many have been previously married.

Meanings Attached to Cohabitation

A wide variety of meanings are associated with, and motivations for, cohabitation.

Arrangements Without Commitment

Sometimes, cohabitation arrangements are hastily or informally decided. After a weekend of fun and a short acquaintance, for example, the young man decides to move into his girlfriend's apartment. He ends up staying the rest of the semester. Other times, the arrangement is carefully worked out over a period of time. The individuals simply want to live, sleep, and have fun together. They are good friends and lovers but want no permanent commitment. Their living arrangement includes sharing expenses, dividing housekeeping chores, and sleeping together. This type

of arrangement usually is of short duration. Either it develops into a greater commitment or the couple breaks up.

Intimate Involvements with Emotional Commitment

Most cohabiting college couples place themselves in this category. These individuals describe themselves as having a strong, affectionate relationship. Although some permit dating and sexual relationships outside the primary relationship, monogamy is the rule. Even though there is a strong emotional commitment, there are no long-range plans for the future or for marriage. Such couples intend to continue the relationship indefinitely, but most involvements end up being of fairly short duration. Although dated, the only study of cohabitation in college found no statistically significant association between cohabitation and marrige (Risman, Hill, Rubin, et al., 1981). Cohabiting couples were not less likely to have married or more likely to have broken up by the end of the two-year study in contrast to those couples that had not cohabited.

Living Together as a Prelude to Marriage

In this type of relationship, the couple has already committed to legal marriage. The partners are engaged, formally or informally, but find no reason to live apart while they are waiting to be married or while they are making arrangements for their marriage. Many times, their living arrangements just develop over time, without conscious intent. Under these circumstances, there is never an intention that cohabitation will replace marriage or even be a trial period before marriage. It is just something the couple decides to do before they get married.

Living Together as a Trial Marriage

In this type of arrangement, the couple decides to live together to test their relationship—to discover if they are compatible and want to enter into legal marriage.

IN THEIR OWN WORDS

"My boyfriend and I never really decided we were going to live together before marriage. It just happened. He would come over to my apartment weekends. It would be late, so I'd put him up for the night. Then several weekends he stayed the whole time, it was easier than driving all that distance back home. After a while, we got thinking: 'Isn't this silly, why should we be separated, why can't he just move in with me?' So he did. Finally, he gave up his own place, because it was cheaper for us to maintain only one apartment. Six months later we got married. If someone would ask: 'What made you decide to live together before marriage?' my answer would be: 'I don't know. It just happened.'"

Couples who cohabit may attach any of several meanings to their relationship. It might be a temporary arrangement without commitment, an emotionally committed relationship without long-range plans, a prelude to marriage, a test trial for marriage, or an alternative to marriage.

This arrangement is "the little marriage before the big marriage that will last." Perhaps due to the fact that they report having less confidence in and commitment to their relationship, those who cohabit for this reason report less satisfaction with the arrangement than those who do so for other reasons (Rhoades, Stanley, & Markman, 2009).

Living Together as an Alternative to Marriage

This arrangement is a proxy for marriage; it is intended not as a prelude to marriage but as a substitute for it. This situation is more common among older adults than adolescents. It is not uncommon, for example, for someone who has been through a messy divorce to want to avoid any possibility of repeating that experience; such an individual may live with a partner indefinitely and never marry. In addition, elderly persons, especially widows and widowers, may find it economically more feasible to cohabitate without marriage than to get married. If they marry, their pension or Social Security benefits may decrease, and there may also be complications with maintaining individual assets and setting up wills.

Cohabitation Versus Dating

There has been little research comparing the satisfaction of those who are cohabiting with those who are dating while living separately. One study that did compare perceptions of relationship problems in dating and cohabiting couples found similar frequencies for most types of problems; notable exceptions were that cohabiting couples argued more often and that dating couples felt less secure about their relationships (Hsueh, Morrison, & Doss, 2009).

The benefits of cohabitation that have been identified include the convenience, the cost sharing, the increased amount of time spent together, the opportunity for more meaningful interaction, and enhanced sex lives; in one recent study, convenience and extra time together were the two most common reasons cited by cohabitors (Rhoades, Stanley, & Markman, 2009). The downsides to cohabitation are mismatched expectations (e.g., one partner is more committed to the relationship than the other), arguments about dividing chores and sharing resources, the potential for feeling used, and lack of privacy.

Still, the majority of college students who have cohabited indicate positive feelings about the experience. Students report the experience as "pleasant," "successful," "highly productive." Many students indicate that it fostered personal growth and maturity, resulting in a deeper understanding of themselves or of what marriage requires (Rice, 1993). Cohabiting men were more likely to say that having sexual intercourse with their partner was satisfying. Cohabiting couples report seeing each other more often, having sexual intercourse more often, feeling greater love for each other, and disclosing more to their partners than dating couples (Risman, Hill, Rubin, et al., 1981). They also reported having higher levels of general well-being and happiness (Kamp Dush & Amato, 2005).

Cohabitation Versus Marriage

Cohabitation is similar to marriage in many ways, but there are also significant differences. People who cohabit do not, as a group, seem as happy or well adjusted as people who are married—although much but not all of the group differences can be accounted for by demographic variables (Hsue, Morrison, & Doss, 2009). Intimate partner violence is more common among cohabitors (Kline, Stanley, Markman, et al., 2004), and cohabitors are more likely to be depressed (Marcussen, 2005). Although most cohabiting individuals are happy with their living arrangement, they are significantly *less* happy than married people, even equating for demographic factors and the duration of the relationship (Brown & Booth, 1996).

Cohabiting relationships are less likely to endure than marriages, for several reasons. Normally, people who are cohabiting have lower levels of commitment than do those who are married (Stanley, Whitton, & Markman, 2004). (Remember, though, that some cohabitors never planned to remain together.) Those who cohabit eschew tradition and are less committed to a traditional lifestyle. Also, it is simply more difficult to dissolve a marriage than a cohabiting partnership; in marriage, more forces hold the relationship together (e.g., property interests).

One similarity between married couples and cohabiting couples is their likelihood of having children. More than 40 percent of cohabiting couples today have children; this is a large increase from the past (Fields & Casper, 2001). Having children is, of course, less true of cohabiting adolescents than adults.

Effects on Subsequent Marriage

What effects does premarital cohabitation have on subsequent marital adjustment? One of the arguments used for cohabitation is that it weeds out incompatible couples and prepares people for a more successful marriage. Is this true? According to several studies, no.

Compared to couples who do not cohabit prior to marriage, those who do score significantly lower on measures of marital quality (Dush, Cohen, & Amato, 2003) and have a significantly higher risk of marital dissolution at any given marital duration (Phillips & Sweeney, 2005). The newest data suggest that the higher divorce rate occurs only when the spouses have

ANSWERS WOULDN'T YOU LIKE TO KNOW ...

Is living together a good test of marital compatibility?

No. Couples who live together before they are married are no more likely to have happy, stable marriages than couples who do not live together.

cohabited multiple times with several different individuals prior to marriage (Lichter & Qian, 2008). Those who have cohabitated only with the person they eventually marry are no more likely to divorce than those who do not cohabit. This is most likely true because premarital cohabitation has become a normative behavior in modern American society. Therefore, those who are thoughtful and cautious in deciding to live with the person whom they eventually wed are no more likely to have a poor attitude toward marriage or a low ability to commit than those who do not live together.

It is important to remember that comparisons between people who have and have not cohabited prior to marriage are correlational in nature. People *choose* whether to live with one another without getting married. This self-selection quite likely accounts for the differences in relationship satisfaction and divorce statistics that have been observed. For example, persons who live together without marriage are likely to be less religious and have lower educational levels than people who do marry. These factors might contribute their own negative outcomes, independent of or in addition to the experience of cohabiting per se.

Adolescent Marriage

To evaluate whether adolescent marriage is wise or unwise, desirable or undesirable, we must ask how successful these marriages are. If they are strong, happy, satisfying marriages, there is no cause for complaint or alarm. But if they are weak, unhappy, frustrating marriages, causing personal suffering and social problems, there is ample cause for concern.

Trends and Incidence

Figure 10.2 illustrates the median age at first marriage by sex. As can be seen, there have been steady increases in the ages at first marriage for both men and women since 1950. This increase was most pronounced between 1980 and 2000. Men now first marry when they are 27.2 years old and women first marry when they are 26.0 years old. In keeping with this trend, the teenage marriage rate has been declining. Given that numerous studies indicate that the younger people are when they marry, the greater the chance of unhappy

FIGURE 10.2
MEDIAN AGE
AT FIRST
MARRIAGE
BY SEX

Source: U.S. Bureau of the Census, Current Population Survey, Annual Social and Economic Supplements, 2008 and earlier.

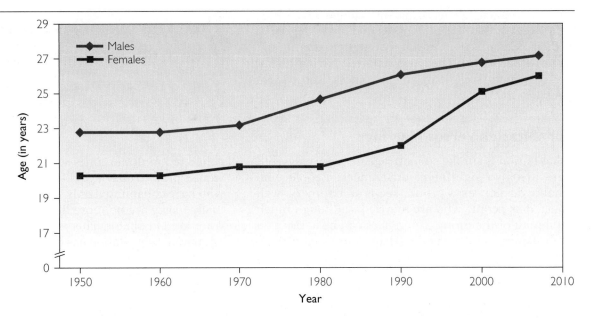

marriage and thus of divorce (e.g., Raley & Bumpus, 2003), this is likely a positive change.

Even so, a small number of youths—especially girls—still marry young. The Census Bureau reports that in 2008 5.1 percent of girls and 2.3 percent of boys ages 18 and 19 were or had been married; 21.1 percent of young women and 12.7 perdent of young men were or had been married by age 24. Hispanic youths were much more likely to be or have been married than non-Hispanic White or Black youths.

A Profile of the Young Married

Very young married couples are usually from low socioeconomic backgrounds. As a group, low-SES youths are less interested in high school and postsecondary education, so they see no need to delay marriage to finish their schooling. Lower-SES parents are less likely to object to early marriage. Furthermore, premarital pregnancy, one of the principal causes of early marriage, is more common among youths from low-SES families.

Similarly, adolescents who get poor grades in school more often marry early. Furthermore, those who marry during school are more likely to drop out. It becomes a

ANSWERS WOULDN'T YOU LIKE TO KNOW ...

How many adolescents get married?

Fewer and fewer adolescents are getting married—less than 5 percent nowadays—probably because of the greater acceptability of nonmarital pregnancy. Regardless, this is a positive trend, since adolescent marriages are rarely happy or long lasting.

vicious cycle: the academically challenged marry earlier, and once married, they are less likely to continue their education. This is especially true of those who have children soon after marriage.

Reasons for Adolescent Marriage

The primary reason for early marriage, particularly while still in school, is pregnancy. Pregnancy rates vary from study to study according to the age of the youths. The younger the adolescent is at the time of marriage, the more likely pregnancy is to be involved. Pregnancy rates may be as high as 50 percent when at least one of the partners is still in high school. Teenage pregnancy and parenthood are discussed in the next chapter.

Adolescents often hold magical views of marriage. Marriage is seen as a fairytale in which a man and woman fall in love, marry, and live in bliss for eternity. Even adolescents whose parents are divorced and/or remarried may have idealized concepts of marriage. Being in love in our culture is held to be so romantic and wonderful that many youths do not want to wait to enter this blissful state. The concept of marriage for love leads youths to believe that the goal of life is to find love, and that once found, they must hurry up and marry, at all costs, before it escapes. Girls who marry early often believe that marriage is their goal in life.

Marriage is also sometimes used as a means of escape from an unhappy home situation, lack of school achievement, personal insecurities or inadequacies, or unsatisfactory social adjustment with one's peers. The less attractive one's present situation is and the more attractive marriage seems, the more the emotionally insecure or socially maladjusted individual feels pushed toward marriage.

The primary reason for early marriage, especially while still in school, is pregnancy. Many problems can be associated with these early marriages, including financial worries, lack of maturity, and resentment at being tied down.

Adjustments and Problems

Many of the adjustments young couples must make or the problems they must solve are no different from those of other couples, but they are aggravated by immaturity. The less mature are less likely to make a wise choice of mate. When the time span between first date and marriage is shortened, youths have less chance to gain experience in knowing and understanding the kind of person with whom they are compatible. The young adolescent girl or boy in the throes of a first love affair is at a distinct disadvantage in making an informed choice of spouse. Youths who marry young have spent insufficient time in the marital search process and tend to marry spouses who are relatively poor matches on a variety of unexamined traits (South, 1995).

The personalities of immature individuals are fluid and not yet completely developed. Youths change as they mature and they may find they have little in common with their partners as they grow older. Two young people who might genuinely find common interests and a good reciprocal interaction at a particular point in time could easily grow away from each other in the ensuing four or five years as their personalities unfold.

In addition, most youths have not yet become responsible enough for marriage. The average teenager is not ready to settle down. He or she wants to go out, have fun, be with the gang, and be free to do as he or she pleases. He or she may resent being tied down. Many teenagers are not ready to manage a family budget or to handle their share of the responsibility for the home-making tasks.

Another major problem of early marriage is financial worry. Little education, inexperience, and youth do not bring high wages. Some couples marry without any income. With little or no income, couples receive part or all of their financial assistance from parents or from the government. Not only low income but also inexperience in financial management and naively optimistic expectations get young marrieds into financial trouble. Teenagers often unrealistically expect to be able to purchase immediately many of the items that probably took their parents years to acquire.

Finally, many of these young couples face discord with one or both sets of their in-laws. It is not unusual for one or both sets of their parents to be unhappy that a marriage has taken place, and hence to be critical of their child's spouse. Since so many young married couples either live with one of their sets of parents or rely on their parents for financial or support or child care assistance, they must interact with these often hostile family members. In-laws, therefore, although a source of aid, can also be a source of tension.

Material Concerns of Adolescent Culture

Let's circle back to where we began this chapter: the topic of youth culture. One way we can try to understand it is by examining the material artifacts that youths buy and use in their daily lives. Four items—clothes, cars, computers, and cell phones—have been selected for discussion because they are so important in the adolescent's life. First, though, is an overview of the total spending power that adolescents have.

Adolescents as Consumer Forces

Teenagers have more disposable income than ever before. From both higher earnings from their own jobs and the fact that families are spending more money on their adolescent children, the buying power of American teens reached $190 billion in 2006. To put that in perspective, it is more than a 25 percent increase since 2001, and it is more than the gross domestic product of Russia (MarketResearch.com, 2005). This translates to about $74 dollars per week for each and every adolescent in America (Newspaper Association of America, 2005).

Where do teens get all this money? There are a number of sources. The majority of adolescents report getting money from their parents, whether it is in the form of irregular payments or a steady allowance or both. The majority of younger teens (ages 12–14) who receive an allowance get $20–$50 per month. The amount for older teens (ages 15–17) is more variable: about one-third get $20–$30 per month whereas about 20 percent get $50–$100 per month. Many adolescents also get cash as gifts for birthdays and other occasions. In addition, a large minority of teens work at any given time. Note that males are more likely to have money from employment and females because it was given to them. It is interesting that a significant number of teenagers reported getting money by collecting spare change from around the house. This foraging typically yields about $14 per month (Coinstar, 2003; Newspaper Association of America, 2005) (see Figure 10.3).

On what do teenagers spend their money? One poll found that the 10 most common (major) purchases that adolescents said they planned to make within the next year were, in order, an MP3 player, a cell phone, a digital camera, a used car, contact lenses, a DVD burner, a car stereo, a video camera, sunglasses, and a digital video recorder (Newspaper Association of America, 2005). In fact, teenagers spend the most money in an average week on clothing and accessories (about one-third of their spending) and food (about one-fifth of their spending). A substantial number also buy prepaid minutes for their cell phones (Coinstar, 2003), and video games now take up 8 percent of their disposable income (PiperJaffray, 2009). It is clear from this list that little adolescent income goes either to savings or to help with basic household expenses.

Teens are also exhibiting increasing influence on their *parents'* purchases (Belch & Willis, 2002). Forty-seven percent of teens have been asked by their parents to surf the Web and give recommendations as to which brand of product to buy (Magazine Publishers of America, 2004). And, unlike in previous decades, adolescents are having a say at the end of the process—making the final decision—rather than only earlier in the exploratory or initiation stage (Wang, Holloway, Beatty, et al., 2007). Teens living in single-parent households have more impact on parents' decisions than teens living in two-parent households (LaChance, Legault, & Bujold, 2000).

So far we've been discussing middle and high school students. Does the situation change once teenagers head off to college? College students generally have more disposable income than secondary students. Most hold part-time jobs during the academic year and work during the summer. College students make, on average, about $169 per week. In addition, their parents continue to give them money. College students average about $210 per week discretionary spending money. Like younger teens, they spend a large portion on their money on technology (cell phones, the latest computers, digital cameras, etc.) and another large portion on entertainment. College students spend almost

FIGURE 10.3 TEENAGERS' SOURCES OF INCOME

Source: Newspaper Association of America (2005).

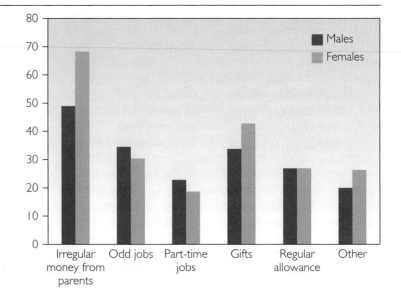

PERSONAL ISSUES   ADOLESCENT CREDIT CARD DEBT

Going to college brings many new challenges, not the least of which, for many older teenagers, is the responsibility of owning their own credit card. Eighty-three percent of college students have at least one credit card, and most acquired them during their first college year. Almost half of undergraduates leave college saddled with credit card debt—on average more than $3,000 (Akaka, 2004). This, of course, is on top of any student loans they have taken out.

Credit card companies aggressively target college students. They offer sign-up gifts, and they flood student mailboxes with easy credit offers. Invitations are plastered in dorm hallways and in classroom buildings. These companies are not being altruistic; for them it makes good business sense to do so. For one, people often develop "brand loyalty" to their credit card; in other words, they tend to stick with whichever card they get first. Second, many if not most of the cards students acquire have annual fees. Third, because college students use their cards but then don't pay off the full balance at the end of the month, they rack up late payment penalties and interest debt. Because credit card interest rates are high, this means

large profits for the credit card companies. Credit card companies encourage cardholders to accrue interest charges by having a minimum monthly payment that is insufficient to reduce the principal quickly.

Credit cards are useful to own if used wisely. They let you avoid carrying large sums of cash, are good sources of emergency funds, help you build up a good credit rating, and allow online purchases. On the other hand, they can become traps if used poorly. Carrying a large balance, delaying your payments, or defaulting on your credit card bill will adversely affect your credit rating, making it harder for you to take out loans in the future if you need them.

In order to try to avoid getting in over your head, it is often a good idea to own only one major credit card. Shop around to get the best terms (such as the interest rate you are being charged). It is also important to read your monthly statements carefully to make sure that the terms have not been changed. Never make purchases that you can't afford. Unless you have good reason, don't assume that you will be able to afford something next month that is out of your price range today (NellieMae Corporation, 2006). You'll sleep better!

$3 billion each year on movies, music, and video games, and they spend more than twice as much on movie theater tickets as the average American (Harris Interactive, 2004).

As the preceding discussion should make clear, there *are* material elements to youth culture. In order to fit in better with peers, teenagers are prepared to spend considerable sums of money to look right and own trendy gadgets. Some of these items—clothing, cars—have been around for some time; others, such as cell phones, MP3 players, and computers, are relatively new.

Clothing

One of the most noticeable aspects of adolescent culture is the preoccupation with clothing. Teens are, in fact, more concerned with their clothing than are most other subgroups (Wilson & MacGillivray, 1998). Adolescents consciously use clothing as a means of self-expression and as a way of judging others (Piacentini & Mailer, 2004). Wearing the right clothing gives a youth a sense of confidence and can boost his or her self-esteem.

Clothing is an important means by which individual adolescents discover and express their identities. As adolescent boys and girls search for self-images with which they can be comfortable, they are preoccupied

with experimentation with their appearance (Littrell, Damhorst, & Littrell, 1990). The clothing they select helps them control the impressions that they make on others. Clothing is a visual means of communicating to others the kind of person an individual wishes to be. Teens are very brand conscious (Moses, 2000), and by choosing which of the current popular brands to wear—for instance, Hollister, PacSun, Forever 21, Abercrombie and Fitch, Zumiez—or by avoiding all of them, teens make a statement about who they are and how they would like to be seen. Several rules seem to guide their clothing selection: avoid appearing childish, call attention to your maturing body, select brands that adults would avoid, and develop an individual look (Konig, 2008).

Clothing can be a medium of rebellion against the adult world. Adolescents who are hostile or rebellious toward their parents may express their contempt by wearing clothes or hairstyles they know their parents dislike. The more fuss the parents make, the more determined adolescents are to stick to their own styles. Similarly, clothing and hairstyles have been used by some youths as an expression of rebellion against particular mores and values of adult society. If adult culture emphasizes that cleanliness is next to godliness, then teenagers can express their rejection of what they perceive as a hypocritical, materialistic culture by choosing to remain unclean and unkempt. Clothing

Clothing helps adolescents discover and express their identities as well as ensure their sense of belonging in their peer group. A number of studies have shown a positive correlation between adolescents' appearance and their social acceptance.

ANSWERS WOULDN'T YOU LIKE TO KNOW ...

Why are fads important to teens?

Following fads—whether in clothing, slang, or music—makes individuals feel secure. (You won't get teased about your taste in clothing if you wear the same thing everyone else does.) Following fads also lets others know something about you, such as which group you are in. Finally, having unique styles of dress and the like separates teens from adults and makes them feel independent.

can be a visible emblem of one's personality, lifestyle, and political philosophy.

Research has shown that females are more concerned about clothes and are more involved in shopping than males (e.g., Chen-yu & Seock, 2002). This reflects differences in their socialization. Females are taught to place more emphasis on dress than are males.

One function of adolescent clothing is to indicate the clique to which an adolescent belongs. Therefore, it stands to reason that peers are a major influence on what a teen will choose to wear (Wilson & MacGillivray, 1998). Individuals who do not wear clothing a teen considers stylish and appropriate are spurned (Liskey-Fitzwater, Moore, & Gurel, 1993).

The importance of clothing wanes over the course of adolescence. One study found that 12- to 14-year-olds were more concerned than 15- to 18-year-olds about wearing the latest fashions, being in style, and

having famous-label clothing (Simpson, Douglas, & Schimmel, 1998). By college, late adolescents generally dress in whatever style is most comfortable for them and are less concerned overall with their image.

Automobiles

Another material aspect of adolescent culture is the automobile. It has become important in the lives of adolescents for a number of reasons:

1. *The automobile is a status symbol.* Owning or having access to a car adds to one's prestige in the eyes of one's peers. The type of car one owns or drives is important, and the status attached to various types changes over the years. Not long ago, to drive the family car—especially if it was a new, large, and expensive one—added greatly to prestige. Later, the big car was out, and the small, fast, expensive sports car was in. Now, sport utility vehicles (SUVs) are filtering down into the adolescent market. For the majority of youths—male and female—owning a car is still one of the most coveted symbols of status.

    Owning a car is becoming ever more common among high school students. Among 15- to 20-year-olds, ownership nearly doubled between 1985 and 2002, jumping from 22 percent to 42 percent. More than 500,000 new cars were sold to teenagers in 2002. This increase can be attributed to the fact that parents are more willing to purchase cars for their teens and to pay their insurance premiums, as well (Higgins, 2003).

2. *The automobile is a means of freedom and mobility.* A car allows adolescents the opportunity to get away from home and drive to the neighboring town, to the big city, or to Florida during the spring break from school. It provides adolescents with a home away from home. If particularly devoted to a car, an adolescent may spend hours in it each day, eating, talking with friends, or even having sex in it. In addition, owning a car means adolescents don't have to rely on the school bus. They can stay after school for extracurricular activities and can get themselves to and from their job.

3. *For a number of youths, an automobile has become a hobby.* Fixing up an old clunker can be a satisfying way to spend a Saturday afternoon. Many adolescent boys share a love for power and speed. Drag-strip or stock-car races are opportunities to compete in socially sanctioned ways to see who can build the fastest engine or soup up an old car. Such races provide opportunities for boys to prove themselves as men and as expert mechanics.

4. *The automobile has become a symbol of glamour and sexuality, of romantic conquest and acceptability.* Madison Avenue has been quick to use not only snob appeal but also sex appeal in promoting automobiles. Advertisements imply that any man who drives a certain car will automatically fill it with beautiful women or that any girl who drives up in a car with leather upholstery will be considered as glamorous and beautiful as the model in the ad. The automobile has also become a favorite lovers' retreat. It allows for mobility, a fair degree of privacy, and even some degree of comfort and warmth.

Cell Phones

Adolescents love to use phones, as any parent will attest. They can spend literally hours and hours on their cell talking about every conceivable subject. Adolescents who receive a number of phone calls take this as an indication of their social standing. Those who don't get many phone calls experience feelings of rejection and sometimes loneliness. It used to be a common joke that parents had to constantly yell at their adolescent children to get off the phone because they were tying up the family's only telephone line. With the expansion of cell phone use, adolescents spend even more time communicating with friends, but at least they are not annoying their parents.

In 2008, 77 percent of all American teenagers owned their own cell phone, and an additional 11 percent regularly borrowed someone else's to use (Nielsen Company, 2009). Slightly more than half of 12- and 13-year-olds have their own cell phones, and 84 percent of 17-year-olds do (Lenhart, 2009). A large majority of adolescent cell phone owners (83 percent) text their friends as well as call them, and more than half send pictures over their phones. The average American teenage cell phone user now sends or receives almost 2,900 text messages each month—that's 96 per day, or almost 35,000 per year!—yet makes only about 190 calls. The number of texts has gone up astronomically in the past few years. They are, in effect, the modern equivalent of "note passing" in that they are private and cannot be overheard (Davie, Panting, & Charlton, 2004).

One benefit of cell phones is the sense of security they provide both adolescents and their parents (Williams & Williams, 2005). With a cell phone, help is only a few button pushes away, regardless of one's location. Ten years ago, pagers and beepers were standard in some high schools. The cell phone has replaced these devices because it guarantees access, allowing a parent the possibility of speaking with their teen at any time (Ribak, 2009). Because of this, parents are often willing to give their adolescents more freedom than they would if the teens did not have cell phones. For example, they let them stay out later or go places without clearing it first as long as they call in. Paradoxically, adolescents have given up a certain amount of true autonomy for this "increased freedom": they are never truly on their own, independent of their parents' supervision. There is always a safety line, a tether, to home.

Because many cell phones represent cutting-edge technology and not everyone has one, they are a new status symbol among youths (Srivastava, 2005). Adolescents can choose models in various colors and designs and with an array of features. For example, some models let you record your voice and e-mail it to someone; others let you download and play movies. Cell phones have become a new fashion accessory (Katz & Sugiyama, 2006).

One downside of cell phones is that they can disturb others when they go off. Some schools have banned cell phones because they are too disruptive during class. A second downside is that it is more dangerous to drive when using a cell phone (see Personal Issues box). There appears to be some risk of adolescents becoming addicted to cell phone use: teens report being anxious when phoneless and feeling driven to compulsively check their phone for missed messages even when it is inappropriate to do so (Walsh, White, & Young, 2008). Even with these caveats, however, it is clear that cell phones are a part of the adolescent

Talking on the phone is an important pastime for most adolescents and can occupy a large part of their day. The prevalence of the cell phone has only reinforced this behavior.

scene and that they will likely be used more and more in the years to come.

Adolescent cell phone use is by no means limited to the United States. In fact, the teenagers in many European and Asian countries are even more likely to use cell phones than their American counterparts. This is because they do not need parental consent for service, and calling rates are relatively less expensive (compared to fixed-line service) than in the United States (Anderson, 2002; Nielsen Company, 2009).

Computers and the Internet

Virtually all adolescents have access to computers and the Internet: if they do not have them at home (and most do), nearly every school in America not only has multiple computers for student use but is wired to the Web. More than 90 percent of teens say they have an Internet connection at home (more than half of them say it is wireless), and about 75 percent can get on the Web at school (Nielsen, 2009). Black youth are somewhat less likely to go online than other adolescents, but even they use the Internet at higher rates than adults. This pattern is likely partially a product of socioeconomic differences, since adolescents whose parents earn more money and went to college are more likely to use the Web than those whose parents do not have those attributes (Lenhart, Madden, & Hitlin, 2005).

Not only do adolescents use the Web, but they use it frequently. About 60 percent of teens say that they

connect to the Internet at least once per day; about one-third say they get on several times per day (Lenhart, Madden, MacGill, et al., 2007). Still, they do not spend as much time on the Internet each day as adults. In fact, they spend less than half as much time: 23 minutes per day for teens versus 59 minutes a day for their elders (Nielsen, 2009), who spend a lot of time on the Internet while at work.

What do teens do while on the Web? How do they spend their Internet time? The general-purpose search engines Google and Yahoo are the most commonly visited sites by teens as well as adults (Nielson, 2009). Almost 60 percent of all teens (two-thirds of Internet users) create their own content and post it for others to view. The most common posting is of some artistic work, such as a drawing or piece of music (40 percent), followed by blogs (28 percent) and personal Web pages (27 percent). Girls and older teens are more likely to post their own content (Lenhart, Madden, MacGill, et al., 2007). In addition, more than half of American teens not only visit social networking sites such as MySpace and Facebook but have a profile on one as well (Madden, Fox, Smith, et al., 2007). Teens use these sites to stay in touch both with friends with whom they are regularly in contact and those they see more sporadically; about half use the sites to make new friends. Other activities include playing games (81 percent), getting news (76 percent), making purchases (43 percent), and getting health information (43 percent) (Lenhart, Madden, & Hitlin, 2005). (See Figure 10.4.) They are more likely to download music or videos and less likely to use e-mail

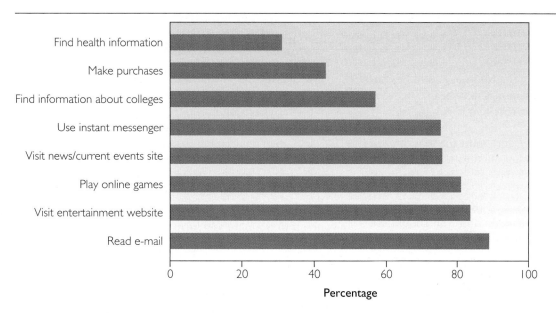

FIGURE 10.4
PERCENTAGE OF
ADOLESCENTS
WHO ENGAGE
IN VARIOUS
INTERNET
ACTIVITIES

Source: Lenhart, Madden, and
Hitlin (2005). From *Teens &
technology.* Washington, DC: Pew
Internet and American Life Project.
Copyright © by Pew.

than their parents (Fox & Madden, 2006). Older girls use the Web more than younger girls or boys.

Besides being able to keep in touch with friends from school, the Internet also allows adolescents to interact with strangers, some of whom may become friends or part of their support network. This may be particularly useful for adolescents who find themselves in a minority in their community or who have some special interest or problem that is not widely shared by those around them. Adolescents can go on chat rooms and "speak" with others who share a hobby, root for the same sports team, share their lifestyle (e.g., bisexual, goth), have the same medical condition as themselves, have the same ethnicity, or share their religious or political beliefs. At present, there is little cause to worry that electronically mediated communication adversely affects adolescents' social skills or prompts them toward antisocial behavior. Mikani, Szwedo, Allen, et al. (2010), for example, found that those who were socially well adjusted as young teens were *more* likely to be heavy users of online communication when older than those who were not. Of course, it cannot be forgotten that interacting with strangers is not all good. There are chat rooms in which teenagers encourage one another to engage in harmful activities, such as eating-disordered behavior or self-mutilation. Also, several studies have revealed that about 15 percent of adolescents have actually met face-to-face with persons whom they have initially had contact with online (e.g., Staksrud, 2003). This clearly carries significant risk, since there is no guarantee that a person is actually who he or she claims to be online.

Another concern (of parents, if not of teens) is the availability of sexually explicit material on the Web. About one-third of adolescents say that they have been exposed to *unwanted* sexual materials while browsing the Internet, an increase over the past five years. About 4 percent have been asked by strangers to transmit nude photos of themselves (Mitchell, Wolak, & Finkelhor, 2007). About half of teens have received e-mails directing them to X-rated Web sites (Symantec Corporation, 2004). Since many youth actively search the Web for sexual material, it is not surprising that 90 percent say that they have viewed sexually explicit materials online (Fox, 2006, cited in Strasburger, Wilson, & Jordan, 2009).

Psychologists have another worry: the anonymity of the Web and its effect upon adolescent identity development. This anonymity offers unprecedented opportunity to experiment with one's identity (Katz & Rice, 2002). You can present yourself in different ways, with minimal "real-life" consequences, to see how others react to you. You can pretend to be things you are not, and no one can know that you are not being truthful. Adolescents do seem to take advantage of the Web for identity experimentation (Calvert, 2002). Early adolescents experiment more than older ones, who spend more of their time communicating with their friends. Girls and boys both alter their personas to be more sexually stereotyped (i.e., girls describe themselves as more beautiful than they are, boys as more hypermasculine). The most common motivation for this deception appears to be to see how others react to you when aspects of yourself are changed; facilitating relationship formation is a secondary concern (Valkenberg, Schouten, & Peter, 2005).

PERSONAL ISSUES   INTERNET AND CELL PHONE ADDICTION

It is so common for high school and college students to spend long hours using the Internet and to be constantly checking their cell phones that the line between normal and abnormal use can be unclear. Internet or cell phone use can be problematic if it becomes compulsive and begins to interfere with the rest of your life. It's not really the number of hours that you log on, chat, or text that matter; it's the attitude you have about those hours and the priority they have in your life.

If you are at all concerned that you are lapsing into Internet or cell phone addiction, you should ask yourself the following questions:

1. Are you in control of the time you spend on the Internet and your phone, or do you find yourself logging on or checking your messages more than you'd like? Do answering calls or messages interfere with other activities?

2. Do you frequently stay online longer than you intended, even if it means missing an appointment or losing needed sleep? Do you ignore the people you are with to speak on your cell?

3. Do you neglect schoolwork or employment responsibilities so that you can stay online or chat or text?

4. Do you cancel social activities so that you can spend more time on the Web or talking on your cell?

5. Do you daydream about being online or talking with someone on your cell phone when you are not?

6. Do you find yourself lying about your Internet or cell phone use, or minimizing it when you talk to others?

7. Have your friends complained to you about your computer or cell phone use, or suggested to you that you spend too much time online or on the phone?

8. Do you get irritated when you can't be online or on your phone as much as you'd like?

These questions are analogous to those you would ask yourself to evaluate any form of addiction, be it drug use or gambling or exercising.

People who are addicted to their cell phones can't bear to feel alone, to miss a message, or fail to know what's going on. Those with Internet addictions are more variable, since there are so many different things one can do on the Web. Some people participate in online gambling, interact with others in chat rooms, shop, surf for information, view pornography, and play online games. It is the desperation and need to be on the Web, rather than the activity itself, that makes the behavior hurtful.

Internet and cell phone addictions can be treated, just as any other compulsive behavior can be treated. If you are worried about your Internet or cell phone use, speak to a counselor in your college or university's counseling center.

Nonmaterial Concerns of Adolescent Culture

Not all aspects of the adolescent subculture involve possessions. Using the latest slang terms and listening to peer-approved music also help teens feel part of a subculture. Both also encourage others to perceive a teen as "cool/groovy/with it/crazy/a bull brahma/all that/bad/phat," depending on the era.

Slang

People in subgroups often use their own variety of slang terms. *Slang* is a shorthand way of expressing a concept that would take longer to express using conventional language. For instance, it takes less time to say *hot* than to say *sexually attractive*. The correct use of slang identifies one as a member of a subculture, just as clothing does. Using slang also provides teens a certain degree of privacy, since the adults around them may have difficulty understanding what they are saying to one another. Slang terms express the values of the subgroup; for example, in the 1960s, hippies used the word *psychedelic*, which refers to hallucinogenic drugs, to express approval for nondrug items. Using slang fosters a sense of cohesion among subgroup members.

Music

Music is an important part of adolescent culture. A large majority of adolescents spend a lot of time listening to music. Most studies reveal that adolescents spend somewhat more than three hours per day listening to music (e.g., Gentile, Lynch, Linder, et al., 2004). Much of that time, the music provides a background for other activities. With the widespread availability of MP3 players—with their small size and huge storage capacity—constant, on-demand access to music is more possible than ever before; teens are no longer constrained by the need for an electric outlet or forced to carry a large "boom box."

Strasburger (1995) has identified four reasons why youths listen to music:

1. Music can help one relax and improve one's mood.

2. Music can enhance a social event, such as a party or gathering of friends.

3. Music can help pass the time and relieve boredom.

4. Music can allow one to express feelings about various issues and can provide something or someone (the singer) to identify with.

Given that it fills so many needs, it is really not surprising that music takes up so much of many adolescents' time.

Although different genres of music emphasize different themes, in mainstream rock, pop, and country and western music, songs about love predominate (Christenson & Roberts, 1998). Many songs depict love in a romantic fashion, suggesting that true love can conquer all or that love is the greatest pleasure in life. Other songs deal with the downsides of love: breaking up, unrequited love, and betrayal. Moreover, songs have become more and more sexually explicit; it is not unusual for songs to be blatantly suggestive and to extol the joys of sexual contact. Both male and female singers frequently describe how good making love feels.

In addition to love and sexual themes, popular music sometimes addresses the problems that teenagers confront. Some artists sing about loneliness or being unable to find a job. Some urge listeners to reject the authority of their parents, their teachers, or the police. Song lyrics may encourage violence against perceived oppressors or rail against societal or world problems, such as war and hatred. Drinking and drugs are also frequently mentioned, either celebrating the fun in getting drunk or high or emphasizing the problems these behaviors can cause. So-called party songs encourage adolescents to let loose and have a good time.

Rock Music

When rock music became popular in the 1950s, it was the music of youth. Prior to this time, adults and adolescents listened to the same types of music, such as the crooners of earlier eras. Although jazz was once viewed as scandalous, it never had an exclusively adolescent audience. But beginning with Little Richard, Elvis, and Chuck Berry, teenagers had their own music and it often met with their parents' disapproval.

Although much rock consisted (and continues to consist) of rather gentle love songs, some of it extolled the virtues of sex, drug use, and rebellion. Early on, Elvis's gyrating hip movements were cause for alarm. In the 1960s, the Beatles' John Lennon scandalized the adult world by claiming that the group was more popular than Jesus (inspiring public record burnings), and the Rolling Stones were prevented from singing "Let's spend the night together" on television. (They had to change the lyrics to "Let's spend some time together.") Later on, the Jefferson Airplane and the Grateful Dead recommended drug use to their listeners, and Country Joe sang out against the war in Vietnam. Heavy metal performers such as Mötley Crüe and Metallica presented themselves as dangerous sexual predators, while glam rockers gloried in sexual ambiguity. The Seattle-based grunge bands of the early 1990s, such as Alice in Chains and Nirvana, were angry and full of despair. At the turn of the new century, new metal bands such as Linkin Park and Limp Bizkit continued the tradition of provocative lyrics.

Rock has lost much of its ability to shock the adult world, since the parents of today's teens grew up listening to some version of it. Many, if not most, adults still tune their radios to rock stations (even if they play hits from the 1970s or 1980s) and attend rock concerts. Because rock became so mainstream, a new type of youth sound was needed.

Rap Music

Rap has now been in existence for about 30 years. Its hallmark is its spoken lyrics, which are accompanied by a rhythmic beat. Rap music is now by far the most popular music with Black, White, and Latino adolescents (Roberts, Foehr, & Rideout, 2005). Rap is the backbone of hip-hop culture. With its roots in African and Caribbean music, rap was invented in New York City by two disc jockeys, Afrika Bambaata and Kool Herc, who had immigrated from the islands. The first large

Attending rock concerts has been a tradition among youths for more than 60 years.

commercial rap recording was the Sugar Hill Gang's "Rapper's Delight," released in 1979. As rap became more established, it diversified. Artists began to experiment with fusing rap with rock (especially metal), Latin, and techno sounds. One branch in particular, gangsta rap—exemplified by rappers such as Ice T, Tupac Shakur, and Public Enemy—became violent, sexist, and homophobic. Throughout the 1980s and the 1990s, rap had a growing tendency to contain pro-drug messages (Herd, 2008).

Inevitably, the same kinds of concerns about antisocial messages that had been reserved for rock music spilled over onto rap. Are these concerns justified? Does listening to music with violent or overtly sexual lyrics negatively affect teens?

The Effects of Antisocial Music

The principles of social learning theory suggest that being exposed to music with antisocial themes, especially when performed by one's heroes or idols, will be harmful. What is known about the effects of television exposure—a different form of media—also argues for caution. What does the research that directly examines the effects of antisocial music on adolescents indicate?

There is a good deal of research demonstrating a correlation between preference for antisocial music and alienation. Scheel and Westefeld (1999), for example, found that heavy metal fans had more positive views of suicide and saw less reason for living than did nonfans. Atkin, Smith, Roberto, et al. (2002) found that adolescents who were aggressive or most prone to engaging in antisocial acts were also most likely to say that heavy metal was their favorite type of music. Similarly, other studies (e.g., Chen, Miller, Grube, et al., 2006) have linked listening to rap with drug use and aggression. Other studies have linked alienation from school and preference for heavy metal music (e.g., Roe, 1995).

However, no study to date has demonstrated a direct causal link between the preference for songs with antisocial lyrics and harmful behavior (Kirsh, 2006). Stack (1998), for instance, found that even though heavy metal fans were more accepting of suicide, this was no longer the case when differences in the religiosity of heavy metal fans and nonfans was taken into account. In other words, it was religious ideation, not the listener's preference for heavy metal, that influenced attitudes toward suicide. Other research has found that when heavy metal fans listen to their preferred music, their mood improves, not darkens (e.g., Scheel & Westefeld, 1999). Heavy metal music serves a purgative function, dissipating accumulative frustration and anger. Nonfans who were new to heavy metal lyrics were likely to react with anger, however. Ballard and Coates (1995) failed to demonstrate that listening to heavy metal or rap had even a short-term effect on youths' suicide ideation.

Still, some studies are troubling. For example, a recent study with Dutch youths found that preference for rap music predicted later externalizing, antisocial behavior in girls, and that preference for either rap or heavy metal predicted later externalizing problems in boys. Conversely, having externalizing problems did not predict becoming rap or heavy metal fans in the future (Selfhout, Delsing, terBogt, et al., 2008). Although it is certainly plausible that a confounding factor is responsible for the correlation, the fact that the relationship existed in only one direction (music taste to problem behavior, not vice versa) bolsters the arguments of those who oppose this type of music.

In sum, the role of antisocial music in the lives of adolescents who like and listen to it is complex, reflecting their concern with the condition of the world and a certain pessimism with regard to the future, but it is also used by them to assuage unpleasant and unruly emotions. Songs about suicide, murder, radical despair, and the destruction of the world are the result. But rather than being the cause of recklessness and despair among adolescents, heavy metal music is a reflection of these concerns and of the socialization environment.

Similarly, there are correlational data showing that adolescents who listen to music that contains sexually degrading lyrics (but not sexual, non-degrading lyrics) are more likely to engage in early sexual intercourse than adolescents who do not listen to music with sexually degrading lyrics (Martino, Collins, Elliott, et al., 2006). This appears to be true even when numerous other factors that could be responsible for the findings are statistically controlled. Although this kind of analysis is more persuasive than a more typical purely correlational research design, it is still premature to conclude that listening to sexually degrading lyrics directly leads to increased early sexual activity (i.e., that there is a causal relationship between the two).

It is important to remember that preferences for violent rock and rap music are associated with participation in reckless behavior but do not necessarily *cause* adolescents to behave recklessly. Rather, both reckless behavior and heavy metal or rap music may appeal to adolescents who have an especially high propensity for sensation seeking. It is equally important to remember that only a few studies have tried to find causal links between music listening and antisocial outcomes. It is quite possible that these links will be demonstrated in the future, especially for those individuals who are subjected to antisocial

> **ANSWERS WOULDN'T YOU LIKE TO KNOW ...**
>
> Does listening to antisocial music cause antisocial behavior?
>
> There are no causal data linking teen depression, suicide, and antisocial behavior to antisocial music. However, adolescents who are depressed or aggressive tend to listen to music that reflects those themes. In addition, exposure to music and music videos that depict stereotypes of women and minorities tends to increase belief in those stereotypes.

music against their will. Also, even if there is no causal connection between rap or heavy metal listening and antisocial behavior, the correlation is important because listening can serve as a marker, or predictor, of risk for future problematic behavior.

Music Videos

With the advent of MTV (Music Television) in August 1981, an immensely popular new form of entertainment was spawned. No one can dispute the huge commercial success of MTV and its residual impact on the music industry. Still, today's adolescents do not spend nearly as much time watching music videos as did those in the 1980s: most watch only 15–30 minutes per day (Roberts, Christianson, & Gentile, 2003). MTV itself devotes little time to music videos. Adolescents now watch videos on other television stations and on their computers. However, 15–30 minutes each day adds up to 90–180 hours each year, so it is worthwhile to consider what we know about music videos' effects.

Targeted at teenagers and containing more violence and sex than conventional television, the music video industry attracted a notable group of critics. For example, the American Academy of Pediatrics, Women against Pornography, National Coalition on Television Violence, Parents Music Resource Center, National Parent Teachers Association, and others all expressed concern about the possible harmful effects of music videos on youths. Content analyses have revealed that more than half of concept videos (those that depict imagery other than that of a musical performance) have violent or sexual imagery or both (Strasburger, 1995). Rap videos, as a group, are more violent, more profane, and more sexual than even rock or heavy metal videos (Kandakai, Price, Telljohann, et al., 1999; Smith & Boyson, 2002).

Johnson and colleagues demonstrated several negative effects of videos with these antisocial themes. In one study, African American male adolescents were exposed to violent rap videos, nonviolent rap videos, or no videos (the control condition). Afterward, the adolescents were presented with a scenario in which violence occurred. Those subjects who had watched the violent rap videos found the violence in the scenario more acceptable than did the other subjects. Moreover, they said that they were more likely to use violence themselves (Johnson, Jackson, & Gatto, 1995). A second study demonstrated that girls who watched videos in which females were sexually subordinate were less likely to disapprove of a scenario involving sexual violence than girls who had not been shown such videos (Johnson, Adams, Ashburn, et al., 1995). Finally, a third study showed that adolescents who watched violent rap videos developed more negative stereotypes about African American males than subjects who did not watch such videos (Johnson, Trawalter, & Dovidio, 2000).

The U.S. Senate held hearings in 1985 to examine the rock music industry and its effect on youthful consumers, but at the time, there was insufficient research to support the allegation of the critics or to allay the anxieties of concerned parents. There are good reasons, however, why music videos have the potential to affect youths more than any other popular medium. Consider the following (Strouse, Buerkel-Rothfuss, & Long, 1995):

1. Music can evoke very strong feelings; the mood-altering effects of music make people more susceptible to behavioral and attitudinal changes.
2. It is well known that a combined audio and visual presentation enhances learning and has a greater impact on attitudes and behavior than music alone.
3. Rock music often contains rebellious, antisocial, and sexually provocative messages.
4. Concept music videos are frequently interspersed with unconnected segments of violence.
5. Some research reveals that a relatively short exposure to music videos can result in desensitization to violence and an increased acceptance of socially violent behavior.

Research on the effects of music videos on adolescents reveals some interesting gender differences. Females tend to listen to more music and prefer soft, romantic, danceable music, whereas males prefer hard rock (Toney & Weaver, 1994). Females describe music as being more important to them than do boys, and they pay more attention to a song's lyrics than do boys. Therefore, they report more personal involvement and participation in music imagery and are more likely to recall the images of the videos when listening to a song on the radio. Survey research finds a stronger association between the amount of exposure to music videos and premarital sexual permissiveness for females than for males (Strouse, Buerkel-Rothfuss, Long, 1995).

Another important consideration is the environment of the family. Parental absence is associated with an increased use of television and radio by adolescents. Furthermore, adolescents who are heavy consumers of rock music tend to be more involved with their peers and less with their families than are adolescents who are light users of rock music. Thus, the family environment is an important moderator of the impact of music videos on youth. Thus, adolescents' perceptions and feelings about their level of satisfaction with their family may be a better moderator of the potential effects of music video exposure than other more objective indices of actual family functions. Unsatisfactory conditions in a family promote an affective need for youthful members to select and attend to music programming that enables them to escape into the fantasies of a seductive video. In summary, the potential effect of music videos as a dynamic, interactional process has a greater impact on youths who are at risk. Adolescents from family environments with a high level of satisfaction may be relatively unaffected by the sexual messages of music videos (Strouse, Buerkel-Rothfuss, & Long, 1995).

SUMMARY

1. Adolescent society consists of the organized networks of social interaction among adolescents. Adolescent culture is the sum of adolescents' ways of living.

2. Some adults believe that adolescents have their own subculture; others believe that adolescent culture is a reflection of adult culture. Actually, both views are partially true. Certain aspects of adolescent culture (such as premarital sexual behavior and use of marijuana) are subcultural because they run counter to adult culture. In many ways, however, adolescent culture reflects adult values.

3. Adolescent societies may be divided into formal (primarily in-school) and informal (friendship) groups. The formal in-school subsystem may be further divided into the formal academic subsystem and the activities subsystem.

4. Involvement in extracurricular activities benefits teens. The benefits may not be as great for athletics as for some other activities.

5. In addition to friendship pairs, adolescents arrange themselves into cliques and crowds. Not everyone belongs to a clique or a crowd—some by their own choice and others by rejection.

6. Bullying is an all too common experience for many teens. Adolescents who are different and quiet and have few friends are most likely to be targeted. Fortunately, there are programs that can greatly reduce the incidence of bullying.

7. The need for close friends intensifies during adolescence. Having friends helps bridge the gap between being emotionally dependent on one's parents and achieving true emotional independence.

8. It is extremely common for adolescents to experience loneliness.

9. The ability to form close friendships is partly learned in the family. Adolescents who have close relationships with their parents tend to be the most socially adjusted.

10. Young adolescent friends are usually very similar to each other. Teens choose friends who are like themselves to begin with, and once they become friends, they encourage one another to be even more similar.

11. When adolescents leave the confines of their elementary schools, they broaden their friendships. Young adolescents want a lot of friends; as they get older, they become more discriminating and seek fewer but better friends.

12. Adolescents find group acceptance and popularity by conforming, achieving, participating in school activities, developing and exhibiting personal qualities that others admire, and learning social skills that ensure acceptance.

13. Having lots of friends does not necessarily make you "popular." Popular adolescents are the social leaders. They are not always well liked, and they often use relational and reputational aggression to maintain their social standing.

14. Psychosocial development takes place in three stages: autosocial, homosocial, and heterosocial. One of the chief tasks is to develop heterosociality, wherein friendships are chosen from both sexes.

15. Most adolescents develop crushes on or fall in love with real or imagined partners.

16. Loss of love can be a major source of stress in the life of the adolescent.

17. Dating has several important purposes: to have fun, to provide companionship, to gain status, for sexual satisfaction, as a means of mate selection, and as a means of developing intimacy.

18. Dating begins gradually, shifting from mixed-sex group activities to one-on-one, private outings.

19. Dating violence is an unfortunately common occurrence.

20. Cohabitation has become a normative behavior, and more than half of young adults will cohabitate with a partner before they marry.

21. Adolescents cohabitate for a variety of reasons: because it is satisfying, because they feel emotionally committed, as a prelude to marriage, as a trial marriage, and because they do not believe in marriage.

22. Cohabitation before marriage does not improve the quality of the subsequent marriage or decrease the probability of divorce.

23. Fewer adolescents are marrying today. Those who do marry do so because of pregnancy, having an overly romantic view of marriage, and trying to escape from their families. Young married couples face many problems, including unwanted children, immaturity, financial hardships, and arguments with in-laws.

24. Adolescents are a powerful consumer force. They have a great deal of discretionary disposable income, which they largely spend on themselves for luxury items.

25. Clothing is one of the most noticeable aspects of adolescent culture. It is an important means by which adolescents discover and express their identities. It expresses their dependence/independence conflict with adults. It may even express a political philosophy and ensure their sense of belonging with peer groups.

26. The automobile is another important material part of adolescent culture. It is a status symbol, a means of freedom and mobility, a symbol of power and independence, a hobby, and a symbol of glamour and sexuality. Ready access to an automobile has a great influence on the adolescent's daily life, social activity, and freedom.

27. Talking on a phone is a favorite pastime of adolescents. Cell phone use ensures even more constant contact with friends than was possible in the past. Cell phones are also used for text messaging.

28. Almost all teenagers make frequent use of the Internet; on it they communicate with friends, interact with strangers who sometimes become friends, look up information, and play games. They do not always present themselves honestly in online interactions.

29. Adolescents use slang to identify themselves as part of a group, for shorthand, to foster cohesion, and for privacy from adults.

30. Music is an important part of adolescent culture. Adolescents listen primarily to rock and rap.

31. Rock has been criticized by adults since it first began, since it sometimes promotes values considered antithetical to adult culture. It is not uncommon for lyrics to endorse casual sex, drug use, and opposition to authority.

32. Rap music is now more popular with youth than any other type of music. Many adults are equally concerned about the sexist and violent messages found in rap music.

33. Youths listen to antisocial music because it serves a purgative function in dissipating their anger and because it is a reflection of alienation. Listening to heavy metal music or rap music and engaging in reckless behavior are correlated, although the former does not *cause* the latter. Rather, those who do both have a propensity for sensation seeking.

34. Music videos are watched by millions of youths. Many professional organizations are critical of some of these videos because they portray much sex and violence. The data suggest that watching such music videos can foster negative attitudes.

KEY TERMS

adolescent culture 242	hippies 246
adolescent society 242	homosociality 253
adolescent subculture 242	liaisons 245
attachment 249	perceived popularity 252
autosociality 253	relational aggression 252
bullying 247	reputational aggression 252
cliques 245	sociometric popularity 252
crowds 245	subsystems 243
flappers 246	
heterosociality 253	

THOUGHT QUESTIONS

Personal Reflection

1. Do you think that you were ever part of a distinct subculture? Did you feel alienated or just different?
2. Did you belong to a clique, were you a liaison, or were you a loner? How did you treat others who were not part of your "inner circle"? How were you treated by others?
3. Compare the relationships you had/have with your closest friend in middle school, high school, and now. How have your friendships changed?
4. How did you feel about the "popular" students in your middle and high school? Did you like them? Admire them? Were they friendly toward you?
5. Reflect back on your first love. Why did you fall for him/her?
6. Would you cohabitate with someone prior to marriage? If so, under what conditions? If not, why not?
7. Did you have a car in high school? How would your life have been different with or without it?
8. Do you think that you were affected by the music you listened to as a younger adolescent? If not, why not?

Group Discussion

9. Do parents or peers exert the greater influence on the lives of youths?
10. Was there much snobbishness and socioeconomic class discrimination in your high school? Explain.
11. Some of the studies discussed in this chapter present the life and values of high school youths as quite superficial. Are adolescents more serious minded than these studies indicate? In your experience, are they less superficial and more concerned with world problems and academics?
12. Do extracurricular activities contribute to adolescent development? If so, in what ways?
13. How would you answer each of the following questions if you were asked it by a youth in middle school or high school?
    a. How can you get others to like you?
    b. What do you do if your best friend talks about you behind your back?
    c. What do boys look for in a girl?
    d. What do girls look for in a boy?
    e. How can I get over being shy?
    f. How do you know if you're really in love?
14. What are the pros and cons of exclusively dating someone while in high school?
15. Would you advise young people to cohabit? Why or why not?
16. How old do you think people should be before getting married? Explain.
17. Is clothing as important to the adolescent as this chapter claims? Why or why not?

Debate Questions

18. Middle and high school students should be required to participate in some structured extracurricular activity.
19. Little can be done to change the social structure of middle and high schools: there will also be popular and unpopular students.
20. Premarital cohabitation should be discouraged.
21. States should raise the legal age of marriage to 21.
22. Adolescent cell phone use is excessive and should be limited.
23. Songs with antisocial lyrics do have harmful effects on adolescents.

SUGGESTED READING

Bennett, A., and Kahn-Harris, K. (Eds.). (2004). *After Subculture: Critical Studies in Contemporary Youth Culture.* Hampshire, England: Palgrave.

Crampton, L., and Rees, D. (2003). *Rock and Roll Year by Year.* London, England: D.K. Publishing.

Furman, W., Brown, B. B., and Feiring, C. (Eds.). (1999). *The Development of Romantic Relationships in Adolescence.* Cambridge, England: Cambridge University Press.

Garbarino, J., and deLara, E. (2003). *And Words Can Hurt: How to Protect Adolescents from Bullying, Harassment, and Emotional Violence.* New York: Free Press.

Katz, J. E., and Rice, R. E. (2002). *Social Consequences of Internet Use: Access, Involvement, and Interaction.* Cambridge, MA: MIT Press.

Simmons, R. (2004). *Odd Girl Speaks Out: Girls Write about Bullies, Cliques, Popularity, and Jealousy.* Westminster, CO: Harvest Books.

Strasburger, V., Wilson, B. J., & Jordan, A. B. (2009). *Children, Adolescents, and the Media,* 2nd ed. Thousand Oaks, CA: Sage.

Way, N., and Hamm, J. V. (Eds.). (2005). *The Experience of Close Friendship in Adolescence: New Directions for Child & Adolescent Development.* San Francisco: Jossey-Bass.

Wu, S. (2000). *Cohabitation: An Alternative Form of Family Living.* Oxford, England: Oxford University Press.

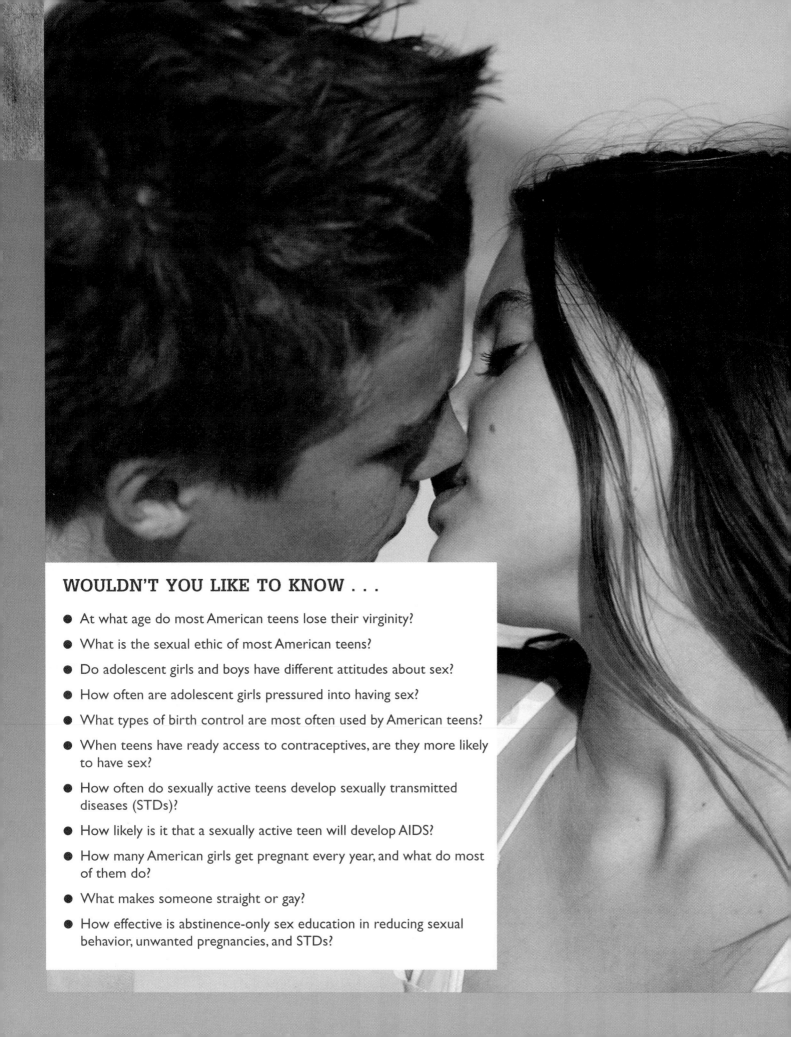

WOULDN'T YOU LIKE TO KNOW . . .

- At what age do most American teens lose their virginity?

- What is the sexual ethic of most American teens?

- Do adolescent girls and boys have different attitudes about sex?

- How often are adolescent girls pressured into having sex?

- What types of birth control are most often used by American teens?

- When teens have ready access to contraceptives, are they more likely to have sex?

- How often do sexually active teens develop sexually transmitted diseases (STDs)?

- How likely is it that a sexually active teen will develop AIDS?

- How many American girls get pregnant every year, and what do most of them do?

- What makes someone straight or gay?

- How effective is abstinence-only sex education in reducing sexual behavior, unwanted pregnancies, and STDs?

Sexual Behaviors

The onset of puberty is accompanied by an increasing interest in sex. At first, this interest is self-centered, focusing on the physical changes happening to the adolescent's body. Most adolescents spend a lot of time looking in the mirror, examining their bodies in detail. This early concern is centered on developing an acceptable body image rather than on erotic sensations or expression.

Gradually, young adolescents become interested not only in their own development but also in that of others. More and more questions arise concerning the development, changes, and sexual characteristics of the opposite sex. Adolescents also become fascinated with basic facts about human reproduction. Both boys and girls slowly become aware of their own developing sexual feelings and drives and how these are aroused and expressed. Most adolescents begin some experimentation: touching themselves, playing with their genitals, exploring new developments. Often by accident, they experience orgasm through self-manipulation. Adolescents begin to spend a lot of time talking about sex, telling crude jokes, viewing pornography, and perhaps even "sexting." Adults are sometimes shocked at this behavior: many parents have been horrified at finding their browser directed to a triple-X Web site. These activities, however, are motivated by a desire to understand human sexuality; they are adolescents' means of comprehending, expressing, and gaining control over their sexual feelings.

Over time, adolescents become more interested in sexual experimentation with others. Part of this interest is motivated by curiosity; part by a desire for sexual stimulation and release; and part by a need for love, affection, intimacy, and acceptance from another person. It is not uncommon for the need for emotional fulfillment and reassurance to be stronger than the need for physical fulfillment.

Sexual ethics in the United States changed greatly during the late 1960s/early 1970s, the time of the so-called sexual revolution. Some of these changes have been positive. For instance, most adolescents today are far more open about sex and are less hesitant in talking about it than were teens in 1962. This attitude should contribute to their having more satisfying sex lives. Along with this new morality have come some changes in sexual attitudes and behavior. Research documents the increasing sexual permissiveness of youths, especially of girls, and the fact that society now is pluralistic as far as sexual morality is concerned. In general, adolescents now accept an individualistic ethic—the belief that all people must decide on their own standards for themselves.

These changes have brought some problems, as well. Along with increased sexual activity have come increases in sexually transmitted diseases, unintended pregnancies, and abortions. The reason for these increases is that adolescents are more sexually active and most do not consistently use effective methods of birth control and disease prevention.

Today's adolescents, like those of past generations, are confronted with the task of making sexual decisions. Youths have the same sexual drives and urges today that other generations have had, but the difference is that these urges are being constantly stimulated and the guidelines for their control or expression are less clearly defined. Despite the abundance of sex seen on television and in movies and the number of discussions of sex in magazines, many adolescents are still uninformed or misinformed about their sexuality. Consequently, there is a need for positive programs of sex education to counteract the half-truths and distortions to which adolescents are exposed and to help adolescents wade through a jungle of moral confusion.

Changing Attitudes and Behavior

How sexually active are American teens? Do most lose their virginity while in high school? Middle school? Apart from intercourse, what else are they doing? This section explores the actual sexual behavior of American teens.

Premarital Sexual Behavior

According to the Centers for Disease Control and Prevention (CDC; 2008), only about 7 percent of teenagers have experienced sexual intercourse by age 13. About 30 percent of 15- to 17-year-olds report that they have engaged in intercourse, and about 66 to 70 percent of 18- to 19-year-olds say that they have lost their virginity (CDC, 2009b). (See Figure 11.1.) Most sexually active adolescents have partners near their own age. About three-quarters of adolescent girls say that their first sexual partner was either the same age as themelves or between 1 and 3 years older than themselves. In other words, most teens have sex with other teens or with very young adults. When asked why they had intercourse the first time, 43 percent of high school males attributed it to opportunity, whereas 23 percent answered that they were in love. Among high school females, 54 percent said they were in love and only 11 percent said that they had the opportunity and were ready (Kaiser Family Foundation, 1998). Most teenage girls who lose their virginity do so with a steady boyfriend (Abma, Martinez, Mosher, et al., 2004)

Other data suggest a distressingly high incidence of unwanted first intercourse, especially on the part of female teenagers. About 9 percent of young women reported having been forced into it, and the younger the girl at age of first intercourse, the more likely that force was involved. Data are unavailable for young men. An additional 13 percent of females and 6 percent of males "really didn't want it to happen" (Abma, Martinex, Mosher, et al., 2004). It is not surprising, then, that males

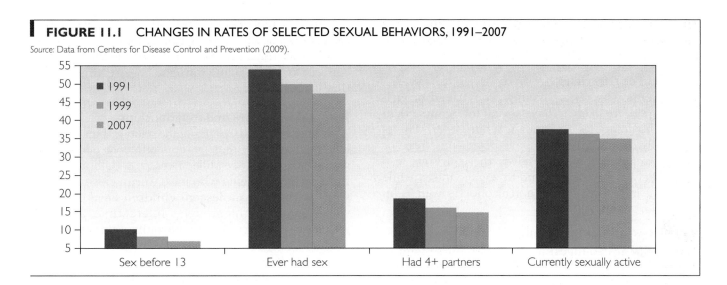

FIGURE 11.1 CHANGES IN RATES OF SELECTED SEXUAL BEHAVIORS, 1991–2007

Source: Data from Centers for Disease Control and Prevention (2009).

generally report that their first experience with intercourse was more satisfying than females do (Sprecher, Barbee, & Schwartz, 1995). Males recall it as being more physically satisfying and less guilt provoking than do females. Both males and females remember the experience as being more emotionally intense if their sexual partner was someone for whom they felt affection.

Overall, today's adolescents are having sex earlier than their grandparents but perhaps not their parents and likely not their older siblings. Today's teens are *less* likely to have sex at a very young age (e.g., 13 or 14), *less* likely to have ever engaged in intercourse, *less* likely to be currently sexually active, and *less* likely to have had four our more sex partners than teens in the early 1990s (CDC, 2009b). Most researchers believe that these declines are mostly due to increased awareness of and fear of sexually transmitted diseases (STDs).

Since the average age of marriage is now in the mid- to late-20s, few Americans are waiting until they marry to have sex, but most sexually active high school students show no signs of having large numbers of partners. The preferred pattern is *serial monogamy,* in which one dates and has intercourse with only one partner at a time. Most adolescents say that their sexual behavior occurs in the context of a relationship that is important to them. Even so, about 15 percent of high school students are involved in concurrent relationships (Kelley, Borawski, Flocke, et al. 2003), and the percentage is higher in college. (See Personal Issues box "Hooking Up on College Campuses" on page 284.)

ANSWERS WOULDN'T YOU LIKE TO KNOW ...

At what age do most American teens lose their virginity?

Because teenage intercourse rates have declined, most American teens now remain virgins until they are 18.

Correlates

Not all teens are equally likely to be sexually active. Let's look at what factors are associated with adolescent sexual activity.

Age

The older they are, the more likely adolescents are to have had premarital **coitus,** or sexual intercourse (CDC, 2009b).

Race/Ethnicity

Other things being equal, African Americans report a higher incidence of premarital intercourse than Caucasians. African Americans are more likely to have experienced intercourse as high schoolers (67 percent vs. 44 percent), to have become sexually active at a young age (16 percent vs. 4 percent), to have had a relatively large number of partners (28 percent vs. 12 percent), and to report that they are currently sexually active (46 percent vs. 33 percent) than Whites (CDC, 2009b). Latinos fall midway between Blacks and Whites on these measures. Asian American adolescents are less likely to be sexually active than teens from other racial and ethnic groups and often postpone even kissing and petting until their twenties (Okazaki, 2002). When differences in socioeconomic status are taken into account, differences in race and ethnicity become less significant (Bingham, Miller, & Adams, 1990).

Religion

Religiosity and a lower level of sexual permissiveness go together (e.g., Edwards, Fehring, Jarrett, et al., 2008). However, it is less clear that religiosity itself is *causally* related to lessened sexual activity; the relationship might be merely correlational (Rostosky,

coitus   sexual intercourse.

Wilcox, Wright, et al., 2004). Still, a large number of adolescents who indicate that they are abstinent claim to be so because of religious reasons.

Boyfriend or Girlfriend

Adolescents who report having a boyfriend or girlfriend are more likely to have sexual intercourse than those who do not (Scott-Jones & White, 1990). This is especially true of girls who have boyfriends three or more years older than themselves; these girls are also more likely to be coerced and to engage in sex while under the influence of drugs and alcohol (Gowen, Feldman, Diaz, et al., 2004).

Young Age at First Intercourse

Those who are youngest at first intercourse tend to engage in more sexual behavior later in adolescence than those who report older ages at first intercourse. In addition, they are more likely to be the victim of sexual violence and partner abuse (Watson, Taft, & Lee, 2007) and to develop substance abuse and conduct problems (Pedersen, Samuelsen, & Wichstrom, 2003). The upshot: early intercourse is an indicator of an adolescent in trouble.

Age at Puberty

The earlier a girl reaches menarche, the younger she will likely be when she first has intercourse (Edgardh, 2000). Similarly, boys who reach puberty at an early age are more likely to become sexually active sooner than boys who do not (Edgardh, 2002). Given the fact that hormones are partially responsible for both self-concept as an adult and for sexual desire, this correlation is reasonable.

Parental Behaviors and Relationships

A number of characteristics of the relationships that adolescents have with their parents influence adolescents' sexual behaviors. (See Miller, Benson, & Galbraith, 2001, for a review.) Parents who have warm, close relationships with their adolescent children have offspring who remain abstinent, delay intercourse, and have fewer sex partners. This is partially a direct effect—the teen's attitude matches that of his or her parents—and partially an indirect effect in that the teen has better overall impulse control, doesn't associate with deviant peers, avoids drug use, and is involved in prosocial activities, all of which help reduce teenage sexual activity rates. Similarly, parents who regulate and monitor their children's behavior, such as by setting rules and enforcing curfews, are less likely to have sexually active teens. (Parents who are perceived as being *excessively* strict have children who are *more* sexually active, though.) Also, contrary to some folk wisdom, talking to adolescents about sex does not implicitly give them permission to be sexually active (a point to which we will return later): parents who

CROSS-CULTURAL CONCERNS   ADOLESCENT SEXUAL BEHAVIOR IN PREINDUSTRIAL SOCIETIES

American adolescents are about as sexually active as those in most Westernized, industrial countries, but how does their behavior compare to that of adolescents in preindustrial, nontechnological societies? Although there are profound differences in the values among these various societies, it is fair to conclude that American adults are *less* tolerant of adolescent sexual behavior than adults in the majority of nontechnological cultures.

When Schlegel and Barry (1991) reviewed accounts of 186 diverse, non-Western societies, they found that 60 to 65 percent of preliterate societies tolerated heterosexual intercourse for both male and female adolescents, at least with a limited number of other adolescents. Eventual spouses were usually included among individuals' early sex partners. Allowance of complete promiscuity was rare. Some groups, such as the Kikuyu of East Africa, allowed mutual masturbation and petting but forbade intercourse.

Schlegel and Barry also found that cultures that were tolerant of adolescent heterosexual activity were characterized as being the least technologically advanced, as having egalitarian relationships between the sexes, as being matrilineal, as being places where women contributed significantly to the family's wealth, and as allowing individuals to choose their own spouses. Restrictive societies, in contrast, had the opposite traits as well as the custom of exchanging wealth at the time of marriage.

In a minority of the cultures, homosexual behaviors were either tolerated or encouraged. The Kimam of Melanesia, for instance, believe that young boys need semen to mature into mature men; boys in this and other similar societies fellate older males in order to ingest their semen.

In sum, the cultures studied exhibited wide variation in tolerance of adolescent sexual activity. Some were completely restrictive and disallowed any contact between adolescent boys and girls. The most common pattern, however, was to view adolescent sexual behavior as merely another aspect of teenage life. Amusement was a more common reaction than anger.

clearly speak to their children about their sexual values have children who delay intercourse and have fewer sexual partners (e.g., Sneed, 2008).

In addition, family constellation can have an effect on adolescent sexual activity. Girls who grow up in a father-absent home are more likely to seek sexual relationships as a means of finding affection and social approval than are girls in father-present homes (Miller, Norton, Curtis, et al., 1997). Also, adolescents from reconstituted families report more sexual experience than those from intact families (Upchurch, Aneshensel, Sucoff, et al., 1999).

Peer Standards

Adolescent peers certainly speak to one another about sex, and, in general, provide more positive, affirming messages about sexual activity than parents (Epstein & Ward, 2008). They often discuss their own sexual exploits or the exploits of friends. (Not all of the tales are true, of course.) These discussions increase the likelihood that a listener will become sexually active (Martens, Page, Mowry, et al., 2006), because the stories foster an erroneous view that

Many variables correlate with adolescent premarital sexual behavior. Being able to discuss sexual matters with one's parents has the highest influence in early adolescence, whereas the influence of friends has a greater effect in later adolescence.

sexual activity is more common than it is and that "everyone is doing it."

Siblings

Many studies have verified a link between an older sibling's sexual behavior and a younger's (see East, 2009). This is more true the closer their relationship, the more friends they have in common, and if the older sibling exerts pressure on the younger. For example, younger sisters of a teenage mother are five times more likely to become pregnant themselves than girls from similar backgrounds who do not have an older sister who is a mother (East, Reyes, & Horn, 2007).

Gender

Adolescent girls are more likely to link sex and romance or love than boys. (Occassionally stereotypes *are* accurate.) They are more willing to become sexually involved in order to express love, intimacy, and commitment (Patrick, Maggs, & Abar, 2007). Gender differences in sexual motivations diminsh in late adolescence (Feldman, Turner, & Araujo, 1999).

Problem Behaviors

Problem behaviors—such as delinquency, drug use, and promiscuity—are typically clustered, so that a teenager who engages in one problem behavior is more likely to engage in others, as well. Given this pattern, it is not surprising that those youths who engage in early sexual activity are more likely to abuse drugs than are those who do not (Cornelius, Clark, Reynolds, et al., 2007). One of the strongest predictors of high-risk sexual activity is alcohol use (e.g., Santelli, Kaiser, Hirsch, et al., 2004).

Educational Expectations

The higher the adolescents' educational expectations, the less likely they are to have premarital sexual intercourse (Slicker, Patton, & Fuller, 2004). It is not surprising, then, that adolescents who spend a lot of time studying, especially girls, are less likely to be sexually active (Whitbeck, Yoder, Hoyt, et al., 1999) than those who do not. Adolescents who are out of school and employed have a higher frequency of premarital intercourse than do adolescent students (Huerta-Franco, deLeon, & Malacara, 1996). Similarly, the higher the parents' educational aspirations for their children, the less sexually active those children tend to be (Slicker, Patton, & Fuller, 2004).

Socioeconomic Status

There is a higher instance of early coital behavior among youths of low socioeconomic status who have less-educated parents (Sieving, McNeely, & Blum, 2000). These youths tend to have lower educational aspirations and are less likely to be in school, factors, as just noted, also associated with higher rates of sexual activity.

Other Mutual Sexual Behaviors

In many people's minds, the term *virgin* conjures up someone with little or no sexual experience. This is not and has not been the case with many virginal adolescents for some time, however. In one study of 2,000 high school students conducted in the 1990s, approximately 30 percent of the virgins reported that they had either masturbated a partner or been masturbated by a partner (Schuster, Bell, & Kanouse, 1996). More recently, a flurry of press reports have suggested that oral sex has become a much more common recreational activity for adolescents (see the Research Highlight box). Although neither of these behaviors carries much risk of pregnancy, many STDs can be transmitted without intercourse.

Masturbation

Masturbation refers to any type of self-stimulation that produces erotic arousal, regardless of whether that arousal proceeds to orgasm. It is commonly practiced by males and females, dating and unattached, married and unmarried. The reported incidences of masturbation vary somewhat among studies.

In a study of female and male college students, twice as many males as females said they had masturbated, and of the males who masturbated, they did so more frequently than the females (Leitenberg, Detzer, & Srebnik, 1993). This and other studies indicate that a greater percentage of males than females masturbate.

Among those who masturbate, males do so more often than females and more frequently fantasize erotic experiences (Smith, Rosenthal, & Reichler, 1996). It is difficult to get reliable numbers about the frequency and prevalence of masturbation because adolescents are embarrassed by their behavior and so may underreport it. In one study (Halpern Udry, Suchindram, et al., 2000), fewer than one-third of the 13-year-old boys surveyed reported masturbating; when questioned again as young adults, more than two-thirds stated that they had masturbated as 13-year-olds. Apparently the middle-schoolers who underreported their behavior believed that masturbating indicated that they were oversexed, out of control, or social losers.

To the contrary, practically all competent health, medical, and psychiatric authorities now say that masturbation is a normal part of growing up. It does not have any harmful physical and mental effects nor does it interfere with normal sexual adjustment. In fact, women who have never masturbated to orgasm before marriage have more difficulty reaching orgasm during coitus in the first year of marriage than do those who have masturbated to orgasm. Masturbation serves as a useful function in helping the individual learn about his or her body, learn how to respond sexually, develop sexual identity, and achieve sexual release. The only ill effect from masturbation comes not from the act itself but from guilt, fear, or anxiety when an adolescent believes the practice will do harm or create problems. These negative emotions can do a great deal of psychological

RESEARCH HIGHLIGHT   JUST HOW COMMON IS ORAL SEX?

During the past several years, a number of well-respected newspapers and magazines have reported that a large percentage of middle school students are engaging in oral sex (e.g., Jarrell, 2000; Stepp, 1999). Is this, in fact, true?

Unfortunately, there is little credible data about middle school oral sexual activity. However, several studies have examined high schoolers' participation in oral sex. The most recent large study (Lindberg, Jones, & Santelli, 2008) indicates that oral sex rates are significant: 54 percent of the females and 55 percent of the males reported having had oral sex, making oral sex a more common activity than vaginal intercourse. Virgins were significantly less likely to have engaged in oral sex than nonvirgins, and virgins were more likely to have engaged in oral sex with only one partner. White teens and teens from higher socioeconomic backgrounds were more likely to have engaged in oral sex than other teens, and girls were more likely than boys to have given oral sex.

There are also some data suggesting that, like President Bill Clinton, adolescents do not consider oral sex "sex." (If you recall, Clinton claimed that he had not had sex with Monica Lewinsky, even though they had engaged in oral sex.) A survey conducted by a popular teen magazine found that only 60 percent of male and female 15- to 19-year-olds considered oral sex to be "sex" (Remez, 2000). To the remaining 40 percent of sampled teens, *virginity* was equivalent to "never having had vaginal sexual intercourse."

Having oral sex does pose fewer risks than having intercourse; namely, pregnancy is unlikely and the chances of contracting some, but not all, STDs are reduced. However, because many teens erroneously believe that oral sex is risk free—which it is not—they may be putting themselves at risk for gonorrhea, chlamydia, genital herpes, and genital warts. Furthermore, because they do not perceive themselves as vulnerable, youths might be slow to seek treatment for these conditions.

damage. Youths who continue to believe that masturbation is unhealthy or harmful, yet continue to practice it, will inevitably feel anxiety.

Sex and Its Meaning

Since so many adolescents engage in sexual intercourse, the question arises regarding the meaning attached to this behavior. For years, research had shown that the preferred standard for youths is permissiveness with affection (Christopher & Cate, 1988). However, there are a significant number of adolescents today who engage in coitus without affection or commitment (Manning, Longmore, & Giordano, 2004).

What Are Adolescents Seeking?

When adolescents say they want sex, what are their primary motives? It is easy to say that they want a quick fix to relieve biological drives. But often, adolescent sexuality is driven by needs that have nothing to do with sex (Diamond & Savin-Williams, 2009). These emotional needs include curiosity, the desire to receive affection, loneliness, need to gain status, confirmation of masculinity or femininity, bolstering of self-esteem, or need to express anger or escape from boredom. Sex becomes a means of expressing and satisfying nonsexual emotional needs.

Sexual Pluralism

Americans live in a **pluralistic society:** different individuals accept not one but a number of standards of sexual behavior. Commonly held standards include abstinence until marriage; sex with affection, commitment, and responsibility; sex with affection and commitment but without responsibility; sex with affection but without commitment; or sex without affection.

The exact meaning of *abstinence* varies tremendously from individual to individual. Some adolescents allow kissing only with affection; others kiss without affection. Kissing can be perfunctory, whether light kissing, heavy kissing, or French kissing. Some adolescents feel that necking is allowed (all forms of kissing and embracing) but disallow petting (body caresses below the neck). Others allow caressing of the breasts but not

of the genitals. Others engage in genital stimulation, even mutual masturbation to orgasm, but stop short of actual coitus. Some adolescents are technical virgins—meaning they never allow the penis to enter the vagina but engage in oral-genital, interfemoral stimulation (penis between the thighs), or other activity except vaginal intercourse itself.

Some adolescents will engage in intercourse only with affection, commitment, and responsibility. They are in love; they are committed to each other and accept the responsibility and consequences of their actions. Responsibility in this case can include the use of dependable means of contraception to prevent unwanted pregnancies. In case of accidental pregnancy, they are willing to take responsibility for whatever course of action they decide to pursue. But what does *commitment* mean? Interpretations vary. Some adolescents will have intercourse only if engaged, others only if they have an understanding to marry, others only if they are living together, and others only if they are committed to exclusive dating.

Some adolescents want sex with affection and commitment but without responsibility. They are in love, have committed themselves to each other, usually on a temporary basis only, but assume no real responsibility for their actions. These adolescents are less likely to use birth control and to have thought through what they would do in the case of an unwanted pregnancy.

Sex with affection but without commitment has become the standard of many adolescents. They would not think of making love unless they really loved (or at least really liked) each other. They may or may not show responsibility in the practice of birth control but have made no promises or plans for the future. They are affectionate, are having intercourse, and that's it, at least for the time being. A recently coined term is *friends with benefits.* Friends with benefits are friends with whom one has sex (oral sex or intercourse); there is no implied commitment and no intent to move the relationship into a romantic partnering (Hughes, Morrison, & Asada, 2005). These relationships are quite common on college campuses: research puts the incidence at between 50 and 60 percent of undergraduates (Mongeau, Ramirez, & Vorrell, 2003, cited in Hughes, Morrison, & Asada, 2005).

Sex without affection characterizes people having sexual intercourse without emotional involvement, without the need for affection. They engage in sex for sex's sake because they enjoy it, and do so without any strings attached. Whereas some have sex purely for physical enjoyment, others have different

---

ANSWERS WOULDN'T YOU LIKE TO KNOW ...

What is the sexual ethic of most American teens?

Most American teens believe that "sex with affection" is permissible. Certainly, some teens engage in intercourse with individuals they do not care about, but this is not considered ideal.

---

pluralistic society   a society in which there are many different competing standards of behavior.

motivations. Some of these ulterior motivations may include

- *To punish:* "She made me mad, so just for spite, I did it." In this case, sex becomes an expression of hostility, anger, or revenge. Some adolescents have sex and strive for pregnancy to get even with parents or to punish a former lover.
- *To win or return favors:* "I spent fifteen dollars on you tonight; now what do I get?" "I can't thank you enough for the bracelet." This is really the prostitution of sex: giving sex as payment.
- *To control behavior:* "If I sleep with you, will you stay with me?" "Let's have a baby; then our parents will have to give us permission to marry."
- *To build up the ego:* "Wait until the others find out whom I slept with last night." "I bet you twenty dollars I can score." "I'll show you who's irresistible."

Gender Differences in Sexual Ethics

The *double standard* refers to having one standard of behavior for males, another for females. In 1999, Milhausen and Herold found that 93 percent of university

---

ANSWERS WOULDN'T YOU LIKE TO KNOW . . .

Do adolescent girls and boys have different attitudes about sex?

Most adolescent girls have a more conservative attitude about sexuality than adolescent boys. Girls are more likely to want to care deeply about a person with whom they are sexually involved. Girls are also more likely to be concerned about their reputation (and about getting a bad reputation) if they have multiple partners.

---

women agreed that women were judged more harshly than men if they were sexually active. In keeping with this, university students were more likely to remember positive messages about sexually active males but negative messages about sexually active females (Marks & Fraley, 2006).

Many adolescents continue to believe that sexual activity is more acceptable for males than for females (Crawford & Popp, 2003). Girls are more likely than boys to be concerned about their reputation if it becomes commonly known that they are sexually active (Hillier, Harrison, & Warr, 1997). Their fears are justified, since girls who have multiple sex partners are in fact belittled by their peers (Graber, Brooks-Gunn, & Galen, 1998). This double standard is by no means confined to the United States. Girls in other Western countries, such as Great Britain and Russia, report the same concern (Ivchenkova, Efimova, & Akkuzina, 2001; Jackson & Cram, 2003).

As previously noted, although gender differences in motivation for sexual behavior are diminishing, they are still present. Males generally accept sex without love more readily than females (Feldman, Turner, & Araujo, 1999). When discussing why they are sexually active, women are more likely than men to emphasize a desire for emotional closeness (Diamond & Savin-Williams, 2009). Exacerbating this situation is the fact that male adolescents are more likely than females to describe a relationship they are in as "casual"; what he terms "casual," she views as "steady" or "regular" (Rosenthal, Moore, & Brumer, 1990). Unfortunately, these differences create a formula for feelings of hurt and betrayal.

RESEARCH HIGHLIGHT   HOOKING UP ON COLLEGE CAMPUSES

Hooking up is a fact of life for many college students. Hooking up occurs when two people who either have just met or who are casual acquaintances meet at a bar or a party and leave to engage in some form of sexual behavior with no expectation of a prolonged, future relationship. Hookups usually occur when both parties have been drinking alcohol. Paul, McManus, and Hayes (2000) found that nearly 80 percent of the students on the college campus they studied had hooked up at least once, and that nearly half of the men and one-third of the women had engaged in sexual intercourse during a hookup. But are students really glad they are doing so?

The answer is likely "not as much as you'd think." Lambert, Kahn, and Apple (2003) conducted a study in which they asked college students how comfortable they were

with their college's norm of hooking up, and both women and men reported being uncomfortable with the commonness of the practice (although men were more comfortable than women). In other words, they believed that they were out of step with their peers, who they took to be more liberal than themselves in their attitudes toward hooking up. This discrepancy was greater for men than for women. In short, many students felt that they were engaging in hooking-up behavior primarily because of the need to conform. Furthermore, men were less comfortable with engaging in hooking-up behaviors than women believed them to be, and women were less comfortable with engaging in hooking-up behaviors than men believed them to be. This is troubling, because it means that much unwanted sexual activity is occurring.

Sexual Aggression

It is distressing to read the research about adolescents' experiences with sexual aggression because almost all studies indicate that it is quite common. According to the Centers for Disease Prevention and Control, about 9 percent of high school students reported having been hit or physically hurt by their boyfriend or girlfriend (dating violence) during the previous year. The rates were highest for Black and twelfth-grade students. Almost the same number—7.5 percent—said that they had been physically forced to have sexual intercourse in the same time period. Forcible rape was more commonly experienced by females than males (11 percent vs. 4 percent), more common for Blacks than Whites, and higher among the older students (CDC, 2006b). Rates are much higher when *coercive*, as well as forcible, rape is counted because in many cases physical violence is not used. Instead, for example, threats of violence or severe inebriation prevent a person from legally consenting to sexual activity. In one study, 30 percent of sexually active, female middle and high school students in New England reported having been either forced or coerced into engaging in sexual intercourse (Shrier, Pierce, Emans, et al., 1998).

Rates are much higher yet when *unwanted* sexual activity is considered. This occurs when a person consents to sex even though he or she would rather not. Sometimes the individual feels obligated to his or her partner or is afraid that partner might end the relationship. Sometimes teens are afraid of being labeled as "gay" if they don't take advantage of a heterosexual

opportunity (Rhynard, Krebs, & Glover, 1997). Sometimes they are disinhibited because of drugs or alcohol.

Females use a variety of rejection strategies to avoid unwanted sexual activity (Perper & Weis, 1987). These include avoiding enticing behavior, avoiding intimate situations, ignoring sexual signals the man gives, using diversion and distraction, making excuses ("I have a big exam tomorrow"), saying no, and physical rejection. Women also use delaying themes ("I'm not ready yet"; "I need an emotional relationship!") and threats ("I won't see you again if you don't stop"; "I'll leave!").

Some adolescents are able to say no to unwanted sex more easily than others. A study of almost 2,500 tenth-grade White, Hispanic, and African American adolescents

stranger rape   forced, unwanted sexual intercourse with someone the victim doesn't know.

acquaintance rape   forced, unwanted sexual intercourse with someone the victim knows.

date rape   forced, unwanted sexual intercourse with a date.

RESEARCH HIGHLIGHT   THE NATURE OF RAPE

There are three varieties of rape. **Stranger rape,** the kind of rape most often envisioned, occurs when a person is assaulted by someone he or she does not know. **Acquaintance rape** is rape perpetrated by a person the victim does know: perhaps a coworker, someone who lives in the same apartment building or on the same block, or a cashier at a frequented grocery store. **Date rape** is a form of sexual assault that occurs on a voluntary, prearranged date or after a woman meets a man on a social occasion and voluntarily goes somewhere with him. Date rape has become an increasing problem in high schools and on college campuses (Casey & Nurius, 2006) and is the most common form of rape (Basile, Chen, Lynberg, et al., 2007).

Victims are often blamed for their rape. Males are more likely to blame victims than females, and they are less likely to view the crime as serious (Newcombe, van den Eynde, Hafner, et al., 2008). Women who dress provocatively or who drink to the point of intoxication are

more likely to be blamed than other women (Maurer & Robinson, 2008). College men who belong to fraternities or sports teams are more likely to endorse rape myths and blame victims, and they are in fact somewhat more likely to engage in sexual aggression (Murnen & Kohlman, 2007).

Rape is a traumatic experience for the victims and for their families as well. A rape victim often becomes acutely disorganized and experiences much distress, which she shows through words and tears. As she tries to put her life back to normal, she may experience depression, fear, and anxiety for months or even years (Howard, Wang, & Yan, 2007). About one-fifth of rape victims have made a suicide attempt—a rate eight times higher than that of women who have not been raped. Unfortunately, fewer than 10 percent of adolescent sexual assault victims turn to parents or other adults for help (Black, Tolman, Callahan, et al., 2008), making it difficult for them to get the aid that they need.

found no racial or ethnic differences in the ability to say no. Females said they were more likely than males to believe they could say no to unwanted sex. Having a less permissive attitude toward sex; giving low importance ratings to peer influence; and, for females, having a generalized sense of self-efficacy are all predictors of the ability to say no (Zimmerman, Sprecher, Langer, et al., 1995).

Contraceptives and Sexually Transmitted Diseases

Given that the majority of American females have premarital coitus, the rate of use of contraceptives is extremely important. Estimates are that 90 percent of adolescent girls who are sexually active and who do not use contraception will become pregnant within one year (Guttmacher Institute, 1999). Countless more will develop STDs that might have been prevented.

Use of Contraceptives Among Adolescents

What percentage of sexually active young people are using some form of protection against pregnancy and sexually transmitted diseases? The good news is that more and more are doing so than in the past.

In 1988, the National Survey of Family Growth revealed that only 35 percent of 15- to 19-year-old females or their partners used any method of contraception (including withdrawal) at first intercourse (Forrest & Singh, 1990). In that same year, only 32 percent

of 15- to 19-year-old females or their partners reported currently using contraceptives (Mosher, 1990). More recent figures indicate that more than three-fourths of teenage couples used some form of birth control, mostly condoms, when they last had intercourse (Centers for Disease Prevention and Control, 2008) and that 96 percent of adolescent girls use contraception at least sporadically (Martinez, Mosher, & Dawson, 2004). Still, adolescent girls are significantly less likely to consistently use birth control than older women, and sporadically is not good enough. These figures indicate that a large number of youths are not protected against unwanted pregnancy and STDs.

The most common contraceptive method used by American adolescents is the condom (94 percent); next most common is the birth control pill (61 percent). Withdrawal, an unreliable method, is the next most popular method (55 percent). All other means—the rhythm method, injectables, IUDs, and the like—are used by only a small number of teens (Martinez, Mosher, & Dawson, 2004). (See Figure 11.2.) Many health officials believe that condoms should be the contraceptive of choice for adolescents because they not only greatly reduce the risk of pregnancy but also substantially decrease the probability of contracting an STD. In contrast, the pill and other hormonal methods do not reduce the chances of disease transmission. Condoms are being used increasingly by sexually active teenagers, probably because of the fear of contracting the human immunodeficiency virus (HIV), which causes acquired immune deficiency syndrome (AIDS). This use is sporadic, however: only about one-fourth of female teens use condoms each time they have sex.

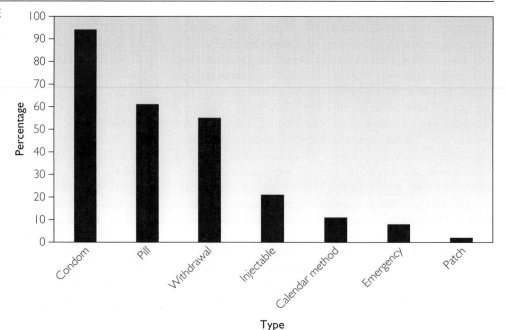

FIGURE 11.2 PERCENTAGE OF SEXUALLY ACTIVE HIGH SCHOOL STUDENTS WHO HAVE USED DIFFERENT TYPES OF BIRTH CONTROL

Source: Martinez, A. J. C., Mosher, W. D., & Dawson, B. S. (2004). Teenagers in the United States: Sexual activity, contraceptive use, and child bearing, 2002. National Center for Health Statistics. *Vital Health Statistic, 23.*

Several types of contraceptives, including condoms, are openly sold in drug and grocery stores. Despite their availability, many sexually active adolescents fail to use contraceptives, increasing the rates of both adolescent pregnancy and STDs.

An individual's use of birth control is a function of race/ethnicity, age, and sexual orientation. Black teens, for example, are relatively more likely to favor condoms than birth control pills; the reverse is true for White teens (Grunbaum, Kann, Kinchen, et al., 2002). Older teens are more likely than younger teens to use oral contraceptives (Santelli, Warren, Lowry, et al., 1997). Gay teens are less likely to use condoms than their heterosexual peers (Blake, Ledsky, Lehman, et al., 2001).

Why aren't condoms used more often? Reasons include negative experiences with them (breakage, decreased sensation, etc.) (Furby, Ochs, & Thomas, 1997), a generalized disregard for risk, a lack of self-efficacy and an unwillingness to take responsibility for oneself, and the perception that condoms are ineffective (Christ, Raszka, & Dillon, 1998). Condoms are used more frequently in casual sexual relationships than in long-term relationships (Landry & Camelo, 1994).

It is interesting that one study found that if an adolescent suggested using a condom during sex, the odds were better than 50:50 that his or her partner would assume that this meant the teen knew he or she had an STD. Moreover, about half of the teens said they would believe that their partner was specifically suspicious of them and about 20 percent said they would feel insulted if their partner suggested wanting to use a condom (Kaiser Family Foundation, 2000).

Why Contraceptives Are Not Used

Getting sexually active teenagers to consistently use effective contraceptives is a challenge. Even sexually active teenagers who say they do not want pregnancy to occur often do not use contraceptives consistently. Users have to be knowledgeable of the method and willing to admit that they are sexually active. They must be willing and able to obtain contraceptives as needed. Some students are misinformed about what are supposedly safe times to have sex and the likelihood of pregnancy (Ryan, Franzetta, & Manlove, 2007). Many do not believe pregnancy will happen to them. A small percentage of unmarried adolescents really want to get pregnant because they believe they are in love and that pregnancy will ensure long-term commitment from their partner. Some hesitate to obtain help for fear of parental disapproval (Zavodny, 2004).

ANSWERS WOULDN'T YOU LIKE TO KNOW ...

What types of birth control are most often used by American teens?

Condoms are the most widely used birth control method used by American teens; birth control pills run a close second. (For many years, the order was reversed.) Although long-lasting hormonal methods, such as patches and injections, are becoming more widely used, they are still much less likely to be used than condoms or the pill.

ANSWERS WOULDN'T YOU LIKE TO KNOW ...

When teens have ready access to contraceptives, are they more likely to have sex?

No! Access to contraception does *not* increase sexual activity rates among teens. It does, however, reduce pregnancy rates.

Should Adolescents Have Contraceptives?

On June 9, 1977, the U.S. Supreme Court affirmed that no state could legally restrict the distribution of contraceptives to minors, that nonprescription devices could be dispensed by those other than registered pharmacists, and that such devices could be openly displayed and advertised (Beiswinger, 1979). A lower court case also determined that clinics do not have to notify parents before prescribing contraceptives for adolescents, regardless of their age (*T.H. v. Jones*, 1975).

Whether adolescents should have access to contraceptives has been a controversial subject. Some adults are worried that the availability of contraceptives will increase teen promiscuity. Nevertheless, most adults agree that contraceptives should be made available to everyone, including teenagers (Princeton Survey Research Associates, 1997).

The availability of contraceptives, then, has almost no influence on whether youths have sex, but it may be a major determinant as to whether they are used and whether pregnancy results (Blake, Ledsky, Goodenow, et al., 2003). One of the major goals of sex education should be to provide information about contraception. Some who oppose sex education argue that they are afraid that if teenagers "know too much," they will use their knowledge to "get into trouble." Evidence indicates, however, that contraceptive knowledge has no influence on sexual behavior. What really influences behavior are the values and morals accepted by individuals and by the groups to which they belong. The fact remains that nonprescription contraceptives are readily available to teenagers, but youths all too frequently fail to use them.

Sexually Transmitted Diseases

People of any age may be exposed to sexually transmitted diseases through sexual contact, but STDs are very much an adolescent problem. Essentially, all sexually active teens are at risk of contracting a sexually transmitted disease because of biological vulnerability and a variety of risk-taking behaviors. Many STDs, such as genital warts and gonorrhea, are more widespread among adolescents than adults. A full 50 percent of the new cases of STDs contracted by persons in this country each year are contracted by individuals 15 to 24 years of age (Weinstock, Berman, & Cates, 2004).

There are more than 25 different infectious organisms that can be transmitted sexually. Chlamydia, gonorrhea, syphilis, and hepatitis B are all among the 10 most frequently reported infections in the United States (Donovan, 1997). Unfortunately, few adolescents are aware how very susceptible they are to STD infection.

As shown in Figure 11.3, HPV (human papillomavirus) is the most commonly contracted STD with more than 4.5 million new cases each year. Fortunately, most infections are asymptomatic, do not require treatment, and clear up on their own. Sometimes HPV causes

ANSWERS WOULDN'T YOU LIKE TO KNOW ...

How often do sexually active teens develop sexually transmitted diseases (STDs)?

Estimates are that as many as one in four sexually active teens will develop an STD *each year.*

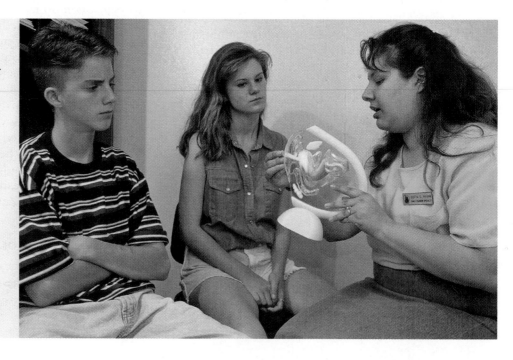

Family-planning clinics are a good source of information about contraceptives for adolescents engaging in sexual intercourse. However, adolescents often do not go to clinics until after they are sexually active or even pregnant.

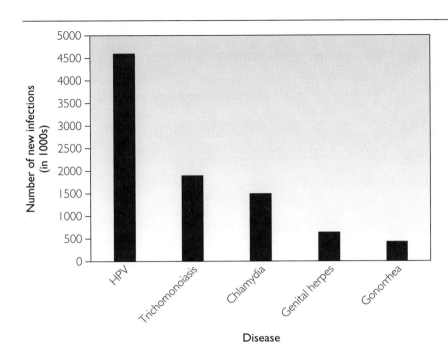

FIGURE 11.3   YEARLY INCIDENCE OF THE FIVE MOST COMMON STDS IN THE AMERICAN 15- TO 24-YEAR-OLD POPULATION

Source: Data from Weinstock, Berman, and Cates (2004).

genital warts, which are contagious and unsightly but painless. More seriously, HPV is associated with cervical cancer in women, and so for that if for no other reason it is best to minimize one's chance of infection. In 2006, the U.S. Food and Drug Administration approved the vaccine Gardasil for use among girls and women ages 9–26. The vaccine prevents infection with the types of HPV most likely to lead to cervical cancer. Use of the vaccine by young teens would virtually eliminate their risk of cervical cancer, but its use is controversial because some adults believe that it will encourage promiscuity.

The second most likely STD for an adolescent to contract is trichomoniasis, which is caused by a single-celled protozoan. The vagina is the most common site of infection in women, and the urethra (urine canal) is the most common site of infection in men. Most men with trichomoniasis do not have noticeable symptoms; women are likely to have a vaginal discharge with a strong odor.

Adolescent girls are more at risk for STDs than boys, since a boy is less likely to develop an STD after having sex with an infected girl than vice versa (Rosenthal, Biro, Succop, et al., 1997). In addition, females are more likely than males to develop serious complications from STDs, because females are more often asymptomatic and the symptoms they do have are often not obvious; hence, they are less likely to seek treatment until serious harm has been done to their bodies.

African American females are more likely to develop an STD than White females, and White females are at more risk than Latino females (CDC, 2004b). The two best predictors of STD risk are the number of sexual partners one has and regularity of condom use (Rosenthal, Biro, Succop, et al., 1997).

Many STDs do not always cause symptoms, which means individuals frequently have STDs but don't know it. These individuals may unwillingly infect others. Because of the rapid increase in and high fatality rate of AIDS, much of the public focus during the past twenty-five years has been on this disease. Other untreated STDs can also lead to infertility and death and should be taken seriously. Table 11.1 illustrates some of the main symptoms and outcomes of untreated STDs.

AIDS

AIDS is the sixth-leading cause of death of Americans 15 to 24 years old. Although the actual AIDS rate among adolescents is relatively low, most young adults who have AIDS most likely acquired the virus during their teenage years (MacKay, Fingerhut, & Duran, 2000). Also, the actual adolescent HIV infection rate is most likely significantly higher than can be inferred from the young adult AIDS prevalence, since many HIV-infected young adults will not have developed symptoms (National Institute of Allergy and Infectious Diseases, 2002). African American youths are more likely to become infected with HIV than either Caucasian or Latino youths.

Causation and Diagnosis of AIDS

AIDS is caused by the human immunodeficiency virus. When HIV gets into the bloodstream, it attacks particular white blood cells, called *T-lymphocytes*. T-lymphocytes stimulate the body's immune system and ability to fight disease. As HIV multiplies, more and more T-lymphocytes are destroyed. The immune system progressively weakens, leaving the body vulnerable to a variety of other so-called opportunistic

TABLE 11.1 FACTS ABOUT COMMON STDS

DISEASE	CAUSE	SYMPTOMS	TREATMENT	OUTCOMES
Chlamydia	Bacterium	Thin, clear discharge in males; females are generally asymptomatic	Antibiotics	Urethral damage in males; infertility and pelvic inflammatory disease in females if untreated
Gonorrhea	Bacterium	Thick, pus-like discharge in males; often asymptomatic in females	Antibiotics	Pelvic inflammatory disease and infertility in females
Syphilis	Bacterium	Chancre sore followed by a rash	Antibiotics	About half of untreated individuals die of heart disease
Genital warts	Papilloma-virus	Warts around and inside the genitals	Topical treatments, lasers	Linked to cervical cancer in women
Genital herpes	Herpes virus	Small, painful blisters on the genitals	No cure; acyclovir moderates symptoms	Narrowing of urethra; meningitis in rare cases; increases susceptibility to HIV virus

diseases. Not everyone who is exposed to the virus gets AIDS, however. About three months after exposure, the presence of HIV in the body can be detected by a blood test that determines whether HIV antibodies are present in one's blood (the ELISA or EIA test).

A person is considered to have AIDS when symptoms develop. The incubation period for AIDS may be from a few years to up to 10 years. The average latency time from viral infection to time of illness is about 5 to 7 years (Ahlstrom, Richmond, Townsend, et al., 1992). Adolescents can be exposed to the human immunodeficiency virus and carry it for years without knowing it. Even at this stage, however, they can spread the virus to others.

Treatment and Transmission of HIV/AIDS
To date, there is no cure for AIDS. However, increasingly better drug therapies are being developed that slow the onset of immunodeficiency and its related symptoms. The most successful treatment is called HAART, which stands for *highly active anti-retroviral therapy*. It is composed of a combination of antiviral drugs. These drugs greatly reduce the virus's ability to replicate itself. HAART is not a cure or an ideal solution; it is extremely costly and can cause major side effects (U.S. Department of Health & Human Services, 2008).

HIV may be found in the semen, blood, vaginal secretions, urine, saliva, tears, and breast milk of an infected individual. The disease may be transmitted from an infected mother to her unborn child, to her child at the time of birth, and after birth through breastfeeding. HIV can also be acquired by contact with infected blood or blood products, usually through needle sharing by intravenous (IV) drug users. Finally, the virus can be

ANSWERS WOULDN'T YOU LIKE TO KNOW ...
How likely is it that a sexually active teen will develop AIDS?

Adolescents rarely develop AIDS because the disease often takes many years to develop after someone has been infected with HIV. However, a large percentage of the people who develop AIDS while in their twenties (which is a large percentage of AIDS cases) became infected with HIV while in their teens.

passed between individuals engaging in either hetero- or homosexual activity in which body fluids are exchanged, especially blood and semen. The skin itself is a barrier against the virus. However, small, unseen tears in the lining of the vagina or rectum may occur during intercourse, thus providing an opening for the virus to enter directly into the bloodstream.

It is important to know that infected students can remain in school as long as they feel well enough to attend and are not infectious with other diseases such as chicken pox. If an open cut or sore on one child is exposed to the blood or body fluids of a child infected with AIDS, there is a possible occurrence of infection. People who have AIDS can remain in virtually any occupation without special restriction as long as they do not have associated symptoms such as open sores. They can share telephones, computers, office equipment, desks, tools, papers, vehicles, toilets, showers, uniforms, eating facilities, coffee pots, and water fountains. Remember: AIDS cannot be contracted by casual contact.

Other than total abstinence, condoms have been widely promoted as the best method of preventing the spread of AIDS. Only latex condoms, not natural skin condoms, provide protection against HIV. Before use, a condom should be inspected for holes and imperfections; if any irregularities are detected, the condom should not be used. In addition, care must be taken when putting on a condom to be sure that it is not snagged on a fingernail or torn. The user should also hold on to the top of the condom when withdrawing the penis from the vagina or anus to prevent leakage and slippage. When correctly used, condoms greatly reduce the chance of spreading HIV and other STDs. However, they do not reduce this risk to zero.

Unwed Pregnancy and Abortion

A high rate of premarital sexual intercourse accompanied by a lack of consistent use of contraceptives results in a large number of out-of-wedlock pregnancies.

Incidence of Teen Pregnancy

With the exception of the Russian Federation, the United States has the highest rate of teen pregnancy among industrialized societies (Singh & Darrock, 2000), and more than 80 percent of pregnancies among American teens are unplanned (Finer & Henshaw, 2006). Adolescent pregnancy is widely recognized in U.S. society as one of the most complex and serious public health problems.

The good news is that the teenage pregnancy rate fell throughout the 1990s and early 2000s, although there was a small upturn in 2006 and 2007. Teenage pregnancy rates dropped an enormous 38 percent from 1990 to 2004; in 2004, the rate was lower than it had been at any time since records were first collected in 1976 (see Figure 11.4). Declines were steeper for 15- to 17-year-olds than for 18- to 19-year-olds. Throughout the 1970s and 1980s, more than 1 million American teenagers became pregnant each year; in 2004, only about 750,000 did (Guttmacher Institute, 2006). Of this total, 14 percent resulted in miscarriages or stillbirths, 29 percent ended in induced abortions, and the remaining 57 percent resulted in live births (see Figure 11.5). The decline in adolescent pregnancies that occurred in the past two decades differed among girls by race/ethnicity. Pregnancy rates declined most markedly for African American teenagers (40 percent). Still, African American girls are about three times as likely to get pregnant as Caucasian girls.

Causation Theories

Why are American adolescents so much more likely to get pregnant than their counterparts in other Western countries? Darroch and her colleagues (2001) compared

The United States has the second highest rate of teen pregnancy in the industrialized world. Most girls decide to keep their children and either drop out of school or juggle motherhood and school responsibilities.

the situation in the United States with those in four other developed nations and drew the following conclusions:

1. American teens are no more likely to be sexually active than European teens. Thus, differences in pregnancy rates are *not* due to higher rates of intercourse.

2. American adolescents are less likely to use contraceptives than adolescents in other countries. And when they do use contraceptives, they are less likely to rely on the methods that most reliably prevent pregnancy: the birth control pill and long-lasting hormonal methods (injectables and implants). European teens are more likely to "double up" and use both condoms and hormonal methods simultaneously, thus minimizing their risks of both pregnancy and STDs.

3. The poverty rate is higher in the United States than in many developed countries. This is significant

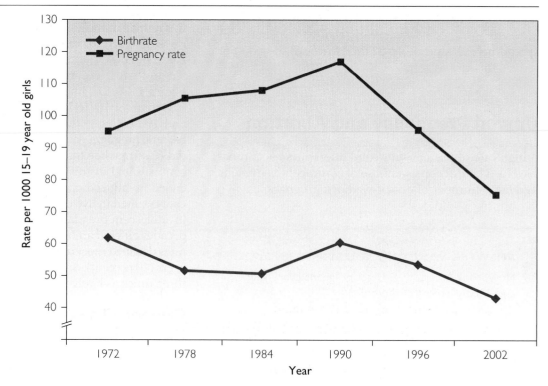

FIGURE 11.4 NUMBER OF PREGNANCIES AMONG AMERICAN TEENAGERS: 1974 TO 1999

Source: Data from Henshaw (2003).

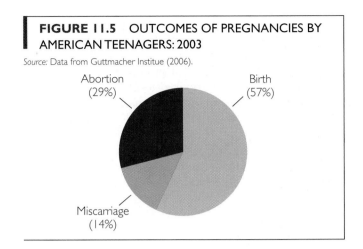

FIGURE 11.5 OUTCOMES OF PREGNANCIES BY AMERICAN TEENAGERS: 2003

Source: Data from Guttmacher Institue (2006).

because in all of the studied nations, poverty was associated with a higher pregnancy rate.

4. The U.S. government provides fewer health care services to middle-class citizens than do other Western countries. Thus, because American teens do not uniformly have access to free or low-cost prescription contraceptives, they are less likely to use them and more likely to become pregnant.

5. Primary-care physicians in the United States are less likely to concern themselves with birth control than primary-care physicians in other nations. American adolescent girls must often go to a gynecologist or separate clinic to receive prescription birth control.

6. Youths in other countries are more likely to receive assistance from outside sources as they make the transition from adolescence to adulthood. For example, they are more likely to receive vocational training and get help finding jobs. Such assistance

reduces the rate of poverty, which in turn reduces the rate of teenage pregnancy.

7. Parental leave policies in the other nations provide incentives to postpone childbearing. In particular, the wages one receives while on leave are proportional to one's regular salary. Since it is much easier to subsist on 60 percent of a higher salary than on a lower one, many couples decide to put off having children. There is therefore a real economic incentive to delay childbearing.

8. Attitudes toward adolescent sexual behavior are more accepting in many European nations. Because there is less shame associated with being sexually active, adolescents feel freer to admit to themselves that they intend to have sex and hence to prepare for it by obtaining birth control.

9. American society is more tolerant of adolescent childbearing than other nations.

10. In contrast to the abstinence-only approach to sex education adopted by many American school districts, comprehensive sex education is favored in other nations. (Sex education is discussed in more detail later in this chapter.)

It is clear from this review that many things could be done to reduce the rate of teenage pregnancy in the United States.

Pregnancy Outcomes

As Figure 11.6 illustrates, the U.S. adolescent birthrate is much higher than that in *all* other Western, industrialized nations. A decline in the teenage birthrate has resulted from a reduction in second births to teenage mothers to 20 percent (Black, Bentley, Papas, et al.,

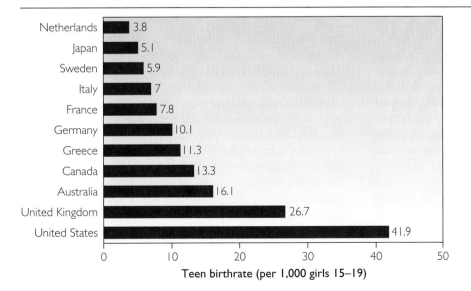

FIGURE 11.6 BIRTHRATES AMONG ADOLESCENTS IN SELECTED COUNTRIES

Source: Data from United Nations (2006).

2006). Birthrates are higher for Latinas and Black teens than for Caucasian teens (131, 134, and 48 births/ 1000, respectively) (Guttmacher Institute, 2006).

There are four possible outcomes to an adolescent pregnancy: (1) The adolescent can choose to have and keep her baby, (2) the adolescent can elect to have an abortion, (3) the adolescent might miscarry, and (4) the adolescent can have the baby and then give it up for adoption. These options are arranged in order from most to least common.

Motherhood

About 97 percent of adolescent mothers decide to keep their babies (Namerow, Kalmuss, & Cushman, 1993). Teenage mothers are more likely than other adolescents to be poor, to have had poor relationships with their parents, to have experienced child abuse, to have parents who are substance abusers, and to have parents who fail to monitor their behavior. These young women tend to be followers with poor social skills. They falsely believe that having a baby will improve their relationship with their baby's father. In addition, they desire the love that a baby will give them (Garrett & Tidwell, 1999). Regardless, the reality of motherhood is rarely what these young women expect: babies are demanding, not giving, and adolescent co-parents rarely live happily every after.

Most Americans consider young teenage motherhood a tragedy (Zachry, 2005). The single mother who decides to keep her baby may become entrapped in a downward spiral. If she marries, the chances of her remaining married are only about one in five (Hanson, 1992). And although most adolescent mothers now complete high school, they are unlikely to go on to college (Hofferth, Reid, & Mott, 2001). Finally, teen mothers are unlikely to get good jobs to support themselves and their families and are likely to require public assistance (Ahn, 1994).

The costs of adolescent childbearing are enormous, and members of three generations generally share in these costs. First, there are direct costs to the young mother in terms of loss or delayed education, abrupt changes in her developmental trajectory, and lost economic opportunities. Many young fathers are also negatively affected by early pregnancies. Second, the parents of these young mothers are also affected: they usually feel immediate disappointment and shock, face disruption of their own life plans, often share a large portion of the child care responsibilities for a child not their own, and have the burden of additional costs (Cross & Aday, 2006). Third, for the children born to adolescent mothers, the cost often includes increased likelihood of life in poverty in a single-parent family, a poor educational prognosis, poor developmental prognosis, and increased probability of becoming adolescent parents themselves (Pogarsky, Thornberry, & Lizotte, 2006). Most

adolescents simply do not know how to be good parents, which harms their children's development.

More recently, a new perspective has been gaining ground: that although it is indisputably true that teenage mothers fare poorly compared to other teenage girls, motherhood is not the *reason* for their poor outcomes. Instead, the theory is that these girls were more distressed than average to begin with—that motherhood is a symptom of their distress, rather than a cause of their problems (e.g., Oxford, Gilchrist, Gillmore, et al., 2006). They are more likely to have used drugs, been abused, been delinquent, and so on. The theory is that these young women would have problems whether or not they were trying to raise children. As an example, one author recently argued that the unwed teenage mothers she studied became more interested, not less interested, in their education after they had children to care for (Zachry, 2005). Still, even given that these adolescents are largely coping with numerous problems before they become mothers, motherhood is for most an additional stress.

Fatherhood

Since most adolescent mothers became pregnant by having sexual intercourse with male teenagers only two to three years older than themselves (Coley & Chase-Lansdale, 1998), there are a substantial number of teenage fathers as well as teenage mothers. Who are these adolescents? What kind of relationships do they have with their children and the mothers of their children?

In many ways, adolescent boys who become fathers are demographically similar to adolescent girls who become mothers. They are more often poor, live in low-income neighborhoods, and have done poorly in school. They are often dropouts and have engaged in delinquent behavior (Fagot, Pears, Capaldi, et al., 1998).

Many teenage fathers say they want to maintain contact with and support their children and the mothers of their children (Glikman, 2004). In reality, though, contact usually steadily decreases after the child's birth. For example, researchers conducting one study (Larson, Hussey, Gilmore, et al., 1996) found that fewer than 40 percent of teenage fathers were living with their child and the child's mother when that child was one year of age; only about one-fourth had been living constantly together as a family unit since the child was born.

Why such low levels of involvement? Teenage mothers and fathers have somewhat different views on this issue. Adolescent fathers cite maternal resistance as the major barrier to their participation; adolescent mothers, on the other hand, are more likely to cite paternal disinterest. It is possible that *both* viewpoints are correct: the fathers may perceive the mothers' frustration and anger at lack of financial support as a more generalized lack of desire for their presence, and the mothers may interpret

Adolescent boys who father children find their lives profoundly changed. Some help the mothers with child care responsibilities, and others drop out of school to help support their children.

the fathers' embarrassment at being unable to contribute more money and their discomfort at handling children as an unwillingness to be involved (Rhein, Ginsburg, Schwartz, et al., 1997). Both parents also frequently give the father's involvement with drugs as a reason for his lack of involvement.

Teenage fathers are usually poor, which makes it impossible for many of them to contribute substantial amounts of money to their children. Typically, teenage fathers leave school earlier, have lower earnings, and work fewer weeks per year than other teenage males in their neighborhoods (Nock, 1998). Also, the adolescents who father children frequently have problems that began before the pregnancy. Compared with non-fathers, teenage fathers are twice as likely to be delinquents (Stouthamer-Loeber & Wei, 1998) and more than three times as likely to be drug users (Guagliardo, Huang, & D'Angelo, 1999). Unfortunately, antisocial behavior prior to fatherhood is a strong predictor of poor parenting (Florsheim, Moore, Zollinger, et al., 1999). Teenage fathers are often the sons of absent fathers themselves; they may or may not have a male parental model and, in fact, may have numerous models of pregnancy outside of marriage (Leadbetter, Way, & Raben, 1994).

In light of these considerations, society needs to increase its attempt to assist teenage fathers. It is fruitless to demand that teenage fathers become responsible parents without providing them with the guidance and resources needed to successfully managing premature parenthood. There is documented evidence that teenage fathers respond favorably to appropriate outreach initiatives, and that such efforts enable teenage fathers to enhance their own lives and to contribute positively to society and to the well-being of their children (e.g., Philliber, Brooks, Lehrer, et al., 2003).

Abortion

Teenagers obtain approximately 20 percent of the abortions performed in the United States (Jones, Darroch, & Henshaw, 2002). As would be expected, the adolescent abortion rate dropped during the 1990s and early 2000s as the adolescent pregnancy rate fell. The abortion rate, however, fell more sharply than the pregnancy rate. Some of this drop occurred because fewer pregnant adolescents opted to abort their fetuses, but a much greater contributor to the decline was the greater availability of emergency contraception—the so-called morning-after pill.

Which teens choose abortion? The strongest correlate of abortion is income level; namely, the higher the adolescent's socioeconomic status, the more likely it is that she will choose abortion over childbirth. Most minors who have an abortion do so with at least one parent's knowledge, and a large majority of parents support their daughter's abortion decision (Henshaw & Kost, 1992). In fact, most states have passed laws requiring parental involvement in a minor's abortion decision. Table 11.2 details these different restrictions. Differing state parental notification or consent requirements have not systematically affected adolescent abortion rates (Gius, 2007).

Adoption

The small number of teens who place infants for adoption limits the information on these adolescents. It does appear, though, that those who decide to place their babies for adoption generally feel quite comfortable with this decision. Certainly, they fare somewhat better than adolescent girls who keep their babies. For example, one study compared the coping responses and psychosocial adjustments of pregnant adolescents

TABLE 11.2   STATE LAWS REGULATING PARENTAL INVOLVEMENT IN MINORS' ABORTIONS

CONSENT REQUIREMENTS	NOTIFICATION REQUIREMENTS
States That Require Consent of Both Parents	**States That Require Notification of Both Parents**
Mississippi, North Dakota	Minnesota
States That Require Consent of One Parent	**States That Require Notification of One Parent**
Alabama, Arizona, Arkansas, Idaho, Indiana, Kentucky, Louisiana, Massachusetts, Michigan, Missouri, North Carolina, Ohio, Oklahoma, Pennsylvania, Rhode Island, South Carolina, Tennessee, Texas, Utah, Virginia, Wisconsin, Wyoming (Laws in Alaska, California, and New Mexico are currently enjoined.*)	Colorado, Delaware, Florida, Georgia, Iowa, Kansas, Maryland, Nebraska, Ohio, Oklahoma, South Dakota, West Virginia (Laws in Illinois, Montana, Nevada, and New Jersey are currently enjoined.*)
States That Allow Relatives Other Than Parents to Give Consent	**States That Allow Notification of Relatives Other Than Parents**
North Carolina, South Carolina, Virginia, Wisconsin	Delaware, Iowa
States That Do Not Require Parental Consent or Notification	
Connecticut, District of Columbia, Hawaii, Maine, New Hampshire, New York, Oregon, Vermont, Washington	

*If a state's laws are currently enjoined, the state legislature passed a law requiring parental consent or notification, but the law has been rejected by the state's court system and is not in effect.

Source: Data from the Alan Guttmacher Institute (2009).

who intended to relinquish their infants with parenting adolescents who wanted to keep their infants (Stern & Alvarez, 1992). Pregnant adolescents who intended to relinquish their infants showed better overall levels of self-image than pregnant adolescents intending to parent. Other research has found that adolescents who choose to raise their babies are more likely to be clinically depressed prior to their pregnancy than those who give their babies up for adoption or have an abortion (Miller-Johnson, Winn, Coie, et al., 1999) and are more likely to have low self-esteem (Plotnick & Butler, 1991).

Gay and Lesbian Youth

Homosexuality refers to a sexual orientation in which one has a sexual interest in those of the same biological sex. Alfred Kinsey was one of the first social scientists to emphasize that there are degrees of **heterosexuality** (sexual orientation to those of the opposite sex) and homosexuality. Figure 11.7 shows Kinsey's seven-level continuum of sexual behavior. Kinsey found that many persons have a mixture of homosexuality and heterosexuality and so are to some degree *bisexual.* Some of these persons, for example, live a typical heterosexual life with a spouse and children and yet enjoy homosexual sex as well.

Homosexuality does not describe physical appearance, sex roles, or personality any more than does heterosexuality. Many homosexual men are stereotypically masculine in appearance and actions; some are outstanding athletes. Many lesbians are stereotypically feminine in appearance and behavior. A person cannot tell by physical or behavioral characteristics if someone is homosexual. Some may display stereotyped heterosexual sex roles in society and in their family life; others may exhibit some of the physical and personality characteristics of the opposite sex and assume opposite-sex roles.

How many individuals are *exclusively* homosexual? Different researchers give somewhat different figures (in part, because they use different definitions of homosexuality), but most estimates fall into the range of 2 to 5 percent of adult males and 1 to 2 percent of adult females (e.g., Laumann, Gagnon, Michael, et al., 1994). However, three times as many individuals report having had at least one homosexual encounter in their lives. How many adolescents are homosexual? About the same percentage of adolescent and adult males are gay, as the majority of gay men recognized their homosexual orientation early in life (Bailey & Zucker, 1995). It is less typical for lesbians to be aware of their homosexuality during adolescence, and so fewer adolescent females know that they are, or label themselves as, lesbians (Diamond & Savin-Williams, 2000). A larger number of adolescents—13 percent of girls and 6 percent of boys—report some degree of homosexual attraction or activity (Savin-Williams, 2005).

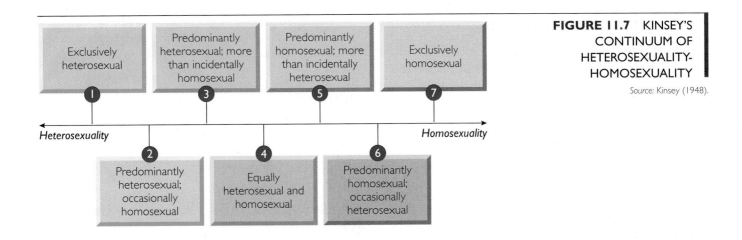

FIGURE 11.7 KINSEY'S CONTINUUM OF HETEROSEXUALITY-HOMOSEXUALITY

Source: Kinsey (1948).

Determinants of Sexual Orientation

Although the question of causation is usually posed as "What causes homosexuality?" it could just as well be asked, "What causes heterosexuality?" The answer is an interplay of biological, personal, and social factors. There is no single determinant of sexual orientation. Also, sexual orientation in females is likely determined by a different constellation of causes than sexual orientation in males (Baumeister, 2000).

Biological Theories

One's biology can influence one's sexual orientation in any of three ways: (1) genetic differences, (2) exposure to atypical concentrations of prenatal sex hormones, and (3) differences in brain structure. These three avenues are not unrelated or mutually exclusive. The presence of a certain pattern of genes, for instance, could influence brain growth or response to prenatal hormonal levels; similarly, prenatal hormones could affect brain development. What do the data suggest?

Most researchers agree that sexual orientation is, in part, a genetic phenomenon, at least in some individuals. (For a review, see Rahman, Glenn, & Wilson, 2003.) For example, in one study, the sexual orientation of individuals whose twin was homosexual was examined. The researchers found that if an individual had an identical twin who was gay, there was approximately a two-thirds probability that the individual was also gay. However, if an individual had a fraternal twin who was gay, the likelihood of his or her also being gay was less than one-third. Identical twins, who developed from the same egg, are genetically more similar than fraternal twins, who are no more closely related than different-aged siblings. The fact that identical twin pairs are more likely than fraternal twin pairs to share the same sexual orientation suggests a genetic component to this phenomenon. However, since not all of the identical twins in the research who had a homosexual twin themselves had a homosexual orientation, environmental factors must be partially involved as well.

Another possibility is that prenatal hormone levels affect sexual orientation. Research has demonstrated that elevated and lowered testosterone levels can affect brain development in human fetuses (e.g., Reiner, 1997). In particular, an elevated prenatal testosterone level causes the developing hypothalamus (the part of the brain most involved with sex drive) to develop specialized receptor cells that are sensitive to androgens, the class of hormones most associated with sex drive (Fernandez-Guasti, Kruijver, Fodor, et al., 2000).

This leads to a discussion of whether differences in brain anatomy can lead to differences in sexual orientation. The most well-known research in this area was conducted by Simon LeVay (1991), who found a bundle of nerve fibers in the hypothalamus that were three times as large in heterosexual males as in homosexual males and females. His research was imperfect, however; he had only a small sample of hypothalamuses to study and many of them had been collected from the brains of individuals who had died of AIDS. LeVay's findings, therefore, are not considered conclusive. Other researchers have continued to pursue similar lines of investigation. For example, studies have shown that several parts of the hypothalamus are indeed larger in homosexual than in heterosexual men. Swaab and Hofman (1995) found that the suprachiasmic nucleus, a region involved in sexual behavior, is larger and more elongated in homosexual men; this shape is more characteristic of women. Allen and Goski (1992) found that a portion of the anterior commisure that is larger in women than in men is also larger in gay men than in straight men. Finally, Scamvougeas, Witelson, Branskill, et al. (1994) found that a part of the corpus callosum, the band of nerve fibers that connects the left and right hemispheres of the cerebrum, is larger in homosexual men than in

homosexuality sexual orientation to those of the same sex.

heterosexuality sexual orientation to those of the opposite sex.

heterosexual men; it is also larger in women than in men. To date, these studies are correlational only and do not prove that neuroanatomical differences cause differences in sexual orientation; they are, however, intriguing and suggestive.

Psychoanalytic Theories/Parenting Theories

Traditionally, homosexuality was thought to be caused by problems in parent-child relationships within the family. The troubled relationships were thought to cause problems in identifying with the parent of the same sex. However, a study of 322 gay men and women from different sections of the country revealed that two-thirds perceived their relationships with their fathers as extremely satisfactory or satisfactory; three-fourths perceived their relationships with their mothers as extremely satisfactory or satisfactory (Robinson, Skeen, Flake-Hobson, et al., 1982). Only 4 percent never or hardly ever felt loved by their mothers, and 11 percent did not feel loved by their fathers.

In fact, there is little evidence that parents have much effect upon their children's sexual orientation.

More than 90 percent of the sons of gay fathers are heterosexual, as are more than 90 percent of women raised by lesbians (Golombok and Tasker, 1996).

Social Learning Theories

Behaviorists would emphasize that homosexuality is simply the result of learning. According to behavioral theories, psychological conditioning through reinforcement or punishment of early sexual thoughts, feelings, and behavior is what influences sexual preference.

ANSWERS WOULDN'T YOU LIKE TO KNOW . . .

What makes someone straight or gay?

Sexual orientation is a complex phenomenon, and many factors work together to determine whether someone is gay or straight. Moreover, the factor that seems to determine sexual orientation in one individual may not be important for another. Most experts agree that a combination of biology, personal experiences, and societal values contributes to the determination of sexual orientation.

CROSS-CULTURAL CONCERNS GAY ADOLESCENTS FROM RACIAL/ETHNIC MINORITY GROUPS

As difficult as it may be for gay Caucasian adolescents to find acceptance, it is often even more difficult for gay adolescents from racial/ethnic minority groups, whether they are African American, Hispanic American, or Asian American (Savin-Williams, 1996). The reasons for this additional difficulty vary by group.

The African American community is relatively negative toward homosexuality (e.g., Heath & Goggin, 2009), and this attitude is likely rooted in two sources: the strong influence of conservative Christian doctrine (Gallagher, 1997) and the reluctance to in any way reinforce the negative stereotype of Blacks being hypersexual. Given that many African Americans (like Americans from other culture groups) believe the stereotype that gays are promiscuous, they disparage homosexual behavior out of fear that it will encourage the perception of Blacks as sexually immoral (Collins, 1990).

Cultures that endorse strictly defined gender roles are also generally less tolerant of homosexual behavior because of the common misunderstanding that masculinity and femininity are closely tied to sexual orientation. Hispanic culture proscribes different gender roles for males and females (*machismo* versus *etiqueta*) and so is relatively intolerant of homosexuality (e.g., Long & Millsap, 2008). For example, it is considered shameful for a man to assume

the "receptive" role in a homosexual encounter, although it is more permissible for a man to assume the "inserter" role (Carrier, 1995).

Within the Asian American community, there is the commonly held belief that individuals should subsume their desires to the well-being of their families. Homosexuality is seen as a violation of that tradition, since exclusive homosexuality precludes marriage. Refusing to marry has implications for the family as a whole, since it prevents the conception of heirs and negates the possibility of solidifying families' ties within the community (Chan, 1992). It is not surprising, therefore, to find relatively high levels of homophobia among Asian Americans (e.g., Span & Vidal, 2003).

In contrast, many Native American tribes have traditionally accepted homosexual behavior. In fact, research going back to the 1960s found that more than 50 percent of all Native American tribes condoned male homosexuality and that more than 15 percent condoned lesbianism (Pomeroy, 1965). This level of acceptance was explained by the belief that each individual is considered to have been given a unique life quest by the gods; therefore, individual differences have generally been well tolerated. This acceptance has continued today, and Native American gay youths are less likely to experience family strain than youths from other ethnic/racial groups.

Thus, a person may lean toward homosexuality if he or she has unpleasant heterosexual experiences and rewarding same-sex experiences. According to this view, a girl who is raped or whose first attempts at heterosexual intercourse are quite painful might turn to homosexuality.

In one pioneering study, 686 homosexual men, 293 homosexual women, 337 heterosexual men, and 140 heterosexual women were interviewed intensively for three to five hours (Bell, Weinberg, & Hammersmith, 1981). The researchers tried to gain data that would uncover the causes of homosexuality. They then analyzed the data statistically using a technique called *path analysis* to establish cause and effect. They could not find any common threads running through the backgrounds of their homosexual participants. Some had negative heterosexual experiences; many had not. Some got along well with their parents; others did not. Some had a positive homosexual experience that triggered their recognition of their own homosexuality; others knew they were gay long before they had any same-sex contact. The lack of any consistent environmental factors led these researchers—and most researchers today—to conclude that homosexuality must have a biological basis.

The fact is that no one knows for certain the causes of homosexuality. There are a number of plausible causative factors, but no single factor emerges as a consistent reason. Perhaps one explanation may be that there are many different types of homosexuals. They are not a homogeneous group, so what contributes to one person's homosexuality may not contribute to another's (Diamond & Savin-Williams, 2003). The tendency in some people seems to be there from childhood. They recognize that they are gay by early adolescence. In most cases, the children of homosexuals do not grow up to be homosexuals, indicating that modeling and imitation alone cannot account for individuals becoming homosexuals or heterosexuals. Most homosexuals do not choose their sexual preference. In fact, many deny it and fight against it for years because they are afraid of public and personal recrimination. In all probability, there is no single cause of homosexuality.

Adjustment

Because homophobia is an unfortunate fact in American society, gay teens may find it more difficult than heterosexual youth to come to grips with their sexuality. Of course, many gay youths accept their orientation fairly readily. Others go through a period of denial after which they accept their preferences, establish intimate relationships with members of their own sex, and are much happier and psychologically better adjusted because of it. The unhappiest are those who are never able to accept their condition but lead separate, secretive lifestyles, seeking fleeting, anonymous sexual encounters. They are often isolated, lonely, unhappy people—terribly afraid of rejection—even by other homosexuals. There is no one consistent "coming out" process followed by gay youth (Rosario, Schrimshaw, & Hunter, 2008).

Unfortunately, many gay and lesbian adolescents find it extremely difficult to come out to their parents. They fear abandonment or even abuse (Cohen & Savin-Williams, 1996), especially from their fathers (Savin-Williams & Dubé, 1998). Regrettably, these fears do not appear to be unrealistic. Some 60 to 80 percent of gay and lesbian teens eventually disclose to their mothers but only 50 to 65 percent disclose to their fathers. Rarely, though, is a parent the first to be told; more commonly, a same-sex friend is selected (Savin-Williams, 1998).

Gay and lesbian adolescents experience additional stressors, as well. They are at heightened risk for harassment and victimization in school (Williams, Connolly, Peplar, et al., 2005). When these stressors are

IN THEIR OWN WORDS

"I realized that I was attracted to girls at quite a young age: in fact, I was 11. Now, this is not very typical for lesbians. What can I say: I always liked to do things differently. The bad thing is the shock I felt when I realized that not everyone saw homosexuality was normal; I was unprepared. I remember that kids used words like fag and dyke very loosely and they directed them toward feminine guys and masculine girls. It became clear that gays were considered abnormal and strange people. I was floored by this realization.

"Research says parents are usually the last people that gay teens come out to; I think they are right. I was feeling very isolated as is typical of many gay teens, and so I turned to the Internet. I found communities of gay teens who were just looking for someone to relate to. I saw a posting of a girl who was bisexual, so I e-mailed her. I was not aware at the time that my mother was reading my e-mails. She called me into her room and asked me to sit down and unfolded a piece of paper that happened to be the e-mail I sent to the girl. My mother went on to tell me that I was too young to make that decision, that I would never really be happy, and that my friends would probably not hang out with me. She suggested therapy.

"Unsurprisingly, I started high school deep in the closet. Then, when I was 16, my friends and I were just discussing life one night and I cautiously brought up my bisexuality. The conversation grew and by the end of it my friends were assuring me that they were my friends no matter what and that nothing would change that. That started a change in me. I stopped feeling so hopeless and lost. My friends enabled me to feel comfortable with who and what I am."

Some adolescent homosexuals readily accept their sexual orientation. Others do so after a period of denial. Still others are never able to accept their sexual preference. Becoming involved in the gay/lesbian community may help encourage these individuals in the expression of their identity.

coupled with rejection by family and friends and the pain of acknowledging an atypical identity, it is not surprising that homosexual teens are much more likely than straight teens to be depressed (Galliher, Rostosky, & Hughes, 2004), to attempt suicide (Morrison & L'Heureux, 2001), and to develop eating disorders (Austin, Ziyadch, Kahn, et al., 2004).

Sex Knowledge and Sex Education

With the large number of adolescent pregnancies and the increased incidence of HIV and other STDs, it has become even more important for adolescents to receive adequate sex education. From where do adolescents receive their information about sex?

Sources of Sex Information

Researchers surveyed 700 male and female respondents ranging in age from 9 to 73 to determine, among other things, the source of their sexuality information. About a fourth of the respondents said their primary source of information was a sibling, about 20 percent said a teacher; about 12 percent said their parents, about 5 percent said their relatives, and about a third of the respondents said they received their sexual information from other, miscellaneous sources (e.g., friends, mass media, literature) (Ansuini, Fiddler-Woite, & Woite, 1996). Similarly, another study, in which 13- to 15-year-olds were asked from whom they learned a lot about sex, found that the two most common responses were "media" such as television and

magazines (61 percent) and "friends" (60 percent). Teachers were more important sources than parents (45 percent vs. 40 percent, respectively). Religious institutions were of minor importance (13 percent) (Shibley-Hyde & DeLamater, 2000). Physicians were not mentioned by many adolescents as a source of information about sexuality.

The Role of Parents

Some people believe that the proper place for sex education is in the adolescent's own home. Unfortunately, as indicated earlier, many parents do not speak with their children about sexual matters (Raffaelli, Bogenschneider, & Flood, 1998). And when they do, the conversation is all too often limited to the physical changes associated with puberty, such as menstruation, and impersonal topics such as pregnancy and STDs (Baumeister, Flores, & Marin, 1995). The topics that most teenagers want to hear about—masturbation, nocturnal emission, how to use contraceptives, and orgasm—are rarely mentioned (Rosenthal & Feldman, 1999).

Mothers are much more likely than fathers to discuss sex with their children (DeIorio, Kelley, & Hockenberry-Eaton, 1999), and mothers spend more time talking with their daughters about sex than with their sons (Noller & Callin, 1990). Adolescents feel better about discussing sex with their mothers (Sneed, 2008), most likely because mothers are more open, they are more likely to try to make teens comfortable, they encourage questions, and they treat sexual matters as they would any other health issue (Feldman & Rosenthal, 2000). These are the characteristics common to all

PERSONAL ISSUES   ADOLESCENT SEXUAL FOLKLORE

Over the years, students in the Adolescent Psychology and Human Sexuality classes at Ohio Wesleyan University have been asked to relate the sexual myths that they had heard in the corridors of their middle and high schools. Here is a sampling of the misinformation shared among American youths:

1. You can't get a girl pregnant if you have sex standing up.
2. You can't get pregnant if you douche with cola after having sex.
3. Plastic food wrap makes a workable condom.
4. You can't get a girl pregnant if you have sex in a hot tub.
5. A girl can't get pregnant the first time she has intercourse.
6. A girl can't get pregnant if her period is irregular.
7. Wearing "tighty whities" can make a guy sterile.
8. If a male masturbates frequently, then he won't have enough sperm stored to cause a pregnancy.
9. The withdrawal method works.

Needless to say, even modern adolescents don't have all the facts they need about sex and reproduction. Sadly, erroneous beliefs such as these explain, in part, the high levels of adolescent pregnancies and STDs.

individuals who have meaningful conversations about sex with teens.

Most research reveals that parents are an important source of transmission of values and attitudes and do have an influence on adolescent attitudes and behavior, especially by way of example. As far as providing formal sex education is concerned, however, many parents are deficient, for a number of reasons:

1. *Some parents are too embarrassed to discuss the subject, or they deal with it in negative ways.* Many parents have been brought up to feel that sex is wrong and dirty, and they become intensely uncomfortable any time the subject is mentioned. (One of my students once told me: "You're right, Dr. D., parents really do get uncomfortable discussing sex with their children. My parents both teach sex ed in my local high school—and neither one of them ever sat me down and had the talk with me.") If parents do discuss sex, the messages they give their children are often negative ones. Some adolescents also feel embarrassed talking to their parents and do not discuss the subject with them.

2. *Some parents are uninformed and do not know how to explain sexuality to their children.* In one study, 90 adolescents and 73 mothers were asked to define in their own words seven terms related to sexual development: *ejaculation, hormones, menstruation, copulation, puberty, semen,* and *wet dreams.* Results suggested that the mothers were not able to adequately define the sexual development terms and thus were poorly prepared to teach their children about sex or to reinforce information the adolescents learned in school (Hockenberry-Eaton, Richman, Dilorio, et al., 1996). One mother remarked, "I don't understand menstruation myself, so how can I explain it to my daughter?"

3. *Some parents are afraid that knowledge will lead to sexual experimentation; they do not tell their children because they want to keep them innocent.* The old argument "Keep them ignorant and they won't get into trouble" couldn't be more wrong. Youths who are uninformed are more likely to get into trouble. There is no evidence to show that sexual knowledge per se leads to sexual experimentation. There is a lot of evidence, however, to show that ignorance leads to trouble.

4. *Some parents tell too little too late.* Most parents are shocked to learn that the time to explain the basic physical facts about reproduction is *before* puberty. Most children ought to know about fertilization and how it takes place in humans by ages 7 to 9. The parent who says "Wait until you are older" is running the risk of telling too little too late. The time to explain about menstruation is before the girl starts her menses, not after. As one boy said, "All the way through my childhood, whenever I asked questions about sex, my parents would say: 'Wait until you're older.' Now that I'm 18 and I ask them something, they remark, 'For Pete's sake, you're 18 years old, you ought to know that!'"

5. *Some parents set a negative example at home.* It is not just the words parents use that are important; it is also the lives they lead and the examples they set. One adolescent remarked, "My parents never came out and actually told me the facts of life. . . . But indirectly they told me plenty. They made me feel that sex was dirty and something to be ashamed of or embarrassed about."

Of course, some parents talk more to their teens about sex than others. Politically conservative, religious parents report more discussion with their teens about the negative consequences of sex than their liberal and nonreligious counterparts. In general, nonreligious parents report more discussion about where to obtain birth control than religious parents do. Parents who have daughters, older teens, and teens in romantic relationships are more likely to speak with their children about sex than those whose children are males, are younger teens, and are not in romantic relationships (Swain, Ackerman, & Ackerman, 2006).

Parents can do a better job by becoming more informed and more comfortable when talking about sexuality. Reading or attending classes in human sexuality can help parents tremendously. The schools can play an important role by teaching parents so they can do a better job instructing their children. Parents can also help support family life and sex education programs in the schools to supplement their own efforts.

The Role of Schools

Nationwide surveys have revealed that the vast majority of American adults (93 percent) favor teaching sex education in the schools (e.g., Kaiser Family Foundation, 2004). According to these respondents, sex education courses should contain information about puberty, abstinence, HIV and other STDs, relationships, contraception, sexual orientation, and abortion. The most controversial topics—oral sex and places to obtain prescription birth control without parental knowledge—were favored by more than 70 percent of the respondents. (See Figure 11.8.) Because so many parents do an inadequate job and adolescents need more reliable sources of information than their peers, the public schools have a responsibility, for several reasons:

1. *Family life and sex education are natural parts of numerous courses already offered to adolescents.* To fail to cover the reproductive system when human anatomy is taught in biology courses gives a negative message and is hypocritical. It is difficult to study social problems without including a study of the family as the basic social unit or to include issues such as illegitimacy, early marriage, or divorce. Discussions of sex or sexual behavior are hard to avoid in a course in the modern novel or in poetry. Thus, if existing courses are taught honestly, family life and sex education will have a place in many of them.

2. *Preparing youths for successful marriage and responsible parenthood is an important progressive educational goal.* It is certain that having a happy marriage and being a good parent are among the most important personal goals of the average person. If the school does not prepare youths for this goal, as well as for a vocation, is it preparing them for living as well as for making a living?

3. *The school is the only social institution that reaches all youths and therefore has a unique opportunity to reach youths who need family life and sex education the most.* Some parents do an excellent job, but the majority of parents do not. Are their children to be deprived of proper information, attitudes, examples, and guidance? One would hope not. Other community youth-service organizations, such as churches and scouts, have a responsibility also, for family life and sex education of youths are a community responsibility. None of these groups, however, reaches as many youths as schools.

FIGURE 11.8 PARENTS' PREFERENCES FOR TOPICS IN HIGH SCHOOL SEX EDUCATION

Source: Data from Kaiser Family Foundation (2004).

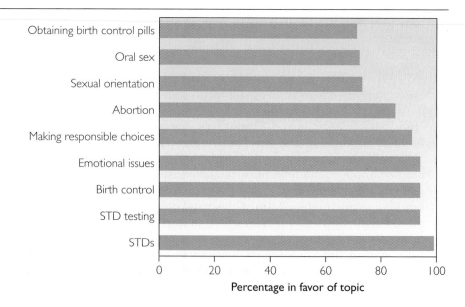

Percentage in favor of topic

4. *The school, as the professional educational institution, is or can be equipped to do a fine job.* This does not mean that all teachers are qualified to teach or that the individual school already has the expertise and resources to develop a program, but it does mean that the school is able to train teachers, develop curricula, and provide the necessary resources once priorities and needs are established.

Does Sex Education Encourage Promiscuity?

Some individuals are opposed to sex education in the schools because they believe that talking about sex tacitly gives adolescents permission to engage in sexual behaviors. Are they correct? The answer is a resounding no! In a review of 47 studies about the effects of teaching sex education, Grunseit and colleagues (Grunseit, Kippax, Aggleton, et al., 1997) found that only 3 reported an increase in student sexual activity after having taken such a course. Seventeen of the studies reported modest *decreases* in early intercourse, number of sex partners, and rates of pregnancy and STDs. Most of the courses seemed to have little effect on teenage sexual activity. More recent research has confirmed these findings: participation in sex education classes (of the right sort, see next section) delays onset of intercourse and increases use of birth control (e.g., Manlove, Ikramullah, & Terry-Humen, 2008; Mueller, 2008).

ANSWERS WOULDN'T YOU LIKE TO KNOW ...

How effective is abstinence-only sex education in reducing sexual behavior, unwanted pregnancies, and STDs?

Although abstinence-only sex education is becoming more and more common, it is *not* as effective as more comprehensive approaches at reducing sexual behavior, unwanted pregnancies, and STDs.

Approaches to Sex Education

To what extent are the schools providing sex education programs? The number of states that mandate sex education has increased in the past 20 years, largely because of concern over HIV/AIDS. There are, however, wide differences in how sex education is approached and what information is presented. For many years, a large majority of schools employed an *abstinence-preferred model* of sex education. These schools attempted to teach students that practicing celibacy during their teenage years is the most desirable behavior. They provided some information about STDs and birth control as well as the basic biology of reproduction. Increasingly common is the the *abstinence-only model,* in which teachers stress that all individuals should remain celibate until marriage. No information about birth control is provided (except perhaps to emphasize its unreliability) and discussions about sex focus on the harmful consequences that can result. A third model is *comprehensive* sex education, in which abstinence is presented as one option but other broader, more inclusive curricula are also typically included.

Currently, more than one-third of the school districts with sex education policies mandate abstinence-only programs, and this number is growing—even though this is not what parents or students want. The federal government alone earmarked $176 million in fiscal year 2006 to fund these programs (Guttmacher Institute, 2006). It is therefore legitimate to ask how successful this type of curriculum is compared to the other models. In actuality, essentially no research supports the abstinence-only approach. Virtually all studies show that it is less effective than abstinence-preferred or comprehensive sex education programs (e.g., Kohler, Manhart, & Lafferty, 2008; Trenholm, Devamy, Fortson, et al., 2008). Some of the research has even found that adolescents who completed abstinence-only sex education courses, because they were less likely to use birth control, were actually *more* likely to acquire an STD or be involved in an early pregnancy than those who did not.

SUMMARY

1. According to the best available data, about 30 percent of 15- to 17-year-olds have lost their virginity, whereas that is true of about 70 percent of 18- and 19-year-olds. Fewer teens are sexually active than in the 1990s.
2. When asked why they had intercourse the first time, about half of the males attributed it to curiosity and readiness for sex and 25 percent answered affection for their partner. Among the females, it was the reverse: about half cited affection for their partner, and many fewer attributed it to curiosity and readiness for sex.
3. Most sexually active young people show no signs of having large numbers of partners.
4. Premarital sexual behavior is correlated with age, race/ethnicity, religiosity, having a boyfriend or girlfriend, early dating and steady dating, age at first intercourse, liberality, age at menarche, parental relationships, peer standards, sibling influence, gender, drug usage, father absence, education expectations, and socioeconomic status.
5. Adults in preindustrial societies are generally tolerant of adolescent heterosexual activity. This is most true in groups in which women have high status.
6. Many adolescents who have never experienced sexual intercourse do engage in other intense forms of sexual

activity. Many report that they have either masturbated a partner or been masturbated by a partner. More than that report that they have either given or received oral sex.

7. Almost all adolescent boys and many girls masturbate regularly. The practice is not harmful and should be considered normal.

8. Although the preferred standard of sexual activity among youths is permissiveness with affection, many adolescents engage in coitus without affection or commitment. Generally speaking, women are less likely to have sex without affection than are men.

9. Not all adolescents have the same sexual standards. American society is pluralistic; it accepts not one but a number of different standards of sexual behavior.

10. Although the sexual double standard is slowly becoming obsolete, American adolescents still endorse it. That is, sexual activity is still more acceptable for males than females.

11. Both male and female adolescents report participating in unwanted sexual activity. Although little of this activity is due to the threat of physical force or harm, the incidence of sexual aggression is disturbingly high.

12. Sexually active adolescents are more likely to use contraceptives now than in the past. Still, most use them only sporadically. Most contraceptive-using adolescents rely on condoms.

13. Getting sexually active teenagers to use effective contraceptives is a huge challenge. There are various reasons why contraceptives are not used: anxiety, ignorance, lack of responsibility, ambivalent feelings about sex, a desire to get pregnant, and rape. The availability of contraceptives does not increase promiscuity, but it does decrease unwanted pregnancy and STD rates.

14. The incidence of STDs among adolescents has reached epidemic proportions. These diseases can have lifelong health consequences if not treated; unfortunately, STDs may be asymptomatic, especially in females.

15. AIDS is the most serious sexually transmitted disease. Adolescents can and do contract HIV, the virus that causes AIDS, but they will not likely exhibit the symptoms of AIDS until they are adults.

16. About 750,000 teenage girls became pregnant in each of the past five years; this is down from a high of more than 1 million adolescent pregnancies/year in the 1990s. About 30 percent of pregnant teenage girls get an abortion.

17. American teens are far more likely to get pregnant or to cause a pregnancy than European teens, even though they are no more sexually active. The reason is that European teens are more likely to use birth control consistently.

18. The future outlook for teenagers who have and keep their children is bleaker than that of teens who do not. Teenage parents are more likely to be poor for much of their lives, and their children will not fare well, either. Children born to and raised by adolescent mothers are unlikely to do well in school and are less apt to be healthy than other children.

19. Adolescent fathers are generally either unwilling or unable to contribute much care to their children. These fathers are often poor, and many have histories of drug use or delinquency.

20. There are three major categories of theories of the causes of homosexuality: biological theories, psychoanalytical theories, and social learning theories. In all probability, there is no single cause of homosexuality. Support is strongest for biological theories.

21. Gay and lesbian adolescents face many hardships, including being frequently harassed. These youths' families often fail to offer them emotional support, especially when the families first learn of the youths' sexual orientation.

22. Peers and the media contribute more to adolescents' sexual knowledge than either parents or teachers.

23. Parents are not doing a good job of sex education for various reasons: they are too embarrassed, they are uninformed, they are afraid knowledge will lead to sexual experimentation, they tell too little too late, or they set a negative example at home.

24. More than 90 percent of parents support offering sex education in the schools. An increasing number of schools offer sex education, but an abstinence-only approach has become more common. This is unfortunate, since abstinence-preferred and comprehensive programs are more successful at reducing teenage pregnancy.

25. Teaching sex education does not increase sexual activity or pregnancy rates among adolescents. The best programs decrease those the rates.

KEY TERMS

acquaintance rape 285	homosexuality 296
coitus 279	pluralistic society 283
date rape 285	stranger rape 285
heterosexuality 296	

THOUGHT QUESTIONS

Personal Reflection

1. How have your sexual values and behaviors changed as you've matured? Why?

2. How closely do your own sexual behaviors match your sexual ethics? If there is a mismatch, why?

3. Did the availability of birth control or abortion affect your own sexual decisions as a high school or middle school student? How?

4. Have you ever felt pressured to have sex when you didn't want to? Have you ever pressured anyone else?

5. Did your parents tell you about sex when you were growing up? What did they tell you? How did they tell you?

6. Did you have sex education in school? Comment on the program.

Group Discussion

7. Do parents have much influence over the sexual behavior of their adolescents?

8. What are some myths about masturbation that you heard while you were growing up?

9. Has the increase in premarital sexual intercourse been accompanied by lessening of emotional intimacy, loving feelings, and decreasing commitment in relationships? Support your answer.

10. Was sexual harassment by peers a problem in the high school that you attended? Explain.

11. Why don't more sexually active adolescents consistently use effective contraceptives? What can be done to improve this situation?

12. Has the AIDS epidemic made any differences in the sexual behavior of your friends? Why or why not?

13. What can be done to reduce the number of unwed pregnancies?

14. What are the alternatives to abortion for teenage pregnancy? What do you think of them?

15. Do you know any gay men or lesbians? What are the most serious problems they face?

16. Comment on this statement: "Adolescents' primary source of sex information is their friends." How do you feel about this?

Debate Questions

17. High school health clinics should distribute contraceptive information and condoms.

18. Middle and high school students should be required to attend a comprehensive sex education class.

19. Oral sex is sex and should be strongly discouraged for high school students.

20. Parental consent should be required before adolescents can obtain abortions.

21. Pediatricians should routinely question their adolescent patients about their sex lives and screen them for STDs if they are sexually active.

SUGGESTED READING

Doan, A. E., & Williams, J. C. (2008). *The Politics of Virginity: Abstinence in Sex Education.* New York: Praeger.

Evans, R. (2006). *Teenage Pregnancy and Parenthood.* New York: Routledge.

Farber, N. (2009). *Adolescent Pregnancy: Policy and Prevention Services.* New York: Springer.

Florsheim, P. (Ed.). (2003). *Adolescent Romantic Relations and Sexual Behavior: Theory, Research, and Practical Implications.* Mahwah, NJ: Erlbaum.

Huegel, K. (2003). *GLBTQ: The Survival Guide for Queer and Questioning Teens.* Minneapolis, MN: Free Spirit Publishing.

Irvine, J. (2004). *Talk About Sex: The Battles over Sex Education in the United States.* Berkeley: University of California Press.

Kiselica, M. S. (2008). *When Boys Become Parents.* New Brunswick, NJ: Rutgers University Press.

Savin-Williams, R. (2005). *The New Gay Teenager.* Cambridge, MA: Harvard University Press.

USEFUL WEB SITES

Alan Guttmacher Institute
www.agi-usa.org

A nonprofit organization dedicated to tracking and improving sexual and reproductive health; it publishes three journals, all available online. The site provides information about topics such as sexual education, adolescent pregnancy, law and public policy, contraception, and sexual behavior. One section of the site is devoted solely to adolescent sexuality.

Henry J. Kaiser Family Foundation
www.kff.org

This well-known philanthropic organization is concerned with major health care issues, including sexual health. Its site contains reports of survey research conducted by the foundation, as well as fact sheets and research reviews about topics such as sex education, sexually transmitted diseases, adolescent health, and abortion.

Sexuality Information and Education Council of the United States (SEICUS)
www.seicus.org

SEICUS is a nonprofit organization that promotes comprehensive sex education. On the site is information about sexually transmitted diseases and current legislative initiatives concerning sex education. The organization also produces an e-newsletter.

WOULDN'T YOU LIKE TO KNOW . . .

- What is the purpose of public education?
- What is the difference between a *middle school* and a *junior high school*?
- Does fostering competition among students make them work harder and learn more?
- Do students fare better in large schools or small schools?
- What can teachers do to help students be successful in school?
- How many students drop out of high school?
- What can parents do to help their children be successful in school?
- Why do students drop out of school?
- What is the relationship between getting pregnant and dropping out of school?

Education and School

Most American youths spend the bulk of their waking hours not at home but at school. And while there, they are exposed to the wide-ranging influence of peers and teachers. A successful school experience is the stepping stone to financial security. Most good jobs require a high school diploma at the very least, and the best-paying jobs usually require even more education. Why do some students succeed whereas others do not? How are American schools structured? How satisfied are adolescents with the schooling they receive?

Trends in U.S. Education

Let's take a look at the evolution of educational trends in the United States, particularly during the last half of the twentieth century through the present.

Traditionalists Versus Progressives

Traditionalists argue that the purpose of education is to teach the basics—English, science, math, history, and foreign languages—so as to increase student knowledge and intellectual powers. **Progressives** urge that the purpose of education is to prepare students for life by teaching citizenship, home and family living, a vocation, physical health, gratifying use of leisure time, and effective personality growth. As envisioned by educational philosopher John Dewey and others (Westbrook, 1991), schools are to prepare students to be active, critical, engaged citizens. Progressive educators believe that students should be recognized as individuals, that they should be treated in a culturally sensitive manner, and that they should be trained to be capable of participating in the community.

The traditionalist-progressive debate has continued partly because of the insistence by both sides that education has an important role in reforming society and solving social problems. Each time a social problem has arisen, a new school program has been designed to deal with it. When traffic fatalities rose, driver education was introduced. A rise in premarital pregnancies and in divorce rates was followed by courses in family life education. Demands for racial integration led to African American studies and school busing. Feminists' demands for equality and liberation resulted in women's and gender studies. A fear that we are failing to compete in highly technological industries has led to a call for increased emphasis upon math and science education. Throughout history, as social needs have changed, the educational pendulum has been pushed first in one direction and then another.

Rise of Progressive Education

Until the 1930s, traditionalism held sway in U.S. schools. Then came the Great Depression, which destroyed the job market for adolescents, so that many

who would have gone to work stayed in school instead (Ravitch, 1983). Most of these youths were not college bound, uninterested in traditional academic subjects, and in need of different programs to deal with the issues they were confronting in their own lives.

Progressive educators such as John Dewey believed that the classroom should be a laboratory that prepares students for life. Under the progressive influence, many schools introduced vocational and personal service courses (e.g., driver's ed), restricting academic courses to the college-preparatory program. Life-adjustment education centered on vocation, leisure activities, health, personal concerns, and community problems. Principals boasted that their programs prepared students for the demands of real life, freeing them from dry academic studies. Developing an effective personality became as important as improving reading skills (Wood, Wood, & McDonald, 1988).

Sputnik and After

The United States was shocked when the Soviet Union launched *Sputnik*, the first space satellite, in the 1950s. Almost overnight, Americans became obsessed with the failure of our schools to keep pace with the technological advances of the Soviet Union. The schools were blamed for a watered-down curriculum that left U.S. youths unprepared to face the challenge of communism. As a result, Congress passed the National Defense Education Act and appropriated nearly $1 billion in federal aid to education, which supported the teaching of math, science, and foreign languages. Schools modernized their laboratories, and courses in physical sciences and math were rewritten by leading scholars to reflect advances in knowledge.

1960s and 1970s

By the mid-1960s, the "cold war" with the Soviet Union had abated. The United States was swamped with a rising tide of social unrest, racial tension, and antiwar protests. Once again, society was in trouble and schools were called upon to meet the challenge. Major school aid legislation was passed, primarily to benefit poor children, as part of the Johnson administration's War on Poverty. Once more, the educational clamor was for relevance. Educators claimed that schools were not preparing young people for adult roles and that adolescents needed to spend more time in community and work settings as well as in the classroom. Academic programs gave way to career and experimental education so that adolescents could receive hands-on experience. Elementary schools adopted open education, knocked down classroom walls, and gave students more choices as to what to do each day. High schools lowered graduation requirements. Enrollments in science, math, and foreign languages fell as traditional subjects gave way to independent study, student-designed courses, and hosts of electives. By the late 1970s, more than 40 percent of all high school students were taking a general rather than college-preparatory or vocational courses of study, and 25 percent of their educational credits came from work experience outside school, remedial course work, and classes aimed at personal growth and development (National Commission on Excellence in Education, 1983).

Soon, the nation became alarmed at the steady, slow decline in academic indicators. **Scholastic Assessment Test (SAT)** scores showed a steady decline from 1963 to 1980. Verbal scores fell more than 50 points and average math scores nearly 40 points. The College Entrance Examination Board, which administered the tests, cited grade inflation, absenteeism, frivolous courses, absence of homework, and decline in reading and writing assignments as reasons for falling test scores. (Psychologists, sociologists, and educators cited other reasons as well, such as increased family instability.) It became obvious that high school students were taking more nonacademic courses and fewer courses necessary for college preparation.

1980s

Parental and public outcry grew in the early 1980s, resulting in the appointment of the National Commission on Excellence in Education (1983). The commission drew a number of bleak conclusions, including that achievement had declined in science and English and that nearly half of high school seniors could not draw inferences from written materials. This time, the reason given for demanding a back-to-basics education was not a threat from the Soviets but a fear that the nation was falling behind the economic competition from Japan and Western Europe and was losing its competitive edge in world markets. Educational reformers demanded more academic rigor in the schools, more required courses, longer school days, and tougher standards for graduation. Thus, the

pendulum again swung back to a more traditionalist posture.

1990s

Education in the 1990s was marked by a move toward *alternative forms* of instruction. Continuing dissatisfaction with public education and acknowledgment of the diversity of the U.S. student population encouraged parents and educators to experiment with a variety of novel approaches to teaching. In addition to the traditional public and private schools, a plethora of options were offered. Magnet schools had existed for decades, but enrollment in these schools jumped dramatically in the 1990s. **Magnet schools** are theme schools within public school systems; for instance, a magnet school might specialize in the arts or in African culture. Newer in concept were charter schools. **Charter schools** are a hybrid between public and private schools. They are public in the sense that they are supported by tax dollars and accountable to the government. They are private in the sense that they are free from most district-level rules and regulations, they are founded and run by corporations or individuals who devise their own curricula, and parents choose for their children to attend them. Charter schools are even more varied than magnet schools in terms of curricula and teaching format.

The distinction between public and private schools has become even more blurred by school districts' increasing use of vouchers. In a **voucher** system, the school district subsidizes the cost of a student attending a private school. Vouchers have existed for a long time, but their use grew and expanded in the 1990s. Formerly, the only students who were given vouchers were those who lived in rural areas with no public schools or those who needed special services because of disabilities. Another type of program, called a **tech-prep program,** is designed for students who are not

traditionalists   educators who emphasize that the purpose of education is to teach the basics.

progressives   educators who emphasize that the purpose of education is to prepare pupils for life.

Scholastic Assessment Test (SAT)   a test that measures aptitude to do academic work.

magnet schools   theme schools that serve students within public school systems.

charter schools   public schools that are funded and run by private corporations or individuals; accountable to government but relatively regulation free.

vouchers   a method by which the public schools subsidize the cost of private school education.

tech-prep schools   high schools that partner with community colleges to provide career preparation for non-college bound students.

interested in obtaining a four-year bachelor's degree after high school. High schools have developed partnerships with community colleges so that their graduates can work on a career-focused, two-year associate's degree along with their high school diploma.

In addition, **open enrollment** policies were established across the nation. Under these policies, students may attend any public school they wish, even if it is outside their own school district. In other words, if you live in Minneapolis but prefer to go to a St. Paul middle school because it offers a foreign language that is not available in your own middle school, you can. Proponents of open enrollment believe that the policy will improve public education because of increased competition for students. Since government financial grants are often based on numbers of students, schools have more of an incentive to do well under open enrollment conditions.

Perhaps the most well-known educational innovation involves *home schooling*. The home-schooling movement began in the 1980s and was originally endorsed primarily by conservative Christians who wanted to shield their children from what they perceived to be immoral, secular influences. Today, it is a broad-based movement, and approximately 2 million American children are home schooled (Ray, 2008). The experiences of home-schooled students vary widely. Some parents follow an established curriculum; some do not. Some parents keep their children home all day, whereas others strive to provide social opportunities for them. Many home-schooled children go to public school for part of the day so that they can participate in activities such as drama, band, or team sports. Although some research has suggested that home-schooled children do well on standardized tests, those studies are inconclusive because of poor methodology. Given the variability of their experiences, it is likely that some home-schooled students will do well in college and the workplace but others will not.

Early Twenty-First Century

Dissatisfaction with public schools continued unabated, in part fueled by new data demonstrating that American students were not learning as much as their European or Asian peers. For example, American 15-year-olds scored 24th (out of 29) in the PISA test, an international assessment given to students mostly from developed nations around the globe. The test measures basic knowledge in science, math, and reading and also examines students' ability to apply their knowledge in problem-solving situations. The call for reform continues.

The most significant piece of educational policy to occur thus far in the twenty-first century was launched by President George W. Bush in 2001: the No Child Left Behind Act. It is based on four principles: (1) schools should be made accountable for the success of their students and rewarded or punished commensurate with their success or failure, (2) local control of the schools should be increased, (3) parents and students should have expanded options, and (4) specific teaching methods should be promoted. Another requirement of this law is yearly testing of all students in grades three through eight to measure their abilities in core content areas. In addition, states are given more leeway in choosing how they will spend federal education dollars, parents are granted more choices as to which schools their children attend, and reading has become more of a priority in early education. In a sense, the No Child Left Behind legislation is a swing toward back-to-basics traditionalism in that it emphasizes achievement in reading and other core subjects.

The No Child Left Behind Act is controversial. Opponents claim that testing is stressful and actually decreases the quality of education, since teachers "teach to the test." In addition, it has been claimed that weak students—those who are believed incapable of passing the tests regardless of how they much they are tutored—and strong students—those who will pass under any circumstances—are ignored by teachers who are motivated to work most closely with those children who might be moved from a failing to a passing score. There is also the fear that schools that are below acceptable standards will lose funding and fall even further behind. The act has not been adequately funded, and so many claim that the assessment requirements are actually draining money that could be spent on enhancing instruction. Others complain that the legislation shifts control of education from state authority, where it has traditionally resided, too far into federal hands. Finally, not everyone agrees with the specific reading methods that are being promoted. In any case, at this point in time it remains the law of the land. (As this text goes to press—in February 2010—President Obama announced that he planned to propose revisions to the NCLB law. While fundamentally leaving it intact, he indicated that he intends to recommend changing the metric by which schools are rated, so that their students need only to show improvement in order for them to be deemed "successful" rather than that designation coming only if students are at grade level.)

Middle Schools

As we have discussed throughout this book, adolescents are considerably different from children, and early adolescents are considerably different from older adolescents. As the U.S. population increased, it was natural to progress from a one-room schoolhouse, which housed students of all ages, to a system in which the older students were separated from the younger ones. Perhaps the earliest model was to divide schools into *elementary schools* (grades one through six) and *secondary schools* (seven through twelve). Later, the most common model was to have *elementary schools, junior high schools,* and *high schools.* As the name implies, junior high schools were meant to be high schools for more junior adolescents. They were therefore structured much the same as high schools: students changed teachers with every class period, the schools had larger enrollments, and students were more likely to be tracked according to ability level.

More recently, there has been recognition that this junior high school model is not well suited to the special needs of early adolescents. Because of this, *middle schools* were developed. There is no single agreed-upon structure for middle schools. Depending on the community, middle schools can include grades five through seven, five through eight, six and seven, six through eight, seven and eight, or seven through nine. The 6th- through 8th-grade configuration has become increasingly popular, growing from fewer than 2,000 schools in the 1970s to more than 8,000 schools in the year 2000 (Banks, 2004). There has also been a call for a return to a two-school model, in this case K–8 and 9–12 (e.g., Juvonen, Le, Kaganoff, et al., 2004), since some research shows that this model is more successful than any three-school configuration. Why might this be so? Elmore (2009) suggests that it is due both to the smaller number of adolescents in K–8 schools and to the way that the presence of younger children changes the interaction patterns between adolescents and teachers.

Ideally, middle schools should not merely be renamed and reshuffled junior high schools; rather, they should be different in concept. This has generally not been the case, however, and so many students still go into a slump when they enter middle school. They exhibit large declines in academic motivation, in perception of their own academic abilities, and in achievement after they leave elementary school (Eccles & Roeser, 2009; Roeser, Eccles, & Freedman-Doan, 1999).

Why does this happen? One factor is that middle schools are larger and more impersonal than elementary schools. Given middle schools' larger size, adolescents spend less time in the company of friends and more

time with relative strangers than children do. In addition, old peer networks break down and friends often no longer see one another at all. This is exacerbated by individual scheduling. Rather than spending all day with the same 30 peers, as in elementary school, students in middle school often have little peer continuity during the seven or eight periods in their day.

Students are less close to their teachers, too. A middle school math teacher might instruct 180 different students each day, as opposed to the 30 or so served by an elementary school teacher. Thus, middle school teachers do not have the time to get to know all of their students and to develop close relationships with them. In fact, large student enrollments usually mean that teachers don't even know all of their students by name. This lack of familiarity may also mean less effective supervision of student misbehavior (Carlo, Fabes, Laible, et al., 1999). Given these changes, it is no wonder that many middle school students come to feel alienated and discouraged.

How might these problems be avoided? Many researchers have called for middle schools to recognize early adolescents' special needs, including that young teens are extremely self-conscious, that they desire autonomy, and that they need support from nonparental adults as they strive to break away from their parents. Eccles and Midgley (1989), as well as others, have suggested that the **performance goal structure** of most schools does not meet these needs and is actually detrimental to many adolescents. Schools with performance goal structures foster competition among students; the goal is to get the highest grade in the class. In contrast, schools with a **task mastery structure** are less competitive and highly value effort and improvement, rather than meeting preset standards (Middleton & Midgley, 1997). Data suggest that adolescents generally experience fewer problems in schools with task mastery structures (Eccles & Roeser, 2009; Felner, Seitsinger, Brand, et al., 2007). For example, students who are motivated by task mastery are more likely than goal-focused students to ask for help (and hence learn the subject matter) when they are confused; goal-focused students don't seek help because they are reluctant to seem ignorant (Ryan & Pintrich, 1997). In addition, students whose teachers use task mastery standards come to value the academic subjects more and show an increased desire to learn

ANSWERS WOULDN'T YOU LIKE TO KNOW . . .

What is the difference between a *middle school* and a *junior high school?*

The term *junior high* really says it all. Junior high schools are high schools for younger students. The term *middle school* was created to indicate that younger adolescents need a different kind of education—one intended to help them in their transition to adolescence. In reality, the terms are used loosely, and many junior highs and middle schools are similar in nature.

open enrollment a policy that allows students to choose from among a large number of public schools, sometimes even those outside their own district.

performance goal structure schooling in a competitive atmosphere in which the goal is to get the highest grade in the class.

task mastery structure schooling in a less competitive setting in which individual effort and improvement are rewarded.

them (Anderman, Eccles, Yoon, et al., 2001). Moreover, as a result of the frustrations they feel, students in schools with a performance goal structure are more likely than students in schools that emphasize task mastery to feel angry and depressed and to be truant (Kaplan & Maehr, 1999).

Drawing on the work of a large group of specialists, Jackson and Davis (2000) summarized the attributes most characteristic of successful middle schools, including the following:

- Teachers who work with early adolescents should have special training in interacting with this age group as well as opportunities for ongoing professional development.
- The curriculum should be rigorous, and there should be high learning expectations.

ANSWERS WOULDN'T YOU LIKE TO KNOW ...

Does fostering competition among students make them work harder and learn more?

Many researchers believe that fostering competition *among* students is less effective than fostering competition *within* students. That is, students do better if they are competing against themselves and trying to improve their own performance. According to this task mastery approach, students' grades should be based on their own improvement, not on how well they do in comparison with others.

- The curriculum should be presented so that the students understand its relevance to their own lives.

RESEARCH HIGHLIGHT TRACKING

Tracking, or *ability grouping,* is an educational technique whereby students are separated into different classes based on their competency in a given subject area. (It differs from being placed in a curriculum, as discussed in the text, in that it refers to individual classes, not an entire program of course work.) Some classes, such as mathematics and science, are more commonly tracked than others.

Tracking, although practiced, is viewed with suspicion by many. One concern is that students are unfairly placed in lower tracks because of race, socioeconomic status, or other personal characteristics (Kubitschek & Hallinan, 1996). To compound that problem, once a student is placed in a lower-track class, it is hard to ever move into a higher track since the material is easier, the pace is slower, and the student is viewed as less competent (Lucas & Good, 2001). Furthermore, it is widely feared that lower-tracked students will suffer from decreased self-esteem, since they (and others) have been given evidence that they are not talented in a subject.

On the other hand, tracking is believed by some to have benefits as well. The students in the higher tracks can learn more because the material is covered more quickly than would be otherwise possible; conversely, students in the lower tracks can actually master material because they are given the time to do so. Students in the lower tracks are not subjected to daily feelings of discomfort as they struggle in front of their more-able peers.

Ultimately, however, one would want to know the long-term effects on achievement and self-esteem for students in both higher and lower tracks. Unfortunately, until recently truly excellent data were not available since most of the research that examined these issues used cross-sectional designs and lacked adequate control groups. However, in

2005 Mulkey and her colleagues (Mulkey, Catsambis, Steelman, et al., 2005) published an excellent longitudinal study that tracked 24,000 students over a six-year period, from middle school through the end of high school. Some of these students were in schools that tracked mathematics; others were not. Some of these students were in high tracks; others were in low.

Mulkey and colleagues' counterintuitive findings were that tracking benefited lower-tracked students more than higher-tracked students. Although *all* students in the tracked schools demonstrated higher mathematics achievement than comparable students in the nontracked schools, the gains were greater for the initially weaker students. In addition, it was the higher-tracked students whose self-esteem suffered, not the lower-tracked students. Because the higher-tracked students shifted from being the best in regular math classes to being average in the high-track classes, they had less and less trust in their math ability as time wore on; the lower-tracked students, in contrast, were now in with same-ability peers and so felt better about themselves. Tracking seemed to benefit males more than females.

One should always be cautious about jumping to conclusions based on any single study, however well designed and executed. Other researchers believe that tracking is in fact deleterious to those in the lower tracks. They cite the fact that teachers in the lower tracks are often of poorer quality than those in the higher ones (Oakes, 2005), and that in the lower tracks a student is more likely to be surrounded by disengaged peers than in the advanced groups (Dryfoos, 1990). Mulkey's results, though, if replicated, indicate that tracking may not be detrimental to lesser-ability students after all, or at least not inevitably.

- The atmosphere of the school should be caring and supportive. Students should feel that they share a community with their peers and teachers.
- Middle-schoolers need to feel that their opinions and thoughts are respected.
- The school should strive to ensure the success of all students—the academically weak and strong.
- Parents should be involved in the school.
- The school should be part of the larger civic community, and there should be interaction with businesses, community service centers, and the like.
- Students should be encouraged to develop good health habits.

Characteristics of Good Schools

Jackson and Davis's list provides a good starting point for a discussion of what constitutes an ideal learning environment for middle and high school students. Other features have also been identified.

Size

As noted earlier, students do better and are more engaged in school if they feel part of a caring, supportive community. This is more likely to occur if the school is relatively small in size (less than 1,000 students) but not extremely small (Lee & Smith, 2001).

Students fare better in smaller schools for two reasons (Elder & Conger, 2000). First, in a small school, students will more likely be able to enjoy active, meaningful participation in activities. Clearly, there are only so many roles in the school play, running backs on the football team, and slots on the student council. This means that in larger schools, more students watch from the sidelines. Denied the opportunity to learn through doing, students may have feelings of disengagement.

The second reason students fare better in smaller schools is that the quality of monitoring by teachers is less adequate in larger schools. In small schools, most teachers know nearly all students by name; students are not as anonymous as they often are in larger schools. It is obviously harder to slip through the cracks if teachers know you as an individual and frequently check on how

you are doing. To address this issue, some large schools have started to divide themselves into self-contained subschools. Schools that are too small, however, may be problematic because of a lack of opportunities and because students cannot avoid peers and teachers they dislike.

Unfortunately, impoverished, inner-city youth are most likely to be in the most overcrowded, largest schools (Wasley, 2002).

Atmosphere

Although the teacher is in control of what happens in his or her individual classroom, the principal sets the tone for the entire school, and schools do have an overall climate (Darling-Hammond & Bransford, 2005). A strong, competent principal who uses her or his leadership position to set high standards, to establish fair rules and discipline for those students who break them, to make connections with the outside community, and to foster an upbeat spirit of cooperation and achievement is an enormous asset to the entire school. Students will be distracted if they do not feel safe in the hallways. They will be unhappy and uncooperative if they believe that they are constantly under scrutiny and suspicion. They will be angry if they believe that some students are treated preferentially. Thus, a school's overall climate can enhance or detract from achievement.

To enhance achievement, the school must create an atmosphere of learning. Too often, students do not perceive school as being primarily a place to go and learn. In many cases, even students who enjoy school do not like it because of the educating that takes place there but because of the opportunity to see friends and participate in activities (Anderson & Young, 1992). When parents ask their adolescent children, "How was school today?" they are more likely to hear about who was fighting with whom and how they had to go outside during that day's fire drill than about what material was covered in their classes. An important aspect of school climate is how invested students are in learning. It is crucial that the school's curriculum be perceived by students as both relevant and challenging, for only then will learning become a priority.

A school is more likely to have an atmosphere of learning if students believe that *they are responsible* for their own learning rather than that they are *being held responsible* for it. Students who feel responsible for their own learning and who are interested in the course material do not need to be constantly prodded to work; they

tracking an organizational technique that permits schools to create homogeneous groupings of students within a heterogeneous student population in order to facilitate instruction.

In an atmosphere of learning, students feel they are responsible for their own learning, not held responsible for it. As such, they are interested in the course material and are willing to work.

choose to do so on their own. Students feel responsible when they are given sufficient autonomy and control (NRC, 2004).

Teachers

Teachers can use many strategies to make students feel responsible for their own learning (Roeser, Galloway, Casey-Cannon, et al., 2008). For instance, students generally do better and are more interested if they are allowed to discover answers for themselves rather than be expected to memorize large quantities of information. In addition, teachers can directly instruct their students about how best to learn. They can give students frequent feedback as to how they are doing, highlighting both accomplishments and areas that still need improvement. Teachers can also give students options for how to master course material and then demonstrate that mastery, allowing students to use their own individual strengths and learning styles.

In addition, good teachers engage their students. They make information seem relevant and meaningful to their students and show them how to apply the course

material and skills they are learning to their daily lives. When they do so, they prevent boredom (Finn, 2006). Good teachers encourage students' questions, alternative points of view, and self-reflection. They allow students some time to explore areas of interest to them (National Middle School Association, 2005).

It is also important for teachers to demonstrate support and caring. Students do best when they believe that their teachers like them, care about them, and have faith in their ability to do well. Teachers can demonstrate such concern by being warm and friendly and by spending time with students. They can demonstrate their belief in students' abilities by having high expectations, demanding high-quality work, having patience, and giving students the chance to redo work that is substandard (Wigfield, Byrnes, & Eccles, 2006). Teachers can undermine students' achievement if they indicate that they dislike them or lack faith in them. Negative teacher expectations fall disproportionately on girls, children from racial/ethnic minority groups, and children from lower-income families (Juvenon, Le, Kaganoff, et al., 2004). Unfortunately, as a whole, middle school teachers exhibit less faith in their students than elementary school teachers (Midgley, Feldlaufer, & Eccles, 1989) and are less warm and caring (Roeser, Peck, & Nasir, 2006).

ANSWERS WOULDN'T YOU LIKE TO KNOW ...

What can teachers do to help students be successful in school?

Teachers can help students succeed by being flexible and patient yet demanding high-quality work. To do well, students need to know that their teachers believe in their ability to master the course material and care about their success.

Curriculum

The *curriculum* of a school consists of the aggregate of the courses of study offered. Most comprehensive high schools today offer three basic curricula: college preparatory/academic, vocational, and general.

College Preparatory

Approximately half of high school students are enrolled in the college preparatory curriculum. Its goal is to prepare students for success college work that leads to a four-year degree and perhaps graduate school. Some high schools, particularly in middle- and upper-middle-class suburban communities, are particularly successful, boasting that 80 to 90 percent of their students go to college. Other schools, although sometimes enrolling large numbers of students in the college prep program, are unsuccessful because the majority of these students do not get into college (Elmore, 2009). In such cases, the college prep program does not meet the needs of the majority of students who are not employable without additional training.

Vocational

The vocational curriculum is designed to prepare students for gainful employment. Students spend about half of their time in general education; the rest in

In order to prepare students for gainful employment, most high schools offer a vocational curriculum that combines general education with specialized courses and possibly on-the-job training.

specialized courses; and, in many cases, in on-the-job training. Vocational teachers usually have work experience in the vocation they are teaching. The quality of the program varies from superb to mediocre. (More information on vocational education is presented in Chapter 13.)

General

Students in the general curriculum are often the castoffs from the other two curricula or are not committed either to college or to one of the vocations taught in the vocational curriculum. The curriculum has no goals other than to provide basic skills for those who may be able to go on to some type of job or some type of vocational school after graduation. Most dropouts and unemployed youths come from the general curriculum. Although students are assigned general education courses because of perceived low ability or motivation, all too often once placed there they are left to flounder. Numerous studies have shown that students in general education courses are taught by less experienced teachers who have low expectations of them (e.g., Pallas, Entwisle, Alexander, et al., 1994). They are surrounded by lackadaisical peers. If "no child is to be left behind," then extra attention must be paid to these students. We must find ways to motivate them to learn.

Private Versus Public Schools

As Figure 12.1 indicates, about 70 percent of American high school students attend public schools. The majority of them attend their regular, neighborhood school; a much smaller percentage attend charter, magnet, or public schools in neighboring districts (Broughman, Swaim, & Keaton, 2009). About 23 percent attend private schools, most of them church affiliated; about 7 percent are home schooled.

What determines which kind of education students receive? Ultimately, it is their and their parents' choice. Parents who choose private, religious schools tend to be devout, have higher incomes, be well educated, be older, be from the Northeast or Midwest, and be foreign born. Parents who select nonsectarian private schools tend to be wealthy and are more likely to be from the South than from the West (Yang & Kayaardi, 2004). Home-schoolers are at present a diverse group, but they are more likely to be religious, conservative, White, better educated, and part of a two-parent family compared to the average American family. They are likely to have three or more children and be middle class (Bielick, Chandler, & Broughman, 2001).

How good is each of these alternatives? Since the backgrounds of the students who utilize the different choices are dissimilar—and we know that socioeconomic

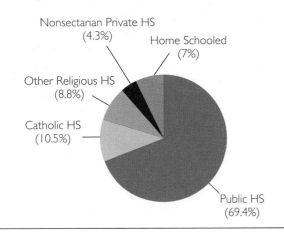

FIGURE 12.1 DISTRIBUTION OF HIGH SCHOOL STUDENTS, 2005

Source: Broughman, Swaim, & Keaton, 2009.

Nonsectarian Private HS (4.3%)
Home Schooled (7%)
Other Religious HS (8.8%)
Catholic HS (10.5%)
Public HS (69.4%)

status, parent involvement, parents' educational level, and so on all help predict a student's academic success— it is actually not as simple to answer that question as you might imagine. We know that on average students who attend private schools, whether or not they are religiously affiliated, tend to do well on college entrance examinations and achievement tests (Hoffer, 1998). As of yet, no large-scale studies have reported on the effectiveness of charter high schools—and by their nature, they vary tremendously from one another. The most comprehensive study that has been completed looked at elementary and middle school achievement. It concluded that students learned more if they were taught by certified teachers than by uncertified ones. (Charter schools are permitted to employ uncertified teachers.) In addition, the study determined that, on average, charter school students did not perform as well as students in traditional public schools (Nelson, Rosenberg, & van Meter, 2004). Although this might be partially due to the result of self-selection in that parents whose children were already struggling opted to switch to charter schools, it is clearly not a strong endorsement. Those who are home schooled, however, appear to do well academically (Lines, 2001). There is some concern, however, that home schooling may hinder social development because home-schooled students spend less time than other adolescents interacting with peers. Many parents, though, ensure that their children have the opportunity to interact with peers by enrolling them in clubs, sports teams, and the like. Also, many states allow home-schooled students to attend classes part time.

Achievement and Dropping Out

In this section, we discuss the reasons that some students fail to graduate from high school.

CROSS-CULTURAL CONCERNS   JAPANESE EDUCATION

The Japanese educational system is known to be one of the finest in the world. Japan boasts high literacy rates, and its students excel in international math and science competitions. Why does the Japanese system work so well?

One reason is that the Japanese take education seriously. Teachers have a higher professional status and enjoy higher salaries than in the United States. Another reason is that Japanese students spend more time in school; their school year is longer, and until very recently, they attended a half-day of school on Saturday. In addition, the Japanese people believe that academic success is more a function of hard work than innate ability, which fosters the belief that all children can learn successfully.

Three criticisms are regularly leveled against the Japanese educational model. First, it is extremely stressful on students. Japanese adolescents must take placement exams in order to get into the high school of their choice, and the competition for the best schools is fierce. Many students study long hours and attend *juku*, or "cram schools," to help them prepare for these tests. Students are well aware that the job they will eventually get and the university they will eventually attend (if any) is very much determined by which high school they go to. The second criticism against the Japanese system is that it is impersonal and rigid; little attention is paid to students' individuality. Finally, the Japanese schools have a tradition of emphasizing rote memorization rather than creative problem solving.

In order to address the latter two concerns, massive curricular changes were implemented in 2002. (Since the Japanese educational system is overseen by the national government, rather than at the local level, these changes were implemented nationwide.) A new subject, *integrated studies*, was introduced. Essentially, this provides a free time slot in which students are encouraged to learn about those topics that interest them. In addition, there has been discussion about making community service mandatory for high school students. These changes would move Japanese education from the traditional end of the continuum to the more progressive, but only time will tell whether they will prove successful.

Sources: Ellington (2001); Letendre (2000).

Enrollment Figures

Education for all youths has not always been the philosophy of the American people. A famous decision in Kalamazoo, Michigan, in 1874 established the now-accepted principle that public education need not be restricted to elementary schools. Prior to that, in 1870, the country's teenagers could choose from among only 800 public high schools. Most adolescents who were preparing for college attended private secondary schools, often called preparatory (or prep) schools. In 1970, 52 percent of Americans under the age of 25 had completed high school; in 2008, that figure stood at 86 percent (U.S. Bureau of the Census, 2009). There has been little overall change in dropout rates in the past 30 years. About 10 percent of those individuals with diplomas did not graduate from high school per se but instead received graduation equivalency degree (GED) certificates after dropping out.

Note that the figures given represent individuals who receive diplomas by age 25. This masks the fact that that approximately *one-third* of U.S. high school first-year students do not earn their high school diploma on time. For African American and Hispanic students, this figure reaches nearly *one-half* (Sweeten, Bushway, & Paternoster, 2009). It is clear, then, that many students struggle with high school, even if they ultimately graduate.

Who Drops Out and Why

A constellation of causes has been offered for why adolescents drop out of school or underachieve. The problem may begin early, even before birth. Children who are born prematurely or with low birth weight may be at high risk because of both biological and social factors. It is known that low-birth-weight children are at risk for subtle neurological defects that may interfere with school functioning. Specific cognitive processes such as attention and short-term memory may be affected, and these, in turn, have an impact on reading and arithmetic ability and social adaptation. A number of studies of elementary schoolchildren indicate that low-birth-weight children have more learning problems, visual-motor deficits, and grade retention than normal-birth-weight children (Cohen, Beckwith, Parmelee, et al., 1996). The fact that many researchers have concluded that poor reading level in third grade—regardless of cause—is strongly predictive of failure to complete high school (e.g., Heinrich, Hickman, Bartholomew, et al., 2008) leads to the conclusion that for many dropouts, their academic problems did not begin with adolescence.

So very many factors can contribute to academic success or failure: socioeconomic status, racial and ethnic prejudice and discrimination, parental influence and relationships, home responsibilities, personality problems, social adjustment, activities and associations, financial problems, health concerns, early pregnancy, intellectual difficulties, learning disabilities, poor grades, misconduct, expulsion, and lack of interest in school (Connell, Halpern-Felsher, Clifford, et al., 1995). Usually, problems accumulate over the years until withdrawal occurs, often after the legal requirement of age or number of years of schooling have been met.

The actual event or circumstance that precipitates withdrawal may be minor: a misunderstanding with a teacher, a disciplinary action, a blowup with peers, tension at home, or other reasons. For instance, one boy known to the author withdrew after he was refused admittance to a class because he did not have a late pass from another teacher. The boy got angry, quit school, and never came back. An incidents like this following a whole series of prior events, such as poor grades, grade retention, and social maladjustment, led to the final withdrawal.

A 2006 survey asked dropouts themselves to give their their reasons for leaving school. The most common causes cited by these adolescents included (1) classes weren't interesting, 47 percent; (2) they had missed too much school and were far behind, 43 percent; (3) they had many friends who were not in school, 42 percent; (4) they had been given too much freedom and perceived the school as chaotic, 38 percent; (4) they were failing, 35 percent; (5) they needed to make money, 32 percent; (6) they were pregnant or had become a parent, 26 percent; and (7) they had to care for a family member, 22 percent. (The numbers do not sum to 100 percent because respondents could provide multiple reasons.) The majority said that they had not been motivated to work hard (69 percent), and that they would have worked harder had they been made to (66 percent) (Bridgeland, DiIulio, & Morison, 2006). Let's examine these motivations.

Boredom and Alienation

A number of the dropouts' responses include elements of boredom (uninteresting classes) and disengagement from school (friends not in school). Individuals often begin to feel alienated and disengaged when they are *powerless*, they perceive the tasks being assigned to them as *meaningless*, and they feel *normless*. People feel powerless when they are controlled or manipulated by authority figures according to rules not of their own making. In schools, students may experience powerlessness when they cannot control or change school policies, the classes into which they have been placed, or their marginal academic positions. They choose not to compete for rewards such as praise and academic grades and instead miss class, rebel, or merely attend but not truly participate. *Meaninglessness* may result when students are unclear on the connection between the subjects taught at school and their own futures. They may have observed graduates who failed to find good jobs or who found jobs that did not seem to require any skill learned in school. *Normlessness* occurs when individuals have little sense that there are uniform goals and standards across their school. School norms reward students who achieve academically and who intend to pursue higher education. Many struggling students perceive these school norms as unfair. This sets the stage for them to embrace peer and/or counter-school norms (Mau, 1992).

There are numerous ways to decrease boredom and enhance feelings of engagement: for example, curricula can be made more relevant, with clear ties to an individual's future, and stronger, more personal relationships can be forged between teachers and students. In addition, students can be encouraged to develop their talents and interests through participation in extracurricular clubs and activities. Students who join the band or go out for sports are more likely to feel connected to their school (Brown & Evans, 2002).

Family Responsibilities

Many students cited the need to care for a family member, including a spouse or a child. Teenage pregnancy, then, is a significant contributor to dropping out. Thirty percent of teenage mothers drop out of school (Whitman, Bokowski, Keogh, & Weed, 2001). In fact, leaving high school because of pregnancy is one of the most common reasons that girls fail to graduate. Not only does pregnancy encourage girls to drop out, but once they have dropped out, they are more likely to become pregnant (Manlove, 1998), and so decreasing the high school dropout rate would have the additional benefit of decreasing the teenage pregnancy rate. Federal law

Title IX requires that schools make reasonable accommodations for pregnant teenage girls and teenage mothers (National Women's Law Center, 2007), and so they are not forced out by the system; more commonly, they drop out because they were disinterested to begin with or need to make money to support their child.

Teenage pregnancy affects high school boys' graduation rates as well. Fatherhood is a factor in the decision to leave school for more than one-fourth of male dropouts; 19 percent say it is a major factor (Peter D. Hart Research Associates, 2005). Teen fathers enter the labor market earlier and initially earn more money than do other young men, but by the time teen fathers reach their mid-twenties they earn less. Teen fathers fare poorly in comparison to men who postpone having children until age 20 or later (Pirog-Good, 1996).

Even if a pregnancy is not involved, financial considerations are often important in an individual's decision about staying in school. High school is expensive: students may think they must have the "right" clothes to wear and many schools have participation fees for at least some of their courses and extracurricular activities. Sometimes parents pressure youths to go to work to help support the family. At other times, there is the lure of being financially independent, having spending money for social activities, or saving to buy a car. If at-risk students are able to get fairly good jobs without an education, they are more likely to drop out (Stallmann & Johnson, 1996).

Truancy

Those who drop out of school often have a high rate of truancy from school prior to their dropping out (Sheldon & Epstein, 2004). Truancy is both a *symptom* of

Pregnancy and marriage are among the most common reasons for girls to drop out of school. Schools that provide special programs to meet the needs of teen mothers play an important role in keeping them in school.

disengagement and a *cause* of academic failure. As such, there are different reasons for it. Bimler and Kirkland (2001) identified five types of truants. The first two types consist of adolescents who miss school because their parents either condone or actively encourage the behavior; for example, the truants' parents may wish them to stay home to care for younger siblings. The difference between the two groups is whether the truants are themselves intrinsically rebellious when they do attend school. Bimler and Kirkland term the third group "unmotivated loners": poorly adjusted social isolates who simply are uninterested in school. The fourth group is equally unmotivated and poorly adjusted but is part of a rebellious social group. Finally, the fifth group is composed of "well-socialized delinquents." They are well adjusted and popular with other deviant youth, but their priorities do not include school.

School Failure
Many academic factors have been associated with dropping out of school. Among these are poor reading ability, improper placement, and low grades (Goldschmidt & Wang, 1999). Students with learning disabilities and who have low IQs are disproportionally likely to drop out (Dunn, Chambers, & Rabren, 2004). Students who continuously get bad grades find class work punishing and unpleasant to complete. They are also likely to be held back, a factor in and of itself known to be associated with dropping out (Hickman & Garvey, 2006).

In addition to these issues, which were identified by dropouts, there are a number of other factors associated with failure to graduate from high school.

Socioeconomic Factors
Research overwhelmingly indicates that low socioeconomic status (SES) correlates positively with early withdrawal from school. Students from low-income families are almost 2.5 times more likely to drop out of high school than middle-income students (Coalition for Juvenile Justice, 2001). Why is the dropout rate higher among students from low-SES families? There are a number of considerations (Simons, Finley, & Yang, 1991):

1. *Students from low-SES families often lack positive parental influences and examples.* Most parents want their children to have more education than they did. But if parents finished only fifth grade, they may consider graduating from junior high school sufficient. In general, sons of low-SES families receive more encouragement to finish school than do daughters.

2. *Teachers are often prejudiced against youths from low-SES families, showing preferential treatment to students from higher-status families.* Students of higher social-class backgrounds are chosen more often for little favors (e.g., running errands, monitoring, chairing committees), whereas students from lower-status groups receive more than their share of discipline. Teachers are usually from middle-class backgrounds and therefore often find it difficult to understand and accept the goals, values, and behavior of pupils from other social backgrounds.

3. *Low-SES students receive fewer rewards for doing well and for staying in school than do students from higher-status families.* Rewards may take the form of academic grades, favors by teachers, social acceptance by peers, offices in school government, participation in extracurricular activities, or school prizes and awards. Lower-status students receive these types of rewards less often than do higher-status students. Their grades are not as good, nor do they enjoy as much social acceptance and prestige from peers; they seldom are elected to positions of leadership; they are not joiners in extracurricular activities; and they are not often given special prizes or awards by the school.

4. *Low-socioeconomic-status students do not as often possess the reading and writing skills of their middle-class peers.* This in itself presents a handicap in almost all academic subjects. Insofar as lack of reading and writing skills is associated with low socioeconomic status, lower-status youths do not do as well in school and are therefore more prone to drop out.

5. *Peer influences on low-SES youths are often anti-school.* Low-SES youths often have severed their ties with adult institutions and values, becoming involved instead with groups composed of jobless dropouts.

Race and Ethnicity
Hispanic American, African American, and Native American students have a higher dropout rate than Caucasian students do (U.S. Bureau of the Census, 2009b). Rates for Latino students are especially high. In addition, Latinos are more likely to drop out at a younger age than others. Only about 20 percent of adolescent dropouts leave school by eighth grade (most leave during tenth grade); however, 40 percent of Hispanic dropouts do so by eighth grade (Schwartz, 1995). Latino students, of course, often face a language barrier that makes academic success more difficult for them. Because of this, they are held back and made to repeat grades more often than other students, and any student who repeats one or more grades is at increased risk for dropping out (Carpenter & Ramirez, 2008). A variety of negative social, cultural, and psychological

forces interfere with minority students' achievement and academic orientation. Therefore, even though minority parents value and encourage education (Steinberg, Dornbusch, & Brown, 1992), their children are less apt to succeed.

The highest dropout rates are among non-White students from inner-city high schools. In fact, the average dropout rate in the inner-city high schools of the nation's largest cities is 50 percent (Orfield, Losen, Wald, et al., 2004). The trying economic, social, and familial conditions faced by these youths are not conducive to continuing education. (See the Research Highlight box: "Factories of Failure?")

Congruence between School and Home
Both economically disadvantaged and minority adolescents are likely to experience a lack of congruence between school and home (Arunkumar, Midgley, & Urdan, 1999). That is, the values and attitudes these students experience at home don't match those of their teachers; this is generally not a problem for middle-class, majority students.

Some areas of incongruence include attitudes toward competition, impulse control, and the appropriateness of emotional display (Trumbull, Rothstein-Fisch, Greenfield, et al., 2001). For example, expressions of anger are more tolerated among low-SES African American families than they are at school. Native American students may feel that it is boastful to raise your hand to indicate that you know the correct answer. When students feel this incongruence, they find themselves getting into trouble for behaviors they have been taught are appropriate and acceptable. This leads to feelings of frustration, alienation, and anger. Students whose homes are dissonant from their schools are less hopeful about the future, have lower self-esteem, have less faith in their academic talents, and have lower grade point averages than students whose homes and schools are more congruent.

Family Relationships
The quality of interaction among members of the adolescent's family has a marked influence on his or her school success (Paulson, Marchant, & Rothlisberg, 1998). Studies of the family relationships of bright, high-achieving versus underachieving high school students show that the high achievers more often than the underachievers describe their parents as typically sharing recreation and ideas; as understanding, approving, trusting, affectionate, and encouraging (but not pressuring) with respect to achievement; and as not overly restrictive or severe in discipline. Parents of high achievers provide their children with learning opportunities at home, monitor their children's homework and achievement, and take time to volunteer at their children's schools.

A large number of studies have examined the impact of parenting style on children's school success. Authoritative parents are most likely to have children who value school and get good grades (e.g., Spera, 2005). Authoritative parents are somewhat more likely than authoritarian parents and much more likely than permissive parents to be engaged in their children's education; they also have more contact with their children's teachers, spend more time helping their children do homework, and spend more time talking to their children about their school day (Melby & Conger, 1996).

Social Adjustment and Peer Associations
Peer associations often are a major factor in influencing a particular student to achieve in school. Most adolescents want to do what their friends are doing. If friends are dropping out of school to earn "big money" or to get married, a teen may be persuaded to do likewise (Schwartz, 1995). Similarly, the student who becomes acculturated into a subgroup that rejects education or into a delinquent group rebelling against the established system of education is strongly encouraged by his or her peers to drop out of school. Ream and Rumberger (2008), for example, found that the more boys' friends valued education, the more likely they were to graduate from high school.

Stress
A large body of research has demonstrated that continual high levels of stress debilitate psychological well-being, physical health, and task performance. A number of studies have focused on the many sources of students' stress while in school.

One source of stress comes from a lack of personal safety. Significant numbers of students report that someone hit, kicked, pushed, or even threatened them with a knife or gun; hence, they feel unsafe in their schools. Often students feel safe in parts of their school building but unsafe in others, such as certain corridors or in the restrooms (Astor, Meyer, & Behre, 1999).

Fear of psychological or social harm can be stressful as well. Students become anxious if they fear being made fun of in front of other students or if they think a teacher is going to criticize them. Being made to feel inferior and ashamed, not being able to finish classroom work, and doing worse on a test than one should or than others did are stressful. Having to meet different teacher expectations in different classrooms can be a source of stress. Other stressful situations include having something stolen from your locker and seeing other students fighting in the lunchroom.

Anything that upsets the school's harmony and interferes with ongoing classroom activities may be a source of stress and certainly can affect academic functioning in school (Ainslie, Shafer, & Reynolds, 1996).

Misconduct

Students may misbehave because they are frustrated at school or because they face stressors at home. In either case, there is a strong negative correlation between misconduct and graduation. In one study, adolescent boys who exhibited severe behavioral problems were 17 times more likely to drop out of high school than boys without those problems (Gluek, 2005, cited in Heinrich, Hickman, Bartholomew, et al., 2008).

Changing Schools

Changing schools is sometimes a factor in pupils' dropping out. When an adolescent changes schools, the ability of the adolescent and his or her parents to make wise decisions about schooling is reduced. They have less information about the new school and its teachers, classes, and norms. Also, they may be less able to take advantage of resources that the new school and teachers can provide. Additionally, teachers may be less committed to a youth who has only recently moved into the system and may be less willing to devote additional time and energy to that student. Such an adolescent may feel separated from the educational process and may be more likely to seek marginalized social contacts (Teachman, Paasch, & Carver, 1996). This is especially true if a student moves several times (Rumberger & Larson, 1998).

It may also be difficult for adolescents to merge into the social scene if they have moved from a distant geographic location, especially in the middle of an academic year. The author still shudders when she remembers how well her out-of-style clothes, Southern accent, and overly polite manners were received when she moved up North "to the big city." School was a nightmare, and academics were the last thing on her mind.

Sense of Academic Competence

Adolescents who do well in school *believe* that they can succeed academically (Cadieux, 1996). Students who have faith in their academic ability are willing to expend the effort needed to do well, persist even when learning is difficult, are resilient and bounce back from

---

RESEARCH HIGHLIGHT   FACTORIES OF FAILURE?

High schools vary widely in their graduation rates. Although a small number do very well—fewer than 15 percent graduate more than 90 percent of their entering first-year students; 20 percent graduate fewer than 60 percent of their entering first-year students (Elmore, 2009). These "factories of failure" are largely found, as might be expected, in areas of concentrated poverty and they enroll disproportionately high numbers of minority students: 46 percent of Black and 39 percent of Latino students attend schools in which the graduation rates are below 50 percent (Balfanz & Legters, 2004). Because they are physically concentrated in particular geographic areas, the students who attend these schools usually have no choice but to attend high schools at which they are likely to fail.

Although many of the students who attend these low graduation-rate schools are at heightened risk of dropping out because of personal characteristics (see body of the text), are there features of the schools themselves that are exacerbating the problem? Christle, Jolivette, and Nelson (2007) tried to determine whether this is the case. Using interviews, observations, and questionnaires, they compared the characteristics of high schools in Kentucky with high graduation rates with those that had low graduation rates.

The authors did find differences among the schools at the school level. Administrators in the high dropout-rate schools had, on average, only half as much experience as administrators in the low dropout-rate schools. The schools with the lowest graduation rates were in worse physical condition and were less clean and orderly. The staff dressed in a less professional manner in these schools. There were less favorable staff-to-student ratios and the overall mood in these schools was more negative.

In addition, numerous differences could be attributed to either school policy or student characteristics or a mixture of both. Students in the high dropout-rate schools were more likely to be held back in a grade, to be suspended, and to be truant. They got lower grades and did not score as well on achievement tests. Family involvement was dramatically lower in the high dropout-rate schools. There were fewer teacher-student interactions, and these interactions were more likely to be authoritarian in nature than in the low dropout-rate schools.

Finally, the schools could be differentiated on the basis of student characteristics. As expected from previous research, there were strong correlations between graduation rates and family income level and percentage of minority students. Students in the less successful schools were more likely to engage in delinquent acts, and they behaved more negatively toward one another in school.

The reasons, then, for the wide disparity in graduation rates are complex and multifaceted. The students attending these schools are often less academically prepared than their peers and may have fewer resources at home to draw upon. At the same time, the schools themselves are less inviting and underfunded and perhaps engage in harsher policies.

failure, and get better grades than students who feel incapable (Patrick, Hicks, & Ryan, 1997). This sense of competence stems from many sources: feedback from parents, encouragement by teachers, a sense of fitting in, and a history of prior school success. Students who lack this sense of competence, or self-efficacy, are more likely to drop out (Lehr, Sinclair, & Christenson, 2004).

ANSWERS WOULDN'T YOU LIKE TO KNOW ...

How many students drop out of high school?

Only about one in eight Americans does not complete high school or earn a GED, and this number has remained quite steady since the mid-1990s. Hispanic American students are much more likely to drop out than either Black or non-Hispanic White students, and they are more likely to drop out at an earlier age. The dropout rate for African Americans has decreased over the years, making it more similar to that of White students.

ANSWERS WOULDN'T YOU LIKE TO KNOW ...

What can parents do to help their adolescents be successful in school?

Parents can best help their adolescents do well in school by being enthusiastic, providing encouragement, and taking an active interest in their education. For instance, parents can make sure that their teens get their homework done, and they can get to know their children's teachers. Parents should avoid putting too much pressure on their children, however, as this makes schoolwork unpleasant.

Dropouts and Employment

Contrary to the stereotype, many high school dropouts work (albeit at primarily unpleasant, low-wage jobs). Still, in 2008 the unemployment rate for dropouts was nearly 1.5 times as high as it was for high school graduates (9 vs. 5.7 percent). White dropouts are more likely to find work than Black dropouts, and male

RESEARCH HIGHLIGHT SCHOOL VIOLENCE

Highly publicized school shootings have caused many adolescents to wonder if they are safe in school. Are they?

The good news is that, relatively speaking, they are. A total of 57 American children and teens were killed in elementary or secondary schools from 1996 to 2008 (Infoplease.com); although even one death or injury is too many, the number is a tiny fraction of the total U.S. student enrollment over that 13-year period. In 2006–2007, the rate was approximately 1 death per 2 million pupils, and the number of school deaths made up less than 2 percent of all youth homicides (Dinkles, Kemp, & Baum, 2009). The risk of other serious violent crime (e.g., rape, aggravated assault) is also less at school than away from it: whereas about 1 percent of American teenagers are the victims of serious violent crime away from school each year, about half that number are assaulted at school or on the way to or from school.

Adolescents are, however, more likely to be robbed than they are to be assaulted, and robberies are more common inside of school than outside of it. Adolescents are about half again as likely to be robbed while at school than elsewhere. In 2007, about 3.5 percent of high school students had something stolen from them while on school grounds. Often these thefts are from lockers or desks.

More common yet is being threatened or injured with a weapon. About 5 percent of female students and 10 percent of male students report having experienced this while at school during 2007. (Threats are more common than injuries.) Black and Latino students were more likely to

have been exposed to weapons than Caucasian students. About 9 percent of male students admit to carrying a weapon on school property; about 3 percent of female students report doing so.

The data indicate that schools are generally as safe or safer now than they were in the 1990s. Still, many students are afraid for their own safety at school. Wallace and May (2005) found that one-third of students had been afraid that someone would hurt them at school, that 17 percent were afraid of being hurt on the way to or from school, and that 14 percent avoided certain areas of the school because of fear of injury. Fearful students often report that their anxiety affects their grades and sometimes causes them to skip school (Bowen & Bowen, 1999).

Schools are responding to their students' fears in several ways. Most middle and high school teachers and administrators are more alert to potential problems. Almost 80 percent of schools now provide some sort of formal violence prevention program (Heaviside, Rowand, Williams, et al., 1998). Many have instituted peer-mediation programs to resolve student conflicts. A growing number of schools employ security guards or have teachers monitor the school grounds. A small number of schools conduct periodic locker checks or have metal detectors installed inside the doors.

Fear of school violence is a problem that will not likely disappear soon. Fueled by alienation, the availability of weapons, and violence in the media, it is not a problem that can be solved by the schools alone.

PERSONAL ISSUES   IS IT WORTHWHILE TO GET A COLLEGE DEGREE?

Since you are reading this text, it seems safe to assume that you are currently enrolled in college. You (and perhaps your parents) must be willing to invest what is likely a considerable amount of money in a college education, so you must believe that getting a degree will benefit you. Will it? The answer is an unequivocal yes.

The most obvious benefits concern knowledge and cognitive ability. Individuals who graduate from college certainly know more than they did before they entered college and likely more than they would if they had not continued their education. In addition, verbal and mathematical skills are enhanced, critical-thinking skills are improved, and the ability to engage in higher-order reasoning increases.

Many students go to college primarily because they believe that having a degree will help them get a good job. In fact, having a bachelor's degree does increase your chance of landing a desirable job along with increasing your earning power. A college graduate can expect to earn $500,000 to $1,000,000 more over his or her lifetime than someone with only a high school diploma. This benefit applies to those who pursued liberal arts as well as more career-targeted programs. The earning power of women and minorities is particularly improved by having a bachelor's degree (Montgomery & Coté, 2003).

In addition, going to college changes people's attitudes. Students tend to leave college with a greater sense of civic responsibility (Ehrlich, 2000). They also tend to become more politically liberal (Lopez, Gurin, & Nagda, 1998), perhaps because they interact with politically liberal professors. (You may or may not view this change as positive.)

How many high school graduates continue on to earn a college degree? You may be surprised to learn that even in the United States, it is relatively rare for a young adult to obtain a college degree. According to the U.S. Bureau of the Census (2009), almost half of American 18- to 24-year-olds have completed at least some college. Only about 57 percent of these (or about one-fourth of all adolescents) will graduate within six years with a bachelor's degree; others will take longer but eventually earn their college degree. Putting it all together, only about one-third of U.S. adolescents in your cohort will earn a B.A. or B.S. The trend is for more and more students to enter and complete college, and so this number will likely rise in the next decade. Right now, however, possessing a bachelor's degree places you in a privileged minority.

ANSWERS WOULDN'T YOU LIKE TO KNOW ...
Why do students drop out of school?

In short, students drop out of school because they are unhappy there. They may feel out of place socially or academically. Perhaps they are receiving too much negative and too little positive feedback from teachers and peers. Students may think that school is not meeting their needs if the education they are receiving seems irrelevant to their lives. They may want to work full time and earn more money than they can at a part-time job.

ANSWERS WOULDN'T YOU LIKE TO KNOW ...
What is the relationship between getting pregnant and dropping out of school?

For a girl, becoming pregnant increases the likelihood that she will drop out of school, and dropping out of school increases the likelihood that she will subsequently become pregnant. Adolescent boys who father children are also less likely to complete high school.

dropouts are more likely to be employed than female dropouts (U.S. Bureau of Labor Statistics, 2009). This makes sense because many girls who drop out of school do because they have had a baby. Assuming they can find a job, at first dropouts earn almost as much as high school graduates. However, dropouts find themselves in dead-end jobs and their salaries do not rise, whereas those of graduates do; the wage gap, therefore, widens with age. The median salary for high school dropouts of all ages was $22,152 in 2008; for high school graduates it was $30,732 and for those with a bachelor's degree it was $50,856. In part because of their poor employment situation, a large majority of dropouts come to regret their decision to leave high school without a diploma (Bridgeland, DiIulio, & Morison, 2006).

SUMMARY

1. There are two opposing perspectives in American educational practice: traditionalism, which emphasizes teaching the basic academic subjects, and progressivism, which encourages the fostering of life skills and independent thought. These two perspectives wax and wane in popularity, depending on political and historical events.
2. Throughout the 1990s and continuing into the present, dissatisfaction with the U.S. educational system has led to experimentation with new methods and tools that are intended to improve student learning and retention. Charter schools, open enrollment, and home schooling, for example, have all become more common. In 2001, Congress passed the No Child Left Behind Act, which mandates stronger local control of schools, compulsory standardized testing, and an increased emphasis on reading and literacy. The measure is controversial.
3. Middle schools were developed to meet the special needs of early adolescents. Although the grades served by these schools vary, most are similar to high schools in structure. The larger size and more impersonal nature of middle schools, as compared with elementary schools, mean that students' achievement and engagement often decrease when they reach middle school.
4. The most successful middle schools share a number of features: a task mastery structure, specially trained teachers, a rigorous curriculum that is presented as relevant to students' lives, a caring and supportive atmosphere, and involved parents and community institutions.
5. All adolescents—high school students as well as those in middle school—benefit from attending smaller schools, where they feel safe, have opportunities to participate, and are treated fairly and with respect.
6. The average comprehensive high school offers three basic curricula: college preparatory, vocational, and general. Students in the general track tend to be more dissatisfied with their schools than students in the other two tracks.
7. As a whole, students who attend private schools or who are home schooled fare better academically than those who attend public schools. Charter schools have not yet proved to be more effective overall than more traditional public schools.
8. There are a number of reasons that pupils drop out of school, including truancy, socioeconomic factors, racial and ethnic prejudices and discrimination, disturbed family situations and negative parental influences, incongruence between home and school, emotional problems, negative social adjustments and peer associations, financial concerns, school failure, school stress, apathy, student alienation and dissatisfactions, and pregnancy and marriage.
9. Well-publicized incidents of school violence have focused attention on this issue. Students' fear is largely unjustified in that students are safer from physical harm at school than away from it. There is a real likelihood

that they will have something stolen from them while at school, however. Schools have become more security conscious in response to students' and parents' concerns.
10. Many dropouts find jobs, but they earn considerably less than high school graduates. The wage gap continues to grow as they get older.
11. College attendance has a number of real benefits, such as becoming a better critical thinker and increasing one's social conscience. In addition, having a bachelor's degree is valuable in acquiring a good job and earning a good salary.

KEY TERMS

charter schools 309
magnet schools 309
open enrollment 310
performance goal structure 311
progressives 308
Scholastic Assessment Test (SAT) 309
task mastery structure 311
tech-prep programs 309
tracking 312
traditionalists 308
vouchers 309

THOUGHT QUESTIONS

Personal Reflection
1. Describe your middle school. Was it modeled after a high school? Do you feel that it was developmentally appropriate for you? Why or why not?
2. Describe your transition to middle school. Were you excited and pleased or anxious and distressed? What factors influenced your feelings?
3. Would you have benefited from an alternative type of middle or high school education? If you had had the options available today, what kind of school would you have selected and why?
4. In what ways did your high school program prepare you for college? In what ways was it deficient in preparing you for college?
5. What did you think of the teachers in your high school? What qualities did you most admire? What qualities did you like the least?
6. Did your high school have many dropouts? Why did these students leave school? What kept you in school when you sometimes felt you would rather leave and go to work?

Group Discussion
7. Do you believe that grades should be based on overall achievement or individual improvement? What are the pros and cons of each approach?
8. Describe the characteristics of the high school you attended. Evaluate the good things about it.

9. Which curriculum options were available in your high school? Did these meet the needs of the students?

10. What are the most important attributes of a good teacher?

11. What sort of grade arrangements do you feel work best? That is, what grade levels should be placed in each building to achieve the maximum amount of learning and satisfactory adjustments of students?

12. What is your opinion of attending a private versus public school? Give examples from your own experience or the experience of others.

13. What, if any, aspects of the Japanese educational system would you like to see instituted in the United States? Why?

14. What can schools do to reduce the risk of violence on their grounds? What measures are counterproductive? Why?

Debate Questions

15. The progressive approach to education is superior to the traditional approach.

16. High schools cater too much to the students who are planning on going to college.

17. Middle schools and high schools are too lax in regard to discipline.

18. Students should help evaluate middle school and high school teachers.

19. Students should have a voice in the selection of their high school's curriculum.

SUGGESTED READING

Harris, S. (2006). *Best Practices of Award-Winning Secondary School Principals.* Thousand Oaks, CA: Corwin Press.

Krovetz, M. L., and Gilberto, A. (2006). *Collaborative Teacher Leadership: How Teachers Can Foster Equitable Schools.* Thousand Oaks, CA: Corwin Press.

Orfield, G. (Ed.). (2004). *Dropouts in America: Confronting the Graduation Rate Crisis.* Boston: Harvard Education Press.

San Antonio, D. M. (2004). *Adolescent Lives in Transition: How Social Class Influences the Adjustment to Middle School.* Albany: State University of New York Press.

Wilcox, K C., and Angelis, J. I. (2009). *Best Practices from High-Performing Middle Schools: How Successful Schools Remove Obstacles and Create Pathways to Learning.* New York: Teachers College Press.

USEFUL WEB SITES

National Education Association (NEA)
www.nea.org

Probably best known for its "Read Across America" program, the NEA is an advocacy group dedicated to improving public education in the United States. Designed primarily for teachers and education students, the site contains position statements on educational issues and news releases. It also contains a section devoted to concerned parents. Quite useful is a "Legal Action Center," which makes it easy for interested individuals to contact their congressional representatives about educational issues.

National Middle School Association
www.nmsa.org

As its name implies, the National Middle School Association is concerned with the education of young adolescents. The site contains numerous online research articles and research summaries as well as current news about middle school education. It also provides position statements and has a useful online bookstore.

U.S. Department of Education
www.ed.gov

The Department of Education Web page contains separate sections for students, parents, teachers, and administrators. You can find information about current federal programs and initiatives, planners to help students decide how much college will cost and what kinds of financial aid are available, tips as to how to succeed in school, information about successful teaching strategies, and No Child Left Behind policy.

WOULDN'T YOU LIKE TO KNOW . . .

- How do you know whether a career will suit you?
- Do most teens think that their parents should have a say in their career plans?
- Who besides his or her parents can influence an adolescent's career choice?
- Do men and women today have equal career opportunities?
- Do most teenagers have jobs?
- Which teens are most likely to work?
- Is it good or bad for adolescents to have paying jobs?
- Do adolescents like doing unpaid volunteer work?
- What's the best thing you can do to avoid being unemployed later in life?

chapter 13

Work and Vocation

The choice of a vocation is one of the most important decisions that an adolescent has to make. In this chapter, we examine the factors that do influence that choice as well as other factors that should. We also examine the major theories of vocational choice that have grown out of research discoveries and discuss the influence of parents, peers, school personnel, sex-role concepts, aptitudes, interests, job opportunities, socioeconomic status, and race/ethnicity on career development. We take a look at adolescents' work experiences, both salaried and volunteer, and discuss adolescent unemployment. The chapter concludes with a section on career education.

Motives for Choice

There are some basic psychological reasons why the task of vocational choice is so important. All people need to meet their emotional needs for recognition, praise, acceptance, approval, and independence. One way individuals do this is by taking on a vocational identity, by becoming "somebodies" whom others can recognize and which grants them emotional fulfillment. High career aspirations are both a consequence of high self-esteem and a contributor to having a satisfying self-image (Chiu, 1990). To the extent that adolescents succeed in their own and others' eyes, they gain self-acceptance and recognition. In their search for identity and self-satisfaction, they are strongly motivated to make a vocational choice that will contribute to their fulfillment (see Chapter 6).

For adolescents who are of a philosophical frame of mind, their vocation is one channel through which their life goals and purposes might be fulfilled. It is the reason for their existence, the niche they feel compelled to fill in the world (Homan, 1986). If adolescents believe life has meaning and purpose, they strive to find and to live out that meaning and purpose by the way they expend their time, talents, and energy. One way is through the work they perform. Vocational choice not only involves asking "How can I make a living?" It also involves asking "What am I going to do with my life?"

For adolescents whose concern is one of service—for meeting the needs of others or bettering the society in which they live—the choice of career will depend on the needs they recognize as most important and they thus seek a vocation in which they can help others. For adolescents who try to be practical, the choice involves discovering the types of work in which there are the most vacant positions, in which the best money and benefits packages are offered, in which they are most interested, and for which they are best qualified. Such choices are based primarily on economic motives, practical considerations, and personal interests and qualifications. For other youths, seeking a vocation becomes a means by which they show they are grown up, financially independent, emancipated from their parents, and able to make it on their own. For them, going to work becomes a means of gaining entrance into the adult world.

Sometimes, however, no rational choice of vocation is made at all. Adolescents just go out and get the first job they can find that pays well, or they accept a job because a friend has recommended them for it or because it happens to be the only one that opens up and that they hear about. Under such circumstances, vocational choice results from happenstance rather than from a thoughtful process. Adolescents may temporarily enjoy economic and other benefits such employment brings. Only later do they likely discover they are unhappy, ill suited to the tasks they are asked to perform, and sacrificing their freedom and lives for doubtful benefits. They need to back up; reassess their goals, talents, and opportunities; and discover the ways these might be combined in meaningful, rewarding work.

Under the best of circumstances, choosing a vocation is an increasingly difficult task as society becomes more complex. The *Occupational Outlook Handbook* (U.S. Bureau of Labor Statistics, 2008), available on the Web, lists more than 1,000 different occupations, most of which are unfamiliar to most teenagers. If at all possible, adolescents need to make rational, considered choices of vocations. If they fail to identify themselves with the kind of work for which they are suited and in which they can find fulfillment, their vocational nonidentity will make it difficult to find overall life satisfaction. In a sense, they will have failed to discover what their own lives are all about.

Theories of Vocational Choice

A number of theorists have sought to describe the process of vocational development. The particular theories that we discuss are those of Eli Ginzberg (1988), John Holland (1985), and Robert Lent (Lent, Brown, & Hackett, 1994, 2000).

Ginzberg's Compromise with Reality Theory

In his **compromise with reality theory,** Eli Ginzberg (1988) emphasized that making a vocational choice is a developmental process that occurs not at a single moment, but over a long period. It involves a series of *subdecisions* that together add up to a final vocational selection. Each subdecision is important because it limits the individual's subsequent freedom of choice and the ability to achieve his or her original goal. For example, a decision to take a vocational track in high school makes it more difficult to decide later to go to college. Extra time, effort, and sometimes money must be expended to make up for a lack of preparation. As children mature, they gain knowledge and exposure to alternatives; they learn to understand themselves and their environment; and they are better able to make rational choices. Most of these choices involve making comparisons between an ideal and reality. Ginzberg divided the process of occupational choice into three stages: fantasy, tentative, and realistic.

Fantasy Stage

The fantasy stage generally occurs up to age 11. During this time, children imagine the workers they want to be without regard to needs, abilities, training, employment opportunities, or any realistic considerations. They want to be airline pilots, teachers, quarterbacks, ballerinas, and so forth. Most commonly, the careers they select are glamorous and easily identifiable because of particular costumes the workers wear.

Tentative Stage

The tentative stage spans ages 11 through 17 and is subdivided into four periods or substages. During the *interest period,* from ages 11 to 12, children make their choices primarily based on their likes and interests. This stage represents a transition between fantasy choice and tentative choice. The second period, the *capacities period,* occurs between ages 13 and 14. During this period, adolescents become aware of job requirements, occupational rewards, and needed levels of preparation. They are primarily thinking of their own abilities in regard to career success. During the third period, the *values period,* from ages 15 to 16, adolescents attempt to relate occupational roles to their own interests and values, to synthesize job requirements

with their own values and capacities. They consider both the occupation and their own interests. The fourth and last stage, which occurs at around age 17, is a *transition period,* in which adolescents make transitions from tentative to realistic choices in response to pressures from school, peers, parents, colleges, and the circumstances of graduating from high school.

Realistic Stage

During the realistic stage, from age 17 on, adolescents seek further clarification and resolution of their vocational choice. This stage is subdivided into a period of *exploration* (ages 17 to 18), during which they make an intensive search to gain greater knowledge and understanding; a period of *crystallization* (between ages 19 and 21), in which they narrowly define a single set of choices and commit themselves to a general area of employment; and a period of *specification,* in which a general choice, such as physicist, is further limited to a particular type of physicist.

Ginzberg's interviews were conducted primarily with adolescents from upper-income families, who no doubt had a considerably great range of choices. The process would likely take longer for these youths than for others because they perceive themselves as having multiple and diverse opportunities. Lower-income youths often have an earlier crystallization of occupational choice, although the steps they follow still seem to parallel those of the theoretical model. Also, Ginzberg's observations were primarily of boys, although he concluded

compromise with reality theory the theory of vocational choice proposed by Ginzberg.

During the fantasy stage, young children imagine the type of work they want to do without regard to training, ability, opportunity, or other realistic considerations.

that girls parallel the first two stages—fantasy and tentative. Other research indicates that the transition to realism applies to both boys and girls, but that girls tend to keep their vocational plans more tentative and flexible than do boys.

Ginzberg's theory suffers from rigidity with respect to the exact sequence, nature, and timing of the stages; thus, it may be too artificial and contrived. Much research, however, generally supports the broad outlines of the hypothesis, but not always the chronological ages, associated with Ginzberg's different stages (e.g., Blanchard & Lichtenberg, 2003; Hartung, Porfeli, & Vondracek, 2005).

Gottfredson (1996) proposed a theory of career development similar to that of Ginzberg. She suggested that early career development involves **circumscription** and then **compromise.** When quite young, children are intrigued by large, powerful individuals. They gradually realize that men and women tend to have different jobs and work roles. By late childhood, they are attuned to the values of society and the people around them, and they recognize that different careers express different values. At this age they are also beginning to realize that some careers require abilities that they do not possess or require efforts that they are not willing to expend, and so they *circumscribe* their choices and begin rejecting careers on these bases. By early adolescence, personal interests and needs become the primary concern in career selection, as are prestige and status (Gottfredson, 2005). However, adolescents *compromise* by modifying

their choices to bring them in line with reality. Adolescents typically make *anticipatory* compromises, meaning that the modifications they make are based on expectations, not actual experiences.

Armstrong and Crombie (2000) conducted a longitudinal study of eighth- through tenth-graders and found support for the movement toward realism theorized by both Ginzberg and Gottfredson. Namely, adolescents who perceived a discrepancy between their ideals and their assessment of what was possible for them changed their career goals; the changes generally made their career selections more gender stereotyped and more realistic. Those who did not perceive a discrepancy did not modify their aspirations.

Similarly, Helwig's (2001) research also supported Ginzberg's and Gottfredson's theories. Helwig found that the tendency to select fantasy careers diminished over childhood and adolescence. It is interesting that boys lagged behind girls in this, in part because a number of them held onto the fantasy career of being a professional athlete into high school. In addition, careers that matched societal values peaked in eighth grade and then diminished. From this point onward, individual concerns began to take on more importance.

Ginzberg reformulated his theory to take new data and criticisms into account. He acknowledged that career choices do not necessarily end with the first job and that some people remain occupationally mobile throughout their work histories. He emphasized that some people—those who are economically

RESEARCH HIGHLIGHT DEVELOPMENTAL-CONTEXTUAL CONCEPTS

Research on career development emphasizes the dynamic interaction between individuals and their environments in their vocational quests. Specifically, there are three types of influences on development (Vondracek & Schulenberg, 1986, 1992):

1. *Normative, age-graded influences:* These influences, which vary with chronological time, might be biological or environmental. For example, certain types of careers, such as professional sports, demand requisite particular physical characteristics. One usually must be quite tall to be a basketball player.
2. *Normative, historical-cohort influences:* These influences may be biological or environmental in nature, too. They could include historical events such as depression, war, famine, or even the launching of *Sputnik.*
3. *Nonnormative, life-event influences:* These idiosyncratic influences might include an unexpected death of a family breadwinner, an illness, an injury, or a loss of scholarship, forcing alteration of career plans.

In other words, there may be significant influences on career choice over which the individual has minimal control. According to some researchers, *chance* plays a large role in shaping career decisions (Cabral & Salomone, 1990). Career decisions are rarely purely rational; nor are they, in most instances, based purely on chance. Some combination of planning and happenstance seems to influence the decision. Individuals are most vulnerable to the effects of chance during life transitions, particularly those that occur early in one's career and that are not anticipated. However, the ability to cope with unforeseen events depends a great deal on the strength of the individual's self-concept and the sense of internal (or enabling) control. The accident theory of vocational choice emphasizes the effect of unexpected personal events on career development but would still emphasize that some individuals are better able than others to overcome negative contingencies and to take advantage of positive developments (Scott & Hatalla, 1990).

disadvantaged and who belong to minority groups especially—do not have as many choices as people in the upper classes do. He also emphasized that there is variability in choice patterns and in the timing of crystallization, acknowledging that some people may make a stable choice from the time they are young, whereas others are never able to make an unwavering choice (Ginzberg, 1988).

Holland's Occupational Environment Theory

According to Holland's (1996) **occupational environment theory** of vocational choice, people select occupations that afford environments consistent with their personality types; they are more likely to choose and remain in a field, and be happy in it, when personal characteristics and the work environment mesh. Holland outlined six personality types—realistic, intellectual, social, conventional, enterprising, and artistic—and occupational environments compatible with these types (see Table 13.1). Thus, individuals striving for a suitable career should seek out those environments compatible with their personal orientations.

Subsequent research has generally supported Holland's theory, and it serves as the basis of much career counseling (Staff, Messersmith, & Schulenberg, 2009). It appears to work well for both males and females (Anderson, Tracey, & Rounds, 1997). It may not work as well, however, for individuals from different cultural backgrounds (e.g., Flores, Spanierman, Armstrong, et al., 2006 found it was not as effective with Mexican American high school students). Also, even though personality often does influence vocational choice, individuals sometimes elect and stay in occupations in which their personality does not match the vocational environment (Wallace-Broscious, Serafica, & Osipow, 1994): individuals may stay in a job because it offers more security, higher wages, or less travel; because it requires less education; because they are close to retirement; or because they don't want to move geographically. Also, many workers stay in jobs for which they are not perfectly suited because of personal or family obligations (Salomone & Sheehan, 1985).

ANSWERS WOULDN'T YOU LIKE TO KNOW ...

How do you know whether a career will suit you?

A career will most likely suit you if it matches your interests, abilities, and values (Ginsberg & Gottfredson) and your personality (Holland). It is also more likely to be a good match if you can count on the support of others around you (Lent et al.).

circumscription limiting one's career aspirations to a set of acceptable choices based on interests and values.

compromise modifying one's career choices to bring them in line with reality.

occupational environment theory the theory of vocational choice proposed by Holland.

TABLE 13.1	HOLLAND'S OCCUPATIONAL ENVIRONMENT THEORY	
PERSONALITY TYPE	**CHARACTERISTICS**	**SUGGESTED CAREERS**
Artistic	Likes creative activities and the arts: music, drama, drawing. Views self as expressive and independent.	Composer, fashion designer, book editor, physician, art teacher, graphic designer
Conventional	Likes structure and order and working with numbers. Views self as systematic and organized.	Bookkeeper, bank teller, postal worker, court clerk, title examiner, secretary
Enterprising	Likes to lead, persuade, and be successful. Views self as ambitious and outgoing.	City manager, lawyer, real estate agent, salesperson, school principal
Investigative	Likes math and science. Views self as intellectual and exacting.	Architect, biologist, dentist, meteorologist, pharmacist, surveyor, veterinarian
Realistic	Likes to work with machines and animals, not people. Views self as practical.	Carpenter, police officer, electrician, firefighter, pilot, locksmith, mechanic

Lent et al.'s Social-Cognitive Career Theory

Social-cognitive career theory was developed by Robert Lent, Steven Brown, and Gail Hackett (1994, 2000). They based their work on the social-cognitive theory of Albert Bandura (1986). Bandura had suggested that when deciding upon long-term goals, individuals weigh their abilities and their chances of success, but that they do this in the context of their environment. Do they have a mentor to help them and give them an "in"? Are there any barriers, such as lack of parental support, to their quest? Lent and his colleagues took these general premises and delineated how they applied to the career search process.

Social-cognitive career theory is dynamic in nature. Individuals are constantly revising and rethinking their goals based upon changes in resources and opportunities. It not only takes into account individual attributes, but also idiosyncratic environmental influences (e.g., a neighbor who owns a particular type of business) and broader societal conditions (e.g., an economic downturn).

People Influencing Vocational Choice

Parents

Parents influence their adolescent's choice of vocation in a number of ways (Whiston & Keller, 2004). One way is through direct inheritance: a son or daughter inherits the parents' business, and it seems easier and wiser to continue in it than to go off on his or her own. Similarly, parents also exert influence by providing apprenticeship training. For example, a father who is a carpenter teaches his trade to his child by taking him or her along on the job or by arranging an apprenticeship with another carpenter. In the case of low-socioeconomic-status families, the adolescent may not have many other choices.

Parents influence children's interests and activities from the time they are young by the play materials they provide, by the encouragement or discouragement of hobbies and interests, and by the activities in which they encourage their children to participate (Lent, Brown, & Hackett, 2000). A parent who is a musician exerts an influence on the child to take music lessons and to like music in a way that a nonmusician parent could never do. Parents also provide role models for their children to follow. A mother who is a lawyer, for example, exposes her child to that profession from the time the child is little. Regardless of whether parents try to exert any conscious, direct influence, the influence by example is there. Furthermore, parents provide general messages about the appropriate role of work in one's life (Bryant, Zvonkovic, & Reynolds, 2006).

Parents can certainly influence their teenagers' career interests by direct encouragement (e.g., Turner, Steward, & Lapan, 2004), and they can even direct, order, or limit their children's choices by insisting they not go to school or go to a certain school, enroll in a particular major, or start out on a predetermined career. Parents who do so without regard for the talents, interests, and desires of their adolescent may be condemning the youth to a life of work to which she or he is unsuited. Often, an adolescent has no strong objections and accedes to parental wishes from a desire to please them, from inertia, and from not knowing what else to do. One of the motives of parents for taking such a course of action is to try to get the child to take up an occupation that the parents were always interested in but never got to do; the parents live vicariously through the child. Another motive is that the parents have a vocation in which they have found satisfaction, and so they urge the adolescent to share their goals because they are sure she or he would like it, too. Stories are legion of the father who insists his son attend his alma mater, join the same fraternity, play football as he did, and become a professional like himself. Some parents exert pressure by offering or withholding money or by getting their child into their alma maters. Other parents have low educational and occupational expectations for their children, thus limiting the child's possible vocational choices (Galambos & Silbereisen, 1987).

Teenagers believe that their parents have the right to try to influence their career decisions (Young, 1994), at least within limits. Although they believe that the decision should ultimately be theirs, adolescents think that it is appropriate for parents to intervene if their child is making an important vocational choice for a bad reason (e.g., because it is the easiest path or he or she wants to stay with a boyfriend or girlfriend). Teens do not think, however, that parents should use punishment or the threat of punishment when trying to change their children's minds (Bregman & Killen, 1999).

One study found that when two parents agree on educational expectations and career goals for their adolescents, their children are more inclined to adopt the orientations held by both parents than are those who are supported by one parent and denied by the other (Smith, 1991). This same study indicated that agreement with the perceived educational and career goal of the mother is positively associated with the mother's formal education. In the case of the father, high occupational status—professional, managerial, or substantial business ownership—appears to increase adolescent agreement with perceived paternal educational and career goals. In summary, when the mother's education or the father's occupational status is high enough, it promotes adolescent agreement with the perceived educational and career goals of the parents (Smith, 1991).

One way that parents can influence their adolescent's choice of vocation is by acting as a role model. "Take Your Children to Work" day gives a child the opportunity to see his or her parent on the job.

the adolescents in the family (Kracke & Schmitt-Rodermund, 2001). Other research has confirmed that adolescents who have strong attachments to their parents experience enhanced career development (Ketterson & Blustein, 1997). One study, for example, found that family functioning, as evaluated by eleventh-grade students and their parents, was a more frequent and stronger predictor of career development than gender, socioeconomic status, or educational achievement (Penick & Jepsen, 1992). In this study, *family functioning* was measured by factors such as cohesion, emotional expression, degree of conflict, organization, sociability, democratic government, and enmeshment.

Peers

Studies of the relative influence of parents and peers on the educational plans of adolescents (relating to the level of vocation rather than to the particular job) reveal somewhat contradictory findings. Actually, the majority of adolescents hold plans in agreement with those of both their parents and their friends. Thus, friends reinforce parental aspirations because adolescents associate with peers whose goals are consistent with parental goals.

It has been found that the extent of upward mobility of working-class adolescents depends on the influences of both parents and peers. Working-class adolescents are most likely to aspire to high-ranking occupations if they are influenced in this direction simultaneously by both parents and peers and are least likely to be high aspirers if they are subjected to neither of these influences. In addition, Kracke (2002) found that friends could positively influence one another to think about career choices and to actively seek information about careers.

Research has found that parents who are warm and supportive are more likely to have adolescent children who are more focused in their career explorations and more certain of their career choices (e.g., Constantine, Wallace, & Kindaichi, 2005). Families that exhibit a democratic family style and are able to resolve conflict exert strong influences on career development of

School Personnel

To what extent do school personnel influence adolescents' educational plans? In some instances, they have a great deal of influence. For example, a teacher or coach who acts as a student's mentor can provide information and advice about careers. Sometimes, a student's personal connection with a teacher makes him or her want to emulate that teacher, and a new career interest is born. Encouragement and praise from mentors can give students a feeling of self-efficacy and competence with a particular subject, opening up the possibility of a related career (Quimby & DeSantis, 2006).

Conversely, we probably all knew students who had the opposite experience: They were so bored or frightened by a teacher that they never pursued any more courses related to that teacher's topic. I personally know several girls who in high school stopped taking upper-level math courses because they were intimidated by a

ANSWERS WOULDN'T YOU LIKE TO KNOW ...

Do most teens think that their parents should have a say in their career plans?

Most teens believe that their parents should have *some* say in their career plans and are entitled to use gentle persuasion to guide them. Teens also believe, however, that unless they are being foolish, their parents should respect their choices.

ANSWERS WOULDN'T YOU LIKE TO KNOW ...

Who besides his or her parents can influence an adolescent's career choice?

Friends, teachers, coaches, and guidance counselors can all help influence an adolescent's career decision. Whether through encouragement or discouragement, such individuals can make a strong and lasting impression.

frankly sexist math teacher. He made them feel so stupid and self-conscious that they were convinced that they couldn't do math. The girls' ongoing refusal to take additional courses that even touched on mathematics (such as chemistry or physics) prevented them from being able to pursue science careers. Clearly, discouragement can be as powerful a tool as encouragement.

Teachers, coaches, and guidance counselors can help (or hinder!) students in conducting a realistic appraisal of their skills and abilities. These school personnel are likely to have knowledge about the types of skills needed for various occupations related to their disciplines. Given that, they can help students develop alternative, related goals if the students' initial goals do not seem plausible. In the field of psychology, for example, students should learn about the range of careers that exist in the helping profession. There are many alternative routes to working with people in need that most students don't know about. Giving these students advice as to how to build their résumés so that they will ultimately be employable is a large and enjoyable part of what college advisors do. Most colleges have a career services office that also can provide this sort of assistance.

Gender Roles and Vocational Choice

Adolescents are strongly influenced by societal expectations as to the type of work that men and women should do (Jozefowicz, Barber, & Mollasis, 1994). Women have traditionally been channeled into a narrow range of careers: teacher, secretary, librarian, waitress, and so on. In 2007, only 30 percent of physicians but 92 percent of nurses were women (U.S. Bureau of Labor Statistics, 2008c). See Figure 13.1 for a list of the jobs most and least likely to be held by American women.

Three types of barriers have been identified in efforts to explain why women are underrepresented in many high-paying professions (Fiorentine, 1988): *structural barriers, normative barriers,* and *cognitive differences.* **Structural barriers** are externally imposed limits on a woman's career success that result from gender discrimination. Some firms refuse to hire women for important

FIGURE 13.1   OCCUPATIONS WITH THE HIGHEST AND LOWEST PERCENTAGES OF FEMALE WORKERS

Source: Data from U.S. Bureau of Labor Statistics (2008c).

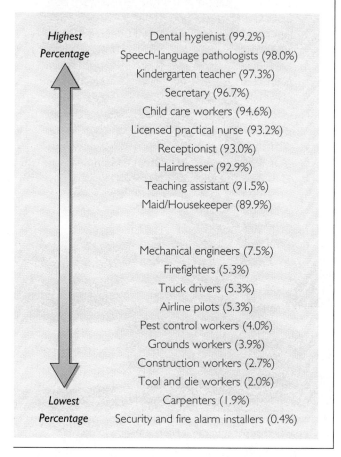

jobs, deny them promotions even if they do well in the jobs they have, and deny them perks granted to male employees.

Normative barriers stem from how girls are socialized to be feminine, which for most includes valuing motherhood and placing great importance on the relationships in their lives (e.g., Cinamon & Rich, 2002). Having these goals can channel women away from high-powered careers, since caring for children while putting in 10-hour days at the office is a daunting prospect. Also, many women believe that their husbands' jobs come first, and so they make decisions that hurt their own career prospects. For example, many wives relocate so that their husbands can get a promotion even if it means that they themselves lose seniority.

The third barrier to women's professional success, cognitive differences, implies that women don't make it into executive and other high-level positions because they are psychologically different from men. Specifically, women are supposed to be less talented in certain domains or lack other traits, such as assertiveness, that are needed to climb to the top of the corporate ladder or make important scientific discoveries. If these views seem hopelessly old-fashioned, recall that the president of Harvard University, Larry Summers, was forced to resign in the summer of 2006 after he stated that he believed it's possible that women are cognitively incapable of being top-notch scientists.

Although diminishing, structural and normative barriers still affect girls in high school and college. If girls are aware of these barriers or believe they exist (even if they do not), many will avoid career paths they perceive as problematic (Messersmith, Garrett, Davis-Kean, et al., 2008). Also, perhaps because in most cases the burdens of child care continue to fall more heavily on women than men, adolescent girls tend to value careers that allow them flexibility (Rottinghaus & Zytowski, 2006), thus ruling out time-intensive careers or those with unpredictable hours.

Adolescents are strongly influenced by societal expectations of what types of work women and men should do. That explains, in part, why there are many women kindergarten teachers but few women construction workers.

ANSWERS WOULDN'T YOU LIKE TO KNOW ...

Do men and women today have equal career opportunities?

Although the situation is gradually improving, many careers are still less available to women than men. Structural barriers include various types of gender discrimination, such as not promoting women to high-level positions. Normative barriers still exist, too. Women shoulder the bulk of family responsibilities and hence many shy away from having an intense, time-demanding career.

As to cognitive differences, no significant gender differences in intelligence exist (see Chapter 5). Similarly, other potential differences—such as achievement motivation and self-confidence—are largely tied to how individuals perceive tasks. Both boys and girls are motivated to succeed when they believe that a given task is appropriate for their gender; both are more confident in their abilities when they perceive the task to be gender appropriate. Cognitive differences, such as they are, are not intrinsic to the sexes but result from gender stereotypes (Brannon, 1999).

Initially, girls have higher career aspirations than boys, perhaps because they are stronger students in their early years (Mau & Bikos, 2000). But after high school, girls' vocational aspirations drop, becoming more traditional and less prestigious. Many young women ultimately opt for careers that underutilize their talents and abilities (O'Brien, Friedman, Tipton, et al., 2000). The interplay of socialization, role expectations, discrimination (real or perceived), and different interests contributes to this drop.

Other Crucial Determinants of Vocational Choice

Aptitudes and Special Abilities

Different occupations require different aptitudes and special abilities. For instance, some occupations require strength, others speed, and still others good eye-hand coordination or good spatial visualization. Some require special talent such as artistic, musical, or verbal skills. Some fields require creativity, originality, and autonomy; others require conformity,

structural barriers   externally imposed limits on a woman's career success that result from sex discrimination.

normative barriers   limitations on career choice that stem from how girls are socialized to be feminine.

cooperation, and ability to take direction. Possession or lack of certain aptitudes may be crucial in immediate job success or in the possibility of success with training and experience. Certainly, increasing technology requires more and more specialized training and abilities.

A person must not only possess a needed skill to successfully perform a job but must also *believe* that he or she possesses that skill or has the ability to master it. Psychologists term this **self-efficacy** (Bandura, 2001), and research has shown that perceived self-efficacy influences teenagers' career choices (Bandura, Barbaranelli, Caprara, et al., 2001). For example, one study demonstrated that Mexican American middle-schoolers who believe that they are academically strong in math and science are more likely to pursue careers in the sciences (Navarro, Flores, & Worthington, 2007).

Interests

Interest is another factor considered important to vocational success. The more interested people are in their work, the more likely they will succeed. To put it another way, all other things being equal, the more a person's interests parallel those of people who are already successful in a field, the more likely they are to be successful, too. Vocational interest tests are based on this last principle: they measure clusters of interests

RESEARCH HIGHLIGHT   WHY SO FEW WOMEN SCIENTISTS?

The path to becoming a scientist begins early—at the latest, while one is in high school. In order to pursue a science career, one must learn how to do science by taking the appropriate courses. Girls start off fine, succeeding as well or better than boys in math and science during elementary school. This begins to change in junior high school, although the differences at this point are small (American Association of University Women, 1992). Boys begin spending more time working on science activities during these years (Lee & Burkam, 1996), and by high school, boys have more positive attitudes than girls toward science (Weinburgh, 1995). When girls do elect to take science courses, they tend to limit themselves to biology, avoiding physics and chemistry. This trend continues in college. Although 58 percent of both the bachelor's and master's degrees earned in the United States went to women in 2002–2003 (National Center for Education Statistics, 2005), women earn only 28 percent of the graduate degrees in math, 41 percent in chemistry, 25 percent in computer science, and 5 percent in physics (National Science Foundation, 2008). The backgrounds of most women in high school and college who drop out of science suggest that they have the *ability* to succeed in science; what they seem to lack is the *desire* (Ware & Lee, 1988).

Why do girls avoid science? Many factors contribute, including sexism and discouragement from others. Girls who plan to pursue science are first and foremost interested in the topic but also have had a positive history with it: good grades, friends' support, extracurricular experiences, and encouraging mothers (Jacobs, Finken, Griffen, et al., 1998). Girls who shun science have not had this support. In addition, they perceive themselves as being different from "scientists" or "science students" (Lee, 1998); the career does not match their self-image, usually because the field is perceived as a masculine endeavor. They often do not believe that they are "good" at math, regardless of their grades (Simpkins, Davis-Kean, & Eccles, 2006). In addition, many young women believe that science careers are not right for them because they desire careers that let them have warm interactions with coworkers and help others. Women generally do not perceive science careers as being as conducive to these values as other types of careers and hence are less interested in them (Morgan, Isaac, & Sansone, 2001).

Furthermore, girls tend to score lower than boys on measures of Holland's realistic personality type (Turner, Conkel, Starkey, et al., 2008). Persons with realistic personalities like to tinker with objects, use their hands, and fix things. It follows that these individuals will likely gravitate toward careers in engineering and the natural sciences. Even when girls are interested in mechanical objects and manipulative kinds of activities, they often feel less competent at them than boys.

Betz and Schilano (1999) demonstrated that it is possible to raise young women's low levels of self-efficacy concerning mechanical objects. They devised a seven-hour intervention based on Bandura's (1977) four-part social learning model. During three sessions, college women were shown how to use various tools and to read blueprints. They were also given tasks with equipment and coached so that they succeeded in them, they were encouraged and rewarded for their efforts, and they practiced relaxation and anxiety reduction techniques. At the end of the intervention, the women felt more mechanically competent. This study demonstrated that even a relatively short-term intervention can erase some of the negative feelings that limit women's occupational choices. If these sorts of activities were paired with encouragement, exploration opportunities, and female role modeling, more women would likely choose science careers.

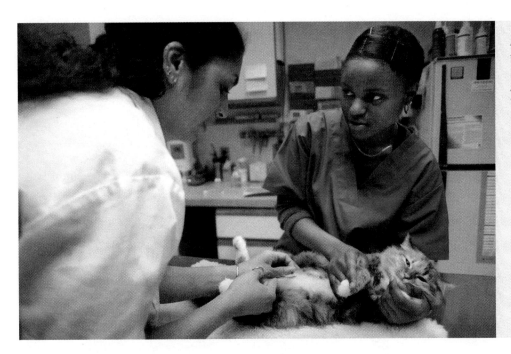

Adolescent girls are less likely than adolescent boys to be interested in science careers, in good part because working in the sciences is perceived as a masculine endeavor.

similar to those of successful people in the field to predict the possibility of success. The individual is counseled to consider vocations in the fields of greatest interest.

Perhaps the most commonly used of these tests is the **Strong Interest Inventory** (Strong, 1943). In its current form, it is based in part upon Holland's occupational environment theory. The test contains approximately 300 multiple-choice questions and takes about 25 minutes to complete. In addition to providing information about work style preferences (e.g., willingness to assume

self-efficacy   the belief that one is competent to master a task.

Strong Interest Inventory   a test that measures suitability for different vocations according to interests.

CROSS-CULTURAL CONCERNS   THE SCHOOL-TO-WORK TRANSITION FOR AMERICAN VERSUS EUROPEAN ADOLESCENTS

Kerckhoff (2002) has described a number of aspects of American adolescents' school-to-work transition that are unique to these youths or at least different from those faced by adolescents in most European countries. How do the American and European experiences differ?

- Most American students pursue general courses of study that are not tied to specific careers, whereas European students tend to be more career focused.
- American adolescents generally have less institutional support for their job searches.
- In the United States, the two criteria that are most important in getting a job are having a high school diploma and having a college degree. These two accomplishments are usually separated by at least four years and often more, and many adolescents begin but then drop out of college. Unfortunately for current students and dropouts, a little bit of college does little for

one's job prospects, which is not the case in most European nations. Furthermore, those who do graduate from college find that further study does not dramatically increase their employment prospects.

- American adolescents are generally older than European adolescents when they begin working full time.
- Having a college degree is more important for American than European adolescents. The gap in the kinds of jobs, pay scales, benefits, and promotional opportunities available to those with a bachelor's degree and those without is greater in the United States than in Europe.
- American adolescents without a college degree are more likely to face periods of unemployment than their European counterparts.
- American adolescents are more likely to return to school after they have been working full time than European adolescents.

**FIGURE 13.2
OCCUPATIONS
PROJECTED TO
GAIN THE MOST
NEW JOBS, 2006–2016**

Source: Data from U.S. Bureau of
Labor Statistics (2008b).

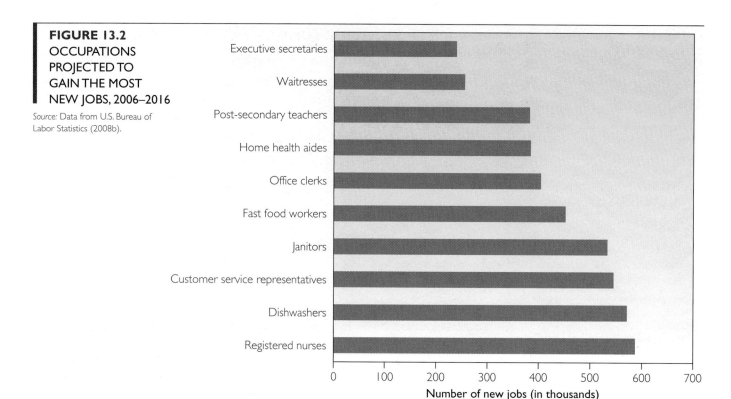

Number of new jobs (in thousands)

Job Opportunities

Being interested in a field does not mean that jobs are available in it. Some employment fields, such as agricultural work, are becoming smaller; others, such as clerical work, are becoming larger. There has been a continued shift toward white-collar and service occupations. This means youths need to control interests as well as be controlled by them, for interests and job availability are not synonymous (Mitchell, 1988).

What are the employment opportunities in various occupations? Figure 13.2 shows projected increases from 2006 to 2016 in selected occupations (U.S. Bureau of Labor Statistics, 2008b). Most of the jobs showing the greatest numbers of openings do not require a bachelor's degree. Figure 13.3 lists the careers that *do* require a college degree and are projected to have the most openings through 2016. Note that postsecondary teachers, general operations managers, and accountants head the list.

leadership), the test matches the characteristics of the taker with those of individuals in more than 100 different occupations.

**FIGURE 13.3   PROJECTED GAINS
IN CAREERS REQUIRING COLLEGE
DEGREES, 2006–2016**

Source: Data from U.S. Bureau of Labor Statistics (2008b).

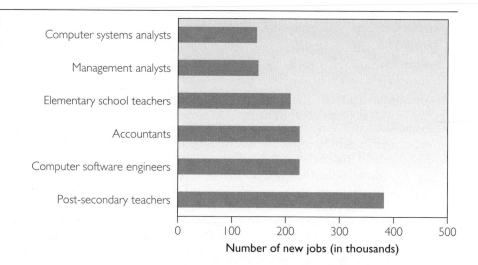

Number of new jobs (in thousands)

TABLE 13.2 AVERAGE STARTING SALARIES OFFERED TO GRADUATES WITH BACHELOR'S DEGREES, 2007

FIELD	AVERAGE STARTING SALARY
Actuary	$53,754
Electrical engineer	$55,292
Web designer	$47,000
Chemist	$41,506
Biologists	$34,953
Teacher	$31,753
Forester	$28,862
Graphic designer	$35,000

Source: Data from *Occupational Outlook Handbook*, U.S. Bureau of Labor Statistics (2009).

Salary

One factor that plays a role in vocational selection is the salary that can be expected. Salaries, of course, vary widely by profession; there are also regional variations in compensation. Table 13.2 shows the average starting salaries for 2007 graduates with bachelor's degrees in different fields.

Socioeconomic Factors

Familiarity

Socioeconomic status (SES) tends to influence the knowledge and understanding youths have of different occupations (Weinger, 2000). Middle-class teenagers are more able than teenagers from lower-SES groups to develop broad vocational interests and an awareness of opportunities beyond the local community. Adolescents from lower-SES families have seen less, read less, and heard less about different careers. They have experienced less variety in their environment in general and have had fewer work and apprenticeship opportunities than youths from higher SES levels. As a result, low-SES adolescents are inclined to take the only jobs they know about at the time they enter the labor market.

Social Status and Aspirations

Middle-class youths tend to choose occupations with higher status than do lower-SES youths (Rojewski & Kim, 2003). A number of considerations determine why this is so. To aspire to a position is one thing; to expect to actually achieve it is another. Poverty-level youths more often than middle-SES youths aspire to jobs they do not expect to achieve, but the fact that lower-SES youths realize the remoteness of reaching

their goal often makes them lower their level of aspirations (Chang, Chen, Greenberger, et al., 2006). Of course, sometimes guidance counselors, teachers, parents, or others try to persuade lower-status youths to attempt to break into higher-paying jobs. These youths can succeed if they have the drive to work hard and have been provided with the basic skills they need to succeed in their chosen field of employment.

Still another factor enters in: a correlation between academic ability and socioeconomic status. In general, the higher the status, the higher is the academic performance; and the better the students' academic performances, the more prestigious is the occupations to which they aspire (Watson, Quatman, & Edler, 2002). Apparently, students see their high academic ability as providing access to high-prestige occupations. Occupational aspiration is thereby related to both social class and academic aptitude.

Race/Ethnicity and Aspirations

When race and ethnicity are considered apart from socioeconomic status, there is little evidence that race or ethnicity alone is a large determinative factor in occupational aspirations (Fouad & Byars-Winston, 2005). However, African American youths of lower socioeconomic status have lower aspirations, just as do White youths of lower status. Regardless of aspirations, there are fewer employment opportunities for youths than for adults and fewer opportunities for African Americans than for Whites—and they know it (Gloria & Hird, 1999).

Some studies have found differences between Asian Americans and White Americans in their occupational aspirations. Asian Americans place greater emphasis on extrinsic and security occupational value clusters (e.g., making more money and having a stable, prestigious, secure future) in comparison with White Americans

"Am I glad I worked at a fast-food restaurant? Yeah, I definitely am (though I probably would have had a different answer if you had asked me that at six in the morning before work). I wasn't planning on working there—let me start with that. However, I learned very quickly that freedom of choice in the job market for precollege teens is basically nonexistent. So my good friend got me a job and that was that.

"What an eye-opener. It was a great thing to do before heading off to college. To be blunt, that is not a job I would want to wake up to every day of my life, so I had better not screw up the next four years because I need that degree. You know, I think one major fault in today's society is in what types of careers receive respect. World-famous doctors and lawyers and successful businesspeople all deserve a whole bunch of kudos for their talent, tenacity, and hard work. But at least when they drive off to work every morning in their BMWs from their nice homes, they are going to do something that not only pays well but that they genuinely enjoy doing. Fast-food workers, on the other hand, get a crappy job, no appreciation, and a whole lot less money for what they do. Now tell me, which would you prefer? I have enormous admiration for people who get up every day for a job they hate that doesn't even pay well but do it anyways so that they can support themselves and their families.

"I have no brilliant philosophy to sum it all up, but I seriously think the country would be a better place if everyone had to work fast food at least once in their lives. I learned a lot about the real world."

ANSWERS WOULDN'T YOU LIKE TO KNOW . . .
Do most teenagers have jobs?

Yes. If we count freelance jobs such as baby-sitting and lawn mowing, most teens begin working by age 14. More than 90 percent of teens work at some point before they graduate from high school.

(Leung, Ivey, & Susuki, 1999). This effect is much more pronounced for Asian American women than Asian American men (Song & Glick, 2004).

Youth Employment

The vast majority of today's American teenagers work before they graduate from high school. Is this a good trend? Do the short- and long-term benefits of working outweigh the costs? How much work is too much?

How does uncompensated work (volunteering) benefit adolescent development? These are the questions we address in this section.

Working for Wages

Scope of Youth Employment

The number of adolescents who work outside the home for wages has increased dramatically in the past few decades. In 1987, about one-third of American high school sophomores and two-thirds of high school seniors held jobs during the school year. In the mid- to late-1990s, however, more than three-fourths worked by age 16 (Mihalic & Elliott, 1997). Nowadays, nearly 90 percent of high school students hold down formal jobs before they graduate (Hirschman & Voloshin, 2007). And when irregular freelance work, such as baby-sitting and lawn mowing, are included, that figure rises even higher.

Many teenagers begin working even before they enter high school, especially when those with irregular jobs are included in the count. In one study, more than half of 14-year-olds reported having had some kind of job, and among 15-year-olds, that figure rose to about 65 percent. In all, nearly 3 million 15- to 17-year-old adolescents work during the academic year, and 4 million work during the summer months (Herman, 2000).

What kinds of work do adolescents do? Many jobs are forbidden to adolescents, especially those younger than 16. Table 13.3 lists some of federal limits on adolescent employment.

Most adolescent girls work in restaurants and retail stores, especially grocery stores. They also work in entertainment venues (such as movie theaters), serve as maids and child care workers, and are employed by construction firms. Most boys also work in restaurants, retail stores, and construction, but they are more likely than girls to work as landscaping aides, with livestock, in factories, and in gas stations. Girls are more likely to work freelance than boys, and they are more likely to be employed by private individuals rather than by companies. Figure 13.4 illustrates the breakdown of school-year employment for male and female adolescents.

Other gender differences in employment include that boys are more likely to work during the school year than girls, and boys work longer hours. However, these gender differences decrease as teenagers get older.

How long do adolescents work and how much do they get paid? Fifteen- to 17-year-olds who have jobs work an average of 17 hours a week during the school year (Herman, 2000), and 29 hours a week during the summer months (Stringer, 2003). In 2006, they earned an average of $7.23 an hour, which was more than the minimum wage (Morisi, 2008).

TABLE 13.3 FEDERAL LIMITS ON ADOLESCENT EMPLOYMENT

LIMITS ON 14- AND 15-YEAR-OLDS	LIMITS ON 16- AND 17-YEAR-OLDS
Cannot work in manufacturing, processing, and mining jobs	Cannot work with hazardous materials
Cannot work in transportation, construction, and warehouse jobs	Cannot operate motor vehicles
Cannot use power-driven machinery	Cannot operate most power-driven machinery

During academic year:
  Cannot work during school hours
  Cannot work more than 18 hours/week
  Cannot work more than 3 hours/day
  Hours restricted to 7 A.M. through 7 P.M.
	Cannot work in most excavating or demolition jobs
	
	Cannot work in mines
	
	Cannot work in slaughterhouses

During summer months
  Cannot work more than 40 hours/week
  Cannot work more than 8 hours/day
  Hours restricted to 7 A.M. through 9 P.M.	

Source: http://www.dol.gov/elaws/esa/flsa/docs/haznonag.asp

FIGURE 13.4 JOBS HELD BY 15- TO 17-YEAR-OLD MALES AND FEMALES DURING THE ACADEMIC YEAR

Source: Herman (2000), p. 36.

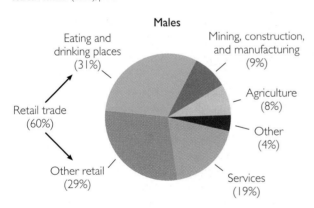

Males

Eating and drinking places (31%)
Retail trade (60%)
Other retail (29%)
Mining, construction, and manufacturing (9%)
Agriculture (8%)
Other (4%)
Services (19%)

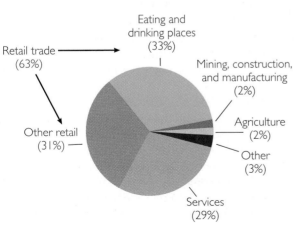

Females

Eating and drinking places (33%)
Retail trade (63%)
Other retail (31%)
Mining, construction, and manufacturing (2%)
Agriculture (2%)
Other (3%)
Services (29%)

It had been common for the number of teenagers who worked for wages to dramatically increase during the summer months. (Adolescents obviously have more free time once school is no longer is session.) In recent years, this trend has become less evident. In July 2008, the proportion of 16- to 19-year-olds who were either employed or looking for work was 65.1 percent; this was the lowest percentage since 1989. Most economists attribute this to the fact that more and more students are attending summer school. Whereas summer school used to be something of a last resort for students who had fallen behind, summer courses are now taken by a much broader range of students (e.g., those who wish to be able to fit in additional science courses before they graduate). Students who are enrolled in summer school are quite a bit less likely also to work than students who do not take summer classes (Bureau of Labor Statistics, 2008a).

Correlates of Adolescent Employment

In addition to gender, other factors predict which adolescents will and will not work. White adolescents are more likely to be employed than minority adolescents.

● **ANSWERS WOULDN'T YOU LIKE TO KNOW ...**

Which teens are most likely to work?

White, middle-SES-level teenagers from intact families are more likely to work than adolescents from other SES and racial/ethnic groups. Why? They have more access to jobs, as it's easer for them to get hired and to have the transportation needed to get to work. These teens do not have a greater desire to work than others.

Adolescents from higher-SES homes are more likely to work than those from lower-SES homes, and those from intact families are more likely to work than those from single-parent families (U.S. Bureau of Labor Statistics, 2000). Since teenagers living in lower-SES neighborhoods likely cannot find work as readily as middle-class teenagers, each of these differences is probably a matter of job availability rather than motivation. When they can find work, disadvantaged teens tend to work more hours than their middle-class counterparts (Staff & Mortimer, 2008).

Effects of Employment

Most people believe that working is good for teenagers (Mortimer, 2003). After all, it teaches them responsibility, exposes them to the world of work, and gives them the opportunity to manage their own money. Are these people correct? The cost/benefit ratio seems to depend on three factors: how many hours per week are spent at the job, the nature of the job itself, and how many weeks per year are spent working.

Most researchers agree that youths should not spend too many hours working. By any standard, however, American teens spend a lot of time working compared to teens in other industrialized nations. Whereas most American high school students work part time, only about 25 percent of Japanese and Taiwanese students do (Fuligni & Stevenson, 1995); almost no French or Russian teenagers work (Alsaker & Flammer, 1999). Moreover, U.S. adolescents work longer hours:, more than three times as many, as Northern European students (Larson & Verma, 1999).

The question is, how much is *too* much? There are two competing views. The first is that any employment is bad since it takes adolescents away from other, more important activities, such as schoolwork or family time. The second is that work is good in small doses, even though too much overall is harmful. Again, most adults believe this. If this were true, then teenagers who work only a few hours per week should look better in terms of grades or social adjustment than teenagers who do not work at all, but teens who work many hours should look worse.

Which view is correct? Although the data are somewhat contradictory, the best research converges

RESEARCH HIGHLIGHT   WORK, MILITARY, OR COLLEGE?

After leaving high school, adolescents have to choose among going to college, working as a civilian, or joining the military. (Very few want to, or can afford to be, unemployed indefinitely.) Research has attempted to identify the factors that lead youth to decide to enter the workforce, enlist in the military, or matriculate in college after graduation from high school. An especially fine study on this topic was conducted by Jerald Bachman and his colleagues at the University of Michigan (Bachman, Segal, Freedman-Doan, et al., 2000).

They found that *work* is chosen by boys from large families in the lower socioeconomic strata, who were enrolled in high school vocational tracks, and who worked more hours in their senior year than those in the college-bound group. Compared with enlisters or matriculators, workers tended to have the lowest intellectual ability and to have friends who were the least impressed by going to college. Boys who early on believed that their parents wanted them to enter the workforce after high school were significantly more likely to do so.

Approximately 200,000 young adults annually enlist in the armed forces (Segal & Segal, 2004); many more, in fact, two-thirds of all adolescents, consider doing so (Gibson, Griepentrog, & Marsh, 2007). Bachman et al. found that the *military* was chosen by boys who tended to express little desire to attend college, were generally from large families in the lower socioeconomic strata, were enrolled in a vocational track, and were poor students when contrasted to the boys headed for college. The military bound, as opposed to those headed for one of the other choices, were most likely to come from nonfarming backgrounds, to have failed a grade, and to believe their parents would be happy if they served in the military. The military group tended to be more vocal about their attitudes but was not significantly more hawkish than the college-bound group. African American teens are more likely to enlist than either Latino or non-Hispanic Caucasian youth, and Latinos are more likely to enlist than Caucasians. Those who join the military are more likely to come from one-parent homes and to be from the South.

The *college* choice was selected by boys who came from the smallest families and the highest socioeconomic-status backgrounds, who had the highest grade point averages and were in a college track, who had a strong intention of going to college, and who worked the least number of hours in twelfth grade. In addition, boys with higher intellectual ability and friends who were impressed by going to college were more likely to go to college instead of to work (Owens, 1992).

The first real job for many adolescents is at a fast-food restaurant. The boring nature of the work, the rapid pace, and the low pay may sour some adolescents' attitudes toward work but prompt others to continue with their education and prepare themselves for a better career.

on the same answer: the common wisdom is wrong. In most cases, *any* amount of working does more harm than good. For example, Marsh and Kleitman (2005) analyzed data collected on 12,000 students from the time they entered middle school until two years after high school graduation. Even after taking into account the effects causes by socioeconomic status, ethnicity, family constellation, and so on, the researchers found a strong, negative pattern of effects of working in grades 8, 10, and 12 on twelfth-grade and postsecondary outcomes. For example, those who worked were less likely to have assumed leadership roles, were more likely to have developed bad habits such as smoking cigarettes or drinking alcohol, had worse grades, participated in fewer extracurricular activities, took easier courses, and were less likely to go to college. It was somewhat surprising that working as a senior was more harmful than working as a sophomore or as a middle school student. Fifteen of the 23 outcomes the researchers examined were adversely affected by working as a senior. The only positive effect was that those who worked were more likely to be employed after they left high school than those who had not. Furthermore, the hill-shaped function that one would expect with the commonsense model (a little is good, a lot is bad) was not seen for any of the variables the researchers examined; instead, the effects were largely linear and cumulative. In other words, two hours were worse than one, three hours were worse than two, and so on.

ANSWERS WOULDN'T YOU LIKE TO KNOW ...

Is it good or bad for adolescents to have paying jobs?

It's more good than bad for lower-income adolescents, as having had a job will help them get another job after high school. But working is more bad than good for middle-class adolescents, especially if they work long hours.

Other studies have had similar results in analyzing other outcome variables. Other negative outcomes that have been associated with working include increased absenteeism from school, less time spent with family, diminished parental control, increased probability of dropping out, and increased use of alcohol and marijuana (Lee & Staff, 2007; Manning, 1990; Steinberg & Dornbusch, 1991; Warren, 2002).

What explains the negative outcomes of employment? Since most of the studies were correlational rather than experimental—that is, they compared self-selected groups of working adolescents with self-selected nonworkers—it is legitimate to wonder the degree to which the differences in substance abuse, poor grades, and the like existed before the employed adolescents began working or if they resulted from working. The causality does appear to go in both directions: that is, students who are disengaged from school and family are more likely to work, and those who work are more likely to see their grades drop, engage in illegal activities, and so forth (Apel, Bushway, Brame, et al., 2007; Mihalic & Elliott, 1997).

Still, working directly contributes to problem behavior by providing youths the income to spend on alcohol and drugs, the time away from home to privately engage in undesirable behaviors, and the opportunity to be with peers who are uninterested in school and prove to be delinquent (Osgood, 1999). In addition, it allows for less involvement in sports, music, or community service activities, opportunities known to be beneficial to youth (Barber, Eccles, & Stone, 2001). Teens who work long hours get less sleep and more frequently skip breakfast than their peers, and this, too, can contribute to lack of academic success (Safron, Bachman, & Schulenberg, 2001).

Steinberg and his colleagues (Steinberg, Greenberger, Garduque, et al., 1982) were the first to suggest that adolescents who work are likely to develop cynical, negative attitudes about working, including tolerance for petty theft and for lying to the boss. Many adolescents develop negative attitudes when they work at stressful, fast-paced, unpleasant jobs that they feel are irrelevant to their future career goals (Mortimer, Pimentel, Ryu, et al., 1996; Ritzer, 2000). When adolescents work in interesting, agreeable jobs, they don't become cynical. Unfortunately, even brief exposure to a noxious workplace can increase cynicism (Loughlin & Barling, 1998), and the longer one spends working in unsatisfying conditions, the more likely one will develop a pessimistic, unethical attitude (Mihalic & Elliott, 1997).

From the adolescents' point of view, of course, working has benefits. First and foremost, it provides them with money to buy things. (Most of the money that teenagers earn goes to buying themselves luxury items rather than to helping support the family or to saving for college.) Besen (2006) claims that jobs also give adolescents a sense of control over their lives (due, in part, to having disposable income that is under their own control), a time when they can be in charge, outlets for creativity, and a time to be with and talk to friends. (This may explain why one often has to wait 10 minutes to check out when trying to buy clothing in a teen-oriented shop.)

Several studies have suggested that although working while in high school may be detrimental to middle-class youth, it might not be a risk factor for impoverished youth (National Research Council, 1998); in fact, it appears to help them find jobs once they leave school. (This ties back to Marsh and Kleitman's findings.) In addition, working during high school significantly increases impoverished students' earning power after high school (Staff & Mortimer, 2008). This is, in part,

because students from low-income homes who work are more likely to complete high school than those who do not work (Carr, Wright, & Brody, 1996). Impoverished male adolescents who work are more likely to go on to college than their nonworking counterparts (Leventhal, Graber, & Brooks-Gunn, 2001), which might suggest that working during high school is indicative of high aspirations in poverty-class youth.

Volunteerism

Just as youths' participation in paid employment has increased over the past 30 years, so has their participation in *unpaid employment*. Between 50 and 65 percent of high school students do at least some volunteer work each year (Niemi, Hepburn, & Chapman, 2000). And given the benefits that volunteerism brings to self

ANSWERS WOULDN'T YOU LIKE TO KNOW ...
Do adolescents like doing unpaid volunteer work?
Most adolescents who do volunteer work find it a good experience and say that they plan to continue volunteering in the future.

IN THEIR OWN WORDS

"I would strongly agree that a real problem with adolescent employment is the large number of stressful, boring, and irrelevant jobs. I worked one summer as a cashier at a pharmacy, and I spent a lot of my time there dealing with a hung-over manager, sweeping the floors, and getting yelled at by little old ladies because Revlon stopped making their favorite color lipstick. I never got any positive feedback, and I felt like a monkey could have done my job with enough training.

"The pharmacy job wasn't completely awful, but I had a much better experience doing occasional volunteer work during the school year. I worked with kids at Volunteers of America, and I actually felt useful there. I also got exposure to a lot of different kinds of people and situations, whereas the pharmacy only exposed me to other bored and frustrated teenagers. It would have been nice to do the volunteer-type work while also getting paid!"

and society, it is not surprising that support for volunteer programs is high. For example, in 2009, the federal government earmarked $97 million to fund summer community service programs for middle and high school students. Many high schools now require students to engage in some community service work (Reinders & Youniss, 2006).

Research has found that adolescents from two-parent homes, especially those in which the mother is a full-time homemaker, are most likely to donate their time (Raskoff & Sundeen, 1994). Adolescents are more likely to engage in public service work if their parents also do so, if they are from higher-level socioeconomic backgrounds, and if they have high grade point averages (Mustillo, Wilson, & Lynch, 2004). Most studies have found that girls are more likely than boys to volunteer.

Community service appears to provide a number of benefits. Volunteers gain skills and knowledge. Identity development is stimulated when individuals reflect on their place in society, their moral values, and their role in social change (Yates & Youniss, 1996). Community service is correlated with high self-esteem (Johnson, Beebe, Mortimer, et al., 1998) and low levels of problematic behaviors (Eccles & Barber, 1999). Volunteering also increases the likelihood of attending college (Eccles & Barber, 1999). It encourages interest in politics and prompts political discussions with parents and others (Niemi, Hepburn, & Chapman, 2000). Equally important, of course, is that volunteering helps others in the community. One study found that 90 percent of the adolescent volunteers surveyed believed they had benefited from their service and would do it again (Hamilton & Fenzel, 1988).

Research into adolescent community service is only beginning. However, it is clear that some volunteer opportunities are more useful than others. Whereas some teenagers stuff envelopes for a political candidate in a room with other students, others go out into the community and mingle with people different from themselves. Metz, McLellan, and Youniss (2003) compared adolescents who participated in social cause service (e.g., providing meals for elderly shut-ins) with those who participated in more standard youth service (e.g., tutoring fellow students; helping with office work). Although almost all of the volunteers found their experience enjoyable and planned to volunteer in the future, only those who had actively interacted with needy individuals showed enhanced social concern.

In any case, schools can enhance the benefits of community service by preparing the students beforehand and giving them opportunities for reflection afterward (Blyth, Saito, & Berkas, 1997).

Adolescents and Unemployment

One of the major social problems in the United States is unemployment among youths.

Numbers of Unemployed Youths

In 2008, 16.8 percent of White 16- to 19-year-old adolescents were unemployed. Rates were even higher among minority youths: for example, 31.2 percent of African American adolescents were unable to find work (Bureau of Labor Statistics, 2009). Figure 13.5 shows comparable figures for young adults ages 20 to 24. Altogether, this means that 2.8 million young people, ages 16 to 24, were out of work in 2008.

The highest unemployment is among African American teenagers, and this is true whether they are in school or not. Also, the jobless rate of Hispanic American youths is above the rate for their Caucasian counterparts but much lower than that for African Americans. These statistics probably underestimate the extent of the problem, for many adolescents who get discouraged and stop looking for work are not counted as unemployed. This high rate of joblessness means more crime, more drug addiction, more social unrest, and less income for many poor families.

FIGURE 13.5 UNEMPLOYMENT RATE BY AGE AND RACE/ETHNICITY: 2002

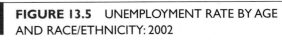
Source: U.S. Bureau of Labor Statistics (2009).

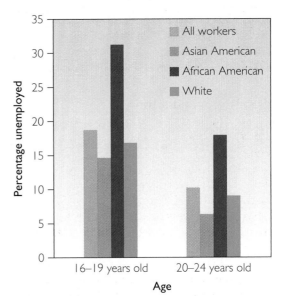

Causes of Unemployment

Why is the rate of unemployment among youths so high? One reason is that they have little training and skill, little experience, and many are able to take only part-time jobs while in school. They are confined to a narrower range of the less-skilled occupations, at which many can work only part time. Youths with a high school diploma have better chances in the labor market than do dropouts, as is reflected by lower unemployment rates among graduates. Figure 13.6 shows the employment status of high school graduates and dropouts in the labor force in 2001. Many employers require educational degrees that have little relationship to job skills; dropouts are often denied work not because they cannot do the job but because they do not have the necessary credentials.

Many unemployed youths are recent college graduates who are searching for their first jobs. Some of these graduates have majored in subjects that do not directly prepare them for employment. For some, it is fairly normative to be out of work for a while before they can find something that is compatible with their education.

State licensing boards often operate to restrict entry into business. The Colorado Board of Cosmetology, for example, requires that a prospective hairdresser take 1,450 hours of instruction, including 100 hours of supervised practice at shampooing. Such requirements hit the young hardest, especially those who seek to combine work with schooling.

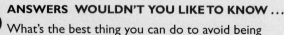

ANSWERS WOULDN'T YOU LIKE TO KNOW ...

What's the best thing you can do to avoid being unemployed later in life?

The best way to avoid unemployment is to graduate from college! The unemployment rate is much lower for college graduates than for people with less education.

Union requirements also limit participation of the young. It takes time and experience to acquire membership in a union; therefore, adolescents are not able to accept jobs in the construction industry, for example, which could be an important source of part-time and summer employment. Many unions also limit the number of apprentices who can be trained. In cases of layoffs, seniority rules work in favor of the older, more experienced workers; youths are the first to lose their jobs.

Minimum wage legislation may sometimes affect unemployment. When the minimum wage goes up relative to the low productivity of inexperienced youths, employers hesitate to hire them, often preferring older people if they are available. Furthermore, job turnover among youths is higher than among older, more stable workers. Some employers will not hire anybody younger than 21 for steady jobs; they want those who have a greater degree of stability.

FIGURE 13.6 UNEMPLOYMENT RATE AS A FUNCTION OF EDUCATIONAL LEVEL AND RACE/ETHNICITY: 2001

Source: U.S. Bureau of Labor Statistics (2009).

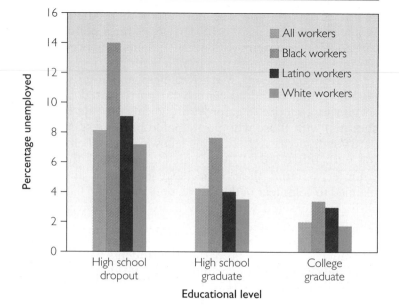

On the other hand, the average period of unemployment among youths is shorter than among older workers. Females average somewhat shorter periods of unemployment than males, and Whites shorter periods than non-Whites. The fact that half of all unemployed youths have no more than four weeks without work reflects the seasonal and intermittent nature of their unemployment and the rapid turnover of jobs.

Career Education

Almost all Americans, men and women, work for wages for a significant portion of their adult lives. Individuals work to earn money, to achieve autonomy, and to enjoy self-fulfillment. Society needs workers to produce goods and perform services. It is crucial, therefore, that schools help prepare adolescents for careers. As discussed in Chapter 12, high schools offer different curricular tracks. Some students are college bound. Although the basic skills they will eventually need in the workplace are learned, in part, during primary and secondary school (reading, math, oral skills, etc.), it is expected that their college educations will prepare them for their careers. Many students, however, never go on to college. The job training and career skills they need must be acquired largely, if not exclusively, in high school.

In fact, many non–college-bound youths are at a disadvantage when they try to enter the job market.

CROSS-CULTURAL CONCERNS   INTERNATIONAL PERSPECTIVES ON YOUTH EMPLOYMENT

Although many American young people are currently feeling understandably worried about their employment prospects given the world's present economic downturn, it might be comforting to remember that youth in developed market economies such as the United States have better labor market prospects than do youth in most parts of the world. This is in good part because our adolescents have unprecedented educational opportunities and in good part because the young adult population is not rapidly rising (which would increase competition for jobs). Females in the developed world are especially advantaged in terms of employment opportunities relative to their sisters across the globe. Even though unemployment rates are relatively high right now, most youth who are looking *will* find a job, albeit not necessarily the job of their dreams.

According to the United Nations (2007), young persons face some employment-related problems that are near-global in scope. Other concerns are more isolated to particular regions of the planet. As a whole, each region faces unique challenges.

Sub-Saharan Africa

Young people in sub-Saharan Africa are the most rapidly growing labor force in the world today; however, the number of youth who are unemployed is growing quickly and the rate is extremely high. As a result, many youth—upward of 90 percent in some countries—live in dire poverty. Unemployment rates are especially high in urban areas, since many rural youth migrate to cities in the mistaken belief that they will be able to find higher paying jobs there. Instead, even if they do find work, it is often exploitive and unpleasant. Females in Africa are more likely to work or to desire to work than females in most other geographic areas, perhaps because African children of both genders are expected to actively help maintain their family's household and girls acquire domestic and trading skills at an early age.

Northern Africa/Middle East

This area has the highest rate of youth unemployment in the world, largely because of booming birthrates and large declines in infant mortality rates . Only one-third of youth have a job. Paternalistic cultural traditions lead to female employment rates that are the lowest in the world; even when young women do work outside the home, they usually stop once they are married. However, unmarried young women are responsible for most of the (unpaid) agricultural labor in the region.

Asia

More than half of the world's youth (55 percent) live in Asia. Asian youth have benefited from the creation of millions of new jobs as Western companies have internationalized and shifted their operations to this region. Many of these jobs, however, are low skill and low paying. Youth unemployment levels, therefore, tend to be higher for those with more, rather than less, education.

Eastern Europe

Many nations in Eastern Europe have been in some degree of economic crisis for the past several decades as they have negotiated the transition from socialism to capitalism. Young people are among the individuals hardest hit by this economic decline: overall approximately one-third of Eastern European youth are neither employed nor in school.

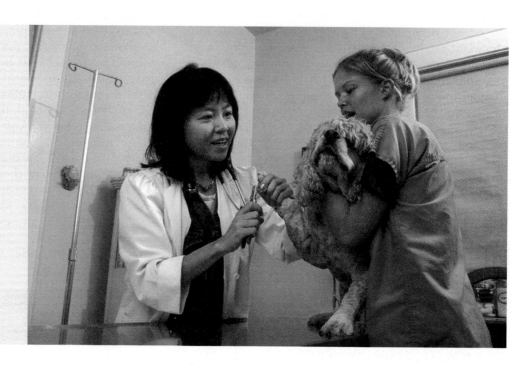

Internships offer adolescents great opportunities to learn about different careers.

Employers complain that teenagers lack basic academic skills and are unable to find information when they need it. Some are said to lack interpersonal skills, initiative, and effective work habits initiative (Taylor, 2005). To try to remedy this situation, Congress passed the School-to-Work Opportunities Act (1994) and the Carl D. Perkins Career and Technical Education Act (revised in 2006), which provide federal funds to schools that attempt to develop more effective job training and to those that build bridges with technical and community colleges.

Several types of programs have been developed to better link school with work and to improve the employment prospects of high school graduates (Lewis, Stone, Shipley, et al., 1998) (see Table 13.4). **Tech-prep programs** involve partnerships between high schools and two-year, postsecondary vocational institutions. In this type of program, the student selects a career at the end of his or her sophomore year and then takes classes in the last two years of school that are directly applicable to that career. Upon high school graduation, he or she transfers to the technical school. One problem with these programs is that students must choose a career path before beginning their junior year. An alternative model, based on the system used in Germany, involves **apprenticeships** or **internships.** Students split their week among working at a company, taking career-related classes, and doing

TABLE 13.4	TYPES OF SCHOOL-TO-WORK PROGRAMS
PROGRAM	**DESCRIPTION**
Job shadowing	Spending time with someone at his or her worksite
Mentoring	Being matched with an individual in a certain occupation
Cooperative education	Combining academic and vocational studies with a job in a related field
School-sponsored enterprise	Producing goods or services for sale or use by others
Technical preparation	Participating in a planned program of study with a defined career focus that links secondary and postsecondary education
Apprenticeship/Internship	Working for an employer to learn about a particular occupation or industry
Career major	Taking a defined sequence of courses to prepare for a specific occupation

Source: U.S. Bureau of Labor Statistics (2000).

regular academic coursework. Again, students must make early, limiting career decisions. Finally, there are **school-based enterprises,** in which schools essentially set up shop and simulate small businesses. Although these enterprises do not get students into the real workplace, they allow students to participate in many aspects of a business and provide them with decision-making opportunities.

Stern and his colleagues (Stern, Rahn, & Chung, 1998) have differentiated between those programs that are "learn-and-stay" and those that are "learn-and-go." In learn-and-stay programs, students are channeled into a particular industry or company; in learn-and-go programs, students learn more general skills that can be transferred to any number of businesses. Stern and colleagues have recommended that schools convert students' existing part-time jobs to learn-and-go experiences. Since most students are employed in dead-end, low-paying work, the focus must shift to providing

transferable job skills. Incentives would have to be provided to companies to secure their participation. Stern et al. also have suggested that schools work to create more firm-based learn-and-stay opportunities in industries that pay high wages. Finally, they have recommended an expansion of school-based enterprises, both learn and stay and learn and go.

tech-prep programs partnerships between high schools and two-year, postsecondary vocational institutions to provide career education.

apprenticeships or **internships** programs in which students split their time among working at a company, taking career-related classes, and doing regular academic coursework.

school-based enterprises programs in which schools set up small businesses to teach job skills.

SUMMARY

1. Choosing and preparing for a vocation is one of the most important developmental tasks of adolescence. Done wisely and realistically, it enables individuals to enter vocations for which they are well suited, in which they find satisfaction and fulfillment, and which are needed by society. Done haphazardly, it leads to frustration, discontent, unhappiness, and social disapproval.

2. The process of choosing a job or career is often a complicated one. Choices made early in high school affect the availability of later options. Adolescents from higher-socioeconomic-status groups are more fortunate because they have more options and more resources to use in taking advantage of options.

3. Ginzberg divides the process of occupational choice into three stages: fantasy stage (up to age 11), tentative stage (ages 11 to 17), and realistic stage (age 17 on). Research generally supports the broad outlines of this theory, although the sequence, nature, and timing of the stages may not always be the same. Also, one's career choices do not always end with one's first job.

4. Gottfredson proposed a theory of career development based on circumscription and then compromise.

5. Influences on development have been divided into three categories: normative, age-graded influences; normative, history-graded influences; and nonnormative, life-event influences.

6. Holland theorized that people select occupations that afford environments consistent with their personality types. He outlined six personality types: realistic, intellectual, social, conventional, enterprising, and artistic.

7. Lent and his colleagues proposed that individuals base their career choices on a combination of personal factors, such as interests, and environmental factors, such as job availability and social support.

8. Parents exert a strong influence on their teenagers' career choices, especially those parents whose teens are strongly attached to them. Parents provide their children with opportunities, model certain behaviors, exhibit satisfaction or dissatisfaction with teens' careers, and encourage or discourage education.

9. Peers, teachers, and coaches also influence adolescents' career decisions.

10. Girls have traditionally been more narrowly channeled into careers than boys because of structural and normative barriers. The notion that cognitive differences restrict girls' and women's occupational success is rooted in stereotypes.

11. Women are underrepresented in careers involving mathematics and the natural sciences.

12. Adolescent career decisions are influenced by interests, aptitudes, job opportunities, job familiarity, prestige, socioeconomic status, and, to some extent, race and ethnicity.

13. Almost all adolescents work at some point before they graduate from high school, primarily as cashiers and food servers. Working even only a few hours per week has harmful ramifications for most adolescents.

14. Community service, or volunteer work, has increased greatly in the past 30 years. It appears to be quite beneficial for everyone involved.

15. One of the major social problems in the United States is unemployment among youths. Rates

among African Americans and Latinos are higher than among Whites for numerous reasons. Lack of training, skills, and experience; restrictive licensing and union requirements; minimum wage legislation; and lack of education all contribute to adolescent unemployment.

16. Patterns of youth employment vary in different regions of the world. In general, youth unemployment is higher than adult unemployment.

17. A variety of school-to-work programs have been developed to help adolescents develop job skills and become employable, including tech-prep programs, apprenticeships, and school-based enterprises.

KEY TERMS

apprenticeships or internships 348	school-based enterprises 349
circumscription 330	self-efficacy 336
compromise 330	Strong Interest Inventory 337
compromise with reality theory 328	structural barriers 334
normative barriers 334	tech-prep programs 348
occupational environment theory 331	

THOUGHT QUESTIONS

Personal Reflection

1. What careers have you wanted at different points in your life, beginning in childhood? Why these careers?
2. Identify some of the normative age-graded, normative historical, and nonnormative events that have affected your career plans.
3. Which of Holland's personality types best describes you? Are you planning to go into the kind of career he would suggest for you? If not, why not?
4. Have you ever attended a career education class? What was the result? In what ways was it helpful? In what ways was it not helpful?
5. How influential were or are your peers regarding your vocational choice?
6. Has any person at school been particularly influential in your choice of vocation?
7. If you worked while in high school, how did the experience affect you? What, if any, valuable lessons did you learn from your job? How could the situation have been more instructive?

Group Discussion

8. Why is making a wise vocational choice one of the most important developmental tasks of adolescence?
9. Why do some adolescents make poor vocational choices?
10. Should parents have any voice about the vocation their adolescent chooses? What's the parental role in this regard?

11. Do you think that some vocations are unsuitable for women? For men? Explain.
12. Just because a person is interested in a particular vocation, does this mean he or she should go into it? What other factors ought to be taken into consideration?
13. How should you go about finding out if you have an aptitude or special ability suitable for a particular vocation?
14. Do you currently or did you perform any community service while in high school? How did the experience affect you?
15. What can be done about the high unemployment rate among adolescents, especially African American adolescents?
16. What kinds of school-to-work programs did your high school offer? How satisfied were the students who participated in these programs?
17. Is having a good education necessary to get a good job? Explain.

Debate Questions

18. Job prestige is a valid concern when selecting a career.
19. The military is a good option for adolescents who are uncertain what to do with their lives.
20. Getting a good education is necessary to getting a good job.
21. All high school students should be required to do community service.
22. All high schools should offer career exploration courses as part of their curriculum to teach students about available careers.

SUGGESTED READING

Booth, A., Crouter, A. C., and Shanahan, M. J. (Eds.). (2007). *Transitions to Adulthood in a Changing Economy: No Work, No Family, No Future?* Westport, CT: Praeger.

Cress, J., Collier, P., and Reitenauer, V. L. (2005). *Learning Through Serving: A Student Guidebook for Service-Learning Across the Disciplines.* Sterling, VA: Stylus.

Howard, C. M., and Ill, P. J. (2003). *Career Pathways: Preparing Students for Life.* Thousand Oaks, CA: Sage.

Jacobsen, M. H. (1999). *Hand-Me-Down Dreams: How Families Influence Our Career Paths and How We Can Reclaim Them.* Bourbon, IN: Harmony Books.

Mortimer, J. (2003). *Working and Growing Up in America.* Cambridge, MA: Harvard University Press.

Siegel, S. (Ed.). (2003). *Career Ladders: Transitions from High School to Adult Life.* Austin, TX: Pro-Ed.

United Nations. (2008). *World Youth Report 2007: Young People's Transition to Adulthood—Progress and Challenges.* New York: United Nations.

Watkins, M., and Braun, L. (2005). *Service Learning: From Classroom to Community to Career.* Indianapolis, IN: Jist.

Wilczenski, F. L., and Coomey, S. M. (2007). *A Practical Guide to Service Learning: Strategies for Positive Development in Schools.* New York: Springer.

USEFUL WEB SITE

United States Bureau of Labor Statistics
www.bls.gov

This site contains several different, helpful kinds of information. First, you can download The Occupational Outlook Handbook; *it details more than 1,000 careers, specifying the qualifications needed, employment prospects, salary ranges, and so on. You can browse or search specific careers. Second, you can download the bureau's report on youths in the labor force. Finally, in addition to reviewing myriad statistics about working and unemployment, you can explore links to other sites concerned with this topic.*

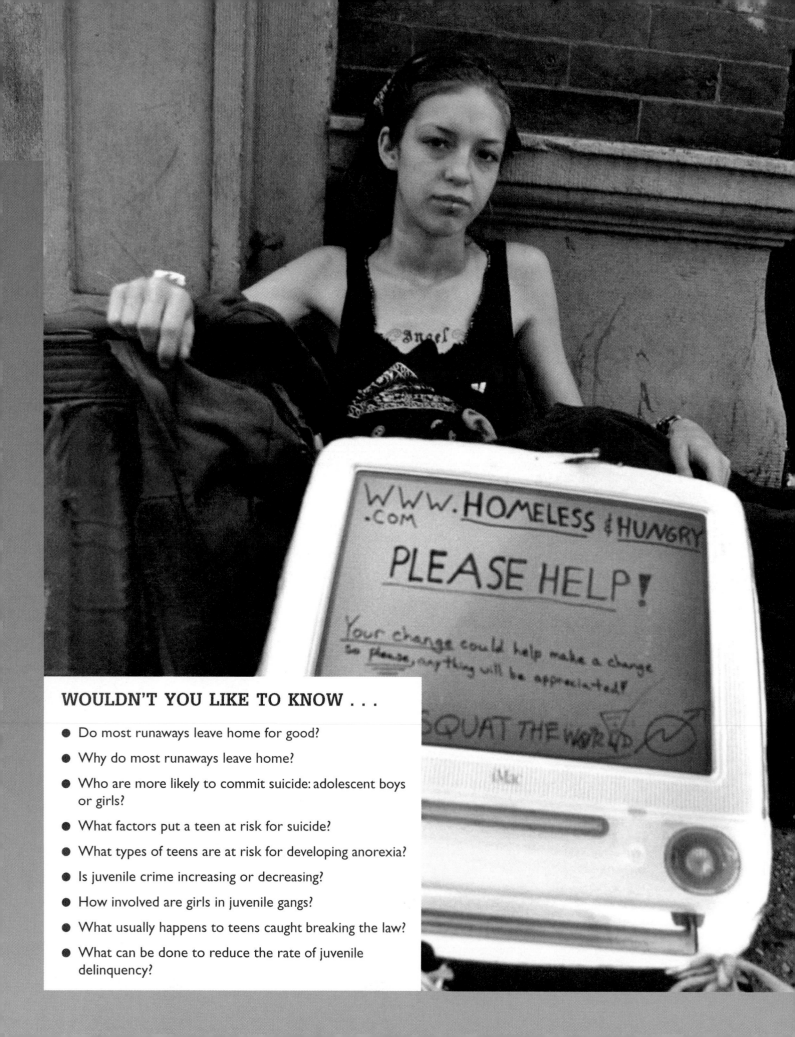

WOULDN'T YOU LIKE TO KNOW . . .

- Do most runaways leave home for good?
- Why do most runaways leave home?
- Who are more likely to commit suicide: adolescent boys or girls?
- What factors put a teen at risk for suicide?
- What types of teens are at risk for developing anorexia?
- Is juvenile crime increasing or decreasing?
- How involved are girls in juvenile gangs?
- What usually happens to teens caught breaking the law?
- What can be done to reduce the rate of juvenile delinquency?

chapter 14

Adolescent Stress and Alienation

Sometimes, adolescents who are angry or unhappy turn outward, expressing pent-up emotions through various forms of acting-out behavior: truancy, aggression, promiscuity, theft, or assault. Sometimes the anger or unhappiness turns against the self, which can result in depression or self-harm. For the most part, these distressed youths feel alienated from family and school; they do not function in the mainstream of adolescent or adult society. Their actions are an expression of their feelings of alienation, which they have found difficult to deal with in socially approved ways (Calabrese & Adams, 1990).

In this chapter, we discuss several manifestations of disturbed, acting-out behavior: running away, depression, suicide, eating disorders, and juvenile delinquency. Although these problems are quite different from one another, they stem from many of the same fundamental causes. There is a growing understanding that although the expressions of disturbance may vary, the root causes are often the same. Furthermore, adolescent problem behaviors—whether they involve substance abuse, pregnancy, delinquency, suicide, or dropping out—tend to *cluster*. In other words, teenagers who engage in one of these activities tend to engage in several of them (Ozer, Park, Paul, et al., 2003).

Clustering occurs for two reasons. The first is common causation. Family discord, association with deviant peers, poverty, and school failure all contribute to a host of behavioral problems (and, therefore, are mentioned multiple times throughout this and other chapters). The second reason for clustering is that one problem can directly trigger another. For example, the stresses caused by running away can lead a youth to substance abuse, promiscuity, and criminal activity.

Running Away

Running away from home is more common than most persons imagine. National estimates indicate that the number of adolescents who run away from home each year ranges from 1 to 2 million (Hammer, Finkelhor, & Sedlak, 2002). It is believed that one in seven adolescents will run away at least once before his or her eighteenth birthday (Sedlak, Finkelhor, Hammer, et al., 2002). Caucasian teenagers are more likely to flee home than their Latino or African American peers (Tyler & Bersani, 2008). Adolescents raised in single-parent or blended family homes are many times as likely to run away than those being raised by both of their biological parents (Sanchez, Waller, & Greene, 2006). A minority of adolescents who run away are running from foster care, group homes, or residential treatment facilities. Runaways are likely to have been victimized either at home or at school (Tyler & Bersani, 2008), and they are more likely to be female than male (Sanchez,

Waller, & Greene, 2006). Teens who leave home are more likely to come from urban rather than rural or suburban areas and to be from the Western half of the country.

Most runaways are 16 or older, but one-third are 15 or younger (Snyder & Sickmund, 2006). These young teenagers find it particularly hard to cope with life on the street—even more so than their older counterparts. Young teens' small size leaves them especially vulnerable to victimization and makes it impossible for them to find legitimate work. They are unlikely to take advantage of social services (shelters, food banks, etc.) because they are afraid they will be turned over to their parents.

Classes of Runaways

There are many reasons for running away and many typologies that classify runaways based upon their motivation for leaving home. However, there are two primary classes of runaways: *intent runaways* and *transient runaways*. Intent runaways are those who really mean to flee. They want to be gone—if not forever, then for a long time. Transient runaways are those who leave more at the spur of the moment and do not intend to stay away for more than a few hours or a day or two. These teens often leave home because they are afraid: perhaps they think that their parents will beat them for getting failing grades, or maybe they have violated their curfew and are terrified to return home. Other teens are angry, perhaps over having been denied permission to do something or having been disciplined.

The reason it is worthwhile at the outset of this discussion to distinguish these two groups is that about *half* of all runaways—the transient runaways—return home within two days (Finkelhor, Hotaling, & Sedlak, 1990). The vast majority run to friends' or relatives' houses, and often their parents know where they are (Snyder & Sickmund, 2006). The fact that an adolescent would take the rather extreme measure of running away for even a short time does not speak particularly well of his or her family's dynamics, and it is quite possible that this behavior is an early warning of more serious problems to come. Still, transient running is a far less serious and less risky behavior than intent running with no plans of returning.

ANSWERS WOULDN'T YOU LIKE TO KNOW ...

Do most runaways leave home for good?

No. About half stay away for only a day or two and go to a friend's or relative's house. Most of the more intent runaways, who are gone for long periods of time, eventually go home as well.

PERSONAL ISSUES PREVENTING TEENS FROM RUNNING AND FINDING THEM WHEN THEY DO

Most teens do not run away on the spur of the moment with the intent of staying away. Rather, their leaving is a dramatic move that they have usually considered for some time. This means that an alert parent or teacher who is aware of the warning signs might be able to speak with the adolescent and head off the behavior.

The most direct and obvious sign of planning to run is that the teen will have begun to accumulate the resources he or she will need to live on the street. He or she may be hoarding money or have packed a suitcase or backpack. In addition, he or she may gather personal mementos, such as photos of close friends.

Some runaways hint at or even directly state their intent to leave home. They sometimes confide their plans to friends. Hints, direct statements, and rumors reported by others should be taken seriously.

Other possible signs are less specific to running away but signal trouble. Changes in behavior, rebelliousness, a need for solitude, switching friends, and truancy often indicate that a problem is brewing and is worth looking into.

If an adolescent has disappeared and is believed to have run away from home, the Office of Juvenile Justice and Delinquency Prevention (1998) recommends the following actions:

1. Check with persons who may know the teenager's whereabouts: friends, neighbors, and so on.
2. Check locations that the adolescent frequents to see if he or she is there.
3. Examine the youth's bedroom and school locker for clues (such as notes or maps) as to where he or she may have gone.
4. Check past telephone bills for unexplained long-distance calls the youth may have made.
5. Examine the adolescent's e-mail account.
6. Call the police and make a report. Ask the police to put out a "Be on the lookout" alert.
7. Disseminate the news that the youth is missing, including a photo of him or her.
8. Contact national runaway help hotlines and the National Center for Missing and Exploited Children to see if the child has been in contact with them.

So, keeping in mind that a full 50 percent of runaways are gone only a night or two, let us examine the more serious intent runaways.

Reasons for Running Away

Rotheram-Borus and her colleagues (1996) have identified six reasons for youths' running away:

- Deserted by their parents as a result of parental death or divorce
- Thrown out of their homes by their parents
- Left home because their parents could not cope with their homosexuality
- Left home after having been sexually abused by their parent(s)
- Left home or thrown out because they have substance abuse problems
- Left home or thrown out because they have long-standing mental health problems

It is widely agreed that the most common thread running through the backgrounds of intent runaways is that they come from dysfunctional homes. They have a history of having been sexually or physically abused, neglected, and rejected by their parents. Their parents constantly fight and are frequently substance abusers (Baron, 1999; Terrell, 1997). Some estimates

have suggested that as many as 70 percent of runaways have been abused in some way (Jencks, 1994).

Most adolescents, then, have been *pushed out* of their homes. They flee from what they perceive to be an intolerable situation. The majority of intent runaway adolescents say that they tried to make their family situation work but failed in their attempt (Schaffner, 1998). Other teens are **throwaways;** that is, their parents have actively encouraged them to leave or have actually thrown them out of their homes (Gullotta, 2003). Only a relatively small number of youths are pulled toward a glamorous vision of life on the street.

Runaway girls generally view their parents as controlling and punitive of their behavior in the home, whereas many runaway boys report minimal family control and supervision, which leads to outside forces, such as peers, becoming causal agents in running away. Thus, low levels of control allow boys opportunities to leave. Many parents of runaways are so absorbed with their own problems that they have little time to consider their children. Such youths report they are not wanted by their parents.

Given their poor family relationships, it is not surprising that most adolescents who run away exhibit a

throwaways adolescents who have been told to leave home.

host of problem behaviors before they leave home (e.g., Robert, Pauzé, & Fournier, 2005). They often commit delinquent acts, do not get along well with peers, and are anxious or depressed. Many have experienced difficulties in school. Children who are slow learners, left back to repeat grades, or ostracized by school personnel seek to escape the school environment that rejects them. An examination of the prevalence of arithmetic and reading difficulties in 16- to 21-year-old clients of a shelter for runaway and homeless street youths found that 52 percent had reading disabilities, 29 percent had trouble with arithmetic and written work, and only 20 percent were normal achievers (Barwick & Siegel, 1996).

Throwaways

One of the largest studies of runaways to date, the NISMART study (Hammer, Finkelhor, & Sedlak, 2002), found that not all runaways had, in fact, run away. Forty-four percent had been thrown out of their homes or asked to leave by their parents, and a large number of other teens had left voluntarily but then were not permitted to return when they wanted to. As noted earlier, these youths are more properly called *throwaways*.

What motivates a family to sever all ties with an adolescent child? Sometimes, the parents are distressed at their child's incorrigible behavior, whether it is substance abuse, promiscuity, delinquency, or the like. Sometimes, the child has a long-standing mental illness, such as conduct disorder, that makes him or her difficult to live with. Sometimes, the child has engaged in incest with a sibling or with one of the parents (Gullotta, 2003). Regardless of the reason, the parents of a throwaway are not making a good, mature decision when they decide to abandon their child. If the family had been strong and healthy, the child's behaviors either would not have occurred or would have been dealt with in a more proactive, healing manner. Shutting the door in a child's face may reduce the parents' problems, but it will only exacerbate the child's.

Another reason that parents ask their children to leave home is dire poverty. Some parents simply cannot afford to feed and clothe all their children. In these cases, the parents will sometimes ask the older children to fend for themselves so that the parents can concentrate on caring for the younger ones (Shinn & Weitzman, 1996). Similarly, some youths are on the street because they have outgrown foster care and been discharged with no means of support (National Coalition of the Homeless, 2008).

Life on the Street

Adolescents who have run away quickly find that life on the street is extremely difficult. Homeless youths are likely to be victimized by others. One study found that 43 percent of the street-living adolescent boys and 39 percent of the adolescent girls they sampled had been assaulted with a weapon (Whitbeck & Simons, 1990). Boys were more often robbed and beaten whereas girls were more commonly sexually assaulted.

The most common way that runaway teens support themselves is to get money from friends or relatives (Benoit-Bryan, 2008). However, in order to get enough money for food, clothes, and shelter, adolescents who have been on the street for more than a few days are usually forced to turn to drug dealing, shoplifting, and theft (Terrell, 1997). Significant numbers engage in prostitution, taking money for sex, or in so-called **survival sex,** swapping sexual favors for food or shelter. An estimated 75 percent of hard-core street youths engage in some form of crime and 25 to 50 percent engage in either prostitution or survival sex (Greene, Ennet, & Ringwalt, 1999; Kipke, O'Connor, Palmer, et al., 1995; Kipke, Palmer, LaFrance, et al., 1997). Even so, street youths often go hungry (Antoniades & Tarasuk, 1998).

Engaging in these activities causes runaways to associate with deviant individuals who draw them further into unhealthy lifestyles. The fact that many hard-core runaways use drugs and engage in sex with multiple partners, usually without condoms, puts them at high risk for contracting human immunodeficiency virus (HIV), which causes acquired immune deficiency syndrome (AIDS) (Booth, Zhang, & Kwiatkowski, 1999). It also leads to extremely high pregnancy rates: homeless adolescent girls are more than 10 times as likely to become pregnant as their at-home peers (Thompson, Bender, Lewis, et al., 2008). Homeless youths are subject to high rates of psychological problems, as well. They experience low self-esteem and depression, engage in various forms of self-injurious behavior, and are at high risk for suicide (Molnar, Shade, Kral, et al. 1999; Yoder, 1999). One study of homeless youths in Los Angeles found that two-thirds were clinically depressed; in comparison, about 7 percent of the overall adolescent population is depressed (Unger, Kipke, Simon, et al., 1997). Most studies report an attempted suicide rate of between 20 and 40 percent (Kidd, 2003). The mortality rate of street youths is estimated to be 40 times as high as that of at-home adolescents (Shaw & Dorling, 1998).

ANSWERS WOULDN'T YOU LIKE TO KNOW ...
Why do most runaways leave home?

Most intent runaways leave home because of intolerable conditions, such as abuse. Almost half of runaways, however, are told to leave or are thrown out by their parents.

Help for Runaways

Runaway youths need a variety of services to help with their many problems. These services include but are not limited to short-term emergency shelters where they can find temporary food and shelter; medical, including psychological, care; access to social workers who can try to reunite them with their families if that is appropriate or help them make arrangements to live on their own; educational programs so that they can attend class and graduate from high school; long-term, stable residential placements; and job training and placement. Unfortunately, the services available to runaway and throwaway youths are, at the current time, inadequate.

Worldwide Scope

Homeless youths are not just an American phenomenon. An estimated 100 million children and adolescents are homeless across the globe. Like their American counterparts, these children and adolescents suffer from malnutrition, self-destructive behaviors, and substance abuse. They eat out of garbage cans and steal or prostitute themselves to survive. Most of these children are from families living deep in poverty. Some have run away, some have been abandoned, and some have lost parents to death.

Le Roux and Smith (1998) blame the increase in the numbers of street children on a combination of industrialization/urbanization and drought with its resulting famine. Urbanization breaks down the traditional extended family structure in rural communities, leaving mothers and fathers to care for children on their own. Famine destroys villages, kills parents, and forces families to make difficult choices when there is simply not enough food to feed them all. In some locales, AIDS has decimated the adult population, leaving large numbers of children and teens to fend for themselves.

Depression and Suicide

Depression

Depression would be an important enough topic to cover in some depth even if it were not related to suicide. Clinical depression is a serious condition that can make a person's life miserable—even unbearable—and trigger a host of other problems. When people are depressed, they feel both helpless—that there is nothing they can do to improve their terrible situation—and hopeless—that their situation will never change for the better. They feel sad and are self-critical; they also believe that others are critical of them. Depressed individuals feel overwhelmed at having to make even simple decisions. They often neglect their appearance and may act out their frustrations in an aggressive fashion (American Psychiatric Association, 2000).

Depression is quite common during adolescence: between 15 and 20 percent of teenagers have been clinically depressed at least once by the time they enter

survival sex swapping sexual favors for food or shelter.

depression a serious psychological disorder marked by sadness, helplessness, and hopelessness.

Homeless youths around the world sleep on the streets, eat out of garbage cans, and steal or prostitute themselves to survive.

young adulthood (Lewinsohn & Essau, 2002). Furthermore, episodes of depression are frequently recurrent, with each bout usually lasting seven to nine months. About two-thirds of adolescents who are clinically depressed have at least one other psychological disorder, as well—often substance abuse.

Depression runs in families. Depressed adolescents are three times more likely to have a close family member with depression than adolescents who are not depressed. The families of depressed youths are also more likely to be filled with discord, and divorce is more common. Depressed teen parents often have a history of overprotecting them (Nilzon & Palmérus, 1997).

Depression is equally common in boys and girls during childhood. However, girls' depression rates increase during adolescence whereas boys' rates do not (Wade, Cairney, & Pevalin, 2002), so that by adulthood, women are twice as likely as men to experience depression (Graber & Sontag, 2009). Depression in boys and girls is typically triggered by different events. Girls are more likely than boys to become depressed because of problems with social relationships. For example, whereas unpopular girls are more likely to be depressed than popular girls, this relationship is not true for boys (Oldenburg & Kerns, 1997). Girls are also more likely to feel others' pain and to become depressed because of the stresses that those they care about are experiencing (Eberhart, Shih, Hammen, et al., 2006). Also, when boys have a problem, they tend to cope with it through denial and avoidance; that is, they try to distract themselves and not think about it. Girls, conversely, tend to ruminate on their problems. This latter coping strategy is more likely to lead to depression whenever it is used (U.S. Department of Health and Human Services, 1999). Girls who experience depression are more likely than boys to have that depression continue into adulthood (Gjerde & Westenberg, 1998). (For other suggestions as to why adolescent girls have higher depression rates than adolescent boys, see the Personal Issues box on p. 360.)

Most kinds of stress increase the likelihood of depression. For example, students who do poorly in school are at heightened risk. It follows, then, that students with attention-deficit hyperactivity disorder, learning disabilities, and conduct disorder are especially vulnerable. Loss of a loved one—whether a family member, close friend, boyfriend, or girlfriend—can also trigger depression, as can traumas such as assault (National Institute of Mental Health, 2000).

Some question remains as to whether depression in adolescents is the same condition as depression in adults. Although many commonalities have been identified, there are a few differences in how the disorder is manifested in the two age groups. For example, adolescents are more likely to have physical ailments as part of their depression than are adults, but they are less likely to be tired or to lose their appetite (Carlson & Kashini, 1988). In addition, some antidepressants that relieve symptoms in adults have much less effect on adolescents (Birmaher, Ryan, Williamson, et al., 1996). To some, these variations suggest a possible difference in the biological foundations of the disorders.

There are two links that tie depression to suicide. First, as mentioned before, depressed youths are at significantly increased risk for suicide (Birmaher, Arbelaez, & Brent, 2002). Second, there is concern that one of the most common treatments for depression—prescription SSRIs (selective serotonin reuptake inhibitors), which include antidepressants such as Prozac—can trigger suicidal thoughts and behavior in adolescents. This is a real cause for alarm: in 2002, American physicians wrote nearly 11 million prescriptions for SSRIs for youths younger than age 17 (Hampton, 2004). Concern grew to the point that in October 2004, the U.S. Food and Drug Administration issued a "black box" warning, stating that these medications put minors at increased risk for suicide and that they should be used with extreme caution in this population. (A number of European countries had previously restricted the use of SSRI antidepressants to adult patients.) The government's panelists determined that using these drugs doubled the risk of suicidal thoughts and behaviors in depressed adolescents who were using them.

Not all researchers are convinced that the dangers outweigh the benefits, however. For example, Vasa, Carlino, and Pine (2006) believe that the suicidal link has been exaggerated; they agree that the risk does double, but they note that the increase is from 2 to 4 percent and so is still small. In addition, they point out that the suicide risk of adolescents who are on psychotropic medications and are under treatment is still much less than that of untreated depressed adolescents. They also point to an inverse negative correlation between the number of prescriptions for these medications and the adolescent suicide rate in any given geographical region, a negative relationship that weakens the argument for a strong causal relationship between taking SSRIs and adolescent suicide. This linkage is under great scrutiny right now, and more will be known in a few years.

Suicide

Suicide is an important topic because it is the third-leading cause of adolescent death (behind accidents and homicides) (Anderson & Smith, 2003). In 2007, 15 percent of American adolescents had seriously considered suicide and 11 percent had gone so far as to make a suicide plan (Centers for Disease Control, 2008). The incidence of suicide among children, especially those younger than 13, is rare (Brent, Baugher, Bridge, et al., 1999) because adolescents are more

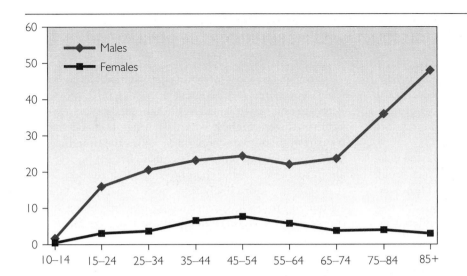

FIGURE 14.1   SUICIDE MORTALITY
BY SEX AND AGE GROUP: 2002

Source: Data from Centers for Disease Control (2004c).

likely than children to have a psychological disorder, which is a significant risk factor for suicide. Also, adolescents have more mature cognitive skills than children and can thus make more effective suicide plans (Shaffer, Gould, Fisher, et al., 1996).

Contrary to popular belief, the suicide mortality rate increases with age, reaching a peak in males older than 85 and in females ages 45 to 54 (Centers for Disease Control, 2004c). Teens are *not* more likely to commit suicide than older persons. Figure 14.1 shows these trends. As Figure 14.2 indicates, the suicide rate in the 15- to 24-year-old age group tripled from 1950 to 1995—from about 4.5 deaths per 100,000 adolescents to more than 13. Since then, the adolescent suicide rate has declined to about 10 deaths per 100,000 (U.S. Bureau of the Census, 2008).

Only a small percentage of people who attempt suicide succeed in killing themselves. Estimates of the ratio of adolescent suicide attempts to fatalities vary from 100 to 1 to 350 to 1 (Seroczynski, Jacquez, & Cole,

2003). About 4,500 young people between ages 15 and 24 successfully commit suicide each year (Centers for Disease Control, 2008). Girls are about twice as likely as boys to attempt suicide, but 85 percent of successful suicides are committed by boys (Anderson & Smith, 2003). One of the reasons males succeed more often is that they frequently use more violent means—hanging, jumping from heights, single-vehicle automobile accidents, or shooting or stabbing themselves—whereas females more often use passive and less dangerous methods, such as taking pills. Females more often make multiple threats but less often really want to kill themselves or actually do it (Peck & Warner, 1995).

Suicide rates also vary by race and ethnicity. Native American adolescents have the highest suicide rate—four times that of Caucasian adolescents. Caucasian adolescents have a higher suicide rate than African American adolescents, and African Americans have a higher rate than Hispanic Americans (National Adolescent Health Information Center, 2006).

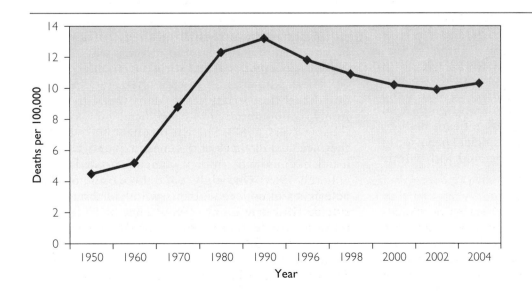

FIGURE 14.2
ADOLESCENT SUICIDE
RATES: 1950 TO 2004

Source: Data from U.S. Bureau
of the Census (2008).

PERSONAL ISSUES WHY ARE ADOLESCENT GIRLS MORE LIKELY TO BE DEPRESSED THAN ADOLESCENT BOYS?

During childhood, boys and girls are equally likely to be depressed, but by adulthood, women are twice as likely to be depressed as men. It is thus during adolescence that this gender difference in the rates of depression first emerges. But why?

An obvious explanation would seem to be the hormonal fluctuations associated with women's menstrual cycle. Evidence for this hypothesis is weak, however (Seroczynski, Jacquez, & Cole, 2003). A second explanation for this difference has to do with gender differences in body satisfaction. Both males and females become less satisfied with their bodies during adolescence, but females' dissatisfaction increases more than males'. Since discontent with one's physique is associated with depression, this could account for the higher depression rate in adolescent females (Kostanski & Gullone, 1998).

Perhaps the most intriguing explanation has come from work linking biological and societal factors. Petersen and her colleagues (1993) noted that depression rates were highest when adolescents made the transition to middle school on or about the time they were experiencing puberty. Because girls hit puberty about two years earlier than boys, in most communities, girls are more likely than boys to begin middle school and to begin experiencing pubertal change at the same time. Experiencing these two significant stressors at once could be overwhelming. It is therefore likely that a confluence of factors—those described here and the social issues described in the body of the text—work together to contribute to girls' higher depression rates.

ANSWERS WOULDN'T YOU LIKE TO KNOW . . .

Who are more likely to commit suicide: adolescent boys or girls?

Girls are much more likely to attempt suicide, but boys are much more likely to succeed.

Causes and Motives of Suicide

Why do adolescents attempt to take their own lives? What are their motives? Many people are surprised to learn that 90 percent of persons who commit suicide have one or more psychological disorders. Most commonly, they are depressed, but they also are likely to have a substance abuse problem or an anxiety disorder. In fact, the two best predictors of suicide are clinical depression and a previous suicide attempt (U.S. Department of Health and Human Services, 1999).

To put this in context, remember that although psychological disorders have a biological component, they are primarily caused by negative experiences and stressors in the environment. Thus, there are some commonalities in the backgrounds of most youths who commit suicide. In particular, a significant body of empirical literature suggests that suicidal behavior in the teenage years is largely associated with family processes (Koopmans, 1995).

Family Relationships

Impaired family relationships are the second common factor observed in suicidal youth. Studies have indicated that many different aspects of family life can be implicated in suicide ideation, attempts, and completions

(e.g., Bridge, Goldstein, & Brent, 2006). For example, parental psychopathology and substance abuse are correlated with attempted and completed adolescent suicide (Brent, 1995); in addition, suicidal behavior runs in families, and this appears to be at least in part from genetic causes (Brent & Mann, 2005). Poor parent-child relationships clearly contribute to adolescent suicidal behavior (e.g., Yuen, Andrade, Nahulu, et al., 1996); the degree to which the child gets along and communicates with his or her father seems especially important (Gould, Fisher, Parides, et al., 1996). Parents who fail to monitor their children also put their children at increased risk (King, Schwab-Stone, Flisher, et al., 2001). Adolescents from one-parent homes are more likely to attempt and commit suicide than adolescents from intact families (Weitoft, Hjern, Haglund, et al., 2003), in part because of lessened monitoring and in part because of poorer parent-child relationships.

All of these factors sum to an absence of any warm, parental figure with whom to identify, with a resulting sense of emotional and social isolation.

Those who attempt suicide often state that they do not feel close to any adult. Many times, they have trouble communicating with significant others around them (Stivers, 1988). There is no one to turn to when they need to talk. Lack of closeness to parents leads to a lack of emotional support when it is needed (Dukes & Lorch, 1989). One study found three common characteristics of college students who had thoughts of suicide (Dukes & Lorch, 1989). They had poor relationships with parents, poor relationships with peers, and a sense of personal helplessness regarding their future. When social integration is high, suicide rates for all age groups are lower (Lester, 1991).

PERSONAL ISSUES   PREVENTING SUICIDE

Recognize the Precipitating Conditions

- The loss of a close friend or family member through death or relocation
- Other significant loss, such as a loss of job, home, status, and so on
- Substance abuse
- Depression
- A long-standing but recently exacerbated problem
- Feelings of worthlessness
- Social isolation

Recognize the Signs That Suicide May Be Imminent

- Depression that disappears for no reason
- Declining school or work performance
- Lack of interest in formerly enjoyed activities
- Deteriorating physical appearance
- Self-abusive, self-injurious behavior
- Explicit or veiled statements that the person is going to die or go away
- Preparation of a will or verbal statements giving away possessions
- Sentimental visits to favorite places
- Acquisition of lethal means, such as a gun, pills, poison, and so on

What You Can Do

- Do *not* ignore these signs. Speak to your friend. You will *not* encourage someone to commit suicide by asking about his or her problems or whether he or she has contemplated suicide.
- Listen to what your friend has to say. Be empathic and sympathetic. Do *not* belittle or trivialize his or her problems.
- Let your friend know that you care.
- Try to diminish feelings of hopelessness by helping your friend brainstorm solutions to his or her problem.
- Do *not* leave your friend alone if you believe that he or she is suicidal.
- Get rid of any means the person has to kill himself or herself. Ask to hold the means until you have had more time to try to help.
- Get help. Encourage your friend to speak to a counselor or call a crisis hotline. Let your friend know that you will not abandon him or her if he or she speaks to someone else.
- If you cannot get your friend to contact someone with training in this area, make the contact yourself.

ANSWERS WOULDN'T YOU LIKE TO KNOW ...

What factors put a teen at risk for suicide?

Most, but not all, teens who commit suicide are depressed. Many of them use drugs or alcohol, and many have a history of sexual abuse. Suicide is often triggered by the loss of someone or something important in the teen's life.

The background of social isolation makes these adolescents particularly vulnerable to the loss of a love object, which may trigger the suicide attempt. The loss of a parent in childhood makes any subsequent loss of a family member, peer, boyfriend, or girlfriend particularly hard to accept (Agerbo, Nordentoft, & Mortensen, 2002). Many studies have found that loss and low family support are good predictors of an adolescent's suicide attempt (e.g., Morano, Cisler, & Lemerond, 1993).

Other Psychological Correlates

The risk of suicide among adolescents, especially males, increases with alcohol and drug abuse (Brent, Baugher, Bridge, et al., 1999). Under the influence of drugs or alcohol, adolescents are more likely to act on impulse or to overdose and kill themselves without intending to do so. Other psychological problems—conduct disorder, post-traumatic stress syndrome, anxiety disorders, and eating disorders—also increase the likelihood of suicidal behavior (Bridge, Goldstein, & Brent, 2006).

A disproportionate number of adolescents who commit suicide have a history of sexual abuse (Pompili, Mancinelli, Girardi, et al., 2004).

Sexual Orientation

Gay and lesbian teens are more likely to attempt and actually complete suicide than heterosexual teens (Lester, 2006). As many as 30 percent of homosexual adolescents attempt suicide (Safren & Heimberg, 1999). These youths have the same risk factors as their straight peers: substance abuse, depression, loss, family discord, and so on. The rates among homosexual teens are higher because, as a group, they face the additional stressors of acknowledging their sexual orientation, of experiencing negative reactions by parents and friends, and of being victimized by hate-motivated individuals (Garland & Zigler, 1993; Savin-Williams, 1994).

Copycat Suicides

Copycat suicide is a real phenomenon (U.S. Department of Health and Human Services, 1999). Knowing someone who commits suicide not only increases one's feelings of loss, but also disinhibits one's own restraints about suicide. One person's suicide, in effect, "gives permission" for others to commit suicide, too. This is especially true if the suicide is well publicized and results in extensive media coverage (Stack, 2003). In fact, fictional accounts of suicides presented on television or in movies can trigger copycat attempts (Gould, 2001).

Unsuccessful Attempts

Sometimes, attempted suicide is a cry for help to get attention or sympathy or an attempt to manipulate other people. Attempted suicide is not necessarily an effort to die but rather a communication to others in an effort to improve one's life. These attempts that seem destined to fail—for example, an overdose of pills taken 10 minutes before a parent is due home from work—are called **suicide gestures.** As a matter of fact, desired changes in one's life situation as a result of attempted suicide may be accomplished. However, many suicidal gestures for help misfire and lead to death.

RESEARCH HIGHLIGHT   A RAPID RISE IN SELF-INJURIOUS BEHAVIOR

An unfortunate behavior appears to be gaining ground with adolescents: self-injurious, or self-mutilating, behavior. Self-injurious behavior is defined as behavior that intentionally causes harm to the body for purposes not socially sanctioned (e.g., not for cosmetic purposes, such as body piercing) and without the apparent intent to commit suicide (Alderman, 1997). Self-injury most often takes the form of cutting with a knife or razor blade, but it also includes burning, picking at wounds, swallowing sharp objects, biting, inserting sharp objects into one's body cavities, scratching oneself, punching hard objects, and purposefully falling down stairs (Burrows, 1992; Styer, 2006).

There is not a great deal of research on the prevalence of self-mutilation in the adolescent population. The relatively few studies that have been conducted have yielded results ranging from 14 to 39 percent for the general, non-clinical population and 40 to 61 percent in clinical, inpatient samples (cited in Nock & Prinstein, 2005). In some but not all of these studies girls have been found to self-injure more than boys (e.g., Kirkcaldy, Richardson-Vejlgaard, & Siefen, 2009, who also found that middle children were more likely than eldest or youngest children to self-injure). The behavior is so newly widespread in persons without other forms of psychopathology that it is not included in the American Psychological Association's *Diagnostic and Statistical Manual*, although some clinicians are calling for its inclusion in the next edition.

What motivates self-injurious behavior? It is closely linked to adolescent depression (e.g., Briere & Gil, 1998), borderline personality disorder (Sansone, Gaither, & Songer, 2002), suicide attempts (Jacobson & Gould, 2007), and eating disorders (Paul, Schroeter, Dahme, et al., 2002), but clearly many adolescents who have not been diagnosed with full-blown psychological disorders are injuring themselves. Adolescents who have been sexually abused have high rates of self-harm (Zlotnick, Shea, Pearlstein, et al.,

1996). In general, self-harm seems to be a response to high levels of stress and unhappiness. Therefore, any adolescent who is coping with substantial problems—for example, homeless youth (Tyler, Whitbeck, Hoyt, et al., 2003)—are at heightened risk.

Why has this behavior surfaced now? We can only speculate. It might be because body piercing "opened the door" to the practice. We know that it, like suicide, is a copycat phenomenon, spreading once it has been identified in a community or given publicity (Yates, 2004).

Self-mutilation can help an adolescent deal with overwhelming stress in multiple ways (Suyemoto, 1998). First, it can be used to express one's pain in a visible form to oneself and to others. Second, it can be a means of achieving control over emotions that would otherwise be devastating. Nock and Prinstein (2005) found evidence for both of these motivations—cries for help and emotional control—but reported that the majority of the self-injurers they studied did so to "stop feeling bad" or "to become numb." These effects last for at least 24 hours (Kamphuis, Ruyling, & Reijntjes, 2007). Most self-mutilators feel little or no pain when they injure themselves (Zila & Kiselica, 2001) because they have elevated endogenous endorphin levels (Sher & Stanley, 2008).

Fortunately, a variety of therapies have proven effective in helping self-mutilators stop their harmful behavior. Yaryura-Tobias, Neziroglu, and Kaplan (1995), for example, had success with an exposure then response prevention technique. This is an approach most commonly used to treat obsessive-compulsive disorder. Clients are monitored when they desire to injure themselves and are not permitted to do so; eventually, the urge diminishes and the habit is broken. Other forms of behavior modification and cognitive therapy can also be beneficial (reviewed by Zila & Kiselica, 2001). Most therapists use a multi-pronged approach (Suyemoto & MacDonald, 1995).

IN THEIR OWN WORDS

"I feel out of control. I reach for my car keys, press one deep in the pale flesh of my forearm, and slowly drag it across my skin. As the metal carves through my arm, the tension increases to an almost unbearable level. When I finally pull the key away, I am rushed with a tremendous feeling of relief. My breathing slows and my muscles relax. All the tension I felt before is completely relieved and I sink into an almost catatonic calm.

"I don't do it to mutilate myself; I do it to hurt myself. I think that is the most misunderstood aspect of self-injury. It's not a cry for help; it's not a suicide attempt. It is a way to deal with stress, a coping mechanism no different from drinking or cigarette smoking. It's a way to overwhelm emotional pain with physical pain. The relief is temporary but instant; it pours over you like warm rain and you feel nothing but quiet euphoria. It's a drugless high."

IN THEIR OWN WORDS

"A year and a half ago, a friend of mine killed herself. We had known each other since seventh grade, and she and I became closer during college. Carrie was always a troubled girl, but no one knew the extent of her pain until it was too late. She had always been dramatic and a little eccentric, and people knew she loved attention. About a year before she killed herself, she became strangely morbid. She would talk about what her funeral would be like, who would come, who would be sorry, etc. She also became fairly promiscuous, sleeping with boyfriends of girls she knew casually. When we would be out, she would burn herself with cigarettes. Because her behavior was exhibitory, we all figured she was just doing it for attention.

"Apparently, Carrie had been diagnosed with depression. Little did we know she had stopped taking her medication a week before she killed herself. That week, she prepared herself. She apologized to our friend for not picking her for kickball in fourth grade. The next day, she got up, went for a run with her dog (her favorite thing to do), returned, and hung herself in her barn with her dog's leash.

"Not only was her suicide very sad, but I have realized how selfish it was, too. Not only did she leave behind two younger siblings (one of whom found her), but she left all her friends a mess. Her mother is now a chain smoker and drinks regularly."

Contrary to common opinion, suicide attempts in a great majority of cases are considered in advance and weighed rationally against other alternatives. The attempter may have tried other means: rebellion, running away from home, lying, stealing, or other attention-getting devices. Having tried these methods and failed, the person turns to suicide attempts. Most adolescents who attempt suicide talk about it first. If others are alerted in time, if they pay attention to these developments and take them seriously enough to try

suicide gestures   suicide attempts that seem destined to fail and that really are cries for help rather than true attempts.

Adolescent suicide is particularly difficult for the family and friends who are left behind. They may suffer from loss and emptiness as well as from feelings of responsibility for not recognizing the problem.

to remedy the situation, a death may be prevented (Ghang & Jin, 1996).

Survivors

Adolescent suicide is particularly devastating for family and peers who are left behind. Survivors typically experience fear, rage, guilt, and depression, as well as shock, disbelief, and numbness. They feel responsible for not recognizing the signals that might have been given and preventing the suicide, and they feel angry at the victim for deserting them. Feelings of loss and emptiness and a sense of disbelief are often followed by bouts of self-doubt and recrimination. Recovering from the loss may take one to two years, depending on the survivor's personality and the events surrounding the suicide. Intense feelings have to be worked through as survivors come to terms with the loss (Baugher, 1999).

Eating Disorders

Societal stereotypes of physical attractiveness cause most adolescent girls to desire to be slim. In fact, it has become the norm for girls to begin dieting in early adolescence if not before (Tyrka, Graber, & Brooks-Gunn, 2000). Sometimes the desire to be thin is carried to such an extreme that an eating disorder develops. No longer a rarity, eating disorders are the third most common chronic illness among adolescent girls (Rosen, 2003). Two of these disorders are discussed here: anorexia nervosa and bulimia.

Anorexia Nervosa

Anorexia nervosa is a life-threatening emotional disorder characterized by an obsession with food and weight. It is sometimes referred to as the *starvation sickness* or *dieter's disease*. In order to be diagnosed as anorexic, an individual must be at least 15 percent under normal body weight for his or her height and build. In addition, an individual must show an excessive fear of gaining weight and becoming fat; he or she must have a distorted body image such that he or she does not perceive himself or herself as being

---

ANSWERS WOULDN'T YOU LIKE TO KNOW ...

What types of teens are at risk for developing anorexia?

Early adolescent Caucasian girls who are perfectionists and who have controlling, overly protective parents are at the highest risk for developing anorexia.

---

underweight. Furthermore, a female must experience *amenorrhea*, or the absence of menstrual cycling (American Psychiatric Association, 2000). It is not uncommon for anorexics to be clinically depressed (Kennedy, Kaplan, Garfinkel, et al., 1994) and to exhibit obsessive-compulsive traits (Fisher, Fornari, Waldbaum, et al., 2002). Some anorexics also engage in binging and purging behaviors.

Anorexia is also associated with numerous medical conditions: slow heartbeat, cardiac arrest (potentially a cause of death), low blood pressure, dehydration, hypothermia, electrolyte abnormalities, metabolic changes, constipation, and abdominal distress (Becker, Grinspoon, Klibanski, et al., 1999). Once the illness has progressed, anorexics become thin and emaciated in appearance. They feel cold, even in warm weather. The body grows fine silky hair (lanugo) to conserve body heat. A potassium deficiency may cause malfunction of the kidneys. Researchers have also found brain abnormalities coupled with impaired mental and memory performance in anorexic girls, a result of the malnutrition they suffer (e.g., Seed, Dixon, McClusky, et al., 2000).

Although some anorexics have only one bout with the condition, between 30 and 40 percent relapse (Herzog, Dorer, Keel, et al., 1999). Ultimately, more than 10 percent of anorexics die because of medical problems associated with malnutrition (Reijonen, Pratt, Patel, et al., 2003). Their obsession with dieting is frequently combined with a compulsion to exercise (Davis, 1999). Hunger and fatigue are usually denied, and any attempt to interfere with their eating and exercising regimen is angrily resisted. Anorexics are very difficult to treat (Woodside, 2005).

Anorexia is less common among African American than Caucasian girls, even though African American girls tend to be heavier (Walcott, Pratt, & Patel, 2003). (Recall from Chapter 4 that African American girls tend to be more satisfied with their bodies than Caucasian girls.) Anorexia is also much less common in males. Those males who do develop the disorder are often athletes, dancers, or models who have reason to control their weight (Rolls, Federoff, & Guthrie, 1991). Wrestlers, body builders, and long-distance runners are especially at risk (Garner, Rosen, & Barry, 1998). Some 90 to 95 percent of anorexics are female, usually between the ages of 12 to 18. The disorder became more common through the 1970s and 1980s, but the prevalence has leveled off at about 0.3 percent in adolescent and young adult females (Hoek, 2006). Although it is most common in middle- and upper-middle class adolescent girls, it has been known to occur among individuals from all economic classes and a wide variety of age groups.

Much of the recent research into the cause of anorexia has focused on anorexics' relationships with their families. Families with anorexic daughters are often described as noncohesive and unsupportive (Tyrka, Graber, & Brooks-Gunn, 2000). They raise their daughters to be full of guilty feelings (Berghold & Lock, 2002), and mothers transfer their own excessive concerns about weight and attractiveness to their daughters (Hirokane, Tokomura, Nanri, et al., 2005). In other words, girls are more likely to diet if their mothers do as well, and they are more likely to engage in extreme weight-loss measures if their mothers are dissatisfied with their own bodies (Benedikt, Wertheim, & Love, 1998; Hill & Pallin, 1998). Eating disorders have also been linked to sexual abuse (Fornari & Dancyger, 2003).

Some of this research is longitudinal, and so it is possible to say that impaired family relationships are a strong predictor of disordered eating symptoms— stronger even than being overweight (Archibald, Graber, & Brooks-Gunn, 1999). This association between disordered family relationships and anorexia holds true in early adolescence but not in middle and late adolescence (Archibald, Linver, Graber, et al., 2002).

The fact that anorexia nervosa appears at puberty after the development of sexual characteristics suggests that sexual conflict is a central issue in the illness. Apparently, anxiety develops over feminine physiological changes. The girl's developing body demands that she comes to terms with her female sexual identification. She has the task of integrating her new body image with her concept of female sexual and gender roles. If she cannot accept her female sexual identity, she may seek to repress her physical development to a stage of prepubertal development. She then actually distorts her body through extreme weight loss and takes on a slim, masculine appearance. She may become severely emaciated in appearance, removing all outward signs of her secondary sex characteristics. In addition, she stops menstruating. These efforts represent the girl's desperate attempt to halt her sexual development. Instead of progressing forward through adolescence, she regresses to a prepubertal stage of development and delays the maturation process.

Anorexics have a pervasive sense of inadequacy and distorted body images and this often leads to depression. They have low self-esteem (Surgenor, Maguire, Russell, et al., 2007), reflecting negative attitudes about their physical attractiveness (Canals, Carbajo, Fernandez, et al., 1996). Anorexics are often described as compliant, self-doubting, dependent, perfectionistic, and anxious (McVey, Pepler, Davis, et al., 2002). They are not very attuned to their body's internal signals of hunger (Wonderlich, Lilenfeld, Riso, et al., 2005). Adolescents with anorexia nervosa rarely look at themselves and, even when forced to, rarely perceive their body images accurately. They view their bodies with disgust, which is a projection of how they actually feel about themselves.

What are the various forms of treatment for anorexia nervosa? Medical treatment involves monitoring the physical condition of the anorexic and trying to return her weight to the safe range. Behavior modification uses rewards and deprivation, contingent on eating behavior and weight gain. Family therapy seeks to solve underlying family interaction

anorexia nervosa   an eating disorder characterized by an obsession with food and with being thin.

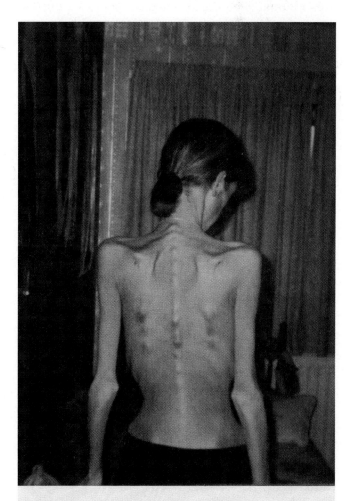

Individuals with anorexia go way beyond becoming slim. They have distorted body images and lose weight to the point that they do considerable damage to their health.

problems and to improve relationships with the anorexic (Dare, Eisler, Russell, et al., 1990). Individual counseling can be used to help the individual resolve her emotional conflicts. One review found that family therapy was most effective overall (Le Grange & Lock, 2005). The goals are to eliminate the anorexic symptoms and to enable the patient to feel and act as an independent person who likes herself, is confident about her capabilities, and is in control of her life. Accomplishing these goals may require lengthy therapy (Lask, Waugh, & Gordo, 1997).

Bulimia

Bulimia is the binge-purge syndrome. The name comes from the Greek *bous limos,* which means "ox hunger" (Ieit, 1985). The first cases of bulimia that appeared in the literature were in connection with anorexia nervosa (Vandereycken, 1994). Originally, bulimia was diagnosed as a subtype of anorexia; however, bulimia is now designated a separate eating disorder (American Psychiatric Association, 2000).

In order to be diagnosed with bulimia, an individual must (1) participate in repeated episodes of binge eating over which he or she has no control; (2) engage in excessive compensatory behaviors to avoid gaining weight, such as fasting, vomiting, and abusing laxatives; and (3) unduly allow his or her weight to influence self-esteem. Moreover, the binging must occur at least twice per week over a period of at least three months (American Psychiatric Association, 2000).

Bulimia is characterized by a compulsive and rapid consumption of large quantities of high-calorie food in a short period of time (Holleran, Pascale, & Fraley, 1988). One study of the frequency and duration of binging episodes among bulimic clients in an outpatient setting revealed an average of 13.7 hours spent in binge eating each week (Mitchell, Pyle, & Eckert, 1981). Binging and purging may occur many times daily. Caloric consumption can range from 1,200 to 11,500 calories per episode, with carbohydrates as the primary food. Many bulimic individuals report losing the ability to perceive a sense of fullness. Episodes usually take place secretly, often in the afternoon or evening and sometimes at night. Induced vomiting is the usual aftermath of binge-eating episodes. Bulimics use laxatives, diuretics, enemas, amphetamines, compulsive exercising, or fasting to offset the huge food intake.

Bulimics are unhappy with the appearance of their bodies and yearn to attain the thin shape glamorized by society (Ruuska, Kaltiala-Heino, Rantanen, et al., 2005). However, they lack control over eating. The bulimic feels driven to consume food and, because of a concern about body size, to purge afterward. Binges usually follow periods of stress and are accompanied by anxiety, depressed mood, and self-deprecating thoughts during and after the episode (Davis & Jamieson, 2005; Wegner, Smyth, Crosby, et al., 2002).

Who develops bulimia? It is more common, by far, in girls than boys; only about 10 percent of bulimics are male (Nye & Johnson, 1999). Bulimia tends to develop in middle to late adolescence and lasts into the twenties, which is a somewhat later age range than for anorexia (Reijonen, Pratt, Patel, et al., 2003). Girls from lower-income families are relatively more likely to develop bulimia than girls from upper-income families (Gard & Freeman, 1996).

Bulimics wish to be perfect, yet they have a poor self-image, are shy, and lack assertiveness (Bardone, Vohs, Abramson, et al., 2000). Like anorexics, they are often perfectionistic and unsatisfied with the way they look. They believe themselves to be unattractive (Young, Clopton, & Bleckley, 2004). They feel pressured by others to be thin.

Because of unrealistic standards, compulsive dieting, and the drive for perfection, pressure builds up, which is relieved through lapses of control during binge-purge episodes. This is followed by feelings of shame and guilt, which contribute to a sense of low self-esteem and depression. Bulimics are often difficult to treat because they resist seeking help or sabotage their treatment.

The families of bulimics are somewhat different from those of anorexics. Whereas the families of anorexics tend to be overprotective, repressed, and enmeshed, the families of bulimics are better described as chaotic, stressful, disengaged (Tyrka, Graber, & Brooks-Gunn, 2000) and to exhibit poor communication (Moreno, Selby, Aved, et al., 2000). Even so, the parents of bulimics are typically intrusive about their daughter's weight and appearance (Rorty, Yager, Rossotto, et al., 2000).

Some of the most promising treatment programs involve cognitive-behavioral approaches that help clients identify unrealistic and self-defeating cognitions and assumptions (Phillips, Greydanus, Pratt, et al., 2003). Correcting these irrational beliefs is an essential step toward changing the bulimic's behavior. Family therapy has also been found useful (e.g., Paulson-Karlsson, Engstron, & Nevonen, 2009). Therapists have found that antidepressants can reduce binging and purging behaviors (Freeman, 1998).

Many individuals find it difficult to distinguish between anorexia nervosa and bulimia. To help clarify the differences, Table 14.1 provides a point-by-point comparison of these two disorders.

TABLE 14.1   COMPARISON OF ANOREXIA NERVOSA AND BULIMIA

CHARACTERISTIC	ANOREXIA NERVOSA	BULIMIA
Weight	Emaciated	Near normal
Prevalence	1% of adolescent girls	2% to 3% of adolescent girls
Age of Onset	Teens	Late teens, early twenties
Race/Ethnicity	Primarily Caucasian	No racial/ethnic differences
Eating Behavior	Barely eats	Periodically consumes large quantities and then purges
Personality	Dependent, anxious, perfectionistic	Moody, impulsive, unable to tolerate frustration
Emotional State	Denial	Guilt and shame
Desire to Change	No desire to change	Great desire to change
Behavior Motivation	Desire for control and rejection of femininity	Desire to be perceived as attractive
Family Background	Enmeshed and repressed	Conflicted and stress filled
Treatment Success	Very difficult to treat	Somewhat easier to treat

Juvenile Delinquency

The term *juvenile delinquency* refers to the violation of the law by a juvenile, which in most states means anyone younger than 18. The legal term **juvenile delinquent** was established for young lawbreakers so that they could avoid the disgrace and stigma of being classified in legal records as criminals and to separate underage people and treat them differently from adult criminals. Most are tried in juvenile courts where the intent is to rehabilitate them.

A young person may be labeled a *delinquent* for breaking any of a number of laws, ranging from murder to truancy from school. Violations of laws that apply only to minors—for instance, underage drinking, curfew violations, and truancy—are called **status crimes.** Because laws are inconsistent, a particular action may be considered delinquent in one community but not in another. Furthermore, law enforcement officials differ in the method and the extent to which they enforce the law. In some communities, the police may simply talk to adolescents who are accused of minor crimes; in others, the police refer youths to their parents; and in still others, they may arrest them and refer them to juvenile courts. As with adults, many crimes adolescents commit are never discovered or, if discovered, are not reported or prosecuted. Most statistics, therefore, understate the extent of juvenile crime (Flannery, Hussey, Biebelhausen, et al., 2003).

Incidence of Delinquency

According to the Office of Juvenile Justice and Delinquency Prevention, in 2006, juveniles were responsible for 15 percent of all violent crime arrests and 29 percent of all property crime arrests in the United States (Snyder & Sickmund, 2006). As Figure 14.3 indicates, juveniles contribute most to the total incidence rates of arson, vandalism, and motor vehicle theft; they are less involved in murder and aggravated assault. The rate at which juveniles commit violent crimes remained fairly constant between the mid-1970s and the mid-1980s but then rose sharply between 1985 and 1993. Since then, the juvenile violent crime rate has dropped and is, in fact, now lower than it has been since 1980 (see Figure 14.4, p. 369).

This trend also holds true for the juvenile homicide rate in particular. As a result of the increasing societal attention paid to killings by youths, there is the widespread misconception that the adolescent homicide rate has continued to rise. Instead, the juvenile homicide rate has dropped dramatically

bulimia   an eating disorder characterized by binge-eating episodes and purging.

juvenile delinquent   a juvenile who violates the law.

status crimes   violations of laws that apply only to minors, such as underage drinking, violating curfews, and truancy.

Many youths engage in status crimes, such as underage drinking.

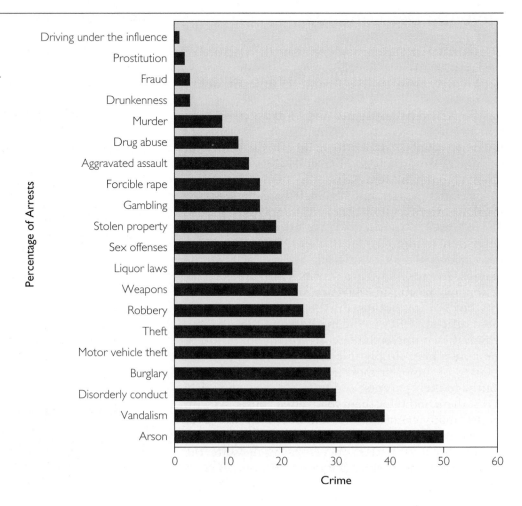

FIGURE 14.3 ARRESTS INVOLVING JUVENILES BY TYPE OF CRIME: 2006

Source: Data from Snyder & Sickmund (2006).

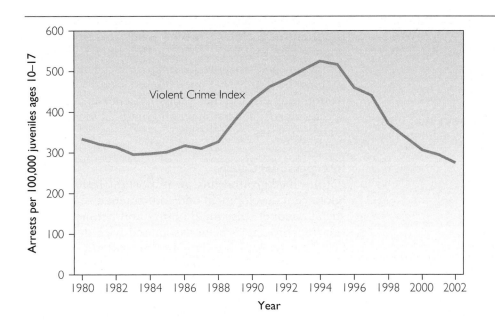

FIGURE 14.4 JUVENILE CRIME RATE: 1980–2002

Source: Data from Snyder (2004).

since it peaked in 1993. Most of this drop has resulted from a decrease in the use of firearms. Juvenile murders committed with other types of weapons have remained nearly constant, unfortunately. Still, the 2003 juvenile murder rate was at a 30-year low (Snyder & Sickmund, 2006).

African American youths are more likely to commit murder than their White counterparts. The vast majority of adolescents who murder kill someone of their own race or ethnic group, which means African American adolescents are also far more likely to be the victims of homicide than White youths. Adolescent males are considerably more likely than females to murder and to be murdered (Fox & Zawitz, 2006).

Teenagers are two and a half times more likely than adults to be the victims of violent crimes. Teens are more likely to be the victims of property crimes, too. Crimes with juvenile victims are committed both by adults and by other teenagers. In fact, only about one in four juvenile homicide victims is killed by another adolescent (Synder & Sickmund, 2006).

Currently, girls account for about 25 percent of all juvenile arrests. However, for many years, the girls' arrest rate has been climbing faster than that for boys, and so the gap continues to narrow. In addition, boys who are involved in the juvenile justice system are likely to be referred for violations of the law, whereas girls are more likely to be referred for truancy, runaway behaviors, and social/personal problems. Boys tend to engage in a broad range of serious delinquent behaviors, whereas the behaviors of girls tend to be more narrowly constrained (Lahey, Van Hulle, Waldman, et al., 2006). For example, girls are more likely to restrict assaults to family members than to acquaintances or strangers; the reverse is true for boys (Roe-Sepowitz, 2009).

Adolescents are more likely to commit crimes and to be victimized when away from school than when at school. On school days, most crimes involving juveniles occur during the hours after school lets out, between 3 P.M. and 6 P.M. On weekends and holidays, most juvenile crime occurs between 8 P.M. and 10 P.M. This suggests that providing after-school programs would reduce crime more than enforcing curfews (Snyder & Sickmund, 2006).

Causes of Delinquency

Antisocial behavior usually begins early in life (Tolan, Guerra, & Kendall, 1995). Much research has been dedicated to trying to determine its cause. In general, the causes of delinquency may be grouped into three major categories:

- *Environmental causes* include elements in the adolescent's neighborhood and community.
- *Interpersonal causes* refer to the influences of family, friends, siblings, and peers.
- *Personal causes* refer to personality traits and biological predispositions to antisocial behavior found within the delinquent.

ANSWERS WOULDN'T YOU LIKE TO KNOW …

Is juvenile crime increasing or decreasing?

Juvenile crime has been decreasing since the mid-1990s. This is true for both violent and nonviolent offenses.

Also, as Bronfenbrenner (1979) explained in his ecological analysis of behavior, these three types of factors interact with one another in synergistic ways; they are not independent.

Environmental Causes

The most important environmental factors that have been investigated in relation to juvenile delinquency are the following:

- Poverty
- Living in a high-crime area
- The presence of gangs
- The availability of drugs
- Having substandard schools
- Living in a fragmented, noncohesive neighborhood
- Exposure to media violence
- Rapid social change

Many of these factors, of course, typically co-occur. That is why youths raised in impoverished areas are more likely to commit delinquent acts and to participate in violent offenses than middle-class youths (Farrington, 2009). Keep in mind, though, that some middle-class adolescents do get involved in crime, and that many poor teenagers do not.

What distinguishes those poverty-stricken teens who become delinquents from those who do not? This is where the interrelations among the different types of risk factors come into play. Chung and his colleagues (Chung, Hawkins, Gilchrist, et al., 2002) tried to answer this question by looking broadly at the lives of poor children and seeing who later became delinquent. They found, for example, that adolescents who avoided becoming delinquent had different temperaments, were closer to their parents, were more closely monitored by their parents, were less involved with antisocial peers, did better in school, and lived in neighborhoods in which drugs were not as ubiquitous than did those adolescents who began to break the law. Furthermore, the circumstances of those youths who were delinquent only for a short time differed along many of the same dimensions, to a lesser degree, than those youth who were chronically delinquent. In a similar study, Fergusson, Swin-Campbell, and Horwood (2004) found that only those lower-income youth who were physically disciplined by their parents, lacked maternal care, frequently missed school, and associated with delinquent peers got into trouble themselves.

Other research has shown that some school environments foster antisocial attitudes and behaviors. In particular, *disorganized schools*—in which rules are only sporadically enforced, there are problems with overcrowding, and after-school programs are unavailable— are the ones most prone to promote delinquency (Flannery, Hussey, Biebelhausen, et al., 2003).

Today's adolescents are also living in a period of rapid cultural change, which tends to foster delinquency (see Chapter 1). Values that once were commonly accepted are now questioned. Social institutions such as the family that once offered security and protection may exert an upsetting influence instead. The specter of social, economic, and political unrest stimulates anxieties and rebellion.

Interpersonal Causes

Family background has an important influence on adolescent development and adjustment and hence on social conduct. Disrupted homes and strained family relationships have been associated with delinquent behavior. Lack of family cohesion and angry family relationships are particularly important correlates of delinquency (Bischof, Stiph, & Whitney, 1995). Parents who model aggression or who reinforce the violent behavior that they observe in their children are most likely to have delinquent children (Patterson, DeBarysne, & Ramsey, 1989). Poor parental monitoring and inconsistent discipline are also associated with children's aggression and antisocial behavior (Herrenkohl, Hawkins, Chun, et al., 2001). Parents who physically abuse their children or their spouses model aggression most acutely, and so it is little wonder that their children are often aggressive (Flannery, Huff, & Manos, 1998).

One of the strongest predictors of criminal behavior by a teenager is that a close relative has also been involved in criminal activity (e.g., Odgers, Milne, Caspi, et al., 2007). Farrington and his colleagues (2001) provide six mechanisms for this association: (1) intergenerational continuities in exposure to the risk factors of poverty, toxic neighborhoods, and so on; (2) self-selection, so that antisocial individuals choose other antisocial individuals as friends; (3) shared genetic tendencies; (4) modeling and social learning within the home; (5) poor parenting practices by the antisocial parent; (6) labeling and bias by the authorities against known criminal families.

An adolescent's peers also have a large influence upon whether he or she becomes involved in delinquency. Adolescents become delinquent in part because they are socialized into it, both intentionally and unintentionally, by peers. For example, Coie and Miller-Johnson (2001) found that boys who were both aggressive and rejected by their peers were the ones who were most likely to become delinquent at a later age. Youths who have a high degree of peer orientation— with the wrong peers—are also more likely to have a high level of delinquency involvement (Elliott & Menard, 1996). For example, teens who begin to associate with antisocial youth—who join a gang, for example—show increased amounts of antisocial activity (Gatti, Tremblay, Vitraro, et al., 2005). Even so, close

Involvement in school and community organizations, such as the teen club shown here, is often a deterrent to delinquent activity.

association with deviant peers usually occurs only after there are both established negative family interactions and a history of rejection by mainstream peers. In other words, peers can exacerbate and encourage delinquency in youths who are already unhappy and poorly adjusted.

Personal Causes

There have also been efforts to determine whether certain personality factors predispose adolescents to delinquency. No single personality type can be associated with delinquency, but it is known that those who become delinquent are more likely to be socially assertive, defiant, ambivalent to authority, resentful, hostile, and impulsive or lacking in self-control (Caspi, Lynan, Moffitt, et al., 1993; Feldman & Weinberger, 1994). Self-control tends to be associated with an entire constellation of personality and behavioral traits, each of which by itself is negatively related to delinquency. Namely, these traits are (1) ability to delay gratification, (2) persistence, (3) caution, (4) ability to set long-term goals, (5) awareness of the importance of academic skills, and (6) sensitivity to others' feelings (Gottfredson & Hirshi, 1990).

Some delinquents consistently exhibit low self-esteem and a negative self-image. Others maintain high self-esteem through denial of their problems and by failure to admit the incongruity between their behaviors and their self-perceptions. Such adolescents become adept at denial. They refuse to accept responsibility for their actions and continually blame other people or circumstances for getting them into trouble. In many cases, delinquents have a psychological disorder such as ODD, conduct disorder, or ADHD (see the Research Highlight box).

Research has studied the extent to which delinquency is related to alcohol or drug use (Watts & Wright, 1990). Several studies have found that drinking is strongly associated with serious delinquency, especially when other factors are present, such as previous arrests, association with criminals or drug users, or heroin use by the adolescent. Furthermore, there is a strong relationship between adolescents who are raised by substance-abusing parents and juvenile delinquency. Adolescents from substance-abusing homes have been found to suffer from low self-esteem, depression, anger, and a variety of acting-out behaviors (McGaha & Leoni, 1995).

School performance is also an important factor in delinquency (Maguin & Loeber, 1996). In particular, a lack of school success—poor grades, classroom misconduct, and an inability to adjust to the school program and to get along with administrators, teachers, and parents—is associated with delinquency (Huizinga & Jakob-Chien, 1998). Delinquent youths have also been found to score lower on social cognitive skills than nondelinquent youths (Edwards, 1996).

Delinquents experience greater conflict in all relationships, which reduces the quality and stability of friendships. Lochman and Dodge (1994), for example, found that aggressive adolescents are more likely than nonaggressive adolescents to perceive others as being hostile. If a person interprets others' behavior as threatening, then he or she will more likely behave aggressively.

Although most delinquency is believed to have environmental causes, in some cases, organic or biological factors may be directly or indirectly influential. It has been found, for example, that some juvenile delinquents show evidence of a maturational lag in the development of the frontal lobe system of the brain (Chretien & Persinger, 2000). It is not that their cognition is impaired; rather, these juveniles cannot act on the basis of the knowledge they have or think through the consequences of their actions.

Other researchers have emphasized the role of biological influences in delinquency, as well. There is some evidence to show that tendencies toward delinquency may be inherited, although it is often difficult to determine whether family influences are rooted in the environment in which a child is raised or their genetic inheritance (Rowe, Rodgers, & Meseck-Bushey, 1992). It is true that certain personality characteristics, such as temperament, are genetically influenced, so that a child may have a predisposition to behave poorly. If the parents do not know how to cope, psychological disturbance in the adolescent may result.

High levels of testosterone and low levels of the neurotransmitter serotonin are also associated with aggressive behavior (Flannery, Hussey, Biebelhausen, et al., 2003). Furthermore, some research has linked these chemical imbalances with criminal activity. These chemicals likely work in conjunction with environmental and situational inputs; for example, having a low level of serotonin might make one less prone to feel happy and content, opening the door for destructive behavior.

Juvenile Gangs

During the 1980s and 1990s, youth gangs again surfaced as a major crime problem in the United States. News stories about violent crimes committed by youth gang members—crimes that often seemed to involve random victims—appeared frequently in the mass media. What does research say about youth gang crime today?

According to the most recent National Youth Gang Survey (Egley & O'Donnell, 2009), there are about 27,000 youth gangs in the United States. This figure is lower than in the mid-1990s, but higher than earlier this century: gang membership, which had been falling has been rising for the past seven or eight years. About 25 percent more police jurisdictions now report gang problems than in 2002. Gangs are most common in large cities; suburbs are the next most likely location, followed by small cities. Rural areas are least likely to have a gang problem (National Youth Gang Center, 2009).

A large body of research has characterized the typical gang member as a lower-income, minority male adolescent who does not get along with his family (Duke, Martinez, & Stein, 1997). In 2006, about 45 percent of all gang members were Latino and one-third were African American (National Youth Gang Center, 2009). Although the number of gang members who are female has held constant at about 6 to 7 percent for quite some time, more gangs have female members and there are more all-female gangs. Because gang

RESEARCH HIGHLIGHT   CONDUCT DISORDER, ODD, AND ADHD

Conduct disorder is the psychological disorder most associated with juvenile delinquency. It can be described as a chronic behavior pattern in which the individual violates age-appropriate societal norms and tramples on others' rights. These long-standing disruptive behaviors impair the adolescent's ability to function in social, occupational, and academic settings.

In order to be diagnosed with conduct disorder, an individual must exhibit at least three different disruptive symptoms. The *Diagnostic and Statistical Manual of Mental Disorders* (4th ed., revised.) clusters these symptoms in four broad groups:

1. Aggression toward people or animals (e.g., hitting or threatening classmates, throwing rocks at others' pets)
2. Destruction of property (e.g., vandalism, arson, graffiti)
3. Theft and/or deceitfulness (e.g., lying, conning, cheating, stealing)
4. Serious rule violations (e.g., repeated truancy, staying out all night) (American Psychiatric Association, 2000)

These symptoms may appear prior to adolescence or after it has begun.

Adolescents with conduct disorder often have poor social skills and don't know how to get along with others. They aren't good at handling frustration and can explode with anger. They are likely to begin using drugs at an early age and to be sexually precocious (Altepeter & Korger, 1999).

Conduct disorder is similar to both **oppositional defiant disorder (ODD)** and **attention-deficit hyperactivity disorder (ADHD)** in that persons with these disorders behave disruptively. But conduct disorder is different from both, as well. Persons with ODD are less likely to actually hurt others than are those with conduct disorder. Individuals with ODD argue and get angry. They blame others and may be defensive or disobedient, especially when interacting with authority figures. Youths with ODD go out of their way to annoy their teachers and parents but are less likely to pester peers. Individuals with ADHD often exhibit low frustration tolerance and poor impulse control, and so they may verbally or physically attack others when aroused. These antisocial behaviors, however, are more by-products of their other symptoms than symptoms in themselves. Still, meta-analyses indicate a strong linkage between delinquency and ADHD (e.g., Pratt, Cullen, Blevins, et al., 2002).

Inner-city males comprise the largest group of street gang members. They join gangs for a variety of emotional and social needs, including companionship, protection, and excitement.

membership is satisfying and profitable, many members do not want to quit as they get older: more than 60 percent of gang members are 18 or older.

Why do some individuals join gangs whereas others with similar backgrounds reject them? One theory says that a self-selection process is involved, such that youths who are already dysfunctional join gangs. A competing theory claims that normal adolescents join gangs and are then coerced into deviant behavior by their gang mates. These theories are not mutually exclusive, and both postulates appear correct: adolescents who elect to join gangs are troubled to start with, but their level of delinquency increases once they join a gang. In particular, adolescents who join gangs often have poor relationships with their parents and unresolved ethnic identities (Duke, Martinez, & Stein, 1997). They engage in antisocial activities to raise money, to gain status and approval, to bond with their gang peers, and to protect themselves.

It is generally accepted that gang membership is a primarily male activity. It appears that when girls do join gangs, they are kept more-or-less on the periphery; one role they do play is to serve as sex partners for the male gang members. Some self-report data, though, place the number of female gang members much higher

(as high as 38 percent) (Snyder & Sickmund, 2006) than the usually cited government statistics. Regardless, the conclusion remains that female gang members are less likely than male members to engage in violent activities and to be arrested, but they are as likely to engage in criminal activity (Egley, Howell, & Major, 2006). In addition, girls tend both to join and leave gangs at younger ages than boys. Finally, girls, even more than boys, join gangs to fulfill a need for connections and relationships.

Youths who are members of gangs are more likely than nonmembers to steal, to commit assaults, to carry weapons, and to kill. Gang members are also more likely to be involved in an early pregnancy, to use drugs, to be assaulted, to be injured in a drive-by shooting, and to be killed at an early age (Flannery, Huff, & Manos, 1998). Thus, for some youths, joining a gang is a last-ditch effort to improve their lives that backfires.

The Juvenile Justice System

Each state determines its own process for handling juvenile delinquents. Although this process varies among states, each system consists of three distinct

---

ANSWERS WOULDN'T YOU LIKE TO KNOW ...

How involved are girls in juvenile gangs?

As many as one-third of gangs contain female members, but fewer than 10% of gang members are female.

---

conduct disorder a psychological order typified by aggressive, hurtful, deceitful behavior.

oppositional defiant disorder (ODD) a psychological disorder that causes a person to get angry and argue, blame and annoy others, and disobey authority figures.

attention-deficit hyperactivity disorder (ADHD) a behavioral disorder characterized by impulsivity, an inability to pay attention, and an inability to sit still.

entities: the police, the juvenile court, and the correctional system.

The Police

The first contact any adolescent has with the juvenile justice system is the local police department. Charged with maintaining and enforcing the law, the police screen cases that may go before the courts. When offenses are discovered, the police may take any one of several actions: (1) ignore the offenses; (2) let the juvenile go with a warning; (3) report the problem to parents; (4) refer the case to the school, a social welfare agency, clinic, or counseling or guidance center; (5) take the juvenile into custody for questioning, to be held or reprimanded by a juvenile officer; or (6) after investigation, arrest the juvenile and turn the matter over to juvenile court. If arrested and awaiting trial, the juvenile may be released with or without bail or kept in a special detention center.

One problem is that in the beginning of the process, police exercise a good deal of discretion; this opens the door to bias and inconsistency. Some police officers enforce the law differently. An individual officer may arrest adolescents who come from the "wrong section" of town or have the wrong color skin but may release adolescents who come from well-to-do families or are neatly dressed. Some officers are far harder on juveniles than are other officers. One of the reasons adolescent offenders become bitter toward the police is because of perceived unfair and discriminatory treatment or harassment.

Many communities hire juvenile officers who are specialists in dealing with youths. Such officers go far beyond law enforcement functions and strive to assist adolescents and their families in solving problems. Some large cities have separate juvenile bureaus with four basic functions:

1. To protect juveniles

2. To prevent juvenile delinquency

3. To investigate cases of juveniles who are delinquents or involved as accessories by association with adult criminals

4. To dispose of juvenile cases

Police in many communities now go far beyond law enforcement, from sponsoring boys' and girls' clubs to offering drug education programs and safety education in local schools.

RESEARCH HIGHLIGHT   THE CASE THAT CHANGED JUVENILE COURT

Prior to the 1900s, the legal system treated juveniles as adults. If arrested, they appeared in adult courts; if sentenced, they went to adult prisons. Reformers working at the turn of the twentieth century were effective in changing this policy. They argued that minors could and should be rehabilitated rather than punished. The courts, they claimed, should assume the role of *parens patriae* and act in the best interests of the child. Although this was a noble intent, in practice it meant that juveniles were treated inconsistently and that their constitutional rights were often violated.

The case that changed the system involved a 15-year-old boy named Gerald Gault. In 1964, Gerald was arrested and detained by the police after a neighbor complained that he had made obscene phone calls to her. The police failed to notify Gerald's parents of his arrest. Neither Gerald's father nor the complainant was present at the hearing.

Witnesses were neither sworn in nor cross-examined, and no official record was kept of the proceedings. The judge ordered that Gerald be sent to a juvenile detention center until his twenty-first birthday, a six-year sentence. In contrast, the maximum penalty that an adult could have received for the same offense would have been a $50 fine and two months in jail.

The case was appealed in the Arizona Supreme Court, but the appeal was denied. When presented to the U.S. Supreme Court in 1967, the Court found in Gerald's favor in a narrow 5 to 4 ruling. It decreed that minors are entitled to due process as outlined in the Bill of Rights and the Fourteenth Amendment. Since that time, even though juvenile court remains separate from adult court, minors are guaranteed the same judicial rights as adults; for example, they have the right to an attorney, they may cross-examine witnesses, and they cannot be made to incriminate themselves.

The Juvenile Court

Even if a juvenile's case is remanded to juvenile court, there are several possible outcomes. First, the case may be dismissed (e.g., for lack of evidence). Second, the case can be handled informally in private hearings. These private hearings often occur in the judge's chambers. The judge can choose to let the juvenile go without penalty or can assign specific conditions that the juvenile must follow for a set period of time. These conditions often include obeying a curfew, regularly attending school, meeting with a counselor, and victim restitution. If the juvenile agrees to the conditions and follows them, then all is well. If he or she does not, the case is reopened and the third option, a formal hearing in juvenile court, is invoked. (Of course, some cases immediately are assigned a formal hearing.) The best juvenile court systems hire judges or magistrates with special qualifications for juvenile court work, who understand not only the law but also child psychology and social problems.

A fourth option exists in many states as well: the juvenile might be transferred to adult criminal court. This usually occurs only if the crime was especially violent or if the juvenile was a repeat offender.

The Correctional System

The majority of juvenile offenders brought to court, especially those charged for the first time, are placed on probation, given suspended sentences, and/or ordered to get help from the proper medical, psychological, or social service agency. The purpose of the court is not just to punish but also to ensure proper treatment and rehabilitation of the delinquent. Thus, the judge often must make thoughtful decisions regarding the best treatment.

The backbone of the correctional procedure is the probation system, whereby the juvenile is placed under the care of a probation officer to whom she or he must report and who strives to regulate and guide his or her conduct. About two-thirds of convicted delinquents are placed on probation (Snyder & Sickmund, 2006).

Probation based entirely on threat of punishment is poor rehabilitation, and so most juveniles placed on probation are also required to attend counseling sessions and make restitution to their victims. Studies show that juvenile offenders who are placed on probation have lower rearrest rates and generally better records than those detained in juvenile facilities. However, this occurs in part because the most serious offenders—those least likely to be rehabilitated—are not placed on probation in the first place.

Most juvenile correction systems include detention centers. Many of these are reception and diagnostic centers that place juveniles under temporary restraint while awaiting a hearing. If hearings have already been held, the individuals are placed in the center for further diagnosis and evaluation before more permanent action is taken. About one-tenth of adolescents in detention centers are not delinquents (Snyder & Sickmund, 2006). They are juveniles in need of supervision (JINS) who are wards of the court because their parents cannot, will not, or should not care for them. Some of the parents are ill or deceased; others have neglected, rejected, or abused the juveniles to the point that they have been taken out of the home. Some adolescents in detention facilities have run away from home. Many are awaiting disposition by the court. Critics charge that overcrowded detention centers are no place for these juveniles. They have done nothing wrong—indeed, they have been victimized—and they are mixed in with juveniles who may have committed serious assaults or even homicides. Similarly, one can question the wisdom of mixing the comparatively innocuous status offenders with more seriously criminal peers, as the potential for intimidation, harassment, and even inappropriate modeling seems substantial.

If a juvenile is sentenced to be held in a facility, there are a number of options. These include detention centers, long-term secure training schools, group homes, shelters, boots camps, and wilderness/ranch camps. About 30 percent of incarcerated juveniles are held in private, rather than public, facilities. The majority of incarcerated youths are in either detention centers or secure training schools (Snyder & Sickmund, 2006).

The system has been improved greatly by the use of *token economies*, which place the emphasis on a 24-hour positive learning environment (Miller, Cosgrove, & Doke, 1990). In this system, students earn points for good behavior, with points convertible to money that can be used to purchase goods or privileges. Money can be spent for room rental, for fines for misconduct, in the commissary or snack bar, or for recreation. Students earn points for academic accomplishments and schoolwork, for proper social behavior, for doing chores or other jobs, or for social development. Under this system, adolescents make great gains in academic achievement; on-the-job training; or eliminating assaultive, disruptive, and antisocial behavior.

One of the criticisms of these correctional institutions is that once the juveniles are released to the community, they often come under the same influences and face many of the same problems that led to detention in the first place. One suggestion has been to use more halfway houses and group homes where youths may live, going from there to school or to work. In this way, some control can be maintained over the

parens patriae   the philosophy that the juvenile court is to act in the best interests of the child.

Of all the options available in the juvenile correction system, sending a youth to an adult prison is the worst way to rehabilitate him or her.

adolescents until they have learned self-direction. One of the most important needs is to prepare youths for employment after discharge.

Only a small number of juvenile delinquents end up serving time in adult prisons. In 2003, 1 percent of persons admitted to adult prisons were younger than 18 (Snyder & Sickmund, 2006). This percentage climbed greatly in the 1990s, peaking in 1996, and has consistently dropped since then. The vast majority of adolescents incarcerated in adult facilities have committed serious person offenses, such as assault or homicide.

It is good that this number is so small, since sending adolescents to adult prisons is the worst way to rehabilitate them. A percentage of inmates of a prison population are violent individuals who prefer antisocial behavior, have no regard for the interests of others, and show little or no remorse. They contrast with adolescents, who are young and still developing. In spite of this, the average sentence for a juvenile is greater than for an adult who has committed the same crime (Cullen & Wright, 2002).

Once in prison, youths have no adequate adult male or female role models with whom they can have significant relationships. Furthermore, once they have a prison record, their chances of finding a useful life are jeopardized. They learn that fear, bribery, cheating, and violence are acceptable ways of dealing with problems. In addition, many prisoners are harassed and bullied by fellow prisoners, who may use them in any number of ways, including for

homosexual activities. If adolescents were not antagonistic toward authority and the system on arrival in prison, they soon become so.

Counseling and therapy, both individually and in groups, are important parts of any comprehensive program of treatment and correction of juvenile offenders. Individual therapy on a one-to-one basis is time consuming, with too few professionals and too many delinquents, but it can be effective. Some therapists believe that group therapy reaches a juvenile sooner than individual therapy because the delinquent feels less anxious and defensive in the group situation. Group therapy is sometimes offered to both juvenile offenders and their parents, in which case it becomes similar to other types of family therapy. Work with parents is especially important in correcting family situations that contribute to the delinquency in the first place.

The Restorative Justice Movement

A new approach to juvenile justice has gained momentum during the past 20 years: the **restorative justice movement.** This approach tries to balance the needs of the victim (for reparation and confrontation), the community at large (for security and protection), and the juvenile perpetrator (to learn skills so he or she has alternatives to crime). To be sure, offenders are held accountable for their crimes: they are expected to understand the harm they have caused, to accept responsibility for that harm, and to repair the damage they have caused. In theory, by meeting with their victim and making restitution and by having opportunities for education, counseling, and community service, offenders become not only more morally mature but gain a feeling of integration into the community and the desire and skills to become productive members of that community (Okimoto, Wenzel, & Feather, 2009).

The restorative justice approach is not without its critics (see Cullen & Wright, 2002). For example, it is unclear how such an approach could be implemented in the case of a serious crime, such as rape or murder, in which the victim might be understandably unwilling to confront the offender. Also, what happens if an offender promises to cooperate and then does not? What if he or she goes through the program and then commits additional offenses? To date, research on the effectiveness of the restorative justice approach has been mixed. More time will be needed to tell whether restorative justice is more effective than other rehabilitative approaches.

ANSWERS WOULDN'T YOU LIKE TO KNOW . . .

What can be done to reduce the rate of juvenile delinquency?

Programs that build life skills, create hope for the future, provide mentors, and instill prosocial values can and do reduce juvenile delinquency.

restorative justice movement   an approach to juvenile justice that addresses the needs of the victim, the community, and the perpetrator; it focuses on restitution for the victim and personal development for the offender.

SUMMARY

1. Alienated adolescents feel estranged from family, friends, and school. They turn away from the mainstream youth and adult society and express their feelings through various types of acting-out or self-destructive behavior, including running away, depression, suicide, eating disorders, and juvenile delinquency.

2. Adolescents run away from home for a number of reasons. Most runaways come from dysfunctional families. Runaways may also have problems with delinquency, academics, and peer relationships.

3. About half of all runaways, called *transient runaways,* are gone only for a night or two. *Intent runaways* are generally more serious about leaving home and are gone for longer periods of time.

4. About half of intent runaways did not leave home voluntarily; rather, they were thrown out by their parents because of poverty, their own misbehavior, or family disintegration.

5. The consequences of running away may be disastrous. Runaways are likely to be victimized by others. They must often resort to drug dealing, theft, and prostitution to earn money for food and shelter. Because of unsafe sex practices and intravenous drug use, many are at risk for HIV and AIDS.

6. Assistance to runaway youths is inadequate. More emergency shelters, more comprehensive services, stable residential placements, and transitional programs for older adolescents are all needed.

7. Adolescent homelessness is a worldwide, rather than a national, problem.

8. Between 15 and 20 percent of adolescents will experience major clinical depression before they are out of their teens. Adolescent girls are twice as likely to suffer from depression as adolescent boys, and girls' depression is more often triggered by social factors. Teenagers who have suffered a personal loss or who are having trouble at school are at heightened risk for depression.

9. Suicide is the third leading cause of death among adolescents (after accidents and homicide). Girls are more likely to attempt suicide than boys, but boys are more likely to succeed because they use more violent means.

10. Most adolescents who commit suicide are clinically depressed or are substance abusers.

11. Adolescents who commit suicide often have dysfunctional family backgrounds. In addition, these youths often lack impulse control. Because of the extra stresses they experience, gay and lesbian teens are especially likely to attempt or commit suicide.

12. Adolescent suicide is especially hard on survivors, who suffer fear, rage, guilt, and depression.

13. Anorexia nervosa is a life-threatening emotional disorder characterized by an obsession with food and weight. Symptoms include constant preoccupation with food and dieting; body image disturbances; excessive weight loss; amenorrhea; hyperactivity; moodiness; isolation; and strong feelings of insecurity, helplessness, depression, and loneliness. Anorexia is also associated with numerous medical conditions.

14. Anorexia is found primarily in teenage girls and usually appears at puberty. Anorexics often have disturbed relationships with their parents.

15. Bulimia is a binge-purge syndrome characterized by compulsive and rapid consumption of large quantities of high-calorie food, followed by efforts to purge the food.

16. Bulimics are unhappy with the appearance of their bodies, yet they are impulsive, lack control over eating, and are anxious and depressed with low self-esteem. Bulimics usually come from families that are characterized by strife and conflict.

17. Juvenile delinquency is the violation of the law by anyone under legal age. From the mid-1980s to the mid-1990s, the juvenile crime rate rose sharply. It has since been declining. Boys are more likely to commit offenses than girls, but girls' rates are rising faster than boys' rates.

18. The causes of delinquency may be grouped into three major categories: environmental, interpersonal, and personal.

19. Environmental factors leading to delinquency include poverty, living in a gang-infested neighborhood, and attending substandard schools. Not all delinquents are poor, however.

20. Interpersonal factors leading to delinquency include coming from an abusive, dysfunctional family and associating with deviant peers.

21. Personal factors leading to delinquency include poor self-control, psychological disorders, substance abuse, poor academic performance, and low social-cognitive skills.

22. Individuals may be predisposed to antisocial behavior because of maturation lags in the brain, genetic endowment, and biochemical imbalances.

23. Adolescents often organize themselves into juvenile gangs for protection, companionship, excitement, or status. Such gangs are a problem because they force members to engage in antisocial and illegal acts that they would not participate in if acting on their own. Dysfunctional youths are more prone to join gangs than psychologically healthy youths; after they join, youths are more likely to engage in deviant activities than they were before.

24. The juvenile justice system consists of the police, the juvenile court, and the correctional system (including the probation system, detention centers, training schools, ranches, forestry camps, farms, halfway houses, group homes, treatment centers, and prisons).

25. The newest approach to juvenile rehabilitation is the restorative justice approach. This model addresses the needs of the victim, the offender, and the community and incorporates both rehabilitation and punishment.

KEY TERMS

anorexia nervosa 364	*parens patriae* 374
attention-deficit hyperactivity disorder (ADHD) 372	restorative justice movement 376
bulimia 366	status crimes 367
conduct disorder 372	suicide gestures 362
depression 357	survival sex 356
juvenile delinquent 367	throwaways 355
oppositional defiant disorder (ODD) 372	

THOUGHT QUESTIONS

Personal Reflection

1. Do you know an adolescent who ran away from home? What were the circumstances?

2. Have you or someone you've been close to battled with depression? Was there a specific cause? How were you or how was he or she helped?

3. Have you ever known anyone who had an eating disorder? Describe the person and explain why you think he or she became that way.

4. Did you commit any status or criminal offenses when you were younger? Why? Were you ever caught? What happened, and how did the consequences affect you?

5. Have you known a juvenile offender who was sent to a training school or correctional institution who became a productive, law-abiding citizen? What factors made the difference?

Group Discussion

6. Should runaways be forced to return home? When should they? When should they not?

7. To what do you attribute gender differences in depression rates? Can anything be done about it?

8. Have you known an adolescent who committed suicide? What were the circumstances? What crisis intervention steps did your school take (if any)?

9. How do you account for the fact that the percentage of those younger than 18 who are arrested is decreasing?

10. Why do far greater number of males than females become delinquent? What factors may be exerting an influence?

11. Why do some adolescents who are brought up in crime-prone neighborhoods not become delinquent?

12. What should parents do if their adolescent is running around with a group whose members are known to be delinquent?

13. How can society decrease the appeal of joining a gang? How can we discourage youths from doing so?

14. What is your opinion of the juvenile justice system? How could it be improved? What do you think is needed to reform known juvenile offenders?

Debate Questions

15. Parents whose children run away from home for more than a day or two should be required to receive counseling.

16. Most teens occasionally have suicidal thoughts. They shouldn't be taken seriously.

17. The media contributes greatly to eating disorders and should be held responsible for them to some degree.

18. Schools should take an active role in preventing delinquency.

19. Delinquents who have been diagnosed with conduct disorder should be treated differently by the system than delinquents who do not have this disorder.

SUGGESTED READING

Al-Rawashdeh, A. (2009). *Runaway Youth: Psychosocial Characteristics.* Saarbrücken, Germany: VDM.

Bartol, C. R., and Bartol, A. M. (2008). *Juvenile Delinquency and Antisocial Behavior: A Developmental Perspective.* Upper Saddle River, NJ: Prentice Hall.

Berman, A. L., Jobes, D. A., and Silverman, M. M. (2005). *Adolescent Suicide: Assessment and Intervention.* Washington, DC: American Psychological Association.

Heibrun, K., Goldstein, N. E. S., and Redding, R. E. (Eds.). (2005). *Juvenile Delinquency: Prevention, Assessment, and Intervention.* New York: Oxford University Press.

Howell, J. C. (2003). *Preventing and Reducing Juvenile Delinquency: A Comprehensive Framework.* Thousand Oaks, CA: Sage.

Jackson, R. K., and McBride, W. D. (2000). *Understanding Street Gangs.* Belmont, CA: Wadsworth.

Kalodner, C. R. (2003). *Too Fat or Too Thin? A Reference Guide to Eating Disorders.* Westport, CT: Greenwood.

Koplewicz, H. (2003). *More Than Moody: Recognizing and Treating Adolescent Depression.* New York: Perigee.

Nixon, M. K., & Heath, N. L. (Eds.). (2009). *Self-injury in Youth: The Essential Guide to Assessment and Intervention.* New York: Routledge.

Noel-Hoeksema, S., and Hilt, L. M. (Eds.). (2008). *Handbook of Depression in Adolescents.* New York: Routledge.

USEFUL WEB SITES

Anorexia Nervosa and Related Eating Disorders (ANRED)
www.anred.com

This site, which is especially clearly written, contains information on the three most well-known eating disorders (anorexia, bulimia, and obesity) as well as information on less common disorders.

National Center for Missing and Exploited Children
http://missingkids.org

The site of this private, nonprofit organization has separate information sections for professionals and parents. It details the steps to take to report a missing adolescent and what to do if someone you love is missing. It also has an FAQs page and a newsroom.

National Eating Disorder Association (NEDA)
www.edap.org/p.asp?webpage_10=294

Click on the button at the top of the page, labeled "Eating Disorder Information." This site is especially useful for those interested in information about eating disorders in males and body image.

National Strategy for Suicide Prevention
www.mentalhealth.org/suicideprevention/default.asp

This site, administered by the U.S. Department of Health and Human Services, contains facts, information about prevention programs, databases, and a newsroom.

Office of Juvenile Justice and Delinquency Prevention
www.ojjdp.ncjrs.org

This federal agency has an extensive Web site filed with the most current facts, statistics, and reports available on all aspects of juvenile delinquency.

WOULDN'T YOU LIKE TO KNOW . . .

- What distinguishes *drug use* from *drug abuse?*
- What are the levels of risk for different types of drug users?
- What are the major types of drugs?
- Which drugs are most commonly used by adolescents?
- Does drug use increase or decrease in college?
- How many adolescents today use drugs?
- What demographic factors distinguish drug users from nonusers?
- What kinds of prevention and treatment programs are effective with adolescents?
- Why do teens smoke cigarettes when they know it's harmful?
- Why do so many adolescents begin to drink?
- Do most students who drink heavily in college keep drinking so heavily as adults?

chapter

15

Substance Abuse, Addiction, and Dependency

This chapter focuses on a major health problem confronting adolescents: drug abuse. This particular problem has been selected because of its frequency and its importance in the lives of adolescents. Drug abuse is considered by many to be the greatest social health problem relating to youths. It is also significantly related to delinquency and other high-risk behaviors. We take a look at the problem and answer a number of questions: Which drugs are most commonly abused? Has drug abuse been overestimated? Who uses drugs and for what reasons?

In addition to illegal drugs, large numbers of youths also smoke tobacco and drink alcohol. What can be done to prevent them from starting? What are the harmful consequences of these behaviors? Because tobacco and alcohol use are so common, each is given its own section later in this chapter. But first, we need to distinguish between *drug use* and *drug abuse.*

Drug Use and Abuse

The fact is, most of us use drugs all the time: we take a couple of aspirin when we have a headache, and we use a decongestant to dry up a stuffy nose. Virtually *all* drugs have the potential for abuse; even aspirin is lethal if taken in a sufficiently large quantity. How, then, can we distinguish between *use* and *abuse?*

There is no single, absolute heuristic for separating the two. But in commonsense terms, drug use qualifies as **drug abuse** when two criteria are met: (1) using the drug puts someone at significantly increased risk for negative consequences and (2) taking the drug interferes in some way with an individual's normal, daily responsibilities and accomplishments. Unfortunately, depending on the drug in question, the first criterion is met quite readily. The second criterion is usually met with higher doses and more frequent use.

To be honest, most adolescents who experiment with drugs suffer no lasting negative consequences. The problem, however, is that we never know when we will be one of the people in the minority—the rare individual who has a heart attack the first time he or she tries crack or the more common individual who gets into the driver's seat drunk and causes a serious car accident. Likewise, no one knows before trying a drug if he or she is particularly susceptible to addiction and dependency. Added to this, of course, is the fact that most of the drugs used by adolescents are illegal for them to possess. Therefore, any adolescent who tries these drugs runs the risk of arrest, fine, probation, or even jail time.

In many ways, using drugs is like playing Russian roulette: if there is only one bullet in the eight chambers, the odds are that you will be fine. But if you get unlucky, the consequences can be serious or even fatal.

Physical Addiction and Psychological Dependency

As an individual continues to take a drug, he or she runs the risk of developing a physical addiction or a psychological dependency. A **physical addiction** to a drug results because the body builds up a physiological need for the drug, so that its sudden denial results in withdrawal symptoms such as nausea, pain, or even seizures. In general, psychoactive drugs work by affecting the neurotransmitters that facilitate communication between nerve cells: they either enhance or diminish the effects of the neurotransmitters. Depending on which neurotransmitters are affected and whether their effects are increased or decreased, the neurons will fire more often than they should, firing when they should not, or they will fail to fire or fire only weakly. **Psychological dependency** is the development of a persistent, sometimes overpowering psychological need for a drug, resulting in a compulsion to take it. A well-established habit of psychological dependency may be more difficult to overcome than one involving physical addiction, especially if someone becomes so dependent on a drug that he or she cannot function without it. A physical addiction to heroin, for example, may be broken in a matter of weeks, but individuals go back to it because of their psychological dependence. It is a mistake, therefore, to assume that the only dangerous drugs are those that are physically addictive.

In either case, an addicted or dependent individual finds that his or her drug use interferes with daily life. He or she may miss class, skip work, or do poorly on a test, for instance. Even someone who is not addicted or dependent can experience these consequences if he or she has a hangover or feels fuzzy headed the day after using the drug.

Patterns and Intensity of Drug Use

Most persons who use drugs can be fit into one of five categories, based upon their motivation for taking the drug:

1. **Experimental use** is defined as the short-term, investigational trial of one or more drugs. It is motivated primarily by curiosity or by a desire to experience new feelings.

ANSWERS WOULDN'T YOU LIKE TO KNOW ...

What are the levels of risk for different types of drug users?

Obviously, the risk increases as the user moves up the scale from experimental to compulsive use. As both the frequency and intensity of drug use increase, so do the nature and extent of the problems a person faces. Compulsive users, by definition, have serious problems.

2. **Social-recreational use** occurs in public settings among friends or acquaintances who wish to share an experience. This type of use tends to vary in frequency, intensity, and duration but not to escalate in either frequency or intensity to patterns of uncontrolled use. Social-recreational users typically do not use highly addictive drugs such as heroin, but instead use "softer" drugs such as marijuana; they are therefore able to exercise control over their behavior.

3. **Circumstantial-situational use** is motivated by the desire to achieve a known and anticipated effect. This would include the student who takes stimulants to stay awake or the person who takes sedatives to relieve tension and sleep. Five common psychological conditions may lead to circumstantial-situational use of illicit drugs by adolescents: a depressed mood, normlessness (not having definite values, opinions, or rules to live by), social isolation, stress, and low self-esteem. The greatest danger from circumstantial drug use is that the person will become accustomed to relying upon drugs to solve or mitigate problems, and the habit will ultimately escalate to intensified use.

4. **Intensified drug use** is generally a long-term pattern of using drugs at least once daily to achieve relief from a persistent problem or stressful situation. Drug use becomes a customary activity of daily life, with people ordinarily remaining socially and economically integrated in the life of the community. Some change in functioning may occur, depending on the frequency and dosage taken.

5. **Compulsive drug use** is use at high frequency and high dosage and of relatively long duration; the use produces physiological addiction or psychological dependence, with disuse resulting in physiological discomfort or psychological stress. Motivation to continue comes from the physical or psychological comfort or relief obtained by using the drug. Users in this category include not only the street junkie or skid-row alcoholic but also the opiate-dependent physician, the barbiturate-dependent homemaker, and the alcohol-dependent business executive.

Types of Drugs

The drugs most commonly abused may be grouped into four categories: *narcotics, stimulants, depressants,* and *hallucinogens.* Some drugs bridge the categories.

Narcotics

Included in the **narcotics** category are *opium* and its derivatives, such as *morphine, heroin,* and *codeine.* They work by mimicking **endogenous endorphins:** chemicals naturally produced by the body to dull the sensation of pain. Opium is a dark, gummy substance extracted from the juice of unripe seed pods of the opium poppy. Opium is usually taken orally or sniffed—that is, it is heated and its vapor inhaled.

Morphine, the chief active ingredient in opium, is extracted as a bitter, white powder with no odor. Each grain of opium contains about one-tenth of a grain of morphine. Morphine is used medicinally to relieve extreme pain because of its depressant effect on the central nervous system. Addicts refer to it as "M" or "monkey." It may be sniffed, but the powder is usually mixed with water and injected under the skin with a hypodermic needle ("skin popping"). For maximum effect, it is injected directly into a vein ("mainlined").

Codeine is the mildest morphine derivative. Often used in cough syrups or to relieve mild body aches, it has the same but milder analgesic properties as other narcotics. Codeine is often used by young people who mistakenly think it is not addictive.

Heroin ("H," "horse," or "smack") was first refined from morphine in 1874. Like its relative, it is a white,

drug abuse   the use of drugs to the point of causing risk or harm, either legal risk or the risk of harming oneself and others.

physical addiction   a condition that develops from abusing a drug that forms a chemical dependency.

psychological dependency   the development of a persistent, sometimes overpowering psychological need for a drug.

experimental use   occasional drug use motivated by curiosity.

social-recreational use   drug use primarily to relax and have fun at parties.

circumstantial-situational use   drug use to produce a desired psychological mood.

intensified drug use   daily drug use.

compulsive drug use   drug use motivated by physical addiction or psychological dependency.

narcotics   a class of opiate-based drugs that depresses the central nervous system and thus relieves pain and induces sleep; in large doses, produces unconsciousness, stupor, coma, and possibly death; most are habit forming.

endogenous endorphins   chemicals similar to narcotics that are produced by the body and cause euphoria and depress pain.

odorless, bitter-tasting powder. It was originally believed to be nonaddictive and hence a beneficial substitute for morphine. It is rarely sold in pure form but is instead "cut," or mixed with, other white substances, such as powdered milk or corn starch. Unfortunately, it is sometimes mixed with quinine. Since quinine is bitter, like heroin, the user cannot tell by tasting how potent the mixture is. Heroin is not always white, however. Impurities can discolor it; in fact, black tar heroin, which ranges in color from dark brown to black, has become popular in the western United States. One reason heroin is so dangerous is that the amount of heroin in a "bag," or single dose, varies widely and an overdose can easily kill.

The heroin being sold today is generally purer than that sold in previous decades, which has changed usage patterns. In the past, heroin was injected, either intravenously (into one's veins) or subcutaneously (under the skin). Although many current users still inject heroin, more and more are snorting it or smoking it. Both of these options are perceived by many adolescents as safer ways to use the drug, since they eliminate the risk of contracting the human immunodeficiency virus (HIV) or hepatitis from shared needles. Still, given that the amount of heroin needed to get high is close to the lethal dosage, use of this drug is dangerous in any form. It is particularly dangerous to mix heroin with alcohol and other depressants. Although it is the most widely used illicit opiate, only a small minority of adolescents experiment with heroin. Heroin use rose over the course of the 1990s, but today fewer than 1 percent of high school students report having taken the drug within the past year (Johnson, O'Malley, Bachman, et al., 2009).

The synthetic opiates, *Demerol* (meperidine) and *Dolophine* (methadone), were created as chemical substitutes for the natural opiates and are used in medicine as pain relievers. They are addictive and restricted by law to medical use.

The consequences of morphine and heroin use are severe. They are the most physically addictive of all drugs. Users quickly develop *tolerance*—diminished response to a given repeated drug dose—and physical as well as psychological dependence and must therefore gradually increase the dosage. Because dependence becomes total and heroin is expensive (addicts spend several hundred dollars daily), many users turn to crime or prostitution to support their habits. Without the drug, withdrawal symptoms begin to appear within six to eight hours. The first symptoms are running eyes and nose, yawning, sweating, dilation of the pupils, and appearance of goose bumps on the skin (from which the expression "cold turkey" originated). Within 24 hours, addicts develop leg, back, and abdominal cramps; violent muscle spasms; vomiting; and diarrhea. The expression "kicking the habit" developed as a result of the muscle spasms during withdrawal. Bodily functions such as respiration,

blood pressure, temperature, and metabolism, which have been depressed, now become hyperactive. These symptoms gradually diminish over a period of a week or more. In addition, women who have babies while addicted deliver infants who are themselves addicts or who are born dead from drug poisoning.

Addiction may have other effects, too. Addicts usually lose their appetite for food, which leads to extreme weight loss and severe malnutrition. They neglect their health, suffer chronic fatigue, and are in a general devitalized condition. Sexual interest and activity decline. Addicts become accident prone—they may fall frequently, drown, or even set themselves on fire if they drop off to sleep while smoking. They lose the willpower to carry on daily functions and they pay little attention to their appearance. Their whole lives center on getting the next fix.

Because the prognosis for curing heroin addiction is so discouraging, methadone is now given as a substitute drug through medically recognized methadone maintenance programs. The drug blocks the hunger for heroin and the effects of it, with the result that the majority of addicts no longer have a constant desire to obtain heroin. Methadone users do not get high or drowsy and can therefore function normally (Joseph, Stancliff, & Langrod, 2000). Studies show outstanding success with methadone maintenance. The majority of patients who are regularly given medically prescribed doses of methadone become productive citizens, returning to work or school and avoiding any drug-related arrests (Gossop, Marsden, Stewart, et al., 2000). Despite the success of these programs, only a small minority of American heroin addicts receive methadone (American Methadone Treatment Association, 1999; Centers for Diseases Control and Prevention, 2002a). Because it is currently the most effective treatment, in 1997 the National Institutes of Health recommended that the law be changed to make access to methadone easier.

A growing form of opiate use is a rise in the number of youths who are acquiring and taking prescription painkillers such as Vicodin or OxyContin. Vicodin is a blend of hydrocodone, a semisynthetic opioid and acetaminophen; OxyContin contains a different semisynthetic opioid and is found in Percodan. Six percent of high school students admitted to illicit use of Vicodin during the previous year; 3.4 percent admitted using OxyContin.

Stimulants
The term **stimulants** refers to a wide variety of drugs that "rev up" the central nervous system; they energize rather than tranquilize. Most work by increasing the amount of norepinephrine and/or **dopamine** available to the brain's neurons (McKim, 1997). Dopamine, in particular, is associated with feelings of pleasure.

One of the most well-known stimulants is *cocaine* ("coke," "snow," or "blow"). It is extracted from the leaves of the South American coca plant and is available as an odorless, fluffy, white powder. Even though it is expensive, it is used by youths as well as by more affluent, older adults. Cocaine depresses the appetite and increases alertness. It is not effective when taken orally, so users sniff or inject it intravenously into the bloodstream. Aside from financial depletion, the primary undesirable effects are nervousness, irritability, restlessness, mild paranoia, physical exhaustion, mental confusion, loss of weight, fatigue, depression when "coming down," and various afflictions of the nasal mucous membranes and cartilage. Taking large doses can lead to a severe psychosis while the person is still on the drug. Large doses can produce headaches, cold sweats, hyperventilation, nausea, tremors, convulsions, unconsciousness, and even death. Psychological dependence is severe; withdrawal is characterized by a profound depression for which cocaine itself appears to be the only remedy. One of the most famous cocaine addicts was Sigmund Freud, who used the drug for many years.

In 2008, about 4 percent of high school seniors reported ever having used cocaine; about 2.5 percent of them had used it within the past year (Johnson, O'Malley, Bachman, et al., 2009). Fewer than 1 percent of young adults used cocaine in 2007 (Johnson, O'Malley, Bachman, et al., 2008c). Hispanic students are significantly more likely to use cocaine than Caucasian students; African American students are less likely to use cocaine than students in the other two groups (Johnson, O'Malley, Bachman, et al., 2008a).

Cocaine can be further processed by heating it with ammonia or sodium bicarbonate to produce "crack," a form of the drug that can be smoked. (The name comes from the crackling sound it makes when heated.) Smoking crack produces a more intense but shorter-lasting high than ingesting powder cocaine. Crack is one of the most addictive of all drugs. It is so potent that users develop a craving for the drug very quickly. The craving can be so demanding that users will resort to theft, deceit, and violence to procure it. The health consequences of its use may be severe, because the drug has destructive effects on brain neurotransmitters and acts as an excessive stimulant on the heart and other organs. Adolescent crack users are likely to make poor grades, be depressed, and be alienated from family and friends (Ringwalt & Palmer, 1989). Crack use is less widespread among adolescents than its parent drug, cocaine (Johnson, O'Malley, Bachman, et al., 2009).

Amphetamines are stimulants that include drugs such as Benzedrine, Dexedrine, Ritalin, and methedrine ("speed"). They are used medically for treating obesity, mild depression, and fatigue, as well as other conditions. The drugs are usually taken orally in the form of tablets or capsules. Because they are stimulants, they increase alertness, elevate mood, and produce a feeling of well-being. Large doses may produce a temporary rise in blood pressure, palpitations, headache, dizziness, sweating, diarrhea, pallor, dilation of the pupils, vasomotor disturbances, agitation, confusion, apprehension, or delirium. Regular amphetamine users usually do not develop physical dependence, but they do soon develop an intense psychological need to continue taking the drug and require larger doses as their tolerance develops. Mental depression and fatigue are experienced after the drug has been withdrawn, so psychological dependence develops quickly because the "high" is so enticing and the "low" so depressing. Heavy users, especially those who inject the drugs into their veins, usually need to be treated in hospitals. Some users end up swallowing whole handfuls of tablets instead of only one or two. The outcome of this or injecting the drugs intravenously can be amphetamine psychosis.

One of the amphetamines, *methedrine* or *methamphetamine* ("speed," "meth," or "chalk"), is particularly dangerous because it is commonly injected under the skin or directly into a vein, sometimes causing rupturing of the blood vessels and death. Other hazards are infections such as tetanus, HIV, syphilis, or hepatitis from dirty needles. The heavy user displays a potential for violence, paranoia, physical dependence, or bizarre behavior. Suicides are frequent during the periods of deep depression following withdrawal. Methedrine works by stimulating the release of dopamine; in the process, it damages the terminal branches of neurons that produce dopamine and another neurotransmitter **serotonin.** Serotonin is found in the digestive tract and effects appetite (hence, destruction of serotonin producing neurons explains amphetamines' effect upon appetite) as well as mood. Methedrine is also available in a smokable, crystallized form ("crystal meth," "ice," "crystal," or "glass"). Fewer than 2 percent of high school seniors report having used methedrine within the past year (Johnson, O'Malley, Bachman, et al., 2009), continuing a downward trend in this drug's popularity that has lasted for a number of years now.

Ritalin (methylphenidate) and Adderall (a mixture of amphetamine and dextroamphetamine) are stimulants that are readily available to teenagers, since both are widely prescribed to help children and adolescents who have **attention-deficit hyperactivity disorder (ADHD).**

---

stimulants agents that produce a temporary increase in the functioning of the body.

dopamine a neurotransmitter whose effects are enhanced by stimulants.

serotonin a neurotransmitter that is chemically similar to the hallucinogens.

attention-deficit hyperactivity disorder (ADHD) a behavioral disorder characterized by impulsivity, an inability to pay attention, and an inability to sit still.

PERSONAL ISSUES   ECSTASY

One drug whose use has increased since the mid-1990s, when it first emerged as a so-called club drug, is *ecstasy* (also known as MDMA, XTC). Ecstasy is an amphetamine, but it also has hallucinogenic effects. It is derived from methamphetamine, and most of the ecstasy found in the United States is imported from the Netherlands. Ecstasy comes in tablets that cost about $25 apiece; these tablets are often impure, containing methamphetamine, ephedrine, and cocaine (all other stimulants) in addition to the ecstasy. Each pill produces a four- to six-hour high, with peak effects about two hours after the pill is taken (Powell, 2003).

Ecstasy works by increasing the body's release of the neurotransmitters dopamine and norepinephrine (like other stimulants) as well as serotonin (like hallucinogens). It produces feelings of enhanced self-confidence and well-being, provides a burst of energy, and causes a loss of inhibitions. In the short run, ecstasy can also lead to confusion, depression, insomnia, anxiety, and paranoia. Blood pressure and heart rate often increase dramatically, and users may experience nausea, faintness, and blurred vision. A particularly dangerous effect of ecstasy is that it destroys the body's ability to regulate temperature, such that body temperature could rise to an unhealthy level. Since it can kill brain cells, it is not surprising that nonhuman primates exposed to ecstasy have been shown to exhibit learning and memory deficits, even after several years have passed (NIDA, 2001). Ecstasy users can quickly become addicted (Stone, Storr, & Anthony, 2006).

Unfortunately, the majority of high school seniors report that ecstasy is easy to obtain. Use of this drug increased from the mid-1990s until 2001 when usage peaked at about 9 percent of high school seniors annually and then began declining in 2002. In 2008, approximately 4 percent of high school seniors and 2 percent of eighth-graders reported having used ecstasy during the previous year (Johnson, O'Malley, Bachman, et al., 2009).

When prescribed and taken at low doses, these medications are effective in helping youths with ADHD concentrate and sit still. When taken in high doses, however, these two drugs have the same negative effects as other amphetamines and can be quite dangerous. About 7 percent of high school students report having illicitly used amphetamines during the past 12 months (Johnson, O'Malley, Bachman, et al., 2009).

Depressants

In contrast to stimulants, **depressants** slow the functioning of the central nervous system. Barbiturates, tranquilizers, inhalants, and alcohol are all depressants. Because they slow heartbeat and respiration rates, they can all be fatal if taken in large enough quantities.

Barbiturates are depressants that decrease the activity of the central nervous system, usually producing sedation, intoxication, and sleep. They are less available now, as they have been replaced by another class of sedatives known as benzodiazepines. Barbiturates include drugs that had commonly been used as sleeping pills, such as *quaaludes, Nembutal, Seconal,* and *phenobarbital*. Some of these drugs—Nembutal, Tuinal, and Seconal, for example—are short acting, meaning the effects set in soon and wear off quickly. Others, such as phenobarbital, are long acting. Barbiturates were widely prescribed medicinally for epilepsy and anxiety as well as insomnia. When taken as directed, in small doses, there is no evidence that the long-acting barbiturates are addictive. There is a greater chance of addiction with the short-acting drugs. All barbiturates are dangerous when abused because they create total addiction: both physical and psychological dependence. Dosages must be increased as tolerance develops. Barbiturates appear to work by making some of the brain's cells more susceptible to the effects of **GABA,** an inhibitory neurotransmitter.

Barbiturate users exhibit slurred speech, staggering gait, and sluggish reactions. They may be easily moved to tears or laughter, are emotionally erratic, and are frequently irritable and antagonistic. They are prone to stumble and drop objects and are often bruised or have cigarette burns on their bodies.

When the abuser has become physically dependent, withdrawal symptoms become severe in about 24 hours. Increasing nervousness, headache, muscle twitching, weakness, insomnia, nausea, and a sudden drop of blood pressure occur. Convulsions that can be fatal are an ever-present danger with barbiturate withdrawal. Delirium and hallucinations may develop. When barbiturates are taken in combination with alcohol or narcotics, the sedative effect is multiplied and can result in coma or death.

Tranquilizers such as Xanax, Equanil, Placidyl, Librium, and Valium (generic: diazepam) are similar to barbiturates in their effects, for they, too, act to slow the central nervous system by enhancing the inhibitory effects of GABA. In short, these products, when abused, have the same dangers as barbiturates.

Inhalants are a subclass of depressants. There are three types of inhalants: (1) *solvents,* such as paint thinner, dry-cleaning fluid, gasoline, and some glues; (2) *gases,* such as the propellants used in spray paints and whipped cream dispensers ("whippets"); and (3) *nitrites,* such as amyl nitrite. Solvents and gases are primarily used by young adolescents to get high; nitrites are largely used by adults to enhance sexual experience. All three types of inhalants slow down the body's functions and, in large quantities, can cause coma and death. In addition, the use of inhalants can produce hearing loss, bone marrow damage, and liver and kidney damage (National Institute on Drug Abuse [NIDA], 1999c). Some users increase the concentration of the drug they breathe by placing a plastic bag over their head when they inhale. This is especially dangerous, since if the user passes out, he or she can easily suffocate. Others stuff an inhalant-soaked rag into their mouth and inhale ("huffing"). Unlike nearly every other drug, young children and early adolescents are more likely to use inhalants than older adolescents, probably because they are inexpensive and easy to buy. About 9 percent of eighth-graders, 6 percent of tenth-graders, and 4 percent of high school seniors reported using inhalants in 2008 (Johnson, O'Malley, Bachman, et al., 2009). Use of inhalants has been holding steady or slightly declining in the past few years.

Finally, several depressants are now being used as so-called *date rape drugs.* Rohypnol ("roofies") and GHB ("scoop," "grievous bodily harm," "Vita-G") are sedatives that produce stupor, coma, or death when consumed with alcohol. Because these drugs are colorless, odorless, and tasteless, they can be slipped into a woman's drink without her knowledge, leaving her vulnerable to sexual assault. Spurred by reports of rape and death, in 1996 Congress passed the Drug-Induced Rape Prevention and Punishment Act, which increased federal criminal penalties for the use of any controlled substance as an aid to sexual assault (NIDA, 1999a). Rohypnol and GHB, together with ecstasy (see the Personal Issues box) and ketamine, are sometimes termed **club drugs.** Ketamine ("Vitamin K," "Special K") is an anesthetic that is primarily used by veterinarians. It can be injected or snorted.

Hallucinogens

Hallucinogens, or psychedelic drugs, include a broad range of substances that act on the central nervous system to alter perception and one's state of consciousness. The most widely used and mildest hallucinogen is *marijuana.* Another well-known hallucinogen is *LSD (lysergic acid diethylamide),* a synthetic drug that must be prepared in a laboratory. Other hallucinogens include *peyote* and *mescaline* (derived from the peyote cactus plant) and *psilocybin* (derived from a species of mushroom). Hallucinogens cause perceptual distortions because they are chemically similar to the neurotransmitter serotonin. When these substances are taken, parts of the brain that are involved in sensation and perception are activated.

Each compound has users who claim unique effects from ingesting it. In general, the drugs produce unpredictable results, including distortions of color, sound, time, and speed. A blurring of the senses in which colors are "heard" and sounds are "seen" is common. Some people experience "bad trips" that are intensely frightening and characterized by panic, terror, and psychosis. A majority of those who experience a bad trip report the feeling that no one anywhere can help, that they are no longer able to control their perceptions, or that they are afraid they have destroyed part of themselves with the drug. Users have been driven to suicide, violence, and murder and have been hospitalized as psychotic.

LSD, or "acid," is the most potent hallucinogen. Derived from a fungus, it was first produced in 1938. It is sold in many forms but most commonly as "tabs," or squares of paper soaked with single doses of the drug. The purity and dosage vary, and thus so do the effects. Nonetheless, LSD is always a slow-acting, long-lasting drug. Its effects are generally not felt until 30 to 90 minutes after it's been ingested, and the "trip" lasts for 8 to 16 hours. Particularly problematic are "flashbacks"—hallucinogenic episodes that occur at a later time even though no additional LSD has been used. Flashbacks are most common in but are not confined to heavy users. They occur when LSD that has been stored in fat cells is released into the bloodstream. LSD users may develop psychological but not physical dependency. In 2008, fewer than 2 percent of high school seniors reported having used LSD at least once during the previous year; this represents the lowest rate of use since statistics have been collected (Johnson, O'Malley, Bachman, et al., 2009).

Marijuana (cannabis; also "grass," "pot," "dope," or "weed") is by far the most widely used illegal substance in America. More than 94 million Americans over the age of 12 have tried marijuana at least once (National Institute on Drug Abuse [NIDA], 2005), and in 2008, 47 percent of high school seniors reported

depressants   a class of drugs that works by slowing the functioning of the central nervous system (alcohol, inhalants).

GABA   an inhibitory neurotransmitter; depressants increase its effectiveness.

club drugs   collectively, ecstasy, rohypnol, GHB, and ketamine; they are part of the rave scene and are used in bars.

hallucinogens   a class of drugs that acts on the central nervous system to alter perception and states of consciousness, causing hallucinations; so-called psychedelic drugs.

having used marijuana during the past year, as did 20 percent of eighth-graders (Johnson, O'Malley, Bachman, et al., 2009). Marijuana is made from the dried leaves of the wild hemp plant. The plant is hardy and useful: it thrives in virtually every country of the world and produces a strong fiber for making cloth, canvas, and rope. The oil serves as a fast-drying paint base. For these reasons, U.S. farmers grew cannabis, and as late as World War II, the federal government licensed production of cannabis in the South and the West. Although 14 states sanction marijuana's use for medicinal purposes, federal law now forbids individuals to grow marijuana. Still, illegal production in the United States continues at a high level; for example, estimates are the $14 billion of marijuana are grown each year in the state of California alone—double the value of their fruit and vegetable harvest (Gettman, 2006).

The principal acting ingredient in cannabis is the chemical delta-9-THC, which is usually referred to as simply **THC.** The THC content of cannabis varies depending on the variety of the plant and the conditions under which it was grown. In 1975, the THC content of "street" marijuana rarely exceeded 1 percent. More recently, new varieties have been produced, commonly containing THC content in the 15 to 25 percent range (Drug Enforcement Administration, 2005). These have more noticeable effects on users than did weaker strains. The THC content also varies with the part of the plant utilized. There is very little THC in the stem, roots, or seeds; the flowers and leaves contain more. *Ganja* or *sinsemilla,* which comes from the flower tops and small leaves, has especially high THC content. *Hashish,* derived from the resin extracted

from unfertilized female flowers, may have a THC content as high as 28 percent. *Hashish oil,* a concentration of resin, has been found to have a THC content as high as 43 percent, with typical samples containing 16 percent (NIDA, 1998). The most common way to use marijuana is to roll it into a cigarette known as a "joint." It can also be smoked in a pipe or a water pipe, called a "bong," and in recent years, it has been made into "blunts," cigars whose contents have been replaced with marijuana.

This variability in the THC content of different varieties of plants, and in the different parts and preparations made from them, has made it difficult for scientists to determine the physical and psychological effects of marijuana use. Studies often yield conflicting results because of a lack of standardized procedures. Still, what do research studies show concerning the effects of marijuana?

Tolerance to cannabis, or diminished response to a given repeated drug dose, has now been well substantiated. Users are able to ingest ever larger quantities without disruptive effects. Physical addiction, as indicated by withdrawal symptoms, does not occur in ordinary users ingesting small or weak amounts. However, withdrawal symptoms can occur following discontinuance of high-dose chronic administration of THC. These symptoms include irritability, decreased appetite, sleep disturbance, sweating, vomiting, tremors, and diarrhea. It should be emphasized that these symptoms most often occur only after unusually high doses of orally administered THC under controlled conditions. Psychological dependency may develop over a period of time and may make it difficult for chronic users to break the marijuana habit.

Marijuana use remains popular with some adolescents. Although not as imminently destructive as other drugs, chronic heavy marijuana use may result in negative outcomes such as psychological dependency, damage to the lining of the lungs, and impairment of the immune system.

An increase in heart rate and reddening of the eyes are the most consistently reported physiological effects of marijuana. The heart rate increase is closely related to dosage. The risk of heart attack in the hour after smoking marijuana is approximately four times what it would normally be due to an increase in blood pressure (NIDA, 2005). However, the drug produces only minimal changes in heart function of young, healthy subjects.

Clinical studies have begun to point to various harmful effects of marijuana on the lungs and implicate it as a cause of lung cancer. The smoke contains much stronger tars and irritants than do regular cigarettes; smoking one joint is the equivalent of smoking four tobacco cigarettes, so heavy usage over a long period may harm the lungs. The tar from marijuana produces tumors when applied to the skin of test animals. Following exposure to marijuana smoke, the lung's defense systems against bacterial invasion have been shown to be impaired (NIDA, 2005).

Marijuana impairs the functioning of the **hippocampus,** a region in the brain responsible for learning, memory, and motivation. It is not surprising, therefore, that heavy users experience memory loss and that children exposed prenatally to marijuana suffer from poor memory and impaired learning abilities. In the short run, marijuana use interferes with a wide range of intellectual tasks in a manner that impairs classroom learning among student users. Marijuana also alters time and space sense, impairs vision, and retards reaction time and performance abilities.

Research has also suggested that heavy marijuana use may impair reproductive functioning in humans. Chronic use is associated with reduced levels of the male hormone testosterone in the bloodstream, which, in turn, may reduce potency and sexual drive and diminish sperm count and motility. It is also associated with possible interference with fertility in females. These preliminary findings may have greater significance for those whose fertility is low to begin with. In addition, there is now substantial research evidence that marijuana use during pregnancy can harm fetal development. In one study, babies born to mothers who smoked marijuana while pregnant had unusual cries and atypical perceptual responses (Lester & Dreher, 1989). Even later, during preschool and grade school, the children born to these mothers were more likely to exhibit lower intelligence than other children (Fried, 1995).

How can a parent or teacher tell if an adolescent is using marijuana? When a person is high, he or she may appear uncoordinated and have trouble walking; be silly and giggly; have difficulty remembering things that were just said; and have red, bloodshot eyes. To disguise their red eyes, users may rely on eye drops, and in order to disguise pot's characteristic odor, they may use perfume or incense.

ANSWERS WOULDN'T YOU LIKE TO KNOW . . .

What are the major types of drugs?

In sum, there are four major types of mind-altering drugs: (1) *narcotics*, which cause euphoria by mimicking naturally occurring endorphins; (2) *stimulants*, which energize the central nervous system; (3) *depressants*, which slow down the functioning of the central nervous system; and (4) *hallucinogens*, which cause perceptual distortions.

Frequency of Adolescent Drug Use

Research studies on adolescent drug use have consistently indicated that the drugs most frequently used by adolescents are alcohol, tobacco, and marijuana, in that order. Figures 15.1 and 15.2 show lifetime and 30-day drug use, respectively, among high school seniors from 1991 to 2008. Both graphs show the same basic pattern: alcohol and tobacco use have declined in the past 15 years, whereas illicit drug use overall has declined or held steady and marijuana use has risen somewhat. If you compare these graphs with the one in Figure 15.3, which illustrates 30-day use of other drugs by high school seniors, you will immediately notice a difference in the frequencies: fewer than 5 percent of seniors use any other type of drugs on a monthly basis, and this has been true for more than 15 years.

One piece of bad news is that the reductions in drug use have been smaller for girls than for boys. Historically, males have not only been more likely to use most drugs than females, but they have been more likely to use drugs heavily. This is changing. Eighth-grade girls are now as likely to use illicit drugs as eighth-grade boys; they are as likely to have experimented with LSD, crack, and cocaine, and they are more likely to have used amphetamines. Their 30-day alcohol use rates are identical with those of boys, and they are as likely to report that they have gotten drunk in a one-month time frame. They are also now smoking cigarettes in similar rates as boys (Johnson, O'Malley, Bachman, et al., 2008a).

Are college students more likely than high school students to use drugs? College students are more likely than high school students to drink alcohol, but they are less likely to smoke cigarettes and about as likely to use illicit drugs (Johnson, O'Malley, Bachman, et al., 2008c). (See Figure 15.4.)

How do current rates of college student drug use compare with those from the past? In fact, drug use

---

THC   the active ingredient in marijuana.

hippocampus   a part of the brain involved with learning, memory, and motivation.

FIGURE 15.1 LIFETIME DRUG USE AMONG HIGH SCHOOL SENIORS: 1991 TO 2008

Source: Data from Johnson, O'Malley, Bachman, et al. (2008b).

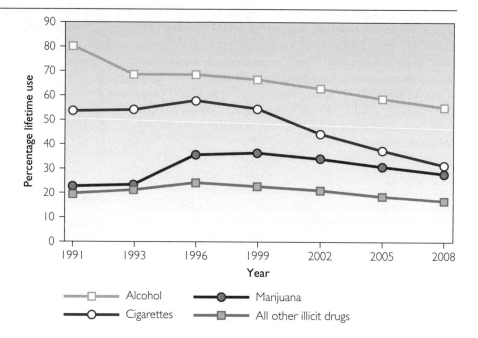

Alcohol   Marijuana
Cigarettes   All other illicit drugs

has been declining. Students in the 1970s and 1980s were generally more likely to use drugs, especially marijuana and cocaine, than college students today (Johnson, O'Malley, Bachman, et al., 2008c). Use of all illicit drugs bottomed out in the early 1990s and has been rising slowly since. This is true, for example, for marijuana, cocaine, heroin, amphetamines, barbiturates, and tranquilizers. Not every drug follows this pattern; inhalant use, for instance, has gradually decreased since the early 1990s.

ANSWERS WOULDN'T YOU LIKE TO KNOW …

Which drugs are most commonly used by adolescents?

About one-third of all American high school seniors report drinking within the past 30 days, and about one-eighth report using tobacco or marijuana during the same time period. All other types of drugs are used by only a small minority of adolescents on a regular basis.

FIGURE 15.2 THIRTY-DAY DRUG USE AMONG HIGH SCHOOL SENIORS: 1991 TO 2008

Source: Data from Johnson, O'Malley, Bachman, et al. (2009).

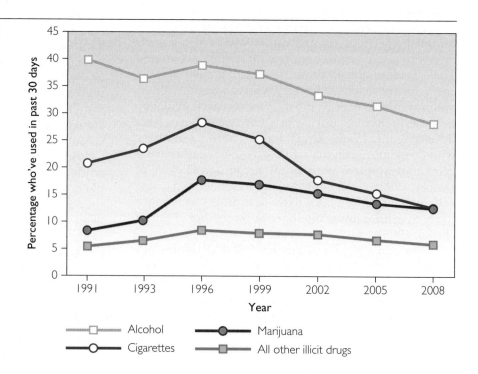

Alcohol   Marijuana
Cigarettes   All other illicit drugs

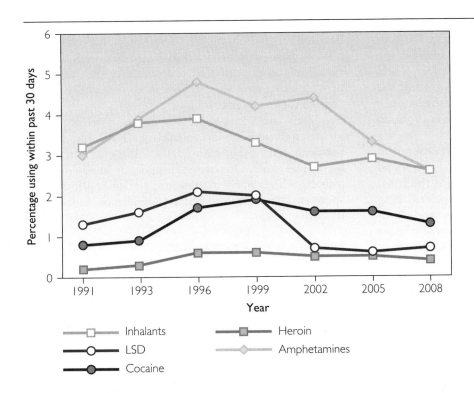

FIGURE 15.3   THIRTY-DAY DRUG USE OF LESS COMMON DRUGS BY HIGH SCHOOL SENIORS: 1991 TO 2008

Source: Data from Johnson, O'Malley, Bachman, et al. (2009).

Reasons for First Drug Use

Why do adolescents first use drugs? The overwhelming majority try drugs out of curiosity—to see what they are like. If adolescents are more attracted by the promise of a drug than repelled by its potential harm, they may be led to experiment. Other adolescents begin using drugs as a means of rebellion, protest, and expression of dissatisfaction with traditional norms and values. This group includes activists and protestors whose lifestyles include involvement with drugs (Pedersen, 1990).

ANSWERS WOULDN'T YOU LIKE TO KNOW ...

Does drug use increase or decrease in college?

With the exception of alcohol, drug use does not increase in college.

Another reason for trying drugs is for fun or sensual pleasure. Users may be seeking an exciting experience. Adolescents are growing up in a fun-oriented culture that emphasizes the need for and value of

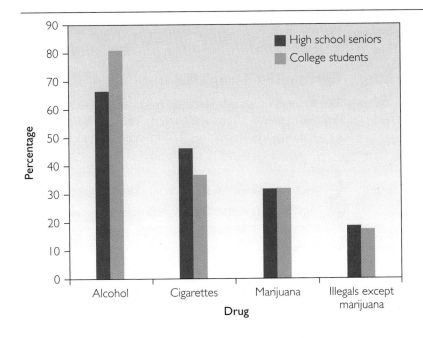

FIGURE 15.4   A COMPARISON OF DRUG USE BY HIGH SCHOOL SENIORS AND COLLEGE STUDENTS: 2007

Source: Data from Johnson, O'Malley, and Bachman (2008).

having a good time. If smoking weed is thought to be fun, this becomes a strong motive for its use. Another aspect of having fun is to experience sensual pleasure. This pleasure may be sexual; many adolescents feel that drinking alcohol makes their exploration of sex less inhibited and more enjoyable. The pleasure motive may involve seeking an increased sensitivity of touch or taste.

Another strong motive for trying drugs is the social pressure to be like one's friends or to be part of a social group. Whether friends use drugs is one of the most significant factors in determining adolescent drug usage (Hart, Robinson, & Kerr, 2001). Research findings indicate that youths who use specific drugs almost invariably have friends who also use the same drugs (Dinges & Oetting, 1993). Adolescents say, "Many of my friends tried it and I didn't want to be different," or "Everybody is doing it." This motive is especially strong among immature adolescents who are seeking to belong to a crowd or gang (Johnson, Bachman, & O'Malley, 1994).

Motives for trying drugs include to relieve tensions and anxieties, to escape from problems, or to be able to deal with or face those problems (Eisen, Youngman, Grob, et al., 1992). Students have cited the following reasons for using drugs:

> "I needed to get away from the problems that were bugging me."
> "I felt tired and depressed and needed a lift."
> "I had to stay awake to study for exams."
> "When I'm on grass, I have more self-confidence and can do anything."

One study found that adolescents who were shy but sociable were more likely to use drugs than those who were not shy. Drugs became a means of feeling more comfortable in social situations (Page, 1990). Those who use drugs as an escape from tension, anxiety, problems, or reality or to make up for personal inadequacies are more likely than others to eventually find themselves dealing with a drug habit (Simons, Whitbeck, Conger, et al., 1991).

There are those uses whose primary motive for trying a drug is to gain self-awareness, increased awareness of others, or more religious insight or to become more creative. The sense of increased awareness or greater creativity may be more imagined than real, but the person may truly believe that the drug provides this awareness. This is an especially strong motive for using psychedelic drugs.

There are some youths who begin selling drugs at an early age, prior to taking them. The bridge between drug dealing and drug using may eventually form. The motive for drug selling is obviously to make money, which may or may not, in the beginning, be spent on drugs for the seller (Feigelman, Stanton, & Ricardo, 1993).

Demographic Differences

If you ask many White, middle-income Americans to visualize a drug user, they will imagine a poor, inner-city adolescent of color. But quite to the contrary, African American youths are significantly less likely than White youths to use drugs, whether one considers overall illicit drug use or the use of alcohol, cigarettes, or most specific illicit drugs. By late adolescence, Hispanic Americans fall midway between the other two groups. In early adolescence, however, they are the group most likely to use drugs. (It is unclear whether this change reflects either earlier initiation rates or a tendency of users to drop out of school.) Urban youths are not more likely than suburban or rural youths to use drugs, including "crack" and heroin, and there are few socioeconomic differences in drug use (Johnson, O'Malley, Bachman, et al., 2009). As mentioned, gender differences for substance use in high school, once quite substantial, have all but disappeared.

In one sense, *all* American adolescents are at risk for substance use, since no demographic pockets are immune. As the following section illustrates, however, certain factors do distinguish experimental and social-recreational users from those who become abusers.

Compulsive Drug Use

The reasons that adolescents first use drugs and then continue to use them are varied. Those who continue to use nonaddictive drugs as a means of trying to solve

ANSWERS WOULDN'T YOU LIKE TO KNOW ...
How many adolescents today use drugs?

Drug use among adolescents peaked in the 1970s and 1980s and then declined. During the 1990s, drug use generally held steady, with some increases for drugs such as cocaine and marijuana. Use of many drugs has gone down in the 2000s. Unfortunately, youths are trying drugs at an increasingly younger age, and girls are catching up to the boys in patterns of use.

ANSWERS WOULDN'T YOU LIKE TO KNOW ...
What demographic factors distinguish drug users from nonusers?

Demographic factors such as gender, socioeconomic status, and residential area do not greatly distinguish drug users from nonusers, which is indicative of the fact that substance use is widespread among American teens.

emotional problems become psychologically dependent on them since drugs become a means of finding security, comfort, or relief (Andrews, Hops, Ary, et al., 1993). When individuals become psychologically dependent on drugs that are also physiologically addicting—such as alcohol, barbiturates, and heroin—dependence is secondarily reinforced by the desire to avoid the pain and distress of physical withdrawal.

Of all the risk factors that contribute to substance abuse, familial factors may be most important. The need to use drugs excessively originates within the families in which children grow up (Repetti, Taylor, & Seeman, 2002). Drug abusers are not as close to their parents and are more likely to have negative adolescent-parental relationships and a low degree of supportive interaction with them than are nonusers (Smart, Chibucos, & Didier, 1990). They are more likely to come from homes in which the parents have been divorced (Doherty & Needle, 1991), including those in which the parents have remarried (Jenkins & Zunguze, 1998). The parents of drug abusers are less likely to be authoritative than the parents of nonabusers (Adalbjarnardottir & Hafsteinsson, 2001). Drug abusers' parents are more likely either to use drugs themselves or to condone drug use (Chassin, Presson, Pitts, et al., 2000). In addition, such parents less closely monitor their children (Svensson, 2003). Overall, research has found that the family relationships of adolescents who abuse drugs are similar to those of adolescents who are emotionally disturbed. The net effect of these family situations is to create personality problems that cause individuals to be more likely to run to drugs.

A different kind of family contributor is genetic vulnerability: the ease by which one can become addicted to a drug is in good part genetic. Heritability estimates for addiction susceptibility range from 25 to 60 percent, depending upon the study and the specific drug (Chassin, Hussong, & Beltran, 2009). The heritability for susceptibility to nicotine addiction is especially high.

The other most commonly cited contributor to adolescent substance abuse (especially by parents) is peer influence. Many studies have found strong, positive correlations between peers' substance abuse patterns. In other words, users have friends and acquaintances who are users or at least they *believe* that their friends are users (Thornberry & Krohn, 1997). It seems likely, however, that peer influence is only indirectly related to an adolescent's substance use (Bauman & Ennett, 1994, 1996). There is good reason to believe that teenagers choose friends who are like themselves. So if an adolescent plans to use drugs, he or she will find friends who approve of drug use. If he or she chooses to abstain, he or she will select friends from among the abstainers. Adolescents with

strong, healthy family ties are less likely to select substance-abusing friends (Bahr, Marcos, & Maughan, 1995). Peer influence is apt to be more powerful for adolescents living in extreme poverty (McGee, 1992) for all of the reasons discussed in Chapter 3. Also, older adolescents are more likely than younger adolescents to listen to their peers (Bush, Weinfurt, & Iannotti, 1994). Finally, once adolescents have become drugs users, peer influence increases (Halebsky, 1987).

Some of these contributing factors, such as parenting style and poverty, appear to affect adolescents of both genders equally (Amaro, Blake, Schwartz, et al., 2001), whereas others differ by gender. Boys, for example, are more influenced by deviant peers than girls (Svensson, 2003). Girls are more motivated by having poor self-esteem (Crump, Lillie-Blanton, & Anthony, 1997), by wanting to lose weight (French & Perry, 1996), and by having been physically or sexually abused (Sarigiani, Ryan, & Peterson, 1999).

Prevention and Treatment

Before an adolescent begins to use drugs, preventive steps can be taken. Prevention programs target the risk factors that make drug use more likely. The National Institute on Drug Abuse has pulled together the results of numerous prevention efforts to develop a set of core principles that underlie the best programs (NIDA, 2003). Some of the most important are that prevention programs should

- seek to enhance protective factors, such as good family functioning
- work to decrease risk factors, such as poverty school failure
- address all forms of substance abuse, including underage use of legal drugs
- focus on what is happening in the local community
- be targeted to the specific needs of the target population's age, ethnicity, and so on
- seek to have a positive effect on a wide variety of parenting issues
- begin early, perhaps as early as preschool
- target social skills
- seek to increase academic success
- be multipronged and long term
- include a teacher training component
- use interactive techniques, such as peer discussions or role-playing

(Note that this list is virtually identical to the characteristics of programs effective at preventing delinquency or adolescent pregnancy or school dropout that you have seen before; effective programs all share the same features.)

Once an adolescent has become a drug abuser, different, more intrusive tactics are needed. Most teenagers (about 70 percent) who receive treatment do so as outpatients (Dennis, Muck, Dawud-No, et al., 2003); this means that they do not live full time in a hospital or treatment facility but instead go home between treatment sessions. Unfortunately, fewer than 10 percent of adolescents who report symptoms of substance use disorder receive any treatment (Muck, Zempolich, Titus, et al., 2001).

Adolescents who have a drug abuse problem differ from adults in several ways. For instance, youths are more likely than adults to develop a psychological dependency and to have comorbid (i.e., co-occurring) psychological problems that existed before the drug abuse began (Winters, 1999) and do not disappear when it stops (Kandel, Johnson, Bird, et al., 1997). Adolescents are also less motivated than adults to stop using drugs and are usually referred by others for treatment, rather than voluntarily choosing to work on their drug use (Muck, Zempolich, Titus, et al., 2001). In order for a youth treatment program to be successful, it must take these differences into account.

There are various approaches to treating chemical dependency. These include the 12-step program of **Alcoholics Anonymous (AA)**; behavioral therapy; professional counseling, medical treatment, and psychiatric care; family systems therapy; and therapeutic treatment. Let's look at these more in detail.

Alcoholics Anonymous

The most widely used approach in treating chemical dependency is the 12-step or Alcoholics Anonymous (AA) model. Sometimes called the *disease perspective*, it emphasizes the individual's inability to control drug consumption. The approach involves group therapy, individual counseling, education, family counseling, homework exercises, and attendance at meetings (Winters, Stinchfield, Opland, et al., 2000).

Willful attempts at stopping on one's own are seen as futile and counterproductive. Recovery is thus largely a spiritual awakening process that is achieved by working through the 12 steps. The 12-step program begins by accepting one's powerlessness over drugs and then developing a sense of one's higher power, which enables one to control the drug habit.

Behavioral Therapy

Whether it is called **behavioral therapy** or *cognitive-behavioral therapy*, this approach is based on learning theory and focuses on building the skills needed to refuse drugs, resist peer pressure, and make good decisions. Two techniques are used in combination by behavioral therapists: *modeling* and *role-playing*. The therapist first models (or demonstrates) a desired behavior, and then the adolescent tries acting out that behavior. The practicing continues until the client is comfortable and can respond effectively to challenging

CROSS-CULTURAL CONCERNS   SUBSTANCE USE BY NATIVE AMERICAN ADOLESCENTS

Substance abuse is an especially large problem among Native American youths. Numerous studies have shown that drinking rates are higher among Native American adolescents than any other racial or ethnic group. Native American teenagers are also more likely than others to smoke marijuana and use inhalants. In fact, compared to youths from other racial and ethnic groups, Native American adolescents are more likely to use all of the major illegal drugs, with the exception of cocaine (see Novins, Spicer, Deals, et al., 2004).

Native Americans don't use drugs for different reasons than other people, and nothing inherent in their cultural traditions especially encourages drug use (Beauvais & LaBoueff, 1985). Instead, as discussed in Chapter 3, Native Americans are subjected to intense pressures as a result of their unique historical situation and generally low socioeconomic status. Native American youths are, as a whole, confronted with more risk factors than adolescents of other races and ethnicities. They are more likely to be economically disadvantaged, to feel alienated at school, to feel distant from both their own Native American and common American heritages, to feel hopeless and depressed, to associate with both parental and peer substance-using models, and to experience social and physical isolation. Moreover, due to significant cultural differences prevention and intervention programs designed for other races and ethnicities may not work well among Native Americans.

The high alcoholism rate takes a high toll in health costs within the Native American community. Among adults, the death rate is high from liver damage associated with drinking. Frequent intoxication also puts people into poverty, which makes getting good health care less likely. Also, a disproportionately large number of Native American children are born with *fetal alcohol syndrome (FAS)*, which results in learning disabilities and behavioral problems that decrease their chance of success in school and life.

situations. A third technique, *behavioral contracting,* involves creating clear, specific agreements between the adolescent and his or her therapist or parents that detail what behaviors are acceptable, the rewards and privileges that will be earned by completing those behaviors, and the punishments that will accrue if the behaviors are not completed.

Professional Counseling, Medical Treatment, and Psychiatric Care

Rather than viewing chemical dependency as a disease in and of itself, traditional psychiatric and counseling approaches have tended to emphasize a

host of emotional disorders as causal factors. Therefore, treatment is focused on understanding and resolving the emotional problems that underlie drug use, as well as medical treatment to restore health.

Alcoholics Anonymous (AA)   an approach that uses a 12-step model and peer support to help people stop abusing alcohol.

behavioral therapy   an approach that uses modeling, reinforcement, and situational inducement to alter behavior.

RESEARCH HIGHLIGHT   FAMILIES OF DRUG ABUSERS

Many studies have delineated the relationship between family factors and drug abuse. The following family factors have an impact on drug use:

Family Closeness

Isolation of adolescent from family
Lack of closeness with parents
Little parental support
Lack of love
Adolescent's need for recognition not filled
Parental rejection and hostility
Closeness bordering on enmeshment
Father not actively involved with family
Lack of supervision and monitoring

Conflict

Marital conflict
Husband irresponsible
Wife unhappy
Disharmony in family
Children as pawns in marital discord
High degree of stress, trauma

Scapegoating

Adolescent used as a scapegoat for family problems

Role Model

Parents are inadequate role models
Parents are drug users
Lack of emulation of parents by adolescent

Divorce, Family Breakup

Broken home
One or both parents absent much of time
Father absence especially harmful

Discipline

Parents showing lack of coping skills
Inconsistent discipline
Discipline too autocratic or laissez-faire
Lack of clear rules, limits, guidance
Excessive use of punishment

Hypocritical Morality

Double standard of behavior: one for selves, another for the adolescent
Parental denial of own problems

Psychological Crutches

Parents lacking confidence in coping with life; using drugs as psychological crutch
No effective coping skills learned from parents; adolescent follows parental model of coping by using drugs, alcohol

Communication Gap

Lack of ability to communicate
Lack of parental understanding
Lack of communication by parents for fear of hearing anything negative
Unheard cries for help from the adolescent
Lack of communication about substance use

Religiosity

Lack of a religious orientation

Source: Based on Chassin, Hussong, & Beltran (2009); Dunn (2005); Melby, Conger, Conger, et al. (1993).

IN THEIR OWN WORDS

"My first experiences with peers using substances happened in middle school. My best friend started smoking and experimenting with alcohol in about seventh grade, and over the next two years, she started using them more regularly and also started using marijuana. It was a very weird time. I still felt like a little kid, and she was telling me all these crazy things that she was doing with her other friends.

"I don't think there's any way I could've gotten away with drinking in seventh grade; my friend's mom never knew where she was or what she was doing, but mine did. It was obvious to me, even at that age, that the biggest factor in how much kids got involved with substance use was how much unsupervised time they had. If your parents knew where you were, drove you there, and picked you up, there was no way you were going to come stumbling in drunk at the age of 12."

Family Systems Therapy

This approach focuses on family-of-origin conflicts and issues as central in developing and maintaining chemical dependency. **Family systems therapy** seeks to help families address separation issues and to help the family system adapt more effectively as the addict gives up drug-using behavior. A central goal is to help family members communicate more effectively and address conflicts that may have been ignored because of the members' focusing on the adolescent's drug-using and antisocial behavior.

Therapeutic Community Treatment

The **therapeutic community treatment** model strongly emphasizes both abstaining from drug consumption and addressing emotional factors associated with drug use. This is a residential treatment model, and clients are typically expected to live in the facility for at least one year. At the center of the therapeutic community philosophy is the critical importance of involvement with one's peer group. Clients are involved in process groups, confrontation groups, support groups, and community meeting groups.

In sum, the drug treatment field seems to be moving in the direction of using multimodal approaches, which incorporate several different models simultaneously. This shift may reflect the increasing recognition that chemically dependent clients require a broad-based approach because of the various needs they present.

Effectiveness of Treatments

How effective are these treatments? All of them appear effective, at least in the short term (Muck, Zempolich, Titus, et al., 2001). However, little research has examined

ANSWERS WOULDN'T YOU LIKE TO KNOW ...

What kinds of prevention and treatment programs are effective with adolescents?

The best programs improve the overall quality of adolescents' lives, give them hope for the future, and help them get along with their parents. Unfortunately, only a small fraction of adolescents have the opportunity to participate in the most successful kinds of programs, whether for prevention or treatment.

RESEARCH HIGHLIGHT   PROJECT DARE

Project DARE (Drug Abuse Resistance Education) is one of the most popular drug prevention programs in existence today. It employs trained police officers who come in weekly over a four-month period to teach students the skills needed to resist peer pressure to use drugs. DARE also provides information about specific drugs and works on students' self-esteem and lifestyle choices. It is utilized in three-fourths of our nation's school districts (D.A.R.E., 2009).

Despite its popularity, there is little evidence that Project DARE is at all effective. For example, Donald Lynam and his colleagues conducted a 10-year follow-up study of 1,000 sixth-graders who had either gone through DARE training or had received other, much briefer forms of drug education (Lynam, Milich, Zimmerman, et al., 1999). At age 20, students who had experienced the DARE curriculum were no more likely to abstain from cigarettes, alcohol, or illicit drugs than other students. Moreover, they were not more immune to peer pressure nor did they have higher self-esteem than other students.

Given the results of this and other studies, why does DARE continue to be so popular? The authors offer two reasons. First, DARE is an innocuous, "feel good" program that is easy to support. In addition, Project DARE may appear to be working, since most adolescents who go through the program don't use drugs. The fact that most adolescents who do not go through the program also do not use drugs is less obvious.

Given the abundance of data that suggest that the roots of drug abuse lie within the family, it is not surprising that Project DARE—which does not address family relations—is so unsuccessful in preventing the problem.

how former drug users fare two or five years after treatment, and so it is difficult to say whether the positive outcomes are sustained.

Are any of the approaches superior to the others? Each has its adherents, but there has been relatively little research directly comparing the effectiveness of these main approaches. Rather, in most research, patients completing these treatments are compared to controls who received no treatment, controls who received only minor interventions (such as education), or individuals who began but did not complete the program. There does seem to be some good, relatively long-term evidence in favor of both the family systems and cognitive-behavioral therapies (Ozechowski & Liddle, 2000; Vaughn & Howard, 2004).

After reviewing the effectiveness of a large number of studies, Williams and colleagues (2000) concluded that the most successful programs were those that (1) minimized dropout rates, (2) provided follow-up and aftercare, (3) were comprehensive in nature, and (4) included family therapy. These authors also emphasized the need to develop successful programs that could serve large numbers of adolescents, since the need is so great.

Tobacco and Smoking

Incidence of Tobacco Use

Adolescent tobacco use rose sharply during the early and mid-1990s and has been decreasing since then. In fact, in 2008, twelfth-graders' smoking rates were lower than at any point since records began being kept in the mid-1970s (University of Michigan News Service, 2008). Seven percent of eighth-graders and 20 percent of twelfth-graders indicated that they had smoked during the previous month, a rate two-thirds and nearly one-half lower, respectively, than students had reported in the mid-1990s. Even so, tobacco is the second most widely used drug by youths ages 12 to 17. About 3 percent and 11 percent, respectively, of the youths in these groups smoke on a daily basis. Disapproval of cigarette smoking has increased: about 80 percent of all high school students say that they do not like to be around smokers and that they have no interest in dating someone who smokes. Caucasian teenagers are more likely to smoke than Hispanic American teenagers, and members of both groups are more likely to smoke than African American teens. Rates for boys and girls are similar.

About 80 percent of adult smokers began to smoke before they were age 18 (Smith & Stutts, 1999), and another 10 percent began between ages 18 and 21 (American Academy of Pediatrics, 1994). Although many adolescents believe that they will eventually quit, they are deluding themselves: most will not "grow out

family systems therapy   an approach to helping adolescents in which the emphasis is on enhancing family communication and improving family relationships.

therapeutic community treatment   treatment in a residential situation with others who have similar problems; includes individual and group therapy and skills training.

Treatment for chemical dependency is beginning to use multiple approaches simultaneously. A component of many of these multiple approaches is group counseling, such as shown here.

of it" and, in fact, will smoke more and more as they age (Perry & Staufacker, 1996). Generally, the heaviest adult smokers are those who began at the youngest age (Escabedo, Marcus, Holtzman, et al., 1986). Also, tobacco is an important "gateway drug"; smokers are about three times more likely to use alcohol and at least ten times more likely to use illegal drugs than nonsmokers (De Civita and Pagani, 1994).

Reasons Adolescents Start Smoking

Most youths are aware of the dangers of smoking. If so, why do they start and continue to smoke? Typical answers include the following:

"Because the rest of my crowd smokes."
"To feel sophisticated."
"I was curious."
"Because I was tense and nervous."
"Because I enjoy smoking."
"Because I wasn't supposed to."

These answers reflect the results of a study in which teenagers were asked to describe their first smoking experiences (Delorme, Kreshel, & Reid, 2003). "Peer influence" was the most often cited reason to start smoking (see also Prince, 1995). Almost as many teens explained that they wanted to "define their image." The two reasons are not unrelated, since image tending is often related to trying to enhance one's social status. Almost half of the respondents claimed that "being rebellious" was part of their motivation to smoke.

Girls and boys begin smoking for somewhat different reasons. Girls are much more likely to report that the reason they had their first cigarette was to feel mature or to enhance their image; boys were more likely to indicate that they enjoyed being rebellious and that smoking made them feel relaxed. Girls are less likely than boys to stop smoking once they begin (Van Roosmalen & McDaniel, 1992).

In addition, many youths imitate their parents, older siblings, and other adults who smoke. There is little hope of changing teenage smoking habits unless the habits of parents and older siblings are changed. One of the primary reasons so many adolescents smoke is that they see adults smoking and they are striving to imitate adult behavior. Adolescents whose parents and older siblings smoke are far more likely to take up the habit than those whose parents do not (Bricker, Peterson, Leroux, et al., 2006).

Effects of Cigarette Advertising

Adolescents are brainwashed from the early years of childhood by the advertising industry. Ads have identified cigarette smoking with masculinity, independence, nature, beauty, youth, sex appeal, sociability, wealth, and the good life. Every conceivable gimmick has been used by the advertising industry to encourage smoking. The appeal is always to the emotions and to a person's desire for acceptability, popularity, and sexual allure. The sultry woman's voice, the high society setting, the back-to-nature promises—all offer rewards the teenager seeks. As a result, adolescents are more

One of the primary reasons so many adolescents start smoking is that they see adults smoking. Parents are especially influential.

strongly affected by tobacco advertising than adults (Strasburger, 1995).

It has been recognized for decades that cigarette advertising influences adolescents. As far back as 1969, Congress passed a law that prohibited cigarette advertising on television. (That law, the Public Health Cigarette Smoking Act, took effect in 1971.) Since that time, tobacco companies have spread their message in other ways. In 1998, the tobacco industry spent nearly $7 billion—more than $18 million per day—to promote its products; only automobile manufacturers spent more money on product promotion (U.S. Department of Health and Human Services, 2000). Cigarettes are heavily advertised in magazines, and the manufacturers also hawk their brands using various promotional activities: sponsoring sporting events and musical concerts and producing clothing and other items carrying logos and brand names.

In November 1998, the tobacco industry agreed, as part of a settlement with a number of states, to stop advertising to minors. (The industry also agreed to pay $206 billion over 25 years to help those states recoup the cost of Medicare payments for tobacco-related illnesses, an indication of the magnitude of the health costs of tobacco use.) You might imagine, then, that there is less tobacco advertising than there was before. If so, you would be wrong. Between 1998 and 2003, the amount of money spent on tobacco advertising rose 125 percent (Campaign for Tobacco Free Kids, 2005). In addition, after the settlement the companies increased the number of ads they placed in magazines with large youth readership (Biener & Siegel, 2000). Instead of reducing advertisements, the industry shifted ads away from the prohibited billboards and into stores and magazines.

Do these advertisements matter? Yes, they do. Youths smoke the most heavily advertised brands (Arnett, 2001), and the advertisements for these brands feature models who look younger than those in advertisements targeted at older adults (Arnett, 2005). In one study, teenagers who could name a tobacco ad that had attracted their attention were twice as likely to begin smoking as those who could not (Biener & Siegel, 2000). Another study found that advertising had an even greater effect than peer pressure on smoking initiation (Evans, Farkas, Gilpin, et al., 1995). A meta-analysis concluded that exposure to cigarette advertising more than doubles the likelihood that a teenager will begin to smoke (Wellman, Sugarman, DiFranza, et al., 2006).

Reasons Adolescents Continue Smoking

Once they begin to smoke, youths continue for the same reasons that adults do:

1. *Relief of tension:* Heavy smokers tend to be tense and restless people.

2. *Development of an unconscious habit:* A reflex action develops that is hard to break—the action of reaching for a cigarette.

3. *Association with sociability and pleasure:* Smokers associate the activity with after-dinner coffee, conversation, a social gathering, or pleasant surroundings.

4. *Social coping mechanism:* Smoking gives people something to do with their hands. In addition, inhaling and lighting up can provide several-second pauses in which to gather one's thoughts before speaking.

5. *Physical addiction to nicotine:* Numerous studies support the conclusion that smokers not only become psychologically dependent on smoking but also physically addicted.

This final point bears elaboration. First, the body develops a physical craving for nicotine that can be alleviated by injecting nicotine, by increasing the

---

RESEARCH HIGHLIGHT   THE HARMFUL EFFECTS OF LEGAL DRUGS

Whereas the majority of Americans would say that it is bad to use crack or ecstasy or LSD, they would most likely also say that it is *less bad* to use tobacco and even *fine* to use alcohol (at least in moderation if you are over 21). After all, tobacco and alcohol are legal, whereas the other drugs are not. There must be some reason for this. Right?

A set of reasons—historical, cultural, and economic—can be offered as to why alcohol and tobacco are legal in the United States, but cocaine, heroine, and marijuana are not. But *safety* does not enter into the discussion. Many people therefore incorrectly assume that legal drugs are less harmful and less risky to use than illicit drugs. The fact is, both nicotine and alcohol are addictive and can cause serious harm to the body. The message is not that illicit drugs are safe but rather that nicotine and alcohol are not entirely safe, either.

nicotine content of cigarettes smoked, or by smoking more cigarettes. Second, only about 2 percent of smokers are able to use cigarettes intermittently or occasionally. The typical pattern of nicotine use is not only daily but hourly. Third, withdrawal of nicotine produces nervousness, anxiety, lightheadedness, headaches, fatigue, constipation or diarrhea, dizziness, sweating, cramps, tremors, and palpitations. Fourth, smokers become tolerant of nicotine. Youthful smokers can tolerate only a few puffs. Gradually, they can tolerate one, then two, then three or more cigarettes. If they exceed their tolerance level, they show signs of acute anxiety. As tolerance levels rise, smokers may reach levels that would have been disastrous earlier in their smoking careers.

Also, when the supply of cigarettes is curtailed, smokers evidence unreasonable, antisocial behavior similar to that of heroin addicts. When the tobacco ration for men in Germany was cut to two packs per month after World War II, for example, it was noted that

> the majority of habitual smokers preferred to do without food even under extreme conditions of nutrition rather than to forgo tobacco. Thus, when food rations in prisoner-of-war camps were down to 900–1,000 calories, smokers were still willing to barter their food rations for tobacco. Of 300 German civilians questioned, 256 had obtained tobacco at the black market. . . . In disregard of considerations of personal dignity, conventional decorum, and esthetic-hygienic feelings, cigarette butts were picked up out of the street dirt by people who . . . would in other circumstances have felt disgust at such contact. Smokers also condescended to beg for tobacco, but not for other things. . . .

Eighty percent of those questioned declared that it felt worse to do without nicotine than without alcohol. (Brill & Christie, 1974)

The conclusion is that cigarette smoking is a highly addictive habit that is difficult to break. Once started, it is not a habit that the majority of smokers can break by an effort of will.

Smokeless Tobacco

The use of chewing tobacco and snuff by American adolescents increased from the 1970s into the 1990s, but fortunately it has been on the decline since that time (Johnson, O'Malley, Bachman, et al., 2008b). Southern, lower SES, rural White males are the most common users. Use of smokeless tobacco usually begins at an earlier age than cigarette smoking (Boyle, Claxton, & Forster, 1997). Nicotine can be absorbed through the mucous membranes in the mouth, and so chewing tobacco is addictive and it is harmful to one's health. Although it is not associated with lung cancer, since no smoke is inhaled into the lungs, it does cause increases in mouth and throat cancer, coronary heart disease, ulcers, and neuromuscular diseases.

Keeping Adolescents from Starting

Clearly, the ideal is to keep adolescents from starting to use tobacco in the first place. A number of different programs have been developed to prevent teenage smoking; they differ widely in their success. Most of these programs are designed to be implemented by schools, since students form a captive audience and

Since cigarette smoking is highly addictive and very difficult to stop, it is important to keep adolescents from starting to smoke.

large numbers of teens can be reached. La Torre and his colleagues (2005) reviewed many in-school programs to determine the elements common to the most successful ones. Among their conclusions:

- Peer-led programs are greatly superior to adult-led programs. These programs rely upon peer reinforcement and changing students' perceptions of peer norms.
- Group discussion is a useful strategy.
- Programs based primarily upon increasing knowledge about the hazards of smoking are ineffective. Although they do increase information and change attitudes, they do not greatly influence behavior. When increased knowledge was found to have an effect upon behavior, that effect was found to be short-lived.
- Although knowledge alone is insufficient to enact behavioral change, some information is necessary. This information includes social influences on tobacco use (e.g., media, peer effects); refusal skills (how to say "no" effectively); short-term physiological effects of tobacco.

In addition, they found that it was helpful for schools to have and uphold a schoolwide policy prohibiting tobacco use. In addition, it was important to begin the antismoking messages in kindergarten.

Other measures can be taken by the government to keep adolescents from starting to smoke. Many states have passed laws making the smoking of cigarettes illegal before age 18. Also, cigarette taxes have been raised to make it harder for adolescents to afford them. More and more, smoking is being banned in public places. Together, these measures should reduce the use of cigarettes.

Alcohol and Excessive Drinking

Alcohol is the drug of choice among youths, yet it is often not recognized as the serious drug that it is.

ANSWERS WOULDN'T YOU LIKE TO KNOW ...
Why do teens smoke cigarettes when they know it's harmful?
Teens start smoking because it makes them look cool, because they want to be daring and rebellious, and because their friends encourage them to smoke. They keep smoking because they enjoy it, because it helps them feel at ease, and because they have become addicted to nicotine.

Incidence of Alcohol Use

Studies of middle school, senior high school, and college students reveal that a substantial proportion of adolescents drink. Findings from the 2008 Monitoring the Future Survey indicate that 39 percent of eighth-graders and 72 percent of high school seniors have had alcohol at some point in their lives, and that 16 percent and 43 percent of the same groups, respectively, have consumed alcohol within the past month (Johnson, O'Malley, Bachman, et al., 2009). Given that drinking is so common in the United States, it is no surprise that a vast majority of adolescents have been introduced to alcohol.

The problem lies not so much in the drinking per se but in the frequent drinking of large quantities of alcohol. In 2007, about 26 percent of high school seniors and 10 percent of eighth-graders reported at least one episode of **binge drinking** in the previous two weeks (Johnson, O'Malley, Bachman, et al., 2008b). Binge drinking is defined as five drinks in a two-hour period. The standard was set because research has shown that this is the quantity at which various risks greatly increase. In addition, a typical 160-pound man who has five drinks within two hours will attain a blood alcohol level of 0.08, a level high enough to qualify him as legally drunk in all 50 states (Substance Abuse and Mental Health Services Administration, 2003).

As noted, binge drinkers are at increased risk for many negative outcomes, and they place others at risk as well. For example, alcohol is a major contributor to traffic accidents and fatalities, and almost half of the persons who die each year in car crashes caused by drunk drivers were not the person driving the vehicle (Hingston & Winter, 2003). Alcohol is also involved in more than 1,500 homicides involving minors each year, and nearly 40 percent of people younger than 21 who are victims of fatal drownings, burns, and falls test positive for alcohol (Bonnie & O'Connell, 2004). The majority of sexual assaults involving youths take place when one or both participants are inebriated, and intoxicated individuals are less likely to follow safe sexual practices when engaging in consensual sexual behavior (Flanigan, McLean, Hall, et al., 1990). (One can only guess at the number of unwanted pregnancies that begin as a result of alcohol consumption.) Finally, drunken adolescents also damage other people's property, wake them up at night, and pick fights.

What do teens drink? It depends upon their age, and for older teens, their gender (Johnson, O'Malley,

binge drinking the consumption of five or more drinks within a two-hour period.

One of the biggest problems with alcohol is binge drinking, or the frequent drinking of large quantities. This is especially prevalent on college campuses.

Bachman, et al., 2008b). Eighth-graders are equally likely to drink beer; wine coolers; and flavored, sweet alcohol beverages; there is no available data about their choice of distilled spirits (hard liquor) or wine. Twelfth-graders are most likely to drink beer (37 percent do so monthly) and hard liquor (34 percent). Flavored, sweet beverages also make a strong showing (29 percent drink them during a 30-day period). Wine and wine coolers are less favored (14 percent and 13 percent, respectively). Senior boys are significantly more likely to reach for beer than senior girls (44 percent vs. 29 percent), and senior girls are more likely to opt for wine coolers (16 percent vs. 9 percent).

Although there are legal sanctions against underage drinking, many teenagers drink before they can legally buy alcoholic beverages or patronize licensed premises. Most who begin to drink do so at home under parental supervision. Much of this drinking occurs on holidays and other special occasions. As youths grow older, they tend to drink more often

outside the home, until the most likely drinking places are those where adults are not present. Common locations for teenage drinking are parties, the outdoors, and cars—all places where teens' activities will likely not be observed.

The prevalence of drinking among middle school and senior high youths motivated many states to reexamine their laws regulating legal drinking ages. After the Vietnam War, many states lowered the drinking age to 18. The argument was "if they're old enough to fight, they're old enough to vote and to drink." But authorities complained that giving 18-year-olds the right to purchase alcoholic beverages also made alcohol available to their younger friends in middle and senior high school (the older seniors purchased it for their younger schoolmates). As a result, many states that had lowered their drinking age raised it again to age 21 (Newman, 1987). Today, the drinking age in all 50 states is 21.

Raising the minimum legal drinking age to 21 has had several positive effects. First, it has produced lower adolescent drinking rates and problems (see Wagenaar & Toomi, 2002, for a review of this literature). Second, it has prevented thousands of traffic fatalities (NHTSA, 1998). Finally, adolescents who do not begin to drink until they are 21 tend to drink less as adults than those who begin earlier (Grant & Dawson, 1997).

Reasons for Drinking during Adolescence

Why do so many adolescents begin to drink? And why does drinking so often begin at this point in life, rather than later or earlier? Schulenberg and Maggs (2002) suggest that a convergence of developmental changes sparks teenage alcohol consumption. Among the most important are the following:

- The physical changes associated with puberty cause a person's tolerance of alcohol to increase, and so he or she can begin to drink in larger quantities without feeling ill.
- Adolescents, who no longer view themselves as children, want to look more mature and adultlike. They believe that having a drink in their hand will make them appear grown up.
- The cognitive skills that emerge after puberty allow teenagers to view issues—including whether or not to drink—in relative rather than absolute terms. They move beyond thinking about alcohol consumption in terms of "yes" or "no" and begin to think about "when" and "how much"
- Cognitive conceit makes youths more likely to question the wishes of authority figures.
- Increased inferential skills make teens more aware of adult hypocrisy. Teens may lose respect for adults who drink themselves but then tell their children or students that drinking is risky.

PERSONAL ISSUES   DRINKING ON COLLEGE CAMPUSES

In the past decade, much good research has been conducted on the magnitude of college drinking. In 2007, two-thirds of college students (male and female) reported drinking at some point in the previous month (Johnson, O'Malley, Bachman, et al., 2008a). Not all of these students drank heavily, however. About 41 percent reported binge drinking at least once during the preceding two-week period; men were more likely to binge than women, with binge rates of 49 percent and 36 percent, respectively. Factors that are associated with high consumption of alcohol by college students include membership in a sorority or fraternity; race/ethnicity (Blacks drink less than Whites); participation in athletics; going to a small college; going to a school located in the Northeast; and living in a dorm as opposed to off campus (Presley, Meilman, & Leichliter, 2002).

Nearly half (48 percent) of all the alcohol consumed by students attending four-year colleges is consumed by underage students (Wechsler, Lec, Kuo, et al., 2002). Young adults who are enrolled full time in college are more likely to drink heavily than their nonstudent peers (Johnson, O'Malley, Bachman, et al., 2008c).

Binge drinkers are far more likely to experience negative consequences from their drinking than those who do not binge. Binge drinkers' grades frequently suffer because they are too fuzzy headed to study and because they miss class. Their athletic performance declines, as well. Many experience blackouts and do not remember what they did or what others did to them. Students who binge drink are more likely to physically injure themselves by falling, fighting, or being in a car accident. Bingers more frequently develop colds and other short-term illnesses, and they are more likely to develop serious, long-term health problems. Heavy drinkers are more likely to engage in unintended and unprotected sexual activity, which causes increased risk for sexually transmitted diseases and pregnancy (Cooper, 2002; Perkins, 2002).

It is worth noting that bingers not only cause significant problems for themselves, but they cause problems for other students, as well. About 75 percent of students report having at least one unwanted, unpleasant encounter with a drunken student (Wechsler, Lee, Kuo, et al., 2000). Although most of these encounters are merely annoying (being interrupted while studying, being awakened, having to take care of a drunk friend), some are assaultive (being pushed or hit, experiencing unwanted sexual advances, or even experiencing date rape) (Abbey, 2002; Perkins, 2002).

Colleges, too, suffer because of student binging. Town-gown relationships can become strained, there may be increased legal fees and maintenance costs from alcohol-related problems, and student service personnel experience higher burnout rates because of the increased demands on their services. The negative impact truly can go beyond the drinking individual.

These findings may seem to document what many college students already feel: that most students they know are heavy drinkers. Yet these data indicate that *more than half of college students do not drink heavily*, at least on a regular basis. Students do not have to binge to be part of the crowd.

- The process of finding an identity involves trying new experiences.
- Adolescents have more freedom and independence than children; they are less closely supervised and monitored.
- Adolescents spend more time with their peers and less with their families. This serves to increase peer influence and decrease family influence on behavior.
- Teenagers mistakenly believe that the drinking rate is higher than it really is. The perception that "everyone drinks" encourages them to drink, too.
- Adolescents are interested in romance and sex; this encourages them to frequent locations such as bars and parties, where alcohol is served.

- Adolescents face many stresses, and drinking is perceived as a means of relaxing.

Dermen, Cooper, and Agocha (1998) would add that alcohol reduces inhibitions and can provide an excuse for behaving wildly. Drinking may allow a teenager to do something that he or she would not normally do—such as have sex with a stranger or vandalize school property.

Adult and Peer Influences

Because drinking is a widespread adult custom, drinking by adolescents reflects their perceptions of the attitudes and behavior of adults in American society (Stevens, Mott, & Youells, 1996). Adolescents use alcohol as an integral part of adult role-playing, as a rite of passage into the adult community.

As discussed earlier regarding substance abuse in general, family factors play a significant role in alcohol misuse. Adolescents who drink to excess are more distant from their families than adolescents who do not (Crowe, Philbin, Richards, et al., 1998). Youths who drink spend less time with their families and do not enjoy the time they do spend at home as much as non-drinking peers.

Parents who are moderate to heavy drinkers are more likely to have adolescents who are moderate to heavy drinkers (Barnes, Reifman, Farrell, et al., 2000); parents who do not drink or who disapprove of drinking are more likely to have children who follow their example. Furthermore, chronic alcoholism is likely to run in families (Lieb, Merikangas, Hofler, et al., 2002). Children who are exposed to drinking by their parents, however, do not necessarily grow up to be problem drinkers. The highest rates of alcoholism among adolescents are found in groups that are under great pressure to refrain from drinking or who are in families that themselves have high rates of alcoholism, such as the Irish or Native Americans (Gfellner & Hundelby, 1994; Huston, Hoberman, & Nugent, 1994). Recent research on family influences has focused on the role of parental monitoring: not surprisingly, parents who monitor their children's behavior and set limits on their children's actions are less likely to have children who drink (DiClemente, Wingood, Crosby, et al., 2001).

Youths also drink because of peer-group pressure and the need for peer identification, sociability, and friendship (Sieving, Perry, & Williams, 2000). Drinking becomes a social custom of a particular group. Therefore, the adolescent who wants to be part of the group drinks as well. Many youths drink because they perceive it as normative (Olds & Thombs, 2001). One effective way to reduce underage drinking, then, is to spread the word that *not everyone drinks, and not all teens think that it is okay to get drunk*. A second peer-related tactic that has proven effective in reducing

adolescent drinking is to teach refusal skills (the ability to say "no" in the face of peer pressure). Some research suggests that this may be even more effective than changing perceptions of norms (e.g., Connor, Young, Williams, et al., 2000).

Not all adolescents who sometimes get drunk become problem drinkers. Problem drinkers start to drink in excess for psychological rather than social reasons. Heavy, escapist drinking is symptomatic of serious adjustment problems. Such youths do not get along at home or at school; they receive more failing grades, are more prone to delinquency, participate less often in extracurricular activities, spend more nights out away from home, and are not as close to their parents as non-problem drinkers. Only some youths who drink are problem drinkers, but they are already evidencing the psychological imbalance that prompts them to rebel or to seek escape through alcohol (Ralph & Morgan, 1991).

Physical Consequences of Alcohol Use

There is absolutely no doubt that the long-term, heavy consumption of alcohol harms the body. Most people know that alcohol abuse is associated with a type of liver damage known as **cirrhosis,** which is a potentially fatal illness. In addition, chronic heavy drinking impairs the functioning of the immune system; this means that abusers cannot fight off infections, including serious ones such as tuberculosis, as readily as people who do not drink. Long-term heavy alcohol use is also associated with high blood pressure, heart arrhythmia (irregular heartbeat), weakened heart muscle, and stroke. Women who drink large amounts of alcohol appear even more susceptible to its detrimental effects than men. Although heavy female drinkers typically consume less than heavy male drinkers, it takes less alcohol to harm a woman's body. In addition, heavy alcohol consumption is associated with an elevated rate of breast cancer. The National Institute on Alcohol Abuse and Alcoholism (NIAAA) has prepared an excellent, detailed summary of what is known about the health consequences of consuming alcohol (NIAAA, 2000).

Alcohol also has well-documented behavioral and cognitive effects. Many behavioral effects—such as engaging in unprotected sex, missing classes, and so on—have already been discussed. Here, we will turn to alcohol's effects on more basic cognitive functioning.

Given that the brains of heavy drinkers actually become physically smaller, it is not surprising that most alcoholics exhibit a mild to moderate loss of intelligence. Most cell loss occurs in the cortex of the **frontal lobe,** the part of the brain most involved in higher-order thinking, such as planning and impulse control; in the hippocampus, and in the **cerebellum,** a part of the brain that helps control balance, coordination, and learning. This cell damage leaves heavy drinkers with deficits in the ability to lay down new memories, to solve complex problems, and to perceive and remember the locations of objects. How about light and moderate drinkers? The data are mixed, but some studies have found that a long-term pattern of light to moderate consumption does decrease cognitive abilities (NIAAA, 2001).

Since the adolescent brain is still growing, it is reasonable to ask if alcohol exposure alters brain development. Studies with both lab animals (see Spear, 2002) and humans suggest that alcohol may have that effect—at least if an adolescent drinks heavily. Adolescents who abuse alcohol have been found to have smaller hippocampi than those who do not use alcohol, and the heavier their drinking and the earlier they began, the smaller this area of the brain becomes (De Bellis, Clark, Beers, et al., 2000). Since the hippocampus is a part of the brain that contributes to memory, it makes sense that research has linked memory deficits to heavy drinking in adolescence (Brown, Tapert, Granhom, et al., 2000).

Drinking in Young Adulthood

Drinking tends to decrease as individuals move out of adolescence and into young adulthood (Bachman, O'Malley, Johnson, et al., 2008a). This is true of both youths who attend college and those who move directly from high school to the working world. Many if not most individuals who binge as college students cut down their consumption greatly once they graduate. Entering the workforce is associated with decreased

ANSWERS WOULDN'T YOU LIKE TO KNOW ...
Do most students who drink heavily in college keep drinking so heavily as adults?

No. The responsibilities of adult life and changes in socialization seem to reduce drinking among young adults.

alcohol use (Wood, Sherman, & McGowen, 2000), although this is less true for post–high school students than for post–college students (Schulenberg, O'Malley, Bachman, et al., 2000). Getting married further drops the drinking rate (Bachman, Wadsworth, O'Malley, et al., 1997).

At least two factors may be at play in these trends. First, the increased responsibilities of adult life may make it more difficult to sustain heavy drinking. One usually needs to get up earlier and work longer hours after graduation; there is also a house or apartment to keep clean, food to buy, and so on. Second, less time is spent socializing after graduation and after

cirrhosis   an often fatal disease of the liver caused by heavy and chronic alcohol consumption.

frontal lobe   the cerebral lobe that is the center for higher-order thinking, such as planning and impulse control.

cerebellum   a part of the brain that controls balance, coordination, and learning.

alcohol abuse   excessive use of alcohol so that functioning is impaired.

alcoholism   chemical dependency on alcohol accompanied by compulsive and excessive drinking.

RESEARCH HIGHLIGHT   ALCOHOL ABUSE AND ALCOHOLISM

Alcohol abuse is the use of alcohol to a degree that causes physical damage; impairs physical, social, intellectual, or occupational functioning; or results in behavior harmful to others. A person does not have to be an alcoholic to have problems with alcohol. The individual who drinks only once a month but drives while intoxicated and has an accident is an alcohol abuser—so is someone who gets drunk and beats up his or her children.

Alcoholism is dependence on alcohol—drinking compulsively and excessively, leading to functional impairment. Some alcoholics drink large amounts daily. Others drink heavily only on weekends. Still others may go through long periods of sobriety interspersed with binges of daily heavy drinking lasting for weeks or months. On some occasions, heavy drinking is limited to periods of stress.

PERSONAL ISSUES   ADOLESCENT CHILDREN OF ALCOHOLIC PARENTS

Another way that alcohol can impact an adolescent is that she or he can live in a family in which a parent or other close family member abuses alcohol. This is distressingly common: more than 17 million Americans suffer from alcohol abuse or dependence (NIAAA, 2006), and many of them are parents. The result is that 1 in 4 children in the United States have been exposed to alcohol abuse or dependency within their own families (Grant, 2000). Being reared in this environment puts them at increased risk for a variety of problems, including anxiety, depression, substance abuse, and academic failure (Rice, Dandreaux, Handley, et al., 2006).

To begin with, children born to alcohol dependent mothers run a risk of acquiring fetal alcohol syndrome. This condition leads to long-lasting brain anomalies at both the structural (Willoughby, Sheard, Nash, et al., 2008) and biochemical levels (Fagerlund, Heikkinen, Autti-Ramo, et al., 2006). It can lead to learning disabilities, memory impairments, and poor executive control—which in turn

are associated with poor decision making, delinquency, and disruptive behavior (Rasmussen & Wyper, 2007).

Alcoholic parents are often unable to fulfill their responsibilities as parents. They discipline only inconsistently and fail to monitor their children's whereabouts (Brody, Ge, Conger, et al., 2001). They also give their children reason to feel stress; for example, they cannot hold down steady jobs or manage to run the household. They often suffer from depression and are not available for emotional support (Fals-Stewart, Kelley, Cooke, et al., 2003). Children frequently feel overwhelmed by the additional responsibilities that are placed upon them as they need to care for their parents and their siblings.

Fortunately, help is available. One resource is Alateen (http://www.al-anon.alateen.org). More information can be found at the Children of Alcoholics Foundation (http://coaf.org). College students can also speak to the counselors in their university's mental health center.

---

marriage, especially with exclusively same-age peers. Most people go out less and stay home more. If they do go out, it is more often with smaller groups of friends and couples, rather than to large parties. Some of that socializing might be with coworkers, who might be older and who might disapprove of heavy drinking.

In sum, although a portion of the adolescent drinkers who became addicted to or dependent on alcohol while in college will continue to drink heavily, most will greatly cut back their consumption.

The following are some warning signals that indicate a drinking problem is developing:

- You drink more than you used to and tend to gulp your drinks.
- You try to have a few extra drinks before or after drinking with others.
- You have begun to drink alone.
- You are noticeably drunk on important occasions.
- You drink the "morning after" to overcome the effects of previous drinking.
- You drink to relieve feelings of boredom, depression, anxiety, or inadequacy.
- You have begun to drink at certain times, to get through difficult situations, or when you have problems.

- You have weekend drinking bouts and Monday hangovers.
- You are beginning to lose control of your drinking; you drink more than you planned and get drunk when you did not want to.
- You promise to drink less but do not.
- You often regret what you have said or done while drinking.
- You are beginning to feel guilty about your drinking.
- You are sensitive when others mention your drinking.
- You have begun to deny your drinking or lie about it.
- You have memory blackouts or pass out while drinking.
- Your drinking is affecting your relationship with friends or family.
- You have lost time at work or school because of drinking.
- You begin to stay away from people who do not drink.

SUMMARY

1. A distinction needs to be made between *physical addiction* and *psychological dependency*. Some drugs are physically habit forming, meaning the body builds up a physical need for the drug. Psychological dependency is the development of an overpowering psychological need for a drug. Both physical addiction and psychological dependency are hard to break.

2. Teens who use drugs occasionally are less likely to develop a substance abuse problem than teens who use drugs to cope with the problems in their lives.

3. Abused drugs (in addition to alcohol and tobacco) may be grouped into a number of categories:
   ▶ Narcotics—opium, morphine, heroin, codeine, and methadone
   ▶ Stimulants—cocaine, amphetamines (Benzedrine, Dexedrine, methedrine), and ecstasy
   ▶ Depressants—barbiturates (Quaalude, Nembutal, Seconal, and phenobarbital), tranquilizers (Xanax, Librium, and Valium), inhalants, and alcohol
   ▶ Hallucinogens—LSD, peyote, mescaline, psilocybin; and marijuana in various forms (the plant cannabis, hashish, hashish oil)

4. The most frequently abused drugs among adolescents in the United States are alcohol, tobacco, and marijuana, in that order. Alcohol continues to be the drug of choice of all age groups.

5. Drug use is widespread throughout the adolescent population. However, White youths are more likely to use drugs than adolescents from other racial and ethnic groups.

6. Adolescents begin to use drugs for a number of reasons: curiosity; fun and sensual pleasure; social pressure to be like friends; desire to relieve tensions, anxiety, and pressures; escape from problems; and desire to gain increased awareness, insight, and creativity. Those who continue to use drugs may build up addictions and/or dependencies. Chronic abusers often have troubled family relationships and personal problems and turn to drugs to lessen pain and conflict and as a substitute for meaningful human relationships.

7. Treatment approaches to drug abuse include Alcoholics Anonymous, behavioral therapy, professional counseling and psychiatric care, family systems therapy, and therapeutic community treatment. Present approaches use several models simultaneously.

8. About 20 percent of high school seniors smoke cigarettes. Adolescents are influenced to start smoking by cigarette advertising, by modeling adults who smoke, by peer-group pressure, and by their own need for status. Some smoke as an expression of rebellion and autonomy and a desire to be grown up. Once they start, they continue to smoke to relieve tension; because smoking becomes an unconscious habit, as a means of social coping; and because of a physical addiction to nicotine. The best solution is to keep adolescents from starting in the first place by antismoking education.

9. Substantial portions of adolescents drink; 80 percent of high school seniors have had a drink. Frequent drinking of large quantities is a major factor in crime, homicides, traffic accidents, violence, pedestrian injuries, and unwed pregnancy. Binge drinking—having five or more drinks at one sitting—is especially frequent on college campuses.

10. Pubertal growth, cognitive development, the identity search, increased peer attachments, and the presence of more intense stressors all contribute to adolescents' desire and ability to drink.

11. Teens' drinking is highly influenced by cultural norms, their parents' behavior (both toward them and toward alcohol), their peers' behavior, and their own personalities.

12. Heavy alcohol consumption carries with it great physical health risks as well as the likelihood of cognitive impairment.

KEY TERMS

alcohol abuse 405	experimental use 382
Alcoholics Anonymous (AA) 394	family systems therapy 396
	frontal lobe 405
alcoholism 405	GABA 386
attention-deficit hyperactivity disorder (ADHD) 385	hallucinogens 387
	hippocampus 389
behavioral therapy 394	intensified drug use 383
binge drinking 401	narcotics 383
cerebellum 405	physical addiction 382
circumstantial-situational use 383	psychological dependency 382
cirrhosis 404	serotonin 385
club drugs 387	social-recreational use 383
compulsive drug use 383	stimulants 384
depressants 386	THC 388
dopamine 384	therapeutic community treatment 396
drug abuse 382	
endogenous endorphins 383	

THOUGHT QUESTIONS

Personal Reflection

1. Was drug abuse a problem in the high school you attended? Explain. What drugs were most commonly used? Was drug abuse limited to any particular type of student? From what type of family background did abusers generally come?

2. What effect did drug abuse have on the lives of adolescents—both users and abstainers—in the school in which you were brought up?

3. Do you smoke regularly? How old were you when you started? Why do you smoke? Have you ever tried to stop? With what effect?

4. Do you drink to excess? On page 406 is a list of symptoms of problem drinking behavior. Do any of these characteristics fit you?

5. Have you ever tried any illegal drug? What was your motivation for doing so? Did the rewards outweigh the risks?

Group Discussion

6. What types of drugs are most commonly used among students you know?

7. What should parents do if they discover their adolescent is using marijuana? Narcotics? LSD? Speed? Cocaine? Inhalants?

8. Did your high school offer drug education? What type of program? With what effect?

9. What approaches do you think should be taken to combat drug abuse among adolescents?

10. How have cigarette advertisements or product placements influenced you or your friends? Which kinds of advertisements have been (or are) most persuasive? Why? Have ads affected the fact that you or your friends smoked (or smoke) or merely the brand chosen?

11. Discuss ways and means of how to quit smoking, such as attending smoking clinics or joining antismoking campaigns. Which way works the best?

12. What are some of the best ways of keeping adolescents from starting to smoke?

13. How common was drinking alcohol in your high school? Was the drinking level high enough to have noticeable consequences? Explain.

14. Discuss binge drinking on your college campus. What steps could college administrations take to reduce binge drinking? What steps would be ineffective? Why?

15. On pages 402–403, there is a list of reasons as to why drinking often begins during adolescence. How many of these do you think apply to smoking? To the use of illicit drugs? Which apply only to alcohol?

Debate Questions

16. Given all the problems that it causes, alcohol use should be outlawed.

17. Marijuana use should be legalized.

18. Tobacco companies should be prohibited from advertising.

19. All middle school students should be required to take a comprehensive drug education course.

SUGGESTED READING

Babbit, N. (2000). *Adolescent Drug and Alcohol Abuse: How to Spot It, Stop It, and Get Help for Your Family.* Cambridge, England: O'Reilly.

Bonnie, R. J., and O'Connell, M. E. (Eds.). (2004). *Reducing Underage Drinking: A Collective Responsibility.* Washington, DC: National Academies Press.

Faupel, C. E., Horowitz, A. M., and Weaver, G. (2003). *The Sociology of American Drug Use.* New York: McGraw-Hill.

Marczinski, C. A., Grant, E. C., & Grant, V. J. (Eds.). (2009). *Binge Drinking in Adolescents and College Students.* Hauppauge, NY: Nova Science Publishers.

Ross, G. R. (2002). *Treating Adolescent Substance Abuse: Understanding the Fundamental Elements.* Portland, OR: Resource Publications.

Wechsler, H., and Wuethrich, B. (2003). *Dying to Drink: Confronting Binge Drinking on College Campuses.* New York: Rodale.

USEFUL WEB SITES

Core Institute
www.siu.edu/~coreinst

This is the Web Site of the Center for Alcohol and Drug Studies Program at Southern Illinois University at Carbondale. It contains data from the Core Alcohol and Drug Survey, which provides information about students' beliefs regarding alcohol consumption, the risks of alcohol use, and the secondary effects of drinking.

Higher Education Center for Alcohol and Other Drug Prevention
www.edc.org/hec

This site was developed by the U.S. Department of Education to assist colleges and universities in developing, implementing, and evaluating alcohol and other drug prevention programs.

Monitoring the Future Study
www.monitoringthefuture.org

This site, provided by the University of Michigan's Institute for Social Research, reports the findings of the Monitoring the Future Study, which has been annually tracking substance use by eighth- and tenth-graders since 1991 and by twelfth-graders since 1975.

National Clearinghouse on Alcohol and Drug
Information (NCADI)
www.health.org

> *This site contains information from the Center for
> Substance Abuse Prevention of the U.S. Department of
> Health and Human Services and provides links to
> several alcohol and drug prevention databases.*

National Institute on Drug Abuse (NIDA)
www.nida.nih.gov

> *A branch of the National Institutes of Health, NIDA's
> mission is to support the scientific investigation of
> substance abuse and to disseminate that information to
> the medical community as well as to legislators and the
> public.*

EPILOGUE

After reading this text, you have likely learned a lot about adolescents and the experiences they typically have. I wanted to end the text on a positive note; since the text also details the many problems experienced by adolescents, I begin by describing what we have learned about *preventing* those problems. A tremendous effort in recent years has focused upon what is termed **positive youth development.** This perspective looks at strengths and constructive attributes of youth. It recognizes that development is not predetermined and that providing individuals with opportunities that foster healthy growth can have a tremendous, beneficial impact. Then, to close this book, I briefly discuss the stages of life that follow adolescence and that youth will experience next.

Positive Youth Development

There is no one accepted definition of positive youth development (Lerner, Phelps, Forman, et al., 2009). To some, it is synonymous with healthy adjustment (e.g., Shek, Siu, & Lee, 2007), whereas to others it means avoidance of harmful activities (Tebes, Feinn, Vanderploeg, et al., 2007). Indeed, much of what we know about positive youth development comes from analyzing prevention programs that were designed to provide skills, establish relationships, and increase self-esteem so that adolescents avoid harmful behaviors and become well-functioning adults.

Prevention efforts are aimed at eliminating problem behaviors before they even occur. Many experts believe that greater efforts should be placed on prevention, for several reasons. First, a single program can effectively and concurrently reduce the risks of several undesirable behaviors, such as substance abuse and dropping out. (This makes sense, as has been said before, because the same stressors are responsible for multiple problems.) In addition, prevention measures eliminate or reduce the trauma experienced by adolescents as well as their families and their victims (if any). Finally, prevention programs can eliminate the spiral of defeat, whereby one problem leads to or at least exacerbates others. Positive youth development prevention efforts differ from more narrowly focused prevention efforts (such as informational lectures on the dangers of unsafe sexual practices or substance abuse) as the latter do not give students the life skills they need for success (Roth, 2000).

What makes a successful youth development program? By examining the literature and 71 existing successful programs, Roth and Brooks-Gunn (2003) identified a triad of attributes. First, the programs must contain the right goals. That is, they work not only to prevent high-risk activities but also to build skills and competencies and to foster connections with others. Second, they accomplish these goals by providing the right activities. Most of the successful programs allowed participants opportunities to practice decision making, feel challenged, and perform community service. The third leg of the triad was that the programs had the right atmosphere, which involved feelings of safety and support. Most of these programs encourage the formation of mentoring relationships between adults and teens. In order to be successful, services must be sustained rather than short term (Roth, 2000).

Lerner and her colleagues (2009) combined the work of a number of researchers in this field to develop the "5 Cs" model of positive youth development. Specifically, positive youth development involves helping teens develop *competence, confidence, connection, character,* and *compassion.* Certainly, youth who have developed these attributes are on the right path to leading productive, satisfying lives!

Successful programs must engage youth and attract them to participate. According to Anderson-Butcher (2005), teens express an interest in taking part in programs that are accessible in terms of location and time, expand their horizons and increase the quality of their lives, help them with their schoolwork or meet their needs in other ways, challenge them and let them experience a sense of mastery, enhance their physical fitness, give them choices, and let them make and be with friends.

The take-away message is that these programs do exist, and we have the means to help ensure that adolescents navigate the teenage years successfully. It *is* within our power to substantially reduce delinquency, teenage pregnancy, substance abuse, and academic disengagement. We have the know-how to help teens feel good about themselves and have faith in their futures. What we need is the resolution and the resources to make this happen.

positive youth development programs   programs designed to provide skills, establish relationships, and increase self-esteem so that adolescents avoid delinquency and become well-functioning adults.

Emerging Adulthood

Traditionally, we expected adolescents to move from adolescence into young adulthood—and, certainly, many still do. Ever greater numbers of adolescents, however, are moving into what has become a distinct, new stage of life: *emerging adulthood*. Since emerging adulthood precedes young adulthood, we discuss it first.

Emerging adulthood was first conceptualized by J. J. Arnett (2000, 2004). It typically lasts from about age 18 through the middle (or even late) twenties. Its existence came about because of the kinds of demographic changes we have already discussed: people are waiting longer to marry, they are more likely to continue their educations, and so on. They are postponing settling down and making permanent choices. Their lives are in constant flux; they move frequently, change jobs, and start and stop and restart their education. Emerging adults are a hard group to characterize: whereas almost all middle-aged Americans are employed and almost all adolescents live with their families, "almost all" emerging adults don't have much in common. They are unique in their diversity.

Another reason to consider emerging adulthood a distinct time of life is that emerging adults themselves feel that they are neither adolescents nor adults. When directly asked if they feel grown up, they are more likely to answer "yes and no" than "yes." This is most likely because they do not yet feel as if they are completely self-reliant, either financially or emotionally.

One appealing aspect of treating emerging adulthood as a separate stage of life is that it provides a time for the identity search to be completed. As you surely remember, Erikson believed that finding an identity was the singular achievement of adolescence. However, most individuals do not fully form their identities by the end of adolescence (unless you feel comfortable stretching adolescence into the twenties). If you are not planning to marry until you are nearly 30, you are not inclined to think seriously about what you are looking for in a life partner at 17. If college and even graduate school are on your horizon, you ruminate about career choices differently than if you plan to get a full-time job right after high school. Emerging adulthood is an extension of the psychological moratorium, the period of time in which one is actively thinking about one's goals and choices but has not yet come to any decisions.

Emerging adulthood is not universal. It exists only in societies in which human development has been prolonged. This is likely to be true in Westernized rather than traditional cultures. Emerging adulthood may not endure as a phenomenon in industrialized societies. But, for now, it seems a fine way to conceptualize that betwixt-and-between period that many people go through in their twenties.

Young Adulthood

More customarily, individuals move from adolescence into young adulthood. Robert Havighurst (1972), who so elegantly described the life tasks of adolescents, also outlined the life tasks of young adulthood. Clearly, they are quite different from those of adolescents:

1. *Selecting a mate.* Dating takes on a different flavor for many people once they reach their twenties: it becomes more serious—more focused on finding a partner. It becomes common, when you are out with someone, to ask yourself: Would this person make a good spouse? A good mother/father someday? During adolescence, you date someone because he or she is fun, attractive, and available, but in young adulthood, that may not be enough.

2. *Learning to live with a marriage partner.** Living with someone requires making many adjustments. In addition to the mundane disagreements about whether the toilet seat should be left up or down and whether it really is important to put the cap back on the toothpaste tube, it is important to learn how to juggle household tasks and integrate personal preferences: How much money should you be saving? How late should you stay up? How do you deal with the fact that your spouse is a complete grouch before having his or her morning coffee? Compromise is usually needed to balance the tastes and desires of both partners. It is extremely unusual for two persons to join their lives effortlessly.

3. *Starting a family.* Not everyone has children; however, most people do. Having children causes profound changes in a couple's lifestyle: money is tighter, sleep deprivation increases, time for romance decreases, spontaneity disappears, and stress skyrockets. Although there are few joys in life equal to that of holding a wanted, loved infant, it is unrealistic to expect that life will otherwise go on as usual. Many adjustments must be made.

4. *Rearing children.* Life does not return to "pre-children normal" for quite some time. Most parents admit that parenting is the most difficult, most time-consuming, most rewarding job they have ever had. Trying to juggle a career or two; keeping up a household; and managing the chauffeuring, added shopping, tutoring, reading time, play time, coaching, and so on that make up a parent's job can be exhausting. Personal needs often

---

*Writing in the early 1970s, Havighurst did not consider the possibility of a long-term, committed, nonmarital relationship.

seem to take a backseat to the demands of being a spouse and a parent. Most parents would say that the time and effort are well worth it and that they would become parents again in a second. Even so, rearing children is undoubtedly a major focus of life in early and mid-adulthood.

5. *Managing a home.* Many college students take great satisfaction in the fact that they can fit everything they own into a car and drive off whenever they want. But when they go from living at home with their folks or in a dorm room to living on their own, they quickly discover that having a lot of material goods is, well, necessary. They come to covet items that they never even thought about before: dish towels, a lawn mower, and a dishwasher. They not only have to acquire some possessions that they did not previously own, but they also have to learn to perform all the little chores that keep a house running. They need to learn about circuit breakers and lint traps. Plus, they need to budget their money so that they can pay the electric bill. There is more to running a household than many youths probably imagine.

6. *Getting started in an occupation.* This life task is self-explanatory. Once schooling is over (however long that is), most people begin to work in earnest. They must learn to interact with their coworkers, master the job itself, and go to work every day. They need to impress the boss so as not to get fired and, maybe, someday get promoted. Quite a large percentage of an adult's waking hours are spent at his or her place of employment.

7. *Taking on civic responsibilities.* Havighurst deemed this a life task of young adulthood, but it is becoming more common for adolescents to do this, as well. This task means becoming a member of a neighborhood and community. You might join the PTA, become a Girl/Boy Scout troop leader, take meals to infirm shut-ins, or volunteer to keep a stretch of road clear of trash. The longer you participate in an activity, the more responsibility you are usually given. Doing community service not only helps others, but it also provides personal satisfaction and strengthens ties to others.

8. *Finding a congenial social group.* When you are in school, you are surrounded mostly by people who are your own age and who are at the same point of life as you are. A sea of ready-made friends is available. Once you leave school, however, it becomes more difficult to find others like yourself. You may go to work in a business with only six other employees, all of whom are older than 40. You may spend most of your day working alone. You may move to a new city and be the only unmarried, childless individual on your block. Therefore, it becomes necessary to learn how to seek out friends. Whether you do it by joining social organizations, by belonging to a religious institution, or simply by learning to introduce yourself to strangers, finding friends is often less automatic once you reach young adulthood.

Although not described by Havighurst, another change that is supposed to occur during young adulthood is becoming psychologically mature, which goes beyond being independent and having an identity (although both of those are necessary). In addition, it entails taking responsibility for your decisions and actions and accepting yourself for who you are. It means that you can look at both yourself and the world *realistically.* It involves being able to handle setbacks and bounce back from them. It involves caring for others, not only for yourself. Not everyone becomes psychologically mature during young adulthood, but it is a fine goal to strive for.

In addition to the issues just described, many people say that young adulthood *feels* different from adolescence. Adolescence has a flavor of "becoming" and "working toward." Many college students use phrases such as "When I join the real world . . . " and "When I'm grown up . . . " Late adolescence is future oriented; you feel as if you are preparing for the life you will someday have. Young adulthood, in contrast, feels more like you have arrived; you are not becoming—you are. Enjoy it!

KEY TERM

positive youth development programs   411

GLOSSARY

accommodation   adjusting to new information by creating new structures to replace old ones.

achievement tests   tests designed to assess mastery of specific subject matter or skills.

acne   pimples on the skin caused by overactive sebaceous glands.

acquaintance rape   forced, unwanted sexual intercourse with someone the victim knows.

adaptation   including and adjusting to new information that increases understanding.

adolescence   the period of growth from childhood to maturity.

adolescent culture   sum of the ways that adolescents behave.

adolescent society   the adolescent social system.

adolescent subculture   values and way of life that are contrary to those found in adult society.

adrenal glands   ductless glands, located just above the kidneys, that secrete androgens and estrogens in both men and women, in addition to secreting adrenaline.

affect   emotions, feelings.

affirmation   a strategy used to confirm beliefs or hypotheses.

Alcoholics Anonymous (AA)   an approach that uses a 12-step model and peer support to help people stop abusing alcohol.

alcohol abuse   excessive use of alcohol so that functioning is impaired.

alcoholism   chemical dependency on alcohol accompanied by compulsive and excessive drinking.

alternating biculturalism   the state in which one vacillates between following one's ethnic beliefs and those of the societal mainstream.

amygdala   the part of the brain that creates primitive emotional responses to the environment.

anabolic steroids   the masculinizing hormone testosterone taken by athletes to build muscle mass.

anal stage   the second psychosexual stage in Sigmund Freud's theory of development: the second year of life, during which the child seeks pleasure and satisfaction through anal activity and the elimination of waste.

analysis   an approach to moral education that emphasizes using logical reasoning to solve social dilemmas.

androgens   a class of masculinizing sex hormones produced by the testes and, to a lesser extent, by the adrenals.

androgyny   a blending of male and female characteristics and roles.

animism   the preoperational belief that inanimate objects have humanlike properties and emotions.

anorexia nervosa   an eating disorder characterized by an obsession with food and with being thin.

anovulatory   without ovulation.

antiprostaglandins   drugs that destroy prostaglandins and can reduce menstrual distress.

apocrine   sweat glands located primarily in the armpits and groin whose secretions cause body odor.

apprenticeships or internships   programs in which students split their time among working at a company, taking career-related classes, and doing regular academic coursework.

assimilation   incorporating a feature of the environment into an existing mode or structure of thought.

attachment   the early emotional bond formed between child and parent.

attention-deficit hyperactivity disorder (ADHD)   a behavioral disorder characterized by impulsivity, an inability to pay attention, and an inability to sit still.

authoritarian parents   parents who set many rules and harshly enforce them.

authoritative parents   parents who respect their children's wishes but maintain control in the home.

autonomy   independence or freedom.

autosociality   the period during which a child plays alongside other children, not with them.

Bartholin's glands   glands on either side of the vaginal opening that secrete fluid during sexual arousal.

behavioral autonomy   becoming independent and free enough to act on one's own without excessive dependence on others.

behavioral therapy   an approach that uses modeling, reinforcement, and situational inducement to alter behavior.

binge drinking   the consumption of five or more drinks at a sitting.

blended biculturalism   the state in which one finds the commonalities between one's ethnic and mainstream identities.

bulimia   an eating disorder characterized by binge-eating episodes and purging.

bullying   repetitive, unprovoked aggression against another.

centering   the tendency of children to focus attention on one detail and their inability to shift attention to other aspects of the situation.

cerebellum   the part of the brain that controls balance, coordination, and learning.

cerebrum   the largest part of the human brain.

charter schools   public schools that are funded and run by private corporations or individuals; accountable to government but relatively regulation free.

child abuse   may include not only physical assault of a child but also malnourishment, abandonment, neglect, emotional abuse, and sexual abuse.

child neglect   failure to provide even minimal care of a child, including adequate food, clothing, shelter, and medical care, as well as for the child's emotional, social, intellectual, and moral needs.

circumscription   limiting one's career aspirations to a set of acceptable choices based on interests and values.

circumstantial-situational use   drug use to produce a desired psychological mood.

cirrhosis   an often fatal disease of the liver caused by heavy and chronic alcohol consumption.

class inclusion relationships   understanding that objects can be fit into different levels of hierarchies.

cliques   relatively small, tightly knit groups of friends that spend a lot or even all of their time together.

clitoris   a small shaft containing erectile tissue, located above the vaginal and urethral openings, that is highly responsive to sexual stimulation.

club drugs   collectively, ecstasy, rohypnol, GHB, and ketamine. They are part of the rave scene and are used in bars.

cognition   the act or process of knowing.

cognitive monitoring   thinking about what you are doing, what you are going to do next, how the problem is going to be solved, and the approaches that you are going to take.

cognitive priming   the activation of neural pathways so that ambiguous or neutral stimuli are perceived as similar to what has been previously perceived.

cohesion   the degree to which family members are connected to one another.

cohort   a group of individuals who are born at approximately the same time and who share traits because they experienced the same historical events.

cohort effects   differences among individuals that are caused by historical events rather than by maturation or development.

coitus   sexual intercourse.

collectivism   an emphasis upon the family rather than upon the individual.

colonias or barrios   colonies or districts of Spanish-speaking people.

comparator   the component of the identity control system that compares one's self-concept with one's identity standards.

compromise   modifying one's career choices to bring them in line with reality.

compromise with reality theory   the theory of vocational choice proposed by Ginzberg.

compulsive drug use   drug use motivated by physical addiction or psychological dependency.

concrete operational stage   the third stage of cognitive development, according to Piaget, lasting from 7 to 11 or 12 years of age.

conduct disorder   a psychological order typified by aggressive, hurtful, deceitful behavior.

confirmation strategy   looking for examples that match a hypothesis.

connection   the presence of a warm, stable, loving, attentive bond between parents and child.

conservation problems   tests used by Piaget to determine whether children had mastered concrete operations, such as understanding that changing an object's appearance does not alter its fundamental properties.

control   the degree to which parents manage their child's behavior.

conventional moral reasoning   according to Kohlberg, the second level of development of moral thought, based on the desire to conform to social convention.

corpus callosum   a fibrous band of tissue that connects the two cerebral hemispheres of the brain.

corpus luteum   a yellow body that grows from the ruptured follicle of the ovary and becomes an endocrine gland that secretes progesterone.

correlation   a description of a relationship between two factors that does not imply a causal relationship between them.

Cowper's glands   small twin glands that secrete a fluid to neutralize the acid environment of the urethra.

cross sectional study   a quasi experimental study in which a group of persons who are one age is compared with a group of persons who are another age.

cross-sequential design   a research method in which subjects at several different ages are tracked over time

crowds   loose associations of cliques that usually meet on weekends.

cultural determinism   the influence of a particular culture in determining the personality and behavior of a developing individual.

cultural relativism   variations in social institutions, economic patterns, habits, mores, rituals, religious beliefs, and ways of life from one culture to another.

cysts   large, deep pimples that can cause scarring.

date rape   forced, unwanted sexual intercourse with a date.

deductive reasoning   beginning with a hypothesis or premise and breaking it down to see if it is true.

defense mechanisms   according to Anna Freud, unrealistic strategies used by the ego to protect itself and to discharge tension.

defensive realists   believing that there are absolute truths but people are biased; differentiates between opinion and fact.

depressants   a class of drugs that works by slowing the functioning of the central nervous system (alcohol, inhalants).

depression   a serious psychological disorder marked by sadness, helplessness, and hopelessness.

developmental tasks   the skills, knowledge, functions, and attitudes that individuals have to acquire at certain points in their lives in order to function effectively as mature persons.

dialectics   an advanced form of reasoning that allows one to create new and better insights by integrating conflicting data.

disengaged families   those whose members are isolated from one another.

dogmatists   those who cling rigidly to one belief.

dopamine   a neurotransmitter whose effects are enhanced by stimulants.

drug abuse   the use of drugs to the point of causing risk or harm, either legal risk or the risk of harming oneself and others.

dual process theory   a theory of decision making that says that adolescents can logically and analytically make choices, but that they often rely upon intuition and short-term benefits instead.

ectomorph   tall, slender body build.

ego   according to Sigmund Freud, the rational mind that seeks to satisfy the id in keeping with reality.

egocentricism   the inability to take the perspective of another or to imagine the other person's point of view.

elimination strategy   looking for evidence that disproves a hypothesis.

emerging adulthood   the stage of life, generally extending through one's twenties, in which one is between adolescence and full adulthood.

emotional abuse   may include constant screaming at the child, calling him or her foul names, giving constant criticism and put-downs, making fun, constantly comparing the child with siblings, ignoring the child, and refusing to talk or listen to him or her.

emotional autonomy   becoming free of childish emotional dependence on parents.

empathy   the ability to identify with the thoughts, attitudes, and feelings of another person.

endocrine glands   structures in the body that produce hormones.

endogenous endorphins   chemicals similar to narcotics that are produced by the body and cause euphoria and depress pain.

endomorph   short, heavy body build.

enmeshed families   those whose members are too heavily connected with one another.

epididymis   a system of ducts, running from the testes to the vas deferens, in which sperm mature and are stored.

epistemology   one's beliefs about knowledge.

equilibrium   according to Piaget, achieving a balance between schemas and accommodation.

estrogens   feminizing hormones produced by the ovaries and, to some extent, by the adrenal glands.

exosystem   that part of an ecological system that includes settings in which the adolescent does not have an active role as a participant but that influence him or her nevertheless.

expected selves   the people we think we will likely be in the future.

experimental use   occasional drug use motivated by curiosity.

fallopian tubes   tubes that transport the ova from the ovaries to the uterus.

familialism   devotion to one's family and respect for one's parents and grandparents.

family systems therapy   an approach to helping adolescents in which the emphasis is on enhancing family communication and improving family relationships.

fatalism   the belief that one cannot change one's destiny or fate.

feared selves   the people we are afraid of becoming in the future.

feminine   having the personality and behavior characteristics of a female according to culturally defined standards of femaleness.

flappers   teenage girls in the late 1910s–1920s who dated, wore short skirts, and drank alcohol.

follicle-stimulating hormone (FSH)   a pituitary hormone that stimulates the maturation of the follicles and ova in the ovaries and of sperm in the testes.

foreclosure   according to Marcia, establishing an identity without search or exploration, usually according to what has been handed down by parents.

formal operational stage   the fourth stage of cognitive development, according to Piaget, during which people develop abstract thought independent of concrete objects.

frontal lobe   the cerebral lobe that is the center for higher-order thought processes, such as planning and impulse control.

fusion   the state in which one has merged one's ethnic traditions and those of the cultural mainstream into a new whole.

GABA   an inhibitory neurotransmitter; depressants increase its effectiveness.

gender   the psychological/sociological construct of what it means to be a man or a woman.

gender roles   the behaviors that are supposedly characteristic of men and women.

gender schema theory   a revised cognitive-developmental approach to gender that emphasizes the effects of labeling, attention, and interest in developing gender beliefs.

genital stage   the last psychosexual stage in Sigmund Freud's theory of development, during which sexual urges result in seeking other persons as sexual objects to relieve sexual tension.

gonadotropic hormones   hormones that are secreted by the pituitary and that influence the gonads, or sex glands.

gonadotropin-releasing hormone (GnRH)   a hormone secreted by the hypothalamus that controls the production and release of FSH and LH from the pituitary.

gonads   the sex glands: testes and ovaries.

good girl—good boy orientation   the first of the two levels of conventional moral reasoning, in which one acts so as to win others' approval.

gynecomastia   a phenomenon experienced by some young male adolescents in which their breasts temporarily swell as they enter puberty.

hallucinogens   a class of drugs that acts on the central nervous system to alter perception and state of consciousness, causing hallucinations; so-called psychedelic drugs.

heterosexuality   sexual orientation to those of the opposite sex.

heterosociality   the period during which adolescents and adults enjoy the company of both sexes.

heuristics   "rules of thumb," strategies that usually work to give you the correct answer.

hierarchical classification   the ability to divide objects into nested series of categories.

hippies   youth in the late 1960s who held pro-drug, pacifistic, antimaterialistic values.

hippocampus   a part of the brain involved with learning, memory, and motivation.

homosexuality   sexual orientation to those of the same sex.

homosociality   the period during which children prefer the company of those of the same sex.

hoped-for selves   the people we hope to be in the future.

hormones   biochemical substances secreted into the bloodstream by the endocrine glands that act as an internal communication system that tells the different cells what to do.

human growth hormone (HGH)   a pituitary hormone that regulates body growth.

hymen   the tissue partly covering the vaginal opening.

hypocrisy   discrepancy between what people say and do.

hypothalamus   a small area of the brain that controls motivation, emotion, pleasure, and pain in the body; it controls eating, drinking, hormonal production,

menstruation, pregnancy, lactation, and sexual response and behavior.

hypothetico-deductive reasoning   a way to solve problems using the scientific method; only one factor at a time is varied while all else is held constant.

id   according to Sigmund Freud, those instinctual urges that a person seeks to satisfy according to the pleasure principle.

ideal self   the kind of person an individual would like to be.

idealistic   insisting upon high standards of behavior.

identification   the process by which an individual ascribes to himself or herself the characteristics of another person, usually one's parent.

identity achieved   according to Marcia, those adolescents who have undergone a crisis in their search for an identity and who have made commitments to choices they have made.

identity control system   a construct that describes the process of developing an identity.

identity diffused   according to Marcia, those adolescents who have not experienced a crisis and explored meaningful alternatives or made any commitments in finding an acceptable identity.

identity standards   one's beliefs about how one should behave.

imaginary audience   adolescents' belief that others are constantly paying attention to them.

immanent justice   the child's belief that immoral behavior inevitably brings pain or punishment as a natural consequence of the transgression.

immigrants   people who leave their native land to come to live in the United States for any reason.

inculcation   an approach to moral education that teaches students to accept specific moral values, such as honesty and trustworthiness.

individuation   the formation of personal identity by the development of the self as a unique person separate from parents and others.

induction   parental control through offering alternative choices.

inductive reasoning   gathering individual items of information and putting them together to form hypotheses or conclusions.

inference   development of new thoughts from old information.

information-processing approach   an approach to studying cognition that focuses on the perception, attention, retrieval, and manipulation of information.

inhibin   a hormone produced in the testes to regulate FSH secretion and sperm production.

instrumental hedonism orientation   the more advanced of the two preconventional reasoning levels, in which one acts so as to gain a future reward.

intelligence quotient (IQ) calculated by dividing the mental age (MA) by the chronological age (CA) and multiplying by 100.

intensified drug use daily drug use.

introspection thinking about one's thoughts and feelings.

joint custody when two parents share decision-making privileges (joint legal custody) and/or living with a child (joint residential custody).

juvenile one who is not yet considered an adult in the eyes of the law.

juvenile delinquent a juvenile who violates the law.

labia majora major or large lips of tissue on either side of the vaginal opening.

labia minora smaller lips or tissue on either side of the vagina.

latency stage the fourth psychosexual stage in Sigmund Freud's theory of development: from about ages 6 to 12, during which sexual interests remain hidden while the child concentrates on school and other activities.

law and order orientation the more advanced type of conventional moral reasoning, in which one unquestioningly obeys society's rules and laws.

legal custody the parent has the right to make important decisions about the child's life, such as which school he or she will attend.

leptin a hormone that helps trigger puberty.

liaisons individuals who have friends from several cliques but belong to none.

long-term storage (long-term memory) the process by which information is perceived and processed deeply so it passes into the layers of memory below the conscious level (also called secondary memory).

longitudinal study a quasi-experimental study in which a group of people are tracked over time as they age.

luteinizing hormone (LH) a pituitary hormone that stimulates the development of the ovum and estrogen and progesterone in females and of sperm and testosterone in males.

machismo Spanish term for maleness or manhood.

macrosystem the ideologies, attitudes, mores, customs, and laws of a particular culture that influence the individual.

magnet schools theme schools that serve students within public school systems.

marianismo in Puerto Rican society, the implication that a woman finds her greatest satisfaction through motherhood.

masculine having the personality and behavioral characteristics of a male according to culturally defined standards of maleness.

matrilineal descent through the mother's line.

melatonin the hormone that the brain produces to induce sleep.

menarche first menstruation.

mental operations logical processes that allow children to think logically.

merocrine glands sweat glands distributed over the entire body.

mesomorph medium, athletic body build.

mesosystem the reciprocal relationships among microsystem settings.

metabolic rate the rate at which the body utilizes food and oxygen.

metacognition the ability to think about one's own thought processes.

microsystem includes those persons with whom the adolescent has immediate contact and who influence him or her.

modeling learning by observing and imitating the behavior of another.

mons veneris mound of flesh (literally "mound of Venus") in the female located above the vagina, over which pubic hair grows.

moral courage the ability to stand up for one's values, especially those concerning fairness.

moral development an approach to moral education that uses moral dilemmas and the like to give youths experience in higher-level reasoning.

moral relativism the latter of Piaget's two stages of moral development, in which individuals make their own moral judgments rather than blindly following rules.

moral rules social rules that are concerned with how people behave toward one another.

morality of constraint conduct that is coerced by rules or authority.

morality of cooperation conduct that is regulated by mutual respect and consent.

moratorium according to Marcia, a period of time in the life of adolescents who are in a continual crisis, continue to search for an identity, and have not made any commitments.

mortality the probability of dying.

naive realists believing that there are absolute, universal truths; creates difficulty in distinguishing fact from opinion.

narcotics a class of opiate-based drugs that depresses the central nervous system and thus relieves pain and induces sleep; in large doses, narcotics produce unconsciousness, stupor, coma, and possibly death; most are habit forming.

naturalistic intelligence the ability to identify plants and animals.

negation a strategy used to disprove.

negative affect negative feelings of emotional coldness, rejection, hostility, anger, and insensitivity among family members.

negative correlation a description of a relationship in which when one factor increases, the other decreases.

negative identity an identity based on rejecting parenting and societal values.

nocturnal emissions male ejaculation during sleep.

normative barriers limitations on career choice that stem from how girls are socialized to be feminine.

nurturance rights the right to be protected by adults and societal institutions.

obesity overweight; excessively fat.

objective judgments judgments based solely on the consequences of wrongdoing.

open enrollment a policy that allows students to choose from among a large number of public schools, sometimes even those outside their own district.

oppositional defiant disorder (ODD) a psychological disorder that causes a person to get angry and argue, to blame and annoy others, and to disobey authority figures.

oral stage the first psychosexual stage in Sigmund Freud's theory of development: from birth to one year, during which the child's chief source of pleasure and satisfaction comes from oral activity.

organismic psychologist someone like Piaget, who believes that both brain maturation and environmental experience are needed for cognitive development.

osteoporosis a condition in which the bones become brittle as a result of calcium loss

ovaries female gonads, or sex glands, that secrete estrogen and progesterone and produce mature egg cells.

papules tender, raised red bumps that are precursors to pimples.

parens patriae the philosophy that the juvenile court is to act in the best interests of the child.

parietal lobe the cerebral lobe that is the center for solving problems involving spatial relationships.

penis the male organ for coitus and urination.

performance goal structure schooling in a competitive atmosphere in which the goal is to get the highest grade in the class.

permissive parents parents who exercise little control over their children's behavior.

personal fable adolescents' belief that they are invulnerable and that their feelings are special and unique.

personal preferences aspects of behavior that involve independent choices with which others have no right to interfere.

phallic stage the third psychosexual stage in Sigmund Freud's theory of development: from about the fourth to the sixth year, during which the genital area is the chief source of pleasure and satisfaction.

physical addiction a condition that develops from abusing a drug that forms a chemical dependency.

pituitary gland master gland of the body located at the base of the brain.

pluralistic society a society in which there are many different competing standards of behavior.

positive affect emotional warmth, affection, love, empathy, care, sensitivity, and emotional support provided in a relationship.

positive correlation a description of a relationship in which when one factor increases, so does the other.

positive youth development programs programs designed to provide skills, establish relationships, and increase self-esteem so that adolescents avoid delinquency and become well-functioning adults.

possible selves the different selves we envision ourselves becoming.

postconventional moral reasoning according to Kohlberg, the third level of development of moral thought, based on adherence to universal principles.

post-skeptical rationalism the belief that truth is constructed but that some beliefs are more valid than others.

practical ability the aspect of creativity that involves turning abstract ideas into practical applications.

preconventional moral reasoning according to Kohlberg, the first level of development of moral thought, based on reward and punishment.

preoperational stage the second stage of cognitive development, according to Piaget, lasting from 2 to 7 years of age.

principles abstract, theoretical guidelines.

processing speed the pace at which the brain perceives and manipulates information.

progesterone a female sex hormone produced by the corpus luteum of the ovary.

progressives educators who emphasize that the purpose of education is to prepare pupils for life.

proprium the self-identity that is developing in time.

prosocial behavior actions that benefit, help, and bolster others.

prostaglandins hormones that cause smooth muscle contractions and contribute to dysmenorrhea and menhorrhagia.

prostate gland gland containing two lobes that secrete a portion of the seminal fluid.

pseudostupidity the tendency to approach problems at much too complex a level and to fail, not because the tasks are difficult, but because they're too simple. Adolescents appear stupid when they are, in fact, bright but not yet experienced.

psychoanalytical theory Freud's theory that the structure of personality is composed of the id, ego, and superego and that mental health depends on keeping the balance among them.

psychological autonomy the freedom to form one's own opinions, have privacy, and make decisions for oneself.

psychological dependency the development of a persistent, sometimes overpowering psychological need for a drug.

psychometric approach an approach to cognitive development that focuses on the measurement of knowledge and thinking ability.

psychosocial moratorium a socially sanctioned period between childhood and adulthood during which an individual is free to experiment to find a socially acceptable identity and role.

puberty the developmental stage at which one becomes capable of reproduction.

punishment orientation the more primitive level of preconventional moral reasoning, in which one acts so as to avoid negative consequences.

pustules the medical term for pimples.

quasi-experiment a study in which the researcher compares preexisting groups.

reasoning logical, constrained, useful thinking.

refugees people who leave their native land to come to live in the United States or another country because they are fleeing political oppression or death.

regulation parental monitoring, supervision, and rule setting.

reinforcement positive reinforcements are influences that increase the probability that the preceding response will occur again; negative reinforcements are influences that increase the probability that the preceding response will stop.

relational aggression using your friends to help socially hurt another.

reputational aggression spreading rumors or doing other actions to hurt another's reputation.

residential custody where and with which parent the child will live.

resiliency an individual's ability to succeed in spite of adversity and hardship.

restorative justice movement an approach to juvenile justice that addresses the needs of the victim, the community, and the perpetrator; it focuses on restitution for the victim and personal development for the offender.

role strain the stress individuals experience when they are faced with competing demands and expectations.

scaffolding the assistance provided to help a child master a task; it is gradually withdrawn as the child gains competence.

schema original patterns of thinking; the mental structures that people use for dealing with what happens in the environment.

Scholastic Assessment Test (SAT) a test that measures aptitude to do academic work.

school-based enterprises programs in which schools set up small businesses to teach job skills.

scrotum the pouch of skin containing the testes.

sebaceous glands oil-producing skin glands whose secretions can cause acne if the glands' pores become blocked.

secondary sexual characteristics features not directly related to reproduction that distinguish male from female bodies.

secular trend the trend to mature sexually at earlier ages.

self a person's personality or nature of which that person is aware.

self-concept a person's conscious, cognitive perception and evaluation of himself or herself; one's thoughts and opinions about oneself.

self-determination the right to have one's own opinions and make one's own decisions

self-efficacy the belief that one is competent to master a task.

self-enhancement thesis an explanation for delinquency based on the need for troubled youths to enhance their self-esteem.

self-esteem a person's impression or opinion of himself or herself.

self-reinforcement the act of learners rewarding themselves for activities or responses that they consider of good quality.

self-serving bias looking at the world in a way that favors one's own opinion.

semenarche a recently coined term for a boy's first ejaculation; derived from the term *menarche*.

seminal vesicles twin glands that secrete fluid into the vas deferens to enhance sperm viability.

sensorimotor stage the first stage of cognitive development, according to Piaget, lasting from birth to about age 2.

sensory storage (sensory memory) the process by which information is received and transduced by the senses, usually in a fraction of a second.

separation-individuation the process by which the adolescent separates from parents and becomes a unique individual.

seriate to line things up in order from large to small or small to large.

serotonin a neurotransmitter that is chemically similar to the hallucinogens.

Sertoli cells cells in the testes that produce the hormone inhibin.

service learning an approach to moral education that emphasizes community service.

sex one's biological endowment as a male or a female.

sexual abuse may include suggestive language, use of pornography, fondling, petting, masturbation, exhibitionism, voyeurism, oral sex, or full vaginal or anal intercourse.

short-term storage (short-term memory) the process by which information is still in the conscious mind, being rehearsed and focused on (also called *primary memory*).

skeptics   those who reject rationality.

social capital   the resources available to an individual through his or her interpersonal connections.

social contract orientation   the type of postconventional moral reasoning in which one believes that individual actions should serve the greater good.

social conventions   social rules that dictate what is appropriate and expected.

social-cognitive domain model   an approach to moral development that stresses the contextual nature of moral decisions and distinguishes social conventions from moral rules.

social-recreational use   drug use primarily to relax and have fun at parties.

sociometric popularity   a measure of how many friends you have, how many people think you are nice.

spermatogenesis   the process by which sperm are developed.

status crimes   violations of laws that apply only to minors, such as underage drinking, violating curfews, and truancy.

stimulants   agents that produce a temporary increase in the functioning of the body.

stranger rape   forced, unwanted sexual intercourse with someone the victim doesn't know.

Strong Interest Inventory   a test that measures suitability for different vocations according to interests.

structural barriers   externally imposed limits on a woman's career success that result from sex discrimination.

sturm und drang   "storm and stress"; used to describe the volatile adolescent temperament.

subjective judgments   judgments that take into account intentions or motives.

subsystems   smaller segments of adolescent society within the larger social system.

suicide gestures   suicide attempts that seem destined to fail and that really are cries for help rather than true attempts.

superego   according to Sigmund Freud, that part of the mind that opposes the desires of the id by enforcing moral restrictions that have been learned to try to attain a goal of perfection.

survival sex   swapping sexual favors for food or shelter.

syncretism   the act of trying to link ideas.

synthetic ability   the aspect of creativity that involves generating new ideas.

task mastery structure   schooling in a less competitive setting in which individual effort and improvement are rewarded.

tech-prep programs   partnerships between high schools and two-year, postsecondary vocational institutions to provide career education.

tech-prep schools   high schools that partner with community colleges to provide career preparation for non-college-bound students.

teenager   in a strict sense, includes only the teen years: ages 13 to 19.

temporal lobe   the cerebral lobe that is the center for producing and understanding language.

testes   the male gonads that produce sperm and male sex hormones.

testing effects   a change in subject performance resulting not from age or maturation, but from repeated exposure to test materials.

testosterone   a masculinizing sex hormone produced by the testes and, to a lesser extent, by the adrenals.

THC   the active ingredient in marijuana.

therapeutic community treatment   treatment in a residential situation with others who have similar problems; includes individual and group therapy and skills training.

thinking   the conscious, deliberate manipulation of information.

throwaways   adolescents who have been told to leave home.

tracking   an organizational technique that permits schools to create homogeneous groupings of students within a heterogeneous student population in order to facilitate instruction.

traditionalists   educators who emphasize that the purpose of education is to teach the basics.

transductive reasoning   proceeding from particular to particular in thought, without making generalizations.

transitive inferences   the ability to solve problems such as "Tom is taller than Fred, and Fred is taller than Marty. Is Tom taller than Marty?"

true experiment   a study in which the researcher maintains control to ensure there are no significant differences among his or her groups of participants before the study begins and that the different groups of participants have identical experiences (except for the one issue of interest).

uninvolved parents   parents who seem disinterested in their children and thus do not supervise them or give them much affection.

universal principled reasoning   the highest form of moral reasoning, in which one acts according to his or her abstract moral principles.

urethra   the tube carrying the urine from the bladder to the outside; in males, it also carries the semen to the outside.

uterus   the womb in which the baby grows and develops.

vagina   the canal from the cervix to the vulva that receives the penis during intercourse and acts as the birth canal through which the baby passes to the outside.

values clarification   a method of teaching values that helps students become aware of their own beliefs and values.

vas deferens   the tubes running from the epididymis to the urethra that carry semen and sperm to the ejaculatory duct.

vestibule   the opening cleft region enclosed by the labia minora.

vicarious reinforcement   learning from observing the positive or negative consequences of another person's behavior.

vouchers   a method by which the public schools subsidize the cost of private school education.

vulva   collective term referring to the external genitalia of the female.

warmth   the love, approval, and emotional support that parents give their children.

youth or youths   terms used synonymously with "adolescent."

youth development programs   programs designed to provide skills, establish relationships, and increase self-esteem so that adolescents avoid delinquency and become well-functioning adults.

zone of proximal development   the level of learning at which a task that is too difficult for a child to complete by himself or herself is manageable with help.

parenting and remarriage: A risk and resiliency perspective (pp. 295–319). Hillsdale, NJ: Erlbaum.

Anderson, H. L., & Young, B. M. (1992). Holistic attitudes of high school students towards themselves and their school experiences. *Adolescence, 27,* 719–729.

Anderson, M. Z., Tracey, T. J., & Rounds, J. (1997). Examining the invariance of Holland's Vocational Interest Model across gender. *Journal of Vocational Behavior, 50,* 349–364.

Anderson, R. E. (2002). Youth and information technology. In J. T. Mortimer & R. W. Larson (Eds.), *The changing adolescent experience* (pp. 175–207). Cambridge, England: Cambridge University Press.

Anderson, R. E., & Ronnkvist, A. (1999). Teaching, learning, and computing, 1998. Retrieved from University of California, Irvine, Web site: http://www.crito.uci.edu/tlc/html/findings.html.

Anderson, R. N., & Smith, B. L. (2003). Deaths: Leading causes for 2001. *National Vital Statistics Report, 52,* 1–86.

Anderson, S., Dallal, G., & Must, A. (2003). Relative weight and racial background influence average age at menarche: Results from two nationally representative surveys of U.S. girls studied 25 years apart. *Pediatrics, 111,* 844–850.

Anderson-Butcher, D. (2005). Recruitment and retention in youth development programming. *The Prevention Researcher, 12,* 3–6.

Andersson, T. A., & Magnusson, D. (1990). Biological maturation in adolescence and the development of drinking habits and alcohol abuse among young males: A prospective longitudinal study. *Journal of Youth and Adolescence, 19,* 33–41.

Andrews, J. A., Hops, H., Ary, D., Tildesley, E., & Harris, J. (1993). Parental influence on early adolescent substance use: Specific and nonspecific effects. *Journal of Early Adolescence, 13,* 285–310.

Ansuini, C. G., Fiddler-Woite, J., & Woite, R. S. (1996). The source, accuracy, and impact of the National Sexual Information on Lifetime Wellness Survey. *Adolescence, 31,* 283–289.

Anthony, K. H. (1985). The shopping mall: A teenage hangout. *Adolescence, 20,* 307–312.

Antoniades, M., & Tarasuk, V. (1998). A survey of food problems experienced by Toronto street youth. *Canadian Journal of Public Health, 89,* 371–375.

Apel, R., Bushway, S., Brame, R., Haviland, M. A., Nagin, D., & Paternoster, R. (2007). Unpacking the relationship between adolescent employment and antisocial behavior: A matched samples comparison. *Criminology, 45,* 67–97.

Apfel, N. H., & Seitz, V. (1991). Four models of adolescent mother-grandmother relationships in Black inner-city families. *Family Relations, 40,* 421–429.

Aquilino, W. S., & Supple, A. J. (2001). Long-term effects of parenting practices during adolescence on well-being outcomes in young adulthood. *Journal of Family Issues, 22,* 289–308.

Arbona, C., & Power, G. (2003). Parental attachment, self-esteem, and antisocial behaviors among African American, European American, and Mexican American adolescents. *Journal of Counseling Psychology, 50,* 40–51.

Archer, S. L., & Waterman, A. S. (1990). Varieties of identity diffusions and foreclosures: An exploration of subcategories of the identity statuses. *Journal of Adolescent Research, 5,* 96–111.

Archibald, A. B., Graber, J. A., & Brooks-Gunn, J. (1999). Parental relations and pubertal development as predictors of dieting and body image in early-adolescent girls: A short term longitudinal study. *Journal of Research on Adolescence, 9,* 395–415.

Archibald, A. B., Linver, M. R., Graber, J. A., & Brooks-Gunn, J. (2002). Parent-adolescent relationships and girls' unhealthy eating: Testing reciprocal relationships. *Journal of Research on Adolescence, 12,* 451–461.

Ardelt, M., & Day, L. (2002). Parents, siblings, and peers: Close social relationships and adolescent deviance. *Journal of Early Adolescence, 22,* 310–349.

Ardila, A., Rosselli, M., Matute, E., & Guajardo, S. (2005). The influence of the parents' educational level on the development of executive functions. *Developmental Neuropsychology, 28,* 539–560.

Arellano, A. R., & Pedilla, A. M. (1996). Academic invulnerability among a select group of Latino university students. *Hispanic Journal of Behavioral Sciences, 18,* 485–507.

Armstrong, P. I., & Crombie, G. (2000). Compromises in adolescents' occupational aspirations and expectations from grades 8 to 10. *Journal of Vocational Behavior, 56,* 82–98.

Arnett, J. J. (1997). Young people's conceptions of the transition to adulthood. *Youth and Society, 29,* 3–23.

Arnett, J. J. (1999). Adolescent storm and stress, reconsidered. *American Psychologist, 54,* 317–326.

Arnett, J. J. (2000). Emerging adulthood: A theory of development from the late teens through the twenties. *American Psychologist, 55,* 469–480.

Arnett, J. J. (2001). Adolescents' responses to cigarette advertisements for five "youth brands" and one "adult brand." *Journal of Research on Adolescence, 11,* 425–443.

Arnett, J. J. (2004). *Emerging adulthood: The winding road from the late teens through the twenties.* New York: Oxford University Press.

Arnett, J. J. (2005). Talk is cheap: The tobacco companies' violations of their own cigarette advertising code. *Journal of Health Communication, 10,* 419–431.

Arnsten, A. F., & Shansky, R. M. (2004). Adolescence: Vulnerable period for stress-induced prefrontal cortical function? Introduction to Part IV. In R. E. Dahl & L. P. Spear (Eds.), *Adolescent brain development: Vulnerabilities and opportunities* (pp. 145–147). New York: New York Academy of Science.

Aronson, E. (2000). *Nobody left to hate: Teaching compassion after Columbine.* New York: Worth.

Arunkumar, R., Midgley, C., & Urdan, T. (1999). Perceiving high or low home-school dissonance: Longitudinal effects of adolescent emotional and academic well-being. *Journal of Research on Adolescence, 9,* 441–466.

Asendorph, J. B., & van Aken, M. A. G. (1999). Resilient, overcontrolled, and undercontrolled personality prototypes in childhood: Replicability, predictive power, and the trait-type issue. *Journal of Personality and Social Psychology, 77,* 815–832.

Astor, R. A., Meyer, H. A., & Behre, W. J. (1999). Unowned places and times: Maps and interviews about violence in high schools. *American Educational Research Journal, 36,* 3–42.

Atkin, C. K., Smith, S. W., Roberto, A. J., Fediuk, T., & Wagner, T. (2002). Correlates of verbally aggressive communication in adolescents. *Journal of Applied Communication Research, 30,* 251–266.

Attar-Schwartz, S., Tan, J., Buchanan, A., Flouri, E., & Griggs, J. (2009). Grandparenting and adolescent adjustment in two-parent biological, lone-parent, and step-families. *Journal of Family Psychology, 23,* 67–75.

Austin, S. B., Ziyadch, M., Kahn, J. A., Camargo, C. A., Colditz, G. A., & Field, A. E. (2004). Sexual orientation, weight concerns, and eating-disordered behaviors in adolescent girls and boys. *Journal of the American Academy of Child & Adolescent Clinical Psychiatry, 43,* 1115–1123.

Azevedo, R., Cromley, J. G., Winters, F. I., Moos, D. C., & Greene, J. A. (2005). Adaptive human scaffolding facilitates adolescents' self-regulated learning with hypermedia. *Instructional Science, 33,* 381–412.

Bachman, J. G., Segal, D. R., Freedman-Doan, P., & O'Malley, P. M. (2000). Who chooses military service? Correlates of propensity and enlistment in the U.S. armed forces. *Military Psychology, 12,* 1–30.

Bachman, J. G., Wadsworth, K. N., O'Malley, P. M., Johnson, L. D., & Schulenberg, J. E. (1997). *Smoking, drinking, and drug use in young adulthood: The impacts of new freedoms and new responsibilities.* Mahwah, NJ: Erlbaum.

Baham, M. E., Weimer, A. A., Braver, S. L., & Fabricius, W. V. (2008). Sibling relationships in blended families. In J. Pryor (Ed.), *The international handbook of stepfamilies: Policy and practice in legal, research, and clinical environments* (pp. 175–207). Hoboken, NJ: Wiley.

Bahr, S. J., Marcos, A. C., & Maughan, S. L. (1995). Family, educational and peer influences on the alcohol use of female and male adolescents. *Journal of Studies on Alcohol, 56,* 457–469.

Bailey, J. M., & Zucker, K. J. (1995). Childhood sex-typed behavior and sexual orientation: A conceptual analysis and quantitative review. *Developmental Psychology, 31,* 43–55.

Baines, E. T., & Slade, P. (1998). Attributional patterns, moods, and the menstrual cycle. *Psychosomatic Medicine, 50,* 469–476.

Baird, A. L., & Grieve, G. (2006). Exposure to male models in advertisements leads to a decrease in men's body satisfaction. *North American Journal of Psychology, 8,* 115–121.

Baldry, A. C., & Farrington, D. P. (2000). Bullies and delinquents: Personal characteristics and parental styles. *Journal of Community and Applied Social Psychology, 10,* 17–31.

Balfanz, R., & Legters, N. (2004). *Locating the dropout crisis.* Baltimore: Johns Hopkins University, Center for Social Organization of Schools.

Ballard, M. E., & Coates, S. (1995). The immediate effects of homicidal, suicidal, and nonviolent heavy metal and rap songs on the moods of college students. *Youth and Society, 27,* 148–168.

Bandura, A. (1973). *Aggression: A social learning analysis.* Englewood Cliffs, NJ: Prentice Hall.

Bandura, A. (1977). Self-efficacy: Toward a unifying theory of behavioral change. *Psychological Review, 84,* 191–215.

Bandura, A. (1986). *Social foundations of thought and action: A social cognitive theory.* Englewood Cliffs, NJ: Prentice Hall.

Bandura, A. (1989). Human agency in social cognitive theory. *American Psychologist, 44,* 1175–1184.

Bandura, A. (2001) Social cognitive theory: An agentic perspective. *Annual Review of Psychology, 52,* 1–26.

Bandura, A., Barbaranelli, C., Caprara, G. V., & Pastorelli, C. (2001). Self-efficacy beliefs as shapers of children's aspirations and career trajectories. *Child Development, 72,* 187–206.

Banks, I. W., & Wilson, P. I. (1989). Appropriate sex education for Black teens. *Adolescence, 24,* 233–245.

Banks, J. A. (2004). *Diversity and citizenship education: Global perspectives.* San Francisco: Jossey-Bass.

Bankston, C. L. III, & Zhou, M. (1997). Valedictorians and delinquents: The bifurcation of Vietnamese American youth. *Deviant Behavior, 18,* 343–364.

Bar-On, R., Tranel, D., Denberg, N. L., & Bechara, A. (2003). Exploring the neurological substrate of emotional and social intelligence. *Brain, 126,* 1790–1800.

Barber, B. K. (1997). Introduction: Adolescent socialization in context—The role of connection, regulation, and autonomy in the family. *Journal of Adolescent Research, 12,* 5–11.

Barber, J. G., & Delfabbro, P. (2000). Predictors of adolescent adjustment: Parent–peer relationships and parent–child conflict. *Child & Adolescent Social Work Journal, 17,* 275–288.

Barber, B. K., Eccles, J. S., & Stone, M. R. (2001). Whatever happened to the jock, the brain, and the princess? Young adult pathways linked to adolescent activity involvement and social identity. *Journal of Adolescent Research, 16,* 429–455.

Barber, B. K., Maughan, S. L., Olsen, J. A., & Thomas, D. L. (2002, April). *Parental support, psychological control, and behavioral control: Assessing the nature of effects*. Paper presented at the biennial meeting of the Society for Research in Adolescence, New Orleans, LA.

Bardone, A. M., Vohs, K. D., Abramson, L. Y., Heatherton, T. F., & Joiner, T. E. (2000). The confluence of perfectionism, body dissatisfaction, and low self-esteem predicts bulimic symptoms: Clinical implications. *Behavior Therapy, 31*, 265–280.

Barker, E. T., & Galambos, N. L. (2003). Body dissatisfaction of adolescent girls and boys: Risk and resources factors. *Journal of Early Adolescence, 23*, 141–165.

Barker, E. T., & Galambos, N. L. (2005). Adolescents' implicit theories of maturity: Ages of adulthood, freedom, and fun. *Journal of Adolescent Research, 20*, 557–576.

Barkowski, J. P., & Xu, X. (2007). Religiosity and teen drug use reconsidered: A social capital perspective. *American Journal of Preventative Medicine, 32*, 182–194.

Barnes, G. M., Reifman, A. S., Farrell, M. P., & Dintcheff, B. A. (2000). The effects of parenting on the development of adolescent alcohol misuse: A six-wave latent growth model. *Journal of Marriage and Family, 62*, 175–186.

Barnes, M. A., Dennis, M., & Haefele-Kalvaitis, J. (1996). The effects of knowledge availability and knowledge accessibility on coherence and elaborative inferencing in children from six to fifteen years of age. *Journal of Experimental Child Psychology, 61*, 216–241.

Baron, S. (1999). Street youths and substance abuse: The role of background, street lifestyle, and economic factors. *Youth and Society, 31*, 3–26.

Barry, C. T., Grafeman, S. J., Adler, K. K., & Pickard, J. D. (2007). The relations among narcissism, self-esteem, and delinquency in a sample of at-risk adolescents. *Journal of Adolescence, 30*, 933–942.

Barry, H. (2007). Corporal punishment and other formative experiences associated with violent crimes. *Journal of Psychohistory, 35*, 71–81.

Barwick, N. A., & Siegel, L. S. (1996). Learning difficulties in adolescent clients of a shelter for runaway and homeless street youths. *Journal of Research on Adolescence, 6*, 649–670.

Basile, K. C., Chen, J. L., Lynberg, M., & Saltzman, L. E. (2007). Prevalence and characteristics of sexual violence victimization. *Violence and Victims, 22*, 437–448.

Basseches, M. (1980). Dialectical schemata: A framework for the empirical study of the development of dialectical thinking. *Human Development, 23*, 200–221.

Batalova, J. P., & Fix, M. (2008). College-educated immigrant workers in the United States. Retrieved from the Migration Policy Institute Web site: http://www.migrationinformation.org/USFocus/display.cfm?ID=702.

Batalova, J., & Terrazas, A. M. (2007). *The recently arrived foreign-born in the United States*. Washington, DC: Migration Policy Institute.

Batsche, G. M., & Knoff, H. M. (1994). Bullies and their victims: Understanding a pervasive problem in schools. *School Psychology Review, 23*, 165–174.

Baugher, R. (1999). *A guide for the bereaved survivor*. Philadelphia: Caring People Press.

Bauman, K. E., & Ennett, S. T. (1994). Peer influence on adolescent drug use. *American Psychologist, 49*, 820–822.

Bauman, K. E., & Ennett, S. T. (1996). On the importance of peer influence for adolescent drug use: Commonly neglected considerations. *Addiction, 91*, 185–198.

Baumeister, L. M., Flores, E., & Marin, B. V. (1995). Sex information given to Latina adolescents by parents. *Health Education Research, 10*, 233–239.

Baumeister, R. (2000). Gender differences in erotic plasticity: The female sex drive as socially flexible and responsive. *Psychological Bulletin, 126*, 347–374.

Baumeister, R. F., Campbell, J. D., Krueger, J. I., & Vohs, K. D. (2003). Does high self-esteem cause better performance, interpersonal success, happiness, or healthier lifestyles? *Psychological Science in the Public Interest, 4*, 1–44.

Baumrind, D. (1971). Current patterns of parental authority. *Developmental Psychology, 4*, 1–103.

Bauserman, R. (2002). Child adjustment in joint-custody versus sole-custody arrangements: A meta-analytic review. *Journal of Family Psychology, 16*, 91–102.

Bearman, S. K., Martinez, E., & Stice, E. (2006). The skinny on body dissatisfaction: A longitudinal study of adolescent girls and boys. *Journal of Youth and Adolescence, 35*, 217–229.

Beaumont, S. L. (1996). Adolescent girls' perceptions of conversations with mothers and friends. *Journal of Adolescent Research, 11*, 325–346.

Beauvais, F., & Laboueff, S. (1985). Drug and acohol abuse intervention in American Indian communities. *International Journal of Addictions, 20*, 139–171.

Becker, A. E., Grinspoon, S. K., Klibanski, A., & Herzog, D. B. (1999). Eating disorders. *New England Journal of Medicine, 340*, 1092–1098.

Beer, W. R. (1992). *American stepfamilies*. New Brunswick, NJ: Transaction.

Beiswinger, G. L. (1979). The high court, privacy, and teenage sexuality. *Family Coordinator, 28*, 191–198.

Belch, M. A., & Willis, A. (2002). Family decision at the turn of the century: Has the changing structure of households impacted the family decision-making process? *Journal of Consumer Behavior, 2*, 111–124.

Bell, A. P., Weinberg, M. S., & Hammersmith, K. S. (1981). *Sexual preference—Its development in men and women*. Bloomington: Indiana University Press.

Bem, S. L. (1974). The measurement of psychological androgyny. *Journal of Consulting and Clinical Psychology, 41*, 155–162.

Ben-Arieh, A., & Haj-Yahia, M. (2008). Corporal punishment of children: A multi-generational perspective. *Journal of Family Violence, 23*, 687–695.

Benedict, R. (1938). Continuities and discontinuities in cultural conditioning. *Psychiatry, 1,* 161–167.

Benedikt, R., Wertheim, E. H., & Love, A. (1998). Eating attitudes and weight-loss attempts in female adolescents and their mothers. *Journal of Youth and Adolescence, 27,* 43–57.

Benoit-Bryan, J. (2008). *National Runaway Switchboard 2008 reporter's sourcebook on runaway and homeless youth.* Chicago: National Runaway Switchboard.

Beran, T., & Li, Q. (2005). Cyber-harassment: A new method for an old behavior. *Journal of Educational Computing Research, 32,* 265–277.

Berge, Z. L. (2000). Designing discussion questions for online, adult learning. *Educational Technology, 37,* 35–47.

Berger, L. M. (2007). Socioeconomic factors and substandard parenting. *Social Service Review, 81,* 485–522.

Berghold, K. M., & Lock, J. (2002). Assessing guilt in adolescents with anorexia nervosa. *American Journal of Psychotherapy, 56,* 378–390.

Berzonsky, M. D. (1989). Identity style: Conceptualization and measurement. *Journal of Adolescence, 4,* 268–282.

Berzonsky, M. D., & Kuk, L. (2000). Identity status, identity processing style, and the transition to university. *Journal of Adolescent Research, 15,* 81–98.

Berzonsky, M. D., Macek, P., & Nurmi, J.-E. (2003). Interrelationships among identity process, content, and structure: A cross-cultural investigation. *Journal of Adolescent Research, 18,* 112–130.

Berzonsky, M. D., Nurmi, J.-E., Kinney, A., & Tammi, K. (1999). Identity processing style and cognitive attributional strategies: Similarities and differences across different contexts. *European Journal of Personality, 13,* 251–263.

Besen, Y. (2006). Exploitation or fun? The lived experience of teenage employment in suburban America. *Journal of Contemporary Ethnography, 35,* 319–340.

Betz, N., & Shilano, R. (1999). Evaluation of an intervention to increase realistic self-efficacy and interests in college women. *Journal of Vocational Behavior, 56,* 35–52.

Bianchi, S. M., Subaiya, L., & Kahn, J. (1999). The gender gap in the economic well-being of nonresident fathers and custodial mothers. *Demography, 36,* 195–203.

Bielick, S., Chandler, K., & Broughman, S. (2001). *Homeschooling in the United States: 1999.* NCES Technical Report, 2001–033. Washington, DC: U.S. Department of Education, National Center for Education Statistics.

Biener, L., & Siegel, M. (2000). Tobacco marketing and adolescent smoking: More support for a causal inference. *American Journal of Public Health, 90,* 407–411.

Bimler, D., & Kirkland, J. (2001). School truants and truancy motivation sorted out with multidimensional scaling. *Journal of Adolescent Research, 16,* 75–102.

Bing, N. M., Nelson, W. M., & Wesolowski, K. L. (2009). Comparing the effects of amount of conflict on children's adjustment following parental divorce. *Journal of Divorce & Remarriage, 50,* 159–171.

Bingham, C. R., Miller, B. C., & Adams, G. R. (1990). Correlates of age at first intercourse in a national sample of young women. *Journal of Adolescent Research, 5,* 18–33.

Birkeland, M. S., Torsheim, T., & Wold, B. (2009). A longitudinal study of the relationship between leisure-time physical activity and depressed mood among adolescents. *Psychology of Sport & Exercise, 10,* 25–34.

Birmaher, B., Arbelaez, C., & Brent, D. (2002). Course and outcome of child and adolescent major depressive disorder. *Child Adolescent Psychiatric Clinics of North America, 11,* 619–637.

Birmaher, B., Ryan, N., Williamson, D. E., Brent, D., Kaufman, J., Dahl, R., et al. (1996). Childhood and adolescent depression: A review of the past ten years. Part 1. *Journal of the American Academy of Child and Adolescent Psychiatry, 35,* 1427–1439.

Biro, F. M., Khoury, P., & Morrison, J. A. (2006). Influence of obesity on timing of puberty. *International Journal of Andrology, 29,* 272–277.

Bishaw, A., & Semega, J. (2008). American Community Survey Reports, ACS-09, *Income, earnings, and poverty data from the 2007 American Community Survey.* Washington, DC: U.S. Government Printing Office.

Bischof, G. T., Stiph, S. N., & Whitney, M. L. (1995). Family environment in adolescent sex offenders and other juvenile delinquents. *Adolescence, 30,* 157–170.

Bjorklund, D. F., & Harnishfeger, K. K. (1990). The resources construct in cognitive development: Diverse sources of evidence and a theory of inefficient inhibition. *Developmental Review, 10,* 48–71.

Black, B. M., Tolman, R. M., Callahan, M., Saunders, D. G., & Weisz, A. N. (2008). When will adolescents tell someone about dating violence victimization? *Violence Against Women, 14,* 741–758.

Black, M. M., Bentley, M. E., Papas, M. A., Oberlander, S., Teti, L. O., McNary, S., Le, K., & O'Connell, M. (2006). Delaying second births among adolescent mothers: A randomized, controlled trial of a home-based mentoring program. *Pediatrics, 118,* e1087–e1099.

Blake, S. M., Ledsky, R., Goodenow, C., Sawyer, R., Lohrmann, D., & Windsor, R. (2003). Condom availability programs in Massachusetts high schools: Relationship with condom use and sexual behavior. *American Journal of Public Health, 93,* 955–962.

Blake, S. M., Ledsky, R., Lehman, T., Goodenow, C., Sawyer, R., & Hack, T. (2001). Preventing sexual risk behaviors among gay, lesbian, and bisexual adolescents: The benefits of gay-sensitive HIV instruction in schools. *American Journal of Public Health, 91,* 940–946.

Blakemore, J. E. O., & Centers, R. E. (2005). Characteristics of boys' and girls' toys. *Sex Roles, 53,* 619–633.

Blanchard, C. A., & Lichtenberg, J. W. (2003). Compromise in career decision making: A test of Gottfredson's theory. *Journal of Vocational Behavior, 62,* 250–271.

Bleske, A. L., & Buss, M. (2000). Can men and women be just friends? *Personal Relationships, 7,* 131–151.

Blyth, D. A., Hill, J. P., & Thiel, K. S. (1982). Early adolescents' significant others: Grade and gender differences in perceived relationships with familial and nonfamilial adults and young people. *Journal of Youth and Adolescence, 11,* 425–450.

Blyth, D. A., Saito, R., & Berkas, T. (1997). A quantitative study of the impact of service-learning programs. In A. S. Waterman (Ed.), *Service learning: Applications from the research* (pp. 39–56). Mahwah, NJ: Erlbaum.

Bock, J. (2005). Farming, for aging, and children's play in the Okavango Delta, Botswana. In D. A. Pellegrini & P. K. Smith (Eds.), *The nature of play: Great apes and humans* (pp. 254–285). New York: Guilford Press.

Boehnke, K. (2001). Parent-offspring value transmission in a societal context: Suggestions for a utopian research design—with empirical underpinnings. *Journal of Cross-Cultural Psychology, 32,* 241–255.

Bogart, A. F. (2008). Menarche and father absence in a national probability sample. *Journal of Biosocial Science, 40,* 623–636.

Boivin, M., Hymel, S., & Bukowski, W. M. (1995). The role of social withdrawal, peer rejection, and victimization by peers predicting loneliness and depressed mood in childhood. *Development and Psychopathology, 7,* 765–785.

Bolognini, M., Plancherel, B., Bellschart, W., & Halfon, O. (1996). Self-esteem and mental health in early adolescence: Development and gender differences. *Journal of Adolescence, 19,* 233–245.

Bomar, J. A., & Sabatelli, R. M. (1996). Family system dynamics, gender, and psychosocial maturity in late adolescence. *Journal of Adolescent Research, 11,* 421–439.

Bond, L., Carlin, J. B., Thomas, L., Rubin, K., & Patton, G. (2001). Does bullying cause emotional problems? A prospective study of young teenagers. *British Medical Journal, 323,* 480–484.

Bonnie, R. J., & O'Connell, M. E. (2004). *Reducing underage drinking: A collective responsibility.* Washington, DC: National Academies Press.

Booth, R. E., Zhang, Y., & Kwiatkowski, C. F. (1999). The challenge of changing drug and sex risk behaviors of runaway and homeless adolescents. *Child Abuse and Neglect, 23,* 1295–1306.

Bosacki, S. L. (2003). Psychological pragmatics in preadolescents: Sociomoral understanding, self-worth, and school behavior. *Journal of Youth and Adolescence, 32,* 141–155.

Bosma, H. A., & Kunnen, E. S. (2001). Determinants and mechanisms in ego-identity development: A review and synthesis. *Developmental Review, 21,* 39–66.

Bosma, H. A., Jackson, S. E., Zijsling, D. H., Zani, B., Cicognani, E., Lucia Xerri, M., Honess, T. M., & Charman, L. (1996). Who has the final say? Decisions on adolescent behavior within the family. *Journal of Adolescence, 19,* 277–291.

Bourget, D., Gagne, P., & Labelle, M. (2007). Parricide: A comparative study of matricide versus patricide. *Journal of the American Academy of Psychiatry and the Law, 35,* 306–312.

Bowen, N. K., & Bowen, G. L. (1999). Effects of crime and violence in neighborhoods and schools on the school behavior and performance of adolescents. *Journal of Adolescent Research, 14,* 319–342.

Bowman, S. A., Gortmaker, S. L., Ebbeling, C. B., Pereira, M. A., & Ludwig, D. (2004). Effects of fast-food consumption on energy intake and diet quality among children in a national household survey. *Pediatrics, 113,* 112–118.

Boyatzis, C. J., Baloff, P., & Durieux, C. (1998). Effects of perceived attractiveness and academic success on early adolescent peer popularity. *Journal of Genetic Psychology, 159,* 337–344.

Boyatzis, C. J., Dollahite, D., & Marks, L. (2006). The family as a context for religious and spiritual development in children and youth. In E. C. Roehlkepartain, P. E. King, L. Wagener, & P. L. Benson (Eds.), *Handbook of spiritual development in childhood and adolescence* (pp. 297–309). Thousand Oaks, CA: Sage.

Boyes, M. C., & Allen, S. G. (1993). Styles of parent-child interaction and moral reasoning in adolescence. *Merrill-Palmer Quarterly, 39,* 551–570.

Boyes, M. C., & Chandler, M. (1992). Cognitive development, epistemic doubt, and identity formation in adolescence. *Journal of Youth and Adolescence, 21,* 277–304.

Boyes, M. C., Giordano, R., & Galperyn, K. (1993, April). *Moral orientation and interpretative contexts of moral deliberation.* Paper presented at the biennial meeting of the Society for Research in Child Development, New Orleans, LA.

Boyle, R. G., Claxton, A. J., & Forster, J. L. (1997). The role of social influences and tobacco availability on adolescent chewing tobacco use. *Journal of Adolescent Health, 20,* 279–285.

Bracey, J. R., Bámaca, M. Y., & Umaña-Taylor, A. J. (2004). Examining ethnic identity and self-esteem among biracial and monoracial youth. *Journal of Youth and Adolescence, 33,* 123–132.

Bradford-Brown, B., & Klute, C. (2003). Friendships, cliques, and crowds. In G. R. Adams & M. D. Berzonsky (Eds.), *Blackwell handbook of adolescence* (pp. 330–348). Oxford, England: Blackwell Publishing.

Braet, C., Claus, L., Goossens, L., Moens, E., van Vlierberghe, L., & Soetens, B. (2008). Differences in eating style between overweight and normal-weight youngsters. *Journal of Health Psychology, 13,* 733–743.

Brage, D., Meredith, W., & Woodward, J. (1993). Correlates of loneliness among midwestern adolescents. *Adolescence, 111,* 685–693.

Bramlett, M. D., & Mosher, W. D. (2002). Cohabitation, divorce, and remarriage in the United States. National Center for Health Statistics, *Vital Health Statistics 23* (22). Retrieved from http://www.cdc.gov/nchs/data/series/sr_23/sr23_022.pdf.

Branje, S. J. T., van Lieshout, C. F. M., van Aiken, M. A. G., & Haselager, G. J. T. (2004). Perceived support in sibling relationships and adolescent adjustment. *Journal of Child Psychology and Psychiatry, 45,* 1385–1396.

Brannon, L. (1999). *Gender: Psychological perspectives.* Boston: Allyn & Bacon.

Braver, S. L., Ellman, I. M., & Fabricius, W. V. (2003). Relocation of children after divorce and children's best interests: New evidence and legal considerations. *Journal of Family Psychology, 17,* 206–219.

Bregman, G., & Killen, M. (1999). Adolescents' and young adults' reasoning about career choice and the role of parental influence. *Journal of Research on Adolescence, 9,* 253–275.

Breivik, K., & Olweus, D. (2006). Adolescents' adjustment in four post-divorce family structures: Single mother, stepfather, joint physical custody and single father families. *Journal of Divorce & Remarriage, 44,* 99–124.

Brendgen, B. J., Markiewicz, D., Doyle, A., & Bukowski, W. M. (2002). The relations bewteen friendship quality, ranked friendship preference, and adolescents' behavior with their friends. *Merrill-Palmer Quarterly, 47,* 396–415.

Brent, D. A. (1995). Risk factors for adolescent suicide and suicidal behavior: Mental and substance abuse disorders, family environmental factors, and life stress. *Suicide and Life-Threatening Behavior, 25* (Supplement), 52–63.

Brent, D. A., Baugher, M., Bridge, J., Chen, T., & Chiappetta, L. (1999). Age and sex-related risk factors for adolescent suicide. *Journal of the American Academy of Child and Adolescent Psychiatry, 38,* 1497–1505.

Brent, D. A., & Mann, J. J. (2005). Family genetic studies, suicide, and suicidal behavior. *American Journal of Medical Genetics, 133C,* 13–24.

Bricker, J. B., Peterson, A. V., Leroux, B. G., Andersen, M. R., Rajan, K. B., & Sarason, I. G. (2006). Prospective prediction of children's smoking transitions: Role of parents' and older siblings' smoking. *Addiction, 101,* 128–136.

Bridge, J. A., Goldstein, T. R., & Brent, D. A. (2006). Adolescent suicide and suicidal behavior. *Journal of Child Psychology and Psychiatry, 47,* 372–394.

Bridgeland, J. M., DiIulio, J. J., Jr., & Morison, K. B. (2006). *The silent epidemic: Perspectives of high school dropouts.* Washington, DC: Civic Enterprises.

Briere, J., & Gil, E. (1998). Self-mutilation in clinical and general population samples: Prevalence, correlates, and functions. *American Journal of Orthopsychiatry, 68,* 609–620.

Brill, H. Q., & Christie, R. L. (1974). Marijuana use and psychological adaptation: Follow-up study of a collegiate population. *Archives of General Psychiatry, 31,* 713–719.

Brody, G. H., Ge, X., Conger, R., Gibbons, F., Murray, V. M., Gerrard, M., & Simons, R. (2001). The influence of neighborhood disadvantage, collective socialization, and parenting on African American children's affiliation with deviant peers. *Child Development, 72,* 1231–1246.

Brody, G. H., Stoneman, V., & Flor, D. (1995). Linking family processes and academic confidence among rural African American youths. *Journal of Marriage and Family, 57,* 567–579.

Bronfenbrenner, U. (1979). *The ecology of human development.* Cambridge, MA: Harvard University Press.

Bronfenbrenner, U. (1987). *Recent advances in theory and design.* Paper presented at the American Psychological Association, New York City.

Brooks-Gunn, J., & Markman, L. B. (2005). The contribution of parenting to ethnic and racial gaps in school readiness. *The Future of Children, 15,* 139–168.

Broughman, S. P., Swaim, N. L., & Keaton, P. W. (2009). *Characteristics of private schools in the United States: Results from the 2007–2008 Private School Universe Survey (NCES 2009-313).* Washington, DC: National Center for Education Statistics, U.S. Department of Education.

Brown, B. B., & Larson, J. (2009). Peer relationships in adolescence. In R. M. Lerner & L. Steinberg (Eds.), *Handbook of adolescent psychology* (Vol. 2, 3rd ed., pp. 74–103). New York: Wiley.

Brown, B. B., Larson, R. W., & Saraswathi, T. S. (2002). *The world's youth: Adolescence in eight regions of the globe.* Cambridge, England: Cambridge University Press.

Brown, B. V., & Theobald, W. E. (1999). *How peers matter: A research synthesis on peer influences on adolescent pregnancy.* Washington, DC: National Campaign to Prevent Teen Pregnancy.

Brown, R., & Evans, W. E. (2002). Extracurricular activity and ethnicity: Creating greater school connection among diverse student populations. *Urban Education, 17,* 41–58.

Brown, S. A., Tapert, S. F., Granholm, E., & Delis, D. C. (2000). Neurocognitive functioning of adolescents: Effects of protracted alcohol use. *Alcoholism: Clinical Experimental Research, 24,* 164–171.

Brown, S. L., & Booth, A. (1996). Cohabitation versus marriage: A comparison of relationship quality. *Journal of Marriage and Family, 58,* 668–678.

Brown, U. M. (2001). *The interracial experience: Growing up Black/White racially mixed in the United States.* Westport, CT: Praeger.

Browning, C. R., Leventhal, T., & Brooks-Gunn, J. (2004). Neighborhood context and racial differences in early adolescent sexual activity. *Demography, 41,* 697–720.

Bryant, B. K., Zvonkovic, A. M., & Reynolds, P. (2006). Parenting in relation to child and adolescent vocational development. *Journal of Vocational Behavior, 69,* 149–175.

Buchanan, C. M., Eccles, J. S., Flanagan, C., Midgley, C., Feldlaufer, J., & Harold, R. D. (1990). Parents' and teachers' beliefs about adolescents: Effects of sex and experience. *Journal of Youth and Adolescence, 19,* 363–394.

Buchholz, E. S., & Catton, R. (1999). Adolescents' perceptions of aloneness and loneliness. *Adolescence, 34,* 203–213.

Buchman, D., & Funk, J. (1996). Children's time commitment and game preference. *Children Today, 24.*

Bulcroft, R. A., Carmody, D. C., & Bulcroft, K. A. (1996). Patterns of parental independence given to adolescents: Variations by race, age, and gender of child. *Journal of Marriage and Family, 58,* 866–883.

Bumpass, L., Raley, R., & Sweet, J. (1995). The changing character of stepfamilies: Implications of cohabitation and non-marital childbearing. *Demography, 32,* 425–436.

Bureau of Indian Education. (2009) Retrieved from http://bie.edu.[2005.]

Burger, J. M. (1995). Individual differences in preference for solitude. *Journal of Research in Personality, 29,* 85–108.

Buri, J. R. (1989). Self-esteem and appraisals of parental behavior. *Journal of Adolescent Research, 4,* 33–49.

Burke, P. J. (1991). Identity processes and social stress. *American Sociological Review, 56,* 836–849.

Burns, A., & Dunlop, R. (1999). "How did you feel about it?" Children's feelings about their parents' divorce at the time and three and ten years later. *Journal of Divorce & Remarriage, 31,* 19–35.

Burrows, S. (1992). Nursing management of self-mutilation. *British Journal of Nursing, 17,* 138–148.

Bush, P. J., Weinfurt, K. P., & Iannotti, R. J. (1994). Families versus peers: Developmental influences on drug use from grade 4–5 to grade 7–8. *Journal of Applied Developmental Psychology, 15,* 437–456.

Bussiere, A. (1998). The development of adoption law. *Adoption Quarterly, 1,* 1–36.

Button, E. (1990). Self-esteem in girls aged 11–12: Baseline findings from a planned prospective study of vulnerability to eating disorders. *Journal of Adolescence, 13,* 407–413.

Byrne, B. (2000). Relationships between anxiety, fear, self-esteem, and coping strategies in adolescence. *Adolescence, 35,* 201–215.

Byrnes, J. P. (2003). Cognitive development during adolescence. In G. R. Adams & M. D. Berzonsky (Eds.), *The Blackwell handbook of adolescence* (pp. 227–246). Oxford, England: Blackwell Publishing.

Byrnes, J. P., & Overton, W. F. (1988). Reasoning about logical connectives: A developmental analysis. *Journal of Experimental Child Psychology, 46,* 194–218.

Cabral, A. C., & Salomone, P. R. (1990). Chance and careers: Normative versus contextual development. *The Career Development Quarterly, 39,* 5–17.

Cacciopo, J. T., Ernst, J. M., Burleson, M. H., McClintock, M. K., Malarkey, W. B., Hawkley, L. C., Kowalewski,

R. B., Paulsen, A., Hobson, J. A., Hugdahl, K., Spiegel, D., & Bernston, G. G. (2000). Lonely traits and concomitant physiological processes. *International Journal of Psychophysiology, 35,* 143–154.

Cadieux, A. (1996). Relationship between self-concept and classroom behavior among learning and non-learning disabled students in regular classrooms. *Perceptual and Motor Skills, 82,* 1043–1050.

Cairns, R., & Cairns, B. (1994). *Lifelines and risks: Pathways of youth in our time.* New York: Cambridge University Press.

Calabrese, R. L., & Adams, J. (1990). Alienation: A cause of juvenile delinquency. *Adolescence, 25,* 435–440.

Call, K. T., Aylin, A. R., Hein, K., McLoyd, V., Petersen, A., & Kipke, M. (2002). Adolescent health and well-being in the twenty-first century: A global perspective. *Journal of Research on Adolescence, 12,* 69–98.

Callahan, D., & Callahan, S. (1981, April). Seven pillars of moral wisdom. *Psychology Today,* 84ff.

Calvert, S. (1999). *Children's journeys through the information age.* New York: McGraw-Hill.

Calvert, S. L. (2002). Identity construction on the Internet. In S. L. Calvert, A. B. Jordan, & R. R. Cocking (Eds.), *Children in the digital age: Influences of electronic media on development* (pp. 57–70). Westport, CT: Greenwood Publishing Group.

Campaign for Tobacco Free Kids. (2005). *Tobacco company marketing to kids.* Retrieved from http://www.tobaccofreekids.org/research/factsheets/pdf/0008.pdf.

Canals, J., Carbajo, G., Fernandez, J., Marti-Henneberg, C., & Domenech, E. (1996). Biopsychopathologic risk profile of adolescents with eating disorder symptoms. *Adolescence, 31,* 443–450.

Canavan, M., Meyer, W., & Higgs, D. (1992). The female experience of sibling incest. *Journal of Marital and Family Therapy, 18,* 129–142.

Cancian, M., & Meyer, D. (1998). Who gets custody? *Demography, 35,* 147–157.

Cantor, J. (1998). Children's attraction to violent television programming. In J. H. Goldstein (Ed.), *Why we watch: The attractions of violent entertainment* (pp. 88–115). New York: Oxford University Press.

Cantor, J. (2000). Media violence. *Journal of Adolescent Health, 27* (Supplement 2), 30–34.

Card, N. A. (2003, April). *Victims of peer aggression: A meta-analytic review.* Presented at the biennial meeting of the Society for Research in Child Development, Tampa, FL.

Carey v. Population Services International. (1977). Retrieved from http://www.law.cornell.edu/supct/html/historics/USSC_CR_0431_0678_ZS.html.

Carlo, G., Fabes, R. A., Laible, D., & Kupanoff, K. (1999). Early adolescence and prosocial/moral behavior II: The role of social and contextual influences. *Journal of Early Adolescence, 19,* 133–147.

Carlo, G., Roesch, S. C., & Melby, J. (1998). The multiplicative relations of parenting and temperament on prosocial and antisocial behaviors in adolescence. *Journal of Early Adolescence, 18,* 148–170.

Carlson, G. A., & Kashini, J. H. (1988). Phenomenology of major depression from childhood through adulthood: Analysis of three studies. *American Journal of Psychiatry, 145,* 1222–1225.

Carlson, W., & Rose, A. J. (2007). The role of reciprocity in romantic relationships in middle childhood and early adolescence. *Merill-Palmer Quarterly, 53,* 262–290.

Carlson Jones, D., & Crawford, J. K. (2005). Adolescent boys and body image: Weight and muscularity concerns as dual pathways to body dissatisfaction. *Journal of Youth and Adolescence, 34,* 629–636.

Carpenter, D. M., & Ramirez, A. (2008). More than one gap: Dropout rate gaps between and among Black, Hispanic, and White students. *Journal of Advanced Academics, 19,* 32–64.

Carpenter, P. A., Just, M. A., & Shell, P. (1990). What one intelligence test measures: A theoretical account of the processing in the Raven Progressive Matrices Test. *Psychological Review, 97*(3), 404–431.

Carr, R. V., Wright, J. D., & Brody, C. J. (1996). Effects of high school work experience a decade later: Evidence from the National Longitudinal Survey. *Sociology of Education, 69,* 66–81.

Carrier, J. (1995). *De los ostros: Intimacy and homosexuality in Mexican men.* New York: Columbia University Press.

Carskadon, M. A. (2002a). Factors influencing sleep patterns of adolescents. In M. A. Carskadon (Ed.), *Adolescent sleep patterns: Biological, social, and psychological influences* (pp. 4–26). New York: Cambridge University Press.

Carskadon, M. A. (2002b). Risks of driving while sleepy in adolescents and young adults. In M. A. Carskadon (Ed.), *Adolescent sleep patterns: Biological, social, and psychological influences* (pp. 148–158). New York: Cambridge University Press.

Carskadon, M. A., Harvey, M. K., & Duke, P. (1980). Pubertal changes in daytime sleepiness. *Sleep, 2,* 453–460.

Carskadon, M. A., Vieira, C., & Acebo, C. (1993). Association between puberty and delayed phase preference. *Sleep, 16,* 258–262.

Carskadon, M. A., Wolfson, A. R., Acebo, C., Tzischinsky, O., & Seifer, R. (1998). Adolescent sleep patterns, circadian timing, and sleepiness at a transition to early school days. *Sleep, 21,* 871–881.

Carver, K., Joyner, K., & Udry, J. R. (2003). National estimates of adolescent romantic relationships. In P. Florsheim (Ed.), *Adolescent romantic relationships and sexual behavior: Theory, research, and practical implications* (pp. 23–56). Mahwah, NJ: Erlbaum.

Casey, B. J., Giedd, J. N., & Thomas, K. M. (2000). Structural and functional brain development and its relation to cognitive development. *Biological Psychology, 54,* 241–257.

Casey, F. A., & Nurius, P. S. (2006). Trends in the characteritics and prevalence of sexual violence: A cohort analysis. *Violence and Victims, 21,* 629–644.

Caspi, A., Lynan, D., Moffitt, T. E., & Silva, P. A. (1993). Unraveling girls' delinquency: Biological, dispositional, and contextual contributions to adolescent misbehavior. *Developmental Psychology, 29,* 19–30.

Caughlin, J. P., & Malis, R. S. (2004). Demand/withdraw communication between parents and adolescents: Connections with self-esteem and substance use. *Journal of Social and Personal Relations, 21,* 125–148.

Cella, D. F., DeWolfe, A. S., & Fitzgibbon, M. (1987). Ego identity status, identification, and decision-making style in late adolescents. *Adolescence, 22,* 849–861.

Centers for Disease Control and Prevention (CDC). (2002a). *Methadone maintainance treatment.* Washington, DC: Author.

Centers for Disease Control and Prevention (CDC). (2003). Injury mortality among American Indian and Alaskan Native children and youth—United States, 1989–1998. *Morbidity and Mortality Weekly Reports, 52,* 697–701.

Centers for Disease Control and Prevention (CDC). (2004a). *Trends in reportable sexually transmitted diseases in the United States, 2004.* Retrieved from http://www.cdc.gov/std/stats/trends2004.htm.

Centers for Disease Control and Prevention (CDC). (2004b). *WISQARS injury mortality reports, 1999–2003.* Retrieved from http://webappa.cdc.gov/sasweb/ncipc/mortrate10_sy.html.

Centers for Disease Control and Prevention (CDC). (2005). Deaths: Leadings causes for 2003. *National Vital Statistics Reports, 53*(17).

Centers for Disease Control and Prevention (CDC). (2006a). Deaths: Final data for 2003. *National Vital Statistics Reports, 54*(13).

Centers for Disease Control and Prevention (CDC). (2006b). *Health, United States, 2006.* Retrieved from http://www.cdc.gov/nchs/data/hus/hus06.pdf#074.

Centers for Disease Control and Prevention (CDC). (2006c). Youth risk behavior surveillance—United States 2005. *Morbidity and Mortality Weekly Report, 55*(SS-5). Washington, DC: Author.

Centers for Disease Control and Prevention (CDC). (2008). Youth risk behavior surveillance—United States, 2007. *Morbidity and Mortality Weekly Report Surveillance Summary, 57*(SS-4). Retrieved from http://www.cdc.gov/healthyyouth/yrbs/pdf/yrbss07_mmwr.pdf.

Centers for Disease Control and Prevention (2009a). Deaths: Final data for 2006. *National Vital Statistics Reports, 57.* Publication No. 2009-1120.

Centers for Disease Control and Prevention. (2009b). Sexual and reproductive health of persons aged 10–24 years—United States, 2002–2007. *Morbidity & Mortality Weekly Report, 58*(SS-6).

Cerel, J., Fristad, M. A., Verducci, J., Weller, E. B., & Weller, R. A. (2006). Childhood Bereavement: Psychopathology in the 2 Years Postparental Death. *Journal of the American Academy of Child & Adolescent Psychiatry*, *45*, 681–690.

Cerel, J., Fristad, M. A., Weller, E. B., & Weller, R. A. (2000). Suicide-bereaved children and adolescents: A controlled longitudinal examination. *Journal of the American Academy of Child and Adolescent Psychiatry*, *38*, 672–679.

Chamorro-Premuzic, T., & Furnham, A. (2006). Self-assessed intelligence and academic performance. *Educational Psychology*, *26*, 769–779.

Chan, C. G., & Elder, G. H., Jr. (2000). Matrilineal advantage in grandchild-grandparent relations. *The Gerontologist*, *40*, 179–190.

Chan, C. S. (1992). Cultural considerations in counseling Asian American lesbians and gay men. In S. Dworkin & E. Gutierrez (Eds.), *Counseling gay men and lesbians: Journey to the end of the rainbow* (pp. 115–124). Alexandria, VA: American Association for Counseling and Development.

Chan, S. (Ed.). (1991). *Entry denied: Exclusion and the Chinese community in America, 1882–1943*. Philadelphia: Temple University Press.

Chandler, C. R., Tsai, Y.-M., & Wharton, R. (1999). Twenty years after: Replicating a study of Anglo- and Mexican-American cultural values. *Social Science Journal*, *36*, 353–367.

Chang, E. S., Chen, C., Greenberger, E., Dooley, D., & Heckhausen, J. (2006). What do they want in life? The life goals of a multi-ethnic, multi-generational sample of high school seniors. *Journal of Youth and Adolescence*, *35*, 321–332.

Chapin, J. (2001). Self-protective pessimism: Optimistic bias in reverse. *North American Journal of Psychology*, *3*, 253–262.

Chaplin, L. N., & John, D. R. (2007). Growing up in a material world: Age differences in materialism in children and adolescents. *Journal of Consumer Research*, *34*, 480–493.

Chassin, L., Hussong, A., & Beltran, I. (2009). Adolescent substance use. In R. Lerner & L. Steinberg (Eds.), *Handbook of adolescent psychology* (Vol. 1, 3rd ed., pp. 723–763). New York: Wiley.

Chassin, L., Presson, C. C., Pitts, S., & Sherman, S. J. (2000). The natural history of cigarette smoking from adolescence to adulthood in a midwestern community sample: Multiple trajectories of parenting and smoking. *Developmental Psychology*, *34*, 1189–1201.

Chassin, L. C., & Young, R. D. (1981). Salient self-conceptions in normal and deviant adolescents. *Adolescence*, *16*, 613–620.

Chatard, A., Selimbegović, L., & Konan, P. N. (2009). Self-esteem and suicide rates in 55 nations. *European Journal of Personality*, *23*, 19–32.

Chen, M.-J., Miller, B., Grube, J. W., & Waiters, E. D. (2006). Music, substance use, and aggression. *Journal of Studies on Alcohol*, *67*, 373–381.

Chen-Yu, J. H., & Seock, Y. (2002). Adolescents' clothing purchase motivations, information sources, and store selection criteria: A comparison of male/female and impulse/nonimpulse shoppers. *Family & Consumer Sciences Research Journal*, *31*, 50–77.

Cherlin, A. J., Chase-Lansdale, P. L., & McRae, C. (1998). Effects of parental divorce on mental health throughout the life course. *American Sociological Review*, *63*, 239–249.

Cherlin, A. J., & Furstenberg, F. F. (1989). Divorce doesn't always hurt the kids. *The Washington Post*, p. C1.

Cherney, I. D., Greteman, A. J., & Travers, B. G. (2008). A cross-cultural view of adults' perceptions of children's rights. *Social Justice Research*, *21*, 432–456.

Cherney, I. D., & Shing, L. (2008). Children's nurturance and self-determination rights: A cross-cultural perspective. *Journal of Social Issues*, *64*, 35–56.

Children Now. (2001). *Fair Play: Violence, Race, and Gender in Video Games*. Retrieved from http://publications.childrennow.org/assets/pdf/cmp/fairplay/fair-play-video-01.pdf.

Chipuer, H. M., Bramston, P., & Pretty, G. (2003). Determinants of subjective quality of life among rural adolescents: A developmental persepcctive. *Social Indicators Research*, *61*, 79–95.

Chiu, L. (1990). The relationship of career goals and self-esteem among adolescents. *Adolescence*, *25*, 593–597.

Chiu, M. L., Feldman, S. S., & Rosenthal, D. A. (1992). The influence of immigration on parental behavior and adolescent distress in Chinese families residing in two Western nations. *Journal of Research on Adolescence*, *2*, 205–239.

Choi, I., Land, S. M., & Turgeon, A. J. (2005). Scaffolding peer-questioning strategies to facilitate metacognition during online small group discussion. *Instructional Science*, *33*, 483–511.

Choi, Y., Harachi, T. W., Gillmore, M. R., & Catalano, R. F. (2006). Are multiracial adolescents at greater risk? Comparisons of rates, patterns, and correlates of substance use and violence between monoracial and multiracial adolescents. *American Journal of Orthopsychiatry*, *76*, 86–97.

Chretien, R. D., & Persinger, M. A. (2000). "Prefrontal deficits" discriminate young offenders from age-matched cohorts: Juvenile delinquency as an expected feature of the normal distribution of prefrontal cerebral development. *Psychological Reports*, *87*, 1196–1202.

Chrisler, J. C., & Zittel, C. B. (1998). Menarche stories: Reminiscences of college students from Lithuania, Malaysia, Sudan, and the United States. *Health Care for Women International*, *19*, 101–110.

Christ, G. H., Siegel, K., & Christ, A. E. (2002). Adolescent grief: "It never really hit me . . . until it actually happened."

Journal of the American Medical Association, 288, 1269–1278.

Christ, M. J., Raszka, W. V., Jr., & Dillon, C. A. (1998). Prioritizing education about condom use among sexually active adolescent females. *Adolescence, 33,* 735–744.

Christenson, P. G., & Roberts, D. F. (1998). *It's not only rock & roll: Popular music in the lives of adolescents.* Cresskill, NJ: Hampton.

Christle, C. A., Jolivette, K., & Nelsom, C. M. (2007). School characteristics related to high school dropout rates. *Remedial and Special Education, 28,* 325–339.

Christopher, F. S., & Cate, R. M. (1988). Premarital sexual involvement: A developmental investigation of relational correlates. *Adolescence, 23,* 793–803.

Chung, I.-J., Hawkins, J. D., Gilchrist, L. D., Hill, K. G., & Nagin, D. S. (2002). Identifying and predicting offending trajectories among poor children. *Social Service Review, 76,* 663–685.

Cillessen, A. H. N., & Rose, A. J. (2005). Understanding popularity in the peer system. *Current Directions in Psychological Science, 14,* 102–105.

Cinamon, R. G., & Rich, Y. (2002). Gender differences in the importance of work and family roles: Implications for work-family conflict. *Sex Roles, 47,* 531–541.

Claman, F., Miller, T., Cromwell, P. F., & Yetman, R. J. (2006). Premenstrual syndrome and premenstrual dysphoric disorder in adolescence. *Journal of Pediatric Health Care, 20,* 329–333.

Clark, K. B. (1953). Desegregation: An appraisal of the evidence. *Journal of Social Issues, 9,* 2–76.

Clarke, J. I., Dawson, C. M., & Bredehoft, D. J. (2004). *How much is enough? Everything you need to know to steer clear of overindulgence and raise likeable, responsible, and respectful children.* New York: Marlow and Company.

Clay, D., Vignoles V. L., & Dittmar, H. (2005). Body image and self-esteem among adolescent girls: Testing the influence of sociocultural factors. *Journal of Research on Adolescence, 15,* 451–477.

Coalition for Juvenile Justice. (2001). *Abandoned in the back row: New lessons in education and delinquency prevention.* Washington, DC: Author.

Cochran, J. K., Wood, P. B., Sellers, C.S., Wilkerson, W., & Chamlin, M. B. (1998). Academic dishonesty and low self-control: An empirical test of a general theory of crime. *Deviant Behavior, 19,* 227–255.

Cohen, K. M., & Savin-Williams, R. C. (1996). Developmental perspectives on coming out to self and others. In R. C. Savin-Williams & K. M. Cohen (Eds.), *The lives of lesbians, gays, and bisexuals: Children to adults* (pp. 113–151). Fort Worth, TX: Harcourt Brace.

Cohen, S. E., Beckwith, L., Parmelee, A. H., Sigman, M., Asarnow, R., & Espinosa, M. P. (1996). Prediction of low and normal school achievement in early adolescents born pre-term. *Journal of Early Adolescence, 16,* 46–70.

Coie, J. D., & Miller-Johnson, S. (2001). Peer factors and interventions. In R. Loeber & D. P. Farrington (Eds.), *Child delinquents: Development, interventon, and service needs* (pp. 191–209). Thousand Oaks, CA: Sage.

Coinstar, Inc. (2003). *First Coinstar TEENS Talk Poll reveals that teens spend at least $264 each month.* Press release. Retrieved from http://www.coinstar .com/US/PressReleases/453946?OpenDocument.

Colby, A., & Damon, W. (1983). Listening to a different voice: A review of Gilligan's *A different voice. Merrill-Palmer Quarterly, 29,* 473–481.

Cole, A., & Kerns, A. (2001). Perceptions of sibling qualities and activities of early adolescents. *The Journal of Early Adolescence, 21,* 204–226.

Cole, D. A., Maxwell, S. E., Martin, J. M., Lachlin, G. P., Seroczynski, A. D. Tram, J. M., et al. (2001). The development of multiple domains of child and adolescent self-concept: A cohort sequential longitudinal design. *Child Development, 72,* 1723–1746.

Cole, M. (1990). Cognitive development and formal schooling: The evidence from cross-cultural research. In L. C. Moll (Ed.), *Vygotsky and education* (pp. 89–110). New York: Cambridge University Press.

Coley, R. L., & Chase-Lansdale, P. L. (1998). Adolescent pregnancy and parenthood: Recent evidence and future directions. *American Psychologist, 53,* 152–166.

College Board. (2008). *College bound seniors, yearly report 2008.* Retrieved from http://professionals.collegeboard .com/profdownload/Total_Group_Report.pdf.

Collins, P. H. (1990). Homophobia and Black lesbians. In P. H. Collins (Ed.), *Black feminist thought: Knowledge, consciousness, and the politics of empowerment* (pp. 192–196). New York: Routledge.

Collins, R. L., Elliott, M. N., Berry, S. H., Kanouse, D. E., Kunkel, D., Hunter, S. B., & Miu, A. (2004). Watching sex on television predicts adolescent initiation of sexual behavior. *Pediatrics, 114,* 280–289.

Collins, W. A., Laursen, B., Mortensen, N., Luebker, C., & Ferreira, M. (1997). Conflict processes and transitions in parent and peer relationships: Implications for autonomy and regulation. *Journal of Adolescent Research, 12,* 178–198.

Commons, M. L., Richards, F. A., & Kuhn, D. (1982). Systematic and metasystematic reasoning: A case for levels of reasoning beyond Piaget's stage of formal operations. *Child Development, 53,* 1058–1069.

Compas, B. E., Connor-Smith, J. K., Saltzman, H., Thomsen, A. H., & Wadsworth, M. E. (2001). Coping with stress during childhood and adolescence: Progress, problems, and potential in theory and research. *Psychological Bulletin, 127,* 87–127.

Comstock, G., & Paik, H. (1999). *Television and the American child.* San Diego, CA: Academic Press.

Comstock, J. (1994). Parent-adolescent conflict: A developmental approach. *Western Journal of Communication, 58,* 263–283.

Conger, R. D., Cu, M., Bryan, C., & Eider, G. H. (2000). Competence in early adult romantic relationships: A developmental perspective on family influences. *Journal of Personality and Social Psychology, 79,* 224–237.

Conley, T. D., Ghavami, N., VonOhlen, J., & Foulkes, P. (2007). General and domain-specific self-esteem among regular education and special education students. *Journal of Applied Social Psychology, 37,* 775–789.

Connolly, J., & McIsaac, C. (2009). Adolescents' explanations for romantic dissolutions: A developmental perspective. *Journal of Adolescence, 32,* 1209–1223.

Connolly, J., Craig, W., Goldberg, A., & Pepler, D. (2004). Mixed-gender groups, dating, and romantic relationships in early adolescence. *Journal of Research on Adolescence, 14,* 185–207.

Connolly, J., Furman, W., &Konarski, R. (2000). The role of peers in the emergence of heterosexual romantic relatinships in adolescence. *Child Development, 71,* 1395–1408.

Connell, J. P., Halpern-Felsher, B. L., Clifford, E., Crichlow, W., & Usinger, P. (1995). Hanging in there: Behavioral, psychological, and contextual factors affecting whether African-American adolescents stay in high school. *Journal of Adolescent Research, 10,* 41–63.

Connor, J. P., Young, R. M., Williams, R. J., & Ricciardelli, L. A. (2000). Drinking restraint versus alcohol expectancies: Which is the better indicator of alcohol problems? *Journal of Studies on Alcohol, 61,* 352–359.

Constantine, M. G., Wallace, B. C., & Kindaichi, M. M. (2005). Examining contextual factors in the career decision status of African-American adolescents. *Journal of Career Assessment, 13,* 307–319.

Cookston, J. T. (1999). Parental supervision and family structure: Effects on adolescent problem behaviors. *Journal of Divorce & Remarriage, 32,* 107–122.

Cooper, M. L. (2002). Alcohol use and risky sexual behavior among college students and youth: Evaluating the evidence. *Journal of Studies on Alcohol, 14* (Supplement), 101–117.

Cornelius, J. R., Clark, D. B., Reynolds, M., Kirisci, L., & Tarter, R. (2007). Early age of first sexual intercourse and affiliation with deviant peers predict development of SUD: A prospective longitudinal study. *Addictive Behaviors, 32,* 850–854.

Cornell, S., & Kalt, J. P. (2004). *Reloading the dice: Improving the chances for economic development on American Indian reservations.* Paper prepared for the Harvard Project on American Indian Economic Development. Retrieved from http://www.hks.harvard.edu/hpaied/key.htm.

Corsana, P., Majorano, M., & Champretavy, L. (2006). Psychological well-being in adolescence: The contribution of interpersonal relations and experience of being alone. *Adolescence, 41,* 341–353.

Coté, J. E., & Levine, C. G. (1992). The genesis of the humanistic academic. A second test of Erikson's theory of ego identity formation. *Youth in Society, 23,* 387–410.

Crawford, E., Wright, M. O., & Masten, A. (2004). Resilience and spirituality in youth. In E. Roehlkepartain, P. King, L. Wagener, & P. Benson (Eds.), *The handbook of spiritual development in children and adolescents* (pp. 355–370). Thousand Oaks, CA: Sage.

Crawford, M., & Popp, D. (2003). Sexual double standards: A review and methodological critique of two decades of research. *Journal of Sex Research, 40,* 13–26.

Crick, N. R. (1997). Engagement in gender alternative versus nonnormative forms of aggression: Links to social-psychological adjustment. *Developmental Psychology, 33,* 610–617.

Crick, N. R., & Dodge, A. (1996). Social information-processing mechanisms in reactive and proactive aggression. *Child Development, 67,* 993–1002.

Crissey, S. R. (2009). Educational attainment in the United States: 2007. *Current Population Reports,* #P20-560. Washington DC: U.S. Government Printing Office.

Crockett, L. J., Brown, J., Russell, S. T., & Shen, Y. (2007). The meaning of good parent-child relationships for Mexican American adolescents. *Journal of Research on Adolescence, 17,* 639–668.

Crone, E., Somsen, R., Zanolie, K., & Van der Molen, M. (2006). A heart rate analysis of developing change in feedback processing and rule shifting from childhood to early adulthood. *Journal of Experimental Child Psychology, 95,* 99–116.

Crooks, R. L., & Baur, K. (2007). *Our sexuality* (10th ed.). Belmont, CA: Wadsworth.

Crosnoe, R. (2001). The social world of male and female athletes in high school. *Sociological Studies of Children and Youth, 8,* 87–108.

Crosnoe, R. (2002). Academic and health-related trajectories in adolescence: The intersection of gender and athletics. *Journal of Health and Social Behavior, 43,* 317–336.

Crosnoe, R., & Elder, G. H., Jr. (2002). Life course transitions, the generational stake, and grandparent-grandchild relationships. *Journal of Marriage and Family, 64,* 1089–1096.

Crouter, A. C., & Head, M. R. (2002). Parental monitoring and knowledge of children. In M. H. Bornstein (Ed.), *Handbook of parenting: Being and becoming a parent* (Vol. 3, pp. 461–483). Mahwah, NJ: Erlbaum.

Crowe, P. A., Philbin, J., Richards, M. H., & Crawford, I. (1998). Adolescent alcohol involvement and the experience of social environments. *Journal of Research on Adolescence, 8,* 403–422.

Crump, R. L., Lillie-Blanton, M., & Anthony, J. C. (1997). The influence of self-esteem on smoking among African-American school children. *Journal of Drug Education, 27,* 277–291.

Cullen, F. T., & Wright, J. P. (2002). Criminal justice in the lives of American adolescents. In J. T. Mortimer & R. W. Larson (Eds.), *The changing adolescent experience: Societal trends and the transition to adulthood* (pp. 88–128). Cambridge, England: Cambridge University Press.

Cyr, M., McDuff, P., Wright, J., Theriault, C., & Cinq-Mars, C. (2005). Clinical correlates and repetition of self-harming behaviors among female adolescent victims of sexual abuse. *Journal of Child Sexual Abuse, 14,* 49–68.

Daire, A. P., LaMothe, S., & Fuller, D. P. (2007). Differences Between Black/African American and White College Students Regarding Influences on High School Completion, College Attendance, and Career Choice. *The Career Development Quarterly, 55,* 275–279.

Daly, R. C., Su, T., Schmidt, P. J., Pagliaro, M., Pickar, D., & Rubinow, D. R. (2003). Neuroendocrine and behavioral effects of high-dose anabolic steroid administration in male normal volunteers. *Psychoneuroendocrinology, 28,* 317–331.

Danielson, C. K., de Arellano, M. A., Kilpatrick, D. G., Saunders, B. E., & Resnick, H. S. (2005). Child maltreatment in depressed adolescents: Differences in symptomatology based on history of abuse. *Child Maltreatment, 10,* 37–48.

D.A.R.E. (2009). *About D.A.R.E.* Retrieved from http://www.dare.com/home/about_dare.asp.

Dare, C., Eisler, I., Russell, G. F. M., & Szmukler, G. I. (1990). The clinical and theoretical impact of a controlled trial of family therapy in anorexia nervosa. *Journal of Marriage and Family Therapy, 16,* 39–57.

Darling-Hammond, L., & Bransford, J. (2005) *Preparing teachers for a changing world: What teachers should learn and be able to do.* San Francisco: Jossey-Bass.

Darroch, J. E., Frost, J. J., & Singh, S. (2001). *Teenage sexual and reproductive behavior in developed countries: Can more progress be made?* Occasional Report no. 3. New York: Alan Guttmacher Institute.

Darroch, J. E., Landry, D. J., & Singh, S. (2000). Changing emphasis in sexuality education in U.S. public secondary schools, 1988–1999. *Family Planning Perspectives, 32,* 204–211.

Davie, R., Panting, C., & Charlton, T. (2004). Mobile phone ownership and usage among pre-adolescents. *Telematics and Informatics, 4,* 359–373.

Davies, P. T., & Windle, M. (2000). Middle adolescents' dating pathways and psychosocial adjustment. *Merrill-Palmer Quarterly, 46,* 90–118.

Davis, C. (1999). Excessive exercise and anorexia nervosa: Addictive and compulsive behaviors. *Psychiatric Annals, 29,* 221–224.

Davis, K. (1944). Adolescence and the social structures. *Annuals of the American Academy of Political and Social Science, 263,* 1–168.

Davison, T. E., & McCabe, M. P. (2006). Adolescent body image and psychosocial functioning. *The Journal of Social Psychology, 146,* 15–30.

De Bellis, M. D., Clark, D. B., Beers, S. R., Soloff, P. H., Boring, A. M., Hall, J., Kersh, A., & Keshavan, M. S. (2000). Hippocampal volume in adolescent-onset alcohol use disorders. *American Journal of Psychiatry, 157,* 737–744.

de Bruyn, E. H., & Cillessen, N. (2006). Popularity in early adolescence: Prosocial and antisocial subtypes. *Journal of Adolescent Research, 21,* 607–627.

de Bruyn, E. H., & Cillessen, A. H. N. (2008). Leisure activity preferences and perceived popularity in early adolescence. *Journal of Leisure Studies, 40,* 442–457.

de Bruyn, E. H., & van den Boom, D. C. (2005). Interpersonal behavior, peer popularity, and self-esteem in early adolescence. *Social Development, 14,* 555–573.

De Civita, M., & Pagani, L. (1996). Familial constraints on the initiation of cigarette smoking among adolescents: An elaboration of social bonding theory and differential association theory. *Canadian Journal of School Psychology, 12,* 177–190.

De Mey, L., Baartman, H. E. M., & Schulze, H.-J. (1999). Ethnic variation and the development of moral judgment of youth in Dutch society. *Youth and Society, 31,* 54–75.

Decety, J., & Jackson, P. L. (2004). The functional architecture of human empathy. *Behavioral and Cognitive Neuroscience Reviews, 3,* 406–412.

Dekovic, M., & Meeus, W. (1997). Peer relations in adolescence: Effects of parenting and adolescents' self-concept. *Journal of Adolescence, 20,* 163–176.

Delgado-Gaitan, C. (1994). Socializing young children in Mexican-American families: An intergenerational perspective. In P. M. Greenfield & A. R. Cocking (Eds.), *Cross-cultural roots of minority child development* (pp. 55–86). Hillsdale, NJ: Erlbaum.

Delorme, D. E., Kreshel, P. J., & Reid, L. N. (2003). Lighting up: Young adults' autobiographical accounts of their first smoking experiences. *Youth and Society, 34,* 468–496.

Demerath, E. W., Towne, B., Chumlea, W. C., Sun, S. S., & Czerwinski, S. A. (2004). Recent declines in age at menarche: The Fels Longitudinal Study. *American Journal of Human Biology, 16,* 453–457.

Demetriou, A., Christou, C., Spanoudis, G., & Platsidou, M. (2002). The development of mental processing: Efficiency, working memory, and thinking. *Monographs of the Society for Research in Child Development, 67,* 1–154.

Demick, J. (2002). Stages of parental development. In M. H. Bornstein (Ed.), *Handbook of parenting: Being and becoming a parent* (Vol. 3, 2nd ed., pp. 389–413). Mahwah, NJ: Erlbaum.

Demuth, S., & Brown, S. L. (2004). Family structure, family processes, and adolescent delinquency: The significance of parental absence versus parental gender. *Journal of Research in Crime and Delinquency, 14,* 58–81.

DeNavas-Walt, C., Proctor, B. D., & Smith, J. (2007). *Income, poverty, and health insurance coverage in the*

United States: 2006. Current Population Reports, P60-233. Washington, DC: U.S. Government Printing Office.

Dennis, M. L., Muck, R. D., Dawud-Noursi, S., & McDermeit, M. (2003). The need for developing and evaluating adolescent treatment models. In S. J. Stevens & A. R. Morral (Eds.), *Adolescent substance abuse treatment in the United States: Exemplary models from a national evaluation study* (pp. 3–35). New York: Haworth Press.

Dermen, K. H., Cooper, M. L., & Agocha, V. B. (1998). Sex-related alcohol expectancies as moderators of the relationship between alcohol use and risky sex in adolescence. *Journal of Studies on Alcohol, 59*, 71–77.

Diamond, L. M., & Savin-Williams, R. C. (2003). Explaining diversity in the development of same-sex sexuality among young women. In L. D. Garnets & D. C. Kimmel (Eds.), *Psychological perspectives on lesbian, gay, and bisexual experiences* (2nd ed., pp. 130–148). New York: Columbia University Press.

Diamond, L. M., Savin-Williams, R. C., & Dubé, E. M. (1999). Sex, dating, passionate friendships, and romance: Intimate peer relations among lesbian, gay, and bisexual adolescents. In W. Furman & C. Feiring (Eds.), *The development of relationships during adolescence* (pp. 175–210). New York: Cambridge University Press.

DiCario, V. (2005). NFI releases report on national marriage survey. *Fatherhood Today, 10*, 4–5.

DiClemente, R. J., Wingood, G. M., Crosby, R., Sionean, C., Cobb, B. K., Harrington, K., Davies, S., Hook, E. W. III, & Oh, M. K. (2001). Parental monitoring: Association with adolescents' risk behaviors. *Pediatrics, 107*, 1363–1368.

Dietz, T. (1998). An examination of violence and gender role portrayals in video games: Implications for gender socialization and aggressive behavior. *Sex Roles, 38*, 425–442.

Dijkstra, J. K., Lindenberg, S., Verhulst, F. C., Ormel, J., & Veenstra, R. (2009). The relation between popularity and aggressive, destructive, and norm-breaking behaviors: Moderating effects of athletic abilities, physical attractiveness, and prosociality. *Journal of Research on Adolescence, 19*, 401–413.

Dilorio, C., Kelley, M., & Hockenberry-Eaton, M. (1999). Communication about sexual issues: Mothers, fathers, and friends. *Journal of Adolescent Health, 24*, 181–189.

DiMeglio, G. (2000). Nutrition in adolescence. *Pediatrics in Review, 21*, 32–33.

Dinges, M. M., & Oetting, E. R. (1993). Similarity in drug use patterns between adolescents and their friends. *Adolescence, 28*, 253–266.

Dinkles, R., Kemp, J., & Baum, K. (2009). *Indicators of school crime and safety: 2008*. National Center for Education Statistics. Washington, DC: U.S. Department of Justice.

Dixon, J. A., & Moore, C. F. (1996). The developmental role of intuitive principles in choosing mathematical strategies. *Developmental Psychology, 32*, 241–253.

D'Onofrio, B. M., Turkheimer, E., Emery, R. E., Slutske, W. S., Heath, A. C., Madden, P. A., & Martin, N. G. (2006). A genetically informed study of the processes underlying the association between parental marital instability and offspring adjustment. *Developmental Psychology, 42*, 486–499.

Dobson, H., Ghuman, S., Prabhakar, S., & Smith, R. (2003). A conceptual model of the influence of stress on female reproduction. *Reproduction, 125*, 151–163.

Doherty, W. J., & Needle, R. H. (1991). Psychological adjustment and substance use among adolescents before and after a parental divorce. *Child Development, 62*, 328–337.

Dolgin, K. G., & Kim, S. (1994). Adolescents' disclosure to best and good friends: The effects of gender and topic intimacy. *Social Development, 3*, 146–157.

Donnellan, M. B., Trzesniewski, K. H., Robins, R., Moffitt, T. E., & Caspi, A. (2005). Low self-esteem is related to aggression, antisocial behavior, and delinquency. *Psychological Science, 16*, 328–335.

Donnelly, J., Young, M., Pearson, R., Penhollow, T. M., & Hernandez, A. (2008). Area specific self-esteem, values, and adolescent substance use. *Journal of Drug Education, 38*, 389–403.

Donovan, P. (1997). Confronting a hidden epidemic: The Institute of Medicine's report on sexually transmitted diseases. *Family Planning Perspectives, 29*, 87–89.

Doty, R. L. (2001). Olfaction. *Annual Review of Psychology, 52*, 423–452.

Douvan, E., & Adelson, J. (1966). *The adolescent experience*. New York: Wiley.

Dowdney, L. (2000). Annotation: Childhood bereavement following parental death. *Journal of Child Psychology & Psychiatry, 41*, 819–830.

Dowdney, L., Wilson, R., Maughan, B., Allerton, M., Schofield, P., & Skuse, D. (1999). Bereaved children: Psychological disturbance and service provision. *British Medical Journal, 319*, 354–357.

Dowdy, B. B., & Kliewer, W. (1998). Dating, parent-adolescent conflict, and behavioral autonomy. *Journal of Youth and Adolescence, 27*, 473–492.

Dowling, E. M., Gestsdottir, S., Anderson, P. M., von Eye, A., Almerigi, J., & Lerner, R. M. (2004). Structural relations among spirituality, religiosity, and thriving in adolescence. *Applied Developmental Science, 8*, 7–16.

Downey, D. B., Ainsworth-Darnell, J. W., & Dufur, M. J. (1998). Sex of parent and children's well-being in single-parent households. *Journal of Marriage and Family, 60*, 878–893.

Doyle, J. A., & Paludi, M. A. (1995). *Sex and gender: A human experience* (3rd ed.). Dubuque, IA: Brown and Benchmark.

Drevets, R. K., Benton, S. L., & Bradley, F. O. (1996). Students' perceptions of parents' and teachers' qualities of interpersonal relationships. *Journal of Youth and Adolescence, 25*, 787–802.

Drug Enforcement Administration. (2005). *Drugs of abuse*. Washington, DC: U.S. Government Printing Office.

Dryfoos, J. G. (1991). *Adolescents at risk: Prevalence and prevention.* New York: Oxford University Press.

DuBois, D. L., Felner, R. D., Brand, S., Phillips, R. S., & Lease, A. N. (1996). Early adolescent self-esteem: A developmental-ecological framework and assessment strategy. *Journal of Research on Adolescence, 6,* 543–579.

DuBois, D. L., & Hirsch, B. J. (1993). School/non-school friendship patterns in early adolescence. *Journal of Early Adolescence, 13,* 102–122.

Dudley, R. L. (1999). Youth religious commitments over time: A longitudinal study of retention. *Review of Religious Research, 41,* 110–121.

Due, P., Merlo, J., Harel-Fisch, Y., Damsgaard, M. T., Holstein, B. E., Hetland, J., et al. (2009). Socioeconomic inequality in exposure to bullying during adolescence: A comparative, cross-sectional, multilevel study in 35 countries. *American Journal of Public Health, 99,* 907–914.

Duke, R. L., Martinez, R. O., & Stein, J. A. (1997). Precursors and consequences of membership in youth gangs. *Youth and Society, 29,* 139–165.

Dukes, R. L., & Lorch, B. D. (1989). The effects of school, family, self-concept, and deviant behavior on adolescent suicide ideation. *Journal of Adolescence, 12,* 239–251.

Dunn, C., Chambers, D., & Rabren, K. (2004). Variables affecting students' decisions to drop out of school. *Remedial and Special Education, 25,* 314–323.

Dunn, J. (2005). Daddy doesn't live here anymore. *The Psychologist, 18,* 28–31.

Dunn, J., Slomkowski, C., & Beardsall, L. (1994). Sibling relationships from the preschool period through middle childhood and early adolescence. *Developmental Psychology, 30,* 163–172.

Dunphy, D. (1963). The social structure of urban adolescent peer groups. *Sociometry, 26,* 230–246.

Durston, S., Hulshoff, P., Hilleke, E., Casey, B. J., Giedd, J. N., Buitelaar, J. K., & van Engeland, H. (2001). Anatomical MRI of the developing human brain: What have we learned? *Journal of the American Academy of Child and Adolescent Psychiatry, 40,* 1012–1020.

Dusek, J. B., & McIntyre, J. G. (2003). Self-concept and self-esteem development. In G. R. Adams & M. D. Berzonsky (Eds.), *The Blackwell handbook of adolescence* (pp. 290–309). Oxford, England: Blackwell Publishing.

Dush, C. M., Cohen, C. L., & Amato, P. R. (2003). The relationship bewteen cohabitation and marital quality and stability: Change across cohorts? *Journal of Marriage and Family, 65,* 539–549.

Dye, J. L. (2005). Fertility of American women: June 2004. *Current Population Reports,* P20-555. Washington, DC: Bureau of the Census.

Egley, A., Jr., Howell, J. C., & Major, A. K. (2006). *National Youth Gang Survey 1999–2001.* Washington, DC: Office of Juvenile Justice and Delinquency Prevention.

East, P. L. (2009). Adolescents' relationships with siblings. In R. M. Lerner & L. Steinberg (Eds.), *Handbook of adolescent psychology* (Vol. 2, 3rd ed., pp. 43–73). Hoboken, NJ: Wiley.

East, P. L., Reyes, B. T., & Horn, E. J. (2007). Association between adolescent pregnancy and a family history of teenage births. *Perspectives on Sexual and Reproductive Health, 39,* 108–115.

Eaton, Y. M., Mitchell, M. L., & Jolley, J. M. (1991). Gender differences in the development of relationships during late adolescence. *Adolescence, 26,* 565–568.

Ebbeling, C. B., Sinclair, K. B., Periera, M. A., Garcia-Lago, E., Feldman, H. A., & Ludwig, D. S. (2004). Compensation for energy intake from fast food among overweight and lean adolescents. *Journal of the American Medical Association, 291,* 2828–2833.

Eberhart, N. K., Shih, J. H., Hammen, C. L., & Brennan, P. A. (2006). Understanding the sex difference in vulnerability to adolescent depression: An examination of child and parent characteristics. *Journal of Abnormal Child Psychology, 34,* 495–508.

Eccles, J. S., & Barber, B. (1999). Student council, volunteering, basketball, or marching band: What kind of extracurricular involvement matters? *Journal of Adolescent Research, 14,* 10–34.

Eccles, J. S., & Midgley, C. (1989). Stage-environment fit: Developmentally appropriate classrooms for young adolescents. In C. Ames & R. Ames (Eds.), *Research on motivation in education: Goals and cognitions* (Vol. 3, pp. 13–44). New York: Academic Press.

Eccles, J. S., & Roeser, R. W. (2009). Schools, academic motivation, and stage-environment fit. In R. M. Lerner & L. Steinberg (Eds.), *Handbook of adolescent psychology* (Vol. 1, 3rd ed., pp. 404–434). Hoboken, NJ: Wiley.

Eder, D., Evans, C. C., & Parker, S. (1995). *School talk: Gender and adolescent culture.* New Brunswick, NJ: Rutgers University Press.

Edgardh, K. (2000). Sexual behavior and early coitarche in a national sample of 17 year old Swedish girls. *Sexually Transmitted Infections, 76,* 98–102.

Edgardh, K. (2002). Sexual behavior and early coitarche in a national sample of 17 year old Swedish boys. *Acta Paediatrica, 91,* 985–991.

Edwards, L. M., Fehring, R. J., Jarrett, K. M., & Haglund, K. A. (2008). The influence of religiosity, gender, and language preference acculturation on sexual activity among Latino/a adolescents. *Hispanic Journal of Behavioral Sciences, 30,* 447–462.

Edwards, W. J. (1996). A measurement of delinquency differences between delinquent and nondelinquent youths between a delinquent and nondelinquent sample: What are the implications? *Adolescence, 31,* 973–989.

Egley, A., & O'Donnell, C. E. (2009). *Highlights of the 2007 National Youth Gang Survey.* Washington, DC: Office of Juvenile Justice.

Ehrlich, T. (2000). *Civic responsibility and college education*. Phoenix, AZ: Oryx Press.

Eisenberg, M. E., Neumark-Sztainer, D., Haines, J., & Wall, M. (2006). Weight-teasing and emotional well-being in adolescents: Longitudinal findings from Project EAT. *Journal of Adolescent Health, 38*, 675–683.

Eisenberg, N. (1986). *Altruistic emotion, cognition, and behavior*. Hillsdale, NJ: Erlbaum.

Eisenberg, N. (1998). Prosocial development. In N. Eisenberg (Vol. Ed.) and W. Damon (Series Ed.), *Handbook of child psychology: Social, emotional, and personality development* (Vol. 3, 5th ed., pp. 701–778). New York: Wiley.

Eisenberg, N., Carlo, G., Murphy, B., & Van Court, P. (1995). Prosocial development in late adolescence: A longitudinal study. *Child Development, 66*, 1179–1197.

Eisenberg, N., Cumberland, A., Guthrie, I. K., Murphy, B. C., & Shepard, S. A. (2005). Age changes in prosocial responding and moral reasoning in adolescence and early adulthood. *Journal of Research on Adolescence, 15*, 235–260.

Eisenberg, N., Guthrie, I., Cumberland, A., Murphy, B. C., Shepard, S. A., Zhou, Q., & Carlo, G. (2002). Prosocial development in early adulthood: A longitudinal study. *Personality and Social Psychology, 82*, 993–1006.

Eisenberg, N., & McNally, S. (1993). Socialization and mothers' and adolescents' empathy-related characteristics. *Journal of Research on Adolescence, 3*, 171–191.

Eisenberg, N., Morris, A. S., McDaniel, B., & Spinrad, T. L. (2009). Moral cognitions and prosocial responding in adolescence. In R. M. Lerner & L. Steinberg (Eds.), *Handbook of adolescent psychology* (Vol. 1, pp. 229–265). New York: Wiley.

Elder, G. H., Jr., & Conger, R. D. (2000). *Children of the land*. Chicago: University of Chicago Press.

Elkind, D. (1967). Egocentrism in adolescence. *Child Development, 38*, 1025–1034.

Elkind, D. (1975). Recent research on cognitive development in adolescence. In S. E. Dragastin & G. H. Elder Jr. (Eds.), *Adolescence in the life cycle*. New York: Wiley.

Ellington, L. (2001). Japanese education. *The Japan Digest*. Retrieved from http://www.indiana.edu/~japan.

Elliott, D. S., & Menard, S. (1996). Delinquent friends and delinquent behavior: Temporal and developmental patterns. In J. D. Hawkinds (Ed.), *Delinquency and crime: Current theories* (pp. 28–67). New York: Cambridge University Press.

Elliott, G. C., Avery, R., Fishman, E., & Hoshiko, B. (2002). The encounter with family violence and risky sexual activity among young adolescent females. *Violence and Victims, 17*, 569–591.

Ellis, B. J. (2004). Timing of pubertal maturation in girls: An integrated life history approach. *Psychological Bulletin, 130*, 920–958.

Ellis, B. J., & Essex, M. J. (2007). Family environments, adrenarche, and sexual maturation: A longitudinal test of a life history model. *Child Development, 78*, 1799–1817.

Ellis, B. J., & Garber, J. (2000). Psychosocial antecedents of variation in girls' pubertal timing: Maternal depression, stepfather presence, and marital and family stress. *Child Development, 71*, 485–501.

Ellison, C. G. (1992). Are religious people nice people? Evidence from the National Survey of Black Americans. *Social Forces, 71*, 411–430.

Elmore, R. F. (2009). Schooling adolescents. In R. M. Lerner & L. Steinberg (Eds.), *Handbook of adolescent psychology* (Vol. 2, 3rd ed., pp. 193–227). New York: Wiley.

Emick, M., & Hayslip, B. (1999). Custodial grandparenting: Stress, coping and relationships with grandchildren. *International Journal of Aging and Human Development, 48*, 35–61.

Employment Policies Institute. (2006). *June report*. Retrieved from http://www.epionline.org/index_gi.cfm.

Engles, R. C. M. E., Knibble, R. A., Drop, M. J., & de Haan, Y. T. (1997). Homogeneity of cigarette smoking within peer groups: Influence or selection. *Health Education and Behavior, 24*, 801–811.

Ennett, S. T., & Bauman, K. E. (1996). Adolescent social networks: School, demographics, and longitudinal considerations. *Journal of Adolescent Research, 11*, 194–215.

Epstein, M., & Ward, M. (2008). "Always use protection": Communication boys receive about sex from parents, peers, and the media. *Journal of Youth and Adolescence, 37*, 113-126.

Erath, S. A., Flanagan, K. S., & Bierman, K. L. (2008). Early adolescent school adjustment: Associations with friendship and peer victimization. *Social Development, 17*, 853–870.

Erbert, L. A., & Aleman, W. (2008). Taking the grand out of grandparent: Dialectical tensions in grandparent perceptions of surrogate parenting. *Journal of Social and Personal Relationships, 25*, 671–695.

Erikson, E. H. (1950). *Childhood and society*. New York: W. W. Norton.

Erikson, E. H. (1959). *Identity and the life cycle*. New York: International Universities Press.

Erikson, E. H. (1968). *Identity: Youth, and crisis*. New York: W. W. Norton.

Erikson, E. H. (1982). *The life cycle completed*. New York: W. W. Norton.

Erwin, P. (1993). *Friendship and peer relations in children*. New York: Wiley.

Escabedo, L. G., Marcus, S. E., Holtzman, D., & Giovino, G. A. (1986). Sports participation, age at smoking initiation, and the risk of smoking among U.S. high school students. *Journal of the American Medical Association, 256*, 2859–2862.

Evans, G. W., Kim, P., Ting, A. H., Tesher, H. B., & Shannas, D. (2007). Cumulative risk, maternal responsiveness, and allostatic load in young adolescents. *Developmental Psychology, 43*, 341–351.

Evans, N., Farkas, A., Gilpin, E., Berry, C., & Pierce, J. P. (1995). The influence of tobacco marketing and exposure to smokers on adolescent susceptibility to smoking. *Journal of the National Cancer Institute, 87,* 1538–1545.

Fabes, R. A., Carlo, G., Kupanoff, K., & Laible, D. (1999). Early adolescence and prosocial/moral behavior. I: The role of individual processes. *Journal of Early Adolescence, 19,* 5–16.

Fagan, A. A. (2005). The relationship between adolescent physical abuse and criminal offending: Support for an enduring and generalized cycle of violence. *Journal of Family Violence, 20,* 279–290.

Fagerlund, A., Heikkinen, S., Autti-Ramo, I., Korkman, M., Timonen, M., Kuusi, T., Riley, E. P., & Lundbon, N. (2006). Brain metabolic alterations in adolescents and young adults with fetal alcohol spectrum disorders. *Alcoholism: Clinical and Experimental Research, 30,* 2097–2104.

Fagot, B., Pears, K., Capaldi, M., Crosby, L., & Leve, C. (1998). Becoming an adolescent father: Precursors and planning. *Developmental Psychology, 34,* 1209–1219.

Fairtest.org. (2009). *Test score optional list.* Retrieved from http://www.fairtest.org/university/optional.

Faith, M. S., Scanlon, K. S., Birch, L. L., Francis, L. A., & Sherry, B. (2004). Parent-child feeding strategies and their relationships to child eating and weight status. *Obesity Research, 12,* 1711–1722.

Fallone, G., Acebo, C., Arnedt, T. J., Seifer, R., & Carskadon, M. A. (2001). Effects of acute sleep restriction on behavior, sustained attention, and response inhibition in children. *Perceptual and Motor Skills, 93,* 213–229.

Fals-Stewart, W., Kelley, M. L., Cooke, C. G., & Golden, J. (2003). Predictors of the psychosocial adjustment of children living in households of parents in which fathers abuse drugs: The effects of postnatal parental exposure. *Addictive Behaviors, 28,* 1013–1031.

Farmer, T. W., Estell, D. B., Bishop, J. L., O'Neal, K. K., & Cairns, B. D. (2003). Rejected bullies or popular leaders? The social relations of aggressive subtypes of rural African American early adolescents. *Developmental Psychology, 39,* 992–1004.

Farrington, D. P. (2009). Conduct disorder, aggression, and delinquency. In R. M. Lerner & L. Steinberg (Eds.), *Handbook of adolescent psychology* (Vol. 1, 3rd ed., pp. 683–722). New York: Wiley.

Farruggia, S. P., Chen, C., Greenberger, E., Dhitrieva, J., & Macek, P. (2004). Adolescent self-esteem in cross-cultural perspective. *Journal of Cross-Cultural Psychology, 15,* 719–733.

Feigelman, S., Stanton, B. F., & Ricardo, I. (1993). Perceptions of drug selling and drug use among urban youths. *Journal of Early Adolescence, 13,* 267–284.

Feiring, C. (1996). Concepts of romance in 15-year-old adolescents. *Journal of Research on Adolescence, 6,* 181–200.

Feldman, A. F., & Matjasko, J. L. (2005). The role of school-based extracurricular activities in adolescent development: A comprehensive review and future directions. *Review of Educational Research, 75,* 159–210.

Feldman, S. A., & Rosenthal, D. A. (1994). Culture makes a difference . . . or does it? A comparison of adolescents in Hong Kong, Australia, and the United States. In R. K. Silbereisen & E. Todt (Eds.), *Adolescence in context* (pp. 99–124). New York: Springer.

Feldman, S. S., Mont-Reynaud, R., & Rosenthal, D. A. (1992). When East moves West: The acculturation of values of Chinese adolescents in the U.S. and Australia. *Journal of Research on Adolescence, 2,* 147–173.

Feldman, S. S., & Quatman, T. (1988). Factors influencing age expectations for adolescent autonomy: A study of early adolescents and parents. *Journal of Early Adolescence, 8,* 325–343.

Feldman, S. S., & Rosenthal, D. A. (2000). The effect of communication characteristics on family members' perceptions of parents as sex educators. *Journal of Research on Adolescence, 10,* 119–150.

Feldman, S. S., Turner, R. A., & Araujo, K. (1999). Interpersonal context as an influence on sexual timetables of youths: Gender and ethnic effects. *Journal of Research on Adolescence, 9,* 25–52.

Feldman, S. S., & Weinberger, D. A. (1994). Self-restraint as a mediator of family influences on boys' delinquent behavior: A longitudinal study. *Child Development, 65,* 195–211.

Feldman, S. S., & Wood, D. N. (1994). Parents' expectations for preadolescent sons' behavioral autonomy: A longitudinal study of correlates and outcomes. *Journal of Research on Adolescence, 4,* 45–70.

Felner, R. D., Seitsinger, A. M., Brand, S., Burns, A., & Bolton, N. (2007). Creating small learning communities: Lessons from the project on high-performing learning communities about "what works" in creating productive, developmentally enhancing, learning contexts. *Educational Psychologist, 42,* 209–221.

Fenzel, L. M. (2000). Prospective study of changes in global self-worth and strain during the transition to middle school. *Journal of Early Adolescence, 20,* 93–116.

Fergusson, D. M., Lynskey, M., & Horwood, L. J. (1995). The adolescent outcomes of adoption: A 16-year longitudinal study. *Journal of Child Psychology and Psychiatry and Allied Disciplines, 36,* 597–615.

Fergusson, D. M., Swain-Campbell, N., & Horwood, L. J. (2004). How does childhood economic disadvantage lead to crime? *Journal of Child Psychology and Psychiatry, 45,* 956–966.

Fernandez-Guasti, A., Kruijver, F. P. M., Fodor, M., & Swaab, D. F. (2000). Sex differences in the distribution of androgen receptors in the human hypothalamus. *Journal of Comparative Neurology, 425,* 422–435.

Field, A. E., & Kitkos, N. R. (2009). Social and interpersonal influences of obesity on youth: Family, peers, society. In L. J. Heinberg & J. K. Thompson (Eds.), *Obesity in youth: Causes, consequences, and cures* (pp. 59–76). Washington, DC: American Psychological Association.

Fields, J. (2004). America's families and living arrangements: 2003. *Current Population Reports* no. P20-553. Washington, DC: U.S. Bureau of the Census.

Fields, J., & Casper, L. M. (2001). American families and living arrangements: March, 2000. *Current Population Reports*, no. P20-537. Washington, DC: U.S. Bureau of the Census.

Fields, J. M. (2003). Children's living arrangements and characteristics: March 2002. *Current Population Reports*, no. P20-547. Washington, DC: U.S. Bureau of the Census.

Finer, L. B., & Henshaw, S. K. (2006). Disparities in rates of unintended pregnancy in the United States, 1994 and 2001. *Perspectives on Sexual and Reproductive Health, 38,* 90–96.

Finkelhor, D. (2003). The legacy of the clergy abuse scandal. *Child Abuse & Neglect, 27,* 1225–1229.

Finkelhor, D., Hotaling, G., & Sedlak, A. (1990). *Missing, abducted, runaway, and throwaway children in America.* Washington, DC: U.S. Department of Justice.

Finkelhor, D., Mitchell, K. J., & Wolak, J. (2000). [2005 in text] *Online victimization: A report on the nation's youth.* Alexandria, VA: National Center for Missing and Exploited Children. Retrieved from http://missingkids.com/download/nc62.pdf.

Finkelstein, M. J., & Gaier, E. L. (1983). The impact of prolonged student status on late adolescent development. *Adolescence, 18,* 115–129.

Finn, J. D. (2006). *The adult lives of at-risk students: The roles of attainment and engagement in high schools* (NCES-2006-328). Washington, DC: National Center for Education Statistics.

Fiorentine, R. (1988). Sex differences in success expectancies and causal attributions: Is this why fewer women become physicians? *Social Psychology Quarterly, 51,* 236–249.

Fishbein, D., Herman-Stahl, M., & Eldreth, D. (2006). Mediators of the stress-substance-use relationship in urban male adolescents. *Prevention Science, 7,* 113–126.

Fisher, M., Fornari, V., Waldbaum, R., & Gold, R. (2002). Three case reports on the relationship between anorexia nervosa and obsessive compulsive disorder. *International Journal of Adolescent Medicine and Health, 14,* 329–334.

Fixico, D. L. (2000). *The urban Indian experience in America.* Albuquerque: University of New Mexico Press.

Flanigan, B., McLean, A., Hall, C., & Propp, V. (1990). Alcohol use as a situational influence on young women's pregnancy risk-taking behavior. *Adolescence, 25,* 205–214.

Flannery, D. J., Huff, C. R., & Manos, M. (1998). Youth gangs: A developmental perspective. In T. P. Gullotta,

G. R. Adams, & R. Montemayor (Eds.), *Youth violence: Prevention, intervention, and social policy* (pp. 175–204). Thousand Oaks, CA: Sage.

Flannery, D. J., Hussey, D. L., Biebelhausen, L., & Wester, K. L. (2003). Crime, delinquency, and youth gangs. In G. R. Adams & M. D. Berzonsky (Eds.), *The Blackwell handbook of adolescence* (pp. 502–522). Oxford, England: Blackwell Publishing.

Flavell, J. H., Miller, P. A., & Miller, S. A. (1993). *Cognitive development* (3rd ed.). Englewood Cliffs, NJ: Prentice Hall.

Fletcher, A., Steinberg, L., & Sellers, E. (1999). Adolescents' well-being as a function of perceived interparental consistency. *Journal of Marriage and Family, 61,* 599–610.

Flett, G. L., & Hewitt, P. L. (Eds.). (2002). *Perfectionism: Theory, research, and treatment.* Washington, DC: American Psychological Association.

Flint, L. (1992). Adolescent parental affinity-seeking: Age- and gender-mediated strategy use. *Adolescence, 27,* 417–434.

Flores, L. Y., Spanierman, L. B., Armstrong, P. I., & Velez, A. D. (2006). Validity of the Strong Interest Inventory and Skills Confidence Inventory with Mexican American high school students. *Journal of Career Assessment, 14,* 183–202.

Florsheim, P., Moore, D., Zollinger, L., MacDonald, J., & Sumida, E. (1999). The transition to parenthood among adolescent fathers and their partners: Does antisocial behavior predict problems in parenting? *Applied Developmental Science, 3,* 178–191.

Foltz, C., Overton, W. F., & Ricco, R. B. (1995). Proof construction: Adolescent development from inductive to deductive problem-solving strategies. *Journal of Experimental Child Psychology, 59,* 179–195.

Fornari, V., & Dancyger, I. F. (2003). Psychosexual development and eating disorders. *Adolescent Medicine, 14,* 61–75.

Forrest, J. D., & Singh, S. (1990). The sexual reproductive behavior of American women, 1982–1988. *Family Planning Perspectives, 22,* 206–214.

Fors, J., Gibson, J. L., Marsh, J., Griepentrog, B. K., Marsh, S., & Boehmer, M. (2006). *Influencer poll wave 5—December 2005.* Arlington, VA: Defense Human Resources Activity.

Fouad, N. A., & Byars-Winston, M. (2005). Cultural context of career choice: Meta-analysis of race/ethnicity differences. *Career Development Quarterly, 53,* 223–233.

Fox, J. (2006). *Sex differences in college students' Internet pornography use.* Unpublished M.A. thesis, University of Arizona.

Fox, G. L., & Kelly, R. F. (1995). Determinants of child custody arrangements at divorce. *Journal of Marriage and Family, 57,* 693–708.

Fox, J. A., & Zawitz, M. W. (2006). *Homicide trends in the United States.* Bureau of Justice Statistics. Retrieved from http://www.ojp.usdoj.gov/bjs/homicide/homtrnd.htm#contents.

Fox, S., & Madden, M. (2006). *Generations online*. Data Memo. Washington, DC: Pew Internet and American Life Project.

Frazao, E. (1999). The high costs of poor eating patterns in the United States. In E. Frazao (Ed.), *America's eating habits: Changes and consequences* (pp. 5–32). Washington, DC: U.S. Department of Agriculture.

Fredricks, J. A., & Eccles, J. A. (2004). Parental influences on youth involvement in sports. In M. R. Weiss (Ed.), *Developmental sport and exercise psychology: A lifespan perspective* (pp. 145–164). Morgantown, WV: Fitness Information Technology.

Freeman, D. (1983). *Margaret Mead and Samoa: The making and unmaking of an anthropological myth*. Cambridge, MA: Harvard University Press.

Freeman, S. F. N., & Alkin, M. C. (2000). Academic and social attainments of children with mental retardation in general education and special education settings. *Remedial and Special Education, 21*, 3–18.

Freisthler, B., Svare, G. M., & Harrison-Jay, S. (2003). It was the best of times, it was the worst of times: Young adult stepchildren talk about growing up in a stepfamily. *Journal of Divorce & Remarriage, 38*(3–4), 83–102.

French, S. A., & Perry, C. L. (1996). Smoking among adolescent girls: Prevalence and etiology. *Journal of the American Medical Women's Association, 51*, 25–28.

Freud, A. (1946). *The ego and the mechanism of defence*. New York: International Universities Press.

Freud, A. (1958). *Psychoanalytic study of the child*. New York: International Universities Press.

Freud, S. A. (1953). *Three essays on the theory of sexuality* (Vol. 7). London: Hogarth Press.

Friedman, H. S., Martin, L. R., Tucker, J. S., Criqui, M. H., Kern, M. L., & Reynolds, C. A. (2008). Stability of physical activity across the lifespan. *Journal of Health Psychology, 13*, 1092–1104.

Frijns, T., Finkenauer, C., Vermulst, A. A., & Engels, C. M. E. (2005). Keeping secrets from parents: Longitudinal associations of secrecy in adolescence. *Journal of Youth and Adolescence, 34*, 137–148.

Froman, R. D., & Owen, S. V. (1991). High school student's perceived self-efficacy in physical and mental health. *Journal of Adolescent Research, 6*, 181–196.

Frost, J., & McKelvie, S. (2004). Self-esteem and body satisfaction in male and female elementary school, high school, and university students. *Sex Roles, 51*, 45–54.

Fry, A. F., & Hale, S. (1996). Processing speed, working memory, and fluid intelligence: Evidence for a developmental cascade. *Psychological Science, 7*, 237–241.

Fu, V. R., Hinkle, D. E., Shoffner, S., Furman, W., & Buhrmester, D. (1992). Age and sex differences in perceptions of networks of personal relationships. *Child Development, 63*, 103–115.

Fuligini, A. J., & Hardway, C. (2004). Preparing diverse adolescents for the transition to adulthood. *Future of Children, 14*, 99–119.

Fuligni, A. J., & Stevenson, H. W. (1995). Time use and mathematics achievement among American, Chinese, and Japanese high school students. *Child Development, 66*, 830–842.

Funk, J. B. (2000). *The impact of interactive violence on children*. U.S. Senate Committee on Commerce, Science, and Transportation hearing of "The Impact of Interactive Violence on Children." Retrieved from http://www.utoledo.edu/psychology/funktestimony.html.

Furby, L., Ochs, L. M., & Thomas, C. W. (1997). Sexually transmitted disease prevention: Adolescents' perceptions of possible side effects. *Adolescence, 32*, 781–810.

Furman, W., & Shaffer, L. (2003). The role of romantic relationships in adolescent development. In P. Florsheim (Ed.), *Adolescent romantic relations and sexual behavior: Theory, research, and practical implications* (pp. 3–22). Mahwah, NJ: Erlbaum.

Furnham, A., Badmin, N., & Sneade, I. (2002). Body image dissatisfaction: Gender differences in eating attitudes, self-esteem, and reasons for exercise. *Journal of Psychology, 136*, 581–596.

Furrow, J. L., King, P. E., & White, K. (2004). Religion and positive youth development: Identity, meaning, and prosocial concerns. *Applied Developmental Science, 8*, 17–26.

Fussell, E. (2002). Youth in aging societies. In J. T. Mortimer & R. W. Larson (Eds.), *The changing adolescent experience: Societal trends and the transition to adulthood* (pp. 18–51). Cambridge, England: Cambridge University Press.

Galambos, N. C., & Silbereisen, R. K. (1987). Income change, parental life outlook, and adolescent expectations for job success. *Journal of Marriage and Family, 49*, 141–149.

Galambos, N. L., Barker, E. V., & Tilton-Weaver, L. C. (2003). Canadian adolescents' implicit theories of immaturity: What does "childish" mean? In J. Arnett & N. Galambos (Eds.), *New directions for child and adolescent development: Exploring cultural conceptions for the transition to adulthood* (pp. 77–89). San Francisco: Jossey-Bass.

Galambos, N. L., Kolaric, G. C., Sears, H. A., & Maggs, J. L. (1999). Adolescents; subjective age: An indicator of perceived maturity. *Journal of Research on Adolescence, 9*, 309–337.

Galambos, N. L., Sears, H. A., Almeida, D. M., & Kolaric, G. C. (1995). Parents' work overload and problem behavior in young adolescents. *Journal of Research on Adolescence, 5*, 201–223.

Galambos, N. L., & Vitunski, E. T. (April, 2000). *Fun, freedom and responsibility: Adolescents' expectations for their futures*. Paper presented at the eighth biennial meeting of the Society for Research on Adolescence, Chicago, IL.

Gallagher, J. (1997, December 9). Blacks and gays: The unexpected divide. *The Advocate*, 37–41.

Gallatin, J. (1980). Political thinking in adolescence. In J. Adelson (Ed.), *Handbook of adolescent psychology* (pp. 344–382). New York: Wiley.

Galliher, R. V., Rostosky, S. S., & Hughes, H. K. (2004). School belonging, self-esteem, and depressive symptoms in adolescents: An examination of sex, sexual attraction status, and urbanicity. *Journal of Youth and Adolescence, 33,* 235–245.

Gallup, G., Jr., & Lindsay, D. M. (1999). *Surveying the religious landscape: Trends in U.S. beliefs.* Harrisburg, PA: Morehouse.

Galotti, K. M., Komatsu, L. K., & Voelz, S. (1997). Children's differential performance on deductive and inductive syllogisms. *Developmental Psychology, 33,* 70–78.

Galvan, A., Hare, T. A., Parra, C. E., Penn, J., Voss, H., Glover, G., & Casey, B. (2006). Earlier development of the accumbens relative to orbitofrontal cortex might underlie the risk-taking behavior in adolescents. *Journal of Neuroscience, 26,* 6885–6892.

Ganong, L. H., Coleman, M., Thompson, A., & Goodwin-Watkins, C. (1996). African American and European American college students' expectations for self and for future partners. *Journal of Family Issues, 17,* 758–775.

Gantz, W., Schwartz, N., Angelini, J. R., & Rindeout, V. (2007). *Food for thought: Television food advertising to children in the United States.* Menlo Park, CA: Henry J. Kaiser Family Foundation.

Garavalia, L., Olson, E., Russell, E., & Christensen, L. (2007). How do students cheat? In E. M. Anderman & T. B. Murdock (Eds.), *Psychology of academic cheating* (pp. 33–55).

Garbarino, J. (2008). *Children and the dark side of human experience: Confronting global realities and rethinking child development.* New York: Springer.

Gard, M. C. E., & Freeman, C. P. (1996). The dismantling of a myth: A review of eating disorders and socioeconomic status. *International Journal of Eating Disorders, 20,* 1–12.

Gardner, H. (1993). *Frames of mind: The theory of multiple intelligences* (10th ed.). New York: Basic Books.

Gardner, H. (1999). *Intelligence reframed: Multiple intelligences for the twenty-first century.* New York: Basic Books.

Gardner, H. (2006). *Multiple intelligences: New horizons in theory and practice.* New York: Basic Books.

Gardner, R. M., Friedman, B. N., & Jackson, N. A. (1999). Hispanic and White children's judgments of perceived and ideal body size in self and others. *Psychological Record, 49,* 555–564.

Garland, A. F., & Zigler, E. (1993). Adolescent suicide prevention: Current research and social policy implications. *American Psychologist, 48,* 169–182.

Garland, A. F., & Zigler, E. (1999). Emotional and behavioral problems among highly intellectually gifted youth. *Roeper Review, 22,* 41–44.

Garnefski, N., & Diekstra, R. (1997). Child sexual abuse and emotional and behavioral problems in adolescence: Gender differences. *Journal of the Academy of Child and Adolescent Psychiatry, 36,* 323–329.

Garner, D. M., Rosen, L. W., & Barry, D. (1998). Eating disorders among athletes: Research and recommendations. *Child and Adolescent Psychiatric Clinics of North America, 7,* 839–857.

Garrett, S. C., & Tidwell, R. (1999). Differences between adolescent mothers and nonmothers: An interview study. *Adolescence, 34,* 91–105.

Garrod, A. C., Smulyan, L., Powers, S. I., & Kilkenny, R. (2005). *Adolescent portraits: Identity, relationships, and challenges* (5th ed.). Auckland, New Zealand: Pearson Education.

Gatti, U., Tremblay, R E., Vitraro, F., & McDuff, P. (2005). Youth gangs, delinquency, and drug use: A test of the selection, enhancement, and facilitation hypotheses. *Journal of Child Psychology & Psychiatry, 46,* 1178–1190.

Gavazzi, S. M., & Sabatelli, R. M. (1990). Family system dynamics, the individuation process and psychosocial development. *Journal of Adolescent Research, 5,* 500–519.

Ge, X., Conger, D., & Elder, G. H. (1996). Coming of age too early: Pubertal influences on girls' vulnerability to psychological distress. *Child Development, 67,* 386–340.

Ge, X., Conger, R. D., & Elder, G. H., Jr. (2001). The relation between puberty and psychological distress in adolescent boys. *Journal of Research on Adolescence, 11,* 49–70.

Gentile, B., Grabe, S., Dolan-Pascoe, B., Twenge, J. M., Wells, B. E., & Maitino, A. (2009). Gender differences in domain-specific self-esteem: A meta-analysis. *Review of General Psychology, 13,* 34–45.

Gentile, D. A., Lynch, P. J., Linder, J. R., & Walsh, J. A. (2004). The effects of violent video game habits on adolescent hostility, aggressive behaviors, and school performance. *Journal of Adolescence, 27,* 5–22.

Gerber, M., & Puhse, U. (2008). "Don't crack under pressure"—Do leisure time physical activity and self-esteem moderate the relationship between school-based stress and psychosomatic complaints? *Journal of Psychosomatic Research, 65,* 363–369.

Gerbner, G., Gross, L., Morgan, M., & Signorielli, N. (1994). Growing up with television: The cultivation perspective. In J. Bryant & D. Zillmann (Eds.), *Media effects: Advances in theory and research* (pp. 17–41). Hillsdale, NJ: Erlbaum.

Gesell, A., & Ames, L. B. (1956). *Youth: The years from ten to sixteen.* New York: Harper and Row.

Gettman, J. (2006). *Marijuana production in the United States.* Retrieved from http://www.drugscience.org/Archive/bcr2/cashcrops.html.

Gfellner, B. M., & Hundelby, J. D. (April, 1994). *Patterns of drug use and social activities among Native Indian and White adolescents*. Paper presented at the Society for Research on Adolescence, San Diego, CA.

Ghang, J., & Jin, S. (1996). Determinants of suicide ideation: A comparison of Chinese and American college students. *Adolescence, 31,* 451–467.

Gibbons, J. L., Brusi-Figueroa, R., & Fisher, S. L. (1997). Gender-related ideals of Puerto Rican adolescents: Gender and school content. *Journal of Early Adolescence, 17,* 349–370.

Gibbs, J. C. (2003). *Moral development and reality: Beyond the theories of Kohlberg and Hoffman.* Thousand Oaks, CA: Sage.

Gibbs, J. C., Basinger, K. S., & Fuller, D. (1992). *Moral maturity: Measuring the development of sociomoral reflection.* Hillsdale, NJ: Erlbaum.

Gibbs, J. C., Basinger, K. S., Grime, R. L., & Snarey, J. R. (2007). Moral judgment development across cultures: Revisiting Kohlberg's universality claims. *Developmental Review, 27,* 443–500.

Gibson, J. L., Griepentrog, B. K., & Marsh, S. M. (2007). Parental influence on youth propensity to join the military. *Journal of Vocational Behavior, 70,* 525–541.

Giedd, J. N., Blumenthal, J., Jeffries, N. O., Rajapakse, J. C., Vaituzis, C., Hung, L., Berry, Y., Tobin, M., Nelson, J., & Castellanos, F. X. (1999). Development of the human corpus callosum during childhood and adolescence: A longitudinal MRI study. *Progress in Neuro-Psychopharmacology and Biological Psychiatry, 23,* 571–588.

Giedd, J. N., Castellanos, F. X., Rajapakse, J. C., Vaituzis, A. C., & Rapaport, J. L. (1997). Sexual dimorphism of the developing human brain. *Progress in Neuro-Psychopharmacology and Biological Psychiatry, 21,* 1185–1201.

Gilligan, C. (1977). In a different voice: Women's conceptions of self and of morality. *Harvard Educational Review, 47,* 481–517.

Gilligan, C. (1982). *In a different voice: Psychological theory and women's development.* Cambridge, MA: Harvard University Press.

Gilligan, C. (1984, June). *Remapping the moral domain in personality research and assessment.* Invited address presented to the American Psychological Association Convention, Toronto, Ontario, Canada.

Gilliland, H. (1995). *Teaching the Native American* (3rd ed.). Dubuque, IA: Kendall/Hall.

Ginzberg, E. (1988). Toward a theory of occupational choice. *The Career Development Quarterly, 36,* 358–363.

Gius M. P. (2007). The impact of provider availability and legal restrictions on the demand for abortions by young women. *Social Science Journal, 44,* 495–506.

Gjerde, P. F., & Westenberg, P. M. (1998). Dysphoric adolescents as young adults: A prospective study of the psychological sequelae of depressed mood in adolescence. *Journal of Research on Adolescence, 8,* 377–402.

Glikman, H. (2004). Low-income young fathers: Contexts, connections, and self. *Social Work, 49,* 195–206.

Glodis, K. A., & Blasi, A. (1993). The sense of self and identity among adolescents and adults. *Journal of Adolescent Research, 8,* 356–380.

Gloria, A. M., & Hird, J. S. (1999). Influences of ethnic and nonethnic variables on the career decision-making self-efficacy of college students. *Career Development Quarterly, 48,* 157–174.

Gloria-Bottini, F., Cervelli, V., Giarrizzo, G. F., Martinoli, R., Di Renzo, L., & De Lorenzo, A. (2007). Sex differences in body fat parameters from the early reproductive to the postreproductive period of life: A multivariate analysis. *Human Biology, 79,* 373–379.

Gluckman, P. D., & Hanson, M. A. (2006). Changing times: The evolution of puberty. *Molecular & Cellular Endocrinology, 254,* 26–31.

Goff, L. (1999). Don't miss the bus! *American Demographics, 21,* 48–54.

Goff, M., & Ackerman, P. L. (1997). Personality-intelligence relations: Assessment of typical intellectual engagement. *Journal of Educational Psychology, 84,* 537–552.

Goldscheider, F., & Goldscheider, C. (1999). *The changing transition to adulthood: Leaving and returning home.* New York: Berkeley Press.

Goldschmidt, L., Richardson, G. A., Willford, J., & Day, N. L. (2008). Prenatal marijuana exposure and intelligence test performance at age 6. *Journal of the American Academy of Child & Adolescent Psychiatry, 47,* 254–263.

Goldschmidt, P., & Wang, J. (1999). When can school affect dropout behavior? A longitudinal multilevel analysis. *American Educational Research Journal, 36,* 715–738.

Goldstein, J. (1999). *Why we watch: The attraction of violent entertainment.* New York: Oxford University Press.

Golombok, S., & Tasker, F. (1996). Do parents influence the sexual orientation of their children? Findings from a longitudinal study of lesbian families. *Developmental Psychology, 32,* 3–11.

Golub, S. (1992). *Periods: From menarche to menopause.* Newbury Park, CA: Sage.

Gonzales, N. A., & Kim, L. S. (1997). Stress and coping in an ethnic minority context. In I. N. Sandler & S. A. Wolchik (Eds.), *Handbook of children's coping: Linking theory and intervention* (pp. 481–511). New York: Wiley.

Goodman, C., & Pickens, J. (2001). Self-blame and self-esteem in college-aged children from divorced families. *Journal of Divorce & Remarriage, 34,* 119–135.

Goodman, G. (2006). Acne and acne scarring: The case for active and early intervention. *Australia Family Physician, 35,* 503–4.

Goosby, B. J. (2007). Poverty duration, maternal psychological resources, and adolescent socioeconomic outcomes. *Journal of Family Issues, 28,* 1113–1134.

Goossens, L., & Marcoen A. (1999). Adolescent loneliness, self-reflection, and identity: From individual differences to developmental processes. In K. J. Rotenberg & S. Hymel (Eds.), *Loneliness in childhood and adolescence* (pp. 225–243). Cambridge, England: Cambridge University Press.

Gordon, R. M. (2005). The doom and gloom of divorce research. Comment on Wallerstein and Lewis (2004). *Psychoanalytic Psychology, 22,* 450-451.

Gore, S., Farrell, F., & Gordon, J. (2001). Sport involvement as protection against depressed mood. *Journal of Research on Adolescence, 11,* 119–130.

Gossop, M., Marsden, J., Stewart, D., & Rolfe, A. (2000). Patterns of improvement after methadone treatment: 1 year follow-up results from the national treatment outcome research study. *Drug & Alcohol Dependency, 60,* 275–286.

Gottfredson, D. C., Gerstenblith, S. A., Soulé, D. A., Worne, S. C., & Lu, S. (2004). Do after-school programs reduce delinquency? *Prevention Science, 5,* 253–266.

Gottfredson, L. S. (2005). Applying Gottfredson's theory of circumscription and compromise in career guidance and counseling. In S. D. Brown & R. W. Lent (Eds.), *Career development and counseling: Putting theory and research to work* (pp. 71–100). Hoboken, NJ: Wiley.

Gottfredson, M., & Hirshi, T. (1990). *A general theory of crime.* Stanford, CA: Stanford University Press.

Gould, M. S. (2001). Suicide and the media. *Annals of the New York Academy of Sciences, 932,* 200–221.

Gould, M. S., Fisher, P., Parides, M., Flore, M., & Shaffer, D. (1996). Psychosocial risk factors of child and adolescent completed suicide. *Archives of General Psychiatry, 53,* 1155–1162.

Gowen, L. K., Feldman, S. S., Diaz, R., & Yisrael, D. S. (2004). A comparison of the sexual behaviors and attitudes of adolescent girls with older vs. similar-aged boyfriends. *Journal of Youth and Adolescence, 33,* 167–175.

Graber, J. A., Brooks-Gunn, J., & Galen, B. R. (1998). Betwixt and between: Sexuality in the context of adolescent transitions. In R. Jessor (Ed.), *New perspectives of adolescent risk behavior* (pp. 270–316). Cambridge, England: Cambridge University Press.

Graber, J. A., Seeley, J. R., Brooks-Gunn, J., & Lewinsohn, P. M. (2004). Is pubertal timing associated with psychopathology in young adulthood? *Journal of the American Academy of Child & Adolescent Psychiatry, 43,* 718–726.

Graber, J. A., & Sontag, L. M. (2009). Internalizing problems during adolescence. In R. M. Lerner & L. Steinberg (Eds.), *Handbook of adolescent psychology* (Vol. 1, 3rd ed., pp. 642–682). New York: Wiley.

Grant, B. F. (2000). Estimates of U.S. children exposed to alcohol use and dependence in the family. *American Journal of Public Health, 90,* 112–115.

Grant, B. F., & Dawson, D. A. (1997). Age at onset of alcohol use and its association with DSM-IV alcohol abuse and dependence: Results from the National Longitudinal Alcohol Epidemiological Survey. *Journal of Substance Abuse, 9,* 103–110.

Gray, M. R., & Steinberg, L. (1999). Adolescent romance and the parent-child relationship: A contextual perspective. In W. Furman, B. B. Brown, & C. Feiring (Eds.), *The development of romantic relationships in adolescence* (pp. 235–265). Cambridge, England: Cambridge University Press.

Gray, P. (2007). *Psychology* (5th ed.). New York: Worth Publishers.

Greene, A. L. (1990). Age and gender differences in adolescents' preference for parental advice: Mum's the word. *Journal of Adolescent Research, 5,* 396–413.

Greene, B., & Land, S. M. (2000). A qualitative analysis of scaffolding use in a resource-based learning environment involving the World Wide Web. *Journal of Educational Computing Research, 23,* 151–179.

Greene, J. M., Ennett, S. T., & Ringwalt, C. L. (1999). Prevalence and correlates of survival sex among runaway and homeless youth. *American Journal of Public Health, 89,* 1406–1409.

Greene, M. B. (2006). Bullying in schools: A plea for a measure of human rights. *Journal of Social Issues, 62,* 63–79.

Greene, M. L., & Way, N. (2005). Self-esteem trajectories among ethnic minority adolescents: A growth curve analysis of the patterns and predictors of change. *Journal of Research on Adolescence, 15,* 151–178.

Greeno, C. G., & Maccoby, E. E. (1986). How different is the "different voice"? *Signs, 11,* 310–312.

Grieser, M., Vu, M. B., Bedimo-Rung, A. L., Neumark-Sztainer, D., Moody, J., Young, D. R., & Moe, S. G. (2006). Physical activity attitudes, preferences, and practices in African American, Hispanic, and Caucasian girls. *Health Education & Behavior, 33,* 40–51.

Grieve, F. G., Jackson, L., Reece, T., Marklin, L., & Delaney, A. (2008). Correlates of social physique anxiety in men. *Journal of Sport Behavior, 31,* 329–337.

Griffin, N., Chassin, L., & Young, R. D. (1981). Measurement of global self-concept versus multiple role-specific self-concept in adolescents. *Adolescence, 16,* 49–56.

Griffin, R. S., & Gross, M. (2004). Childhood bullying: Current empirical findings and future directions for research. *Aggression and Violent Behavior, 9,* 379–400.

Grossman, J. B., & Bulle, M. J. (2006). Review of what youth programs do to increase the connectedness of youth with adults. *Journal of Adolescent Health, 39,* 788–799.

Grotevant, H. D. (1987). Toward a process model of identity formation. *Journal of Adolescent Research, 2,* 203–222.

Grotevant, H. D. (1992). Assigned and chosen identity components: A process perspective on their integration. In G. R. Adams, T. P. Gullotta, & R. Montemayor

(Eds.), *Adolescent identity formation: Advances in adolescent development* (pp. 73–90). Newbury Park, CA: Sage.

Grotevant, H. D., & Cooper, C. R. (1985). Patterns of interaction in family relationships and the development of identity exploration in adolescence. *Child Development, 56,* 415–428.

Grotevant, H. D., Wrobel, G. M., Von Korff, L., Skinner, B., Newell, J., Friese, S., et al. (2007). Many faces of openness in adoption: Perspectives of adopted adolescents and their parents. *Adoption Quarterly, 10,* 79–101.

Grube, J. W. (1995). Television alcohol portrayals, alcohol advertising and alcohol expectancies among children and adolescents. In S. E. Martin & P. Mail (Eds.), *Effects of the mass media on the use and abuse of alcohol* (pp. 105–121). Bethesda, MD: National Institute on Alcohol Abuse and Alcoholism.

Grunbaum, J. A., Kann, L., Kinchen, S. A., Williams, B., Ross, J. G., & Lowry, R. (2002). Youth risk behavior surveillance—United States, 2001. *Morbidity and Mortality Weekly Report, 51,* 1–62.

Grunseit, A., Kippax, S., Aggleton, P., Baldo, M., & Slutkin, G. (1997). Sexuality education and young people's sexual behavior: A review of studies. *Journal of Adolescent Research, 12,* 421–453.

Guagliardo, M. F., Huang, Z., & D'Angelo, L. J. (1999). Fathering pregnancies: Marking health-risk behaviors in urban adolescents. *Journal of Adolescent Health, 24,* 10–15.

Guay, F., Boivin, M., & Hodges, E.V. E. (1999). Predicting change in academic achievement: A model of peer experiencees and self-system processes. *Journal of Educational Psychology, 91,* 105–115.

Gullotta, T. P. (2003). Leaving home: The runaway and the forgotten throwaway. In G. R. Adams & M. D. Berzonsky (Eds.), *The Blackwell handbook of adolescence* (pp. 494–501). Oxford, England: Blackwell Publishing.

Guroglu, B., van Lieshout, C. F. M., Haselager, G. J. T., & Scholte, R. H. J. (2007). Similarity and complementarity of behavioral profiles of friendship types and types of friends: Friendships and psychosocial adjustment. *Journal of Research on Adolescence, 17,* 357–386.

Gutman, I. M., Sameroff, A. J., & Cole, R. (2003). Academic growth curve trajectories from 1st grade to 12th grade: Effects of multiple social risk factors and preschool child factors. *Developmental Psychology, 39,* 777–790.

Guttmacher Institute. (2006). *U.S. teenage pregnancy statistics: National and state trends and trends by race and ethnicity.* Retrieved from http://www.guttmacher.org/pubs/2006/09/11/USTPstats.pdf.

Guttman, L. M., & Eccles, J. S. (1999). Financial strain, parenting behaviors, and adolescent achievement: Testing model equivalence between African American and European American single- and two-parent families. *Child Development, 70,* 1464–1476.

Guzmán, B. (2001). *The Hispanic population.* Census 2000 Brief. Publication No. C2KBR/01-3. Washington DC: U.S. Bureau of the Census.

Hafen, B. Q., & Frandsen, K. J. (1986). *Youth suicide: Depression and loneliness.* Provo, UT: Behavioral Health Associates.

Hafez, E. S. E. (Ed.). (1980). *Human reproduction: Conception and contraception.* Hagerstown, MD: Harper and Row.

Hajat, A., Lucas, J. B., & Kington, R. (2000). Health outcomes among Hispanic subgroups: Data from the National Health Interview Survey, 1992–1995. National Center for Health Statistics, *Advance Data, 310.*

Hale, S. (1990). A global, developmental trend in cognitive processing speed. *Child Development, 61,* 653–663.

Halebsky, M. A. (1987). Adolescent alcohol and substance abuse: Parent and peer effects. *Adolescence, 22,* 961–967.

Hall, G. S. (1904). *Adolescence: Its psychology and its relation to physiology, anthropology, sociology, sex, crime, religion and education* (2 vols.). New York: D. Appleton.

Hall, H. I., Song, R., Rhodes, P., Prejean, J., An, Q., Lee, L. M., Karon, J., Brookmeyer, R., Kaplan, E. H., McKenna, M. T., & Janssen, R. S. (2008). Estimation of HIV incidence in the United States. *Journal of the American Medical Association, 300,* 520–529.

Halpern, C. J. T., Udry, J. R., Suchindran, C., & Campbell, B. (2000). Adolescent males' willingness to report masturbation. *Journal of Sex Research, 37,* 327–332.

Halpern-Felsher, B. L. (2009). Adolescent decision making: An overview. *The Prevention Researcher, 16,* 3–7.

Hamilton, B. E., Ventura, S. J., Martin, J. A., & Sutton, P. D. (2005). *Preliminary births for 2004.* Hyattsville, MD: National Center for Health Statistics.

Hamilton, S. F., & Fenzel, L. M. (1988). The impact of volunteer experience on adolescent social development: Evidence of program effects. *Journal of Adolescent Research, 3,* 65–80.

Hammer, H., Finkelhor, D., & Sedlak, A. J. (2002). *Runaway/Thrownaway children: National estimates and characteristics.* Bulletin of the Office of Juvenile Justice and Delinquency Prevention. Washington, DC: U.S. Department of Justice.

Hampton, T. (2004). Suicide caution stamped on antidepressants. *Journal of the American Medical Association, 291,* 2060–2061.

Hanson, S. L. (1992). Involving families in programs for pregnant teens: Consequences for teens and their families. *Family Relations, 41,* 303-311.

Hanson, T. L., McLanahan, S. S., & Thomson, E. (1996). Double jeopardy: Parental conflict and stepfamily outcomes for children. *Journal of Marriage and Family, 58,* 141–154.

Harding, C. G., & Snyder, K. (1991). Tom, Huck, and Oliver Stone as advocates in Kohlberg's Just Community: Theory-based strategies for moral education. *Adolescence, 26,* 319–329.

Hardy, S. A., & Carlo, G. (2005). Religiosity and prosocial behaviors in adolescence: The mediating influence of prosocial values. *Journal of Moral Education, 34,* 231–249.

Harkness, S., & Super, C. (1985). The cultural context of gender segregation in children's peer groups. *Child Development, 56,* 219–224.

Harris Interactive. (2004). *College students tote $122 billion in spending power back to campus this year.* Press release. Retrieved from http://www.harrisinteractive.com/news/allnewsbydate.asp?NewsID=835.

Harris-Britt, A., Valrie, C. R., Kurtz-Costes, B., & Rowley, S. J. (2007). Perceived racial discrimination and self-esteem in African American youth: Racial socialization as a protective factor. *Journal of Research on Adolescence, 17,* 669–682.

Harrison, K. S., & Cantor, J. (1999). Tales from the screen: Enduring fright reactions to scary media. *Media Psychology, 1,* 97–116.

Hart, D., Atkins, R., & Fegley, S. (2003). Personality and development in childhood: A person-centered approach. *Monographs for the Society for Research in Child Development, 68,* vii–109.

Hart, J. L., & Helms, L. (2003). Factors of parricide: Allowance of the use of battered child syndrome as a defense. *Aggression and Violent Behavior, 8,* 671–683.

Hart, S., Robinson, S. E. K., & Kerr, B. (June, 2001). *Adolescent at-risk behaviors: Effects of parents, older siblings, and peers.* Paper presented at the annual convention of the American Psychological Association, San Francisco.

Harter, S. (1990). Self and identity development. In S. S. Feldman & G. R. Elliott (Eds.), *At the thresholds: The developing adolescent* (pp. 352–387). Cambridge, MA: Harvard University Press.

Harter, S., Stocker, C., & Robinson, N. S. (1996). The perceived directionality of the link between approval and self-worth: The liabilities of a looking gladd self-orientation among young adolescents. *Journal of Research on Adolescence, 6,* 285–308.

Hartman, A., & Laird, J. (1990). Family treatment after adoption: Common themes. In D. Brodzinsky & M. Schechter (Eds.), *The psychology of adoption* (pp. 221–239). New York: Oxford University Press.

Hartos, J. L., & Power, T. G. (2000). Relations among single-mothers' awareness of their adolescents' stressors, maternal monitoring, mother-adolescent communication, and adolescent adjustment. *Journal of Adolescent Research, 15,* 546–563.

Hartung, P. J., Porfeli, E. J., & Vondracek, E. W. (2005). Child vocational development: A review and reconsideration. *Journal of Vocational Development, 66,* 385–419.

Hartup, W. (1983). Peer relations. In E. M. Hetherington (Ed.), *Handbook of child psychology: Socialization, personality, and social development.*(Vol. 4). New York: Wiley.

Hartup, W. W., & Stevens, N. (1999). Friendships and adaptation across the lifespan. *Current Directions in Psychological Science, 8,* 76–79.

Harwood, J., Hewstone, M., Paolini, S., & Voci, A. (2005). Grandparent-grandchild contact and attitudes towards older adults: Moderator and mediator effects. *Personality and Social Psychology Journal, 31,* 393–406.

Hassler, M. (1992). The critical teens—Musical capacities change in adolescence. *European Journal for High Ability, 3,* 89–98.

Hatfield, E., & Rapson, R. L. (1996*). Love and sex: Cross-cultural perspectives.* Boston: Allyn & Bacon.

Haugaard, J. J., & Hazan, C. (2003). Adoption as a natural experiment. *Development and Psychopathology, 15,* 909–926.

Havighurst, R. J. (1972). *Developmental tasks and education* (3rd ed). New York: David McKay.

Hawley, P. H. (2003). Prosocial and coercive configurations of resource control in early adolescence: A case for the well-adapted Machiavellian. *Merrill-Palmer Quarterly, 49,* 279–309.

Haynie, D. (2003). Context of risk? Explaining the link between girls' pubertal development and their delinquency involvement. *Social Forces, 82,* 355–397.

Heath, J., & Goggin, K. (2009). Attitudes towards male homosexuality, bisexuality, and the down low lifestyle: Demographic differences and HIV implications. *Journal of Bisexuality, 9,* 17–31.

Heaviside, K., Rowand, L., Williams, F., & Farris, K. (1998). *Violence and discipline problems in U.S. public schools: 1996–1997.* Washington, DC: Department of Education, National Center for Education Statistics.

Hebebrand, J., & Hinney, A. (2009). Environmental and genetic risk factors in obesity. *Child and Adolescent Psychiatric Clinics of North America, 18,* 83–94.

Heide, K. M., & Petee, A. (2007). Weapons used by juveniles and adult offenders in U.S. parricide cases. *Journal of Interpersonal Violence, 22,* 1400–1414.

Heiman, T. (2000). Friendship quality among children in three educational settings. *Journal of Intellectual and Developmental Disability, 25,* 1–12.

Heinrich, R. S., Hickman, G. P., Bartholomew, M., & Mathwig, J. (2008). Differential developmental pathways of high school dropouts and graduates. *The Journal of Educational Research, 102,* 3–14.

Heller, C. G., & Clermont, Y. (1963). Spermatogenesis in man: An estimate of its duration. *Science, 140,* 184–186.

Helms, J. E. (June, 1990). *Black and White racial identity theory and professional interracial collaboration.* Paper presented at the meeting of the American Psychological Association, Boston, MA.

Helsen, M., Vollebergh, W., & Meeus, W. (2000). Social support from parents and friends and emotional problems in adolescence. *Journal of Youth and Adolescence, 29,* 319–335.

Helwig, A. (2001). A test of Gottfredson's theory using a ten-year longitudinal study. *Journal of Career Development, 28,* 77–95.

Helwig, C. C., Arnold, M. L., Tan, D., & Boyd, D. (2007). Mainland Chinese and Canadian adolescents' judgments and reasoning about the fairness of democratic and other forms of government. *Cognitive Development, 22,* 96–109.

Henninger, D., & Esposito, N. (1971). Indian schools. In D. Gottlieb & A. L. Heinsohn (Eds.), *America's other youth: Growing up poor.* Englewood Cliffs, NJ: Prentice Hall.

Henshaw, S. K. (2003). *U.S. teenage pregnancy statistics with comparative statistics for women aged 20–24.* New York: Alan Guttmacher Institute.

Henshaw, S. K., & Kost, K. (1992). Parental involvement in minors' abortion decisions. *Family Planning Perspectives, 24,* 196–207.

Herd, D. (2008). Changes in drug use prevalence in rap music songs, 1979–1997. *Addiction Research & Theory, 16,* 167–180.

Herman, A. M. (2000). *Report on youth labor force.* Washington, DC: U.S. Department of Labor.

Herman, M. R., Dornbusch, S. M., Herron, M. C., & Herting, J. R. (1997). The influence of family regulation, connection, and psychological autonomy on six measures of adolescent functioning. *Journal of Adolescent Research, 12,* 34–67.

Hernandez, D. (2004). Demographic change and the life circumstances of the children from immigrant families. *The Future of Children, 14,* 17–47.

Herrenkohl, T., Hawkins, J. D., Chung, I.-J., Hill, K. G., & Battin-Pearson, S. (2000). School and community risk factors and interventions. In R. Loeber & D. P. Farrington (Eds.), *Child delinquents: Development, intervention, and service needs* (pp. 211–246). Thousand Oaks, CA: Sage.

Herzog, D. B., Dorer, D. J., Keel, P., Selwyn, S. E., Ekeblad, E. R., Flores, A. T., Greenwood, D. N., Burwell, R, A., & Keller, M. (1999). Recovery and relapse in anorexia and bulimia nervosa: A 7.5 year follow-up study. *Journal of the American Academy of Child and Adolescent Psychiatry, 38,* 829–837.

Hetherington, E. M. (1972). Effects of father-absence on personality development in adolescent daughters. *Developmental Psychology, 7,* 313–326.

Hetherington, E. M. (1991). The role of individual differences and family relationships in children's coping with divorce and remarriage. In P. A. Cowan & E. M. Hetherington (Eds.), *Family transitions* (pp. 165–194). Hillsdale, NJ: Erlbaum.

Hetherington, E. M. (1993). An overview of the Virginia Longitudinal Study of Divorce and Remarriage with a focus on early adolescence. *Journal of Family Psychology, 7,* 39–56.

Hetherington, E. M. (1999a). Family functioning and the adjustment of adolescent siblings in diverse types of families. In E. M. Hetherington, S. H. Henderson, & D. Reiss (Eds.), *Adolescent siblings in stepfamilies: Family functioning and adolescent adjustment* (pp. 1–25). *Monographs of the Society for Research in Child Development, 64*(4).

Hetherington, E. M. (1999b). Family functioning in non-stepfamilies and different kinds of stepfamilies: An integration. In E. M. Hetherington, S. H. Henderson, & D. Reiss (Eds.), *Adolescent siblings in stepfamilies: Family functioning and adolescent adjustment* (pp. 184–191). *Monographs of the Society for Research in Child Development, 64*(4).

Hetherington, E. M., & Clingempeel, W. G. (1992). Coping with marital transitions: A family systems perspective. *Monographs of the Society for Research in Child Development, 57*(2–3).

Hetherington, E. M., & Jodl, K. M. (1994). Stepfamilies as settings for child development. In A. Booth & J. Dunn (Eds.), *Stepfamilies: Who benefits? Who does not?* (pp. 55–79). Hillsdale, NJ: Erlbaum.

Hetherington, E. M., & Kelly, J. (2002). *For better or for worse.* New York: Norton.

Hetherington, E. M., & Stanley-Hagan, M. (1999). The adjustment of children with divorced parents: A risk and resiliency perspective. *Journal of Child Psychology and Psychiatry, 40,* 129–140.

Hickman, G. P., & Garvey, I. (2006). Analyses of academic achievement and school behavior problems as indices of program effectiveness among at-risk adolescents enrolled in a youth-based mentoring program. *Journal of At-Risk Issues, 12,* 1–15.

Higgins, J. (2003, March 4). More high school students driving nicer, bigger cars. *Detroit Free Press,* p. 4.

Hill, A. J., & Pallin, V. (1998). Dieting awareness and low self-worth: Related issues in 8-year-old girls. *International Journal of Eating Disorders, 24,* 405–413.

Hill, R. B. (1998). Understanding Black family functioning: A holistic perspective. *Journal of Comparative Family Studies, 29,* 15–25.

Hilliard, P. J. (2008). Menstruation in adolescents—What's normal, what's not. In C. M. Gordon, C. Welt, R. W. Rebar et al. (Eds.), *Annals of the New York Academy of Sciences, 2008* (pp. 29–35). Oxford, England: Blackwell Publishing.

Hillier, L., Harrison, L., & Warr, D. (1997). "When you carry a condom, all the boys think you want it": Negotiating competing discourses about safe sex. *Journal of Adolescence, 21,* 15–29.

Hines, A. M. (1997). Divorce-related transitions, adolescent development, and the role of the parent–child relationship: A review of the literature. *Journal of Marriage and Family, 59,* 375–388.

Hingston, R., & Winter, M. (2003). Epidemiology and consequences of drinking and driving. *Alcohol Research & Health, 27,* 63–78.

Hirokane, K., Tokomura, M., Nanri, S., Kimura, K., & Saito, I. (2005). Influences of mothers' dieting behaviors on their junior high school daughters. *Eating and Weight Disorders, 10,* 162–167.

Hirschman, C., & Voloshin, I. (2007). The structure of teenage employment: Social background and the jobs held by high school seniors. *Research in Social Stratification and Mobility, 25,* 189–203.

Ho, C. S., Lempers, J. D., & Clark-Lempers, D. S. (1995). Effects of economic hardship on adolescent self-esteem: A family mediation model. *Adolescence, 30,* 117–131.

Hobbs, F., & Stoops, N. (2002). Demographic trends in the 20th century. *Census 2000 Special Report.* Publication No. CENSR-4. Washington DC: U.S. Bureau of the Census.

Hockenberry-Eaton, M., Richman, M. J., DiIorio, C., Rivero, T., & Maibach, E. (1996). Mothers and adolescent knowledge of sexual development: The effects of gender, age, and sexual experience. *Adolescence, 31,* 35–46.

Hoek, H. W. (2006). Incidence, prevalence and mortality of anorexia nervosa and other eating disorders. *Current Opinion in Psychiatry, 19,* 389–394.

Hoff, E., Laursen, B., & Tardif, T. (2002). Socioeconomic status and parenting. In M. H. Bornstein (Ed.), *Handbook of parenting: Biology and ecology of parenting* (Vol. 2, 2nd ed., pp. 231–252). Mahwah, NJ: Erlbaum.

Hoffer, T. B. (1998). Social background and achievement in public and Catholic high schools. *Social Psychology of Education, 2,* 7–23.

Hofferth, S. L., & Anderson, G. (2003). Are all dads equal? Biology versus marriage as a basis for paternal investment. *Journal of Marriage and Family, 65,* 213–232.

Hofferth S. L., Reid, L., & Mott, F. L. (2001). The effects of early childbearing on schooling over time. *Family Planning Perspectives, 33,* 259–267.

Hoffman, M. L. (1994). Discipline and internalization. *Developmental Psychology, 30,* 26–28.

Hoffman, M. L. (2000). *Empathy and moral development: Implications for caring and justice.* Cambridge, England: Cambridge University Press.

Hoffner, C. A., & Levine, K. J. (2005). Enjoyment of mediated fright and violence: A meta-analysis. *Media Psychology, 7,* 207–237.

Holden, G., Geffner, R., & Jouriles, E. (Eds.). (1998). *Children exposed to marital violence.* Washington, DC: American Psychological Association.

Holifield, J. E., Nelson, W. M. III, & Hart, K. J. (2002). MMPI profiles of sexually abused and nonabused outpatient adolescents. *Journal of Adolescent Research, 17,* 188–195.

Holland, J. D., & Klaczynski, P. A. (2009). Intuitive risk taking during adolescence. *The Prevention Researcher, 16,* 8–11.

Holland, J. L. (1985). *Making vocational choices: A theory of vocational personalities and work environments* (2nd Ed.). Englewood Cliffs, NJ: Prentice Hall.

Holland, J. L. (1996). Exploring careers with a typology: What we have learned and some new directions. *American Psychologist, 51,* 397–406.

Holleran, P. R., Pascale, J., & Fraley, J. (1988). Personality correlates of college-age bulimics. *Journal of Counseling and Development, 66,* 378–381.

Holmbeck, G. N., Paikoff, R. L., & Brooks-Gunn, J. (1995). Parenting adolescents. In M. Bornstein (Ed.), *Handbook of parenting: Children and parenting* (Vol. 1, pp. 91–118). Hillsdale, NJ: Erlbaum.

Homan, K. B. (1986). Vocation as the quest for authentic existence. *The Career Development Quarterly, 35,* 14–23.

Hope, R. M., & Hodge, D. M. (2006). Factors affecting children's adjustment to the death of a parent: The social work professional's perspective. *Child and Adolescent Social Work Journal, 23,* 107–126.

Horowitz, J. A., Vessey, J. A., Carlson, K. L., Bradley, J. F., Montoya, C., McCullough, B., & David, J. (2004). Teasing and bullying experiences of middle school students. *Journal of the American Psychiatric Nurses Association, 10,* 165–172.

Hortacsu, N. (1989). Target communication during adolescence. *Journal of Adolescence, 12,* 253–263.

Howard, D. E., & Qi Wang, M. (2003). Risk procedures of adolescent girls who were victims of dating violence. *Adolescence, 38,* 1–14.

Howard, D. E., Wang, M. Q., & Yan, F. (2007). Prevalence and psychological correlates of forced sexual intercourse among U.S. high school adolescents. *Adolescence, 42,* 629–643.

Howard, D. E., Wang, M. Q., & Yan, F. (2008). Psychosocial factors associated with reports of physical dating violence victimization among U.S. adolescent males. *Adolescence, 43,* 449–460.

Hoza, B., Bukowski, W. M., & Beery, S. (2000). Assessing peer network and dyadic loneliness. *Journal of Clinical Child Psychology, 29,* 119–128.

Hsueh, A. C., Morrison, K. R., & Doss, B. D. (2009). Qualitative reports of problems in cohabiting relationships: Comparisons to married and dating relationships. *Journal of Family Psychology, 23,* 236–246.

Huerta-Franco, R., deLeon, J. D., & Malacara, J. M. (1996). Knowledge and attitudes towards sexuality in adolescence and their association with the family and other factors. *Adolescence, 31,* 179–191.

Hughes, D., Hagelskamp, C., Way, N., & Foust, M. D. (2009). The role of mothers' and adolescents' perceptions of ethnic-racial socialization in shaping ethnic-racial identity among early adolescent boys and girls. *Journal of Youth and Adolescence, 38,* 605–626.

Hughes, M., Morrison, K., & Asada, K. J. K. (2005). What's love got to do with it? Exploring the maintenance rules, love attitudes, and network support on friends with benefits relationships. *Western Journal of Communication, 69,* 49–66.

Huitt, W. (2003). *Values.* Retrieved July 11, 2003, from http://chiron.valdosta.edu/whuitt.

Huizinga, D., & Jakob-Chien, C. (1998). The contemporaneous co-occurrence of serious and violent juvenile offending and other behavior problems. In R. Loeber & D. P. Farrington (Eds.), *Serious and violent juvenile offenders: Risk factors and successful intervention* (pp. 47–67). Thousand Oaks, CA: Sage.

Hulanicka, B. (1999). Acceleration of menarcheal age of girls from dysfunctional families. *Journal of Reproductive and Infant Psychology, 17,* 119–132.

Hunt, G. P., & Laidler, K. J. (2001). Alcohol and violence in the lives of gang members. *Alcohol Research & Health, 25,* 66–71.

Hunter, A. (1997). Counting on grandmothers: Black mothers' and fathers' reliance on grandmothers for parenting support. *Journal of Family Issues, 18,* 251–269.

Hussong, A. M. (2000). Distinguishing mean and structural sex differences in adolescent friendship quality. *Journal of Social and Personal Relationships, 17,* 223–243.

Huston, A. C., & Alvarez, M. M. (1990). The socialization context of gender role development in early adolescence. In R. Montemayor, G. R. Adams, & T. P. Gullota, (Eds.), *From childhood to adolescence: A transitional period?* (pp. 156–179). Newbury Park, CA: Sage.

Huston, A. C., Donnerstein, E., Fairchild, H., Freshback, N. D., Katz, P. A., Murray, J. P., Rubenstein, E. A., Wilcox, B. L., & Zuckerman, D. (1992). *Big world, small screen: The role of television in American society.* Lincoln: University of Nebraska Press.

Huston, L., Hoberman, H., & Nugent, S. (1994, April). *Alcohol use and abuse in Native American adolescents.* Paper presented at the meeting of the Society for Research on Adolescence, San Diego, CA.

Hutchinson, R. L., Valutis, W. E., Brown, D. T., & White, J. S. (1989). The effects of family structure on institutionalized children's self-concepts. *Adolescence, 94,* 303–310.

Huurre, T., Junkkari, H., & Aro, H. (2006). Long-term psychosocial effects of parental divorce: A follow-up study from adolescence to adulthood. *European Archives of Psychiatry and Clinical Neuroscience, 256,* 256–263.

Hwang, Y. S., Echols, C., & Vrongistinos, K. (2002). Multidimensional academic motivation of high achieving African American students. *College Student Journal, 36,* 544–554.

Iceland, J., Weinberg, D. H, & Steinmetz, E. (2002). *Racial and ethnic residential segregation in the United States: 1980–2000.* Series no. CENSR-3. Washington, DC: U.S. Government Printing Office.

Ieit, D. (1985, February). *Anxiety, depression, and self-esteem in bulimia: The role of the school psychologist.* Paper presented at the annual meeting of the Educational Research Association, Virginia Beach, VA.

Infoplease.com. *Timeline of worldwide school shootings.* Retrieved from http://www.infoplease.com/ipa/A0777958 .html.

Inhelder, B., & Piaget, J. (1958). *The growth of logical thinking from childhood to adolescence.* New York: Basic Books.

Internet World Stats. (2009). *Internet usage stats: The big picture.* Retrieved from http://www.internetworldstats .com/stats.htm.

Issacs, J. (2007). *Economic mobility of Black and White families.* Retrieved from the PEW Charitable Trust Web site: http://www.pewtrusts.org/uploadedFiles/ wwwpewtrustsorg/Reports/Economic_Mobility/EMP% 20Black%20and%20White%20Families%20ES+ Chapter.pdf.

Ivchenkova, N. P., Efimova, A. V., & Akkuzina, O. P. (2001). Teenage attitudes towards the beginning of sex life. *Voprosy Psikologii, 3,* 49–57.

Jablonska, B., & Lindberg, L. (2007). Risk behaviours, victimisation and mental distress among adolescents in different family structures. *Social Psychiatry and Psychiatric Epidemiology, 42,* 656–663.

Jackson, A. W., & Davis, G. A. (2000). *Turning points 2000: Educating adolescents in the 21st century.* New York: Teachers College Press.

Jackson, D. N., & Rushton, P. (2006). Males have greater *g:* Sex differences in general mental ability from 100,000 17- to 18-year-olds on the Scholastic Assessment Test. *Intelligence, 34,* 479–486.

Jackson, L. M., Pratt, M. W., Hunsberger, B., & Pancer, S. M. (2005). Optimism as a mediator of the relation between perceived parental authoritativeness and adjustment among adolescents: Finding the sunny side of the street. *Social Development, 14,* 273–304.

Jackson, S. M., & Cram, F. (2003). Disrupting the sexual double standard: Young women's talk about heterosexuality. *British Journal of Social Psychology, 42,* 113–127.

Jackson, S. M., Cram, F., & Seymour, F. W. (2000). Violence and sexual coercion in high school students' dating relationships. *Journal of Family Violence, 15,* 23–36.

Jacobs, J. E., Finken, L. L., Griffen, N. L., Lindsley, J. A., & Wright, J. D. (1998). The career plans of science talented rural adolescent girls. *American Educational Research Journal, 35,* 681–704.

Jacobs, J. F., & Potenza, M. T. (1991). The use of judgment heuristics to make social and object decisions: A developmental perspective. *Child Development, 62,* 166–178.

Jacobson, C. M., & Gould, M. (2007). The epidemiology and phenomenology of non-suicidal self-injurious behavior among adolescents: A literature review. *Archives of Suicide Research, 11,* 129–147.

Jacobson, K. C., & Crockett, L. J. (2000). Parental monitoring and adolescent adjustment: An ecological perspective. *Journal of Research on Adolescence, 10,* 65–97.

Jaffee, S., & Hyde, J. S. (2000). Gender differences in moral orientation: A meta-analysis. *Psychological Bulletin, 126,* 703–726.

Jankauskiene, R., Kardelis, K., Sukys, S., & Kardeliene, L. (2008). Associations between school bullying and psychosocial factors. *Social Behavior and Personality, 36,* 145-162.

Janssen, D. F. (2007). First stirrings: Cultural notes on orgasm, ejaculation, and wet dreams. *Journal of Sex Research, 44,* 122–134.

Jarrell, A. (2000, April 2). The face of teenage sex grows younger. *New York Times.*

Jencks, C. (1994). *The homeless.* Cambridge, MA: Harvard University Press.

Jenkins, J. E., & Zunguze, S. T. (1998). The relationship of family structure to adolescent drug use, peer affiliation, and perception of peer acceptance of drug use. *Adolescence, 33,* 811–822.

Jensen, L. (1995, April). *The moral reasoning of orthodox and progressivist Indians and Americans.* Paper presented at the meeting of the Society for Research in Child Development, Indianapolis, IN.

Jensen, L. A., Arnett, J. J., Feldman, S. S., & Cauffman, E. (2002). It's wrong, but everybody does it: Academic dishonesty among high school and college students. *Contemporary Educational Psychology, 27,* 209–228.

Jensen, L. A., Arnett, J. J., Feldman, S. S., & Cauffman, E. (2004). The right to do wrong: Lying to parents among adolescents and emerging adults. *Journal of Youth and Adolescence, 33,* 101–112.

Joe, J., & Malach, R. (1992). Families with Native American roots. In E. Lynch & M. Hanson (Eds.), *Developing cross-cultural competence: A guide for working with young children and their families* (pp. 89–116). Baltimore: Brookes Publishing Co.

Johnsen, K. P., & Medley, M. L. (1978). Academic self-concept among Black high school seniors: An examination of perceived agreement with selected others. *Phylon, 39,* 264–274.

Johnson, C. L., & Flach, R. A. (1985). Family characteristics of 105 parents with bulimia. *American Journal of Psychiatry, 142,* 1321–1324.

Johnson, H., & Durrell, T. (2004). Gender, grade, and relationship differences in emotional closeness within adolescent friendships. *Adolescence, 39,* 243–255.

Johnson, J. D., Adams, M. S., Ashburn, L., & Reed, W. (1995). Differential gender effects of exposure to rap music on African American adolescents' acceptance of teen dating violence. *Sex Roles, 33,* 597–605.

Johnson, J. D., Jackson, L. E., & Gatto, L. (1995). Violent attitudes and deferred academic aspirations: Deleterious effects of exposure to rap music. *Basic and Applied Social Psychology, 16,* 27–41.

Johnson, J. D., Trawalter, S., & Dovidio, J. F. (2000). Converging interracial consequences of exposure to violent rap music on stereotypical attributions of Blacks. *Journal of Experimental Social Psychology, 36,* 233–251.

Johnson, J. G., Cohen, P., Kotler, L., Kasen, S., & Brook, J. S. (2002). Psychiatric disorders associated with risk for the development of eating disorders during adolescence and early adulthood. *Journal of Consulting and Clinical Psychology, 70,* 1119–1128.

Johnson, L., Bachman, J., & O'Malley, P. (1994). *Drug use rises among American teenagers.* News Release, Institute of Social Research, University of Michigan, Ann Arbor.

Johnson, L. D., O'Malley, P. M., Bachman, J. G., & Schulenberg, J. E. (2008a). *Demographic subgroup trends for various licit and illicit drugs, 1975–2007* (Monitoring the Future Occasional Paper No, 69). Ann Arbor, MI: Institute for Social Research.

Johnson, L. D., O'Malley, P. M., Bachman, J. G., & Schulenberg, J. E. (2008b). *Monitoring the Future national survey results on drug use, 1975–2007: Volume I, Secondary school students* (NIH Publication No. 08-6418a). Bethesda, MD: National Institute on Drug Abuse.

Johnson, L. D., O'Malley, P. M., Bachman, J. G., & Schulenberg, J. E. (2008c). *Monitoring the Future national survey results on drug use, 1975–2007: Volume II: College students and adults ages 19–45* (NIH Publication No. 08-6418b). Bethesda, MD: National Institute on Drug Abuse.

Johnson, L. D., O'Malley, P. M., Bachman, J. G., & Schulenberg, J. E. (2009). *Monitoring the Future national results on adolescent drug use: Overview of key findings, 2009* (NIH Publication No. 09-7401). Bethesda, MD: National Institute on Drug Abuse.

Johnson, M. K., Beebe, T., Mortimer, J. T., & Snyder, M. (1998). Volunteerism in adolescence: A process perspective. *Journal of Research on Adolescence, 8,* 309–332.

Jolliffe, D. (2004). Extent of overweight among U.S. children and adolescents from 1971 to 2000. *International Journal of Obesity and Related Metabolic Disorders, 28,* 4–9.

Jones, D. C., & Crawford, K. (2005). Adolescent boys and body image: Weight and muscularity concerns as dual pathways to body dissatisfaction. *Journal of Youth and Adolescence, 34,* 629–636.

Jones, R. K., Darroch, J. E., & Henshaw, S. K. (2002). Patterns in the socioeconomic characteristics of women obtaining abortions in 2000–2001. *Perspectives on Sexual and Reproductive Health, 34,* 226–235.

Jorm, A. F., Christensen, H., Rogers, B., Jacomb, P. A., & Easteal, S. (2004). Association of adverse childhood experiences, age of menarche and adult reproductive behavior: Does the androgen receptor gene play a role?

American Journal of Medical Genetics Part B: Neuropsychiatric Genetics, 125, 105–111.

Joseph, H., Stancliff, S., & Langrod, J. (2000). Methadone maintenance treatment (MMT): A review of historical and clinical issues. *Mt. Sinai Journal of Medicine, 67,* 347–364.

Josephson Institute of Ethics. (2002). *The Six Pillars of Character.* Retrieved from http://www.josephsoninstitute.org/MED/MED-2sixpillars.htm.

Joyner, K., & Udry, J. R. (2000). You don't bring me anything but down: Adolescent romance and depression. *Journal of Health and Social Behavior, 41,* 369–391.

Jozefowicz, D. M., Barber, B. L., & Mollasis, C. (April, 1994). *Relations between maternal and adolescent values and beliefs: Sex differences and implications for vocational choice.* Paper presented at the meeting of the Society for Research on Adolescence, San Diego, CA.

Juffer, F., & van IJzendoorn, M. H. (2005). Behavior problems and mental health referrals of international adoptees: A meta-analysis. *Journal of the American Medical Association, 293,* 2501–2515.

Juffer, F., & van IJzendoorn, M. H. (2007). Adoptees do not lack self-esteem: A meta-analysis of studies on self-esteem of transracial, international, and domestic adoptees. *Psychological Bulletin, 133,* 1067–1083.

Juvenon, J., Le, V. N., Kaganoff, T., Augustine, C., & Constantine, L. (2004). *Focus on the wonder years: Challenges facing the American middle school.* Santa Monica, CA: The Rand Corporation.

Kacerguis, M. A., & Adams, G. R. (1980). Erikson stage resolution: The relationship between identity and intimacy. *Journal of Youth and Adolescence, 9,* 117–126.

Kaczmarek,n M. G., & Backlund, V. A. (1991). Disenfranchised grief: The loss of an adolescent romantic relationship. *Adolescence, 26,* 253–259.

Kahneman, D., & Tversky, A. (1973). On the psychology of prediction. *Psychological Review, 80,* 237–251.

Kail, R. (1991). Developmental change in speed of processing during childhood and adolescence. *Psychological Bulletin, 109,* 490–501.

Kail, R. (1997). The neural noise hypothesis: Evidence from processing speed in adults with multiple sclerosis. *Aging, Neuropsychology, and Cognition, 4,* 157–165.

Kail, R. (2000). Speed of information processing: Developmental change and links to intelligence. *Journal of School Psychology, 38,* 51–61.

Kaiser Family Foundation. (1998). *National survey of teens: Teens talk about dating, intimacy, and their sexual experiences.* Publication No. 1373. Retrieved from http://www.kff.org/youthhivstds/1373-datingrep.cfm.

Kaiser Family Foundation. (2000). *Safer sex, condoms, and "the pill": A series of national surveys of teens about sex.* Menlo Park, CA: Author.

Kaiser Family Foundation. (2004). *Sex education in America.* Washington, DC: Author.

Kalman, M. B. (2003). Adolescent girls, single-parent fathers, and menarche. *Holistic Nurse Practitioner, 17,* 36–40.

Kamp Dush, C. M., & Amato, R. (2005). Consequences of relationship status and quality for subjective well-being. *Journal of Social and Personal Relationships, 22*(5), 607–627.

Kamphuis, J. H., Ruyling, S. B., & Reijntjes, A. H. (2007). Testing the emotion regulation hypothesis among self-injuring females: Evidence for differences across mood states. *Journal of Nervous and Mental Disease, 195,* 912–918.

Kanazawa, S. (2001). Why father absence might precipitate early menarche: The role of polygyny. *Evolution and Human Behavior, 22,* 329–334.

Kandakai, T. L., Price, J. H., Teejohann, S. K., & Wilson, C. A. (1999). Mothers' perceptions of factors influencing violence in schools. *Journal of School Health, 69,* 189–195.

Kandel, D. B., Johnson, J. G., Bird, H. R., Canino, G., Goodman, S. H., Lahey, B. B., Regier, D. A., & Schwab-Stone, M. (1997). Psychiatric disorders associated with substance use among children and adolescents: Findings from the Methods for the Epidemiology of Child and Adolescent Mental Disorders (MECA) study. *Journal of Abnormal Child Psychology, 25,* 121–132.

Kaplan, H. B. (1980). Deviant behavior and self-enhancement in adolescence. *Journal of Youth and Adolescence, 7,* 253–277.

Kaplan, J. (2005). The effectiveness of SAT coaching on math SAT scores. *Chance, 18,* 25–34.

Kaplan, A., & Maehr, L. (1999). Enhancing the motivation of African American students: An achievement goal theory perspective. *Journal of Negro Education, 68,* 23–41.

Kaplowitz, P. B., Slora, E. J., Wasserman, R. C., Pedlow, S. E., & Herman-Giddens, M. E. (2001). Earlier onset of puberty in girls: Relation to increased body mass index and race. *Pediatrics, 108,* 347–353.

Karatzias, A., Power, K. G., & Swanson, V. (2002). Bullying and victimization in Scottish secondary schools: Same or separate entities? *Aggressive Behavior, 28,* 45–61.

Kaskutas, L. A. (2000). Understanding drinking during pregnancy among urban American Indians and African Americans: Health messages, risk beliefs, and how we measure consumption. *Alcoholism: Clinical and Experimental Research, 24,* 1241–1250.

Katchadourian, H. (1977). *The biology of adolescence.* San Francisco: W. H. Freeman.

Katz, J. E., & Rice, R. E. (2002). *Social consequences of Internet use: Access, involvement, and interaction.* Cambridge, MA: MIT Press.

Katz, J. E., & Sugiyama, S. (2006). Mobile phones as fashion statements: Evidence from student surveys in the U.S. and Japan. *New Media & Society, 8,* 321–337.

Katzer, C., Fetchenhauer, D., & Belschak, F. (2009). Cyberbullying: Who are the victims?: A comparison of victimization in Internet chatrooms and victimization in school. *Journal of Media Psychology: Theories, Methods, and Applications, 21*, 25–36.

Katzmarzyk, P. T., Tremblay, A., Pérusse, L., Després, J. P., & Bouchard, C. (2003). The utility of the child and adolescent overweight guidelines for predicting coronary heart disease risk factors. *Journal of Clinical Epidemiology, 56*, 456–462.

Kaufman, A. S., & Lichtenberger, E. O. (2002). *Assessing adolescent and adult intelligence* (2nd ed.). Boston: Allyn & Bacon.

Kaufmann, D., Gesten, E., & Santa Lucia, R. C. (2000). The relationship between children's adjustment and parenting style: The parents' perspective. *Journal of Child and Family Studies, 9*, 231–245.

Keating, D. (2004). Cognitive and brain development. In R. Lerner & L. Steinberg (Eds.), *Handbook of adolescent psychology* (pp. 45–84). Chichester, England: Wiley.

Keefe, K., & Berndt, T. J. (1996). Relations of friendship quality to self-esteem in early adolescence. *Journal of Early Adolescence, 16*, 110–129.

Kelley, S. S., Borawski, E. A., Flocke, S. A., & Keen, K. J. (2003). The role of sequential and concurrent sexual relationships in the risk of sexually transmitted diseases among adolescents. *Journal of Adolescent Health, 32*, 296–305.

Kelly, J. (2003). Changing perspectives on children's adjustment following divorce: A view from the United States. *Childhood, 10*, 237–254.

Kendler, K. S., Sheth, K., Gardner, C. O., & Prescott, C. A. (2002). Childhood parental loss and risk for first-onset of major depression and alcohol dependence: The time-decay of risk and sex differences. *Psychological Medicine, 32*, 1187–1194.

Keniston, K. (1971). Youth: A new stage of life. *American Scholar, 39*, 4.

Keniston, K. The tasks of adolescence. In *Developmental psychology today*. Del Mar, CA: CRM Books.

Kennedy, A. C. (2007). Homelessness, violence exposure, and school participation among urban adolescent mothers. *Journal of Community Psychology, 35*, 639–654.

Kennedy, S. H., Kaplan, A. S., Garfinkel, P. E., Rockert, W., Toner, B., & Abbey, S. E. (1994). Depression in anorexia nervosa and bulimia nervosa: Discriminating depressive symptoms and episodes. *Journal of Psychosomatic Research, 38*, 773–782.

Kerber, C. S. (2005). Problem and pathological gambling among college athletes. *Annals of Clinical Psychiatry, 17*, 243–247.

Kerckhoff, A. C. (2002). The transition from school to work. In J. T. Mortimer & R. W. Larson (Eds.), *The changing adolescent experience: Societal trends and the transition to adulthood* (pp. 52–87). Cambridge, England: Cambridge University Press.

Kerpelman, J. L., Pittman, J. F., & Lamke, L. K. (1997). Toward a microprocess perspective on adolescent identity development: An identity control theory approach. *Journal of Adolescent Research, 12*, 325–346.

Kerr, M., Stattin, H., & Trost, K. (1999). To know you is to trust you: Parents' trust is rooted in child disclosure of information. *Journal of Adolescence, 22*, 737–752.

Keshna, R. (1980). Relevancy of tribal interests and tribal diversity in determining the educational needs of American Indians. In *Conference on the education and occupational needs of American Indian work*. Washington, DC: U.S. Department of Education, National Institute of Education.

Keski-Rahkonen, A., Viken, R. J., Kapiro, J., Rissanen, A., & Rose, R. J. (2004). Genetic and environmental factors in breakfast eating patterns. *Behavior Genetics, 90*, 503–514.

Ketterson, T. U., & Blustein, D. L. (1997). Attachment relationships and the career exploration process. *Career Development Quarterly, 46*, 167–177.

Kibler, W. L. (1993). Academic dishonesty: A student development perspective. *NASPA Journal, 30*, 252–267.

Kidd, S. A. (2003). Street youth: Coping and interventions. *Child & Adolescent Social Work Journal, 20*, 235–261.

Kidwell, J. S., Dunham R. M., Bacho, R. A., Pastorino, E., & Portes, P. R. (1995). Adolescent identity exploration: A test of Erikson's theory of transitional crisis. *Adolescence, 30*, 785–793.

Killen, M., Lee-Kim, J., McGlothlin, H., & Stangor, C. (2002). How children and adolescents evaluate gender and racial exclusion. *Monograph of the Society for Research in Child Development, 67*(4), 118.

Kim, J., McHale, S. M., Osgood, D. W., & Crouter, A. C. (2006). Longitudinal course and family correlates of sibling relationships from childhood through adolescence. *Child Development, 77*, 1746–1761.

Kim, B. S. K., Yang, P. H., Atkinson, D. R., Wolfe, M. M., & Hong, S. (2001). Cultural value similarities and differences among Asian American ethnic groups. *Cultural Diversity and Ethnic Minority Psychology, 7*, 343–361.

Kim, J. L., & Ward, L. M. (2007). Silence speaks volumes. *Journal of Adolescent Research, 22*, 3–31.

Kim, K. G., Conger, R. D., & Lorenz, F. O. (2001). Parent-adolescent reciprocity in negative affect and its relation to early adult social development. *Developmental Psychology, 37*, 775–790.

Kim-Cohen, J., Moffett, T. E., Caspi, A., & Taylor, A. (2004). Genetic and environmental processes in young children's resilience and vulnerability to socioeconomic deprivation. *Child Development, 75*, 651–668.

King, A., Staffieri, A., & Adelgais, A. (1998). Mutual peer tutoring: Effects of structuring tutorial interaction to scaffold peer learning. *Journal of Educational Psychology, 90,* 134–152.

King, M. L., Jr. (1964). *Why we can't wait.* New York: Harper and Row.

King, P. E. (2008). Spirituality as fertile ground for positive youth development. In R. M. Lerner, R. W. Roesner, & E. Phelps (Eds.), *Positive youth development and spirituality: From theory to research* (pp. 55–73). West Conshohocken, PA: Templeton Foundation Press.

King, P. E., & Furrow, J. L. (2004). Religion as a resource for positive youth development: Religion, social capital, and moral outcomes. *Developmental Psychology, 40,* 703–713.

King, P. M., Kitchener, K. S., Davidson, M. L., Parker, C. A., & Wood, P. K. (1983). The justification of beliefs in young adults: A longitudinal study. *Human Development, 26,* 106–118.

King, R. A., Schwab-Stone, M., Flisher, A. J., Greenwald, S., Kramer, R. A., Goodman, S. H., Lahey, B. B., Shaffer, D., & Gould, M. S. (2001). Psychosocial and risk behavior correlates of youth suicide attempts and suicidal ideation. *Journal of the American Academy of Child & Adolescent Psychiatry, 40,* 837–846.

King, V., Elder, G. H., Jr., & Whitbeck, L. B. (1997). Religious involvement among rural youth: An ecological and life-course perspective. *Journal of Research on Adolescence, 7,* 431–456.

King, V., Harris, K. M., & Heard, H. E. (2004). Racial and ethnic diversity in nonresident father involvement. *Journal of Marriage and Family, 66,* 1–21.

King, V., & Sobolewski, M. (2006). Nonresident fathers' contributions to adolescent well-being. *Journal of Marriage and Family, 68,* 537–557.

Kingston, S., & Raghavan, C. (2009). The relationship of sexual abuse, early initiation of substance use, and adolescent trauma to PTSD. *Journal of Traumatic Stress, 22,* 65–68.

Kinsey, A., Pomeroy, W., & Martin, C. (1948). *Sexual behavior in the human male.* Philadelphia: Saunders.

Kinze, J. D., Frederickson, R. H., Ben, R., Fleck, J., & Karls, W. (1984). Post-traumatic stress disorder among survivors of Cambodian concentration camps. *American Journal of Psychiatry, 141,* 645–650.

Kipke, M. D., O'Connor, S., Palmer, R. F., & MacKenzie, R. G. (1995). Street youth in Los Angeles: Profile of a group at high risk for HIV. *Archives of Pediatric and Adolescent Medicine, 149,* 513–519.

Kipke, M. D., Palmer, R. F., LaFrance, S., & O'Connor, S. (1997). Homeless youths' descriptions of their parents' child-rearing practices. *Youth and Society, 28,* 415–431.

Kirkcaldy, B., Richardson-Vejlgaard, R., & Siefen, G. (2009). Birth order: Self-injurious and suicidal behavior among adolescents. *Psychology, Health & Medicine, 14,* 9–16.

Kirkcaldy, B. D., Shephard, R. J., & Siefen, R. G. (2002). The relationship between physical activity and self-image and problem behavior among adolescents. *Social Psychiatry and Psychiatric Epidemiology, 37,* 544–550.

Kirschner, D. (1996). Adoption psychopathology and the "adopted child syndrome." In *The Hatherleigh guide to child and adolescent therapy* (pp. 103–123). New York: Hatherleigh Press.

Kirsh, S. J. (2006). *Children, adolescents, and media violence: A critical look at the research.* Thousand Oaks, CA: Sage.

Klaczynski, P. A. (2001). The influence of analytic and heuristic processing on adolescent reasoning and decision making. *Child Development, 72,* 844–861.

Klaczynski, P., & Cottrell, J. (2004). A dual-process approach to cognitive development: The case of children's understanding of sunk-cost decisions. *Thinking and Reasoning, 10,* 147–174.

Klaczynski, P. A., & Gordon, D. H. (1996). Self-serving influences on adolescents' evaluations of belief-relevant evidence. *Journal of Experimental Child Psychology, 62,* 317–339.

Klacznski, P. A., & Narasimhan, G. (1998). Representations as mediators of adolescent deductive reasoning. *Developmental Psychology, 34,* 865–881.

Klacznski, P. A., Schuneman, M., & Daniel D. (2004). Development of conditional reasoning: A test of competing theories. *Developmental Psychology, 40,* 559–571.

Klahr, D. (2000). *Exploring science: The cognition and development of discovery processes.* Cambridge, MA: MIT Press.

Kline, G. H., Stanley, S. M., Markman, H. J., Olmos-Gallo, P. A., St. Peters, M., Whitton, S. W., et al. (2004). Timing is everything: Pre-engagement at cohabitation and increased risk for poor marital outcomes. *Journal of Famiy Psychology, 18,* 311–318.

Knapp, M., & Shields, P. (1990). Recovering academic instruction for the children of poverty. *Phi Delta Kappan, 71,* 753–758.

Kochenderfer, B. J., & Ladd, G. W. (1997). Victimized children's responses to peers' aggression: Behaviors associated with reduced versus continued victimization. *Developmental Psychopathology, 9,* 59–73.

Koenig, L. J., & Abrams, R. F. (1999). Adolescent loneliness and adjustment—A focus on gender differences. In K. J. Rotenberg & S. Hymel (Eds.), *Loneliness in childhood and adolescence* (pp. 296–322). Cambridge, England: Cambridge University Press.

Koerner, S. S., Rankin, L. A., Kenyon, D. B., & Korn, M. (2004). Mother-repartnering after divorce: Diverging perceptions of mothers and adolescents. *Journal of Divorce & Remarriage, 41,* 25–38.

Koff, E., & Rierdan, J. (1995). Preparing girls for menstruation: Recommendations from adolescent girls. *Adolescence, 30,* 795–811.

Kohlberg, L. (1963). The development of children's orientations toward a moral order. *Vita Humana, 6,* 11–33.

Kohlberg, L. (1969). *Stages in the development of moral thought and action.* New York: Holt, Rinehart and Winston.

Kohlberg, L. (1970). Moral development and the education of adolescents. In R. F. Purnell (Ed.), *Adolescents and the American high school* (pp. 56–87). New York: Holt, Rinehart and Winston.

Kohlberg, L. (1994). *Moral reasoning in adolescence.* Boston: Allyn & Bacon.

Kohlberg, L., & Gilligan, C. (Fall, 1971). The adolescent as a philosopher: The discovery of the self in a post-conventional world. *Daedalus,* 1051–1086.

Kohlberg, L., & Kramer, R. (1969). Continuities and discontinuities in childhood and adult development. *Human Development, 12,* 93–120.

Kohlberg, L., & Turiel, E. (Eds.). (1972). *Recent research in moral development.* New York: Holt, Rinehart and Winston.

Kohler, P. K., Manhart, L. E., & Lafferty, W. E. (2008). Abstinence-only and comprehensive sex education and the initiation of sexual activity and teen pregnancy. *Journal of Adolescent Health, 42,* 344–351.

Konig, A. (2008). Which clothes suit me?: The presentation of the juvenile self. *Childhood, 15,* 225–237.

Koopmans, M. (1995). A case of family dysfunction and teenage suicide attempt: Applicability of a family system's paradigm. *Adolescence, 30,* 87–94.

Kopera-Frye, K., & Wiscott, R. (2000). Intergenerational continuity: Transmission of beliefs and culture. In B. Hayslip Jr. & R. Goldberg-Glen (Eds.), *Grandparents raising grandchildren: Theoretical, empirical, and clinical perspectives* (pp. 65–84). New York: Springer-Verlag.

Kostanski, M., & Gullone, E. (1998). Adolescent body image dissatisfaction: Relationships with self-esteem, anxiety, and depression controlling for body mass. *Journal of Child Psychiatry, 39,* 255–262.

Kracke, B. (2002). The role of personality, parents and peers in adolescents' career exploration. *Journal of Adolescence, 25,* 19–30.

Kracke, B., & Schmitt-Rodermund, E. (2001). Adolescents' career exploration in the context of educational and occupational transitions. In J. E. Nurmi (Ed.), *Navigating through adolescence: European perspectives* (pp. 137–161). New York: Garland.

Krcmar, M., & Hight, A. (2007). The development of aggressive mental models in young children. *Media Psychology, 10,* 250–269.

Kreider, R. M. (2008). *Living arrangements of children: 2004.* Current Population Reports, P70-114. Washington, DC: U.S. Bureau of the Census.

Kreider, R. M., & Fields, J. M. (2002). Number, timing, and duration of marriages and divorces: 1996. *Current Population Reports,* P70–80. Washington, DC: U.S. Bureau of the Census.

Krettenauer, T. (2004). Metaethical cognition and epistemic reasoning development in adolescence. *International Journal of Behavioral Development, 28,* 461–470.

Kroger, J. (1990). Ego structuralization in late adolescence as seen through early memories and ego identity status. *Journal of Adolescence, 13,* 65–77.

Kroger, J. (1995). The differentiation of "firm" and "developmental" foreclosure identity statuses: A longitudinal study. *Journal of Adolescent Research, 10,* 317–337.

Kroger, J. (2003). Identity development during adolescence. In G. R. Adams & M. D. Berzonsky (Eds.), *The Blackwell handbook of adolescence* (pp. 205–226). Oxford, England: Blackwell Publishing.

Krohn, F. B., & Bogan, Z. (2001). The effects absent fathers have on female development and college attendance. *College Student Journal, 35,* 598–608.

Kubitschek, W. N., & Hallinan, M. T. (1996). Race, gender, and track inequity in track assignment. *Research in Sociology of Education, 11,* 121–146.

Kuhn, D. (1989). Children and adults as intuitive scientists. *Psychological Review, 96,* 674–689.

Kuhn, D. (2006). Do cognitive changes accompany development in the adolescent brain? *Perspectives on Psychological Science, 1,* 59–67.

Kuhn, D. (2009). Adolescent thinking. In R. M. Lerner & L. Steinberg (Eds.), *Handbook of adolescent psychology* (Vol. 1, 3rd ed., pp. 152–186). Hoboken, NJ: Wiley.

Kuhn, D., & Dean, D. (2004). Connecting scientific reasoning and causal inference. *Journal of Cognition & Development, 5,* 261–288.

Kuhn, D., & Dean, D. (2005). Is developing scientific thinking all about learning to control variables? *Psychological Science, 16,* 866–870.

Kuhn, D., Katz, J., & Dean, D. (2004). Developing reason. *Thinking & Reasoning, 10,* 197–219.

Kuhn, D., Langer, J., Kohlberg, L., & Haan, N. S. (1977). The development of formal operations in logical and moral judgment. *Genetic Psychology Monographs, 95,* 97–188.

Kuhn, D., & Pease, M. (2006). Do children and adults learn differently? *Journal of Cognition and Development, 7,* 279–293.

Kunkel, D., Keren, E., Finnety, K., Biely, E., & Donnerstein, E. (2005). *Sex on TV: 2005.* Menlo Park, CA: Kaiser Family Foundation.

Kuperminc, G. P., Allen, J. P., & Arthur, M. W. (1996). Autonomy, relatedness, and male adolescent delinquency. *Journal of Adolescent Research, 11,* 397–420.

Kuttler, A. F., & La Greca, A. M. (2004). Linkages among adolescent girls' romantic relationships, best friendships, and peer networks. *Journal of Adolescence, 27,* 395–414.

La Torre, G., Chiaradia, G., & Ricciardi, G. (2005). School-based smoking prevention in children and adolescents: Review of the scientific literature. *Journal of Public Health, 13,* 285–290.

LaChance, M. J., Legault, F., & Bujold, N. (2000). Family structure, parent-child communication, and adolescent participation in family consumer tasks and decisions. *Family & Consumer Sciences Research Journal, 29,* 125–152.

LaFromboise, T. D., & Dixon, M. R. (2003). American Indian children and adolescents. In J. Taylor Gibbs & L. N. Huang (Eds.), *Children of color: Psychological interventions with culturally diverse youth* (2nd ed., pp. 45–90). San Francisco: Jossey-Bass.

Lachman, M. E., & Burack, O. R. (1993). Planning and control processes across the life span: An overview. *International Journal of Behavioral Development, 16,* 131–143.

LaFontana, K. M., & Cillessen, K. H. N. (2002). Children's perceptions of popular and unpopular peers: A multimethod assessment. *Developmental Psychology, 38,* 635–647.

LaFromboise, T. D., & Dixon, M. R. (2003). American Indian children and adolescents. In J. T. Gibbs & L. H. Huang (Eds.), *Children of color: Psychological interventions with culturally diverse youth* (pp. 45–90). San Francisco: Jossey-Bass.

Lahey, B. B., Van Hulle, C. A., Waldman, I. D., Rodgers, J. L., D'Onofrio, B. M., Pedlow, S., et al. (2006). Testing descriptive hypotheses regarding sex differences in the development of conduct problems and delinquency. *Journal of Abnormal Child Psychology, 34,* 737–755.

Laird, R. (2005). What is it we think we are trying to fix and how should we fix it? A view from the admissions office. In W. J. Camara & E. W. Kimmel (Eds.), *Choosing students: Higher education admissions tools for the 21st century* (pp. 13–32). Mahwah, NJ: Erlbaum.

Lam, C-M. (2003). Covert parental control: Parent-adolescent interaction and adolescent development in a Chinese context. *International Journal of Adolescent Medicine & Health, 15,* 63–77.

Lambert, T. A., Kahn, A. S., & Apple, K. J. (2003). Pluralistic ignorance and hooking up. *Journal of Sex Research, 40,* 129–133.

Land, S. M. (2000). Cognitive requirements for learning with open-ended learning environments. *Educational Technology: Research and Development, 48,* 61–78.

Landry, B. (2000). *Black working wives.* Berkeley: University of California Press.

Landry, D. J., & Camelo, T. M. (1994). Young unmarried men and women discuss men's role in contraceptive practice. *Family Planning Perspectives, 26,* 222–227.

Landsheer, H., Maasen, G. H., Bisschop, P., & Adema, L. (1998). Can higher grades result in fewer friends? A reexamination of the relation between academic and social competence. *Adolescence, 33,* 185–191.

Lanza, S. T., & Collins, M. (2002). Pubertal timing and the onset of substance use in females during early adolescence. *Prevention Science, 3,* 69–82.

Larson, J. H., & Lowe, W. (1990). Family cohesion and personal space in families with adolescents. *Journal of Family Issues, 11,* 101–108.

Larson, J. H., Peterson, D. J., Heath, V. A., & Birch, P. (2000). The relationship between perceived dysfunctional family-of-origin rules and intimacy in young adult dating relationships. *Journal of Sex and Marital Therapy, 26,* 161–175.

Larson, N. C., Hussey, J. M., Gilmore, J. R., & Gilchrist, L. D. (1996). What about dad? Fathers of children born to school mothers. *Families in Society ,77,* 279–289.

Larson, R. W., & Verma, S. (1999). How children and adolescents spend time across the world: Work, play, and developmental opportunities. *Psychological Bulletin, 125,* 701–736.

Larson, R., Csikszentmihalyi, M., & Graef, R. (1982). Time alone in daily experience: Loneliness or renewal? In L. A. Peplau & D. Perlman (Eds.), *Loneliness: A sourcebook of current theory, research and therapy* (pp. 40–53). New York: Wiley.

Lask, B., Waugh, R., & Gordo, I. (1997). Childhood-onset anorexia nervosa is a serious illness. *Annals of the New York Academy of Sciences, 817,* 120–126.

Lau, M., Markham, C., Lin, H., Flores, G., & Chacko, M. R. (2009). Dating and sexual attitudes in Asian-American adolescents. *Journal of Adolescent Research, 24,* 91–113.

Laumann, E., Gagnon, J., Michael, R., & Michaels, S. (1994). *The social organization of sexuality: Sexual practices in the United States.* Chicago: University of Chicago Press.

Laursen, B. (1993). The perceived impact on conflict on adolescent relationships. *Merrill Palmer Quarterly, 39,* 535–550.

Laursen, B. (1995). Conflict and social interaction in adolescent relationships. *Journal of Research on Adolescence, 5,* 55–70.

Laursen, B., & Collins, W. A. (1994a). Interpersonal conflict during adolescence. *Psychological Bulletin, 115,* 197–209.

Laursen, B., & Collins, W. A. (1994b). Parent-child communication during adolescence. In A. Vangelisti (Ed.), *Handbook of family communication* (pp. 333–348). Mahwah, NJ: Erlbaum.

Laursen, B., & Collins, W. A. (2009). Parent-child relationships during adolescence. In R. M. Lerner & L. Steinberg (Eds.), *Handbook of adolescent psychology* (Vol. 2, 3rd ed., pp. 3–42). New York: Wiley.

Laursen, B., Coy, K. C., & Collins, W. C. (1998). Reconsidering changes in parent-child conflict across adolescence: A meta-analysis. *Child Development, 69,* 817–832.

Laursen, B., & Mooney, S. (2008). Relationship network quality: Adolescent adjustment and perceptions of relationships with parents and friends. *American Journal of Orthopsychiatry, 78*, 47–53.

Lee, P. A., & Houk, C. P. (2008). Disorders of sexual differentiation in the adolescent. *Annals of the New York Academy of Sciences, 1135*, 67–75.

Le Gall, A., Mullet, C., & Shafighi, R. (2002). Age, religious beliefs, and sexual attitudes. *Journal of Sex Research, 39*, 207–216.

Le Grange, D., & Lock, J. (2005). The dearth of psychological treatment studies for anorexia nervosa. *International Journal of Eating Disorders, 37*, 79–91.

Le Roux, J., & Smith C. S. (1998). Causes and characteristics of the street child phenomenon: *A global perspective. Adolescence, 33*, 683–688.

Leadbetter, D. J., Way, M., & Raben, A. (April, 1994). *Barriers to involvement of fathers of the children of adolescent mothers.* Paper presented at the meeting of the Society for Research on Adolescents, San Diego, CA.

Lease, A. M., Musgrove, K. T., & Axelrod, J. L. (2002). Dimensions of social status in preadolescent peer groups: Likability, perceived popularity, and social dominance. *Social Development, 11*, 508–533.

Lederman, L. C. (1993). Gender and the self. In L. P. Arliss & D. J. Borisoff (Eds.), *Women and men communicating* (pp. 139–162*).* Fort Worth, TX: Harcourt Brace Jovanovich.

Lee, J. C., & Staff, J. (2007). When work matters: The varying impact of adolescent work intensity on high school drop out. *Sociology of Education, 80*, 158–178.

Lee, J. D. (1998). Which kids can "become" scientists? Effects of gender, self-concepts, and perceptions of scientists. *Social Psychology Quarterly, 61*, 199–219.

Lee, M.-Y. (2002). A model of children's postdivorce behavioral adjustment in maternal- and dual-residence arrangements. *Journal of Family Issues, 23*, 672–697.

Lee, S. M., Daniels, M. H., & Kissinger, D. B. (2006). Parental influences on adolescent adjustment: Parenting styles versus parenting practices. *Family Therapy: Counseling and Therapy for Couples and Families, 14*, 253–259.

Lee, V. E., & Smith, J. (2001). *Restructuring high schools for equity and excellence: What works.* New York: Teachers College Press.

Lehman, E. B., Morath, R., Franklin, K., & Elbaz, V. (1998). Knowing what to remember and forget: A developmental study of cue memory in intentional forgetting. *Memory and Cognition, 26*, 860–868.

Lehr, C. A., Sinclair, M. F., & Christenson, S. L. (2004). Addressing student engagement and truancy prevention during the elementary school years: A replication study of the check & connect model. *Journal of Education for Students Placed At Risk, 9*, 279–301.

Leitenberg, H., Detzer, M. J., & Srebnik, D. (1993). Gender differences in the relation of masturbation experience in preadolescence and/or early adolescence to sexual behavior and adjustment in young adulthood. *Archives of Sexual Behavior, 22*, 87–98.

Lempers, J. D., & Clark-Lempers, D. G. (1992). Young, middle, and late adolescents' comparisons of the functional importance of five significant relationships. *Journal of Youth and Adolescence, 21*, 53–96.

Lenhart, A. (2009). *Teens and social media: An overview.* PEW Internet and American Life Project. Retrieved from http://www.pewinternet.org/Presentations/2009/17-Teens-and-Social-Media-An-Overview.aspx.

Lenhart, A., Madden, M., & Hitlin, P. (2005). Teens and technology. Washington, DC: Pew Internet and American Life Project.

Lenhart, A., Madden, M., MacGill, A. R., & Smith, A. (2007). *Teens and social media.* Washington, DC: Pew Internet and American Life Project.

Lent, R. W., Brown, S. D., & Hackett, G. (1994). Towards a unifying social cognitive theory of career and academic interest, choice, and performance. *Journal of Vocational Behavior, 45*, 79–122.

Lent, R. W., Brown, S. D., & Hackett, G. (2000). Contextual supports and barriers to career choice: A social cognitive analysis. *Journal of Counseling Psychology, 47*, 36–49.

Leong, F. T. L. (1991). Career development attributes and occupational values of Asian-American and White-American college students. *Career Development Quarterly, 39*, 221–230.

Leong, F. T. L., & Hayes, T. J. (1990). Occupational stereotyping of Asian Americans. *The Career Development Quarterly, 39*, 143–154.

Lerner, R. M., Delaney, M., Hess, L. E., Jovanovic, J., & et al, . (1990). Early adolescent physical attractiveness and academic competence. *Journal of Early Adolescence, 10*, 4–20.

Lerner, J. V., Phelps, E., Forman, Y., & Bowers, E. P. (2009). Positive youth development. In R. M. Lerner & L. Steinberg (Eds.), *Handbook of adolescent psychology* (Vol. 1, pp. 524–589). New York: Wiley.

Lerner, R. M., Lerner, J. V., Almerigi, J. B., Theokas, C., Phelps, E., Gestsdottir, et al. (2005). Positive youth development, participation in community development programs, and community contributions of fifth-grade adolescents: Finds from the first wave of the 4-H study of positive youth development. *Journal of Early Adolescence, 25*, 17–71.

Lerner, R. M., Lerner, J. V., Hess, L. E., Schwab, J., Jovanovic, J., Talwar, R., & Kucher, J. (1991). Physical attractiveness and psychosocial functioning among early adolescents. *Journal of Early Adolescence, 11*, 300–320.

Lester, B. M., & Dreher, M. (1989). Effects of marijuana use during pregnancy on newborn cry. *Child Development, 60*, 764–771.

Lester, D. (1991). Social correlates of youth suicide rates in the United States. *Adolescence, 26*, 55–58.

Lester, D. (2006). Sexual orientation and suicidal behavior. *Psychological Reports, 99*, 923–924.

Letendre, G. K. (2000). *Learning to be adolescent: Growing up in U.S. and Japanese middle schools.* New Haven, CT: Yale University Press.

Leung, S., A., Ivey, D., & Susuki, L. (1994. Factors affecting the career aspirations of Asian Americans. *Journal of Counseling and Development, 72,* 401–410.

LeVay, S. (1991). A difference in hypothalamic structure between heterosexual and homosexual men. *Science, 253,* 1034–1037.

Levenson, M. R., Aldwin, C. M., & D'Mello, M. (2005). Religious development from adolescence to middle adulthood. In R. F. Paloutzian & C. L. Park (Eds.), *The psychology of religion and spirituality* (pp. 144–161). New York: Guilford Press.

Leventhal, T., Dupéré, V., & Brooks-Gunn, J. (2009). Neighborhood influences on adolescent development. In R. M. Lerner & R. Steinberg (Eds.), *Handbook of adolescent psychology* (3rd ed., pp. 411–443). New York: Wiley.

Leventhal, T., Graber, J. A., & Brooks-Gunn, J. (2001). Adolescent transitions to adulthood: Antecedents, correlates, and consequences of adolescent employment. *Journal of Research on Adolescence, 11,* 297–323.

Levine, M., & Harrison, K. (2004). Media's role in the perpetuation and prevention of negative body image and disordered eating. In J. K. Thompson (Ed.), *Handbook of eating disorders and obesity* (pp. 695–717). New York: Wiley.

Lewin, K. (1939). Field theory and experiment in social psychology: Concepts and methods. *American Journal of Sociology, 44,* 868–897.

Lewinsohn, P. M., & Essau, C. A. (2002). Depression in adolescents. In I. Gotlib & C. Hammen (Eds.), *Handbook of depression* (pp. 541–559). New York: Guilford Press.

Lewis, R. E. (2004). Resilience: Individual, family, school, and community perspectives. In D. Capuzzi & D. Gross (Eds.), *Youth at risk: A prevention resource for counselors, teachers and parents* (pp. 35–68). Upper Saddle River, NJ: Pearson.

Leyendecker, B., Harwood, R. L., Comparini, L., & Yalcinkaya, A. (2005). Socioeconomic status, ethnicity, and parenting. In T. Luster & L. Okagaki (Eds.), *Parenting: An ecological perspective* (2nd ed., pp. 319–341). Mahwah, NJ: Erlbaum.

Li, Q. (2006). Cyberbullying: A research of gender differences. *School Psychology International, 27,* 157–170.

Li, S., Naveh-Benjamin, M., & Lindenberger, U. (2005). Aging neuromodulation impairs associative binding: A neurocomputational account. *Psychological Science, 16,* 445–450.

Lichter, D. T., & Qian, Z. (2008). Serial cohabitation and the marital life course. *Journal of Marriage and Family, 70,* 861–878.

Lidz, C. S. (2001). Multicultural issues and dynamic assessment. In L. A. Suzuki & J. G. Ponterotto (Eds.), *Handbook of multicultural assessment: Clinical, psychological, and educational applications* (2nd ed., pp. 523–539). San Francisco: Jossey-Bass.

Lieb, R., Merikangas, K. R., Hofler, M., Pfister, H., Isensee, B., & Wittchen, H.-U. (2002). Parental alcohol use disorders and alcohol use and disorders in offspring: A community study. *Psychological Medicine, 32,* 63–78.

Lindberg, L. D., Jones, R., & Santelli, J. S. (2008). Non-coital sexual activities among adolescents. *Journal of Adolescent Health, 43,* 231–238.

Lines, P. M. (2001). Homeschooling. *ERIC Digest, 151,* 1–7.

Linver, M. R., & Silverberg, S. B. (1995). Parenting as a multidimensional construct: Differential prediction of adolescents' sense of self and engagement in problem behavior. *International Journal of Adolescent Medicine and Health, 8,* 29–40.

Liskey-Fitzwater, M., Moore, C. L., & Gurel, L. M. (1993). Clothing importance and self-perception of female adolescents with and without scoliosis. *Clothing and Textiles Research Journal, 11,* 16–22.

Littrell, M. A., Damhorst, M. L., & Littrell, J. M. (1990). Clothing interests, body satisfaction, and eating behavior of adolescent females: Belated or independent dimensions? *Adolescence, 25,* 77–95.

Lochman, J. E., & Dodge, K. A. (1994). Social-cognitive processes of severely violent, moderately aggressive, and nonaggressive boys. *Journal of Counseling and Clinical Psychology, 62,* 366–374.

LoCicero, K. A., & Ashby, J. S. (2000). Mulitdimensional perfectionism in middle school age gifted students: A comparison to peers from the general cohort. *Roeper Review, 22,* 182–185.

Long, W., & Millsap, A. (2008). Fear of AIDS and Homophobia Scales in an ethnic population of university students. *Journal of Social Psychology, 148,* 637–640.

Lopez, G. E., Gurin, P., & Nagda, B. A. (1998). Education and understanding structural causes for group inequalities. *Political Psychology, 19,* 305–329.

Lopez, N. L., Bonenberger, J. L., & Schneider, H. G. (2001). Parental disciplinary history, current levels of empathy, and moral reasoning in young adults. *North American Journal of Psychology, 3,* 193–204.

Loughlin, C. A., & Barling, J. (1998). Teenagers' part-time employment and their work-related attitudes and aspirations. *Journal of Organizational Behavior, 19,* 197–207.

Lowenstein, L. (2006). Aspects of young sex abusers—A review of the literature concerning young sex abusers (1996–2004). *Clinical Psychology & Psychotherapy, 13,* 47–55.

Lucas, J. R., & Stone, L. (1994). Acculturation and competition among Mexican-Americans: A reconceptualization. *Hispanic Journal of Behavioral Sciences, 16,* 129–142.

Lucas, S. R., & Good, A. D. (2001). Race, class, and tournament track mobility. *Sociology of Education, 74,* 139–156.

Lussier, G., Deater-Deckard, K., Dunn, J., & Davies, L. (2002). Support across two generations: Children's closeness to parents following parental divorce and remarriage. *Journal of Family Psychology, 16,* 363–376.

Luyckx, K., Schwartz, S. J., Goossens, L., & Pollock, S. (2008). Employment, sense of coherence, and identity formation: Contextual and psychological processes on the pathway to sense of adulthood. *Journal of Adolescent Research, 23,* 566–591.

Lynam, D. R., Milich, R., Zimmerman, R., Novak, S. P., Logan, T. K., Martin C., Leukefeld, C., & Clayton, R. (1999). Project DARE: No effects at 10-year follow-up. *Journal of Consulting and Clinical Psychology, 67,* 590–593.

Lynch, W. C., Heil, D. P., Wagner, E., & Havens, M. (2007). Ethnic differences in BMI, weight concerns, and eating behaviors: Comparison of Native American, White, and Hispanic adolescents. *Body Image, 4,* 179–190.

Ma, H. K. (1989). Moral orientation and moral judgment in adolescents in Hong Kong, mainland China, and England. *Journal of Cross-Cultural Psychology, 20,* 152–177.

Maccoby, E. E., & Mnookin, R. H. (1992). *Dividing the child: Social and legal dilemmas of custody.* Cambridge, MA: Harvard University Press.

MacKay, A. P., Fingerhut, L. A., & Duran, C. R. (2000). *Adolescent health chartbook. Health, United States, 2000.* Hyattsville, MD: National Center for Health Statistics.

Madden, M., Fox, S., Smith, A., & Vitak, J. (2007). *Digital footprints: Online identity management and search in the age of transparency.* Washington, DC: Pew Internet and American Life Project.

Magazine Publishers of America. (2004). *Teen market profile.* New York: Author.

Maguin, E., & Loeber, R. (1996). Academic performance and delinquency. In M. Tonry (Ed.), *Crime and justice: A review of research* (pp. 145–264). Chicago: University of Chicago Press.

Mahon, N.E., Yarcheski, A., Yarcheski, T. J., Cannella, B. L., & Hanks, M. M. (2006). A meta-analytic study of predictors for loneliness during adolescence. *Nursing Research, 55,* 308–315.

Mahoney, J. L. (2000). School extracurricular activity participation as a moderator in the development of antisocial patterns. *Child Development, 71,* 502–516.

Mahoney, J. L., Cairns, B. D., & Farmer, T. W. (2003). Promoting interpersonal competence and educational success through extracurricular activity participation. *Journal of Educational Psychology, 95,* 409–418.

Mahoney, J. L., Schweder, A. E., & Stattin, H. (2002). Structured after-school activities as a moderator of depressed-mood for adolescents with detached relations to their parents. *Journal of Community Psychology, 30,* 69–86.

Malmberg, L. E. (2001). Future-orientation in educational and interpersonal contexts. In J. E. Nurmi (Ed.), *Navigating through adolescence: European perspectives* (pp. 119–140). New York: Routledge.

Mandara, J., Murray, C. B., & Joyner, T. N. (2005). The impact of fathers' absence on African American adolescents' gender role development. *Sex Roles, 53,* 207–220.

Manlove, J. (1998). The influence of high school dropout and school disengagement on the risk of school-age pregnancy. *Journal of Research on Adolescence, 8,* 187–220.

Manlove, J., Ikramullah, E., & Terry-Humen, E. (2008). Condom use and consistency among male adolescents in the United States. *Journal of Adolescent Health, 43,* 325–333.

Manning, W. D., Longmore, M. A., & Giordano, P. C. (2004). Adolescents' involvement in non-romantic sexual activity. *Social Science Research, 34,* 384–407.

Manning, W. D., Longmore, M. A., & Giordano, P. C. (2007). The changing institution of marriage: Adolescents' expectations to cohabit and to marry. *Journal of Marriage and Family, 69,* 559–575.

Mannion, A. F., & Dolan, P. (1994). EMG median frequency changes during isometric contraction of the back extensors to fatigue. *Spine, 19,* 1223–1229.

Marcia, J. E. (1966). Development and validation of ego identity status. *Journal of Personality and Social Psychology, 3,* 551–558.

Marcia, J. E. (1976). Identity six years after: A follow up study. *Journal of Youth and Adolescence, 5,* 145–160.

Marcia, J. E. (1991). Identity and self development. In R. M. Lerner, A. D. Petersen, & J. Brooks-Gunn (Eds.), *Encyclopedia of adolescence* (Vol. 1). New York: Garland.

Marcia, J. E. (1994). The empirical study of ego identity. In H. A. Bosma, T. L. G. Graafsma, H. D. Grotebanc, & D. J. DeLivita (Eds.), *Identity and development: An interdisciplinary approach* (pp. 98–116). Newbury Park, CA: Sage.

Marcus, M. D., & Kalarchian, M. A. (2003). Binge eating in children and adolescents. *International Journal of Eating Disorders, 34,* S47–S57.

Marcussen, K. (2005). Explaining differences in mental health between married and cohabiting individuals. *Social Psychology Quarterly, 68,* 239–257.

MarketResearch.com. (2005). By 2006, U.S. teens can buy and sell Russia. Press release. Retrieved from http://www.marketresearch.com/Corporate/aboutus/Press_view.asp?SID=54650555-228592314-249687041&Article=143.

Markiewicz, D., Doyle, A. B., & Bregden, M. (2001). The quality of adolescents' friendships: Associations with mothers' interpersonal relationships, attachment to parents and friends, and prosocial behaviors. *Journal of Adolescence, 24,* 429–445.

Marks, M. J., & Fraley, C. (2006). Confirmation bias and the sexual double standard. *Sex Roles, 54,* 19–26.

Markstrom-Adams, C. (1990). Coming-of-age among contemporary American Indians as portrayed in adolescent fiction. *Adolescence, 25,* 225–237.

Markus, H. R., & Kitayama, S. (1994). A collective fear of the collective: Implications for selves and theories of selves. *Personality and Social Psychology Bulletin, 20,* 568–579.

Marquart, B. S., Nannini, D. K., Edwards, R. W., Stanley, L. R., & Wayman, J. C. (2007). Prevalence of dating violence and victimization: Regional and gender differences. *Adolescence, 42,* 645–657.

Marsh, H. (1989). Age and sex effects in multiple dimensions of self-concept: Preadolescence to early adulthood. *Journal of Educational Psychology, 81,* 417–430.

Marsh, H. W., & Kleitman, S. (2003). School athletic participation: Mostly gain with little pain. *Journal of Sport & Exercise Psychology, 25,* 205–228.

Marsh, H. W., & Kleitman, S. (2005). Consequences of employment during high school: Character building, subversion of academic goals, or a threshold? *American Educational Research Journal, 42,* 331–369.

Martens, M. P., Page, J. C., Mowry, E. S., Damann, K. M., Taylor, K. K., & Cimini, M. D. (2006). Differences between actual and perceived student norms: An examination of alcohol use, drug use, and sexual behavior. *Journal of American College Health, 54,* 295–300.

Martin, C.L., & Fabes, R. A. (2001). The stability and consequences of young children's same sex peer interactions. *Developmental Psychology, 37,* 431–446.

Martin, C. L., Ruble D. N., & Szkrybalo, J. (2002). Cognitive theories of early gender development. *Psychological Bulletin, 128,* 903–933.

Martin, J. A., Hamilton, B. E., Sutton, P. D., Ventura, S. J., Menacker, F., Kimeyer, S., & Matthews, T. J. (2009). Births: Final data for 2006. *National Vital Statistics Reports, 57*(7). Hyattsville, MD: National Center for Health Statistics.

Martin, Q., Peters, R. J., Amos, C. E., Yacoubian, G. S., Johnson, R. G., Meshack, A., & Essien, E. J. (2005). The relationship between sexual abuse and drug use: A view of African-American college students in Texas. *Journal of Ethnicity in Substance Abuse, 4,* 23–33.

Martinez, A. J. C., Mosher, W. D., & Dawson, B. S. (2004). Teenagers in the United States: Sexual activity, contraceptive use, and child bearing, 2002. *Vital Health Statistic, 23.* Washington, DC: National Center for Health Statistics.

Martinez, E. A. (1988). Child behavior in American/Chicano families: Maternal teaching and child-rearing practices. *Family Relations, 37,* 275–280.

Martinez, M. E. (2000). *Education as the cultivation of intelligence.* Mahwah, NJ: Erlbaum.

Martino, S. C., Collins, R. L., Elliott, M. N., Strachman, A., Kanouse, D. E., & Berry, S. H. (2006). Exposure to degrading versus nondegrading music lyrics and sexual behavior among youth. *Pediatrics, 118,* 430–441.

Martyn-Nemeth, P., Penckofer, S., Gulanick, M., Velsor-Friedrich, B., & Bryant, F. B. (2009). The relationships among self-esteem, stress, coping, eating behavior, and depressive mood in adolescents. *Research in Nursing & Health, 32,* 96–109.

Mascie-Taylor, C. G. N., & Lasker, W. (2005). Biosocial correlates of stature in a British national cohort. *Journal of Biosocial Science, 37,* 245–251.

Maslow, A. (1943). A theory of human motivation. *Psychological Review, 50,* 370–396.

Masselam, V. S., Marcus, R. F., & Stunkard, C. L. (1990). Parent–adolescent communication, family functioning, and school performance. *Adolescence, 25,* 725–737.

Masters, W. H., & Johnson, V. (1966). *Human sexual response.* Boston: Little, Brown.

Mattis, J. S., Jagers, R. J., Hatcher, C. A., Lawhon, G. D., Murphy, E. J., & Murray, Y. F. (2000). Religiosity, volunteerism, and community involvement among African American men: An exploratory analysis. *Journal of Community Psychology, 28,* 391–406.

Matton, L., Duvigneaud, N., Wijndaele, K., Philippaerts, R., Duquet, W., Beunen, G., et al. (2007). Secular trends in anthropometric characteristics, physical fitness, physical activity, and biological maturation in Flemish adolescents between 1969 and 2005. *American Journal of Human Biology, 19,* 345–357.

Mau, R. Y. (1992). The validity and devolution of a concept: Student alienation. *Adolescence, 27,* 731–741.

Mau, W.-C., & Bikos, L. H. (2000). Educational and vocational aspirations of minority and female students: A longitudinal study. *Journal of Counseling and Development, 78,* 186–194.

Maurer, T. W., & Robinson, W. (2008). Effects of attire, alcohol, and gender on perceptions of date rape. *Sex Roles, 58,* 423–434.

Mazor, A., & Enright, R. D. (1988). The development of the individuation process from a social-cognitive perspective. *Journal of Adolescence, 11,* 29–47.

McAdams, D. P. (2001). The psychology of life stories. *Review of General Psychology, 5,* 100–122.

McCabe, D. L. (1999). Academic dishonesty among high school students. *Adolescence, 34,* 681–687.

McCabe, D. L., & Trevino, L. K. (1997). Individual and contextual influences on academic dishonesty: A multi-campus investigation. *Research in Higher Education, 38,* 379–396.

McCabe D. L., Trevino L. K., & Butterfield K. D. (2001). Cheating in academic institutions: A decade of research. *Ethics and Behavior, 11,* 219–232.

McCabe, M. P., & Ricciardelli, L. A. (2004). A longitudinal study of pubertal timing and extreme body change behaviors among adolescent boys and girls. *Adolescence, 39,* 145–166.

McCartt, A. T., Shabanova, V. I., & Leaf, W. A. (2003). Driving experience, crashes and traffic citations of teenage beginning drivers. *Accident Analysis and Prevention, 35,* 311–320.

McCurdy, S. J., & Scherman, E. (1996). Effects of family structure on the adolescent separation-individuation process. *Adolescence, 31,* 307–319.

McEvoy, M., Chang, J., & Coupey, S. M. (2004). Common menstrual disorders in adolescence: Nursing interventions. *MCN: The American Journal of Maternal/Child Nursing, 29,* 41–49.

McGaha, J. E., & Leoni, E. L. (1995). Family violence, abuse, and related family issues of incarcerated delinquents of alcoholic parents compared with those of nonalcoholic parents. *Adolescence, 30,* 473–482.

McGee, Z. T. (1992). Social class differences in parental and peer influence on adolescent drug use. *Deviant Behavior, 13,* 349–372.

McGrory, A. (1990). Menarche: Responses of early adolescent females. *Adolescence, 25,* 265–270.

McGue, M., Elkins, I., Walden, B., & Iacono, W. G. (2005). Perceptions of the parent-child relationship: A longitudinal investigation. *Developmental Psychology, 41,* 971–984.

McHale, S. M., Updegraff, K. A., Shanahan, L., & Killoren, S. E. (2005). Siblings' differential treatment in Mexican American families. *Journal of Marriage and Family, 67,* 1259–1274.

McIntosh, J., & Chisholm, R. (2008). Cautionary notes on the shared care of children in conflicted parental separation. *Journal of Family Studies, 14,* 37–52.

McKim, W. A. (1997). *Drugs and behavior: An introduction to behavioral pharmacology* (3rd ed.). Upper Saddle River, NJ: Prentice Hall.

McKinnon, J. D., & Bennett, C. E. (2005). *We the people: Blacks in the United States.* Census 2000 Special Reports. Washington DC: U.S. Bureau of the Census.

McLanahan, S. S. (1999). Father absence and the welfare of children. In E. M. Hetherington (Ed.), *Coping with divorce, single parenting, and remarriage: A risk and resiliency perspective* (pp. 117–145). Mahwah, NJ: Erlbaum.

McLanahan, S. S., & Sandefur, G. (1994). *Growing up with a single parent: What hurts, what helps.* Cambridge, MA: Harvard University Press.

McLoyd, V. C. (1990). Minority children: Introduction to the special issue. *Child Development, 61,* 260–263.

McLoyd, V. C. (1998). Socioeconomic disadvantage and child development. *American Psychologist, 53,* 185–204.

McLoyd, V. C., Kaplan, R., Purtell, K. M., Bagley, E., Hardaway, C. R., & Smalls, C. (2009). Poverty and socioeconomic disadvantage in adolescence. In R. M. Lerner & R. Steinberg (Eds.), *Handbook of adolescent psychology* (3rd ed., pp. 444–491). New York: Wiley.

McRoy, R. G., Grotevant, H. D., Ayers-Lopez, S., & Henney, S. (2007). Open adoptions: Longitudinal outcomes for the adoption triad. In R. A. Javier, A. L. Baden, R. A. Biafora, & A. Comacho-Gingerich (Eds.), *Handbook of adoption* (pp. 175–189) Thousand Oaks, CA: Sage.

McShane, D. (1988). An analysis of mental health research with American Indian youth. *Journal of Adolescence, 11,* 87–116.

McVey, G. L., Pepler, D., Davis, R., Flett, G. L., & Abdolell, M. (2002). Risk and protective factors associated with disordered eating during early adolescence. *Journal of Early Adolescence, 22,* 75–95.

Mead, M. (1950). *Coming of age in Samoa.* New York: New American Library.

Mead, M. (1970). *Culture and commitment: A study of the generation gap.* Garden City, NY: Doubleday.

Mead, M. (1974). Adolescence. In H. V. Kraemer (Ed.), *Youth and culture: A human development approach.* Monterey, CA: Brooks/Cole.

Medora, N., & Woodward, J. C. (1986). Loneliness among adolescent college students at a midwestern university. *Adolescence, 21,* 391–402.

Meer, J. (1986). Yours, mine, and divorce. *Psychology Today, 20,* 13.

Meer, J. (1985). Loneliness. *Psychology Today, 19,* 28–33.

Meeus, W., Iedama, M., Helsen, M., & Vollebergh, W. (1999). Patterns of adolescent identity development: Review of literature and longitudinal analysis. *Developmental Review, 19,* 419–461.

Meeus, W., Iedema, J. Maasem, G., & Engels, R. (2005). Separation-individuation revisited: On the interplay of parent-adolescent relations, identity and emotional adjustment in adolescence. *Journal of Adolescence, 28,* 89–106.

Melby, J. N., & Conger, R. D. (1996). Parental behaviors and adolescent academic performance: A longitudinal analysis. *Journal of Research on Adolescence, 6,* 113–137.

Melby, J. N., Conger, R. D., Conger, K. J., & Lorenz, F. O. (1993). Effects of parental behavior on tobacco use by young male adolescents. *Journal of Marriage and Family, 55,* 439–454.

Meneses, L. M., Orrell-Valente, J. K., Guendelman, S. R., Oman, D., & Irwin, C. E. (2006). Racial/ethnic differences in mother-daughter communication about sex. *Journal of Adolescent Health, 39,* 128–131.

Mercer, R. J. Merritt, S. L., & Cowell, J. M. (1998). Differences in reported sleep needs among adolescents. *Journal of Adolescent Health, 23,* 259–263.

Messersmith, E. E., Garrett, J. L., Davis-Kean, P. E., Malanchuk, O., & Eccles, J. S. (2008). Career development from adolescence through emerging adulthood. *Journal of Research on Adolescence, 23,* 206–227.

Metz, E., McLellan, J., & Youniss, J. (2003). Types of voluntary service and adolescents' civic development. *Journal of Adolescent Research, 18,* 188–203.

Meyer-Bahlburg, H., Dolezal, C., Baker, S., Ehrhardt, A., & New, M. (2006). Gender development in women with congenital adrenal hyperplasia as a function of disorder severity. *Archives of Sexual Behavior, 35,* 667–684.

Michaels, M. L. (2006). Factors that contribute to stepfamily success: A qualitative analysis. *Journal of Divorce & Remarriage, 44,* 53–66.

Middleton, M., & Midgley, C. (1997). Avoiding the demonstration of lack of ability: An underexplored aspect of goal theory. *Journal of Educational Psychology, 89,* 710–718.

Midgley, C., Feldlaufer, H., & Eccles, J. S. (1989). Student/teacher relations and attitudes toward mathematics before and after the transition to junior high school. *Child Development, 60,* 981–992.

Midgley, C., & Urdan, T. (1995). Predictors of middle school students' views of self-handicapping strategies. *Journal of Early Adolescence, 15,* 389–411.

Migration Policy Institute. (2007). Annual immigration to the United States: The real numbers. Retrieved from http://www.migrationpolicy.org/pubs/FS16_USImmigration_051807.pdf.

Mihalic, S. W., & Elliott, D. (1997). Short- and long-term consequences of adolescent work. *Youth and Society, 28,* 464–498.

Mikami, A. Y., Szwedo, D. E., Allen, J. P., Evans, M. A., & Hare, A. L. (2010). Adolescent peer relationships and behavior problems predict young adults' communication on social networking websites. *Developmental Psychology, 46,* 46–56.

Milevsky, A. (2004). Perceived parental marital satisfaction and divorce: Effects on sibling relations in emerging adults. *Journal of Divorce & Remarriage, 41,* 115–128.

Milhausen, R. R., & Herold, E. S. (1999). Does the sexual double standard still exist? Perceptions of university women. *Journal of Sex Research, 36,* 361–368.

Miller, B. C., Benson, B., & Galbraith, K. A. (2001). Family relationships and adolescent pregnancy risk: A research synthesis. *Developmental Review, 21,* 1–38.

Miller, B. C., Norton, M. C., Curtis, T., Hill, E. J., Schvanveldt, P., & Young, M. H. (1997). The timing of sexual intercourse among adolescents: Family, peer, and other antecedants. *Youth & Society, 29,* 54–83.

Miller, J. G. (1997). Culture and self: Uncovering the cultural grounding of psychological theory. In J. G. Snodgrass & R. Thompson (Eds.), *Annals of the New York Academy of Sciences, 18* (pp. 217–231). New York: New York Academy of Sciences.

Miller, K. E. (1990). Adolescents' same-sex and opposite-sex peer relations: Sex differences in popularity, perceived social competence, and social cognitive skills. *Journal of Adolescent Research, 5,* 222–241.

Miller, K. E., Sabo, D. F., Farrell, M. P., Barnes, G. M., & Melnick, M. J. (1998). Athletic participation and sexual behavior in adolescents: The different worlds of boys and girls. *Journal of Health and Social Behavior, 39,* 108–123.

Miller, K. E., Sabo, D. F., Farrell, M. P., Barnes, G. M., & Melnick, M. J. (1999). Sports, sexual behavior, contraceptive use, and pregnancy among female and male high school students: Testing cultural resource theory. *Sociology of Sport Journal, 16,* 366–387.

Miller, R. P., Cosgrove, J. M., & Doke, L. (1990). Motivating adolescents to reduce their fines in a token economy. *Adolescence, 25,* 97–104.

Miller-Johnson, S., Winn, D. M., Coie, J., Maumary-Gremaud, A., Hyman, C., Terry, R., & Lochman, J. (1999). Motherhood during the teenage years: A developmental perspective on risk factors for childbearing. *Development and Psychopathology, 11,* 85–100.

Mills, B., Reyna, V. F., & Estrada, S. (2008). Explaining contradictory relations between risk perception and risk taking. *Psychological Science, 19,* 429–433.

Mills, R. K. (1988). Using Tom and Huck to develop moral reasoning in adolescents: A strategy for the classroom. *Adolescence, 23,* 325–329.

Millstein, S. G., & Halpern-Felsher, B. L. (2002. Perceptions of risk and vulnerability. *Journal of Adolescent Health, 31,* 10–27.

Minkler, M., & Fuller-Thomson, E. (1999). The health of grandparents raising grandchildren: Results of a national study. *American Journal of Public Health, 89,* 1384–1389.

Mintz, L. B., & Kashubeck, S. (1999). Body-image and disordered eating among Asian American and Caucasian college students: An examination of race and gender differences. *Psychology of Women Quarterly, 23,* 781–796.

Misra, M. (2008, June). *Teenage athletes: Hormones, periods, and bone density.* Paper presented at the 30th annual meeting of the Endocrinology Society, San Francisco, CA.

Mitchell, C. E. (1988). Preparing for vocational choice. *Adolescence, 23,* 331–334.

Mitchell, J. E., Pyle, R. L., & Eckert, E. D. (1981). Frequency and duration of binge-eating episodes in patients with bulimia. *America Journal of Psychiatry, 138,* 835, 836.

Mitchell, K. J., Wolak, J., & Finkelhor, D. (2007). Trends in youth reports of sexual solicitations, harassment, and unwanted exposure to pornography on the Internet. *Journal of Adolescent Health, 40,* 116–126.

Molitor, F., & Hirsch, K. W. (1994). Children's toleration of real-life aggression after exposure to media violence: A replication of the Drabman and Thomas studies. *Child Studies Journal, 24,* 191–207.

Molnar, B. E., Shade, S. B., Kral, A. H., Booth, R. H., & Watters, J. K. (1999). Suicidal behavior and sexual/physical abuse among street youth. *Child Abuse and Neglect, 22,* 213–222.

Monroe, S. M., & Reid, W. (2008). Gene-environment interactions in depression research: Genetic polymorphisms and life-stress polyprocedures. *Psychological Science, 19,* 947–956.

Monsour, M. (2002). *Women and men as friends: Relationships across the lifespan in the 21st century.* Mahwah, NJ: Erlbaum.

Montemayor, R., & Flannery, D. J. (1991). Parent-adolescent relations in middle to late adolescence. In R. Lerner, A. Petersen, & J. Brooks-Gunn (Eds.), *Encyclopedia of adolescence* (pp. 729–734). New York: Garland.

Montepare, J. M., & Lachman, M. E. (1989). "You're only as old as you feel": Self-perceptions of age, fears of aging, and life satisfaction from adolescence to old age. *Psychology and Aging, 4,* 73–78.

Montgomery, M. J., & Coté, J. E. (2003). College as a transition to adulthood. In G. R. Adams & M. D. Berzonsky (Eds.), *The Blackwell handbook of adolescence* (pp. 149–172). Oxford, England: Blackwell Publishing.

Montgomery, M. J., & Sorell, G. T. (1998). Love and dating experience in early and middle adolescence: Grade and gender comparisons. *Journal of Adolescence, 21,* 677–689.

Mooney, K. S., Laursen, B., & Adams, R. E. (2006). Social support and positive development: Looking on the bright side of adolescent close relationships. In R. K. Silbereisen & R. M. Lerner (Eds.), *Approaches to positive youth development* (pp. 189–203). Thousand Oaks, CA: Sage.

Moore, J. W., Jensen, B., & Hauck, W. E. (1990). Decision-making processes of youth. *Adolescence, 25,* 583–592.

Moore, S., & Cartwright, C. (2005). Adolescents' and young adults' expectations of parental responsibilities in stepfamilies. *Journal of Divorce & Remarriage, 43,* 109–127.

Moran, P. B., Vuchinich, S., & Hall, N. K. (2004). Associations between types of maltreatment and substance use during adolescence. *Child Abuse & Neglect, 28,* 565–574.

Morano, C. D., Cisler, R. A., & Lemerond, J. (1993). Risk factors for adolescent suicidal behavior: Loss, insufficient family support, and hopelessness. *Adolescence, 28,* 851–865.

Moreno, J. K., Selby, M. J., Aved, K., & Besse, C. (2000). Differences in family dynamics among anorexic, bulimic, obese and normal women. *Journal of Psychotherapy in Independent Practice, 1,* 75–87.

Morgan, C., Isaac, J. D., & Sansone, C. (2001). The role of interest in understanding the career choices of female and male college students. *Sex Roles, 44,* 295–320.

Morisi, T. L. (2008). Youth enrollment and employment during the school year. *Monthly Labor Review,* 51–63.

Morris, B., & Sloutsky, V. (2002). Children's solutions to logical vs. empirical problems: What's missing and what develops? *Cognitive Development, 116,* 907–928.

Morrison, D. A., & Coiro, M. J. (1999). Parental conflict and marital disruption: Do children benefit when high conflict marriages are dissolved? *Journal of Marriage and Family, 61,* 626–637.

Morrison, L. L., & L'Heureux, J. (2001). Suicide and gay/lesbian/bisexual youth: Implications for clinicians. *Journal of Adolescence, 42,* 39–49.

Mortimer, J. (2003). *Working and growing up in America.* Cambridge, MA: Harvard University Press.

Mortimer, J. T., Pimentel, E. E., Ryu, S., Nash, K., & Lee, C. (1996). Part-time work and occupational value formation in adolescence. *Social Forces, 74,* 1405–1418.

Moser, M. R., Paternite, C. E., & Dixon, W. E., Jr. (1996). Late adolescents' feelings toward parents and siblings. *Merrill-Palmer Quarterly, 42,* 537–553.

Moses, E. (2000). *The $100 billion allowance: Accessing the global ten market.* New York: Wiley.

Mosher, W. D. (1990). Contraceptive practice in the United States, 1982–1988. *Family Planning Perspectives, 22,* 198–205.

Moshman, D. (1993). Adolescent reasoning and adolescent rights. *Human Development, 36,* 27–40.

Moshman, D. (1994). Reason, reasons, and reasoning: A constructivist account of human rationality. *Theory and Psychology, 4,* 245–260.

Moshman, D. (1997). Cognitive development beyond childhood. In W. Damon, D. Kuhn, & R. Siegler (Eds.), *Handbook of child psychology* (Vol. 2, pp. 947–978). New York: Wiley.

Moshman, D. (1999). *Adolescent psychological development: Rationality, morality, and identity.* Mahwah, NJ: Erlbaum.

Moshman, D., & Franks, B. F. (1986). Development of the concept of inferential validity. *Child Development, 57,* 153–165.

Moulton, P., Moulton, M., Housewright, M., & Bailey, K. (1998). Gifted and talented: Exploring the positive and negative aspects of labeling. *Roeper Review, 21,* 153–154.

Muck, R., Zempolich, K. A., Titus, J. C., Fishman, M., Godley, M. D., & Schwebel, R. (2001). An overview of the effectiveness of adolescent substance abuse treatment models. *Youth and Society, 33,* 143–168.

Mueller, M. M., Wilhelm, B., & Elder, G. H., Jr. (2002). Variations in grandparenting. *Research on Aging, 24,* 360–388.

Mueller, T. (2008). The association between sex education and youth's engagement in sexual intercourse, age at first intercourse, and birth control use at first sex. *Journal of Adolescence, 42,* 89–96.

Mueller, U., Sokol, B., & Overton, W. F. (1999). Developmental sequences in class reasoning and propositional reasoning. *Journal of Experimental Child Psychology, 74,* 69–106.

Mulkey, L. M., Catsambis, S., Steelman, L. C., & Crain, R. L. (2005). The long-term effects of ability grouping in mathematics: A national investigation. *Social Psychology of Education, 8,* 137–177.

Mullis, A. K., Mullis, R. L., & Normandin, D. (1992). Cross-sectional and longitudinal comparisons of adolescent self-esteem. *Adolescence, 27,* 51–61.

Murnen, S. K., & Kohlman, H. (2007). Athletic participation, fraternity membership, and sexual aggression among college men: A meta-analytic review. *Sex Roles, 57,* 145–157.

Murray, A., & Sandkvist, K. (1990). Father absence and children's achievement from age 13 to 21. *Scandinavian Journal of Educational Research, 34,* 3–28.

Mustillo, S., Wilson, J., & Lynch, S. M. (2004). Legacy volunteering: A test of two theories of intergenerational transmission. *Journal of Marriage and Family, 66,* 530–541.

Myers, S. M. (1996). An interactive model of religiosity inheritance: The importance of family context. *American Sociological Review, 61,* 858–866.

Nadeem, E., & Graham, S. (2005). Early puberty, peer victimization, and internalizing symptoms in ethnic minority adolescents. *Journal of Early Adolescence, 25,* 197–222.

Nævdal, F., & Thuen, F. (2004). Residence arrangements and well-being: A study of Norwegian adolescents. *Scandinavian Journal of Psychology, 45,* 363–371.

Nail, J. M., & Evans, J. G. (1997). The emotional adjustment of gifted adolescents: A view of global functioning. *Roeper Review, 20,* 18–21.

Najman, J. M., Aird, R., Bor, W., O'Callaghan, M., Williams, G. M., & Shuttlewood, G. J. (2004). The generational transmission of socioeconomic inequalities in child cognitive development and emotional health. *Social Science & Medicine, 58,* 1147–1158.

Nakajima, Y., & Hotta, M. (1989). A developmental study of cognitive processes in decision-making: Information searching as a function of task complexity. *Psychological Reports, 64,* 67–79.

Namerow, P. B., Kalmuss, D. S., & Cushman, L. F. (1993). The determinants of young women's pregnancy-resolution choices. *Journal of Research on Adolescence, 3,* 193–215.

Nathanson, C., Paulhus, D. L., & Williams, K. M. (2006). Predictors of a behavioral measure of scholastic cheating: Personality and competence but not demographics. *Contemporary Educational Psychology, 31,* 97–122.

National Adolescent Health Information Center. (2006). *2006 fact sheet on suicide: Adolescents and young adults.* San Francisco: University of California, San Francisco.

National Campaign to Prevent Teenage Pregnancy. (2008). *Policy brief: Racial and ethnic differences in teenage pregnancy.* Retrieved from http://www.thenationalcampaign.org/resources/pdf/Briefly_PolicyBrief_RacialEthnicDisparities.pdf.

National Center for Education Statistics. (2001). *National mathematics achievement-level results by race/ethnicity for grade 12: 1990–2000.* Retrieved from http://nces.ed.gov/nationsreportcard/mathematics/results/natachieve-g12RE.asp.

National Center for Education Statistics. (2002). *Table 146: Percent of high school seniors who participate in selected school-sponsored extracurricular activities, by student characteristics: 1980 and 1992.* Retrieved from http://nces.ed.gov.proxy.lib.ohio-state.edu/programs/digest/d02/dt145.asp.

National Center for Education Statistics. (2005). *Postsecondary institutions in the United States: Fall 2003 and degrees and other awards conferred: 2002–03* (NCES 2005-154). Washington, DC: U.S. Department of Education.

National Center for Education Statistics. (2005a). *Status and trends in the education of American Indian and Alaska Natives.* Retrieved from http://nces.ed.gov/pubs2005/nativetrends/index.asp.

National Center for Health Statistics. (2001). *Healthy people 2000: Final review.* Hyattsville, MD: Public Health Service.

National Center for Health Statistics. (2002). *Vital statistics of the United States, 2001, Volume I: Natality.* Washington, DC: Author.

National Center for Health Statistics. (2004). Summary health statistics for U.S. children: National health interview survey. *Vital and Health Statistics, 10,* 7–8.

National Center for Tobacco Free Kids. (2000). Tobacco company marketing to kids Retrieved from http://www.tobaccofreekids.org/research/factsheets/pdf/0008.pdf.

National Children's Home. (2002). *NCH 2002 Survey.* Retrieved from http://www.nch.org.uk/itok/showquestion.asp?faq=9andfldAuto=145.

National Coalition of the Homeless. (2006). *Why are people homeless?* Fact Sheet no. 1. Retrieved from http://www.nationalhomeless.org/publications/facts/Why.pdf.

National Coalition of the Homeless. (2008). *Homeless youth.* Fact Sheet no. 13. Retrieved from http://www.nationalhomeless.org/factsheets/youth.html.

National Commission on Excellence in Education. (1983). *A nation at risk: The imperative for educational reform.* Washington, DC: U.S. Government Printing Office.

National Consumer League. (2000). *An overview of federal labor laws*. Retrieved from http://www.neinet.org/child%20labor/factI.htm.

National Highway Traffic Safety Administration (NHTSA). (1998). *Traffic safety facts 1997: Alcohol*. Report no. DOT HS 808 806. Washington, DC: U.S. Department of Transportation.

National Highway Traffic Safety Administration (NHTSA). (2001). *Traffic safety facts 2000: A compilation of motor vehicle crash data from the fatality analysis reporting system and the general estimates system*. Washington, DC: U.S. Department of Transportation.

National Indian Gaming Commission. (2009). *NIGC announced 2008 revenues*. Retrieved from http://www.nigc.gov/ReadingRoom/PressReleases/PressReleasesMain/PR113062009/tabid/918/Default.aspx.

National Institute of Allergy and Infectious Diseases. (2002). *HIV infection in adolescents: Fact sheet*. Rockville, MD: National Institutes of Health.

National Institute of Arthritis and Musculoskeletal and Skin Diseases. (2006). *Questions and answers about acne*. Retrieved from http://www.nih.gov/niams/health-info/acne/acne.htm.

National Institute of Mental Health. (2000). *Depression in children and adolescents*. NIH Publication no. 00-4744. Retrieved from http://www.nimh.gov/publicat/dechildresfact.cfm.

National Institute on Alcohol Abuse and Alcoholism (NIAAA). (2000). *Tenth special report to the U.S. Congress on alcohol and health*. Rockville, MD: Author.

National Institute on Alcohol Abuse and Alcoholism. (2001). *Cognitive impairment and recovery from alcoholism*. Publication no. 53. Rockville, MD: Author.

National Institute on Alcohol Abuse and Alcoholism. (2006). *National epidemiological survey of alcohol and related conditions*. Retrieved from http://niaaa.census.gov/index.html.

National Institute on Drug Abuse (NIDA). (1999). *Infofax: Inhalants*. Report no. 13549. Retrieved from http://www.nida.nih.gov/infofax/inhalants.html.

National Institute on Drug Abuse (NIDA). (2001). *Ecstasy: What we know and don't know about MDMA*. Retrieved from http://www.drugabuse.gov/Meetings/MDMA/MDMAExSummary.

National Institute on Drug Abuse. (2003). *Preventing drug use among children and adolescents* (2nd ed.). NIH Publication no. 04-4212(A). Bethesda, MD: Author.

National Institute on Drug Abuse. (2005). *Marijuana abuse*. NIH Publication no. 05-3859. Bethesda, MD: Author.

National Institute on Drug Abuse. (2006). *Anabolic steroid abuse and addiction*. NIH Publication no. 06-3721. Bethesda, MD: Author.

National Marriage Project. (2005). *The state of our unions 2005: The social health of marriage in America*. Piscataway, NJ: Rutgers University Press.

National Middle School Association. (2005). *Position statement on curriculum, instruction, and assessment*. Retrieved from http://www.nmsa.org/AboutNMSA/PositionStatements/Curriculum/tabid/767/Default.aspx.

National Science Foundation. (2008). *Graduate students and postdoctorates in science and engineering: Fall 2006*. NSF 08-306. Arlington, VA: Author.

National Women's Law Center. (2007). *How to keep pregnant and parenting teens from dropping out: A primer for schools*. Retrieved from http://www.nwlc.org/details.cfm?id=3566&section=education.

National Youth Gang Center. (2009). *National Youth Gang Survey analysis*. Retrieved from http://www.iir.com/nygc/nygsa/.

Navarro, R. L., Flores, L. Y., & Worthington, R. L. (2007). Mexican American middle school students' goal intentions in mathematics and science: A test of social cognitive career theory. *Journal of Counseling Psychology, 54*, 320–335.

Necessary, J. R., & Parish, T. S. (1995). Relationships of parents' perceived actions toward their children. *Adolescence, 30*, 175–176.

Niemann, Y. F., Romero, A. J., Arredondo, J., & Rodrieguez, V. (1999). What does it mean to be "Mexican"? Social construction of an ethnic identity. *Hispanic Journal of Behavioral Sciences, 21*, 47–60.

Neimark, E. D. (1975). Longitudinal development of formal operations thought. *Genetic Psychology Monographs, 91*, 171–225.

NellieMae Corporation. (2006). *Credit card tips*. Retrieved from http://www.nelliemae.org/managingmoney/cc_tips.html.

Nelson, E., Leibenluft, E., McClure, E., & Pine, D. (2005). The social re-orientation of adolescence: A neuroscience perspective on the process and its relation to psychopathology. *Psychological Medicine, 35*, 163–174.

Nelson, F. H., Rosenberg, B., & van Meter, N. (2004). *Charter school achievement on the 2003 National Assessment of Educational Progress*. Washington, DC: American Federation of Teachers.

Nelson, T. F., & Wechsler, H. (2001). Alcohol and college athletes. *Medicine and Science in Sports and Exercise, 33*, 43–47.

Newcombe, P. A., van den Eynde, J., Hafner, D., & Jolly, L. (2008). Attributions of responsibility for rape: Differences across familiarity of situation, gender, and acceptance of rape myths. *Journal of Applied Social Psychology, 38*, 1736–1754.

Newman, B. M. (1989). The changing nature of the parent-adolescent relationship from early to late adolescence. *Adolescence, 24*, 915–924.

Newman, J. (1987). Psychological effects on college students on raising the drinking age. *Adolescence, 22*, 503–510.

Newspaper Association of America. (2005). *Targeting teens*. Retrieved from http://www.naa.org/marketscope/TargetingTeensBrief.pdf.

Nieder, T., & Seiffge-Krenke, I. (2001). Coping with stress in different phases of romantic development. *Journal of Adolescence, 24*, 297–311.

Nielson Company. (2009). *How teens use media*. New York: Author.

Nielsen S. J., & Popkin B. M. (2003). Patterns and trends in food portion sizes, 1977–1998. *Journal of the American Medical Association, 289*, 450–453.

Niemi, R. G., Hepburn, M. A., & Chapman, C. (2000). Community service by high school students: A cure for civic ills? *Political Behavior, 22*, 45–69.

Nilzon, K. R., & Palmérus, K. (1997). The influence of familial factors on anxiety and depression in childhood and early adolescence. *Adolescence, 32*, 935–943.

Nippold, M. (1994). Third-order verbal analogical reasoning: A developmental study of children and adolescents. *Contemporary Educational Psychology, 19*, 101–107.

Noack, P., & Buhl, H. M. (2004). Relations with parents and friends during adolescence and early adulthood. *Marriage & Family Review, 36*, 31–51.

Noble, P. S., Adams, G. R., & Openshaw, D. K. (1989). Interpersonal communication in parent–adolescent dyads: A brief report on the effects of a social skills training program. *Journal of Family Psychology, 2*, 483–494.

Nock, M. K., & Prinstein, M. J. (2005). Contextual features and behavioral functions of self-mutilation among adolescents. *Journal of Abnormal Psychology, 114*, 140–146.

Nock, S. L. (1998). The consequences of premarital fatherhood. *American Sociological Review, 63*, 250–263.

Noller, P., & Callan, V. J. (1986). Adolescent and parent perception of family cohesion and adaptability. *Journal of Adolescence, 9*, 97–106.

Nosek, M. A., Hughes, R. B., Swedlund, N., Taylor, H. B., & Swank, P. (2003). Self-esteem and women with disabilities. *Social Science & Medicine, 56*, 1737–1747.

Novins, D. K., Spicer, P., Beals, J., & Spero, M. M. (2004). Preventing underage drinking in American Indian and Alaska Native communities: Contexts, epidemiology, and culture. In R. J. Bonnie & M. E. O'Connell (Eds.), *Reducing underage drinking: A collective responsibility* (pp. 678–696). Washington, DC: National Academies Press.

Nussey, S. S., & Whitehead, S. A. (2001). *Endocrinology: An integrated approach*. Oxford, England: BIOS Scientific Publishers. Retrieved from http://www.ncbi.nlm.nih.gov/bookshelf/br.fcgi?book=endocrin.

Nwadiora, E., & McAdoo, H. (1996). Acculturative stress among Amerasian refugees: Gender and racial differences. *Adolescence, 31*, 477–487.

Nyborg, H., & Jensen, R. (2001). Occupation and income related to psychometric g. *Intelligence, 29*, 45–55.

Nye, S. S., & Johnson, C. L. (1999). Eating disorders. In S. D. Netherton, D. Holmes, & C. E. Walker (Eds.), *Child and adolescent psychological disorders: A comprehensive textbook* (pp. 397–414). New York: Oxford University Press.

O'Brien, K. M., Friedman, S. M., Tipton, L. C., & Linn, S. G. (2000). Attachment, separation, and women's vocational development: A longitudinal analysis. *Journal of Counseling Psychology, 47*, 301–315.

O'Brien, S. (1989). *American Indian tribal governments*. Norman: University of Oklahoma Press.

O'Connor, T. G., Pickering, K., Dunn, J., & Golding, J. (1999). Frequency and predictors of relationship dissolution in a community sample in England. *Journal of Family Psychology, 13*, 436–439.

O'Keefe, M., & Treister, L. (1998). Victims of dating violence among high school students: Are the predictors different for males and females? *Violence Against Women, 4*, 195–223.

O'Neill, R., Welsh, M., Parke, R. D., Wang, S., & Strand, C. (1997). A longitudinal assessment of the academic correlates of early peer acceptance and rejection. *Journal of Clinical Child Psychology, 26*, 290–303.

Oakes, J. (2005). *Keeping track: How schools structure inequality*. New Haven, CT: Yale University Press.

Odgers, C. L., Milne, B. J., Caspi, A., Crump, R., Poulton, R., & Moffitt, T. E. (2007). Predicting prognosis for the conduct-problem boy: Can family history help? *Journal of the American Academy of Child & Adolescent Psychiatry, 46*, 1240–1249.

Offer, D., & Schonert-Reichl, A. (1992). Debunking the myths of adolescence: Findings from recent research. *Journal of the American Academy of Child & Adolescent Psychiatry, 31*, 1003–1014.

Office of Economic Cooperation and Development. (2004). *Employment outlook 2004: How does the U.S. compare?* Retrieved from http://www.oecd.org/dataoecd/41/15/32504422.pdf.

Office of Juvenile Justice and Delinquency Prevention. (1998). *When your child is missing: A family survival guide*. Washington, DC: Author.

Office of Juvenile Justice and Prevention. (2006). *Juvenile offenders and victims: 2006 National Report*. Washington, DC: Author.

Office of Minority Health. (2006). *American Indian and Alaska Native populations*. Retrieved from http://www.cdc.gov/omh/Populations/AIAN/AIAN.htm.

Ogden, C. I., Carroll, M. D., Curtin, L. R., McDowell, M. A., Tabak, C. J., & Flegal, K. M. (2006). Prevalence of overweight and obesity in the United States, 1999–2004.

Journal of the American Medical Association, 295, 1549–1555.

Ogunwole, S. U. (2006). *We the people: American Indians and Alaska Natives in the United States.* Census 2000 Special Reports. Washington, DC: U.S. Bureau of the Census.

Ohannesian, C. M., & Lerner, R. M. (1995). Discrepancies in adolescents' and parents' perceptions of family functioning and adolescent emotional development. *Journal of Early Adolescence, 15,* 490–516.

Okazaki, S. (2002). Influences of culture on Asian Americans' sexuality. *Journal of Sex Research, 39,* 34–41.

Okimoto, T. G., Wenzel, M., & Feather, N. T. (2009). Beyond retribution: Conceptualizing restorative justice and exploring its determinants. *Social Justice Research, 22,* 156–180.

Oldenburg, C. M., & Kerns, K. A. (1997). Associations between peer relationships and depressive symptoms: Testing moderator effects of gender and age. *Journal of Early Adolescence, 17,* 319–337.

Olds, R. S., & Thombs, D. L. (2001). The relationship of adolescent perceptions of peer norms and parent involvement to cigarette and alcohol use. *Journal of School Health, 71,* 223–228.

Olson, D. (1988). Family assessment and intervention: The circumplex model of family systems. *Child and Youth Services, 11,* 9–48.

Olweus, D. (1991). Bully-victim problems among school children: Basic facts and effects of a school-based intervention program. In D. Pepler & K. Rubin (Eds.), *The development and treatment of childhood aggression* (pp. 411–448). Hillsdale, NJ: Erlbaum.

Olweus, D. (1993). *Bullying in schools: What we know and what we can do.* Oxford, England: Basil Blackwell.

Olweus, D. (1994). Annotation: Bullying at school: Basic facts and effects of a school-based intervention program. *Journal of Child Psychology and Psychiatry, 35,* 1171–1190.

Orfield, G., Losen, D., Wald, J., & Swanson, C. B. (2004). *Losing our future: How minority youth are being left behind by the graduation rate crisis.* Cambridge, MA: The Civil Rights Project at Harvard University.

Ormond, C., Luszez, M. A., Mann, L., & Beswick, G. (1991). Metacognitive analysis of decision making in adolescence. *Journal of Adolescence, 14,* 275–291.

Osgood, D. W. (1999). Having the time of their lives: All work and no play? In A. Booth, A. C. Crouter, & M. J. Shanahan (Eds.), *Transitions to adulthood in a changing economy: No work, no family, no future?* (pp. 176–186). Westport, CT: Praeger.

Ostermann, J., Sloan, F. A., & Taylor, D. H. (2005). Heavy alcohol use and marital dissolution in the USA. *Social Science & Medicine, 61,* 2304–2316.

Owens, J. A., Stahl, J., Patton, A., Reddy, U., & Crouch, M. (2006). Sleep practices, attitudes, and beliefs in inner city middle school children: A mixed-methods study. *Behavioral Sleep Medicine, 4,* 114–134.

Owens, T. J. (1992). Where do we go from here? Post-high school choices of American men. *Youth and Society, 23,* 452–477.

Oxford, M. L., Gilchrist, L. D., Gillmore, M. R., & Lohr, M. J. (2006). Predicting variation in the life course of adolescent mothers as they enter adulthood. *Journal of Adolescent Health, 39,* 20–26.

Oyserman, D., & Markus, H. R. (1990a). Possible selves and delinquency. *Journal of Personality and Social Psychology, 59,* 112–125.

Oyserman, D., & Markus, H. R. (1990b). Possible selves in balance: Implications for delinquency. *Journal of Social Issues, 46,* 141–157.

Ozarak, E. W. (1989). Social and cognitive influences on the development of religious beliefs and commitment in adolescence. *Journal for the Scientific Study of Religion, 28,* 448–463.

Ozechowski, T. J., & Liddle, H. A. (2000). Family-based therapy for adolescent drug abuse: Knowns and unknowns. *Clinical and Family Psychology Review, 3,* 269–298.

Ozer, E. M., Park, M. J., Paul, T., Brindis, C. D., & Irwin, C. E., Jr. (2003). *America's adolescents: Are they healthy?* San Francisco: University of California, San Francisco, National Adolescent Health Information Center.

Padilla-Walker, L. M., & Carlo, G. (2004). "It's not fair!" Adolescents' constructions of appropriateness of parental reactions. *Journal of Youth and Adolescence, 33,* 389–401.

Page, R. M. (1990). Shyness and sociability: A dangerous combination for illicit substance use in adolescent males? *Adolescence, 25,* 803–806.

Page, R. M., & Suwanteerangkul, J. (2007). Dieting among Thai adolescents: Having friends who diet and pressure to diet. *Eating and Weight Disorders, 12,* 114–124.

Pagliuso, S. (1976). *Understanding stages of moral development: A programmed learning workbook.* New York: Paulist Press.

Pallas, A. M., Entwisle, D. R., Alexander, K. L., & Stluka, M. F. (1994). Ability-group effects: Instructional, social, or institutional? *Sociology of Education, 67,* 27–46.

Paolucci, E. O., Genius, M. L., & Violato, C. (2001). A meta-analysis of the published research on the effects of child sexual abuse. *Journal of Psychology, 135,* 17–36.

Papini, D. R., Mucks, J. C., & Barnett, J. K. (1989). Perceptions of intrapsychic and extrapsychic functioning as bases of adolescent ego identity statuses. *Journal of Adolescent Research, 4,* 462–482.

Parent, A., Teilmann, G., Juul, A., Skakkebaek, N. E., Toppari, J., & Bourguignon, J. (2003). The timing of normal puberty and the age limits of sexual precocity: Variations around the world, secular trends, and changes after migration. *Endocrine Reviews, 24,* 668–693.

Parker, J. G., Low, C. M., Walker, A. R., & Gamm, B. K. (2005). Friendship jealousy in young adolescents: Individual differences and links to sex, self-esteem, aggression, and social adjustment. *Developmental Psychology, 29,* 611–621.

Parker, J. S., & Benson, M. J. (2005). Parent-adolescent relations and adolescent functioning: Self-esteem, substance abuse, and delinquency. *Family Therapy, 32,* 131–142.

Patrick, H., Hicks, L., & Ryan, A. M. (1997). Relations of perceived social efficacy and social goal pursuit to self-efficacy for academic work. *Journal of Early Adolescence, 17,* 109–128.

Patrick, H., Ryan, A. M., Alfeld-Liro, C., Fredricks, J. A., Hruda, L., & Eccles, J. (1999). Adolescents' commitment to developing talent: The role of peers in continuing motivation for sports and the arts. *Journal of Youth and Adolescence, 28,* 741–763.

Patrick, M. E., Maggs, K. L., & Abar, C. C. (2007). Reasons to have sex, personal goals, and sexual behavior during the transition to college. *Journal of Sex Research, 44,* 240–249.

Patterson, G. R., DeBarysne, B. D., & Ramsey, E. (1989). A developmental perspective on antisocial behavior. *American Psychologist, 44,* 329–335.

Paul, E. L., McManus, B., & Hayes, A. (2000). Hookups: Characteristics and correlates of college students' spontaneous and anonymous sexual experiences. *Journal of Sex Research, 37,* 76–88.

Paulson, S. E., Marchant, G. J., & Rothlisberg, B. A. (1998). Early adolescents' perceptions of patterns of parenting, teaching, and school atmosphere: Implications for achievement. *Journal of Early Adolescence, 18,* 5–26.

Paulson-Karlsson, G., Engstrom, I., & Nevonen, L. (2009). A pilot study of a family-based treatment for adolescent anorexia nervosa: 18- and 36-month follow-ups. *Eating Disorders: The Journal of Treatment & Prevention, 17,* 72–88.

Paus, T., Zijdenbos, A., Worsley, K., Collins, D. L., Blumenthal, J., Giedd, J. N., Rapoport, J. L., & Evans, A. C. (1999). Structural maturation of neural pathways in children and adolescents: In vivo study. *Science, 283,* 1908–1911.

Paxton, S. J., Norris, M., Wertheim, E. H., Durkin, S. J., & Anderson, J. (2005). Body dissatisfaction, dating, and importance of thinness to attractiveness in adolescent girls. *Sex Roles, 53,* 663–675.

Pearlman, M. (1995). The role of socioeconomic status in adolescent literature. *Adolescence, 30,* 223–231.

Pearson, C. A., & Gleaves, D. H. (2006). The multiple dimensions of perfectionism and their relation with eating disorder features. *Personality and Individual Differences, 41,* 225–235.

Peck, D. L., & Warner, K. (1995). Accident or suicide? Single-vehicle car accident and the intent hypothesis. *Adolescence, 30,* 463–472.

Pedersen, W. (1990). Adolescents initiating cannabis use: Cultural opposition or poor mental health? *Journal of Adolescence, 13,* 327–339.

Pedersen, W., Samuelsen, S. O., & Wichstrom, L. (2003). Intercourse debut age: Poor resources, problem behavior, or romantic appeal? A population-based longitudinal study. *Journal of Sex Research, 40,* 333–345.

Penick, N. I., & Jepsen, D. A. (1992). Family functioning and adolescent career development. *Career Development Quarterly, 40,* 208–222.

Perkins, D. F., & Lerner, R. M. (1995). Single and multiple indicators of physical attractiveness and psychosocial behaviors among young adolescents. *Journal of Early Adolescence, 15,* 269–298.

Perkins, H. W. (2002). Surveying the damage: A review of research on consequences of alcohol misuse in college populations. *Journal of Studies on Alcohol, 14,* 91–100.

Perper, T., & Weis, D. L. (1987). Proceptive and rejective strategies of U.S. and Canadian college women. *Journal of Sex Research, 23,* 455–480.

Perry, C. L., & Staufacker, M. J. (1996). Tobacco use. In R. J. DiClemente, W. B. Hansen, & L. E. Ponton (Eds.), *Handbook of adolescent health risk behavior* (pp. 53–81). New York: Plenum Press.

Perry, J. L., Coursey, D., Brudney, J. L., & Littlepage, L. (2008). What drives morally committed citizens? A study of the antecedents of public service motivation. *Public Administration Review, 68,* 445–458.

Peter D. Hart Research Associates. (2005). *Gates Foundation dropouts survey.* Seattle, WA: The Gates Foundation.

Petersen, A. C., Compas, B. E., Brooks-Gunn, J., & Stemmler, M. (1993). Depression in adolescence. *American Psychologist, 48,* 155–168.

Peterson, K. L., & Roscoe, B. (1991). Imaginary audience behavior in older adolescent females. *Adolescence, 26,* 195–200.

Pettingell, S. L., Bearinger, L. H., Skay, C. L., Resnick, M. D., Potthoff, S. J., & Eichhorn, J. (2008). Protecting urban American Indian young people from suicide. *American Journal of Health Behavior, 32,* 465–476.

Pew Hispanic Center. (2009). *Statistical portrait of Hispanics in the United States, 2007.* Retrieved from http://pewhispanic.org/factsheets/factsheet.php?FactsheetID=46.

Philliber, S., Brooks, L., Lehrer, L. P., Oakley, M., & Waggoner, S. (2003). Outcomes of teen parenting programs in New Mexico. *Adolescence, 38,* 535–553.

Phillips, E. L., Greydanus, D. E., Pratt, H. D., & Patel, D. P. (2003). Treatment of bulimia nervosa: Psychological and psychopharmacologic considerations. *Journal of Adolescent Research, 18,* 261–279.

Phillips, J. A., & Sweeney, M. A. (2005). Premarital cohabitation and marital disruption among White, Black and Mexican American women. *Journal of Marriage and Family, 67,* 296–314.

Phinney, J. S. (1992). The Multigroup Ethnic Identity Measure. A new scale for use with diverse groups. *Journal of Adolescent Research, 7,* 156–176.

Phinney, J. S., & Alipuria, L. L. (1996). At the interface of cultures: Multiethnic/multiracial high school and college students. *Journal of Social Psychology, 136,* 139–158.

Phinney, J. S., & Chavira, V. (1995). Parental ethnic socialization and adolescent coping with problems related to ethnicity. *Journal of Research on Adolescence, 5,* 31–63.

Phinney, J. S., Chavira, V., & Williamson, L. (1992). Acculturation attitudes and self-esteem among high-school and college students. *Youth and Society, 23,* 299–312.

Phinney, J. S., & Devich-Navarro, M. (1997). Variations in bicultural identification among African American and Mexican American adolescents. *Journal of Research on Adolescence, 7,* 3–32.

Phinney, J. S., Jacoby, B., & Silva, C. (2007). Positive intergroup attitudes: The role of ethnic identity. *International Journal of Behavioral Development, 31,* 478–490.

Piacentini, M., & Mailer, G. (2004). Symbolic consumption in teenagers' clothing choices. *Journal of Consumer Behaviour, 3,* 251–262.

Piaget, J. (1948/1932). *The moral judgment of the child.* Glencoe, IL: Free Press.

Piaget, J. (1951). *Psychology of intelligence.* London: Routledge and Kegan Paul.

Piaget, J. (1963/1936). *The origins of intelligence in the child.* New York: Norton.

Piaget, J. (1967). *Six psychological studies* (A. Tenzer & D. Elkind, Trans.). New York: Random House.

Piaget, J. (1971). The theory of stages in cognitive development. In D. R. Green (Ed.), *Measurement and Piaget* (pp. 5–38). New York: McGraw-Hill.

Piaget, J. (1972). Intellectual evolution from adolescence to adulthood. *Human Development, 15,* 1012.

Piaget, J., & Inhelder, B. (1969). *The psychology of the child* (H. Weaver, Trans.). New York: Basic Books.

Pino, N. W., & Smith, W. L. (2003). College students and academic dishonesty. *College Student Journal, 37,* 490–500.

Pinquart, M. (2003). Loneliness in married, widowed, divorced, and never-married older adults. *Journal of Social and Personal Relationships, 20,* 31–53.

Pipher, M. (1996). *The shelter of each other: Rebuilding our families.* New York: Grosset/Putnam Book.

PipperJaffray. (2009). *Challenging economy leads to decline in teen spending.* Retrieved from http://www.piperjaffray.com/2col_largeright.aspx?id=1284.

Pirog-Good, M. A. (1996). The education and labor market outcomes of adolescent fathers. *Youth and Society, 28,* 236–262.

Plastic Surgery Information Service. (2000). *Most popular surgeries among teenagers: Nose reshaping and breast reduction.* Retrieved from http://www.plastic-surgery.org.

Pleck, J. H. (1976). The male sex role: Definitions, problems, and sources of change. *Journal of Social Issues, 32,* 155–164.

Plotnick, R., & Butler, S. (1991). Attitudes and adolescent nonmarital childbearing. *Journal of Adolescent Research, 6,* 470–492.

Plunkett, M., & Mitchell, C. M. (2000). Substance abuse rates among American Indian adolescents: Regional comparisons with Monitoring the Future high school seniors. *Journal of Drug Issues, 30,* 575–591.

Pogarsky, G., Thornberry, T. P., & Lizotte, A. J. (2006). Developmental outcomes for children of young mothers. *Journal of Marriage and Family, 68,* 332–344.

Pomeroy, W. (1965). Why we tolerate lesbians. *Sexology, May,* 652–654.

Pompili, M., Mancinelli, I., Girardi, P., Ruberto, A., & Taterelli, R. (2004). Suicide in anorexia nervosa: A meta-analysis. *International Journal of Eating Disorders, 36,* 99–103.

Popenoe, D. (1996). *Life without father.* New York: Martin Kessler Books.

Popenoe, D., & Whitehead, B. D. (2005). *The state of our unions 2005.* Piscataway, NJ: The National Marriage Project.

Poulin, F., & Pedersen, S. (2007). Developmental changes in gender composition of friendship networks in adolescent girls and boys. *Developmental Psychology, 43,* 1484–1496.

Powell, A. (2003). *Infofacts resources: Campuses and the club drug ecstasy.* Higher Education Center for Alcohol and Other Drug Prevention. Retrieved from http://www.campusblues.com/drgus3.shtml.

Powers, D. E., & Rock, D. A. (1999). Effects of coaching on SAT I: Reasoning test scores. *Journal of Educational Measurement, 36,* 93–118.

Pratt, M. W., Arnold, M. L., Pratt, A. T., & Diessner, R. (1999). Predicting adolescent formal reasoning from family climate: A longitudinal study. *Journal of Early Adolescence, 19,* 148–175.

Pratt, M. W., Hunsberger, B., Pancer, S. M., & Alicat, S. (2003). A longitudinal analysis of personal values socialization: Correlates of a moral self-ideal in late adolescence. *Social Development, 12,* 563–585.

Pratt, T. C., Cullen, F. T., Blevins, K. R., Daigle, L., & Unnever, J. D. (2002). The relationships of attention deficit hyperactivity disorder to crime and delinquency: A meta-analysis. *International Journal of Police Science & Management, 4,* 344–360.

President's Advisory Commission on Educational Excellence for Hispanic Americans. (1996). *Hispanic American education.* Washington, DC: U.S. Government Printing Office.

Presley, C. A., Meilman, P. W., & Leichliter, J. S. (2002). College factors that influence drinking. *Journal of Studies on Alcohol, 14,* 82–90.

Prince, F. (1995). The relative effectiveness of a peer-led and adult-led smoking intervention program. *Adolescence, 30,* 187–194.

Princeton Survey Research Associates for the Association of Reproductive Health Professionals and the National Campaign to Prevent Teen Pregnancy. (1997). *National Omnibus Survey questions about teen pregnancy.* Washington, DC: Author.

Prokopcakova, A. (1998). Drug experimenting and pubertal maturation in girls. *Studia Psychologica, 40,* 287–290.

Pruchno, R. (1999). Raising grandchildren: The experiences of Black and White grandmothers. *The Gerontologist, 39,* 209–221.

Pryor, J., & Rogers, B. (2001). *Children in changing families: Life after parental separation.* Oxford, England: Blackwell Publishing.

Public Agenda. (1999). *Kids these days '99.* Retrieved from http://publicagenda.org/research/pdfs/kids_these_days_99.pdf.

Quatman, T., Sokolik, E., & Smith, K. (2000). Adolescent perception of peer success: A gendered perspective over time. *Sex Roles, 43,* 61–84.

Quimby, J. L., & DeSantis, A. M. (2006). The influence of role models on women's career choices. *Career Development Quarterly, 54,* 297–306.

Quintana, S. M., Casteñeda-English, P., & Ybarra, V. C. (1999). Role of perspective-taking abilities and ethnic socialization in development of adolescent ethnic identity. *Journal of Research on Adolescence, 9,* 161–184.

Quintana, S. M., & Lapsley, D. K. (1990). Rapprochement in late adolescent separation-individuation: A structure equations approach. *Journal of Adolescence, 13,* 371–385.

Radmacher, K., & Azmitia, M. (2006). Are there gendered pathways to intimacy in early adolescents' and emerging adults' friendships? *Journal of Adolescent Research, 21,* 415–448.

Raffielli, M. (2005). Adolescent dating experiences described by Latino college students. *Journal of Adolescence, 28,* 559–572.

Raffaelli, M., Bogenschneider, K., & Flood, M. F. (1998). Parent-teen communication about sexual topics. *Journal of Family Issues, 19,* 316–334.

Raffaelli, M., & Ontai, L. L. (2004). Gender socialization in Latino/a families: Results from two retrospective studies. *Sex Roles, 50* 287–299.

Rahman, Q. Q., Glenn, G. D., & Wilson, D. (2003). Born gay? The psychobiology of human sexual orientation. *Personality and Individuals Differences, 34,* 1337–1382.

Raley, K., & Bumpus, L. (2003). The topography of the divorce plateau: Levels and trends in unity stability in the United States after 1980. *Demographic Research, 8,* 245–259.

Ralph, N., & Morgan, K. A. (1991). Assessing differences in chemically dependent adolescent males using the Child Behavior Check List. *Adolescence, 26,* 183–194.

Ramirez, R. R. (2004). *We the people: Hispanics in the United States.* Census 2000 Special Report. Washington DC: U.S. Bureau of the Census.

Raphael, B., Cubis, J., Dunne, M., Lewin, T., & Kelly, S. (1990). The impact of parental loss on adolescents' psychosocial characteristics. *Adolescence, 25,* 689–700.

Raskoff, S., & Sundeen, R. (1994). *The ties that bind: Teenage volunteers in the United States.* Paper presented at the International Sociological Association Meetings, Bielefeld, Germany.

Rasmussen, C., & Wyper, K. (2007). Decision making, executive functioning and risky behaviors in adolescents with prenatal alcohol exposure. *International Journal on Disability and Human Development, 6,* 405–416.

Ravitch, D. (1983). The educational pendulum. *Psychology Today, 17,* 62–71.

Ray, B. D. (2008). *Research facts on homeschooling.* Retrieved from National Home Education Research Institute, http://www.nheri.org/content/view/199/.

Ream, G. L., & Savin-Williams, R. C. (2003). Religious development in adolescence. In G. R. Adams & M. D. Berzonsky (Eds.), *The Blackwell handbook of adolescence* (pp. 51–59). Oxford, England: Blackwell Publishing.

Ream, R. K., & Rumberger, R. W. (2008). Student engagement, peer social capital, and school dropout among Mexican American and non-Latino White students. *Sociology of Education, 81,* 109–139.

Redmond, G. P. (1998). Androgens and women's health. *International Journal of Fertility & Women's Medicine, 43,* 91–97.

Reeves, T. J., & Bennett, C. E. (2004). *We the people: Asians in the United States.* Census Bureau Special Report. Washington, DC: U.S. Bureau of the Census.

Regnerus, M. D. (2000). Shaping schooling success: Religious socialization and educational outcomes in metropolitan public schools. *Journal for the Scientific Study of Religion, 39,* 363–370.

Regnerus, M. D. (2005). Talking about sex: Religion and patterns of parent-child communication about sex and contraception. *Sociological Quarterly, 46,* 79–105.

Regnerus, M. D., & Elder, G. H. (2003). Staying on track in school: Religious influences in high- and low-risk settings. *Journal for the Scientific Study of Religion, 42,* 189–203.

Regnerus, M. D., Smith, C., & Smith, B. (2004). Social Context in the Development of Adolescent Religiosity. *Applied Developmental Science, 8*(1), 27–38.

Reijonen, J. H., Pratt, H. D., Patel, D. R., & Greydanus, D. E. (2003). Eating disorders in the general population: An overview. *Journal of Adolescent Research, 18,* 209–222.

Reinders, H., & Youniss, J. (2006). School-based required community service and civic development in adolescence. *Applied Developmental Science, 10,* 2–12.

Reinemann, D. H., Stark, K. D., & Swearer, S. M. (2003). Family factors that differentiate sexually abused and nonabused adolescent psychiatric inpatients. *Journal of Interpersonal Violence, 18,* 471–489.

Reiner, W. (1997). To be male or female—That is the question. *Archives of Pediatric and Adolescent Medicine, 151,* 224–225.

Reinking, M. F., & Alexander, L. E. (2005). Prevalence of disordered-eating behaviors in undergraduate female collegiate athletes and nonathletes. *Journal of Athletic Training, 40,* 47–51.

Reis, O., & Buhl, M. (2008). Individuation during adolescence and emerging adulthood: Five German studies. *International Journal of Behavioral Development, 32,* 369–371.

Reisch, S. K., Bush, L., Nelson, C. J., Ohm, B. J., Portz, P. A., Abell, B., et al. (2000). Topics of conflict between parents and young adolescents. *Journal of the Society of Pediatric Nurses, 5,* 27–40.

Remez, L. (2000). Oral sex among adolescents: Is it sex or is it abstinence? *Family Planning Perspective, 32,* 298–304.

Rende, R., Slomlkowski, C., Lloyd-Richardson, E., & Niaura, R. (2005). Sibling effects on substance use in adolescence: Social and genetic relatedness. *Journal of Family Psychology, 19,* 611–618.

Renk, K., Liljequist, L., Simpson, J. E., & Phares, V. (2005). Gender and age differences in the topics of parent-adolescent conflict. *The Family Journal: Counseling and Therapy for Couples and Families, 13,* 139–149.

Repetti, R., Taylor, S., & Seeman, T. (2002). Risky families: Family social environments and the mental and physical health of offspring. *Psychological Bulletin, 128,* 330–366.

Reyna, V. F., & Farley, F. (2006). Risk and rationality in adolescent decision making: Implications for theory, practice, and public policy. *Psychological Science in the Public Interest, 7,* 1–44.

Reyna, V. F., & Rivers, E. (2008). Current theories of risk and rational decision making. *Developmental Review, 28,* 1–11.

Reyes, O., Kobus, K., & Gillock, K. (1999). Career aspirations of urban, Mexican American adolescent females. *Hispanic Journal of Behavioral Sciences, 21,* 366–382.

Rhein, L. M., Ginsburg, K. R., Schwartz, D., Pinto-Martin, J. A., Zhao, H., Morgan, A. P., & Slap, G. B. (1997). Teen father participation in child rearing: Family perspectives. *Journal of Adolescent Health, 21,* 244–252.

Rhoades, G. K., Stanley, S. M., & Markman, H. J. (2009). Couples' reasons for cohabitation: Associations with individual well-being and relationship quality. *Journal of Family Issues, 30,* 233–258.

Rhynard, J., Krebs, M., & Glover, J. (1997). Sexual assault in dating relationships. *Journal of School Health, 67,* 89–93.

Ribak, R. (2009). Remote control, umbilical cord and beyond: The mobile phone as a transitional object. *British Journal of Developmental Psychology, 27,* 183–196.

Ricciardelli, L. A., & McCabe, M. P. (2001). Children's body image concerns and eating disturbance: A review of the literature. *Clinical Psychology Review, 21,* 325–344.

Ricciardelli, L. A., & McCabe, M. P. (2004). A biopsychosocial model of disordered eating and the pursuit of muscularity in adolescent boys. *Psychological Bulletin, 130,* 179–205.

Ricciardelli, L. A., McCabe, M. P., Holt, K. E., & Finemore, J. (2003). A biopsychosocial model for understanding body image and body change strategies among children. *Applied Developmental Psychology, 24,* 475–495.

Rice, C. E., Dandreaux, D., Handley, E. D., & Chassin, L. (2006). Children of alcoholics: Risk and resilience. *The Prevention Researcher, 13,* 3–6.

Rice, F. P. (1975–1996). *Counselling notes.* Provided by former first author of this text from his collection.

Rice, F. P. (1980). *Morality and youth.* Philadelphia: Westminster Press.

Rice, K. G. (1993). Separation-individuation and adjustment in college: A longitudinal study. *Journal of Counseling Psychology, 39,* 203–213.

Richards, L. N., & Schmiege, C. J. (1993). Problems and strengths of single-parent families. *Family Relations, 42,* 277–285.

Richards, M. H., Crowe, P. A., Larson, R., & Swarr, A. (1998). Developmental patterns and gender differences in the experience of peer companionship during adolescence. *Child Development, 69,* 154–163.

Richards, M. H., & Larson, R. (1993). Pubertal development in the daily subjective states of young adolescents. *Journal of Research on Adolescence, 3,* 145–169.

Richardson, K. (2002). What IQ tests test. *Theory & Psychology, 12,* 283–314.

Richtel, M. (2009). In study, texting lifts crash risk by large margin. *New York Times,* July 29.

Rideout, V., Foehr, U. G., & Roberts, D. F. (2010). *Generation M²: Media in the lives of 8- to 18-year-olds.* Menlo Park, CA: Kaiser Family Foundation.

Rideout, V., Roberts, D. F., & Foehr, U. G. (2005). *Generation M: Media in the lives of 8–18 year olds.* Washington, DC: Kaiser Family Foundation.

Riegel, K. F. (1973). Dialectical operations: The final period of cognitive development. *Human Development, 16,* 346–370.

Rigby, K. (2002). *New perspective on bullying.* Philadephia: Kingsley.

Riggio, H. R. (2001). Relations between parental divorce and the quality of adult sibling relationships. *Journal of Divorce & Remarriage, 36,* 67–82.

Rind, B., & Tromovitch, P. (1997). A meta-analytic review of findings from national samples of psychological correlates of child sexual abuse. *Journal of Sex Research, 34,* 237–255.

Ringwalt, C. L., & Palmer, J. H. (1989). Cocaine and crack users compared. *Adolescence, 24,* 851–859.

Risman, B. J., Hill, C. T., Rubin, Z., & Peplau, L. A. (1981). Living together in college: Implications for courtship. *Journal of Marriage and Family, 43,* 77–83.

Ritchey, P. N., & Fishbein, H. D. (2001). The lack of an association between adolescents' friends' prejudices and stereotypes. *Merrill-Palmer Quarterly, 47,* 188–206.

Ritzer, G. (2000). *The McDonaldization of society.* Thousand Oaks, CA: Pine Forge Press.

Robert, M. M., Pauzé R., & Fournier, L. (2005). Factors associated with homelessness of adolescents under supervision of the youth protection system. *Journal of Adolescence, 28,* 215–230.

Roberto, L. G. (1986). Bulimia: The transgenerational view. *Journal of Marital and Family Therapy, 12,* 231–240.

Roberts, D. F. (2000). Media and youth: Access, exposure, and privatization. *Journal of Adolescent Health, 27,* 8–14.

Roberts, D. F., Christianson, P. G., & Gentile, D. A. (2003). The effects of violent music on children and adolescents. In D. A. Gentile (Ed.), *Media violence and children: A complete guide for parents and professionals* (pp. 153–170). Westport, CT: Praeger.

Robinson, B. E., Skeen, P., Flake-Hobson, C., & Herman, M. (1982). Gay men's and women's perceptions of early family life and their relationships with parents. *Family Relations, 31,* 79–83.

Robinson, N. S. (1995). Evaluating the nature of perceived support and its relation to perceived self-worth in adolescents. *Journal of Research on Adolescence, 5,* 253–280.

Roe, K. (1995). Adolescents' use of socially devalued media: Towards a theory of media delinquency. *Journal of Youth and Adolescence, 24,* 617–631.

Roe-Sepowitz, D. E. (2009). Comparing male and female juveniles charged with homicide: Child maltreatment, substance abuse, and crime details. *Journal of Interpersonal Violence, 24,* 601–617.

Roeser, R. W., Eccles, J. S., & Freedman-Doan, C. (1999). Academic functioning and mental health in adolescence: Patterns, progressions, and routes from childhood. *Journal of Adolescent Research, 14,* 135–174.

Roeser, R. W., Galloway, M., Casey-Cannon, S., Watson, C., Keller, L., & Tan, E. (2008). Identity representations in patterns of school achievement and well-being among early adolescent girls: Variable- and person-centered approaches. *Journal of Early Adolescence, 28,* 115–152.

Roeser, R. W., Peck, S. C., & Nasir, N. S. (2006). Self and identity processes in school motivation, learning and achievement. In P. A. Alexander & P. H. Winne (Eds.), *Handbook of educational psychology* (2nd ed., pp. 391–424). Mahwah, NJ: Erlbaum.

Rogers, C. R. (1961). *On becoming a person: A therapist's view of psychotherapy.* Boston: Houghton Mifflin.

Rohner, R. P., & Britner, P. A. (2002). Worldwide mental health correlates of parental acceptance-rejection: Review of cross-cultural and intracultural evidence. *Journal of Cross-Cultural Research, 36,* 15–47.

Roig, M. (1999). When college students' attempts at paraphrasing become instances of potential plagiarism. *Psychological Reports, 84,* 973–982.

Roig, M., & Caso, M. (2005). Lying and cheating: Fraudulent excuse making, cheating, and plagiarism. *Journal of Psychology: Interdisciplinary and Applied, 139,* 485–494.

Rojewski, J. W., & Kim, H. (2003). Career choice patterns and behaviors of work-bound youth during early adolescence. *Journal of Career Development, 30,* 89–108.

Rolls, B. J., Federoff, I. C., & Guthrie, J. F. (1991). Gender differences in eating behavior and body weight regulation. *Health Psychology, 10,* 133–142.

Romans, S. E., Martin, M., Gendall, K., & Herbison, G. P. (2003). Age of menarche: The role of some psychosocial factors. *Psychological Medicine, 33,* 933–939.

Rosario, M., Schrimshaw, E. W., & Hunter, J. (2008). Predicting different patterns of sexual identity development over time among lesbian, gay, and bisexual youths: A cluster analytic approach. *American Journal of Community Psychology, 42,* 266–282.

Rorty, M., Yager, J., Rossotto, E., & Buckwalter, G. (2000). Parental intrusiveness in adolescence recalled by women with a history of bulimia nervosa and comparison women. *International Journal of Eating Disorders, 28,* 202–208.

Rose, A. J., Swenson, L. P., & Waller, E. M. (2004). Overt and relational aggression and perceived popularity: Developmental differences in concurrent and prospective relations. *Developmental Psychology, 40,* 378–387.

Rosen, D. (2003). Eating disorders in childhood and early adolescence: Etiology, classification, clinical features, and treatment. *Adolescent Medicine, 14,* 49–59.

Rosenblum, G. D., & Lewis, M. (1999). The relations among body image, physical attractiveness, and body mass in adolescence. *Child Development, 70*, 50–64.

Rosenthal, D. A., Biro, F. M., Succop, P. A., Bernstein, D. I., & Stanberg, L. (1997). Impact of demographics, sexual history, and psychological functioning on the acquisition of STDs in adolescents. *Adolescence, 32*, 757–770.

Rosenthal, D. A., & Feldman, S. S. (1991). The influence of perceived family and personal factors on self-reported school performance of Chinese and Western high school students. *Journal of Research on Adolescence, 1*, 135–154.

Rosenthal, D. A., & Feldman, S. S. (1999). The importance of importance: Parent-adolescent communication about sexuality. *Journal of Adolescence, 22*, 835–852.

Rosenthal, D. A., Moore, S. M., & Brumer, I. (1990). Ethnic group differences in adolescent responses to AIDS. *Australian Journal of Social Science, 25*, 77–88.

Rosenthal, S. L., Biro, F. M., Succop, P. A., Bernstein, D. I., & Stanberry, L. R. (1997). Impact of demographics, sexual history, and psychological functioning on the acquisition of STDS in adolescents. *Adolescence, 32*, 757–769.

Rosenthal, S. L., Lewis, L. M., & Cohen, S. S. (1996). Issues related to the sexual decision making of inner-city adolescent girls. *Adolescence, 31*, 731–739.

Ross, J. A. (1981). Improving adolescent decision-making skills. *Curriculum Inquiry, 11*, 279–295.

Ross, M. E. T., & Aday, M. L. (2006). Stress and coping in African American grandparents who are raising their grandchildren. *Journal of Family Issues, 27*, 912–932.

Rostosky, S. S., Wilcox, B. L., Wright, M. L. C., & Randall, B. A. (2004). The impact of religiosity on adolescent sexual behavior: A review of the evidence. *Journal of Adolescent Research, 19*, 677–697.

Roth, J. (2000, April). *What we know and what we need to know about youth development programs.* Paper presented at the biennial meeting for the Society for Research on Adolescence, Chicago, IL.

Roth, J., & Brooks-Gunn, J. (2003). What exactly is a youth development program? Answers from research and practice. *Applied Developmental Science, 7*, 94–111.

Rotheram-Borus, M. J., Lightfoot, M., Moraes, A., Dopkins, S., & LaCouer, J. (1998). Developmental, gender, and ethnic differences in ethnic identity among adolescents. *Journal of Adolescent Research, 13*, 487–507.

Rotheram-Borus, M. J., Parra, M., Cantwell, C., Gwadz, M., & Murphy, D. A. (1996). Runaway and homeless youths. In R. J. Diclemente, W. B. Hansen, & L. E. Ponton (Eds.), *Handbook of adolescent health risk behavior* (pp. 369–391). New York: Plenum Press.

Rottinghaus, P. J., & Zytowski, D. G. (2006). Commonalities between adolescents' work values and interests. *Measurement and Evaluation in Counseling and Development, 38*, 211–221.

Rowe, D. C. (2002). On genetic variation at menarche and age at first sexual intercourse: A critique of the Belsky-Draper hypothesis. *Evolution and Human Behavior, 23*, 365–372.

Rowe, D. C., Rodgers, J. L., & Meseck-Bushey, S. (1992). Sibling delinquency and the family environment: Shared and unshared influences. *Child Development, 63*, 59–67.

Rubin, K. H., Bukowski, W., & Parker, J. G. (1998). Peer interactions, relationships, and groups. In W. Damon (Series Ed.) & N. Eisenberg (Vol. Ed.), *Handbook of child psychology: Social, emotional, and personality development* (Vol. 3, 5th ed., pp. 619–700). New York: Wiley.

Rubin, L. R., Fitts, M. L, & Baker, A. E. (2003). "Whatever feels good in my soul": Body ethics and aesthetics among African American and Latina women. *Culture, Medicine, and Psychiatry, 27*, 49–75.

Ruble, D. N., & Martin, C. L. (2000). Gender development. In W. Damon (Series Ed.) & N. Eisenberg (Vol. Ed.), *Handbook of child psychology: Social, emotional, and personality development* (Vol. 3, pp. 933–1016). New York: Wiley.

Rueda, M. R., Fan, J., McCandliss, B. D., Halparin, J. D., Gruber, D. B., Pappert Lecari, L., & Posner, M. L. (2004). Development of attentional networks in childhood. *Neuropsychologia, 42*, 1029–1040.

Rueter, M. A., & Conger, R. D. (1995). Antecedents of parent-adolescent disagreements. *Journal of Marriage and Family, 57*, 435–448.

Rumberger, R. W., & Larson, A. (1998). Student mobility and the increased risk of high school dropout. *American Journal of Education, 107*, 1–35.

Russell, S. T., & Consolacion, T. B. (2003). Adolescent romance and emotional health in the United States: Beyond binaries. *Journal of Clinical Child and Adolescent Psychology, 32*, 499–508.

Ruuska, J., Kaltiala-Heino, R., Rantanen, P., & Koivisto, A.-M. (2005). Are there differences in the attitudinal body image between adolescent anorexia nervosa and bulimia nervosa? *Eating and Weight Disorders, 10*, 98–106.

Ryan, A. M., & Pintrich, P. R. (1997). "Should I ask for help?" The role of motivation and attitudes in adolescents' help-seeking in math class. *Journal of Educational Psychology, 89*, 1–13.

Ryan, S., Franzetta, K., & Manlove, J. (2007). Knowledge, perceptions, and motivations for contraception: Influence on teens contraceptive consistency. *Youth & Society, 39*, 182–208.

Sacks, J. H. (1994). A new age of understanding: Allowing self-defense claims for battered children who kill their abusers. *Journal of Contemporary Health Law and Policy, 10*, 349–388.

Safren, S. A., & Heimberg, R. G. (1999). Depression, hopelessness, suicidality, and related factors in sexual minority and heterosexual adolescents. *Journal of Consulting and Clinical Psychology, 67*, 859–866.

Safron, D., Bachman, J. G., & Schulenberg, J. E. (2001). Part-time work and hurried adolescence: The links among work intensity, sexual activities, health behaviors, and substance use. *Journal of Health and Social Behavior, 42*, 425–449.

Sallis, J. F., Prochaska, J. J., Taylor, W. C., Hill, J. O., & Geraci, J. C. (1999). Correlates of physical activity in a national sample of girls and boys in grades 4 through 12. *Health Psychology, 18*, 410–415.

Salmon, C. A., & Daly, M. (1998). Birth order and familial sentiment: Middleborns are different. *Evolution and Human Behavior, 19*, 299–312.

Salomone, P. R., & Sheehan, M. C. (1985). Vocational stability and congruence: An examination of Holland's proposition. *The Vocational Guidance Quarterly, 34*, 91–98.

Sanchez, R. P., Waller, M. W., & Greene, J. M. (2006). Who runs? A demographic profile of runaway youth in the United States. *Journal of Adolescent Health, 39*, 778–781.

Sandler, I. (2001). Quality and ecology of adversity as common mechanisms of risk and resilience. *American Journal of Community Psychology, 29*, 19–42.

Sansone, R. A., Gaither, G. A., & Songer, D. A. (2002). Self-harm behaviors across the life cycle: A pilot study of inpatients with borderline personality disorder. *Comprehensive Psychiatry, 43*, 215–218.

Santelli, J. S., Kaiser, J., Hirsch, L., Radosh, A., Simkin, L., & Middlestadt, S. (2004). Initiation of sexual intercourse among middle school adolescents: The influence of psychosocial factors. *Journal of Adolescent Health, 34*, 200–208.

Santelli, J. S., Warren, C. W., Lowry, R., Sogolow, E., Collins, J., Kann, L., Kaufmann, R. B., & Celentano, D. D. (1997). The use of condoms with other contraceptive methods among young men and women. *Family Planning Perspectives, 29*, 261–267.

Sappington, A. A., Phrr, R., Turnstall, A., & Rickert, E. (1997). Relationships among child abuse, date abuse, and psychological problems. *Journal of Clinical Psychology, 53*, 319–329.

Sarigiani, P. A., Ryan, R. M., & Peterson, J. (1999). Prevention of high-risk behaviors in adolescent women. *Journal of Adolescent Health, 25*, 109–119.

Savin-Williams, R. C. (1990). *Gay and lesbian youth: Expressions of identity.* New York: Hemisphere.

Savin-Williams, R. C. (1994). Verbal and physical abuse as stressors in the lives of lesbians, gay male and bisexual youth: Associations with school problems, running away, substance abuse, prostitution, and suicide. *Journal of Consulting and Clinical Psychology, 62*, 261–269.

Savin-Williams, R. C. (1996). Ethnic- and sexual-minority youth. In R. C. Savin-Williams & K. M. Cohen (Eds.), *The lives of lesbians, gays, and bisexuals: Children to adults* (pp. 152–165). Orlando: Harcourt, Brace College.

Savin-Williams, R. C. (1998). The disclosure to families of same-sex attractions by lesbian, gay, and bisexual youths. *Journal of Research on Adolescence, 8*, 49–68.

Savin-Williams, R. (2005). *The new gay teenager.* Cambridge, MA: Harvard University Press.

Savin-Williams, R. C., & Dubé, E. M. (1998). Parental reactions to their child's disclosure of same-sex attractions. *Family Relations, 47*, 1–7.

Scamvougeras, A., Witelson, S. F., Branskill, M., Stanchev, P., Black, S., Cheung, G., Steiner, M., & Buck, B. (1994). Sexual orientation and anatomy of the corpus callosum. *Society for Neuroscience Abstracts, 20*, 1425.

Scarr, S. (1997). Behavior-genetic and socialization theories of intelligence: Truce and reconciliation. In R. J. Sternberg & E. L. Grigorenko (Eds.), *Intelligence, heredity, and environment* (pp. 3–41). Cambridge, England: Cambridge University Press.

Schab, F. (1991). Schooling without learning: Twenty years of cheating in high school. *Adolescence, 26*, 839–847.

Schaffner, L. (1998). Searching for connection: A new look at teenaged runaways. *Adolescence, 33*, 619–628.

Schaie, K. W. (1996). *Intellectual development in adulthood: The Seattle Longitudinal Study.* New York: Cambridge University Press.

Schaller, M. (1992). In-group favoritism and statistical reasoning in social inference: Implications for formation and maintenance of group stereotypes. *Journal of Personality and Social Psychology, 63*, 61–74.

Scheel, K. R., & Westefeld, J. S. (1999). Heavy metal music and adolescent suicidality: An empirical investigation. *Adolescence, 34*, 253–273.

Schlegel, A., & Barry, H. II. (1991). *Adolescence: An anthropological inquiry.* New York: Free Press.

Schneider, B. H., & Younger, A. K. (1996). Adolescent-parent attachment in adolescents' relations with their peers. *Youth and Society, 28*, 95–108.

Schneider, F. W., & Couts, L. M. (1985). Person orientation of male and female high school students: To the educational disadvantage of males? *Sex Roles, 13*, 47–63.

Schneider, W., Perner, J., Bullock, M., Stefanick, J., & Zeigler, A. (1999). Development of intelligence and thinking. In F. E. Weinert & W. Schneider (Eds.), *Individual development from 3 to 12: Findings from the Munich Longitudinal Study* (pp. 9–28). Cambridge, England: Cambridge University Press.

Schonert-Reichl, K. A. (1999). Relations of peer acceptance, friendship adjustment, and social behavior to moral reasoning during early adolescence. *Journal of Early Adolescence, 19*, 249–279.

Schulenberg, J., O'Malley, P. M., Bachman, J. G., & Johnson, L. D. (2000). "Spread your wings and fly": The course of well-being and substance use during the transition to young adulthood. In L. J. Crockett & R. K. Silbereisen (Eds.), *Negotiating adolescence in times of social change* (pp. 224–255). New York: Cambridge University Press.

Schwartz, S. J. (2005). A new identity for identity research: Recommendations for explanding and refocusing the identity literature. *Journal of Adolescent Research, 20*, 293–308.

Schwartz, W. (1995). School dropouts: New information about an old problem. *ERIC Clearinghouse on Urban Education Digest, 109.*

Scott, J., & Hatalla, J. (1990). The influence of chance and contingency factors on career patterns of college-educated women. *The Career Development Quarterly, 39*, 19–30.

Scott-Jones, D., & White, A. B. (1990). Correlates of sexual activity in early adolescence. *Journal of Early Adolescence, 10*, 221–238.

Sedlak, A. J., Finkelhor, D., Hammer, H., & Schultz, D. (2002). *National estimates of missing children: An overview.* Office of Juvenile Justice and Delinquency Prevention Bulletin Series. Washington, DC: U.S. Department of Justice.

Seed, J. A., Dixon, R. A., McCluskey, S. E., & Young, A. H. (2000). Basal activity of the hypothalamic-pituitary-adrenal axis and cognitive function in anorexia nervosa. *European Archives of Psychiatry and Clinical Neuroscience, 250*, 11–15.

Segal, D. R., & Segal, M. W. (2004). America's military population, *Population Bulletin, 59*, 3–40

Seiffge-Krenke, I. (1999). Families with daughters, families with sons: Different challenges for family relationships and marital satisfaction? *Journal of Youth and Adolescence, 28*, 325–342.

Seiffge-Krenke, I. (2003). Testing theories of romantic development from adolescence to young adulthood: Evidence of a developmental sequence. *International Journal of Behavioral Development, 27*, 519–531.

Selah-Shayovits, R. (2006). Adolescent preferences for violence in television shows and music video clips. *International Journal of Adolescence and Youth, 13*, 99–112.

Selfhout, M. H. W., Delsing, M. J. M. H., ter Bogt, T. F. M., & Meeus, W. H. J. (2008). Heavy metal and hip-hop style preferences and externalizing problem behavior: A two-wave longitudinal study. *Youth & Society, 39*, 435–452.

Selwyn, N. (2008). "Not necessarily a bad thing . . .": A study of online plagiarism amongst undergraduate students. *Assessment & Evaluation in Higher Education, 33*, 465–479.

Sequin, J., Arseneault, L., & Tremblay, R. (2007). The contribution of "cool" and "hot" components of decision making in adolescence: Implications for developmental psychopathology. *Cognitive Development, 22*, 530–543.

Seroczynski, A. D., Jacquez, F. M., & Cole, D. A. (2003). Depression and suicide during adolescence. In G. R. Adams & M. D. Berzonsky (Eds.), *The Blackwell handbook of adolescence* (pp. 550–572). Oxford, England: Blackwell Publishing.

Sexuality Information and Education Council of the United States (SEICUS). (1996). Media recommendations for more realistic, accurate images concerning sexuality. *SIECUS Report, 24*, 22–23.

Shaffer, D., Gould, M. S., Fisher, P., Trautmant, P., Moreau, D., Kleinman, M., & Flory, M. (1996). Psychiatric diagnosis in child and adolescent suicide. *Archives of General Psychiatry, 53*, 339–348.

Shanahan, L., McHale, S. M., Crouter, A. C., & Osgood, D. W. (2007). Warmth with mothers and fathers from middle childhood to late adolescence: Within- and between-families comparisons. *Developmental Psychology, 43*, 551–563.

Shaw, M., & Dorling, D. (1998). Mortality among street youth in the UK. *Lancet, 352*, 743.

Sheehan, G., Darlington, Y., Noller, P., & Feeney, J. (2004). Children's perceptions of their sibling relationships during parental separation and divorce. *Journal of Divorce & Remarriage, 41*, 69–94.

Shek, D. T. L. (2001). Chinese adolescents and their parents' views on a happy family: Implications for family therapy. *Family Therapy, 28*, 73–104.

Shek, D. T. L., Siu, A. M. H., & Lee, T. Y. (2007). The Chinese positive youth development scale: A validation study. *Research on Social Work Practice, 17*, 380–391.

Sheldon, S. B., & Epstein, L. (2004). Getting students to school: Using family and community involvement to reduce chronic absenteeism. *School Community Journal, 14*, 39–56.

Sher, L., & Stanley, H. (2008). The role of endogenous opioids in the pathophysiology of self-injurious and suicidal behavior. *Archives of Suicide Research, 12*, 299–308.

Sherman, A. M., Lansford, J. E., & Volling, B. L. (2006). Sibling relationships and best friendships in young adulthood: Warmth, conflict, and well-being. *Personal Relationships, 13*, 151–165.

Shibley-Hyde, J., & Delamater, J. D. (2000). *Understanding human sexuality.* New York: McGraw-Hill.

Shinn, M., & Weitzman, B. (1996). Homeless families are different. In J. Baumohl (Ed.), *Homelessness in America* (pp. 109–122). Westport, CT: Greenwood Press.

Shon, P. C., & Targonski, R. (2003). Declining trends in U.S. parricides, 1976–1998: Testing the Freudian assumptions. *International Journal of Law and Psychiatry, 26*, 387–402.

Shrier, L., Pierce, J., Emans, S., & DuRant, R. (1998). Gender differences in risk behaviors associated with forced or pressured sex. *Archives of Pediatric and Adolescent Medicine, 152,* 57–63.

Shrum, W., & Cheek, N. H. (1987). Social structure during the school years: Onset of the degrouping process. *American Sociological Review, 52,* 218–223.

Siann, G., Callaghan, M. Glissov, P., Lockhart, R., & Rawson, L. (1999). Who gets bullied? The effect of school, gender, and ethnic group. *Educational Research, 36,* 123–134.

Siegel, J. M., Yancy, A. K., Aneshensel, C. S., & Schuler, R. (1999). Body image, perceived pubertal timing, and adolescent mental health. *Journal of Adolescent Health, 25,* 155–165.

Sieving, R., McNeely, C., & Blum, R. (2000). Maternal expectations, mother-child connectedness, and adolescent sexual debut. *Archives of Pediatrics and Adolescent Medicine, 154,* 809–816.

Sieving, R. E., Perry, C. L., & Williams, C. L. (2000). Do friendships change behaviors, or do behaviors change friendships? Examining paths of influence in young adolescents' alcohol use. *Journal of Adolescent Health, 26,* 27–35.

Sikkema, K. J., Hansen, N. B., Meade, C. S., Kochman, A., & Fox, A. M. (2009). Psychosocial predictors of sexual HIV transmission risk behavior among HIV-positive adults with a sexual abuse history in childhood. *Archives of Sexual Behavior, 38,* 121–134.

Sim, T. N. (2000). Adolescent psychosocial competence: The importance and role of regard for parents. *Journal of Research on Adolescence, 10,* 49–64.

Simes, M. R., & Berg, D. H. (2001). Surreptitious learning: Menarche and menstrual product advertisements. *Health Care for Women International, 22,* 455–469.

Simons, J. M., Finley, R., & Yang, A. (1991). *The adolescent and young adult fact book.* Washington, DC: Children's Defense Fund.

Simons, R. L., Lin, K.-H., Gordon, L. C., Conger, R. D., & Lorenz, F. O. (1999). Explaining the higher incidence of adjustment problems among children of divorce compared with those in two-parent families. *Journal of Marriage and Family, 61,* 1020–1033.

Simons, R. L., Whitbeck, L. B., Conger, R. D., & Melby, J. N. (1991). The effect of social skills, values, peers, and depression on adolescent substance use. *Journal of Early Adolescence, 11,* 466–481.

Simpkins, S. D., Davis-Kean, P. E., & Eccles, J. S. (2006). Math and science motivation: A longitudinal examination of the links between choices and beliefs. *Developmental Psychology, 42,* 70–83.

Simpson, L., Douglas, S., & Schimmel, J. (1998). Teen consumers: Catalog clothing purchase behavior. *Adolescence, 33,* 637–644.

Simsek, F., Ulukol, B., & Gulnar, S. B. (2005). The secular trends in height and weight of Turkish school children during 1993–2003. *Child: Care, Health, and Development, 31,* 441–447.

Singh, S., & Darrock, J. E. (2000). Adolescent pregnancy and childbearing: Levels and trends in developed countries. *Family Planning Perspectives, 32,* 14–23.

Sirgy, M. J., Lee, D.-J., Kosenko, R., Meadow, H. L., Rahtz, D., Cicic, M., Jin, G. X., Yarsuvat, D., Blenkhorn, D. L., & Wright, N. (1998). Does television viewership play a role in the perception of quality of life? *Journal of Advertising, 27,* 125–142.

Sirin, S. R. (2005). Socioeconomic status and academic achievement: A meta-analytic review of research. *Review of Educational Research, 75,* 417–453.

Sisk, C. L., & Foster, J. L. (2004). The neural basis of puberty and adolescence. *Nature Neuroscience, 7,* 1040–1047.

Skinner, B. F. (1938). *The behavior of organisms.* New York: Appleton-Century-Crofts.

Slater, M. D. (2003). Alienation, aggression, and sensation seeking as predictors of adolescent use of violent film, computer, and website content. *Journal of Communication, 53,* 105–121.

Slicker, E. K., Patton, M., & Fuller, D. K. (2004). Parenting dimensions and adolescent sexual initiation: Using self-esteem, academic aspiration, and substance use as mediators. *Journal of Youth Studies, 7,* 295–314.

Smart, L. S., Chibucos, T. R., & Didier, L. A. (1990). Adolescent substance use and perceived family functioning. *Journal of Family Issues, 11,* 208–227.

Smetana, J. G. (1995). Context, conflict, and constraint in adolescent-parent authority relationships. In M. Killen & D. Hart (Eds.), *Morality in everyday life: Developmental perspectives* (pp. 225–255). Cambridge, England: Cambridge University Press.

Smetana, J. G. (2002). Culture, autonomy, and personal jurisdiction in adolescent-parent relationships. In H. W. Reese & R. Kail (Eds.), *Advances in child development and behavior* (Vol. 2, pp. 51–87). New York: Academic Press.

Smetana, J. G., & Asquith, P. (1994). Adolescents' and parents' conceptions of parental authority and adolescent autonomy. *Child Development, 65,* 1147–1162.

Smetana, J. G., Crean, H. F., & Campione-Barr, N. (2005). Adolescents' and parents' changing conceptions of parental authority. In J. G. Smetana (Ed.), *Changing boundaries of parental authority* (pp. 31–46). San Francisco: Jossey-Bass.

Smetana, J. G., Metzger, A., Gettman, D. C., & Campione-Barr, N. (2006). Disclosure and secrecy in parent-adolescent relationships. *Child Development, 77,* 201–217.

Smetana, J. G., & Turiel, E. (2003). Moral development during adolescence. In G. R. Adams & M. D. Berzonsky

(Eds.), *The Blackwell handbook of adolescence* (pp. 247–268). Oxford, England: Blackwell Publishing.

Smith, A. M. A., Rosenthal, D. A., & Reichler, H. (1996). High schoolers' masturbatory practices: Their relationship to sexual intercourse and personal characteristics. *Psychological Reports, 79,* 499–509.

Smith, C. (2003). Theorizing religious effects among American adolescents. *Journal for the Scientific Study of Religion, 42,* 259–267.

Smith, C., & Denton, M. (2005). *Soul searching: The religious and spiritual lives of American teenagers.* New York: Oxford University Press.

Smith, E. J. (1991). Ethnic identity development: Toward the development of a theory within the context of majority/minority status. *Journal of Counseling and Development, 770,* 181–188.

Smith, K. H., & Stutts, M. A. (1999). Factors that influence adolescents to smoke. *Journal of Consumer Affairs, 33,* 321–357.

Smith, S. L., & Boyson, A. R. (2002). Violence in music videos: Examining the prevalence and context of physical aggression. *Journal of Communication, 52,* 61–83.

Snarey, J. R. (1995). In a commutarian voice: The sociological expansion of Kohlbergian theory, research, and practice. In W. R. Kurtines & J. L. Gewirtz (Eds.), *Moral development: An introduction* (pp. 109–134). Boston: Allyn & Bacon.

Sneddon, H. (2003). The effects of maltreatment on children's health and well-being. *Child Care in Practice, 9,* 236–250.

Sneed, C. D. (2008). Parent-adolescent communication about sex: The impact of content and comfort on adolescent sexual behavior. *Journal of HIV/AIDS Prevention in Children & Youth, 9,* 70–83.

Snell, J. C., & Marsh, M. (2008). Life cycle loneliness curve. *Psychology and Education: An Interdisciplinary Journal, 45,* 26–28.

Snyder, H. N. (2004). *Juvenile arrests 2002.* Washington, DC: Office of Juvenile Justice and Prevention.

Snyder, H., & Sickmund, M. (2006). *Juvenile offenders and victims: 2006 national report.* Washington, DC: Office of Juvenile Justice and Delinquency Prevention.

Snyder, L. B., Milici, F. F., Slater, M., Sun, H., & Strizhakova, Y. (2006). Effects of alcohol advertising exposure on drinking among youth. *Archives of Pediatrics and Adolescent Medicine, 160,* 18–24.

Song, C., & Glick, E. (2004). College attendance and choice of college majors among Asian-American students. *Social Science Quarterly, 85,* 1401–1421.

South, S. J. (1995). Do you need to shop around? *Journal of Family Issues, 16,* 432–449.

Span, S. A., & Vidal, A. (2003). Cross-cultural differences in female university students' attitudes toward homosexuals: A preliminary study. *Psychological Reports, 92,* 565–572.

Sparks, G. G. (2001). *Media effects research: A basic overview.* Belmont, CA: Wadsworth.

Spear, L. P. (2002). The adolescent brain and the college drinker: Biological basis of propensity to use and misuse alcohol. *Journal of Studies on Alcohol, 14,* 71–81.

Spera, C. (2005). A review of the relationship among parenting practices, parenting styles, and adolescent school achievement. *Educational Psychology Review, 17,* 125–146.

Sprecher, S., Barbee, A., & Schwartz, P. (1995). "Was it good for you, too?": Gender differences in first sexual intercourse experiences. *Journal of Sex Research, 32,* 3–15.

Spruijt, E., Degoede M., & Vandervalk, I. (2001). The well-being of youngsters coming from six different family types. *Patient Education and Counselling, 45,* 285–294.

Srivastava, L. (2005). Mobile phones and the evolution of social behaviour. *Behaviour & Information Technology, 24,* 111–129.

St-James, M. B., de Man, A. F. & Stout, D. (2006). Athletic style of dress and perceived social distance. *North American Journal of Psychology, 8,* 541–546.

Stack, S. (1998). Heavy metal, religiosity, and suicide acceptability. *Suicide and Life-Threatening Behavior, 28,* 388–394.

Stack, S. (2003). Media coverage as a risk factor in suicide. *Journal of Epidemiology and Community Health, 57,* 238–240.

Staff, J., Messersmith, E. E., & Schulenberg, J. E. (2009). Adolescents and the world of work. In R. M. Lerner & L. Steinberg (Eds.), *Handbook of adolescent psychology* (3rd ed., pp. 270–313). Hoboken, NJ: Wiley.

Staff, J., & Mortimer, J. T. (2008). Social class background and the "school to work" transition. *New Directions for Child and Adolescent Development, 119,* 55–69.

Staksrud, E. (2003). Parents believe, kids act. Presented at the 2003 SAFT Conference: *Future kids online: How to promote safety, awareness, facts, and tools.* Sweden. Retrieved from http://www.saftonline.org.

Stallmann, J. I., & Johnson, T. G. (1996). Community factors in secondary educational achievement in Appalachia. *Youth and Society, 27,* 469–484.

Stanley, S. M., Whitton, S. W., & Markman, H. J. (2004). Maybe I do: Interpersonal commitment and remarital or nonmarital cohabitation. *Journal of Family Issues, 25,* 496–519.

Stapley, J. C., & Haviland, J. M. (1989). Beyond depression: Gender differences in normal adolescents' emotional experiences. *Sex Roles, 20,* 295–308.

Stattin, H., & Kerr, M. (2000). Parental monitoring: A reinterpretation. *Child Development, 71,* 1072–1085.

Steinberg, L. (2001). We know some things: Parent-adolescent relationships in retrospect and prospect. *Journal of Research on Adolescence, 11,* 1–19.

Steinberg, L. (2007). Risk taking in adolescence: New perspectives from brain and behavioral science. *Current Directions in Psychological Science, 16,* 55–59.

Steinberg, L., Blatt-Eisengart, I., & Cauffman, E. (2006). Patterns of competence and adjustment among adolescents from authoritative, authoritarian, indulgent, and neglectful homes: A replication in a sample of serious juvenile offenders. *Journal of Research on Adolescence, 16,* 47–58.

Steinberg, L., & Dornbusch, S. M. (1991). Negative correlates of part-time employment during adolescence: Replication and elaboration. *Developmental Psychology, 27,* 304–313.

Steinberg, L., Dornbusch, S. M., & Brown, B. B. (1992). Ethnic differences in adolescent achievement: An ecological perspective. *American Psychologist, 47,* 723–729.

Steinberg, L., Greenberger, E., Garduque, L., Ruggiero, M., & Vaux, A. (1982). Effects of working on adolescent development. *Developmental Psychology, 18,* 385–395.

Steinberg, L., & Steinberg, W. (1994). *Crossing paths: How your child's adolescence triggers your own crisis.* New York: Simon and Schuster.

Steinmayr, R., & Spinath, B. (2008). Sex differences in school achievement: What are the roles of personality and achievement motivation? *European Journal of Personality, 22,* 185–209.

Stepp, L. S. (1999). Parents are alarmed by an unsettling new fad in middle school: Oral sex. *Washington Post,* July 8.

Stern, D., Rahn, M. L., & Chung, Y.-P. (1998). Design of work-based learning for students in the United States. *Youth and Adolescence, 29,* 471–502.

Stern, M., & Alvarez, A. (1992). Pregnant and parenting adolescents. A comparative analysis of coping response and psychosocial adjustment. *Journal of Adolescent Research, 7,* 469–493.

Sternberg, R. J. (1997). *Successful intelligence.* New York: Plume.

Sternberg, R. J., & Girgorenko, E. L. (2002). *Dynamic testing.* New York: Cambridge University Press.

Sternberg, R. J., & Wagner, R. K. (Eds.). (1986). *Practical intelligence: Nature and origins of competence in the everyday world.* Cambridge, England: Cambridge University Press.

Sternberg, R. J., Torff, B., & Grigorenko, E. L. (1998). Teaching triarchically improves school achievement. *Journal of Educational Psychology, 90,* 374–384.

Stevens, N. M., Mott, L. A., & Youells, F. (1996). Rural adolescent drinking behavior: Three-year follow-up on the New Hampshire Substance Abuse Prevention Study. *Adolescence, 31,* 159–166.

Stivers, C. (1988). Parent-adolescent communication and its relationship to adolescent depression and suicide proneness. *Adolescence, 23,* 291–295.

Stoltz, J. M., Shannon, K., Kerr, T., Zhang, R., Montaner, J. S., & Wood, E. (2007). Associations between childhood maltreatment and sex work in a cohort of drug-using youth. *Social Science & Medicine, 65,* 1214–1221.

Stolzenberg, R. M., Blair-Loy, M., & Waite, L. J. (1995). Religious participation in early adulthood: Age and family life cycle effects on church membership. *American Sociological Review, 60,* 84–103.

Stone, A. L., Storr, C. L., & Anthony, J. C. (2006) Evidence for a hallucinogen dependence syndrome developing soon after onset of hallucinogen use during adolescence. *International Journal of Methods in Psychiatric Research, 15,* 116–130.

Storch, E. A., & Storch, J. B. (2002). Fraternities, sororities, and academic dishonesty. *College Student Journal, 36,* 247–252.

Stouthamer-Loeber, M., & Wei, E. H. (1998). The precursors of young fatherhood and its effects on delinquency of teenage males. *Journal of Adolescent Health, 22,* 56–65.

Strasburger, V. C. (1995). *Adolescents and the media: Medical and psychological impact.* Thousand Oaks, CA: Sage.

Strasburger, V. C., & Donnerstein, E. (1999). Children, adolescents, and the media: Issues and solutions. *Pediatrics, 103,* 129–139.

Strasburger, V., Wilson, B. J., & Jordan, A. B. (2009). *Children, adolescents, and the media* (2nd ed.). Thousand Oaks, CA: Sage.

Straugh, B. (2003). *The primal teen: What new discoveries about the teenage brain tell us about our kids.* New York: Doubleday.

Strayer, D. L., Drews, F. A., & Crouch, D. J. (2006). A comparison of the cell phone driver and the drunk driver. *Human Factors, 48,* 381–391.

Streib, H. (1999). Off-road religion? A narrative approach to fundamentalist and occult orientations of adolescents. *Journal of Adolescence, 22,* 255–267.

Stringer, T. (2003, Winter). *Summer time, summer teens.* Occupational Outlook Quarterly. Washington, DC: National Bureau of Labor Statistics.

Strong, E. K. (1943). *Vocational interests of men and women.* Palo Alto, CA: Stanford University Press.

Strouse, J. S., Buerkel-Rothfuss, N., & Long, E. C. J. (1995). Gender and families as moderators of the relationship between music video exposure and adolescent sexual permissiveness. *Adolescence, 30,* 505–521.

Stubbs, M. M. (2008). Cultural perceptions and practices around menarche and adolescent menstruation in the United States. *Annals of the New York Academy of Sciences, 1135,* 58–66.

Styer, D. M. (2006). An understanding of self-injury and suicide. *The Prevention Researcher, 13,* 10–12.

Styne, D. M. (2002). The testes: Disorders of sexual differentiation and puberty in the male. In M. A. Sperling

(Ed.), *Pediatric endocrinology* (2nd ed., pp. 565–628). Philadelphia: Saunders.

Suárez-Orozco, C., & Suárez-Orozco, M. M. (2001). *Children of immigration.* Cambridge, MA: Harvard University Press.

Subrahmanyam, K., Greenfield, P., Kraut, R., & Gross, E. (2001). The impact of computer use on children's and adolescents' development. *Journal of Applied Developmental Psychology, 22,* 7–30.

Substance Abuse and Mental Health Services Administration. (2003). *Results from the 2002 National Survey on Drug Use and Health: National findings* (Office of Applied Studies, NHSDA Series H-22, DHHS Publication No. SMA 03-3836). Rockville, MD: Author.

Sue, D. W., Bucceri, J., Lin, A. I., Nadal, K. L., & Torino, G. C. (2009). Racial microaggressions and the Asian American experience. *Asian American Journal of Psychology, 5,* 88–101.

Sun, S. S., Schubert, C. M., Liang, R., Roche, A. F., Kulin, H. E., Le, P. A., Himes, J. H., & Chumlea, W. C. (2005). Is sexual maturity occurring earlier among U.S. children? *Journal of Adolescent Health, 37,* 345–355.

Sun, Y., & Li, Y. (2008). Parents' marital disruption and its uneven effect on children's academic performance—A simulation model. *Social Science Research, 37,* 449–460.

Surgenor, L. J., Maguire, S., Russell, J., & Touyz, S. (2007). Self-liking and self-competence relationship to symptoms of anorexia nervosa. *European Eating Disorders Review, 15,* 139–145.

Susman E. J., & Dorn, L. D. (2009). Puberty. In R. M. Lerner & R. Steinberg (Eds.), *Handbook of adolescent psychology* (3rd ed., pp. 116–151). New York: Wiley.

Suyemoto, K. L. (1998). The functions of self-mutilation. *Clinical Psychology Review, 18,* 531–554.

Suyemoto, K. L., & MacDonald, M. L. (1995). Self-cutting in female adolescents. *Psychotherapy, 32,* 162–171.

Svensson, R. (2003). Gender differences in adolescent drug use: The impact of parental monitoring and peer deviance. *Youth and Society, 34,* 300–329.

Swaab, D. F., & Hofman, M. A. (1995). Sexual differentiation of the human hypothalamus in relation to gender and sexual orientation. *Trends in Neurosciences, 18,* 264–270.

Swain, C. R., Acherman, L. K., & Ackerman, M. A. (2006). The influence of individual characteristics and contraceptive beliefs on parent-teen sexual communications: A structural model. *Journal of Adolescent Health, 38,* 753e.9–753e.18.

Swanson, H. L. (1999). What develops in working memory? A life span perspective. *Developmental Psychology, 35,* 986–1000.

Swanson, H. L., & Hill, G. (1993). Metacognitive aspects of moral reasoning and behavior. *Adolescence, 28,* 711–735.

Sweeten, G., Bushway, S. D., & Paternoster, R. (2009). Does droppng out of school mean dropping into delinquency? *Criminology, 47,* 47–91.

Sweeting, H., & West, P. (2001). Being different: Correlates of the experience of teasing at age 11. *Research Paper in Education, 16,* 225–246.

Symantec Corporation. (2004). *Symantec survey shows seniors are the most spam savvy online demographic.* Retrieved from http://www.symantec.com/press/2004.

Szabo, A., & Underwood, J. (2004). Cybercheats: Is information and communication technology fueling academic dishonesty? *Active Learning in Higher Education, 5,* 180–199.

Szinovacz, M. E. (1998). Grandparent research: Past, present, and future. In M. E. Szinovacz (Ed.), *Handbook on grandparenthood* (pp. 1–20). Westport, CT: Greenwood Press.

Tamborini, R. (1996). A model of empathy and emotional reactions to horror. In J. Weaver & R. Tamborini (Eds.), *Horror films: Current research on audience preference and reactions* (pp. 103–123). Mahwah, NJ: Erlbaum.

Tanaka, T. (2001). The identity formation of the victim of shunning. *School Psychology International, 22,* 464–476.

Tang, S., & Zuo, J. (2000). Dating attitudes and behaviors of American and Chinese college students. *Social Science Journal, 37,* 67–78.

Tanner, J. M. (1968). Earlier maturation in man. *Scientific American, 218,* 21–27.

Tanner, J. M. (1990). *Foetus into man* (2nd ed.). Cambridge, MA: Harvard University Press.

Tarnowski, K. J., Brown, R. T., & Simonian, S. J. (1999). Social class. In W. K. Silverman & T. H. Ollendick, (Eds.), *Developmental issues in the clinical treatment of children* (pp. 213–230). Boston: Allyn & Bacon.

Tasker, F. (2005). Lesbian mothers, gay fathers, and their children: A review. *Journal of Developmental & Behavioral Pediatrics, 26,* 224–240.

Taylor, A. (2005). What employers look for: The skills debate and the fit with youth perceptions. *Journal of Education and Work, 18,* 201–218.

Taylor, L. D. (2005). Effects of visual and verbal sexual content and perceived realism on attitudes and beliefs. *Journal of Sex Research, 42,* 130–137.

Taylor, R. (2000). Diversity within African American families. In D. H. Demo, K. R. Allen, & M. A. Fine (Eds.), *Handbook of family diversity* (pp. 232–251). New York: Oxford University Press.

Teachman, J. D., Paasch, K., & Carver, K. (1996). Social capital and dropping out of school early. *Journal of Marriage and Family, 58,* 773–783.

Tebes, J. K., Feinn, R., Vanderploeg, J. J., Chinman, M. J., Shepard, J., Brabham, T., et al. (2007). Impact of a positive youth development program in urban after-school settings on the prevention of adolescent substance abuse. *Journal of Adolescent Health, 41,* 219–220.

Teitelman, A. M. (2004). Adolescent girls' perspectives of family interactions related to menarche and sexual health. *Qualitative Health Research, 14,* 1292–1308.

Terrell, N.-E. (1997). Aggravated and sexual assaults among homeless and runaway adolescents. *Youth and Society, 28,* 267–290.

Thanasiu, P. L. (2004). Childhood sexuality: Discerning healthy from abnormal sexual behaviors. *Journal of Mental Health Counseling, 26,* 309–319.

The Oyez Project. (2009). *Carcieri v. Salazar.* Retrieved from http://oyez.org/cases/2000-2009/2008/2008_07_526.

Thomas, P., Schroeter, K., Dahme, B., & Nutzinger, D. O. (2002). Self-injurious behavior in women with eating disorders. *The American Journal of Psychiatry, 159*(3), 408–411.

Thompson, S. J., Bender, K. A., Lewis, C. M., & Watkins, R. (2008). Runaway and pregnant: Risk factors associated with pregnancy in a national sample of runaway/homeless female adolescents. *Journal of Adolescent Health, 4,* 125–132.

Thornberry, T. P., & Krohn, M. D. (1997). Peers, drug use, and delinquency. In D. M. Stoff, J. Breiling, & J. D. Maser (Eds.), *Handbook of antisocial behavior* (pp. 218–233). New York: Wiley.

Thorne, B. (1986). Girls and boys together . . . but mostly apart: Gender arrangements in elementary schools. In W. Hartup & Z. Rubin (Eds.), *Relationships and development* (pp. 167–184). Hillsdale, NJ: Erlbaum.

Tietjen, A. (1982). The social networks of preadolescent children in Sweden. *International Journal of Behavioral Development, 5,* 111–130.

Tietz, C. C., Hu, S. S., & Arendt, E. A. (1997). The female athlete: Evaluation and treatment of sports-related problems. *Journal of the Academy of Orthopaedic Surgeons, 5,* 87–96.

Tiggemann, M. (2005). Body dissatisfaction and adolescent self-esteem: Prospective findings. *Body Image, 2,* 129–135.

Tisak, M. S., & Tisak, J. (1996). My sibling's but not my friend's keeper: Reasoning about responses to aggressive acts. *Journal of Early Adolescence, 16,* 324–339.

Titus, D. N. (1994). *Values education in American secondary schools.* Paper presented at the Kutztown University Education Conference, Kutztown, PA.

Tolan, P. H., Guerra, N. G., & Kendall, P. (1995). A developmental-ecological perspective on antisocial behavior in children and adolescents: Towards a unified risk and intervention framework. *Journal of Consulting and Clinical Psychology, 63,* 579–584.

Toney, G. T., & Weaver, B. (1994). Effects of gender and gender role self-perceptions on affective reactions to rock music videos. *Sex Roles, 30,* 567–583.

Trenholm, C., Devamy, B., Fortson, K., Clark, M., Quay Bridgespan, L., & Wheeler, J. (2008). Impacts of abstinence education on teen sexual activity, risk of pregnancy, and risk of sexually transmitted diseases. *Journal of Policy Analysis and Management, 27,* 255–276.

Trinder, L. (2008). The relationship between contact and child adjustment in high conflict cases after divorce or separation. *Child and Adolescent Mental Health, 13,* 181–187.

Trumbull, E., Rothstein-Fisch, C., Greenfield, P., & Quiroz, B. (2001). *Bridging cultures between home and school: A guide for teachers.* Mahwah, NJ: Erlbaum.

Tsunokai, G. T. (2005). Beyond the lenses of the "model" minority myth: A descriptive portrait of Asian gang members. *Journal of Gang Research, 12,* 37–58.

Tucker, C. J., Barber, B. L., & Eccles, J. S. (1997). Advice about life plans and personal problems in late adolescent sibling relationships. *Journal of Youth and Adolescence, 26,* 63–76.

Turiel, E. (1998). Moral development. In W. Damon (Series Ed.) and N. Eisenberg (Vol. Ed.), *Handbook of child psychology: Social, emotional and personality development* (Vol. 3, 5th ed., pp. 863–932). New York: Wiley.

Turner, S. L., Conkel, J. L., Starkey, M., Landgraf, R., Lapan, R. T., Siewert, J. J., et al. (2008). Gender differences in Holland vocational personality types: Implications for school counselors. *Professional School Counseling, 11,* 317–326.

Tyler, C., Johnston, C. A., Dalton, W. T., & Foreyt, J. P. (2009). Relationships between weight and body dissatisfaction, body esteem, and teasing in African American girls. *Journal of Black Psychology, 35,* 125–132.

Tyler, K. A., & Bersani, B. E. (2008). A longitudinal study of early adolescent precursors to running away. *Journal of Early Adolescence, 28,* 230–251.

Tyler, K. A., Whitbeck, L. B., Hoyt, D. R., & Johnson, K. (2003). Self-mutilation and homeless youth: The role of family abuse, street experiences, and mental disorders. *Journal of Research on Adolescence, 13,* 457–474.

Tyrka, A. R., Graber, J. A., & Brooks-Gunn, J. (2000). The development of disordered eating: Correlates and predictors of eating in the context of adolescence. In A. J. Sameriff, M. Lewis, & S. Miller (Eds.), *Handbook of developmental psychopathology* (2nd ed., pp. 607–627). New York: Plenum.

U.S. Bureau of Labor Statistics. (2000). *Report on the youth labor force.* Retrieved from http://www.stats.bls.gov/opub/rylf/pdf.chapter3.pdf.

U.S. Bureau of Labor Statistics. (2009a) [2009a in text, ch. 1]*Current Population Survey.* Retrieved from http://www.bls.gov/cps/demographics.htm.

U.S. Bureau of the Census. (2000a). *Poverty rate lowest in 20 years, household income at record high*. Census Bureau Reports. Press Release, Department of Commerce News, September 26, 2000. Retrieved from http://www.census.gov/pressrelease/www/2000/cb00-158.html.

U.S. Bureau of the Census. (2002). *Statistical abstract of the United States: 2002*. Washington, DC: U.S. Government Printing Office.

U.S. Bureau of the Census. (2003). *School enrollment: 2000*. C2KBR-26. Washington, DC: U.S. Government Printing Office.

U.S. Bureau of the Census. (2003b). *Computer use in 2003: Population profile of the United States*. Retrieved from http://www.census.gov/population/pop-profile/dynamic/Computers.pdf.

U.S. Bureau of the Census. (2004). *U.S. interim projections by age, sex, race, and Hispanic origin*. Retrieved from http://www.census.gov/ipc/www/usinterimproj/natprojtab02a.pdf.

U.S. Bureau of the Census. (2005a). *Poverty: 2004 highlights*. Retrieved from http://www.census.gov/hhes/www/poverty/poverty04/pov04hi.html.

U.S. Bureau of the Census. (2005d). *Statistical abstract of the United States: 2004*. Washington, DC: Author.

U.S. Bureau of the Census. (2006). *Current Population Survey*, March 2006.

U.S. Bureau of the Census. (2007a). *Current Population Survey*, March 2007.

U.S. Bureau of the Census. (2007b). *The American community—American Indians and Alaskan Natives: 2004*. ACS-07. Washington, DC: Bureau of the Census.

U.S. Bureau of the Census. (2008). *Current Population Survey, Annual Social and Economic Supplements*. Retrieved from http://www.census.gov/apsd/techdoc/cps/cpsmar08.pdf.

U.S. Bureau of the Census. (2008a). Population projections of the United States by age, sex, race, and Hispanic origin: 1995–2000. *Current Population Report* # P25-1130. Washington, DC: U.S. Government Printing Office.

U.S. Bureau of the Census. (2008b). *Women in the labor force: A databook 2008*. Washington, DC: U.S. Government Printing Office.

U.S. Bureau of the Census. (2009). *Annual estimates of the resident population by sex, race, and Hispanic origin for the United States: April 1, 2000 to July 1, 2008* (NC-EST2008-03). Retrieved from http://www.census.gov/popest/national/asrh/NC-EST2008-srh.html.

U.S. Bureau of the Census. (2009a). *Current Population Survey, 2008 Annual Social and Economic Supplement*.

U.S. Bureau of the Census. (2009b). *Statistical abstract of the United States: 2002*. Washington, DC: U.S. Government Printing Office.

U.S. Department of Commerce. (1999). *Falling through the net: Defining the digital divide*. Retrieved from http://www.ntia.doc.gov/ntiahome/fttn99/contents.html.

U.S. Department of Health and Human Services. (1999). *Mental health: A report of the Surgeon General*. Washington, DC: U.S. Government Printing Office.

U.S. Department of Health and Human Services. (2000). *Reducing tobacco use: A report of the Surgeon General*. Washington, DC: U.S. Government Printing Office.

U.S. Department of Health and Human Services. (2001). *The Surgeon General's call to action to prevent and decrease overweight and obesity*. Rockville, MD: U.S. Government Printing Office.

U.S. Department of Health and Human Services. (2008). *Recommended HIV treatment regimens*. Retrieved from http://aidsinfo.nih.gov/contentfiles/RecommendedHIVTreatmentRegimens_FS_en.pdf.

U.S. Department of Health and Human Services. (2009). *Fiscal year 2007 refugee arrivals*. Retrieved from http://www.acf.hhs.gov/programs/orr/data/fy2007RA.htm.

Uhlenberg, P., & Hammill, B. G. (1998). Frequency of grandparent contact with grandchild sets: Six factors that make a difference. *The Gerontologist, 38*, 276–285.

Underwood, R. C., & Patch, C. (1999). Siblicide: A descriptive analysis of sibling homicide. *Homicide Studies: An Interdisciplinary & International Journal, 3*, 333–348.

Unger, J. B., Kipke, M. D., Simon, T. R., Montgomery, S. B., & Johnson, C. J. (1997). Homeless youths and young adults in Los Angeles: Prevalence of mental health problems and the relationship between mental health and substance abuse disorders. *American Journal of Community Psychology, 25*, 371–394.

United Nations. (2005). *World youth report 2005*. New York: Author.

United Nations. (2006). *Demographic yearbook 2006*. New York: Author.

United Nations. (2007). *World youth report 2007: Young people's transition to adulthood*. New York: Author.

United Nations High Commissioner for Refugees. (2005). *Refugees by the numbers, 2005 edition*. New York: Author.

United Nations Population Fund. (2003). *Making 1 billion count: Investing in adolescents' health and rights. The state of the world's population: 2003*. Retrieved from http://www.unfpa.org/swp/2003/english/ch1/page2.htm.

United Nations Population Fund. (2007). *Change, choice, and power:Young women, livelihoods, and HIV prevention*. New York: Author

University of California at Los Angeles Medical Center. (2000). *Acne*. Retrieved from http://www.mednet.ucla.edu/healthtopics/pls/acne.htm.

University of Michigan News Service. (2008). *More good news on teen smoking: Rates at or near record lows*.

Retrieved from http://www.monitoringthefuture.org/pressreleases/08cigpr_complete.pdf.

Upchurch, D. M., Aneshensel, C. S., Sucoff, C. A., & Levy-Storms, L. (1999). Neighborhood and family contexts of adolescent sexual activity. *Journal of Marriage and Family, 61*, 920–933.

Urberg, K. A., Degirmencioglu, S. M., & Tolson, J. M. (1998). Adolescent friendship selection and termination: The role of similarity. *Journal of Social and Personal Relationships, 15*, 703–710.

Vachon, J., Vtaro, F., Wanner, B., & Tremblay, R. E. (2004). Adolescent gambling: Relationships with parent gambling and parenting practices. *Psychology of Addictive Behaviors, 18*, 398–401.

Vakil, E., Blachstein, H., Sheinman, M., & Greenstein, Y. (2009). Developmental changes in attention tests norms: Implications for the structure of attention. *Child Neuropsychology, 15*, 21–39.

Valentine, S., & Mosley, G. (1999). Acculturation and sex-role attitudes among Mexican Americans: A longitudinal analysis. *Hispanic Journal of Behavioral Sciences, 22*, 104–113.

Valkenburg, P. M., Schouten, A. P., & Peter, J. (2005). Adolescents' identity experiments on the Internet. *New Media & Society, 7*, 383–402.

Van der Meij, H. (1990). Question asking: To know that you do not know is not enough. *Journal of Educational Psychology, 82*(3), 505–512.

Van der Meij, H. (1998). The great divide between teacher and student questioning. In S. A. Karabenick (Ed.), *Strategic help seeking: Implications for learning and teaching* (pp. 195–218). Mahwah, NJ: Erlbaum.

van Jaarsveld, C. H. M., Fidler, J. A., Simon, A. E., & Wardle, J. (2007). Persistent impact of pubertal timing on trends in smoking, food choice, activity, and stress in adolescence. *Psychosomatic Medicine, 69*, 798–806.

van Roosmalen, E. H., & McDaniel, S. A. (1992). Adolescent smoking intentions. Gender differences in peer context. *Adolescence, 27*, 87–105.

Vandereycken, W. (1994). Emergence of bulimia nervosa as a separate diagnostic entity: Review of the literature from 1960 to 1979. *International Journal of Eating Disorders, 16*, 105–116.

Vartanian, L. R., & Herman, C. P. (2006). Beliefs about the determinants of body weight predict dieting and exercise behavior. *Eating Behavior, 7*, 176–179.

Vasa, R. A., Carlino, A. R., & Pine, D. S. (2006). Pharmacotherapy of depressed children and adolescents: Current issues and potential directions. *Biological Psychiatry, 59*, 1021–1028.

Vaughn, M. G., & Howard, M. O. (2004). Adolescent substance abuse treatment: A synthesis of controlled evaluations. *Research on Social Work Practice, 14*, 325–335.

Vazsonyi, A. T., Hibbert, J. R., & Snider, J. B. (2003). Exotic enterprise no more? Adolescent reports of family and parenting processes from youth in four countries. *Journal of Research on Adolescence, 13*, 129–160.

Venkdeswaran, R. (2000). Nutrition for youth. *Clinical Family Practice, 2*, 791–822.

Ventura, S. J., Abma, J. C., Mosher, W. D., & Henshaw, S. K. (2008). *Estimated pregnancy rates by outcome for the United States, 1990–2004*. National Vital Statistics Reports, 56, No. 15. Hyattsville, MD: National Center for Health Statistics.

Villarruel, A. M. (1998). Cultural influences on the sexual attitudes, beliefs, and norms of young Latina adolescents. *Journal of the Society of Pediatric Nurses, 3*, 69–79.

Vincenzo, R., Bruno, M., Matteo, F., Elena, V., & Cesare, C. (2005). Estrogens and male reproduction. In R. McLachlin (Ed.), *Endocrinology of male reproduction*. Retrieved from http://www.endotext.org/male/male17/maleframe17.htm.

Visser, J., & Geuze, R. H. (2000). Kinesthetic acuity in adolescent boys: A longitudinal study. *Developmental Medicine and Child Neurology, 42*, 93–96.

Vitaro, F., Brendgen, M., & Tremblay, R. E. (2000). Influence of deviant friends on delinquency: Searching for moderator variables. *Journal of Abnormal Child Psychology, 28*, 313–325.

Voight, J. (1999). Moving target. *Mediaweek, 9*, 38–39.

Vondracek, F. W., & Schulenberg, J. E. (1986). Career development in adolescence: Some conceptual and intervention issues. *The Vocational Guidance Quarterly, 34*, 247–254.

Vondracek, F. W., & Schulenberg, J. E. (1992). Counseling for normative and nonnormative influences on career development. *The Career Development Quarterly, 40*, 291–301.

Vygotsky, L. S. (1978). *Mind in society: The development of higher mental processes*. Cambridge, MA: Harvard University Press.

Wade, T. J., Cairney, J., & Pevalin, D. J. (2002). Emergence of gender differences in depression during adolescence: National panel results from three countries. *Journal of the American Academy of Child & Adolescent Psychiatry, 41*, 190–198.

Wadsworth, M. E., & Compas, B. E. (2002). Coping with economic strain and family conflict: The adolescent perspective. *Journal of Research on Adolescence, 12*, 243–274.

Wagenaar, A. C., & Toomey, T. L. (2002). Effects of minimum drinking age laws: Review and analyses of the literature from 1960 to 2000. *Journal of Studies on Alcohol, 14*, 206–225.

Wainright, J. L., & Patterson, J. (2008). Peer relations among adolescents with female same-sex parents. *Developmental Psychology, 44*, 117–126.

Waizenhofer, R. N., Buchanan, C. M., & Jackson-Newsom, J. (2004). Mothers' and fathers' knowledge of adolescents' daily activities: Its sources and its links with adolescent adjustment. *Journal of Family Psychology, 18,* 348–360.

Walcott, D. D., Pratt, H. D., & Patel, D. R. (2003). Adolescents and eating disorders: Gender, racial, ethnic, sociocultural, and socioeconomic issues. *Journal of Adolescent Research, 18,* 223–243.

Walker, L. J. (2006). Gender and morality. In M. Killen & J. G. Smetana (Eds.), *Handbook of moral development* (pp. 93–115). Mahwah, NJ: Erlbaum.

Walker, L. J., & Henning, K. H. (1997). Moral development in the broader context of personality. In S. Hala (Ed.), *The development of social cognition* (pp. 297–327). Hove, England: Psychology Press.

Walker, L. J., & Richards, B. S. (1979). Stimulating transitions in moral reasoning as a function of stage of cognitive development. *Developmental Psychology, 15,* 95–103.

Walker, L. J., & Taylor, H. (1991). Family interactions and the development of moral reasoning. *Child Development, 62,* 264–283.

Walker-Barnes, C. J., & Mason, C. A. (2004). Delinquency and substance use among gang-involved youth: The moderating role of parenting practices. *American Journal of Community Psychology, 34,* 235–250.

Wallace, J. M., Jr., & Forman, T. A. (1998). Religion's role in promoting health and reducing risk among American youth. *Health Education & Behavior, 25,* 721–741.

Wallace, L. H., & May, C. (2005). The impact of parental attachment and feelings of isolation on adolescent fear of crime at school. *Family Therapy, 32,* 157–173.

Wallace-Broscious, A., Serafica, F. C., & Osipow, S. H. (1994). Adolescent career development: Relationships to self-concepts and identity status. *Journal of Research on Adolescence, 4,* 127–150.

Wallerstein, J. S. (1991). The long-term effects of divorce on children: A review. *Journal of the Academy of Child Adolescence Psychiatry, 30,* 349–360.

Wallerstein, J. S., & Blakeslee, S. (1989). *Second chances: Men, women, and children a decade after divorce.* New York: Ticknor and Fields.

Wallerstein, J. S., & Lewis, J. (1998). The long-term impact of divorce on children: A first report from a 25-year study. *Family and Conciliation Courts Review, 36,* 368–383.

Wallerstein, J. S., & Lewis, J. M. (2004). The unexpected legacy of divorce: Report of a 25-year study. *Psychoanalytic Psychology, 21,* 353–370.

Wang, S., Holloway, B. B., Beatty, S. E., & Hill, W. W. (2007). Adolescent influence in family purchase decisions: An update and cross-national extension. *Journal of Business Research, 60,* 1117–1124.

Ward, L. M. (2002). Does television exposure affect emerging adults' attitudes and assumptions about sexual relationships? Correlational and experimental confirmation. *Journal of Youth and Adolescence, 24,* 595–615.

Ward, S. L., & Overton, W. F. (1990). Semantic familiarity, relevance, and the development of deductive reasoning. *Developmental Psychology, 26,* 488–493.

Ware, N. C., & Lee, V. E. (1988). Sex differences in choice of college science majors. *American Educational Research Journal, 25,* 593–614.

Wark, G. R., & Krebs, D. L. (1996). Gender and dilemma differences in real-life moral judgment. *Developmental Psychology, 32,* 220–230.

Warner, P. E., Critchley, H., Lumsden, M. A., Campbell-Brown, M., Douglas, A., & Murray, G. D. (2004). Menorrhagia I: Measured blood loss, clinical features, and outcome in women with heavy periods: A survey with follow-up data. *American Journal of Obstetrics and Gynecology, 190,* 1216–1223.

Warren, J. R. (2002). Reconsidering the relationship between student employment and academic outcomes. *Youth and Society, 33,* 366–393.

Warren, M. P., & Perlroth, N. E. (2001). The effects of intense exercise on the female reproductive system. *Journal of Endocrinology, 170,* 3–11.

Warshak, R. A. (1986). Father-custody and child development: A review of analysis of psychological research. *Behavioral Science and the Law, 4,* 185–202.

Washington State Department of Health. (2000). *Adolescent nutrition.* Publication no. 910-117. Tacoma: Author.

Wasley, P. A. (2002). Small classes, small schools, etc. *Educational Leadership, 59,* 6–10.

Waterman, J. (1986). Overview of treatment issues. In K. MacFarlane & J. Waterman (Eds.), *Sexual abuse of young children: Evaluation and treatment* (pp. 197–203). New York: Guilford Press.

Waters, E., & Cummings, M. (2000). A secure base from which to explore close relationships. *Child Development, 71,* 164–172.

Watson, C. M., Quatman, T., & Edler, E. (2002). Career aspirations of adolescent girls: Effects of achievement level, grade, and single-sex school environment. *Sex Roles, 46,* 323–335.

Watson, L. F., Taft, A. J., & Lee, C. (2007). Associations with self-reported violence with age at menarche, first intercourse, and first birth among a national population sample of young Australian women. *Women's Health Issues, 17,* 281–289.

Watts, W. D., & Wright, L. S. (1990). The relationship of alcohol, tobacco, marijuana, and other illegal drug use to delinquency among Mexican-American, Black, and White adolescent males. *Adolescence, 25,* 171–181.

Way, N., & Chen, L. (2000). Close and general friendships among African American, Latino, and Asian American adolescents from low-income families. *Journal of Adolescent Research, 15,* 274–301.

Way, N., & Greene, M. (2005, April). *Exploring adolescents' perceptions of parental attitudes and rules about friendships*. Paper presented at the biennial meeting of the Society for Research on Child Development, Seattle, WA.

Wechsler H., Lee, J. E., Kuo, M., Seibring, M., Nelson, T. F., & Lee, H. P. (2002). Trends in college binge drinking during a period of increased prevention efforts: Findings from four Harvard School of Public Health Study surveys, 1993–2001. *Journal of American College Health, 50*, 203–217.

Wegner, K. E., Smyth, J. M., Crosby, R. D., Wittrock, D., Wonderlich, S. A., & Mitchell, J. E. (2002). An evaluation of the relationship between mood and binge eating in the natural environment using ecological momentary assessment. *International Journal of Eating Disorders, 32*, 352–361.

Wehmeyer, M. L., & Palmer, S. B. (1997). Perceptions of control of students with and without cognitive disabilities. *Psychological Reports, 81*, 195–206.

Weinberg, R. A., Waldman, I., van Dulmen, M. H. M., & Scarr, S. (2004). The Minnesota Transracial Adoption Study: Parent reports of psychosocial adjustment at late adolescence. *Adoption Quarterly, 8*, 27–44.

Weinger, S. (2000). Opportunities for career success: Views of poor and middle-class children. *Children and Youth Services Review, 22*, 13–35.

Weinstock, H., Berman, S., & Cates, W., Jr. (2004). Sexually transmitted diseases among American youth: Incidence and prevalence estimates, 2000. *Perspectives on Sexual and Reproductive Health, 36*, 6–10.

Weisfeld, G. (1997). Puberty rites as clues to the nature of human adolescence. *Cross-Cultural Research: The Journal of Comparative Social Science, 31*, 27–54.

Weitoft, G. R., Hjern, A., Haglund, B., & Rosén, M. (2003). Mortality, severe morbidity, and injury in children living with single parents in Sweden: A population-based study. *Lancet, 361*, 289–295.

Wellman, H. M., & Gellman, S. A. (1998). Knowledge acquisition in fundamental domains. In W. Damon (Ed.), *Handbook of child psychology: Cognition, language, and perception* (Vol. 2, pp. 524–573). New York: Wiley.

Wellman, R. J., Sugarman D. R., DiFranza, J. R., & Winickoff, J. P. (2006). The extent to which tobacco marketing and tobacco use in films contribute to children's use of tobacco. *Archives of Pediatric & Adolescent Medicine, 160*, 1285–1296.

Wells, J. C. (2007). Sexual dimorphism of body composition. *Best Practice & Research in Clinical Endocrinology, 21*, 415–430.

Wentzel, K. R., & McNamara, C. C. (1999). Interpersonal relationships, emotional distress, and prosocial behavior in middle school. *Journal of Early Adolescence, 19*, 114–125.

Werner, E. E. (1998). Resilience and the lifespan perspective: What we have learned—so far. *Resiliency in Action, 3*, 1–9.

Werner, E. E., & Smith, R. (2001). *Journeys from childhood to midlife: Risk, resilience, and recovery*. Ithaca, NY: Cornell University Press.

Wertheim, W. H., Paxton, S. J., & Blaney, S. (2009). Body image in girls. In J. K. Thompson & L. Smolak (Eds.), *Body image, eating disorders, and obesity in youth: Assessment, prevention, and treatment* (pp. 463–494). Washington, DC: American Psychological Association.

Westbrook, R. B. (1991). *John Dewey and the American democracy*. Ithaca, NY: Cornell University Press.

Wetzel, N., & Schroger, E. (2007). Cognitive control of involuntary attention and distraction in children and adolescents. *Brain Research, 1155*, 134–146

Whitbeck, L. B., & Simons, R. L. (1990). Life on the streets: The victimization of runaway and homeless adolescents. *Youth and Society, 22*, 108–125.

Whitbeck, L. B., Yoder, K. A., Hoyt, D. R., & Conger, R. D. (1999). Early adolescent sexual activity: A developmental study. *Journal of Marriage and Family, 61*, 934–946.

White, M. A., Kohlmaier, J. R., Varnado-Sullivan, P., & Williamson, D. A. (2003). Racial/ethnic differences in weight concerns: Protective and risk factors for the development of eating disorders and obesity among adolescent females. *Eating and Weight Disorders, 8*, 20–25.

Whiston, S. C., & Keller, B. K. (2004). The influences of the family of origin on career development: A review and analysis. *Counseling Psychologist, 32*, 493–568.

Whitley, B. E., & Keith-Spiegel, P. (2002). *Academic dishonesty: An educator's guide*. Mahwah, NJ: Erlbaum.

Whitman, T., Bokowski, J., Keogh, D., & Weed, K. (2001). *Interwoven lives: Adolescent mothers and their children*. Mahwah, NJ: Erlbaum.

Whitton, S. W., Rhoades, G. K., Stanley, S. M., & Markman, H. J. (2008). Effects of parental divorce on marital commitment and confidence. *Journal of Family Psychology, 22*, 789–793.

Wichstrøm, L. (2001). The impact of pubertal timing on adolescents' alcohol use. *Journal of Research on Adolescence, 11*, 131–150.

Wickens, C. D. (1974). Limits of human information processing: A developmental study. *Psychological Bulletin, 81*, 739–755.

Widmer, E. D., & Weiss, C. C. (2000). Do older siblings make a difference? The effects of older sibling support and older sibling adjustment on the adjustment of socially disadvantaged adolescents. *Journal of Research on Adolescents, 10*, 1–27.

Wigfield, A., Byrnes, J. P., & Eccles, J. S. (2006). Development during early and middle adolescence. In P. A. Alexander & P. H. Winne (Eds.), *Handbook of educational psychology* (2nd ed., pp. 87–113). Mahwah, NJ: Erlbaum.

Wilcox, B., Cantor, J., Dowrick, P., Kunkel, D., Linn, S., & Palmer, E. (2004). *Report of the APA Task Force on Advertising and Children: Summary of findings and conclusions*. Washington, DC: American Psychological Association.

Willard, N. (2004). *Cyberbullying*. Retrieved from http://cyberbully.org/.

Williams, J. M., & Currie, C. (2000). Self-esteem and physical development in early adolescence: Pubertal timing and body image. *Journal of Early Adolescence, 20*, 129–149.

Williams, J. M., & Dunlop, L. C. (1999). Pubertal timing and self-reported delinquency among male adolescents. *Journal of Adolescence, 22*, 157–171.

Williams, M., Himmel, K. F., Sjoberg, A. F., & Torrez, D. J. (1995). The assimilation model, family life, and race and ethnicity in the United States. *Journal of Family Issues, 16*, 380–405.

Williams, R. J., Chang, S. Y., & Addiction Centre Adolescent Research Group. (2000). A comprehensive and comparative review of adolescent substance abuse treatment outcome. *Clinical Psychology: Science and Practice, 7*, 138–166.

Williams, S., Conger, K. J., & Blozis, S. A. (2007). The development of interpersonal aggression during adolescence: The importance of parents, siblings, and family economics. *Child Development, 78*, 1526–1542.

Williams, S., & Williams, L. (2005). Space invaders: The negotiation of teenage boundaries through the mobile phone. *The Sociological Review, 53*, 314–331.

Williams, T., Connolly, J., Peplar, D., & Craig, W. (2005). Peer victimization, social support, and psychosocial adjustment of sexual minority adolescents. *Journal of Youth and Adolescence, 34*, 471–482.

Willoughby, K. A., Sheard, E. D., Nash, K., & Rovet, J. (2008). Effects of prenatal alcohol exposure on hippocampal volume, verbal learning, and verbal and spatial recall in late childhood. *Journal of the International Neuropsychological Society, 14*, 1022–1033.

Wilson, B. J., Smith, S. L., Potter, J. W., Kunkel, D., Linz, D., Covlin, C. M., et al. (2002). Violence in children's television programming: Assessing the risks. *Journal of Communication, 52*, 5–35.

Wilson, J. (2001). Hi-tech plagiarism: New twist on a perennial problem. *Acumen, 1*, 1–4.

Wilson, J. D., & MacGillivray, M. S. (1998). Self-perceived influences of family, friends, and media on adolescent clothing choice. *Family and Consumer Sciences Research Journal, 26*, 425–443.

Winters, K. (1999). Treating adolescents with substance abuse disorders: An overview of practice issues and treatment outcomes. *Substance Abuse, 20*, 203–223.

Winters, K., Stinchfield, R. D., Opland, E., Weller, C., & Latimer, W. W. (2000). The effectiveness of the Minnesota Model approach in the treatment of adolescent drug abusers. *Addiction, 95*, 601–612.

Wissow, L. S. (2001). Ethnicity, income, and parenting contexts of physical punishment in a national sample of families with young children. *Child Maltreatment, 6*, 118–129.

Wolfson, A. R., & Carskadon, M. A. (1998). Sleep schedules and daytime functioning in adolescents. *Child Development, 69*, 875–887.

Wolke, D., Woods, S., Bloomfield, L., & Karstadt, L. (2000). The association between direct and relational bullying and behavior problems among primary school children. *Journal of Child Psychology and Psychiatry, 41*, 989–1002.

Wonderlich, S. A., Lilenfeld, L. R., Riso, L. P., Engel, S., & Mitchell, J. E. (2005). Personality and anorexia nervosa. *International Journal of Eating Disorders, 37*, s68–s71.

Wood, D., Kaplan, R., & McLoyd, V. C. (2007). Gender differences in the educational expectations of urban, low-income African American youth: The role of parents and the school. *Journal of Youth and Adolescence, 36*, 417–427.

Wood, M. D., Sherman, K. J., & McGowen, A. K. (2000). Collegiate alcohol involvement and role attainment in early adulthood: Findings from a prospective high-risk study. *Journal of Studies of Alcohol, 61*, 278–289.

Wood, N. L., Wood, R. A., & McDonald, T. D. (1988). Integration of student development theory into the academic classroom. *Adolescence, 23*, 349–356.

Woodside, D. B. (2005). Treatment of anorexia nervosa: More questions than answers. *International Journal of Eating Disorders, 37*, s41–s42.

Woodward, J. C., & Kalyan-Masih, V. (1990). Loneliness, coping strategies and cognitive styles of the gifted rural adolescent. *Adolescence, 25*, 977–988.

Wright, R. (1937). The ethics of living Jim Crow. In *American Stuff*. New York: Harper and Row.

Wright, V. R., & Chau, M. (2009). *Basic facts about low-income children: Children aged 12–17*. Fact sheet from the National Center for Children in Poverty, Columbia University.

Wrobel, G. M., Grotevant, H. D., & McRoy, R. G. (2004). Adolescent search for birth parents: Who moves forward? *Journal of Adolescent Research, 19*, 132–151.

Wyatt, G. E., & Newcomb, M. (1990). Internal and external mediators of women's sexual abuse in childhood. *Journal of Consulting and Clinical Psychology, 58*, 758–767.

Wynne, E. (1989). Transmitting traditional values in contemporary schools. In L. Nucci (Ed.), *Moral development and character education: A dialogue* (pp. 19–36). Berkeley, CA: McCutchan.

Xie, H., Swift, D. J., Carins, R. B., & Cairns, B. D. (2002). Aggressive behaviors in social interaction and developmental adaptation: A narrative analysis of interpersonal conflicts during early adolescence. *Social Development, 11*, 205–224.

Yang, K. (2004). Southeast Asian American children: Not the "model minority." *Future of Children, 14*, 127–133.

Yang, P. Q., & Kayaardi, N. (2004). Who chooses non-public schools for their children? *Educational Studies, 30*, 231–249.

Yaryura-Tobias, J. A., Neziroglu, F. A., & Kaplan, S. (1995). Self-mutilation, anorexia, and dysmenorrhea in obsessive-compulsive disorder. *International Journal of Eating Disorders, 17*, 33–38.

Yates, M., & Youniss, J. (1996). Community service and political-moral identity in adolescents. *Journal of Research in Adolescence, 6*, 271–284.

Yates, T. M. (2004). The developmental psychology of self-injurious behavior: Compensatory regulation in post-traumatic adaptation. *Clinical Psychological Review, 24*, 35–74.

Yoder, K. A. (1999). Comparing suicide attempters, suicide ideators, and nonsuicidal homeless and runaway adolescents. *Suicide and Life-Threatening Behavior, 29*, 23–36.

Young, E. A., Clopton, J. R., & Bleckley, M. K. (2004). Perfectionism, low self-esteem, and family factors as predictors of bulimic behavior. *Eating Behaviors, 5*, 273–283.

Young, J. F., & Mroczek, K. (2003). Predicting intraindividual self-concept trajectories during adolescence. *Journal of Adolescence, 26*, 586–600.

Young, M. H., Miller, B. C., Norton, M. C., & Hill, E. J. (1995). The effect of parental supportive behaviors on life satisfaction of adolescent offspring. *Journal of Marriage and Family, 57*, 813–822.

Young, R. A. (1994). Helping adolescents with career development: The active role of parents. *Career Development Quarterly, 42*, 195–203.

Youniss, J., & Smollar, J. (1985). *Adolescent relations with mothers, fathers, and friends.* Chicago: University of Chicago Press.

Yu, J. (2007). British born Chinese teenagers: The influence of Chinese ethnicity on their attitudes towards sexual behavior. *Nursing and Health Sciences, 9*, 69–75.

Yuan, A. S. V. (2007). Gender differences in the relationship of puberty with adolescents' depressive symptoms: Do body perceptions matter? *Sex Roles, 57*, 69–80.

Yuen, N., Andrade, N., Nahulu, L., Makini, G., McDermott, J. F., Danko, G., et al. (1996). The rate and characteristics of suicide attempters in the Native Hawaiian adolescent population. *Suicide and Life-Threatening Behavior, 26*, 27–36.

Zachry, E. M. (2005). Getting my education: Teen mothers' experiences in school before and after motherhood. *Teachers College Record, 107*, 2566–2598.

Zald, D. H., & Iacono, W. G. (1998). The development of spatial working memory abilities. *Developmental Neuropsychology, 14*, 563–578.

Zavodny, M. (2004). Fertility and parental consent for minors to receive contraceptives. *American Journal of Public Health, 94*, 1347–1351.

Zebrowitz, L. A., Hall, J. A., Murphy, N. A., & Rhodes, G. (2002). Looking smart and looking good: Facial cues to intelligence and their origins. *Personality and Social Psychology Bulletin, 28*, 238–249.

Zeidner, M. (1995). Personality trait correlates of intelligence. In D. H. Saklofske & M. Zeidner (Eds.), *International handbook of personality and intelligence* (pp. 299–319). New York: Plenum Press.

Zelkowitz, P. (1987). Social support and aggressive behavior in young children. *Family Relations, 36*, 129–134.

Zila, L. M., & Kiselica, M. (2001). Understanding and counseling self-mutilation in female adolescents and young adults. *Journal of Counseling and Development, 79*, 46–52.

Zillman, D. (1996). The psychology of suspense in dramatic exposition. In P. Vorderer, H. J. Wulff, & M. Friedrichsen (Eds.), *Suspense: Conceptualizations, theoretical analyses, and empirical explorations* (pp. 199–231). Mahwah, NJ: Erlbaum.

Zillman, D. (2000). Influence of unrestrained access to erotica on adolescents' and young adults' dispositions toward sexuality. *Journal of Adolescent Health, 27*(2), 41–44.

Zimmerman, P. (1999). Structure and functioning of internal models of attachment and their role in emotional regulation. *Attachment and Human Development, 1*, 55–71.

Zimmermann, P. (2004). Attachment representations and characteristics of friendship relations during adolescence. *Journal of Experimental Child Psychology, 88*, 83–101.

Zimmerman, R. S., Sprecher, S., Langer, L. M., & Holloway, C. D. (1995). Adolescents' perceived ability to say "no" to unwanted sex. *Journal of Adolescent Research, 10*, 383–399.

Zlotnick, C., Shea, M. T., Pearlstein, T., Simpson, E., Costello, E., & Begin, A. (1996). The relationship between dissociative symptoms, alexithymia, impulsivity, sexual abuse, and self-mutilation. *Comprehensive Psychiatry, 37*, 12–16.

Zuckeman, D., & Abraham, A. (2008). Teenagers and cosmetic surgery: Focus on breast augmentation and liposuction. *Journal of Adolescent Health, 43*, 318–324.

PHOTO CREDITS

NAME INDEX

SUBJECT INDEX

H

HAART, 290
Hackett, Gail, 332
Hall, G. Stanley, 32, 33
Hallucinogens, 387–89
Havighurst, Robert, 42, 43–44, 412–13
Health. *See also* Physical health and development
decisions, 104–5
Latino, 65
mental, 59
Native American, 68–69
poverty and, 59–60
in third world countries, 105
Health concerns, 105–12
acne, 111–12
exercise, 107–8
nutrition, 106–7
obesity, 108–10
sleep, 110–11
Health status, 103–5
health decisions and, 104–5
mortality and, 103–4
in Third World countries, 105
Herd life, 252
Heroin, 383–84
Heterosexuality, 296, 297
Heterosociality, 253–56
adolescent love and crushes, 254–55
cross-sex friendships and, 254
loss of love and, 255, 256
psychosocial development and, 253–54
Heuristics, 135
Hierarchical classification, 119–20
Higher-order thought processes, 132–34
Highly active anti-retroviral therapy (HAART), 290
High schools, 311
Hippies, 246
Hippocampus, 138, 139, 389
HIV. *See* Human immunodeficiency virus (HIV)
Holland, J. L., 331
Homelessness, 57–58
Home schooling, 310
Homosexuality, 296, 297. *See also* Gays and lesbians
Homosociality, 253
Hoped-for selves, 151
Hormones. *See also* Sex hormone regulation
androgens, 83–84
biological sex and, 166
defined, 82
estrogens, 83–84, 97
follicle-stimulating hormone (FSH), 83
gonadotropic hormones, 83
gonadotropin-releasing hormone (GnRH), 82
human growth hormone (HGH), 83
luteinizing hormone (LH), 83
menstrual cycle and, 89–91
testosterone, 83–84, 97
Human growth hormone (HGH), 83
Human immunodeficiency virus (HIV)
causation and diagnosis of, 289–90
contraceptive use and, 286
knowledge of (quiz), 291
premarital sexual activity and, 8
shared needles and, 87
in Third World countries, 105
treatment and transmission of, 290–91
Human rights, adolescents' views of, 190
Hymen, 88, 89
Hypocrisy, 124–25
Hypothalamus, 82, 83
Hypothetico-deductive reasoning, 122–23

I

Iconic memory, 131
Id, 35
Idealism, 124
Idealistic, 124, 125
Ideal self, 151
Identification
defined, 34, 35
parental, 169–70
Identity, 120–21, 157–66. *See also* Ethnic identity
achieved, 160–61
components of, 162–63
conflicts, 157–58
control system, 162, 163
diffused, 158–59
diffusion, 38, 39
formation, 36–37
as a process, 162
standards, 162, 163
status, 158–62
Identity status
critique, 161–62
foreclosure, 159–60
identity achieved, 160–61
identity diffused, 158–59
moratorium, 160, 161
If/then statements, 133
Imaginary audience, 125
Immanent justice, 176–77
Immigrants, 74–77. *See also* Refugees
Impulsive behavior, 136
Incest, 215
Income, African American, 63
Inculcation, 193
Independence, 187
Indian Education Act (Title IV), 69
Indian Health Service, 69
Indifferent behavior, 136
Individuation, 34–35, 40
Induction, 133, 206, 207
Inductive reasoning, 119
Informal subsystem, 245–46
Informational style, 162
Information processing, 129–34
barriers to good decision making, 135
higher-order thought processes, 132–34
knowledge in, role of, 134
processing speed, 132, 133
process of, 134–35
risky decision making, 135
steps in, 130–32
Information technologies, 9–12
cell phones, 12
Internet, 10–12
Inhalants, 387
Inhibin, 84, 85
Integrated studies, 316
Integration, 163
Intellectual neglect, 216
Intelligence
analytic, 139, 140
artificial, 130
body-kinesthetic, 140
creative, 139
interpersonal/intrapersonal, 140
linguistic, 139, 140
logical-mathematical, 139, 140
musical, 140
naturalistic, 140, 141
practical, 139
spatial, 139–40
testing, 140–41
theories of, 139–40
Intelligence quotient (IQ), 139, 142, 143
Intensified drug use, 383
Intent runaways, 354
Intercourse, 279–80
Internalized imitation, 119
Internet, 10–12, 268–70
Interpersonal competence, 153
Interpersonal feedback, 162
Interpersonal intelligence, 140
Intrapersonal intelligence, 140
Introspection, 126, 127
Intuitionists, 180–81
Intuitive behavior, 136
IQ tests, 139, 142, 143

J

Japanese education, 316
Joint custody, 228, 229
Josephson Institute of Ethics, 193
Junior high schools, 311
Juvenile, defined, 4
Juvenile court, 375
Juvenile delinquency, 367–77
conduct disorder and, 372
environmental causes of, 369, 370
gangs, 372–73
incidence of, 367–69
interpersonal causes of, 369, 370–71
personal causes of, 369, 371–72
self-concept and, 153–54
status crimes, 367
Juvenile delinquent, defined, 367
Juvenile justice system, 373–77
correctional system, 375–76
juvenile court, 375
parens patriae role of courts in, 374
police, 374
restorative justice movement, 376–77
Juveniles in need of supervision (JINS), 375

K

Knowledge in information processing, 134
Kohlberg, Lawrence, 177–81
Kohlberg's levels of moral development, 177–81
conventional moral reasoning, 179
criticisms of, 181
postconventional moral reasoning, 179–80
preconventional moral reasoning, 178–79
stagelike, 181
thinking ability and, 180–81
universality of, 181
vs. Gilligan's, 182–83

L

Labia majora, 88, 89
Labia minora, 88, 89
Latency stage, 34, 35
Latino adolescents, 64–68. *See also* Mexican American adolescents; Puerto Rican adolescents
culture, 66
educational attainment, 64–65, 68
health, 65
Law and order orientation, 179
Legal custody, 228, 229
Lent, Robert, 332
Leptin, 93
Lesbians. *See* Gays and lesbians
Lewin, Kurt, 44–45
Life space, 44
Linguistic intelligence, 139, 140
Locker-room syndrome, 94
Logical-mathematical intelligence, 139, 140
Loneliness, 248–49
Longitudinal study, 26
Long-term storage (long-term memory), 131–32
Loss of love, 255, 256
Love
and crushes, 254–55
loss of, 255, 256
Low socioeconomic status (low SES), 55–60
defined, 55
limitations of, 55–56
poverty and deprivation, cycle of, 56–60
vs. middle class status, 59
LSD, 387
Luteal phase, 89–90
Luteinizing hormone (LH), 83

M

Machismo, 67
Macrosystem, 46
Magnet schools, 319
Maladaptive perfectionists, 152
Male sex organs, maturation of, 86–88
Cowper's glands, 88, 89
early-maturing boys, 100, 102
late-maturing boys, 102
nocturnal emissions, 88, 89
penis, 86, 87
results of, 95
secondary sexual characteristics, 92, 93–94, 95
spermatogenesis, 84, 85, 86
Maltreatment, 214–16
incest, 215
neglect, 215–16
physical abuse, 214–15
sexual abuse, 215
Marginality, 163
Marginal man, adolescent as, 44–45
Marianismo, 67
Marijuana, 387–89